Fodor's 2015

CALIFORNIA

WELCOME TO CALIFORNIA

California's endless wonders, from Yosemite National Park to Disneyland, are both natural and man-made. Soul-satisfying wilderness often lies close to urbane civilization. With the iconic Big Sur coast, dramatic Mojave Desert, and majestic Sierra Nevada mountains, sunny California indulges those in search of great surfing, hiking, and golfing. Other pleasures await, too: superb food in San Francisco, studio tours in Los Angeles, winery visits and spas in Napa and Sonoma. Follow a beach picnic with a city stroll and live the California dream.

TOP REASONS TO GO

★ **Stunning Scenery:** Picture-perfect backdrops from the Golden Gate Bridge to redwoods.

★ **Beaches:** For surfing, swimming, or sunbathing, the state's beaches can't be beat.

★ **Cool Cities:** San Francisco, Los Angeles, San Diego, Palm Springs, and more.

★ **Feasts:** Cutting-edge restaurants, food trucks, fusion flavors, farmers' markets.

★ **Wine Country:** Top-notch whites and reds in Napa, Sonoma, and beyond.

★ **Road Trips:** The Pacific Coast Highway offers spectacular views and thrills aplenty.

Fodor's CALIFORNIA 2015

Publisher: Amanda D'Acierno, *Senior Vice President*

Editorial: Arabella Bowen, *Editor in Chief*; Linda Cabasin, *Editorial Director*

Design: Fabrizio La Rocca, *Vice President, Creative Director*; Tina Malaney, *Associate Art Director*; Chie Ushio, *Senior Designer*; Ann McBride, *Production Designer*

Photography: Melanie Marin, *Associate Director of Photography*; Jessica Parkhill and Jennifer Romains, *Researchers*

Maps: Rebecca Baer, *Senior Map Editor*; Mark Stroud (Moon Street Cartography), David Lindroth, *Cartographers*

Production: Linda Schmidt, *Managing Editor*; Evangelos Vasilakis, *Associate Managing Editor*; Angela L. McLean, *Senior Production Manager*

Sales: Jacqueline Lebow, *Sales Director*

Marketing & Publicity: Heather Dalton, *Marketing Director*; Katherine Punia, *Senior Publicist*

Business & Operations: Susan Livingston, *Vice President, Strategic Business Planning*; Sue Daulton, *Vice President, Operations*

Fodors.com: Megan Bell, *Executive Director, Revenue & Business Development*; Yasmin Marinaro, *Senior Director, Marketing & Partnerships*

Copyright © 2015 by Fodor's Travel, a division of Random House LLC

Writers: Sarah Amandalore, Jim Arnold, Cindy Arora, Michele Bigley, John Blodgett, Cheryl Crabtree, Alene Dawson, Dianne de Guzman, Denise M. Leto, Kathy A. McDonald, Daniel Mangin, Jenie Skoy, Claire Deeks van der Lee, Christine Vovakes, Clarissa Wei, Sharron Wood, Bobbi Zane

Editors: Luke Epplin *(lead project editor)*, Salwa Jabado

Editorial Contributors: Linda Cabasin, Andrew Collins, Daniel Mangin, Steven Montero, Jacinta O'Halloran, Amanda Sadlowski, Mark Sullivan

Production Editor: Evangelos Vasilakis

ISBN 978-0-8041-4273-1

ISSN 0192-9925

All details in this book are based on information supplied to us at press time. Always confirm information when it matters, especially if you're making a detour to visit a specific place. Fodor's expressly disclaims any liability, loss, or risk, personal or otherwise, that is incurred as a consequence of the use of any of the contents of this book.

SPECIAL SALES

This book is available at special discounts for bulk purchases for sales promotions or premiums. For more information, e-mail specialmarkets@randomhouse.com

PRINTED IN THE UNITED STATES OF AMERICA

10 9 8 7 6 5 4 3 2 1

CONTENTS

Fodor's Features

CONTENTS

CONTENTS

CONTENTS

ABOUT
THIS GUIDE

Fodor's Recommendations

Everything in this guide is worth doing—we don't cover what isn't—but exceptional sights, hotels, and restaurants are recognized with additional accolades. **Fodor's**Choice★ indicates our top recommendations; and **Best Bets** call attention to notable hotels and restaurants in various categories. Care to nominate a new place? Visit Fodors.com/contact-us.

Trip Costs

We list prices wherever possible to help you budget well. Hotel and restaurant price categories from **$** to **$$$$** are noted alongside each recommendation. For hotels, we include the lowest cost of a standard double room in high season. For restaurants, we cite the average price of a main course at dinner or, if dinner isn't served, at lunch. For attractions, we always list adult admission fees; discounts are usually available for children, students, and senior citizens.

Hotels

Our local writers vet every hotel to recommend the best overnights in each price category, from budget to expensive. Unless otherwise specified, you can expect private bath, phone, and TV in your room. *For expanded hotel reviews and deals, visit Fodors.com.*

Restaurants

Unless we state otherwise, restaurants are open for lunch and dinner daily. We mention dress code only when there's a specific requirement and reservations only when they're essential or not accepted. *To make restaurant reservations, visit Fodors.com.*

Credit Cards

The hotels and restaurants in this guide typically accept credit cards. If not, we'll say so.

Top Picks
★ **Fodor's**Choice

Listings
⊠ Address
⊠ Branch address
☎ Telephone
🖷 Fax
⊕ Website
✉ E-mail
🎟 Admission fee
🕐 Open/closed times
Ⓜ Subway
✛ Directions or Map coordinates

Hotels & Restaurants
🏨 Hotel
🛏 Number of rooms
🍽 Meal plans
✗ Restaurant
🔖 Reservations
👔 Dress code
▭ No credit cards
Ⓢ Price

Other
⇨ See also
☞ Take note
⛳ Golf facilities

EXPERIENCE
CALIFORNIA

WHAT'S NEW IN CALIFORNIA

Foodie's Paradise

Great dining is a staple of the California lifestyle, and a new young generation of chefs is challenging old ideas about preparing and presenting great food. Food-truck frenzy has created a movable feast up and down the state. Esteemed chefs and urban foodies follow the trucks on Twitter as they move around cities 24/7 purveying delicious, cheap, fresh meals. In L.A., chef Roy Choi started the movement when he began serving his Korean/Mexican Pacman burgers from his Kogi BBQ truck. In SoCal, you can find food-laden trucks at sports and entertainment venues, near parks and attractions, and on busy roads and boulevards—and the ensuing lines of hungry patrons. You can keep up with the trucks in L.A. and San Francisco through ⊕ *www.foodtruckmaps.com*.

California chefs continue to shop locally for produce and farmer-sourced meat. Tender Greens (with locations in Hollywood, Pasadena, San Diego, and Walnut Creek) sets the bar high by serving hand-raised produce; grain-fed, hormone-free beef; hand-raised chickens; and line-caught tuna.

Kid-ding Around

California's theme parks work overtime to keep current and attract patrons of all ages. LEGOLAND California Resort keeps expanding with new attractions such as Pirate Reef and LEGOLAND Water Park. And LEGOLAND opened its 250-room LEGO-theme hotel in 2013.

Disneyland continues to grow. The newest attraction, Car's Land, is a must for big and little kids. The Disneyland Hotel also has a new look, with water features galore and family-friendly accommodations.

With trees as tall as they come, the Children's Redwood Forest in Humboldt Redwoods State Park is a great place for kids to romp through some awe-inspiring landscapes.

Grape Expectations

Evidence that California wine culture is alive and well comes from Temecula, which is emerging as an exciting wine destination in the Inland Empire. The number and quality of the wineries continue to grow: Thornton, Ponte, and Mount Palomar wineries offer fine dining to pair with their delicious Rhône-style wines. Hotels are springing up among the vineyards, and events such as the Balloon and Wine Festival draw thousands of visitors to the region. Winemaking is also expanding in the Central Valley and Shasta Cascade areas.

In SoCal, vineyards are going up in unlikely places, such as in the hillsides of San Diego County, where Escondido-based Orfila keeps snagging awards, and on Catalina Island, where the Rusack family planted the first wine grapes ever on the historic Escondido Ranch. The Turkovich Family Winery opened in the Central Valley town of Winters just west of Sacramento. The Truckee River Winery, near Lake Tahoe, claims to be the highest and coldest winery in the nation.

Suite Dreams

Hotels are coming back to life in a big way. The luxurious JW Marriott and Ritz-Carlton stand side by side in the burgeoning L.A. LIVE sports and entertainment complex. The W Hollywood now occupies the famed corner of Hollywood and Vine, another hot spot just steps from the Pantages Theatre. Visitors to Yountville in the Napa Valley have another lodging choice, the Bardessono, a LEED-certified hotel that sports an eco spa and an underground geothermal system.

All Aboard

Riding the rails can be a satisfying experience, particularly in California where the distances between destinations sometimes run into the hundreds of miles. You can save money on gas and parking, avoid freeway traffic, and see some of the best the state has to offer.

The best trip is on the luxuriously appointed Coast Starlight, a long-distance train with sleeping cars that runs between Seattle and Los Angeles, passing some of California's most beautiful coastline as it hugs the beach. For the best surfside viewing, get a seat or a room on the left side of the train and ride south to north from San Diego to Oakland.

Amtrak has frequent Pacific Surfliner service between San Diego and Los Angeles, and San Diego and Santa Barbara. These are coach cars, but many of the trains have been upgraded and are comfortable and convenient, especially if you want to get off and on the train at several destinations—Anaheim near Disneyland, Downtown Los Angeles, coastal Ventura and Santa Barbara, San Luis Obispo, and Oakland (just a BART ride to San Francisco).

It's Easy Being Green

The Golden State is glowing green all over. It's the only state in the nation to mandate green building codes for all new construction to reduce greenhouse emissions. Palm Desert is also pushing green, not only in sustainable construction but also in encouraging use of golf carts for local transportation.

Homegrown Hospitality

Agritourism in California isn't new (remember, Knott's Berry Farm once *was* a berry farm), but it is on the rise, with farm tours and agricultural festivals sprouting up everywhere.

Wine country is a particularly fertile area—spurred by the success of vineyards, the area's lavender growers and olive-oil producers have started welcoming visitors. Sonoma Farm Trail Tours include walking the land and a farm-driven dinner with paired wines.

In the Central Valley, America's number-one producer of stone fruit, you can travel themed tourist routes (like Fresno County's Blossom Trail) and tour herb gardens, fruit orchards, organic dairies, and pumpkin patches.

State of the Arts

California's beauty-obsessed citizens aren't the only ones opting for a fresh look these days: its esteemed art museums are also having a bit of work done.

Following a trend set by the de Young Museum in San Francisco and the Getty Villa in L.A., Long Beach's Museum of Latin American Art doubled its exhibition space. Meanwhile, San Jose's Institute of Contemporary Art and the Museum of Contemporary Art in San Diego (MCASD Downtown) have both expanded into new digs. And the Palm Springs Museum of Art, a world-class showcase for contemporary work, has opened a satellite venue in Palm Desert. The L.A. County Museum of Art keeps expanding its Wilshire Boulevard campus; the latest addition is the Renzo Piano–designed Resnick Pavilion, where changing shows display works by David Hockney and Chinese paintings.

WHAT'S WHERE

The following numbers refer to chapters.

2 **San Diego.** San Diego's Gaslamp Quarter and early California–themed Old Town have a human scale—but it's big-ticket animal attractions like SeaWorld and the San Diego Zoo that pull in visitors.

3 **Orange County.** A diverse destination with premium resorts and restaurants, strollable waterfront communities, and kid-friendly attractions.

4 **Los Angeles.** Go for the glitz of the entertainment industry, but stay for the rich cultural attributes and communities.

5 **The Central Coast.** Three of the state's top stops— swanky Santa Barbara, Hearst Castle, and Big Sur—sit along the scenic 200-mile route.

6 **Channel Islands National Park.** Only 60 miles northwest of Los Angeles, this park seems worlds away from urban sprawl.

13 **The Inland Empire.** The San Bernardino Mountains provide seasonal escapes, and the Temecula Valley will challenge your ideas of "California Wine Country."

14 **Palm Springs and the Desert Resorts.** Golf on some of the West's most challenging courses, lounge at fabulous resorts, check out

midcentury-modern architectural gems, and trek through primitive desert parks.

15 **Joshua Tree National Park.** Proximity to major urban areas—as well as world-class rock climbing and nighttime celestial displays—help make this one of the most visited national parks.

16 **The Mojave Desert.** Material pleasures are in short supply here, but Mother Nature's stark beauty more than compensates.

17 **Death Valley National Park.** America's second-largest national park is vast, beautiful, and often the hottest place in the nation.

19 **The Southern Sierra.** In the Mammoth Lakes region, sawtooth mountains and deep powdery snowdrifts create the state's premier conditions for skiing and snowboarding.

20 **Yosemite National Park.** The views immortalized by photographer Ansel Adams—towering granite monoliths, verdant glacial valleys, and lofty waterfalls— are still camera-ready.

21 **Sequoia and Kings Canyon National Parks.** The sight of ancient redwoods towering above jagged mountains is breathtaking.

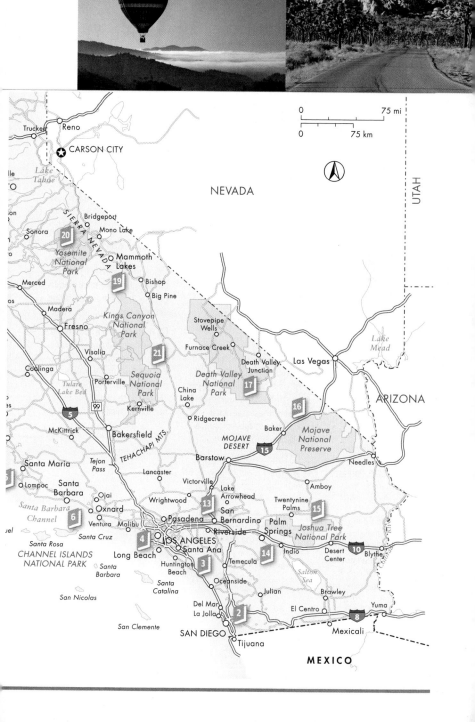

WHAT'S WHERE

The following numbers refer to chapters.

7 Monterey Bay Area. Postcard-perfect Monterey, Victorian-flavored Pacific Grove, and exclusive Carmel all share this stretch of California coast. To the north, Santa Cruz boasts a board-walk, a UC campus, ethnic clothing shops, and plenty of surfers.

8 San Francisco. To see why so many have left their hearts here, you need to visit the city's iconic neighbor-hoods—posh Pacific Heights, the Hispanic Mission, and gay-friendly Castro.

9 The Bay Area. The area that rings San Francisco is nothing like the city—but it is home to some of the nation's great universities, fabulous bay views, Silicon Valley, and Alice Waters' Chez Panisse.

10 The Wine Country. Napa and Sonoma counties retain their title as *the* California Wine Country, by virtue of award-winning vintages, luxe lodgings, and epicurean eats.

11 The North Coast. The star attractions here are natural ones, from the secluded beaches and wave-battered bluffs of Point Reyes National Seashore to the towering redwood forests.

12 Redwood National Park. More than 200 miles of trails, ranging from easy to strenuous, allow visitors to see these spectacu-lar trees in their primitive environments.

18 The Central Valley. Travelers along Highway 99 will enjoy attractions like Fresno's Forestiere Under-ground Gardens, the winer-ies of Lodi, and white-water rafting on the Stanislaus River.

22 Sacramento and the Gold Country. The 1849 gold rush that built San Francisco and Sacramento began here, and the former mining camps strung along 185 miles of Highway 49 replay their past to the hilt.

23 Lake Tahoe. With miles of crystalline water reflecting the peaks of the High Sierra, Lake Tahoe is the perfect setting for activities like hiking and golfing in summer and skiing and snowmobiling in winter.

24 The Far North. California's far northeast corner is home to snowcapped Mount Shasta, the pristine Trinity Wilderness, and abundant backwoods character that appeals to outdoorsy types.

Crescent
City
Klamath
Redwood
National Park
Trinidad
12
Arcata
Eureka
Ferndale
Garberville
Leggett
Fort Bragg   Willits
Mendocino
Boonville   Ukiah
Point Arena
Gualala   11
Jenner
Santa Rosa
Novato
Point Reyes
National Seashore
8
SAN FRANCISCO
9
Palo
Alto
Santa Cruz
Castroville
Monterey
Pacific Grove
Carmel   7
Big Sur

San Simeon

PACIFIC
OCEAN

Yreka

Mt. Shasta
Burney
Weaverville   Shasta
Lake
Redding
24
Lassen Volcanic
National Park
Susanville
Red Bluff

Chico   Paradise
Willows
Oroville
99
Grass
Valley   Truckee
Yuba City   49
80   23   Lake
Auburn   Tahoe
Woodland   Placerville
Heldsburg   10
SACRAMENTO
Napa   Elk Grove
Sonoma   Fairfield   22
Jackson
Berkeley   Lodi
Oakland   Stockton   Sonora
9   Modesto
Fremont   Turlock
San Jose   Merced
Gilroy   Chowchilla
San Luis   Los Banos   Madera
Res.
Salinas   18
Soledad   5   Fresno
Coalinga

Paso Robles
San Luis
Obispo   McKittrick
Santa Maria
Lompoc   Santa
Barbara   Ojai
Santa Barbara   Ventura   Oxnard
Channel

Goose
Lake

CASCADE RANGE

Alturas

NEVADA

Pyramid
Lake

Reno

CARSON CITY

South Lake
Tahoe

Bridgeport
Mono
Lake
Yosemite
Village   Mammoth
Lakes
Bishop

Big Pine

Visalia
Tulare
Lake Bed   Porterville
Kernville   China
Lake
99
Bakersfield   Ridgecrest

TEHACHAPI MTS.
Tejon
Pass   Lancaster

Pasadena

Sacramento Valley
Clear
Lake
Feel R.

San Joaquin Valley

SIERRA NEVADA

0   75 mi
0   75 km

CALIFORNIA PLANNER

Car Travel

Driving may be a way of life in California, but it isn't cheap (gas prices here are usually among the highest in the nation). It's also not for the fainthearted; you've surely heard horror stories about L.A.'s freeways, but even the state's scenic highways and byways have their own hassles. For instance, on the dramatic coastal road between San Simeon and Carmel, twists, turns, and divinely distracting vistas frequently slow traffic; in rainy season, mudslides can close the road altogether. ⚠ Never cross the double line to pass a slower car ahead of you. If you see that cars are backing up behind you, stop at the first available pullout to allow faster drivers to pass.

On California's notorious freeways, other rules apply. Nervous Nellies must resist the urge to stay in the two slow-moving lanes on the far right, used primarily by trucks. To drive at least the speed limit, get yourself in a middle lane. If you're ready to bend the rules a bit, the second (lanes are numbered from 1 starting at the center) lane moves about 5 mph faster. But avoid the far-left lane (the one next to the carpool lane), where speeds range from 75 mph to 90 mph.

Air Travel

Air travelers beginning or ending their vacation in San Francisco have two main airports to choose from: San Francisco International (SFO) or Oakland International (OAK) across the bay. The former lands you closer to the city core (ground transportation will take about 20 minutes versus 35), but the latter is less heavily trafficked and less prone to pesky fog delays. BART, the Bay Area's affordable rapid-transit system, serves both airports. So your decision will probably rest on which one has the best fares and connections for your particular route.

If your final destination is Monterey or Carmel, San Jose International Airport (SJC), about 40 miles south of San Francisco, is another alternative.

Around Los Angeles, the options grow exponentially. LAX, the world's sixth-busiest airport, gets most of the attention—and not usually for good reasons. John Wayne Airport (SNA), about 25 miles south in Orange County, is a solid substitute—especially if you're planning to visit Disneyland or Orange County beaches. Depending on which part of L.A. you're heading to, you might also consider Bob Hope Airport (BUR) in Burbank (close to Hollywood and its studios) or Long Beach Airport (LGB), convenient if you're catching a cruise ship. If your trip plan includes a backtrack to a major airport, you might consider arriving at one airport and departing from the closest one to the end of your trip. The smaller size of these airports means easier access and shorter security lines. Another advantage is that their lower landing costs often attract budget carriers (like Southwest and JetBlue).

Convenience is the allure of San Diego's recently renovated Lindbergh International Airport (SAN), located minutes from the Gaslamp Quarter, Balboa Park and Zoo, SeaWorld, and the cruise ship terminal.

WHEN TO GO

Because they offer activities indoors and out, the top California cities rate as all-season destinations. Ditto for Southern California's coastal playgrounds. Dying to see Death Valley or Joshua Tree National Park? They are best appreciated in spring when desert blooms offset their austerity and temperatures are still manageable. Early spring—when the gray-whale migration overlaps with the end of the elephant-seal breeding season and the start of the bird migration—is the optimal time to visit Point Reyes National Seashore. Yosemite is ideal in the late spring because roads closed in winter are reopened, and the park's waterfalls—swollen with melting snow—run fast.

Autumn is "crush time" in all the wine destinations, from Napa/Sonoma in the north, central coast, and Temecula in the south. Snowfall makes winter peak season for skiers in Mammoth Mountain and Lake Tahoe, where runs typically open around Thanksgiving (they sometimes remain in operation into June.)

Climate

It's difficult to generalize about the state's weather beyond saying that precipitation comes in winter and summer is dry in most places. As a rule, inland regions are hotter in summer and colder in winter, compared with coastal areas, which are relatively cool year-round. Fog is a potential hazard any day of the year in coastal regions. As you climb into the mountains, seasonal variations are more apparent: winter brings snow (at elevations above 3,000 feet), autumn is crisp, spring can go either way, and summer is sunny and warm, with an occasional thundershower in the southern part of the state.

Microclimates

Mountains separate the California coastline from the state's interior, and the weather can sometimes vary dramatically within a 15-minute drive. On a foggy summer day in San Francisco, you'll be grateful for a sweater—but head 50 miles north inland to Napa Valley, and you'll likely be content in short sleeves. Day and nighttime temperatures can also vary greatly. In August, Palm Springs' thermometers can soar to 110°F at noon, and drop to 75°F at night. Temperature swings elsewhere can be even more extreme. Take Sacramento: on August afternoons the mercury hits the 90s and occasionally exceeds 100°F. Yet as darkness falls, it sometimes plummets to 40°F.

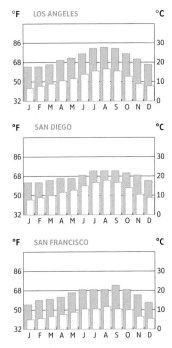

CALIFORNIA TODAY

The People

California is as much a state of mind as a state in the union—a kind of perpetual promised land that has represented many things to many people. In the 18th century, Spanish missionaries came seeking converts and gold. In the 19th, miners rushed here to search for gold. And, in the years since, a long line of Dust Bowl farmers, land speculators, Haight-Ashbury hippies, migrant workers, dotcommers, real estate speculators, and would-be actors has come chasing their own dreams.

The result is a population that leans toward idealism—without necessarily being as liberal as you might think. (Remember, this is Ronald Reagan's old stomping ground.) And despite the stereotype of the blue-eyed, blond surfer, California's population is not homogeneous either. Ten million people who live here (more than 27% of Californians) are foreign born. Almost half hail from Latin American countries; another third emigrated from Asia, following the waves of Chinese workers who arrived in the 1860s to build the railroads and subsequent waves of Indochinese refugees from the Vietnam War.

The Politics

What's blue and red and green all over? California: a predominantly Democratic state with an aggressive "go green" agenda. Democratic Governor Jerry Brown, who was elected to the office for the second time in 30 years, is moving the progressive agenda ahead with policies that make California the greenest state in the nation supporting more green construction, wind farms, and solar panels.

The Economy

Leading all other states in terms of the income generated by agriculture, tourism, entertainment, and industrial activity, California has the country's most diverse state economy. Moreover, with a gross state product of nearly $2 trillion, California would be one of the top ten economies *in the world* if it were an independent nation. But due to its wealth ($61,400 median household income) and productivity, California took a large hit in the recession that began in 2007, although the state has shown signs of recovery recently.

But the Golden State's economic history is filled with boom and bust cycles—beginning with the mid-19th-century gold rush that started it all. Optimists already have their eyes on the next potential boom: high-tech and bioresearch, "green companies" focused on alternative energy, renewables, electric cars, and the like.

The Culture

Cultural organizations thrive in California. San Francisco—a city with only about 825,000 residents—has well-regarded ballet, opera, and theater companies, and is home to one of the continent's most noteworthy orchestras. Museums like San Francisco Museum of Modern Art (SFMOMA) and the de Young also represent the city's ongoing commitment to the arts. Art and culture thrive farther south in San Diego as well. Balboa Park alone holds 15 museums, opulent gardens, and three performance venues, in addition to the San Diego Zoo. The Old Globe Theater and La Jolla Playhouse routinely originate plays that capture coveted Tony Awards in New York.

But California's *real* forte is pop culture, and L.A. and its environs are the chief arbiters. Movie, TV, and video production have been centered here since the early 20th century. Capitol Records set up shop in L.A. in the 1940s, and this area has been instrumental in the music industry ever since. And while these industries continue to influence national trends, today they are only part of the pop culture equation. Websites are also a growing part of that creativity—Facebook, YouTube, and Google are California companies.

The Parks and Preserves

Cloud-spearing redwood groves, snow-tipped mountains, canyon-slashed deserts, primordial lava beds, and a seemingly endless coast: California's natural diversity is staggering—and efforts to protect it started early. Yosemite, the first national park, was established here in 1890, and the National Park Service now oversees 30 sites in California (more than in any other state). When you factor in 280 state parks—which encompass underwater preserves, historic sites, wildlife reserves, dune systems, and other sensitive habitats—the number of acres involved is almost as impressive as the topography itself.

Due to encroaching development and pollution, keeping these natural treasures in pristine condition is an ongoing challenge. For instance, Sequoia and Kings Canyon (which is plagued by pesticides and other agricultural pollutants blown in from the San Joaquin Valley) has been named America's "smoggiest park" by the National Parks Conservation Association, and the Environmental Protection Agency has designated it as an "ozone nonattainment area with levels of ozone pollution that threaten human health."

There is no question that Californians love their 280 state parks. Nearly every park has its grass-roots supporters, who volunteer to raise money, volunteer as rangers, and work other jobs to keep the parks open.

The Cuisine

California gave us McDonald's, Denny's, Carl's Jr., Taco Bell, and, of course, In-N-Out Burger. Fortunately for those of us with fast-clogging arteries, the state also kick-started the organic food movement. Back in the 1970s, California-based chefs put American cuisine on the culinary map by focusing on freshly prepared seasonal ingredients.

Today, this focus has spawned the "locavore" or sustainable food movement—followers try to only consume food produced within a 100-mile radius of where they live, since processing and refining food and transporting goods over long distances is bad for both the body and the environment. This isn't much of a restriction in California, where a huge variety of crops grow year-round. Some 350 cities and towns have certified farmers' markets—and their stalls are bursting with a variety of goods. California has been America's top agricultural producer for the last 50 years, growing more fruits and vegetables than any other state. Dairies and ranches also thrive here, and fishing fleets harvest fish and shellfish from the rich waters offshore.

CALIFORNIA TOP ATTRACTIONS

San Diego

(A) San Diego is a thoroughly modern metropolis set on the sunny Pacific, filled with tourist attractions (think the Zoo, Balboa Park, SeaWorld, and LEGO-LAND) and blissful beaches. But this is also a city steeped in history—in 1769 Spaniards established a settlement here near Old Town, site of the first Spanish outpost and now a state park dedicated to illustrating San Diego's raucous early days. The city's rousing Downtown dining and entertainment district, the Gaslamp Quarter, is a contemporary re-creation of bawdy Stingaree of the late 1800s.

Channel Islands National Park

(B) This five-island park northwest of Los Angeles is a remote eco escape accessible by boat. There are no phones, no cars, and no services—but there are more than 2,000 species of plants and animals (among them blue whales and brown pelicans), plus ample opportunities for active pursuits. On land, hiking tops the itinerary. Underwater preserves surround the park, so snorkeling, scuba diving, fishing, and kayaking around lava tubes and natural arches are other memorable options.

Los Angeles

(C) Tinseltown, Lala Land, City of Angels: L.A. goes by many names and has many personas. Recognized as America's capital of pop culture, it also has highbrow appeal with arts institutions like the Getty Center, the Geffen Contemporary at MOCA, Walt Disney Concert Hall, the Norton Simon Museum, and Huntington Library. But you can go wild here, too—and not just on the Sunset Strip. Sprawling Griffith Park, Will Rogers State Historic Park, and Malibu Lagoon State Beach all offer a natural break from the concrete jungle.

Palm Springs and Beyond

(D) Celebrities used to flee to the desert for rest, relaxation, a few rays of sun, and to indulge in some high jinks beyond the watchful eyes of the media. You don't have to spend much time in Palm Springs to realize those days are *long* gone. In this improbably situated bastion of Bentleys and bling, worldly pleasures rule. Glorious golf courses, tony shops and restaurants, decadent spa resorts—they're all here. Solitude seekers can still slip away to nearby Joshua Tree National Park or Anza-Borrego Desert State Park.

Death Valley

(E) On the surface, a vacation in Death Valley sounds about as attractive as a trip to hell. Yet for well-prepared travelers, the experience is more awe-inspiring than ominous. Within the largest national park in the contiguous United States you'll find the brilliantly colored rock formations of Artists Palette, the peaks of the Panamint Mountains, and the desolate salt flats of Badwater, 282 feet below sea level. You can't get any lower than this in the Western Hemisphere—and, in summer, you can't get much hotter.

San Francisco

(F) Population-wise, San Francisco is smaller than Indianapolis. But when it comes to sites (and soul), this city is a giant. Start working through the standard travelers' "to do" list by strolling across the Golden Gate Bridge, taking a ferry to Alcatraz, and hopping on the Powell–Hyde cable car. Just leave enough time to explore the diverse neighborhoods where San Francisco's distinctive personality—an amalgam of gold-rush history, immigrant traditions, counterculture proclivities, and millennial materialism—is on display.

CALIFORNIA TOP ATTRACTIONS

Yosemite National Park

(G) Nature looms large here, both literally and figuratively. In addition to hulking Half Dome, the park is home to El Capitan (the world's largest exposed granite monolith, rising 3,593 feet above the glacier-carved valley floor) and Yosemite Falls (North America's tallest cascade). In Yosemite's signature stand of giant sequoias—the Mariposa Grove—even the trees are Bunyanesque. Needless to say, crowds can be supersize, too.

Lake Tahoe

(H) Deep, clear, and intensely blue, this forest-rimmed body of water straddling the California–Nevada border is one of the continent's prettiest alpine lakes. That environmental controls can keep it that way is something of a miracle, given Tahoe's popularity. Throngs of outdoor adventurers flock to the California side to ski, hike, bike, and boat. On the Nevada side, where casinos are king, gambling often wins out over fresh-air activities—but natural wonders are never far away.

Point Reyes National Seashore

(I) Aside from the namesake seashore, this Marin County preserve encompasses ecosystems that range from woodlands and marshlands to heathlike grasslands. The range of wildlife here is equally diverse—depending on when you visit, expect to see gray whales, rare Tule elk, and almost 500 species of birds. December through March you can also see male elephant seals compete for mates.

Wine Country

(J) Although the vineyard-blanketed hills of California's original Wine Country are undeniably scenic, the wine itself (preferably accompanied by the area's famed cuisine) remains the big draw here. Budding oenophiles can educate their palettes on scores of tours and tasting sessions.

CALIFORNIA'S TOP EXPERIENCES

Hit the Road

Kings Canyon Highway, Redwood Highway, Tioga Pass, 17-Mile Drive, the Lake Tahoe loop: California has some splendid and challenging roads. You'll drive through a tunnel formed by towering redwood trees on the Redwood Highway. If you venture over the Sierras by way of Tioga Pass (through Yosemite in summer only), you'll see emerald green meadows, gray granite monoliths, and pristine blue lakes—and very few people.

Ride a Wave

Surfing—which has influenced everything from fashion to moviemaking to music—is a quintessential California activity. You can find great surf breaks in many places along the coast between Santa Cruz and San Diego. But one of the best places to try it is Huntington Beach. Lessons are widely available. If you're not ready to hang 10, you can hang out at "Surf City's" International Surfing Museum or stroll the Surfing Walk of Fame.

Pan for Gold

Though California's gold rush ended more than a hundred years ago, you can still feel the forty-nine fever on the western face of the Sierra Nevada in Columbia, a well-preserved town populated by costumed interpreters, where you can pan for gold or tour a mine. Or visit Bodie, an eerie ghost town in the eastern Sierra that remains in a state of "arrested decay."

Think Globally, Eat Locally

Over the years California cuisine has evolved from a mere trend into a respected gastronomic tradition: one that pairs local, often organic or sustainable, ingredients with techniques inspired by European, Asian, and, increasingly, Indian and Middle Eastern cookery.

See Eccentric Architecture

California has always drawn creative and, well, eccentric people. And all that quirkiness has left its mark in the form of oddball architecture that makes for some fun sightseeing. Begin by touring Hearst Castle—the beautifully bizarre estate William Randolph Hearst built above San Simeon. Scotty's Castle, a Moorish confection in Death Valley, offers a variation on the theme, as does Marta Becket's one-woman Amargosa Opera House. And Lake Tahoe's Vikingsholm (a re-created Viking castle) is equally odd.

Get Behind the Scenes

In L.A. it's almost obligatory to do some Hollywood-style stargazing. Cue the action with a behind-the-scenes tour of one of the dream factories. (Warner Bros. Studios' five-hour deluxe version, which includes lunch in the commissary, is just the ticket for cinephiles.) Other must-sees include the Dolby Theater, permanent home to the Cirque du Soleil and Academy Awards; Grauman's Chinese Theatre, where celebs press feet and hands into cement for posterity's sake; Hollywood Boulevard's star-paved Walk of Fame; and the still-iconic Hollywood sign.

People-Watch

Opportunities for world-class people-watching abound in California. Just saunter the rainbow-flagged streets of San Francisco's Castro neighborhood or the century-old boardwalk in time-warped, resiliently boho Santa Cruz. Better yet, hang around L.A.'s Venice Boardwalk, where chain-saw jugglers, surfers, fortune-tellers, and well-oiled bodybuilders take beachfront exhibitionism to a new high (or low, depending on your point of view). The result is pure eye candy.

QUINTESSENTIAL CALIFORNIA

The Beach

California's beach culture is, in a word, legendary. Of course, it only makes sense that folks living in a state with a 1,264-mile coastline (a hefty portion of which sees the sun upward of 300 days a year) would perfect the art of beachgoing. True aficionados begin with a reasonably fit physique, plus a stylish wardrobe consisting of flip-flops, bikinis, wet suits, and such. Mastery of at least one beach skill—surfing, boogie boarding, kayaking, Frisbee tossing, or looking fab while catching rays—is also essential. As a visitor, though, you need only a swimsuit and some rented equipment for most sports. You can then hit the beach almost anywhere, thanks to the California belief in coastal access as a birthright. The farther south you go, the wider, sandier, and sunnier the beaches become; moving north they are rockier and foggier, with colder and rougher surf.

The Automobile

Americans may have a love affair with the automobile, but Californians have an out-and-out obsession. Even when gas prices rev up and freeway traffic slows down, their passion burns as hot as ever. You can witness this ardor any summer weekend at huge classic- and custom-car shows held statewide. Even better, you can feel it yourself by taking the wheel. Drive to the sea following Laguna Canyon Road to Laguna Beach; trace an old stagecoach route through the mountains above Santa Barbara on Highway 154; track migrating whales up the coast to Big Sur; or take 17-Mile Drive along the precipitous edge of the Monterey Peninsula. Glorious for the most part, but authentically congested in some areas in the south, Highway 1 runs almost the entire length of the state, hugging the coast most of the way.

Californians live in such a large and splashy state that they sometimes seem to forget about the rest of the country. They've developed a distinctive culture all their own, which you can delve into by doing as the locals do.

The Wine

If California were a country, it would rank as the world's fourth-largest wine producer, after Italy, France, and Spain. In those countries, where *vino* is barely considered an alcoholic beverage, wine drinking has evolved into a relaxing ritual best shared with friends and family. A modern, Americanized version of that mentality integrates wine into daily life in California, and there are many places to sample it. The Napa and Sonoma valleys come to mind first. But there are other destinations for oenophiles. You can find great wineries around Santa Barbara County, San Luis Obispo, Monterey Bay, Gold Country's Amador County, and the Inland Empire's Temecula Valley, too. All are respected appellations, and their winery tours and tastings will show you what all the buzz is about.

The Outdoors

One of California's greatest assets—the mild year-round weather enjoyed by most of the state—inspires residents to spend as much time outside as they possibly can. They have a tremendous enthusiasm for every imaginable outdoor sport, and, up north especially, fresh-air adventures are extremely popular (which may explain why everyone there seems to own at least one pair of hiking boots). But the California-alfresco creed is more broadly interpreted, and the general rule when planning any activity is "if it can happen outside, it will!" *Plein air* vacation opportunities include dining on patios, decks, and wharves; shopping in street markets or elaborate open-air malls; hearing almost any kind of music at moonlight concerts; touring the sculpture gardens that grace major art museums; and celebrating everything from gay pride to garlic at outdoor fairs.

IF YOU LIKE

One-of-a-Kind Accommodations

Hoteliers statewide have done their utmost to create accommodations that match the glories of the region's landscape, in the process creating lodgings that boast character as well as comfort. Some are unconventional, while others are genuine old-school gems.

Hotel Del Coronado, Coronado. A turreted beauty and veritable Victorian extravaganza, this spot inspired L. Frank Baum's description of Oz. Iconic architecture aside, Hotel Del Coronado is also famous as the filming locale for *Some Like It Hot*, and has hosted most of the U.S. presidents in the last century. Today it caters more to tour groups than Tinseltown stars, but fans remain loyal.

Mission Inn, Riverside. This sprawling Spanish colonial revival estate has welcomed a who's who of politicos. Ronald and Nancy Reagan spent their wedding night here, Richard and Pat Nixon were married in its chapel, and eight U.S. heads of state have patronized its Presidential Lounge.

Movie Colony Hotel, Palm Springs. Hollywood's 1930s heyday comes alive at this glamorous boutique hotel designed by Albert Frey, who created midcentury minimalism in Palm Springs. It now attracts a lively clientele and has a cool vibe.

Fairmont San Francisco, San Francisco. It got off to a shaky start (the 1906 earthquake delayed its opening by exactly a year), but this Nob Hill hotel has hosted groundbreaking events like the drafting of the United Nations Charter and Tony Bennett's debut of "I Left My Heart in San Francisco."

Off-the-Beaten-Path Adventures

Mother Nature has truly outdone herself in California. But at the state's most popular sites, it can be hard to approach her handiwork with a sense of awe when you're encircled by souvenir hawkers and camera-wielding tourists. Step off the beaten path, though, and all you'll be able to hear will be the echo of your own voice saying "wow."

Hiking. Steam is the theme at Lassen Volcanic National Park: especially along the 3-mile Bumpass Hell Trail, which has hot springs, steam vents, and mud pots. If you're looking for a cooler hiking experience (temperature-wise), it's hard to top the rugged beauty of Point Reyes National Seashore.

Climbing. Joshua Tree National Park is California's epicenter for rock climbing; within the park there are hundreds of formations and thousands of routes to choose from. No experience? No problem. J-Tree Outfitters offers crash courses for beginners.

Kayaking. Paddling around the lichen-covered sea caves of Channel Islands National Park or the surreal tufa towers of Mono Lake, you'll feel as if you're on another planet. But kayaking in San Francisco or La Jolla proves you needn't travel far to lose the mob.

Ballooning. Hot-air ballooning—whether over Wine Country, Temecula, Palm Desert, Mammoth Lakes, or Shasta Valley—lets you sightsee from a totally new perspective.

Amusement Parks

You're on vacation, so why not enjoy some carefree pleasures? For concentrated doses of old-fashioned fun, indulge in creaky waterfront amusements—like Musée Mécanique on San Francisco's Fisherman's Wharf and the antique carousel at Santa Monica Pier. Or opt for a full day at an over-the-top theme park.

Disneyland, Anaheim. Walt Disney set the gold standard for theme parks, and his original "magic kingdom" (the only one built during his lifetime) remains at the top of its class due to innovative rides, animatronics, and a liberal sprinkling of pixie dust.

LEGOLAND California, Carlsbad. Dedicated to the plastic bricks that have been a playtime staple for almost 60 years, this park has more than 50 LEGO-inspired attractions (including the popular Driving School, Fun Town Fire Academy, plus get-all-wet Splash Battle and Treasure Falls) and some 15,000 LEGO models ranging from teeny working taxis to a 9-foot-tall dinosaur.

San Diego Zoo Safari Park, Escondido. Get up close and personal with lions and tigers at this huge park where animals appear to be roaming free. You can feed a giraffe, talk to the gorillas, and track herds of elk as they cross the plain. Cheetahs bound, hippos huff, and zebras zip.

Santa Cruz Beach Boardwalk, Santa Cruz. Now well over 100 years old, the state's oldest amusement park is a sentimental favorite. Expect vintage rides (most notably a 1911 carousel and wooden roller coaster) alongside contemporary attractions, as well as corn dogs, cotton candy, and loads of kitsch.

Spas

Ancient Romans coined the word "spa" as an acronym for *solus per aqua* (or "health by water"). There's plenty of the wet stuff in the Golden State, yet California spas—like California kitchens—are known for making the most of any indigenous ingredient. The resulting treatments are at once distinctive, decadent, and most important, relaxing.

The Golden Door, Escondido. Relax and renew at this destination spa tucked into a secluded canyon north of San Diego. Serenity and simplicity rule here, where every moment reflects its Zen-like ambience.

Glen Ivy Hot Springs Spa, Corona. Forget Club Med; in the Inland Empire, it's Club Mud that counts. The outdoor bath at this historic day spa couples red clay from Temescal Canyon with naturally heated, mineral-rich water from its own thermal springs.

Post Ranch Inn & Spa, Big Sur. Like its organic architecture, this luxe retreat's spa treatments are designed to capture the tone of Big Sur—case in point, the Crystal and Gemstone Therapy. It combines Native American tradition (a ceremonial burning of sage) with an aromatherapy massage that employs jade collected from nearby beaches and essences of local wildflowers.

Spa Terra, Napa. While other Wine Country spas often overlook vineyards, the one at the new Meritage Resort occupies an estate cave 40 feet below them. Appropriately, the facility specializes in vinotherapy treatments incorporating—you guessed it—the fruit of the vine.

GREAT ITINERARIES

SOUTHERN CALIFORNIA WITH KIDS, 7 DAYS

SoCal offers many opportunities to entertain the kids beyond the Magic Kingdom. LEGOLAND is a blast for kids 12 and under, and families can't beat SeaWorld, the San Diego Zoo, and San Diego's historic Old Town.

Day 1–2: Disneyland

Get out of Los Angeles International Airport as fast as you can. Pick up your rental car and head south on the I–405 freeway, which can be congested day or night, toward Orange County and **Disneyland.** Skirt the lines at the box office with advance-purchased tickets in hand and storm the gates of the Magic Kingdom. You can cram the highlights into a single day, but if you get a two-day ticket and stay the night you can see the parade and visit **Downtown Disney** before heading south. Highway 39, just west of Disneyland will take you all the way to the coast, just south of surfer's haven at **Huntington Beach,** where you can spend the night in one of several beachfront hotels.

Day 3: LEGOLAND

Get an early start for your next roller-coaster ride at **LEGOLAND**, about an hour's drive south of Huntington Beach via the Pacific Coast Highway. Check into newly opened **LEGOLAND Hotel** or the **Sheraton Carlsbad Resort & Spa;** both offer direct access to the park. LEGOLAND has a water park and aquarium in addition to the LEGO-based rides, shows, and roller coasters. The little ones can live out their fairy-tale fantasies and bigger ones can spend all day on waterslides, shooting water pistols, driving boats, or water fighting with pirates.

TIPS

No matter how carefully you plan your movements to avoid busy routes at peak hours, you will inevitably encounter heavy traffic in L.A., Orange County, and San Diego. All these itineraries start at LAX. If your plans include a trip from L.A. to San Diego or O.C., you can save time (and maybe money) by booking your flight to L.A. and returning from San Diego, O.C., P.S., or LA/Ontario.

Allow yourself twice as much time as you think you'll need to negotiate LAX.

Day 4: La Jolla and San Diego

Take a leisurely drive south to San Diego by using the "old road," the original Pacific Coast Highway that hugs the shore all the way. It's a slow drive through Leucadia, Encinitas, Solana Beach, and Del Mar, all of which are popular surfing beaches. When you get to **La Jolla,** swing around the cove to see one of the area's most beautiful beaches. Look, but don't go in the water at the children's pool, as it's likely to be filled with barking seals. The **Birch Aquarium at Scripps** here offers a look at how scientists study the oceans.

Hop onto I–5 and head for Downtown **San Diego.** Go straight for the city's nautical heart by exploring the restored ships of the **Maritime Museum** at the waterfront in Downtown. Victorian buildings—and plenty of other tourists—surround you on a stroll through the **Gaslamp Quarter,** but the 21st century is in full swing at the **Westfield Horton Plaza** retail and entertainment complex. Plant yourself at a Downtown hotel and graze your way through the neighborhood's many restaurants.

Los Angeles
405
39 Anaheim
Disneyland
Huntington Beach
Joshua Tree
National Park
Twenty Nine Palms
Palm Springs
10
86S
Salton
Sea
Borrego
Springs
86
Catalina
Island
Carlsbad LEGOLAND
Leucadia
Encinitas
Solana Beach
Del Mar
La Jolla
Sea World/
Old Town
San Diego/
San Diego Zoo
78
Anza-Borrego Desert
State Park
PACIFIC
OCEAN
MEXICO

Day 5: San Diego Zoo

Malayan tapirs in a faux-Asian rain forest, polar bears in an imitation Arctic, and pandas frolicking in the trees— the **San Diego Zoo** maintains a vast and varied collection of creatures in a world-renowned facility comprised of meticulously designed habitats. Come early, wear comfy shoes, and stay as long as you like.

Day 6: SeaWorld and Old Town

Resistance is futile: you're going to **SeaWorld**. So what if it screams commercial? This humongous theme park, with its walk-through shark tanks and killer-whale shows, also screams fun. Surrender to the experience and try not to sit in anything sticky. Also touristy, but with genuine historical significance, **Old Town** drips with Mexican and early Californian heritage. Soak it up in the plaza at **Old Town San Diego State Historic Park;** have a bite at one of the Mexican restaurants here, then browse the stalls and shops at **Fiesta de Reyes** and along San Diego Avenue.

Day 7: Departure from San Diego or Los Angeles

Pack up your Mouseketeer gear and give yourself ample time to reach the airport. San Diego International Airport lies within a 10-minute drive from Old Town. Although you'll be driving on freeways the entire way to LAX, traffic is always heavy and you should plan for a full day to get there.

PALM SPRINGS AND THE DESERT, 5 DAYS

The Palm Springs area is paradise for many. Most go for more than a good tan or to play golf on championship courses. Expect fabulous and funky spas, a dog-friendly atmosphere, and sparkling stars at night.

Day 1: Palm Springs

Freeway traffic permitting, you can drive from the middle of L.A. to the middle of the desert in a couple of hours. Somehow in harmony with the harsh environment, midcentury-modern homes and businesses with clean, low-slung lines define the **Palm Springs** style. Although the desert cities comprise a trendy destination with beautiful hotels, fabulous multicultural food, abundant nightlife, and plenty of culture, a quiet atmosphere prevails. The city seems far away when you hike in hushed **Tahquitz** or **Indian Canyon;** cliffs and palm trees shelter rock art, irrigation works, and other remnants of Agua Caliente culture. If your boots aren't

made for walking, you can always practice your golf game or indulge in some sublime or funky spa treatments at an area resort instead.

Day 2: Explore Palm Springs
If riding a tram up an 8,516-foot mountain for a stroll or even a snowball fight above the desert sounds like fun to you, then show up at the **Palm Springs Aerial Tramway** before the first morning tram leaves (later, the line can get discouragingly long). Afterward stroll through the **Palm Springs Art Museum** where you can see a shimmering display of contemporary studio glass, an array of enormous Native American baskets, and significant works of 20th-century sculpture by Henry Moore and others. After all that walking you may be ready for an early dinner. Nearly every restaurant in Palm Springs offers a happy hour, when you can sip a cocktail and nosh on a light entrée, usually for half price. Using your hotel as a base, take a few day trips to discover the natural beauty of the desert.

Day 3: Joshua Tree National Park
Due to its proximity to Los Angeles and the highway between Las Vegas and coastal cities, **Joshua Tree** is one of the most popular and accessible of the national parks. It's about an hour northeast of Palm Springs. You can see most of it in a day, entering the park at the town of Joshua Tree, exploring sites along **Park Boulevard**, and exiting at **Twentynine Palms**. With its signature trees, piles of rocks, glorious spring wildflowers, starlit skies, and colorful pioneer history, the experience is a bit more like the Wild West than Sahara sand dunes.

Day 4: Anza-Borrego Desert State Park and the Salton Sea
There are two worthwhile destinations about two hours south and east of the Palm Springs area, Salton Sea and Anza-Borrego State Park. The **Salton Sea**, about 60 miles south of Palm Springs via I–10 and Highway 86S, is one of the largest inland seas on earth. A new sea, formed by the flooding of the Colorado River in 1905, it attracts thousands of migrating birds and bird-watchers every fall. **Anza-Borrego Desert State Park** is the largest state park in California, with 600,000 acres of mostly untouched wilderness; it offers one of the best spring-wildflower displays in California and also displays a large collection of life-size bronze sculpture of animals that roamed this space millions of years ago. **Borrego Springs**, a tiny hamlet, lies in the center of it all. The desert is home to an archeological site, where scientists continue to uncover remnants of prehistoric animals ranging from mastodons to horses.

Day 5: Return to L.A.
If you intend to depart from LAX, plan for a full day of driving from the desert to the airport. Be prepared for heavy traffic at any time of day or night. If possible, opt to fly out of Palm Springs International or LA/Ontario International Airport instead.

HOORAY FOR HOLLYWOOD, 4 DAYS

If you are a movie fan, there's no better place to see it all than L.A. Always keep your eyes out for a familiar face: you never know when you might spot a celebrity.

Day 1: Los Angeles

As soon as you land at LAX, make like a local and hit the freeway. Even if L.A.'s top-notch art, history, and science museums don't tempt you, the hodgepodge of art deco, Beaux-Arts, and futuristic architecture begs at least a drive-by. Heading east from Santa Monica, Wilshire Boulevard cuts through a historical and cultural cross section of the city. Two stellar sights on its Miracle Mile are the encyclopedic **Los Angeles County Museum of Art** and the fossil-filled **La Brea Tar Pits.** Come evening, the open-air **Farmers Market** and its many eateries hum. Hotels in Beverly Hills or West Hollywood beckon, just a few minutes away.

Day 2: Hollywood and the Movie Studios

Every L.A. tourist should devote at least one day to the movies and take at least one studio tour in the San Fernando Valley. For fun, choose the special-effects theme park at **Universal Studios Hollywood;** for the nitty-gritty, choose **Warner Bros. Studios.** Nostalgic musts in Hollywood include the **Walk of Fame** along **Hollywood Boulevard** and the celebrity footprints cast in concrete outside **Grauman's Chinese Theatre.** When evening arrives, the Hollywood scene boasts a bevy of trendy restaurants and nightclubs.

Day 3 and 4: Beverly Hills and Santa Monica

Even without that extensive art collection, the **Getty Center's** pavilion architecture, hilltop gardens, and frame-worthy L.A. views make it a dazzling destination. Descend to the sea via Santa Monica Boulevard for lunch along **Third Street Promenade,** followed by a ride on the historic carousel on the pier. The buff and the bizarre meet at **Venice Beach Oceanfront Walk** (strap on some Rollerblades if you want to join them!). **Rodeo Drive** in Beverly Hills specializes in exhibitionism with a heftier price tag, but voyeurs are still welcome.

Splurge on breakfast or brunch at a posh café in the **Farmers Market,** then stroll through aisles and aisles of gorgeous produce and specialty food before you take a last look at the Pacific Ocean through the camera obscura at **Palisades Park** in Santa Monica.

SIERRA RICHES: YOSEMITE, GOLD COUNTRY, AND TAHOE, 10 DAYS

This tour will show you why Tony Bennett left his heart in San Francisco. It also includes some of the most beautiful places in a very scenic state, plus gold-rush-era history, and a chance to hike a trail or two.

Day 1: San Francisco

Straight from the airport, drop your bags at the lighthearted **Hotel Monaco** near **Union Square** and request a goldfish for your room. A Union Square stroll packs a wallop of people-watching, window-shopping, and architecture viewing. **Chinatown,** chock-full of dim sum shops, storefront temples, and open-air markets, promises unfamiliar tastes for lunch. Catch a Powell Street **cable car** to the end of the line and get off to see the bay views and the antique arcade games at **Musée Mécanique,** the hidden gem of otherwise mindless **Fisherman's Wharf.** No need to go any farther than cosmopolitan North Beach for cocktail hour, dinner, and live music.

Day 2: Golden Gate Park

In **Golden Gate Park,** linger amid the flora of the **Conservatory of Flowers** and the **San Francisco Botanical Garden at Strybing Arboretum,** soak up some art at the **de Young Museum,** and find serene refreshment at the **San Francisco Japanese Tea Garden.** The Pacific surf pounds the cliffs below the **Legion of Honor** art museum, which has an exquisite view of the **Golden Gate Bridge—** when the fog stays away. Sunset cocktails at the circa-1909 **Cliff House** include a prospect over Seal Rock (actually occupied by sea lions). Eat dinner elsewhere: Pacific Heights, the Mission, and SoMa teem with excellent restaurants.

Day 3: Into the High Sierra

First thing in the morning, pick up your rental car and head for the hills. A five-hour drive due east brings you to **Yosemite National Park,** where **Bridalveil Fall** and **El Capitan,** the 350-story granite monolith, greet you on your way to **Yosemite Village.** Ditch the car and pick up information and refreshment before hopping on the year-round shuttle to explore. Justly famous sights cram Yosemite Valley: massive **Half Dome** and **Sentinel Dome,** thundering **Yosemite Falls,** and wispy **Ribbon Fall** and **Nevada Fall.** Invigorating short hikes off the shuttle route lead to numerous vantage points. Celebrate your arrival in one of the world's most sublime spots with dinner in the dramatic **Ahwahnee Hotel Dining Room** and stay the night there (reserve well in advance).

Day 4: Yosemite National Park

Ardent hikers consider **John Muir Trail to Half Dome** a must-do, tackling the rigorous 12-hour round-trip to the top of Half Dome in search of life-changing vistas. The merely mortal hike downhill from Glacier Point on Four-Mile Trail or **Panorama Trail,** the latter an all-day trek past waterfalls. Less demanding still is a drive to Wawona for a stroll in the **Mariposa Grove of Big Trees** and lunch at the 19th-century **Wawona Hotel Dining Room.** In bad weather, take shelter in the Ansel Adams Gallery and Yosemite Museum; in fair conditions, drive up to **Glacier Point** for a breathtaking sunset view.

Day 5: Gold Country South

Highway 49 traces the mother lode that yielded many fortunes in gold in the 1850s and 1860s. Step into a living gold-rush town at **Columbia State Historic Park,** where you can ride a stagecoach and pan for riches. **Sutter Creek's** well-preserved downtown bursts with shopping opportunities, but the vintage goods displayed at **Monteverde Store Museum** are not for sale. A different sort of vintage powers the present-day bonanza of **Shenandoah Valley,** heart of the Sierra Foothills Wine Country. Taste your way through Rhône-style blended Zinfandels and Syrahs at boutique wineries such as **Shenandoah Vineyards** and **Sobon Estate.** Amador City's 1879 **Imperial Hotel** places you firmly in the past for the night.

Day 6: Gold Country North

In **Placerville,** a mineshaft invites investigation at **Hangtown's Gold Bug Mine,** while **Marshall Gold Discovery State Historic Park** encompasses most of **Coloma** and preserves the spot where James Marshall's 1849 find set off the California gold rush. Old Town **Auburn,** with its museums and courthouse, makes a good lunch stop, but if you hold out until you reach Grass Valley you can try authentic miners' pasties. A tour of **Empire Mine State Historic Park** takes you into a mine, and a few miles away horse-drawn carriages ply the narrow, shop-lined streets

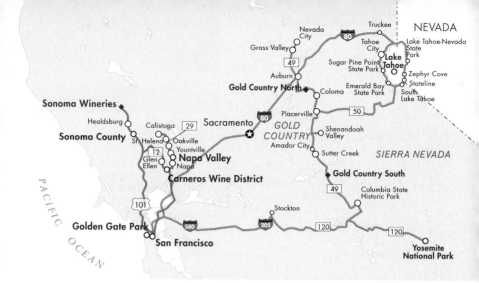

of downtown **Nevada City**. Both Nevada City and **Grass Valley** hold a collection of bed-and-breakfast inns that date back to gold-rush days. For more contemporary accommodations backtrack to Auburn or Placerville.

Day 7: Lake Tahoe

Jewel-like **Lake Tahoe** is a straight shot east of Placerville on Highway 50; stop for picnic provisions in commercial **South Lake Tahoe**. A stroll past the three magnificent estates in **Pope-Baldwin Recreation Area** hints at the sumptuous lakefront summers once enjoyed by the elite. High above a glittering cove, **Emerald Bay State Park** offers one of the best lake views as well as a steep hike down to (and back up from) **Vikingsholm**, a replica 9th-century Scandinavian castle. Another fine, old mansion—plus a nature preserve and many hiking trails—lies in **Sugar Pine Point State Park**. Tahoe City offers more history and ample dining and lodging choices.

Day 8: Exploring Lake Tahoe

The picture-perfect beaches and bays of **Lake Tahoe–Nevada State Park** line the Nevada shoreline, a great place to bask in the sun or go mountain biking. For a different perspective of the lake, get out on the azure water aboard the sternwheeler MS *Dixie II* from **Zephyr Cove**. In South Lake Tahoe, another view unfurls as the **Heavenly Gondola** travels 2½ miles up a mountain. Keep your adrenaline pumping into the evening with some action at the massive casinos clustered in Stateline, Nevada.

Day 9: Return to San Francisco

After a long (five hours) morning of driving, return your rental car in San Francisco and soak up some more urban excitement. Good options include a late lunch at the **Ferry Building,** followed by a visit to the **San Francisco Museum of Modern Art,** or lunch in **Japantown** followed by shopping in **Pacific Heights**. People-watching excels in the late afternoon bustle of the **Castro** and the **Haight**. Say good-bye to Northern California at one of the plush lounges or trendy bars in the downtown hotels.

Day 10: Departure

Check the weather and your flight information before you start out for the airport: Fog sometimes causes delays at SFO. On a clear day, your flight path might give you one last fabulous glimpse of the City by the Bay.

THE ULTIMATE WINE TRIP, 5 DAYS

In these five days of wine tasting, you'll have a chance to see legendary wineries that produce well-known brands, stay in lovely hotels with knowledgeable hosts, and dine at restaurants operated by celebrity chefs.

Day 1: Sonoma County

Begin your wine tour in **Healdsburg,** about 65 miles north of San Francisco on Highway 101. Healdsburg was named one of the Top Small Towns in America by Fodor's editors in 2013 for its charming atmosphere, great restaurants, and lovely B&Bs. The best choices to overnight at are **The Honor Mansion** or **Hôtel Les Mars.** Take your pick of the trendy restaurants that ring the plaza. Stellar choices are **Scopa** and **Spoonbar.** End the day with a stroll around the plaza.

Day 2: Sonoma Wineries

You won't have to travel far to begin your day of wine tasting. Many local wineries have tasting rooms within walking distance of Healdsburg Plaza. You'll find some of the most interesting wineries in the countryside surrounding the town, including **Preston Vineyards, Francis Ford Coppola Winery,** and **Dry Creek Vineyard.** All produce wonderful Cabernet Sauvignon, Chardonnay, and Zinfandel. Most have picnic areas where you can savor a bite while sampling the grape. In the afternoon head south on Highway 101 to scenic Highway 12. Take a break at **Glen Ellen** to visit **Jack London State Historic Park,** the memorabilia-filled home of the famed writer.

Day 3: Napa Valley

Plan to spend two nights in the same lodging in the **Napa Valley,** in the city of **Napa** or a few miles north in **Yountville.** For your Day 3 tasting schedule head north to **Saint Helena,** which has the largest concentration of wineries, like the **Beringer Vineyards, John Phelps Vineyards,** and **Spring Mountain Vineyard,** and most of the well-known names in the region plus the **Culinary Institute of America** and **Wine Spectator Greystone Restaurant.** Yountville has **V Marketplace** where you'll find **Napa-Style,** a luxury food market and deli, and celebrity chef Michael Chiarello's **Bottega** restaurant.

Day 4: North on Hwy 29

After breakfast, head north on Highway 29 to **Oakville,** home of the oldest continually operating grocery store in California, the **Oakville Grocery. Calistoga,** a few miles up the road, dates back more than 100 years and is known for its hot-spring spas. Robert Louis Stevenson and his bride spent their honeymoon in 1880 here. Head south for dinner at one of the Napa Valley's celebrity restaurants.

Day 5: Carneros to San Francisco

Your final day in the Wine Country includes a couple of stops in the Carneros Wine District on the way back to San Francisco. Stop at **Domaine Carneros,** a Taittinger brand that creates perfectly dry sparkling wine in the French tradition. The art-stuffed **di Rosa** preserve nearby is worth a stop as well. Give yourself plenty of time to get to your departure airport; traffic is generally heavy as you close in on the Bay Area.

CALIFORNIA MADE EASY

I'm not particularly active. Will I still enjoy visiting a national park? Absolutely. The most popular parks really do have something for everyone. Take Yosemite. When the ultrafit embark on 12-hour trail treks, mere mortals can hike Cook's Meadow—an easy 1-mile loop that's also wheelchair accessible. If even that seems too daunting, you can hop on a free shuttle or drive yourself to sites like Glacier Point or the Mariposa Grove of Giant Sequoias.

What's the single best place to take the kids? Well, that depends on your children's ages and interests, but for its sheer smorgasbord of activities, San Diego is hard to beat. Between the endless summer weather and sites such as SeaWorld, the San Diego Zoo, and LEGOLAND (about 30 minutes away), California's southernmost city draws families in droves. Once you've covered the mega-attractions, enjoy an easy-to-swallow history lesson in Old Town or the Maritime Museum. Want to explore different ecosystems? La Jolla Cove has kid-friendly tidal pools and cliff caves, while Anza-Borrego Desert State Park is a doable two-hour drive east.

If you're traveling in Northern California, San Francisco is also chockablock with kid-friendly attractions. A cable-car ride is a no-brainer—but if you have a Thomas the Tank engine fan in tow, be sure to also take a spin on the historic F-line trolleys. Other classic kid-friendly SF sights include the Exploratorium, the San Francisco Zoo, Alcatraz, the Ferry Building, and the California Academy of Sciences. Take the kids for dim sum in Chinatown; odds are they'll enjoy picking their dishes from a rolling buffet filled with foods they've likely never seen before. Or head to Musée Mécanique to see what kids played (way) before Nintendo's Wii came out.

That said, there are kid-friendly attractions all over the state—your kids are going to have to try really hard to be bored.

California sounds expensive. How can I save on sightseeing? CityPass (☎ *888/330–5008* ⊕ *www.citypass.com*) includes admission and some upgrades for main attractions in San Francisco, Hollywood, and Southern California (Disneyland, Universal Studios, San Diego Zoo/Safari Park, LEGOLAND, and SeaWorld). Also, many museums set aside free-admission days. Prefer the great outdoors? An $80 America the Beautiful annual pass (☎ *888/275–8747* ⊕ *www.nps.gov*) admits you to every site under the National Park Service umbrella. Better yet, depending on the property, passengers in your vehicle get in free, too.

Any tips for a first-time trip into the desert? The desert's stark, sun-blasted beauty will strip your mind of everyday clutter. But it is a brutal, punishing place for anyone ill-prepared. So whether it's your first or 15th visit, the same do's and don'ts apply. Stick to a state or national park. Pick up pamphlets at its visitor center and follow the instructions they set out. Note that your cell phone may not work. Keep your gas tank full. Bring lots of water and drink at least two gallons a day—even if you're not thirsty. Wear a hat and sunscreen, and don't expect to move too fast at midday when the sun is kiln-hot.

THE ULTIMATE ROAD TRIP

CALIFORNIA'S LEGENDARY HIGHWAY 1

by Cheryl Crabtree

One of the world's most scenic drives, California's State Route 1 (also known as Highway 1, the Pacific Coast Highway, the PCH) stretches along the edge of the state for nearly 660 miles, from Southern California's Dana Point to its northern terminus near Leggett, about 40 miles north of Fort Bragg. As you travel south to north, the water's edge transitions from long, sandy beaches and low-lying bluffs to towering dunes, craggy cliffs, and ancient redwood groves. The ocean changes as well; the relatively tame and surfable swells lapping the Southern California shore give way to the frigid, powerful waves crashing against weatherbeaten rocks in the north.

HIGHWAY 1 TOP 10

- Santa Monica
- Santa Barbara
- Hearst San Simeon State Historical Monument
- Big Sur
- Carmel
- 17–Mile Drive
- Monterey
- San Francisco
- Marin Headlands
- Point Reyes National Seashore

Give yourself lots of extra time to pull off the road and enjoy the scenery

STARTING YOUR JOURNEY

You may decide to drive the road's entire 660-mile route, or bite off a smaller piece. In either case, a Highway 1 road trip allows you to experience California at your own pace, stopping when and where you wish. Hike a beachside trail, dig your toes in the sand, and search for creatures in the tidepools. Buy some artichokes and strawberries from a roadside farmstand. Talk to people along the way (you'll run into everyone from soul-searching meditators, farmers, and beatniks to city-slackers and working-class folks), and take lots of pictures. Don't rush—you could easily spend a lifetime discovering secret spots along this route.

To help you plan your trip, we've broken the road into three regions (Santa Monica to Carmel, Carmel to San Francisco, and San Francisco to Fort Bragg); each region is then broken up into smaller segments—many of which are suitable for a day's drive. If you're pressed for time, you can always tackle a section of Highway 1, and then head inland to U.S. 101 or I-5 to reach your next destination more quickly.

WHAT'S IN A NAME?

Though it's often referred to as the Pacific Coast Highway (or PCH), sections of Highway 1 actually have different names. The southernmost section (Dana Point to Oxnard) is the Pacific Coast Highway. After that, the road becomes the Cabrillo Highway (Las Cruces to Lompoc), the Big Sur Coast Highway (San Luis Obispo County line to Monterey), the North Coast Scenic Byway (San Luis Obispo city limit to the Monterey County line), the Cabrillo Highway again (Santa Cruz County line to Half Moon Bay), and finally the Shoreline Highway (Marin City to Leggett). To make matters more confusing, smaller chunks of the road have additional honorary monikers.

Just follow the green triangular signs that say "California 1."

HIGHWAY 1 DRIVING

- Rent a convertible. (You will not regret it.)
- Begin the drive north from Santa Monica, where congestion and traffic delays pose less of a problem.
- Take advantage of turnouts. Let cars pass you as you take in the ocean view and snap a picture.
- Mind your manners: Don't tailgate or glare at other drivers.
- If you're prone to motion sickness, take the wheel yourself. Focusing on the landscape outside should help you feel less queasy.
- If you're afraid of heights, drive from south to north so you'll be on the mountain rather than the cliff side of the road.
- Driving PCH is glorious during winter, but check weather conditions before you go as landslides are frequent after storms.

HIGHWAY 1: SANTA MONICA TO BIG SUR

Hearst Castle

SANTA MONICA TO MALIBU (approx. 26 mi)
Highway 1 begins in Dana point, but it seems more appropriate to begin a PCH adventure in **Santa Monica.** Be sure to experience the beach culture, then balance the tacky pleasures of Santa Monica's amusement pier with a stylish dinner in a neighborhood restaurant.

MALIBU TO SANTA BARBARA (approx. 70 mi)
The PCH follows the curve of Santa Monica Bay all the way to **Malibu** and **Point Mugu,**

near **Oxnard.** Chances are you'll experience *déjà vu* driving this 27-mile stretch: mountains on one side, ocean on the other, opulent homes perched on hillsides; you've seen this piece of coast countless times on TV and film. Be sure to walk out on the **Malibu Pier** for a great photo opp, then check out **Surfrider Beach,** with three famous points where perfect waves ignited a worldwide surfing rage in the 1960s. After Malibu you'll drive through miles of protected, largely unpopulated coastline. Ride a wave at **Zuma Beach**, scout for offshore whales at **Point Dume State Beach,** or hike the trails at **Point Mugu State Park.** After skirting Point Mugu, Highway 1 merges with U.S. 101 for about 70 mi before reaching **Santa Barbara.** A mini-tour of the city includes a real Mexican lunch at **La Super-Rica,** a visit to the magnificent Spanish **Mission Santa Barbara,** and a walk down hopping **State Street to Stearns Wharf.**

SANTA BARBARA TO SAN SIMEON (approx. 147 mi)
North of Santa Barbara, Highway 1 morphs into the Cabrillo Highway, separating

Santa Barbara

from and then rejoining U.S. 101. The route winds through rolling vineyards and rangeland to **San Luis Obispo,** where any legit road trip includes a photo stop at the quirky **Madonna Inn.** Be sure to also climb the humungous dunes at **Guadalupe-Nipomo Dunes Preserve.**

In downtown San Luis Obispo, the **Mission San Luis Obispo de Tolosa** stands by a tree-shaded creek edged with shops and cafés. Highway 1 continues to **Morro Bay** and up the coast. About 4 mi north of Morro Bay, you'll reach **Cayucos,** a classic old California beach town with an 1875 pier, restaurants, taverns, and shops in historic buildings. The road continues through **Cambria** to solitary **Hearst San Simeon State Historical Monument**—the art-filled pleasure palace at **San Simeon.** Just four miles north of the castle, elephant seals grunt and cavort at the

Santa Monica

Big Sur

TOP 5 PLACES TO LINGER

- Point Dume State Beach
- Santa Barbara
- Hearst San Simeon State Historical Monument
- Big Sur/Julia Pfeiffer Burns State Park
- Carmel

Piedras Blancas Elephant Seal Rookery, just off the side of the road.

SAN SIMEON TO CARMEL (approx. 92 mi) Heading north, you'll drive through **Big Sur,** a place of ancient forests and rugged shoreline stretching 90 mi from San Simeon to **Carmel.** Much of Big Sur lies within several state parks and the 165,000-acre **Ventana Wilderness,** itself part of the **Los Padres National Forest.** This famously scenic stretch of the coastal drive, which twists up and down bluffs above the ocean, can last hours. Take your time.

At **Julia Pfeiffer Burns State Park** one easy but rewarding hike leads to an iconic waterfall off a beach-front cliff. When you reach lovely **Carmel,** stroll around the picture-perfect town's mission, galleries, and shops.

HIGHWAY 1: CARMEL TO SAN FRANCISCO

San Francisco

Davenport cliffs, Devenport

THE PLAN

Distance: approx. 123 mi

Time: 2-4 days

Good Overnight Options: Carmel, Monterey, Santa Cruz, Half Moon Bay, San Francisco

For more information on the sights and attractions along this portion of Highway 1, please see chapters Monterey Bay, San Francisco, and Bay Area.

CARMEL TO MONTEREY
(approx. 4 mi)
Between **Carmel** and **Monterey,** Highway 1 cuts across the base of the Monterey Peninsula. Pony up the toll and take a brief detour to follow famous **17-Mile Drive,** which traverses a surf-pounded landscape of cypress trees, sea lions, gargantuan estates, and the world famous **Pebble Beach Golf Links.** Take your time here as well, and be sure to allow lots of time for pulling off to enjoy the gorgeous views.

If you have the time, spend a day checking out the sights in **Monterey,** especially the kelp forests and bat rays of the **Monterey Bay Aquarium** and the adobes and artifacts of **Monterey State Historic Park.**

MONTEREY TO SANTA CRUZ (approx. 42 mi)
From Monterey the highway rounds the gentle curve of Monterey Bay, passing through sand dunes and artichoke fields on its way to **Moss Landing** and the **Elkhorn Slough National Estuarine Marine Preserve.** Kayak near or walk through the protected wetlands here, or board a pontoon safari boat—don't forget your binoculars. The historic seaside villages of **Aptos, Capitola,** and **Soquel,** just off the highway near the bay's midpoint, are ideal stopovers for beachcombing, antiquing, and hiking through redwoods. In boho **Santa Cruz,** just 7 mi north, walk along the **wharf,** ride the historic roller coaster on the **boardwalk,** and perch on the cliffs to watch surfers peel through tubes at **Steamer Lane.**

SANTA CRUZ TO SAN FRANCISCO (approx. 77 mi)
Highway 1 hugs the ocean's edge once again as it departs Santa Cruz and runs

northward past a string of secluded beaches and small towns. Stop and stretch your legs in the tiny, artsy town of **Davenport,** where you can wander through several galleries and enjoy sumptuous views from the bluffs. At **Año Nuevo State Park,** walk down to the dunes to view gargantuan elephant

FRIGID WATERS

If you're planning to jump in the ocean in Northern California, wear a wetsuit or prepare to shiver. Even in summer, the water temperatures warm up to just barely tolerable. The fog tends to burn off earlier in the day at relatively sheltered beaches near Monterey Bay's midpoint, near Aptos, Capitola and Santa Cruz. These beaches also tend to attract softer waves than those on the bay's outer edges.

Half Moon Bay

TOP 5 PLACES
TO LINGER

- 17-Mile Drive
- Monterey
- Santa Cruz
- Año Nuevo State
  Reserve
- Half Moon Bay

seals lounging on shore,
then break for a meal or
snack in **Pescadero** or **Half
Moon Bay.**

From Half Moon Bay to **Daly
City,** the road includes a
number of shoulderless
twists and turns that de-
mand slower speeds and
nerves of steel. Signs of
urban development soon appear: mansions holding fast
to Pacific cliffs and then, as
the road veers slightly inland
to merge with Skyline Boulevard, boxlike houses sprawling across **Daly City** and
South San Francisco.

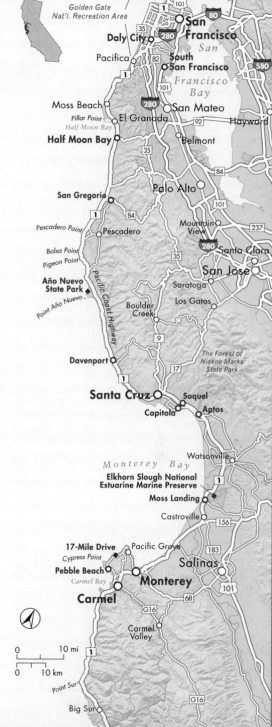

HIGHWAY 1: SAN FRANCISCO TO FORT BRAGG

Mendocino Coast Botanical Garden

THE PLAN

Distance: 177 mi

Time: 2-4 days

Good Overnight Options: San Francisco, Olema, Bodega Bay, Gualala, Mendocino, Fort Bragg

For more information on the sights and attractions along this portion of Highway 1, please see San Francisco, Bay Area, and North Coast chapters

SAN FRANCISCO

The official Highway 1 heads straight through **San Francisco** along 19th Avenue through **Golden Gate Park** and the **Presidio** toward the **Golden Gate Bridge.** For a more scenic tour, watch for signs announcing exits for 35 North/Skyline Boulevard, then Ocean Beach/The Great Highway (past Lake Merced). The Great Highway follows the coast along the western border of San Francisco; you'll cruise past entrances to the **San Francisco Zoo, Golden Gate Park,** and the **Cliff**

Golden Gate Bridge

House. Hike out to **Point Lobos** or **Land's End** for awesome vistas, then drive through **Lincoln Park** and the **Palace of the Legion of Honor** and follow El Camino del Mar/Lincoln Boulevard all the way to the Golden Gate Bridge.

The best way to see San Francisco is on foot and public transportation. A **Union Square** stroll—complete with people-watching, window-shopping, and architecture-viewing—is a good first stop. In **Chinatown,** department stores give way to storefront temples, open-air markets, and delightful dim-sum shops. After lunch in one, catch a **Powell Street cable car** to the end of the line and get off to see the bay views and the antique arcade games at **Musée Mécanique** (the gem of otherwise mindless **Fisherman's Wharf**). For dinner and live music, try cosmopolitan **North Beach.**

SAN FRANCISCO TO OLEMA

(approx. 37 mi)

Leaving the city the next day, your drive across the Golden Gate Bridge and a stop at a **Marin Headlands** overlook will yield memorable views (if fog hasn't socked in the bay). So will a hike in **Point Reyes National Seashore,** farther up Highway 1 (now

Point Reyes National Seashore

called Shoreline Highway). On this wild swath of coast you'll likely be able to claim an unspoiled beach for yourself. You should expect company, however, around the lighthouse at the tip of Point Reyes because year-round views—and seasonal elephant seal- and whale-watching—draw crowds. If you have time, poke around tiny **Olema,** which has some excellent restaurants, and is home to the historic Olema Inn & Restaurant.

OLEMA TO MENDOCINO

(approx. 131 mi)

Passing only a few minuscule towns, this next stretch of Highway 1 showcases the northern coast in all its rugged glory. The reconstructed compound of eerily foreign buildings at **Fort Ross State Historic Park** recalls the era of Russian fur trading in California. Pull into **Gualala** for an espresso, a sandwich, and a little human contact

Point Reyes National Seashore

TOP 5 PLACES TO LINGER

- San Francisco
- Marin Headlands
- Point Reyes National Seashore
- Fort Ross State Historic Park
- Mendocino

before rolling onward. After another 50 mi of tranquil state beaches and parks you'll return to civilization in **Mendocino**.

MENDOCINO TO FORT BRAGG

(approx. 9 mi)

Exploring Mendocino you may feel like you've fallen through a rabbit hole: the weather screams Northern California, but the 19th-century buildings—erected by homesick Yankee loggers—definitely say New England. Once you've browsed around the artsy shops, continue on to the **Mendocino Coast Botanical Gardens;** then travel back in time on the **Skunk Train,** which follows an old logging route from **Fort Bragg** deep into the redwood forest.

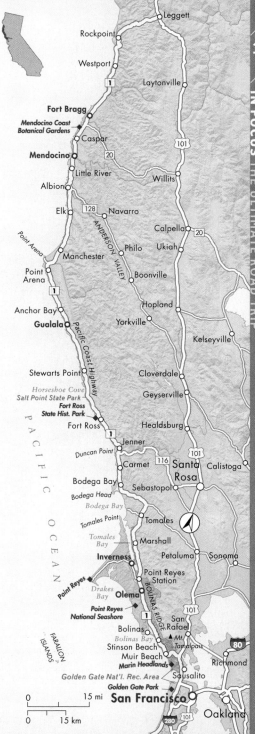

Leggett
Rockpoint
Westport
Laytonville
1
Fort Bragg
Mendocino Coast
Botanical Gardens
Caspar
101
Mendocino
20
Little River
Willits
Albion
Elk
128
Navarro
Calpella
20
Point Arena
Philo
Ukiah
Manchester
ANDERSON VALLEY
Boonville
Point Arena
1
Hopland
Anchor Bay
Yorkville
Gualala
Pacific Coast Highway
Kelseyville
Stewarts Point
Cloverdale
Horseshoe Cove
Salt Point State Park
Geyserville
Fort Ross State Hist. Park
Fort Ross
1
Healdsburg
PACIFIC
Jenner
Duncan Point
101
Carmet
116
Santa Rosa
Calistoga
Bodega Bay
Sebastopol
Bodega Head
Bodega Bay
Tomales Point
Tomales
OCEAN
Tomales Bay
Marshall
Inverness
Petaluma
Sonoma
Point Reyes Station
Point Reyes
BOLINAS RIDGE
Drakes Bay
Olema
101
Point Reyes National Seashore
Bolinas
San Rafael
FARALLON ISLANDS
Bolinas Bay
Mt. Tamalpais
Stinson Beach
Richmond
Muir Beach
Marin Headlands
80
Golden Gate Nat'l. Rec. Area
Sausalito
Golden Gate Park
San Francisco
Oakland
280
101

0   15 mi
0   15 km

SAN DIEGO

WELCOME TO SAN DIEGO

TOP REASONS TO GO

★ **Beautiful beaches:** San Diego's shore shimmers with crystalline Pacific waters rolling up to some of the prettiest stretches of sand on the West Coast.

★ **Good eats:** Taking full advantage of the region's bountiful vegetables, fruits, herbs, and seafood, San Diego's chefs dazzle and delight diners with inventive California-colorful cuisine.

★ **History lessons:** The well-preserved and recon-structed historic sites in California's first European settlement help you imagine what the area was like when explorers first arrived.

★ **Stellar shopping:** The Gaslamp Quarter, Seaport Village, Coronado, Old Town, La Jolla . . . no matter where you go in San Diego, you'll find great places to do a little browsing.

★ **Urban oasis:** Balboa Park's 1,200 acres contain world-class museums and the San Diego Zoo, but also well-groomed lawns and gardens and wild, undeveloped canyons.

1 Downtown. San Diego's Downtown area is delight-fully urban and accessible, filled with walkable A-list attractions like the Gaslamp Quarter and the waterfront.

2 Balboa Park. San Diego's cultural heart is where you'll find most of the city's museums and its world-famous zoo.

3 Old Town and Uptown. California's first permanent European settlement is now preserved as a state historic park in Old Town. Uptown is composed of several smaller neighborhoods that showcase a unique blend of historical charm and modern urban community.

4 Mission Bay, Beaches, and SeaWorld. Home to 27 miles of shoreline, this 4,600 acre aquatic park is San Diego's monument to sports and fitness. SeaWorld, one of the city's most popular attrac-tions, lies south of the bay.

5 La Jolla. This luxe, bluff-top enclave fittingly means "the jewel" in Spanish. Come here for fantastic upscale shopping and unspoiled stretches of the coast.

6 Point Loma and Coronado. Home to the Hotel Del, Coronado's island-like isthmus is a favorite celebrity haunt. Visit the site of the first European landfall on Point Loma.

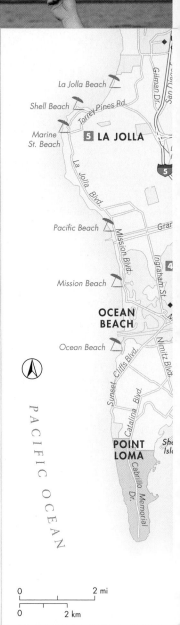

2

GETTING ORIENTED

Exploring San Diego may be an endless adventure, but there are limitations, especially if you don't have a car. San Diego is more a chain of separate communities than a cohesive city, and many of the major attractions are miles apart. Walking is good for getting an up-close look at neighborhoods like the Gaslamp Quarter, but true Southern Californians use the freeways that crisscross the county. Interstate 5 runs a direct north–south route through the coastal communities from Orange County in the north to the Mexican border. Interstates 805 and 15 do much the same inland. Interstate 8 is the main east–west route. Routes 163, 52, and 94 serve as connectors.

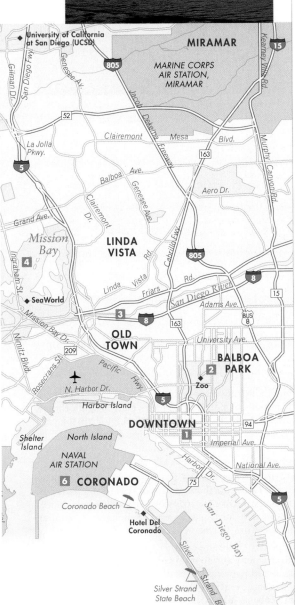

Updated by
Claire Deeks
van der Lee

San Diego is a vacationer's paradise, complete with idyllic year-round temperatures and 70 miles of pristine coastline. Recognized as one of the nation's leading family destinations, with SeaWorld, LEGOLAND, and the San Diego Zoo, San Diego is equally attractive to those in search of art, history, world-class shopping, and culinary exploration. San Diego's beaches are legendary, offering family-friendly sands, killer surf breaks, and spectacular scenery. San Diego's cultural sophistication often surprises visitors, as the city is better known for its laid-back vibe. Tourists come for some fun in the sun, only to discover a city with much greater depth.

San Diego is a big California city—second only to Los Angeles in population—with a small-town feel. San Diego's many neighborhoods offer diverse adventures: from the tony boutiques in La Jolla to the yoga and surf shops of Encinitas; from the subtle sophistication of Little Italy to the flashy nightlife of the Downtown Gaslamp Quarter, each community adds flavor and flair to San Diego's personality.

San Diego County also covers a lot of territory, roughly 400 square miles of land and sea. To the north and south of the city are its famed beaches. Inland, a succession of chaparral-covered mesas is punctuated with deep-cut canyons that step up to forested mountains, separating the coast from the arid Anza-Borrego Desert.

Known as the birthplace of California, San Diego was claimed for Spain by explorer Juan Rodríguez Cabrillo in 1542 and eventually came under Mexican rule. You'll find reminders of San Diego's Spanish and Mexican heritage throughout the region—in architecture and place-names, in distinctive Mexican cuisine, and in the historic buildings of Old Town.

In 1867 developer Alonzo Horton, who called the town's bay front "the prettiest place for a city I ever saw," began building a hotel, a plaza, and prefab homes on 960 Downtown acres. A remarkable number of these buildings are preserved in San Diego's historic Gaslamp Quarter today. The city's fate was sealed in the 1920s when the U.S. Navy, impressed by the city's excellent harbor and temperate climate, decided to build a destroyer base on San Diego Bay. Today, the military operates many bases and installations throughout the county (which, added together, form the largest military base in the world) and continues to be a major contributor to the local economy.

PLANNING

WHEN TO GO

San Diego's weather is so ideal that most locals shrug off the high cost of living and relatively lower wages as a "sunshine tax." Along the coast, average temperatures range from the mid-60s to the high 70s, with clear skies and low humidity. Annual rainfall is minimal, less than 10 inches per year.

The peak season for sun seekers is July through October. In July and August, the mercury spikes and everyone spills outside. From mid-December to mid-March, whale-watchers can glimpse migrating gray whales frolicking in the Pacific. In spring and early summer, a marine layer hugs the coastline for much or all of the day (locals call it "June Gloom"), which can be dreary and disappointing for those who were expecting to bask in Southern California sunshine.

GETTING HERE AND AROUND

AIR TRAVEL

The major airport is San Diego International Airport (SAN), called Lindbergh Field locally. Major airlines depart and arrive at Terminal 1 and Terminal 2; commuter flights identified on your ticket with a 3000-sequence flight number depart from a third commuter terminal. A red shuttle bus provides free transportation between terminals.

Airport San Diego International Airport ✉ *3225 N. Harbor Dr., off I–5* ☎ *619/400–2400* ⊕ *www.san.org.*

Airport Transfers Cloud 9 Shuttle/SuperShuttle ✉ *123 Caminio de la Riena* ☎ *800/974–8885* ⊕ *www.cloud9shuttle.com.* **San Diego Transit** ☎ *619/233–3004* ⊕ *transit.511sd.com.*

BUS AND TROLLEY TRAVEL

Under the umbrella of the Metropolitan Transit System, there are two major transit agencies in the area: San Diego Transit and North County Transit District (NCTD). The bright-red trolleys of the San Diego Trolley light-rail system operate on three lines that serve Downtown San Diego, Mission Valley, Old Town, South Bay, the U.S. border, and East County. The trolley system connects with San Diego Transit bus routes—connections are posted at each trolley station.

San Diego Transit bus fares range from $2.25 to $5; North County Transit District bus fares are $1.75. You must have exact change in coins and/or bills. Pay upon boarding. Transfers are not included; the $5 day pass is the best option for most bus travel and can be purchased on board.

San Diego Trolley tickets cost $2.50 and are good for two hours, but for one-way travel only. For a round-trip journey or longer, day passes are available for $5.

Bus and Trolley Information North County Transit District ☎ *760/966–6500* ⊕ *www.gonctd.com.* **San Diego Transit** ☎ *619/233–3004* ⊕ *transit.511sd.com.* **Transit Store** ✉ *102 Broadway* ☎ *619/234–1060* ⊕ *www.sdmts.com.*

CAR TRAVEL

A car is necessary for getting around greater San Diego on the sprawling freeway system and for visiting the North County beaches, mountains, and Anza Borrego Desert. Driving around San Diego County is pretty simple: most major attractions are within a few miles of the Pacific Ocean. Interstate 5, which stretches from Canada to the Mexican border, bisects San Diego. Interstate 8 provides access from Yuma, Arizona, and points east. Drivers coming from the Los Angeles area, Nevada, and the mountain regions beyond can reach San Diego on I–15. During rush hour there are jams on I–5 and on I–15 between I–805 and Escondido.

There are border inspection stations along major highways in San Diego County. Travel with your driver's license, and passport if you're an international traveler, in case you're asked to pull into one.

TAXI TRAVEL

Fares vary among companies. If you are heading to the airport from a hotel, ask about the flat rate, which varies according to destination; otherwise you'll be charged by the mile (which works out to $15 or so from any Downtown location). Taxi stands are at shopping centers and hotels; otherwise you must call and reserve a cab. The companies listed *below* don't serve all areas of San Diego County. If you're going somewhere other than Downtown, ask if the company serves that area.

Taxi Companies Orange Cab ☎ *619/291–3333* ⊕ *www.orangecabsandiego.com.* **Silver Cabs** ☎ *619/280–5555* ⊕ *www.sandiegosilvercab.com.* **Yellow Cab** ☎ *619/444–4444* ⊕ *www.driveu.com.*

TRAIN TRAVEL

Amtrak serves Downtown San Diego's Santa Fe Depot with daily trains to and from Los Angeles, Santa Barbara, and San Luis Obispo. Amtrak trains stop in San Diego North County at Solana Beach and Oceanside. Coaster commuter trains, which run between Oceanside and San Diego Monday–Saturday, stop at the same stations as Amtrak as well as others. The frequency is about every half hour during the weekday rush hour, with four trains on Saturday. One-way fares are $4 to $5.50, depending on the distance traveled. The Sprinter runs between Oceanside and Escondido, with many stops along the way.

Metrolink operates high-speed rail service between the Oceanside Transit Center and Union Station in Los Angeles.

Information Amtrak ☎ *800/872–7245* ⊕ *www.amtrak.com.* **Coaster** ☎ *760/966–6500* ⊕ *www.gonctd.com/coaster.* **Metrolink** ☎ *800/371–5465* ⊕ *www.metrolinktrains.com.*

TOURS

BIKE TOURS

Biking is popular in San Diego. You can find trails along the beach, in Mission Bay, and throughout the mountains.

Secret San Diego. Taking in spectacular views of the beach, bay, and skyline, these bike rides, offered by Where You Want to Be Tours, cover everything from historic neighborhoods to historic Highway 101. The walking tours and Rent-a-Local custom tours are popular options as well. ⊠ *611 K St., No. B224* ☎ *619/917–6037* ⊕ *www.wheretours. com* ✉ *From $55.*

BOAT TOURS

Visitors to San Diego can get a great overview of the city from the water. Tour companies offer a range of harbor cruises, from one-hour jaunts to dinner and dancing cruises. In season, whale-watching voyages are another popular option.

Flagship Cruises and Events. One and two-hour tours of the San Diego harbor loop north or south from the Broadway Pier throughout the day. Other offerings include dinner and dance cruises, brunch cruises, and winter whale-watching tours. ⊠ *990 N. Harbor Dr., Embarcadero* ☎ *619/234–4111* ⊕ *www.flagshipsd.com* ✉ *From $22.*

H&M Landing. From mid-December to March, this outfitter offers three-hour tours to spot migrating gray whales just off the San Diego coast. From June to October, six-hour cruises search for the gigantic blue whales that visit the California coast in summer. Winter gray-whale cruises are offered daily; summer blue-whale tours are available Thursday, Saturday, and Sunday. ⊠ *2803 Emerson St.* ☎ *619/222–1144* ⊕ *www.hmlanding.com* ✉ *From $45.*

Hornblower Cruises & Events. One- and two-hour cruises around San Diego harbor depart from the Embarcadero several times a day and alternate between the northern and southern portion of the bay. If you're hoping to spot some sea lions, take the North Bay route. Dinner and brunch cruises are also offered, as well as whale-watching tours in winter. ⊠ *970 N. Harbor Dr.* ☎ *619/234–8687, 800/668–4322* ⊕ *www. hornblower.com* ✉ *From $23.*

San Diego Seal Tours. This amphibious tour drives along the Embarcadero before splashing into the San Diego Harbor for a cruise. The 90-minute tours depart from Seaport Village year-round, and from outside the Maritime Museum seasonally. Call for daily departure times and locations. ⊠ *500 Kettner Blvd., Embarcadero* ☎ *619/298–8687* ⊕ *www. sealtours.com* ✉ *$36.*

Seaforth Boat Rentals. For those seeking a private tour on the water, this company can provide a skipper along with your boat rental. Options include harbor cruises, whale-watching, and sunset sails. Seaforth has five locations and a diverse fleet of sail and motorboats to choose from. ⊠ *1641 Quivira Rd., Mission Bay* ☎ *888/834–2628* ⊕ *www.seaforth boatrental.com* ✉ *From $225.*

BUS AND TROLLEY TOURS

For those looking to cover a lot of ground in a limited time, narrated trolley tours include everything from Balboa Park to Coronado. To venture farther afield, consider a coach tour to the desert, Los Angeles or even Baja, Mexico.

DayTripper. Single- and multi-day trips throughout Southern California, the Southwest, and Baja depart from San Diego year-round. Popular day trips include the Getty Museum, and theater performances in Los Angeles. Call or check website for pickup locations. ☎ *619/299–5777, 800/679–8747 ⊕ www.daytripper.com ✉ From $69.*

Five Star Tours. Private and group sightseeing bus tour options around San Diego and beyond include everything from the San Diego Zoo to Brewery tours and trips to Baja, Mexico. ✉ *1050 Kettner Blvd.* ☎ *619/232–5040 ⊕ www.fivestartours.com ✉ From $48.*

Old Town Trolley Tours. Combining points of interest with local history, trivia, and fun anecdotes, this hop-on, hop-off trolley tour provides an entertaining overview of the city and offers easy access to all the highlights. The tour is narrated, and you can get on and off as you please. Stops include Old Town, Seaport Village, the Gaslamp Quarter, Coronado, Little Italy, and Balboa Park. The trolley leaves every 30 minutes, operates daily, and takes two hours to make a full loop. ☎ *619/298–8687 ⊕ www.trolleytours.com/san-diego ✉ From $36.*

San Diego Scenic Tours. Half- and full-day bus tours of San Diego and Tijuana depart daily, and some include a harbor cruise. Tours depart from several hotels around town. ☎ *858/273–8687 ⊕ www. sandiegoscenictours.com ✉ From $38.*

WALKING TOURS

Several fine walking tours are available on weekdays or weekends; upcoming walks are usually listed in the *San Diego Reader.*

Coronado Walking Tours. Deparing from the Glorietta Bay Inn at 11 am Tuesday, Thursday and Saturday, this 90-minute stroll through Coronado's historic district takes in the island's mansions, old Tent City, the Hotel del Coronado, and the castles and cottages that line the beautiful beach. Reservations are recommended. ✉ *1630 Glorietta Blvd.* ☎ *619/435–5993 ⊕ coronadowalkingtour.com ✉ $12.*

Gaslamp Quarter Historical Foundation. Two-hour walking tours of the Downtown historic district depart from the William Heath Davis House at 11 am Tuesdays, Thursdays, and Saturdays. ✉ *410 Island Ave.* ☎ *619/233–4692 ⊕ www.gaslampquarter.org ✉ $15.*

Balboa Park Offshoot Tours. On Saturday at 10 am, free, hour-long walks start from the Balboa Park Visitor Center. The tour's focus rotates weekly, covering topics such as the park's history, palm trees, and desert vegetation. Reservations are not required, but no tours are scheduled between Thanksgiving and the New Year. ✉ *1549 El Prado, Balboa Park* ☎ *619/239–0512 ⊕ www.balboapark.org ✉ Free.*

Urban Safaris. Led by longtime San Diego resident Patty Fares, these two-hour Saturday walks through diverse neighborhoods like Hillcrest, Ocean Beach, and Point Loma are popular with tourists and locals alike. The tours, which always depart from a neighborhood coffee-house, focus on art, history, and ethnic eateries, among other topics. Reservations are required, and private walks can be arranged during the week. ☎ *619/944–9255* ⊕ *www.walkingtoursofsandiego.com* ✉ *$10.*

VISITOR INFORMATION

For general information and brochures before you go, contact the San Diego Tourism Authority, which publishes the helpful *San Diego Visitors Planning Guide.* When you arrive, stop by one of the local visitor centers for general information.

Citywide Contacts San Diego Convention & Visitors Bureau ☎ *619/232–3101* ⊕ *www.sandiego.org.* **San Diego Tourism Authority International Visitor Information Center** ✉ *1140 N. Harbor Dr., Downtown* ☎ *619/236–1212* ⊕ *www.sandiego.org.*

EXPLORING SAN DIEGO

DOWNTOWN

Nearly written off in the 1970s, today Downtown San Diego is a testament to conservation and urban renewal. Once derelict Victorian storefronts now house the hottest restaurants, and the *Star of India,* the world's oldest active sailing ship, almost lost to scrap, floats regally along the Embarcadero. Like many modern U.S. cities, Downtown San Diego's story is as much about its rebirth as its history. Although many consider Downtown to be the 16½-block Gaslamp Quarter, it's actually comprised of eight neighborhoods, including East Village, Little Italy, and Embarcadero.

GASLAMP QUARTER

Considered the liveliest of the Downtown neighborhoods, the Gaslamp Quarter's 4th and 5th avenues are peppered with trendy nightclubs, swanky lounge bars, chic restaurants, and boisterous sports pubs. The Gaslamp has the largest collection of commercial Victorian-style buildings in the country. Despite this, when the move for Downtown redevelopment gained momentum in the 1970s, there was talk of bulldozing them and starting from scratch. In response, concerned history buffs, developers, architects, and artists formed the Gaslamp Quarter Council to clean up and preserve the quarter. The majority of the quarter's landmark buildings are on 4th and 5th avenues, between Island Avenue and Broadway.

WORTH NOTING

Gaslamp Museum at the William Heath Davis House. The oldest wooden house in San Diego houses the Gaslamp Quarter Historical Foundation, the district's curator. Before developer Alonzo Horton came to town, Davis, a prominent San Franciscan, had made an unsuccessful attempt to develop the waterfront area. In 1850 he had this prefab saltbox-style house, built in Maine, shipped around Cape Horn and assembled in San Diego (it originally stood at State and Market streets). Regularly scheduled ninety-minute walking tours of the historic district leave from the house on Tuesday, Thursday, and Saturday at 11 am and cost $15. If you can't time your visit with the tour, a self-guided tour map is available for $2. ⊠ *410 Island Ave., at 4th Ave., Gaslamp Quarter* ☎ *619/233–4692* ⊕ *www.gaslampquarter.org* ⊠ *$5* ⊙ *Tues.–Sat. 10–5, Sun. noon–4.*

EMBARCADERO

The Embarcadero cuts a scenic swath along the harbor front and connects today's Downtown San Diego to its maritime routes. The bustle of Embarcadero comes less these days from the activities of fishing folk than from the throngs of tourists, but this waterfront walkway, stretching from the Convention Center to the Maritime Museum, remains the nautical soul of the city. There are several seafood restaurants here, as well as sea vessels of every variety—cruise ships, ferries, tour boats, and navy destroyers.

TOP ATTRACTIONS

FAMILY
Fodor'sChoice
★

Maritime Museum. From sailing ships to submarines, the Maritime Museum is a must for anyone with an interest in nautical history. This collection of restored and replica ships affords a fascinating glimpse of San Diego during its heyday as a commercial seaport.

The jewel of the collection, the *Star of India,* is often considered a symbol of the city. An iron windjammer built in 1863, the *Star of India* made 21 trips around the world in the late 1800s, when it traveled the East Indian trade route, shuttled immigrants from England to New Zealand, and served the Alaskan salmon trade. Saved from the scrap yard and painstakingly restored, the *Star of India* is the oldest active iron sailing ship in the world.

The popular HMS *Surprise,* purchased in 2004, is a replica of an 18th-century British Royal Navy frigate and was used in the Academy Award–winning *Master and Commander: The Far Side of the World.*

The museum's headquarters are on the *Berkeley,* an 1898 steam-driven ferryboat, which served the Southern Pacific Railroad in San Francisco until 1958. Its ornate detailing carefully restored, the main deck serves as a floating museum, with permanent exhibits on West Coast maritime history and complementary rotating exhibits.

Two submarines are featured at the museum: a *Soviet B-39* "Foxtrot" class submarine and the USS *Dolphin* research submarine. Take a peek at the harbor from a periscope, get up close with the engine control room, and wonder at the tight living quarters onboard.

At Spanish Landing Park, about 2 miles to the west, the museum is constructing a full-scale working replica of the *San Salvador,* the first European ship to land on the western coast of the future United States. To view this work-in-progress (daily 11–4), obtain directions at the Berkeley. Once complete, the San Salvador will be on display at the museum's main location. ⊠ *1492 N. Harbor Dr., Embarcadero* ☎ *619/234–9153* ⊕ *www.sdmaritime.org* ⊠ *$16 includes entry to all ships except Californian, $5 more for Pilot Boat Bay Cruise* ⊙ *Daily 9–8.*

Fodor'sChoice
★

Museum of Contemporary Art San Diego (MCASD). At the Downtown branch of the city's contemporary art museum (the original is in La Jolla), explore the works of international and regional artists in a modern,

Be sure to enjoy a walk along San Diego's lovely waterfront sometime during your visit.

urban space. The Jacobs Building—formerly the baggage building at the historic Santa Fe Depot—features large gallery spaces, high ceilings, and natural lighting, giving artists the flexibility to create large-scale installations. MCASD's collection includes many Pop Art, minimalist, and conceptual works from the 1950s to the present. The museum showcases both established and emerging artists in temporary exhibitions, and has permanent, site-specific commissions by Jenny Holzer and Richard Serra. ■ TIP→ **Admission, good for seven days, includes the Downtown and La Jolla locations.** ⊠ *1100 and 1001 Kettner Blvd., Downtown* ☎ *858/454–3541* ⊕ *www.mcasd.org* ⊠ *$10; free 3rd Thurs. of the month 5–7* ☉ *Thurs.–Tues., 11–5; 3rd Thurs. until 7* ☉ *Closed Wed.*

FAMILY
Fodor's Choice
★
The New Children's Museum (NCM). Opened in May 2008, NCM blends contemporary art with unstructured play to create an environment that appeals to children as well as adults. The 50,000-square-foot structure was constructed from recycled building materials, operates on solar energy, and is convection-cooled by an elevator shaft. It also features a nutritious and eco-conscious café. Interactive exhibits include designated areas for toddlers and teens, as well as plenty of activities for the entire family. Several art workshops are offered each day, as well as hands-on studios where visitors are encouraged to create their own art. The studio projects change frequently and the entire museum changes exhibits every 18 to 24 months, so there is always something new to explore. The adjoining 1-acre park and playground is conveniently located across from the convention center trolley stop. ⊠ *200 W. Island Ave., Embarcadero* ☎ *619/233–8792* ⊕ *www.thinkplaycreate. org* ⊠ *$10; 2nd Sun. each month free 10–4* ☉ *Mon. and Wed.–Sat. 10–4; Sun. noon–4.*

FAMILY   **Seaport Village.** You'll find some of the best views of the harbor at Seaport Village, three bustling shopping plazas designed to reflect the New England clapboard and Spanish mission architectural styles of early California. On a prime stretch of waterfront the dining, shopping and entertainment complex connects the harbor with hotel towers and the convention center. Specialty shops offer everything from a kite store and swing emporium to a shop devoted to hot sauces. You can dine at snack bars and restaurants, many with harbor views. Seaport Village's shops are open daily 10 to 9; a few eateries open early for breakfast, and venues many have extended nighttime hours, especially in summer. Restaurant prices here are high and the food is only average, so your best bet is to go elsewhere for a meal.

Live music can be heard daily from noon to 4 at the main food court. Additional free concerts take place every Sunday from 1 to 4 at the East Plaza Gazebo. If you happen to visit San Diego in late November or early December, you might be lucky enough to catch Surfing Santa's Arrival and even have your picture taken with Santa on his wave. In late March or early April, the Seaport Buskers Fest presents an array of costumed street performers. The **Seaport Village Carousel** (rides $2) has 54 animals, hand-carved and hand-painted by Charles Looff in 1895. ⊠ *849 W. Harbor Dr., Downtown* ☎ *619/235–4014 office and events hotline* ⊕ *www.seaportvillage.com.*

Fodor's Choice   **USS Midway Museum.** After 47 years of worldwide service, the retired
★   USS *Midway* began a new tour of duty on the south side of the navy pier in 2004. Launched in 1945, the 1,001-foot-long ship was the largest in the world for the first 10 years of its existence. The most visible landmark on the north Embarcadero, it now serves as a floating interactive museum—an appropriate addition to the town that is home to one-third of the Pacific fleet and the birthplace of naval aviation. A free audio tour guides you through the massive ship while offering insight from former sailors. As you clamber through passageways and up and down ladder wells, you'll get a feel for how the *Midway*'s 4,500 crew members lived and worked on this "city at sea."

Though the entire tour is impressive, you'll really be wowed when you step out onto the 4-acre flight deck—not only the best place to get an idea of the ship's scale, but also one of the most interesting vantage points for bay and city skyline views. An F-14 Tomcat jet fighter is just one of many vintage aircraft on display. Free guided tours of the bridge and primary flight control, known as "the Island," depart every 10 minutes from the flight deck. Many of the docents stationed throughout the ship served in the navy, some even on the *Midway*, and they are eager to answer questions or share stories. The museum also offers multiple flight simulators for an additional fee, climb-aboard cockpits, and interactive exhibits focusing on naval aviation. There is a gift shop and a café with pleasant outdoor seating. This is a wildly popular stop, with most visits lasting several hours. ⚠ **Despite efforts to provide accessibility throughout the ship, some areas can only be reached via fairly steep steps; a video tour of these areas is available on the hangar deck.** ⊠ *910 N. Harbor Dr., Embarcadero* ☎ *619/544–9600* ⊕ *www.midway. org* 🖃 *$20* ⊙ *Daily 10–5, last admission 4 pm.*

EAST VILLAGE

The most ambitious of the Downtown projects is East Village, not far from the Gaslamp Quarter, and encompassing 130 blocks between the railroad tracks up to J Street, and from 6th Avenue east to around 10th Street. Sparking the rebirth of this former warehouse district was the 2004 construction of the San Diego Padres' baseball stadium, PETCO Park. As the city's largest Downtown neighborhood, East Village is continually broadening its boundaries with its urban design of redbrick cafés, spacious galleries, rooftop bars, sleek hotels, and warehouse restaurants.

LITTLE ITALY

Unlike many tourist-driven communities, the charming neighborhood of Little Italy is authentic to its roots, from the Italian-speaking residents to the imported delicacies. The main thoroughfare—from India Street to Kettner Boulevard—is filled with lively cafés, gelato shops, bakeries, and restaurants. Art lovers can browse gallery showrooms, while shoppers adore the Fir Street cottages. Home to many in San Diego's design community, Little Italy exudes a sense of urban cool.

BALBOA PARK AND SAN DIEGO ZOO

Overlooking Downtown and the Pacific Ocean, 1,200-acre Balboa Park is the cultural heart of San Diego. Ranked as one of the world's best parks by the Project for Public Spaces, it's also where you can find most of the city's museums, art galleries, the Tony Award–winning Old Globe Theatre, and the world-famous San Diego Zoo. Often referred to as the "Smithsonian of the West" for its concentration of museums, Balboa Park is also a series of botanical gardens, performance spaces, and outdoor playrooms endeared to the hearts of residents and visitors alike.

Thanks to the "Mother of Balboa Park," Kate Sessions, who suggested hiring a landscape architect in 1889, wild and cultivated gardens are an integral part of the park, featuring 350 species of trees. What Balboa Park would have looked like had she left it alone can be seen at Florida Canyon (between the main park and Morley Field, along Park Boulevard)—an arid landscape of sagebrush, cactus, and a few small trees.

In addition, the captivating architecture of Balboa's buildings, fountains, and courtyards gives the park an enchanted feel. Historic buildings dating from San Diego's 1915 Panama–California International Exposition are strung along the park's main east–west thoroughfare, El Prado. The parkland across the Cabrillo Bridge, at the west end of El Prado, is set aside for picnics and athletics. East of Plaza de Panama, El Prado becomes a pedestrian mall and ends at a footbridge that crosses over Park Boulevard, to rose and desert gardens.

TOP ATTRACTIONS

Bea Evenson Fountain. A favorite of barefoot children, this fountain shoots cool jets of water upwards of 50 feet. Built in 1972 between the Fleet Center and Natural History Museum, the fountain offers plenty of room to sit and watch the crowds go by. ⊠ *East end of El Prado, Balboa Park* ⊕ *www.balboapark.org.*

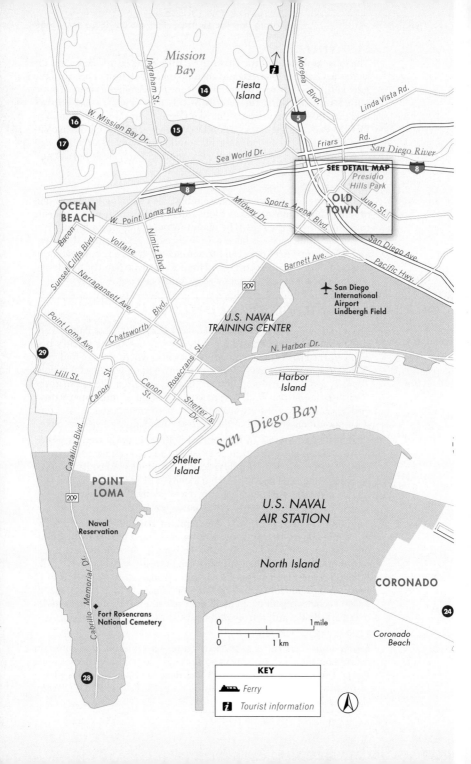

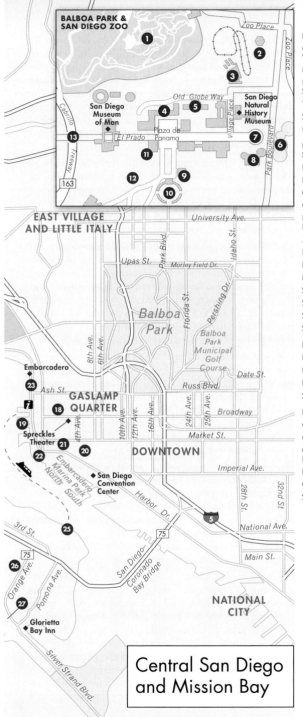

Central San Diego
and Mission Bay

Fodor's Choice
★ **Botanical Building.** The graceful redwood-lath structure, built for the 1915 Panama–California International Exposition, now houses more than 2,000 types of tropical and subtropical plants plus changing seasonal flower displays. Ceiling-high tree ferns shade fragile orchids and feathery bamboo. There are benches beside miniature waterfalls for resting in the shade. The rectangular pond outside, filled with lotuses and water lilies that bloom in spring and fall, is popular with photographers. ✉ *1549 El Prado, Balboa Park* ☎ *619/239–0512* ⊕ *www. balboapark.org* ✉ *Free* ☉ *Fri.–Wed. 10–4* ☉ *Closed Thurs.*

Cabrillo Bridge. The park's official (and pedestrian-friendly) gateway soars 120 feet above a canyon floor. Crossing the 1,500-foot bridge into the park provides awe-inspiring views of the California Tower and El Prado beyond. This is a great spot for a photo capturing a classic image of the park. ✉ *On El Prado, at the 6th Ave. park entrance, Balboa Park* ⊕ *www.balboapark.org.*

FAMILY **Carousel.** Suspended an arm's length away on this antique merry-go-round is the brass ring that could earn you an extra free ride (it's one of the few carousels in the world that continue this bonus tradition). Hand-carved in 1910, the carousel features colorful murals, big-band music, and bobbing animals including zebras, giraffes, and dragons; real horsehair was used for the tails. ✉ *1889 Zoo Pl., behind zoo parking lot, Balboa Park* ☎ *619/239–0512* ✉ *$2.50* ☉ *Mid-June–Labor Day, 11–5:30 daily; Labor Day–Mid-June, 11–5:30 weekends and school holidays.*

Fodor's Choice
★ **Inez Grant Parker Memorial Rose Garden and Desert Garden.** These neighboring gardens sit just across the Park Boulevard pedestrian bridge and offer gorgeous views over Florida Canyon. The formal rose garden contains 2,500 roses representing nearly 200 varieties; peak bloom is usually in April and May. The adjacent Desert Garden provides a striking contrast, with 2.5 acres of succulents and desert plants seeming to blend into the landscape of the canyon below. ✉ *2525 Park Blvd., Balboa Park* ⊕ *www.balboapark.org.*

Japanese Friendship Garden. A koi pond with a cascading waterfall, a tea pavilion, and a large activity center are highlights of the park's authentic Japanese garden, designed to inspire contemplation and evoke tranquility. You can wander the various peaceful paths and meditate in the traditional stone and Zen garden. The development of an additional 9 acres is well under way and will include a traditional teahouse and a cherry orchard. ✉ *2215 Pan American Rd., Balboa Park* ☎ *619/232–2721* ⊕ *www.niwa.org* ✉ *$6* ☉ *10–4:30, last admission at 3:30.*

Mingei International Museum. The name "Mingei" comes from the Japanese words *min*, meaning "all people," and *gei*, meaning "art." Thus the museum's name describes what you'll find under its roof: "art of all people." All ages can enjoy the Mingei's colorful and creative exhibits of folk art, featuring toys, pottery, textiles, costumes, jewelry, and curios from around the globe. Traveling and permanent exhibits in the high-ceilinged, light-filled museum include everything from antique American carousel horses to the latest in Japanese ceramics. The gift shop carries artwork from cultures around the world, from Zulu baskets to Turkish ceramics to Mexican objects, plus special items related to major exhibitions. ⊠ *House of Charm, 1439 El Prado, Balboa Park* ☎ *619/239–0003* ⊕ *www.mingei.org* ⊠ *$8* ⊘ *Tues.–Sun. 10–5.*

Palm Canyon. With more than 450 palms planted in 2 acres within Balboa Park, this lush and tropical oasis offers winding paths, shady palms, and an instant escape. ⊠ *South of the House of Charm, 1549 El Prado, Balboa Park.*

FAMILY **Reuben H. Fleet Science Center.** The center's interactive exhibits are artfully educational. Older kids can get hands-on with inventive projects in the Tinkering Studio, while Kid City entertains the 5-and-under set with interactive play stations like the Ball Wall and Fire Truck. The IMAX Dome Theater, which screens exhilarating nature and science films, was the world's first, as is the Fleet's "NanoSeam" (seamless) dome ceiling that doubles as a planetarium. ⊠ *1875 El Prado, Balboa Park* ☎ *619/238–1233* ⊕ *www.rhfleet.org* ⊠ *Gallery exhibits $13, gallery exhibits and 1 IMAX film $17, or 2 IMAX films $24* ⊘ *Opens daily at 10; closing hrs vary from 5 to 9, so call ahead.*

San Diego Museum of Art. Known primarily for its Spanish baroque and Renaissance paintings, including works by El Greco, Goya, Rubens, and van Ruisdael, San Diego's most comprehensive art museum also has strong holdings of South Asian art, Indian miniatures, and contemporary California paintings. An outdoor Sculpture Court and Garden exhibits both traditional and modern pieces. The museum's exhibits tend to have broad appeal, and if traveling shows from other cities come to town, you can expect to see them here. Free docent tours are offered throughout the day. If you become hungry, head to the **Sculpture Court Café by Giuseppe,** which serves artisan pizzas, gourmet salads and sandwiches, and grilled burgers and steak. ⊠ *1450 El Prado, Balboa Park* ☎ *619/232–7931* ⊕ *www.sdmart.org* ⊠ *$12* ⊘ *Mon., Tues., and Thurs.–Sat. 10–5, Sun. noon–5; Fri. until 9 Memorial Day–Labor Day* ⊘ *Closed Wed.*

FAMILY **San Diego Zoo.**
Fodor'sChoice *See the highlighted listing in this chapter.*
★

Spanish Village Art Center. More than 200 local artists, including glass-blowers, enamel workers, woodcarvers, sculptors, painters, jewelers, and photographers rent space in these red tile–roof studio-galleries that were set up for the 1935–36 exposition in the style of an old Spanish village, and they give demonstrations of their work on a rotating basis. Spanish Village is a great source for memorable gifts. ⊠ *1770 Village Pl., Balboa Park* ☎ *619/233–9050* ⊕ *www.spanishvillageart.com* ⊠ *Free* ⊘ *Daily 11–4.*

Spreckels Organ Pavilion. The 2,400-bench-seat pavilion, dedicated in 1915 by sugar magnates John D. and Adolph B. Spreckels, holds the 4,518-pipe Spreckels Organ, the largest outdoor pipe organ in the world. You can hear this impressive instrument at one of the year-round, free, 2 pm Sunday concerts, regularly performed by civic organist Carol Williams and guest artists—a highlight of a visit to Balboa Park. On Monday evenings from late June to mid-August, internationally renowned organists play evening concerts. At Christmastime the park's Christmas tree and life-size Nativity display turn the pavilion into a seasonal wonderland. ✉ *2211 Pan American Rd., Balboa Park* ☎ *619/702–8138* ⊕ *www.sosorgan.org.*

OLD TOWN AND UPTOWN

San Diego's Spanish and Mexican roots are most evident in Old Town and the surrounding hillside of Presidio Park. Visitors can experience settlement life in San Diego from Spanish and Mexican rule to the early days of U.S. statehood. Nearby Uptown is composed of several smaller neighborhoods near Downtown and around Balboa Park that showcase a unique blend of historical charm and modern urban community.

OLD TOWN

As the first European settlement in Southern California, Old Town began to develop in the 1820s. But its true beginnings took place on a nearby hillside in 1769 with the establishment of a Spanish military outpost and the first of California's missions, San Diego de Alcalá. In 1774 the hilltop was declared a *presidio reál*, a fortress built by the Spanish Empire, and the mission was relocated along the San Diego River. Over time, settlers moved down from the presidio to establish Old Town. A central plaza was laid out, surrounded by adobe and, later, wooden structures. San Diego became an incorporated U.S. city in 1850, with Old Town as its center. In the 1860s, however, the advent of Alonzo Horton's New Town to the southeast caused Old Town to wither. Efforts to preserve the area began early in the 20th century, and Old Town became a state historic park in 1968.

Today Old Town is a lively celebration of history and culture. The Old Town San Diego State Historic Park re-creates life during the early settlement, while San Diego Avenue buzzes with art galleries, gift shops, festive restaurants, and open-air stands selling inexpensive Mexican handicrafts.

TOP ATTRACTIONS

FAMILY
Fodor'sChoice
★

Fiesta de Reyes. North of San Diego's Old Town Plaza lies the area's unofficial center, built to represent a colonial Mexican plaza. This collection of shops and restaurants around a central courtyard in blossom with magenta bougainvillea, scarlet hibiscus, and other flowers in season reflect what it might have looked like in the early California days, from 1821 to 1872, complete with shops stocked with items reminiscent of that era. More than a dozen shops and restaurants line the plaza (Casa de Reyes is a great stop for a margarita and some chips and guacamole), and if you are lucky, you might catch a mariachi band or folklorico dance performance on the plaza stage—check the website for times and upcoming special events. ✉ *4016 Wallace St., Old Town* ☎ *619/297–3100* ⊕ *www.fiestadereyes.com* ☉ *Shops 10–9 daily.*

FAMILY
Fodor'sChoice
★

Old Town San Diego State Historic Park. The six square blocks on the site of San Diego's original pueblo are the heart of Old Town. Most of the 20 historic buildings preserved or re-created by the park cluster around **Old Town Plaza,** bounded by Wallace Street on the west, Calhoun Street on the north, Mason Street on the east, and San Diego Avenue

Continued on page 72

Polar bear, San Diego Zoo

LIONS AND TIGERS AND PANDAS:
The World-Famous San Diego Zoo

From cuddly pandas and diving polar bears to 6-ton elephants and swinging great apes, San Diego's most famous attraction has it all. Nearly 4,000 animals representing 800 species roam the 100-acre zoo in expertly crafted habitats that replicate the animals' natural environments. While the pandas get top billing, there are plenty of other cool creatures to see here, from teeny-tiny mantella frogs to two-story-tall giraffes. But it's not all just fun and games. Known for its exemplary conservation programs, the zoo educates visitors on how to go green and explains its efforts to protect endangered species.

SAN DIEGO ZOO TOP ATTRACTIONS

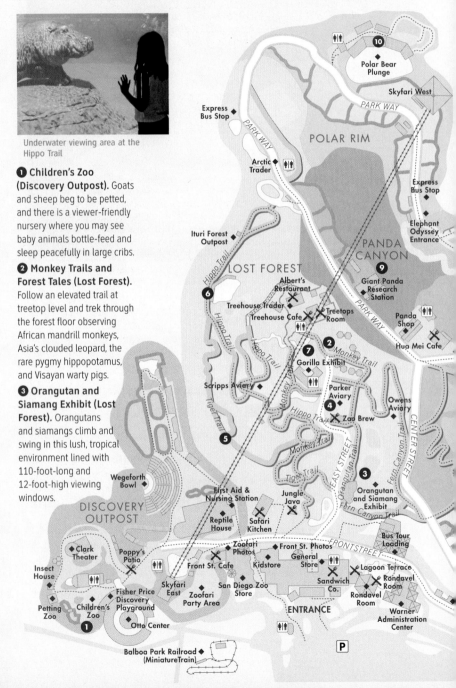

Underwater viewing area at the Hippo Trail

❶ Children's Zoo (Discovery Outpost). Goats and sheep beg to be petted, and there is a viewer-friendly nursery where you may see baby animals bottle-feed and sleep peacefully in large cribs.

❷ Monkey Trails and Forest Tales (Lost Forest). Follow an elevated trail at treetop level and trek through the forest floor observing African mandrill monkeys, Asia's clouded leopard, the rare pygmy hippopotamus, and Visayan warty pigs.

❸ Orangutan and Siamang Exhibit (Lost Forest). Orangutans and siamangs climb and swing in this lush, tropical environment lined with 110-foot-long and 12-foot-high viewing windows.

Polar Bear Plunge

Skyfari West

PARK WAY

POLAR RIM

Express Bus Stop

PARK WAY

PARK WAY

Arctic Trader

Express Bus Stop

Elephant Odyssey Entrance

Ituri Forest Outpost

Hippo Trail

LOST FOREST

PANDA CANYON

Albert's Restaurant

Giant Panda Research Station

Treehouse Trader

Treehouse Cafe

Treetops Room

PARK WAY

Panda Shop

Hua Mei Cafe

❻

❼

❷ Monkey Trail

Gorilla Exhibit

Scripps Aviary

Parker Aviary

Owens Aviary

Hippo Trail

❹

Zao Brew

❺

Tiger Trail

Hippo Trail

Monkey Trail

EASY STREET

Orangutan Trail

Fern Canyon Trail

CENTER STREET

Tiger Trail

❸

Orangutan and Siamang Exhibit

Wegeforth Bowl

First Aid & Nursing Station

Jungle Java

Bus Tour Loading

DISCOVERY OUTPOST

Reptile House

Safari Kitchen

FRONT STREET

Clark Theater

Poppy's Patio

Zoofari Photos

Front St. Photos

General Store

Lagoon Terrace

Insect House

Front St. Cafe

Kidstore

Sandwich Co.

Rondavel Room

Skyfari East

San Diego Zoo Store

Rondavel Room

Petting Zoo

Children's Zoo

Fisher Price Discovery Playground

Zoofari Party Area

ENTRANCE

Warner Administration Center

❶

Otto Center

Balboa Park Railroad ◆ (Miniature Train)

P

4 Scripps, Parker, and Owens Aviaries (Lost Forest). Wandering paths climb through the enclosed aviaries where brightly colored tropical birds swoop between branches inches from your face.

5 Tiger Trail (Lost Forest). The mist-shrouded trails of this simulated rainforest wind down a canyon. Tigers, Malayan tapirs, and Argus pheasants wander among the exotic trees and plants.

6 Hippo Trail (Lost Forest). Glimpse huge but surprisingly graceful hippos frolicking in the water through an underwater viewing window and buffalo cavorting with monkeys on dry land.

7 Gorilla Exhibit (Lost Forest). The gorillas live in one of the zoo's bioclimatic zone exhibits modeled on their native habitat with waterfalls, climbing areas, and an open meadow. The sounds of the tropical rain forest emerge from a 144-speaker sound system that plays CDs recorded in Africa.

8 Sun Bear Forest (Asian Passage). Playful beasts claw apart the trees and shrubs that serve as a natural playground for climbing, jumping, and general merrymaking.

9 Giant Panda Research Station (Panda Canyon). An elevated pathway provides visitors with great access

Lories at Owen's Aviary

to the zoo's most famous residents in their side-by-side viewing areas. The adjacent discovery center features lots of information about these endangered animals and the zoo's efforts to protect them.

10 Polar Bear Plunge (Polar Rim). Watch polar bears take a chilly dive from the underwater viewing room. There are also Siberian reindeer, white foxes, and other Arctic creatures here. Kids can learn about the Arctic and climate change through interactive exhibits.

11 Elephant Odyssey. Get a glimpse of the animals that roamed Southern California 12,000 years ago and meet their living counterparts. The 7.5-acre, multispecies habitat features elephants, California condors, jaguars, and more.

12 Koala Exhibit (Outback). The San Diego Zoo houses the largest number of koalas outside Australia. Walk through the exhibit for photo ops of these marsupials from Down-Under curled up on their perches or dining on eucalyptus branches.

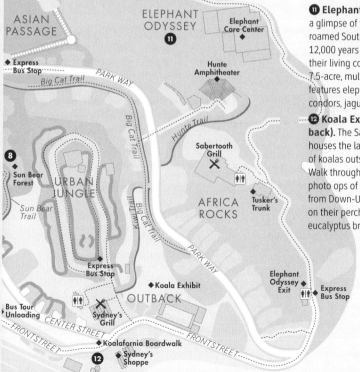

ASIAN PASSAGE

ELEPHANT ODYSSEY
11

Elephant Care Center

Express Bus Stop

Big Cat Trail

PARK WAY

Hunte Amphitheater

Big Cat Trail

Hunte Trail

8
Sun Bear Forest

Sabertooth Grill

URBAN JUNGLE

Sun Bear Trail

Big Cat Trail

AFRICA ROCKS

Tusker's Trunk

Express Bus Stop

Koala Exhibit

PARK WAY

OUTBACK

Elephant Odyssey Exit

Express Bus Stop

Bus Tour Unloading

CENTER STREET

Sydney's Grill

FRONT STREET

FRONT STREET

Koalafornia Boardwalk

12

Sydney's Shoppe

MUST-SEE ANIMALS

❶ GORILLA

This troop of primates engages visitors with their human-like expressions and behavior. The youngsters are sure to delight, especially when hitching a ride on mom's back. Up-close encounters might involve the gorillas using the glass partition as a backrest while peeling cabbage. By dusk the gorillas head inside to their sleeping quarters, so don't save this for your last stop.

❷ ELEPHANT

Asian and African elephants coexist at the San Diego Zoo. The larger African elephant is distinguished by its big flapping ears—shaped like the continent of Africa—which it uses to keep cool. An elephant's trunk has over 40,000 muscles in it—that's more than humans have in their whole body.

❸ GIANT PANDA

The San Diego Zoo is well-known for its giant panda research and conservation efforts, and has had six successful panda births. You'll likely see parents Bai Yun ("White Cloud") and Gao-Gao ("Big-Big") with their youngest baby Xiao Liwu ("little gift").

❹ KOALA

While this collection of critters is one of the cutest in the zoo, don't expect a lot of activity from the koala habitat. These guys spend most of their day curled up asleep in the branches of the eucalyptus tree—they can sleep up to 20 hours a day. Although eucalyptus leaves are poisonous to most animals, bacteria in koalas' stomachs allow them to break down the toxins.

❺ POLAR BEAR

The trio of polar bears is one of the San Diego Zoo's star attractions, and their brand-new exhibit gets you up close and personal. Visitors sometimes worry about polar bears living in the warm San Diego climate, but there is no cause for concern. The San Diego-based bears eat a lean diet, thus reducing their layer of blubber and helping them keep cool.

DID YOU KNOW?

Bamboo is the panda's dietary staple—they can consume 84 pounds of it a day—and the zoo grows 69 species of bamboo to ensure they have plenty of variety.

PLANNING YOUR DAY AT THE ZOO

Left: Main entrance of the San Diego Zoo. Right: Sunbear

PLANNING YOUR TIME

Plan to devote at least a half-day to exploring the zoo, but with so much to see it is easy to stay a full day or more.

If you're on a tight schedule, opt for the guided **35 minute bus tour** that lets you zip through three-quarters of the exhibits. However, lines to board the busses can be long, and you won't get as close to the animals.

Another option is to take the **Skyfari Aerial Tram** to the far end of the park, choose a route, and meander back to the entrance. The Skyfari trip gives a good overview of the zoo's layout and a spectacular view.

The **Elephant Odyssey,** while accessible from two sides of the park, is best entered from just below the Polar Rim. The extremely popular **Panda exhibit** can develop long lines, so get there early.

The zoo offers several entertaining **live shows** daily. Check the website or the back of the map handed out at the zoo entrance for the day's offerings and showtimes.

BEFORE YOU GO

■ To avoid ticket lines, purchase and print tickets online using the zoo's Web site.

■ To avoid excessive backtracking or a potential meltdown, plan your route along the zoo map before setting out. Try not to get too frustrated if you lose your way, as there are exciting exhibits around every turn and many paths intersect at several points.

■ The zoo offers a variety of program extras, including behind-the-scenes tours, backstage pass animal encounters, and sleepover events. Call in advance for pricing and reservations.

AT THE ZOO

■ Don't forget to explore at least some of the exhibits on foot—a favorite is the lush Tiger Trail.

■ If you visit on the weekend, find out when the Giraffe Experience is taking place. You can purchase leaf–eater biscuits to hand feed the giraffes!

■ Splurge a little at the gift shop: your purchases help support zoo programs.

■ The zoo rents strollers, wheelchairs, and lockers; it also has a first-aid office, a lost and found, and an ATM.

Fern Canyon, San Diego Zoo

GETTING HERE AND AROUND

The zoo is easy to get to, whether by bus or car.

Bus Travel: Take Bus No. 7 and exit at Park Boulevard and Zoo Place.

Car Travel: From Downtown, take Route 163 north through Balboa Park. Exit at Zoo/Museums (Richmond Street) and follow signs.

Several options help you get around the massive park: express buses loop through the zoo and the Skyfari Aerial Tram will take you from one end to the other. The zoo's topography is fairly hilly, but moving sidewalks lead up the slopes between some exhibits.

QUICK BITES

There is a wide variety of food available for purchase at the zoo from food carts to ethnic restaurants such as the Pan-Asian **Hua Mei Cafe**.

One of the best restaurants is **Albert's** ($), near the Gorilla exhibit, which features grilled fish, homemade pizza, and fresh pasta along with a full bar.

SERVICE INFORMATION

✉ 2920 Zoo Dr., Balboa Park

☎ 619/234–3153; 888/697–2632 Giant panda hotline

⊕ www.sandiegozoo.org

💳 $46 adult, $36 children (3-11) includes Skyfari and bus tour; 2-Visit Pass ($82 adult, $64 children age 3-11); zoo parking free

▭ AE, D, MC, V

🕑 July–Sept., daily 9–9; Oct.–June, daily 9–dusk. Hours may be extended for holidays and special events, and Children's Zoo and Skyfari ride may have reduced hours—check

SAN DIEGO ZOO SAFARI PARK

online or call for details.

About 45 minutes north of the zoo in Escondido, the 1,800-acre San Diego Zoo Safari Park is an extensive wildlife sanctuary where animals roam free—and guests can get close in escorted caravans and on backcountry trails. This park and the zoo operate under the auspices of the San Diego Zoo's nonprofit organization; joint tickets are available.

on the south. The plaza is a pleasant place to rest, plan your tour of the park, and watch passersby. San Diego Avenue is closed to vehicle traffic here.

Some of Old Town's buildings were destroyed in a fire in 1872, but after the site became a state historic park in 1968, reconstruction and restoration of the remaining structures began. Five of the original adobes are still intact. The tour pamphlet available at Robinson-Rose House gives details about all the historic houses on the plaza and in its vicinity; *a few of the more interesting ones are noted below.* Several reconstructed buildings serve as restaurants or as shops purveying wares reminiscent of those that might have been available in the original Old Town; **Racine & Laramie**, a painstakingly reproduced version of San Diego's first (1868) cigar store, is especially interesting. Free tours depart daily from the Robinson-Rose House at 11 and 2.

Casa de Estudillo. San Diego's first county assessor, Jose Antonio Estudillo, built this home in 1827 in collaboration with his father, the commander of the San Diego Presidio, José Maria Estudillo. The largest and most elaborate of the original adobe homes, it was occupied by members of the Estudillo family until 1887. It was purchased and restored in 1910 by sugar magnate and developer John D. Spreckels, who advertised it in bold lettering on the side as "Ramona's Marriage Place." Spreckels' claim that the small chapel in the house was the site of the wedding in Helen Hunt Jackson's popular novel *Ramona* had no basis; that didn't stop people from coming to see it, however. *4001 Mason St.*

Cosmopolitan Hotel and Restaurant. A Peruvian, Juan Bandini, built a hacienda on this site in 1829, and the house served as Old Town's social center during Mexican rule. Albert Seeley, a stagecoach entrepreneur, purchased the home in 1869, built a second story, and turned it into the Cosmopolitan Hotel, a way station for travelers on the daylong trip south from Los Angeles. It later served as a cannery before being revived (a few times over the years) as a hotel and restaurant. *2660 Calhoun St.*

Robinson-Rose House. Facing Old Town Plaza, this was the original commercial center of Old San Diego, housing railroad offices, law offices, and the first newspaper press. Built in 1853 but in ruins at the end of the 19th century, it has been reconstructed and now serves as the park's visitor center. Inside are a model of Old Town as it looked in 1872, as well as various historic exhibits. Ghosts came with the rebuild, as the house is now considered haunted. Just behind the Robinson-Rose House is a replica of the Victorian-era Silvas-McCoy house, originally built in 1869. *4002 Wallace St.*

Seeley Stable. Next door to the Cosmopolitan Hotel, the stable became San Diego's stagecoach stop in 1867 and was the transportation hub of Old Town until 1887, when trains became the favored mode of travel. The stable houses horse-drawn vehicles, some so elaborate that you can see where the term "carriage trade" came from. Also inside are

Western memorabilia, including an exhibit on the California vaquero, the original American cowboy, and a collection of Native American artifacts. *2630 Calhoun St.*

Also worth exploring: The San Diego Union Museum, Mason Street School, Wells Fargo History Museum, First San Diego Courthouse, Casa de Machado y Silvas Commercial Restaurant Museum, and the Casa de Machado y Stewart. Ask at the visitor center for locations. ⊠ *Visitor Center (Robinson-Rose House), 4002 Wallace St., Old Town* ☎ *619/220–5422* ⊕ *www.parks.ca.gov* ⊠ *Free* ☉ *Oct.–Apr., Mon–Thurs 10–4, Fri–Sun 10–5; May–Sept., daily 10–5; hrs may vary at individual sites.*

WORTH NOTING

Thomas Whaley House Museum. Thomas Whaley was a New York entrepreneur who came to California during the gold rush. He wanted to provide his East Coast wife with all the comforts of home, so in 1857 he had Southern California's first two-story brick structure built, making it the oldest double-story brick building on the West Coast. The house, which served as the county courthouse and government seat during the 1870s, stands in strong contrast to the Spanish-style adobe residences that surround the nearby historic plaza and marks an early stage of San Diego's "Americanization." A garden out back includes many varieties of prehybrid roses from before 1867. The place is perhaps most famed, however, for the ghosts that are said to inhabit it. Starting at 5 pm, admission is by guided tour offered every half hour with the last tour departing at 9:30 pm. The nighttime tours are geared more toward the supernatural aspects of the house than the daytime self-guided tour. ✉ *2476 San Diego Ave., Old Town* ☎ *619/297–7511* ⊕ *www.whaleyhouse.org* ✉ *$6 before 5 pm, $10 after 5* ⊙ *Sept.–May, Sun.–Tues. 10–5, Thurs.–Sat. 10–9:30; June–Aug., daily 10–9:30.*

HILLCREST

The large retro Hillcrest sign over the intersection of University and 5th avenues makes an excellent landmark at the epicenter of this vibrant section of Uptown. Strolling along University Avenue between 4th and 6th avenues from Washington Street to Robinson Avenue will reveal a mixture of retail shops and restaurants. A few blocks east, another interesting stretch of stores and restaurants runs along University Avenue to Normal Street. Long established as the center of San Diego's gay community, the neighborhood bustles both day and night with a mixed crowd of shoppers, diners, and partygoers.

MISSION VALLEY

Although Mission Valley's charms may not be immediately apparent, it offers many conveniences to visitors and residents alike. The Mission Basilica San Diego de Alcalá provides a tranquil refuge from the surrounding suburban sprawl.

TOP ATTRACTIONS

Mission Basilica San Diego de Alcalá. It's hard to imagine how remote California's earliest mission once must have been; these days, it's accessible by major freeways (I–15 and I–8) and by the San Diego Trolley. Mission San Diego de Alcalá, the first of a chain of 21 missions stretching northward along the coast, was established by Father Junípero Serra on Presidio Hill in 1769 and moved to this location in 1774. There was no greater security from enemy attack here: Padre Luis Jayme, California's first Christian martyr, was clubbed to death by the Kumeyaay Indians he was trying to convert in 1775. The present church is the fifth built on the site; it was reconstructed in 1931 following the outline of the 1813 church. It measures 150 feet long but only 35 feet wide because, without easy means of joining beams, the mission buildings were only as wide as the trees that served as their ceiling supports were tall. Father Jayme is buried in the sanctuary; a small museum named for him documents mission history and exhibits tools and artifacts from the early days. From the peaceful palm-bedecked gardens out back you can gaze at the 46-foot-high *campanario* (bell tower), the mission's most distinctive feature; one of its five bells was cast in 1802. ✉ *10818 San Diego Mission Rd., Mission Valley* ✛ *From I–8 east, exit and turn left on Mission Gorge Rd., turn left on Twain Rd. and the mission will be on the right* ☎ *619/281–8449* ⊕ *www. missionsandiego.com* ✉ *$5, $3–5 audio tours* ⊙ *Daily 9–4:30.*

NORTH PARK

Named for its location north of Balboa Park, this evolving neighborhood is home to an exciting array of restaurants, bars, and shops. High-end condominiums and local merchants are often cleverly disguised behind historic signage from barbershops, bowling alleys, and theater marquees.

The stretch of Ray Street near University Avenue is home to several small galleries. With a steady stream of new openings in the neighborhood, North Park is one of San Diego's top dining and nightlife destinations.

MISSION BAY, BEACHES, AND SEAWORLD

Mission Bay and the surrounding beaches are the aquatic playground of San Diego. The choice of activities available is astonishing, and the perfect weather makes you want to get out there and play. At the south end of the bay lies SeaWorld, one of San Diego's most popular attractions. If you're craving downtime after all the activity, there are plenty of peaceful spots to relax and simply soak up the sunshine.

Mission Bay welcomes visitors with its protected waters and countless opportunities for fun. The 4,600-acre Mission Bay Park is the place for water sports like sailing, stand-up paddleboarding, and waterskiing. With 19 miles of beaches and grassy areas, it's also a great place for a picnic. One Mission Bay caveat: swimmers should note signs warning about water pollution; on occasions when heavy rains or other events cause pollution, swimming is dangerous.

Mission Beach is a famous and lively fun zone for families and young people both; if it isn't party time at the moment, it will be five minutes from now. The pathways in this area are lined with vacation homes, many for rent by the week or month.

North of Mission Beach is the college-packed party town of Pacific Beach, or "PB" as locals call it. The laid-back vibe of this surfer's mecca draws in free-spirited locals who roam the streets on skateboards and beach cruisers. The energy level peaks during happy hour, when PB's cluster of nightclubs, bars, and 150 restaurants open their doors to those ready to party.

TOP ATTRACTIONS

FAMILY **Belmont Park.** The once-abandoned amusement park between the bay and Mission Beach Boardwalk is now a shopping, dining, and recreation complex. Twinkling lights outline the **Giant Dipper,** an antique wooden roller coaster on which screaming thrill seekers ride more than 2,600 feet of track and 13 hills (riders must be at least 4 feet, 2 inches tall). Created in 1925 and listed on the National Register of Historic Places, this is one of the few old-time roller coasters left in the United States. The **Plunge,** an indoor swimming pool, also opened in 1925, and was the largest—60 feet by 125 feet—saltwater pool in the world at the time (it's had freshwater since 1951). Johnny Weissmuller and Esther Williams are among the stars who were captured on celluloid swimming here. Other Belmont Park attractions include miniature golf, a video arcade, bumper cars, a tilt-a-whirl, and an antique carousel. The rock wall challenges both junior climbers and their elders. Belmont Park also has the most consistent wave in the county at the **Wave House,** where the FlowRider provides surfers and bodyboarders a near-perfect simulated wave on which to practice their skills. ⊠ *3146 Mission Blvd., Mission Bay* ☎ *858/488–1549 for rides, 858/228–9300 for pool* ⊕ *www. belmontpark.com* ✉ *Unlimited ride day package $27 for 48 in. and over, $16 for under 48 in.; pool $7; pool and fitness center $15* ☾ *Park*

TIP SHEET: SEAWORLD SAN DIEGO

SEAWORLD IN A DAY

The highlights of any visit to SeaWorld are the shows, so review the current performance schedule (available online or when you arrive at the park) and plan accordingly. Shows are fairly short—about 20 minutes—so you can see several.

SeaWorld is busiest in the middle of the day, so tackle the adventure rides either at the beginning or end of your visit. Coaster lovers will want to carve out time for the popular new **Manta** ride. Unless it's very hot, consider braving the soakers—**Journey to Atlantis, Shipwreck Rapids**, and sitting in the arenas' **Splash Zones**—in close secession, and then changing into dry clothes.

For an interactive experience, focus on the feeding stations and touch pools. The friendly bottlenose dolphins at **Dolphin Point** just might let you pet them while the hands-on **California Tide Pool** features San Diego's indigenous marine life. At the **Bat Ray Feeding** pool, the friendly rays pop up to the surface for snacks and a gentle pat on the head, while hungry sea lions await you at **Pacific Point**.

The standouts among the walk-through marine exhibits are the **Penguin** and **Shark Encounters, Turtle Reef,** and **Wild Arctic**. Those with tots 42 inches and under should head to the **Sesame Street Bay of Play**.

It's easy for your SeaWorld visit to become a very full day. Although saving either **One Ocean** or **Blue Horizons** for a finale can be great, if you get too tired you might end up missing a main attraction.

POPULAR ADD-ONS

The 30-minute **Dolphin Interaction Program** ($215) lets you feed, touch, and give behavior signals to bottlenose dolphins. A less expensive treat ($39 adults, $19 children) is the **Dine with Shamu** package, which includes a buffet lunch or dinner. The one-hour **Penguin Up Close Tour** ($60) takes you into backstage exhibit areas.

TIPS

■ Pack a change of clothes for after the soaker rides and shows; you can rent lockers to stow belongings. And bring sunscreen and hats.

■ If you get your hand stamped when exiting the park, you can return later that same day.

■ Arrive at shows at least 30 minutes early to get front-row seats, and be prepared to get wet.

■ Steer kids to the **Under the Sun** gift shop, near the Calypso Smoke House, where all items are $10 or less.

■ Eating options include dining with Shamu next to the pool, or casual spots like the Seaside Coffee and Bakery or the Seaport Market.

Elmo's Flying Fish, in SeaWorld's Sesame Street Bay of Play.

opens at 11 daily, ride operation varies seasonally; pool open weekdays 11 am–4 pm and 6:30–9:45 pm, weekends 11am–7:45 pm.

Mission Bay Park. Mission Bay Park is San Diego's monument to sports and fitness. This 4,600-acre aquatic park has 27 miles of shoreline including 19 miles of sandy beaches. Playgrounds and picnic areas abound on the beaches and low grassy hills. On weekday evenings, joggers, bikers, and skaters take over. In the daytime, swimmers, water-skiers, windsurfers, anglers, and boaters—some in single-person kayaks, others in crowded powerboats—vie for space in the water. ⊠ *2688 E. Mission Bay Dr., off I-5 at Exit 22 East Mission Bay Drive, Mission Bay* ☎ *858/581–7602 Park Ranger's Office* ⊕ *www.sandiego.gov/park-and-recreation* ⊠ *Free.*

Mission Beach Boardwalk. The cement pathway lining the sand from the southern end of Mission Beach north to Pacific Beach is always bustling with activity. Cyclists ping the bells on their beach cruisers to pass walkers out for a stroll alongside the oceanfront homes. Vacationers kick back on their patios, while friends play volleyball in the sand. The activity picks up alongside Belmont Park and the Wavehouse, where people stop to check out the action on the FlowRider wave. ⊠ *Alongside the sand from Mission Beach Park to Pacific Beach, Mission Beach.*

FAMILY
Fodor's Choice
★

SeaWorld San Diego. One of the world's largest marine-life amusement parks, SeaWorld is spread over 189 tropically landscaped bay-front acres—and it seems to be expanding into every available square inch of space with new exhibits, shows, and activities. The park offers a variety of amusement rides, some on dry land and others that will leave riders soaking wet.

The majority of SeaWorld's exhibits are walk-through marine environments. Kids get a particular kick out of the **Shark Encounter,** where they come face-to-face with sand, tiger, nurse, bonnethead, black-tipped, and white-tipped reef sharks by walking through a 57-foot clear acrylic tube that passes through the 280,000-gallon shark habitat. **Turtle Reef** offers an incredible up-close encounter with the green sea turtle, while the moving sidewalk at **Penguin Encounter** whisks you through a colony of nearly 300 macaroni, gentoo, Adelie, and emperor penguins. Various **freshwater and saltwater aquariums** hold underwater creatures from around the world.

SeaWorld's highlights are its large-arena entertainments. You can get front-row seats if you arrive 30 minutes in advance, and the stadiums are large enough for everyone to get a seat in the off-season. **One Ocean,** Sea World's headlining Shamu show, stars a synchronized team of orca whales who leap out of the water to the tunes of surround-sound music, illuminated by brilliantly colored lights. **Blue Horizons** combines dolphins, pilot whales, tropical birds, and aerialists in a spectacular performance.

The **Dolphin Interaction Program** gives guests the chance to interact with SeaWorld's bottlenose dolphins in the water. The hour-long program (20 minutes in the water), during which visitors can feed, touch, and give behavior signals, costs $215. You can also **Breakfast with**

Shamu ($26) or **Dine with Shamu** ($39), buffet meals with great views of the whales at play.

The San Diego 3-for-1 Pass ($149 for adults, $119 for children ages 3 to 9) offers seven consecutive days of unlimited admission to SeaWorld, the San Diego Zoo, and the San Diego Zoo's Safari Park. This is a good idea, because if you try to get your money's worth by fitting everything in on a single day, you're likely to end up tired and cranky. Many hotels, especially those in the Mission Bay area, also offer SeaWorld specials that may include rate reductions or two-day entry for the price of one.

There is no shortage of dining options inside SeaWorld, from sandwiches at the Seaport Market, to Italian fare at Mama Stella's Pizza Kitchen, BBQ at the Calypso Bay Smokehouse, or baked goods at Seaside Coffee and Bakery. ⊠ *500 SeaWorld Dr., near west end of I–8, Mission Bay* ☎ *800/257–4268* ⊕ *www.seaworldparks.com* ⊠ *$84 adults, $78 kids; parking $15* ⊘ *Daily 10–dusk; extended hrs in summer.*

LA JOLLA

La Jollans have long considered their village to be the Monte Carlo of California, and with good cause. Its coastline curves into natural coves backed by verdant hillsides covered with homes worth millions. La Jolla is both a natural and cultural treasure trove. The upscale shops, galleries, and restaurants of La Jolla Village satisfy the glitterati, while secluded trails, scenic overlooks, and abundant marine life provide balance and refuge.

Although La Jolla is a neighborhood of the city of San Diego, it has its own postal zone and a coveted sense of class; the ultrarich from around the globe own second homes here—the seaside zone between the neighborhood's bustling Downtown and the cliffs above the Pacific has a distinctly European flavor—and old-money residents maintain friendships with the visiting film stars and royalty who frequent the area's exclusive luxury hotels and private clubs.

The Native Americans called the site La Hoya, meaning "the cave," referring to the grottoes that dot the shoreline. The Spaniards changed the name to La Jolla (same pronunciation as La Hoya), "the jewel," and its residents have cherished the name and its allusions ever since.

Fodor's Choice   **Museum of Contemporary Art San Diego.** Driving along Coast Boulevard,
★   it is hard to miss the mass of watercraft jutting out from the rear of the Museum of Contemporary Art San Diego (MCASD) La Jolla location. *Pleasure Point* by Nancy Rubins is just one example of the mingling of art and locale at this spectacular oceanfront setting.

The oldest section of La Jolla's branch of San Diego's contemporary art museum was originally a residence, designed by Irving Gill for philanthropist Ellen Browning Scripps in 1916. In the mid-1990s the compound was updated and expanded by architect Robert Venturi, who respected Gill's original geometric structure and clean mission style lines while adding his own distinctive touches. The result is a striking contemporary building that looks as though it's always been here.

Acrobatic dolphins perform in SeaWorld's Dolphin Discovery show.

The light-filled Axline Court serves as the museum's entrance and does triple duty as reception area, exhibition hall, and forum for special events, including the glittering Monte Carlo gala each September, attended by the town's most fashionable folk. Inside, the museum's artwork gets major competition from the setting: you can look out from the top of a grand stairway onto a landscaped garden that contains permanent and temporary sculpture exhibits as well as rare 100-year-old California plant specimens and, beyond that, to the Pacific Ocean.

California artists figure prominently in the museum's permanent collection of post-1950s art, but the museum also includes examples of every major art movement through the present—works by Andy Warhol, Robert Rauschenberg, Frank Stella, Joseph Cornell, and Jenny Holzer, to name a few. Important pieces by artists from San Diego and Tijuana were acquired in the 1990s. The museum also gets major visiting shows. ⊠ *700 Prospect St., La Jolla* ☎ *858/454-3541* ⊕ *www. mcasd.org* ⌲ *$10, good for 1 visit here and at MCASD Downtown within 7 days; free 3rd Thurs. of the month 5–7* ⊙ *Thurs.–Tues. 11–5; 3rd Thurs. of month 11–7* ⊙ *Closed Wed.*

Fodor'sChoice ★ **Torrey Pines State Natural Reserve.** *Pinus torreyana,* the rarest native pine tree in the United States, enjoys a 1,700-acre sanctuary at the northern edge of La Jolla. About 6,000 of these unusual trees, some as tall as 60 feet, grow on the cliffs here. The park is one of only two places in the world (the other is Santa Rosa Island, off Santa Barbara) where the Torrey pine grows naturally. The reserve has several hiking trails leading to the cliffs, 300 feet above the ocean; trail maps are available at the park station. Wildflowers grow profusely in spring, and the ocean

panoramas are always spectacular. When in this upper part of the park, respect the restrictions. Not permitted: picnicking, smoking, leaving the trails, dogs, alcohol, or collecting plant specimens.

You can unwrap your sandwiches, however, at Torrey Pines State Beach, just below the reserve. When the tide is out, it's possible to walk south all the way past the lifeguard towers to Black's Beach over rocky promontories carved by the waves (avoid the bluffs, however; they're unstable). **Los Peñasquitos Lagoon** at the north end of the reserve is one of the many natural estuaries that flow inland between Del Mar and Oceanside. It's a good place to watch shorebirds. Volunteers lead guided nature walks at 10 and 2 on most weekends. ⊠ *N. Torrey Pines Rd. exit off I–5 onto Carmel Valley Rd. going west, then turn left (south) on Coast Hwy. 101, 12600 N. Torrey Pines Rd., La Jolla* ☎ *858/755–2063* ⊕ *www.torreypine.org* ✉ *Parking $12–$15* ☉ *Daily 9–dusk.*

WORTH NOTING

University of California at San Diego. The campus of one of the country's most prestigious research universities spreads over 1,200 acres of coastal canyons and eucalyptus groves, where students and faculty jog, bike, and rollerblade to class. If you're interested in contemporary art, check out the **Stuart Collection of Sculpture**—18 thought-provoking, site-specific works by artists such as Nam June Paik, William Wegman,

Niki de St. Phalle, Jenny Holzer, and others arrayed around the campus. UCSD's **Price Center** has a well-stocked, two-level bookstore—the largest in San Diego—and a good coffeehouse, Perks. Look for the postmodern **Geisel Library**, named for longtime La Jolla residents Theodor "Dr. Seuss" Geisel and his wife, Audrey. For campus culture, political views, vegan dishes, and live music, head to the **Che Café** located in Building 161, painted in bright murals. Bring quarters for the parking meters, or cash or a credit card for the parking structures, since free parking is only available on weekends. ⊠ *Exit I–5 onto La Jolla Village Dr. going west; take Gilman Dr. off-ramp to right and continue on to information kiosk at campus entrance on Gilman Dr., La Jolla* 🕾 *858/534–4414 campus tour information* 🌐 *www.ucsd.edu* ⊗ *90-min campus tours Sun. at 2 from South Gilman Information Pavilion; reserve before 4 pm Thurs.*

POINT LOMA AND CORONADO WITH HARBOR AND SHELTER ISLANDS, AND OCEAN BEACH

Although Coronado is actually an isthmus, easily reached from the mainland if you head north from Imperial Beach, it has always seemed like an island and is often referred to as such. To the west, Point Loma protects the San Diego Bay from the Pacific's tides and waves. Both Coronado and Point Loma have stately homes, sandy beaches, private marinas, and prominent military installations. Nestled between the two, Harbor and Shelter islands owe their existence to dredging in the bay.

POINT LOMA

The hilly peninsula of Point Loma curves west and south into the Pacific and provides protection for San Diego Bay. Its high elevations and sandy cliffs provide incredible views, and make Point Loma a visible local landmark. Its maritime roots are evident, from its longtime ties to the U.S. Navy to its bustling sport fishing and sailing marinas. The funky community of Ocean Beach coexists alongside the stately homes of Sunset Cliffs and the honored graves at Fort Rosecrans National Cemetery.

TOP ATTRACTIONS

FAMILY
Fodor's Choice
★

Cabrillo National Monument. This 160-acre preserve marks the site of the first European visit to San Diego, made by 16th-century explorer Juan Rodríguez Cabrillo. Cabrillo landed at this spot on September 15, 1542. Today the site, with its rugged cliffs and shores and outstanding overlooks, is one of the most frequently visited of all the national monuments.

The **visitor center** presents films and lectures about Cabrillo's voyage, the sea-level tide pools, and migrating gray whales. **Interpretive stations** have been installed along the walkways that edge the cliffs. The moderately steep **Bayside Trail**, 2½ miles round-trip, winds through coastal sage scrub, curving under the cliff-top lookouts and taking you ever closer to the bay-front scenery. You cannot reach the beach from this trail, and must stick to the path to protect the cliffs from erosion and yourself from thorny plants and snakes—including rattlers. You'll see prickly pear cactus and yucca, black-eyed Susans, fragrant sage, and

A surfer prepares to head out before sunset at La Jolla's Torrey Pines State Beach and Reserve.

maybe a lizard, rabbit, or hummingbird. The climb back is long but gradual, leading up to the **Old Point Loma Lighthouse.**

The western and southern cliffs of Cabrillo National Monument are prime whale-watching territory. A sheltered **viewing station** has wayside exhibits describing the great gray whales' yearly migration from Baja California to the Bering and Chukchi seas near Alaska. High-powered telescopes help you focus on the whales' waterspouts. Whales are visible on clear days from late December through early March, with the highest concentration in January and February. More-accessible sea creatures (starfish, crabs, anemones) can be seen in the **tide pools** at the foot of the monument's western cliffs. Drive north from the visitor center to Cabrillo Road, which winds down to the Coast Guard station and the shore. ⊠ *1800 Cabrillo Memorial Dr., Point Loma* ☎ *619/557–5450* ⊕ *www.nps.gov/cabr* ✉ *$5 per car, $3 per person on foot/bicycle, entry good for 7 days* ☉ *Daily 9–5.*

Sunset Cliffs. As the name suggests, the 60-foot-high bluffs on the western side of Point Loma south of Ocean Beach are a perfect place to watch the sun set over the sea. To view the tide pools along the shore, use the staircase off Sunset Cliffs Boulevard at the foot of Ladera Street.

The dramatic coastline here seems to have been carved out of ancient rock. The impact of the waves is very clear: each year more sections of the cliffs are posted with caution signs. Don't ignore these warnings—it's easy to slip in the crumbling sandstone, and the surf can be extremely rough. The small coves and beaches that dot the coastline are popular with surfers drawn to the pounding waves. The homes along the boulevard—pink stucco mansions beside shingled Cape Cod–style cottages—are fine examples of Southern California luxury. ✉ *Sunset Cliffs Blvd., Point Loma.*

OCEAN BEACH

At the northern end of Point Loma lies the chilled-out, hippyesque town of Ocean Beach, commonly referred to as "OB." The main thoroughfare of this funky neighborhood is dotted with dive bars, coffeehouses, surf shops, and 1960s diners. OB is a magnet for everyone from surfers to musicians and artists. Fans of OB applaud its resistance to "selling out" to upscale development, whereas detractors lament its somewhat scruffy edges.

SHELTER ISLAND

In 1950 San Diego's port director decided to raise the shoal that lay off the eastern shore of Point Loma above sea level with the sand and mud dredged up during the course of deepening a ship channel in the 1930s and '40s. The resulting peninsula, **Shelter Island**, became home to several marinas and resorts, many with Polynesian details that still exist today, giving them a retro flair. This reclaimed peninsula now supports towering palms and resorts, restaurants, and side-by-side marinas. A long sidewalk runs past boat brokerages to the hotels and marinas that line the inner shore, facing Point Loma. On the bay side, fishermen launch their boats and families relax at picnic tables along the grass, where there are fire rings and permanent barbeque grills.

HARBOR ISLAND

Following the successful creation of Shelter Island, in 1961 the U.S. Navy used the residue from digging berths deep enough to accommodate aircraft carriers to build **Harbor Island**. Restaurants and high-rise hotels dot the inner shore of this 1½-mile-long man-made peninsula adjacent to the airport. The bay's shore is lined with pathways, gardens, and scenic picnic spots. The east-end point has killer views of the Downtown skyline.

CORONADO

As if freeze-framed in the 1950s, Coronado's quaint appeal is captured in its old-fashioned storefronts, well-manicured gardens, and charming **Ferry Landing Marketplace.** The streets of Coronado are wide, quiet, and friendly, and many of today's residents live in grand Victorian homes handed down for generations. Naval Air Station North Island was established in 1911 on Coronado's north end, across from Point Loma, and was the site of Charles Lindbergh's departure on the transcontinental flight that preceded his famous solo flight across the Atlantic. Coronado's long relationship with the U.S. Navy and its desirable real estate have made it an enclave for military personnel; it's said to have more retired admirals per capita than anywhere else in the United States.

Coronado is accessible via the arching blue 2.2-mile-long San Diego–Coronado Bay Bridge, which handles some 68,000 cars each day. The view of the harbor, Downtown, and the island is breathtaking, day and night. Until the bridge was completed in 1969, visitors and residents relied on the Coronado Ferry, which today has become quite popular

San Diego's myriad coastal trails and paths provide great views of natural and man-made wonders alike.

with bicyclists, who shuttle their bikes across the harbor and ride Coronado's wide, flat boulevards for hours.

TOP ATTRACTIONS

FAMILY **Coronado Ferry Landing.** This collection of shops at Ferry Landing is on a smaller scale than the Embarcadero's Seaport Village, but you do get a great view of the Downtown San Diego skyline. The little bayside shops and restaurants resemble the gingerbread domes of the Hotel Del Coronado. **Bikes and Beyond** (☎ *619/435–7180* ⊕ *hollandsbicycles.com*) rents bikes and surreys, perfect for riding through town and along Coronado's scenic bike path. ⊠ *1201 1st St., at B Ave., Coronado* ☎ *619/435–8895* ⊕ *www.coronadoferrylandingshops.com*.

Fodor's Choice **Hotel Del Coronado.** The Del's distinctive red-tile roofs and Victorian gin-
★ gerbread architecture have served as a set for many movies, political meetings, and extravagant social happenings. It's speculated that the Duke of Windsor may have first met Wallis Simpson here. Eleven presidents have been guests of the Del, and the film *Some Like It Hot*—starring Marilyn Monroe, Jack Lemmon, and Tony Curtis—used the hotel as a backdrop.

The Hotel Del, as locals call it, was the brainchild of financiers Elisha Spurr Babcock Jr. and H. L. Story, who saw the potential of Coronado's virgin beaches and its view of San Diego's emerging harbor. It opened in 1888 and became a National Historic Landmark in 1977.

Although the pool area is reserved for hotel guests, several surrounding dining patios make great places to sit back and imagine the scene during the 1920s, when the hotel rocked with good times. Behind the pool area, an attractive shopping arcade features a classic candy shop as well as several fine clothing and accessories stores. A lavish Sunday brunch is served in the Crown Room, from 9:30 to 1:30 pm. During the holidays, the hotel hosts Skating by the Sea, an outdoor beachfront ice-skating rink open to the public. ■ TIP→ **Even if you don't happen to be staying at the Del, gazing out over the ocean while enjoying a drink at the Sun Deck Bar and Grill makes for a great escape. If it's chilly, the fire pits and sofa seating are very inviting.**

The History Gallery displays photos from the Del's early days, and books elaborating on its history and that of Kate Morgan, the hotel's resident ghost, are sold along with logo apparel and gifts in the hotel's 15-plus shops. Tours of the Del take place on Tuesday and Friday at 10:30, Saturday and Sunday at 2. Reservations are required. ⊠ *1500 Orange Ave., at Glorietta Blvd., Coronado* ☎ *619/435–6611, 619/437– 8788 tour reservations (through Coronado Visitor Center)* ⊕ *www. hoteldel.com* ⊠ *Tours $15.*

Orange Avenue. Coronado's business district and its villagelike heart, this is surely one of the most charming spots in Southern California. Slow-paced and very "local" (the city fights against chain stores), it's a blast from the past, although entirely up to date in other respects. The military presence—Coronado is home to the U.S. Navy Sea, Air and Land (SEAL) forces—is reflected in shops selling military gear and places like **McP's Irish Pub,** at No. 1107. A family-friendly stop for a good, all-American meal, it's the unofficial SEALs headquarters. Many clothing boutiques, home-furnishings stores, and upscale restaurants cater to visitors with deep pockets, but you can buy plumbing sup-plies, too, or get a genuine military haircut at **Crown Barber Shop,** at No. 947. If you need a break, stop for a latte at the sidewalk café of **Bay Books,** San Diego's largest independent bookstore, at No. 1029. ⊠ *Orange Avenue, near 9th St., Coronado.*

WORTH NOTING

Coronado Museum of History and Art. The neoclassical First Bank of Commerce building, constructed in 1910, holds the headquarters and archives of the Coronado Historical Association, a museum, the Coro-nado Visitor Center, and the Coronado Museum Store. The museum's collection celebrates Coronado's history with photographs and displays of its formative events and major sights. *Promenade Through the Past: A Brief History of Coronado and its Architectural Wonders,* available at the museum store, traces a 60-minute walking tour of the area's architecturally and historically significant buildings. A guided tour of them departs from the museum lobby on Wednesday mornings at 10:30 and costs $10 (reservations required). ⊠ *1100 Orange Ave., at Park Pl., Coronado* ☎ *619/435–7242, 619/437–8788 walking tour reservations* ⊕ *www.coronadohistory.org* ⊠ *Free* ☾ *Mon.–Fri. 9–5, Sat.–Sun. 10–5.*

BEACHES

San Diego's beaches have a different vibe from their northern counter-parts in neighboring Orange County and glitzy Los Angeles farther up the coast. San Diego is more laid-back and less of a scene. Cyclists on cruiser bikes whiz by as surfers saunter toward the waves and sunbathers bronze under the sun, be it July or November.

Even at summer's hottest peak, San Diego's beaches are cool and breezy. Ocean waves are large, and the water will be colder than what you experience at tropical beaches—temperatures range from 55°F to 65°F from October through June, and 65°F to 73°F from July through September.

Finding a parking spot near the ocean can be hard in summer, but for the time being, unmetered parking is available at all San Diego city beaches.

Pay attention to signs listing illegal activities; undercover police often patrol the beaches. Smoking and alcoholic beverages are completely banned on city beaches. Drinking in beach parking lots, on boardwalks, and in landscaped areas is also illegal. Glass containers are not permitted on beaches, cliffs, and walkways, or in park areas and adjacent parking lots. Littering is not tolerated, and skateboarding is prohibited at some beaches. Fires are allowed only in fire rings or elevated barbecue grills. Although it may be tempting to take a sea creature from a tide pool as a souvenir, it may upset the delicate ecological balance, and it's illegal, too.

Lifeguards are stationed at city beaches from Sunset Cliffs up to Black's Beach in the summertime, but coverage in winter is provided by roving patrols only. When swimming in the ocean, be aware of rip currents, which are common in California shores.

San Diego's beaches are well maintained and very clean during summertime, when rainfall is infrequent. Pollution is generally worse near river mouths and storm-drain outlets, especially after heavy rainfall. Call San Diego's Lifeguard Services at ☎ 619/221–8824 for a recorded message that includes pollution reports along with surfing and diving conditions.

Beaches are listed geographically, south to north.

CORONADO

FAMILY **Silver Strand State Beach.** This quiet Coronado beach is ideal for families. The water is relatively calm, lifeguards and rangers are on duty year-round, and there are places for boating, watersports, biking, volleyball, and fishing. Picnic tables, grills, and fire pits are available, and the Silver Stand Beach Cafe is open during the summer. The beach sits across the street from Loews Coronado Bay Resort and the Coronado Cays, an exclusive community popular with yacht owners and celebrities. You can reserve RV sites ($65 beach; $50 inland) at ⊕ *www.reserveamerica. com.* Four day-use parking lots provide room for more than 1,000 cars. Foot tunnels under Route 75 lead to a bayside beach with great views of the San Diego skyline. **Amenities:** food and drink, lifeguards, parking (fee), showers, toilets. **Best for:** walking, swimming, surfing. ⊠ *From San Diego–Coronado Bridge, turn left onto Orange Ave., which becomes Rte. 75, and follow signs, Coronado* ☎ *619/435–5184* ⊕ *www.parks.ca.gov/silverstrand* ⊠ *Parking $10.*

FAMILY
Fodor'sChoice
★ **Coronado Beach.** With the famous Hotel Del Coronado as a backdrop, this sandy white beach is one of San Diego County's largest and most picturesque strands. It's perfect for sunbathing, people-watching, and

Experts and beginners alike head to San Diego for its excellent surfing.

Frisbee tossing. Exercisers might include Navy SEAL teams or other military units that conduct training runs on beaches in and around Coronado. There are picnic tables, grills and fire rings, a playground, and (on the northern end) a dog run. Free parking is available along Ocean Boulevard, though it's often hard to snag a space. **Amenities:** food and drink, lifeguards, showers, toilets. **Best for:** walking, swimming. ⊠ *From the San Diego–Coronado bridge, turn left on Orange Ave. and follow signs, Coronado.*

POINT LOMA, MISSION BAY, AND LA JOLLA

POINT LOMA

Sunset Cliffs. Semi-secluded Sunset Cliffs is popular with surfers and locals but offers little in the way of amenities. A few miles long, it lies beneath jagged cliffs on the Point Loma peninsula's western side. Low tide at the southern end, near Cabrillo Point, reveals tide pools teeming with small sea creatures. Farther north the waves lure surfers, and the lonely coves attract sunbathers. Stairs at the foot of Pescadero and Bermuda avenues provide beach access, as do some cliff trails, which are treacherous at points. Osprey Point offers good fishing off the rocks. A visit here is more enjoyable at low tide or at sunset when the views are sensational. Check WaveCast (⊕ *wavecast.com/tides*) for tide schedules. **Amenities:** parking (no fee). **Best for:** solitude, sunset. ⊠ *Take I–8 west to Sunset Cliffs Blvd. and head west, Point Loma.*

Ocean Beach. Much of this mile-long beach south of Mission Bay's channel entrance is a haven for volleyball players, sunbathers, and swimmers. The area around the municipal pier at the southern end is a hangout for surfers and transients. The pier stays open 24 hours a day for fishing and walking. There's a restaurant about halfway out, and more places to grab a snack can be found on the streets near the beach. Swimmers should beware of strong rip currents around the main lifeguard tower. There's a dog beach at the northern end; during summer there can be as many as 100 dogs running in the sand. For picnic areas (with fire rings) and a paved path, check out Ocean Beach Park, across from Dog Beach. **Amenities:** lifeguards, parking (no fee), showers, toilets. **Best for:** surfing, swimming, walking. ⊠ *Take I–8 west to Sunset Cliffs Blvd. and head west; a right turn off Sunset Cliffs Blvd. takes you to the water, Point Loma.*

MISSION BAY

FAMILY   **Mission Beach.** San Diego's most popular beach draws huge crowds on hot summer days, but it's lively year-round. The 2-mile-long stretch extends from the northern entrance of Mission Bay to Pacific Beach. A wide boardwalk paralleling the beach is popular with walkers, joggers, roller skaters, rollerbladers, and bicyclists. Surfers, swimmers, and volleyball players congregate at the southern end. Scantily clad volleyball players practice on Cohasset Court. Toward its northern end, near the Belmont Park roller coaster, the beach narrows and the water becomes rougher. The crowds grow thicker and somewhat rougher as well. For parking, you can try for a spot on the street, but your best bets are the two big lots at Belmont Park. **Amenities:** lifeguards, parking (no fee), showers, toilets. **Best for:** swimming, surfing, walking. ⊠ *Exit I–5 at Grand Ave. and head west to Mission Blvd.; turn south and look for parking near roller coaster at West Mission Bay Dr., Mission Bay.*

Pacific Beach/North Pacific Beach. The boardwalk of Mission Beach turns into a sidewalk here, but there are still bike paths and picnic tables along the beach. Pacific Beach runs from the northern end of Mission Beach to Crystal Pier. The scene here is lively on weekends, with nearby restaurants, beach bars, and nightclubs providing a party atmosphere. North Pacific Beach, extending north from the pier, attracts families. There are designated swimming and surfing areas, and fire rings are available, as are places to eat. Parking can be a challenge. **Amenities:** food and drink, lifeguards, parking (no fee), showers, toilets. **Best for:** partiers, swimming, surfing. ⊠ *Exit I–5 at Grand Ave. and head west to Mission Blvd. Turn north and look for parking, Mission Bay.*

Tourmaline Surfing Park. Offering slow waves and frequent winds, this is one of the most popular beaches for beginning surfers, longboarders, windsurfers, and kiteboarders. Separate areas designated for swimmers and surfers are strictly enforced. The 175-space parking lot at the foot of Tourmaline Street normally fills to capacity by midday. **Amenities:** lifeguards, parking (no fee), showers, toilets. **Best for:** windsurfing, surfing. ⊠ *Take Mission Blvd. north (it turns into La Jolla Blvd.) and turn west on Tourmaline St., 600 Tourmaline St., Mission Bay.*

LA JOLLA

Windansea Beach. Named for a hotel that burned down in the late 1940s, Windansea Beach has become famous for the unusual A-frame waves the reef break here creates—and for the eclectic group of surfers those waves attract. This is one of San Diego County's most popular surf spots, and with its incredible views and secluded sunbathing spots set among sandstone rocks, Windansea is also one of the most romantic of West Coast beaches, especially at sunset. You can usually find nearby street parking. **Amenities:** lifeguards. **Best for:** sunset, surfing, solitude. ☒ *Take Mission Blvd. north (it turns into La Jolla Blvd.) and turn west on Nautilus St., La Jolla.*

> **WORD OF MOUTH**
>
> "The cove at La Jolla…reminds one of the South of France. From there you can easily wander around the very cute/upscale village of La Jolla."
>
> —Tomsd

Marine Street Beach. A wide expanse of white sand, this beach often teems with sunbathers, swimmers, walkers, joggers, and folks just out for the incredible views. This is a great spot for bodysurfing, but be aware that the waves break in extremely shallow water. You'll also need to watch out for riptides. Picnic tables, showers, and toilets are available at the nearby cove. **Amenities:** lifeguards. **Best for:** solitude, swimming, walking. ☒ *Accessible from Marine St., off La Jolla Blvd., La Jolla.*

FAMILY
Fodor'sChoice
★

La Jolla Cove. This shimmering blue inlet is what first attracted everyone to La Jolla, from Native Americans to the glitterati; it's the secret to the village's enduring cachet. You'll find "the Cove"—as locals refer to it, as though it were the only one in San Diego—beyond where Girard Avenue dead-ends into Coast Boulevard, marked by towering palms that line a promenade where people strolling in designer clothes are as common as Frisbee throwers. Ellen Browning Scripps Park sits atop cliffs formed by the incessant pounding of the waves and offers a great spot for picnics with a view. At low tide the pools and cliff caves are a destination for explorers. Divers, snorkelers, and kayakers can check out the underwater delights of the **San Diego–La Jolla Underwater Park Ecological Reserve.** The cove is also a favorite of rough-water swimmers. **Amenities:** lifeguards, showers, toilets. **Best for:** snorkeling, swimming, walking. ☒ *Follow Coast Blvd. north to signs, or take La Jolla Village Dr. exit from I–5, head west to Torrey Pines Rd., turn left, and drive downhill to Girard Ave.; turn right and follow signs, La Jolla.*

FAMILY
La Jolla Shores. This is one of San Diego's most popular beaches, so get here early on summer weekends. The lures are an incredible view of La Jolla peninsula, a wide sandy beach, a grassy park that's adjacent to **San Diego La Jolla Underwater Park Ecological Reserve,** and the gentlest waves in San Diego. Several surf and scuba schools teach here, and kayak rentals are nearby. A concrete boardwalk parallels the beach, and a boat launch for small vessels lies 300 yards south of the lifeguard station at Avenida de Playa. Arrive early to get a parking spot in the lot at the foot of Calle Frescota. **Amenities:** lifeguards, parking (no fee), showers, toilets. **Best for:** surfing, swimming, walking. ☒ *8200 Camino del Oro, From I–5 take La Jolla Village Dr. west and turn left onto La Jolla Shores Dr.; head west to Camino del Oro or Vallecitos St., turn right, La Jolla.*

Black's Beach. The powerful waves at this beach, officially known as Torrey Pines City Park beach, attract world-class surfers, and the strand's relative isolation appeals to nudist nature lovers (although by law nudity is prohibited) as well as gays and lesbians. Backed by cliffs whose colors change with the sun's angle, Black's can be accessed from Torrey Pines State Beach to the north, or by a narrow path descending the cliffs from Torrey Pines Glider Port. Access to parts of the shore coincides with low tide. Lifeguards patrol the area only between spring break and mid-October. Strong rip currents are common—only experienced swimmers should take the plunge. Storms have weakened the cliffs in the past few years; they're dangerous to climb and should be avoided. Part of the fun here is watching hang gliders and paragliders ascend from atop the cliffs. Parking is available at the Torrey Pines Glider Port and La Jolla Farms. **Amenities:** None. **Best for:** solitude, nudists, surfing. ⊠ *Take Genesee Ave. west from I–5 and follow signs to Torrey Pines Glider Port; easier access, via a paved path, available on La Jolla Farms Rd., but parking is limited to 2 hrs., La Jolla.*

Torrey Pines State Beach and Reserve. One of San Diego's best beaches encompasses 2,000 acres of bluffs and bird-filled marshes. A network of meandering trails leads to the wide, sandy shoreline below. Along the way enjoy the rare Torrey pine trees, found only here and on Santa Rosa Island, offshore. Guides conduct tours of the nature preserve on weekends. Torrey Pines tends to get crowded in summer, but you'll find more isolated spots heading south under the cliffs leading to Black's Beach. **Amenities:** lifeguards, parking (fee), showers, toilets. **Best for:** swimming, surfing, walking. ⊠ *Take Carmel Valley Rd. exit west from I–5, turn left on Rte. S21, 12600 N. Torrey Pines Rd.* ☎ *858/755–2063* ⊕ *www.torreypine.org* 🚗 *Parking $12–$15 per vehicle depending on day and season.*

NORTH COUNTY BEACHES

DEL MAR

Del Mar Beach. The numbered streets of Del Mar, from 15th north to 29th, end at a wide beach popular with volleyball players, surfers, and sunbathers. The portion of Del Mar south of 15th Street is lined with cliffs and rarely crowded. Leashed dogs are permitted on most sections of the beach, except Main Beach, where they are prohibited from June 15th through Labor Day. For the rest of the year, dogs may run under voice control at North Beach, also known as Dog Beach. Food, hotels, and shopping are all within an easy walk of Del Mar beach. Parking costs from $1.50 to $3 per hour at meters and pay lots on Coast Boulevard and along Camino Del Mar. **Amenities:** food and drink, lifeguards, parking (fee), showers, toilets. **Best for:** swimming, walking. ⊠ *Take Via de la Valle exit from I–5 west to Rte. S21 (also known as Camino del Mar in Del Mar) and turn left.*

ENCINITAS

Swami's. The palms and the golden lotus-flower domes of the nearby Self-Realization Center temple and ashram earned this picturesque beach, also a top surfing spot, its name. Extreme low tides expose tide pools that harbor anemones, starfish, and other sea life. The only access is by a long stairway leading down from the cliff-top Seaside Roadside Park, where there's free parking. On big winter swells, the bluffs are lined with gawkers watching the area's best surfers take on—and be taken down by—some of the county's best big waves. Offshore, divers do their thing at North County's underwater park, Encinitas Marine Life Refuge. **Amenities:** lifeguards, parking (no fee), showers, toilets. **Best for:** snorkeling, surfing, swimming. ✉ *Follow Rte. S21 north from Cardiff, or Exit I–5 at Encinitas Blvd., go west to Rte. S21, and turn left.*

2

WHERE TO EAT

San Diego's proximity to Mexico makes it an attractive destination for anything wrapped in a tortilla, but there's so much more. While most of the top restaurants offer seasonal California fare, San Diego also boasts excellent ethnic cuisines available at all prices.

As elsewhere in the United States, the San Diego dining scene has moved toward using sustainable, locally sourced meat, seafood, and produce—and providing good value. This emphasis on affordability is often presented as early or late-night dining specials, but also extends to the wine lists, where smart sommeliers are offering more wines from value regions like France's Loire and Languedoc, and countries like Chile and South Africa. *Use the coordinate (⊕ A1) at the end of each listing to locate a site on the corresponding map.*

WHAT IT COSTS

	$	$$	$$$	$$$$
Restaurants	under 18	$18–$24	$25–$35	over $35

Restaurant prices are the average cost of a main course at dinner or, if dinner is not served, at lunch.

DOWNTOWN

GASLAMP QUARTER

$$ SPANISH Fodor's Choice ★

🍴 **Café Sevilla.** Sevilla moved into new digs in 2011, allowing a fresh look for this tapas bar, nightclub, and restaurant. Thursday through Sunday evenings, it's packed with youthful throngs who crowd the ground-floor bar for drinks, tapas, and live music. Others head to the downstairs club for classics from the Spanish kitchen and, on Saturday nights, professional flamenco dancing. The kitchen does a respectable job with the traditional shellfish and chicken paella (there are meat and other seafood versions, too); other good choices are the highly flavorful saffron-infused sea bass and the roasted pork tenderloin. A new favorite is a trio of dramatically presented *brochetas,* or skewers, of spiced shrimp, Spanish sausage, and steak with mushrooms and onions. [$] *Average main: $22* ✉ *353 5th Ave., Gaslamp Quarter, San Diego* ☎ *619/233–5979* 🌐 *www.cafesevilla.com* ⏲ *No lunch* ⊕ *H3.*

$$$ AMERICAN

🍴 **Searsucker.** The much-hyped first restaurant from *Top Chef* finalist Brian Malarkey opened in summer 2010 and has maintained its buzz ever since, attracting patrons with its fun urban decor and experimental dishes like mahimahi with drunken cherries; and beef coulotte with chimichurri and bernaise. The flavor combinations are mostly successful, particularly when paired with comfort-food sides like bacon grits and fried brussels sprouts. [$] *Average main: $30* ✉ *611 5th Ave., Gaslamp Quarter, San Diego* ☎ *619/233–7327* 🌐 *www.searsucker.com* ✍ *Reservations essential* ✥ *H2.*

$$ JAPANESE Fodor's Choice ★

🍴 **Taka.** It may be on a prominent corner, but the pristine fish imported from around the world and the creative presentations are what attracts the crowds each night. Start with one of the sushi chef's appetizers, perhaps the monkfish liver with ponzu, some slices of tender hamachi sashimi, or a special box-press sushi with shrimp, tuna, and crab topped with pickled seaweed and caviar. Hot dishes include salmon teriyaki and an East-meets-West-style New York steak. The restaurant is a favorite with Japanese visitors. [$] *Average main: $18* ✉ *555 5th Ave., Gaslamp Quarter, San Diego* ☎ *619/338–0555* 🌐 *www.takasushi.com* 🕒 *No lunch* ✥ *H2.*

EAST VILLAGE

$$ FRENCH Fodor's Choice ★

🍴 **Café Chloe.** The intersection of 9th and G is the meeting point for San Diego's café society, thanks to the superchic and friendly Café Chloe. Surrounded by luxury high-rises, hotels, and boutiques, this pretty Parisian spot is frequented by the locals for breakfast, lunch, dinner, and weekend brunch. Whole-wheat pancakes with sour-cherry sauce are an excellent way to start the day; lunch might mean a smoked trout and apple salad or a casserole of macaroni, pancetta, and Gorgonzola; and dinner hightlights include duck confit or steak frites. Enjoy wines by the glass, imported teas, and coffee with desserts like seasonal fruit tarts or chocolate pot de crème. It's a particularly lovely place to spend the afternoon. [$] *Average main: $24* ✉ *721 9th Ave., East Village, San Diego* ☎ *619/232–3242* 🌐 *www.cafechloe.com* ✥ *E5.*

$$$$ STEAKHOUSE Fodor's Choice ★

🍴 **Cowboy Star.** Executive chef Victor Jimenez cooks up porterhouses for two and grass-fed fillets along with sautéed brussels sprouts and yellow corn polenta at this modern, urban steak house with a tongue-in-cheek cowboy theme. It's not a place for line dancing or peanut shelling: servers wear stylish plaid shirts and the wood-and-brick decor has leather accents and photography that recalls the Old West. Non–steak eaters can tuck into dishes like crispy seared pheasant or seared amberjack. The high-back booths are comfy; so are the chef's counter and the bar, where mixologists shake up strong bourbon cocktails. The drink selections include artisanal brews paired with the steaks. Street parking is usually available. [$] *Average main: $38* ✉ *640 10th Ave., East Village, San Diego* ☎ *619/450–5880* 🌐 *www.thecowboystar.com* 🕒 *No lunch Sat.–Mon.* ✥ *H2.*

$ GREEK Fodor's Choice ★

🍴 **The Kebab Shop.** Easy to find in Europe but rare in San Diego are kebab shops: fast-food Mediterranean eateries where roasted meats and falafel are served on plates of rice or wrapped in flatbread for consumption at all hours of the day. This East Village shop doesn't have much competition, but that doesn't mean it's not first-rate. The lamb is spicy and filling, and fresh tabouli and Greek salads round out the meals. For a delicious meal on the go, order the *döner* box: a choice of spiced lamb, marinated chicken, or falafel, accompanied by fries or rice, fresh veggies, and creamy garlic yogurt sauce. $ *Average main: $8* ⊠ *630 9th Ave., East Village, San Diego* ☎ *619/525–0055* ⊕ *www.thekebabshop. com* ⚲ *Reservations not accepted* ✛ *H2.*

LITTLE ITALY

$$
ITALIAN
Fodor's Choice
★

✕ **Bencotto.** The Northern Italian team behind Bencotto opened a fine-dining restaurant in Milan and a bistro called Salumeria Rosi in New York before developing this sophisticated addition to Little Italy. Diners linger over wine and meat platters at the friendly bar and the more intimate upstairs dining room. Small plates designed for sharing include fried saffron risotto balls and sliced cantaloupe with prosciutto, but the real draws are the fresh pastas made daily in-house that include Gorgonzola-filled gnocchi, various ravioli, and squid-ink fettuccine. The pastas can be topped with a choice of sauces and chicken, shrimp, or meatballs. ■TIP➔ **Parking can be challenging but the Little Italy valet service is available after 6 pm.** $ *Average main: $18* ⊠ *750 W. Fir St., Little Italy, San Diego* ☎ *619/450–4786* ⊕ *www.lovebencotto. com* ◷ *Closed Mon.* ✛ *E5.*

BALBOA PARK AND BANKERS HILL

BALBOA PARK

$$$
ECLECTIC

✕ **The Prado.** The striking Spanish-Moorish interior of this lovely restaurant in the historic House of Hospitality on Balboa Park's museum row has painted ceilings and elaborate glass sculptures. It also brings a contemporary menu to an area where picnic lunches or hot dogs from a nearby cart are the usual options. The bar is a fashionable pre- and post-theater destination for light nibbles with Latin, Italian, and Asian flavors and creative drinks; in the dining room, reliable dishes range from lunchtime grilled mahimahi tacos and a fancy pressed salad of baby arugula, strawberries, candied walnuts, and asiago cheese to saffron-scented lobster paella and roasted sea bass. $ *Average main: $27* ⊠ *1549 El Prado, Balboa Park, San Diego* ☎ *619/557–9441* ⊕ *www. pradobalboa.com* ◷ *No dinner Mon.* ✛ *E5.*

BANKERS HILL

$
MEXICAN
Fodor's Choice
★

✕ **Barrio Star.** In a colorful, airy Bankers Hill space, chef Isabel Cruz of Isabel's Cantina and up-and-coming chef Todd Camburn put a fresh, distinctive, and rather refined spin on classic Mexican fare. After an afternoon at nearby Balboa Park, swing by for happy hour margaritas and tacos or feast on grilled sweet corn slathered in spicy lime butter, tortilla soup with cotija cheese, slow-roasted pork carnitas tacos with house-made tortillas, flourless Mexican chocolate cake, and Latin-inspired cocktails. On weekends, Barrio Star opens at 9 am for breakfasts of tamales, tortas, and blackberry pancakes. $ *Average main: $16* ⊠ *2706 5th Ave., Bankers Hill, San Diego* ☎ *619/501–7827* ⊕ *www.barriostar.com* ✛ *E5.*

$$
ITALIAN
Fodor's Choice
★

✕ **Cucina Urbana.** Proprietor Tracy Borkum's casual and stylish Cal-Italian spot remains one of the most popular tables in town. Everything is reasonably priced, and diners can pop into the retail wine room, select a bottle, and drink it with dinner for a modest corkage fee. The ricotta gnudi bathed in brown butter and fried sage are the best yet; fried

BEST BETS FOR SAN DIEGO DINING

With hundreds of restaurants to choose from, how will you decide where to eat? We've selected our favorite restaurants by price, cuisine, and experience in the Best Bets list below. In the first column, Fodor's Choice properties represent the "best of the best" in every price category. Bon appétit!

Fodor's Choice ★

A.R. Valentien, $$$$, p. 98
Bali Hai, $$, p. 101
Barrio Star, $, p. 93
Bencotto, $$, p. 93
Bread & Cie, $, p. 95
Café Chloe, $$, p. 92
Café Sevilla, $$, p. 91
Cowboy Star, $$$$, p. 92
Cucina Urbana, $$, p. 93
El Pescador, $, p. 99
George's at the Cove, $$$$, p. 99
Jimmy's Famous American Tavern, $, p. 100
The Kebab Shop, $, p. 92
Lucha Libre, $, p. 95
Nine-Ten, $$$, p. 99
Ortega's Bistro, $$, p. 95
Phil's BBQ, $, p. 100
Sushi on the Rock, $, p. 100
Sushi Ota, $$$, p. 98
Taka, $$, p. 92
Tender Greens, $, p. 101
Whisknladle, $$, 100

By Price

$

Bread & Cie, p. 95
Lucha Libre, p. 95
Tender Greens, p. 101
URBN Coal Fired Pizza, p. 98

$$

Bencotto, p. 93
Café Chloe, p. 92
Taka, p. 92

$$$

1500 Ocean, p. 101
Nine-Ten, p. 99
Searsucker, p. 92
Sushi Ota, p. 98

$$$$

A.R. Valentien, p. 98
Cowboy Star, p. 92
George's at the Cove, p. 99

Best by Cuisine

AMERICAN

A.R. Valentien, $$$$, p. 98

Jimmy's Famous American Tavern, $, p. 100
Nine-Ten, $$$, p. 99
Searsucker, $$$, p. 92

CAFÉS

Bread & Cie, $, p. 95
Café Chloe, $$, p. 92

ITALIAN

Bencotto, $$, p. 93
Cucina Urbana, $$, p. 93

JAPANESE

Sushi Ota, $$$, p. 98
Taka, $$, p. 92

LATIN/MEXICAN

El Agave, $$$, p. 95
Lucha Libre, $, p. 95
Ortega's Bistro, $$, p. 95

PIZZA

Cucina Urbana, $$, p. 93
URBN Coal Fired Pizza, $, p. 98

VEGETARIAN

Tender Greens, $, p. 101

Best By Experience

BRUNCH

Café Chloe, $$, p. 92
Nine-Ten, $$$, p. 99

DINING WITH KIDS

Ortega's Bistro, $$, p. 95
Tender Greens, $, p. 101
URBN Coal Fired Pizza, $, p. 98

GOOD FOR GROUPS

Barrio Star, $, p. 93
Café Sevilla, $$, p. 91
URBN Coal Fired Pizza, $, p. 98

ROMANTIC

A.R. Valentien, $$$$, p. 98
George's at the Cove, $$$$, p. 99

WATER VIEWS

Bali Hai, $$, p. 101
George's at the Cove, $$$$, p. 99
Jimmy's Famous American Tavern, $, p. 100

squash blossoms sing; and polenta boards mixed tableside are creative and satisfying. Also good are the lasagna, the short rib pappardelle, and the mushroom garganelli with goat cheese fonduta. Sit at the cozy bar and watch the chefs turn out bubbly, thin-crust pizzas topped with wild mushroom and taleggio cheese or pancetta and brussels sprout leaf, or find a spot at the main bar for a clever cocktail crafted from seasonal fruit and Italian liqueurs. $ *Average main: $21* ⊠ *505 Laurel St., Bankers Hill, San Diego* ☎ *619/239–2222* ⊕ *www.cucinaurbana. com* ⚲ *Reservations essential* ☽ *No lunch Sat.–Mon.* ✛ *E5.*

OLD TOWN AND UPTOWN

OLD TOWN

$$$ ╳ **El Agave.** The area is a bit touristy so you might not expect to find
MEXICAN such authentic regional Mexican fare at this comfortably upmarket restaurant. Standout options include quesadillas filled with mushrooms, baked halibut in chipotle sauce with rice and vegetables, and chicken in a slow-simmered mole sauce. There are more than 2,000 tequilas to choose from, displayed throughout the brick-walled space (even on shelves suspended from the ceiling), which make El Agave the largest "tequileria" in the United States. The collection includes artisanal tequilas dating to the 1930s and some infused with jalapeño chilis. $ *Average main: $30* ⊠ *2304 San Diego Ave., Old Town, San Diego* ☎ *619/220–0692* ⊕ *www.elagave.com* ✛ *D4.*

$ ╳ **Lucha Libre.** On any given weekday at lunch, you're sure to see a line of
MEXICAN locals from nearby offices waiting for their favorite Lucha Libre picks—
Fodor's Choice and the food here is worth the wait. Named for a form of Mexican
★ wrestling that often involves brightly colored masks, the restaurant's hot-pink walls and shiny booths create a fun and family-friendly atmosphere. There is an array of gourmet tacos and burritos on the menu; the Surfin' California burrito packed with grilled steak, shrimp, french fries, avocado, and chipotle sauce is a favorite. There are also many meatless options. $ *Average main: $7* ⊠ *1810 W. Washington St., Old Town, San Diego* ☎ *619/296–8226* ⊕ *www.tacosmackdown.com* ✛ *D4.*

HILLCREST

$ ╳ **Bread & Cie.** There's an East Coast air to this artsy urban bakery and
CAFÉ café known for being one of San Diego's first and best artisanal bread
Fodor's Choice bakers. Owner Charles Kaufman is a former New Yorker and a film-
★ maker, and he gave Bread & Cie a sense of theater by putting bread ovens imported from France at center stage. Warm focaccia covered in cheese and vegetables, crusty loaves of black olive bread, bear claws, gourmet granola with Mediterranean yogurt, and first-rate cinnamon rolls are served from daybreak to sunset; lunch time also brings options like house-made quiche and panini filled with pastrami, turkey, and pesto, or Brie and honey. $ *Average main: $7* ⊠ *350 University Ave., Hillcrest, San Diego* ☎ *619/683–9322* ⊕ *www.breadandcie.com* ☽ *No dinner* ✛ *E4.*

$$ ╳ **Ortega's Bistro.** Californians have long flocked to Puerto Nuevo, the
MEXICAN "lobster village" south of San Diego in Baja California, so when a mem-
FAMILY ber of the family that operates several Puerto Nuevo restaurants opened
Fodor's Choice Ortega's, it became an instant sensation. The draw is no-nonsense,
★ authentic Mexican fare, and the specialty of choice is a whole lobster

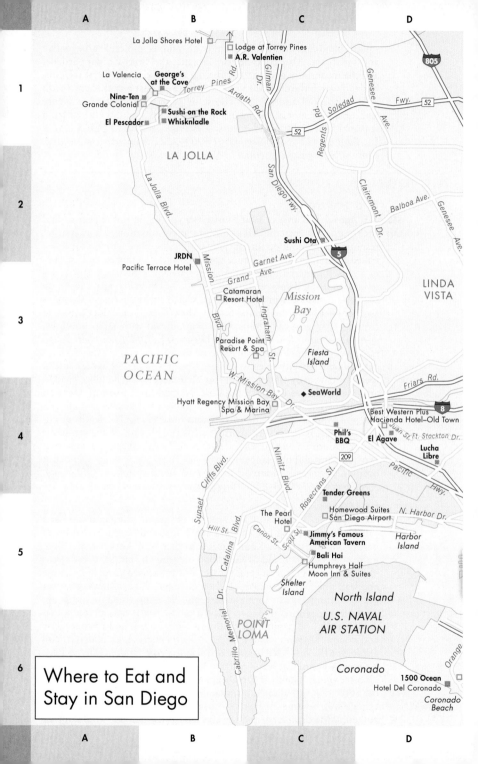

Where to Eat and Stay in San Diego

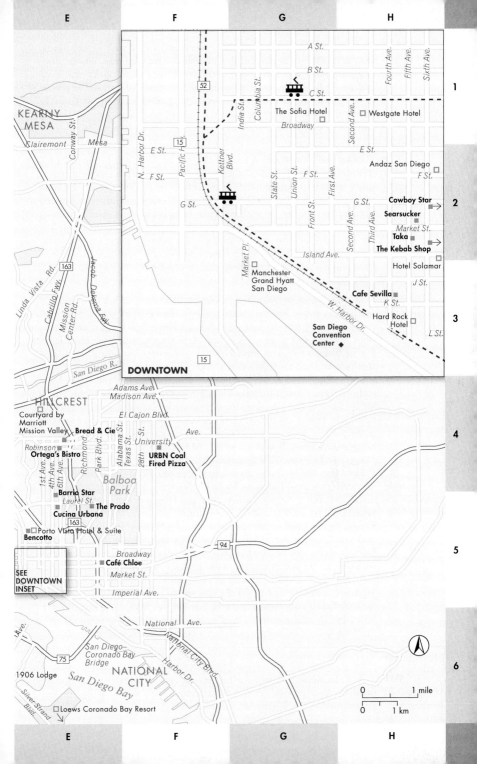

prepared Baja-style (steamed then grilled) and served with superb beans, rice, and made-to-order tortillas. But there are other fine options, too, including melt-in-your-mouth carnitas (slow-cooked pork), made-at-the-table guacamole, and Ensenada-style battered fish tacos. The pomegranate margaritas are a must, as is the special red salsa if you like authentic spice. $ *Average main: $19* ⊠ *141 University Ave., Hillcrest, San Diego* ☎ *619/692–4200* ⊕ *www.ortegasbistro.com* ✛ *E4.*

NORTH PARK

$ ✕ **URBN Coal Fired Pizza.** A few blocks east of 30th Street (North Park's
PIZZA   restaurant row), this 5,000-square-foot warehouse is a chic and casual pizza spot. Hip young locals chow down on coal-fired New Haven–style pies, fresh salads, and cheese boards. Try the carbalicious mashed potato pizza pie topped with pancetta, fresh mozzarella, and Parmesan. Linger with a local brew or a craft cocktail off the extensive drink list. It's a good space for groups so the atmosphere can get quite festive. $ *Average main: $12* ⊠ *3085 University Ave., North Park, San Diego* ☎ *619/255–7300* ⊕ *www.urbnpizza.com* ✛ *F4.*

PACIFIC BEACH

$$$$ ✕ **JRDN.** With some 200 seats, this ocean-facing restaurant (pronounced
AMERICAN   Jordan), in the beach-chic boutique-style Tower23 Hotel might sound overwhelming, but the seating is divided between a long, narrow outdoor terrace and a series of relatively intimate indoor rooms. Chef David Warner prepares modern steak-house fare including chops and steaks with sauces of the diner's choosing, lightened with lots of seasonal produce and a raw bar menu. Weekend brunch and lunch have a similar appeal, with dishes like crab cake eggs Benedict with citrus hollandaise, a blackened mahimahi sandwich, and a hamachi sashimi salad. On Fridays and Saturdays the bar is the place to see and be seen in Pacific Beach for under-30 types, and it's jammed after 9 pm. $ *Average main: $37* ⊠ *Tower 23 Hotel, 723 Felspar St., Pacific Beach, San Diego* ☎ *858/270–5736* ⊕ *www.jrdn.com* ✛ *B3.*

$$$ ✕ **Sushi Ota.** Wedged into a minimall between a convenience store and
JAPANESE   a looming medical building, Sushi Ota's location might seem less than
Fodor'sChoice   auspicious but it helps to know that San Diego–bound Japanese busi-
★   nesspeople frequently call for reservations before boarding their trans-Pacific flights. Look at the expressions on customers' faces as they leave and you can see the satisfied glows that result from dining on San Diego's best sushi. Besides the usual California roll and tuna and shrimp sushi, there are specialties that change daily such as sea urchin or surf clam sushi, a soft-shell crab roll, or the *omakase* tasting menu. Note that Japanese speakers tend to get the best spots, and servers can be abrupt. ■TIP➜ **There's additional parking behind the mall.** $ *Average main: $30* ⊠ *4529 Mission Bay Dr., Pacific Beach, San Diego* ☎ *858/270–5670* ⌒ *Reservations essential* ⊙ *No lunch Sat.–Mon.* ✛ *C2.*

LA JOLLA

$$$$ ✕ **A. R. Valentien.** Known for his insistence on in-season, fresh-today
AMERICAN   produce and seafood, chef Jeff Jackson writes menus daily for this
Fodor'sChoice   cozy room in the luxurious, Craftsman-style Lodge at Torrey Pines.
★

His take on food combinations is simultaneously simple and inventive, as demonstrated in appetizers of smoked trout with horseradish and pickled onion, and porcini mushroom and butternut squash soup with chorizo and spiced pepitas. In addition to the à la carte menu, a nightly three-course tasting menu explores the day's market through the eyes of the talented chef. At lunch on the outdoor terrace, consider the "Drugstore" hamburger: a grilled patty is placed on top of lettuce, tomato, and condiments, and is then topped with cheese before being steamed to perfection on its sesame seed bun. [$] *Average main: $36* ✉ *11480 N. Torrey Pines Rd., La Jolla, San Diego* ☎ *858/777–6635* 🌐 *www.arvalentien.com* 🕐 *No breakfast Mon.–Fri.* ✣ *B1.*

$ SEAFOOD Fodor's Choice ★ 🍴 **El Pescador.** This low-key fish market and café in the heart of La Jolla village is popular with locals for its simply prepared fresh fish. Try a filet—maybe halibut, swordfish, salmon, or tuna—lightly grilled and perched on a soft torta roll with shredded lettuce, tomato, and onions. Other choices include ceviche, sashimi plates, Dungeness crab salad, sautéed mussels with sourdough bread, and excellent fish tacos. Seats are few, and tables often end up being shared, but the food is worth the wait. ■ **TIP→ Order fish sandwiches to go for a tasty oceanfront picnic at La Jolla Cove.** [$] *Average main: $15* ✉ *627 Pearl St., La Jolla, San Diego* ☎ *858/456–2526* 🌐 *www.elpescadorfishmarket.com* ✍ *Reservations not accepted* ✣ *B1.*

$$$$ AMERICAN Fodor's Choice ★ 🍴 **George's at the Cove.** La Jolla's oceanfront destination restaurant includes three dining areas: **California Modern** on the bottom floor, **George's Bar** in the middle, and **Ocean Terrace** on the roof. Hollywood types and other visiting celebrities can be spotted at California Modern, the sleek main dining room with its wall of windows. Simple preparations of fresh seafood, beef, and lamb reign on the menu, which chef Trey Foshee enlivens with produce from local specialty growers. Give special consideration to roasted California lamb with wild mushrooms and sunchokes, smoked Maine lobster, and the legendary fish tacos. For a more casual and inexpensive experience, go to the indoor/outdoor George's Bar, where you can get tacos and watch a sports game, or head upstairs to the outdoor-only Ocean Terrace for spectacular views of La Jolla Cove. [$] *Average main: $36* ✉ *1250 Prospect St., La Jolla, San Diego* ☎ *858/454–4244* 🌐 *www.georgesatthecove.com* ✍ *Reservations essential* ✣ *B1.*

$$$ AMERICAN Fodor's Choice ★ 🍴 **Nine-Ten.** In the sleek, contemporary dining room that occupies the ground floor of the Grande Colonial Hotel, acclaimed chef (and 2011 *Iron Chef* challenger) Jason Knibb serves satisfying seasonal fare at breakfast, lunch, and dinner. The downtown La Jolla location is ideal for travelers but it's just as much a locals spot, attracting professionals for power lunches and foodies for the excellent food. At night the perfectly executed menu may include tantalizing appetizers like Jamaican jerk pork belly or lamb sugo and mains such as a smoked maple leaf duck breast with butternut squash and braised turnips, or beef short ribs braised with Alesmith stout and served with root vegetables. Stand-out desserts include a caramel apple custard and a lemon meringue with olive ice cream. Three- and five-course prix-fixe menus are available for the whole table. [$] *Average main: $33* ✉ *Grande Colonial Hotel,*

910 Prospect St., La Jolla, San Diego ☎ 858/964–5400 🌐 www.nineten.com ✥ B1.

$ 🍴 **Sushi on the Rock.** There's something fun about Sushi on the Rock, from the young friendly chefs to the comically named California-style sushi specialties, like the Slippery When Wet roll featuring tempura shrimp, eel, crab, and cucumber. There are many original rolls to choose from, including the Barrio Roll stuffed with tuna, cilantro, and spicy tomato salsa; the Ashley Roll that pairs seared tuna with soft-shell crab and tangy whole-grain mustard sauce; and the Bruce Lee, with spicy crab, tuna, and avocado. The Japanese-inspired dishes, including pot stickers and an Asian-style Caesar salad are also good, as is the lobster mac and cheese. This popular spot, which has a patio with an ocean view, gets busy in the late afternoon with people wanting to grab a seat for the daily happy hour (4–6:30 pm). [$] *Average main: $16 ✉ 1025 Prospect St., #250, La Jolla, San Diego ☎ 858/459–3208 🌐 www.sushiontherock.com ✍ Reservations not accepted ✥ B1.*

SUSHI
Fodor's Choice ★

$$ 🍴 **Whisknladle.** This hip, popular eatery that doubles as a fashion show of La Jolla ladies who lunch has earned national acclaim with its combination of casual comfort and a menu of ever-changing local fare. In nice weather, request a patio table when reserving. Appetizers include dishes like heirloom tomato salad and savory flatbreads that change daily. Larger plates feature local halibut with Chino Farms vegetables or crab tortellini. And the bar is worth a visit, too, with its original menu of cocktails like the cranberry margarita, cucumber honey mimosa, and pomegranate mojito. [$] *Average main: $23 ✉ 1044 Wall St., La Jolla, San Diego ☎ 858/551–7575 🌐 www.whisknladle.com ✍ Reservations essential ✥ B1.*

SEAFOOD
Fodor's Choice ★

POINT LOMA, SHELTER ISLAND, AND CORONADO

POINT LOMA

$ 🍴 **Jimmy's Famous American Tavern.** Jimmy's is a standout in the wave of recent gastropubs, and while the food is the main draw here, the decor—industrial meets Americana—has an appealing straightforwardness, too. Head through the garage-style doors for a patio seat with a water view or opt for a cozy booth. The menu features elevated takes on backyard BBQ that include the Jimmy, a half-pound burger topped with pimento cheese, applewood smoked bacon, and jalapeño jelly. The buttermilk fried chicken breast and jalapeño deviled eggs are also worth a try. The short rib hash at Sunday brunch is stellar. [$] *Average main: $17 ✉ 4990 N. Harbor Dr., Point Loma, San Diego ☎ 619/226–2103 🌐 www.j-fat.com ✥ C5.*

AMERICAN
FAMILY
Fodor's Choice ★

$ 🍴 **Phil's BBQ.** At peak dining hours, the line can be hours long for diners craving Phil's baby back ribs, the pulled pork, or the huge, crispy onion rings. Adding to the restaurant's reputation and allure is the fact that one of the specialties, the El Toro tri-tip sandwich, was included in Travel Channel celebrity Adam Richman's 2012 list of America's best sandwiches. But don't let the crowds dissuade you: phone in for carry-out, sit at the bar, or bring the family during midafternoon for a messy, chargrilled introduction to barbecue heaven. [$] *Average main: $14 ✉ 3750*

BARBECUE
Fodor's Choice ★

Sports Arena Blvd., Point Loma, San Diego ☎ *619/226–6333* 🌐 *www.philsbbq.net* ✍ *Reservations not accepted* ⏲ *Closed Mon.* ✥ *C4.*

$ AMERICAN FAMILY Fodor's Choice ★

🍴 **Tender Greens.** "Farm-fresh ingredients served up with little fuss" is the ethos behind this casual cafeteria-style spot in Liberty Station. It's very popular at lunch but the line moves quickly. Expect big salads like seared tuna Niçoise; P. Balistreri salumi with housemade feta, pickled vegetables, and roasted peppers; or chipotle chicken salad. Naturally raised beef and chicken are roasted and then tucked into sandwiches or served as a dinner plate with vegetables. Wine and house-made desserts round out the menu. [$] *Average main: $12* ✉ *2400 Historic Decatur Rd., Point Loma, San Diego* ☎ *619/226–6254* 🌐 *tendergreens.com* ✥ *C5.*

SHELTER ISLAND

$$ HAWAIIAN Fodor's Choice ★

🍴 **Bali Hai.** This kitschy-classy waterfront restaurant is loved as much for the strong, sugary drinks served in tiki mugs as it is for the gorgeous views of the San Diego Bay and the Downtown skyline. One of few restaurants within walking distance of Shelter Island hotels, Bali Hai's menu has Hawaiian, Asian, and Californian influences, with an emphasis on seafood. Standouts include the Hawaiian tuna poke, crispy spring rolls, and seared diver scallops. Lounge seating accommodates groups while tables by the window are ideal for quiet, romantic dinners. [$] *Average main: $23* ✉ *2230 Shelter Island Dr., Shelter Island, San Diego* ☎ *619/222-1181* 🌐 *www.balihairestaurant.com* ✥ *C5.*

CORONADO

$$$ AMERICAN

🍴 **1500 Ocean.** The fine-dining restaurant at Hotel Del Coronado, right on the beach, offers a memorable evening showcasing the best organic and naturally raised ingredients the region has to offer. Select ingredients come straight from the hotel's herb and produce garden. Sublimely subtle dishes include a savory butternut squash velouté; and diver scallops with toasted almond, lemon confit, and brown butter. The elegant interior of the restaurant evokes a posh cabana; the terrace has ocean views. An excellent international wine list and clever desserts and artisanal cheeses complete the experience. [$] *Average main: $35* ✉ *Hotel Del Coronado, 1500 Orange Ave., Coronado, San Diego* ☎ *619/522–8490* 🌐 *www.hoteldel.com/1500-ocean* ✍ *Reservations essential* ⏲ *Closed. Sun. and Mon. No lunch* ✥ *D6.*

WHERE TO STAY

In San Diego, you could plan a luxurious vacation, staying at a hotel with 350-thread-count sheets, wall-mounted flat screens, and panoramic Pacific views. But with some flexibility—maybe opting for a partial-view room with standard TVs—it's possible to experience the city's beauty at half the price.

Any local will tell you two things about San Diego: No. 1, the weather really is perfect; and No. 2, the area's neighborhoods and beach communities offer great diversity, from lively urban vacations to laid-back beachfront escapes. You'll need a car if you stay outside Downtown, but the coastal communities are rich with lodging options. For families, Uptown, Mission Valley, and Old Town are close to SeaWorld and the

San Diego Zoo, offering good-value accommodations with extras like sleeper sofas and video games.

Many hotels promote discounted weekend packages to fill rooms after convention and business customers leave town. You can save on hotels and attractions by visiting the San Diego Convention and Visitors Bureau website (🌐 *www.sandiego.org*) for a free Vacation Planning Kit with a Travel Value Coupon booklet. *Hotel reviews have been shortened. For full information, visit Fodors.com.*

Use the coordinate (✣ A1) at the end of each listing to locate a site on the corresponding map.

WHAT IT COSTS

	$	$$	$$$	$$$$
Hotels	under $201	$201–$300	$301–$400	over $400

Hotel prices are the lowest cost of a standard double room in high season.

DOWNTOWN

GASLAMP QUARTER

$$$ HOTEL Fodor's Choice ★ 🏨 **Andaz San Diego.** The lobby of the luxury, Hyatt-managed Andaz—with its sexy vibe, tall columns wrapped in braided leather, buckets of chilled wine awaiting guests, and welcoming service—pretty much sums up the experience here: high-style stay without the attitude. **Pros:** luxurious rooms; thriving nightlife scene; friendly service. **Cons:** noisy on weekends; not a good choice for families. [$] *Rooms from: $315* ✉ *600 F St., Gaslamp Quarter, San Diego* ☎ *619/849–1234* 🌐 *www.sandiego.andaz.hyatt.com* 🛏 *142 rooms, 17 suites* 🍴 *No meals* ✣ *H2.*

$$ HOTEL Fodor's Choice ★ 🏨 **Hard Rock Hotel.** Self-billed as a hip playground for rock stars and people who want to party like them, the Hard Rock is conveniently located near PETCO Park overlooking glimmering San Diego Bay. **Pros:** central location; great scene; luxurious rooms. **Cons:** pricey drinks; some attitude. [$] *Rooms from: $276* ✉ *207 5th Ave., Gaslamp Quarter, San Diego* ☎ *619/702–3000, 866/751–7625* 🌐 *www.hardrockhotelsd.com* 🛏 *244 rooms, 176 suites* 🍴 *No meals* ✣ *H3.*

$$ HOTEL FAMILY Fodor's Choice ★ 🏨 **Hotel Solamar.** The hip Solamar is best known for its pool-side rooftop bar, LoungeSix, and stylish lobby decor. **Pros:** great restaurant; attentive service; upscale rooms. **Cons:** busy valet parking; bars are crowded and noisy on weekends. [$] *Rooms from: $295* ✉ *435 6th Ave., Gaslamp Quarter, San Diego* ☎ *619/819–9500, 877/230–0300* 🌐 *www.hotelsolamar.com* 🛏 *217 rooms, 16 suites* 🍴 *No meals* ✣ *H2.*

$$ HOTEL Fodor's Choice ★ 🏨 **The Sofia Hotel.** This stylish and centrally located boutique hotel may have small rooms, but it more than compensates with pampering extras like motion-sensor temperature controls, a Zen-like 24-hour yoga studio, and in-suite spa services. **Pros:** upscale amenities; historic building; near shops and restaurants. **Cons:** busy area; small rooms. [$] *Rooms from: $259* ✉ *150 W. Broadway, Gaslamp Quarter, San*

BEST BETS FOR
SAN DIEGO LODGING

Fodor's offers a selective listing of quality lodging experiences. Here we've compiled our top recommendations. The very best properties—in other words, those that provide a particularly remarkable experience in their price range—are designated in the listings with a Fodor's Choice logo.

BEST POOL

Andaz San Diego, $$$, p. 102

Hotel Solamar, $$, p. 102

Hyatt Regency Mission Bay Spa & Marina, $$, p. 105

Loews Coronado Bay Resort, $$, p. 107

Manchester Grand Hyatt San Diego, $$, p. 104

BEST FOR ROMANCE

1906 Lodge, $$$, p. 106

Hotel Del Coronado, $$$, p. 107

Hotel Solamar, $$, p. 102

The Lodge at Torrey Pines, $$$, p. 106

Fodor's Choice ★

1906 Lodge at Coronado Beach, $$$, p. 106

Andaz San Diego, $$$, p. 102

Courtyard by Marriott Mission Valley, $, p. 104

Grande Colonial, $$$, p. 105

Hard Rock Hotel, $$, p. 102

Homewood Suites San Diego Airport, $$, p. 106

Hotel Del Coronado, $$$, p. 107

Hotel Solamar, $$, p. 102

Lodge at Torrey Pines, $$$, p. 106

The Pearl Hotel, $, p. 106

The Sofia Hotel, $$, p. 102

Westgate Hotel, $$$, p. 104

Best by Price

$

Best Western Plus Hacienda Hotel–Old Town, p. 104

Courtyard by Marriott Mission Valley, p. 104

The Pearl Hotel, p. 106

Porto Vista Hotel & Suites, p. 104

$$

Catamaran Resort Hotel, p. 105

Hard Rock Hotel, p. 102

Homewood Suites San Diego Airport, p. 106

Hotel Solamar, p. 102

Paradise Point Resort & Spa, p. 105

The Sofia Hotel, p. 102

$$$

Andaz San Diego, p. 102

Grande Colonial, p. 105

Hotel Del Coronado, p. 107

La Valencia, p. 106

Lodge at Torrey Pines, p. 106

$$$$

Pacific Terrace Hotel, p. 105

Best by Experience

BEST BEACH

Catamaran Resort Hotel, $$, p. 105

Hotel Del Coronado, $$$, p. 107

La Jolla Shores Hotel, $$, p. 105

Paradise Point Resort & Spa, $$, p. 105

Diego ☎ *619/234–9200, 800/826–0009* 🌐 *www.thesofiahotel.com* 🛏 *211 rooms, 28 suites* 🍴 *No meals* ✣ *G1.*

$$$ HOTEL Fodor's Choice ★ 🏨 **Westgate Hotel.** A modern high-rise near Horton Plaza hides San Diego's most opulent old-world-style hotel, featuring a lobby that is modeled after the anteroom at Versailles, and outfitted with antiques and Baccarat chandeliers. **Pros:** elegant rooms; grand lobby, near shopping. **Cons:** formal atmosphere; mandatory facility fee. [$] *Rooms from: $394* ✉ *1055 2nd Ave., Gaslamp Quarter, San Diego* ☎ *619/238–1818, 800/522–1564* 🌐 *www.westgatehotel.com* 🛏 *215 rooms, 8 suites* 🍴 *No meals* ✣ *H1.*

LITTLE ITALY

$ HOTEL 🏨 **Porto Vista Hotel & Suites.** A $15 million renovation turned this former budget motel into a contemporary hotel-motel with two additional buildings, a stylish restaurant and lounge, and a fitness center. **Pros:** new decor in common areas, some guest rooms, and the fitness center; airport shuttle. **Cons:** spotty service; small rooms, some still in need of updating. [$] *Rooms from: $149* ✉ *1835 Columbia St., Little Italy, San Diego* ☎ *619/544–0164, 855/504–8986* 🌐 *www.portovistasd.com* 🛏 *189 rooms, 22 suites* 🍴 *No meals* ✣ *E5.*

EMBARCADERO

$$ HOTEL FAMILY 🏨 **Manchester Grand Hyatt San Diego.** Primarily for business travelers, this hotel between Seaport Village and the convention center is San Diego's largest, and its 33- and 40-story towers make it the West Coast's tallest waterfront hotel. **Pros:** great views; conference facilities; good location. **Cons:** very busy; some rooms dated. [$] *Rooms from: $299* ✉ *1 Market Pl., Embarcadero, San Diego* ☎ *619/232–1234, 800/233–1234* 🌐 *www.manchestergrand.hyatt.com* 🛏 *1,552 rooms, 76 suites* 🍴 *No meals* ✣ *G3.*

OLD TOWN, MISSION VALLEY, AND NORTH PARK

OLD TOWN

$ HOTEL FAMILY 🏨 **Best Western Plus Hacienda Hotel–Old Town.** Perched on a hill in the heart of Old Town, this hotel is known for its expansive courtyards, outdoor fountains, and maze of stairs that connect eight buildings of guest rooms. **Pros:** airport shuttle; well-maintained outdoor areas. **Cons:** some rooms need renovating; complicated layout. [$] *Rooms from: $169* ✉ *4041 Harney St., Old Town, San Diego* ☎ *619/298–4707* 🌐 *www.haciendahotel-oldtown.com* 🛏 *178 rooms, 20 suites* 🍴 *No meals* ✣ *D4.*

MISSION VALLEY

$ HOTEL FAMILY Fodor's Choice ★ 🏨 **Courtyard by Marriott Mission Valley.** Amenities abound for families seeking a fun and casual base for trips to SeaWorld and the zoo. **Pros:** easy freeway access to area attractions; good value; nice perks for families and business travelers. **Cons:** few stores and restaurants in walking distance; halls can be noisy with kids. [$] *Rooms from: $149* ✉ *595 Hotel Circle S, Mission Valley, San Diego* ☎ *619/291–5720* 🌐 *www.courtyardsd.com* 🛏 *309 rooms, 8 suites* 🍴 *No meals* ✣ *E4.*

MISSION BAY AND BEACHES

MISSION BAY

$$ RESORT FAMILY **Hyatt Regency Mission Bay Spa & Marina.** This modern property has many desirable amenities, including balconies with excellent views of the garden, bay, ocean, or swimming pool courtyard. **Pros:** modern decor; great pet program; water views; 120-foot waterslides in pools, plus kiddie slide. **Cons:** slightly hard to navigate surrounding roads; thin walls; not centrally located. [$] *Rooms from: $269* ✉ *1441 Quivira Rd., Mission Bay, San Diego* ☎ *619/224–1234, 800/233–1234* 🌐 *www.missionbay.hyatt.com* 🛏 *353 rooms, 76 suites* 🍴 *No meals* ✣ *C4.*

$$ RESORT FAMILY **Paradise Point Resort & Spa.** The beautiful landscape of this 44-acre resort on Vacation Isle has been the setting for a number of movies. **Pros:** water views; pools; good service. **Cons:** not centrally located; summer minimum stays; motel-thin walls; parking and resort fees. [$] *Rooms from: $279* ✉ *1404 Vacation Rd., Mission Bay, San Diego* ☎ *858/274–4630, 800/344–2626* 🌐 *www.paradisepoint.com* 🛏 *462 cottages* 🍴 *No meals* ✣ *C3.*

MISSION BEACH

$$ RESORT FAMILY **Catamaran Resort Hotel.** Tiki torches light the way through grounds thick with tropical foliage to the six two-story buildings and the 14-story high-rise on Mission Bay. **Pros:** spa; bay views; many activities for kids. **Cons:** not centrally located; dated room decor. [$] *Rooms from: $249* ✉ *3999 Mission Blvd., Mission Beach, San Diego* ☎ *858/488–1081, 800/422–8386* 🌐 *www.catamaranresort.com* 🛏 *262 rooms, 50 suites* 🍴 *No meals* ✣ *B3.*

PACIFIC BEACH

$$$$ RESORT **Pacific Terrace Hotel.** Travelers love this terrific beachfront hotel and the ocean views from most rooms; it's a perfect place for watching sunsets over the Pacific. **Pros:** beach views; large rooms; friendly service. **Cons:** busy and sometimes noisy area; lots of traffic. [$] *Rooms from: $428* ✉ *610 Diamond St., Pacific Beach, San Diego* ☎ *858/581–3500, 800/344–3370* 🌐 *www.pacificterrace.com* 🛏 *61 rooms, 12 suites* 🍴 *No meals* ✣ *B3.*

LA JOLLA

$$$ HOTEL Fodor's Choice ★ **Grande Colonial.** This white wedding cake–style hotel in the heart of La Jolla village has ocean views and charming European details that include chandeliers, mahogany railings, and French doors. **Pros:** near shopping; near beach; superb restaurant. **Cons:** somewhat busy street; no fitness center. [$] *Rooms from: $360* ✉ *910 Prospect St., La Jolla, San Diego* ☎ *858/454–2181, 888/828–5498* 🌐 *www.thegrandecolonial.com* 🛏 *52 rooms, 41 suites* 🍴 *No meals* ✣ *B1.*

$$ HOTEL FAMILY **La Jolla Shores Hotel.** One of San Diego's few hotels actually on the beach, this property is part of La Jolla Beach and Tennis Club. **Pros:** on beach; great views; quiet area. **Cons:** not centrally located; some rooms are dated. [$] *Rooms from: $279* ✉ *8110 Camino del Oro, La Jolla, San Diego* ☎ *858/459–8271, 877/346–6714* 🌐 *www.ljshoreshotel.com* 🛏 *127 rooms, 1 suite* ✣ *B1.*

$$$ ⬚ **La Valencia.** This pink Spanish-Mediterranean confection drew Hol-
HOTEL lywood film stars in the 1930s and '40s with its setting and views of
La Jolla Cove; now it draws the Kardashians. **Pros:** upscale rooms;
views; near beach. **Cons:** standard rooms are tiny; lots of traffic out-
side. Ⓢ *Rooms from: $380* ✉ *1132 Prospect St., La Jolla, San Diego*
☎ *858/454–0771, 800/451–0772* ⊕ *www.lavalencia.com* ⤏ *82 rooms,
15 villas, 15 suites* ⦶ *No meals* ✛ *B1.*

$$$ ⬚ **Lodge at Torrey Pines.** This beautiful Craftsman-style lodge sits on
RESORT a bluff between La Jolla and Del Mar and commands a coastal view.
Fodor'sChoice **Pros:** spacious upscale rooms; good service; Torrey Pines Golf Club on
★ property. **Cons:** not centrally located; expensive. Ⓢ *Rooms from: $400*
✉ *11480 N. Torrey Pines Rd., La Jolla, San Diego* ☎ *858/453–4420,
800/995–4507* ⊕ *www.lodgetorreypines.com* ⤏ *164 rooms, 6 suites*
⦶ *No meals* ✛ *B1.*

POINT LOMA AND CORONADO WITH HARBOR AND SHELTER ISLANDS

POINT LOMA

$$ ⬚ **Homewood Suites San Diego Airport.** Families and business travelers
HOTEL on long trips will benefit from the space and amenities at this all-suites
FAMILY hotel. **Pros:** complimentary grocery shopping service; free parking; close
Fodor'sChoice to paths for joggers and bikers. **Cons:** often crowded dining room; far
★ from nightlife. Ⓢ *Rooms from: $289* ✉ *2576 Laning Rd., Point Loma,
San Diego* ☎ *619/222–0500* ⊕ *www.homewoodsuites.com* ⤏ *150
suites* ⦶ *Multiple meal plans* ✛ *C5.*

$ ⬚ **The Pearl Hotel.** This previously vintage motel received a makeover,
HOTEL turning it into a retro-chic beach hangout decorated with kitschy lamps
Fodor'sChoice and original art by local children. **Pros:** near marina; restaurant on-site
★ (dinner only). **Cons:** not centrally located; one bed in rooms. Ⓢ *Rooms
from: $139* ✉ *1410 Rosecrans St., Point Loma, San Diego* ☎ *619/226–
6100* ⊕ *www.thepearlsd.com* ⤏ *23 rooms* ⦶ *No meals* ✛ *C5.*

SHELTER ISLAND

$$ ⬚ **Humphreys Half Moon Inn & Suites.** This sprawling South Seas–style
RESORT resort has grassy open areas with palms and tiki torches; many of the
rooms have water views. **Pros:** water views; near marina; free admission
to Backstage Live music club. **Cons:** resort fee; vast property; not centrally located. Ⓢ *Rooms from: $219* ✉ *2303 Shelter Island Dr., Shelter
Island, San Diego* ☎ *619/224–3411, 800/542–7400* ⊕ *www.halfmoon
inn.com* ⤏ *128 rooms, 54 suites* ⦶ *No meals* ✛ *C5.*

CORONADO

$$$ ⬚ **1906 Lodge at Coronado Beach.** Smaller but no less luxurious than
B&B/INN the sprawling beach resorts of Coronado, this lodge welcomes couples
Fodor'sChoice for romantic retreats two blocks from the ocean. **Pros:** most suites fea-
★ ture Jacuzzi tubs, fireplaces, and porches; historic property; free under-
ground parking. **Cons:** too quiet for families; no pool. Ⓢ *Rooms from:
$309* ✉ *1060 Adella Ave., Coronado, San Diego* ☎ *619/437–1900,
866/435–1906* ⊕ *www.1906lodge.com* ⤏ *6 rooms, 11 suites* ⦶ *Some
meals* ✛ *D6.*

$$$ RESORT FAMILY Fodor's Choice ★ **Hotel Del Coronado.** As much of a draw today as it was when it opened in 1888, the Victorian-style "Hotel Del" is always alive with activity, as guests—including U.S. presidents and celebrities—and tourists marvel at the fanciful architecture and ocean views. **Pros:** romantic; on the beach; hotel spa. **Cons:** some rooms are small; expensive dining; hectic public areas. [$] *Rooms from: $329* ✉ *1500 Orange Ave., Coronado, San Diego* ☎ *800/468–3533, 619/435–6611* 🌐 *www.hoteldel.com* 🛏 *679 rooms, 43 villas, 35 cottages* 🍴 *No meals* ✣ *D6.*

$$ RESORT FAMILY **Loews Coronado Bay Resort.** You can park your boat at the 80-slip marina of this romantic retreat set on a secluded 15-acre peninsula on the Silver Strand. **Pros:** great restaurants; lots of activities; all rooms have furnished balconies with water views. **Cons:** far from anything; confusing layout. [$] *Rooms from: $299* ✉ *4000 Coronado Bay Rd., Coronado, San Diego* ☎ *619/424–4000, 800/815–6397* 🌐 *www.loewshotels.com/Coronado-Bay-Resort* 🛏 *402 rooms, 37 suites* 🍴 *No meals* ✣ *E6.*

NIGHTLIFE

A couple of decades ago, San Diego scraped by on its superb daytime offerings. Those sleepy-after-dark days are over; San Diego now sizzles when the sun goes down. Of particular interest to beer lovers, the city has become internationally acclaimed for dozens of breweries, beer pubs, and festivals.

The most obvious destination for visitors is the Gaslamp Quarter, a 16-block former red-light district gone glam. The debauchery is slightly more modest these days—or at least legal, anyway. Between the Gaslamp and neighboring East Village, there's truly something for everyone, from secretive speakeasies to big, bangin' dance clubs and chic rooftop lounges to grimy dives. If you're staying in the Gaslamp, it's the perfect place to party. If you're driving from elsewhere, prepare to pay. Your best options: parking lots (prices start at $20) or valet (at some restaurants and clubs).

The epicenter of gay culture is Hillcrest, where you'll find bars and clubs catering primarily to the LGBT crowd—though everyone is welcome. East of Hillcrest is North Park, where hip twenty- and thirtysomethings hang out at edgy scenester hot spots. Nearby South Park and University Heights also have a few cool offerings. A cab from Downtown to any of these 'hoods costs about $15.

Pacific Beach tends to draw college kids who don't know when to say when, while Ocean and Mission beaches pull laid-back surfers and their cohorts. La Jolla, for the most part, is a snooze if you're in the mood to booze late at night.

DOWNTOWN

GASLAMP QUARTER

BARS

Fodor's Choice
★
Rooftop 600 @Andaz. At this rooftop bar and lounge atop the Andaz hotel, a fashionable crowd sips cocktails poolside while gazing at gorgeous views of the city. Thursday through Saturday, the scene heats up with a DJ spinning dance music, while velvet ropes and VIP bottle service please the A-listers (like Prince Harry) in the crowd. ✉ *600 F St., Gaslamp Quarter, San Diego* ☎ *619/814–2055* ⊕ *www.rooftop600.com.*

WINE BARS

Fodor's Choice
★
Vin de Syrah. This "spirit and wine cellar" sends you down a rabbit hole (or at least down some stairs) to a whimsical spot straight out of Alice in Wonderland. Behind a hidden door (look for a handle in the grass wall), you'll find visual delights (grapevines suspended from the ceiling, vintage jars with flittering "fireflies," cozy chairs nestled around a faux fireplace and pastoral vista) that rival the culinary ones—the wine list is approachable and the charcuterie boards are exquisitely curated. ■ TIP➔ More than just a wine bar, the cocktails are also worth a try. ✉ *901 5th Ave., Gaslamp Quarter, San Diego* ☎ *619/234–4166* ⊕ *www. syrahwineparlor.com.*

DANCE CLUBS

Stingaree. One could argue that Stingaree was the Gaslamp's first megaclub and, almost a decade later, it's still going strong. Guests can enjoy electro and Top 40 in the main nightclub, a smashing three-story space with translucent "floating" staircases and floor-to-ceiling water walls. Dress nicely. The air of exclusivity at this hangout is palpable, and to reinforce the point, the drink prices are steep. ✉ *454 6th Ave., at Island St., Gaslamp Quarter, San Diego* ☎ *619/544–9500* ⊕ *www. stingsandiego.com.*

MUSIC CLUBS

House of Blues. The local branch of the renowned music chain is decorated floor to ceiling with colorful folk art and features three different areas to hear music. There's something going on here just about every night of the week, and the gospel brunch on select Sundays is one of the most praiseworthy events in town. Can we get a hallelujah? ✉ *1055 5th Ave., Gaslamp Quarter, San Diego* ☎ *619/299–2583* ⊕ *www.houseofblues.com.*

OFF THE
BEATEN
PATH
The Casbah. This small club near the airport, the unofficial headquarters of the city's indie music scene, has a national reputation for showcasing up-and-coming acts of all genres. Nirvana, Smashing Pumpkins, and the White Stripes all played here on the way to stardom. ✉ *2501 Kettner Blvd., Middletown, San Diego* ☎ *619/232–4355* ⊕ *www.casbahmusic.com.*

PIANO BARS

Fodor's Choice
★
Westgate Hotel Plaza Bar. The old-money surroundings, including leather-upholstered seats, marble tabletops, and a grand piano, supply one of the most elegant and romantic settings for a drink in San Diego. ✉ *1055 2nd Ave., Gaslamp Quarter, San Diego* ☎ *619/557-3650* ⊕ *www.west gatehotel.com.*

EAST VILLAGE
PIANO BARS

Fodor's Choice ★ **Noble Experiment.** Speakeasy-style bars have been popping up all over San Diego, and the trend is impeccably realized in this quaint but decidedly swank cocktail lounge hidden in the back of a burger restaurant. Once customers find the hidden door (hint: look for the stack of kegs), they can bask in one of the plush leather booths while enjoying intricately crafted drinks that are second to none in the city. ⚠ Warning: Reservations are almost always a must, so be sure to call ahead. ⊠ *777 G St., East Village, San Diego* ☎ *619/888–4713* ⊕ *nobleexperimentsd.com.*

LITTLE ITALY
BARS

Fodor's Choice ★ **The Waterfront Bar & Grill.** It isn't really *on* the waterfront, but San Diego's oldest bar was once the hangout of Italian fishermen. Most of the collars are now white, and patrons enjoy an excellent selection of beers, along with chili, burgers, fish-and-chips, and other great-tasting grub, including fish tacos. Get here early, as there's almost always a crowd. ⊠ *2044 Kettner Blvd., Little Italy, San Diego* ☎ *619/232–9656* ⊕ *www.waterfrontbarandgrill.com.*

COFFEEHOUSES

Extraordinary Desserts. A delicious visual treat, with a lacy, laser-cut metal façade and elegant teak patio, also satisfies every sort of culinary craving, from savory to sweet and everything in between. The wine, beer, and bubbly list is très chic, too. ⊠ *1430 Union St., Little Italy, San Diego* ☎ *619/294–7001* ⊕ *www.extraordinarydesserts.com.*

OLD TOWN AND UPTOWN

HILLCREST
GAY NIGHTLIFE

Fodor's Choice ★ **Baja Betty's.** Although it draws plenty of gay customers, the festive and friendly atmosphere is popular with just about everyone in the Hillcrest area (and their pets are welcome, too). The bar staff stocks more than 100 brands of tequila and mixes plenty of fancy cocktails. ⊠ *1421 University Ave., Hillcrest, San Diego* ☎ *619/269–8510* ⊕ *www.bajabettyssd.com.*

Urban Mo's Bar and Grill. Cowboys gather for line dancing and two-stepping on the wooden dance floor—but be forewarned, yee-hawers, it can get pretty wild on Western nights. There are also Latin, hip-hop, and drag revues but the real allure is in the creative drinks ("Gone Fishing"—served in a fishbowl, for example) and the breezy patio where love (or something like it) is usually in the air. ⊠ *308 University Ave., Hillcrest, San Diego* ☎ *619/491–0400* ⊕ *www.urbanmos.com.*

MISSION HILLS
PIANO BARS

Fodor's Choice ★ **Starlite.** Bar-goers are dazzled by Starlite's award-winning interior design, which includes rock walls, luxe leather booths, and a massive mirror-mounted chandelier. A hexagonal wood-plank entryway leads to a sunken white bar, where sexy tattooed guys and girls mix creative cocktails, such as the signature Starlite Mule, served in a copper mug.

An iPod plays eclectic playlists ranging from old-timey jazz and blues to obscure vintage rock (and DJs are on hand on certain evenings). During warmer months, procuring a spot on the outside wood-decked patio is an art form. ✉ *3175 India St., Mission Hills, San Diego* ☎ *619/358–9766* ⊕ *www.starlitesandiego.com.*

NORTH PARK
BARS

Toronado. One of San Diego's favorite gathering spots for hop-heads is named in honor of the San Francisco beer bar of the same name. The beer list—both on tap and by the bottle—is hard to beat. The place can get noisy, but the food—a mix of burgers and American-style comfort food—more than makes up for it. ✉ *4026 30th St., North Park, San Diego* ☎ *619/282–0456* ⊕ *www.toronadosd.com.*

MISSION BAY AND THE BEACHES

PACIFIC BEACH
BARS

JRDN. This contemporary lounge (pronounced "Jordan") occupies the ground floor of Pacific Beach's chicest boutique hotel, Tower23, and offers a more sophisticated vibe in what is a very party-happy neighborhood. Sleek walls of windows and an expansive patio overlook the boardwalk. ✉ *723 Felspar St., Pacific Beach, San Diego* ☎ *858/270–5736* ⊕ *www.t23hotel.com.*

THE ARTS

TICKETS

Arts Tix. You can buy advance tickets, many at half price, to theater, music, and dance events at Arts Tix. ✉ *28 Horton Plaza, 3rd Ave. and Broadway, Gaslamp Quarter, San Diego* ☎ *858/381–5595* ⊕ *www.sdartstix.com.*

DANCE

California Ballet Company. The company performs high-quality contemporary and classical works September–May at the **Civic Theatre**. The *Nutcracker* is staged annually around the holiday season. ✉ *1100 3rd Ave., Downtown, San Diego* ☎ *619/570–1100* ⊕ *www.californiaballet.org.*

Balboa Theatre. This historic landmark hosts ballet, music, plays and even stand-up comedy performances. ✉ *868 4th Ave., Downtown, San Diego* ☎ *619/570–1100* ⊕ *www.sandiegotheatres.org.*

MUSIC

Fodor's Choice
★

Copley Symphony Hall. The great acoustics here are surpassed only by the incredible Spanish baroque interior. Not just the home of the San Diego Symphony Orchestra, the renovated 2,200-seat 1920s-era theater has also hosted major stars like Elvis Costello, Leonard Cohen, and Sting. ✉ *750 B St., Downtown, San Diego* ☎ *619/235–0804* ⊕ *www.sandiegosymphony.org.*

San Diego On Tap

The secret is out: San Diego is the nation's best beer town. In addition to more than 60 local breweries, San Diego has a stretch of beer-nerd heaven nicknamed the Belgian Corridor (30th Street in North/South Park). You can find all styles of beer in San Diego, from the meek to the mighty, but many local brewers contend that the specialty is the big, bold Double IPA (also called an Imperial IPA). It's an India Pale Ale with attitude—and lots of hops. Nearly every local brewery has its own version.

Bars with the best microbrew selection: Blind Lady Ale House, Hamilton's Tavern, Live Wire, O'Brien's, Toronado.

Best fests: Want one location and a seemingly endless supply of beer? Try the San Diego Festival of Beers (September ⊕ www.sdbeerfest.org), San Diego Beer Week (November ⊕ www.sdbw.org), and the Strong Ale Fest (December). Find more listings at ⊕ www.sandiegobrewersguild.org.

Best way to sample it all: Sign up for Brewery Tours of San Diego (⊕ www.brewerytoursofsandiego.com) to sample the best craft beers without a second thought about directions or designated drivers.

SAN DIEGO'S BEST BREWERIES
You can also head to the source, where beer is brewed. These are outside the city center, but worth the trek for beer aficionados.

AleSmith Brewing Co. This artisanal microbrewery offers tastings at its out-of-the-way locale in the Miramar area. Just how artisanal is it? The "Kopi Luwak" special edition of AleSmith's popular Speedway Stout is brewed with Civet coffee from Indonesia, made from rare and expensive coffee berries that have been eaten—and passed, undigested—by the Asian Palm Civet. Visitors can tour the entire brewery on Saturdays at 2 pm. ⊠ *9368 Cabot Dr., Scripps Ranch, San Diego* ☎ *858/549–9888* ⊕ *www. alesmith.com.*

Alpine Brewing Co.
Fodor's Choice★ Well worth the mountain drive, this family-owned operation may be itty-bitty, but it's also a big champ: brewmaster Pat McIlhenney, a former fire captain, has won national and international kudos for his hopped-up creations and took the title of the fifth-best brewery in the nation from *Beer Advocate*. Tasters are only a buck each, or fill a growler, which holds a half gallon, for future imbibing. If they're on tap, don't pass up Duet, Pure Hoppiness, or Exponential Hoppiness. Alpine recently opened a pub a few doors down where you can taste flights of their various beers. ⊠ *2351 Alpine Blvd., Alpine, San Diego* ☎ *619/445–2337* ⊕ *www.alpinebeerco.com.*

Stone Brewing World Gardens and Bistro. The Big Daddy of San Diego craft brewing was founded by a couple of basement beer tinkerers in 1996; the company now exports its aggressively hoppy beers—instantly identifiable by their leering gargoyle labels—to bars and stores across the nation. Stone's monumental HQ is off the beaten path, but totally worth a visit for its tours ($3 includes souvenir tasting glass), vast on-tap selection (not just Stone beers), and hard-to-beat bistro eats. ⊠ *1999 Citracado Pkwy., Escondido* ☎ *760/294-7866* ⊕ *www.stonebrew.com.*

San Diego Symphony Orchestra. The orchestra's events include classical concerts and summer and winter pops, nearly all of them at Copley Symphony Hall. The outdoor Summer Pops series is held on the Embarcadero, on North Harbor Drive beyond the convention center. ⊠ *Box office, 750 B. St., Downtown, San Diego* ☎ *619/235–0804* ⊕ *www. sandiegosymphony.org.*

Spreckels Organ Pavilion. Home of a giant outdoor pipe organ donated to the city, the beautiful Spanish baroque pavilion hosts concerts by civic organist Carol Williams and guest organists on most Sunday afternoons and on Monday evenings in summer. Local military bands, gospel groups, and barbershop quartets also perform here. All shows are free. ⊠ *2211 Pan American Rd. E., Balboa Park, San Diego* ☎ *619/702– 8138* ⊕ *sosorgan.com.*

THEATER

Fodor'sChoice
★   **La Jolla Playhouse.** Under the artistic direction of Christopher Ashley, the playhouse presents exciting and innovative plays and musicals on three stages. Many Broadway shows—among them *Memphis*, *Tommy*, and *Jersey Boys*—have previewed here before their East Coast premieres. ⊠ *University of California at San Diego, 2910 La Jolla Village Dr., La Jolla, San Diego* ☎ *858/550–1010* ⊕ *www.lajollaplayhouse.org.*

Fodor'sChoice
★   **The Old Globe.** This complex, comprising the Sheryl and Harvey White Theatre, the Lowell Davies Festival Theatre, and the Old Globe Theatre, offers some of the finest theatrical productions in Southern California. Theater classics such as *The Full Monty* and *Dirty Rotten Scoundrels*, both of which went on to Broadway, premiered on these famed stages. The Old Globe presents the family-friendly *How the Grinch Stole Christmas* around the holidays, as well as a renowned summer Shakespeare Festival with three to four plays in repertory. ⊠ *1363 Old Globe Way, Balboa Park, San Diego* ☎ *619/234–5623* ⊕ *www.oldglobe.org.*

SPORTS AND THE OUTDOORS

BASEBALL

Fodor'sChoice
★   Long a favorite spectator sport in San Diego, where games are rarely rained out, baseball gained even more popularity in 2004 with the opening of PETCO Park, a stunning 42,000-seat facility in the heart of Downtown.

San Diego Padres. The Padres slug it out for bragging rights in the National League West from April into October. Tickets are usually available on game day, but games with such rivals as the Los Angeles Dodgers and the San Francisco Giants often sell out quickly. For an inexpensive day at the ballpark, go for the park pass ($10–$15, depending on demand, available for purchase at the park only) and have a picnic on the grass, while watching the game on one of several giant-screen TVs. ⊠ *100 Park Blvd., East Village* ☎ *619/795–5000, 877/374–2784* ⊕ *sandiego.padres.mlb.com.*

BIKING

San Diego offers bountiful opportunities for bikers, from casual boardwalk cruises to strenuous rides into the hills. The mild climate makes biking in San Diego a year-round delight. Bike culture is respected here, and visitors are often impressed with the miles of designated bike lanes running alongside city streets and coastal roads throughout the county. **Cheap Rentals Mission Beach.** Right by the boardwalk, this place has good daily and weekly prices for bike rentals, which include beach cruisers, tandems, hybrids, and two-wheeled baby carriers. ✉ *3689 Mission Blvd., Mission Beach* ☎ *858/488–9070, 800/941–7761* ⊕ *www. cheap-rentals.com.*

Hike Bike Kayak San Diego. This outfitter offers a wide range of guided bike tours, from easy excursions around Mission Bay and Coronado Island to slightly more rigorous trips through coastal La Jolla. Tours last up to two and a half hours, and cost $30–40. The company also rents bikes, and can even deliver them to your hotel. ✉ *2222 Ave. de la Playa, La Jolla* ☎ *858/551–9510* ⊕ *www.hikebikekayak.com.*

Holland's Bicycles. This great bike rental source on Coronado Island has another store (**Bikes and Beyond** ☎ *619/435–7180)* located at the ferry landing, so you can jump on your bike as soon as you cross the harbor from Downtown San Diego. ✉ *977 Orange Ave., Coronado* ☎ *619/435–3153* ⊕ *www.hollandsbicycles.com.*

Route S21. On many summer days, Route S21, aka Old Highway 101, from La Jolla to Oceanside looks like a freeway for cyclists. About 24 miles long, it's easily the most popular and scenic bike route around, never straying far from the beach. Although the terrain is fairly easy, the long, steep Torrey Pines grade is famous for weeding out the weak. Another Darwinian challenge is dodging slow-moving pedestrians and cars pulling over to park in towns like Encinitas and Del Mar.

DIVING

Ocean Enterprises Scuba Diving. Stop in for everything you need to plan a diving adventure, including equipment, advice, and instruction. ✉ *7710 Balboa Ave., Suite 101, Clairemont Mesa* ☎ *858/565–6054* ⊕ *www. oceanenterprises.com.*

San Diego–La Jolla Underwater Park Ecological Preserve. Diving enthusiasts the world over come to San Diego to snorkel and scuba dive off La Jolla at the underwater preserve. Because all sea life is protected here, this 533-acre preserve (all of La Jolla Cove to La Jolla Shores) is the best place to see large lobster, sea bass, and sculpin (scorpion fish), as well as numerous golden garibaldi damselfish, the state marine fish. It's common to see hundreds of beautiful (and harmless) leopard sharks schooling at the north end of the cove, near La Jolla Shores, especially in summer.

Scuba San Diego. This center is well regarded for its top-notch instruction and certification programs, as well as for guided dive tours. Trips include dives to kelp reefs in La Jolla Cove, and night diving at La Jolla Canyon. ✉ *San Diego Hilton Hotel, 1775 E. Mission Bay Dr., Mission Bay* ☎ *619/260–1880* ⊕ *www.scubasandiego.com.*

FISHING

Fisherman's Landing. You can book space on a fleet of luxury vessels from 57 feet to 124 feet long and embark on multiday trips in search of yellowfin tuna, yellowtail, and other deep-water fish. Half-day fishing and whale-watching trips are also available. ⊠ *2838 Garrison St., Point Loma* ☎ *619/221–8500* ⊕ *www.fishermanslanding.com.*

H&M Landing. Join up for fishing trips, plus whale-watching excursions from December through March. ⊠ *2803 Emerson St., Point Loma* ☎ *619/222–1144* ⊕ *www.hmlanding.com.*

FOOTBALL

San Diego Chargers. The Chargers play their NFL home games at Qualcomm Stadium. Games with AFC West rivals the Oakland Raiders are particularly intense. ⊠ *9449 Friars Rd., Mission Valley* ☎ *858/874–4500 Charger Park, 877/242–7437 Season Tickets* ⊕ *www.chargers.com.*

GOLF

Balboa Park Municipal Golf Course. In the heart of Balboa Park, this public course is convenient to Downtown and offers impressive views of the city and bay. The challenging course weaves among the park's canyons with some tricky drop-offs, and offers players a good value. Finish off your round with a meal or drink at Tobey's 19th Hole Cafe, a classic greasy spoon with excellent views. ⊠ *2600 Golf Course Dr., Balboa Park* ☎ *619/235–1184* ⊕ *www.balboagc.com* ☞ *$18 for 9 holes, $40 for 18 holes on weekdays; $23 for 9 holes, $50 for 18 holes on weekends* ⚐ *18 holes, 6281 yards, par 72.*

Coronado Municipal Golf Course. Spectacular views of San Diego Bay and the Coronado Bridge from the front 9 make this course extremely popular. It's difficult to get on unless you reserve a tee time, 3 to 14 days in advance. The pace of the course is leisurely, and it's a good one to walk. The wide fairways make it a good choice for beginners, but the course is challenging for all levels. ⊠ *2000 Visalia Row, Coronado* ☎ *619/435–3121* ⊕ *www.golfcoronado.com* ☞ *$35 on weekdays; $40 on weekends. Reservations essential* ⚐ *18 holes, 6590 yards, par 72.*

Omni La Costa Resort and Spa. One of the premier golf resorts in Southern California, La Costa is home to the PGA Tour Golf Academy, whose instructors include past and present touring pros and coaches. The resort recently remodeled both its Champions and Legends Courses. After a day on the links you can wind down with a massage, steam bath, and dinner at the resort. ⊠ *2100 Costa del Mar Rd., Carlsbad* ☎ *800/854-5000* ⊕ *www.lacosta.com* ☞ *Champions and Legends, Mon.–Thurs., $210; Fri.–Sun., $230. Reservations essential.* ⚐ *Champions: 18 holes, 6608 yards, par 72. Legends: 18 holes, 6524 yards, par 72.*

Fodor's Choice **Park Hyatt Aviara Golf Club.** Designed by Arnold Palmer, this top-quality
★   course includes views of the protected adjacent Batiquitos Lagoon and the Pacific Ocean. The carts, which are fitted with GPS systems that

tell you the distance to the pin, are included in the cost. ✉ *7447 Batiquitos Dr., Carlsbad* ☎ *760/603–6900* ⊕ *www.golfaviara.com* ✆ *$225 on weekdays; $245 on weekends* ⚑ *18 holes, 7007 yards, par 72.*

Fodor'sChoice
★
Torrey Pines Golf Course. One of the best public golf courses in the United States, Torrey Pines was the site of the 2008 U.S. Open and has been the home of the Buick Invitational (now the Farmers Insurance Open) since 1968. The par-72 South Course receives rave reviews from the touring pros. Redesigned by Rees Jones in 2001, it's longer, more challenging, and more expensive than the North Course. Tee times may be booked from 8 to 90 days in advance (*877/581–7171*) and are subject to an advance booking fee ($43). A full-day or half-day instructional package includes cart, greens fee, and a golf-pro escort for the first 9 holes. ✉ *11480 N. Torrey Pines Rd., La Jolla* ☎ *858/452–3226, 800/985–4653* ⊕ *www.torreypinesgolfcourse.com* ✆ *South: $183 on weekdays, $229 on weekends; North: $100 on weedays, $125 on weekends* ⚑ *South: 18 holes, 7227 yards, par 72; North: 18 holes, 6874 yards, par 72.*

HIKING AND NATURE TRAILS

Fodor'sChoice
★
Bayside Trail at Cabrillo National Monument. Driving here is a treat in itself, as a vast view of the Pacific unfolds before you. The view is equally enjoyable on Bayside Trail (2 miles round-trip), which is home to the same coastal sagebrush that Juan Rodriguez Cabrillo saw when he first discovered the California coast in the 16th century. After the hike, you can explore nearby tide pools, the monument statue, and the Old Point Loma Lighthouse. Don't worry if you don't see everything on your first visit; your entrance receipt ($5 per car) is good for 7 days. ✉ *1800 Cabrillo Memorial Dr., from I–5, take the Rosecrans exit and turn right on Canon St. then left on Catalina Blvd.; continue following signs to the park, Point Loma* ☎ *619/557–5450* ⊕ *www.nps.gov/cabr.*

Torrey Pines State Reserve. Hiking aficionados will appreciate this park's many winning features: a number of modest trails that descend to the sea, an unparalleled view of the Pacific, and a chance to see the Torrey pine tree, one of the rarest pine breeds in the United States. The reserve hosts guided nature walks as well. All food is prohibited at the reserve so save the picnic until you reach the beach below. Parking is $12–15, depending on day and season. ✉ *12600 N. Torrey Pines Rd., exit I–5 at Carmel Valley Rd. and head west toward Coast Hwy. 101 until you reach Torrey Pines State Beach; turn left, La Jolla* ☎ *858/755–2063* ⊕ *www.torreypine.org.*

KAYAKING, SAILING, AND BOATING

Hike Bike Kayak San Diego. This shop offers several kayak tours, from easy excursions in Mission Bay that are well suited to families and beginners on to more advanced jaunts. Tours include kayaking the caves off La Jolla coast, whale-watching (from a safe distance) December through March, moonlight and sunset trips, and a cruise into the bay to see SeaWorld's impressive fireworks shows over the water in the summer. Tours last two to three hours and cost between $50 and $70 per person; cost includes kayak, paddle, life vest, and guide. ✉ *2222 Ave. de la Playa, La Jolla* ☎ *858/551–9510* ⊕ *www. hikebikekayak.com.*

Seaforth Boat Rentals. You can book charter tours and rent kayaks, Jet Skis, fishing skiffs, powerboats, and sailboats at Seaforth's five locations around town. They also can hook you up with a skipper for a deep-sea fishing trip. Seaforth also rents paddleboards at their Mission Bay and Coronado locations. ✉ *1715 Strand Way, Coronado* ☎ *888/834–2628* ⊕ *www.seaforthboatrentals.com.*

SURFING

If you're a beginner, consider paddling in the waves off Mission Beach, Pacific Beach, Tourmaline Surfing Park, La Jolla Shores, Del Mar, or Oceanside. More experienced surfers usually head for Sunset Cliffs, La Jolla reef breaks, Black's Beach, or Swami's in Encinitas. All necessary equipment is included in the cost of all surfing schools. Beach-area Y's offer surf lessons and surf camp in the summer months and during spring break.

Cheap Rentals Mission Beach. Many local surf shops rent both surf and bodyboards. Cheap Rentals Mission Beach is right off the boardwalk, just steps from the waves. They rent wet suits and skimboards in addition to soft surfboards and long and short fiberglass rides. They also have good hourly to weekly pricing on paddleboards and accessories. ✉ *3689 Mission Blvd., Mission Beach* ☎ *858/488–9070, 800/941–7761* ⊕ *www.cheap-rentals.com.*

Hansen's. A short walk from Swami's beach, Hansen's is one of San Diego's oldest and most popular surf shops. It has an extensive selection of boards, wet suits, and clothing for sale, and a rental department as well. ✉ *1105 S. Coast Hwy. 101, Encinitas* ☎ *760/753–6595, 800/480–4754* ⊕ *www.hansensurf.com.*

Surf Diva Surf School. Check out clinics, surf camps, surf trips, and private lessons especially formulated for girls and women. Most clinics and trips are for women only, but there are some co-ed options. Guys can also book private lessons from the nationally recognized staff. ✉ *2160 Ave. de la Playa, La Jolla* ☎ *858/454–8273* ⊕ *www.surfdiva.com.*

SHOPPING

San Diego's retail venues are as diverse as the city's vibrant neighborhoods. From La Jolla's tony boutiques to the outlet malls at San Ysidro, you'll find stores that appeal to every taste and budget.

DOWNTOWN

2

The Gaslamp Quarter, Downtown's trendy hot spot, is where you'll find independent shops selling urban apparel, unique home decor items, and vintage treasures. If you can't find it in the boutiques, head for Westfield Horton Plaza, the Downtown mall with more than 130 stores and 26 eateries.

Just a hop, skip, and a jump from the Gaslamp Quarter, the 130-block East Village neighborhood contains shops catering to local hipsters and visitors looking for edgy street wear, novelty T-shirts, and offbeat accessories. Some of the best shopping can be found from 8th to 10th avenues between Broadway and J Street.

Nearby, Little Italy is the place to find contemporary art, clothing from local designers, and home-decor items. Kettner Boulevard and India Street from Laurel to Date Street are the heart of the Art and Design District.

Into kitschy gifts and souvenirs? Downtown's Seaport Village has an abundance of quirky shops that won't disappoint, plus you'll be able to enjoy the coastal breezes while you shop for that Coronado Bridge snow globe.

Spanning 14 acres and offering more than 50 shops and 18 restaurants, Seaport Village is by far the most popular destination in the waterfront Embarcadero neighborhood.

SHOPPING CENTER

Westfield Horton Plaza. This Downtown shopping, dining, and entertainment mecca fronts Broadway and G Street from 1st to 4th avenues and covers more than six city blocks. Designed by Jon Jerde and completed in 1985, Westfield Horton Plaza is a collage of colorful tile work, banners waving in the air, and modern sculptures. The complex rises in uneven, staggered levels to five floors; great views of Downtown from the harbor to Balboa Park and beyond can be had here.

Macy's and Nordstrom department stores anchor the plaza housing clothing, sporting-goods, jewelry, and gift shops. Other attractions include a movie complex, restaurants, and the respected San Diego Repertory Theatre below ground level. In 2008 the **Balboa Theater,** contiguous with the shopping center, reopened its doors after a $26.5-million renovation. The historic 1920s theater seats 1,400 and offers live arts and cultural performances throughout the week.

The mall has a multilevel parking garage; even so, lines to find a space can be long. ■TIP➜ **Entering the parking structure on G Street rather than 4th Avenue generally means less traffic and more parking space.** Parking validation is complimentary whether you spend a bundle or just window-shop. Validation machines throughout the center allow for three hours' free parking; after that it's $8 per hour (or $2 per 15-minute increment). If you use this notoriously confusing fruit-and-vegetable–themed garage, be sure to remember at which produce level you've left your car. If you're staying Downtown, the Old Town Trolley Tour will drop you directly in front of Westfield Horton Plaza.

✉ *324 Horton Plaza, Gaslamp Quarter* ☎ *619/238–1596* ⊕ *www. westfield.com/hortonplaza* ⊘ *Weekdays 10–9, Sat. 10–8, Sun. 11–6.*

OLD TOWN AND UPTOWN

OLD TOWN

Tourist-focused Old Town, north of Downtown off I–5 has a festival-like ambience that also makes it a popular destination for locals. At Old Town Historic Park, you'll feel like a time traveler as you visit shops housed in restored adobe buildings. Farther down the street you'll find stores selling Mexican blankets, piñatas, and glassware. Old Town Market offers live entertainment, local artists selling their wares from carts, and a market crammed with unique apparel, home-decor items, toys, jewelry, and food.

MARKET

Fodor'sChoice
★
Bazaar del Mundo Shops. An arcade with a Mexican villa theme, the Bazaar hosts riotously colorful gift shops such as **Ariana,** for ethnic and artsy women's fashions; **Artes de Mexico,** which sells handmade Latin American crafts and Guatemalan weavings; and **The Gallery,** which carries handmade jewelry, Native American crafts, collectible glass, and original serigraphs by John August Swanson. The **Laurel Burch Gallerita** carries the complete collection of the Northern California artist's signature jewelry, accessories, and totes. ✉ *4133 Taylor St., at Juan St., Old Town* ☎ *619/296–3161* ⊕ *www.bazaardelmundo.com.*

UPTOWN

Hillcrest has a large gay community and boasts many avant-garde apparel shops alongside gift, book, and music stores. North Park, east of Hillcrest, is a retro buff's paradise with many resale shops, trendy boutiques, and stores that sell a mix of old and new. South Park's 30th, Juniper, and Fern streets have everything from the hottest new denim lines to baby gear and craft supplies. The shops and art galleries in upscale Mission Hills, west of Hillcrest, have a modern and sophisticated ambience that suits the well-heeled residents.

MISSION VALLEY

Northeast of Downtown near I–8 and Route 163, Mission Valley holds two major shopping centers and a few smaller strip malls.

MALL

Fodor'sChoice
★
Fashion Valley. San Diego's best and most upscale mall has a contemporary mission style, lush landscaping, and more than 200 shops and restaurants. Acclaimed retailers like Bloomingdale's, Neiman Marcus, and Tiffany are here, along with boutiques from fashion darlings like Michael Kors, Jimmy Choo, Tory Burch, and James Perse. H&M is a favorite of fashionistas in search of edgy and affordable styles. ■TIP➔ Free wireless Internet service is available throughout the mall. Select "Simon WiFi" from any Wi-Fi–enabled device to log onto the network. ✉ *7007 Friars Rd., Mission Valley* ☎ *619/688–9113* ⊕ *www. simon.com/mall/fashion-valley.*

LA JOLLA

Known as San Diego's answer to Rodeo Drive in Beverly Hills, La Jolla has chic boutiques, art galleries, and gift shops and plenty of celebrity sightings. Prospect Street and Girard Avenue are the primary shopping stretches, and North Prospect is chockablock with art galleries. Parking is tight in the village. Most shops on Prospect Street stay open until 10 pm on weeknights to accommodate evening strollers.

2

CORONADO

Coronado's resort hotels attract tourists in droves, but somehow the town has managed to avoid being overtaken by chain stores. Friendly shopkeepers make the boutiques lining Orange Avenue, Coronado's main drag, a good place to browse for clothes, home-decor and gift items, and gourmet foods.

SHOPPING CENTER

Fodor'sChoice ★ **Coronado Ferry Landing.** A staggering view of San Diego's Downtown skyline across the bay and a dozen boutiques make this a delightful place to shop while waiting for a ferry. La Camisa (☎619/435–8009) is a fun place to pick up kitschy souvenirs, T-shirts, fleece jackets, and postcards. **The French Room** (☎619/889–9004) specializes in comfy women's shoes and affordable casual wear. **Men's Island Sportswear** (☎619/437–4696) sells hats, tropical sportswear, and accessories to complete your seaside getaway outfit. ⊠ *1201 1st St., Coronado* ☎ *619/435–8895* ⊕ *www.coronadoferrylandingshops.com* ⊗ *Shops daily 10–7* ✑ *Farmers' market Tues. 2:30–6; some restaurants daily late-afternoon happy hour.*

La Camisa. This is a fun place to pick up kitschy souvenirs, T-shirts, fleece jackets, and postcards. ⊠ *1201 1st St., between B Ave. and C Ave., Coronado* ☎ *619/435–8009.*

Scottish Treasures. Get in touch with your Celtic roots with imported apparel, gifts, tableware, and jewelry from Ireland, Scotland, England, and Wales. You can even order a custom-made kilt. ☎ *619/435–1880.*

Men's Island Sportswear. Complete your seaside getaway with hats, tropical sportswear, and accessories here. ☎ *619/437–4696.*

Fodor'sChoice ★ **Hotel Del Coronado.** At the dozen gift shops within the peninsula's main historic attraction, you can purchase sportswear, designer handbags, jewelry, and antiques. **Babcock & Story Emporium** (☎ *Ext. 7265*) carries an amazing selection of home-decor items, garden accessories, and classy gifts. **Blue Octopus** (☎ *Ext. 7330*) is a children's store featuring creative toys, gifts, and apparel. **Spreckels Sweets & Treats** (☎ *Ext. 7627*) offers old-time candies, freshly made fudge, and decadent truffles. Women will appreciate the stylish fashions and accessories at **Kate's** (☎ *Ext. 7601*) and **Isabel B** (☎ *Ext. 7384*), while well-dressed men can't go wrong with a shirt or jacket from **Brady's** (☎ *Ext. 7339*). For those celebrating a special occasion, **Crown Jewels Coronado** (☎ *Ext. 7340*) features fine jewelry, some inspired by the sea. ⊠ *1500 Orange Ave., Coronado* ☎ *619/435–6611 plus extension* ⊕ *www.hoteldel.com/shopping.*

SIDE TRIPS TO NORTH COUNTY

DEL MAR

23 miles north of Downtown San Diego on I–5, 9 miles north of La Jolla on Rte. S21.

Del Mar is best known for its quaint old section west of Interstate 5 marked with a glamorous racetrack, half-timber buildings, chic shops, tony restaurants, celebrity visitors, and wide beaches.

EXPLORING

FAMILY **Del Mar Fairgrounds.** The Spanish mission–style fairground is the home of the **Del Mar Thoroughbred Club** (☎☎ *858/755–1141* 🌐 *www.dmtc.com*). Crooner Bing Crosby and his Hollywood buddies—Pat O'Brien, Gary Cooper, and Oliver Hardy, among others—organized the club in the 1930s, and the racing here (usually July–September, Wednesday–Monday, post time 2 pm) remains a fashionable affair. Del Mar Fairgrounds hosts more than 100 different events each year, including the San Diego County Fair, which draws more than a million visitors annually. ✉ *2260 Jimmy Durante Blvd.* ☎ *858/793–5555* 🌐 *www.delmarfairgrounds.com.*

WHERE TO EAT

$$$$ FRENCH Fodor's Choice ★ 🍴 **Addison.** The sophisticated and stylish dining room and adjacent bar feel Italian and clubby, with intricately carved dark-wood motifs, and the tables, by contrast, are pure white, adorned with a single flower. Acclaimed chef William Bradley serves up explosive flavors in his four, seven, and ten-course prix-fixe dinners, such as Prince Edward Island mussels with champagne sabayon and lemon verbena *jus* or foie gras de canard with Le Puy lentils, port wine, and smoked bacon mousse. Entrées might include spring lamb *persille* (parsely and garlic topping) with pistachio pâté brisée and caramelized garlic purée or wild Scottish salmon with sauce *vin jaune* (white wine from France's Jura region). Addison challenges wine lovers with 160 pages of choices. [$] *Average main: $98* ✉ *5200 Grand Del Mar Way* ☎ *858/314–1900* 🌐 *www.addisondelmar.com* ✍ *Reservations essential* 🕒 *Closed Sun. and Mon. No lunch.*

$$$ AMERICAN Fodor's Choice ★ 🍴 **Market Restaurant + Bar.** Carl Schroeder, one of California's hottest young chefs, draws well-heeled foodies to sample his creative and fun California fare, much of it with an Asian flare. The menu changes regularly depending upon what's fresh. Schroeder's seasonally inspired dishes have a playful spirit, whether it's a blue cheese soufflé with seasonal fruit, a Maine lobster salad with mango, or coriander-spiced red snapper with prawn dumplings. A well-edited wine list offers food-friendly wines by the best and brightest young winemakers around the world. Desserts are exquisite, such as the salty-sweet "Market Bar" or the chocolate butterscotch trio. [$] *Average main: $30* ✉ *3702 Via de la Valle* ☎ *858/523–0007* 🌐 *www.marketdelmar.com* ✍ *Reservations essential* 🕒 *No lunch.*

WHERE TO STAY

$$$$ RESORT FAMILY Fodor's Choice ★ **The Grand Del Mar.** Mind-blowing indulgence in serene surroundings, from drop-dead beautiful guest accommodations to outdoor adventures, sets the opulent Mediterranean-style Grand Del Mar apart from any other luxury hotel in San Diego. **Pros:** ultimate luxury; secluded, on-site golf course. **Cons:** service can be slow; hotel is not on the beach. [$] *Rooms from: $595* ✉ *5200 Grand Del Mar Ct., San Diego* ☎ *858/314–2000, 888/314–2030* 🌐 *www.thegranddelmar.com* 🛏 *218 rooms, 31 suites* 🍴 *No meals.*

CARLSBAD

6 miles north of Encinitas on Rte. S21, 36 miles north of Downtown San Diego on I–5.

Once-sleepy Carlsbad has long been popular with beachgoers and sun seekers. On a clear day in this village, you can take in sweeping ocean views that stretch from La Jolla to Oceanside by walking the 2-mile-long seawalk running between the Encina power plant and Pine Street. En route, you'll find several stairways leading to the beach and quite a few benches. Inland are LEGOLAND California and other attractions in its vicinity.

EXPLORING

FAMILY Fodor's Choice ★ **Flower Fields at Carlsbad Ranch.** In spring the hillsides are abloom on this, the largest bulb production farm in Southern California, when thousands of giant Tecolote ranunculus produce a stunning 50-acre display of color against the backdrop of the blue Pacific Ocean. Other knockouts include the rose gardens—with examples of every All-American Rose Selection award-winner since 1940—and a historical display of Paul Ecke poinsettias. Family activities include a LEGO Flower Garden and a kids' playground. ✉ *5704 Paseo del Norte, east of I–5* ☎ *760/431–0352* 🌐 *www.theflowerfields.com* 🎟 *$12* 🕒 *Mar.–May, daily 9–6.*

FAMILY Fodor's Choice ★ **LEGOLAND California Resort.** The centerpiece of a development that includes resort hotels, a designer discount shopping mall, an aquarium, and a waterpark, LEGOLAND has rides and diversions geared toward kids ages 2 to 12. Bring bathing suits; there are lockers at the entrance and at Pirate Shores. The main events are as follows:

Lost Kingdom Adventure: Armed with a laser blaster, you'll journey through ancient Egyptian ruins in a desert roadster, scoring points as you hit targets.

***Star Wars* Miniland:** Follow the exploits of Yoda, Princess Leia, Obi-Wan, Anakin, R2, Luke, and the denizens of the six *Star Wars* films. Some kids loop back several times to take it all in.

Miniland U.S.A.: This miniature, animated, interactive collection of U.S. icons was constructed out of 24 million LEGO bricks!

Soak-N-Sail: Hundreds of gallons of water course through 60 interactive features including a pirate shipwreck–theme area. You'll need your swimsuit for this one.

A LEGOLAND model worker puts the finishing touches on the San Francisco portion of Miniland U.S.A.

Dragon Coaster: Little kids love this popular indoor/outdoor steel roller coaster that goes through a castle. Don't let the name frighten you—the motif is more humorous than scary.

Volvo Driving School: Kids 6–13 can drive speed-controlled cars (not on rails) on a miniature road; driver's licenses are awarded after the course. Volvo Junior is the pint-sized version for kids 3–5.

■ TIP→ **The best value is one of the Hopper Tickets that give you one admission to LEGOLAND plus Sea Life Aquarium and/or the LEGOLAND Water Park. These can be used on the same day or on different days. Purchase tickets online for discounted pricing. Go midweek to avoid the crowds.**

LEGOLAND Hotel: Opened in 2013, this is the place for the family that eats, sleeps, and lives LEGO. Family rooms are themed Pirate, Adventure, and Kingdom, with corresponding LEGO-style decor. Each room has sleeping quarters for up to three kids. The hotel has interactive play areas, a restaurant, bar, and swimming pool but best of all, guests get early admission to the park.

Be sure to try Granny's Apple Fries, Castle Burgers, and Pizza Mania for pizzas and salads. The Market near the entrance has excellent coffee, fresh fruit, and yogurt. ⊠ *5885 The Crossings Dr.* ✛ *Exit I–5 at Cannon Rd. and follow signs east ¼ mile* ☎ *760/918–5346* ⊕ *california.legoland.com* ✉ *LEGOLAND $83 adults, $73 children; parking $15* ☉ *Late May–early Sept. daily (hrs vary), early Sept.–late May closed Tues. and Wed. except holiday weeks. Water Park closed Nov. to spring; check website or call for specifics.*

WHERE TO EAT

$$$
MEDITERRANEAN
Fodor's Choice
★

✕ **BlueFire Grill.** Fire and water drama defines this signature restaurant that's part of La Costa resort complex. The centerpiece of the resort's entrance plaza, the grill holds an outdoor patio with fire pits, fountains, and a year-round floral display. Inside is a contemporary mission-style room surrounding a green bottle glass fountain that extends the length of the main dining room. The menu features local seafood and vegetables combined in exciting ways. As a starter, try the heirloom field green salad with handpicked La Costa Resort herbs, followed by a California lamb barbacoa slow baked in banana leaves. Tantalizing desserts include luscious Carlsbad strawberries marinated in balsamic and lemon herb crème brûlée. $ *Average main: $31* ✉ *2100 Costa Del Mar Rd.* ☎ *760/929–6306* ⊕ *www.dinebluefire. com* & *Reservations essential* ☻ *Closed Sun.–Tues. No lunch.*

WHERE TO STAY

$$$
RESORT
FAMILY
Fodor's Choice
★

⌂ **Omni La Costa Resort and Spa.** This chic Spanish colonial oasis on 400 tree-shaded acres has ample guest rooms, in shades of brown and sand with oversize chairs and sofas; public rooms filled with dark wood, open-beam ceilings, paneling, crystal chandeliers, and leather and wrought-iron furnishings. **Pros:** huge glamorous spa; excellent kids' facilities; popular restaurant. **Cons:** very spread out, making long walks necessary; lots of kids, so if you're not in the market for a family-friendly stay, look elsewhere. $ *Rooms from: $399* ✉ *2100 Costa del Mar Rd.* ☎ *760/438–9111, 800/854–5000* ⊕ *www.lacosta.com* ➹ *607 rooms, 137 villas* ⏧ *No meals.*

$$$
RESORT
FAMILY
Fodor's Choice
★

⌂ **Park Hyatt Aviara Resort.** The quietly elegant hilltop retreat is one of the most luxurious hotels in the San Diego area, where rooms have every possible amenity (including private terraces and deep soaking tubs) and one of the most sublime views in Southern California, overlooking Batiquitos Lagoon and the Pacific. **Pros:** unbeatable location; great golf course; many nature trails. **Cons:** a little stiff; some complaints about service; $25 resort fee. $ *Rooms from: $324* ✉ *7100 Aviara Resort Dr.* ☎ *800/233–1234, 760/448–1234* ⊕ *www.parkhyattaviara.com* ➹ *329 rooms, 44 suites* ⏧ *No meals.*

OCEANSIDE

8 miles north of Carlsbad on Rte. S21, 37 miles north of Downtown San Diego on I–5.

EXPLORING

FAMILY
Fodor's Choice
★

Old Mission San Luis Rey. Known as the King of the Missions, the 18th and largest and most prosperous of California's missions was built in 1798 by Franciscan friars under the direction of Father Fermin Lasuen to help educate and convert local Native Americans. The *sala* (parlor), the kitchen, a friar's bedroom, a weaving room, and a collection of religious art and old Spanish vestments convey much about early mission life. A location for filming Disney's 1950's *Zorro* TV series, the well-preserved mission is still owned by the Franciscans. ✉ *4050 Mission Ave.* ☎ *760/757–3651* ⊕ *www.sanluisrey.org* ✉ *$5* ☻ *Weekdays 9:30–5; weekends 10–5.*

ESCONDIDO

8 miles north of Rancho Bernardo on I–15, 31 miles northeast of Downtown San Diego on I–15.

EXPLORING

FAMILY

Fodor's Choice

★

San Diego Zoo Safari Park. A branch of the San Diego Zoo, 35 miles to the south, the 1,800-acre preserve in the San Pasqual Valley is designed to protect endangered species from around the world. Exhibit areas have been carved out of the dry, dusty canyons and mesas to represent the animals' natural habitats in various parts of Africa and Asia. The best way to see these preserves is to take the 25-minute, 2½-mile Africa tram safari, included with admission. As you pass in front of the large, naturally landscaped enclosures, you can see animals bounding across prairies and mesas as they would in the wild. More than 3,500 animals of more than 400 species roam or fly above the expansive grounds. Predators are separated from prey by deep moats, but only the elephants, tigers, lions, and cheetahs are kept in enclosures. Photographers with zoom lenses can get spectacular shots of zebras, gazelles, and rhinos. In summer, when the park stays open late, the trip is especially enjoyable in the early evening, when the heat has subsided and the animals are active and feeding. When the bus travels through the park after dark, sodium-vapor lamps illuminate the active animals.

For a more focused view of the park, you can take one of several other safaris at an extra charge. You can choose from several behind-the-scenes safaris, fly above it all via the zip-line safari, or get up close to giraffes and rhinos on a caravan safari.

The park is as much a botanical garden as a zoo, serving as a "rescue center" for rare and endangered plants. Unique gardens include cacti and succulents from Baja California, a bonsai collection, a fuchsia display, native plants, and protea.

The **Lion Camp** gives you a close-up view of the king of beasts in a slice of African wilderness complete with sweeping plains and rolling hills. As you walk through this exhibit, you can watch the giant cats lounging around through a 40-foot-long window. The last stop is a research station where you can see them all around you through glass panels.

The ticket booths at **Nairobi Village,** the park's center, are designed to resemble the tomb of an ancient king of Uganda. Animals in the **Petting Kraal** here affectionately tolerate tugs and pats and are quite adept at posing for pictures with toddlers. At the **Congo River Village** 10,000 gallons of water pour each minute over a huge waterfall into a large lagoon. **Hidden Jungle,** an 8,800-square-foot greenhouse, is a habitat for creatures that creep, flutter, or just hang out in the tropics. Gigantic cockroaches and bird-eating spiders share the turf with colorful butterflies and hummingbirds and oh-so-slow-moving two-toed sloths. **Lorikeet Landing** holds 75 of the loud and colorful small parrots—you can buy a cup of nectar at the aviary entrance to induce them to land on your hand. Along the trails of the 32-acre **African Outpost** you can travel in the footsteps of an early explorer through forests and lowlands, across a floating bridge to a research station, where an expert is on hand to answer questions; finally you arrive at Kilima Point for an up-close-and-personal view of cheetahs, and a distant glimpse of the expansive savanna where rhinos, impalas, wildebeest, oryx, and beautiful migrating birds reside. At **Condor Ridge**, the Safari Park, which conducts captive breeding programs to save rare and endangered species, shows off one of its most successful efforts, the California condor. The exhibit, perched like one of the ugly black vultures it features, occupies nearly the highest point in the park, and affords a sweeping view of the surrounding San Pasqual Valley. Also on exhibit here is a herd of rare desert bighorn sheep. The park's newest project is the **Tiger Trail**, a Sumatran tiger habitat set to open in mid-2014. The 5-acre exhibit features a waterfall and swimming hole, and addresses poaching and other environmental threats to the species.

All the park's walk-to exhibits and animal shows (included in admission) are entertainingly educational. The gift shops are well worth a visit for their limited-edition items. Rental lockers, strollers, and wheelchairs are available. You can also arrange to stay overnight in the park in summer on a Roar and Snore Sleepover (adults $140–$220, kids 3–11 $120–$160, plus admission). ⊠ *15500 San Pasqual Valley Rd.* ✛ *Take I-15 north to Via Rancho Pkwy. and follow signs, 6 miles* 📞 *760/747–8702* ⊕ *www.sdzsafaripark.org* 🖅 *$46 one-day pass including Africa tram ride; multipark and multiday passes are available; special safaris are extra; parking $10* ☾ *Daily 9–dusk.*

ORANGE COUNTY AND CATALINA ISLAND

With Disneyland and Knott's Berry Farm

WELCOME TO ORANGE COUNTY AND CATALINA ISLAND

TOP REASONS TO GO

★ **Disney Magic:** Walking down Main Street, U.S.A., with Cinderella's Castle straight ahead, you really will feel that you're in one of the happiest places on Earth.

★ **Beautiful Beaches:** Surf, swim, paddleboard, or just relax on one of the state's most breathtaking stretches of coastline. Keep in mind, the water may be colder than you expect.

★ **Island Getaways:** Just a short high-speed catamaran ride away, Catalina Island feels 1,000 miles away from the mainland. Wander around charming Avalon, or explore the unspoiled beauty of the island's wild interior.

★ **The Fine Life:** Some of the state's wealthiest communities are in coastal Orange County, so spend at least part of your stay here experiencing how the other half lives.

★ **Family Fun:** Spend some quality time with the kids riding roller coasters, eating ice cream, fishing off ocean piers, and bodysurfing.

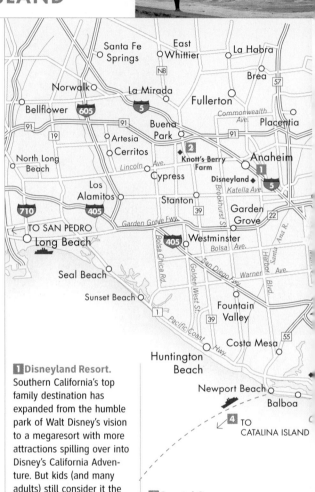

1 Disneyland Resort. Southern California's top family destination has expanded from the humble park of Walt Disney's vision to a megaresort with more attractions spilling over into Disney's California Adventure. But kids (and many adults) still consider it the happiest place on Earth.

2 Knott's Berry Farm. Amusement park lovers should check out this Buena Park attraction, with thrill rides, the *Peanuts* gang, and lots of fried chicken and boysenberry pie.

3 Coastal Orange County. The OC's beach communities may not be quite as glamorous as seen on TV, but coastal spots like Huntington Beach, Newport Harbor, and Laguna Beach are perfect for chilling out in a beachfront hotel.

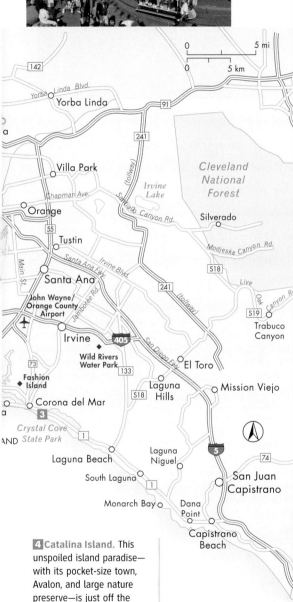

GETTING ORIENTED

3

Like Los Angeles, Orange County stretches over a large area, lacks a singular focal point, and has limited public transportation. You'll need a car and a sensible game plan to make the most of your visit. Anaheim, home of Disneyland, has every style of hotel imaginable, from family-friendly motels to luxurious high-rises. The coastal cities are more expensive but have cooler weather in summer and marvelous beaches that you can enjoy throughout the year.

4 Catalina Island. This unspoiled island paradise—with its pocket-size town, Avalon, and large nature preserve—is just off the Orange County coast.

Updated by Kathy A. McDonald

With its tropical flowers and palm trees, the stretch of coast between Seal Beach and San Clemente is often called the California Riviera. Exclusive Newport Beach, artsy Laguna, and the surf town of Huntington Beach are the stars, but lesser-known gems on the glistening coast—such as Corona del Mar—are also worth visiting. Offshore, meanwhile, lies gorgeous Catalina Island, a terrific spot for diving, snorkeling, and hiking.

Few of the citrus groves that gave Orange County its name remain. This region south and east of Los Angeles is now ruled by tourism and high-tech business instead of farmers. Despite a building boom that began in the 1990s, the area is still a place to find wilderness trails, canyons, greenbelts, and natural environs. And just offshore, is a deep-water wilderness that's possible to explore via daily whale-watching excursions.

PLANNING

GETTING HERE AND AROUND
AIR TRAVEL
Orange County's main facility is John Wayne Airport Orange County (SNA), which is served by 10 major domestic airlines and two commuter lines. Long Beach Airport (LGB) is served by four airlines, including its major player, JetBlue. It's roughly 20 to 30 minutes by car from Anaheim.

Super Shuttle and Prime Time Airport Shuttle provide transportation from John Wayne and LAX to the Disneyland area of Anaheim. Round-trip fares average about $20 per person from John Wayne and $16 to $42 from LAX.

BUS TRAVEL

The Orange County Transportation Authority will take you virtually anywhere in the county, but it will take time; OCTA buses go from Knott's Berry Farm and Disneyland to Huntington Beach and Newport Beach. Bus 1 travels along the coast; buses 701 and 721 provide express service to Los Angeles.

Information Orange County Transportation Authority ☎ *714/636-7433* ⊕ *www.octa.net.*

CAR TRAVEL

The San Diego Freeway (Interstate 405), the coastal route, and the Santa Ana Freeway (Interstate 5), the inland route, run north–south through Orange County. South of Laguna, Interstate 405 merges into Interstate 5 (called the San Diego Freeway south from this point). A toll road, Highway 73, runs 15 miles from Newport Beach to San Juan Capistrano; it costs $5.25–$6.25 (lower rates are for weekends and off-peak hours) and is usually less jammed than the regular freeways. Do your best to avoid all Orange County freeways during rush hours (6–9 am and 3:30–6:30 pm). Highway 55 leads to Newport Beach. The Pacific Coast Highway (Highway 1) allows easy access to beach communities and is the most scenic route but expect it to be crowded, especially on summer weekends.

FERRY TRAVEL

There are two ferries that service Catalina Island; Catalina Express runs from Long Beach (about 90 minutes) and from Newport Beach (about 75 minutes). Reservations are advised for summers and weekends. During the winter months, ferry crossings are not as frequent as in the summer high season.

TRAIN TRAVEL

Amtrak makes daily stops in Orange County at all major towns. Metrolink is a weekday commuter train that runs to and from Los Angeles and Orange County.

Information Amtrak ☎ *800/872-7245* ⊕ *www.amtrak.com.* **Metrolink** ☎ *800/371-5465* ⊕ *www.metrolinktrains.com.*

RESTAURANTS

Much like L.A., restaurants in Orange County are generally casual, and you'll rarely see men in jackets and ties. Nevertheless, at top resort hotel dining rooms, many guests choose to dress up.

Of course, there's also a swath of casual places along the beachfronts—seafood takeout, taquerias, burger joints—that won't mind if you wear flip-flops. Reservations are recommended for the nicest restaurants.

Many places don't serve past 11 pm, and locals tend to eat early. Remember that according to California law, smoking is prohibited in all enclosed areas.

HOTELS

Along the coast there are remarkable luxury resorts; if you can't afford a stay, pop in for the view at Laguna Beach's Montage or the always welcoming Ritz-Carlton at Dana Point. For a taste of the OC glam life, have lunch overlooking the yachts of Newport Bay at the Balboa Bay Resort.

As a rule, lodging prices tend to rise the closer the hotels are to the beach. If you're looking for value, consider a hotel that is inland along the Interstate 405 freeway corridor.

In most cases, you can take advantage of some of the facilities of the high-end resorts, such as restaurants and spas, even if you aren't an overnight guest. *Hotel reviews have been shortened. For full information, visit Fodors.com.*

WHAT IT COSTS				
	$	$$	$$$	$$$$
Restaurants	under $16	$16–$22	$23–$30	over $30
Hotels	under $121	$121–$175	$176–$250	over $250

Restaurant prices are the average cost of a main course at dinner or, if dinner is not served, at lunch, excluding sales tax. Hotel prices are the lowest cost of a standard double room in high season, excluding service charges and tax.

VISITOR INFORMATION

The Anaheim-Orange County Visitor and Convention Bureau is an excellent resource for both leisure and business travelers and can provide materials on many area attractions. It's on the main floor of the Anaheim Convention Center.

The Orange County Tourism Council's website is also a useful source of information.

Information Anaheim/Orange County Visitor & Convention Bureau
⊠ *Anaheim Convention Center, 800 W. Katella Ave., Anaheim* ☎ *714/765–8888* ⊕ *www.anaheimoc.org.* **Orange County Tourism Council** ⊕ *www.visittheoc.com.*

DISNEYLAND RESORT

26 miles southeast of Los Angeles, via I-5.

The snowcapped Matterhorn, the centerpiece of the Magic Kingdom, punctuates the skyline of Anaheim. Since 1955, when Walt Disney chose this once-quiet farming community for the site of his first amusement park, Disneyland has attracted more than 600 million visitors and tens of thousands of workers, and Anaheim has been their host.

To understand the symbiotic relationship between Disneyland and Anaheim, you need only look at the $4.2 billion spent in a combined effort to revitalize Anaheim's tourist center and run-down areas, and to expand and renovate the Disney properties into what is known now as Disneyland Resort.

The resort is a sprawling complex that includes Disney's two amusement parks; three hotels; and Downtown Disney, a shopping, dining, and entertainment promenade. Anaheim's tourist center includes Angel Stadium of Anaheim, home of baseball's 2002 World Series Champion Los Angeles Angels of Anaheim; the Honda Center (formerly the Arrowhead Pond), which hosts concerts and the Anaheim Ducks hockey team; and the enormous Anaheim Convention Center.

3

GETTING THERE

Disney is about a 30-mile drive from either LAX or Downtown. From LAX, follow Sepulveda Boulevard south to the Interstate 105 freeway and drive east 16 miles to the Interstate 605 north exit. Exit at the Santa Ana Freeway (Interstate 5) and continue south for 12 miles to the Disneyland Drive exit. Follow signs to the resort. From Downtown, follow Interstate 5 south 28 miles and exit at Disneyland Drive. **Disneyland Resort Express** (☎ *800/828–6699* ⊕ *graylineanaheim.com*) offers daily nonstop bus service between LAX, John Wayne Airport, and Anaheim. Reservations are not required. The cost is $30 one-way from LAX; and $20 from John Wayne Airport.

SAVING TIME AND MONEY

If you plan to visit for more than a day, you can save money by buying two- three-, four-, and five-day Park Hopper tickets that grant same-day "hopping" privileges between Disneyland and Disney's California Adventure. You get a discount on the multiple-day passes if you buy online through the Disneyland website.

A one-day Park Hopper pass costs $137 for anyone 10 or older, $131 for kids ages 3–9. Admission to either park (but not both) is $92 or $86 for kids 3–9; kids 2 and under are free.

In addition to tickets, parking is $16–$22 (unless your hotel has a shuttle or is within walking distance), and meals in the parks and at Downtown Disney range from $10 to $30 per person.

DISNEYLAND

FAMILY
Fodor's Choice
★

Disneyland. One of the biggest misconceptions people have about Disneyland is that they've "been there, done that" if they've visited either Florida's mammoth Walt Disney World or one of the Disney parks overseas. But Disneyland, which opened in 1955 and is the only one of the parks to have been overseen by Walt himself, has a genuine historic feel and occupies a unique place in the Disney legend. Expertly run, with polite and helpful staff ("cast members" in the Disney lexicon), the park has plenty that you won't find anywhere else—such as the Indiana Jones Adventure ride and Storybook Land, with its miniature replicas of animated Disney scenes from classics such as *Pinocchio* and *Alice in Wonderland*. Characters appear for autographs and photos throughout the day; times and places are posted at the entrances. Live shows, parades, strolling musicians, nightly fireworks, and endless snack choices add to the carnival atmosphere. You can also meet some of the animated icons at one of the character meals served at the three Disney hotels (open to the public). Belongings can be stored in lockers just off Main Street; stroller rentals at the entrance gate are a convenient option for families with small tykes. ⊠ *1313 S. Disneyland Dr., between Ball Rd. and Katella Ave., Anaheim* ☎ *714/781–4636 guest information* ⊕ *www. disneyland.com* ✉ *$92; parking $16* ⊙ *Hrs vary.*

PARK NEIGHBORHOODS
Neighborhoods for Disneyland are arranged in geographic order.

MAIN STREET, U.S.A. Walt's hometown of Marceline, Missouri, was the inspiration behind this romanticized image of small-town America, circa 1900. The sidewalks are lined with a penny arcade and shops that sell everything from tradable pins to Disney-theme clothing, an endless supply of sugar confections, and a photo shop that offers souvenirs created via Disney's PhotoPass (on-site photographers capture memorable moments digitally—you can access in person or online). Main Street opens a half hour before the rest of the park, so it's a good place to explore if you're getting an early start to beat the crowds (it's also open an hour after the other attractions close, so you may want to save your shopping for the end of the day). **Main Street Cinema** offers a cool respite from the crowds and six classic Disney animated shorts, including *Steamboat Willie.* There's rarely a wait to enter. Grab a cappuccino and fresh-made pastry at the Jolly Holiday bakery to jump-start your visit. Board the **Disneyland Railroad** here to save on walking; it tours all the lands plus offers unique views of Splash Mountain and the Grand Canyon and Primeval World dioramas.

NEW ORLEANS SQUARE This mini–French Quarter, with narrow streets, hidden courtyards, and live street performances, is home to two iconic attractions and the Cajun-inspired Blue Bayou restaurant. **Pirates of the Caribbean** now features Jack Sparrow and the cursed Captain Barbossa, in a nod to the blockbuster movies of the same name, plus enhanced special effects and battle scenes (complete with cannonball explosions). Nearby **Haunted Mansion** continues to spook guests with its stretching room and "doombuggy" rides (plus there's now an expanded storyline for the beating-heart bride). Its *Nightmare Before Christmas* holiday overlay is an annual tradition. This is a good area to get a casual bite to eat; the clam chowder in sourdough bread bowls, sold at the French Market Restaurant and Royal Street Veranda, is a popular choice. Food carts offer everything from just-popped popcorn to churros, and even fresh fruit.

FRONTIERLAND Between Adventureland and Fantasyland, Frontierland transports you to the wild, wild West with its rustic buildings, shooting gallery, mountain range, and foot-stompin' dance hall. The marquee attraction, **Big Thunder Mountain Railroad,** is a relatively tame roller coaster ride (no steep descents) that takes the form of a runaway mine car as it rumbles past desert canyons and an old mining town. Tour the Rivers of America on the **Mark Twain Riverboat** in the company of a grizzled old river pilot or circumnavigate the globe on the **Sailing Ship Columbia,** though its operating hours are usually limited to weekends. From here, you can raft over to Pirate's Lair on **Tom Sawyer Island,** which

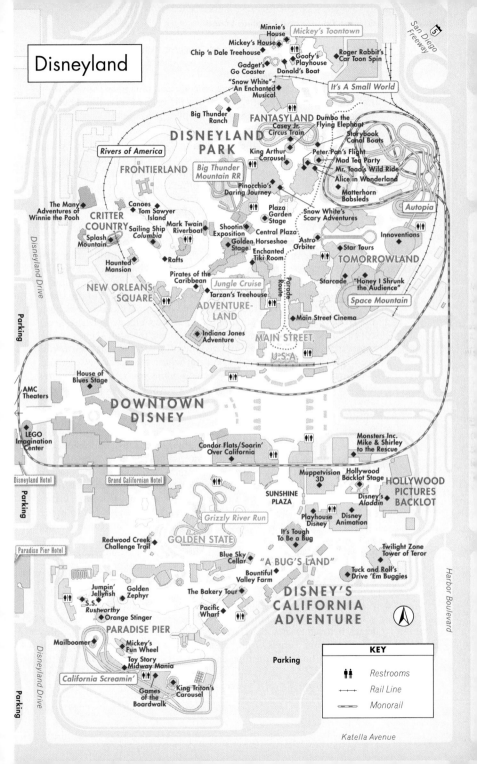

now features pirate-theme caves, treasure hunts, and music, along with plenty of caves and hills to climb and explore. If you don't mind tight seating, have a snack at the Golden Horseshoe Restaurant while enjoying the always-entertaining comedy and bluegrass show of Billy Hill and the Hillybillies. Children won't want to miss **Big Thunder Ranch,** a small petting zoo featuring pigs, goats, and cows, beyond Big Thunder Mountain.

CRITTER COUNTRY
Down-home country is the theme in this shady corner of the park, where Winnie the Pooh and Davy Crockett make their homes. Here you can find **Splash Mountain,** a classic flume ride accompanied by music and appearances by Brer Rabbit and other characters from *Song of the South.* Don't forget to check out your photo (the camera snaps close-ups of each car just before it plunges into the water) on the way out. The patio of the popular Hungry Bear Restaurant has great views of Tom Sawyer's Island and Davy Crockett's Explorer Canoes.

ADVEN-TURELAND
Modeled after the lands of Africa, Polynesia, and Arabia, this tiny tropical paradise is worth braving the crowds that flock here for the ambience and better-than-average food. Sing along with the animatronic birds and tiki gods in the **Enchanted Tiki Room,** sail the rivers of the world with joke-cracking skippers on **Jungle Cruise,** and climb the *Disneyodendron semperflorens* (aka always-blooming Disney tree) to **Tarzan's Treehouse,** where you can walk through scenes, some interactive, from the 1999 animated film. Cap off the visit with a wild Jeep ride at **Indiana Jones Adventure,** where the special effects and decipherable hieroglyphics distract you while you're waiting in line. The skewers (some vegetarian options available) at Bengal Barbecue and pineapple whip at Tiki Juice Bar are some of the best fast-food options in the park.

FANTASYLAND
Sleeping Beauty Castle marks the entrance to Fantasyland, a visual wonderland of princesses, spinning teacups, flying elephants, and other classic storybook characters. Rides and shops (such as the princess-theme Once Upon a Time and Gepetto's Toys and Gifts) take precedence over restaurants in this area of the park, but outdoor carts sell everything from churros to turkey legs. Tots love the **King Arthur Carousel, Casey Jr. Circus Train,** and **Storybook Land Canal Boats:** This is also home to **Mr. Toad's Wild Ride, Peter Pan's Flight,** and **Pinocchio's Daring Journey,** classic, movie-theater-dark rides that immerse riders in Disney fairy tales and appeal to adults and kids alike. The Abominable Snowman pops up on the **Matterhorn Bobsleds,** a roller coaster that twists and turns up and around on a made-to-scale model of the real Swiss mountain. Anchoring the east end of Fantasyland is **It's a Small World,** a smorgasbord of dancing animatronic dolls, cuckoo clock–covered walls, and variations of the song everyone knows, or soon *will* know, by heart. Beloved Disney characters like Ariel from *Under the Sea* are also part of the mix. Fantasy Faire is a fairy tale-style village that collects all the Disney princesses together. Each has her own reception nook in the Royal Hall. Condensed retellings of *Tangled* and *Beauty and the Beast* take place at the Royal Theatre.

BEST TIPS FOR DISNEYLAND

Buy entry tickets in advance. Many nearby hotels sell park admission tickets; you can also buy them through the Disney website. If you book a package deal, such as those offered through AAA, tickets are included, too.

The lines at the ticket booths can take more than an hour on busy days, so you'll definitely save time by buying in advance, especially if you're committed to going on a certain day regardless of the weather.

Come midweek. Weekends, especially in summer, are a mob scene. Holidays are crowded, too. A rainy winter weekday is often the least crowded time to visit.

Plan your times to hit the most popular rides. Fodorites recommend getting to the park as early as possible. If you're at the park when the gates open, make a beeline for the top rides before the crowds reach a critical mass. Another good time is the late evening, when the hordes thin out somewhat, and during a parade or other show. Save the quieter attractions for midafternoon.

Use FASTPASS. These passes allow you to reserve your place in line at some of the most crowded attractions (only one at a time). Distribution machines are posted near the entrances of each attraction. Feed in your park admission ticket, and you'll receive a pass with a printed time frame (generally up to 1–1½ hours later) during which you can return to wait in a much shorter line.

Plan your meals to avoid peak mealtime crowds. Start the day with a big breakfast so you won't be too hungry at noon, when restaurants and vendors get swarmed. Wait to have lunch until after 1.

If you want to eat at the **Blue Bayou** in New Orleans Square, you can make a reservation up to six months in advance online. Another (cheaper) option is to bring your own food. There are areas just outside the park gates with picnic tables set up for this. And it's always a good idea to bring water.

Check the daily events schedule online or at the park entrance. During parades, fireworks, and other special events, sections of the parks clog with crowds. This can work for you or against you. An event could make it difficult to get around a park—but if you plan ahead, you can take advantage of the distraction to hit popular rides.

Send the Teens Next Door. Disneyland's newer sister park, California Adventure, features more intense rides suitable for older kids (Park Hopper passes include admission to both parks).

MICKEY'S TOONTOWN Geared toward small fries, this lopsided cartoonlike downtown, complete with cars and trolleys that invite exploring, is where Mickey, Donald, Goofy, and other classic Disney characters hang their hats. One of the most popular attractions is **Roger Rabbit's Car Toon Spin,** a twisting, turning cab ride through the Toontown of *Who Framed Roger Rabbit?* You can also walk through **Mickey's House** to meet and be photographed with the famous mouse, take a low-key ride on **Gadget's Go Coaster,** or bounce around the fenced-in playground in front of **Goofy's House.**

TOMOR-
ROWLAND

This popular section of the park continues to tinker with its future, adding and enhancing rides regularly. One of the newest attractions, Star Tours, is a 3-D immersive experience in the world of *Star Wars*. Finding Nemo's **Submarine Voyage** updates the old Submarine Voyage ride with the exploits of Nemo, Dory, Marlin, and other characters from the Disney Pixar film. Try to visit this popular ride early in the day if you can and be prepared for a wait. The interactive **Buzz Lightyear Astro Blasters** lets you zap your neighbors with laser beams and compete for the highest score. Hurtle through the cosmos on **Space Mountain** or check out mainstays like the futuristic **Astro Orbiter** rockets, **Innoventions,** a self-guided tour of the latest toys and gadgets of tomorrow, and **Caption EO,** a 3-D film featuring the music and talents of the late Michael Jackson. Disneyland Monorail and Disneyland Railroad both have stations here. There's also a video arcade and dancing water fountain that makes a perfect playground for kids on hot summer days. The Jedi Training Academy spotlights future Luke Skywalkers in the *Star Wars*–theme show's crowd.

Besides the eight lands, the daily live-action shows and parades are always crowd-pleasers. *Fantasmic!* is a musical, fireworks, and laser show in which Mickey and friends wage a spellbinding battle against Disneyland's darker characters. ■TIP→ **Arrive early to secure a good view; if there are two shows scheduled for the day, the second one tends to be less crowded.** A fireworks display sparks up most evenings. Brochures with maps, available at the entrance, list show and parade times.

DISNEY CALIFORNIA ADVENTURE

FAMILY
Fodor's Choice
★

Disney California Adventure. The sprawling Disney California Adventure, adjacent to Disneyland (their entrances face each other), pays tribute to the Golden State with eight theme areas that re-create vintage architectural styles and embrace several hit Pixar films via engaging attractions. In 2012, the front gate was revamped—visitors now enter through the art deco–style Buena Vista Street—and the 12-acre Cars Land and Radiator Springs Racers, an immediate blockbuster hit (FASTPASS tickets for the ride run out early most days), was added. Other popular attractions include *World of Color*, a nighttime water-effects show, and Toy Story Mania!, an interactive adventure ride hosted by Woody and Buzz Lightyear. At night, the park takes on neon-color hues as glowing signs light up Route 66 in Cars Land and Mickey's Fun Wheel, a mega-size Ferris wheel on the Paradise Pier. Unlike at Disneyland, cocktails, beer, and wine are available, and there's even an outdoor dance spot, the Mad T Party. Live nightly entertainment also features a 1930s jazz troupe that arrives in a vintage jalopy. ✉ *1313 S. Disneyland Dr., between Ball Rd. and Katella Ave., Anaheim* ☎ *714/781–4636* ⊕ *www.disneyland. com* ⬛ *$92; parking $16* ⊙ *Hrs vary.*

PARK NEIGHBORHOODS

BUENA VISTA
STREET

California Adventure's grand entryway re-creates the lost 1920s of Los Angeles that Walt Disney encountered when he moved to the Golden State. There's a **Red Car trolley** (modeled after Los Angeles's bygone streetcar line); hop on for the brief ride to Hollywood Land. Buena Vista

DID YOU KNOW?

Apparently, the plain purple teacup in Disneyland's Mad Tea Party ride spins the fastest—though no one knows why.

Street is also home to a Starbucks outlet—within the Fiddler, Fifer & Practical Café—and the upscale Carthay Circle Restaurant and Lounge, which serves modern craft cocktails and beer.

CONDOR FLATS Dive into California's history and natural beauty with nature trails, a winery, and a tortilla factory (with free samples). Condor Flats has **Soarin' Over California,** a spectacular simulated hang-glider ride over California terrain.

GRIZZLY PEAK Test your outdoorsman skills on the **Redwood Creek Challenge Trail,** a challenging trek across net ladders and suspension bridges. **Grizzly River Run** mimics the river rapids of the Sierra Nevadas; be prepared to get soaked.

HOLLYWOOD LAND With a main street modeled after Hollywood Boulevard, a fake blue-sky backdrop, and real soundstages, this area celebrates California's most famous industry. **Disney Animation** gives you an insider's look at the work of animators and how they create characters. **Turtle Talk with Crush** lets kids have an unrehearsed talk with computer-animated Crush, a sea turtle from *Finding Nemo.* The Hyperion Theater hosts **Aladdin—A Musical Spectacular,** a 45-minute live performance with terrific visual effects. ■TIP➔ **Plan on getting in line about half an hour in advance: the show is worth the wait.** On the film-inspired ride, **Monsters, Inc. Mike & Sulley to the Rescue,** you climb into taxis and travel the streets of Monstropolis on a mission to safely return Boo to her bedroom. A major draw for older kids is the looming **Twilight Zone Tower of Terror,** which drops riders 13 floors. Their screams can be heard throughout the park!

A BUG'S LAND Inspired by the 1998 film *A Bug's Life,* this section skews its attractions to an insect's point of view. Kids can spin around in giant takeout Chinese food boxes on **Flik's Flyers,** and hit the bug-shaped bumper cars on **Tuck and Roll's Drive 'Em Buggies.** The short show *It's Tough to Be a Bug!* gives a 3-D look at insect life.

CARS LAND Amble down Route 66, the main thoroughfare of Cars Land, a pitch-perfect re-creation of the vintage highway. Quick eats are found at the Cozy Cone Motel (in a teepee-shape motor court) while Flo's V8 café serves hearty comfort food. Start your day at Radiator Springs Racers, the park's most popular attraction, where waits can be two hours or longer. Strap into a nifty sports car and meet the characters of Pixar's *Cars*; the ride ends in a speedy auto race through the red rocks and desert of Radiator Springs.

PACIFIC WHARF The Wine Country Trattoria at the Golden Vine Winery is a great place for Italian specialties paired with California wine; relax outside on the restaurant's terrace for a casual bite. Mexican cuisine and potent margaritas are available at the Cocina Cucamonga Mexican Grill and Rita's Baja Blenders.

PARADISE PIER This section re-creates the glory days of California's seaside piers. If you're looking for thrills, the **California Screamin'** roller coaster takes its riders from 0 to 55 mph in about four seconds and proceeds through scream tunnels, steeply angled drops, and a 360-degree loop. **Goofy's Sky School** is a rollicking roller coaster ride that goes up three stories and covers more than 1,200 feet of track. **Mickey's Fun Wheel,** a giant

3

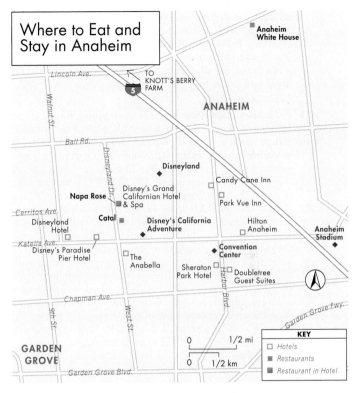

Ferris wheel, provides a good view of the grounds at a more leisurely pace. There are also carnival games, a fish-theme carousel, and Ariel's Grotto, where future princesses can dine with the mermaid and her friends (reservations are a must). Get a close-up look of Ariel's world on the **Little Mermaid—Ariel's Undersea Adventure.** The best views of the nighttime music, water, and light show, *World of Color,* are from the paths along Paradise Bay. Book a picnic dinner at the Golden Vine Winery that includes a ticket to a viewing area to catch all the show's stunning visuals.

OTHER ATTRACTIONS

FAMILY **Downtown Disney.** This 20-acre promenade of dining, shopping, and entertainment connects the resort's hotels and theme parks. Restaurant-nightclub **House of Blues** spices up its Delta-inspired ribs and seafood with various live music acts on an intimate two-story stage. At **Ralph Brennan's Jazz Kitchen** you can dig into New Orleans–style food and music. Sports fans gravitate to **ESPN Zone,** with American grill food, interactive video games, and 175 video screens telecasting worldwide sports events. An **AMC** multiplex movie theater with stadium-style seating plays the latest blockbusters and, naturally, a couple of kid flicks. Shops sell everything from Disney goods to antique jewelry—don't miss **Vault 28,** a hip boutique that sells one-of-a-kind vintage and couture clothing and accessories. At the mega-sized **LEGO Store,** there are hands-on demonstrations and space to play with the latest LEGO creations. Parking is a deal: the first three hours are free, with two extra hours with validation. ✉ *1580 Disneyland Dr., Anaheim* ☎ *888/262–4386* 🌐 *disneyland.disney.go.com/downtown-disney* 🎫 *Free* 🕐 *Daily 7 am–2 am; hrs at shops and restaurants vary.*

WHERE TO EAT

$$$$ NORTHERN ITALIAN 🍴 **Anaheim White House.** Several small dining rooms are set with crisp linens and candles in this flower-filled 1909 mansion. The northern Italian menu includes steak, rack of lamb, and fresh seafood. Try the signature ravioli *arragosta*, lobster-filled pasta in a ginger-and-citrus sauce. A three-course prix-fixe low-calorie lunch, served weekdays, costs $23. [$] *Average main: $35* ✉ *887 S. Anaheim Blvd., Anaheim* ☎ *714/772–1381* 🌐 *www.anaheimwhitehouse.com* 🕐 *No lunch Sat.*

$$$ MEDITERRANEAN 🍴 **Catal Restaurant & Uva Bar.** Famed chef Joachim Splichal and his staff take a relaxed approach at this bi-level Mediterranean spot. People-watch at the colorful, outdoor Uva (Spanish for "grape") bar on the ground floor, where there are specialty cocktails, craft beers, and more than 40 wines by the glass. Burgers here are crowd-pleasers, as are appetizers from corn arepas to lemony hummus. Upstairs, Catal's menu has tapas, a variety of flavorful paellas (lobster is worth the splurge), and charcuterie. **■ TIP→ Reserve a table on the outdoor terrace for an awesome view of the Disneyland fireworks.** [$] *Average main: $30* ✉ *Downtown Disney, 1580 S. Disneyland Dr., Suite 103, Anaheim* ☎ *714/774–4442* 🌐 *www.patinagroup.com.*

$$$$ AMERICAN 🍴 **Napa Rose.** Done up in a lovely Arts and Crafts style, this eatery overlooks a woodsy corner of Disney's California Adventure park. The contemporary cuisine is matched with an extensive wine list, with 1,000 labels and 80 available by the glass. For a look into the open kitchen, sit at the counter and watch the chefs as they whip up such signature dishes as pan-roasted diver scallops in a sauce of lobster, lemon, and vanilla, and slowly braised beef short rib in a Cabernet *jus*. There's also a list of kid-friendly dishes. A cocktail on the outdoor patio with a fire pit is a pleasant way to end the night. The four-course, $95 prix-fixe menu changes weekly. [$] *Average main: $40* ✉ *Disney's Grand Californian Hotel, 1600 S. Disneyland Dr., Anaheim* ☎ *714/300–7170* 🌐 *disneyland.disney.go.com/grand-californian-hotel/napa-rose* ✍ *Reservations essential.*

WHERE TO STAY

$ HOTEL 🏨 **The Anabella.** At the Anaheim Convention Center, this hotel's Spanish mission–style exterior and leafy landscaping set it apart from other budget properties. **Pros:** 15-minute walk to Disneyland and California Adventure entrance; extended happy hour at hotel bar; free Wi-Fi. **Cons:** some complaints about thin walls. [$] *Rooms from: $120* ✉ *1030 W. Katella Ave., Anaheim* ☎ *714/905–1050, 800/863–4888* 🌐 *www.anabellahotel.com* 🛏 *234 rooms, 124 suites* 🍽 *No meals.*

$$ HOTEL 🏨 **Candy Cane Inn.** One of the Disneyland area's first hotels, the Candy Cane is one of Anaheim's most relaxing properties, with spacious and understated rooms and an inviting palm-fringed pool. **Pros:** proximity to everything Disney; friendly service; well-lighted property.

Cons: rooms and lobby are on the small side; all rooms face parking lot. [$] *Rooms from: $149* ✉ *1747 S. Harbor Blvd., Anaheim* ☎ *714/774–5284, 800/345–7057* 🌐 *www.candycaneinn.net* 🛏 *171 rooms* 🍴 *Breakfast.*

$$$$ RESORT FAMILY Fodor's Choice ★ 🏨 **Disney's Grand Californian Hotel & Spa.** The most opulent of Disneyland's three hotels, the Craftsman-style Grand Californian offers views of Disney California Adventure and Downtown Disney. **Pros:** gorgeous lobby; plenty for families; direct access to theme parks. **Cons:** the self-parking lot is across the street; standard rooms are on the small side. [$] *Rooms from: $482* ✉ *1600 S. Disneyland Dr., Anaheim* ☎ *714/635–2300, 714/956–6425 reservations* 🌐 *disneyland.disney.go.com/grand-californian-hotel* 🛏 *904 rooms, 44 suites, 50 villas* 🍴 *No meals.*

$$ HOTEL 🏨 **Doubletree Guest Suites Anaheim Resort-Convention Center.** This upscale hotel near the Anaheim Convention Center and a 20-minute walk from Disneyland caters to business travelers and vacationers alike. **Pros:** huge suites; elegant lobby; walking distance to a variety of restaurants. **Cons:** a bit far from Disneyland; pool area is small. [$] *Rooms from: $139* ✉ *2085 S. Harbor Blvd., Anaheim* ☎ *714/750–3000, 800/215–7316* 🌐 *doubletree3.hilton.com* 🛏 *50 rooms, 202 suites* 🍴 *No meals.*

$$ HOTEL FAMILY 🏨 **Hilton Anaheim.** Next to the Anaheim Convention Center, this busy Hilton is one of the largest hotels in Southern California with a restaurant and food court, cocktail lounges, a full-service gym, and its own Starbucks. **Pros:** efficient service; great children's programs; some rooms have views of the nightly fireworks. **Cons:** huge size can be daunting; fee to use health club. [$] *Rooms from: $159* ✉ *777 Convention Way, Anaheim* ☎ *714/750–4321, 800/445–8667* 🌐 *www.anaheim.hilton.com* 🛏 *1,479 rooms, 93 suites* 🍴 *No meals.*

$$ HOTEL 🏨 **Park Vue Inn.** Watch the nightly fireworks from the rooftop sundeck at this bougainvillea-covered Spanish-style inn, one of the closest lodgings to Disneyland main gate. **Pros:** easy walk to Disneyland, Downtown Disney, and Disney California Adventure; good value; some rooms have bunk beds. **Cons:** all rooms face the parking lot; some complain about early-morning street noise. [$] *Rooms from: $151* ✉ *1570 S. Harbor Blvd., Anaheim* ☎ *714/772–3691, 800/334–7021* 🌐 *www.parkvueinn.com* 🛏 *76 rooms, 8 suites* 🍴 *Breakfast.*

SPORTS

Anaheim Ducks. The National Hockey League's Anaheim Ducks, winners of the 2007 Stanley Cup, play at Honda Center. ✉ *Honda Center, 2695 E. Katella Ave., Anaheim* ☎ *877/945–3946* 🌐 *ducks.nhl.com.*

Los Angeles Angels of Anaheim. Professional baseball's Los Angeles Angels of Anaheim play at Angel Stadium. An "Outfield Extravaganza" celebrates great plays on the field, with fireworks and a geyser exploding over a model evoking the California coast. ✉ *Angel Stadium, 2000 E. Gene Autry Way, Anaheim* ☎ *714/940–2000* 🌐 *www.angelsbaseball.com* [M] *Metrolink Angels Express.*

3

KNOTT'S BERRY FARM

25 miles south of Los Angeles, via I-5, in Buena Park.

FAMILY **Knott's Berry Farm.** The land where the boysenberry was invented (by crossing raspberry, blackberry, and loganberry bushes) is now occupied by Knott's Berry Farm. In 1934 Cordelia Knott began serving chicken dinners on her wedding china to supplement her family's income—or so the story goes. The dinners and her boysenberry pies proved more profitable than husband Walter's farm, so the two moved first into the restaurant business and then into the entertainment business. The park is now a 160-acre complex with 40 rides, dozens of restaurants and shops, a brick-by-brick replica of Philadelphia's Independence Hall, and loads of Americana. Although it has plenty to keep small children occupied, the park is best known for its awesome rides. The boardwalk area was expanded in 2013, adding two coasters—the stomach-churning Rip Tide turns thrill seekers upside down and around several times—water features to cool things off on hot days, and a lighted promenade. And, yes, you can still get that boysenberry pie (and jam, juice—you name it). ⊠ *8039 Beach Blvd.* ✚ *Between La Palma Ave. and Crescent St., 2 blocks south of Hwy. 91* ☎ *714/220–5200* ⊕ *www.knotts.com* ✉ *$62.*

PARK NEIGHBORHOODS

THE Not-for-the-squeamish thrill rides and skill-based games dominate the
BOARDWALK scene at the **boardwalk.** New roller coasters—Coast Rider, Surfside Glider, and Pacific Scrambler—were added in 2013 and surround a pond that keeps things cooler on hot days. Go head over heels on the **Boomerang** roller coaster, then do it again—backward. The boardwalk is also home to a string of test-your-skill games that are fun to watch whether you're playing or not, and Johnny Rockets, the park's newest restaurant.

CAMP SNOOPY It can be gridlock on weekends, but small fries love this miniature High Sierra wonderland where the *Peanuts* gang hangs out. Tykes can push and pump their own mini–mining cars on **Huff and Puff,** zip around a pint-size racetrack on **Charlie Brown Speedway,** and hop aboard **Woodstock's Airmail,** a kids' version of the park's Supreme Scream ride. Most of the rides here are geared toward kids only, leaving parents to cheer them on from the sidelines. **Sierra Sidewinder,** a roller coaster near the entrance of Camp Snoopy, is aimed at older children, with spinning saucer-type vehicles that go a maximum speed of 37 mph.

FIESTA Over in **Fiesta Village** are two more musts for adrenaline junkies: **Mon-**
VILLAGE **tezooma's Revenge,** a roller coaster that goes from 0 to 55 mph in less than five seconds, and **Jaguar!,** which simulates the motions of a cat stalking its prey, twisting, spiraling, and speeding up and slowing down as it takes you on its stomach-dropping course. There's also **Hat Dance,** a version of the spinning teacups but with sombreros, and a 100-year-old **Dentzel Carousel,** complete with an antique organ and menagerie of hand-carved animals.

GHOST TOWN Clusters of authentic old buildings relocated from their original mining-town sites mark this section of the park. You can stroll down the street, stop and chat with a blacksmith, pan for gold (for a fee), crack open a geode, check out the chalkboard of a circa-1875 schoolhouse, and ride an original Butterfield stagecoach. Looming over it all is **GhostRider,** Orange County's first wooden roller coaster. Traveling up to 56 mph and reaching 118 feet at its highest point, the park's biggest attraction is riddled with sudden dips and curves, subjecting riders to forces up to three times that of gravity. On the Western-theme **Silver Bullet,** riders are sent to a height of 146 feet and then back down 109 feet. Riders spiral, corkscrew, fly into a cobra roll, and experience overbanked curves. The **Calico Mine** ride descends into a replica of a working gold mine. The **Timber Mountain Log Ride** is a visitor favorite—the flume ride underwent a complete renovation in 2013. Also found here is the park's newest thrill ride, the **Pony Express,** a roller coaster that lets riders saddle up on packs of "horses" tethered to platforms that take off on a series of hairpin turns and travel up to 38 mph. Don't miss the **Western Trails Museum,** a dusty old gem full of Old West memorabilia and rural Americana, plus menus from the original chicken restaurant, and an impressive antique button collection. **Calico Railroad** departs regularly from Ghost Town station for a round-trip tour of the park (bandit holdups notwithstanding).

3

This section is also home to **Big Foot Rapids,** a splash-fest of white-water river rafting over towering cliffs, cascading waterfalls, and wild rapids. Don't miss the visually stunning show at **Mystery Lodge,** which tells the story of Native Americans in the Pacific Northwest with lights, music, and beautiful images.

INDIAN TRAILS

Celebrate Native American traditions through interactive exhibits like tepees and daily dance and storytelling performances.

Knott's Soak City Water Park is directly across from the main park on 13 acres next to Independence Hall. It has a dozen major water rides; the latest is **Pacific Spin,** an oversize waterslide that drops riders 75 feet into a catch pool. There's also a children's pool, 750,000-gallon wave pool, and funhouse. Soak City's season runs mid-May to mid-September. It's open daily after Memorial Day, weekends only after Labor Day, and then closes for the season.

WHERE TO EAT AND STAY

$$
AMERICAN
FAMILY

🍴 **Mrs. Knott's Chicken Dinner Restaurant.** Cordelia Knott's fried chicken and boysenberry pies drew crowds so big that Knott's Berry Farm was built to keep the hungry customers occupied while they waited. The restaurant's current incarnation (outside the park's entrance) still serves crispy fried chicken, along with fluffy hand-made biscuits, mashed potatoes, and Mrs. Knott's signature chilled cherry-rhubarb compote. On a busy day the restaurant will cook up 1,200 chickens. The wait, unfortunately, can be an hour or more on weekends and longer on holidays (Mother's Day is crazy busy!). To beat the lines, order from the adjacent takeout counter and enjoy a picnic at the duck pond. Jump-start a visit to the park with a hearty breakfast here. There's three hours of free parking in the lot across from the restaurant. [$] *Average main: $17* ✉ *Knott's Berry Farm Marketplace, 8039 Beach Blvd.* ☎ *714/220–5080.*

$ RESORT FAMILY **Knott's Berry Farm Hotel.** Knott's Berry Farm runs this convenient high-rise hotel, which sits on the park grounds surrounded by graceful palm trees. **Pros:** easy access to Knott's Berry Farm; plenty of family activities; basketball court. **Cons:** lobby and hallways can be noisy; public areas show significant wear-and-tear. [$] *Rooms from: $89* ✉ *7675 Crescent Ave.* ☎ *714/995–1111, 866/752–2444* 🌐 *www.knottshotel.com* 🛏 *320 rooms* 🍴 *No meals.*

THE COAST

Running along the Orange County coastline is scenic Pacific Coast Highway (Highway 1, known locally as the PCH). Older beachfront settlements, with their modest bungalow-style homes, are joined by posh gated communities. The pricey land between Newport Beach and Laguna Beach is where Laker Kobe Bryant, novelist Dean Koontz, and a slew of Internet and finance moguls live.

Though the coastline is rapidly being filled in, there are still a few stretches of beautiful, protected open land. And at many places along the way you can catch an idealized glimpse of the Southern California lifestyle: surfers hitting the beach, boards under their arms.

LONG BEACH AND SAN PEDRO

About 25 miles southeast of Los Angeles, via I-110 south.

EXPLORING

FAMILY **Aquarium of the Pacific.** Sea lions, nurse sharks, and penguins, oh my!—this aquarium focuses on creatures of the Pacific Ocean. The main exhibits include large tanks of sharks, stingrays, and ethereal sea dragons, which the aquarium has successfully bred in captivity. The Great Hall features the multimedia attraction *Penguins,* a panoramic film that captures the world of this endangered species. Be sure to say hello to Betty, one of the recent rescues at the engaging sea otter exhibit. For a nonaquatic experience, head to Lorikeet Forest, a walk-in aviary full of the friendliest parrots from Australia. Buy a cup of nectar and smile as you become a human bird perch. If you're a true tropical animal lover, book an up-close-and-personal Animal Encounters Tour ($109) to learn about and assist in the care and feeding of the animals; or find out how the aquarium functions with the extensive Behind the Scenes Tour ($42.95, including admission). Certified divers can book a supervised dive in the aquarium's Tropical Reef Habitat ($299). Twice daily whale-watching trips on the *Harbor Breeze* depart from the dock adjacent to the aquarium; summer sightings of blue whales are an unforgettable thrill. ✉ *100 Aquarium Way, Long Beach* ☎ *562/590–3100* 🌐 *www.aquariumofpacific.org* 🎟 *$28.95* 🕒 *Daily 9–6.*

Cabrillo Marine Aquarium. Dedicated to the marine life that flourishes off the Southern California coast, this Frank Gehry–designed center gives an intimate and instructive look at local sea creatures. Head to the Exploration Center and S. Mark Taper Foundation Courtyard for kid-friendly interactive exhibits and activity stations. Especially fun is

A mural at Huntington Beach

the "Crawl In" aquarium, where you can be surrounded by fish without getting wet. From March through July the aquarium organizes a legendary grunion program, when you can see the small, silvery fish as they come ashore at night to spawn on the beach. ■ TIP➔ After visiting the museum, stop for a picnic or beach stroll along Cabrillo Beach. ✉ 3720 Stephen M. White Dr., San Pedro, Los Angeles ☎ 310/548–7562 ⊕ www.cabrilloaq.org ✉ $5 suggested donation, parking $1 per hr ☉ Tues.–Fri. noon–5, weekends 10–5.

FAMILY **Queen Mary.** This impressive example of 20th-century cruise ship opulence is the last of its kind. And there's a saying among staff members that the more you get to know the *Queen Mary,* the more you realize she has an endearing personality to match her wealth of history. The beautifully preserved art deco–style ocean liner was launched in 1936 and made 1,001 transatlantic crossings before finally berthing in Long Beach in 1967. Today there's a popular Princess Diana exhibit and a daily British-style high tea.

On board, you can take one of a dozen tours, such as the informative Behind the Scenes walk or the downright spooky Haunted Encounters tour. (Spirits have reportedly been spotted in the pool and engine room.) You could stay for dinner at one of the ship's restaurants, listen to live jazz in the original first-class lounge, or even spend the night in one of the 346 wood-panel cabins. The ship's neighbor, a geodesic dome originally built to house Howard Hughes's *Spruce Goose* aircraft, now serves as a terminal for Carnival Cruise Lines, making the *Queen Mary* the perfect pit stop before or after a cruise. Anchored next to the *Queen* is the *Scorpion,* a Russian submarine you can tour for a look at Cold War history. ✉ *1126 Queens Hwy., Long Beach* ☎ *877/342–0742* 🌐 *www.queenmary.com* 🎟 *Tours $28–$75, including a self-guided audio tour* ⏱ *Hrs vary for tours.*

WHERE TO STAY

$$ HOTEL 🏨 **Hotel Maya–a Doubletree Hotel.** Formerly the Coast Long Beach, this waterfront property set on 11 acres, on the edge of a man-made beach, gets a second lease on life as Hotel Maya. **Pros:** low-key vibe; dedicated staff; waterfront location. **Cons:** location is slightly confusing for first-time visitors. [$] *Rooms from: $129* ✉ *700 Queensway Dr., Long Beach* ☎ *562/435–7676* 🌐 *www.hotelmaya.doubletree.com* 🛏 *196 rooms, 1 suite* 🍴 *No meals.*

$$ HOTEL FAMILY 🏨 **Hotel Queen Mary.** Experience the golden age of transatlantic travel without the seasickness: a 1936–art deco style reigns on the *Queen Mary,* from the ship's mahogany paneling to its nickel-plated doors to the majestic Grand Salon. **Pros:** a walkable historic promenade deck; views from Long Beach out to the Pacific; art deco details. **Cons:** spotty service; no soundproofing makes for a challenging night's sleep. [$] *Rooms from: $139* ✉ *1126 Queens Hwy., Long Beach* ☎ *562/435–3511, 877/342–0742* 🌐 *www.queenmary.com* 🛏 *346 staterooms, 9 suites* 🍴 *No meals.*

$ B&B/INN 🏨 **The Varden.** Constructed in 1929 to house Bixby Knolls Sr.'s mistress, Dolly Varden, this small historic European-style hotel, on the metro line in downtown Long Beach, now caters to worldly budget travelers. **Pros:** great value for downtown location; discount passes to Gold's Gym across the street; complimentary Continental breakfast. **Cons:** no resort services; small rooms. [$] *Rooms from: $119* ✉ *335 Pacific Ave., Long Beach* ☎ *562/432–8950* 🌐 *www.thevardenhotel.com* 🛏 *35 rooms.*

HUNTINGTON BEACH

40 miles southeast of Los Angeles, I-5 south to I-605 south to I-405 south to Beach Blvd.

Once a sleepy residential town with little more than a string of rugged surf shops, Huntington Beach has transformed itself into a resort destination. The town's appeal is its broad white-sand beaches with often-towering waves, complemented by a lively pier, shops and restaurants on Main Street, and a growing collection of resort hotels.

A draw for sports fans and partiers of all stripes is the U.S. Open professional surf competition, which brings a festive atmosphere to town annually in late July. There's even a Surfing Walk of Fame, with plaques set in the sidewalk around the intersection of PCH and Main Street.

ESSENTIALS

Visit Huntington Beach ✉ *301 Main St., Suite 212* ☎ *714/969–3492, 800/729–6232* 🌐 *www.surfcityusa.com.*

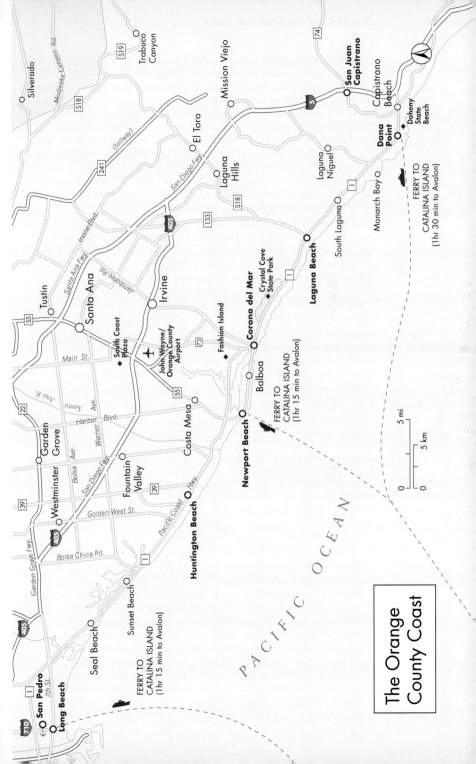

The Orange County Coast

EXPLORING

Bolsa Chica Ecological Reserve. Wildlife lovers and bird-watchers flock to Bolsa Chica Ecological Reserve, which has a 1,180-acre salt marsh where 321 of Orange County's 420 bird species—including great blue herons, snowy and great egrets, and brown pelicans—have been spotted in the past decade. Throughout the reserve are trails for bird-watching, including a comfortable 1½-mile loop. Free, guided tours depart from the walking bridge on the second Saturday of each month at 10 am. There are two entrances off the Pacific Coast Highway: one close to the Interpretive Center and a second 1 mile south on Warner Avenue, opposite Bolsa Chica State Beach. ⊠ *Bolsa Chica Wetlands Interpretive Center, 3842 Warner Ave.* ☎ *714/846–1114* ⊕ *www.bolsachica.org* 🎟 *Free* ⊙ *Interpretive Center daily 9–4.*

Bolsa Chica State Beach. In the northern section of the city, Bolsa Chica State Beach is usually less crowded than its southern neighbors. The sand is somewhat gritty and not the cleanest, but swells make it a hot surfing spot. Picnic sites and barbecue pits can be reserved in advance. **Amenities:** food and drink; lifeguards; parking; showers; toilets. **Best for:** sunset; surfing; swimming; walking. ⊠ *Pacific Coast Hwy., between Seapoint St. and Warner Ave.* ☎ *714/846–3460* ⊕ *www.parks. ca.gov/?page_id=642* 🅿 *$15 parking.*

Huntington Pier. This pier stretches 1,800 feet out to sea, well past the powerful waves that gave Huntington Beach the title of "Surf City U.S.A." A farmers' market and arts fair is held on Friday afternoons; an informal car show sets up most weekends. ⊠ *Pacific Coast Hwy.* ⊕ *www.huntingtonbeachca.gov.*

◼ NEED A BREAK?

Ruby's. At the end of Huntington Pier sits Ruby's, part of a California chain of 1940s-style burger joints. Try the Cobb, with bacon and slices of avocado. ⊠ *1 Main St.* ☎ *714/969–7829* ⊕ *www.rubys.com.*

Huntington City Beach. Stretching for 3½ miles from Bolsa Chica State Beach to Huntington State Beach, Huntington City Beach is most crowded around the pier; amateur and professional surfers brave the waves daily on its north side. Fire pits, numerous concession stands, an area for dogs, and well-raked white sand make this a popular beach come summertime. **Amenities:** food and drink; lifeguards; parking; showers; toilets. **Best for:** sunset; surfing; swimming; walking. ⊠ *Pacific Coast Hwy., from Beach Blvd. to Seapoint St.* ☎ *714/536–5281* ⊕ *www.ci.huntington-beach.ca.us* 🅿 *Parking $15 weekdays, $17 weekends, $20–$27 holidays.*

Huntington State Beach. This state beach also has 200 fire pits, so it's popular day and night. There are changing rooms, concession stands, lifeguards, Wi-Fi access, and ample parking. A 6-mile bike path connects to the area's other stretches of sand. Picnic areas can be reserved in advance for a $150 fee; otherwise it's first come, first served. On hot days, expect crowds at this broad, soft sandy beach. **Amenities:** food and drink; lifeguards; parking; showers; toilets. **Best for:** sunset; surfing; swimming; walking. ⊠ *Pacific Coast Hwy., from Beach Blvd. south to Santa Ana River* ☎ *714/536–1454* ⊕ *www.parks. ca.gov/?page_id=643* 🅿 *$15 parking.*

International Surfing Museum. Just up Main Street from Huntington Pier, the International Surfing Museum pays tribute to the sport's greats with an impressive collection of surfboards and related memorabilia. They've even got the Bolex camera used to shoot the 1966 surf documentary *Endless Summer.* ✉ *411 Olive Ave.* ☎ *714/960–3483* ⊕ *www. surfingmuseum.org* ⌫ *$2* ⊘ *Sun. noon–5, Mon. and Wed.–Fri. noon–7, Tues. noon–9, Sat. 11–7.*

WHERE TO EAT

$$$$ ✕ **Duke's.** Freshly caught seafood reigns supreme at this homage to surf-
SEAFOOD ing legend Duke Kahanamoku; it's also a prime people-watching spot right at the beginning of Huntington Pier. Choose from several fish-of-the-day selections—many with Hawaiian flavors—prepared in one of five ways. Or try the crispy coconut shrimp or tuna tacos with Maui onions. Duke's mai tai is not to be missed. $ *Average main: $34* ✉ *317 Pacific Coast Hwy.* ☎ *714/374–6446* ⊕ *www.dukeshuntington.com.*

$$ ✕ **Lou's Red Oak BBQ.** You won't find any frills at Lou's Red Oak BBQ—
AMERICAN just barbecue pork, grilled linguica, rotisserie chicken, and a lot of beef. Try the tri-tip (either as an entrée or on a toasted bun smothered with traditional Santa Maria-style salsa) or the smoked turkey plate for a hearty nosh. $ *Average main: $17* ✉ *21501 Brookhurst St.* ☎ *714/965–5200* ⊕ *www.lousbbq.com.*

$ ✕ **Wahoo's Fish Taco.** Proximity to the ocean makes this eatery's
MEXICAN mahimahi-filled tacos taste even better. This healthy fast-food chain—
FAMILY tagged with dozens of surf stickers—brought Baja's fish tacos north of the border to quick success. $ *Average main: $7* ✉ *120 Main St.* ☎ *714/536–2050* ⊕ *www.wahoos.com.*

WHERE TO STAY

$$$$ ⌂ **Shorebreak Hotel.** Across the street from the beach, this boutique hotel
HOTEL attracts a mix of couples, families, and the hipster-surfer crowd. **Pros:** proximity to beach and shops; comfortable beds; quiet rooms despite central location. **Cons:** steep valet parking fee; courtyard rooms have uninspiring alley views. $ *Rooms from: $289* ✉ *500 Pacific Coast Hwy.* ☎ *714/861–4470, 877/744–1117* ⊕ *www.shorebreakhotel.com* ⌫ *157 rooms* ⦿ *No meals.*

SPORTS AND THE OUTDOORS

SURFING

Corky Carroll's Surf School. This surf school organizes lessons, weeklong workshops, and international surf camps at Bolsa Chica State Beach. Private lessons are available year-round. ☎ *714/969–3959* ⊕ *www. surfschool.net.*

Dwight's. You can rent wet suits as well as surf and boogie boards at Dwight's, one block south of Huntington Pier. ✉ *201 Pacific Coast Hwy.* ☎ *714/536–8083.*

SHOPPING

HSS Pierside. The best surf-gear source is HSS Pierside, across from Huntington Pier. It's staffed by true surf enthusiasts. ✉ *300 Pacific Coast Hwy.* ☎ *714/841–4000* ⊕ *www.hsssurf.com.*

NEWPORT BEACH

6 miles south of Huntington Beach via the Pacific Coast Highway.

Newport Beach has evolved from a simple seaside village to an icon of chic coastal living. Its ritzy reputation comes from megayachts bobbing in the harbor, boutiques that rival those in Beverly Hills, and spectacular homes overlooking the ocean.

Newport is said to have the highest per-capita number of Mercedes-Benzes in the world; inland Newport Beach's concentration of high-rise office buildings, shopping centers, and luxury hotels drive the economy. But on the city's Balboa Peninsula, you can still catch a glimpse of a more innocent, down-to-earth beach town scattered with taco spots, tackle shops, and sailor bars.

ESSENTIALS

Visitor and Tour Information Visit Newport Beach ⊠ *401 Newport Center Dr.* ☎ *855/569–7678* ⊕ *www.visitnewportbeach.com.*

EXPLORING

Balboa Island. This sliver of terra firma in Newport Harbor boasts quaint streets tightly packed with impossibly charming multimillion-dollar cottages. The island's main drag, Marine Avenue, is lined with equally picturesque cafés and shops.

NEED A
BREAK?

Sugar & Spice. Stop by ice cream parlor Sugar & Spice for a Balboa Bar—a slab of vanilla ice cream dipped first in chocolate and then in a topping of your choice such as hard candy or Oreo crumbs. Other parlors serve the concoction, but Sugar & Spice claims to have invented it back in 1945. ⊠ *310 Marine Ave., Balboa Island* ☎ *949/673–8907.*

Balboa Peninsula. Newport's best beaches are on Balboa Peninsula, where many jetties pave the way to ideal swimming areas. The most intense bodysurfing place in Orange County and arguably on the West Coast, known as the **Wedge,** is at the south end of the peninsula. It was created by accident in the 1930s when the Federal Works Progress Administration built a jetty to protect Newport Harbor. ■ **TIP→** Rip currents mean it's strictly for the pros—but it sure is fun to watch an experienced local ride it. ⊕ *www.visitnewportbeach.com/vacations/balboa-peninsula.*

FAMILY **ExplorOcean.** This destination has exhibits on the history of the harbor, ocean explorers, and scientific aspects of the Pacific Ocean. There's a fleet of ship models: some date to 1798, and one is made entirely of gold and silver. Another fun feature is a touch tank holding local sea creatures. ⊠ *600 E. Bay Ave.* ☎ *949/675–8915* ⊕ *www.explorocean.org* 🖅 *$5* ⊙ *Mon.–Thurs. 11–3:30, Fri. and Sat. 11–6, Sun. 11–5.*

Newport Harbor. Sheltering nearly 10,000 small boats, Newport Harbor may seduce even those who don't own a yacht. Spend an afternoon exploring the charming avenues and surrounding alleys. Several grassy areas on the primarily residential Lido Isle have views of the water. ⊠ *Pacific Coast Hwy.*

Newport Pier. Jutting out into the ocean near 20th Street, Newport Pier is a popular fishing spot. Street parking is difficult, so grab the first space

Riding the waves at Newport Beach

you find and be prepared to walk. On weekday mornings, you're likely to encounter dory fishermen hawking their predawn catches, as they've done for generations. On weekends the area is alive with kids of all ages on in-line skates, skateboards, and bikes dodging pedestrians and whizzing past fast-food joints and classic dive bars. ✉ *72 McFadden Pl.*

Orange County Museum of Art. The Orange County Museum of Art gathers a collection of modernist paintings and sculpture by California artists like Richard Diebenkorn, Ed Ruscha, Robert Irwin, and Chris Burden. There are also cutting-edge international works. ✉ *850 San Clemente Dr.* ☎ *949/759–1122* ⊕ *www.ocma.net* ✉ *$12* ⊙ *Wed. and Fri.–Sun. 11–5, Thurs. 11–8.*

WHERE TO EAT

$$$

AMERICAN

✕ **3-Thirty-3.** If there's a nightlife "scene" to be had in Newport Beach, this is it. This stylish eatery attracts a convivial crowd—both young and old—for midday, sunset, and late-night dining. A long list of small, shareable plates heightens the camaraderie. Pair a cocktail with charred lollipop lamb chops or chicken satay while you check out the scene, or settle in for a dinner of Kobe flatiron steak or sesame-topped ahi tuna. $ *Average main: $25* ✉ *333 Bayside Dr.* ☎ *949/673–8464* ⊕ *www.3thirty3nb.com.*

$$$

BRASSERIE

✕ **Basilic.** This intimate French-Swiss bistro adds a touch of old-world elegance to the island with its white linen and flower-topped tables. Chef Bernard Althaus grows the herbs used in his classic French dishes. Head here for charcuterie, steak *au poivre*, and a fine Bordeaux. $ *Average main: $28* ✉ *217 Marine Ave., Balboa Island* ☎ *949/673–0570* ⊕ *www.basilicrestaurant.com* ⊙ *Closed Sun. and Mon. No lunch.*

$ ✕**Bear Flag Fish Co.** Expect long lines in summer at this indoor/out-
SEAFOOD   door dining spot serving up the freshest local fish (swordfish, sea bass, halibut, and tuna) and a wide range of creative seafood dishes (the Hawaiian-style *poke* salad with ahi tuna is a local favorite). Order at the counter, which doubles as a seafood market, and sit at one of the many shared tables in the dining room or on the small patio. One of the few restaurants in Southern California with its own fishing boat, there's a good chance some line-caught local fish will be on the menu. Oysters are a great choice, and the fish tacos topped with the house-made hot sauce are not to be missed. $ *Average main: $10* ⌧ *407 31st St.* ☎ *949/673–3474* ⊕ *www.bearflagfishco.com.*

$$$$ ✕**The Cannery.** This 1920s cannery building still teems with fish, but
SEAFOOD   now they go into dishes on the eclectic Pacific Rim menu rather than being packed into crates. Settle in at the sushi bar, dining room, or patio before choosing between sashimi, seafood platters, or the upscale surf-and-turf with bone-in rib eye steaks and grilled Maine lobsters. The menu includes a selection of steaks, ribs, and seafood from the world's waters. Many diners arrive by boat, as there's a convenient dock off the front entrance. $ *Average main: $35* ⌧ *3010 Lafayette Rd.* ☎ *949/566–0060* ⊕ *www.cannerynewport.com.*

WHERE TO STAY

$$$$ 🛏**Balboa Bay Resort.** Sharing the same frontage as the private Balboa
RESORT   Bay Club that once hosted Humphrey Bogart, Lauren Bacall, and the Reagans, this hotel has one of the best bay views around. **Pros:** exquisite bay-front views; comfortable beds; a raked beach for guests. **Cons:** not much within walking distance; high nightly hospitality fee. $ *Rooms from: $309* ⌧ *1221 W. Coast Hwy.* ☎ *949/645–5000* ⊕ *www. balboabayresort.com* ↩ *149 rooms, 10 suites* ⏀⏀ *No meals.*

$$$$ 🛏**The Island Hotel.** Across the street from stylish Fashion Island, this
HOTEL   20-story tower caters to business types during the week and luxury seekers weekends. **Pros:** 24-hour exercise facilities; first-class spa; great location. **Cons:** steep valet parking prices; some rooms have views of mall; pricey rates. $ *Rooms from: $259* ⌧ *690 Newport Center Dr.* ☎ *949/759–0808, 866/554–4620* ⊕ *www.theislandhotel.com* ↩ *295 rooms, 83 suites* ⏀⏀ *No meals.*

SPORTS AND THE OUTDOORS

BOAT RENTALS

Balboa Boat Rentals. You can tour Lido and Balboa isles with kayaks ($15 an hour), sailboats ($45 an hour), small motorboats ($70 an hour), and electric boats ($75 to $95 an hour) at Balboa Boat Rentals. ⌧ *510 E. Edgewater Ave.* ☎ *949/673–7200* ⊕ *www.boats4rent.com.*

BOAT TOURS

Catalina Flyer. At Balboa Pavilion, the Catalina Flyer operates a 90-minute daily round-trip passage to Catalina Island for $70. Reservations are required. ⌧ *400 Main St.* ☎ *800/830–7744* ⊕ *www.catalinainfo.com.*

Gondola Company of Newport. Try a one-hour Venetian-style gondola cruise with the Gondola Company of Newport. It costs $85 for two and is frequently voted as the best place to take a date in Orange County. ⌧ *Lido Marine Village, 3400 Via Oporto* ☎ *949/675–1212* ⊕ *www.gondolas.com.*

A whimbrel hunts for mussels at Crystal Cove State Park.

Hornblower Cruises & Events. This operator books three-hour weekend dinner cruises with dancing for $82. The two-hour Sunday brunch cruise starts at $63. ✉ *2431 West Coast Hwy.* ☎ *949/631–2469* ⊕ *www. hornblower.com.*

FISHING

Davey's Locker. In addition to a complete tackle shop, Davey's Locker offers half-day sportfishing trips starting at $41.50. ✉ *Balboa Pavilion, 400 Main St.* ☎ *949/673–1434* ⊕ *www.daveyslocker.com.*

SHOPPING

Balboa Pavilion. On the bay side of the peninsula, Balboa Pavilion was built in 1905. Today it is home to a restaurant and shops and serves as a departure point for Catalina Island ferries and whale-watching cruises. In the blocks around the pavilion you can find restaurants, shops, and the small Balboa Fun Zone, a local kiddie hangout with a Ferris wheel. On the other side of the narrow peninsula is Balboa Pier. ✉ *400 Main St.* ☎ *800/830–7744* ⊕ *www.balboapavilion.com.*

Fashion Island. Shake the sand out of your shoes to head inland to the ritzy Fashion Island outdoor mall, a cluster of arcades and courtyards complete with koi pond, fountains, and a family-friendly trolley—plus some awesome ocean views. It has the luxe department stores Neiman Marcus and Bloomingdale's plus expensive spots like Jonathan Adler, Kate Spade, and Michael Stars. ✉ *401 Newport Center Dr., between Jamboree and MacArthur Blvds., off PCH* ☎ *949/721–2000, 855/658–8527* ⊕ *www.shopfashionisland.com.*

CORONA DEL MAR

2 miles south of Newport Beach, via PCH.

A small jewel on the Pacific Coast, Corona del Mar (known by locals as "CDM") has exceptional beaches that some say resemble their majestic Northern California counterparts. South of CDM is an area referred to as the Newport Coast or Crystal Cove—whatever you call it, it's another dazzling spot on the California Riviera.

EXPLORING

Corona del Mar State Beach. This beach is actually made up of two beaches, Little Corona and Big Corona, separated by a cliff. Both have soft, golden-hue sand. Facilities include fire pits and volleyball courts. Two colorful reefs (and the fact that it's off-limits to boats) make Corona del Mar great for snorkelers and for beachcombers. Parking in the lot is a steep $15 and $25 on holidays, but you can often find a spot on the street on weekdays. **Amenities:** lifeguards; parking; showers; toilets. **Best for:** snorkeling; sunset; swimming. ✉ *3100 Ocean Blvd., Newport Beach* ☎ *949/644–3151* ⊕ *www.parks.ca.gov.*

FAMILY
Fodor's Choice
★

Crystal Cove State Park. Midway between Corona del Mar and Laguna, Crystal Cove State Park is a favorite of local beachgoers and wilderness trekkers. It encompasses a 3.2-mile stretch of unspoiled beach and has some of the best tide pooling in Southern California. Here you can see starfish, crabs, and other sea life on the rocks. The park's 2,400 acres of backcountry are ideal for hiking, horseback riding, and mountain biking, but stay on the trails to preserve the beauty. **Crystal Cove Historic District** holds a collection of 46 handmade historic cottages (16 of which are available for overnight rental), decorated and furnished to reflect the 1935 to 1955 beach culture that flourished here. On the sand above the high-tide line and on a bluff above the beach, the cottages offer a funky look at beach life 50 years ago. ✉ *8471 N. Coast Hwy., Laguna Beach* ☎ *949/494–3539* ⊕ *www.crystalcovestatepark. com* 🅿 *$15 parking* ⊙ *Daily 6–dusk.*

NEED A
BREAK?

Beachcomber at Crystal Cove Café. Beach culture flourishes in the Crystal Cove Historic District's restaurant, the Beachcomber at Crystal Cove Café. The umbrella-laden deck is just a few steps above the white sand. ✉ *Crystal Cove, 15 Crystal Cove, Newport Coast* ☎ *949/376–6900* ⊕ *www.thebeachcombercafe.com.*

Sherman Library and Gardens. This 2½-acre botanical garden and library specializes in the history of the Pacific Southwest. You can wander among cactus gardens, rose gardens, a wheelchair-height touch-and-smell garden, and a tropical conservatory. There's a good gift shop, too. Café Jardin serves lunch on weekdays and Sunday brunch. ✉ *2647 E. Pacific Coast Hwy.* ☎ *949/673–0033* ⊕ *www.slgardens.org* 🅿 *$3* ⊙ *Daily 10:30–4.*

WHERE TO EAT AND STAY

$
AMERICAN

✗ **Pacific Whey Cafe.** The ovens rarely get a break here; everything is made from scratch daily. Pick up a BLTA (a BLT with avocado) for a picnic across the street at Crystal Cove State Park. Or stay—at a communal table inside or in the courtyard, which has an ocean view—for organic buckwheat pancakes or grilled salmon with citrus sauce. $\boxed{\$}$ *Average main: $10* ⊠ *Crystal Cove Promenade, 7962 E. Coast Hwy., Newport Coast* ☏ *949/715–2200* ⊕ *www.pacificwhey.com.*

$\$$

MEDITERRANEAN

✕ **Panini Cafe.** For reasonably priced food and outstanding espresso drinks, this link of a local chain packs a lot of punch for your dining dollars. Think straight-from-the-oven breads, pizzas, and pastas, as well as grilled panini stuffed with roast beef, onions, and provolone cheese. This is a breakfast favorite among locals; at dinner, entrées include Mediterranean classics like moussaka and kebabs. $\boxed{\$}$ *Average main: $10* ⊠ *2333 E. Coast Hwy.* ☏ *949/675–8101* ⊕ *www.mypaninicafe.com.*

$\$\$\$\$

RESORT

FAMILY

The Resort at Pelican Hill. Adjacent to Crystal Cove State Park, this Mediterranean-style resort has spacious bungalow suites, each with Italian limestone fireplaces and marble baths, built into terraced hillsides overlooking the Pacific. **Pros:** paradise for golfers; gracious, attentive staff. **Cons:** sky-high prices; common areas can feel cold. $\boxed{\$}$ *Rooms from: $595* ⊠ *22701 Pelican Hill Rd. S, Newport Coast* ☏ *949/612–0332, 888/507–6427* ⊕ *www.pelicanhill.com* ⮑ *204 suites, 128 villas* ⏃ *No meals.*

3

SHOPPING

Crystal Cove Promenade. Adding to Orange County's overwhelming supply of high-end shopping and dining is Crystal Cove Promenade, which might be described as the toniest strip mall in America. The storefronts and restaurants of this Mediterranean–inspired center are lined up across the street from Crystal Cove State Park, with the shimmering Pacific waters in plain view. ⊠ *7772–8112 E. Coast Hwy., Newport Beach* ⊕ *www.crystalcove.com/beach-living/shopping.*

LAGUNA BEACH

10 miles south of Newport Beach on PCH, 60 miles south of Los Angeles, I-5 south to Hwy. 133, which turns into Laguna Canyon Rd.

Fodor'sChoice

★

Even the approach tells you that Laguna Beach is exceptional. Driving in along Laguna Canyon Road from the Interstate 405 freeway gives you the chance to cruise through a gorgeous coastal canyon, large stretches of which remain undeveloped. You'll arrive at a glistening wedge of ocean.

Laguna's welcome mat is legendary. On the corner of Forest and Park avenues is a gate proclaiming, "This gate hangs well and hinders none, refresh and rest, then travel on." A gay community has long been established here. Art galleries dot the village streets, and there's usually someone daubing up in Heisler Park. Along the Pacific Coast Highway you'll find dozens of clothing boutiques, jewelry shops, and cafés.

ESSENTIALS

Visitor and Tour Information Laguna Beach Visitors Center ⊠ *381 Forest Ave.* ☏ *949/497–9229, 800/877–1115* ⊕ *www.lagunabeachinfo.com.*

Looking for shells on Laguna Beach, one of the nicest stretches of sand in Southern California

EXPLORING

1,000 Steps Beach. Off South Coast Highway at 9th Street, 1,000 Steps Beach is a hard-to-find spot tucked away in a neighborhood with great waves and hard-packed, white sand. There aren't really 1,000 steps down (but when you hike back up, it'll certainly feel like it). **Amenities:** parking. **Best for:** sunset; surfing; swimming. ✉ *South Coast Hwy., at 9th St.*

Laguna Art Museum. The Laguna Art Museum displays American art, with an emphasis on California artists from all periods. Special exhibits change quarterly. ✉ *307 Cliff Dr.* ☎ *949/494–8971* ⊕ *www. lagunaartmuseum.org* 🎟 *$7* ⊙ *Fri.–Tues. 11–5, Thurs. 11–9.*

Laguna Coast Wilderness Park. The Laguna Coast Wilderness Park is spread over 7,000 acres of fragile coastal territory, including the canyon. The 40 miles of trails are great for hiking and mountain biking and are open daily, weather permitting. Docent-led hikes are given regularly. ✉ *18751 Laguna Canyon Rd.* ☎ *949/923–2235* ⊕ *www.ocparks.com/ parks/lagunac* 🎟 *$3 parking.*

FAMILY **Main Beach Park.** A stocky 1920s lifeguard tower marks Main Beach Park, where a wooden boardwalk separates the sand from a strip of lawn. Walk along this soft-sand beach, or grab a bench and watch people bodysurfing, playing volleyball, or scrambling around two half-basketball courts. The beach also has children's play equipment. Most of Laguna's hotels are within a short (but hilly) walk. **Amenities:** lifeguards; parking; showers; toilets. **Best for:** sunset; swimming; walking. ✉ *Broadway at S. Coast Hwy.*

Wood's Cove. Off South Coast Highway, Wood's Cove is especially quiet during the week. Big rock formations hide lurking crabs. This is a prime scuba diving spot, and at high tide much of the beach is underwater. Climbing the steps to leave, you can see a Tudor-style mansion that was once home to Bette Davis. Street parking is limited. **Amenities:** none. **Best for:** snorkeling; scuba diving; sunset. ✉ *Diamond St. and Ocean Way.*

WHERE TO EAT

$$$ INTERNATIONAL 🍴 **Sapphire Laguna.** This Laguna Beach establishment is part gourmet pantry (a must-stop for your every picnic need) and part global dining adventure. Iranian-born chef Azmin Ghahreman takes you on a journey through Europe and Asia with dishes ranging from a Korean monkfish hot pot to Spanish-style seafood paella. Nearly a dozen beers from around the world and a fittingly eclectic wine list round out the experience. The dining room is intimate and earthy but infused with local style. Brunch is a favorite with locals, as well—enjoy it on the patio in good weather. [$] *Average main: $27* ✉ *The Old Pottery Place, 1200 S. Coast Hwy.* ☎ *949/715–9888* 🌐 *www.sapphirellc.com.*

$$$$ MODERN AMERICAN Fodor's Choice ★ 🍴 **Studio.** In a nod to Laguna's art history, Studio has house-made specialties that entice the eye as well as the palate. You can't beat the location, atop a 50-foot bluff overlooking the Pacific Ocean. And because the restaurant occupies its own Craftsman-style bungalow, it doesn't feel like a hotel dining room. Under the deft direction of executive chef Craig Strong, the menu changes seasonally and features the finest seafood and the freshest locally grown produce (some herbs come from a small garden just outside the kitchen). You might begin with paper-thin charred shrimp carpaccio or black pepper seared hamachi before moving on to a perfectly cooked King salmon in subtle cardamom sauce or lamb chops on a bed of pomegranate quinoa. The wine list here is bursting with nearly 2,500 labels. Service is crisp and attentive. [$] *Average main: $55* ✉ *Montage Laguna Beach, 30801 S. Coast Hwy.* ☎ *949/715–6420* 🌐 *www.studiolagunabeach.com* ✍ *Reservations essential* ⏲ *Closed Mon. No lunch.*

$ VEGETARIAN 🍴 **Zinc Café & Market.** Families flock to this small Laguna Beach institution for reasonably priced breakfast and lunch options. Try the signature quiches or poached egg dishes in the morning, or swing by later in the day for healthy salads, house-made soups, quesadillas, or pizzettes. The café also has great artisanal cheeses and gourmet goodies you can take with you or savor on the outdoor patio. All the sweets are house-made, including the mega-size brownies. [$] *Average main: $12* ✉ *350 Ocean Ave.* ☎ *949/494–6302* 🌐 *www.zinccafe.com* ⏲ *No dinner Nov.–Apr.*

WHERE TO STAY

$$$ HOTEL 🏨 **La Casa del Camino.** This historic Spanish-style hotel opened in 1929 and was once a favorite of Hollywood stars. **Pros:** breathtaking views from rooftop lounge; personable service; close to beach. **Cons:** some rooms face the highway; frequent events can make hotel noisy; some rooms are very small. [$] *Rooms from: $229* ✉ *1289 S. Coast Hwy.* ☎ *949/497–2446, 888/367–5232* 🌐 *www.lacasadelcamino.com* 🛏 *26 rooms, 10 suites* 🍽 *No meals.*

$$$$ RESORT FAMILY Fodor's Choice ★ **Montage Laguna Beach.** Laguna's connection to the Californian plein air artists is mined for inspiration at this head-turning, lavish hotel. **Pros:** top-notch, enthusiastic service; idyllic coastal location; special programs cover everything from art to marine biology. **Cons:** multinight stays required on weekends and holiday; expensive valet parking. [$] *Rooms from: $595* ✉ *30801 S. Coast Hwy.* ☎ *949/715–6000, 866/271–6953* 🌐 *www.montagelagunabeach.com* 🛏 *188 rooms, 60 suites* 🍴 *No meals.*

SPORTS AND THE OUTDOORS

WATER SPORTS

Hobie Sports. In summer, rent bodyboards at Hobie Sports. ✉ *294 Forest Ave.* ☎ *949/497–3304* 🌐 *www.hobiesurfshop.com.*

SHOPPING

Coast Highway, Forest and Ocean avenues, and Glenneyre Street are full of art galleries, fine jewelry stores, and clothing boutiques.

Candy Baron. Get your sugar fix at the time-warped Candy Baron, filled with old-fashioned goodies like gumdrops, bull's-eyes, and more than a dozen barrels of saltwater taffy. ✉ *231 Forest Ave.* ☎ *949/497–7508* 🌐 *www.thecandybaron.com.*

DANA POINT

10 miles south of Laguna Beach, via the Pacific Coast Highway.

Dana Point's claim to fame is its small-boat marina tucked into a dramatic natural harbor and surrounded by high bluffs. The early-March Dana Point Festival of the Whales celebrates the passing gray-whale migration with two weekends full of activities.

EXPLORING

Dana Point Harbor. Dana Point Harbor was first described more than 100 years ago by its namesake, Richard Henry Dana, in his book *Two Years Before the Mast.* At the marina are docks for private boats and yachts, shops, restaurants, and boat, kayak, stand-up paddleboard, and bike rentals. ✉ *Dana Point Harbor Dr.* ☎ *949/923–2255* 🌐 *www.danapointharbor.com.*

Doheny State Beach. At the south end of Dana Point, Doheny State Beach is one of Southern California's top surfing destinations, but there's a lot more to do within this 61-acre area. There are five indoor tanks and an interpretive center devoted to the wildlife of the Doheny Marine Refuge, as well as food stands, picnic facilities, and volleyball courts. Divers and anglers hang out at the beach's western end, and during low tide, the tide pools beckon both young and old. The water quality occasionally falls below state standards—signs are posted if that's the case. **Amenities:** food and drink; lifeguards; parking; showers; toilets. **Best for:** partiers; sunset; surfing; swimming; walking. ✉ *25300 Dana Point Harbor Dr.* ☎ *949/496–6172* 🌐 *www.dohenystatebeach.org* 🎟 *$15 parking.*

WHERE TO EAT

$$$ FRENCH ✕ **Gemmell's.** Accomplished chef Byron Gemmell's moderately priced bistro is a welcome change from the fish houses that dominate this town, particularly around the harbor. In a laid-back but romantic

setting, you can begin with escargots or French onion soup before moving on to rack of lamb with thyme demi-glace or roasted duck in a seductive rum–banana liqueur reduction. Finish with a soufflé—either classic chocolate or Grand Marnier. The wine list includes some reasonably priced Bordeaux. The food is rich, but a meal here won't break the bank. $\boxed{S}$ *Average main: $25* ✉ *34471 Golden Lantern St., Dana Point* ☎ *949/234–0063* ⊕ *www.gemmellsrestaurant.com.*

$$$
AMERICAN

✗ **Wind & Sea.** Unobstructed marina views make this a particularly appealing place for lunch or a sunset dinner. On warm days, patio tables beckon you outside, and looking out on the Pacific might put you in the mood for a retro cocktail like a mai tai. Among the entrées, the macadamia-crusted mahimahi and the grilled teriyaki shrimp stand out. The Sunday breakfast buffet is a good value at $15 per person. $\boxed{S}$ *Average main: $25* ✉ *Dana Point Harbor, 34699 Golden Lantern St.* ☎ *949/496–6500* ⊕ *www.windandsearestaurants.com.*

WHERE TO STAY

$$$
B&B/INN

🏠 **Blue Lantern Inn.** Combining New England–style architecture with a Southern California setting, this white-clapboard B&B rests on a bluff overlooking the harbor and ocean. **Pros:** bikes to borrow; one room welcomes pets; free Wi-Fi and parking. **Cons:** nearby restaurant can be noisy. $\boxed{S}$ *Rooms from: $235* ✉ *34343 St. of the Blue Lantern* ☎ *949/661–1304, 800/950–1236* ⊕ *www.bluelanterninn.com* ⬎ *29 rooms* ❏ *Breakfast.*

$$$$
RESORT
FAMILY
Fodor's Choice
★

🏠 **Ritz-Carlton, Laguna Niguel.** Combine the Ritz-Carlton's top-tier level of service with an unparalleled view of the Pacific and you're in the lap of luxury at this resort. **Pros:** beautiful grounds and views; luxurious bedding; seamless service. **Cons:** some rooms are small for the price; culinary program has room to grow. $\boxed{S}$ *Rooms from: $475* ✉ *1 Ritz-Carlton Dr.* ☎ *949/240–2000, 800/542–8680* ⊕ *www.ritzcarlton.com* ⬎ *367 rooms, 29 suites* ❏ *No meals.*

$$$$
RESORT

🏠 **St. Regis Monarch Beach Resort and Spa.** Grand and sprawling, the St. Regis can satisfy your every whim with its 172 acres of grounds, private beach club, 18-hole Robert Trent Jones Jr.–designed golf course, three swimming pools, and tennis courts. **Pros:** immaculate rooms; big bathrooms with deep tubs; beautiful spa. **Cons:** hotel layout is somewhat confusing; high resort fee. $\boxed{S}$ *Rooms from: $495* ✉ *1 Monarch Beach Resort, off Niguel Rd.* ☎ *949/234–3200, 800/722–1543* ⊕ *www.stregismb.com* ⬎ *325 rooms, 75 suites.*

SPORTS AND THE OUTDOORS

Capt. Dave's Dolphin & Whale Watching Safari. You have a good chance of getting a water's-eye view of resident dolphins and migrating whales if you take one of these tours on three deluxe catamarans. Dave Anderson, a marine naturalist and filmmaker, and his wife run the safaris year-round. The endangered blue whale is sometimes spotted in summer. Reservations are required for the safaris, which last 2½ hours and cost $65. ✉ *24440 Dana Point Harbor Dr.* ☎ *949/488–2828* ⊕ *www. dolphinsafari.com.*

Mission San Juan Capistrano

SAN JUAN CAPISTRANO

5 miles north of Dana Point, Hwy. 74, 60 miles north of San Diego, I-5.

San Juan Capistrano is best known for its historic mission, where the swallows traditionally return each year, migrating from their winter haven in Argentina, but these days they are more likely to choose other local sites for nesting. St. Joseph's Day, March 19, launches a week of fowl festivities. Charming antiques stores, which range from pricey to cheap, line Camino Capistrano.

GETTING HERE AND AROUND

If you arrive by train, which is far more romantic and restful than battling freeway traffic, you'll be dropped off across from the mission at the San Juan Capistrano depot. With its appealing brick café and preserved Santa Fe cars, the depot retains much of the magic of early American railroads. If driving, park near Ortega and Camino Capistrano, the city's main streets.

EXPLORING

FAMILY

Fodor'sChoice

★

Mission San Juan Capistrano. Founded in 1776 by Father Junípero Serra, Mission San Juan Capistrano was one of two Roman Catholic outposts between Los Angeles and San Diego. The Great Stone Church, begun in 1797, is the largest structure created by the Spanish in California. Many of the mission's adobe buildings have been preserved to illustrate mission life, with exhibits of an olive millstone, tallow ovens, tanning vats, metalworking furnaces, and the padres' living quarters. The gardens, with their fountains, are a lovely spot in which to wander. The bougainvillea-covered Serra Chapel is believed to be the oldest church still standing in California and is the only building remaining in which Fr. Serra actually led Mass. Mass takes place weekdays at 7 am in the chapel. Enter via a small gift shop in the gatehouse. ⊠ *Camino Capistrano and Ortega Hwy.* ☎ *949/234–1300* ⊕ *www.missionsjc.com* ☞ *$9* ⊙ *Daily 9–5.*

WHERE TO EAT

$$ ✕ **The Ramos House Cafe.** It may be worth hopping the Amtrak to San

AMERICAN Juan Capistrano just for the chance to have breakfast or lunch at one of Orange County's most beloved restaurants. Here's your chance to visit one of Los Rios Historic District's board-and-batten homes dating back to 1881. This café sits practically on the railroad tracks across from the depot—nab a table on the patio and dig in to a hearty breakfast, such as the smoked bacon scramble. The weekend brunch includes Champagne, memorable mac and cheese with wild mushrooms, and huckleberry coffee cake. Every item on the menu illustrates chef-owner John Q. Humphreys' creative hand. $ *Average main: $18* ⊠ *31752 Los Rios St.* ☎ *949/443–1342* ⊕ *www.ramoshouse.com* ⊙ *Closed Mon. No dinner.*

NIGHTLIFE

Swallow's Inn. Across the way from Mission San Juan Capistrano you'll spot a line of Harleys in front of the Swallow's Inn. Despite a somewhat tough look, it attracts all kinds—bikers, surfers, modern-day cowboys, grandparents—for a drink, a casual bite, and some rowdy live music. ⊠ *31786 Camino Capistrano* ☎ *949/493–3188* ⊕ *www.swallowsinn.com.*

CATALINA ISLAND

Fodor'sChoice Just 22 miles out from the L.A. coastline, across from Newport Beach
★ and Long Beach, Catalina has virtually unspoiled mountains, canyons, coves, and beaches; best of all, it gives you a glimpse of what undeveloped Southern California once looked like.

Water sports are a big draw, as divers and snorkelers come for the exceptionally clear water surrounding the island. Kayakers are attracted to the calm cove waters and thrill seekers have made the eco-themed zip line so popular, there are nighttime tours via flashlight in summer. The main town, Avalon, is a charming, old-fashioned beach community, where yachts and pleasure boats bob in the crescent bay. Wander beyond the main drag and find brightly painted little bungalows fronting the sidewalks; golf carts are the preferred mode of transport.

In 1919, William Wrigley Jr., the chewing-gum magnate, purchased a controlling interest in the company developing Catalina Island, whose most famous landmark, the Casino, was built in 1929 under his orders. Because he owned the Chicago Cubs baseball team, Wrigley made Catalina the team's spring training site, an arrangement that lasted until 1951.

In 1975, the Catalina Island Conservancy, a nonprofit foundation, acquired about 88% of the island to help preserve the area's natural flora and fauna, including the bald eagle and the Catalina Island fox. These days the conservancy is restoring the rugged interior country with plantings of native grasses and trees. Along the coast you might spot oddities like electric perch, saltwater goldfish, and flying fish.

GETTING HERE AND AROUND

FERRY TRAVEL   Two companies offer ferry service to Catalina Island. The boats have both indoor and outdoor seating and snack bars. Excessive baggage is not allowed, and there are extra fees for bicycles and surfboards. The waters around Santa Catalina can get rough, so if you're prone to seasickness, come prepared. Winter, holiday, and weekend schedules vary, so reservations are recommended.

Catalina Express makes an hour-long run from Long Beach or San Pedro to Avalon and a 90-minute run from Dana Point to Avalon with some stops at Two Harbors. Round-trip fares begin at $74.50, with discounts for seniors and kids. On busy days, a $15 upgrade to the Commodore Lounge, when available, is worth it. Service from Newport Beach to Avalon is available through the Catalina Flyer. Boats leave from Balboa Pavilion at 9 am (in season), take 75 minutes to reach the island, and cost $70 round-trip. Return boats leave Catalina at 4:30 pm. Reservations are required for the Catalina Flyer and recommended for all weekend and summer trips. ■TIP➔ **Keep an eye out for dolphins, which sometimes swim alongside the ferries.**

GOLF CARTS   Golf carts constitute the island's main form of transportation for sightseeing in the area, however some parts of town are off limits as is the island's interior. You can rent them along Avalon's Crescent Avenue and Pebbly Beach Road for about $40 per hour with a $40 deposit, payable via cash or traveler's check only.

HELICOPTER TRAVEL   Island Express helicopters depart hourly from San Pedro, Santa Ana, and Long Beach next to the Queen Mary (8 am–dusk). The trip from Long Beach takes about 15 minutes and costs $125 one-way, $250 round-trip (plus tax). Reservations a week in advance are recommended (☏ 800/228–2566).

TIMING

Although Catalina can be seen in one very hectic day, several inviting hotels make it worth extending your stay for one or more nights. A short itinerary might include breakfast on the pier, a tour of the interior, a snorkeling excursion at Casino Point, or beach day at the Descanso Beach Club and a romantic waterfront dinner in Avalon.

After late October, rooms are much easier to find on short notice, rates drop dramatically, and many hotels offer packages that include transportation from the mainland and/or sightseeing tours. January to March you have a good chance of spotting migrating gray whales on the ferry crossing.

TOURS

Santa Catalina Island Company runs 16 Discovery Tours, including the *Flying Fish* boat trip (summer evenings only); a comprehensive inland motor tour; a tour of Skyline Drive; several Casino tours; a scenic tour of Avalon; a glass-bottom-boat tour; an undersea tour on a semi-submersible vessel; an eco-themed zip-line tour that traverses a scenic canyon; a speedy Dolphin Quest that searches for all manner of sea creatures. Reservations are highly recommended for the inland tours. Tours cost $10 to $178. There are ticket booths on the Green Pleasure Pier, at the Casino, in the plaza, and at the boat landing. Catalina

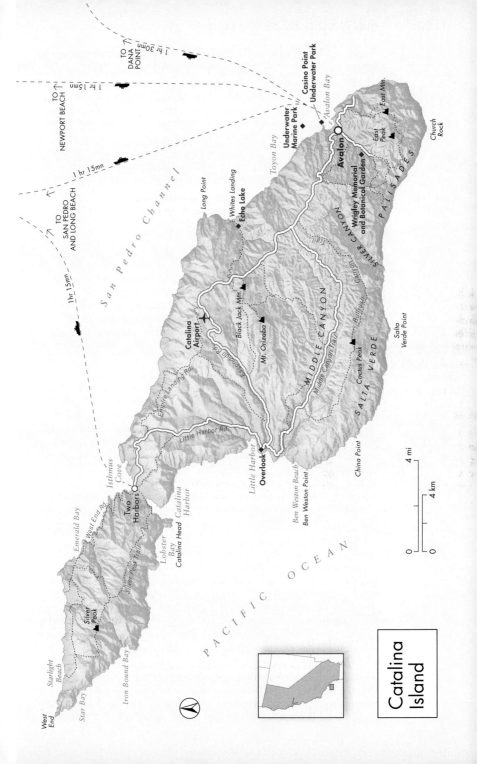

Catalina Island

Adventure Tours, which has booths at the boat landing and on the pier, arranges similar excursions at comparable prices.

The Catalina Island Conservancy organizes custom ecotours and hikes of the interior. Naturalist guides drive open Jeeps through some gorgeously untrammeled parts of the island. Tours start at $70 per person for a two-hour trip (two-person minimum); you can also book half- and full-day tours. The tours run year-round.

ESSENTIALS

Ferry Contacts Catalina Express ☎ 800/481–3470 ⊕ www.catalinaexpress. com. **Catalina Flyer** ☎ 949/673–5245, 800/830–7744 ⊕ www.catalinainfo.com.

Golf Cart Rentals Island Rentals ✉ 125 Pebbly Beach Rd., Avalon ☎ 310/510–1456 ⊕ www.catalinagolfcartrentals.com.

Helicopter Contacts Island Express ☎ 800/228–2566 ⊕ www.islandexpress.com.

Visitor and Tour Information Catalina Adventure Tours ☎ 877/510–2888 ⊕ www.catalinaadventuretours.com. **Catalina Island Chamber of Commerce & Visitors Bureau** ✉ #1 Green Pleasure Pier, Avalon ☎ 310/510–1520 ⊕ www.catalinachamber.com. **Santa Catalina Island Company** ☎ 877/778–8322 ⊕ www.visitcatalinaisland.com. **Catalina Island Conservancy** ✉ 125 Claressa Ave., Avalon ☎ 310/510–2595 ⊕ www.catalinaconservancy.org.

AVALON

A 1- to 2-hour ferry ride from Long Beach, Newport Beach, or San Pedro; a 15-minute helicopter ride from Long Beach or San Pedro, slightly longer from Santa Ana.

Avalon, Catalina's only real town, extends from the shore of its natural harbor to the surrounding hillsides. Its resident population is about 3,800, but it swells with tourists on summer weekends. Most of the city's activity, however, is centered on the pedestrian mall on Crescent Avenue, and most sights are easily reached on foot. Private cars are restricted and rental cars aren't allowed, but taxis, trams, and shuttles can take you anywhere you need to go. Bicycles, electric bikes, and golf carts can be rented from shops along Crescent Avenue.

EXPLORING

Fodor'sChoice **Casino.** This circular white structure is one of the finest examples of art
★ deco architecture anywhere. Its Spanish-inspired floors and murals gleam with brilliant blue and green Catalina tiles. In this case, *casino*, the Italian word for "gathering place," has nothing to do with gambling. To the right of the theater's grand entrance is the quaint Catalina Island Museum, which examines and chronicles 7,000 years of island history. First-run movies are screened nightly at the Avalon Theatre, noteworthy for its classic 1929 theater pipe organ and art deco wall murals.

The Santa Catalina Island Company leads two tours of the Casino—the 30-minute basic tour ($10) and the 90-minute behind-the-scenes tour ($25), which leads visitors through the green room and into the Wrigleys' private lounge. ✉ 1 Casino Way ☎ 310/510–2414 museum, 310/510–0179 theater ⊕ www.catalinamuseum.org ⊠ Museum $5 ☉ Daily 10–5.

Casino Point Dive Park. In front of the Casino are the crystal clear waters of the Casino Point Dive Park, a protected marine preserve where moray eels, bat rays, spiny lobsters, harbor seals, and other sea creatures cruise around kelp forests and along the sandy bottom. It's a terrific site for scuba diving, with some shallow areas suitable for snorkeling. Equipment can be rented on and near the pier. The shallow waters of Lover's Cove, east of the boat landing, are also good for snorkeling.

Green Pleasure Pier. Head to the Green Pleasure Pier for a good vantage point of Avalon. On the pier you can find the visitor information, snack stands, and scads of squawking seagulls. It's also the landing where visiting cruise ship passengers catch tenders back out to their ship. ✉ *End of Catalina Ave.*

Wrigley Memorial and Botanic Garden. Two miles south of the bay is Wrigley Memorial and Botanic Garden, home to plants native to Southern California. Several grow only on Catalina Island—Catalina ironwood, wild tomato, and rare Catalina mahogany. The Wrigley family commissioned the garden as well as the monument, which has a grand staircase and a Spanish-style mausoleum inlaid with colorful Catalina tile. The mausoleum was never used by the Wrigleys, who are buried in Pasadena. ✉ *Avalon Canyon Rd.* ☎ *310/510–2897* 🌐 *www.catalinaconservancy.org* 🎟 *$7* 🕒 *Daily 8–5.*

WHERE TO EAT

$$$ SEAFOOD

🍴 **Bluewater Avalon.** Overlooking the ferry landing and the entire harbor, the open-to-the-salt-air Bluewater Avalon offers freshly caught fish, savory chowders, and all manner of shellfish. If they're on the menu, don't miss the swordfish steak or the sand dabs. Opened in 2013, the dining room has an understated nautical vibe. Fishing rods serve as room dividers, and plank floors lend a casual feel inside and out. Vintage black-and-white photos acknowledge the island's famed sports fishing legacy. The wraparound patio is the preferred spot to dine, but beware of aggressive seagulls that may try to snatch your food. Happy hour attracts a crowd for the craft beers, potent cocktails, and tasty bites like popcorn shrimp and oyster shooters. [$] *Average main: $25* ✉ *306 Crescent Ave.* ☎ *310/510–3474* 🌐 *www.bluewateravalon.com.*

$ AMERICAN FAMILY

🍴 **Descanso Beach Club.** Set on an expansive deck overlooking the water, Descanso Beach Club serves a wide range of favorites: peel-and-eat shrimp, hamburgers, salads, nachos, and wraps are all part of the selection. Watch the harbor seals frolic just offshore while sipping the island's super-sweet signature cocktail, the Buffalo Milk, a mix of fruit liqueurs, vodka, and whipped cream. Fire pits and colorful beach cabanas add to the scene, as does the sound of happy and terrified screams from the zip-liners in the canyon above the beach. [$] *Average main: $15* ✉ *Descanso Beach, 1 Descanso Ave.* ☎ *310/510-7410.*

$$$ SEAFOOD

🍴 **The Lobster Trap.** Seafood rules at the Lobster Trap—the restaurant's owner has his own boat and fishes for the catch of the day and, in season, spiny lobster. Ceviche is a great starter, always fresh and brightly flavored. Locals (you'll see many at the small counter) come for the relaxed atmosphere, large portions, draft beer, and live music on weekend nights. [$] *Average main: $24* ✉ *128 Catalina St.* ☎ *310/510–8585* 🌐 *catalinalobstertrap.com.*

WHERE TO STAY

$$$ HOTEL **Aurora Hotel & Spa.** In a town dominated by historic properties, the Aurora is refreshingly contemporary, with a hip attitude and sleek furnishings. **Pros:** trendy design; quiet location off main drag; close to restaurants. **Cons:** standard rooms are small, even by Catalina standards; no elevator. [$] *Rooms from: $219* ✉ *137 Marilla Ave., Avalon* ☎ *310/510–0454, 800/422–6836* 🌐 *www.auroracatalina.com* 🛏 *15 rooms, 3 suites* 🍴 *Breakfast.*

$$$ HOTEL **Hotel Villa Portofino.** Steps from the Green Pleasure Pier, this European-style hotel creates an intimate feel with brick courtyards and walkways and suites named after Italian cities. **Pros:** romantic; close to beach; incredible sundeck. **Cons:** ground-floor rooms can be noisy; some rooms are on small side; no elevator. [$] *Rooms from: $235* ✉ *111 Crescent Ave.* ☎ *310/510–0555, 888/510–0555* 🌐 *www.hotelvillaportofino.com* 🛏 *35 rooms* 🍴 *Breakfast.*

$$$ HOTEL **Hotel Vista del Mar.** On the bay-facing Crescent Avenue, this third-floor property is steps from the beach, where complimentary towels, chairs, and umbrellas await guests. **Pros:** comfortable beds; central location; modern decor. **Cons:** no restaurant or spa facilities; few rooms with ocean views; no elevator. [$] *Rooms from: $250* ✉ *417 Crescent Ave.* ☎ *310/510–1452, 800/601–3836* 🌐 *www.hotel-vistadelmar.com* 🛏 *12 rooms, 2 suites* 🍴 *Breakfast.*

SPORTS AND THE OUTDOORS

BICYCLING

Brown's Bikes. Look for rentals on Crescent Avenue and Pebbly Beach Road, where Brown's Bikes is located. Beach cruisers and mountain bikes start at $20 per day. Electric bikes are also on offer. ✉ *107 Pebbly Beach Rd.* ☎ *310/510–0986* 🌐 *www.catalinabiking.com.*

DIVING AND SNORKELING

The Casino Point Underwater Park, with its handful of wrecks, is best suited for diving. Lover's Cove is better for snorkeling (but you'll share the area with glass-bottom boats). Both are protected marine preserves.

Catalina Divers Supply. Head to Catalina Divers Supply to rent equipment, sign up for guided scuba and snorkel tours, and attend certification classes. It also has an outpost at the Dive Park at Casino Point. ✉ *No. 7 Green Pleasure Pier* ☎ *310/510–0330* 🌐 *www.catalinadiverssupply.com.*

LOS ANGELES

WELCOME TO
LOS ANGELES

TOP REASONS
TO GO

★ **People-watching:**
Celeb spotting in Beverly
Hills, trying to get past the
velvet rope at hip clubs,
hanging out on the Venice
Boardwalk . . . there's
always something (or someone) interesting to see.

★ **Trendy restaurants:**
Celebrity is big business
here, so it's no accident
that the concept of the
celebrity chef is a key part
of the city's dining scene.

★ **Hollywood magic:**
A massive chunk of the
world's entertainment is
developed, written, filmed,
edited, distributed, and
sold here; you'll hear
people discussing "the
Industry" wherever you go.

★ **The beach:** Getting
some sand on the floor of
your car is practically a
requirement here, and the
beach is an integral part
of the SoCal lifestyle.

★ **Chic shopping:** From
Beverly Hills's Rodeo Drive
and Downtown's Fashion
District to the funky boutiques of Los Feliz, Silver
Lake, and Echo Park, L.A.
is a shopper's paradise.

1 Downtown. Downtown
L.A. shows off spectacular
modern architecture with
the swooping Walt Disney
Concert Hall and the stark
Cathedral of Our Lady
of the Angels. The Music
Center and the Museum of
Contemporary Art anchor a
world-class arts scene, while
Olvera Street, Chinatown,
and Little Tokyo reflect the
city's history and diversity.

**2 Hollywood and the
Studios.** Glitzy and
tarnished, good and bad—
Hollywood is just like the
entertainment business
itself. The Walk of Fame, TCL
Chinese Theatre, Paramount
Pictures studio, and the
Hollywood Bowl keep the
neighborhood's romantic
past alive. Universal Studios
Hollywood, Warner Bros.,
and NBC Television Studios
are in the Valley.

**3 Beverly Hills and the
Westside.** Go for the
glamour, the restaurants,
and the scene. Rodeo Drive
is particularly good for a
look at wretched or ravish-
ing excess. But don't forget
the Westside's cultural
attractions—especially
the dazzling Getty Center.
West Hollywood's an area
for urban indulgences—
shopping, restaurants,
nightspots—rather than
sightseeing. Its main arteries

are the Sunset Strip and
Melrose Avenue, lined with
shops ranging from punk to
postmodern.

**4 Santa Monica and the
Beaches.** These desirable
beach communities move
from ultrarich, ultracasual
Malibu to bohemian/transi-
tioning Venice, with liberal,
Mediterranean-style Santa
Monica in between.

5 Pasadena. Its own
separate city, Pasadena is a
quiet area with outstanding
Arts and Crafts homes, good
dining, and a pair of exceptional museums.

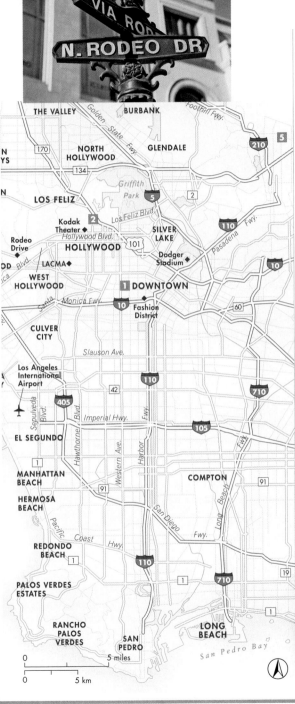

GETTING ORIENTED

4

Looking at a map of sprawling Los Angeles, first-time visitors are sometimes overwhelmed. Where to begin? What to see first? And what about all those freeways? Here's some advice: relax. Begin by setting your priorities—movie and television buffs should first head to Hollywood, Universal Studios, and a taping of a television show. Beach lovers and nature types might start out in Santa Monica, Venice, or Malibu, or spend an afternoon in Griffith Park, one of the largest city parks in the country. Culture vultures should make a beeline for the twin Gettys (the center in Brentwood and the villa near Malibu) or the Los Angeles County Museum of Art (LACMA). And urban explorers might begin with Downtown L.A.

SOUTH-OF-THE-BORDER FLAVOR

From Cal-Mex burritos to Mexico City–style tacos, Southern California is a top stateside destination for experiencing Mexico's myriad culinary styles.

Many Americans are surprised to learn that the Mexican menu goes far beyond Tex-Mex (or Cal-Mex) favorites like burritos, chimichangas, enchiladas, fajitas, and nachos—many of which were created or popularized stateside. Indeed, Mexico has rich, regional food styles, like the complex *mole* sauces of Puebla and Oaxaca and the fresh *ceviches* of Veracruz, as well as the trademark snack of Mexico City: tacos.

In Southern California, tacos are an obsession, with numerous blogs and websites dedicated to the quest for the perfect taco. They're everywhere—in ramshackle taco stands, roving taco trucks, and strip-mall taquerias. Whether you're looking for a cheap snack or a lunch on-the-go, SoCal's taco selection can't be beat. But be forewarned: there may not be an English menu. Here we've noted unfamiliar taco terms, along with other potentially new-to-you items from the Mexican menu.

THIRST QUENCHERS

Spanish for "fresh water," *agua fresca* is a nonalcoholic Mexican drink made from fruit, rice, or seeds that are blended with sugar and water. Fruit flavors like lemon, lime, and watermelon are common. Other varieties include *agua de Jamaica*, flavored with red hibiscus petals; *agua de horchata*, a cinnamon-scented rice milk; and *agua de tamarindo*, a bittersweet variety flavored with tamarind. If you're looking for something with more kick, try a *Michelada*, a beer with a mixture of lime juice, chili sauce, and other savory ingredients. It's typically served in a salt-rimmed glass with ice.

DECODING THE MENU

Ceviche—Citrus-marinated seafood appetizer from the Gulf shores of Veracruz. Often eaten with tortilla chips.

Chile relleno—Roasted poblano pepper that is stuffed with ingredients like ground meat or cheese, then dipped in egg batter, fried, and served in tomato sauce.

Clayuda—A Oaxacan dish similar to pizza. Large corn tortillas are baked until hard, then topped with ingredients like refried beans, cheese, and salsa.

Fish taco—A specialty in Southern California, the fish taco is a soft corn tortilla stuffed with grilled or fried white fish (mahimahi, tilapia, or wahoo), pico de gallo, *crema*, and shredded cabbage.

Gordita—"Little fat one" in Spanish, this dish is like a taco, but the cornmeal shell is thicker, similar to pita bread.

Mole—A complex, sweet sauce with Aztec roots made from more than 20 ingredients, including chilis, cinnamon, cumin, anise, black pepper, sesame seeds, and Mexican chocolate. There are many types of mole using various chilis and ingredient combinations, but the most common is *mole poblano* from the Puebla region.

Quesadilla—A snack made from a fresh tortilla that is folded over and stuffed with simple fillings like cheese, then toasted on a griddle. Elevated versions

of the quesadilla may be stuffed with sautéed *flor de calabaza* (squash blossoms) or *huitlacoche* (corn mushrooms).

Salsa—A class of cooked or raw sauces made from chilis, tomatoes, and other ingredients. Popular salsas include *pico de gallo*, a fresh sauce made from chopped tomatoes, onions, chilis, cilantro, and lime; *salsa verde*, made with tomatillos instead of tomatoes; and *salsa roja*, a cooked sauce made with chilis, tomatoes, onion, garlic, and cilantro.

Sopes—A small, fried corn cake topped with ingredients like refried beans, shredded chicken, and salsa.

Taco—In Southern California, as in Mexico, tacos are made from soft, palm-sized corn tortillas folded over and filled with meat, chopped onion, cilantro, and salsa. Common taco fillings include *al pastor* (spiced pork), *barbacoa* (braised beef), *carnitas* (roasted pork), *cecina* (chili-coated pork), *carne asada* (roasted, chopped beef), *chorizo* (spicy sausage), *lengua* (beef tongue), *sesos* (cow brain), and *tasajo* (spiced, grilled beef).

Tamales—Sweet or savory corn cakes that are steamed, and may be filled with cheese, roasted chilis, shredded meat, or other fillings.

Torta—A Mexican sandwich served on a crusty sandwich roll. Fillings often include meat, refried beans, and cheese.

Updated by Sarah Amandalore, Jim Arnold, Cindy Arora, Michele Bigley, Alene Dawson, Dianne de Guzman, and Clarissa Wei

Los Angeles is as much a fantasy as it is a physical city. A mecca for face-lifts, film noir, shopping starlets, beach bodies, and mind-numbing traffic, it is a true urban mash-up, equal parts glamour and grit.

Yes, you'll encounter traffic-clogged freeways, but there are also palm tree–lined, walkable pockets like Venice's Abbot Kinney. You'll drive past Beverly Hills mansions and spy palaces perched atop hills, but you'll also see the roots of midcentury modern architecture in Silver Lake. You'll soak up the sun in Santa Monica and then find yourself barhopping in the city's revitalized Downtown while chomping on scrumptious fish tacos along the way.

You might think that you'll have to spend most of your visit in a car, but that's not the case. In fact, getting out of your car is the only way to really get to know the various entertainment-industry-centered financial, beachfront, wealthy, and fringe neighborhoods and mini-cities that make up the vast L.A. area. But remember, no single locale—whether it be Malibu, Downtown, Beverly Hills, or Burbank—fully embodies Los Angeles. It's in the mix that you'll discover the city's character.

PLANNING

WHEN TO GO
Almost any time of the year is the right time to go to Los Angeles; the climate is mild and pleasant year-round. Winter brings crisp, sunny, unusually smogless days from about November to May (expect brief rains from December to April). Los Angeles summers, which are virtually rainless, can lead to air-quality alerts. Prices skyrocket and reservations are a must when tourism peaks from July through early October.

GETTING HERE AND AROUND
AIR TRAVEL
It's generally easier to navigate the secondary airports than to get through sprawling LAX, the city's major gateway. Bob Hope Airport in Burbank is closest to Downtown, and domestic flights to it can be cheaper than those to LAX—it's definitely worth checking out. From Long Beach Airport it's equally convenient to go north to central Los

Angeles or south to Orange County. Flights to Orange County's John Wayne Airport are often more expensive than those to the other secondary airports. Parking at the smaller airports is cheaper than at LAX.

At LAX, SuperShuttle allows walk-on shuttle passengers without prior reservations. FlyAway buses travel between LAX and Van Nuys, Westwood, La Brea, and Union Station in Downtown.

Airports Bob Hope Airport *(BUR).* ☎ *818/840–8840* ⊕ *www.bobhopeairport. com.* **John Wayne Airport** *(SNA).* ✉ *18601 Airport Way* ☎ *949/252–5006* ⊕ *www.ocair.com.* **LA/Ontario International Airport** *(ONT).* ☎ *909/937–2700* ⊕ *www.lawa.org/welcomeont.aspx.***Long Beach Airport** *(LGB).* ✉ *4100 Donald Douglas Dr.* ☎ *562/570–2600* ⊕ *www.lgb.org.* **Los Angeles International Airport** *(LAX).* ☎ *310/646–5252* ⊕ *www.lawa.org.*

Shuttles FlyAway ☎ *866/435–9529* ⊕ *www.lawa.org.* **SuperShuttle** ☎ *323/775–6600, 310/782–6600, 800/258–3826* ⊕ *www.supershuttle.com.*

BUS TRAVEL

Inadequate public transportation has plagued L.A. for decades. That said, many local trips can be made, with time and patience, by buses run by the Los Angeles County Metropolitan Transit Authority. In certain cases—visiting the Getty Center, for instance, or Universal Studios—buses may be your best option. There's a special Dodger Stadium Express that shuttles passengers between Union Station and the world-famous ballpark for home games. It's free if you have a ticket in hand, and saves you parking-related stress.

Metro Buses cost $1.50, plus 35¢ for each transfer to another bus or to the subway. A one-day pass costs $5, and a weekly pass is $20 for unlimited travel on all buses and trains. Passes are valid from Sunday through Saturday. For the fastest service, look for the red-and-white Metro Rapid buses; these stop less frequently and are able to extend green lights. There are 25 Metro Rapid routes, including along Wilshire and Vermont boulevards.

Other bus services make it possible to explore the entire metropolitan area. DASH minibuses cover six different circular routes in Hollywood, Mid-Wilshire, and Downtown. You pay 50¢ every time you get on. The Santa Monica Municipal Bus Line, also known as the Big Blue Bus, is a pleasant and inexpensive way to move around the Westside. Trips cost $1, and transfers are free. An express bus to and from Downtown L.A., run by Culver CityBus, costs $1.

Bus Information Culver CityBus ☎ *310/253–6510* ⊕ *www.culvercity.org.* **DASH** ☎ *310/808–2273* ⊕ *www.ladottransit.com/dash.* **Los Angeles County Metropolitan Transit Authority** ☎ *323/466–3876* ⊕ *www.metro.net.* **Santa Monica Municipal Bus Line** ☎ *310/451–5444* ⊕ *www.bigbluebus.com.*

CAR TRAVEL

If you're used to driving in a congested urban area, you shouldn't have too much trouble navigating the streets of Los Angeles. If not, L.A. can be unnerving. Nevertheless, the city evolved with drivers in mind. Streets are wide and parking garages abound, so it's more car-friendly than many older big cities.

Remember that most freeways are known by a name and a number; for example, the San Diego Freeway is Interstate 405, the Hollywood Freeway is U.S. 101, the Ventura Freeway is a different stretch of U.S. 101, the Santa Monica Freeway is Interstate 10, and the Harbor Freeway is Interstate 110. It helps, too, to know which direction you're traveling; say, west toward Santa Monica or east toward Downtown Los Angeles. Distance in miles doesn't mean much, depending on the time of day you're traveling: the short 10-mile drive between the San Fernando Valley and Downtown Los Angeles might take an hour to travel during rush hour but only 20 minutes at other times.

There are plenty of identical or similarly named streets in L.A. (Beverly Boulevard and Beverly Drive, for example), so be as specific as you can when asking directions. Expect sudden changes in addresses as streets pass through neighborhoods, then incorporated cities, then back into neighborhoods. This can be most bewildering on Robertson Boulevard, an otherwise useful north–south artery that, by crossing through L.A., West Hollywood, and Beverly Hills, dips in and out of several such numbering shifts in a matter of miles.

Information California Highway Patrol ☎ *800/427-7623 for road conditions.*

Emergency Services Metro Freeway Service Patrol ☎ *213/922-2957 general information, 323/982-4900 for breakdowns* ⊕ *www.mta.net.*

METRO RAIL TRAVEL

Metro Rail covers only a small part of L.A.'s vast expanse, but it's convenient, frequent, and inexpensive. Most popular with visitors is the underground Red Line, which runs from Downtown's Union Station through Mid-Wilshire, Hollywood, and Universal City on its way to North Hollywood, stopping at the most popular tourist destinations along the way.

The light-rail Green Line stretches from Redondo Beach to Norwalk, while the partially underground Blue Line travels from Downtown to the South Bay. The monorail-like Gold Line extends from Union Station to Pasadena and Sierra Madre. The Orange Line, a 14-mile bus corridor, connects the North Hollywood subway station with the western San Fernando Valley.

Most recently unveiled was the Expo Line, which connects Downtown to Culver City. When completed, it will reach nearly to the Pacific Ocean.

There's daily service from about 4:30 am to 12:30 am, with departures every 5 to 15 minutes. On weekends trains run until 2 am. Buy tickets from station vending machines; fares are $1.50, or $5 for an all-day pass.

Metro Rail Information Los Angeles County Metropolitan Transit Authority (LACMTA) ☎ *323/466-3876* ⊕ *www.metro.net.*

TAXI AND LIMOUSINE TRAVEL

Instead of trying to hail a taxi on the street, phone one of the many taxi companies. The metered rate is $2.70 per mile, plus a $2.85 perfare charge. Taxi rides from LAX have an additional $4 surcharge. Be aware that distances are greater than they might appear on the map so fares add up quickly.

On the other end of the price spectrum, limousines come equipped with everything from full bars to nightclub-style sound-and-light systems. Most charge by the hour, with a three-hour minimum.

Limo Companies ABC Limo ☏ *818/637-2277* ⊕ *www.abclimola.com.* **American Executive** ☏ *800/927-2020* ⊕ *www.americanexecutiveairportlimo.com.* **Dav El Chauffeured Transportation Network** ☏ *800/922-0343* ⊕ *www.davel. com.* **First Class Limousine Service** ☏ *800/400-9771* ⊕ *www.first-classlimo. com.* **ITS** ☏ *800/487-4255* ⊕ *www.itslimo.com.*

Taxi Companies Beverly Hills Cab Co. ☏ *800/398-5221* ⊕ *www. beverlyhillscabco.com.* **Checker Cab** ☏ *800/300-5007* ⊕ *www.ineedtaxi.com.* **United Independent Taxi** ☏ *800/822-8294* ⊕ *www.unitedtaxi.com.* **Yellow Cab Los Angeles** ☏ *800/200-1085, 877/733-3305* ⊕ *www.layellowcab.com.* **Independent Cab Co.** ☏ *800/521-8294* ⊕ *www.taxi4u.com.*

TRAIN TRAVEL

Downtown's Union Station is one of the great American railroad terminals. The interior includes comfortable seating, a restaurant, and several snack bars. As the city's rail hub, it's the place to catch an Amtrak or Metrolink commuter train. Among Amtrak's Southern California routes are 22 daily trips to San Diego and five to Santa Barbara. Amtrak's luxury *Coast Starlight* travels along the spectacular coastline from Seattle to Los Angeles in just a day and a half (though it's often a little late). The *Sunset Limited* arrives from New Orleans, and the *Southwest Chief* comes from Chicago.

Information Amtrak ☏ *800/872-7245* ⊕ *www.amtrak.com.* **Metrolink** ☏ *800/371-5465* ⊕ *www.metrolinktrains.com.* **Union Station** ✉ *800 N. Alameda St.* ☏ *213/683-6979* ⊕ *www.amtrak.com.*

VISITOR INFORMATION

Discover Los Angeles publishes an annually updated general information packet with suggestions for entertainment, lodging, and dining, as well as a list of special events. There are two visitor information centers, both accessible to Metro stops: the Hollywood & Highland entertainment complex and Union Station.

Contacts Beverly Hills Conference and Visitors Bureau ☏ *310/248-1000, 800/345-2210* ⊕ *www.lovebeverlyhills.com.* **Discover Los Angeles** ☏ *213/624-7300, 800/228-2452* ⊕ *www.discoverlosangeles.com.* **Hollywood Chamber of Commerce** ☏ *323/469-8311* ⊕ *www.hollywoodchamber.net.* **Long Beach Area Convention and Visitors Bureau** ☏ *562/436-3645* ⊕ *www. visitlongbeach.com.* **Pasadena Convention and Visitors Bureau** ☏ *626/795-9311* ⊕ *www.pasadenacal.com.* **Santa Monica Convention & Visitors Bureau** ☏ *310/393-7593, 800/544-5319* ⊕ *www.santamonica.com.* **Visit California** ☏ *916/444-4429, 800/862-2543* ⊕ *www.visitcalifornia.com.* **Visit West Hollywood** ☏ *310/289-2525, 800/368-6020* ⊕ *www.visitwesthollywood.com.*

4

EXPLORING LOS ANGELES

Star-struck . . . excessive . . . smoggy . . . superficial. There's a modicum of truth to each of the adjectives regularly applied to L.A. But Angelenos—and most objective visitors—dismiss their prevalence as signs of envy from people who hail from places less blessed with fun and sun.

Pop culture, for instance, *does* permeate life in LaLaLand: A massive economy employing millions of Southern Californians is built around it. Nevertheless, this city also boasts highbrow appeal, having amassed an impressive array of world-class museums and arts venues. America's second-largest city has more depth than paparazzi shutters can ever capture.

DOWNTOWN

If there's one thing Angelenos love, it's a makeover, and city planners have put the wheels in motion for a dramatic revitalization. Downtown is both glamorous and gritty and is an example of Los Angeles's complexity as a whole. There's a dizzying variety of experiences not to be missed here if you're curious about the artistic, historic, ethnic, or sports-loving sides of L.A.

Downtown Los Angeles isn't just one neighborhood: it's a cluster of pedestrian-friendly enclaves where you can sample an eclectic mix of flavors, wander through world-class museums, and enjoy great live performances or sports events.

TOP ATTRACTIONS

FAMILY **California Science Center.** You're bound to see excited kids running up to the dozens of interactive exhibits here that illustrate the relevance of science to everyday life. Clustered in different "worlds," this center keeps them busy for hours. They can design their own building and learn how to make it earthquake-proof, or watch Tess, the 50-foot animatronic star of the exhibit "Body Works," dramatically demonstrate how the body's organs work together. Air and Space Exhibits show what it takes to go to outer space with Gemini 11, a real capsule flown into space by Pete Conrad and Dick Gordon in 1966. The museum is also home to NASA's Space Shuttle Endeavor. ■TIP➜ **A timed ticket is needed to visit the massive spacecraft.** An IMAX theater shows large-format releases. ⊠ *700 Exposition Park Dr., Exposition Park* ☎ *213/744–7400, 323/724–3623* ⊕ *www.californiasciencecenter.org* ⊠ *Free; IMAX ticket prices vary* ⊗ *Daily 10–5.*

Fodor's Choice **Cathedral of Our Lady of the Angels.** A half-block away from the giant
★ rose-shaped steel grandeur of Frank Gehry's curvaceous Disney Concert Hall sits Cathedral of Our Lady of the Angels. It is both a spiritual draw as well as an architectural attraction. The exterior is all strict soaring angles and the building is as heavy, solid, and hunkering as the Gehry building is feminine and ethereal.

Controversy surrounded Spanish architect José Rafael Moneo's unconventional, costly, austere design for the seat of the Archdiocese of Los Angeles. But judging from the swarms of visitors and the standing-room-only holiday masses, the church has carved out a niche for itself in Downtown L.A.

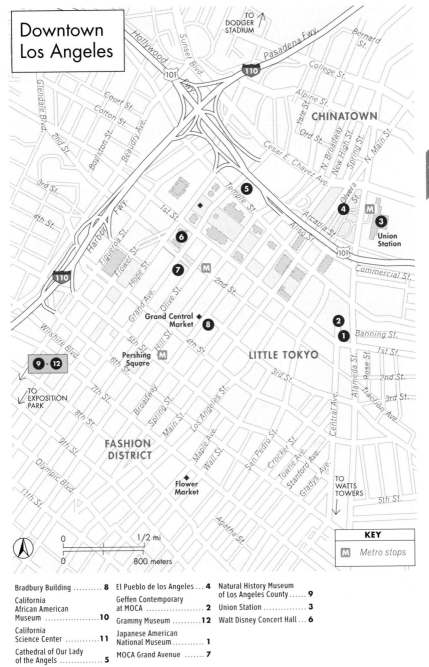

Downtown Los Angeles

Opened in 2002, the ocher-concrete cathedral looms up by the Hollywood Freeway. The plaza in front is relatively austere, glaringly bright on sunny days; a children's play garden with bronze animals helps relieve the stark space. Imposing bronze entry doors, designed by local artist Robert Graham, are decorated with multicultural icons and New World images of the Virgin Mary. The canyon-like interior of the church is spare, polished, and airy. By day, sunlight illuminates the sanctuary through translucent curtain walls of thin Spanish alabaster, a departure from the usual stained glass.

Artist John Nava used residents from his hometown of Ojai, California, as models for some of the 135 figures in the tapestries that line the nave walls. Make sure to go underground to wander the bright, maze-like white-marble corridors of the mausoleum.

Free, guided tours start at the entrance fountain at 1 pm on weekdays. Check for free concerts inside the cathedral on Wednesdays at 12:45 p.m. There's plenty of underground visitor parking; the vehicle entrance is on Hill Street. ■ TIP➔ **The café in the plaza has become one of Downtown's favorite lunch spots. You can pick up a fresh, reasonably priced meal to eat at one of the outdoor tables.** ⊠ *555 W. Temple St., Downtown* ☎ *213/680–5200* ⊕ *www.olacathedral.org* ▨ *Free, parking $4 every 15 min, $18 maximum* ☉ *Weekdays 6–6, Sat. 9–6, Sun. 7–6.*

El Pueblo de Los Angeles. The oldest section of the city, known as El Pueblo de Los Angeles, represents the rich Mexican heritage of L.A. It had a close shave with disintegration in the early 20th century, until the socialite Christine Sterling walked through in 1926. Jolted by the historic area's decay, Sterling fought to preserve key buildings and led the transformation of Olvera Street into a Mexican-American marketplace. Today this character remains; vendors sell puppets, leather goods, sandals, and woolen shawls from stalls that line the center of the narrow street. You can find everything from donkey-shape salt and pepper shakers to gorgeous glassware and pottery.

At the beginning of Olvera Street is the Plaza, a wonderful Mexican-style park with plenty of benches and walkways shaded by a huge Moreton Bay fig tree. On weekends, mariachi bands and folkloric dance groups perform. Not to be missed is one of the city's top sites—Cathedral of Our Lady of the Angels, designed by architect José Rafael Moneo.

Two annual events particularly worth seeing: the Blessing of the Animals and Las Posadas. On the Saturday before Easter, Angelenos bring their pets (not just dogs and cats, but horses, pigs, cows, birds, hamsters) to be blessed by a priest. For Las Posadas (every night between December 16 and 24), merchants and visitors parade up and down the street, led by children dressed as angels, to commemorate Mary and Joseph's search for shelter on Christmas Eve. For information, stop by the Olvera Street Visitors Center at 622 N. Main Street, a Victorian built in 1887 as a hotel and boardinghouse. The center is open weekdays and weekends 9 to 4. Free hour-long walking tours leave here at 10, 11, and noon Tuesday to Saturday. ⊠ *125 Paseo De La Plaza, Downtown* ☎ *213/628–1274* ⊕ *elpueblo.lacity.org.*

Grammy Museum. For a unique experience, head to the wildly entertaining interactive Grammy Museum—a space that brings the music industry's history to life. The museum, which has 30,000 square feet of space, has four floors of films and interactive exhibits on performers ranging from pop stars to opera divas. ⊠ *800 W. Olympic Blvd., Downtown* ☎ *213/765–6800* ⊕ *www.grammymuseum.org* ⊠ *$12.95* ⊙ *Weekdays 11:30–7:30, weekends 10–7:30.*

Geffen Contemporary at MOCA. A Frank Gehry creation, the Geffen Contemporary is one of the architect's boldest pieces. The space used to be a police car warehouse in Little Tokyo. This location, the largest of the three MOCA branches, boasts more than 40,000 square feet of exhibition space and features enterprising pieces that are typically larger in size and more recent. ⊠ *152 N. Central Ave., Downtown* ☎ *213/626–6222* ⊕ *www.moca.org/museum/moca_geffen.php* ⊠ *$12* ⊙ *Mon. and Fri. 11–5, Thurs. 11–8, weekends 11–6.*

MOCA Grand Avenue. The main branch of the Museum of Contemporary Art Grand Avenue, MOCA Grand Avenue features underground galleries and elegant exhibitions. With thousands of pieces dating back to 1940, the galleries are inundated with works by groundbreakers like Jean-Michel Basquiat and Cindy Sherman. Take advantage of the free audio tour. ⊠ *250 S. Grand Ave., Downtown* ☎ *213/626-6222* ⊕ *www. moca.org/museum/moca_grandave.php* ⊠ *$12* ⊙ *Mon. and Fri. 11–5, Thurs. 11–8, weekends 11–6.*

Fodor'sChoice ★ **Walt Disney Concert Hall.** One of the architectural wonders of Los Angeles, the 2,265-seat Walt Disney Concert Hall is a sculptural monument of gleaming, curved steel designed by master architect Frank Gehry. It's part of a complex that includes a public park, gardens, and shops, as well as two outdoor amphitheaters. This is the home of Los Angeles Master Chorale as well as Los Angeles Philharmonic, under the baton of Music Director Gustavo Dudamel, an international celebrity in his own right. Audio tours and guided tours are available. The complimentary walking tours, which start at noon, take an hour and begin in the lobby. ⊠ *111 S. Grand Ave., Downtown* ☎ *323/850–2000* ⊕ *www.laphil.org.*

WORTH NOTING

Bradbury Building. Stunning wrought-iron railing, blond-wood and brick interior, ornate moldings, pink marble staircases, Victorian-style skylighted atrium that rises almost 50 feet, and a birdcage elevator: it's easy to see why the Bradbury leaves visitors awestruck.

Designed in 1893 by a novice architect who drew his inspiration from a science-fiction story and a conversation with his dead brother via a Ouija board, the office building was originally the site of turn-of-the-20th-century sweatshops, but now houses a variety of businesses that try to keep normal working conditions despite the barrage of daily tourist visits and filmmakers. *Blade Runner, Chinatown,* and *Wolf* were filmed here.

Frank Gehry's Walt Disney Concert Hall was an instant L.A. icon.

For that reason, visits (and photo taking) are limited to the lobby and the first-floor landing. The building is open daily 9–5 for a peek, as long as you don't wander beyond visitor-approved areas. ✉ *304 S. Broadway, southeast corner Broadway and 3rd St., Downtown* ☎ *213/626–1893.*

California African American Museum. Works by 20th-century African-American artists and contemporary art of the African Diasporas are the backbone of this museum's permanent collection. Its exhibits document the African-American experience from Emancipation and Reconstruction through the 20th century, especially as expressed by artists in California and elsewhere in the West. ✉ *600 Exposition Park, Exposition Park* ☎ *213/744–7432* ⊕ *www.caamuseum.org* ✉ *Free, parking $10* ☉ *Tues.–Sat. 10–5, Sun. 11–5.*

Japanese American National Museum. What was it like to grow up on a sugar plantation in Hawaii? How difficult was life for Japanese-Americans interned in concentration camps during World War II? These questions are addressed by changing exhibits at this museum in Little Tokyo. Insightful volunteer docents are on hand to share their own stories and experiences. The museum occupies an 85,000-square-foot adjacent pavilion as well as its original site in a renovated 1925 Buddhist temple. ✉ *100 North Central Ave., off E. 1st St., next to Geffen Contemporary, Downtown* ☎ *213/625–0414* ⊕ *www.janm.org* ✉ *$9, free Thurs. 5–8 and 3rd Thurs. of month* ☉ *Tues.–Wed., and Fri.–Sun. 11–5; Thurs. noon–8.*

FAMILY **Natural History Museum of Los Angeles County.** This 1913-built Beaux-Arts museum has the same quaint feel of many natural history museums, with enclosed dioramas of animals in their natural habitats. But it mixes it up with interactive displays such as a seasonal Butterfly Pavilion in a separate small building in front of the museum; the Discovery Center, where kids can touch real animal pelts; the Insect Zoo; and the Dino Lab, where you can watch actual paleontologists work on dinosaur fossils. In addition, there are exhibits typifying various cultural groups, including pre-Columbian artifacts and a display of crafts from the South Pacific, as well as marine-life exhibits. Dinosaur Hall features more than 300 fossils, 20 full-body specimens, manual and digital interactivity, and large-format video, as well as a *T. rex* series that includes adult, juvenile, and baby specimens. And at the time of this writing, a new gardens complex was set to debut. ⊠ *900 Exposition Blvd., Exposition Park* ☎ *213/763–3466* ⊕ *www.nhm. org* ⊠ *$12, free 1st Tues. of month except July and Aug.* ☉ *Daily 9:30–5.*

Union Station. Even if you don't plan on going anywhere, head to Union Station to soak up the ambience of one of the country's last great rail stations. Envisioned by John and Donald Parkinson, the architects who also designed the grand City Hall, the 1939 masterpiece combines Spanish colonial revival and art deco elements that have retained their classic warmth and quality. The waiting hall's commanding scale and enormous chandeliers have provided the setting for countless films, TV shows, and music videos. ⊠ *800 N. Alameda St., Downtown.*

HOLLYWOOD AND THE STUDIOS

The Tinseltown mythology of Los Angeles was born in Hollywood. Daytime attractions can be found on foot around the home of the Academy Awards at the Dolby Theatre, part of the Hollywood & Highland entertainment complex. The adjacent TCL Chinese Theatre delivers silver screen magic with its cinematic facade and ornate interiors from a bygone era. Walk the renowned Hollywood Walk of Stars to find your favorite celebrities' hand- and footprints. In summer, visit the crown jewel of Hollywood, the Hollywood Bowl, which features shows by the Los Angeles Philharmonic.

To the north there's Studio City, a thriving strip at the base of the Hollywood Hills that's home to many smaller film companies; Universal City, where you'll find Universal Studios Hollywood; and bustling Burbank, home of several of the major studios. Los Feliz, to the east, where you'll find Griffith Park and the hip and trendy Vermont Avenue area. Beyond that you'll find Silver Lake and Echo Park.

TOP ATTRACTIONS

Dolby Theatre. Formerly the Kodak Theatre, the Dolby's interior design was inspired by European opera houses, but underneath all the trimmings, the space has one of the finest technical systems in the world. The half-hour tour of this theater that hosts the Academy Awards is a worthwhile expense for movie buffs who just can't get enough insider information. Tour guides share plenty of behind-the-scenes tidbits about Oscar ceremonies as they take you through the theater. You'll get to step into the VIP lounge where celebrities mingle on the big night and get a bird's-eye view from the balcony seating. ■ TIP→ **If you have the Hollywood CityPass, the tour is included.** ⊠ *6801 Hollywood Blvd., Hollywood* ☎ *323/308–6300* ⊕ *www.dolbytheatre.com* ⊠ *Tours $17* ☉ *Daily 10:30–4.*

Griffith Observatory. High on a hillside overlooking the city, the Griffith Observatory is one of the most celebrated icons of Los Angeles. And now, its interior is as impressive as its exterior after a massive expansion and cosmic makeover. Highlights of the building include the Foucault's pendulum hanging in the main lobby, the planet exhibitions on the lower level, and the playful wall display of galaxy-themed jewelry along the twisty indoor ramp.

In true L.A. style, the Leonard Nimoy Event Horizon Theater presents guest speakers and shows on current space-related topics and discoveries. The planetarium now features a new dome, laser digital projection system, theatrical lighting, and a stellar sound system. Shows are $7.

Grab a meal at the Café at the End of the Universe, which serves up dishes created by celebrity chef Wolfgang Puck. For a fantastic view, come at sunset to watch the sky turn fiery shades of red with the city's skyline silhouetted. ⊠ *2800 E. Observatory Rd., Griffith Park* ☎ *213/473–0800* ⊕ *www.griffithobservatory.org* ☽ *Wed.–Fri. noon–10, Sat.–Sun. 10–10.*

Griffith Park. The country's largest municipal park, the 4,210-acre Griffith Park is a must for nature lovers. It's the perfect spot for quiet respite from the hustle and bustle of the surrounding urban areas. Bronson Canyon (where the Batcave from the classic *Batman* TV series is located) and Crystal Springs are favorite picnic spots. A variety of plants and animals native to Southern California can be found within the park's borders, including deer, coyotes, and even a reclusive mountain lion.

The park is named after Colonel Griffith J. Griffith, a mining tycoon who donated 3,000 acres to the city in 1896. As you might expect, the park has been used as a film and television location since the industry's early days. Here you'll find the Griffith Observatory, the Los Angeles Zoo, the Greek Theater, two golf courses, hiking and bridle trails, a swimming pool, a merry-go-round, and an outdoor train museum. ⊠ *4730 Crystal Springs Dr., Griffith Park* ☎ *323/913–4688* ⊕ *www.laparks.org/dos/ parks/griffithpk* ⊡ *Free; attractions inside park have separate admission fees* ☽ *Daily 5 am–10:30 pm. Mountain roads close at sunset.*

Fodor's Choice   **Hollywood Museum.** Lovers of Hollywood's glamorous past will be sing-
★   ing "Hooray for Hollywood" when they stop by this gem of cinema history. It's inside the Max Factor Building, purchased in 1928. Factor's famous makeup was made on the top floors and on the ground floor was a salon. After its renovation, this art deco landmark now holds more than 10,000 bits of film memorabilia.

The extensive exhibits inside include those dedicated to Marilyn Monroe and Bob Hope and to costumes and set props from such films as *Moulin Rouge, The Silence of the Lambs,* and *Planet of the Apes.* There's an impressive gallery of photos showing movie stars frolicking at such venues as the Brown Derby, Ciro's, the Trocadero, and the Mocambo.

Hallway walls are covered with the stunning autograph collection of ultimate fan Joe Ackerman; aspiring filmmakers will want to check out an exhibit of early film equipment. The museum's showpiece, however, is the Max Factor exhibit, where separate dressing rooms are dedicated to Factor's "color harmony": creating distinct looks for "brownettes"

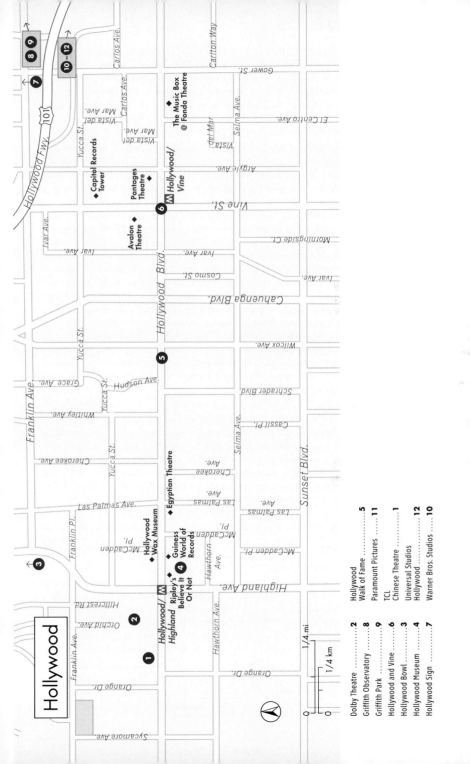

Hollywood

The Music Box @ Fonda Theatre

Capitol Records Tower

Pantages Theatre

Hollywood/Vine Ⓜ❻

Avalon Theatre

❺

Egyptian Theatre

Hollywood Wax Museum

Guiness World of Records ❹

Ripley's Believe It Or Not

Hollywood/Highland Ⓜ

❶ ❷ ❸

❼

❽ ❾
❿ – 12

Carlos Ave.
Carlos Ave.
Carlton Way
Carlton Way
Gower St.
Yucca St.
Vista del Mar Ave.
Vista del Mar Ave.
Selma Ave.
El Centro Ave.
Vista del Mar
Argyle Ave.
Vine St.
Ivar Ave.
Ivar Ave.
Ivar Ave.
Morningside Ct.
Cosmo St.
Cahuenga Blvd.
Hollywood Blvd.
Wilcox Ave.
Schrader Blvd.
Hudson Ave.
Yucca St.
Grace Ave.
Whitley Ave.
Franklin Ave.
Cherokee Ave.
Yucca St.
Cassil Pl.
Selma Ave.
Cherokee Ave.
Sunset Blvd.
Las Palmas Ave.
Cherokee Ave.
Las Palmas Ave.
Las Palmas Ave.
Franklin Pl.
McCadden Pl.
McCadden Pl.
McCadden Pl.
Hawthorn Ave.
Highland Ave.
Hillcrest Rd.
Orchid Ave.
Hawthorn Ave.
Franklin Ave.
Orange Dr.
Orange Dr.
Sycamore Ave.
Hollywood Fwy.
Hollywood Fwy. 101

1/4 mi
1/4 km
0

Dolby Theatre **2**
Griffith Observatory **8**
Griffith Park **9**
Hollywood and Vine **6**
Hollywood Bowl **3**
Hollywood Museum **4**
Hollywood Sign **7**

Hollywood
Walk of Fame **5**
Paramount Pictures **11**
TCL
Chinese Theatre **1**
Universal Studios **12**
Hollywood **12**
Warner Bros. Studios **10**

(Factor's term), redheads, and of course, bombshell blondes. You can practically smell the peroxide of Marilyn Monroe getting her trademark platinum look here, and see makeup cases owned by Lucille Ball, Lana Turner, Ginger Rogers, Bette Davis, Rita Hayworth, and others who made the makeup as popular as the starlets who wore it. ⊠ *1660 N. Highland Ave., Hollywood* ☎ *323/464–7776* ⊕ *www.thehollywoodmuseum.com* ⊠ *$15* ⊙ *Wed.–Sun. 10–5.*

Hollywood Walk of Fame. Along Hollywood Boulevard runs a trail of affirmations for entertainment-industry overachievers. On this mile-long stretch of sidewalk, inspired by the concrete handprints in front of Grauman's Chinese Theatre, names are embossed in brass, each at the center of a pink star embedded in dark-gray terrazzo. They're not all screen deities; many stars commemorate people who worked in a technical field. The first eight stars were unveiled in 1960 at the northwest corner of Highland Avenue and Hollywood Boulevard: Olive Borden, Ronald Colman, Louise Fazenda, Preston Foster, Burt Lancaster, Edward Sedgwick, Ernest Torrence, and Joanne Woodward (some of these names have stood the test of time better than others). Since then, more than 2,000 others have been immortalized, though that honor doesn't come cheap—upon selection by a special committee, the personality in question (or more likely his or her movie studio or record company) pays about $30,000 for the privilege. To aid you in spotting celebrities you're looking for, stars are identified by one of five icons: a motion-picture camera, a radio microphone, a television set, a record, or a theatrical mask. Contact the **Hollywood Chamber of Commerce** (⊠ *7018 Hollywood Blvd.* ☎ *323/469–8311*) for celebrity-star locations and information on future star installations. ⊕ *www.walkoffame.com.*

Fodor's Choice
★   **Paramount Pictures.** With a history dating to the early 1920s, this studio was home to some of Hollywood's most luminous stars, including Rudolph Valentino, Mae West, Mary Pickford, and Lucille Ball, who filmed episodes of *I Love Lucy* here. The lot still churns out memorable movies and TV shows, such as *Forrest Gump, Titanic,* and *Star Trek.* You can take a studio tour (reservations required; ages 12 and up) led by guides who walk and trolley you around the back lots. As well as gleaning some gossipy history (see the lawn where Lucy and Desi broke up), you'll spot the sets of TV and film shoots in progress. You can also be part of the audience for live TV tapings. Tickets are free; call for listings and times. ⊠ *5555 Melrose Ave., Hollywood* ☎ *323/956–1777* ⊕ *www.paramountstudiotour.com* ⊠ *$48* ⊙ *Tours daily by reservation only.*

TCL Chinese Theatre. A place that inspires the phrase "only in Hollywood," these stylized Chinese pagodas and temples have become a shrine to stardom. Although you have to buy a movie ticket to appreciate the interior trappings, the courtyard is open to the public. The main theater itself is worth visiting, if only to see a film in the same seats as hundreds of celebrities who have attended big premieres here.

And then, of course, outside in front are the oh-so-famous cement hand- and footprints. This tradition is said to have begun at the theater's opening in 1927, with the premiere of Cecil B. DeMille's *King of Kings,* when actress Norma Talmadge just happened to step into wet cement.

Now more than 160 celebrities have contributed imprints for posterity, including some oddball specimens, such as ones of Whoopi Goldberg's dreadlocks. ✉ *6925 Hollywood Blvd., Hollywood* ☎ *323/464–8111* ⊕ *www.tclchinesetheatres.com.*

FAMILY **Universal Studios Hollywood.** While most first-time Los Angeles visitors consider this to be a must-see stop, bear in mind there are many other attractions that define Hollywood that aren't a tourist trap with steep prices. ■ TIP→ **If you get here when the park opens, you'll likely save yourself from long waits in line.**

The first-timer favorite is the tram tour, during which you can experience the parting of the Red Sea; duck from spitting creatures in Jurassic Park; visit Dr. Seuss's "Whoville"; see the airplane wreckage of *War of the Worlds* and the still-creepy *Psycho* house; be attacked by the ravenous killer shark of *Jaws* fame. The trams have audiovisual monitors that play video clips of TV shows and movies shot on the sets you pass. ■ TIP→ **This tram ride is usually the best place to start, since it's on the lower level of the park, which gets really crowded in the afternoon.**

Many attractions are based on Universal films and TV shows, designed to give you a thrill in one form or another. Take your pick from the bone-rattling roller coaster Revenge of the Mummy, The Ride; or see Shrek 4-D, a 15-minute trailer of 3-D animation shown in an action simulation theater. Fear Factor Live and the House of Horrors are guaranteed to provide screams, while the Animal Actors show offers milder entertainment courtesy of some talented furry friends. The attraction based on *The Simpsons* animated series takes you on a journey like no other through their Springfield neighborhood in a ride that only the beloved, albeit cantankerous, Krusty the Klown could dream up. Look for the most recent thrill ride based on the popular *Transformers* movies.

Throughout the park you can wander through prop-style settings of a French village or travel back in time to the 1950s, as costumed characters mingle with guests and pose for photos. Aside from the park, City-Walk is a separate venue, with shops, restaurants, nightclubs, and movie theaters, including IMAX 3-D. ✉ *100 Universal City Plaza, Universal City* ☎ *818/622–3801* ⊕ *www.universalstudioshollywood.com* ✉ *$80, parking $15 ($10 after 3)* ☉ *Contact park for seasonal hrs.*

Warner Bros. Studios. This major studio center wins hands down for the most authentic behind-the-scenes look at how films and TV shows are made.

You start with a short film on Warner Bros. movies and TV shows, then hop into a tram for a ride through the sets and soundstages of such favorites as *Casablanca* and *Rebel Without A Cause.* You'll see the bungalows where icons such as Marlon Brando and Bette Davis spent time between shots, and the current production offices for Clint Eastwood and George Clooney. You might even spot a celeb or see a shoot in action—tours change from day to day depending on the productions taking place on the lot.

Reservations are required. Call at least one week in advance and ask about provisions for people with disabilities; children under 8 are not admitted. Tours are given at least every hour, more frequently from

May to September, and last 2 hours and 15 minutes. A five-hour deluxe tour, $250 including a VIP lunch, allows visitors to spend more time on the sets, with more ops for behind-the-scenes peeks and star spotting. ✉ *3400 W. Riverside Dr., Burbank* ☎ *877/492–8687* ⊕ *vipstudiotour. warnerbros.com* 🎫 *$52 for the VIP tour, $250 for the Deluxe tour* ⊙ *Mon.–Sat. 8:15–4, limited availability on Sun.*

WORTH NOTING

Hollywood and Vine. The mere mention of this intersection inspires images of a street corner bustling with movie stars, hopefuls, and moguls arriving on foot or in Duesenbergs and Rolls-Royces. In the old days this was the hub of the radio and movie industry: film stars like Gable and Garbo hustled in and out of their agents' office buildings (some now converted to luxury condos) at these fabled cross streets. Even the Red Line Metro station here keeps up the Hollywood theme, with a *Wizard of Oz*–style yellow brick road, vintage movie projectors, and old film reels on permanent display. Sights visible from this intersection include the Capitol Records Building, the Avalon Theater, the Pantages Theatre, and the W Hollywood Hotel. ✉ *Hollywood Ave. and Vine St.*

Hollywood Sign. With letters 50 feet tall, Hollywood's trademark sign can be spotted from miles away. The sign, which originally read "Hollywoodland," was erected on Mt. Lee in the Hollywood Hills in 1923 to promote a real-estate development. In 1949 the "land" portion of the sign was taken down. By 1973, the sign had earned landmark status, but since the letters were made of wood, its longevity came into question. A makeover project was launched and the letters were auctioned off (rocker Alice Cooper bought the "o" and singing cowboy Gene Autry sponsored an "l") to make way for a new sign made of sheet metal. Inevitably, the sign has drawn pranksters who have altered it over the years, albeit temporarily, to spell out "Yollyweed" (in the 1970s, to commemorate lenient marijuana laws), "go navy" (before a Rose Bowl game), and "Perotwood" (during the 1992 presidential election). A fence and surveillance equipment have since been installed to deter intruders. Use caution if driving up to the sign on residential streets since many cars speed around the blind corners. ⊕ *www.hollywoodsign.org.*

BEVERLY HILLS AND THE WESTSIDE

If you only have a day to see L.A., see Beverly Hills. Love it or hate it, it delivers wealth and excess on a dramatic, cinematic scale. West Hollywood is not a place to see things (like museums or movie studios) as much as it is a place to *do* things—like go to a nightclub, eat at a world-famous restaurant, or attend an art gallery opening.

The three-block stretch of Wilshire Boulevard known as Museum Row, east of Fairfax Avenue, features intriguing museums and a prehistoric tar pit to boot. Wilshire Boulevard itself is something of a cultural monument—it begins its grand 16-mile sweep to the sea in Downtown L.A.

For some privileged Angelenos, the city begins west of La Cienega Boulevard, where keeping up with the Joneses becomes an epic pursuit. Chic, attractive neighborhoods with coveted postal codes—Bel Air, Brentwood, Westwood, West Los Angeles, and Pacific Palisades—are

A mural depicting Hollywood's legends (John Wayne, Elvis Presley, and Marilyn Monroe) adorns a wall of West Hollywood's Stella Adler Academy on Highland Avenue.

home to power couples pushing power kids in power strollers. Still, the Westside is rich in culture—and not just entertainment-industry culture. It's home to the monumental Getty Center and the engrossing Museum of Tolerance.

TOP ATTRACTIONS

FAMILY

Fodor'sChoice

★

The Getty Center. With its curving walls and isolated hilltop perch, the Getty Center resembles a pristine fortified city of its own. You may have been lured up by the beautiful views of L.A. (on a clear day stretching all the way to the Pacific Ocean), but the architecture, uncommon gardens, and fascinating art collections will be more than enough to capture and hold your attention. When the sun is out, the complex's rough-cut travertine marble skin seems to soak up the light.

J. Paul Getty, the billionaire oil magnate and art collector, began collecting Greek and Roman antiquities and French decorative arts in the 1930s. He opened the J. Paul Getty Museum at his Malibu estate in 1954, and in the 1970s, he built a re-creation of an ancient Roman village to house his initial collection. When Getty died in 1976, the museum received an endowment of $700 million that grew to a reported $4.5 billion. The Malibu villa, reopened in 2006, is devoted to the antiquities. The Getty Center, designed by Richard Meier, opened in 1998 and pulled together the rest of the collections, along with the museum's affiliated research, conservation, and philanthropic institutes.

Getting to the center involves a bit of anticipatory lead-up. At the base of the hill, a pavilion disguises the underground parking structure. From there you either walk or take a smooth, computer-driven tram up the steep slope, checking out the Bel Air estates across the humming 405 freeway.

The five pavilions that house the museum surround a central courtyard and are bridged by walkways. From the courtyard, plazas, and walkways, you can survey the city from the San Gabriel Mountains to the ocean.

In a ravine separating the museum and the Getty Research Institute, conceptual artist Robert Irwin created the playful Central Garden in stark contrast to Meier's mathematical architectural geometry.

Inside the pavilions are the galleries for the permanent collections of European paintings, drawings, sculpture, illuminated manuscripts, and decorative arts, as well as American and European photographs. The Getty's collection of French furniture and decorative arts, especially from the early years of Louis XIV (1643–1715) to the end of the reign of Louis XVI (1774–92), is renowned for its quality and condition; you can see a pair of completely reconstructed salons. In the paintings galleries, a computerized system of louvered skylights allows natural light to filter in, creating a closer approximation of the conditions in which the artists painted. Notable among the paintings are Rembrandt's *The Abduction of Europa,* Van Gogh's *Irises,* Monet's *Wheatstack, Snow Effects,* and *Morning,* and James Ensor's *Christ's Entry into Brussels.*

If you want to start with a quick overview, pick up the brochure in the entrance hall that guides you to 15 highlights of the collection. There's also an instructive audio tour ($5) with commentaries by art historians. Art information rooms with multimedia computer stations contain more details about the collections. The Getty also presents lectures, films, concerts, and special programs for kids and families. The complex includes an upscale restaurant and downstairs cafeteria with panoramic window views, and two outdoor coffee bar cafés. ■ TIP→ On-site parking is subject to availability and can fill up by late afternoon on holidays and summer weekends, so try to come early in the day. You may also take public transportation (MTA Bus 761). ⊠ *1200 Getty Center Dr., Brentwood* ☎ *310/440–7300* ⊕ *www.getty.edu* ⊠ *Free, parking $15* ☉ *Tues.–Fri. 10–5:30, Sat. 10–9, Sun. 10–5:30.*

Fodor's Choice ★ **Los Angeles County Museum of Art (LACMA).** Without a doubt, LACMA is the focal point of the museum district that runs along Wilshire Boulevard. Chris Burden's *Urban Light* sculpture, composed of more than two hundred restored cast iron antique street lamps, elegantly illuminates the building's facade.

Inside, visitors will find one of the country's most comprehensive collections of more than 100,000 objects dating from ancient times to the present. Since opening in 1965, the museum has grown into a complex of several different buildings interconnected via walkways, stretching across a 20-acre campus.

Works from the museum's rotating permanent collection include Latin American artists such as Diego Rivera and Frida Kahlo, prominent Southern California artists, collections of Islamic and European art, paintings by Henri Matisse and Rene Magritte, as well as works by Paul Klee and Wassily Kandinsky. There's also a solid collection of art representing the ancient civilizations of Egypt, the Near East, Greece, and Rome, plus a vast costume and textiles collection dating back to the 16th century.

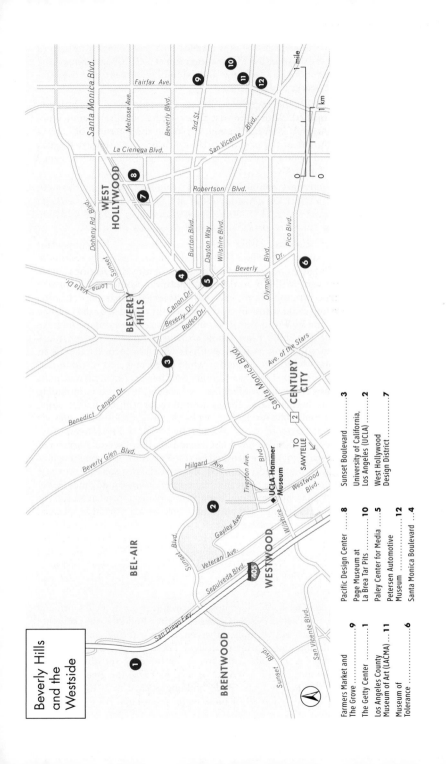

Beverly Hills
and the
Westside

SANTA MONICA BLVD.

Fairfax Ave.

Melrose Ave.

Beverly Blvd.

3rd St.

San Vicente Blvd.

La Cienega Blvd.

WEST
HOLLYWOOD

Robertson Blvd.

Doheny Rd. Blvd.

Sunset

Loma Vista Dr.

BEVERLY
HILLS

Burton Blvd.

Dayton Way

Wilshire Blvd.

Canon Dr.

Beverly Dr.

Rodeo Dr.

Benedict Canyon Dr.

Beverly Glen Blvd.

Beverly

Olympic Blvd.

Pico Blvd.

Dr.

CENTURY
CITY

Ave. of the Stars

Santa Monica Blvd.

Hilgard Ave.

Tiverton Ave.

UCLA Hammer
Museum

BEL-AIR

Gayley Ave.

Veteran Ave.

Sunset Blvd.

Wilshire

Westwood
Blvd.

WESTWOOD

TO
SAWTELLE

Sepulveda Blvd.

San Diego Fwy.

BRENTWOOD

Sunset

San Vicente Blvd.

1 mile

1 km

Farmers Market and
The Grove **9**

The Getty Center **1**

Los Angeles County
Museum of Art (LACMA) ... **11**

Museum of
Tolerance **6**

Pacific Design Center **8**

Page Museum at
La Brea Tar Pits **10**

Paley Center for Media **5**

Petersen Automotive
Museum **12**

Santa Monica Boulevard ...**4**

Sunset Boulevard.........**3**

University of California,
Los Angeles (UCLA) **2**

West Hollywood
Design District..............**7**

As part of an ambitious 10-year face-lift plan that is becoming a work of art on its own, entitled "Transformation: The LACMA Campaign," the museum is adding buildings and exhibition galleries, and redesigning public spaces and gardens.

In early 2008, the impressive Broad Contemporary Art Museum (BCAM) opened. With three vast floors, BCAM integrates contemporary art into LACMA's collection, exploring the interplay of current times with that of the past. In 2010, the Lynda and Stewart Resnick Exhibition Pavilion was added, a stunning, light-filled space designed by Renzo Piano.

■**TIP**→ Temporary exhibits sometimes require tickets purchased in advance, so check the calendar ahead of time. ✉ *5905 Wilshire Blvd., Miracle Mile* ☎ *323/857–6000* ⊕ *www.lacma.org* 💲 *$15* ⊗ *Mon., Tues., and Thurs. noon–8, Fri. noon–9, weekends 11–8.*

FAMILY **Museum of Tolerance.** Using interactive technology, this important museum (part of the Simon Wiesenthal Center) challenges visitors to confront bigotry and racism. One of the most affecting sections covers the Holocaust, with film footage of deportation scenes and simulated sets of concentration camps. Each visitor is issued a "passport" bearing the name of a child whose life was dramatically changed by the German Nazi rule and by World War II; as you go through the exhibit, you learn the fate of that child. Anne Frank artifacts are part of the museum's permanent collection as is Wiesenthal's Vienna office, set exactly as the famous "Nazi hunter" had it while performing his research that brought more than 1,000 war criminals to justice. Interactive exhibits include the "Millennium Machine," which engages visitors in finding solutions to human rights abuses around the world; Globalhate.com, which examines hate on the Internet by exposing problematic sites via touch-screen computer terminals; and the "Point of View Diner," a re-creation of a 1950s diner, red booths and all, that "serves" a menu of controversial topics on video jukeboxes. Renovations brought a new youth action floor and revamped 300-seat theater space. To ensure a visit to this popular museum, make reservations in advance (especially for Friday, Sunday, and holidays) and plan to spend at least three hours here. Testimony from Holocaust survivors is offered at specified times. Museum entry stops at least two hours before the actual closing time. Although every exhibit may not be appropriate for children, school tours regularly visit the museum. ✉ *9786 W. Pico Blvd., just south of Beverly Hills* ☎ *310/553–8403* ⊕ *www.museumoftolerance. com* 💲 *$15.50* ⊗ *Sun. 11–5 year-round; Mon.–Fri.10–5 Apr.–Oct. and 10–3 Nov.–Mar.*

Pacific Design Center. World-renowned architect Cesar Pelli's original vision for the Pacific Design Center was three buildings that together housed designer showrooms, office buildings, parking, and more—a virtual multibuilding shrine to design. These architecturally intriguing buildings were built years apart: the building sheathed in blue glass (known as the Blue Whale) opened in 1975; the green building opened in 1988. The final "Red" building opened in 2013, completing Pelli's grand vision all of these many years later. All together the

1.2 million-square-foot vast complex covers more than 14 acres, housing more than 120 design showrooms as well as 2,100 interior product lines; it's the largest interior design complex in the western United States. You'll also find restaurants such as Red Seven by Wolfgang Puck, the Silverscreen movie theater, and an outpost of the Museum of Contemporary Art. ⊠ *8687 Melrose Ave., West Hollywood* ☏ *310/657–0800* ⊕ *www.pacificdesigncenter.com* ⊙ *Weekdays 9–5.*

FAMILY **Page Museum at the La Brea Tar Pits.** Do your children have prehistoric animals on the brain? Show them where Ice Age fossils come from by taking them to the stickiest park in town. The area formed when deposits of oil rose to the earth's surface, collected in shallow pools, and coagulated into asphalt. In the early 20th century, geologists discovered that all that goo contained the largest collection of Pleistocene, or Ice Age, fossils ever found at one location: more than 600 species of birds, mammals, plants, reptiles, and insects. Roughly 100 tons of fossil bones have been removed in excavations during the last 100 years, making this one of the world's most famous fossil sites. You can see most of the pits through chain-link fences. (La Brea Tar Pits can be a little smelly, but your kids are sure to love it.)

Pit 91 and Project 23 are ongoing excavation projects; tours are available, and you can volunteer to help with the excavations in summer. There are several pits scattered around Hancock Park and the surrounding neighborhood; construction in the area has often had to accommodate them, and in nearby streets and along sidewalks, little bits of tar occasionally ooze up, unstoppable. The museum displays fossils from the tar pits and has a glass-walled laboratory that allows visitors a rare look at where paleontologists and volunteers work on specimens. ⊠ *5801 Wilshire Blvd., Miracle Mile* ☏ *323/857–6300* ⊕ *www.tarpits. org* 🎫 *$12* ⊙ *Daily 9:30–5.*

Santa Monica Boulevard. From La Cienega Boulevard in the east to Doheny in the west, Santa Monica Boulevard is the commercial core of West Hollywood's gay community, with restaurants and cafés, bars and clubs, bookstores and galleries, and other establishments catering largely to gays and lesbians. Twice a year—during June's L.A. Pride and on Halloween, in October, the boulevard becomes an open-air festival. ⊠ *Santa Monica Blvd., between La Cienega and Doheny* ⊕ *weho.org/.*

Sunset Boulevard. One of the most fabled avenues in the world, Sunset Boulevard began humbly enough in the 18th century as a route from El Pueblo de Los Angeles (today's Downtown L.A.) to the ranches in the west and then to the Pacific Ocean. Now as it winds its way across the L.A. basin to the ocean, it cuts through gritty urban neighborhoods and what used to be the working center of Hollywood's movie industry. In West Hollywood, it becomes the sexy and seductive Sunset Strip, then slips quietly into the tony environs of Beverly Hills and Bel Air, twisting and winding past gated estates. Continuing on past UCLA in Westwood, through Brentwood and Pacific Palisades, Sunset finally descends to the beach, the edge of the continent, and the setting sun.

WORTH NOTING

Paley Center for Media. Formerly the Museum of Television and Radio, this institution changed its name in 2007 with a look toward a future that encompasses all media in the ever-evolving world of entertainment and information. Reruns are taken to a curated level in this sleek stone-and-glass building, designed by Getty architect Richard Meier. A sister to the New York location, the Paley Center carries a duplicate of its collection: more than 100,000 programs spanning eight decades. Search for your favorite commercials and television shows on easy-to-use computers. A radio program listening room provides cozy seats supplied with headphones playing snippets of a variety of programming from a toast to Dean Martin to an interview with John Lennon. Frequent seminars with movers 'n' shakers from the film, television, and radio world are big draws, as well as screenings of documentaries and short films. Free parking is available in the lot off Santa Monica Boulevard. ⊠ *465 N. Beverly Dr., Beverly Hills* ☎ *310/786–1000* ⊕ *www.paleycenter.org* ⊘ *Wed.–Sun. noon–5.*

FAMILY **Petersen Automotive Museum.** You don't have to be a gearhead to appreciate this building full of antique and unusual cars. The Petersen is likely to be one of the coolest museums in town with its take on some of the most unusual creations on wheels and rotating exhibits of the icons who drove them. Lifelike dioramas and street scenes spread through the ground floor help to establish a local context for the history of the automobile. The second floor may include displays of Hollywood-celebrity and movie cars, "muscle" cars (like a 1969 Dodge Daytona 440 Magnum), alternative-powered cars, motorcycles, and a showcase of the Ferrari. You can also learn about the origins of our modern-day car-insurance system, as well as the history of L.A.'s formidable freeway network. A children's interactive Discovery Center illustrates the mechanics of the automobile and fun child-inspired creations; there is also a gift shop. ⊠ *6060 Wilshire Blvd., Miracle Mile* ☎ *323/930–2277* ⊕ *www.petersen.org* 🖃 *$10* ⊘ *Tues.–Sun. 10–6.*

University of California, Los Angeles (UCLA). With spectacular buildings such as a Romanesque library, the parklike campus of UCLA makes for a fine stroll through one of California's most prestigious universities. In the heart of the north campus, the **Franklin Murphy Sculpture Garden** contains more than 70 works by artists such as Henry Moore and Gaston Lachaise. The **Mildred E. Mathias Botanic Garden,** which contains some 5,000 species of plants from all over the world in a 7-acre outdoor garden, is in the southeast section of the campus and is accessible from Tiverton Avenue. West of the main-campus bookstore, the **J.D. Morgan Center and Athletic Hall of Fame** displays the sports memorabilia and trophies of the university's athletic departments and championship teams.

Campus maps and information are available daily at kiosks at major entrances, and free two-hour walking tours of the campus are given most weekdays at 10:15 and 2:15 and Saturday at 10:15. The main-entrance gate is on Westwood Boulevard. Campus parking costs $12 but there's also a lot at UCLA Parking Structure 4 off Sunset Boulevard that only charges you according to the time you stay—starting at as little as $1 for about 20 minutes. ✉ *Bordered by Le Conte, Hilgard, and Gayley Aves. and Sunset Blvd., Westwood* ☎ *310/825–8764* ⊕ *www.ucla.edu.*

West Hollywood Design District. More than 200 businesses—art galleries, antiques shops, fashion outlets (including Rag & Bone and Christian Louboutin), and interior design stores—are found in the West Hollywood Design District. There are also about 40 restaurants, including the famous paparazzi magnet, the Ivy. They are all clustered within walking distance of each other—a rare L.A. treat. ✉ *Melrose Ave. and Robertson and Beverly Blvds.* ☎ *310/289–2534* ⊕ *wehodesigndistrict.com.*

SANTA MONICA AND THE BEACHES

Hugging the Santa Monica Bay in an arch, the desirable communities of Malibu, Santa Monica, and Venice move from ultrarich, ultracasual Malibu to bohemian, borderline seedy Venice. What they have in common is cleaner air, mild temperatures, horrific traffic, and an emphasis on the beach-focused lifestyle that many people consider the hallmark of Southern California.

TOP ATTRACTIONS

Fodor'sChoice ★ **Getty Villa Malibu.** Feeding off the cultures of ancient Rome, Greece, and Etruria, the remodeled Getty Villa opened in 2006 with much fanfare—and some controversy concerning the acquisition and rightful ownership of some of the Italian artifacts on display. The antiquities are astounding, but on a first visit even they take a backseat to their environment. This megamansion sits on some of the most valuable coastal property in the world. Modeled after an Italian country home, the Villa dei Papiri in Herculaneum, the Getty Villa includes beautifully manicured gardens, reflecting pools, and statuary. The largest and most lovely garden, the Outer Peristyle, gives you glorious views over a rectangular reflecting pool and geometric hedges to the Pacific. The new structures blend thoughtfully into the rolling terrain and significantly improve the public spaces, such as the new outdoor amphitheater, gift store, café, and entry arcade. Talks and educational programs are offered at an indoor theater. ■ TIP→ **An advance timed entry ticket is required for admission. Tickets are free and may be ordered from the website or by phone.** ✉ *17985 Pacific Coast Hwy., Pacific Palisades* ☎ *310/440–7300* ⊕ *www.getty.edu* ☜ *Free, tickets required. Parking $15, cash or credit card* ☉ *Wed.–Mon. 10–5.*

Fodor'sChoice ★ **Robert H. Meyer Memorial State Beach.** Part of Malibu's most beautiful coastal area, this beach is made up of three minibeaches: El Pescador, La Piedra, and El Matador—all with the same spectacular view. Scramble down the steps to the rocky coves via steep, steep stairways; all food and water needs to be toted in, as there are no services. Portable toilets at the trailhead are the only restrooms. "El Mat" has a series of caves, Piedra some nifty rock formations, and Pescador a secluded feel; but they're all picturesque and fairly private. **Amenities:** parking (fee); toilets. **Best for:** solitude; sunset; surfing; walking. ⚠ **One warning: watch the incoming tide and don't get trapped between those otherwise scenic boulders.** ✉ *32350, 32700, and 32900 PCH, Malibu* ☎ *818/880–0363* ⊕ *www. parks.ca.gov* ☜ *Parking $8.*

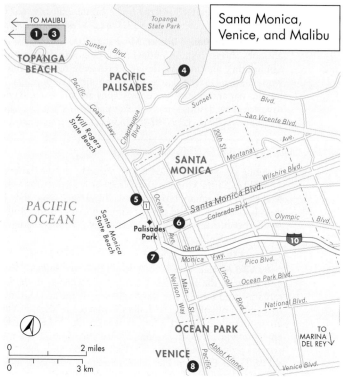

Santa Monica,
Venice, and Malibu

Third Street Promenade. Stretch your legs along this pedestrians-only three-block stretch of 3rd Street, just a whiff away from the Pacific, lined with jacaranda trees, ivy-topiary dinosaur fountains, strings of lights, and branches of nearly every major U.S. retail chain. Outdoor cafés, street vendors, movie theaters, and a rich nightlife make this a main gathering spot for locals, visitors, as well as street musicians and performance artists. Plan a night just to take it all in or take an afternoon for a long people-watching stroll. There's plenty of parking in city structures on the streets flanking the promenade. **Santa Monica Place** reopened in 2010 at the south end of the promenade as a sleek outdoor mall and foodie haven. Its three stories are home to Bloomingdale's, Burberry, Coach, and other upscale retailers. Don't miss the ocean views from the rooftop food court. ⊠ *Third St., between Colorado and Wilshire Blvds., Santa Monica* ⊕ *www. thirdstreetpromenade.com.*

Venice Beach Boardwalk. The surf and sand of Venice are fine, but the main attraction here is the boardwalk scene, which is a cosmos all its own. Go on weekend afternoons for the best people-watching experience. There are also swimming, fishing, surfing, skateboarding, basketball (it's the site of some of L.A.'s most hotly contested pickup games), racquetball, handball, and shuffleboard. You can rent a bike or some in-line skates and hit the Strand bike path. ✉ *1800 Ocean Front Walk, west of Pacific Ave., Venice* ☎ *310/392–4687* ⊕ *www. westland.net/venice.*

Will Rogers State Historic Park and Museum. The humorist, actor, and rambling cowboy, Will Rogers lived on this site in the 1920s and 1930s. His ranch house, a folksy blend of Navajo rugs and mission-style furniture, has become a museum featuring Rogers' memorabilia. A short film presented in the visitor center highlights Rogers' roping technique and homey words of wisdom. Open for docent-led tours, the ranch house features Rogers' stuffed practice calf and the high ceiling he raised so he could practice his famed roping style indoors.

Rogers was a polo enthusiast, and in the 1930s, his front-yard polo field attracted such friends as Douglas Fairbanks Sr. for weekend games. Today, the park's broad lawns are excellent for picnicking, and there are miles of eucalyptus-lined trails for hiking. Free weekend games are scheduled April through October, weather permitting.

Also part of the park is **Inspiration Point Trail.** Who knows how many of Will Rogers' famed witticisms came to him while he and his wife hiked or rode horses along this trail from their ranch. The point is on a detour off the lovely 2-mile loop, which you pick up right by the riding stables beyond the parking lot ($12 per car). On a clear (or even just semiclear) day, the panorama is one of L.A.'s widest and most "wow" inducing, from the peaks of the San Gabriel Mountains in the distant east to the Oz-like cluster of Downtown L.A. skyscrapers to Catalina Island looming off the coast to the southwest. If you're looking for a longer trip, the top of the loop meets up with the 65-mile Backbone Trail, which connects to Topanga State Park.

A new visitor center with displays of the park's history, and a gift shop with books and DVDs on Rogers' life recently opened. ✉ *1501 Will Rogers State Park Rd., Pacific Palisades* ☎ *310/454–8212* ✉ *Free; parking $12* ☽ *Parking daily 8–dusk, house tours Thurs. and Fri. hourly 11–3, weekends, hourly 10–4.*

WORTH NOTING

Malibu Lagoon State Beach. Bird-watchers, take note: in this 5-acre marshy area near Malibu Beach Inn you can spot egrets, blue herons, avocets, and gulls. (You need to stay on the boardwalks so as not to disturb their habitats.) The path leads out to a rocky stretch of Surfrider Beach, and makes for a pleasant stroll. The sand is soft, clean, and white, and you're also likely to spot a variety of marine life. Look for the signs to help identify these sometimes exotic-looking creatures. The lagoon is particularly enjoyable in the early morning and at sunset—and even more so now, thanks to a restoration effort that improved the lagoon's smell. The parking lot has limited hours, but street-side parking is usually available at off-peak times. It's near shops and a theater. **Amenities:** lifeguards; parking (fee); showers; toilets. **Best for:** sunset; walking. ✉ *23200 Pacific Coast Hwy., Malibu* ☎ *310/457–8143* ⊕ *www.parks.ca.gov* ✉ *$12 parking.*

FAMILY **Santa Monica Pier.** Souvenir shops, carnival games, arcades, eateries, an outdoor trapeze school, **Pacific Park,** and more are all part of the festive atmosphere of this truncated pier at the foot of Colorado Boulevard below Palisades Park. The pier's indoor trademark 46-horse Looff Carousel, built in 1922, has appeared in several films, including *The Sting.* Free concerts are held on the pier in summer. ✉ *Colorado Ave. and the ocean, Santa Monica* ☎ *310/458–8900* ⊕ *www.santamonicapier. org* ⊙ *Hrs vary by season; check website before visiting.*

Santa Monica State Beach. It's the first beach you'll hit after the Santa Monica Freeway (I–10) runs into the PCH, and it's one of L.A.'s best known. Wide and sandy, Santa Monica is *the* place for sunning and socializing: be prepared for a mob scene on summer weekends, when parking becomes an expensive ordeal. Swimming is fine (with the usual post-storm pollution caveat); for surfing, go elsewhere. For a memorable view, climb up the stairway over the PCH to Palisades Park, at the top of the bluffs. Free summer-evening concerts are held Thursday nights on the pier. **Amenities:** food and drink; lifeguards; parking; showers; toilets; water sports. **Best for:** sunset; surfing; swimming; walking. ✉ *1642 Promenade, PCH at California Incline, Santa Monica* ☎ *310/458–8573* ⊕ *www.smgov.net/Portals/Beach* 🖘 *$10 parking* ☞ *Parking, lifeguard (year-round), restrooms, showers.*

PASADENA AREA

Although seemingly absorbed into the general Los Angeles sprawl, Pasadena is a separate and distinct city. Noted for its Tournament of Roses, seen around the world each New Year's Day, the city brims with noteworthy spots, from its gorgeous Craftsman homes to its exceptional museums, particularly the Norton Simon and the Huntington Library, Art Collections, and Botanical Gardens. Where else can you see a Chaucer manuscript and rare cacti in one place?

TOP ATTRACTIONS

Gamble House. Built by Charles and Henry Greene in 1908, this is a spectacular example of American Arts and Crafts bungalow architecture. The term *bungalow* can be misleading, since the Gamble House is a huge three-story home. To wealthy Easterners such as the Gambles (as in Procter & Gamble), this type of vacation home seemed informal compared with their mansions back home. What makes admirers swoon is the incredible craftsmanship, including a teak staircase and cabinetry, Greene and Greene–designed furniture, and an Emil Lange glass door. The dark exterior has broad eaves, with sleeping porches on the second floor. An hour-long, docent-led tour of the Gamble's interior will draw your eye to the exquisite details. If you want to see more Greene and Greene homes, buy a self-guided tour map of the neighborhood in the bookstore. ✉ *4 Westmoreland Pl., Pasadena* ☎ *626/793-3334* ⊕ *www. gamblehouse.org* 🖘 *$13.75* ⊙ *Thur.–Sun. noon–3; tickets go on sale Thur.–Sat. at 10, Sun. at 11:30. 1-hr tour every 20–30 min.*

Fodor'sChoice **Huntington Library, Art Collections, and Botanical Gardens.** If you have
★ time for only one stop in the Pasadena area, it should be the Huntington, built in the early 1900s as the home of railroad tycoon Henry E.

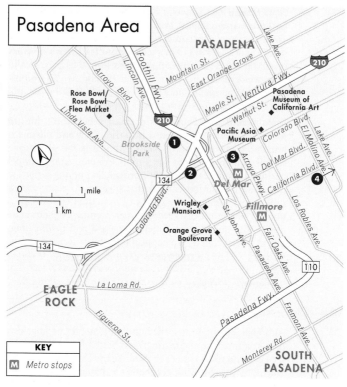

Huntington. Wandering the ground's 150 acres, just over the Pasadena line in San Marino, you can truly forget you're in a city. Henry and his wife, Arabella (who was his aunt by marriage), voraciously collected rare books and manuscripts, botanical specimens, and 18th-century British art. The institution they established became one of the most extraordinary cultural complexes in the world. ■TIP→ Ongoing gallery renovations occasionally require some works from the permanent collection to be shifted to other buildings for display.

Among the highlights are John Constable's intimate *View on the Stour near Dedham* and the monumental *Sarah Siddons as the Tragic Muse*, by Joshua Reynolds. In the Virginia Steele Scott Gallery of American Art, you can see paintings by Mary Cassatt, Frederic Remington, and more.

The library contains more than 700,000 books and 4 million manuscripts, including such treasures as a Gutenberg Bible, the Ellesmere manuscript of Chaucer's *Canterbury Tales*, George Washington's genealogy in his own handwriting, scores of works by William Blake, and a world-class collection of early editions of Shakespeare. You'll find some of these items in the Library Hall with more than 200 important works on display. In 2006 the library acquired more than 60,000 rare books and reference volumes from the Cambridge, Massachusetts–based Bundy Library, making the Huntington the source of one of the biggest history-of-science collections in the world.

Although the art collections are increasingly impressive here, don't resist being lured outside into the stunning Botanical Gardens. From the main buildings, lawns and towering trees stretch out toward specialty areas. The 10-acre Desert Garden, for instance, has one of the world's largest groups of mature cacti and other succulents, arranged by continent. ■ TIP➔ Visit this garden on a cool morning or in the late afternoon, or a hot midday walk may be a little too authentic.

✉ *1151 Oxford Rd., San Marino* ☎ *626/405–2100* ⊕ *www.huntington. org* ✐ *$15 Mon.–Fri., $20 Sat.–Sun., free 1st Thurs. of month (reservations required)* ⊙ *Mon. and Wed.–Fri. noon–4:30, Sat.–Sun. 10:30–4:30; call for summer hours.*

Fodor's Choice **Norton Simon Museum.** Long familiar to TV viewers of the New Year's
★ Day Parade, this low-profile brown building is more than just a background for the passing floats. It's one of the finest small museums anywhere, with an excellent collection that spans more than 2,000 years of Western and Asian art. It all began in the 1950s when Norton Simon (Hunt-Wesson Foods, McCalls Corporation, and Canada Dry) started collecting the works of Degas, Renoir, Gauguin, and Cézanne. His collection grew to include old masters, impressionists, and modern works from Europe as well as Indian and Southeast Asian art. After he retired, Simon reorganized the failing Pasadena Art Institute and continued to assemble one of the world's finest collections.

Today the Norton Simon Museum is richest in works by Rembrandt, Goya, Picasso, and, most of all, Degas—this is one of the only two U.S. institutions to hold the complete set of the artist's model bronzes (the other is New York's Metropolitan Museum of Art). Renaissance, baroque, and rococo masterpieces include Raphael's profoundly spiritual *Madonna with Child with Book* (1503), Rembrandt's *Portrait of a Bearded Man in a Wide-Brimmed Hat* (1633), and a magical Tiepolo ceiling, *The Triumph of Virtue and Nobility Over Ignorance* (1740–50). The museum's collections of impressionist (Van Gogh, Matisse, Cézanne, Monet, Renoir) and cubist (Braque, Gris) works are extensive. Several Rodin sculptures are placed throughout the museum. Head down to the bottom floor to see rotating exhibits and phenomenal Southeast Asian and Indian sculptures and artifacts, where graceful pieces like a Ban Chiang blackware vessel date to well before 1000 BC. Don't miss a living artwork outdoors: the garden, conceived by noted Southern California landscape designer Nancy Goslee Power. The tranquil pond was inspired by Monet's gardens at Giverny. ✉ *411 W. Colorado Blvd., Pasadena* ☎ *626/449–6840* ⊕ *www.nortonsimon.org* ✐ *$10, free 1st Fri. of month 6–9 pm* ⊙ *Wed., Thurs., and Sat.–Mon. noon–6, Fri. noon–9.*

WORTH NOTING

Old Town Pasadena. Once the victim of decay, the area was revitalized in the 1990s as a blend of restored 19th-century brick buildings with a contemporary overlay. A phalanx of chain stores has muscled in, but there are still some homegrown shops and plenty of tempting cafés and restaurants. In the evening and on weekends, streets are packed with people, and Old Town crackles with energy. The 12-block historic district is anchored along Colorado Boulevard between Pasadena Avenue and Arroyo Parkway.

WHERE TO EAT

Dining out in Los Angeles tends to be a casual affair, and even at some of the most expensive restaurants you're likely to see customers in jeans (although this is not necessarily considered in good taste). Despite its veneer of decadence, L.A. is not a particularly late-night city for eating (the reenergized Hollywood dining scene is emerging as a notable exception). The peak dinner times are from 7 to 9, and most restaurants won't take reservations after 10 pm. Generally speaking, restaurants are closed either Sunday or Monday; a few are shuttered both days. Most places—even the upscale spots—are open for lunch on weekdays, when Hollywood megadeals are conceived.

Use the coordinate (✛ 1:A1) at the end of each listing to locate a site on the corresponding map.

WHAT IT COSTS				
	$	$$	$$$	$$$$
Restaurants	under $18	$18–$24	$25–$35	over $35

Prices are the average cost of a main course at dinner or, if dinner is not served, at lunch, excluding 9.75% tax.

DOWNTOWN

DOWNTOWN

$$ ╳ **Bottega Louie.** This former Brooks Brothers suit store was reincarnated
ITALIAN into a lively Italian restaurant and gourmet market in 2008 and quickly
Fodor'sChoice crowned Downtown's new culinary darling. Vast open space, stark
★ white walls and long windows that stretch from floor to ceiling give it a grand and majestic appeal. An army of stylish servers weaves in-and-out of the crowds carrying bowls of pasta, trays of bubbly Prosecco and thin-crust pizzas. Pick and choose from a bevy of salads, pastas, pizzas, and entrées that range from shrimp scampi to a hearty New York strip steak. Or simply order from its small plates menu with favorites: asparagus with fried egg, burrata and roasted vine tomatoes, tomato bruschetta, and fried calamari. Don't let the crowd of people waiting for a table deter you, order a cocktail from the bar, peruse the gourmet *patisserie*, and nibble on a brightly colored macaroon. $ *Average main: $18* ✉ *700 S. Grand Ave.* ☎ *213/802–1470* ⊕ *www.bottegalouie.com* ⌲ *Reservations not accepted* ✛ *1:A3.*

$$ ╳ **Engine Co. No. 28.** A lovingly restored 1912 fire station where
AMERICAN everything—even the original brass sliding pole—has been preserved,
FAMILY Engine Co. No. 28 now rushes out solid, old-fashioned comfort food. The long bar is a popular hangout for Downtown workers delaying their rush-hour commute. The kitchen does a fine job with chili, crab cakes, macaroni and cheese, and thick slabs of meat loaf. Specials showcase recipes inspired by firehouse cooking across the country. $ *Average main: $18* ✉ *644 S. Figueroa St., Downtown* ☎ *213/624–6996* ⊕ *www.engineco.com* ☯ *No lunch weekends* ✛ *1:A3.*

$$ INTERNATIONAL 🍴 **Lazy Ox Canteen.** In the artsy Little Tokyo section of Downtown Los Angeles, Lazy Ox Canteen is a neighborhood favorite often filled with Downtown dwellers who tuck themselves into a communal table for the night. The dimly lit restaurant brings together flavorful food, great wine, and moderate prices, along with an outdoor patio for enjoying L.A.'s great weather. The kitchen is led by Chef Josef Centeno, whose diverse culinary background has resulted in a hodgepodge of seasonal eats that range from caramelized onion soup to porcini rosemary ragu. Try the toad in the hole (crispy pork, brie, and poached egg on a brioche), the seared albacore ratatouille, or the burger with white cheddar and whole grain mustard. They have a lively weekend brunch, and desserts that don't disappoint. [$] *Average main: $20* ✉ *241 S. San Pedro, Downtown* ☎ *213/626–5299* 🌐 *www.lazyoxcanteen.com* ✥ *1:D3.*

4

$$$$ FRENCH 🍴 **Patina.** Formed by chef Joachim Splichal, the Patina Group's flagship restaurant has Downtown's most striking address: inside the Frank Gehry–designed Walt Disney Concert Hall. The contemporary space, surrounded by a rippled "curtain" of rich walnut, is an elegant, dramatic stage for the acclaimed restaurant's contemporary French cuisine. Seasonally changing specialties include copious amounts of foie gras, butter-poached lobster, and medallions of venison served with lady apples. Finish with a hard-to-match cheese tray (orchestrated by a genuine *maître fromager*) and the elegant fromage blanc soufflé served with house-made bourbon ice cream. [$] *Average main: $46* ✉ *Walt Disney Concert Hall, 141 S. Grand Ave.* ☎ *213/972–3331* 🌐 *www.patinagroup.com* ✍ *Reservations essential* ⏲ *Closed Mon.* ✥ *1:B2.*

$ AMERICAN FAMILY Fodor's Choice ★ 🍴 **Philippe the Original.** L.A.'s oldest restaurant (1908), Philippe claims that the French dip sandwich originated here. You can get one made with beef, pork, ham, lamb, or turkey on a freshly baked roll; the house hot mustard is as famous as the sandwiches. Its reputation is earned by maintaining traditions, from sawdust on the floor to long communal tables where customers debate the Dodgers or local politics. The home cooking—orders are taken at the counter where some of the motherly servers have managed their long lines for decades—includes huge breakfasts, chili, pickled eggs, and a generous pie selection. The best bargain: a cup of java for 49¢. [$] *Average main: $7* ✉ *1001 N. Alameda St.* ☎ *213/628–3781* 🌐 *www.philippes.com* ✍ *Reservations not accepted* 💳 *No credit cards* ✥ *1:D1.*

HOLLYWOOD AND THE STUDIOS

BURBANK

$ CUBAN FAMILY 🍴 **Porto's Bakery.** Waiting in line at Porto's is as much as part of the experience as is indulging in a roasted pork sandwich and chocolate-dipped croissant. Locals love this neighborhood bakery and café that has been an L.A. staple for more than 50 years. This is its second location, just minutes away from the studios; it's a great spot to take a stroll and peruse the consignment shops run by former movie stylists. The crowded café bustles with an ambitious lunch crowd, but counter service is quick and efficient. Go for one of its tasty Cuban sandwiches like the *medianoche* or the *pan con lechon* (roasted pork) sandwich,

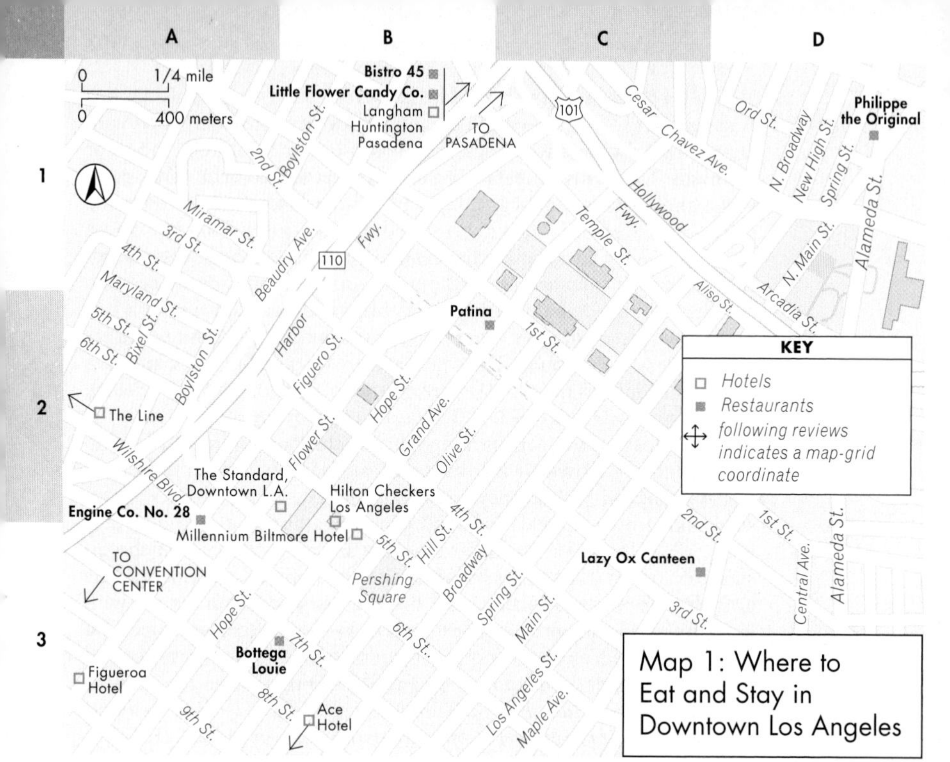
A
B
C
D
1
2
3
0 1/4 mile
0 400 meters
Bistro 45
Little Flower Candy Co.
Langham Huntington Pasadena
TO PASADENA
Philippe the Original
Patina
KEY
Hotels
Restaurants
following reviews indicates a map-grid coordinate
The Line
The Standard, Downtown L.A.
Hilton Checkers Los Angeles
Engine Co. No. 28
Millennium Biltmore Hotel
TO CONVENTION CENTER
Pershing Square
Lazy Ox Canteen
Figueroa Hotel
Bottega Louie
Ace Hotel
101
110
Cesar Chavez Ave.
Ord St.
N. Broadway
New High St.
Spring St.
Alameda St.
Hollywood Fwy.
Temple St.
N. Main St.
Aliso St.
Arcadia St.
1st St.
2nd St.
Boylston St.
Miramar St.
3rd St.
4th St.
Maryland St.
5th St.
Bixel St.
6th St.
Beaudry Ave.
Harbor Fwy.
Figuero St.
Hope St.
Grand Ave.
Flower St.
Olive St.
Wilshire Blvd.
Hill St.
Broadway
Spring St.
Main St.
Central Ave.
7th St.
8th St.
9th St.
Los Angeles St.
Maple Ave.
Map 1: Where to Eat and Stay in Downtown Los Angeles

or try the filling *ropa vieja* (shredded beef) plate. Skipping dessert here would just be wrong. Your sweet tooth will thank you later. [$] *Average main: $10* ✉ *3614 W. Magnolia Blvd.* ☎ *818/846–9100* 🌐 *www.portosbakery.com* ✥ *2:E1.*

HOLLYWOOD

$ AMERICAN 🍴 **25 Degrees.** Named after the difference in temperature between a medium-rare and well-done burger, this upscale burger joint sits in one of Hollywood's hippest hotels. The action at 25 Degrees revolves around a counter constructed of rich oak instead of Formica, and Cabernet is favored over cola. Order the No. 1 (caramelized onions, Gorgonzola and Crescenza cheeses, bacon, arugula, and Thousand Island dressing) or create your own masterpiece from a selection of premium meats, artisanal cheeses, and house-made condiments. A long list of half bottles makes wine pairings easy for solo diners. It's open 24 hours—and does offer other choices, including a good fried egg sandwich, if you're unsure about burgers for breakfast. [$] *Average main: $15* ✉ *Hollywood Roosevelt Hotel, 7000 Hollywood Blvd., Hollywood* ☎ *323/785–7244* 🌐 *www.25degreesrestaurant.com* ✍ *Reservations not accepted* ✥ *2:D1.*

$$ AMERICAN 🍴 **Ammo.** This hip canteen proves that designers and photographers (regulars here) have good taste in food as well as fashion. The ever-evolving menu at this neighborhood favorite changes with the seasons: lunch might be French lentil salad, a perfectly cooked burger, or a prosciutto, mozzarella, and arugula sandwich. Start dinner with one of the kitchen's market-fresh salads, then follow up with a baby artichoke

pizza or a grilled hanger steak. The crisp, minimal setting is cool but not chilly. [$] *Average main: $18* ✉ *1155 N. Highland Ave., Hollywood* ☎ *323/871–2666* 🌐 *www.ammocafe.com* ✣ *2:D2.*

$$$ AMERICAN 🍴 **Animal.** When foodies in Los Angeles need a culinary thrill, they come to this minimalist restaurant in the Fairfax District, which is light on the flash but heavy on serious food. The James Beard Award–winning restaurant is owned by Jon Shook and Vinny Dotolo, two young chefs who shot to fame with a stint on *Iron Chef* and later with their own Food Network show, *Two Dudes Catering*. With a closing time of 1 am, the small restaurant is an L.A. anomaly. The restaurant's diverse clientele ranges from neighborhood dwellers to young Hollywood celebrities to food snobs in search of their new favorite dish. The changing daily menu consists of small plates and entrées that make it easy to explore many items, like barbecue pork belly sandwiches, *poutine* with oxtail gravy, foie gras *loco moco* (a hamburger topped with foie gras, quail egg, and Spam), and grilled quail served with plum *char-siu*. For dessert, the house specialty is a multilayered bacon-chocolate crunch bar. [$] *Average main: $25* ✉ *435 N. Fairfax Ave.* ☎ *323/782–9225* 🌐 *www.animalrestaurant.com* ✍ *Reservations essential* ⏲ *No lunch* ✣ *2:C2.*

$$$ MEDITERRANEAN 🍴 **Cleo.** Hollywood's nightlife and revitalized dining landscape continues to thrive, especially with spots like this hip Mediterranean restaurant that pays homage to Cleopatra. Tucked away in the newly revamped Redbury Hotel, Cleo bumps with energy and life in both its ambience as well as its fresh approach to Mediterranean cuisine. Small-plate offerings allow for plenty of sampling. Start with a trio of dips including hummus with tahini, *lebaneh* (thick yogurt) with feta, and *muhammara* (walnut garlic spread) that comes with fresh-from-the-oven flatbread. Chicken and lamb kebabs are an ideal segue into the proteins, as is a perfectly roasted lamb shank or moussaka made with eggplant, beef ragù, and feta, and sprinkled with pine nuts. Get your veggie allowance with the brussels sprouts made with capers, parsley, and almonds, or mushrooms with hazelnuts and dates. The thoughtful cocktail menu, decent wine list, and enthusiastic staff make Cleo a great place to spend the evening—Hollywood style. [$] *Average main: $30* ✉ *1717 Vine St.* ☎ *323/962–1711* 🌐 *www.cleorestaurant.com* ⏲ *No lunch* ✣ *2:D1.*

$$ ITALIAN Fodor's Choice ★ 🍴 **Cube Café & Marketplace.** Cheese, charcuterie, and pasta lovers take heed: this dark and cozy Italian restaurant will ruin you for all the others. With more than 30 varieties of cheese, an enviable salami selection, pasta made in-house, and a passionate and earnest staff, this former pasta company turned upscale café and gourmet market is one of L.A.'s more affordable culinary gems. Take a seat at the cheese bar, order the cheesemonger's choice, and pair it with a glass of Italian wine. For dinner, order the antipasti of braised octopus, and then move onto the seasonally driven pasta dishes, like the English pea tortellini. [$] *Average main: $22* ✉ *615 N. La Brea Blvd.* ☎ *323/939–1148* 🌐 *www.eatatcube.com* ⏲ *Closed Sun.–Mon.* ✣ *2:D2*

$ AMERICAN FAMILY 🍴 **Pink's Hot Dogs.** Orson Welles ate 18 of these hot dogs in one sitting, and you, too, will be tempted to order more than one. The chili dogs are the main draw, but the menu has expanded to include a Martha Stewart Dog (a 10-inch frank topped with mustard, relish, onions,

BEST BETS FOR LOS ANGELES DINING

With thousands of restaurants to choose from, how will you decide where to eat? Fodor's writers and editors have selected their favorite restaurants by price and cuisine in the Best Bets lists below. You can also search by neighborhood—just peruse the following pages to find specific details about a restaurant in the full reviews later in the chapter.

Fodor's Choice ★

Angelini Osteria, $$$, p. 211
A.O.C. $$$, p. 211
The Apple Pan, $, p. 213
Bouchon Bistro, $$$, p. 210
Bottega Louie, $$, p. 202
Cube Café & Marketplace, $$, p. 205
Little Dom's, $$, p. 209
Mélisse, $$$$, p. 213
Philippe the Original, $, p. 203
Pizzeria Mozza, $$, p. 207
Providence, $$$$, p. 207
Spago Beverly Hills, $$$, p. 210
Urasawa, $$$$, p. 211
Yuca's Hut, $, p. 209

By Price

$

25 Degrees, $, p. 204
The Apple Pan, p. 213
Artisan Cheese Gallery, p. 209
Father's Office, p. 213
Little Flower Candy Company, p. 215
Philippe the Original, p. 203
Pink's Hot Dogs, p. 205
Porto's Bakery, p. 203
Yuca's Hut, p. 209
Zankou Chicken, p. 207

$$

Ammo, $$, p. 204
Bottega Louie, p. 202
Cube Café & Marketplace, p. 205
Gjelina, p. 215
Little Dom's, p. 209
Pizzeria Mozza, p. 207

$$$

Angelini Osteria, p. 211
Animal, p. 205
A.O.C., p. 211
Bouchon Bistro, p. 210
Oliverio, p. 210

$$$$

The Bazaar by José Andrés, p. 209
Gordon Ramsay at the London, p. 211
Patina, $$$$, p. 203
Providence, p. 207
Urasawa, p. 211

By Cuisine

AMERICAN

25 Degrees, $, p. 204
Ammo, $$, p. 204
The Apple Pan, $, p. 213
Engine Co. No. 28, $$, p. 202
Gjelina, $$, p. 215

Philippe the Original, $, p. 203
Pink's Hot Dogs, $, p. 205

FRENCH

Patina, $$$$, p. 203

ITALIAN

Angelini Osteria, $$$, p. 211
Bottega Louie, $$, p. 202
Cube Café & Marketplace, $$, p. 205
Pizzeria Mozza, $$, p. 207
Valentino, $$$$, p. 214

JAPANESE

Urasawa, $$$$, p. 211
Wa Sushi, $$$, p. 212

MEDITERRANEAN

A.O.C., $$$, p. 211
Cleo, $$$, p. 205

MEXICAN

Yuca's Hut, $, p. 209

SPANISH

The Bazaar by José Andrés, $$$$, p. 209

SEAFOOD

Santa Monica Seafood, $$, p. 214
Providence, $$$$, p. 207

tomatoes, sauerkraut, bacon, and sour cream). Since 1939, Angelenos and tourists alike have been lining up to plunk down some modest change for one of the greatest guilty pleasures in L.A. Pink's is open until 3 am on weekends. $ *Average main: $4* ⊠ *709 N. La Brea Ave.* ☎ *323/931–4223* ⊕ *www.pinkshollywood.com* ✍ *Reservations not accepted* ▭ *No credit cards* ✚ *2:D2.*

$$ ✕ **Pizzeria Mozza.** The other, more casual half of Batali, Bastianich, and
ITALIAN Silverton's partnership (the first being Osteria Mozza), this casual venue
Fodor's Choice gives newfound eminence to the humble "pizza joint." With traditional
★ Mediterranean items like white anchovies, lardo, squash blossoms, and Gorgonzola, Mozza's pies—thin-crusted delights with golden, blistered edges—are much more Campania than California, and virtually every one is a winner. Antipasti include simple salads, roasted bone marrow, and platters of *salumi*. All sing with vibrant flavors thanks to superb market-fresh ingredients, and daily specials may include favorites like lasagna. Like the menu, the Italian-only wine list is both interesting and affordable. Walk-ins are welcomed for dining at the bar. $ *Average main: $20* ⊠ *641 N. Highland Ave.* ☎ *323/297–0101* ⊕ *www. pizzeriamozza.com* ✍ *Reservations essential* ✚ *2:D2.*

$$$$ ✕ **Providence.** Chef-owner Michael Cimarusti has elevated Providence
SEAFOOD to the ranks of America's finest seafood restaurants. The elegant dining
Fodor's Choice room, outfitted with subtle nautical accents, is smoothly overseen by co-
★ owner–general manager Donato Poto. Obsessed with quality and freshness, the meticulous chef maintains a network of specialty purveyors, some of whom tip him off to their catch before it even hits the dock. This exquisite seafood then gets the Cimarusti treatment of French technique, traditional American themes, and Asian accents, often presented in elaborate tasting menus. Pastry chef David Rodriguez's exquisite desserts are not to be missed; consider the six-course dessert tasting menu. $ *Average main: $43* ⊠ *5955 Melrose Ave.* ☎ *323/460–4170* ⊕ *www. providencela.com* ✍ *Reservations essential* ☾ *No lunch Mon.–Thurs. and weekends* ✚ *2:D2.*

$ ✕ **Roscoe's House of Chicken 'n Waffles.** Don't be put off by the name of
SOUTHERN this casual eatery, which honors a late-night combo popularized in
FAMILY Harlem jazz clubs. Roscoe's is *the* place for real down-home Southern cooking. Just ask the patrons, who drive from all over L.A. for Roscoe's bargain-price fried chicken, wonderful waffles (which, by the way, turn out to be a great partner for fried chicken), buttery chicken livers, and toothsome grits. Although Roscoe's has the intimate feel of a smoky jazz club, those musicians hanging out here are just taking five. $ *Average main: $10* ⊠ *1514 N. Gower St., Hollywood* ☎ *323/466–7453* ⊕ *www. roscoeschickenandwaffles.com* ✍ *Reservations not accepted* ✚ *2:D1.*

$ ✕ **Zankou Chicken.** Forget the Colonel. Zankou's aromatic, Armenian-
MIDDLE EASTERN style rotisserie chicken with perfectly crisp, golden skin is one of L.A.'s
FAMILY truly great budget meals. It's served with pita bread, veggies, hummus, and unforgettable garlic sauce. If this doesn't do it for you, try the kebabs, falafel, or sensational *shawarma* (spit-roasted lamb or chicken) plates. $ *Average main: $9* ⊠ *5065 W. Sunset Blvd.* ☎ *323/665–7845* ✍ *Reservations not accepted* ✚ *2:F2.*

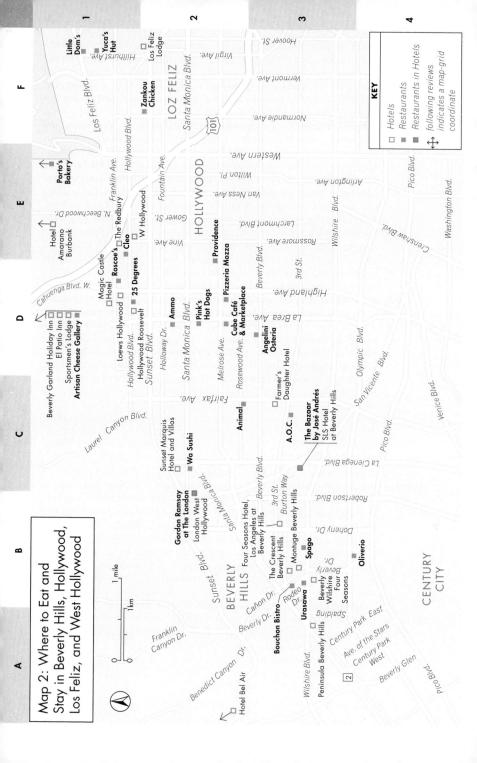

Map 2: Where to Eat and Stay in Beverly Hills, Hollywood, Los Feliz, and West Hollywood

LOZ FELIZ

HOLLYWOOD

BEVERLY HILLS

CENTURY CITY

Little Dom's
Yuca's Hut
Los Feliz Lodge
Zankou Chicken
Porto's Bakery
Hotel Amarano Burbank
Beverly Garland Holiday Inn
El Patio Inn
Sportsmen's Lodge
Artisan Cheese Gallery
Magic Castle Hotel
Roscoe's
The Redbury
Cleo
25 Degrees
Loews Hollywood
Hollywood Roosevelt
Ammo
Pink's Hot Dogs
Providence
Pizzeria Mozza
Cube Café & Marketplace
Angelini Osteria
Animal
Farmer's Daughter Hotel
A.O.C.
The Bazaar by José Andrés
SLS Hotel at Beverly Hills
Sunset Marquis Hotel and Villas
Wa Sushi
Gordon Ramsay at The London
London West Hollywood
Four Seasons Hotel, Los Angeles at Beverly Hills
The Crescent Beverly Hills
Montage Beverly Hills
Spago
Beverly Wilshire Four Seasons
Oliverio
Bouchon Bistro
Urasawa
Peninsula Beverly Hills
Hotel Bel Air

Los Feliz Blvd.
Hillhurst Ave.
Hoover St.
Virgil Ave.
Vermont Ave.
Hollywood Blvd.
Santa Monica Blvd.
Normandie Ave.
Western Ave.
Wilton Pl.
Van Ness Ave.
Arlington Ave.
Wilshire Blvd.
Pico Blvd.
Washington Blvd.
Crenshaw Blvd.
Larchmont Blvd.
Rossmore Ave.
Beverly Blvd.
3rd St.
Highland Ave.
La Brea Ave.
Melrose Ave.
Rosewood Ave.
Fountain Ave.
Gower St.
Vine Ave.
N. Beechwood Dr.
Franklin Ave.
Cahuenga Blvd. W.
Laurel Canyon Blvd.
Fairfax Ave.
Holloway Dr.
Santa Monica Blvd.
Hollywood Blvd.
Sunset Blvd.
Santa Monica Blvd.
La Cienega Blvd.
Robertson Blvd.
Olympic Blvd.
San Vicente Blvd.
Pico Blvd.
Venice Blvd.
Doheny Dr.
Burton Way
3rd St.
Beverly Blvd.
Cañon Dr.
Rodeo Dr.
Beverly Dr.
Spalding
Beverly Dr.
Wilshire Blvd.
Century Park East
Ave. of the Stars
Century Park West
Beverly Glen
Pico Blvd.
Sunset Blvd.
Franklin Canyon Dr.
Benedict Canyon Dr.

1 mile
1 km

2

LOS FELIZ

$$ ✕ **Little Dom's.** With a $15 Monday night supper, a vintage bar with a bar-
ITALIAN keep who mixes up seasonally inspired retro cocktails, and an attached
Fodor'sChoice Italian deli where one can pick up a pork cheek sub, it's not surprising
★ why Little Dom's is a neighborhood favorite. Cozy and inviting with big
leather booths one can sink into for the night, Little Dom's has a menu
that blends classic Italian fare with a modern sensibility, with dishes like
the baked ricotta and wild boar sopressata, rigatoni with homemade
sausage, whitefish piccata, and a New York strip steak with fennel béar-
naise. This is a terrific spot for weekend brunch; order a bottle of the
well-priced house wine and take a seat in the sidewalk patio. ⑤ *Average
main: $24* ✉ *2128 Hillhurst Ave.* ☎ *323/661–0055* ⊕ *www.littledoms.
com* ⌖ *Reservations essential* ✛ *2:F1.*

$ ✕ **Yuca's Hut.** Blink and you can miss this place, whose reputation far
MEXICAN exceeds its size (it may be the tiniest place to have ever won a James
FAMILY Beard Award). It's known for *carne asada,* carnitas, and *cochinita pibil*
Fodor'sChoice (Yucatán-style roasted pork) tacos, burritos, and banana leaf–wrapped
★ tamales (Sat. only). This is a fast-food restaurant in the finest tradi-
tion—independent, family-owned, and sticking to what it does best. The
liquor store next door sells lots of Coronas to Yuca's customers soak-
ing up the sun on the makeshift parking-lot patio. There's no chance
of satisfying a late-night craving, though; it closes at 6 pm. ⑤ *Average
main: $10* ✉ *2056 N. Hillhurst Ave.* ☎ *323/662–1214* ⊕ *www.yucasla.
com* ⌖ *Reservations not accepted* ▭ *No credit cards* ⊘ *Closed Sun. No
dinner* ✛ *2:F1.*

STUDIO CITY

$ ✕ **Artisan Cheese Gallery.** Taste your way through triple creams, blues,
DELI goat's milk, and stinky cheeses from all over the globe at this charm-
FAMILY ing locale that offers cheese and charcuterie plates, sandwiches, over-
size salads, and hot panini sandwiches. Taste testing is encouraged, so
don't be shy to ask. Grab a table on the small outdoor patio and enjoy
the neighborhood scenery; it's a great way to experience the Valley.
⑤ *Average main: $10* ✉ *12023 Ventura Blvd.* ☎ *818/505–0207* ⊕ *www.
artisancheesegallery.com* ⌖ *Reservations not accepted* ✛ *2:D1.*

BEVERLY HILLS AND THE WESTSIDE

BEVERLY HILLS

$$$$ ✕ **The Bazaar by José Andrés.** Celebrity Spanish chef José Andrés con-
SPANISH quers L.A. with a multifaceted concept that includes two dining rooms
(one classic, one modern, each with a tapas bar), a cocktail bar stocked
with liquid nitrogen, and a flashy *pâtisserie.* There are even roaming
pushcarts dispensing foie gras wrapped in cotton candy. Half the menu
is dedicated to traditional Spanish tapas: creamy chicken *croquetas,*
bacalao (salt cod) fritters with honey aïoli, and plates of chorizo or
prized *jamón Ibérico* (Iberian ham). The other half involves some wild
inventions of molecular gastronomy inspired by Andrés' mentor Ferran
Adrià of world-famous El Bulli restaurant in Spain. Among the latter
are "liquid" olives (created through a technique called spherification),
and an ethereal version of the traditional tortilla Española in which an

egg is cooked slowly at 63 degrees, just short of coagulation. A splendid list of Spanish wines is offered. For dessert, items like beet meringue with pistachios and chocolate lollipops await. $ *Average main: $36* ⊠ *SLS Hotel at Beverly Hills, 465 S. La Cienega Blvd.* ☎ *310/246–5555* ⊕ *www.thebazaar.com* ⚑ *Reservations essential* ✛ *2:C3.*

$$$
FRENCH
Fodor's Choice
★

✕ **Bouchon Bistro.** Famed chef Thomas Keller finally made it back to Los Angeles and has set up his French bistro in swanky Beverly Hills. Grand and majestic, but still casual and friendly, there is nothing about an afternoon or night at Bouchon that doesn't make you feel pampered. With little details that separate it from the pack, there's filtered Norwegian water served at every table, a twig-shaped baguette made fresh in the kitchen, and an expansive wine list celebrating California and French wines. It's a foodie scene that welcomes L.A.'s high-profile chefs, celebrities, and locals. Start with its classic onion soup that arrives with a bubbling lid of cheese or the salmon rillettes, which are big enough to share. For dinner, there's a traditional steak and frites, roasted chicken, steamed Maine mussels, and a delicious grilled *croque madame.* Bouchon Bistro is also known for its beautiful French pastries. For a sweet bite, order an espresso and the profiteroles or the Bouchons (bite-size brownies served with homemade vanilla ice cream). Special dining menus can come with a tour of the multimillion-dollar kitchen. $ *Average main: $27* ⊠ *235 N. Canon Dr.* ☎ *310/271–9910* ⊕ *www. bouchonbistro.com* ⚑ *Reservations essential* ✛ *2:B3.*

$$$
ITALIAN

✕ **Oliverio.** This restaurant in the Avalon Hotel, an eco-friendly property in a renovated 1950s apartment complex, feels straight out of the *Valley of the Dolls* movie. Midcentury design gives vintage appeal that blends in with the restaurant's modern Italian cuisine and Californian sensibility. Fresh food concepts are created by chef Mirko Paderno who favors seasonal ingredients. Enjoy a starter of fritto misto or a cauliflower soufflé; for dinner try the classic chicken *fra diavolo,* beef short ribs, or a risotto Milanese. Private poolside cabanas are a favorite for celebratory occasions. $ *Average main: $25* ⊠ *9400 W. Olympic Ave.* ☎ *310/277–5221* ⊕ *www.avalonbeverlyhills.com* ✛ *2:B4.*

$$$
MODERN
AMERICAN
Fodor's Choice
★

✕ **Spago Beverly Hills.** The famed flagship restaurant of Wolfgang Puck is justifiably a modern L.A. classic. Spago centers on a buzzing outdoor courtyard shaded by 100-year-old olive trees. From an elegantly appointed table inside, you can glimpse the exhibition kitchen and, on rare occasions, the affable owner greeting his famous friends (these days, compliments to the chef are directed to Lee Hefter). The people-watching here is worth the price of admission, but the clientele is surprisingly inclusive, from the biggest Hollywood stars to Midwestern tourists to foodies more preoccupied with vintages of Burgundy than with faces from the cover of *People.* Foie gras has disappeared, but the daily-changing menu might offer a pizza with wild mushrooms, baby asparagus, and sun-dried tomatoes, Cantonese-style duck, and some traditional Austrian specialties. Dessert is magical, with everything from an ethereal apricot soufflé to Austrian *kaiserschmarrn* (crème fraîche pancakes with fruit). $ *Average main: $35* ⊠ *176 N. Cañon Dr., Beverly Hills* ☎ *310/385–0880* ⊕ *www.wolfgangpuck.com* ⚑ *Reservations essential* ☾ *No lunch Sun.* ✛ *2:B3.*

LOS FELIZ

$$ · ITALIAN · Fodor's Choice ★

🍴 **Little Dom's.** With a $15 Monday night supper, a vintage bar with a barkeep who mixes up seasonally inspired retro cocktails, and an attached Italian deli where one can pick up a pork cheek sub, it's not surprising why Little Dom's is a neighborhood favorite. Cozy and inviting with big leather booths one can sink into for the night, Little Dom's has a menu that blends classic Italian fare with a modern sensibility, with dishes like the baked ricotta and wild boar sopressata, rigatoni with homemade sausage, whitefish piccata, and a New York strip steak with fennel béarnaise. This is a terrific spot for weekend brunch; order a bottle of the well-priced house wine and take a seat in the sidewalk patio. [$] *Average main: $24* ✉ *2128 Hillhurst Ave.* ☎ *323/661–0055* 🌐 *www.littledoms.com* ✍ *Reservations essential* ✣ *2:F1.*

$ · MEXICAN · FAMILY · Fodor's Choice ★

🍴 **Yuca's Hut.** Blink and you can miss this place, whose reputation far exceeds its size (it may be the tiniest place to have ever won a James Beard Award). It's known for *carne asada*, carnitas, and *cochinita pibil* (Yucatán-style roasted pork) tacos, burritos, and banana leaf-wrapped tamales (Sat. only). This is a fast-food restaurant in the finest tradition—independent, family-owned, and sticking to what it does best. The liquor store next door sells lots of Coronas to Yuca's customers soaking up the sun on the makeshift parking-lot patio. There's no chance of satisfying a late-night craving, though; it closes at 6 pm. [$] *Average main: $10* ✉ *2056 N. Hillhurst Ave.* ☎ *323/662–1214* 🌐 *www.yucasla.com* ✍ *Reservations not accepted* 💳 *No credit cards* ⏲ *Closed Sun. No dinner* ✣ *2:F1.*

STUDIO CITY

$ · DELI · FAMILY

🍴 **Artisan Cheese Gallery.** Taste your way through triple creams, blues, goat's milk, and stinky cheeses from all over the globe at this charming locale that offers cheese and charcuterie plates, sandwiches, oversize salads, and hot panini sandwiches. Taste testing is encouraged, so don't be shy to ask. Grab a table on the small outdoor patio and enjoy the neighborhood scenery; it's a great way to experience the Valley. [$] *Average main: $10* ✉ *12023 Ventura Blvd.* ☎ *818/505–0207* 🌐 *www.artisancheesegallery.com* ✍ *Reservations not accepted* ✣ *2:D1.*

BEVERLY HILLS AND THE WESTSIDE

BEVERLY HILLS

$$$$ · SPANISH

🍴 **The Bazaar by José Andrés.** Celebrity Spanish chef José Andrés conquers L.A. with a multifaceted concept that includes two dining rooms (one classic, one modern, each with a tapas bar), a cocktail bar stocked with liquid nitrogen, and a flashy *pâtisserie*. There are even roaming pushcarts dispensing foie gras wrapped in cotton candy. Half the menu is dedicated to traditional Spanish tapas: creamy chicken *croquetas*, *bacalao* (salt cod) fritters with honey aïoli, and plates of chorizo or prized *jamón Ibérico* (Iberian ham). The other half involves some wild inventions of molecular gastronomy inspired by Andrés' mentor Ferran Adrià of world-famous El Bulli restaurant in Spain. Among the latter are "liquid" olives (created through a technique called spherification), and an ethereal version of the traditional tortilla Española in which an egg is cooked slowly at 63 degrees, just short of coagulation. A splendid list of Spanish wines is offered. For dessert, items like beet meringue with pistachios and chocolate lollipops await. [$] *Average main: $36* ✉ *SLS Hotel at Beverly Hills, 465 S. La Cienega Blvd.* ☎ *310/246–5555* 🌐 *www.thebazaar.com* ✍ *Reservations essential* ✥ *2:C3.*

$$$ FRENCH Fodor's Choice ★ 🍴 **Bouchon Bistro.** Famed chef Thomas Keller finally made it back to Los Angeles and has set up his French bistro in swanky Beverly Hills. Grand and majestic, but still casual and friendly, there is nothing about an afternoon or night at Bouchon that doesn't make you feel pampered. With little details that separate it from the pack, there's filtered Norwegian water served at every table, a twig-shaped baguette made fresh in the kitchen, and an expansive wine list celebrating California and French wines. It's a foodie scene that welcomes L.A.'s high-profile chefs, celebrities, and locals. Start with its classic onion soup that arrives with a bubbling lid of cheese or the salmon rillettes, which are big enough to share. For dinner, there's a traditional steak and frites, roasted chicken, steamed Maine mussels, and a delicious grilled *croque madame*. Bouchon Bistro is also known for its beautiful French pastries. For a sweet bite, order an espresso and the profiteroles or the Bouchons (bite-size brownies served with homemade vanilla ice cream). Special dining menus can come with a tour of the multimillion-dollar kitchen. [$] *Average main: $27* ✉ *235 N. Canon Dr.* ☎ *310/271–9910* 🌐 *www.bouchonbistro.com* ✍ *Reservations essential* ✥ *2:B3.*

$$$ ITALIAN 🍴 **Oliverio.** This restaurant in the Avalon Hotel, an eco-friendly property in a renovated 1950s apartment complex, feels straight out of the *Valley of the Dolls* movie. Midcentury design gives vintage appeal that blends in with the restaurant's modern Italian cuisine and Californian sensibility. Fresh food concepts are created by chef Mirko Paderno who favors seasonal ingredients. Enjoy a starter of fritto misto or a cauliflower soufflé; for dinner try the classic chicken *fra diavolo*, beef short ribs, or a risotto Milanese. Private poolside cabanas are a favorite for celebratory occasions. [$] *Average main: $25* ✉ *9400 W. Olympic Ave.* ☎ *310/277–5221* 🌐 *www.avalonbeverlyhills.com* ✥ *2:B4.*

$$$ MODERN AMERICAN Fodor's Choice ★ 🍴 **Spago Beverly Hills.** The famed flagship restaurant of Wolfgang Puck is justifiably a modern L.A. classic. Spago centers on a buzzing outdoor courtyard shaded by 100-year-old olive trees. From an elegantly appointed table inside, you can glimpse the exhibition kitchen and, on rare occasions, the affable owner greeting his famous friends (these days, compliments to the chef are directed to Lee Hefter). The people-watching here is worth the price of admission, but the clientele is surprisingly inclusive, from the biggest Hollywood stars to Midwestern tourists to foodies more preoccupied with vintages of Burgundy than with faces from the cover of *People*. Foie gras has disappeared, but the daily-changing menu might offer a pizza with wild mushrooms, baby asparagus, and sun-dried tomatoes, Cantonese-style duck, and some traditional Austrian specialties. Dessert is magical, with everything from an ethereal apricot soufflé to Austrian *kaiserschmarrn* (crème fraîche pancakes with fruit). [$] *Average main: $35* ✉ *176 N. Cañon Dr., Beverly Hills* ☎ *310/385–0880* 🌐 *www.wolfgangpuck.com* ✍ *Reservations essential* ⏲ *No lunch Sun.* ✥ *2:B3.*

$$$$
JAPANESE
Fodor's Choice ★

🍴 **Urasawa.** Shortly after celebrated sushi chef Masa Takayama packed his knives for the Big Apple, his soft-spoken protégé Hiroyuki Urasawa settled into the master's former digs. The understated sushi bar has few precious seats, resulting in incredibly personalized service. At a minimum of $375 per person for a strictly *omakase* (chef's choice) meal, Urasawa remains the priciest restaurant in town, but the endless parade of masterfully crafted, exquisitely presented dishes renders few regrets. The maple sushi bar, sanded daily to a satin-like finish, is where most of the action happens. You might be served velvety bluefin toro paired with beluga caviar, slivers of foie gras to self-cook *shabu shabu* style, or egg custard layered with *uni* (sea urchin), glittering with gold leaf. This is also the place to come during *fugu* season, when the legendary, potentially deadly blowfish is artfully served to adventurous diners. [$] *Average main: $375* ✉ *2 Rodeo, 218 N. Rodeo Dr.* ☎ *310/247–8939* ✍ *Reservations essential* ⏲ *Closed Sun. and Mon. No lunch* ✥ *2:B3.*

WEST HOLLYWOOD

$$$
ITALIAN
Fodor's Choice ★

🍴 **Angelini Osteria.** You might not guess it from the modest, rather congested dining room, but this is one of L.A.'s most celebrated Italian restaurants. The key is chef-owner Gino Angelini's thoughtful use of superb ingredients, evident in dishes such as a salad of baby greens, Gorgonzola, and pear; and pumpkin tortelli with butter, sage, and asparagus. An awesome lasagna verde, inspired by Angelini's grandmother, is not to be missed. Whole branzino, crusted in sea salt, and boldly flavored rustic specials (e.g., tender veal kidneys, rich oxtail stew) consistently impress. An intelligent selection of mostly Italian wines complements the menu. [$] *Average main: $32* ✉ *7313 Beverly Blvd.* ☎ *323/297–0070* 🌐 *www.angeliniosteria.com* ✍ *Reservations essential* ⏲ *Closed Mon. No lunch weekends* ✥ *2:D3.*

$$$
MEDITERRANEAN
Fodor's Choice ★

🍴 **A.O.C.** Since it opened in 2002, this restaurant and wine bar has revolutionized dining in L.A., pioneering the small-plate format that has now swept the city. The space is dominated by a long, candle-laden bar serving more than 50 wines by the glass. There's also a charcuterie bar, an L.A. rarity. The tapas-like menu is perfectly calibrated for the wine list; you could pick duck confit, lamb roulade with mint pistou, an indulgent slice of ricotta tartine, or just plunge into one of the city's best cheese selections. Named for the acronym for Appellation d'Origine Contrôlée, the regulatory system that ensures the quality of local wines and cheeses in France, A.O.C. upholds the standard of excellence. [$] *Average main: $35* ✉ *8022 W. 3rd St.* ☎ *323/653–6359* 🌐 *www.aocwinebar.com* ✍ *Reservations essential* ⏲ *No lunch Mon.–Fri.* ✥ *2:C3*

$$$$
FRENCH

🍴 **Gordon Ramsay at the London.** The foul-mouthed celebrity chef from Fox's *Hell's Kitchen* demonstrates why he nevertheless ranks among the world's finest chefs at this fine-dining restaurant in a West Hollywood boutique hotel. Two pastel-color dining rooms with city views flank a formidable white marble bar, creating a space that feels trendy yet surprisingly unpretentious. A menu of small plates accommodates both light suppers and indulgent feasts alike. Highlights include Ramsay's signature beef Wellington for two, filet mignon and braised short

Local Chains Worth Stopping For

It's said that the drive-in burger joint was invented in L.A., probably to meet the demands of an ever-mobile car culture. Burger aficionados line up at all hours outside **In-N-Out Burger** (⊕ *www.in-n-out. com,* multiple locations), still a family-owned operation whose terrific made-to-order burgers are revered by Angelenos. Visitors may recognize the chain as the infamous spot where Paris Hilton got nabbed for drunk driving, but locals are more concerned with getting their burger fix off the "secret" menu, with variations like "Animal Style" (mustard-grilled patty with grilled onions and extra spread), a "4 x 4" (four burger patties and four cheese slices, for big eaters) or the bun-less "Protein Style" that comes wrapped in a bib of lettuce. The company's website lists explanations for other popular secret menu items.

Tommy's sells a delightfully sloppy chili burger; the original location (✉ *2575 Beverly Blvd., Los Angeles*

☎ *213/389–9060*) is a no-frills culinary landmark. For rotisserie chicken that will make you forget the Colonel forever, head to **Zankou Chicken** (✉ *5065 Sunset Blvd., Hollywood* ☎ *323/665–7845* ⊕ *www.zankouchicken.com*), a small chain noted for its golden crispy-skinned birds, potent garlic sauce, and Armenian specialties. Homesick New Yorkers will appreciate **Jerry's Famous Deli** (✉ *10925 Weyburn Ave., Westwood* ☎ *310/208–3354* ⊕ *www. jerrysfamousdeli.com*), where the massive menu includes all the classic deli favorites. With a lively bar scene, good barbecued ribs, and contemporary takes on old favorites, the more upscale **Houston's** (✉ *202 Wilshire Blvd., Santa Monica* ☎ *310/576–7558* ⊕ *www.hillstone.com*) is a popular local hangout. And **Señor Fish** (✉ *422 E. 1st St., Downtown* ☎ *213/625–0566* ⊕ *www.senorfish. net*) is known for its healthy Mexican seafood specialties, such as scallop burritos and ceviche tostadas.

ribs, and a Maine lobster with coconut froth and mushroom ravioli. To maximize the experience, consider one of the flexible tasting menus ($120 on average), artfully crafted by Ramsay's local culinary team and orchestrated by a polished, gracious serving staff. $ *Average main: $38* ✉ *The London, 1020 N. San Vicente Blvd.* ☎ *310/358–7788* ⊕ *www.thelondonwesthollywood.com/gordon-ramsay* ⟁ *Reservations essential* ✛ *2:B2.*

$$$ ✕ **Wa Sushi & Bistro.** Founded by three alums of trendsetting Matsuhisa,
JAPANESE   Wa offers a more personalized experience with high-quality ingredients and intriguing Japanese cooking. Particularly enticing are dishes enhanced with French-inspired sauces. For instance, the Chilean sea bass is layered with foie gras and bathed in a port reduction, while the Santa Barbara prawns are dosed with a perfect *beurre blanc* prepared on a rickety range behind the sushi bar. Wa's hillside location allows for seductive city views from a small handful of tables dressed up with linen and candles. $ *Average main: $35* ✉ *1106 N. La Cienega Blvd., West Hollywood* ☎ *310/854–7285* ⟁ *Reservations essential* ☾ *Closed Mon. No lunch* ✛ *2:C2.*

WEST LOS ANGELES

$ AMERICAN Fodor's Choice ★ 🍴 **The Apple Pan.** A burger-insider haunt since 1947, this unassuming joint with a horseshoe-shaped counter—no tables here—turns out one heck of a good burger topped with Tillamook cheddar, plus an excellent hickory burger with barbecue sauce. You can also find great fries and, of course, an apple pie indulgent enough to christen the restaurant (although many regulars argue that the banana cream deserves the honor). Be prepared to wait, but the veteran countermen turn the stools at a quick pace. In the meantime, grab a cup of Sanka and enjoy a little L.A. vintage. [$] *Average main: $10* ✉ *10801 W. Pico Blvd.* ☎ *310/475–3585* ✍ *Reservations not accepted* 💳 *No credit cards* ⏲ *Closed Mon.* ⊕ *3:D2.*

4

SANTA MONICA AND VENICE

SANTA MONICA

$ AMERICAN 🍴 **Farmshop.** Tucked away inside the Brentwood Country Mart, the new seasonal and California-inspired culinary darling Farmshop was invented by Jeffrey Cerciello, formerly the culinary director of Thomas Keller's casual restaurants. The Southern California native brought a little Napa Valley home with this classic spot that pays attention to the details but also keeps things refreshingly simple. Breads and pastries are made on-site daily, which is one detail that makes breakfast epic. Order the buttermilk biscuits served with quince preserves, French toast with pear marmalade and raisins, and the shirred eggs with wild greens, fennel cream, and flavorful sourdough toast. Lunch is an assortment of farm-fresh salads, soups, and sandwiches. Try the warm Dungeness crab salad made with butter lettuce, sunchokes, and curly mustard greens, or the smoked salmon tartine dressed with caper berries and pickled vegetables on rye bread. [$] *Average main: $14* ✉ *225 26th St.* ☎ *310/566–2400* 🌐 *www.farmshopla.com* ⊕ *3:B2.*

$ AMERICAN 🍴 **Father's Office.** With a facade distinguished only by a vintage neon sign, Father's Office is a congested, gentrified pub famous for handcrafted beers and what has been called L.A.'s best burger. Topped with Gruyère and Maytag blue cheeses, arugula, caramelized onions, and applewood-smoked bacon compote, the "Office Burger" is a guilty pleasure worth waiting in line for (which is usually required). Other options include steak frites and Spanish tapas, with side orders of addictive sweet potato fries served in a miniature shopping cart with aioli—don't even think of asking for ketchup, because FO enforces a strict no-substitutions policy. So popular is the Office Burger that chef-owner Sang Yoon opened a second location in Culver City. Note: Because Father's Office is a bar, it's strictly 21 and older. [$] *Average main: $15* ✉ *1018 Montana Ave.* ☎ *310/393–2337* 🌐 *www.fathersoffice.com* ✍ *Reservations not accepted* ⏲ *No lunch weekdays* ⊕ *3:B2.*

$$$$ FRENCH Fodor's Choice ★ 🍴 **Mélisse.** In a city where informality reigns, this is one of L.A.'s more dressy, but not stuffy, establishments. The dining room is contemporary yet elegant, with well-spaced tables topped with flowers and fine china. Chef-owner Josiah Citrin enhances his modern French cooking with seasonal California produce. Consider white-corn ravioli in brown butter–truffle froth, lobster bolognese, and elegant tableside presentations of Dover sole and stuffed rotisserie chicken. The cheese

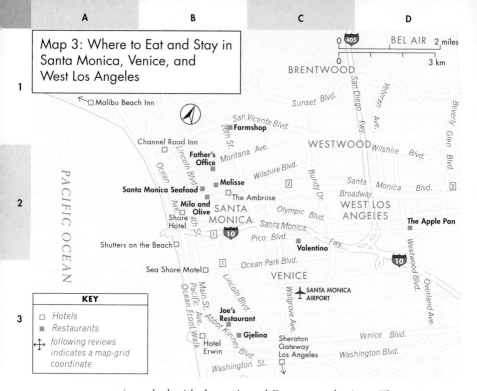

Map 3: Where to Eat and Stay in Santa Monica, Venice, and West Los Angeles

BEL AIR 2 miles

3 km

BRENTWOOD

← Malibu Beach Inn

Sunset Blvd.

San Diego Fwy.

Veteran Ave.

Beverly Glen Blvd.

San Vicente Blvd.

Farmshop

WESTWOOD

Wilshire Blvd.

Channel Road Inn

26th St.

Montana Ave.

Father's Office

Wilshire Blvd.

Bundy Dr.

Santa Monica Blvd.

Melisse

Ocean

Lincoln Blvd.

Santa Monica Seafood

Milo and Olive

The Ambrose

SANTA MONICA

Olympic Blvd.

Santa Monica

WEST LOS ANGELES

The Apple Pan

Shore Hotel

4th St.

Pico Blvd.

Fwy.

Westwood Blvd.

Shutters on the Beach

Valentino

Sea Shore Motel

Ocean Park Blvd.

Lincoln Blvd.

VENICE

Overland Ave.

PACIFIC OCEAN

SANTA MONICA AIRPORT

Main St.

Pacific Ave.

Ocean Front Walk

Abbot Kinney Blvd.

Walgrove Ave.

Joe's Restaurant

Gjelina

Sheraton Gateway Los Angeles

Venice Blvd.

KEY

□ Hotels
■ Restaurants
⊕ following reviews indicates a map-grid coordinate

Hotel Erwin

Blvd.

Washington St.

Washington Blvd.

cart is packed with domestic and European selections. The tasting menus offered here including a creative vegetarian option. $ *Average main: $115* ✉ *1104 Wilshire Blvd., Santa Monica* ☎ *310/395–0881* ⊕ *www.melisse.com* ➘ *Reservations essential* ☾ *Closed Sun. and Mon. No lunch* ⊕ *3:B2.*

$$
SEAFOOD
FAMILY

✕ **Santa Monica Seafood.** The Cigliano family began its modest seafood business on Santa Monica Pier in the early 1930s. The restaurant remains a Southern California favorite in its swankier digs along Wilshire Boulevard. It expanded the retail market and made room for a café where you can enjoy oysters and Champagne while wearing jeans and flip-flops. The simple menu includes Italian flavors in such dishes as the rainbow trout drizzled with olive oil and spices. There are also sandwiches, soups, and a children's menu. Take time to stroll around the market, read up on the history, and enjoy free tastings of the specials. $ *Average main: $22* ✉ *1000 Wilshire Blvd., Santa Monica* ☎ *310/393–5244* ⊕ *www.santamonicaseafood.com* ⊕ *3:B2.*

$$$$
ITALIAN

✕ **Valentino.** Renowned as one of the country's top Italian restaurants, Valentino has a truly awe-inspiring wine list. With nearly 2,800 labels consuming 130 pages, backed by a cellar overflowing with more than 80,000 bottles, this restaurant is nothing short of heaven for serious oenophiles. In the 1970s, suave owner Piero Selvaggio introduced L.A. to his exquisite modern Italian cuisine, and he continues to impress guests with dishes like a timballo of wild mushrooms with rich Parmigiano-Reggiano–saffron *fonduta*, a fresh risotto with farmers' market vegetables, a memorable osso buco, and sautéed branzino with lemon emulsion. A welcome addition to this exalted venue is its more casual wine bar for wine tasting and nibbles like *crudo* and carpaccio. [$] *Average main: $40* ✉ *3115 Pico Blvd.* ☎ *310/829–4313* 🌐 *www.valentinosantamonica.com* ✍ *Reservations essential* ⏲ *No lunch Sat. and Mon.–Thurs. Closed Sun.* ✣ *3:C2.*

VENICE

$$ AMERICAN 🍴 **Gjelina.** This handsome restaurant comes alive with personality the minute you walk through its oversize, rustic wooden door. There are long communal tables, hanging light fixtures that soften the room and make it glow, and an outdoor patio. The menu is smart and seasonal with small plates, cheese and charcuterie, pastas, and pizza. Begin with a mushroom, goat cheese, and truffle oil pizza, heirloom spinach salad, mussels with chorizo, or grilled squid with lentils and salsa verde. For the main course, there's the duck leg confit or the Niman Ranch hanger steak with watercress salsa verde. Typically crowded and noisy, the outdoor patio is the spot. But service is not on a par with the setting. [$] *Average main: $22* ✉ *1429 Abbot Kinney Blvd.* ☎ *310/450–1429* 🌐 *www.gjelina.com* ✍ *Reservations essential* ⏲ *Open until midnight daily* ✣ *3:B3.*

$$$ AMERICAN 🍴 **Joe's Restaurant.** In a century-old beach house, Joe Miller has created the definitive neighborhood restaurant with a citywide reputation. His imaginative French-influenced California cooking focuses on fresh ingredients. Start with tuna tartare or porcini ravioli in a mushroom-Parmesan broth, and continue with Berkshire pork *crépinette* (a type of sausage) or potato-crusted red snapper in port wine sauce. For dessert, try the chocolate crunch cake with hazelnuts and house-made coffee ice cream. Lunch is a terrific value—all entrées are $18 or less and come with soup or salad. [$] *Average main: $30* ✉ *1023 Abbott Kinney Blvd., Venice* ☎ *310/399–5811* 🌐 *www.joesrestaurant.com* ⏲ *Closed Mon.* ✣ *3:B3.*

PASADENA

$$$ FRENCH 🍴 **Bistro 45.** One of Pasadena's most stylish and sophisticated dining spots, Bistro 45 blends traditional French themes with modern concepts to create fanciful California hybrids that delight locals and visitors alike. Seared ahi tuna with a black-and-white-sesame crust, and duck with a tamari-ginger sauce incorporate Pacific Rim accents. The art deco bungalow has been tailored into a sleek environment. Oenophiles, take note: in addition to offering one of the best wine lists in town, owner Robert Simon regularly hosts lavish wine dinners. [$] *Average main: $29* ✉ *45 S. Mentor Ave., Pasadena* ☎ *626/795–2478* 🌐 *www.bistro45.com* ✍ *Reservations essential* ⏲ *Closed Mon. No lunch weekends* ✣ *1:B1.*

$ CAFÉ FAMILY 🍴 **Little Flower Candy Co.** Just off-the-beaten-path of Old Town Pasadena sits this quaint café that charms the hearts and tastebuds of locals with its seasonally driven menu of sandwiches, salads, fresh soups, and incredible baked goods. The café is owned by Christine Moore, who made a name for herself in the candy world as a creator of addicting sea salt caramels and oversize sugar marshmallows. She opened shop a few years ago to sell her sweets and ended up also creating a neighborhood hub for northeast Los Angeles. The café is nestled up against the sloping hills for a small-town feel (even though Downtown L.A. is a few miles away). It's a terrific place to grab a coffee, a fresh berry pastry, or a light lunch before heading out for an afternoon of shopping. $ *Average main: $10* ⊠ *1424 W. Colorado Blvd.* ☎ *626/304–4800* ⊕ *www. littleflowercandyco.com* ⊗ *Closed Sun.* ✛ *1:B1.*

WHERE TO STAY

When looking for a hotel, don't write off the pricier establishments immediately. Price categories are determined by "rack rates"—the list price of a hotel room, which is usually discounted. Specials abound, particularly Downtown on the weekends. Many hotels have packages that include breakfast, theater tickets, spa services, or exotic rental cars. Pricing is very competitive, so always check out the hotel website in advance for current special offers. When making reservations, particularly last-minute ones, check the hotel's website for exclusive Internet specials or call the property directly.

Use the coordinate (✛ 1:B2) at the end of each listing to locate a site on the corresponding map. Hotel reviews have been shortened. For full information, visit Fodors.com.

WHAT IT COSTS			
$	$$	$$$	$$$$
Hotels	under $201	$201–$300	$301–$400	over $400

Hotel prices are the lowest cost of a standard double room in high season, excluding taxes (as high as 14%, depending on the region).

DOWNTOWN

$ ☷ **Ace Hotel.** L.A.'s newest hipster haven wears multiple hats as a hotel,
HOTEL theater, neighborhood diner/coffee shop, and series of lounges, where you can barhop by elevator. **Pros:** lively public areas; great rates; free Wi-Fi. **Cons:** expensive parking rates compared to nightly rates ($36); service needs to get the kinks worked out; compact and somewhat awkwardly designed rooms. $ *Rooms from: $199* ⊠ *929 S. Broadway, Downtown* ☎ *213/623–3233* ⊕ *www.acehotel.com/losangeles* ⤵ *182 rooms, 1 suite* †⊙† *No meals* ✛ *1:B3.*

$ ☷ **Figueroa Hotel.** On the outside, it feels like Spanish colonial; on the
HOTEL inside, this 12-story hotel, built in 1926, is a mix of Mexican, Mediterranean, and Moroccan styles, with earth tones, hand-glazed walls, and wrought-iron beds. **Pros:** a short walk to Nokia Theatre, L.A. Live, Convention Center; well-priced, great poolside bar. **Cons:** somewhat funky room decor; small bathrooms; gentrifying neighborhood. $ *Rooms from: $148* ⊠ *939 S. Figueroa St.* ☎ *213/627–8971, 800/421–9092* ⊕ *www. figueroahotel.com* ⤵ *285 rooms, 6 suites* †⊙† *No meals* ✛ *1:A3.*

$ · HOTEL · Fodor's Choice · ★ **⊤ Hilton Checkers Los Angeles.** Opened as the Mayflower Hotel in 1927, Checkers retains much of its original character; its various-size rooms all have charming period details, although it also has contemporary luxuries like pillow-top mattresses, coffeemakers, 24-hour room service, and plasma TVs. **Pros:** historic charm; business-friendly; rooftop pool and spa. **Cons:** no on-street parking; some rooms compact; urban setting. $ *Rooms from: $189* ⊠ *535 S. Grand Ave.* ☎ *213/624–0000, 800/445–8667* ⊕ *www. hiltoncheckers.com* ⤢ *188 rooms, 5 suites* ⊙ *No meals* ✛ *1:B2.*

$$ · HOTEL **⊤ The Line.** L.A.'s newest boutique hotel pays homage to its Koreatown address with a dynamic new dining concept by superstar Roy Choi, artsy interiors, and a hidden karaoke speakeasy, aptly named Speek. **Pros:** free bikes to explore the area; cheery staff; celebratory atmosphere. **Cons:** design might feel cold and too ambitious for some; expensive parking ($32). $ *Rooms from: $240* ⊠ *3515 Wilshire Blvd., Hollywood* ☎ *213/381–7411* ⊕ *www.thelinehotel.com* ⤢ *362 rooms, 26 suites* ⊙ *No meals* ✛ *1:A2.*

$$$ · HOTEL **⊤ Millennium Biltmore Hotel.** One of Downtown L.A.'s true treasures, the gilded 1923 Beaux-Arts masterpiece exudes ambience and history. **Pros:** historic character; famed filming location; club-level rooms have many hospitable extras. **Cons:** pricey ($40) valet parking; standard rooms are truly compact. $ *Rooms from: $359* ⊠ *506 S. Grand Ave.* ☎ *213/624–1011, 866/866–8086* ⊕ *www.millenniumhotels.com* ⤢ *635 rooms, 48 suites* ⊙ *No meals* ✛ *1:B3.*

$$ · HOTEL **⊤ The Standard, Downtown L.A.** Built in 1955 as Standard Oil's company headquarters, the building was completely revamped under the sharp eye of owner André Balazs, giving it a sleek, cutting-edge feel. **Pros:** on-site Rudy's barbershop for grooming; 24/7 coffee shop for dining; rooftop pool and lounge for fun. **Cons:** disruptive party scene weekends and holidays; street noise; pricey valet parking. $ *Rooms from: $245* ⊠ *550 S. Flower St.* ☎ *213/892–8080* ⊕ *www.standardhotels.com* ⤢ *171 rooms, 36 suites* ⊙ *No meals* ✛ *1:B2.*

HOLLYWOOD AND THE STUDIOS

BURBANK

$$$ · HOTEL **⊤ Hotel Amarano Burbank.** Close to Burbank's TV and movie studios, the smartly designed Amarano feels like a Beverly Hills boutique hotel. **Pros:** boutique style in a Valley location; pleasant breakfast room. **Cons:** Pass Avenue street noise. $ *Rooms from: $365* ⊠ *322 N. Pass Ave.* ☎ *818/842–8887, 888/956–1900* ⊕ *www.hotelamarano.com* ⤢ *108 rooms, 24 suites* ⊙ *No meals* ✛ *2:E1.*

HOLLYWOOD

$$$ · HOTEL · Fodor's Choice · ★ **⊤ Hollywood Roosevelt Hotel.** Think hip bachelor pad when considering the Roosevelt, which is known for its party-centric vibe in the heart of Hollywood and was once the home of the first Academy Awards. **Pros:** in the heart of Hollywood's action and a block from the Metro; lively social scene; great burgers at hotel's restaurant, 25 Degrees. **Cons:** reports of noise and staff attitude; stiff parking charges. $ *Rooms from: $399* ⊠ *7000 Hollywood Blvd., Hollywood* ☎ *323/466–7000, 800/950–7667* ⊕ *www.hollywoodroosevelt.com* ⤢ *305 rooms, 48 suites* ⊙ *No meals* ✛ *2:D2.*

4

BEST BETS FOR
LOS ANGELES LODGING

Fodor's offers a selective listing of lodging experiences at every price range. Here, we've compiled our top recommendations by price and experience. The very best properties are designated in the listings with the Fodor's Choice logo.

By Experience

BEST DESIGN

The Redbury, $$$$, p. 219

The Standard, Downtown L.A., $$, p. 217

BEST SPAS

Four Seasons Hotel, Los Angeles at Beverly Hills, $$$$, p. 220

Shutters on the Beach, $$$$, p. 222

MOST KID-FRIENDLY

Magic Castle Hotel, $$, p. 219

Shutters on the Beach, $$$$, p. 222

Fodor's Choice ★

Channel Road Inn, $$, p. 222

The Crescent Beverly Hills, $$, p. 220

Farmer's Daughter Hotel, $, p. 221

Hilton Checkers Los Angeles, $, p. 217

Hollywood Roosevelt Hotel, $$$, p. 217

Hotel Bel-Air, $$$, p. 220

The Langham Huntington, Pasadena, $$, p. 223

Loews Hollywood, $$, p. 219

Montage Beverly Hills, $$$$, p. 220

Peninsula Beverly Hills, $$$$, p. 220

The Redbury, $$$$, p. 219

Shore Hotel, $$$, p. 222

Shutters on the Beach, $$$$, p. 222

Sunset Marquis Hotel & Villas, $$$, p. 221

By Price

$

Ace Hotel, p. 216

Farmer's Daughter Hotel, p. 221

Figueroa Hotel, p. 216

Hilton Checkers Los Angeles, p. 217

Los Feliz Lodge, p. 219

Sea Shore Motel, p. 222

$$

The Ambrose, p. 222

Channel Road Inn, p. 222

The Crescent Beverly Hills, p. 220

Hotel Erwin, p. 222

The Langham Huntington, Pasadena, p. 223

The Line, p. 217

The London West Hollywood, p. 221

Loews Hollywood, p. 219

Magic Castle Hotel, p. 219

Sportsmen's Lodge, p. 219

The Standard, Downtown L.A., p. 217

$$$

Hollywood Roosevelt Hotel, p. 217

Hotel Amarano Burbank, p. 217

Hotel Bel-Air, p. 220

Millennium Biltmore Hotel, p. 217

Sunset Marquis Hotel & Villas, p. 221

$$$$

Beverly Wilshire, a Four Seasons Hotel, p. 220

Four Seasons Hotel, Los Angeles at Beverly Hills, p. 220

Montage Beverly Hills, p. 220

Peninsula Beverly Hills, p. 220

The Redbury, p. 219

Shutters on the Beach, p. 222

SLS Hotel at Beverly Hills, p. 221

W Hollywood, $$$$, p. 219

$$
HOTEL
FAMILY
Fodor's Choice
★
🖵 **Loews Hollywood.** Part of the massive Hollywood & Highland shopping and entertainment complex, this 20-story luxury hotel is at the center of Hollywood's action. **Pros:** large rooms with new contemporary-styled furniture; Red Line Metro–station adjacent. **Cons:** corporate feeling; very touristy. $ *Rooms from: $299* ✉ *1755 N. Highland Ave.* ☎ *323/856–1200, 800/769–4774* ⊕ *www.loewshotels.com/en/Hollywood-Hotel* 🛏 *604 rooms, 33 suites* ⦿ *No meals* ✥ *2:D1.*

$$
HOTEL
FAMILY
🖵 **Magic Castle Hotel.** Close to the action (and traffic) of Hollywood, this former apartment building faces busy Franklin Avenue and is a quick walk to the nearby Red Line stop at Hollywood & Highland. **Pros:** remarkably friendly and able staff; free Wi-Fi; good value. **Cons:** traffic-y locale; no elevator; small bathrooms. $ *Rooms from: $224* ✉ *7025 Franklin Ave.* ☎ *323/851–0800, 800/741–4915* ⊕ *www.magiccastlehotel.com* 🛏 *7 rooms, 36 suites* ⦿ *Breakfast* ✥ *2:D1.*

$$$$
HOTEL
Fodor's Choice
★
🖵 **The Redbury.** In the heart of Hollywood's nightlife, near the intersection of Hollywood and Vine, the Redbury's dark hues and suites (the smallest is 750 square feet) are designed to appeal to the inner bohemian in most travelers. **Pros:** kitchenette, washer-dryer, and spacious rooms are ideal for those staying a while; excellent dining. **Cons:** no pool or on-site gym; noisy on lower floors; a real Hollywood scene (which can be a pro, depending on your point of view). $ *Rooms from: $500* ✉ *1717 Vine St., Hollywood* ☎ *323/962–1717, 977/962–1717* ⊕ *www.theredbury.com* 🛏 *57 suites* ⦿ *No meals* ✥ *2:E1.*

$$$$
HOTEL
🖵 **W Hollywood.** Just off the historic intersection of Hollywood and Vine and above a busy Metro station, the W Hollywood is ultramodern and outfitted for the wired traveler, though party people will enjoy the central location and rooftop pool deck. **Pros:** Metro stop outside the front door; you'll be equipped for an in-room party—from ice to cocktail glasses. **Cons:** small pool; pricey dining and valet parking; soundproofing issues. $ *Rooms from: $749* ✉ *6250 Hollywood Blvd., Hollywood* ☎ *323/798–1300, 888/625–4955* ⊕ *www.whotels.com/hollywood* 🛏 *265 rooms, 40 suites* ⦿ *No meals* ✥ *2:E1.*

LOS FELIZ

$
RENTAL
🖵 **Los Feliz Lodge.** Checking into this bungalow-style lodge is like crashing at an eco-minded and artsy friend's place: you let yourself into an apartment with fully stocked kitchen, washer and dryer, and a communal patio. **Pros:** homey feel; walking distance to restaurants. **Cons:** no on-site restaurant or pool. $ *Rooms from: $150* ✉ *1507 N. Hoover St.* ☎ *323/660–4150* ⊕ *www.losfelizlodge.com* 🛏 *4 rooms* ⦿ *No meals* ✥ *2:F2.*

STUDIO CITY

$$
HOTEL
FAMILY
🖵 **Sportsmen's Lodge.** The sprawling five-story hotel, an L.A. landmark with a good location, is under new ownership and management and thus has a new contemporary look. **Pros:** close to Ventura Boulevard's plentiful restaurants; free shuttle and discounted tickets to Universal Hollywood; garden-view rooms are quietest. **Cons:** $11 daily self-parking fee. $ *Rooms from: $249* ✉ *12825 Ventura Blvd.* ☎ *818/769–4700, 800/821–8511* ⊕ *www.sportsmenslodge.com* 🛏 *177 rooms, 13 suites* ⦿ *No meals* ✥ *2:D1.*

4

BEVERLY HILLS AND THE WESTSIDE

BEL AIR

$$$ HOTEL Fodor's Choice ★

🏨 **Hotel Bel-Air.** Set on 12 acres of lush gardens, this legendary Spanish mission-style icon—a discreet hillside retreat for celebrities and society types since 1946—recently reopened its pink doors to unveil an updated look courtesy of star designers Alexandra Champalimaud and David Rockwell. **Pros:** country-club feel; lovely pool; spacious rooms. **Cons:** attracts society crowd; hefty price tag; a car is essential. [$] *Rooms from: $395* ✉ *701 Stone Canyon Rd.* ☎ *310/472–1211, 800/648–4097* 🌐 *www.hotelbelair.com* 🛏 *52 rooms, 39 suites* 🍴 *No meals* ✥ *2:A2.*

BEVERLY HILLS

$$$$ HOTEL

🏨 **Beverly Wilshire, a Four Seasons Hotel.** Built in 1928, the Italian Renaissance–style Wilshire wing of this fabled hotel is replete with elegant details: crystal chandeliers, oak paneling, walnut doors, crown moldings, and marble. **Pros:** chic location; top-notch service; refined vibe. **Cons:** small lobby; valet parking backs up at peak times; expensive dining options. [$] *Rooms from: $475* ✉ *9500 Wilshire Blvd.* ☎ *310/275–5200, 800/427–4354* 🌐 *www.fourseasons.com/beverlywilshire* 🛏 *258 rooms, 137 suites* 🍴 *No meals* ✥ *2:B3.*

$$ HOTEL Fodor's Choice ★

🏨 **The Crescent Beverly Hills.** Built in 1926 as a dorm for silent film actors, the Crescent is now a sleek boutique hotel with a great location—within the Beverly Hills shopping triangle. **Pros:** the on-site restaurant CBH's tasty cuisine and convivial happy hour; the lobby is fashionista central. **Cons:** dorm-size rooms; gym an additional fee and only accessed outside hotel via Sports ClubLA; no elevator. [$] *Rooms from: $224* ✉ *403 N. Crescent Dr.* ☎ *310/247–0505* 🌐 *www.crescentbh.com* 🛏 *35 rooms* 🍴 *No meals* ✥ *2:B3.*

$$$$ HOTEL

🏨 **Four Seasons Hotel, Los Angeles at Beverly Hills.** High hedges and patio gardens make this hotel a secluded retreat that even the hum of traffic can't permeate. **Pros:** expert concierge; deferential service; celebrity magnet. **Cons:** Hollywood scene in bar and restaurant means rarefied prices. [$] *Rooms from: $455* ✉ *300 S. Doheny Dr.* ☎ *310/273–2222, 800/332–3442* 🌐 *www.fourseasons.com/losangeles* 🛏 *185 rooms, 100 suites* 🍴 *No meals* ✥ *2:B3.*

$$$$ HOTEL Fodor's Choice ★

🏨 **Montage Beverly Hills.** The nine-story, Mediterranean-style palazzo is dedicated to welcoming those who relish luxury, providing classic style and exemplary service. **Pros:** a feast for the senses; architectural details include crown moldings and muted colors; the highly trained staff is most obliging. **Cons:** all this finery adds up to a hefty tab. [$] *Rooms from: $595* ✉ *225 N. Canon Dr., Beverly Hills* ☎ *310/860–7800, 888/860–0788* 🌐 *www.montagebeverlyhills.com* 🛏 *146 rooms, 55 suites* 🍴 *No meals* ✥ *2:B4.*

$$$$ HOTEL Fodor's Choice ★

🏨 **Peninsula Beverly Hills.** This French Rivera–style palace is a favorite of Hollywood boldface names, but all kinds of visitors consistently describe their stay as near perfect—though expensive. **Pros:** central, walkable Beverly Hills location; stunning flowers; one of the best concierges in the city. **Cons:** serious bucks required to stay here. [$] *Rooms from: $555* ✉ *9882 S. Santa Monica Blvd.* ☎ *310/551–2888,*

800/462–7899 🌐 www.beverlyhills.peninsula.com 🛏 142 rooms, 36 suites, 16 villas 🍴 No meals ✥ 2:A3.

$$$$ HOTEL 🏨 **SLS Hotel at Beverly Hills.** Imagine dropping into Alice in Wonderland's rabbit hole: this is the colorful, textured, and tchotke-filled lobby of the SLS from design maestro Philippe Starck. **Pros:** a vibrant newcomer with lofty ambitions; excellent design and cuisine. **Cons:** standard rooms are compact, but you pay for the scene; pricey hotel dining. [$] *Rooms from: $599 ✉ 465 S. La Cienega Blvd. ☎ 310/247–0400 🌐 www.slshotels.com 🛏 236 rooms, 61 suites 🍴 No meals ✥ 2:C3.*

WEST HOLLYWOOD

$ HOTEL Fodor's Choice ★ 🏨 **Farmer's Daughter Hotel.** A favorite of *The Price Is Right* and *American Idol* hopefuls (both TV shows tape at the CBS studios nearby) as well as local hipsters, this motel has a tongue-in-cheek country style with farm tools as art, a hopping Sunday brunch, and a little pool accented by giant rubber duckies and bean bags. **Pros:** great central city location; across from the cheap eats of the Farmers Market and The Grove's shopping and entertainment mix. **Cons:** shaded pool; no bathtubs. [$] *Rooms from: $189 ✉ 115 S. Fairfax Ave., Farmers Market ☎ 323/937–3930, 800/334–1658 🌐 www.farmersdaughterhotel.com 🛏 63 rooms, 2 suites 🍴 No meals ✥ 2:C3.*

$$ HOTEL 🏨 **The London West Hollywood.** Just off the Sunset Strip, cosmopolitan and chic in design, the London WeHo is a remake of 1984-built Bel Age. **Pros:** perfectly designed interiors; hillside and city views in generous-size suites all with balconies and steps from the strip. **Cons:** too refined for kids to be comfortable; lower floors have mundane views. [$] *Rooms from: $249 ✉ 1020 N. San Vicente Blvd. ☎ 310/854–1111, 866/282–4560 🌐 www.thelondonwesthollywood.com 🛏 200 suites 🍴 No meals ✥ 2:B2.*

$$$ HOTEL Fodor's Choice ★ 🏨 **Sunset Marquis Hotel & Villas.** If you're in town to cut your new hit single, you'll appreciate the two on-site recording studios here. **Pros:** superior service; discreet setting just off the Strip; club-like atmosphere; free passes to Equinox nearby. **Cons:** standard suites are somewhat small. [$] *Rooms from: $315 ✉ 1200 N. Alta Loma Rd. ☎ 310/657–1333, 800/858–9758 🌐 www.sunsetmarquis.com 🛏 102 suites, 52 villas 🍴 No meals ✥ 2:C2.*

SANTA MONICA AND THE BEACHES

LOS ANGELES INTERNATIONAL AIRPORT

$$ HOTEL 🏨 **Sheraton Gateway Los Angeles.** LAX's coolest-looking hotel is so swank that guests have been known to ask to buy the black-and-white photos hanging behind the front desk. **Pros:** weekend rates significantly lower; free LAX shuttle. **Cons:** convenient to airport but not much else. [$] *Rooms from: $219 ✉ 6101 W. Century Blvd. ☎ 310/642–1111, 800/325–3535 🌐 www.sheratonlosangeles.com 🛏 714 rooms, 88 suites ✥ 3:C3.*

4

MALIBU

$$$ B&B/INN **Malibu Beach Inn.** Set right on exclusive and private Carbon Beach, the hotel is home to all manner of the super-rich: the location doesn't get any better than this. **Pros:** live like a billionaire in designer-perfect interiors right on the beach. **Cons:** noise of PCH; no pool, gym, or hot tub; billionaire's travel budget also required. [$] *Rooms from: $385 ✉ 22878 Pacific Coast Hwy., Malibu ☎ 310/456–6444 🌐 www.malibubeachinn.com 🛏 41 rooms, 6 suites 🍴 No meals ⊕ 3:A1.*

SANTA MONICA

$$ HOTEL **The Ambrose.** An air of tranquillity pervades the four-story Ambrose, which blends right into its mostly residential Santa Monica neighborhood. **Pros:** L.A.'s most eco-conscious hotel with nontoxic housekeeping products and recycling bins in each room. **Cons:** quiet, residential area of Santa Monica; no restaurant on-site. [$] *Rooms from: $225 ✉ 1255 20th St. ☎ 310/315–1555, 877/262–7673 🌐 www.ambrosehotel.com 🛏 77 rooms 🍴 Breakfast ⊕ 3:B2.*

$$ B&B/INN Fodor's Choice ★ **Channel Road Inn.** A quaint surprise in Southern California, the Channel Road Inn is every bit the country retreat B&B lovers adore, with four-poster beds with fluffy duvets and a cozy living room with fireplace. **Pros:** quiet residential neighborhood close to beach; free Wi-Fi and evening wine and hors d'oeuvres. **Cons:** no pool. [$] *Rooms from: $235 ✉ 219 W. Channel Rd. ☎ 310/459–1920 🌐 www.channelroadinn.com 🛏 15 rooms 🍴 Breakfast ⊕ 3:B2.*

$ HOTEL **Sea Shore Motel.** On Santa Monica's busy Main Street, the Sea Shore is a throwback to Route 66 and to '60s-style, family-run, roadside motels. **Pros:** close to beach and great restaurants; free Wi-Fi and parking. **Cons:** street noise; motel-style decor and beds. [$] *Rooms from: $160 ✉ 2637 Main St. ☎ 310/392–2787 🌐 www.seashoremotel.com 🛏 19 rooms, 5 suites 🍴 No meals ⊕ 3:B3.*

$$$ HOTEL Fodor's Choice ★ **Shore Hotel.** With views of the Santa Monica Pier, this newly constructed hotel with a friendly staff offers eco-minded travelers stylish rooms with a modern design and scenic views steps from the sand and sea. **Pros:** excellent location near beach and Third Street Promenade; low carbon footprint hotel; free Wi-Fi. **Cons:** expensive rooms and parking fees; fronting the busy Ocean Avenue. [$] *Rooms from: $389 ✉ 1515 Ocean Ave., Santa Monica ☎ 310/458–1515 🌐 shorehotel.com 🛏 144 rooms, 20 suites 🍴 No meals ⊕ 3:B2.*

$$$$ HOTEL FAMILY Fodor's Choice ★ **Shutters on the Beach.** Set right on the sand, this gray-shingle inn has become synonymous with in-town escapism, and while the hotel's service gets mixed reviews from some readers, the beachfront location and show-house decor make this one of SoCal's most popular luxury hotels. **Pros:** romantic; discreet; residential vibe. **Cons:** service not as good as it should be. [$] *Rooms from: $575 ✉ 1 Pico Blvd. ☎ 310/458–0030, 800/334–9000 🌐 www.shuttersonthebeach.com 🛏 186 rooms, 12 suites ⊕ 3:B2.*

VENICE

$$ HOTEL **Hotel Erwin.** Formerly a Best Western, this now bona fide boutique hotel just off the Venice Beach boardwalk has a happening rooftop bar and lounge, appropriately named High, that even attracts locals (weather

permitting). **Pros:** great location, great food; close to Santa Monica without hefty prices. **Cons:** some rooms face a noisy alley; no pool. [$] *Rooms from: $229* ✉ *1697 Pacific Ave.* ☎ *310/452–1111, 800/786–7789* 🌐 *www.hotelerwin.com* 🛏 *119 rooms* 🍴 *No meals* ✣ *3:B3.*

PASADENA

$$
HOTEL
FAMILY
Fodor's Choice ★

🏨 **The Langham Huntington, Pasadena.** An azalea-filled Japanese garden and the unusual Picture Bridge, with murals celebrating California's history, are just two of the picturesque attributes of this grande dame that opened in 1907 and has long been a mainstay of Pasadena's social history. **Pros:** great for romantic escape; excellent restaurant; top-notch spa. **Cons:** set in a suburban neighborhood far from local shopping and dining. [$] *Rooms from: $269* ✉ *1401 S. Oak Knoll Ave.* ☎ *626/568–3900* 🌐 *www.pasadena.langhamhotels.com* 🛏 *342 rooms, 38 suites* 🍴 *No meals* ✣ *1:B1.*

NIGHTLIFE AND THE ARTS

Hollywood and West Hollywood, where hip and happening nightspots liberally dot Sunset and Hollywood boulevards, are the epicenter of L.A. nightlife. The city is one of the best places in the world for seeing soon-to-be-famous rockers as well as top jazz, blues, and classical performers. Movie theaters are naturally well represented here, but the worlds of dance, theater, and opera have flourished in the past few years as well.

Local publications *Los Angeles* magazine (🌐 *www.la.com*) and *LA Weekly* (🌐 *www.laweekly.com*) are great places to discover what's happening in Los Angeles. Lifestyle websites UrbanDaddy (🌐 *www.urbandaddy.com/home/la*) and Flavorpill (🌐 *www.flavorpill.com/losangeles*) do a good job of keeping track of the latest nightlife events and recently opened bars and clubs.

THE ARTS

CONCERT HALLS

Fodor's Choice ★

Dorothy Chandler Pavilion. One of the Music Center's most cherished and impressive music halls, the 3,200-seat landmark remains an elegant space to see performances with its plush red seats and giant gold curtain. It presents an array of music programs and L.A. Opera's classics from September through June. Music director Plácido Domingo encourages fresh work (in 2006, for instance, he ushered in *Grendel,* a new opera staged by the hypercreative director Julie Taymor) as much as old favorites (the 2010 season marked the world-renowned production of Wagner's *Der Ring des Nibelungen*, or *Ring Cycle*, that ran in conjunction with *Ring Festival L.A.*—a celebration of the arts and L.A. style). There's also a steady flow of touring ballet and modern ballet companies. ✉ *135 N. Grand Ave., Downtown* ☎ *213/972–7211* 🌐 *www.musiccenter.org.*

Greek Theatre. In the beautiful tree-enclosed setting of Griffith Park, this open-air auditorium in Los Feliz is in the company of stunning Hollywood Hills' homes and the nearby Griffith Observatory shining atop the hill. The Greek has hosted some of the biggest names in entertainment across all genres. Go for the laid-back California experience and the unique opportunity to experience your favorite performers in the warm western air with a view of the sparkling lights of the city flats splayed at your feet. After the concert, go for a later-night snack or cocktail in the hipster neighborhood hot spots nearby. Open from May through November, the theater celebrated its 82nd year in 2013. ⊠ *2700 N. Vermont Ave., Los Feliz* ☎ *323/665–5857* ⊕ *www.greektheatrela.com.*

Fodor's Choice ★   **Hollywood Bowl.** Ever since it opened in 1920, in a park surrounded by mountains, trees, and gardens, the Hollywood Bowl has been one of the world's largest and most atmospheric outdoor amphitheaters. Its season runs from May through September; the L.A. Philharmonic spends its summers here. There are performances daily except Monday (and some Sundays); the program ranges from jazz to pop to classical. Concertgoers usually arrive early and bring picnic suppers (picnic tables are available). Additionally, a moderately priced outdoor grill and a more upscale restaurant are among the dining options operated by the Patina Group. ■TIP→ Be sure to bring a sweater—it gets chilly here in the evening. You might also bring or rent a cushion to apply to the wood seats. Avoid the hassle of parking by taking one of the Park-and-Ride buses, which leave from various locations around town; call the Bowl for information. ⊠ *2301 Highland Ave., Hollywood* ☎ *323/850–2000* ⊕ *www.hollywoodbowl.com.*

Nokia Theatre L.A. Live. Hosting a variety of concerts and big-name awards shows—the Emmys, American Music Awards, and the BET Awards have all taken place here—this theater and the surrounding L.A. Live complex is a draw for those looking for a fun night out. The emphasis the building places on acoustics and versatile seating arrangements means that all seats are good seats, whether it's an intimate John Legend concert you're attending, or the People's Choice Awards (complete with screaming crowds). Outside, the L.A. Live complex hosts a number of restaurants and attractions (including the Grammy Museum) to keep patrons entertained before, after, or without a concert. ⊠ *777 Chick Hearn Court, Downtown* ☎ *213/763–6030* ⊕ *www.nokiatheatrelalive.com.*

Shrine Auditorium. Former home of the Oscars, the 6,300-seat Arabic-inspired space was built in 1926 as Al Malaikah Temple. Touring companies from all over the world perform here, as do assorted gospel choirs, choral groups, and other musical acts. High-profile awards shows, including SAG and NAACP Image Awards, are still televised on-site. ⊠ *665 W. Jefferson Blvd., Downtown* ☎ *213/748–5116* ⊕ *www.shrineauditorium.com.*

FILM

Watching movies here isn't merely an efficient way to kill time, but it's an *event*. Being in the midst of movie studios makes it extremely easy—and worthwhile—to attend screenings with a major director (or actor) participating in a postfilm discussion. Whether it's a first-run film or a revival, the show will likely be worth the trip out.

The American Cinemathèque at the Aero and Egyptian Theatres. Film enthusiasts will enjoy the roster of movies put on by the American Cinemathèque, with classic and independent films screening on a constantly rotating schedule at its two theaters: the Aero Theatre and the Egyptian Theatre. Expect everything from suspenseful Hitchcock to anime from Hayao Miyazaki, along with occasional question-and-answer sessions with directors and actors following film screenings. The Egyptian Theatre in Hollywood has the distinction of hosting the first-ever movie premiere, back when it opened in 1922, and its Egyptian-themed courtyard and columns have been lovingly restored to preserve its history. The Aero Theatre is in Santa Monica and first opened in 1940. ⊠ *6712 Hollywood Blvd., Hollywood* ☎ *323/466–3456* ⊕ *www. americancinematheque.com.*

Fodor's Choice   **ArcLight.** Beyond the historically important Cinerama Dome on Sunset
★   Boulevard—that impossible-to-miss golf ball-looking structure built in 1963 to show widescreen Cinerama films—ArcLight is the theater that attempts to problem-solve the issues associated with going to the movies. Assigned seating for movies, space for parking, a shopping area, a restaurant, and a bar—the 15-screen ArcLight has a lot going for it. The event calendar is worth paying attention to, as directors and actors stop in from time to time to chat with audiences; for example, Leonardo DiCaprio stopped in for a Q&A for his role in *The Wolf of Wall Street.* ■ TIP→ Evening shows on the weekend feature "21+" shows, where moviegoers can bring alcoholic beverages into the screening rooms. Check the website for show times. ⊠ *6360 Sunset Blvd., Hollywood* ☎ *323/464–4226* ⊕ *www.arclightcinemas.com.*

Cinefamily at The Silent Movie Theatre. A treasure of pretalkies, nonsilent films (the artier the better), and sneak previews of upcoming independent films are screened here. Live musical accompaniment and shorts precede some films. Each show is made to seem like an event in itself, and it's just about the only theater of its kind. The schedule—which also offers occasional DJ and live music performances—varies, but you can be sure to catch silent screenings every week. ⊠ *611 N. Fairfax Ave., Fairfax District* ☎ *323/655–2510* ⊕ *www.cinefamily.org.*

THEATER

Center Theatre Group. Comprising three theaters, Center Theatre Group is the natural go-to for fans of theater in Los Angeles (and, well, Broadway). Each theater has its own style of notable shows, whether they're premieres of plays or touring productions. ⊠ *135 N. Grand Ave., Downtown* ☎ *213/972–7211* ⊕ *www.musiccenter.org.*

Geffen Playhouse. Jason Robards and Nick Nolte got their starts here. This acoustically superior, 522-seat theater offers five new plays each season from September to July—both contemporary works and classics are mixed in with musicals and comedies, and many of the productions are on their way to or from Broadway. ⊠ *10886 Le Conte Ave., Westwood* ☎ *310/208–5454* ⊕ *www.geffenplayhouse.com.*

John Anson Ford Amphitheater. In addition to theater performances, this 1,250-seat outdoor venue in the Hollywood Hills hosts a wide variety of other events, including lectures, children's programs, summer jazz, dance, cabaret, and occasionally Latin and rock concerts. Winter shows are typically staged at the smaller indoor theater, **Inside the Ford.** ⊠ *2580 Cahuenga Blvd. E, Hollywood* ☎ *323/461–3673* ⊕ *www. fordamphitheater.org.*

Montalbán Theatre. Plays, musicals, and concerts all happen here, mostly focusing on Latin culture. This midsize theater collaborates with local arts groups and also hosts the occasional sports-themed event, thanks to a basketball court installed on the rooftop. ⊠ *1615 N. Vine St., Hollywood* ☎ *323/871–2420* ⊕ *www.themontalban.com.*

Pantages Theatre. The home of the Academy Awards telecast from 1949 to 1959, this is a massive (2,600-seat) and splendid example of high-style Hollywood art deco, presenting large-scale Broadway musicals such as *The Lion King* and *Wicked.* ⊠ *6233 Hollywood Blvd., Hollywood* ☎ *323/468–1770* ⊕ *www.broadwayla.org.*

NIGHTLIFE

The focus of nightlife once centered on the Sunset Strip, with its multitude of bars, rock clubs, and dance spots, but more neighborhoods are competing with each other and forcing the nightlife scene to evolve. Although the Strip can be a worthwhile trip, other areas of the city are catching people's attention. Downtown Los Angeles, for instance, is becoming a destination in its own right, drawing cocktail connoisseurs at Seven Grand and rooftop revelers at the Standard.

Parking can be a pain if you're the type who insists on circling the block until you find a space. Most neighborhoods near party-heavy areas like West Hollywood require residential parking permits, so sometimes you're better off with a garage or valet parking. Either option costs anywhere from $5 to $20.

DOWNTOWN

BARS

Fodor'sChoice ★ **Downtown L.A. Standard.** This futuristic hotel has a groovy lounge with pink sofas and DJs, as well as an all-white restaurant that looks like something out of *2001: A Space Odyssey.* But it's the rooftop bar and *biergarten*, with an amazing view of the city's illuminated skyscrapers, a heated swimming pool, and private, podlike water-bed tents, that's worth waiting in line to get into. And wait you probably will, especially on weekends and in summer. On Friday and Saturday nights there's a $20 cover charge after 7 pm. ⊠ *550 S. Flower St., at Sixth St.* ☎ *213/892–8080* ⊕ *www.standardhotels.com.*

HOLLYWOOD

BARS

Fodor'sChoice ★ **Musso & Frank Grill.** The prim and proper vibe of this old-school steak house won't appeal to those looking for a raucous night out, but its appeal lies more in its history and sturdy drinks. Established in 1919, its dark-wood decor, red tuxedo-clad waiters, and bartenders of great skill can easily shuttle you back to its Hollywood heyday when Marilyn Monroe, F. Scott Fitzgerald, and Greta Garbo used to hang around. ⊠ *6667 Hollywood Blvd., Hollywood* ☎ *323/467–7788.*

Three Clubs. This casually hip club is in a strip mall, beneath a sign that simply reads "cocktails." The DJs segue through the many faces and phases of rock-and-roll and dance music. With dark-wood paneling, lamp-lighted tables, and even some sofas, you could be in a giant basement rec room from decades past—no fancy dress required, but fashionable looks suggested. ✉ *1123 Vine St.* ☎ *323/462–6441* ⊕ *www.threeclubs.com.*

Yamashiro. A lovely L.A. tradition is to meet here for cocktails at sunset. In the elegant restaurant, waitresses glide by in kimonos, and entrées can zoom up to $42; on the terrace, a spectacular hilltop view spreads out before you. ■ TIP→ **Valet parking is mandatory and runs $8.** ✉ *1999 N. Sycamore Ave.* ☎ *323/466–5125* ⊕ *www.yamashirorestaurant.com.*

CLUBS

Boardner's. This bar has a multidecade history (in the '20s it was a speakeasy), but with the adjoining ballroom, which was added a couple of years ago, it's now a state-of-the-art dance club. DJs may be spinning electronica, funk, or something else depending on the night—at the popular Saturday Goth event "Bar Sinister," patrons must wear black or risk not getting in. The cover here ranges from $3–$20. ✉ *1652 N. Cherokee Ave.* ☎ *323/462–9621* ⊕ *www.boardners.com.*

COMEDY

Groundlings Theatre. For close to forty years, this renowned theater company has been a breeding ground for *Saturday Night Live* performers; alumni include Will Ferrell, Lisa Kudrow, and *Bridesmaids'* Melissa McCarthy. The primarily sketch and improv comedy shows run Wednesday–Sunday, costing $13–$19. ✉ *7307 Melrose Ave.* ☎ *323/934–4747* ⊕ *www.groundlings.com.*

Upright Citizens Brigade. New York's UCB marched in with a mix of sketch comedy and wild improvisations skewering pop culture. Members of the L.A. Brigade include VH1 commentator Paul Scheer and *Mad TV*'s Andrew Daly. ✉ *5919 Franklin Ave.* ☎ *323/908–8702* ⊕ *www.ucbtheatre.com.*

LIVE MUSIC

Avalon. The multilevel art deco building opposite Capitol Records, the Avalon, formerly known as the Palace, has a fabulous sound system, four bars, and a balcony. Big-name rock and pop concerts hit the stage during the week, but on weekends the place becomes a dance club, with the most popular night the DJ-dominated Avaland on Saturday. Upstairs, but with a separate entrance, you can find celeb hub **Bardot,** a glamorous tribute to Old Hollywood where stars and their entourages are frequent visitors. ✉ *1735 N. Vine St.* ☎ *323/462–8900* ⊕ *www. avalonhollywood.com.*

Fodor'sChoice **El Floridita.** Although the exterior might not look like much, El Floridita
★ is a popular live salsa music spot on Monday, Friday, and Saturday, with dancers ranging from enthusiasts to those just trying to keep up. There's a $10 cover to listen to the band, although admission is free with dinner. Reservations are recommended to guarantee a table. ✉ *1253 N. Vine St., Hollywood* ☎ *323/871–8612* ⊕ *www.elfloridita.com.*

Largo. Musician-producer Jon Brion (Fiona Apple, Aimee Mann, and others) shows off his ability to play virtually any instrument and any song in the rock lexicon—and beyond—as host of a popular evening of music some Fridays at Largo. Other nights, low-key rock and singer-songwriter fare is offered at this cozy venue. And when comedy comes in, about one night a week, it's usually one of the best comedy nights in town, with folks like Sarah Silverman. Cash only. ⊠ *366 N. La Cienega Blvd.* ☎ *310/855–0350* ⊕ *www.largo-la.com.*

WEST HOLLYWOOD

BARS

The Abbey. Don't let the church theme scare you off: this club's fun atmosphere makes it a central gathering point for West Hollywood. Most folks partying in the area often wind up here at one point or another, whether for drinking or dancing (or even a Champagne brunch the next morning). The patio is perfection both day and night, with music keeping everyone in an upbeat mood. ⊠ *692 N. Robertson Blvd., West Hollywood* ☎ *310/289–8410* ⊕ *www.abbeyfoodandbar.com.*

Rainbow Bar & Grill. In the heart of the Strip and next door to the legendary Roxy, the Rainbow is a landmark in its own right as *the* drinking spot of the '80s hair-metal scene—and it still attracts a music-industry crowd. ⊠ *9015 Sunset Blvd.* ☎ *310/278–4232* ⊕ *www.rainbowbarandgrill.com.*

The Standard. This smart, brash-looking hotel for the young, hip, and connected in the happening part of Sunset Strip was formerly a nursing home—how's that for a classic Hollywood makeover? (Check out the live model in the lobby's terrarium.) The bar, at the hotel's 24/7 restaurant, is popular with those in the biz. There is also a Standard in Downtown L.A. (⇨ *Downtown*) ⊠ *8300 Sunset Blvd.* ☎ *323/650–9090* ⊕ *www.standardhotels.com.*

CLUBS

Rage. This spot is a longtime favorite of the "gym boy" set, with DJs following a different musical theme every night of the week (alternative rock, house, dance remixes, etc.). The cover ranges from free to $12. ⊠ *8911 Santa Monica Blvd.* ☎ *310/652–7055* ⊕ *www.theragenightclub.com.*

COMEDY

Comedy Store. A nightly premiere comedy showcase, this venue has been going strong for more than two decades, with three stages (with covers ranging from free to $20) to supply the yucks. Famous comedians occasionally make unannounced appearances. ⊠ *8433 Sunset Blvd.* ☎ *323/650–6268* ⊕ *www.thecomedystore.com.*

Improv. Richard Pryor got his start at this renowned stand-up comedy establishment that has venues throughout the country. Reservations are recommended. Cover is $11–$21, and you need to order a minimum of two items off the menu. ⊠ *8162 Melrose Ave.* ☎ *323/651–2583* ⊕ *www.improv.com.*

Laugh Factory. Look for top stand-ups—and frequent celeb residents—like Bob Saget, or unannounced drop-ins, like Chris Rock. The club has shows Sunday through Thursday nights at 8 pm and 10 pm, plus an additional show on Friday and Saturday at midnight; the cover is

$20–$45 plus a two-drink minimum. ✉ *8001 Sunset Blvd.* ☎ *323/656–1336* ⊕ *www.laughfactory.com.*

LIVE MUSIC

The Troubadour. One of the best and most comfortable clubs in town, this wood-paneled, live music venue has a rich history dating back to the late 1950s when it was a folk club. After surviving the '80s heavy-metal scene, Troubadour caught a second (third? fourth?) wind by booking hot alternative rock acts. There's valet parking, but if you don't mind walking up Doheny a block or three, there's usually ample street parking (check the signs carefully). ✉ *9081 Santa Monica Blvd.* ⊕ *www.troubadour.com.*

Viper Room. Actor Johnny Depp sold his share of the infamous rock venue in 2004, but the place continues to rock with a motley live music lineup, if a less stellar crowd. ✉ *8852 W. Sunset Blvd.* ☎ *310/358–1881* ⊕ *www.viperroom.com.*

Whisky-A-Go-Go. The Whisky, as locals call it, is the most famous rock-and-roll club on the Strip, where back in the '60s, Johnny Rivers cut hit singles and the Doors, Love, and the Byrds cut their musical eyeteeth. It's still going strong, with up-and-coming alternative, hard rock, and punk bands, though mostly of the unknown variety. ✉ *8901 Sunset Blvd.* ☎ *310/652–4202* ⊕ *www.whiskyagogo.com.*

ECHO PARK AND SILVER LAKE

BARS

Cha Cha Lounge. Seattle's coolest rock bar aims to repeat its success with this colorful, red-lighted space. Think part tiki hut, part tacky Tijuana party palace. The tabletops pay homage to the lounge's former performers; they've got portraits of Latin drag queens. ✉ *2375 Glendale Blvd., Silver Lake* ☎ *323/660–7595* ⊕ *www.chachalounge.com.*

Tiki-Ti. This tiny Hawaiian-theme room is one of the most charming drinking huts in the city. You can spend hours just looking at the Polynesian artifacts strewn all about the place, but be careful—time flies in this tropical bar, and the colorful drinks can be so potent that you may have to stay marooned for a while. ✉ *4427 Sunset Blvd., Silver Lake* ☎ *323/669–9381* ⊕ *www.tiki-ti.com.*

LIVE MUSIC

The Echo. This Echo Park mainstay sprang from the people behind the Silver Lake rock joint Spaceland. Most evenings this dark and divey space's tiny dance floor and well-worn booths attract artsy local bands and their followers, but things rev up when DJs spin reggae, rock, and funk. ✉ *1154 Glendale Blvd.* ☎ *213/413–8200* ⊕ *www.attheecho.com.*

The Satellite. The hottest bands of tomorrow, surprises from yesteryear, and unclassifiable bands of today perform at this low-key Silver Lake venue (formerly known as Spaceland), which has two bars, a jukebox, and a pool table. Monday is always free, with month-long gigs by the indie fave du jour. There is a nice selection of beers. ✉ *1717 Silver Lake Blvd., Silver Lake* ☎ *323/661–4380* ⊕ *www.thesatellitela.com.*

Silver Lake Lounge. Neighborhood-y and relaxed, this lounge draws a mixed collegiate and boho crowd. The club is very unmainstream "cool," the booking policy an adventurous mix of local and touring alt-rockers. Bands play three to five nights a week; covers vary but are low. ⊠ *2906 Sunset Blvd., Silver Lake* ☎ *323/663–9636.*

SANTA MONICA

LIVE MUSIC

McCabe's Guitar Shop. This famous guitar shop is rootsy-retro-central, where all things earnest and (preferably) acoustic are welcome—chiefly folk, blues, bluegrass, and rock. It *is* a guitar shop (so no liquor license), with a room full of folding chairs for concert-style presentations. Shows on weekends only. Make reservations well in advance. ⊠ *3101 Pico Blvd.* ☎ *310/828–4497 for concert information* ⊕ *www.mccabes.com.*

SPORTS AND THE OUTDOORS

BASEBALL

Dodgers. You can watch the Dodgers take on its National League rivals while munching on pizza, tacos, or a foot-long "Dodger dog" at one of the game's most comfortable ballparks, Dodger Stadium. ⊠ *Dodger Stadium, 1000 Elysian Park Ave., exit off I–110, Pasadena Fwy.* ☎ *866/363–4377 ticket information* ⊕ *www.dodgers.com.*

Los Angeles Angels of Anaheim. The Los Angeles Angels of Anaheim made headlines when they acquired home-run hitter Josh Hamilton from the Texas Rangers for $125 million in late 2012. In 2002, the Angels won the World Series, the first time since the team formed in 1961. ⊠ *Angel Stadium of Anaheim, 2000 Gene Autry Way, Anaheim* ☎ *714/663–9000* ⊕ *www.angelsbaseball.com.*

BASKETBALL

L.A.'s pro basketball teams play at the Staples Center.

Clippers. L.A.'s "other" team, the much maligned but newly revitalized Clippers, sells tickets that are sometimes cheaper and easier to get than those for Lakers games. ☎ *888/895–8662* ⊕ *www.nba.com/clippers.*

Los Angeles Lakers. See where Magic Johnson once strutted his stuff. It's not easy to get tickets, but if you can, don't miss the chance to see this championship-winning team—especially if the Lakers are playing their rivals, the Boston Celtics. ⊠ *STAPLES Center, 1111 S. Figueroa St., Downtown* ☎ *310/426–6000* ⊕ *www.nba.com/lakers.*

Los Angeles Sparks. After the 2010 retirement of WNBA superstar Lisa Leslie, the Los Angeles Sparks have put the spotlight on forward Candace Parker. ☎ *310/426–6031* ⊕ *www.wnba.com/sparks.*

HOCKEY

L.A. Kings. The National Hockey League's L.A. Kings was the first professional hockey team to make California its home. The team made a name for itself nationally when it cinched the Stanley Cup for the first time in 2012. ⊠ *Staples Center, 1111 S. Figueroa St.* ☎ *213/742–7100* ⊕ *www.lakings.com.*

SHOPPING

DOWNTOWN

Downtown L.A. is dotted with ethnic neighborhoods (Olvera Street, Chinatown, Koreatown, Little Tokyo) and several large, open-air shopping venues (the Fashion District, the Flower Market, Grand Central Market, and the Jewelry District).

MARKETS

Grand Central Market. For almost 100 years, this open-air market has tempted Angelenos with all kinds of produce, fresh meats and seafood, spices, and fresh tortillas. These days, while overstuffed *pupusas,* Cuban sandwiches, and kebabs still satisfy shoppers on the go, the oft-expanding array of vendors make it easy to spend hours browsing and tasting. The market occasionally hosts cultural events, from coffee tastings to film screenings to live music. ✉ *317 S. Broadway, between 3rd and 4th Sts., Downtown* ☎ *213/624–2378* ⊕ *www.grandcentralmarket.com.*

SHOPPING STREETS AND DISTRICTS

Fashion District. Although this 100-block hub of the West Coast fashion industry is mainly a wholesale market, more than 1,000 independent stores sell to the general public. The massive Flower District, featuring the country's largest wholesale flower market, and the Fabric District are also here. Bargaining is expected, but note that most sales are cash-only. Dressing rooms are scarce, as are parking spaces on weekends. ✉ *Roughly between I-10 and 7th St., San Pedro and Main Sts., Downtown* ⊕ *www.fashiondistrict.org.*

Jewelry District. Filled with bargain hunters, these crowded sidewalks resemble a slice of Manhattan. Expect to save big on everything from wedding bands to sparkling belt buckles. The more upscale stores are along Hill Street between 6th and 7th streets. There's a parking garage next door on Broadway. ✉ *Between Olive St. and Broadway from 5th to 8th St., Downtown.*

Fodor'sChoice ★ **Olvera Street.** Historic buildings line this redbrick walkway overhung with grape vines. At dozens of clapboard stalls you can browse south-of-the-border goods—leather sandals, woven blankets, devotional candles, and the like—as well as cheap toys and souvenirs. With the musicians and cafés providing the soundtrack, the area is constantly lively. ✉ *Between Cesar Chavez Ave. and Arcadia St., Downtown* ⊕ *www.olvera-street.com.*

HOLLYWOOD AND THE STUDIOS

From records to lingerie to movie memorabilia, this area is a mixed bag when it comes to shopping.

BOOKS AND MUSIC

Fodor'sChoice ★ **Amoeba Records.** Touted as the "World's Largest Independent Music Store," Amoeba is a playground for music lovers with a knowledge-able staff and a "Homegrown" display to highlight local artists. Catch in-store appearances by artists and bands that play sold-out shows at

The Santa Monica Pier is packed with fun diversions and hosts free concerts in summer.

venues down the road several times a week. Find a rich stock of used CDs and DVDs, an impressive cache of rarities and collectibles (like the Beatles' "Butcher" cover), an encyclopedic range of indie releases, and walls filled with posters for sale. ⊠ *6400 W. Sunset Blvd., at Cahuenga Blvd.* ☎ *323/245–6400.*

CLOTHING

Lost & Found. The owner of this place describes it as "Alice in Wonderland meets Jimi Hendrix." It's actually six storefronts offering clothing for men, women, and children; brass jewelry from France; African silk batiks; and other goodies handpicked from around the world. ⊠ *6320 Yucca St., Hollywood* ☎ *323/856–5872.*

Hollywood & Highland. Dozens of stores, eateries, a bowling alley, and the Dolby Theatre fill this outdoor complex, which mimics cinematic glamour. Find designer shops (Coach, Louis Vuitton) and chain stores (Victoria's Secret, Fossil, Sephora, and the Hard Rock Café).

From the upper levels, there's a camera-perfect view of the famous "Hollywood" sign. On the second level, next to the Dolby Theatre, is a **Visitor Information Center** (☎ *323/467–6412*) with a multilingual staff, maps, attraction brochures, and information about services.

The streets nearby provide the setting for the Sunday Hollywood Farmers Market, where you're likely to spot a celebrity or two picking up fresh produce or stopping to eat breakfast from the food vendors. ⊠ *Hollywood Blvd. and Highland Ave.* ☎ *323/817–0220.*

BEVERLY HILLS AND THE WESTSIDE

The shops of Beverly Hills, particularly Rodeo Drive, are a big draw for window-shopping, and leave visitors awestruck by L.A.'s glitz and excess. It's easy to stroll this area on foot, stopping into big-name luxury jewelers and department stores such as Barneys New York and Cartier.

BEVERLY HILLS

BEAUTY

MAC. This beauty emporium is what's called a "professional" store, with lines of products not available at the chain's regular outlets. This is also a place to arrange makeup lessons or all-out makeovers, or even to prepare for red carpet or other special events. The artists here are fashion show and award-season veterans. ⊠ *133 N. Robertson Blvd., West Hollywood* ☎ *310/271–9137* ⊕ *www.maccosmetics.com.*

BOOKS

Taschen. Philippe Starck designed the space to evoke a cool 1920s Parisian salon—a perfect showcase for the coffee-table books about architecture, travel, culture, and (often racy) photography. A suspended glass-cube gallery space in back hosts rotating art, photo exhibits, and limited edition books. ⊠ *354 N. Beverly Dr., Beverly Hills* ☎ *310/274–4300* ⊕ *www.taschen.com.*

CLOTHING

Theodore. One of the few indie clothing stores in the area, Theodore is a haven for the young and perhaps rebellious to find James Perse T-shirts, jeans of all labels, and hoodies aplenty. Upstairs, browse the avant-garde designer duds from names like Ann Demeulemeester and Jean Paul Gaultier. Next door, Theodore Man has faux-scruffy leather jackets and other items for the guys. ⊠ *336 N. Camden Dr., Beverly Hills* ☎ *310/276–0663* ⊕ *www.theodorebh.com.*

Tory Burch. Preppy, stylish, and colorful clothes appropriate for a road trip to Palm Springs or a flight to Palm Beach fill this flagship boutique. ⊠ *366 N. Rodeo Dr., Beverly Hills* ☎ *310/274–2394* ⊕ *www.toryburch.com.*

DEPARTMENT STORES

Barneys New York. This is truly an impressive one-stop shop for high fashion. The Co-op section introduces indie designers before they make it big. Shop for beauty products, shoes, and accessories on the first floor, then wind your way up the staircase for couture. Keep your eyes peeled for fabulous and/or famous folks eating deli-style lunches at Barney Greengrass on the top floor. ⊠ *9570 Wilshire Blvd., Beverly Hills* ☎ *310/276–4400* ⊕ *www.barneys.com.*

MALLS AND SHOPPING CENTERS

Beverly Center. This is one of the more traditional malls you can find in L.A., with eight levels of stores, including Macy's, Bloomingdale's, and the newer addition: luxury retailer Henri Bendel. Fashion is the biggest draw and there's a little something for everyone, from D&G to H&M, and many shops in the midrange, including Banana Republic, Club Monaco, and Coach. Look for inexpensive accessories at Aldo or edgy dresses at new addition Maje; there's even a destination for the race-car obsessed at the Ferrari Store. Inside there are casual dining choices at the top-floor food court, and several popular chain restaurants are outside on the ground floor. ⊠ *8500 Beverly Blvd., West Hollywood* ☎ *310/854–0071* ⊕ *www.beverlycenter.com.*

SHOPPING NEIGHBORHOODS

Rodeo Drive. New York City has 5th Avenue, but L.A. has famed Rodeo Drive (pronounced Ro-DAY-o). The triangle, between Santa Monica and Wilshire boulevards and Beverly Drive, is one of the city's biggest tourist attractions and is lined with shops featuring the biggest names in fashion. You can see well-coiffed, well-heeled ladies toting multiple packages to their Mercedes and paparazzi staking out street corners. Steep price tags on designer labels make it a "just looking" experience for many residents and tourists alike. ⊠ *Beverly Hills* ⊕ *www. rodeodrive-bh.com.*

WEST HOLLYWOOD

This is prime shopping real estate, with everything from bridal couture design shops to furnishing stores sharing sidewalk space along posh streets like Melrose Place and Robertson Boulevard. It's worth strolling West 3rd Street as well, which is lined with independent but affordable boutiques and several of the city's hottest restaurants and cafés.

CLOTHING

Fodor'sChoice
★
American Rag Cie. Half the store features new clothing from established and emerging labels and of-the-moment denim lines, and the other side is stocked with well-preserved vintage clothing, neatly organized by color and style. Also find shoes and accessories. Adjoining store World Denim Bar stocks jeans galore. ⊠ *150 S. La Brea Ave., Beverly–La Brea* ☎ *323/935–3154.*

Fodor'sChoice
★
Fred Segal. The ivy-covered building and security guards in the parking lot might tip you off that this is *the* place to be. Go during the lunch hour to stargaze at the super-trendy café. This longtime L.A. fashion landmark is subdivided into miniboutiques that range from couture clothing to skateboard fashions. The entertainment industry's fashion fiends are addicted to the exclusive goods here, some from overseas, others from cult L.A. designers just making their marks. ⊠ *8118 Melrose Ave., at Crescent Heights Blvd., near West Hollywood* ☎ *323/651–4129.*

James Perse. The soft cotton tees (and sweaters and fleece) are quintessentially L.A. Find them here in an immaculate gallery-like space, with sleek white- and light-wood furnishings. ⊠ *8914 Melrose Ave., West Hollywood* ☎ *310/276–7277* ⊕ *www.jamesperse.com.*

Fodor'sChoice
★
Maxfield. This modern concrete structure holds one of L.A.'s too-cool-for-school sources for high fashion, with sleek-as-can-be offerings from Chanel, Saint Laurent, Balmain, and Rick Owen. It's for serious shoppers (or gawkers) only. ⊠ *8825 Melrose Ave., at Robertson Blvd., West Hollywood* ☎ *310/274–8800* ⊕ *www.maxfieldla.com.*

Stacey Todd. The newly opened boutique, all wood, white, and natural light, touts a denim bar stocked with brands like Rag & Bone and DSquared. Classic, menswear-inspired clothing by luxe labels, including Helmut Lang and Band of Outsiders, pair with bohemian-tough accessories, like Isabel Marant boots. A selection of lifestyle products features candles, coffee table books, and bath and body products. A second store is in Studio City. ⊠ *454 N. Robertson Blvd., West Hollywood* ☎ *310/659–8633* ⊕ *www.staceytoddboutique.com.*

MALLS AND SHOPPING CENTERS

Fodor'sChoice
★ **Farmers Market.** The granddaddy of L.A. markets dates back to 1935, and the amazing array of clapboard stalls (selling everything from candy to hot sauce, just-picked fruit to fresh lamb), wacky regulars, and a United Nations of food choices must be experienced to be appreciated. Employees from the nearby CBS studios mingle with hungover clubbers and elderly locals at dozens of eateries, movie theaters, and shops under one huge roof. The green trolley shuttles visitors between the Farmers Market and the nearby Grove. ⊠ *6333 W. 3rd St., at Fairfax Ave., Fairfax District* ☎ *323/933–9211 Farmers Market* ⊕ *www.farmersmarketla.com/.*

The Grove. This wildly popular outdoor mall is fabulous for people-watching. Although many of the stores may sound familiar (Abercrombie & Fitch, American Girl Place, Nordstrom), the winding tile walkways, the central fountain with "dancing" water choreographed to music, and the "snow" that falls during the holiday season, put this place over the top. ⊠ *189 The Grove Dr., West Hollywood* ☎ *323/900–8080* ⊕ *www.thegrovela.com.*

SANTA MONICA AND THE BEACHES

The breezy beachside communities of Santa Monica and Venice are ideal for leisurely shopping. Scads of tourists (and some locals) gravitate to Santa Monica Place and the Third Street Promenade, a popular pedestrians-only shopping area that is within walking distance of the beach and historic Santa Monica Pier. ■ TIP→ **Parking in Santa Monica is next to impossible on Wednesday, when some streets are blocked off for the farmers' market, but there are several parking structures with free parking for an hour or two.**

BEAUTY

Strange Invisible Perfumes. A custom-made fragrance by perfumer Alexandra Balahoutis might run you thousands of dollars, but you can pick up ready-made scents, such as citrusy Fair Verona and sultry Black Rosette, for much less. Her exquisitely designed shop is both modern and romantic. ⊠ *1138 Abbot Kinney Blvd., Venice* ☎ *310/314–1505* ⊕ *www.siperfumes.com.*

BOOKS AND MUSIC

Arcana. A treasure trove for art lovers, this store boasts a serious collection of new, rare, and out-of-print books on architecture, design, and fashion—with an especially impressive selection on photography. ⊠ *8675 W. Washington Blvd., Santa Monica* ☎ *310/458–1499* ⊕ *www.arcanabooks.com.*

CLOTHING

Heist. Owner Nilou Ghodsi sends thank-you notes to customers and employs a sales staff that is friendly and helpful but not at all overbearing. The focus at this airy boutique is on elegantly edgy separates from American designers like Nili Lotan and Gary Graham, as well as hard-to-find French and Italian designers. ⊠ *1100 Abbot Kinney Blvd., Venice* ☎ *310/450–6531* ⊕ *shopheist.com.*

MALLS AND SHOPPING CENTERS

Malibu Lumberyard. This shopping complex is a window into beachfront California living. Emblematic Malibu lifestyle stores include James Perse, Maxfield, and one of the chicest J. Crew stores you've ever seen. ⊠ *3939 Cross Creek Rd., Malibu* ⊕ *www.themalibulumberyard.com.*

PASADENA

In Pasadena, the stretch of Colorado Boulevard between Pasadena Avenue and Arroyo Parkway, known as Old Town, is a popular pedestrian shopping destination, with retailers such as Crate & Barrel and H&M, and Tiffany's, which sits a block away from Forever 21.

BOOKS

Fodor's Choice
★
Vroman's Bookstore. Southern California's oldest and largest independent bookseller is justly famous for its great service. A newsstand, café, and stationery store add to the appeal. Some 400 author events annually, plus a fab kids' zone complete with play area, make this a truly outstanding spot. ⊠ *695 E. Colorado Blvd., Pasadena* ☎ *626/449–5320* ⊕ *www.vromansbookstore.com.*

THE CENTRAL COAST

From Ventura to Big Sur

WELCOME TO THE CENTRAL COAST

TOP REASONS TO GO

★ **Incredible nature:** Much of the Central Coast looks as wild and wonderful as it did centuries ago. The area is home to Channel Islands National Park, two national marine sanctuaries, state parks and beaches, and the vast and rugged Los Padres National Forest.

★ **Edible bounty:** Land and sea provide enough fresh regional foods to satisfy even the most sophisticated foodies—grapes, strawberries, seafood, olive oil . . . the list goes on and on. Get your fill at countless farmers' markets, wineries, and restaurants.

★ **Outdoor activities:** Kick back and revel in the casual California lifestyle. Surf, golf, kayak, hike, play tennis—or just hang out and enjoy the gorgeous scenery.

★ **Small-town charm, big-city culture:** Small, friendly, uncrowded towns offer amazing cultural amenities. With all the art and history museums, theater, music, and festivals, you might start thinking you're in L.A. or San Francisco.

1 Ventura County. Ventura is a classic California city with a thriving arts community, miles of beaches, and a vibrant harbor—the gateway to Channel Islands National Park. Eleven miles inland, tiny, artsy Ojai plays host to folks who want to golf, meditate, and commune with tony peers in an idyllic mountain setting.

2 Santa Barbara. Down-home surfers rub elbows with Hollywood celebrities in sunny, well-scrubbed Santa Barbara, 95 miles north of Los Angeles. Its Spanish-Mexican heritage is reflected in the architectural style of its mission, courthouse, and many homes and public buildings.

3 **Santa Barbara County.** Wineries, ranches, and small villages dominate the quintessentially Californian landscape here.

4 **San Luis Obispo County.** Friendly college town San Luis Obispo serves as the hub of a burgeoning wine region that stretches nearly 100 miles from Pismo Beach north to Paso Robles; the 230-plus wineries here have earned reputations for high-quality vintages that rival those of Northern California.

5 **The Big Sur Coast-line.** Rugged cliffs meet the Pacific for more than 60 miles—one of the most scenic and dramatic drives in the world.

6 **Channel Islands National Park.** Home to 145 species of plants and animals found nowhere else on Earth, this relatively undiscovered gem of a park encompasses five islands and a mile of surrounding ocean. *See Chapter 6 for more information.*

GETTING ORIENTED

The Central Coast region begins about 60 miles north of Los Angeles, near the seaside city of Ventura. North along the sinuous coastline from here lie the cities of Santa Barbara and San Luis Obispo, and beyond them the smaller towns of Morro Bay, Cambria, and Big Sur. The nearly 300-mile drive through this region, especially the section of Highway 1 from San Simeon to Big Sur, is one of the most scenic in the state.

5

Updated
by Cheryl
Crabtree

Balmy weather, glorious beaches, crystal clear air, and serene landscapes have lured people to the Central Coast since prehistoric times. Today it's also known for its farm-fresh bounty, from grapes vintners craft into world-class wines to strawberries and other produce chefs incorporate into distinctive cuisine. The scenic variety along the Pacific coast is equally impressive—you'll see everything from dramatic cliffs and grass-tufted bluffs to wildlife estuaries and miles of dunes. It's an ideal place to relax, slow down, and appreciate the sheer abundance of beauty.

Offshore, a pristine national park and a vast marine sanctuary protect the wild, wonderful underwater resources of this incredible corner of the planet. But not all of the Central Coast's top attractions are natural: Ventura, Santa Barbara, and San Luis Obispo are filled with sparkling examples of Spanish-Mediterranean architecture, bustling shopping districts, and first-rate restaurants showcasing regional foods and wines.

PLANNING

WHEN TO GO

The Central Coast climate is mild year-round. If you like to swim in warmer (if still nippy) ocean waters, July and August are the best months to visit. Be aware that this is also high season. Fog often rolls in along the coastal areas in early summer; you'll need a jacket, especially after sunset, close to the shore. It usually rains from December through March. From April to early June and in early fall the weather is almost as fine as in high season, and the pace is less hectic.

GETTING HERE AND AROUND
AIR TRAVEL

Alaska Air, Frontier, and United, and US Airways fly to Santa Barbara Airport (SBA), 9 miles from downtown. United and US Airways provide service to San Luis Obispo County Regional Airport (SBP), 3 miles from downtown San Luis Obispo.

Santa Barbara Airbus shuttles travelers between Santa Barbara and Los Angeles for $50 one-way and $95 round-trip. The Santa Barbara Metropolitan Transit District Bus 11 ($1.75) runs every 30 minutes from the airport to the downtown transit center. A taxi between the airport and the hotel districts costs between $20 and $38.

Airport Contacts San Luis Obispo County Regional Airport ⊠ *903 Airport Dr., off Hwy. 227, San Luis Obispo* ☎ *805/781–5205* ⊕ *www.sloairport.com.* **Santa Barbara Airport** ⊠ *500 Fowler Rd., off U.S. 101 Exit 104B, Santa Barbara* ☎ *805/683–4011* ⊕ *www.flysba.com.* **Santa Barbara Airbus** ☎ *805/964–7759, 800/423–1618* ⊕ *www.sbairbus.com.* **Santa Barbara Metropolitan Transit District** ☎ *805/963–3366* ⊕ *www.sbmtd.gov.*

BUS TRAVEL

Greyhound provides service from Los Angeles and San Francisco to San Luis Obispo, Ventura, and Santa Barbara. Local transit companies serve these three cities and several smaller towns. Buses can be useful for visiting some urban sights, particularly in Santa Barbara; they're less so for rural ones.

Bus Contact Greyhound ☎ *800/231–2222* ⊕ *www.greyhound.com.*

CAR TRAVEL

Driving is the easiest way to experience the Central Coast. U.S. 101 and Highway 1, which run north–south, are the main routes to and through the Central Coast from Los Angeles and San Francisco. Highly scenic Highway 1 hugs the coast, and U.S. 101 runs inland. Between Ventura County and northern Santa Barbara County, the two highways are the same road. Highway 1 again separates from U.S. 101 north of Gaviota, then rejoins the highway at Pismo Beach. Along any stretch where these two highways are separate, U.S. 101 is the quicker route.

The most dramatic section of the Central Coast is the 70 miles between San Simeon and Big Sur. The road is narrow and twisting, with a single lane in each direction. In fog or rain the drive can be downright nerve-racking; in wet seasons mudslides can close portions of the road.

Other routes into the Central Coast include Highway 46 and Highway 33, which head, respectively, west and south from Interstate 5 near Bakersfield.

Road Conditions Caltrans ☎ *800/427–7623, 888/836–0866 Hwy. 1 Visitor Hotline (Cambria north to Carmel)* ⊕ *www.dot.ca.gov.*

TRAIN TRAVEL

The Amtrak *Coast Starlight*, which runs between Los Angeles and Seattle via Oakland, stops in Paso Robles, San Luis Obispo, Santa Barbara, and Oxnard. Amtrak runs several *Pacific Surfliner* trains and buses daily between San Luis Obispo, Santa Barbara, Los Angeles, and San Diego. Metrolink Regional Rail Service trains connect Ventura and Oxnard with Los Angeles and points between.

Train Contacts Amtrak ☎ *800/872-7245* ⊕ *www.amtrak.com.* **Metrolink** ☎ *800/371-5465* ⊕ *www.metrolinktrains.com.*

RESTAURANTS

The cuisine in Ventura and Santa Barbara is every bit as eclectic as it is in California's bigger cities; fresh seafood is a standout. A foodie renaissance has overtaken the entire region from Ventura to Paso Robles, spawning dozens of restaurants touting locavore cuisine made with fresh organic produce and meats. Dining attire on the Central Coast is generally casual, though slightly dressy casual wear is the custom at pricier restaurants.

HOTELS

Expect to pay top dollar for rooms along the shore, especially in summer. Moderately priced hotels and motels do exist—most just a short drive inland from their higher-price counterparts. Make your reservations as early as possible and take advantage of midweek specials to get the best rates. It's common for lodgings to require two-day minimum stays on holidays and some weekends, especially in summer, and to double rates during festivals and other events. *Hotel reviews have been shortened. For full information, visit Fodors.com.*

WHAT IT COSTS				
	$	**$$**	**$$$**	**$$$$**
Restaurants	under 16	$16–$22	$23–$30	over $30
Hotels	under $121	$121–$175	$176–$250	over $250

Restaurant prices are the average cost of a main course at dinner or, if dinner is not served, at lunch, excluding sales tax of 8%–8.25% (depending on location). Hotel prices are the lowest cost of a standard double room in high season, excluding service charges and occupancy 9%–12% tax.

TOUR OPTIONS

Many of the tour companies will pick you up at your hotel or central locations; ask about this when booking.

Central Coast Food Tours. Food and wine destinations are the focus of this outfit's walking tours of shops, restaurants, wineries, and other spots in San Luis Obispo, Paso Robles, and elsewhere. ☎ *800/979-3370, 212/209-3370* ⊕ *www.centralcoastfoodtours.com* 🎫 *From $69.*

Cloud Climbers Jeep and Wine Tours. This outfit conducts trips in open-air, six-passenger jeeps to the Santa Barbara/Santa Ynez mountains and Wine Country. Tour options include wine tasting, mountain, sunset, and a Discovery Adventure for families. The company also offers a four-hour All Around Ojai Tour and arranges horseback-riding and trap-shooting tours. ☎ *805/646-3200* ⊕ *www.ccjeeps.com* 🎫 *From $89.*

The Grapeline Wine Country Shuttle. Wine and vineyard picnic tours in Paso Robles and the Santa Ynez Valley are the Grapeline's specialty. ☎ *888/894–6379, 805/325–0059* ⊕ *www.gogrape.com* ✉ *From $99.*

Santa Barbara Wine Country Cycling Tours. The company leads half- and full-day tours of the Santa Ynez wine region, conducts hiking and cycling tours, and rents bicycles. ✉ *3630 Sagunto St., Santa Ynez* ☎ *888/557–8687, 805/686–9490* ⊕ *www.winecountrycycling.com* ✉ *From $80.*

Spencer's Limousine & Tours. Based in Santa Barbara, Spencer's conducts customized tours of Santa Barbara and the Wine Country via sedan, limousine, or van. ☎ *805/884–9700* ⊕ *www.spencerslimo.com* ✉ *From $90.*

Stagecoach Wine Tours. Locally owned and operated, Stagecoach runs daily wine-tasting excursions through the Santa Ynez Valley in vans, minicoaches, and SUVs. ✉ *Solvang* ☎ *805/686–8347* ⊕ *www. winetourssantaynez.com* ✉ *From $129.*

Sustainable Vine Wine Tours. This green-minded company specializes in eco-friendly Santa Ynez Valley wine tours in nine-passenger Mercedes Sprinter vans. Trips include tastings at limited-production wineries committed to sustainable practices. An organic picnic lunch is served. ☎ *805/698–3911* ⊕ *www.sustainablevine.com* ✉ *$125.*

Wine Edventures. This learning-oriented company conducts Santa Ynez Valley wine tours in vans, minicoaches, and other vehicles. ✉ *Santa Barbara* ☎ *805/965–9463* ⊕ *www.welovewines.com* ✉ *From $105.*

VISITOR INFORMATION
Contact **Central Coast Tourism Council** ⊕ *www.centralcoast-tourism.com.*

VENTURA COUNTY

Ventura County was first settled by the Chumash Indians. Spanish missionaries were the first Europeans to arrive, followed by Americans and other Europeans, who established bustling towns, transportation networks, and highly productive farms. Since the 1920s, agriculture has been steadily replaced as the area's main industry—first by the oil business and more recently by tourism.

VENTURA

60 miles north of Los Angeles.

Like Los Angeles, the city of Ventura enjoys gorgeous weather and sun-kissed beaches—but without the smog and congestion. The miles of beautiful beaches attract athletes—bodysurfers and boogie boarders, runners and bikers—and those who'd rather doze beneath an umbrella all day. Ventura Harbor is home to myriad fishing boats, restaurants, and water-activity centers where you can rent boats and take harbor cruises. Foodies can get their fix all over Ventura—dozens of upscale cafés and wine and tapas bars have opened in recent years. Arts and antiques buffs have long trekked downtown to browse the galleries and shops there.

GETTING HERE AND AROUND

Amtrak and Metrolink trains serve the area from Los Angeles. Greyhound buses stop in Ventura; Gold Coast Transit serves the city and the rest of Ventura County.

U.S. 101 is the north–south main route into town, but for a scenic drive, take Highway 1 north from Santa Monica. The highway merges with U.S. 101 just south of Ventura. ■TIP→ Traveling north to Ventura from Los Angeles on weekdays it's best to depart before 6 am, between 10 and 2, or after 7, or you'll get caught in the extended rush-hour traffic. Coming south from Santa Barbara, depart before 1 or after 6. On weekends, traffic is generally fine except southbound on U.S. 101 between Santa Barbara and Ventura.

ESSENTIALS

Bus Contact **Gold Coast Transit** ☎ 805/643–3158 ⊕ www.goldcoasttransit.org.

Visitor Information **Ventura Visitors and Convention Bureau** ⊠ Downtown Visitor Center, 101 S. California St. ☎ 805/648–2075, 800/483–6214 ⊕ www.ventura-usa.com.

EXPLORING

FAMILY **Lake Casitas Recreation Area.** Lunker largemouth bass, rainbow trout, crappie, redears, and channel catfish live in the waters at this park, one of the country's best bass-fishing areas. Nestled below the Santa Ynez Mountains' Laguna Ridge, Lake Casitas is also a beautiful spot for pitching a tent or having a picnic. The Casitas Water Adventure, which has two water playgrounds and a lazy river for tubing and floating, provides kids with endless diversions in summer. ⊠ 11311 Santa Ana Rd., off Hwy. 33, 13 miles northwest of Ventura ☎ 805/649–2233, 805/649–1122 campground and water park reservations ⊕ www.lakecasitas.info ☞ $10–$15 per vehicle, $13 per boat; Water Adventure $12 ($6 5–7 pm) ⊙ Daily.

Mission San Buenaventura. The ninth of the 21 California missions, Mission San Buenaventura was established in 1782 but burned to the ground in the 1790s. It was rebuilt and rededicated in 1809. A self-guided tour takes you through a small museum, a quiet courtyard, and a chapel with 250-year-old paintings. ⊠ 211 E. Main St., at Figueroa St. ☎ 805/643–4318 ⊕ www.sanbuenaventuramission.org ☞ $4 ⊙ Weekdays 10–5, Sat. 9–5, Sun. 10–4.

Museum of Ventura County. Exhibits in a contemporary complex of galleries and a sunny courtyard plaza tell the story of Ventura County from prehistoric times to the present. A highlight is the gallery that contains Ojai artist George Stuart's historical figures, dressed in exceptionally detailed, custom-made clothing reflecting their particular eras. In the courtyard, eight panels made with 45,000 pieces of cut glass form a historical timeline. ⊠ 100 E. Main St., at S. Ventura Ave. ☎ 805/653–0323 ⊕ ventura-museum.org ☞ $4, free first Sun. of the month ⊙ Tues.–Sun. 11–5.

Ventura Oceanfront. Four miles of gorgeous coastline stretch from the county fairgrounds at the northern border of the city of San Buenaventura, through San Buenaventura State Beach, down to Ventura Harbor in the south. The main attraction here is the San Buenaventura City Pier,

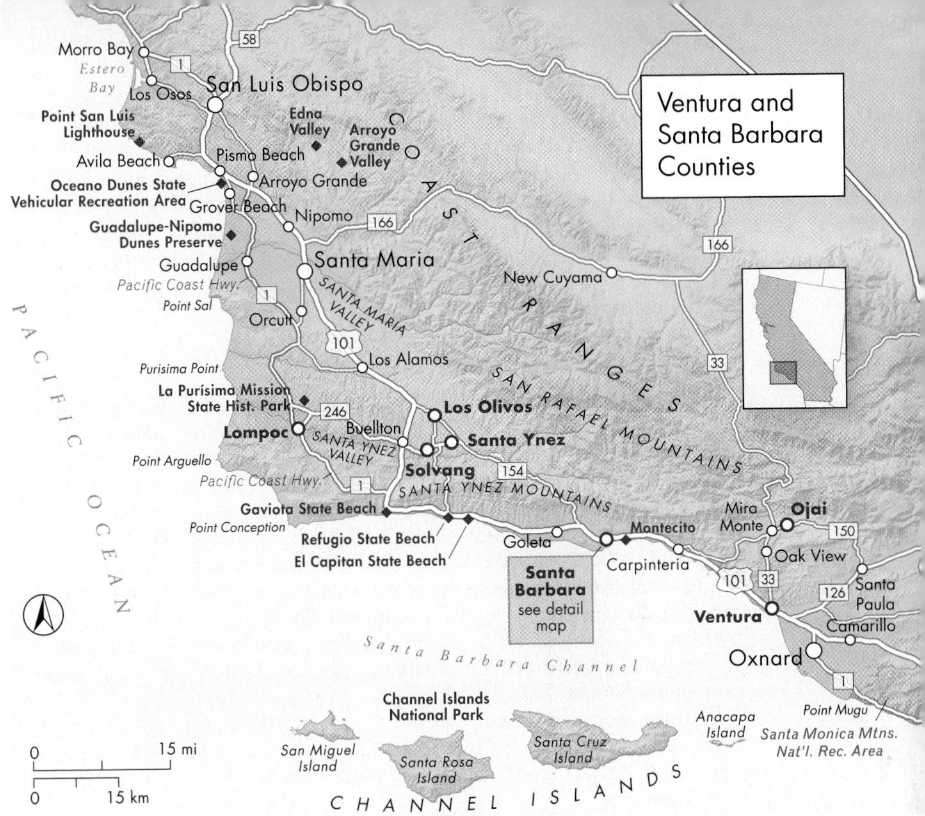
Ventura and Santa Barbara Counties
Morro Bay
Estero Bay
Los Osos
San Luis Obispo
Point San Luis Lighthouse
Edna Valley
Arroyo Grande Valley
Avila Beach
Pismo Beach
Arroyo Grande
Oceano Dunes State Vehicular Recreation Area
Grover Beach
Nipomo
Guadalupe-Nipomo Dunes Preserve
Guadalupe
Santa Maria
Pacific Coast Hwy.
Point Sal
Orcutt
SANTA MARIA VALLEY
New Cuyama
COAST RANGES
Los Alamos
SAN RAFAEL MOUNTAINS
Purisima Point
La Purísima Mission State Hist. Park
Los Olivos
Lompoc
Buellton
Santa Ynez
SANTA YNEZ VALLEY
Solvang
Point Arguello
Pacific Coast Hwy.
SANTA YNEZ MOUNTAINS
Gaviota State Beach
Point Conception
Refugio State Beach
El Capitan State Beach
Goleta
Montecito
Carpinteria
Mira Monte
Ojai
Oak View
Santa Paula
Ventura
Camarillo
Oxnard
Santa Barbara see detail map
PACIFIC OCEAN
Santa Barbara Channel
Channel Islands National Park
San Miguel Island
Santa Rosa Island
Santa Cruz Island
Anacapa Island
Point Mugu
Santa Monica Mtns. Nat'l. Rec. Area
CHANNEL ISLANDS
0 15 mi
0 15 km
58
1
166
101
246
154
33
150
126

a landmark built in 1872 and restored in 1993. Surfers rip the waves just north of the pier, and sunbathers relax on white-sand beaches on either side. The mile-long promenade and the Omer Rains Bike Trail north of the pier attract scores of joggers, surrey cyclers, and bikers throughout the year. ✉ *California St., at ocean's edge.*

WHERE TO EAT

$$ SEAFOOD 🍴 **Brophy Bros.** The Ventura outpost of the wildly popular Santa Barbara restaurant provides the same fresh seafood-oriented meals in a spacious second-story setting overlooking the harbor. Feast on everything from fish-and-chips and crab cakes to chowder and delectable fish—often straight from the boats moored below. [$] *Average main: $22* ✉ *1559 Spinnaker Dr., in Ventura Harbor Village* ☎ *805/639–0865* 🌐 *www.brophybros.com* ✍ *Reservations not accepted.*

$ AMERICAN 🍴 **Busy Bee Cafe.** A local favorite for decades, this classic 1950s diner has a jukebox on every table and serves hearty burgers and comfort food (think meat loaf and mashed potatoes, pot roast, and Cobb salad). For breakfast, tuck into a huge omelet; for a snack or dessert, order a shake or hot fudge sundae from the soda fountain. [$] *Average main: $13* ✉ *478 E. Main St., near S. California St.* ☎ *805/643–4864* 🌐 *www.busybeecafe.biz.*

$ SEAFOOD 🍴 **Lure Fish House.** Fresh, sustainably caught seafood charbroiled over a mesquite grill, a well-stocked oyster bar, specialty cocktails, and a wine list heavy on local vintages lure diners into this slick, nautical-theme space downtown. The menu, which changes daily, centers on the mostly local catch and organic veggies, and also includes tacos, sandwiches, and salads. Grilled entrées come with a choice of unusual farm-to-table sides: quinoa salad, sweet-potato fries, pineapple cole slaw. The regulars rave about the shrimp-and-chips, cioppino, and citrus crab-cake salad. [$] *Average main: $15* ✉ *60 S. California St.* ☎ *805/567–4400* 🌐 *www.lurefishhouse.com.*

WHERE TO STAY

$$ HOTEL 🏨 **Crowne Plaza Ventura Beach.** A 12-story hotel with an enviable location on the beach and next to a historic pier, the Crowne Plaza is also within walking distance of downtown restaurants and nightlife. **Pros:** on the beach; near downtown; steps from waterfront. **Cons:** early-morning train noise; waterfront crowded in summer; most rooms on the small side. [$] *Rooms from: $169* ✉ *450 E. Harbor Blvd.* ☎ *800/842–0800, 805/648–2100* 🌐 *cpventura.com* 🛏 *254 rooms, 4 suites* 🍽 *No meals.*

$$ RESORT 🏨 **Four Points by Sheraton Ventura Harbor Resort.** An on-site restaurant, spacious rooms, and a slew of amenities make this 17-acre property—which includes sister hotel Holiday Inn Express—a popular and practical choice for Channel Islands visitors. **Pros:** close to island transportation; mostly quiet; short drive to historic downtown. **Cons:** not in the heart of downtown; noisy seagulls sometimes congregate nearby. [$] *Rooms from: $160* ✉ *1050 Schooner Dr.* ☎ *805/658–1212, 800/368–7764* 🌐 *www.fourpoints.com/ventura* 🛏 *102 rooms, 4 suites* 🍽 *No meals.*

$$ HOTEL 🏨 **Holiday Inn Express Ventura Harbor.** A favorite among Channel Islands visitors, this quiet, comfortable, lodge-inspired property sits right at the Ventura Harbor entrance. **Pros:** quiet at night; easy access to harbor restaurants and activities; five-minute drive to downtown. **Cons:** busy area on weekends; complaints of erratic service. [$] *Rooms from: $145* ✉ *1080 Navigator Dr.* ☎ *805/856–9533, 888/233–9450* 🌐 *www.holidayinnexpress.com/venturaca* 🛏 *69 rooms* 🍽 *Breakfast.*

$$$ HOTEL 🏨 **Ventura Beach Marriott.** Spacious, contemporary rooms, a peaceful location just steps from San Buenaventura State Beach, and easy access to downtown arts and culture make the Marriott a popular choice. **Pros:** walk to beach and biking/jogging trails; a block from historic pier; great value for location. **Cons:** close to highway; near busy intersection. [$] *Rooms from: $189* ✉ *2055 E. Harbor Blvd.* ☎ *805/643–6000, 888/236–2427* 🌐 *www.marriottventurabeach.com* 🛏 *270 rooms, 15 suites* 🍽 *No meals.*

$$ HOTEL 🏨 **Wyndam Garden Ventura Pierpont Inn.** Back in 1910, Josephine Pierpont-Ginn built the original Pierpont Inn on a hill overlooking Ventura Beach. **Pros:** near the beach; lush gardens; Tempur-Pedic mattresses and pillows. **Cons:** near the freeway and train tracks; difficult to walk to downtown from here. [$] *Rooms from: $129* ✉ *550 Sanjon Rd.* ☎ *805/643–6144* 🌐 *www.pierpontinn.com* 🛏 *65 rooms, 9 suites, 2 cottages* 🍽 *No meals.*

SPORTS AND THE OUTDOORS

The most popular outdoor activities in Ventura are beachgoing and whale-watching. California gray whales migrate offshore through the Santa Barbara Channel from late December through March; giant blue and humpback whales feed here from mid-June through September. The channel teems with marine life year-round, so tours, which depart from Ventura Harbor, include more than just whale sightings. To learn about the spectacular hiking trails on the five islands that comprise Channel Islands National Park, check out its visitor center, also at the harbor.

Island Packers. A cruise through the Santa Barbara Channel with Island Packers will give you the chance to spot dolphins and seals—and sometimes even whales—throughout the year. ⊠ *Ventura Harbor, 1691 Spinnaker Dr.* ☎ *805/642–1393* ⊕ *www.islandpackers.com.*

OJAI

15 miles north of Ventura.

The Ojai Valley, which director Frank Capra used as a backdrop for his 1936 film *Lost Horizon,* sizzles in the summer when temperatures routinely reach 90°F. The acres of orange and avocado groves here evoke postcard images of long-ago agricultural Southern California. Many artists and celebrities have sought refuge from life in the fast lane in lush Ojai.

GETTING HERE AND AROUND

From northern Ventura, Highway 33 veers east from U.S. 101 and climbs inland to Ojai. From Santa Barbara, exit U.S. 101 at Highway 150 in Carpinteria, then travel east 20 miles on a twisting, two-lane road that is not recommended at night or during poor weather. You can also access Ojai by heading west from Interstate 5 on Highway 126. Exit at Santa Paula and follow Highway 150 north for 16 miles to Ojai. Gold Coast Transit provides service to Ojai from Ventura.

Ojai can be easily explored on foot; you can also hop on the Ojai Trolley ($1, or $2 day pass), which until about 5 pm follows two routes around Ojai and neighboring Miramonte on weekdays and one route on weekends. Tell the driver you're visiting and you'll get an informal guided tour.

ESSENTIALS

Bus Contacts Gold Coast Transit ☎ *805/643–3158* ⊕ *www.goldcoasttransit.org.* **Ojai Trolley** ☎ *805/646–5581* ⊕ *www.ojaitrolley.com.*

Visitor Information Ojai Visitors Bureau ⊠ *206 N. Signal St., Ste. P, at E. Ojai Ave.* ☎ *888/652-4669, 805/640-3606* ⊕ *www.ojaivisitors.com* ☼ *Weekdays 8–5.*

EXPLORING

Ojai Art Center. California's oldest nonprofit, multipurpose arts center exhibits visual art from various disciplines and presents theater, dance, and other performances. ⊠ *113 S. Montgomery St., near E. Ojai Ave.* ☎ *805/646–0117* ⊕ *www.ojaiartcenter.org* ☼ *Tues.–Sun. noon–4.*

Ojai Avenue. The work of local artists is displayed in the Spanish-style shopping arcade along the avenue downtown. Organic and specialty growers sell their produce on Sundays between 9 and 1 at the outdoor market behind the arcade.

Ojai Valley Museum. The museum collects, preserves, and exhibits the art, history, and culture of Ojai and Ojai Valley. Walking tours of Ojai depart from here. ⊠ *130 W. Ojai Ave.* ☎ *805/640–1390* ⊕ *www. ojaivalleymuseum.org* ✉ *Museum $5, walking tour $5 ($15 family)* ☉ *Tues.–Sat. 10–4, Sun. noon–4; tour Oct.–July, Sat. 10:30.*

Ojai Valley Trail. The 18-mile trail is open to pedestrians, joggers, equestrians, bikers, and others on nonmotorized vehicles. You can access it anywhere along its route. ⊠ *Parallel to Hwy. 33 from Soule Park in Ojai to ocean in Ventura* ☎ *888/652–4669* ⊕ *www.ojaivisitors.com.*

WHERE TO EAT

$$$
MEDITERRANEAN

✗ **Azu.** Farm-fresh tapas, a full bar, slick furnishings, and piped jazz music draw diners to this artsy Mediterranean bistro. You can also order soups, salads, and bistro fare such as steak frites and paella. Save room for the homemade gelato. Ⓢ *Average main: $24* ⊠ *457 E. Ojai Ave.* ☎ *805/640–7987* ⊕ *azuojai.com.*

$
ITALIAN

✗ **Boccali's.** Edging a ranch, citrus groves, and a seasonal garden that provides produce for menu items, the modest but cheery Boccali's attracts many loyal fans. When it's warm, you can dine alfresco in the oak-shaded patio and lawn area and sometimes listen to live music. The family-run operation, best known for hand-rolled pizzas and home-style pastas (don't miss the eggplant lasagna), also serves a popular seasonal strawberry shortcake. Ⓢ *Average main: $15* ⊠ *3277 Ojai Ave., about 2 miles east of downtown* ☎ *805/646–6116* ⊕ *www.boccalis.com* ▭ *No credit cards* ☉ *No lunch Mon. and Tues.*

$$$
AMERICAN

✗ **The Ranch House.** This elegant yet laid-back eatery has been around for decades. Main dishes such as the broiled-and-roasted rack of lamb with pineapple guava chutney and the grilled diver scallops with curried sweet-corn sauce are not to be missed. The verdant patio is a wonderful place to have Sunday brunch. Ⓢ *Average main: $29* ⊠ *500 S. Lomita Ave.* ☎ *805/646–2360* ⊕ *www.theranchhouse.com* ☉ *Closed Mon. No lunch.*

$$$
EUROPEAN

✗ **Suzanne's Cuisine.** Peppered filet mignon, linguine with steamed clams, and pan-roasted salmon with a roasted mango sauce are among the offerings at this European-style restaurant. Game, seafood, and vegetarian dishes dominate the dinner menu, and salads and soups star at lunchtime. All the desserts are made on the premises. Ⓢ *Average main: $27* ⊠ *502 W. Ojai Ave.* ☎ *805/640–1961* ⊕ *www. suzannescuisine.com* ☉ *Closed Tues.*

WHERE TO STAY

$$
B&B/INN

🛏 **The Blue Iguana Inn & Suites.** Artists run this Southwestern-style hotel, and their work (which is for sale) decorates the rooms. **Pros:** colorful art everywhere; secluded. **Cons:** 2 miles from downtown; on a highway; small. Ⓢ *Rooms from: $129* ⊠ *11794 N. Ventura Ave.* ☎ *805/646–5277* ⊕ *www.iguanainnsofojai.com* ⇄ *4 rooms, 8 suites, 8 cottages* ⦿ *Breakfast.*

$$$ ⊞ **Oaks at Ojai.** Rejuvenation is the name of the game at this destina-
RESORT   tion spa. **Pros:** great place to get fit; peaceful retreat; healthful meals.
Cons: some rooms are basic; on main road through town. $ *Rooms
from: $240 ⊠ 122 E. Ojai Ave. ☎ 805/646–5573, 800/753–6257
⊕ www.oaksspa.com ⤳ 44 rooms, 2 suites ⦿ All meals ⌁ 2-night
minimum stay.*

$$$$ ⊞ **Ojai Valley Inn & Spa.** This outdoorsy, golf-oriented resort and spa
RESORT   is set on beautifully landscaped grounds, with hillside views in nearly
Fodor'sChoice   all directions. **Pros:** gorgeous grounds; exceptional outdoor activities;
★   romantic yet kid-friendly. **Cons:** expensive; areas near restaurants can
be noisy. $ *Rooms from: $400 ⊠ 905 Country Club Rd. ☎ 805/646–
1111, 855/697–8780 ⊕ www.ojairesort.com ⤳ 231 rooms, 77 suites
⦿ No meals.*

$$$ ⊞ **Su Nido Inn.** A short walk from downtown Ojai sights and restau-
B&B/INN   rants, this posh Mission revival–style inn sits in a quiet neighborhood
a few blocks from Libbey Park. **Pros:** walking distance from downtown; homey feel. **Cons:** no pool; can get hot during summer. $ *Rooms
from: $199 ⊠ 301 N. Montgomery St. ☎ 805/646–7080, 866/646–7080
⊕ www.sunidoinn.com ⤳ 3 rooms, 9 suites ⦿ No meals ⌁ 2-night
minimum stay on weekends.*

SANTA BARBARA

27 miles northwest of Ventura and 29 miles west of Ojai.

Santa Barbara has long been an oasis for Los Angelenos seeking respite
from big-city life. The attractions begin at the ocean and end in the foothills of the Santa Ynez Mountains. A few miles up the coast east and
west—but still very much a part of Santa Barbara—are the exclusive
residential districts of Montecito and Hope Ranch. Santa Barbara is on
a jog in the coastline, so the ocean is actually to the south, instead of
the west; for this reason, directions can be confusing. "Up" the coast
toward San Francisco is west, "down" toward Los Angeles is east, and
the mountains are north.

GETTING HERE AND AROUND

U.S. 101 is the main route into Santa Barbara. If you're staying in
town, a car is handy but not essential; the beaches and downtown are
easily explored by bicycle or on foot. Visit the Santa Barbara Car Free
website for bike-route and walking-tour maps, suggestions for car-free
vacations, and transportation discounts.

Santa Barbara Metropolitan Transit District's Line 22 bus serves major
tourist sights. Several bus lines connect with the very convenient electric shuttles that cruise the downtown and waterfront every 10 to 15
minutes (50¢ each way).

Santa Barbara Trolley Co. operates a motorized San Francisco–style
cable car that loops past major hotels, shopping areas, and attractions from 10 to 4. Get off whenever you like, and pick up another
trolley (they come every hour) when you're ready to move on. The
fare is $19 for the day.

Continued on page 256

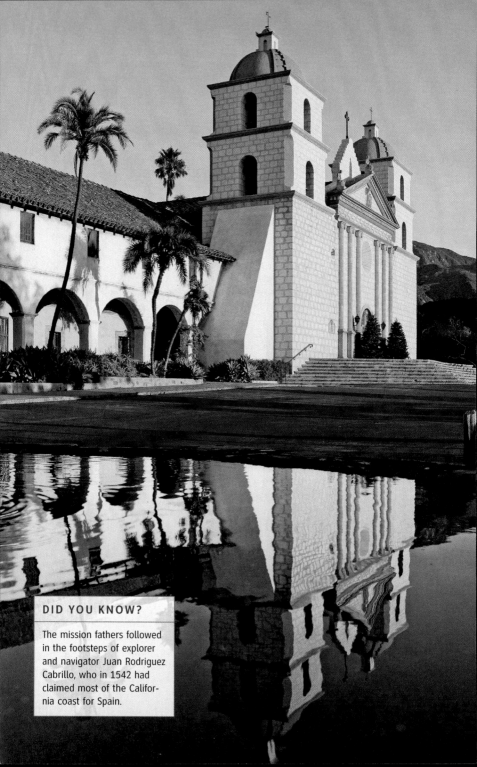

ON A MISSION

Their soul may belong to Spain, their heart to the New World, but the historic missions of California, with their lovely churches, beckon the traveler on a soulful journey back to the very founding of the American West.

by Cheryl Crabtree and Robert I.C. Fisher

California history changed forever in the 18th century when Spanish explorers founded a series of missions along the Pacific coast. Believing they were following God's will, they wanted to spread the gospel and convert as many natives as possible. The process produced a collision between the Hispanic and California Indian cultures, resulting in one of the most striking legacies of Old California: the Spanish mission churches. Rising like mirages in the middle of desert plains and rolling hills, these historic sites transport you back to the days of the Spanish colonial period.

GOD AND MAN IN CALIFORNIA

The Alta California territory came under pressure in the 1760s when Spain feared foreign advances into the territory explorer Juan Rodríguez Cabrillo had claimed for the Spanish crown back in 1542. But how could Spain create a visible and viable presence halfway around the world? They decided to build on the model that had already worked well in Spain's Mexico colony. The plan involved establishing a series of missions, to be operated by the Catholic Church and protected by four of Spain's *presidios* (military outposts). The native Indians—after quick conversion to Christianity—would provide the labor force necessary to build mission towns.

FATHER OF THE MISSIONS

Father Junípero Serra is an icon of the Spanish colonial period. At the behest of the Spanish government, the diminutive padre—then well into his fifties, and despite a chronic leg infection— started out on foot from Baja California to search for suitable mission sites, with a goal of reaching Monterey. In 1769 he helped establish Alta California's first mission in San Diego and continued his travels until his death, in 1784, by which time he had founded eight more missions.

The system ended about a decade after the Mexican government took control of Alta California in the early 1820s and began to secularize the missions. The church lost horses and cattle, as well as vast tracts of land, which the Mexican government in turn granted to private individuals. They also lost laborers, as the Indians were for the most part free to find work and a life beyond the missions. In 1848, the Americans assumed control of the territory, and California became part of the United States. Today, these missions stand as extraordinary monuments to their colorful past.

Mission Santa Barbara Museum

MISSION ACCOMPLISHED

California's Mission Trail is the best way to follow in the fathers' footsteps. Here, below, are its 21 settlements, north to south.

Amazingly, all 21 Spanish missions in California are still visible—some in their pristine historic state, others with modifications made over the centuries. Many are found on or near the "King's Road"—El Camino Real—which linked these mission outposts. At the height of the mission system the trail was approximately 600 miles long, eventually extending from San Diego to Sonoma. Today the road is commemorated on portions of routes 101 and 82 in the form of roadside bell markers erected by CalTrans every one to two miles between San Diego and San Francisco.

San Francisco Solano, Sonoma (1823; this was the final California mission constructed.)

San Rafael, San Rafael (1817)

San Francisco de Asís (aka Mission Dolores), San Francisco (1776). Situated in the heart of San Francisco,

Mission Santa Clara de Asís

these mission grounds and nearby Arroyo de los Dolores (Creek of Sorrows) are home to the oldest intact building in the city.

Santa Clara de Asís, Santa Clara (1777). On the campus of Santa Clara University, this beautifully restored mission contains original paintings, statues, a bell, and hundreds of artifacts, as well as a spectacular rose garden.

San José, Fremont (1797)

Santa Cruz, Santa Cruz (1791)

San Juan Bautista, San Juan Bautista (1797). Immortalized in Hitchcock's *Vertigo*, this remarkably preserved pueblo contains the largest church of all the California missions, as well as 18th- and 19th-century buildings and a sprawling plaza.

San Carlos Borromeo del Río Carmelo, Carmel (1770). Carmel Mission was head-

quarters for the California mission system under Father Serra and the Father Presidents who succeeded him; the on-site museum includes Serra's tiny sleeping quarters (where he died in 1784).

Nuestra Señora de la Soledad, Soledad (1791)

San Antonio de Padua, Jolon (1771)

San Miguel Arcángel, San Miguel (1797). San Miguel boasts the only intact original interior wall painting in any of the missions, painted in 1821 by Native American converts under the direction of Spanish artist Esteban Muras.

Painting from 1818, San Juan Bautista.

Mission Santa Inés

San Luis Obispo de Tolosa, San Luis Obispo (1772). Bear meat from grizzlies captured here saved the Spaniards from starving, which helped convince Father Serra to establish a mission.

La Purísima Concepción, Lompoc (1787). La Purísima is the nation's most completely restored mission complex. It is

now a living-history museum with a church and nearly forty craft and residence rooms.

Santa Inés, Solvang (1804). Home to one of the most significant pieces of religious art created by a California mission Indian.

Santa Bárbara, Santa Barbara (1786). The "Queen of the Missions" has twin bell towers, gorgeous gardens with heirloom plant varietals, a massive collection of rare artworks and artifacts, and lovely stonework.

San Buenaventura, Ventura (1782). This was the last mission founded by Father Serra; it is still an active parish in the Archdiocese of Los Angeles.

Mission San Fernando Rey de España

San Fernando Rey de España, Mission Hills (1797)

San Gabriel Arcángel, San Gabriel (1771)

San Luis Rey de Francia, Oceanside (1798)

San Juan Capistrano, San Juan Capistrano (1776). This mission is famed for its Saint Joseph's Day (March 19) celebration of the return of swallows in the springtime. The mission's adobe walls enclose acres of lush gardens and historic buildings.

San Diego de Alcalá, San Diego (1769). This was the first California missions constructed, although the original was destroyed in 1775 and rebuilt over a number of years.

5

IN FOCUS ON A MISSION

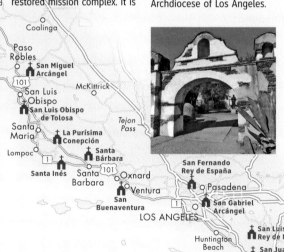

KEY

✝ *Mission*

| 0 | | 50 mi |
| 0 | | 50 km |

SPANISH MISSION STYLE

(left) Mission San Luis Rey de Francia; (right) Mission San Antonio de Padua

The Spanish mission churches derive much of their strength and enduring power from their extraordinary admixture of styles. They are spectacular examples of the combination of races and cultures that bloomed along Father Serra's road through Alta California.

SPIRIT OF THE PLACE
In building the missions, the Franciscan padres had to rely on available resources. Spanish churches back in Europe boasted marble floors and gilded statues. But here, whitewashed adobe walls gleamed in the sun and floors were often merely packed earth.

However simple the structures, the art within the mission confines continued to glorify the Church. The padres imported much finery to decorate the churches and perform the mass— silver, silk and lovely paintings to teach the life of Christ to the Indians and soldiers and settlers. Serra himself commissioned

fine artists in Mexico to produce custom works using the best materials and according to exact specifications. Sculptures of angels, Mary, Joseph, Jesus and the Franciscan heroes and saints—and of course the Stations of the Cross—adorned all the missions.

AN ENDURING LEGACY
Mission architecture reflects a gorgeous blend of European and New World influences. While naves followed the simple forms of Franciscan Gothic, cloisters (with beautiful arcades) adopted aspects of the Romanesque style, and ornamental touches of the Spanish Renaissance— including red-tiled roofs and wrought-iron grilles—added even more elegance. In the 20th century, the Mission Revival Style had a huge impact on architecture and design in California, as seen in examples ranging from San Diego's Union Station to Stanford University's main quadrangle.

Father Junípero Serra statue at Mission San Gabriel

FOR WHOM THE BELLS TOLLED

Perhaps the most famous architectural motif of the Spanish Mission churches was the belltower. These took the form of either a campanile—a single tower called a campanario—or, more spectacularly, of an open-work espedaña, a perforated adobe wall housing a series of bells (notable examples of this form are at San Juan Capistrano and San Diego de Alcalá). Bells were essential to maintaining the routines of daily life at the missions.

MISSION LIFE
Morning bells summoned residents to chapel for services; noontime bells introduced the main meal, while the evening bells sounded the alert to gather around 5 pm for mass and dinner. Many of the natives were happy with their new faith, and even enjoyed putting in numerous hours a week working as farmers, soapmakers, weavers, and masons.

Others were less willing to abandon their traditional culture, but were coerced to abide by the new Spanish laws and mission rules. Natives were sometimes mistreated by the friars, who used a system of punishments typical of the times to enforce submission to the new culture.

NATIVE TRAGEDY
In the end, mission life proved extremely destructive to the Native Californian population. European diseases and contaminated water caused the death of nearly a third, with some tribes—notably the Chumash—suffering disproportionately.

Despite these losses, small numbers did survive. After the Mexican government secularized the missions in 1833, a majority of the native population was reduced to poverty. Some stayed at the missions, while others went to live in the pueblos, ranchos, and countryside.

Many Native Californian people today still work and live near the missions that are monuments to their artistry skills.

FOR MORE INFORMATION

California Missions Foundation

⊠ 123 E. Canon Perdido St. Santa Barbara, CA 93101

☎ 805/963-1633

⊕ www.california missionsfoundation.org

Top, Mission San Gabriel Arcángel
Bottom, Mission San Miguel Arcángel

5

IN FOCUS ON A MISSION

TOURS

Land and Sea Tours. This outfit conducts 90-minute narrated tours in an amphibious 49-passenger vehicle nicknamed the Land Shark. The adventure begins with a drive through the city, followed by a plunge into the harbor for a cruise along the coast. ⊠ *10 E. Cabrillo Blvd., at Stearns Wharf* ☎ *805/683–7600* ⊕ *www.out2seesb.com* 🖃 *From $25* ⊙ *Tours May–Oct., daily noon, 2, and 4; Nov.–Apr., daily noon and 2.*

Segway Tours of Santa Barbara. After a brief training session, a guide leads you around town on electric-powered personal balancing transporters. Tour options include the waterfront (1¼ hours), Butterfly Beach and Montecito (2 hours), historic downtown Santa Barbara (2½ hours), and through town to the mission (3 hours). ⊠ *16 Helena Ave., at Cabrillo Blvd.* ☎ *805/963–7672* ⊕ *www.segwayofsb.com* 🖃 *From $75.*

ESSENTIALS

Transportation Contacts Santa Barbara Car Free ☎ *805/696–1100* ⊕ *www.santabarbaracarfree.org.* **Santa Barbara Metropolitan Transit District** ☎ *805/963–3366* ⊕ *www.sbmtd.gov.* **Santa Barbara Trolley Co.** ☎ *805/965–0353* ⊕ *www.sbtrolley.com.*

Visitor Information Outdoors Santa Barbara Visitor Center ⊠ *113 Harbor Way, off Shoreline Dr.* ☎ *805/456–8752* ⊙ *Daily 11–5.*

Santa Barbara Visitor Center ⊠ *1 Garden St., at Cabrillo Blvd.* ☎ *805/965–3021, 805/568–1811* ⊕ *www.sbchamber.org* ⊙ *Feb.–Oct., Mon.–Sat. 9–5, Sun. 10–5; Nov.–Jan., Mon.–Sat. 9–4, Sun. 10–4.* **Visit Santa Barbara** ⊠ *500 E. Montecito St.* ☎ *805/966–9222* ⊕ *www.santabarbaraca.com.*

EXPLORING

Santa Barbara's waterfront is beautiful, with palm-studded promenades and plenty of sand. In the few miles between the beaches and the hills are downtown, the old mission, and the botanic gardens.

TOP ATTRACTIONS

El Presidio State Historic Park. Founded in 1782, El Presidio was one of four military strongholds established by the Spanish along the coast of California. The park encompasses much of the original site in the heart of downtown. El Cuartel, the adobe guardhouse, is the oldest building in Santa Barbara and the second oldest in California. ⊠ *123 E. Canon Perdido St., at Anacapa St.* ☎ *805/965–0093* ⊕ *www.sbthp.org* 🖃 *$5* ⊙ *Daily 10:30–4:30.*

FAMILY
Fodor'sChoice
★

Lotusland. The 37-acre estate called Lotusland once belonged to the Polish opera singer Ganna Walska, who purchased it in the late 1940s and lived here until her death in 1984. Many of the exotic trees and other subtropical flora were planted in 1882 by horticulturist R. Kinton Stevens. On the two-hour guided tour—the only option for visiting unless you're a member; reserve well ahead in summer—you'll see an outdoor theater, a topiary garden, a huge collection of rare cycads (an unusual plant genus that has been around since the time of the dinosaurs), and a lotus pond. ∎TIP→ Child-friendly family tours are available for groups with children under the age of 10; contact Lotusland for scheduling.

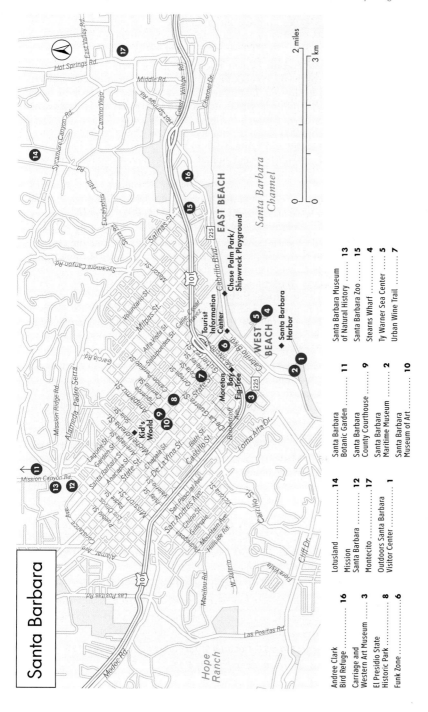

Santa Barbara

5

Hot Springs Rd.

East Valley Rd.

Middle Rd.

Coast Village Rd.

Channel Dr.

Hot Springs Rd.

Camino Viejo

Sycamore Canyon Rd.

Hill Rd.

Eucalyptus Rd.

Serra Rd.

Sycamore Canyon Rd.

Salinas St.

Mason St.

EAST BEACH

Cabrillo Blvd.

225

**Santa Barbara
Channel**

2 miles

3 km

Voluntario St.

Milpas St.

Alta Vista St.

Salsipuedes St.

Calle Cesar Chavez

Tourist
Information
Center

Chase Palm Park/
Shipwreck Playground

Garden St.

Garcia Rd.

Mission Ridge Rd.

Alameda Padre Serra

**Santa Barbara
Harbor**

**WEST
BEACH**

Cabrillo Blvd.

Moreton
Bay
Fig Tree

225

Anapamu St.

Olive St.

State St.

De la Guerra St.

Laguna St.

Santa Barbara St.

Anacapa St.

State St.

Chapala St.

De La Vina St.

Beth St.

Castillo St.

**Kid's
World**

Micheltorena St.

Loma Alta Dr.

Mission Canyon Rd.

Pueblo St.

Los Olivos St.

Padre St.

Mission St.

San Pascual Ave.

San Andrés Ave.

Chino St.

R. Mountain Ave.

Gillespie.

Hillside Rd.

Castillo St.

Cliff Dr.

Constance Ave.

Alamar Ave.

101

Las Positas Rd.

Modoc Rd.

Manitou Rd.

W. Valerio

Flora Vista

Las Positas Rd.

**Hope
Ranch**

101

✉ *695 Ashley Rd., off Sycamore Canyon Rd. (Hwy. 192), Montecito* ☎ *805/969–9990* ⊕ *www.lotusland.org* 💲 *$45* ⊙ *Mid-Feb.–mid-Nov., Wed.–Sat. at 10 and 1:30 by appointment only.*

Fodor'sChoice **Mission Santa Barbara.** Widely referred to as the "Queen of Missions,"
★ this is one of the most beautiful and frequently photographed buildings in coastal California. Dating to 1786, the architecture evolved from adobe-brick buildings with thatch roofs to more permanent edifices as the mission's population burgeoned. An earthquake in 1812 destroyed the third church built on the site. Its replacement, the present structure, is still a functioning Catholic church. Mission Santa Barbara has a splendid Spanish/Mexican colonial art collection, as well as Chumash sculptures and the only Native American–made altar and tabernacle left in the California missions. Docents lead 60-minute tours ($8 adult) Thursday and Friday at 11 and Saturday at 10:30. ✉ *2201 Laguna St., at E. Los Olivos St.* ☎ *805/682–4149 gift shop, 805/682–4713* ⊕ *www. santabarbaramission.org* 💲 *$6* ⊙ *Daily 9–4:15.*

Santa Barbara Botanic Garden. Scenic trails meander through the garden's 78 acres of native plants. The Mission Dam, built in 1806, stands just beyond the redwood grove and above the restored aqueduct that once carried water to Mission Santa Barbara. More than a thousand plant species thrive in various themed sections, including mountains, deserts, meadows, redwoods, and Channel Islands. ✉ *1212 Mission Canyon Rd., north of Foothill Rd. (Hwy. 192)* ☎ *805/682–4726* ⊕ *www.sbbg. org* 💲 *$10* ⊙ *Mar.–Oct., daily 9–6; Nov.–Feb., daily 9–5. Guided tours weekends at 11 and 2, Mon. at 2.*

Fodor'sChoice **Santa Barbara County Courthouse.** Hand-painted tiles and a spiral staircase
★ infuse the courthouse, a national historic landmark, with the grandeur of a Moorish palace. This magnificent building was completed in 1929, part of a rebuilding process after a 1925 earthquake destroyed many downtown structures. At the time, Santa Barbara was also in the midst of a cultural awakening, and the trend was toward an architectural style appropriate to the area's climate and history. The result is the harmonious Mediterranean–Spanish look of much of the downtown area, especially the municipal buildings. An elevator rises to an arched observation area in the courthouse tower that provides a panoramic view of the city. The murals in the ceremonial chambers on the courthouse's second floor were painted by an artist who did backdrops for some of Cecil B. DeMille's films. ✉ *1100 Anacapa St., at E. Anapamu St.* ☎ *805/962–6464* ⊕ *www.santabarbaracourthouse.org* ⊙ *Weekdays 8–4:45, weekends 10–4:30. Free guided tours Mon., Tues., Wed., and Fri. at 10:30, daily at 2.*

QUICK BITES

Jeannine's. Take a break from State Street shopping at Jeannine's, revered locally for its wholesome sandwiches, salads, and baked goods, made from scratch with organic and natural ingredients. Pick up a turkey cranberry or chicken pesto sandwich to go, and picnic in the courthouse gardens a block away. ✉ *La Arcada, 15 E. Figueroa St., at State St.* ☎ *805/966–1717* ⊕ *jeannines.com/restaurants* ⊙ *Daily 6:30–3.*

Santa Barbara Museum of Art. The highlights of this museum's permanent collection include ancient sculpture, Asian art, impressionist paintings, contemporary art, photography, and American works in several media. ⊠ *1130 State St., at E. Anapamu St.* ☎ *805/963–4364* ⊕ *www.sbma.net* 🖃 *$10, free Thurs. 5–8* ☉ *Tues., Wed., Fri. and weekends 11–5, Thurs. 11–8.*

FAMILY **Santa Barbara Museum of Natural History.** The gigantic skeleton of a blue whale greets you at the entrance of this complex. The major draws include the planetarium, space lab, and a gem and mineral display. A room of dioramas illustrates Chumash Indian history and culture. Startlingly alive-looking stuffed specimens, complete with nests and eggs, roost in the bird hall. Many exhibits have interactive components. Outdoors, nature trails wind through the serene oak-studded grounds. ■TIP➔ **A Nature Pass, available at the museum and the associated Ty Warner Sea Center, is good for discounted unlimited two-day admission to both facilities.** ⊠ *2559 Puesta del Sol Rd., off Mission Canyon Rd.* ☎ *805/682–4711* ⊕ *www.sbnature.org* 🖃 *$13 May–Sept.; $12 Oct.–Apr.; free 3rd Sun. of month Sept.–Apr.* ☉ *Daily 10–5.*

FAMILY **Santa Barbara Zoo.** This compact zoo's grounds are so gorgeous people book weddings here long in advance. The palm-studded lawns on a hilltop overlooking the beach are perfect spots for family picnics. The natural settings of the zoo shelter elephants, gorillas, exotic birds like the California condor, and big cats such as the rare snow leopard, a thick-furred, high-altitude dweller from Asia. For small children, there's a scenic railroad and barnyard petting zoo. Three high-tech dinosaurs perform in live stage shows, daily in summer, on weekends the rest of the year (free with admission). ⊠ *500 Niños Dr., off El Cabrillo Blvd.* ☎ *805/962–5339 main line, 805/962–6310 information* ⊕ *www.santabarbarazoo.org* 🖃 *Zoo $15, parking $6* ☉ *Daily 10–5.*

Stearns Wharf. Built in 1872, Stearns Wharf is Santa Barbara's most visited landmark. Expansive views of the mountains, cityscape, and harbor unfold from every vantage point on the three-block-long pier. Although it's a nice walk from the Cabrillo Boulevard parking areas, you can also park on the pier and then wander through the shops or stop for a meal at one of the wharf's restaurants. ⊠ *Cabrillo Blvd. and State St.* ⊕ *www.stearnswharf.org.*

FAMILY **Ty Warner Sea Center.** A branch of the Santa Barbara Museum of Natural History, the center specializes in Santa Barbara Channel marine life and conservation. Though small compared to aquariums in Monterey and Long Beach, this is a fascinating, hands-on marine science laboratory that lets you participate in experiments, projects, and exhibits, including touch tanks. Two-story glass walls here open to stunning ocean, mountain, and city views. You can purchase a Nature Pass, which includes discounted two-day admission to the natural history museum and the Sea Center. ⊠ *211 Stearns Wharf* ☎ *805/962–2526* ⊕ *www.sbnature. org* ☜ *$8* ⊗ *Daily 10–5.*

WORTH NOTING

Andree Clark Bird Refuge. This peaceful lagoon and its gardens sit north of East Beach. Bike trails and footpaths, punctuated by signs identifying native and migratory birds, skirt the lagoon. ⊠ *1400 E. Cabrillo Blvd., near the zoo* ☜ *Free.*

FAMILY **Carriage and Western Art Museum.** The country's largest collection of old horse-drawn vehicles—painstakingly restored—is exhibited here, everything from polished hearses to police buggies to old stagecoaches and circus vehicles. In August the Old Spanish Days Fiesta borrows many of the vehicles for a jaunt around town. ■TIP→ This is one of the city's hidden gems. ⊠ *Pershing Park, 129 Castillo St.* ☎ *805/962–2353* ⊕ *www.carriagemuseum.org* ☜ *Free* ⊗ *Weekdays 9–3, 3rd Sun. of month 1–4 for tours.*

Funk Zone. A formerly run-down industrial neighborhood near the waterfront and train station, the Funk Zone has evolved into a hip hangout filled with wine-tasting rooms, arts-and-crafts studios, murals, breweries, restaurants, and small shops. It's fun to poke around the three-square-block district. ■TIP→ Street parking is limited, so leave your car in a nearby city lot and cruise up and down the alleys on foot. ⊠ *Between State and Garden Sts. and Cabrillo Blvd. and U.S. 101* ⊕ *funkzone.net.*

Montecito. Since the late 1800s the tree-studded hills and valleys of this town have attracted the rich and famous: Hollywood icons, business tycoons, tech moguls, and old-money families who installed themselves years ago. Shady roads wind through the community, which consists mostly of gated estates. Swank boutiques line **Coast Village Road,** where well-heeled residents such as Oprah Winfrey sometimes browse for truffle oil, picture frames, and designer jeans. Residents also hang out in the Upper Village, a chic shopping area with restaurants and cafés at the intersection of San Ysidro and East Valley roads.

FAMILY **Santa Barbara Maritime Museum.** California's seafaring history is the focus here. High-tech, hands-on exhibits, such as a sportfishing activity that lets participants catch a "big one" and a local surfing history retrospective, make this a fun stop for families. The museum's shining star is an extremely rare, 17-foot-tall First Order Fresnel lens from the historic Point Conception Lighthouse. ⊠ *113 Harbor Way, off Shoreline Dr.* ☎ *805/962–8404* ⊕ *www.sbmm.org* ☜ *$7* ⊗ *June–Aug., Thurs.–Tues. 10–6; Sept.–May, Thurs.–Tues. 10–5.*

Urban Wine Trail. Nearly two dozen winery tasting rooms form the Urban Wine Trail; most are within walking distance of the waterfront and the lower State Street shopping and restaurant district. **Santa Barbara Winery,** at 202 Anacapa Street, and **Au Bon Climat,** at 813 Anacapa Street, are good places to start your oenological trek. ⊕ *urbanwinetrailsb.com.*

Santa Barbara's downtown is attractive, but be sure also to visit its beautiful—and usually uncrowded—beaches.

BEACHES

Santa Barbara's beaches don't have the big surf of the shoreline farther south, but they also don't have the crowds. You can usually find a solitary spot to swim or sunbathe. In June and July, fog often hugs the coast until about noon.

Arroyo Burro Beach. The beach's usually gentle surf makes it ideal for families with young children. It's a local favorite, since you can walk for miles in both directions when tides are low. Leashed dogs are allowed on the main stretch of beach and westward; they are allowed to romp off-leash east of the slough at the beach entrance. The parking lots fill early on weekends and throughout the summer, but the park is relatively quiet at other times. Walk along the beach just a few hundreds yards away from the main steps at the entrance to escape crowds on warm-weather days. Surfers, swimmers, standup paddlers, and boogie boarders regularly ply the waves, and photographers come often to catch the vivid sunsets. **Amenities:** food and drink; lifeguard in summer; parking, showers, toilets. **Best for:** sunset; surfing; swimming; walking. ⊠ *Cliff Dr. and Las Positas Rd.* ⊕ *www.countyofsb.org/parks.*

FAMILY **East Beach.** The wide swath of sand at the east end of Cabrillo Boulevard is a great spot for people-watching. East Beach has sand volleyball courts, summertime lifeguard and sports competitions, and arts-and-crafts shows on Sunday and holidays. You can use showers, a weight room, and lockers (bring your own towel) and rent umbrellas and boogie boards at the Cabrillo Bathhouse. Next door, there's an elaborate jungle-gym play area for kids. Hotels line the boulevard across from the beach. **Amenities:** food and drink; lifeguards in summer; parking (fee); showers; toilets; water sports. **Best for:** walking; swimming; surfing. ✉ *1118 Cabrillo Blvd., at Ninos Dr.* ☎ *805/897–2680.*

WHERE TO EAT

$$$ JAPANESE 🍴 **Arigato Sushi.** You might have to wait for a table at this trendy, two-story restaurant and sushi bar—locals line up early for the wildly creative combination rolls and other delectables. Fans of authentic Japanese food sometimes disagree about the quality of the seafood, but all dishes are fresh and artfully presented. The menu includes traditional dishes as well as innovative creations such as jalapeño yellowtail sashimi and ahi carpaccio. [$] *Average main: $25* ✉ *1225 State St., near W. Victoria St.* ☎ *805/965–6074* 🌐 *www.arigatosantabarbara.com* ✍ *Reservations not accepted* ⏲ *No lunch.*

$$ SEAFOOD 🍴 **Brophy Bros.** The outdoor tables at this casual harborside restaurant have perfect views of the marina and mountains. Staffers serve enormous, exceptionally fresh fish dishes—don't miss the seafood salad and chowder—and provide guests with a pager if there's a long wait for a table. Stroll along the waterfront until the beep lets you know your table's ready. Hugely popular, Brophy Bros. can be crowded and loud, especially on weekend evenings. [$] *Average main: $22* ✉ *119 Harbor Way, off Shoreline Dr.* ☎ *805/966–4418* 🌐 *www.brophybros.com.*

$ INDIAN 🍴 **Flavor of India.** Feast on authentic northern Indian dishes like tandoori chicken, lamb biryani, and a host of curries at this local favorite in a residential neighborhood. Best bets include the combination dinners served in a traditional Indian tray and the all-you-can-eat lunch buffet ($9). [$] *Average main: $13* ✉ *3026 State St., at De La Vina St.* ☎ *805/682–6561* 🌐 *www.flavorofindiasb.com* ⏲ *Closed Sun.*

$$$ SEAFOOD 🍴 **The Hungry Cat.** The hip Santa Barbara sibling of a famed Hollywood eatery, run by chefs David Lentz and his wife, Suzanne Goin, dishes up savory seafood in a small but lively nook in the downtown arts district. Feast on sea urchin, addictive peel-and-eat shrimp, and creative cocktails made from farmers' market fruits and veggies. A busy nightspot on weekends, the Cat also awakens for a popular brunch on Sunday. Night or day, come early or be prepared for a wait. [$] *Average main: $28* ✉ *1134 Chapala St., near W. Figueroa St.* ☎ *805/884–4701* 🌐 *www.thehungrycat.com* ⏲ *No lunch Mon. Sept.–Apr.*

$ MEXICAN 🍴 **La Super-Rica.** This food stand on the east side of town serves some of the spiciest and most authentic Mexican dishes between Los Angeles and San Francisco. Fans (the late chef Julia Child was one) fill up on the soft tacos served with yummy spicy or mild sauces and legendary beans. Portions are on the small side; order several dishes and share. [$] *Average main: $10* ✉ *622 N. Milpas St., at Alphonse St.* ☎ *805/963–4940* 💳 *No credit cards* ⏲ *Closed Wed.*

$$$ ITALIAN 🍴 **Olio e Limone.** Sophisticated Italian cuisine (with an emphasis on Sicily) is served at this restaurant near the Arlington Center. The juicy veal chop is popular, but surprises abound here; be sure to try unusual dishes such as ribbon pasta with quail and sausage in a mushroom ragout, or the duck ravioli. Tables are placed close together, so this may not be the best spot for intimate conversations. Next door is the more casual Olio Pizzeria, a combination pizzeria and wine bar, and Olio Crudo, a raw bar. [$] *Average main: $30* ✉ *17 W. Victoria St., at State St.* ☎ *805/899–2699* 🌐 *www.olioelimone.com* ⏲ *No lunch Sun.*

TAKE THE KIDS

Two playful playgrounds provide welcome interludes for the young set. Children love tooling around **Kids' World** (✉ *Garden and Micheltorena Sts.*), a public playground with a castle-shape maze of climbing structures, slides, and tunnels. At **Shipwreck Playground** (✉ *Chase Palm Park, E. Cabrillo Blvd., east of Garden St.*), parents take as much pleasure in the waterfront views as the kids do in the nautical-theme diversions and the antique carousel.

$$$ SOUTHERN

🍴 **Palace Grill.** Mardi Gras energy, team-style service, lively music, and great food have made the Palace a Santa Barbara icon. Acclaimed for its Cajun and creole dishes such as blackened redfish and jambalaya with dirty rice, the Palace also serves Caribbean fare, including a delicious coconut-shrimp dish. If you're spice-phobic, you can choose pasta, soft-shell crab, or filet mignon. Be prepared to wait for a table on Friday and Saturday nights (when reservations are taken for a 5:30 seating only), though the live entertainment and free appetizers, sent out front when the line is long, will whet your appetite for the feast to come. [$] *Average main: $29* ✉ *8 E. Cota St., at State St.* ☎ *805/963–5000* 🌐 *palacegrill.com.*

$$ MODERN AMERICAN

🍴 **Roy.** In a low-key room with a loungelike feel, owner-chef Leroy Gandy serves stylish contemporary cuisine and local wines at reasonable prices. Entrées might include sautéed local fish with an almond crust, lemon-butter sauce, and papaya orange salsa, or bacon-wrapped filet mignon. **■ TIP→ Roy is a favorite spot for late-night dining—it's open until midnight and has a full bar.** [$] *Average main: $20* ✉ *7 W. Carrillo St., near State St.* ☎ *805/966–5636* 🌐 *www.restaurantroy.com* ⏲ *No lunch.*

$$$$ AMERICAN
Fodor's Choice ★

🍴 **The Stonehouse.** The elegant Stonehouse is inside a century-old granite former farmhouse at the San Ysidro Ranch resort. Executive chef Matt Johnson creates outstanding regional cuisine centered around herbs and veggies from the on-site garden and top-quality local ingredients. The menu changes constantly but typically includes favorites such as pan-seared abalone and classic steak Diane flambéed tableside. Dine on the radiant-heated oceanview deck with stone fireplace, next to a fountain under a canopy of loquat trees, or in the romantic, candlelit dining room overlooking a creek. **■ TIP→ The Plow & Angel pub, downstairs, serves casual bistro fare.** [$] *Average main: $49* ✉ *900 San Ysidro La., off San Ysidro Rd., Montecito* ☎ *805/565–1700* 🌐 *www.sanysidroranch.com* ✍ *Reservations essential* ⏲ *No lunch Sun.–Tues.*

$$$ AMERICAN

🍴 **Wine Cask.** A reinvention of a same-named local favorite that closed a few years back, the Wine Cask serves bistro-style meals—many of them made with ingredients from a nearby farmers' market—in a comfortable and classy dining room. The dishes are paired with wines from Santa Barbara's most extensive wine list. The more casual

5

bar-café, Intermezzo, across the courtyard, serves pizzas, salads, small plates, wines, and cocktails and is open late. [$] *Average main: $29* ✉ *El Paseo, 813 Anacapa St., at E. De La Guerra St.* ☎ *805/966–9463* 🌐 *www.winecask.com* ✍ *Reservations essential.*

WHERE TO STAY

$$$$ RESORT 🏨 **Bacara Resort & Spa.** A luxury resort with four restaurants and a 42,000-square-foot spa and fitness center with 36 treatment rooms, the Bacara provides a gorgeous setting for relaxing retreats. **Pros:** serene natural setting; nature trails; first-rate spa; three zero-edge pools. **Cons:** pricey; not close to downtown; sand on beach not pristine enough for some. [$] *Rooms from: $450* ✉ *8301 Hollister Ave., Goleta* ☎ *805/968–0100, 855/817–9782* 🌐 *www.bacararesort.com* 🛏 *306 rooms, 45 suites* 🍴 *No meals.*

$$$$ HOTEL 🏨 **Canary Hotel.** The only full-service hotel in the heart of downtown, this Kimpton property blends a casual, beach-getaway feel with urban sophistication. **Pros:** easy stroll to museums, shopping, dining; friendly, attentive service; adjacent fitness center. **Cons:** across from transit center; some rooms feel cramped. [$] *Rooms from: $400* ✉ *31 W. Carrillo St.* ☎ *805/884–0300, 877/468–3515* 🌐 *www.canarysantabarbara.com* 🛏 *77 rooms, 20 suites* 🍴 *No meals.*

$$$$ HOTEL Fodor's Choice ★ 🏨 **Belmond El Encanto.** Following years of extensive renovations by Orient-Express, this Santa Barbara icon lives on to thrill a new generation of guests with its relaxed-luxe bungalow rooms, lush gardens, and personalized service. **Pros:** revitalized historic landmark; stellar spa facility; drinks and dining with stunning views; friendly and personal service; free use of electric bikes. **Cons:** long walk to downtown; pricey, restaurant menus limited if you are staying for more than a few days. [$] *Rooms from: $650* ✉ *800 Alvarado Pl.* ☎ *805/845–5800, 800/393–5315* 🌐 *elencanto.com* 🛏 *70 rooms, 22 suites* 🍴 *No meals.*

$$$$ RESORT Fodor's Choice ★ 🏨 **Four Seasons Resort The Biltmore Santa Barbara.** Surrounded by lush, perfectly manicured gardens and across from the beach, Santa Barbara's grande dame has long been a favorite for quiet, California-style luxury. **Pros:** first-class resort; historic Santa Barbara character; personal service; steps from the beach. **Cons:** back rooms are close to train tracks; expensive. [$] *Rooms from: $425* ✉ *1260 Channel Dr.* ☎ *805/969–2261, 805/332–3442 reservations* 🌐 *www.fourseasons.com/santabarbara* 🛏 *181 rooms, 26 suites* 🍴 *No meals.*

$$ HOTEL 🏨 **Franciscan Inn.** The friendly staff and the range of cheery, spacious beach-theme rooms, from singles to mini- and family suites, at this family-owned Spanish-Mediterranean motel make this a good choice for all types of travelers; its location just a block from the harbor and West Beach is hard to beat. **Pros:** walking distance from waterfront and harbor; family-friendly; great value. **Cons:** busy lobby; pool can be crowded. [$] *Rooms from: $145* ✉ *109 Bath St.* ☎ *805/963–8845* 🌐 *www.franciscaninn.com* 🛏 *33 rooms, 20 suites* 🍴 *Breakfast.*

$$$ HOTEL 🏨 **Hotel Indigo.** The closest hotel to the train station, artsy Hotel Indigo (opened in 2012) is a great choice for travelers who appreciate contemporary art and want easy access to dining, nightlife, and the beach. **Pros:** multilingual staff; a block from Stearns Wharf; great value for

location. **Cons:** showers only (no bathtubs); train whistles early morning; rooms on small side. *[$] Rooms from: $189 ✉ 121 State St. ☎ 805/966–6586, 877/270–1392 toll-free 🌐 www.indigosantabarbara.com 🛏 41 rooms 🍴 No meals.*

BEST VIEWS

Drive along Alameda Padre Serra, a hillside road that begins near the mission and continues to Montecito, to feast your eyes on spectacular views of the city and the Santa Barbara Channel.

$$$ HOTEL 🏨 **Hyatt Santa Barbara.** A complex of four buildings on three landscaped acres, the Hyatt provides an appealing lodging option in a prime location right across from East Beach. **Pros:** steps from the beach; many room types and rates; walk to the zoo and waterfront shuttle. **Cons:** motelish vibe; busy area in summer. *[$] Rooms from: $229 ✉ 1111 E. Cabrillo Blvd. ☎ 805/882–1234, 800/643–1994 🌐 www.santabarbara.hyatt.com 🛏 171 rooms, 3 suites 🍴 No meals.*

$ HOTEL 🏨 **Motel 6 Santa Barbara Beach.** A half block from East Beach amid fancier hotels sits this basic but comfortable motel—the first Motel 6 in existence and the first in the chain to transform into a contemporary Euro-style abode. **Pros:** very close to zoo and beach; friendly staff; clean. **Cons:** no frills; motel-style rooms; no breakfast. *[$] Rooms from: $119 ✉ 443 Corona Del Mar Dr. ☎ 805/564–1392, 800/466–8356 🌐 www.motel6.com 🛏 51 rooms 🍴 No meals.*

5

$$$$ RESORT Fodor's Choice ★ 🏨 **San Ysidro Ranch.** At this romantic hideaway on a historic property in the Montecito foothills—where John and Jackie Kennedy spent their honeymoon and Oprah sends her out-of-town visitors—guest cottages are scattered among groves of orange trees and flower beds. **Pros:** ultimate privacy; surrounded by nature; celebrity hangout; pet-friendly. **Cons:** very expensive; too remote for some. *[$] Rooms from: $695 ✉ 900 San Ysidro La., Montecito ☎ 805/565–1700, 800/368–6788 🌐 www.sanysidroranch.com 🛏 23 rooms, 4 suites, 14 cottages 🍴 No meals ☞ 2-day minimum stay on weekends, 3 days on holiday weekends.*

$$$$ B&B/INN Fodor's Choice ★ 🏨 **Simpson House Inn.** If you're a fan of traditional B&Bs, this property, with its beautifully appointed Victorian main house and acre of lush gardens, is for you. **Pros:** impeccable landscaping; walking distance from everything downtown; ranked among the nation's top B&Bs. **Cons:** some rooms in main building are small; two-night minimum stay on weekends. *[$] Rooms from: $255 ✉ 121 E. Arrellaga St. ☎ 805/963–7067, 800/676–1280 🌐 www.simpsonhouseinn.com 🛏 11 rooms, 4 cottages 🍴 Breakfast.*

$$$$ B&B/INN 🏨 **Spanish Garden Inn.** A half block from the Presidio in the heart of downtown, this elegant Spanish-Mediterranean retreat celebrates Santa Barbara style, from the tile floors, wrought-iron balconies, and exotic plants, to the original art by local plein-air artists. **Pros:** walking distance from downtown; classic Spanish-Mediterranean style; caring staff. **Cons:** no restaurant. *[$] Rooms from: $379 ✉ 915 Garden St. ☎ 805/564–4700, 866/564–4700 🌐 www.spanishgardeninn.com 🛏 23 rooms 🍴 Breakfast.*

NIGHTLIFE AND THE ARTS

Most major hotels present entertainment nightly during the summer and on weekends all year. The bar, club, and live-music scene centers on lower State Street, between the 300 and 800 blocks. The thriving arts district, with theaters, restaurants, and cafés, starts around the 900 block of State Street and continues north to the Arlington Center for the Performing Arts, in the 1300 block. To see what's scheduled around town, pick up a copy of the free weekly *Santa Barbara Independent* newspaper or visit its website, ⊕ *www.independent.com.*

NIGHTLIFE

Blue Agave. Leather couches, a crackling fire in chilly weather, a cigar balcony, and pool tables draw a fancy crowd here for good food and designer martinis. ⊠ *20 E. Cota St., near State St.* ☎ *805/899–4694* ⊕ *www.blueagavesb.com.*

Dargan's. Lively Dargan's pub has pool tables, great draft beers and Irish whiskeys, and serves a full menu of traditional Irish dishes. ⊠ *18 E. Ortega St., at Anacapa St.* ☎ *805/568–0702* ⊕ *darganssb.com.*

James Joyce. A good place to have a few beers and while away an evening, the James Joyce sometimes hosts folk and rock performers. ⊠ *513 State St., at W. Haley St.* ☎ *805/962–2688* ⊕ *www.sbjamesjoyce.com.*

Joe's Cafe. Steins of beer accompany hearty bar food at Joe's. It's a fun, if occasionally rowdy, collegiate scene. ⊠ *536 State St., at E. Cota St.* ☎ *805/966–4638* ⊕ *www.joescafesb.com.*

Lucky's. A slick sports bar attached to an upscale steak house owned by the maker of Lucky Brand dungarees, this place attracts hip patrons hoping to see and be seen. ⊠ *1279 Coast Village Rd., near Olive Mill Rd., Montecito* ☎ *805/565–7540* ⊕ *www.luckys-steakhouse.com/bar.*

Milk & Honey. Artfully prepared tapas, mango mojitos, and exotic cocktails lure trendy crowds to swank M&H, despite high prices and a reputation for inattentive service. ⊠ *30 W. Anapamu St., at State St.* ☎ *805/275–4232* ⊕ *milknhoneytapas.com.*

SOhO. A hip restaurant, bar, and music club, SOhO books bands, from jazz to blues to rock, nightly. ⊠ *1221 State St., at W. Victoria St.* ☎ *805/962–7776* ⊕ *www.sohosb.com.*

THE ARTS

Arlington Theatre. This Moorish-style auditorium hosts events during the two-week Santa Barbara International Film Festival every winter and presents touring performers and films throughout the year. ⊠ *1317 State St., at Arlington Ave.* ☎ *805/963–4408* ⊕ *www.thearlingtontheatre.com.*

The Granada Theatre. A restored, modernized landmark that dates to 1924, the Granada hosts Broadway touring shows and dance, music, and other cultural events. ⊠ *1214 State St., at E. Anapamu St.* ☎ *805/899–2222 box office* ⊕ *www.granadasb.org.*

Lobero Theatre. A state landmark, the Lobero hosts community theater groups and touring professionals. ⊠ *33 E. Canon Perdido St., at Anacapa St.* ☎ *805/963–0761* ⊕ *www.lobero.com.*

Santa Barbara International Film Festival. The hottest ticket in town in late January, the 11-day festival attracts film enthusiasts and major stars to various downtown venues for screenings, industry panels, and celebrity tributes. ⊕ *sbiff.org.*

SPORTS AND THE OUTDOORS

BIKING

Cabrillo Bike Lane. The level, two-lane, 3-mile Cabrillo Bike Lane passes the Santa Barbara Zoo, the Andree Clark Bird Refuge, beaches, and the harbor. There are restaurants along the way, and you can stop for a picnic along the palm-lined path looking out on the Pacific.

Wheel Fun Rentals. You can rent bikes, quadricycles, and skates here. ⊠ *23 E. Cabrillo Blvd.* ☎ *805/966–2282* ⊕ *www.wheelfunrentalssb.com.*

BOATS AND CHARTERS

Channel Islands Outfitters. A full-service paddle sports center in the harbor, this outfit rents kayaks, stand-up paddleboards, surfboards, boogie boards, and water-sports gear, and conducts guided tours and excursions. Smaller outlets are at Goleta Beach near UC Santa Barbara (year-round) and at West Beach next to Stearns Wharf (summer). ⊠ *117 B Harbor Way, off Shoreline Dr.* ☎ *805/899–4925 tours, 805/617–3425 rentals* ⊕ *www.channelislandso.com.*

Condor Express. From SEA Landing, the *Condor Express,* a 75-foot high-speed catamaran, whisks up to 149 passengers toward the Channel Islands on dinner cruises, whale-watching excursions, and pelagic-bird trips. ⊠ *301 W. Cabrillo Blvd.* ☎ *805/882–0088, 888/779–4253* ⊕ *condorexpress.com.*

Santa Barbara Sailing Center. The center offers sailing instruction; rents and charters sailboats, kayaks, and stand-up paddleboards; and organizes dinner and sunset champagne cruises, island excursions, and whale-watching trips. ⊠ *Santa Barbara Harbor launching ramp* ☎ *805/962–2826* ⊕ *www.sbsail.com.*

FAMILY **Santa Barbara Water Taxi.** Children beg to ride *Lil' Toot,* a cherry yellow water taxi that cruises from the harbor to Stearns Wharf and back again. The fare for kids is $1 each way. ⊠ *Santa Barbara Harbor and Stearns Wharf* ☎ *888/316–9363* ⊕ *sbwatertaxi.com* ⊠ *$4 one-way* ⊙ *June–Aug., daily noon–6, Sept.–May, Fri.–Sun. noon–sunset.*

Truth Aquatics. Truth runs kayaking, paddleboarding, hiking, and scuba excursions to the National Marine Sanctuary and Channel Islands National Park. ⊠ *Departures from SEA Landing, Santa Barbara Harbor* ☎ *805/962–1127* ⊕ *www.truthaquatics.com.*

GOLF

Sandpiper Golf Club. This course sits on the ocean bluffs and combines super-scenic views with a challenging game. ⊠ *7925 Hollister Ave., 14 miles north of downtown off U.S. 101* ☎ *805/968–1541* ⊕ *www. sandpipergolf.com* ⊠ *$140 Mon.–Thurs., $160 Fri.–Sun./holidays* ⅄ *18 holes, 7000 yards, par 72.*

Santa Barbara Golf Club. The well-maintained public club—among the area's most affordable—occupies a hilltop site with sweeping views of mountains, ocean, and islands. Hotel guests receive greens-fee discounts by showing a room key card. ✉ *3500 McCaw Ave., at Las Positas Rd.* 📞 *805/687–7087* ⊕ *www.thesantabarbaragolfclub.com* 💳 *Nonresidents $50 weekdays, $60 weekends* 🚩 *18 holes, 6037 yards, par 70.*

TENNIS
Many hotels in Santa Barbara have courts.

City of Santa Barbara Parks and Recreation Department. The City of Santa Barbara Parks and Recreation Department operates public courts with lighted play until 9 pm weekdays. You can purchase day permits ($8) at the courts, or call the department. 📞 *805/564–5573* ⊕ *www.sbparksandrecreation.com.*

Municipal Tennis Center. The center's 12 hard courts include an enclosed stadium court and three that are lighted on weekdays. ✉ *1414 Park Pl., near Salinas St. and U.S. 101.*

Pershing Park. The eight lighted courts here are available for public play after 5 pm weekdays and all day on weekends and some holidays. ✉ *100 Castillo St., near Cabrillo Blvd.*

SHOPPING

BOOKS
Book Den. Bibliophiles have browsed for new, used, and out-of-print books at this independent shop since 1933. ✉ *15 E. Anapamu St., at State St.* 📞 *805/962–3321* ⊕ *www.bookden.com.*

Chaucer's Bookstore. This well-stocked independent shop is a favorite of many locals. ✉ *Loreto Plaza, 3321 State St., at Los Positas Rd.* 📞 *805/682–6787* ⊕ *www.chaucersbooks.com.*

Granada Books. A nonprofit community bookstore in the arts and culture district, Granada has an excellent collection of local books and regularly hosts lectures and events. ✉ *1224 State St.* 📞 *805/845–1818* ⊕ *www.sbgranadabooks.com.*

CLOTHING
Diani. This upscale, European-style women's boutique dresses clients in designer clothing from around the world. A sibling shoe shop is nearby. ✉ *1324 State St., at Arlington Ave.* 📞 *805/966–3114, 805/966–7175 shoe shop* ⊕ *www.dianiboutique.com.*

Surf N Wear's Beach House. This shop carries surf clothing, gear, and collectibles; it's also the home of Santa Barbara Surf Shop and the exclusive local dealer of Surfboards by Yater. ✉ *10 State St., at Cabrillo Blvd.* 📞 *805/963–1281* ⊕ *surfnwear.com.*

Wendy Foster. This store sells casual-chic women's fashions. ✉ *833 State St., at W. Canon Perdido St.* 📞 *805/966–2276* ⊕ *www.wendyfoster.com.*

SHOPPING AREAS
Brinkerhoff Avenue. Antiques and gift shops are clustered in restored Victorian buildings on Brinkerhoff Avenue. ✉ *2 blocks west of State St., at W. Cota St.*

El Paseo. Shops, art galleries, and studios share the courtyard and gardens of El Paseo, a historic arcade. ⊠ *Canon Perdido St., between State and Anacapa Sts.*

State Street. Between Cabrillo Boulevard and Sola Street, State Street is a shopper's paradise. Chic malls, quirky storefronts, antiques emporia, elegant boutiques, and funky thrift shops abound. You can shop on foot or ride a battery-powered trolley (50¢) that runs between the waterfront and the 1300 block. Nordstrom and Macy's anchor **Paseo Nuevo,** an open-air mall in the 700 block. Shops, restaurants, galleries, and fountains line the tiled walkways of **La Arcada,** a small complex of landscaped courtyards in the 1100 block designed by architect Myron Hunt in 1926.

> **EARTH DAY**
>
> In 1969, 200,000 gallons of crude oil spilled into the Santa Barbara Channel, causing an immediate outcry from residents. The day after the spill, Get Oil Out (GOO) was established; the group helped lead the successful fight for legislation to limit and regulate offshore drilling in California. The Santa Barbara spill also spawned Earth Day, which is still celebrated across the nation today.

Summerland. Serious antiques hunters head southeast of Santa Barbara to Summerland, which is full of shops and markets. Several good ones are along Lillie Avenue and Ortega Hill Road. ⊠ *Summerland.*

SANTA BARBARA COUNTY

Residents refer to the glorious 30-mile stretch of coastline from Carpinteria to Gaviota as the South Coast. The Santa Ynez Mountains divide the county geographically; U.S. 101 passes through a mountain tunnel leading inland. Northern Santa Barbara County used to be known for its sprawling ranches and strawberry and broccoli fields. Today its 100-plus wineries and 22,000 acres of vineyards dominate the landscape from the Santa Ynez Valley in the south to Santa Maria in the north. The hit film *Sideways* was filmed almost entirely in the North County Wine Country; when the movie won Golden Globe and Oscar awards in 2005, it sparked national and international interest in visits to the region.

GETTING HERE AND AROUND

Two-lane Highway 154 over San Marcos Pass is the shortest and most scenic route from Santa Barbara into the Santa Ynez Valley. You can also drive along U.S. 101 north 43 miles to Buellton, then 7 miles east through Solvang to Santa Ynez. Santa Ynez Valley Transit shuttle buses serve Santa Ynez, Los Olivos, Ballard, Solvang, and Buellton. COLT Wine Country Express buses connect Lompoc, Buellton, and Solvang on weekdays except holidays.

ESSENTIALS

Bus Contacts COLT Wine Country Express ⊠ *Lompoc* ☎ *805/736–7666* ⊕ *www.cityoflompoc.com/transit.* **Santa Ynez Valley Transit** ☎ *805/688–5452* ⊕ *www.syvt.com.*

Visitor Information **Santa Barbara Wine Country** ☎ *805/688–0881* 🌐 *www.sbcountywines.com.* **Visit Santa Barbara** 🌐 *www.santabarbaraca.com.* **Visit the Santa Ynez Valley** ☎ *805/686–0053* 🌐 *www.visitthesantaynezvalley.com.*

SANTA YNEZ

31 miles north of Goleta.

Founded in 1882, the tiny town of Santa Ynez still has many of its original frontier buildings. You can walk through the three-block downtown area in a few minutes, shop for antiques, and hang around the old-time saloon. At some of the Santa Ynez Valley's best restaurants, you just might bump into one of the celebrities who own nearby ranches.

GETTING HERE AND AROUND

Take Highway 154 over San Marcos Pass or U.S. 101 north 43 miles to Buellton, then 7 miles east.

WHERE TO EAT AND STAY

$$ ITALIAN 🍴 **Trattoria Grappolo.** Authentic Italian fare, an open kitchen, and festive, family-style seating make this trattoria equally popular with celebrities from Hollywood and ranchers from the Santa Ynez Valley. Thin-crust pizza, homemade ravioli, risottos, and seafood linguine are among the menu favorites. The noise level tends to rise in the evening, so this isn't the best spot for a romantic getaway. [$] *Average main: $22* ✉ *3687-C Sagunto St.* ☎ *805/688–6899* 🌐 *www.trattoriagrappolo.com* 🕒 *No lunch Mon.*

$$$ B&B/INN 🏨 **Santa Ynez Inn.** This posh two-story Victorian inn in downtown Santa Ynez was built from scratch in 2002, and the owners have furnished all the rooms with authentic historical pieces. **Pros:** near restaurants; unusual antiques; spacious rooms. **Cons:** high price for location; building not historic. [$] *Rooms from: $245* ✉ *3627 Sagunto St.* ☎ *805/688–5588, 800/643–5774* 🌐 *www.santaynezinn.com* 🛏 *20 rooms* 🍽 *Breakfast.*

SPORTS AND THE OUTDOORS

Santa Barbara Soaring. Scenic glider rides operated by this outfit last from 10 to 50 minutes. Options include a basic tour of the Santa Ynez Valley; the coastal mountains and part of the Channel Islands, and a glide-by of celebrities' homes. ✉ *Santa Ynez Airport, 900 Airport Rd.* ☎ *805/688–2517* 🌐 *www.sbsoaring.com* 🎟 *$149–$499.*

LOS OLIVOS

4 miles north of Santa Ynez.

This pretty village was once on Spanish-built El Camino Real (Royal Road) and later a stop on major stagecoach and rail routes. Tasting rooms, art galleries, antiques stores, and country markets line Grand Avenue and intersecting streets for several blocks.

GETTING HERE AND AROUND

From U.S. 101 north or south, exit at Highway 154 and drive east about 8 miles. From Santa Barbara, travel 30 miles northwest on Highway 154.

EXPLORING

Carhartt Vineyard Tasting Room. Pinot Noir, Sauvignon Blanc, and Syrah are among the small-lot vintages produced by owner-winemakers Mike and Brooke Carhartt. You'll often find the duo pouring at their intimate tasting room. ✉ *2990-A Grand Ave.* ☎ *805/693–5100* 🌐 *www.carharttvineyard.com* 🎟 *Tasting $10* 🕒 *Daily 11–6.*

Daniel Gehrs Tasting Room. Heather Cottage, built in the early 1900s as a doctor's office, houses winemaker Gehrs's tasting room, where you can sample Port, Chardonnay, Gewürztraminer, Riesling, and other small-lot wines. ✉ *2939 Grand Ave.* ☎ *805/693–9686* 🌐 *www.danielgehrswines.com* 🎟 *Tastings $5–$10* 🕒 *Sun.–Fri. 11–5, Sat. 11–6.*

Firestone Vineyard. Heirs to the Firestone tire fortune developed (but no longer own) this winery known for Chardonnay, Gewürztraminer, Merlot, Riesling, and Syrah—and for the fantastic valley views from its tasting room and picnic area. The tour here is highly informative. ✉ *5017 Zaca Station Rd., off U.S. 101* ☎ *805/688–3940* 🌐 *www.firestonewine.com* 🎟 *Tastings $10–$15* 🕒 *Daily 10–5; tours 11:15, 1:15, and 3:15.*

WHERE TO EAT AND STAY

$$ AMERICAN 🍴 **Los Olivos Cafe.** Part wine store and part social hub, this café that appeared in the film *Sideways* focuses on wine-friendly fish, pasta, and meat dishes, plus salads, pizzas, and burgers. Don't miss the homemade muffuletta and olive tapenade spreads. Other house favorites include an artisanal cheese plate, baked Brie with honey-roasted hazelnuts, and braised short ribs with smashed potatoes. [$] *Average main: $21* ✉ *2879 Grand Ave.* ☎ *805/688–7265* 🌐 *www.losolivoscafe.com.*

$$$ AMERICAN 🍴 **Sides Hardware & Shoes: A Brothers Restaurant.** After renovating a historic Los Olivos storefront, brothers Matt and Jeff Nichols shuttered their highly popular Brothers restaurant and began serving comfort food prepared with their inimitable panache. The Kobe-style burgers make a great lunch, and the dinner favorites include fried chicken and lamb sirloin with herbed gnocchi. [$] *Average main: $24* ✉ *2375 Alamo Pintado Ave.* ☎ *805/688–4820* 🌐 *www.brothersrestaurant.com.*

$$$$ B&B/INN 🏨 **The Ballard Inn & Restaurant.** Set among orchards and vineyards in the tiny town of Ballard, 2 miles south of Los Olivos, this inn makes an elegant Wine Country escape. **Pros:** exceptional food; attentive staff; secluded. **Cons:** some baths could use updating. [$] *Rooms from: $265* ✉ *2436 Baseline Ave., Ballard* ☎ *805/688–7770, 800/638–2466* 🌐 *www.ballardinn.com* 🛏 *15 rooms* 🍽 *Breakfast.*

$$$$ B&B/INN 🏨 **Fess Parker's Wine Country Inn and Spa.** This luxury inn includes an elegant, tree-shaded French country–style main building and an equally attractive annex across the street with a pool and day spa. **Pros:** convenient wine-touring base; walking distance from restaurants and galleries; well-appointed rooms. **Cons:** pricey; not pet-friendly. [$] *Rooms from: $395* ✉ *2860 Grand Ave.* ☎ *805/688–7788, 800/446–2455* 🌐 *www.fessparkerinn.com* 🛏 *15 rooms, 4 suites* 🍽 *Breakfast.*

SOLVANG

5 miles south of Los Olivos.

You'll know you've reached the town of Solvang when the architecture suddenly changes to half-timber buildings and windmills. Danish educators settled the town in 1911—the flatlands and rolling green hills reminded them of home—and even today, more than half the residents are of Danish descent. Although Solvang has attracted tourists for decades, it's lately become more sophisticated, with galleries, upscale restaurants, and wine-tasting rooms. The visitor center on Copenhagen Drive has walking-tour maps (also available online). The Sweet Treats tour covers the town's bakeries, confectionary stores, and ice-cream parlors, all well worth investigating.

GETTING HERE AND AROUND

Highway 246 West (Mission Drive) traverses Solvang, connecting with U.S. 101 to the west and Highway 154 to the east. Alamo Pintado Road connects Solvang with Ballard and Los Olivos to the north. Park your car in one of the free public lots and stroll the town. Or take the bus: Santa Ynez Valley Transit shuttles run between Solvang and nearby towns.

TOURS

Segway Tours of Solvang. After a brief training session, tool around Solvang on a guided tour via electric-powered personal balancing transporters. This company also offers early-evening adventures, and trips high up Figueroa Mountain. ☎ *805/688–8899* ⊕ *www.advoutwest.com* ✉ *$65* ⊙ *Nov.–Mar., tours at 11, 1, and 3; Apr.–Oct., tours at 9, 11, 1, 3, and 5.*

ESSENTIALS

Visitor Information Solvang Conference & Visitors Bureau ✉ *1639 Copenhagen Dr., at 2nd St.* ☎ *805/688–6144* ⊕ *www.solvangusa.com.*

EXPLORING

Alma Rosa Winery. Winemaker Richard Sanford helped put Santa Barbara County on the international wine map with a 1989 Pinot Noir. For Alma Rosa, started in 2005, he crafts wines from grapes grown on 100-plus acres of certified organic vineyards in the Santa Rita Hills. The Pinot Noirs and Chardonnays are exceptional. ✉ *181 C Industrial Way, off Hwy. 246, west of U.S. 101, Buellton* ☎ *805/688–9090* ⊕ *www.almarosawinery.com* ✉ *Tastings $10–$15* ⊙ *Daily 11–4:30.*

Lafond Winery and Vineyards. A rich, concentrated Pinot Noir is the main attention-getter at this winery that also produces noteworthy Chardonnays and Syrahs. Bottles with Lafond's SRH (Santa Rita Hills) label are an especially good value. ✉ *6855 Santa Rosa Rd., west off U.S. 101 Exit 139, Buellton* ☎ *805/688–7921* ⊕ *www.lafondwinery.com* ✉ *Tasting $5 weekdays, $10 weekends (includes logo glass)* ⊙ *Daily 10–5.*

Mission Santa Inés. The mission holds an impressive collection of paintings, statuary, vestments, and Chumash and Spanish artifacts in a serene bluff-top setting. You can tour the museum, sanctuary, and gardens. ✉ *1760 Mission Dr., at Alisal Rd.* ☎ *805/688–4815* ⊕ *www.missionsantaines.org* ✉ *$5* ⊙ *Daily 9–4:30.*

Rideau Vineyard. This winery celebrates its locale's rich history—the King of Spain himself once owned this land, and the tasting room occupies a former guest ranch inn—but fully embraces the area's wine-making present. The Rhône varietals Marsanne, Mourvèdre, Roussanne, Syrah, and Viognier are the specialty. ✉ *1562 Alamo Pintado Rd., 2 miles north of Hwy. 246* ☎ *805/688–0717* 🌐 *www.rideauvineyard.com* 🎫 *Tasting $12* 🕒 *Sun.–Fri. 11–4:30, Sat. 11–5.*

WHERE TO EAT

$$$ AMERICAN 🍴 **The Hitching Post II.** You'll find everything from grilled artichokes to quail at this casual eatery just outside Solvang, but most people come for the smoky Santa Maria–style barbecue. Be sure to try a glass of owner-chef-winemaker Frank Ostini's signature Highliner Pinot Noir, a star in the film *Sideways.* [$] *Average main: $29* ✉ *406 E. Hwy. 246, off U.S. 101, Buellton* ☎ *805/688–0676* 🌐 *www.hitchingpost2.com* 🕒 *No lunch.*

$$$ AMERICAN Fodor's Choice ★ 🍴 **Root 246.** The chefs at this chic restaurant tap local purveyors and shop for organic ingredients at farmers' markets before deciding on the day's menu. Depending on the season, you might feast on boar sausage and other house-cured meats, swordfish or Santa Maria–style tri-tip grilled over an oak fire, or smoky lamb shank served with yogurt and harissa. The well-informed waitstaff can recommend regional wines from the restaurant's 1,800-bottle selection. Root 246's gorgeous design incorporates wood, stone, tempered glass, and leather elements in several distinct areas, including the slick dining room, a more casual bar with sofas and chairs, and a hip lounge. [$] *Average main: $29* ✉ *Hotel Corque, 420 Alisal Rd., at Molle Way* ☎ *805/686–8681* 🌐 *www.root-246.com* 🕒 *Closed Mon. No lunch Tues.–Sat.*

WHERE TO STAY

$$$$ RESORT 🏨 **Alisal Guest Ranch and Resort.** Since 1946 this 10,000-acre ranch has been popular with celebrities and plain folk alike. **Pros:** Old West atmosphere; tons of activities; ultraprivate. **Cons:** isolated; cut off from high-tech world; some units aging. [$] *Rooms from: $515* ✉ *1054 Alisal Rd.* ☎ *805/688–6411, 800/425–4725* 🌐 *www.alisal.com* 🛏 *36 rooms, 37 suites* 🍽 *Some meals.*

$$$ HOTEL 🏨 **Hotel Corque.** Sleek, stunning Hotel Corque—the Santa Ynez Valley's largest hotel—provides a full slate of upscale amenities. **Pros:** front desk staff are trained concierges; short walk to shops, tasting rooms and restaurants; smoke-free. **Cons:** no kitchenettes or laundry facilities; pricey. [$] *Rooms from: $239* ✉ *400 Alisal Rd.* ☎ *805/688–8000, 800/624–5572* 🌐 *www.hotelcorque.com* 🛏 *122 rooms, 10 suites* 🍽 *No meals.*

$$$ B&B/INN 🏨 **Petersen Village Inn.** The canopy beds here are plush, the bathrooms small but sparkling, and the rates include a European buffet breakfast. **Pros:** in the heart of Solvang; easy parking; comfy beds. **Cons:** on highway; some find atmosphere too traditional. [$] *Rooms from: $195* ✉ *1576 Mission Dr.* ☎ *805/688–3121, 800/321–8985* 🌐 *peterseninn.com* 🛏 *37 rooms, 1 suite* 🍽 *No meals.*

$ B&B/INN 🏨 **Solvang Gardens Lodge.** The lush gardens with fountains and waterfalls and the cheery English-country-theme rooms make for a peaceful retreat just a few blocks—but worlds away—from Solvang's main tourist area. **Pros:** homey; family-friendly; colorful gardens. **Cons:** some rooms tiny; some need upgrades. [$] *Rooms from: $119* ✉ *293 Alisal Rd.* ☎ *805/688–4404, 888/688–4404* 🌐 *www.solvanggardens.com* 🛏 *16 rooms, 8 suites* 🍴 *Breakfast.*

LOMPOC

20 miles west of Solvang.

Known as the flower-seed capital of the world, Lompoc is blanketed with vast fields of brightly colored flowers that bloom from May through August.

GETTING HERE AND AROUND

Driving is the easiest way to get to Lompoc. From Santa Barbara, follow U.S. 101 north to Highway 1 exit off Gaviota Pass, or Highway 246 west at Buellton.

5

ESSENTIALS

Visitor Information **Lompoc Valley Chamber of Commerce & Visitors Bureau** ✉ *111 S. I St., at Hwy. 246* ☎ *805/736–4567, 800/240–0999* 🌐 *www.lompoc.com.*

EXPLORING

FAMILY **La Purísima Mission State Historic Park.** The state's most fully restored mission, founded in 1787, stands in a stark and still remote location that powerfully evokes the lives and isolation of California's Spanish settlers. Docents lead tours every afternoon, and vivid displays illustrate the secular and religious activities that formed mission life. Special events include crafts demonstrations by costumed docents. ✉ *2295 Purisima Rd., off Hwy. 246* ☎ *805/733–3713* 🌐 *www.lapurisimamission.org* 🎟 *$6 per vehicle* 🕒 *Daily 9–5; tour daily at 1.*

Lompoc Wine Ghetto. Nearly 20 laid-back tasting rooms with premium wines from the surrounding Santa Rita Hills appellation—among them Fiddlehead Cellars and Longoria (both known for stellar Pinot Noirs)—cluster in a downtown industrial park. ✉ *Take 7th St. north from Hwy. 1/246 and turn east (right), 200 N. 9th St.* ☎ *805/735–8937* 🌐 *www.lompoctrail.com* 🎟 *Tasting fee varies, some free* 🕒 *Most rooms open Thurs.–Sun., 11 or noon until 4 or 5; some also Mon. and by appointment* 🕒 *Closed Tues. and Wed.*

EN ROUTE

Guadalupe-Nipomo Dunes Preserve. This spectacular preserve straddles the coast for 18 miles between Santa Barbara and San Luis Obispo counties. California's largest and most ecologically diverse dune system, this habitat shelters more than 200 species of birds as well as sea otters, black bears, bobcats, coyotes, and deer. The 1,500-foot Mussel Rock is the highest beach dune in the western states. About two-dozen movies have been filmed here, including Cecil B. DeMille's 1923 silent epic *The Ten Commandments*. At the **Dunes Center** (*1065 Guadalupe St.*) in downtown Guadalupe, you can get nature information and view an exhibit about DeMille's movie set. ✉ *Hwy. 166/Main St., west 5 miles from Hwy. 1, Guadalupe* ☎ *805/343–2455* 🌐 *www.dunescenter.org* 🎟 *Free ($3 suggested donation)* 🕒 *Dunes daily sunrise–sunset; center Wed.–Sun. 10–4, Mon. and Tues. by appointment.*

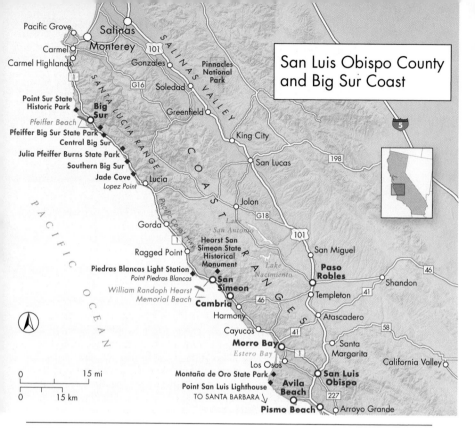

SAN LUIS OBISPO COUNTY

San Luis Obispo County's pristine landscapes and abundant wildlife areas, especially those around Morro Bay and Montaña de Oro State Park, have long attracted nature lovers. In the south, Pismo Beach and other coastal towns have great sand and surf; inland, a booming wine region stretches from the Edna, Arroyo Grande, and Avila valleys and Nipomo in the south to Paso Robles in the north. With historical attractions, a photogenic downtown, and busy shops and restaurants, the college town of San Luis Obispo is at the heart of the county.

GETTING HERE AND AROUND
San Luis Obispo Regional Transit Authority operates buses in San Luis Obispo and serves Paso Robles as well as Pismo Beach and other coastal towns.

ESSENTIALS
Transportation Contact San Luis Obispo Regional Transit Authority
☎ 805/541–2228 ⊕ www.slorta.org.

Visitor Information Visit San Luis Obispo County ✉ 835 12th St., Suite 204, Paso Robles ☎ 805/541–8000, 800/634–1414 ⊕ www.visitsanluisobispocounty. com. **WineCoastCountry** ✉ San Luis Obispo ⊕ winecoastcountry.com.

PISMO BEACH

40 miles north of Lompoc.

About 20 miles of sandy shoreline—nicknamed the Bakersfield Riviera for the throngs of vacationers who come here from the Central Valley—begins at the town of Pismo Beach. The southern end of town runs along sand dunes, some of which are open to cars and off-road vehicles. Sheltered by the dunes, a grove of eucalyptus trees attracts thousands of migrating monarch butterflies from November through February. A long, broad beach fronts the center of town, where a municipal pier extends into the sea at the foot of shop-lined Pomeroy Street. To the north, hotels and homes perch atop chalky oceanfront cliffs. Fewer than 10,000 people live in this quintessential surfer haven, but Pismo Beach has a slew of hotels and restaurants with great views of the Pacific Ocean.

GETTING HERE AND AROUND

Pismo Beach straddles both sides of U.S. 101. If you're coming from the south and have time for a scenic drive, exit U.S. 101 in Santa Maria and take Highway 166 west for 8 miles to Guadalupe and follow Highway 1 north 16 miles to Pismo Beach. South County Area Transit (SCAT; ⊕ *www.slorta.org*) buses run throughout San Luis Obispo and connect the city with nearby towns. On summer weekends, the free Avila Trolley extends service to Pismo Beach.

ESSENTIALS

Visitor Information California Welcome Center ✉ *333 Five Cities Dr.* ☎ *805/773-7924.* **Pismo Beach Visitors Information Center** ✉ *Dolliver St./ Hwy. 1, at Hinds Ave.* ☎ *800/443-7778, 805/773-4382* ⊕ *classiccalifornia.com* ⊗ *Weekdays 9-5, Sat. 11-4 , Sun. 10-2.*

BEACHES

Fodor's Choice ★ **Oceano Dunes State Vehicular Recreation Area.** Part of ⇨ *Guadalupe-Nipomo Dunes,* the largest and most ecologically diverse dunes complex in California, this popular state park offers a huge array of activities in a 3,600-acre coastal playground. This is one of the only places in California where you can drive or ride off-highway vehicles on the beach and sand dunes (1,500 acres are open to OHVs.) Hike, ride horses, kiteboard, join a Hummer tour, or rent an ATV or a dune buggy and cruise up the white-sand peaks for spectacular views. At **Oso Flaco Lake Nature Area**—3 miles west of Highway 1 on Oso Flaco Road—a 1½-mile boardwalk over the lake leads to a platform with views up and down the coast. Leashed dogs are allowed in much of the park except Oso Flaco and Pismo Dunes Natural Reserve. **Amenities:** food and drink; lifeguards (seasonal); parking (fee); showers; toilets; water sports. **Best for:** sunset; surfing; swimming; walking. ✉ *West end of Pier Ave., off Hwy. 1, Oceano* ☎ *805/473-7220* ⊕ *www.parks.ca.gov* ⊠ *$5 per vehicle* ⊗ *Daily 6 am-11 pm; Oso Flaco Lake sunrise-sunset.*

Pismo State Beach. One of the busiest state beaches in the county, Pismo offers a slew of activities along the 17-mile western edges of Oceano, Grover Beach, and Pismo Beach. Hike, surf, golf, ride horses, swim, fish in a lagoon or off the pier, and dig for Pismo clams. From November through late February, one of the nation's largest colonies of monarch butterflies rests in a grove of eucalyptus and Monterey pine trees (Hwy. 1, 3 miles north of Pier Ave.). Entrances to day-use parking areas are off Hwy. 1 (milepost 8) and at Pier Ave. in the south. **Facilities:** food and drink; lifeguards (seasonal); parking (fee); showers; toilets; water sports. **Best for:** sunset; surfing; swimming; walking. ⊠ *555 Pier Ave., Oceano* ☎ *805/489–1869* ⊕ *www.parks.ca.gov* ⊠ *Day use $5 per vehicle if parking at the beach* ⊙ *Day use 6 am–11 pm.*

> **VOLCANOES?**
>
> Those funny looking, sawed-off peaks along the drive from Pismo Beach to Morro Bay are the Seven Sisters—a series of ancient volcanic plugs. Morro Rock, the northernmost sibling and a state historic monument, is the most famous and photographed of the clan.

WHERE TO EAT

$$$
SEAFOOD
✕ **Cracked Crab.** This traditional New England–style crab shack imports fresh seafood daily from Australia, Alaska, and the East Coast. Fish is line-caught, much of the produce is organic, and everything is made from scratch. For a real treat, don a bib and sample a bucket of steamed shellfish with Cajun sausage, potatoes, and corn on the cob, all dumped right onto your table. $ *Average main: $24* ⊠ *751 Price St., near Main St.* ☎ *805/773–2722* ⊕ *www.crackedcrab.com* ⚓ *Reservations not accepted.*

$$
ITALIAN
✕ **Giuseppe's Cucina Italiana.** The classic flavors of southern Italy are highlighted at this lively downtown spot. Most recipes originate from Bari, a seaport on the Adriatic; the menu includes breads and pizzas baked in the wood-burning oven, hearty dishes such as osso buco and lamb, and homemade pastas. The wait for a table can be long at peak dinner hours, but sometimes an accordion player gets the crowd singing. $ *Average main: $22* ⊠ *891 Price St., at Pismo Ave.* ☎ *805/773–2870* ⊕ *www.giuseppesrestaurant.com* ⚓ *Reservations not accepted* ⊙ *No lunch weekends.*

$
SEAFOOD
✕ **Splash Café.** Folks stand in line down the block for clam chowder served in a sourdough bread bowl at this wildly popular seafood stand. You can also order beach food such as fresh steamed clams, burgers, and fried calamari at the counter (no table service). The grimy, cramped, but cheery hole-in-the-wall is open daily for lunch and dinner (plus a rock-bottom basic breakfast), but closes early on weekday evenings during low season. ∎TIP→ Splash also has two locations in San Luis Obispo. $ *Average main: $8* ⊠ *197 Pomeroy St., at Cypress St.* ☎ *805/773–4653* ⊕ *www.splashcafe.com.*

WHERE TO STAY

$$$
RESORT
🛏 **The Cliffs Resort.** Perched dramatically on an oceanfront cliff, this full-service resort is surrounded by lawns and palm trees; the pool, with a cascading fountain, overlooks the sea. **Pros:** beach access via short downhill path; oceanfront restaurant and lounge; bluff-top walking trail. **Cons:** not close to downtown; rooms near service areas and elevator can be noisy. $ *Rooms from: $189* ⊠ *2757 Shell Beach Rd.* ☎ *805/773–5000, 800/826–7827* ⊕ *www.cliffsresort.com* ⤵ *160 rooms* ⦿ *No meals.*

$$$
HOTEL
🛏 **SeaVenture Beachfront Hotel & Restaurant.** The bright, homey rooms at this hotel all have fireplaces and featherbeds; most have balconies with private hot tubs, and some have beautiful ocean views.

Pros: on the beach; excellent food; romantic rooms. **Cons:** touristy area; some rooms and facilities dated; dark hallways. $ *Rooms from: $179* ⊠ *100 Ocean View Ave.* ☎ *805/773–4994* ⊕ *www.seaventure. com* ↪ *50 rooms* |○| *No meals.*

$ ▦ **Shell Beach Inn.** Just 2½ blocks from the beach, this basic but cozy
HOTEL motor court is a great bargain for the area. **Pros:** walking distance from the beach; clean rooms; friendly and dependable service. **Cons:** sits on a busy road; small rooms; tiny pool. $ *Rooms from: $100* ⊠ *653 Shell Beach Rd.* ☎ *805/773–4373, 800/549–4727* ⊕ *www.shellbeachinn.com* ↪ *10 rooms* |○| *No meals.*

AVILA BEACH

4 miles north of Pismo Beach.

FAMILY Because the village of Avila Beach and the sandy, cove-front shoreline for which it's named face south into the Pacific Ocean, they get more sun and less fog than any other stretch of coast in the area. With its fortuitous climate and protected waters, Avila's public beach draws sunbathers and families; weekends are very busy. Downtown Avila Beach has a lively seaside promenade and some shops and hotels, but for real local color, head to the far end of the cove and watch the commercial fishers offload their catch on the old Port San Luis wharf. A few seafood shacks and fish markets do business on the pier while sea lions congregate below. On Friday from mid-April through mid-September, a fish and farmers' market livens up the beach area with music, fresh local produce and seafood, and children's activities.

GETTING HERE AND AROUND
Exit U.S. 101 at Avila Beach Drive and head 3 miles west to reach the beach. The free Avila Trolley operates weekends year-round, plus Friday afternoon and evening from April to September. The minibuses connect Avila Beach and Port San Luis to Shell Beach, with multiple stops along the way. Service extends to Pismo Beach in summer.

ESSENTIALS
Visitor Information Avila Beach Tourism Alliance ⊕ *visitavilabeach.com.*

EXPLORING
Central Coast Aquarium. You'll learn all about local marine plants and animals from the hands-on exhibits at this science center next to the main beach. ⊠ *50 San Juan St., at 1st St., off Avila Beach Dr.* ☎ *805/595–7280* ⊕ *www.centralcoastaquarium.com* ▱ *$5* ☉ *June–Aug., Tues.–Sun. 10–5; Sept.–May, weekends 10–4 and holiday breaks.*

FAMILY **Avila Valley Barn.** An old-fashioned, family-friendly country store jam-packed with local fruits and veggies, prepared foods and gift items, Avila Valley Barn also gives visitors a chance to experience rural American traditions. You can pet farm animals and savor homemade ice cream and pies daily; on weekends, ride a hay wagon out to the fields to pick your own farm-fresh produce. ⊠ *560 Avila Beach Dr., San Luis Obispo* ☎ *805/595–2816* ⊕ *avilavalleybarn.com* ☉ *Daily 9–5* ☉ *Closed Tues. and Wed. Jan.–Mar.*

DID YOU KNOW?

You can unwind in a waterfall pool fed by a hot-mineral-springs waterfall at Avila Beach.

FAMILY **Point San Luis Lighthouse.** Docents lead hikes along scenic Pecho Coast Trail (3½ miles round-trip) to see the historic 1890 lighthouse and its rare Fresnel lens. ■ **TIP→ If you'd prefer a lift out to the lighthouse, join a trolley tour. Hikes and tours require reservations.** ✉ *Point San Luis, 1¾ miles west of Harford Pier, Port San Luis* ☎ *855/533–7843* 🌐 *www.sanluislighthouse.org* 🎟 *Trolley tours $20; hikes free ($5 to enter lighthouse)* 🕓 *Trolley tours Wed. at noon, Sat. at noon, 1, and 2; hikes Wed. and Sat. at 9.*

BEACHES

FAMILY **Avila State Beach.** At the edge of a sunny cove next to downtown shops and restaurants, Avila's ½-mile stretch of white sand lures scores of beachgoers on weekends year-round and daily in summer. It's especially family-friendly, with a playground, barbecue and picnic tables, volleyball and basketball courts, and lifeguards on watch in summer and on many holiday weekends. Limited free beachfront parking is available but fills up fast; otherwise park in a nearby pay lot ($5 for the day, $1 after 4 pm). Dogs are not allowed on the beach from 10 to 5. **Facilities:** food and drink; lifeguards (seasonal); parking; showers; toilets; water sports. **Best for:** sunset; surfing; swimming; walking. ✉ *Avila Beach Dr., at 1st St.* 🌐 *www.visitavilabeach.com* 🎟 *Free* 🕓 *Daily 6 am–10 pm.*

WHERE TO STAY

$$$$ HOTEL 🏨 **Avila Lighthouse Suites.** Families, honeymooners, and business travelers all find respite at this two-story, all-suite luxury hotel. **Pros:** directly across from sand; easy walk to restaurants and shops; free underground parking. **Cons:** noise from passersby can be heard in room; some ocean-view rooms have limited vistas. [$] *Rooms from: $319* ✉ *550 Front St.* ☎ *805/627–1900, 800/372–8452* 📠 *805/627–1909* 🌐 *www.avilalighthousesuites.com* 🛏 *54 suites* 🍴 *Breakfast.*

$$ RESORT 🏨 **Sycamore Mineral Springs Resort.** This wellness resort's hot mineral springs bubble up into private outdoor tubs on an oak-and-sycamore-forest hillside. **Pros:** great place to rejuvenate; nice hiking; incredible spa services. **Cons:** rooms vary in quality; 2½ miles from the beach. [$] *Rooms from: $169* ✉ *1215 Avila Beach Dr., San Luis Obispo* ☎ *805/595–7302, 800/234–5831* 🌐 *www.sycamoresprings.com* 🛏 *26 rooms, 50 suites* 🍴 *No meals.*

SAN LUIS OBISPO

8 miles north of Avila Beach.

About halfway between San Francisco and Los Angeles, San Luis Obispo—nicknamed SLO—spreads out below gentle hills and rocky extinct volcanoes. Its main appeal lies in its architecturally diverse, pedestrian-friendly downtown, which bustles with shoppers, restaurant goers, and students from California Polytechnic State University, known as Cal Poly. On Thursday evening from 6 to 9 a farmers' market fills Higuera Street with local produce, entertainment, and food stalls. A Saturday-morning market in the Cost Plus World Market parking lot includes organic meats and wine tasting.

The wineries of the Edna Valley and Arroyo Grande Valley wine regions lie just south of the city off Highway 227, the parallel (to the east) Orcutt Road, and connecting roads. Wine-touring maps are available around town.

GETTING HERE AND AROUND

U.S. 101/Highway 1 traverses the city for several miles. From the north, Highway 1 merges with U.S. 101 when it reaches the city limits. SLO City Transit buses operate daily; Regional Transit Authority (SLORTA) buses connect with north county towns. The Downtown Trolley provides evening service to the city's hub every Thursday, on Friday from June to early September, and on Saturday from April through October.

ESSENTIALS

Visitor Information San Luis Obispo Chamber of Commerce ⊠ *895 Monterey St.* 🕾 *805/781–2777* ⊕ *www.visitslo.com.* **San Luis Obispo City Visitor Information** ⊕ *www.sanluisobispovacations.com.* **SLO Wine Country** 🕾 *805/541–5868* ⊕ *www.slowine.com.*

EXPLORING
TOP ATTRACTIONS

FAMILY **History Center of San Luis Obispo County.** Across the street from the old Spanish mission, the center presents exhibits that explore topics such as Native American life in the county, the California ranchos, and the impact of railroads. On the center's website are links to free downloadable video-podcast walking tours of historic San Luis Obispo. ⊠ *696 Monterey St., at Broad St.* 🕾 *805/543–0638* ⊕ *historycenterslo.org* 🔁 *Free* ⊙ *Daily 10–4.*

Mission San Luis Obispo de Tolosa. Sun-dappled Mission Plaza fronts the fifth mission established in 1772 by Franciscan friars. A small museum exhibits artifacts of the Chumash Indians and early Spanish settlers. ⊠ *751 Palm St., at Chorro St.* 🕾 *805/543–6850* ⊕ *www. missionsanluisobispo.org* 🔁 *$3* ⊙ *Early Mar.–early Nov. daily 9–5, early Nov.–early Mar. daily 9–4.*

San Luis Obispo Museum of Art. The permanent collection here focuses on the artistic legacy of the Central Coast. Temporary exhibits include traditional and cutting-edge arts and crafts by Central Coast, national, and international artists. ⊠ *Mission Plaza, 1010 Broad St., at Monterey St.* 🕾 *805/543–8562* ⊕ *www.sloma.org* ⊙ *Early Sept.–early July, Wed.– Mon. 11–5; early July–early Sept., daily 11–5.*

Fodor's Choice **Talley Vineyards.** Acres of Chardonnay and Pinot Noir, plus smaller lots
★ of Sauvignon Blanc, Syrah, and other varietals blanket Talley's mountain-ringed dell in the Arroyo Grande Valley. The estate tour ($35), worth a splurge, includes wine and cheese, a visit to an 1860s adobe, and barrel-room tastings of upcoming releases. ⊠ *3031 Lopez Dr., off Orcutt Rd., Arroyo Grande* 🕾 *805/489–0446* ⊕ *www.talleyvineyards. com* 🔁 *Tastings $8–$15; tours $15–$35* ⊙ *Daily 10:30–4:30; tours by appointment.*

WORTH NOTING

Claiborne & Churchill. An eco-friendly winery built from straw bales, C&C makes small lots of Alsatian-style wines such as dry Riesling and Gewürztraminer, plus Pinot Noir and Chardonnay. ✉ *2649 Carpenter Canyon Rd., at Price Canyon Rd.* ☎ *805/544–4066* ⊕ *www.claibornechurchill.com* 🍷 *Tasting $10* ⊙ *Daily 11–5.*

> ### DEEP ROOTS
>
> Way back in the 1700s, the Spanish padres who accompanied Father Junípero Serra planted grapevines from Mexico along California's Central Coast, and began using European wine-making techniques to turn the grapes into delectable vintages.

Edna Valley Vineyard. For sweeping valley views and crisp Sauvignon Blancs and Chardonnays, head to the modern tasting bar here. ■ TIP➜ **The reserve tasting ($15) is the best option here.** ✉ *2585 Biddle Ranch Rd., off Edna Rd.* ☎ *805/544–5855* ⊕ *www.ednavalleyvineyard.com* 🍷 *Tastings $10–$15* ⊙ *Daily 10–5.*

Niven Family Wine Estates. A refurbished 1909 schoolhouse serves as tasting room for six Niven Family wineries: Baileyana, Cadre, Tangent, Trenza, True Myth, and Zocker. The winemaker for all these labels is Christian Roguenant, whose Cadre Pinot Noirs are worth checking out. ✉ *5828 Orcutt Rd., at Righetti Rd.* ☎ *805/269–8200* ⊕ *www.nivenfamilywines.com* 🍷 *Tasting $8–$12* ⊙ *Daily 10–5.*

Old Edna. This peaceful, 2-acre site once *was* the town of Edna. Nowadays you can peek at the vintage 1897 and 1908 farmhouse cottages, taste wines, pick up sandwiches at the gourmet deli, and stroll along Old Edna Lane. ✉ *1655 Old Price Canyon Rd., at Hwy. 227* ☎ *805/544–8062* ⊕ *www.oldedna.com.*

FAMILY **San Luis Obispo Children's Museum.** Activities at this delightful facility geared to kids under age eight include an "imagination-powered" elevator that transports visitors to a series of underground caverns. Elsewhere, simulated lava and steam sputter from an active volcano. Kids can pick rubber fruit at a farmers' market and race in a fire engine to fight a fire. ✉ *1010 Nipomo St., at Monterey St.* ☎ *805/544–5437* ⊕ *www.slocm.org* 🍷 *$8* ⊙ *May–Aug., Mon.–Wed. 10–3, Thurs.–Sat. 10–5, Sun. and some holidays 11–5; Sept.–Apr., Tues. and Wed. 10–3, Thurs.–Sat. 10–5, Sun. and some holidays 1–5.*

WHERE TO EAT

$$ ✕ **Big Sky Café.** Family-friendly Big Sky turns local and organically
ECLECTIC grown ingredients into global dishes, starting with breakfast. Just pick your continent: Brazilian churrasco chicken breast, Thai catfish, North African vegetable stew, Maryland crab cakes. Vegetarians have ample choices. $ *Average main: $17* ✉ *1121 Broad St., at Higuera St.* ☎ *805/545–5401* ⊕ *www.bigskycafe.com* ⌫ *Reservations not accepted.*

$$ ✕ **Café Roma.** Authentic northern Italian cuisine is the specialty at this
NORTHERN Railroad Square restaurant. Beneath a mural of Tuscany or out on the
ITALIAN covered patio, you can dine on squash-filled tortelli with a sage-and-butter sauce or beef tenderloin glistening with porcini butter and a Pinot Noir reduction. $ *Average main: $19* ✉ *1020 Railroad Ave., at Osos St.* ☎ *805/541–6800* ⊕ *www.caferomaslo.com* ⊙ *No lunch weekends.*

5

$$$ INTERNATIONAL 🍴 **Luna Red.** A spacious, contemporary space with a festive outdoor patio, this restaurant near Mission Plaza serves creative tapas and cocktails. The small plates include pork-belly buns, avocado-tuna ceviche, and piquillo peppers stuffed with goat cheese. Roast chicken adobo and Kurobuta pork short ribs are two large plates of note. [$] *Average main: $25* ✉ *1023 Chorro St., at Monterey St.* ☎ *805/540–5243* 🌐 *www.lunaredslo.com.*

$$ ECLECTIC 🍴 **Novo Restaurant & Lounge.** In the colorful dining room or on the large creek-side deck, this animated downtown eatery will take you on a culinary world tour. The salads, small plates, and entrées come from nearly every continent. The wine and beer list also covers the globe and includes local favorites. [$] *Average main: $19* ✉ *726 Higuera St., at Broad St.* ☎ *805/543–3986* 🌐 *www.novorestaurant.com.*

$$ MODERN AMERICAN 🍴 **Sidecar.** Hip Sidecar serves farm-fresh meals and small plates along with classic cocktails and 16 mostly local beers on tap. Burger patties made from grass-fed beef, free-range chicken, or housemade veggies are served on a brioche bun with inventive sauces such as bacon-maple ketchup. The menu includes many vegetarian and vegan options, among them the raw "green zebra" lasagna, made of basil-pistachio pesto, tomato sauce, and pine-nut "ricotta." Happy hour (daily from 4 to 6) and Sunday brunch (live jazz, five types of eggs Benedict) are very popular here. [$] *Average main: $18* ✉ *1127 Broad St., at Marsh St.* ☎ *805/540–5340* 🌐 *sidecarslo.com.*

WHERE TO STAY

$$$ HOTEL 🏨 **Apple Farm.** Decorated to the hilt with floral bedspreads and watercolors by local artists, this Wine Country–theme hotel is highly popular. **Pros:** flowers everywhere; convenient to Cal Poly and U.S. 101; creek-side setting. **Cons:** hordes of tourists during the day; too floral for some people's tastes. [$] *Rooms from: $219* ✉ *2015 Monterey St.* ☎ *800/255–2040, 805/544-2040* 🌐 *www.applefarm.com* 🛏 *104 rooms* 🍽 *No meals.*

$$$ HOTEL 🏨 **Granada Hotel & Bistro.** Built in 1922 and sparkling again after renovations completed in 2012, the Granada is the only full-service hotel in the heart of downtown. **Pros:** free parking; easy walk to downtown; luxurious rooms and amenities. **Cons:** some rooms are tiny; sometimes noisy near restaurant kitchen. [$] *Rooms from: $229* ✉ *1126 Morro St.* ☎ *805/544–9100* 🌐 *granadahotelandbistro.com* 🛏 *17 rooms* 🍽 *No meals.*

$$$ HOTEL 🏨 **Madonna Inn.** From its rococo bathrooms to its pink-on-pink frou-frou steak house, the Madonna Inn is fabulous or tacky, depending on your taste. **Pros:** fun, one-of-a-kind experience. **Cons:** rooms vary widely; must appreciate kitsch. [$] *Rooms from: $189* ✉ *100 Madonna Rd.* ☎ *805/543–3000, 800/543–9666* 🌐 *www.madonnainn.com* 🛏 *106 rooms, 4 suites* 🍽 *No meals.*

$ HOTEL 🏨 **Peach Tree Inn.** Extra touches such as rose gardens, a porch with rockers, and flower-filled vases turn this modest, family-run motel into a relaxing creek-side haven. **Pros:** bargain rates; cozy rooms; decent breakfast. **Cons:** near a busy intersection; basic amenities. [$] *Rooms from: $99* ✉ *2001 Monterey St.* ☎ *805/543–3170, 800/227–6396* 🌐 *www.peachtreeinn.com* 🛏 *37 rooms* 🍽 *Breakfast.*

$$ Petit Soleil. A cobblestone courtyard, country-French custom furnish-
B&B/INN ings, and Gallic music piped through the halls evoke a Provençal mood
at this cheery inn on upper Monterey Street's motel row. **Pros:** French
details throughout; scrumptious breakfasts; cozy rooms. **Cons:** sits on a
busy avenue; cramped parking. $ *Rooms from: $169* ⊠ *1473 Monterey
St.* ☎ *805/549–0321, 800/676–1588* ⊕ *www.psslo.com* ⇛ *15 rooms,
1 suite* ⏀ *Breakfast.*

NIGHTLIFE AND THE ARTS
NIGHTLIFE
SLO's club scene is centered on Higuera Street, off Monterey Street.

Koberl at Blue. A trendy crowd hangs out at this upscale restaurant's slick
bar to sip on exotic martinis and the many local and imported beers
and wines. ⊠ *998 Monterey St., at Osos St.* ☎ *805/783–1135* ⊕ *www.
epkoberl.com.*

SLO Brew. Handcrafted microbrews and live music most nights make for
a winning combination at this downtown watering hole and restaurant
that should be relocated to 736 Higuera St. by 2015. ⊠ *1119 Garden
St.* ☎ *805/543–1843* ⊕ *www.slobrewingco.com.*

THE ARTS
Performing Arts Center, San Luis Obispo. The center hosts live theater,
dance, and music performances. ⊠ *Cal Poly, 1 Grand Ave., off U.S.
101* ☎ *805/756–7222, 805/756–2787 box office, 888/233–2787 toll-
free* ⊕ *www.pacslo.org.*

OFF THE **Montaña de Oro State Park.** West of San Luis Obispo, Los Osos Valley
BEATEN Road winds past farms and ranches to this state park whose miles of
PATH nature trails traverse rocky shoreline, wild beaches, and hills overlook-
ing dramatic scenery. Check out the tide pools, watch the waves roll
into the bluffs, and picnic in the eucalyptus groves. From Montaña de
Oro you can reach Morro Bay by following the coastline along South
Bay Boulevard 8 miles through the quaint residential villages of Los
Osos and Baywood Park. ⊠ *West about 13 miles from downtown San
Luis Obispo on Madonna Rd., to Los Osos Valley Rd., to Pecho Val-
ley Rd.; to continue on to Morro Bay, backtrack east to Los Osos Val-
ley Rd., then head north on S. Bay Blvd., and west on State Park Rd.*
☎ *805/528–0513, 805/772–7434* ⊕ *www.parks.ca.gov.*

MORRO BAY

14 miles north of San Luis Obispo.

Commercial fishermen slog around Morro Bay in galoshes, and beat-
up fishing boats bob in the bay's protected waters. Nature-oriented
activities take center stage here: kayaking, hiking, biking, fishing, and
wildlife-watching around the bay and national marine estuary and
along the state beach.

GETTING HERE AND AROUND
From U.S. 101 south or north, exit at Highway 1 in San Luis Obispo
and head west. Scenic Highway 1 passes through the eastern edge of
town. From Atascadero, two-lane Highway 41 West treks over the
mountains to Morro Bay. San Luis Obispo RTA Route 12 buses travel

year-round between Morro Bay, San Luis Obispo, Cayucos, Cambria, San Simeon, and Hearst Castle. The Morro Bay Shuttle picks up riders throughout the town from Friday through Monday in summer ($1.25 one-way, $3 day pass).

ESSENTIALS

Visitor Information Morro Bay Visitors Center ✉ *255 Morro Bay Blvd., at Morro Ave.* ☎ *805/225–1633, 800/231–0592* 🌐 *www.morrobay.org* 🕒 *Daily 9–5.*

EXPLORING

Embarcadero. The center of the action on land is the Embarcadero, where vacationers pour in and out of souvenir shops and seafood restaurants and stroll or bike along the scenic half-mile Harborwalk to Morro Rock. From here, you can get out on the bay in a kayak or tour boat. ✉ *On waterfront from Beach St. to Tidelands Park.*

FAMILY **Morro Bay State Park Museum of Natural History.** Entertaining interactive exhibits at this spiffy museum explain the natural environment and how to preserve it—in the bay and estuary and on the rest of the planet. **■ TIP→ Children age 16 and under are admitted free here.** ✉ *State Park Rd., south of downtown* ☎ *805/772–2694* 🌐 *www.ccnha.org/morrobay* 🎟 *$3* 🕒 *Daily 10–5.*

Morro Rock. At the mouth of Morro Bay stands 576-foot-high Morro Rock, one of nine small volcanic peaks, or morros, in the area. A short walk leads to a breakwater, with the harbor on one side and crashing ocean waves on the other. You may not climb the rock, where endangered falcons and other birds nest. Sea lions and otters often play in the water below the rock. ✉ *Northern end of Embarcadero.*

WHERE TO EAT

$$ SEAFOOD 🍴 **Dorn's Original Breakers Cafe.** This restaurant overlooking the harbor has satisfied local appetites since 1948. In addition to straight-ahead dishes such as cod or shrimp fish-and-chips or calamari tubes sautéed in butter and wine, Dorn's serves breakfast. [$] *Average main: $22* ✉ *801 Market Ave., at Morro Bay Blvd.* ☎ *805/772–4415* 🌐 *www.dornscafe.com.*

$ SOUTHWESTERN 🍴 **Taco Temple.** This family-run diner serves some of the freshest food around. The seafood-heavy menu includes salmon burritos, superb fish tacos with mango salsa, and other dishes hailing from somewhere between California and Mexico. **■ TIP→ Taco Temple**is in a supermarket parking lot on the frontage road parallel to Highway 1, just north of the Highway 41 junction. [$] *Average main: $15* ✉ *2680 Main St., at Elena St.* ☎ *805/772–4965* ✍ *Reservations not accepted* 💳 *No credit cards* 🕒 *Closed Tues.*

$$$ SEAFOOD 🍴 **Windows on the Water.** Diners at this second-floor restaurant view the sunset through giant picture windows. Meanwhile, fresh fish and other dishes based on local ingredients emerge from the wood-fired oven in the open kitchen, and oysters on the half shell beckon from the raw bar. The California-centric wine list includes about 20 selections poured by the glass. [$] *Average main: $30* ✉ *699 Embarcadero, at Pacific St.* ☎ *805/772–0677* 🌐 *www.windowsmb.com* 🕒 *No lunch.*

WHERE TO STAY

$$$ B&B/INN Fodor's Choice ★ **Anderson Inn.** Friendly, personalized service and an oceanfront setting keep loyal patrons returning to this Embarcadero inn. **Pros:** walk to restaurants and sights; nice rooms; attentive service. **Cons:** not low-budget; waterfront area can get crowded. [$] *Rooms from: $239* ✉ *897 Embarcadero* ☎ *805/772–3434, 866/950–3434 toll-free reservations* 🌐 *www.andersoninnmorrobay.com* 🛏 *8 rooms* 🍴 *No meals.*

$$$ B&B/INN Fodor's Choice ★ **Cass House.** In tiny Cayucos, 4 miles north of Morro Bay, a shipping pioneer's 1867 home is now a luxurious B&B surrounded by rose and other gardens. **Pros:** historic property; some ocean views; excellent meals. **Cons:** away from nightlife and attractions; not good for families. [$] *Rooms from: $200* ✉ *222 N. Ocean Ave., Cayucos* ☎ *805/995–3669* 🌐 *casshouseinn.com* 🛏 *5 rooms* 🍴 *Breakfast.*

$$ RESORT **The Inn at Morro Bay.** Surrounded by eucalyptus trees, this inn abuts a heron rookery and Morro Bay State Park. **Pros:** great for wildlife enthusiasts; stellar views from restaurant and some rooms. **Cons:** some rooms on the small side; birds and seals can wake you early. [$] *Rooms from: $169* ✉ *60 State Park Rd.* ☎ *805/772–5651, 800/321–9566* 🌐 *innatmorrobay.com* 🛏 *97 rooms, 1 cottage* 🍴 *No meals.*

SPORTS AND THE OUTDOORS

Kayak Horizons. This outfit rents kayaks and paddleboards and gives lessons and guided tours. ✉ *551 Embarcadero, near Marina St.* ☎ *805/772–6444* 🌐 *www.kayakhorizons.com.*

Sub-Sea Tours & Kayaks. You can view sea life aboard this outfit's glass-bottom boat, watch whales from its catamaran, or rent a kayak or canoe. ✉ *699 Embarcadero* ☎ *805/772–9463* 🌐 *subseatours.com.*

Virg's Landing. Virg's conducts deep-sea-fishing and whale-watching trips. ✉ *1169 Market Ave.* ☎ *805/772–1222* 🌐 *virgslanding.com.*

PASO ROBLES

30 miles north of San Luis Obispo; 25 miles northwest of Morro Bay.

In the 1860s tourists began flocking to this dusty ranching outpost to "take the cure" in a luxurious bathhouse fed by underground mineral hot springs. An Old West town, complete with opera house, emerged, and grand Victorian homes went up, followed in the 20th century by Craftsman bungalows. A 2003 earthquake demolished or weakened several beloved downtown buildings, but historically faithful reconstruction has helped the district retain its character.

More than 200 wineries pepper the wooded hills of Paso Robles west of U.S. 101 and blanket the flatter, more open land on the east side. The region's hot summer days and cool nights yield grapes that produce robust Cabernet Sauvignon, Merlot, Syrah, and Zinfandel. Pinot Noir does well in some of the cooler, more fog-heavy western sections. Chardonnay, Sauvignon Blanc, and Viognier are among the white-wine grapes that do well here.

Small-town friendliness prevails at most wineries, especially smaller ones. Pick up a regional wine-touring map at lodgings, wineries, and attractions around town. Many lodgings pass out coupons good for discount tastings. Most tasting rooms close at 5 pm; many charge a small fee.

More attracts people to the Paso Robles area than fine wine and fancy tasting rooms, however. Golfers play the four local courses and spandex-clad bicyclists race along the winding back roads. Down-home and upmarket restaurants, bars, antiques stores, and little shops fill the streets around oak-shaded City Park, where special events of all kinds—custom car shows, an olive festival, Friday-night summer concerts—take place on many weekends. Despite its increasing sophistication, Paso (as the locals call it) more or less remains cowboy country. Each year in late July and early August, the city throws the two-week California Mid-State Fair, complete with livestock auctions, carnival rides, and corn dogs.

GETTING HERE AND AROUND

U.S. 101 runs through the city of Paso Robles. Highway 46 West links Paso Robles to Highway 1 and Cambria on the coast. Highway 46 East connects Paso Robles with Interstate 5 and the San Joaquin Valley. Public transit is not convenient for wine touring and sightseeing.

ESSENTIALS

Visitor Information Paso Robles Wine Country Alliance ☎ *805/239–8463* ⊕ *www.pasowine.com.* **Travel Paso Robles Alliance** ✉ *1225 Park St., near 12th St.* ☎ *805/238–0506* ⊕ *www.travelpaso.com.*

EXPLORING

TOP ATTRACTIONS

Fodor's Choice
★
Calcareous Vineyard. Elegant wines, a stylish tasting room, and knockout hilltop views make for a winning experience at this winery along winding Peachy Canyon Road. Cabernet Sauvignon, Syrah, and Zinfandel grapes thrive in the summer heat and limestone soils of the two vineyards near the tasting room, and a third vineyard on cooler York Mountain produces Pinot Noir, Chardonnay, and a Cabernet with a completely different character from the Peachy Canyon edition. ■ TIP➡ The picnic area's expansive eastward views invite lingering. ✉ *3430 Peachy Canyon Rd.* ☎ *805/239–0289* ⊕ *www.calcareous.com* 🍷 *Tasting $10; tour and tasting (reservations required) $25* ☉ *Daily 11–5.*

FAMILY
Estrella Warbirds Museum. An entertaining homage to fighter planes, flyboys, and flygirls, this museum maintains indoor exhibits about wartime aviation and displays retired specimens (of planes) outdoors and in repair shops. Bonus attraction: a huge building with spruced-up autos, drag racers, and "funny cars." ✉ *4251 Dry Creek Rd., off Airport Rd., north off Hwy. 46E* ☎ *805/227–0440* ⊕ *www.ewarbirds.org* 🍷 *$10* ☉ *Thurs.–Sun. 10–4 and Mon. legal holidays.*

Firestone Walker Brewing Company. At this working craft brewery you can sample medal winners such as the Double Barrel Ale and learn about the beer-making process on 30-minute guided tours of the brew house and cellar. ✉ *1400 Ramada Dr., east side of U.S. 101; exit at Hwy. 46 W/Cambria, but head east* ☎ *805/225–5911* ⊕ *www.firestonebeer. com* 🍷 *Tasting $1.50–$3 per sample, tour free* ☉ *Daily 10–5; tours on the half hour Fri.–Sun. 10:30–3:30 and Mon.–Thurs. by appointment.*

Fodor's Choice ★ **Justin Vineyards & Winery.** Suave Justin built its reputation—and, claim some, the Paso Robles wine region's as well—on Isosceles, a hearty Bordeaux blend, usually of Cabernet Sauvignon, Cabernet Franc, and Merlot. Justin's Cabernet Sauvignon is also well regarded, as is the Right Angle blend of Cab and three other varietals. Tastings here take place in an expansive room whose equally expansive windows provide views of Justin's hillside vineyards. ✉ *11680 Chimney Rock Rd., 15 miles west of U.S. 101's Hwy. 46 E exit; take 24th St. west and follow road (name changes along the way) to Chimney Rock Rd.* ☎ *805/238–6932, 800/726–0049* ⊕ *www.justinwine.com* ✉ *Tasting $10, tour $10, tour and tasting $15* ☉ *Daily 10–4:30* ☉ *Tours 10:30 and 2:30.*

> ## LAID-BACK WINE COUNTRY
>
> Hundreds of vineyards and wineries dot the hillsides from Paso Robles to San Luis Obispo, through the scenic Edna Valley and south to northern Santa Barbara County. The wineries offer much of the variety of northern California's Napa and Sonoma valleys—without the glitz and crowds. Since the early 1980s the region has developed an international reputation for high-quality wines, most notably Pinot Noir, Chardonnay, and Zinfandel. Wineries here tend to be small, but most have tasting rooms (some have tours), and you'll often meet the winemakers themselves.

Fodor's Choice ★ **Pasolivo.** While touring the idyllic west side of Paso Robles, take a break from wine tasting by stopping at Pasolivo. Find out how the artisans here make their Tuscan-style olive oils on a high-tech Italian press, and test the acclaimed results. ✉ *8530 Vineyard Dr., west off U.S. 101 (Exit 224) or Hwy. 46 W (Exit 228)* ☎ *805/227–0186* ⊕ *www.pasolivo.com* ✉ *Free* ☉ *Daily 11–5.*

River Oaks Hot Springs & Spa. The lakeside spa, on 240 hilly acres near the intersection of U.S. 101 and Highway 46 East, is a great place to relax after wine tasting or festival-going. Soak in a private indoor or outdoor hot tub fed by natural mineral springs, or indulge in a massage or facial. ✉ *800 Clubhouse Dr., off River Oaks Dr.* ☎ *805/238–4600* ⊕ *www.riveroakshotsprings.com* ✉ *$20–$24 per hr* ☉ *Tues.–Sun. 9–9.*

Tablas Creek Vineyard. Tucked in the western hills of Paso Robles, Tablas Creek is known for its blends of organically grown, hand-harvested Rhône varietals. Roussanne and Viognier are the two standout whites; the Mourvèdre-heavy blend called Panoplie (it also includes Grenache and Syrah) has received high praise in recent years. ■TIP→ There's a fine picnic area here. ✉ *9339 Adelaida Rd., west of Vineyard Dr.* ☎ *805/237–1231* ⊕ *www.tablascreek.com* ✉ *Tasting $10, tour free* ☉ *Daily 10–5; tour 10:30 and 2 by appointment.*

WORTH NOTING

Carnegie Historic Library. Philanthropist and steel magnate Andrew Carnegie funded this sturdy and splendid structure, erected in 1908. The jewel of City Park, it hosts thoughtful exhibits on local history, many of which include quirky products and advertisements from days gone by. ✉ *800 12th St., at Park St.* ☎ *805/238–4996* ⊕ *www.*

pasorobleshistoricalsociety.org ⊙ *Tues. and Thurs.–Sat. 10–4, Sun.
11–4* ⊙ *Closed Mon., Wed., and holidays.*

Eberle Winery. Even if you don't drink wine, stop here for a fascinating
tour of the huge wine caves beneath the vineyards. Eberle produces
wines from Bordeaux, Rhône, and Italian varietals and makes intriguing
blends including Grenache Blanc–Viognier and Cabernet Sauvignon–
Syrah. ⊠ *3810 Hwy. 46 E, 3½ miles east of U.S. 101* ☎ *805/238–9607*
⊕ *www.eberlewinery.com* ☜ *Basic tasting and tour free; weekend
reserve tasting $10* ⊙ *Apr.–Sept. daily 10–6, Oct.–Mar. daily 10–5.*

Paso Robles Pioneer Museum. The museum's one-room schoolhouse and its
displays of ranching paraphernalia, horse-drawn vehicles, hot-springs
artifacts, and photos evoke Paso's rural heritage. ⊠ *2010 Riverside
Ave., at 21st St.* ☎ *805/239–4556* ⊕ *www.pasoroblespioneermuseum.
org* ☜ *Free* ⊙ *Sep.–May Thurs.–Sun. 1–4; Jun.–Aug. Thurs., Fri. and
Sun. 1–4, Sat. 10–4.*

WHERE TO EAT

$$$
AMERICAN

✕ **Artisan.** Innovative variations on traditional American comfort foods,
well-chosen regional wines, and a sophisticated urban vibe have made
this family-run American bistro such a hit with winemakers, locals,
and tourists that it recently relocated to larger quarters. Chef Chris
Kobayashi, a James Beard Award nominee, uses local, organic, wild-
caught ingredients to put a fresh spin on dishes such as rabbit Stroganoff
and scallops with cedar-planked spaghetti squash, sherry brown but-
ter, and pork fried wild rice. Save room for chef's home-style desserts:
sundaes, puddings, cakes, cookies, and other sweet delights. $ *Aver-
age main: $28* ⊠ *843 12th St., at Pine St.* ☎ *805/237–8084* ⊕ *www.
artisanpasorobles.com.*

$$$
FRENCH

✕ **Bistro Laurent.** Owner-chef Laurent Grangien's handsome, welcoming
French bistro occupies an 1890s brick building across from City Park.
He focuses on traditional dishes such as duck confit, rack of lamb,
and onion soup, but always prepares a few au courant daily specials
as well. The wines, sourced from the adjacent wine shop, come from
around the world. $ *Average main: $28* ⊠ *1202 Pine St., at 12th St.*
☎ *805/226–8191* ⊕ *www.bistrolaurent.com* ⊙ *Closed Sun. and Mon.*

$$$
AMERICAN

✕ **McPhee's Grill.** Just south of Paso Robles in tiny Templeton, this casual
chophouse in an 1860s wood-frame storefront serves sophisticated,
contemporary versions of traditional Western fare such as oak-grilled
filet mignon and cedar-planked salmon. The house-label wines, made
especially for the restaurant, are quite good. $ *Average main: $25*
⊠ *416 S. Main St., at 5th St., Templeton* ☎ *805/434–3204* ⊕ *mcphees-
grill.com* ⊙ *No lunch Sun.*

$
FRENCH

✕ **Panolivo Family Bistro.** Scrumptious, affordable French fare draws
patrons to this cheery café just north of the town square. For break-
fast, try a fresh pastry or quiche, or build your own omelet. Lunch and
dinner choices include sandwiches, salads, and fresh pastas—includ-
ing cannelloni stuffed with vegetables or house-made beef—along with
traditional dishes like snails baked in garlic-butter sauce or beef bour-
guignon. $ *Average main: $15* ⊠ *1344 Park St., at 14th St.* ☎ *805/239–
3366* ⊕ *www.panolivo.com.*

$$ MODERN AMERICAN 🍴 **Thomas Hill Organics Market Bistro & Wine Bar.** In casual quarters a block north of City Park, Joe and Debbie Thomas serve inventive locavore cuisine. Much of the produce comes from their nearby 10-acre organic farm, and the meats and fish—even the olive oil and cheeses, not to mention the wines—come mostly from local providers as well. **TIP→ When the weather's fine, ask for a table in the outdoor courtyard.** [$] *Average main: $17* ✉ *1313 Park St., at 13th St.* ☎ *805/226–5888* 🌐 *thomashillorganics.com.*

$$$ SOUTHWESTERN 🍴 **Villa Creek.** With a firm nod to the Rancho and Mission cuisine of California's early settlers, chef Tom Fundero conjures distinctly modern magic with local, organic ingredients. The seasonal menu has included grilled fish with quinoa pilaf, braised pork belly with sweet-potato hash, mussels steamed in coconut milk, and seared chicken with whipped potatoes and preserved-lemon sauce. Central Coast selections dominate the wine list. All brick and bare wood, the dining room can get loud, but the atmosphere is always festive. For lighter appetites or wallets, the bar serves smaller plates—and potent margaritas. [$] *Average main: $26* ✉ *1144 Pine St., at 12th St.* ☎ *805/238–3000* 🌐 *www.villacreek.com* ⏲ *No lunch.*

5

WHERE TO STAY

$ HOTEL 🏨 **Adelaide Inn.** Family-owned and -managed, this clean, friendly oasis with meticulous landscaping offers spacious rooms and everything you need: coffeemaker, iron, hair dryer, and peace and quiet. **Pros:** great bargain; attractive pool area; ideal for families. **Cons:** not a romantic retreat; near a busy intersection. [$] *Rooms from: $104* ✉ *1215 Ysabel Ave.* ☎ *805/238–2770, 800/549–7276* 🌐 *www.adelaideinn.com* 🛏 *108 rooms* 🍽 *Breakfast.*

$$$$ HOTEL 🏨 **Hotel Cheval.** Equestrian themes surface throughout this intimate, European-style inn a half-block from the main square and near some of Paso's best restaurants. **Pros:** near downtown restaurants; sophisticated; personal service. **Cons:** views aren't great; no pool or hot tub. [$] *Rooms from: $330* ✉ *1021 Pine St.* ☎ *805/226–9995, 866/522–6999* 🌐 *www.hotelcheval.com* 🛏 *16 rooms* 🍽 *Breakfast.*

$$$$ B&B/INN 🏨 **JUST Inn.** Fine wines, a destination restaurant, and a vineyard's-edge setting make a stay at Justin winery's on-site inn an exercise in sophisticated seclusion. **Pros:** sophisticated; secluded; vineyard views; destination restaurant. **Cons:** half-hour drive to town; location may be *too* secluded for some. [$] *Rooms from: $400* ✉ *11680 Chimney Rock Rd.* ☎ *805/238–6932, 800/726–0049* 🌐 *www.justinwine.com* 🛏 *4 suites* 🍽 *Breakfast.*

$$ HOTEL 🏨 **La Bellasera Hotel & Suites.** The swankest full-service hotel for miles around, La Bellasera caters to those looking for high-tech amenities and easy access to major Central Coast roadways. **Pros:** new property; tons of amenities. **Cons:** far from downtown; at a major intersection. [$] *Rooms from: $169* ✉ *206 Alexa Court* ☎ *805/238–2834, 866/782–9669* 🌐 *www.labellasera.com* 🛏 *35 rooms, 25 suites* 🍽 *No meals.*

$$$ HOTEL 🏨 **Paso Robles Inn.** On the site of an old spa hotel of the same name, the inn is built around a lush, shaded garden with a pool. **Pros:** private spring-fed hot tubs; historic property; across from town square. **Cons:** fronts a busy street; rooms vary in size and amenities. [$] *Rooms from: $183* ✉ *1103 Spring St.* ☎ *805/238–2660, 800/676–1713* 🌐 *www.pasoroblesinn.com* 🛏 *92 rooms, 6 suites* 🍽 *No meals.*

THE ARTS

Vina Robles Ampitheatre. At this 3,300-seat, mission-style venue that opened in summer 2013, you can wine, dine, and listen to acclaimed musicians in concert. ☒ *Vina Robles winery, 3800 Mill Rd., off Hwy. 46* ☎ *805/286–3680* ⊕ *www.vinarobles.com* ☽ *May–Nov.*

CAMBRIA

28 miles west of Paso Robles; 20 miles north of Morro Bay.

Cambria, set on piney hills above the sea, was settled by Welsh miners in the 1890s. In the 1970s, the gorgeous, isolated setting attracted artists and other independent types; the town now caters to tourists, but it still bears the imprint of its bohemian past. Both of Cambria's downtowns, the original East Village and the newer West Village, are packed with art and crafts galleries, antiques shops, cafés, restaurants, and B&Bs. Late-Victorian homes stand alongside streets, and the hills are filled with redwood-and-glass residences.

Two diverting detours lie between Morro Bay and Cambria. In the laid-back beach town of Cayucos, 4 miles north of Morro Bay, you can stroll the long pier, feast on chowder (at Duckie's), and sample the namesake delicacies of the Brown Butter Cookie Co. Over in Harmony, a cute former dairy town 7 miles south of Cambria, you can take in the glassworks, pottery, and other artsy enterprises.

GETTING HERE AND AROUND

Highway 1 leads to Cambria from the north and south. Highway 246 West curves from U.S. 101 through the mountains to Cambria. San Luis Obispo RTA Route 12 buses stop in Cambria (and Hearst Castle).

ESSENTIALS

Visitor Information Cambria Chamber of Commerce ☎ *805/927–3624* ⊕ *www.cambriachamber.org.*

EXPLORING

Fiscalini Ranch Preserve. Walk along a mile-long coastal bluff trail to spot migrating whales, otters, and shore birds at this 450-acre public open space. Miles of additional scenic trails crisscross the protected habitats of rare and endangered species of flora and fauna, including a Monterey pine forest, western pond turtles, monarch butterflies, and burrowing owls. Dogs are permitted on-leash everywhere and off-leash on all trails except the bluff. ☒ *Hwy. 1, between Cambria Rd. and Main St. to the north, and Burton Dr. and Warren Rd. to the south; access either end of bluff trail off Windsor Blvd.* ☎ *805/927–2856* ⊕ *www.ffrpcambria.org.*

Leffingwell's Landing. A state picnic ground, the landing is a good place for examining tidal pools and watching otters as they frolic in the surf. ☒ *North end of Moonstone Beach Dr.* ☎ *805/927–2070.*

Moonstone Beach Drive. The drive runs along a bluff above the ocean, paralleled by a 3-mile boardwalk that winds along the beach. On this fine walk—a great photo op—you might glimpse sea lions and sea otters, and perhaps a gray whale during winter and spring. Year-round, birds aplenty fly about, and tiny creatures scurry amid the tidepools. ☒ *Off Hwy. 1.*

Nit Wit Ridge. Arthur Beal (aka Captain Nit Wit, Der Tinkerpaw) spent 51 years building a home above Cambria's West Village out of collected junk: beer cans, rocks, abalone shells, car parts, TV antennas—you name it. The site, sometimes signed as Nitt Witt Ridge, is a state landmark. **TIP→ You can drive by and peek in—from the 700 block of Main Street, head southeast on Cornwall Street and east on Hillcrest Drive. Better yet, schedule a guided tour.** ✉ *881 Hillcrest Dr.* ☎ *805/927–2690* 🎟 *$10* ⏲ *Tour daily by appointment.*

WHERE TO EAT

$$$ AMERICAN 🍴 **Black Cat Bistro.** Jazz wafts through the several small rooms of this intimate East Village bistro where stylish cushions line the banquettes. Start with an order of the fried olives stuffed with Gorgonzola, accompanied by a glass of local or imported wine. Mains on offer might include asiago pappardelle (vegetarian or with shrimp) or duck breast with mushroom risotto and cherry duck jus. [$] *Average main: $25* ✉ *1602 Main St.* ☎ *805/927–1600* 🌐 *www.blackcatbistro.com* ✍ *Reservations essential* ⏲ *Closed Tues. and Wed. No lunch.*

$$ AMERICAN FAMILY 🍴 **Linn's Restaurant.** Homemade olallieberry pies, soups, potpies, and other farmhouse comfort foods share the menu with fancier dishes such as free-range chicken cordon bleu at this spacious East Village restaurant. Also on-site are a bakery, a café serving more casual fare (take-out available), and a gift shop that sells gourmet foods. [$] *Average main: $18* ✉ *2277 Main St.* ☎ *805/927–0371* 🌐 *www.linnsfruitbin.com.*

$$ ECLECTIC 🍴 **Robin's.** A multiethnic, vegetarian-friendly dining experience awaits you at this cozy East Village cottage. At dinner, choose from lobster enchiladas, Moroccan duck breast, tandoori chicken, and more. Lunchtime's extensive salad and sandwich menu embraces burgers and tofu alike. **TIP→ Unless it's raining, ask for a table on the secluded (heated) garden patio.** [$] *Average main: $22* ✉ *4095 Burton Dr., at Center St.* ☎ *805/927–5007* 🌐 *www.robinsrestaurant.com.*

$$$ SEAFOOD 🍴 **Sea Chest Oyster Bar and Restaurant.** Cambria's best place for seafood fills up soon after it opens at 5:30. Those in the know grab seats at the oyster bar and take in spectacular sunsets while watching the chefs broil fresh halibut, steam garlicky clams, and fry crispy calamari steaks. If you arrive to a wait, play cribbage or checkers in the game room. [$] *Average main: $26* ✉ *6216 Moonstone Beach Dr., near Weymouth St.* ☎ *805/927–4514* 🌐 *www.seachestrestaurant.com* ✍ *Reservations not accepted* 💳 *No credit cards* ⏲ *Closed Tues. mid-Sept.–May. No lunch.*

WHERE TO STAY

$ HOTEL 🏨 **Bluebird Inn.** This sweet motel in Cambria's East Village sits amid beautiful gardens along Santa Rosa Creek. **Pros:** excellent value; well-kept gardens; friendly staff. **Cons:** few frills; basic rooms; on Cambria's main drag; not on beach. [$] *Rooms from: $78* ✉ *1880 Main St.* ☎ *805/927–4634, 800/552–5434* 🌐 *bluebirdmotel.com* 🛏 *37 rooms* 🍽 *No meals.*

$$ RESORT 🏨 **Cambria Pines Lodge.** This 25-acre retreat up the hill from the East Village is a good choice for families. **Pros:** short walk from downtown; many recreational facilities; verdant gardens; spacious grounds. **Cons:** service and housekeeping not always top-quality; some units need updating. [$] *Rooms from: $169* ✉ *2905 Burton Dr.* ☎ *805/927–4200, 800/966–6490* 🌐 *www.cambriapineslodge.com* 🛏 *77 rooms, 75 suites* 🍽 *Breakfast.*

5

$$ B&B/INN 🏨 **J. Patrick House.** Monterey pines and flower gardens surround this Irish-theme inn, which sits on a hilltop above Cambria's East Village. **Pros:** fantastic breakfasts; friendly innkeepers; quiet neighborhood. **Cons:** few rooms; fills up quickly. [$] *Rooms from: $175* ✉ *2990 Burton Dr.* ☎ *805/927–3812, 800/341–5258* 🌐 *www.jpatrickhouse.com* 🛏 *8 rooms* 🍴 *Breakfast.*

$$ HOTEL 🏨 **Moonstone Landing.** Friendly staff, lots of amenities, and reasonable rates make this up-to-date motel a top pick of readers who like to stay right on Moonstone Beach. **Pros:** sleek furnishings; across from the beach; cheery lounge. **Cons:** narrow property; some rooms overlook a parking lot. [$] *Rooms from: $125* ✉ *6240 Moonstone Beach Dr.* ☎ *805/927–0012, 800/830–4540* 🌐 *www.moonstonelanding.com* 🛏 *29 rooms* 🍴 *Breakfast.*

SAN SIMEON

9 miles north of Cambria; 65 miles south of Big Sur.

Whalers founded San Simeon in the 1850s but had virtually abandoned it by 1865, when Senator George Hearst began purchasing most of the surrounding ranch land. Hearst turned San Simeon into a bustling port, and his son, William Randolph Hearst, further developed the area while erecting Hearst Castle. Today, San Simeon is basically a strip of unremarkable gift shops and so-so motels that straddle Highway 1 about 4 miles south of the castle's entrance, but Old San Simeon, right across from the entrance, is worth a peek.

GETTING HERE AND AROUND

Highway 1 is the only way to reach San Simeon. Connect with the highway off U.S. 101 directly or via rural routes such as Highway 41 West (Atascadero to Morro Bay) and Highway 46 West (Paso Robles to Cambria).

EXPLORING

TOP ATTRACTIONS

Fodor's Choice ★ **Hearst Castle.** Officially known as "Hearst San Simeon State Historical Monument," Hearst Castle sits in solitary splendor atop La Cuesta Encantada (the Enchanted Hill). Its buildings and gardens spread over 127 acres that were the heart of newspaper magnate William Randolph Hearst's 250,000-acre ranch. Hearst devoted nearly 30 years and about $10 million to building this elaborate estate. He commissioned renowned California architect Julia Morgan, but he was very much involved with the final product, a blend of Italian, Spanish, and Moorish styles. The 115-room main building and three huge "cottages" are connected by terraces and staircases and surrounded by pools, gardens, and statuary. In its heyday the castle was a playground for Hearst and his guests—Hollywood celebrities, political leaders, scientists, and other well-known figures. Construction began in 1919 and was never officially completed. Work was halted in 1947 when Hearst had to leave San Simeon because of failing health. The Hearst family donated the property to the State of California in 1958.

Access to the castle is through the visitor center at the foot of the hill, which contains a collection of Hearst memorabilia and a giant-screen theater that shows a 40-minute film giving an overview of Hearst's life and of the castle's construction. Buses from the visitor center zigzag up to the neoclassical extravaganza, where guides conduct three different daytime tours of parts of the estate: grand rooms, upstairs suites, and cottages and kitchen. Daytime tours take about two hours and include the movie and time at the end to explore the castle exteriors. In spring and fall, docents in period costume portray Hearst's guests and staff for the slightly longer evening tour, which begins at sunset. Reservations are recommended for all the tours, which include a ½-mile walk and between 150 and 400 stairs. ⌂ *San Simeon State Park, 750 Hearst Castle Rd.* ☎ *800/444–4445* ⊕ *www.hearstcastle. com* ✉ *Daytime tours $25, evening tours $36* ☉ *Tours daily 9–3:20, later in summer; additional tours take place most Fri. and Sat. evenings Mar.–May and Sept.–Dec.*

FAMILY   **Piedras Blancas Elephant Seal Rookery.** A large colony of elephant seals (at last count 15,000 members) gathers every year at Piedras Blancas Elephant Seal Rookery, on the beaches near Piedras Blancas Lighthouse. The huge males with their pendulous, trunklike noses typically start appearing on shore in late November, and the females begin to arrive in December to give birth—most babies are born in the last two weeks of January. The newborn pups spend about four weeks nursing before their mothers head out to sea, leaving them on their own; the "weaners" leave the rookery when they are about 3½ months old. The seals return in the spring and summer months to molt or rest, but not en masse as in winter. You can watch them from a boardwalk along the bluffs just a few feet above the beach; do not attempt to approach them, as they are wild animals. The nonprofit Friends of the Elephant Seal runs a small visitor center and gift shop at 250 San Simeon Avenue in San Simeon. ⌂ *Off Hwy. 1, 4½ miles north of Hearst Castle, just south of Piedras Blancas Lighthouse* ☎ *805/924–1628* ⊕ *www. elephantseal.org.*

Piedras Blancas Light Station. If you think traversing craggy, twisting Highway 1 is tough, imagine trying to navigate a boat up the rocky coastline (piedras blancas means "white rocks" in Spanish) near San Simeon before lighthouses were built. Captains must have cheered wildly when the beam began to shine here in 1875. Try to time a visit to include a morning tour (reservations not required). ■**TIP**➔ **Do not meet at the gate to the lighthouse—you'll miss the tour. Meet your guide instead at the former Piedras Blancas Motel, a mile and a half north of the light station.** ☎ *805/927–7361* ⊕ *piedrasblancas.org* ✉ *$10* ☉ *Tours at 9:45, mid-June–Aug. Mon–Sat.; Sept.–mid-June Tues., Thurs., and Sat.; no tours on national holidays* ☞ *No pets allowed.*

WORTH NOTING

Old San Simeon. Founded in the 1850s as a whaling village, Old San Simeon morphed into an outpost for employees of Hearst Ranch about two decades later. **Sebastian's General Store,** built in 1852 as a whaling store, was moved by oxen to its present location in 1878. Julia Morgan, William Randolph Hearst's architect, designed some of the village's mission revival–style buildings. **■ TIP→ Sebastian's houses a deli that serves an excellent French dip sandwich (made from Hearst Ranch beef) and the laid-back tasting room of Hearst Ranch Winery, another delight.** ✉ *West of Hwy. 1, across from Hearst Castle entrance.*

BEACHES

William Randolph Hearst Memorial Beach. This wide, sandy beach edges a protected cove on both sides of San Simeon Pier. Fish from the pier or from a charter boat, picnic and barbecue on the bluffs, or boogie board or bodysurf on relatively gentle waves. In summer, you can rent a kayak and paddle out into the bay for close encounters with marine life and sea caves. **Facilities:** food and drink; parking; toilets; water sports. **Best for:** sunset; swimming; walking. ✉ *750 Hearst Castle Rd., off Hwy. 1, west of Hearst Castle entrance* ☎ *805/927–2020* 🌐 *www.slostateparks.com* 🎟 *Free* 🕒 *Daily sunrise–sunset.*

WHERE TO STAY

$$$ HOTEL 🏨 **Best Western Cavalier Oceanfront Resort.** Reasonable rates, an oceanfront location, evening bonfires, and well-equipped rooms—some with wood-burning fireplaces and private patios—make this motel a great choice. **Pros:** on the bluffs; fantastic views; close to Hearst Castle. **Cons:** room amenities and sizes vary; pools are small and sometimes crowded. [$] *Rooms from: $179* ✉ *9415 Hearst Dr.* ☎ *805/927–4688, 800/826–8168* 🌐 *www.cavalierresort.com* 🛏 *90 rooms* 🍴 *No meals.*

$$ HOTEL 🏨 **The Morgan San Simeon.** On Highway 1's ocean side, the Morgan offers motel-style rooming options in two Asian-inspired buildings. **Pros:** fascinating artwork; easy access to Hearst Castle; some ocean views. **Cons:** not right on beach; no fitness room or laundry facilities. [$] *Rooms from: $149* ✉ *9135 Hearst Dr.* ☎ *805/927–3878, 800/451–9900* 🌐 *www.hotel-morgan.com* 🛏 *54 rooms, 1 suite* 🍴 *Breakfast.*

BIG SUR COASTLINE

Long a retreat of artists and writers, Big Sur is a place of ancient forests and rugged shoreline, stretching 90 miles from San Simeon to Carmel. Residents have protected it from overdevelopment, and much of the region lies within several state parks and the more than 165,000-acre Ventana Wilderness, itself part of the Los Padres National Forest.

ESSENTIALS

Visitor Information Big Sur Chamber of Commerce ☎ *831/667–2100* 🌐 *www.bigsurcalifornia.org.*

SOUTHERN BIG SUR

Hwy. 1 from San Simeon to Julia Pfeiffer Burns State Park.

This especially rugged stretch of oceanfront is a rocky world of mountains, cliffs, and beaches.

GETTING HERE AND AROUND

Highway 1 is the only major access route from north or south. From the south, access Highway 1 from U.S. 101 in San Luis Obispo. From the north, take rural route Highway 46 West (Paso Robles to Cambria) or Highway 41 West (Atascadero to Morro Bay). Nacimiento-Fergusson Road snakes through mountains and forest from U.S. 101 at Jolon about 25 miles to Highway 1 at Kirk Creek, about 4 miles south of Lucia; this curving, at times precipitous road is a motorcyclist favorite, not recommended for the faint of heart or during inclement weather.

EXPLORING

Fodor's Choice ★ **Highway 1.** One of California's most spectacular drives, Highway 1 snakes up the coast north of San Simeon. Numerous pullouts along the way offer tremendous views and photo ops. On some of the beaches, huge elephant seals lounge nonchalantly, seemingly oblivious to the attention of rubberneckers. Heavy rain sometimes causes mudslides that block the highway north and south of Big Sur. 🌐 *www.dot.ca.gov.*

Jade Cove. In Los Padres National Forest just north of the town of Gorda is Jade Cove, a well-known jade-hunting spot. Rock hunting is allowed on the beach, but you may not remove anything from the walls of the cliffs. ✉ *Hwy. 1, 34 miles north of San Simeon.*

Julia Pfeiffer Burns State Park. The park provides fine hiking, from an easy ½-mile stroll with marvelous coastal views to a strenuous 6-mile trek through redwoods. The big draw here, an 80-foot waterfall that drops into the ocean, gets crowded in summer; still, it's an astounding place to contemplate nature. Migrating whales, harbor seals, and sea lions can sometimes be spotted just offshore. ✉ *Hwy. 1, 15 miles north of Lucia* ☎ *831/667–2315* 🌐 *www.parks.ca.gov* 🎟 *$10* 🕒 *Daily sunrise–sunset.*

WHERE TO STAY

$$ HOTEL 🏨 **Ragged Point Inn.** At this cliff-top resort—the only inn and restaurant for miles around—glass walls in most rooms open to awesome ocean views. **Pros:** on the cliffs; great food; idyllic views. **Cons:** busy road stop during the day; often booked for weekend weddings. [$] *Rooms from: $169* ✉ *19019 Hwy. 1, 20 miles north of San Simeon, Ragged Point* ☎ *805/927–4502, 805/927–5708 restaurant* 🌐 *raggedpointinn.com* 🛏 *39 rooms* 🍴 *No meals.*

$$$ RESORT 🏨 **Treebones Resort.** Perched on a hilltop, surrounded by national forest and stunning, unobstructed ocean views, this yurt resort provides a stellar back-to-nature experience along with creature comforts. **Pros:** 360-degree views; spacious pool area; comfortable beds. **Cons:** steep paths; no private bathrooms; not good for families with young children. [$] *Rooms from: $225* ✉ *71895 Hwy. 1, Willow Creek Rd., 32 miles north of San Simeon, 1 mile north of Gorda* ☎ *805/927–2390, 877/424–4787* 🌐 *www.treebonesresort.com* 🛏 *16 yurts, 5 campsites, 1 human nest w/campsite* 🍴 *Breakfast* ☞ *Two-night minimum on weekends and Apr.–Oct.*

CENTRAL BIG SUR

Hwy. 1, from Partington Cove to Bixby Bridge.

The countercultural spirit of Big Sur—which instead of a conventional town is a loose string of coast-hugging properties along Highway 1—is alive and well today. Its few residents include the very wealthy, the enthusiastically outdoorsy, and the thoroughly evolved: since the 1960s the Esalen Institute, a center for alternative education and East–West philosophical study, has attracted seekers of higher consciousness and devotees of the property's hot springs. Today, posh and rustic resorts hidden among the redwoods cater to visitors drawn from near and far by the extraordinary scenery and serene isolation.

GETTING HERE AND AROUND
From the north, follow Highway 1 south from Carmel. From the south, continue the drive north from Julia Pfeiffer Burns State Park *(above)* on Highway 1. Monterey-Salinas Transit operates the Line 22 Big Sur bus from Monterey and Carmel to Central Big Sur (the last top is Nepenthe), daily from late May to early September and weekends only the rest of the year.

Bus Contact Monterey-Salinas Transit 🖀 *888/678–2871* ⊕ *www.mst.org.*

EXPLORING
Bixby Creek Bridge. The graceful arc of Bixby Creek Bridge is a photographer's dream. Built in 1932, the bridge spans a deep canyon, more than 100 feet wide at the bottom. From the north-side parking area you can admire the view or walk the 550-foot structure. ⊠ *Hwy. 1, 6 miles north of Point Sur State Historic Park, 13 miles south of Carmel.*

Pfeiffer Big Sur State Park. Among the many hiking trails at Pfeiffer Big Sur, a short route through a redwood-filled valley leads to a waterfall. You can double back or continue on the more difficult trail along the valley wall for views over miles of treetops to the sea. ⊠ *47225 Hwy. 1* 🖀 *831/667–2315* ⊕ *www.parks.ca.gov* 🖃 *$10 per vehicle* ☉ *Daily sunrise–sunset.*

Point Sur State Historic Park. An 1889 lighthouse still stands watch from atop a large volcanic rock at this state park. Four lighthouse keepers lived here with their families until 1974, when the light station became automated. Their homes and working spaces are open to the public only on 2½- to 3-hour ranger-led tours. Considerable walking, including up two stairways, is involved. Strollers are not allowed. ⊠ *Hwy. 1, 7 miles north of Pfeiffer Big Sur State Park* 🖀 *831/625–4419* ⊕ *www.pointsur. org* 🖃 *$12* ☉ *Tours generally Nov.–Mar., weekends at 10, Wed. at 1; Apr.–Oct., Sat. and Wed. at 10 and 2, Sun. at 10; call to confirm.*

BEACHES
Pfeiffer Beach. Through a hole in one of the gigantic boulders at secluded Pfeiffer Beach, you can watch the waves break first on the sea side and then on the beach side. Keep a sharp eye out for the unsigned, ungated road to the beach: it branches west of Highway 1 between the post office and Pfeiffer Big Sur State Park. The 2-mile, one-lane road descends sharply. **Amenities:** parking (fee); toilets. **Best for:** solitude; sunset. ⊠ *Off Hwy. 1, 1 mile south of Pfeiffer Big Sur State Park* 🖃 *$5 per vehicle* ☉ *Daily 9–8.*

WHERE TO EAT

$$$ ECLECTIC 🍴 **Big Sur Roadhouse.** The chef at this colorful bistro perks up California favorites with a pinch of Cajun spice. Zesty mains include stewed leg of lamb with toasted farro, root vegetables, and long-cooked greens, and seafood gumbo with Dungeness crab and andouille sausage. The roadhouse, which serves breakfast, lunch, and dinner, is a good stop for small bites such as oysters, buttermilk biscuits, and fried-chicken "lollipops." The salted caramel panna cotta with chocolate shortbread and blood orange caramel is a popular dessert. [$] *Average main: $25* ✉ *Hwy. 1, 1 mile north of Pfeiffer Big Sur State Park* ☎ *831/667–2370* 🌐 *www.glenoaksbigsur.com/roadhouse.html.*

$$$ AMERICAN 🍴 **Deetjen's Big Sur Inn.** The candle-lighted, creaky-floor restaurant in the main house at the historic inn of the same name is a Big Sur institution. It serves spicy seafood paella, steak, and rack of lamb for dinner and flavorful eggs Benedict for breakfast. The chef sources most ingredients from purveyors known for sustainable practices. [$] *Average main: $30* ✉ *Hwy. 1, 3½ mile south of Pfeiffer Big Sur State Park* ☎ *831/667–2378* 🌐 *www.deetjens.com* ⏲ *No lunch.*

$$$ AMERICAN 🍴 **Nepenthe.** It may be that no other restaurant between San Francisco and Los Angeles has a better coastal view than Nepenthe. The food and drink are overpriced but good; there are burgers, sandwiches, and salads for lunch, and fresh fish and hormone-free steaks for dinner. For the real show, settle on the terraced deck in the late afternoon, order a glass from the extensive wine list, and watch the sun slip into the Pacific Ocean. The less expensive, outdoor Café Kevah serves brunch and lunch. [$] *Average main: $30* ✉ *48510 Hwy. 1, 2½ miles south of Big Sur Station* ☎ *831/667–2345* 🌐 *www.nepenthebigsur.com.*

$$$$ AMERICAN 🍴 **The Restaurant at Ventana.** The redwood, copper, and cedar elements at the Ventana Inn's restaurant pay tribute to the historic natural setting, while gleaming fixtures and dining accoutrements place the facility firmly in the 21st century. Chef Truman Jones's seasonal menu showcases meat, fish, and produce—such as organic chicken breast, wild king salmon, artichokes, and abalone—grown or caught in California. A full slate of regional and international wines complements his dishes. The restaurant is also open for lunch. **■ TIP→ If the day is sunny, ask for a table on the outdoor terrace and take in the ocean views.** [$] *Average main: $36* ✉ *48123 Hwy. 1, 1½ miles south of Pfeiffer Big Sur State Park* ☎ *831/667–4242* 🌐 *www.ventanainn.com* ✍ *Reservations essential.*

$$$$ AMERICAN 🍴 **Sierra Mar.** Ocean-view dining doesn't get much better than this. At cliff's edge 1,200 feet above the Pacific at the ultra-chic Post Ranch Inn, Sierra Mar serves cutting-edge American food made from mostly organic, seasonal ingredients, some from the on-site chef's garden. The four-course prix-fixe option always shines. The nine-course Taste of Big Sur menu centers around ingredients grown and foraged on the property or sourced locally. The restaurant's wine list is among the nation's most extensive. [$] *Average main: $120* ✉ *Hwy. 1, 1½ miles south of Pfeiffer Big Sur State Park* ☎ *831/667–2800* 🌐 *www.postranchinn.com/dining* ✍ *Reservations essential.*

WHERE TO STAY

$$$ HOTEL — [icon] **Big Sur Lodge.** Modern motel-style cottages with mission-style furnishings and vaulted ceilings sit in a meadow, surrounded by trees and flowering shrubbery. **Pros:** near trailheads; good camping alternative. **Cons:** basic rooms; walk to main lodge. [$] *Rooms from: $204* ✉ *Pfeiffer Big Sur State Park, 47225 Hwy. 1* ☎ *831/667–3100, 800/424–4787* 🌐 *www.bigsurlodge.com* 🛏 *61 rooms* 🍴 *No meals.*

$$ B&B/INN — [icon] **Deetjen's Big Sur Inn.** This historic 1930s Norwegian-style property is endearingly rustic, especially if you're willing to go with a camplike flow. **Pros:** tons of character; wooded grounds. **Cons:** thin walls; some rooms don't have private baths. [$] *Rooms from: $160* ✉ *Hwy. 1, 3½ miles south of Pfeiffer Big Sur State Park* ☎ *831/667–2377* 🌐 *www.deetjens.com* 🛏 *20 rooms, 15 with bath* 🍴 *No meals.*

$$$$ HOTEL — [icon] **Glen Oaks Big Sur.** At this rustic-modern cluster of adobe-and-redwood buildings, you can choose between motel-style rooms, cabins, and cottages in the woods. **Pros:** in the heart of town; walking distance of restaurants. **Cons:** near busy road and parking lot; no TVs. [$] *Rooms from: $275* ✉ *Hwy. 1, 1 mile north of Pfeiffer Big Sur State Park* ☎ *831/667–2105* 🌐 *www.glenoaksbigsur.com* 🛏 *16 rooms, 2 cottages, 7 cabins* 🍴 *No meals.*

$$$$ RESORT — Fodor's Choice ★ — [icon] **Post Ranch Inn.** This luxurious retreat, designed exclusively for adult getaways, has remarkable environmentally conscious architecture. **Pros:** world-class resort; spectacular views; gorgeous property with hiking trails. **Cons:** expensive; austere design; not a good choice if heights scare you. [$] *Rooms from: $775* ✉ *Hwy. 1, 1½ miles south of Pfeiffer Big Sur State Park* ☎ *831/667–2200, 888/524–4787* 🌐 *www.postranchinn.com* 🛏 *39 units* 🍴 *Breakfast.*

$$$$ HOTEL — Fodor's Choice ★ — [icon] **Ventana.** Hundreds of celebrities, from Oprah Winfrey to Sir Anthony Hopkins, have escaped to Ventana, a romantic resort on 243 tranquil acres 1,200 feet above the Pacific. **Pros:** nature trails everywhere; great food; secluded. **Cons:** simple breakfast; some rooms have no ocean view. [$] *Rooms from: $650* ✉ *Hwy. 1, almost 1 mile south of Pfeiffer Big Sur State Park* ☎ *831/667–2331, 800/628–6500* 🌐 *www.ventanainn.com* 🛏 *25 rooms, 31 suites* 🍴 *Breakfast.*

CHANNEL ISLANDS
NATIONAL PARK

WELCOME TO CHANNEL ISLANDS NATIONAL PARK

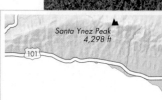

TOP REASONS TO GO

★ **Rare flora and fauna:** The Channel Islands are home to 145 species of terrestrial plants and animals found nowhere else on Earth.

★ **Time travel:** With no cars, phones, or services, these undeveloped islands provide a glimpse of what California was like hundreds of years ago, away from hectic modern life.

★ **Underwater adventures:** The incredibly healthy channel waters rank among the top 10 diving destinations on the planet—but you can also visit the kelp forest virtually via Channel Islands Live, an underwater video program.

★ **Marvelous marine mammals:** More than 30 species of seals, sea lions, whales, and other marine mammals ply the park's waters at various times of year.

★ **Sea-cave kayaking:** Paddle around otherwise inaccessible portions of the park's 175 miles of gorgeous coastline—including one of the world's largest sea caves.

1 Anacapa. Tiny Anacapa is a 5-mile stretch of three islets, with towering cliffs, caves, natural bridges, and rich kelp forests.

2 Santa Barbara. More than 5 miles of scenic trails crisscross this tiny island, known for its excellent wildlife viewing and native plants. It's a favorite destination for diving, snorkeling, and kayaking.

Santa Ynez Peak
4,298 ft

101

Harris Point
Point Bennett
Cuyler Harbor
Cabrillo Monument
Lester Ranch site
Carrington Point
West Point
Santa Cruz Channel
Tyler Bight
Vail & Vickers Ranch
Bechers Bay
San Miguel Island
San Miguel Passage
Sandy Point
4
Torrey Pines
Santa Rosa Island
Soledad Peak
1,574 ft
East Point
Johnsons Lee
South Point

P A C I F I C   O C E A N

3 Santa Cruz. The park's largest island offers some of the best hikes and kayaking opportunities, one of the world's largest and deepest sea caves, and more species of flora and fauna than any other park island.

Santa Barbara Island is approximately 52 miles southeast of Santa Cruz Island

Santa Barbara Island Light Beacon

2 *Santa Barbara Island*

1 Light Station & Museum

Anacapa Island

6

GETTING ORIENTED

Channel Islands National Park includes five of the eight Channel Islands and the one nautical mile of ocean that surrounds them. Six nautical miles of surrounding channel waters are designated a National Marine Sanctuary and are teeming with life, including giant kelp forests, 345 fish species, dolphins, whales, seals, sea lions, and seabirds. The islands range in size from 1-square-mile Santa Barbara to 96-square-mile Santa Cruz. Together they form a magnificent nature preserve with 145 endemic or unique species of plants and animals.

4 **Santa Rosa.** Campers love to stay on Santa Rosa, with its myriad hiking opportunities, stunning white-sand beaches, and rare grove of Torrey pines. It's also the only island accessible by plane.

Updated
by Cheryl
Crabtree

On crystal clear days the craggy peaks of the Channel Islands are easy to see from the mainland, jutting from the Pacific in such sharp detail it seems you could reach out and touch them. The islands really aren't that far away—a high-speed boat will whisk you to the closest ones in less than an hour—yet very few people ever visit them. Those fearless, adventurous types who do will experience one of the most splendid land-and-sea wilderness areas on the planet.

CHANNEL ISLANDS PLANNER

WHEN TO GO

Channel Islands National Park records about 620,000 visitors each year, but many never venture beyond the visitor center. The busiest times are holidays and summer weekends; if you're going then, make your transportation and accommodation arrangements in advance.

The warm, dry summer and fall months are the best time to go camping. Humpback and blue whales arrive to feed from late June through early fall. The rains usually come December through March—but this is also the best time to spot gray whales and to get discounts at area hotels. In the late spring, thousands of migratory birds descend on the islands to hatch their young, and wildflowers carpet the slopes. The water temperature is nearly always cool, so bring a wet suit if you plan to spend much time in the ocean, even in the summer. Fog, high winds, and rough seas can happen any time of the year.

GETTING HERE AND AROUND

BOAT TRAVEL

The visitor center for Channel Islands National Park is on California's mainland, in the town of Ventura, off U.S. 101. From the harbors at Ventura, Santa Barbara, and Oxnard, you can board a boat to one of the islands. If you have your own boat, you can land at any of the islands without a permit, but you should visit the park website for instructions and information on restricted areas. A permit is required to land on the Nature Conservancy property on Santa Cruz Island. Boaters landing at San Miguel must contact the park ranger beforehand.

Island Packers. Sailing on high-speed catamarans from Ventura or a mono-hull vessel from Oxnard, Island Packers goes to Santa Cruz Island daily most of the year, weather permitting. The boats also go to Anacapa several days a week, and to the outer islands from late April through early November. They also cruise along Anacapa's north shore on three-hour wildlife tours (non-landing) several times a week. ⊠ *3550 Harbor Blvd., Oxnard* ☎ *805/642–1393* ⊕ *www.islandpackers. com* ⊠ *$36–$147* ⊠ *1691 Spinnaker Dr., Ventura.*

CAR TRAVEL

To reach the Ventura harbor, exit U.S. 101 in Ventura at Seaward Boulevard or Victoria Avenue and follow the signs to Ventura Harbor/ Spinnaker Drive. To access Channel Islands Harbor in Oxnard, exit U.S. 101 at Victoria Avenue and head south approximately 7 miles to Channel Islands Boulevard. To access dive and whale-watching boats in Santa Barbara, exit U.S. 101 at Castillo Street and head south to Cabrillo Boulevard, then turn right for the harbor entrance. Private vehicles are not permitted on the islands. Pets are also not allowed in the park.

PARK ESSENTIALS

PARK FEES AND PERMITS

There is no fee to enter Channel Islands National Park, but unless you have your own boat, you will pay $36 or more per person for a ride with a boat operator. The cost of taking a boat to the park varies depending on which operator you choose. Also, there is a $15-per-day fee for staying in one of the islands' campgrounds.

If you take your own boat, landing permits are not required to visit islands administered by the National Park Service. Nevertheless, boaters who want to land on the Nature Conservancy preserve on Santa Cruz Island must have a permit. Visit ⊕ *www.nature.org/cruzpermit* for permit information; allow 10 business days to process and return your permit application. If you anchor in a nearby cove at any island, at least one person should remain aboard the boat at all times. To hike beyond the ranger station on San Miguel, you need a reservation and permit; call ☎ *805/658–5711* to be matched up with a ranger, who must accompany you. Anglers must have a state fishing license; for details, call the California Department of Fish and Wildlife at ☎ *916/653–7664* or visit ⊕ *www.wildlife.ca.gov*. More than a dozen Marine Protected Areas (MPAs) with special resource protection regulations surround the islands, so read the guidelines carefully before you depart.

PARK HOURS

The islands are open every day of the year. Channel Islands National Park Visitor Center in Ventura is closed on Thanksgiving and Christmas. Channel Islands National Park is in the Pacific time zone.

VISITOR INFORMATION
PARK CONTACT INFORMATION
Channel Islands National Park Visitor Center ⊠ *1901 Spinnaker Dr., Ventura* ☎ *805/658–5730* ⊕ *www.nps.gov/chis.*

VISITOR CENTERS
Channel Islands National Park Robert J. Lagomarsino Visitor Center. The park's main visitor center has a museum, a bookstore, a three-story observation tower with telescopes, and exhibits about the islands. There's also a marine life exhibit where you can see sea stars clinging to rocks, anemones waving their colorful, spiny tentacles, and a brilliant orange Garibaldi darting around. The center also has full-size reproductions of a male northern elephant seal and the pygmy mammoth skeleton unearthed on Santa Rosa Island in 1994. *Treasure in the Sea*, a 24-minute film narrated by Kevin Costner, shows throughout the day and gives an overview of the islands. Rangers lead various free public programs describing park resources on weekends and holidays at 11 and 3; they can also give you a detailed map and trip-planning packet if you're interested in visiting the actual islands. In summer you can watch live ranger broadcasts of underwater dives and hikes on Anacapa Island, shown at the center Wednesday through Saturday (hike at 11, dive at 2). ⊠ *1901 Spinnaker Dr., Ventura* ☎ *805/658–5730* ⊕ *www.nps.gov/chis* ⊗ *Daily 8:30–5.*

EXPLORING

THE ISLANDS

Anacapa Island. Although most people think of it as an island, Anacapa Island actually comprises three narrow islets. The tips of these volcanic formations nearly touch but are inaccessible from one another except by boat. All three islets have towering cliffs, isolated sea caves, and natural bridges; Arch Rock, on East Anacapa, is one of the best-known symbols of Channel Islands National Park. Wildlife viewing is the reason most people come to East Anacapa—particularly in summer when seagull chicks are newly hatched and sea lions and seals lounge on the beaches. Trips to Middle Anacapa Island require a ranger escort.

The compact **museum** on East Anacapa tells the history of the island and houses, among other things, the original lead-crystal Fresnel lens from the island's 1932 lighthouse.

Depending on the season and the number of desirable species lurking about there, a limited number of boats travel to **Frenchy's Cove** at West Anacapa, where you might see anemones, limpets, barnacles, mussel beds, and colorful marine algae in the pristine tide pools. The rest of West Anacapa is closed to protect nesting brown pelicans.

Santa Barbara Island. At about 1 square mile, Santa Barbara Island is the smallest of the Channel Islands and nearly 35 miles south of the others. Triangular in shape, Santa Barbara's steep cliffs—which offer a perfect nesting spot for the Scripps's murrelet, a rare seabird—are topped by twin peaks. In spring, you can enjoy a brilliant display of yellow coreopsis. Learn about the wildlife on and around the islands at the island's small museum.

Santa Cruz Island. Five miles west of Anacapa, 96-square-mile Santa Cruz Island is the largest of the Channel Islands. The National Park Service manages the easternmost 24% of the island; the rest is owned by the Nature Conservancy, which requires a permit to land. When your boat drops you off on the 70 miles of craggy coastline, you see two rugged mountain ranges with peaks soaring to 2,500 feet and deep canyons traversed by streams. This landscape is the habitat of a remarkable variety of flora and fauna—more than 600 types of plants, 140 kinds of land birds, 11 mammal species, five varieties of reptiles, and three amphibian species live here. Bird-watchers may want to look for the endemic island scrub jay, which is found nowhere else in the world.

One of the largest and deepest sea caves in the world, **Painted Cave,** lies along the northwest coast of Santa Cruz. Named for the colorful lichen and algae that cover its walls, Painted Cave is nearly ¼ mile long and 100 feet wide. In spring a waterfall cascades over the entrance. Kayakers may encounter seals or sea lions cruising alongside their boats inside the cave. The Channel Islands hold some of the richest archaeological resources in North America; all artifacts are protected within the park. Remnants of a dozen Chumash villages can be seen on the island. The largest of these villages, at the eastern end of the island, occupied the area now called **Scorpion Ranch.** The Chumash mined extensive chert deposits on the island for tools to produce shell-bead money, which they traded with people on the mainland. You can learn about Chumash history and view artifacts, tools, and exhibits on native plant and wildlife at the interpretive visitor center near the landing dock. Visitors can also explore remnants of the early-1900s ranching era in the restored historic adobe and outbuildings.

Santa Rosa Island. Set between Santa Cruz and San Miguel, Santa Rosa Island is the second largest of the Channel Islands and has a relatively low profile, broken by a central mountain range rising to 1,589 feet. The coastal areas range from broad sandy beaches to sheer cliffs. The island is home to about 500 species of plants, including the rare Torrey pine. Three unusual mammals—the endemic island fox, spotted skunk, and deer mouse—are among those that make their home here. They hardly compare to the mammoths that once roamed the island; a nearly complete skeleton of a 6-foot-tall pygmy mammoth was unearthed here in 1994.

The island was once home to the **Vail & Vickers Ranch,** where cattle were raised from 1901 to 1998. You can catch a glimpse of what the operation was like when you walk from the landing dock to the campground; the route passes by the historic ranch buildings, barns, equipment, and the wooden pier where cattle were brought onto the island.

SPORTS AND THE OUTDOORS

DIVING

Some of the best snorkeling and diving in the world can be found in the cool waters surrounding the Channel Islands. In the relatively warm water around Anacapa and eastern Santa Cruz, photographers can get great shots of rarely seen giant black bass swimming among the kelp forests. Here you also find a reef covered with red brittle starfish. If you're an experienced diver, you might swim among five species of seals and sea lions, or try your hand at spearing rockfish or halibut near San Miguel and Santa Rosa. The best time to scuba dive is in summer and fall, when the water is often clear up to a 100-foot depth.

KAYAKING

The most remote parts of the Channel Islands are accessible only by a sea kayak. Some of the best kayaking in the park can be found on Anacapa, Santa Barbara, and the eastern tip of Santa Cruz. It's too far to kayak from the mainland out to the islands, but outfitters have tours that take you to the islands. Tours are offered year-round, but high seas may cause trip cancellations between December and March. ⚠ Channel waters can be unpredictable and challenging. Guided trips are highly recommended.

WHALE-WATCHING

About a third of the world's cetacean species (27 to be exact) can be seen in the Santa Barbara Channel. In July and August, humpback and blue whales feed off the north shore of Santa Rosa. From late December through March, up to 10,000 gray whales pass through the Santa Barbara Channel on their way from Alaska to Mexico and back again, and on a whale-watching trip during this time frame, you should see one or more of them. Other types of whales, but fewer in number, swim the channel June through August.

THE MONTEREY BAY AREA

From Carmel to Santa Cruz

WELCOME TO THE MONTEREY BAY AREA

TOP REASONS TO GO

★ **Marine life:** Monterey Bay is the location of the world's third-largest marine sanctuary, home to whales, otters, and other underwater creatures.

★ **Getaway central:** For more than a century, urbanites have come to the Monterey Bay area to unwind, relax, and have fun. It's a great place to browse unique shops and galleries, ride a giant roller coaster, or play a round of golf on a world-class course.

★ **Nature preserves:** More than the sea is protected here: the region boasts nearly 30 state parks, beaches, and preserves—fantastic places for walking, jogging, hiking, and biking.

★ **Wine and dine:** The area's rich agricultural bounty translates into abundant fresh produce, great wines, and fabulous dining. It's no wonder more than 300 culinary events take place here every year.

★ **Small-town vibes:** Even the cities here are friendly, walkable places where you'll feel like a local.

1 Carmel and Pacific Grove. Exclusive Carmel-by-the-Sea and Carmel Valley Village burst with historic charm, fine dining, and unusual boutiques that cater to celebrity residents and well-heeled visitors. Nearby 17-Mile Drive—quite possibly the prettiest stretch of road you'll ever travel—runs between Carmel-by-the-Sea and Victorian-studded Pacific Grove, home to thousands of migrating monarch butterflies between October and February.

2 Monterey. A former Spanish military outpost, Monterey's well-preserved historic district is a hands-on history lesson. Cannery Row, the center of Monterey's once-thriving sardine industry, has been reborn as a tourist attraction with shops, restaurants, hotels, and the Monterey Bay Aquarium.

3 Around Monterey Bay. Much of California's lettuce, berries, artichokes, and brussels sprouts is grown in Salinas and Watsonville. Salinas is also home to the National Steinbeck Center, and Moss Landing and Watsonville encompass pristine wildlife wetlands. Aptos, Capitola, and Soquel are former lumber towns that became popular seaside resorts more than a century ago. Today they're filled with antiques shops, restaurants, and wine-tasting rooms; you'll also find some of the bay's best beaches along the shore here.

4 Santa Cruz. Santa Cruz shows its colors along an old-time beach boardwalk and municipal wharf. A University of California campus imbues the town with arts and culture and a liberal mind-set.

The Forest of
Nisene Marks
State Park

SANTA CRUZ MOUNTAINS

152

Soquel

Aptos

Capitola

Rio
del Mar

*Soquel
Cove*

1

Freedom

Watsonville

129

Pajaro

Las Lomas

1

M
O
N
T
E
R
E
Y

B
A
Y

3

Moss Landing

Prunedale

156

Castroville

101

1

183

Marina

S
A
L
I
N
A
S

V
A
L
L
E
Y

Salinas R.

Salinas

G17

Point
Pinos

Pacific
Grove

Seaside

Sand City

Spreckels

Spanish Bay

17-Mile Dr.

1

Monterey 2

Del Rey Oaks

68

*Cypress
Point*

68

68

Carmel

SIERRA DE SALINAS

*Carmel
Bay*

1

G16

Carmel Valley Rd.

G20

Point
Lobos

Carmel
Highlands

Carmel River

G16

Carmel
Valley

GETTING
ORIENTED

North of Big Sur the coastline
softens into lower bluffs,
windswept dunes, pristine
estuaries, and long, sandy
beaches, bordering one of
the world's most amazing
marine environments—the
Monterey Bay. On the
Monterey Peninsula, at the
southern end of the bay, are
Carmel-by-the-Sea, Pacific
Grove, and Monterey; Santa
Cruz sits at the northern tip
of the crescent. In between,
Highway 1 cruises along
the coastline, passing windswept beaches piled high
with sand dunes. Along the
route are wetlands, artichoke
and strawberry fields, and
workaday towns such as
Castroville and Watsonville.

7

Updated
by Cheryl
Crabtree

Natural beauty is at the heart of the Monterey Bay area's enormous appeal—it's everywhere, from the redwood-studded hillsides to the pristine shoreline with miles of walking paths and bluff-top vistas. Nature even takes center stage indoors at the world-famous Monterey Bay Aquarium, but history also draws visitors, most notably to Monterey's well-preserved waterfront district. Quaint, walkable towns and villages such as Carmel-by-the-Sea and Carmel Valley Village lure with smart restaurants and galleries, while sunny Aptos, Capitola, Soquel, and Santa Cruz, with miles of sand and surf, attract surfers and beach lovers.

Monterey Bay life centers around the ocean. The bay itself is protected by the Monterey Bay National Marine Sanctuary, the nation's largest undersea canyon—bigger and deeper than the Grand Canyon. On-the-water activities abound, from whale-watching and kayaking to sailing and surfing. Bay cruises from Monterey and Moss Landing almost always encounter other enchanting sea creatures, among them sea otters, sea lions, and porpoises.

Land-based activities include hiking, zip-lining in the redwood canopy, and wine tasting along urban and rural trails. Golf has been an integral part of the Monterey Peninsula's social and recreational scene since the Del Monte Golf Course opened in 1897. Pebble Beach's championship courses host prestigious tournaments, and though the greens fees at these courses can run up to $500, elsewhere on the peninsula you'll find less expensive options. And, of course, whatever activity you pursue, natural splendor appears at every turn.

PLANNING

WHEN TO GO

Summer is peak season; mild weather brings in big crowds. In this coastal region, a cool breeze generally blows and fog often rolls in from offshore; you will frequently need a sweater or windbreaker. Off-season, from November through April, fewer people visit and the mood is mellower. Rainfall is heaviest in January and February. Fall and spring days are often clearer than those in summer.

GETTING HERE AND AROUND

AIR TRAVEL

Monterey Regional Airport, 3 miles east of downtown Monterey off Highway 68, is served by Alaska, Allegiant, American, United, and US Airways. Taxi service costs $16 to $18 to downtown, and $24 to $33 to Carmel. Monterey Airbus service between the region and the San Jose and San Francisco airports starts at $40; the Early Bird Airport Shuttle costs $80 to $190 ($195 from Oakland).

Airport Contacts Monterey Regional Airport (MRY). ✉ *200 Fred Kane Dr., at Olmsted Rd., off Hwy. 68, Monterey* ☎ *831/648–7000* ⊕ *www.montereyairport.com.*

Ground Transportation Central Coast Cab Company ☎ *831/626–3333.*
Early Bird Airport Shuttle ☎ *831/462–3933* ⊕ *www.earlybirdairportshuttle.com.*
Monterey Airbus ☎ *831/373–7777* ⊕ *www.montereyairbus.com.*
Yellow Cab ☎ *831/333–1234.*

BUS TRAVEL

Greyhound serves Santa Cruz and Salinas from San Francisco and San Jose. The trips take about 3 and 4½ hours, respectively. Monterey-Salinas Transit (MST) provides frequent service in Monterey County (from $1.50 to $3.50; day pass $10), and Santa Cruz METRO ($2; day pass from $6 to $10) buses operate throughout Santa Cruz County. You can switch between the lines in Watsonville.

Bus Contacts Greyhound ☎ *800/231–2222* ⊕ *www.greyhound.com.*
Monterey-Salinas Transit ☎ *888/678–2871* ⊕ *www.mst.org.*
Santa Cruz METRO ☎ *831/425–8600* ⊕ *www.scmtd.com.*

CAR TRAVEL

Highway 1 runs south–north along the coast, linking the towns of Carmel-by-the-Sea, Monterey, and Santa Cruz; some sections have only two lanes. The freeway, U.S. 101, lies to the east, roughly parallel to Highway 1. The two roads are connected by Highway 68 from Pacific Grove to Salinas; Highway 156 from Castroville to Prunedale; Highway 152 from Watsonville to Gilroy; and Highway 17 from Santa Cruz to San Jose. ⚠ **Traffic near Santa Cruz can crawl to a standstill during commuter hours. In the morning, avoid traveling between 7 and 9; in the afternoon avoid traveling between 4 and 7.**

The drive south from San Francisco to Monterey can be made comfortably in three hours or less. The most scenic way is to follow Highway 1 down the coast. An often faster route is Interstate 280 south from San Francisco to Highway 17, north of San Jose, to Highway 1 south.

The drive from the Los Angeles area takes five or six hours. Take U.S. 101 to Salinas and head west on Highway 68. You can also follow Highway 1 up the coast.

TRAIN TRAVEL

Amtrak's *Coast Starlight* runs between Los Angeles, Oakland, and Seattle. From the train station in Salinas, you can connect with buses serving Carmel, Monterey, and Santa Cruz.

Train Contacts Amtrak ☎ *800/872-7245* ⊕ *www.amtrak.com.*

RESTAURANTS

The Monterey Bay area is a culinary paradise. The surrounding waters are full of fish, wild game roams the foothills, and the inland valleys are some of the most fertile in the country—local chefs draw on this bounty for their fresh, truly Californian cuisine. Except at beachside stands and inexpensive eateries, where anything goes, casual but neat dress is the norm.

HOTELS

Accommodations in the Monterey area range from no-frills motels to luxurious hotels. Pacific Grove, amply endowed with ornate Victorian houses, is the region's bed-and-breakfast capital; Carmel also has charming inns. Lavish resorts cluster in exclusive Pebble Beach and pastoral Carmel Valley.

High season runs from May through October. Rates in winter, especially at the larger hotels, may drop by 50% or more, and B&Bs often offer midweek specials. Whatever the month, some properties require a two-night stay on weekends. *Hotel reviews have been shortened. For full information, visit Fodors.com.* ⚠ **Many of the fancier accommodations aren't suitable for children; if you're traveling with kids, ask before you book.**

WHAT IT COSTS			
$	**$$**	**$$$**	**$$$$**
Restaurants	under $16	$16–$22	$23–$30	over $30
Hotels	under $121	$121–$175	$176–$250	over $250

Restaurant prices are the average cost of a main course at dinner or, if dinner is not served, at lunch, excluding sales tax of 8.25%–9.5% (depending on location). Hotel prices are the lowest cost of a standard double room in high season, excluding service charges and 10%–10.5% tax.

TOUR OPTIONS

Ag Venture Tours & Consulting. Crowd-pleasing half- and full-day wine-tasting, sightseeing, and agricultural tours are Ag Venture's specialty. Tastings are at Monterey and Santa Cruz Mountains wineries; sightseeing opportunities include the Monterey Peninsula, Big Sur, and Santa Cruz; and the agricultural forays take in the Salinas Valley. Customized itineraries can be arranged. ☎ *831/761–8463* ⊕ *www.agventuretours. com* 🖂 *From $75.*

California Parlor Car Tours. This outfit operates motor-coach tours from San Francisco that include one or two days in Monterey and Carmel. The company's three-day San Francisco–Los Angeles tours include stops in Monterey and Carmel. ☎ *415/474–7500, 800/227–4250* ⊕ *www.calpartours.com* ✉ *From $80 (day) and $267 (overnight).*

VISITOR INFORMATION

Contacts Monterey County Convention & Visitors Bureau ☎ *877/666–8373* ⊕ *www.seemonterey.com.* **Monterey County Vintners and Growers Association** ☎ *831/375–9400* ⊕ *www.montereywines.org.* **Santa Cruz County Conference and Visitors Council** ✉ *303 Water St., #100, Santa Cruz* ☎ *831/425–1234, 800/833–3494* ⊕ *www.santacruz.org.* **Santa Cruz Mountain Winegrowers Association** ✉ *725 Front St., #112, Santa Cruz* ☎ *831/685–8463* ⊕ *www.scmwa.com.*

CARMEL AND PACIFIC GROVE

As Highway 1 swings inland about 30 miles north of Big Sur, historic Carmel-by-the Sea anchors the southern entry to the Monterey Peninsula—a gorgeous promontory at the southern tip of Monterey Bay. Just north of Carmel along the coast, the legendary 17-Mile Drive wends its way through private Pebble Beach and the town of Pacific Grove. Highway 1 skirts the peninsula to the east with more direct access to Pebble Beach and Pacific Grove.

7

CARMEL-BY-THE-SEA

26 miles north of Big Sur.

Even when its population quadruples with tourists on weekends and in summer, Carmel-by-the-Sea, commonly referred to as Carmel, retains its identity as a quaint village. Self-consciously charming, the town is populated by many celebrities, major and minor, and has its share of quirky ordinances. For instance, women wearing high heels do not have the right to pursue legal action if they trip and fall on the cobblestone streets, and drivers who hit a tree and leave the scene are charged with hit-and-run.

Buildings have no street numbers—street names are written on discreet white posts—and consequently no mail delivery. One way to commune with the locals: head to the post office. Artists started this community, and their legacy is evident in the numerous galleries.

GETTING HERE AND AROUND

From north or south follow Highway 1 to Carmel. Head west at Ocean Avenue to reach the main village hub. In summer the MST Carmel-by-the-Sea Trolley loops around town to the beach and mission every 30 minutes or so.

TOURS

Carmel Walks. For insight into Carmel's history and culture, join one of these guided two-hour ambles through hidden courtyards, gardens, and pathways. Tours depart from the Pine Inn courtyard, on Lincoln Street. Call to reserve a spot. ✉ *Lincoln St. at 6th Ave.* ☎ *831/642–2700* ⊕ *www.carmelwalks.com* ✉ *$25* ⊙ *Tues.–Fri. at 10, Sat. at 10 and 2.*

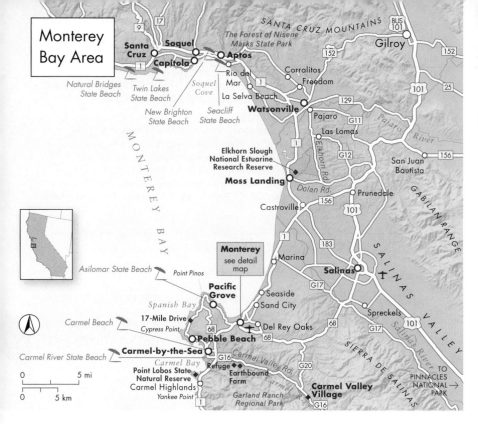

Monterey Bay Area

Santa Cruz · Soquel · Capitola · Aptos · Rio del Mar · Soquel Cove · La Selva Beach

Natural Bridges State Beach · Twin Lakes State Beach · New Brighton State Beach · Seacliff State Beach

The Forest of Nisene Marks State Park · Corralitos · Freedom · Watsonville · Pajaro · Las Lomas

SANTA CRUZ MOUNTAINS · Gilroy

Elkhorn Slough National Estuarine Research Reserve · **Moss Landing** · *Dolan Rd.* · Castroville · Prunedale

San Juan Bautista

M O N T E R E Y   B A Y

Asilomar State Beach · Point Pinos

Monterey see detail map

Marina · **Salinas** · Spreckels

Pacific Grove · Seaside · Sand City · Del Rey Oaks

Carmel Beach · 17-Mile Drive · Cypress Point · Spanish Bay · **Pebble Beach**

Carmel-by-the-Sea · *Carmel Bay* · Point Lobos State Natural Reserve · Carmel Highlands · Yankee Point

Refuge · *Carmel Valley Rd.* · **Earthbound Farm** · Garland Ranch Regional Park

Carmel Valley Village

TO PINNACLES NATIONAL PARK

GABILAN RANGE · SALINAS VALLEY · SIERRA DE SALINAS · *Salinas River* · *Pajaro River*

0   5 mi
0   5 km

ESSENTIALS

Visitor Information Carmel Chamber of Commerce ✉ *Visitor Center, San Carlos, between 5th and 6th* ☎ *831/624–2522, 800/550–4333* ⊕ *www.carmelcalifornia.org* ⊗ *Daily 10–5.*

EXPLORING

TOP ATTRACTIONS

Carmel Mission. Long before it became a shopping and browsing destination, Carmel was an important religious center during the establishment of Spanish California. That heritage is preserved in the Mission San Carlos Borroméo del Rio Carmelo, more commonly known as the Carmel Mission. Founded in 1771, it served as headquarters for the mission system in California under Father Junípero Serra. Adjoining the stone church is a tranquil garden planted with California poppies. Museum rooms at the mission include an early kitchen, Serra's spartan sleeping quarters, and the first college library in California. ✉ *3080 Rio Rd., at Lasuen Dr.* ☎ *831/624–1271* ⊕ *www.carmelmission.org* 🎫 *$6.50* ⊗ *Daily 9:30–4:45.*

Fodor's Choice ★ **Point Lobos State Natural Reserve.** A 350-acre headland harboring a wealth of marine life, the reserve lies a few miles south of Carmel. The best way to explore here is to walk along one of the many trails. The Cypress Grove Trail leads through a forest of Monterey cypress (one of only two natural groves remaining), which clings to the rocks above an emerald-green cove. Sea Lion Point Trail is a good place to view sea lions. From those and other trails you might also spot otters, harbor seals, and (in winter and spring) migrating whales. An additional 750 acres of the reserve is an undersea marine park open to qualified scuba divers. No pets are allowed. ■TIP→ Arrive early (or in late afternoon) to avoid crowds; the parking lots fill up.

✉ *Hwy. 1* ☎ *831/624–4909, 831/624–8413 for scuba-diving reservations* ⊕ *www.pointlobos.org* ✉ *$10 per vehicle* ☉ *Daily 8 am–½ hr after sunset in winter, 8 am–7 pm spring–fall.*

WORTH NOTING

Carmel Wine Walk By-the-Sea. Park the car and sample local wines at tasting rooms and shops in downtown Carmel, all within a few blocks of each other. To do so, purchase a Wine Walk Passport, good for flights in nine tasting rooms and free corkage at local restaurants. There's no expiration date—participating venues will stamp it each time you visit. ✉ *Carmel Chamber of Commerce Visitor Center, San Carlos St., between 5th and 6th Aves.* ☎ *831/624–2522, 800/550–4333* ⊕ *www. carmelcalifornia.org* ✉ *$65.*

Dawson Cole Fine Art. Amazing images of dancers, athletes, and other humans in motion come to life in this gallery that is devoted to the artworks of Monterey Bay resident Richard MacDonald, one of the most famed figurative sculptors of our time. ✉ *Lincoln St., at 6th Ave.* ☎ *800/972–5528* ⊕ *www.dawsoncolefineart.com* ✉ *Free* ☉ *Mon.–Sat. 10–6, Sun. 10–5:30.*

Ocean Avenue. Downtown Carmel's chief lure is shopping, especially along its main street, Ocean Avenue, between Junipero Avenue and Camino Real. The architecture here is a mishmash of ersatz Tudor, Mediterranean, and other styles.

Tor House. Scattered throughout the pines of Carmel-by-the-Sea are houses and cottages originally built for the writers, artists, and photographers who discovered the area decades ago. Among the most impressive dwellings is Tor House, a stone cottage built in 1919 by poet Robinson Jeffers on a craggy knoll overlooking the sea. Portraits, books, and unusual art objects fill the low-ceilinged rooms. The highlight of the small estate is Hawk Tower, a detached edifice set with stones from the Carmel coastline—as well as one from the Great Wall of China. The docents who lead tours (six people maximum) are well informed about the poet's work and life. ■TIP→ To reserve a tour, which is recommended, email thf@torhouse.org. ✉ *26304 Ocean View Ave.* ☎ *831/624–1813, 831/624–1840 direct docent office line, Fri. and Sat. only* ⊕ *www.torhouse.org* ✉ *$10* ☉ *Hourly tours Fri. and Sat. 10–3* ☞ *No children under 12.*

BEACHES

Carmel Beach. Carmel-by-the-Sea's greatest attraction is its rugged coastline, with pine and cypress forests and countless inlets. Carmel Beach, an easy walk from downtown shops, has sparkling white sands and magnificent sunsets. ■ **TIP→ Dogs are allowed to romp off-leash here.** **Amenities:** parking (no fee); toilets. **Best for:** sunset; surfing; walking. ✉ *End of Ocean Ave.*

Carmel River State Beach. This sugar-white beach, stretching 106 acres along Carmel Bay, is adjacent to a bird sanctuary, where you might spot pelicans, kingfishers, hawks, and sandpipers. **Amenities:** none. **Best for:** sunrise; sunset; walking. ✉ *Off Scenic Rd., south of Carmel Beach* ☎ *831/624–4909, 831/649–2836* 🌐 *www.parks.ca.gov* 🎟 *Free* 🕒 *Daily 8 am–½ hr after sunset in winter; 8 am–7 pm spring–fall.*

WHERE TO EAT

$$$ FRENCH 🍴 **Andre's Bouchée.** The food here represents an innovative bistro-style take on local ingredients. A Monterey Bay sea scallop reduction adorns pan-seared veal tenderloin; grilled rib-eye steaks are topped with a shallot–Cabernet Sauvignon sauce. With its copper wine bar, the dining room feels more urban than most of Carmel. The owners operate the adjacent wineshop, which explains the dizzyingly comprehensive, 52-page wine list. [$] *Average main: $28* ✉ *Mission St., between Ocean and 7th Aves.* ☎ *831/626–7880* 🌐 *www.andresbouchee.com* ✍ *Reservations essential* 🕒 *No lunch Mon. and Tues.*

$$$ EUROPEAN 🍴 **Anton and Michel.** Carefully prepared European cuisine is the draw at this airy restaurant. The rack of lamb is carved at the table, the grilled halloumi cheese and tomatoes are meticulously stacked and served with basil and Kalamata olive tapenade, and the desserts are set aflame before your eyes. ■ **TIP→ For lighter fare with a worldwide flair, head to the bar, where small plates such as Dungeness crab ravioli and brochette of filet mignon with chimichurri sauce are served.** [$] *Average main: $30* ✉ *Mission St. and 7th Ave.* ☎ *831/624–2406* 🌐 *antonandmichel.com* ✍ *Reservations essential.*

$$$ MEDITERRANEAN 🍴 **Casanova.** This cozy restaurant inspires European-style celebration and romance—accordions hang from the walls, and tiny party lights dance along the low ceilings. The food consists of delectable seasonal dishes from southern France and northern Italy. Private dining and a special menu are offered at Van Gogh's Table, a special table imported from France's Auberge Ravoux, the artist's final residence. [$] *Average main: $30* ✉ *5th Ave., between San Carlos and Mission Sts.* ☎ *831/625–0501* 🌐 *www.casanovarestaurant.com* ✍ *Reservations essential.*

$ AMERICAN 🍴 **The Cottage Restaurant.** This family-friendly spot serves sandwiches, pizzas, and homemade soups at lunch, but the best meal is breakfast (good thing it's served all day). The menu offers six variations on eggs Benedict, and all kinds of sweet and savory crepes. [$] *Average main: $14* ✉ *Lincoln St., between Ocean and 7th Aves.* ☎ *831/625–6260* 🌐 *www.cottagerestaurant.com* 🕒 *No dinner.*

$$$ SEAFOOD 🍴 **Flying Fish Grill.** Simple in appearance yet bold with its flavors, this Japanese–California seafood restaurant is one of Carmel's most inventive eateries. Among the best entrées is the almond-crusted sea bass served with Chinese cabbage and rock shrimp stir-fry. The warm,

Point Lobos Reserve State Park is home to one of the only two natural stands of Monterey cypress in the world.

wood-lined dining room is broken up into very private booths. $\boxed{\$}$ *Average main: $26* ✉ *Carmel Plaza, Mission St., between Ocean and 7th Aves.* ☎ *831/625–1962* ⊕ *flyingfishgrill.com* ⊘ *No lunch.*

$$$
AMERICAN
✕ **Grasing's Coastal Cuisine.** Chef Kurt Grasing draws from fresh Carmel Coast and Central Valley ingredients to whip up contemporary adaptations of European-provincial and American cooking. Longtime menu favorites include artichoke lasagna in a roasted tomato sauce, duck with fresh cherries and green peppercorns in a red wine sauce, a savory paella, and grilled steaks and chops. $\boxed{\$}$ *Average main: $30* ✉ *6th Ave. and Mission St.* ☎ *831/624–6562* ⊕ *www.grasings.com* ⌖ *Reservations essential.*

$$$
FRENCH
✕ **L'Escargot.** Chef-owner Kericos Loutas personally sees to each plate of food served at this romantic, unpretentious French restaurant. Order the pan-roasted duck breast or the cassoulet de Toulouse; or, if you can't decide, choose the three-course prix-fixe dinner. $\boxed{\$}$ *Average main: $30* ✉ *Mission and 4th Ave.* ☎ *831/620–1942* ⊕ *www.escargot-carmel.com* ⌖ *Reservations essential* ⊘ *No lunch.*

$$
TAPAS
✕ **Mundaka.** The traditional Spanish-style tapas, made with fresh local ingredients, and the full bar attract legions of locals to this cozy downtown spot. The menu changes weekly, but longtime favorites include the lamb slider with truffle fries, the authentic Valencian paella, and a platter of housemade charcuterie. At the adjacent Mundaka Cafe, the breakfast menu includes Spanish tortillas, plus Belgian waffles and homemade baked goods; among the lunchtime choices are sandwiches, soups, and salads. Leashed dogs are welcome at the patio tables. After 4 pm, music livens up the scene at High Tide, the restaurant's separate bar in the same cluster of buildings. $\boxed{\$}$ *Average main: $21* ✉ *San Carlos St., between Ocean and 7th Aves.* ☎ *831/624–7400* ⊕ *www.mundakacarmel.com.*

$ AMERICAN 🍴 **Tuck Box.** This bright little restaurant is in a cottage right out of a fairy tale, complete with stone fireplace. Handmade scones, good for breakfast or afternoon tea, are the specialty. [$] *Average main: $12* ✉ *Dolores St., between Ocean and 7th Aves.* ☎ *831/624–6365* 🌐 *www.tuckbox.com* ✍ *Reservations not accepted* 💳 *No credit cards* 🕐 *No dinner.*

$$$ ITALIAN 🍴 **Vesuvio.** Chef and restaurateur Rich Pèpe heats up the night with his latest venture, a lively trattoria downstairs and a swinging rooftop terrace, Starlight Lounge 65°. Pèpe's elegant take on traditional Italian cuisine yields dishes such as wild-boar Bolognese pappardelle, lobster ravioli, and velvety limoncello mousse cake. Pizzas and small plates are served in the restaurant and two bars. Upstairs, relax in comfy chairs by fire pits and enjoy bird's-eye views of the village. On most nights in summer there's live music. [$] *Average main: $24* ✉ *6th and Junipero Aves.* ☎ *831/625–1766* 🌐 *www.vesuviocarmel.com* 🕐 *No lunch.*

WHERE TO STAY

$$$ B&B/INN 🏨 **Cypress Inn.** A top-to-bottom redecorating project in 2013 gave this luxurious inn a fresh Mediterranean ambience with Moroccan touches. **Pros:** luxury without snobbery; popular lounge; British-style afternoon tea on weekends. **Cons:** not for the pet-phobic. [$] *Rooms from: $235* ✉ *Lincoln St. and 7th Ave.* ☎ *831/624–3871, 800/443–7443* 🌐 *www.cypress-inn.com* 🛏 *39 rooms, 5 suites* 🍽 *Breakfast.*

$$$$ HOTEL 🏨 **Hyatt Carmel Highlands.** High on a hill overlooking the Pacific, this place has superb views; accommodations include king rooms with fireplaces, suites with personal Jacuzzis, and full town houses with all the perks. **Pros:** killer views; romantic getaway; great food. **Cons:** thin walls; must drive to Carmel. [$] *Rooms from: $369* ✉ *120 Highlands Dr.* ☎ *831/620–1234, 800/233–1234* 🌐 *carmelhighlands.hyatt.com* 🛏 *46 rooms, 2 suites.*

$$$$ B&B/INN Fodor's Choice ★ 🏨 **L'Auberge Carmel.** Stepping through the doors of this elegant inn is like being transported to a little European village. **Pros:** in town but off the main drag; four blocks from the beach; full-service luxury. **Cons:** touristy area; not a good choice for families. [$] *Rooms from: $435* ✉ *Monte Verde at 7th Ave.* ☎ *831/624–8578* 🌐 *www.laubergecarmel.com* 🛏 *20 rooms* 🍽 *Breakfast.*

$$$$ HOTEL 🏨 **La Playa Hotel.** A historic complex of lush gardens and Mediterranean-style buildings, La Playa reopened in 2012 after a $3.5 million renovation. **Pros:** residential neighborhood; manicured gardens; two blocks from the beach. **Cons:** four stories (no elevator); busy lobby; some rooms are on the small side. [$] *Rooms from: $279* ✉ *Camino Real, at 8th Ave.* ☎ *831/293–6100, 800/582–8900* 🌐 *www.laplayahotel.com* 🛏 *75 rooms* 🍽 *Breakfast.*

$$ HOTEL 🏨 **Lobos Lodge.** The white-stucco motel units here are set amid cypress, oaks, and pines on the edge of the business district. **Pros:** walking distance from beach and village attractions; inviting lobby; Continental breakfast delivered to your room. **Cons:** no outdoor facilities; sits on a busy avenue. [$] *Rooms from: $145* ✉ *Monte Verde St. and Ocean Ave.* ☎ *831/624–3874* 🌐 *www.loboslodge.com* 🛏 *28 rooms, 2 suites* 🍽 *Breakfast.*

$$ HOTEL 🏨 **Mission Ranch.** Movie star Clint Eastwood owns this sprawling property whose accommodations include rooms in a converted barn, and several cottages, some with fireplaces. **Pros:** farm setting; pastoral views; great for tennis buffs. **Cons:** busy parking lot; must drive to the heart of town. [$] *Rooms from: $140* ✉ *26270 Dolores St.* ☎ *831/624–6436, 800/538–8221, 831/625–9040 restaurant* 🌐 *www.missionranchcarmel.com* 🛏 *31 rooms* 🍴 *Breakfast.*

$$$ B&B/INN 🏨 **Sea View Inn.** In a residential area a few hundred feet from the beach, this restored 1905 home has a double parlor with two fireplaces, oriental rugs, canopy beds, and a spacious front porch. **Pros:** quiet; private; close to the beach. **Cons:** small building; uphill trek to the heart of town. [$] *Rooms from: $200* ✉ *Camino Real, between 11th and 12th Aves.* ☎ *831/624–8778* 🌐 *www.seaviewinncarmel.com* 🛏 *8 rooms, 6 with private bath* 🍴 *Breakfast.*

$$$$ B&B/INN 🏨 **Tickle Pink Inn.** Atop a towering cliff, this inn has views of the Big Sur coastline, which you can contemplate from your private balcony. **Pros:** close to great hiking; intimate; dramatic views. **Cons:** close to a big hotel; lots of traffic during the day. [$] *Rooms from: $299* ✉ *155 Highland Dr.* ☎ *831/624–1244, 800/635–4774* 🌐 *www.ticklepink.com* 🛏 *23 rooms, 10 suites, 1 cottage* 🍴 *Breakfast.*

$$$ B&B/INN 🏨 **Tradewinds Carmel.** This converted motel with sleek decor inspired by the South Seas encircles a courtyard with waterfalls, a meditation garden, and a fire pit. **Pros:** serene; within walking distance of restaurants; friendly service. **Cons:** no pool; long walk to the beach. [$] *Rooms from: $250* ✉ *Mission St., at 3rd Ave.* ☎ *831/624–2776* 🌐 *www.tradewindscarmel.com* 🛏 *26 rooms, 2 suites* 🍴 *Breakfast.*

NIGHTLIFE

BARS AND PUBS

High Tide. Al Capone and other Prohibition-era legends once sidled up to this hip nightspot's carved wooden bar. Rock to DJ music and sit indoors, or head out to the pet-friendly patio. Some menu items pay homage to California's early days, and you can order Spanish tapas and wines from the adjacent Mundaka restaurant, which is under the same ownership. **TIP→ High Tide only takes cash.** ✉ *San Carlos St., between Ocean and 7th Aves.* ☎ *831/624–7400* 🌐 *www.mundakacarmel.com* 💳 *No credit cards.*

Jack London's. Among the few Carmel restaurants that serve food late, this publike hangout is a good stop for a beer or cocktail or to watch sports on TV. On most weekends Jack London's hosts live music. The weekday happy hour (from 4 to 6) is a bargain. ✉ *Su Vecino Court, Dolores St., between 5th and 6th Aves.* ☎ *831/624–2336.*

SHOPPING

ART GALLERIES

Carmel Art Association. The association exhibits the original paintings and sculptures of local artists. ✉ *Dolores St., between 5th and 6th Aves.* ☎ *831/624–6176* 🌐 *www.carmelart.org.*

Galerie Plein Aire. The gallery showcases the oil paintings of a group of local artists. ✉ *Dolores St., between 5th and 6th Aves.* ☎ *831/625–5686* 🌐 *www.galeriepleinaire.com.*

Gallery Sur. Fine art photography of the Big Sur Coast and the Monterey Peninsula, including scenic shots and golf images, is the focus here. ⊠ *6th Ave., between Dolores and Lincoln Sts.* ☏ *831/626–2615* ⊕ *www.gallerysur.com.*

Weston Gallery. Run by the family of the late Edward Weston, this is hands down the best photography gallery around, with contemporary color photography complemented by classic black-and-whites. ⊠ *6th Ave., between Dolores and Lincoln Sts.* ☏ *831/624–4453* ⊕ *www. westongallery.com.*

MALL

Carmel Plaza. Tiffany & Co. and J. Crew are among the name brands doing business at this mall on Carmel's east side, but what makes it worth a stop are homegrown enterprises such as Homescapes, for marvelous and visually stimulating home and garden objects; Madrigal and Sylvie Unique Boutique, for women's fashion; and J. Lawrence Khaki's for debonair menswear. Flying Fish Grill (⇨ *Where to Eat)* and several other restaurants are here, along with the Wrath Wines tasting room (heavenly Chardonnays and Pinot Noirs). ⊠ *Ocean Ave. and Mission St.* ☏ *831/624–0137* ⊕ *www.carmelplaza.com.*

SPECIALTY SHOPS

Bittner. The shop carries collectible and vintage pens from around the world. ⊠ *Ocean Ave., between Mission and San Carlos Sts.* ☏ *831/626–8828* ⊕ *bittner.com.*

Intima. The European lingerie that ranges from lacy to racy. ⊠ *San Carlos St., between Ocean and 6th Aves.* ☏ *831/625–0599* ⊕ *www. intimacarmel.com.*

Jan de Luz. This shops monograms and embroiders fine linens (including bathrobes) while you wait. ⊠ *Dolores St., between Ocean and 7th Aves.* ☏ *831/622–7621* ⊕ *www.jandeluz.com.*

CARMEL VALLEY

10 miles east of Carmel.

Carmel Valley Road, which heads inland from Highway 1 south of Carmel, is the main thoroughfare through this valley, a secluded enclave of horse ranchers and other well-heeled residents who prefer the area's sunny climate to coastal fog and wind. Once thick with dairy farms, the valley has evolved into an esteemed wine appellation. Carmel Valley Village has crafts shops, art galleries, and the tasting rooms of numerous local wineries.

GETTING HERE AND AROUND

From U.S. 101 north or south, exit at Highway 68 and head west toward the coast. Scenic, two-lane Laureles Grade winds west over the mountains to Carmel Valley Road north of the village.

TOURS

The Carmel Valley Grapevine Express, aka MST's Line 24 bus, travels between downtown Monterey and Carmel Valley Village, with stops near wineries, restaurants, and shopping centers. At $10 for a ride-all-day pass, it's an incredible bargain.

Bus Contact Carmel Valley Grapevine Express ☎ *888/678–2871* 🌐 *www.mst.org.*

EXPLORING

TOP ATTRACTIONS

Bernardus Tasting Room. At the tasting room of Bernardus, known for its Bordeaux-style red blend, called Marinus, and Chardonnays, you can sample current releases and library and reserve wines. ✉ *5 W. Carmel Valley Rd., at El Caminito Rd.* ☎ *831/298–8021, 800/223–2533* 🌐 *www.bernardus.com* 🎟 *Tastings $12–$20* 🕒 *Daily 11–5.*

Château Julien. The expansive winery, recognized internationally for its Chardonnays and Merlots, offers tours by appointment only, but the tasting room is open daily. ✉ *8940 Carmel Valley Rd., at Schetter Rd., Carmel* ☎ *831/624–2600* 🌐 *www.chateaujulien.com* 🎟 *Tasting $15 (includes tour), private tours $20–$100* 🕒 *Winery: weekdays 8–5, weekends 11–5. Tours: Tues.–Fri. at 10:30 and 2:30, Sat. at 12:30 and 2:30, Sun. at 2:30, and by appointment.*

Cowgirl Winery. Cowgirl chic prevails in the main tasting building here, and it's just plain rustic at the outdoor tables, set amid chickens, a tractor, and a flatbed truck. The wines include Chardonnay, Cabernet Sauvignon, Rosé, and some blends. You can order wood-fired pizzas from sister business Corkscrew Café down the block for delivery to your tasting table. ✉ *25 Pilot Rd.* ☎ *831/298–7030* 🌐 *cowgirlwinery.com* 🎟 *Tasting $13* 🕒 *Mon.–Thurs. 11:30–4:30, Fri.–Sun. 11:30–5 (until 6 on Sat. Apr.–Oct.).*

7

WORTH NOTING

Earthbound Farm. Pick up fresh veggies, ready-to-eat meals, gourmet groceries, flowers, and gifts at Earthbound Farm, the world's largest grower of organic produce. You can also take a romp in the kid's garden, cut your own herbs, and stroll through the chamomile aromatherapy labyrinth. Special events, on Saturday from April through December, include bug walks and garlic-braiding workshops. ✉ *7250 Carmel Valley Rd., Carmel* ☎ *831/625–6219* 🌐 *www.ebfarm.com* 🎟 *Free* 🕒 *Mon.–Sat. 8–6:30, Sun. 9–6.*

Garland Ranch Regional Park. Hiking trails stretch across much of this park's 4,500 acres of meadows, forested hillsides, and creeks. ✉ *Carmel Valley Rd., 9 miles east of Carmel-by-the-Sea* ☎ *831/659–4488* 🌐 *www.mprpd.org.*

WHERE TO EAT

$$ EUROPEAN

🍴 **Café Rustica.** European country cooking is the focus at this lively roadhouse. Specialties include roasted meats, seafood, pastas, and thin-crust pizzas from the wood-fired oven. It can get noisy inside; for a quieter meal, request a table outside. [$] *Average main: $20* ✉ *10 Delfino Pl., at Pilot Rd., off Carmel Valley Rd.* ☎ *831/659–4444* 🌐 *www.caferusticavillage.com* ✍ *Reservations essential* 🕒 *Closed Mon.*

$$ MODERN AMERICAN

🍴 **Corkscrew Café.** Farm-fresh Wine Country food is the specialty of this casual, Old Monterey–style bistro. Herbs and seasonal produce come from the Corkscrew's own organic gardens, the catch of the day comes from local waters, and the meats are hormone-free. Popular dishes include the fish tacos, chicken salad, and wood-fired pizzas, which come with classic toppings and unusual ones such as Meyer lemon and prosciutto. You can dine indoors near the open kitchen, or outside in the garden patio. ■ **TIP→ Don't miss the collection of corkscrews from the 17th century to the present.** [$] *Average main: $22* ✉ *55 W. Carmel Valley Rd., at Pilot Rd.* ☎ *831/659–8888* 🌐 *www.corkscrewcafe.com.*

$ AMERICAN 🍴 **Wagon Wheel Coffee Shop.** This local hangout decorated with wagon wheels, cowboy hats, and lassos serves terrific hearty breakfasts, including oatmeal and banana pancakes, eggs Benedict, and biscuits and gravy. The lunch menu includes a dozen different burgers and other sandwiches. [$] *Average main: $11* ✉ *Valley Hill Center, 7156 Carmel Valley Rd., next to Quail Lodge, Carmel* ☎ *831/624–8878* 💳 *No credit cards* 🕒 *No dinner.*

WHERE TO STAY

$$$$ RESORT Fodor's Choice ★ 🏨 **Bernardus Lodge.** The spacious guest rooms at this luxury spa resort have vaulted ceilings, featherbeds, fireplaces, patios, and bathtubs for two. **Pros:** exceptional personal service; outstanding food and wine. **Cons:** pricey; some guests can seem snooty. [$] *Rooms from: $475* ✉ *415 W. Carmel Valley Rd.* ☎ *831/658–3400, 888/648–9463* 🌐 *www.bernardus.com* 🛏 *56 rooms, 1 suite.*

$$$ HOTEL 🏨 **Carmel Valley Lodge.** This small inn has rooms surrounding a garden patio as well as separate one- and two-bedroom cottages with fireplaces and full kitchens. **Pros:** peaceful property; good value; friendly staff; close to village. **Cons:** rooms may be too rustic—as in out of date—for some. [$] *Rooms from: $179* ✉ *8 Ford Rd., at Carmel Valley Rd.* ☎ *831/659–2261, 800/641–4646* 🌐 *www.valleylodge.com* 🛏 *19 rooms, 4 suites, 8 cottages* 🍽 *Breakfast.*

$$$$ RESORT 🏨 **Carmel Valley Ranch.** The activity options at this luxury ranch are so varied that the resort provides a program director to guide you through them. **Pros:** stunning natural setting; tons of activities; state-of-the-art amenities. **Cons:** must drive several miles to shops and nightlife; pricey. [$] *Rooms from: $400* ✉ *1 Old Ranch Rd., Carmel* ☎ *831/625–9500* 🌐 *www.carmelvalleyranch.com* 🛏 *139 suites* 🍽 *No meals.*

$$$ HOTEL FAMILY 🏨 **Quail Lodge & Golf Club.** A sprawling collection of ranch-style buildings on 850 acres of meadows, fairways, and lakes, Quail Lodge offers luxury rooms and outdoor activities at surprisingly affordable rates. **Pros:** on the golf course; on-site restaurant. **Cons:** extra fees for athletic passes and some services; 5 miles from the beach and Carmel Valley Village. [$] *Rooms from: $195* ✉ *8205 Valley Greens Dr., Carmel* 📠 *831/624–2888* ☎ *866/675–1101 reservations* 🌐 *www.quaillodge.com* 🛏 *77 rooms, 16 suites* 🍽 *Breakfast.*

$$$$ RESORT Fodor's Choice ★ 🏨 **Stonepine Estate Resort.** Set on 330 pastoral acres, the former estate of the Crocker banking family has been converted to a luxurious inn. **Pros:** supremely exclusive. **Cons:** difficult to get a reservation; far from the coast. [$] *Rooms from: $300* ✉ *150 E. Carmel Valley Rd.* ☎ *831/659–2245* 🌐 *www.stonepineestate.com* 🛏 *10 rooms, 2 suites, 3 cottages.*

SPORTS AND THE OUTDOORS
GOLF
Quail Lodge & Golf Club. Robert Muir Graves designed this championship semiprivate 18-hole course next to Quail Lodge that provides challenging play for golfers of all skill levels. The course, which incorporates 10 lakes, edges the Carmel River. For the most part flat, the walkable course is well maintained, with stunning views, lush fairways, and ultrasmooth greens. ⊠ *8000 Valley Greens Dr., Carmel* ☎ *831/620–8808 golf shop, 831/620–8866 club concierge* ⊕ *www.quaillodge.com* ⌨ *$150 Apr.–Oct., $125 Nov.–Mar.* ⅃. *18 holes, 6500 yards, par 71.*

Rancho Cañada Golf Club. With two 18-hole courses at reasonable rates, this public course is a local favorite. The gently rolling fairways crisscross the Carmel River, and views of the tree-studded Santa Lucia Mountains appear from nearly every vantage point. ⊠ *4860 Carmel Valley Rd., 1 mile east of Hwy. 1, Carmel* ☎ *831/624–0111, 800/536–9459* ⊕ *www.ranchocanada.com* ⌨ *$70* ⅃. *East Course: 18 holes, 6125 yards, par 71; West Course: 18 holes, 6357 yards, par 71.*

SHOPPING
Avant Garden & Home. An eclectic array of garden accents, art, jewelry, home furnishings, and handmade gift items from around the world are on display at this family-run shop. ⊠ *14 Delfino Pl.* ☎ *831/659–9899* ⊕ *www.avantgardenandhome.com.*

SPAS
Refuge. At this co-ed, European-style center on 2 serene acres you can recharge without breaking the bank. Heat up in the eucalyptus steam room or cedar sauna, plunge into cold pools, and relax indoors in zero-gravity chairs or outdoors in Adirondack chairs around fire pits. Repeat the cycle a few times, then lounge around the thermal waterfall pools. Talk is not allowed, and bathing suits are required. ⊠ *27300 Rancho San Carlos Rd., south off Carmel Valley Rd., Carmel* ☎ *831/620–7360* ⊕ *www.refuge.com* ⌨ *$39* ☉ *Daily 10–10* ☞ *$60 50-min massage, $12 robe rental, hot tubs (outdoor), sauna, steam room. Services: Aromatherapy, hydrotherapy, massage.*

PEBBLE BEACH

Off North San Antonio Road in Carmel-by-the-Sea or off Sunset Drive in Pacific Grove.

In 1919 the Pacific Improvement Company acquired 18,000 acres of prime land on the Monterey Peninsula, including the entire Pebble Beach coastal region and much of Pacific Grove. Pebble Beach Golf Links and the Lodge at Pebble Beach opened the same year, and the private enclave evolved into a world-class golf destination with three posh lodges, five golf courses, and some of the West Coast's ritziest homes.

GETTING HERE AND AROUND
If you drive south from Monterey on Highway 1, exit at 17-Mile-Drive/Sunset Drive in Pacific Grove to find the northern entrance gate. Coming from Carmel, exit at Ocean Avenue and follow the road almost to the beach; turn right on North San Antonio Road to the Carmel Gate. You

can also enter through the Highway 1 Gate at Scenic Drive/Sunridge Road. Monterey–Salinas Transit buses provide regular service in and around Pebble Beach.

EXPLORING

Fodor's Choice ★ **17-Mile Drive.** Primordial nature resides in quiet harmony with palatial estates along 17-Mile Drive, which winds through an 8,400-acre microcosm of the Pebble Beach coastal landscape. Dotting the drive are rare Monterey cypress, trees so gnarled and twisted that Robert Louis Stevenson described them as "ghosts fleeing before the wind." Some visitors balk at the $10 per car collected at the gates to drive on the private roads, but most find the drive well worth the price. An alternative is to grab a bike; cyclists tour for free. There are three entrances: the Highway 1 Gate, at Highway 68; the Pacific Grove gate, off Sunset Drive; and the Carmel gate, at San Antonio Road near Carmel Beach. **■ TIP→ If you spend at least $30 on dining or shopping in Pebble Beach and show a receipt at the exit gate, you'll receive a fee refund.** ✉ *West of Hwy. 1 and Hwy. 68 intersection.*

Bird Rock. The largest of several islands at the southern end of the Monterey Peninsula Country Club's golf course, Bird Rock teems with harbor seals, sea lions, cormorants, and pelicans.

Crocker Marble Palace. Many of the stately homes along 17-Mile Drive reflect the classic Monterey or Spanish-mission style typical of the region. A standout is the Crocker Marble Palace, about a mile south of the Lone Cypress *(⇨ below)*. The private waterfront estate, inspired by a Byzantine castle, is easily identifiable by its dozens of marble arches.

The Lone Cypress. The most-photographed tree along 17-Mile Drive is the weather-sculpted Lone Cypress, which grows out of a precipitous outcropping above the waves about 1½ miles up the road from Pebble Beach Golf Links. You can't walk out to the tree, but you can stop for a view of it at a small parking area off the road.

Seal Rock. Sea creatures and birds—as well as some very friendly ground squirrels—make use of Seal Rock, the largest of a group of islands about 2 miles north of the Lone Cypress.

WHERE TO STAY

$$$$ RESORT Fodor's Choice ★ 🏨 **Casa Palmero.** This exclusive boutique hotel evokes a stately Mediterranean villa. **Pros:** ultimate in pampering; sumptuous decor; more private than sister resorts; right on the golf course. **Cons:** pricey; may be *too* posh for some. [$] *Rooms from: $885* ✉ *1518 Cypress Dr.* ☎ *831/622–6650, 800/654–9300* 🌐 *www.pebblebeach.com* 🛏 *20 rooms, 4 suites* 🍴 *Breakfast.*

$$$$ RESORT 🏨 **The Inn at Spanish Bay.** This resort sprawls across a breathtaking stretch of shoreline, and has lush, 600-square-foot rooms. **Pros:** attentive service; tons of amenities; spectacular views. **Cons:** huge hotel; 4 miles from other Pebble Beach Resorts facilities. [$] *Rooms from: $635* ✉ *2700 17-Mile Dr.* ☎ *831/647–7500, 800/654–9300* 🌐 *www.pebblebeach.com* 🛏 *252 rooms, 17 suites.*

$$$$ RESORT 🏨 **Lodge at Pebble Beach.** All rooms have fireplaces and many have wonderful ocean views at this circa-1919 resort. **Pros:** world-class golf; borders the ocean and fairways; fabulous facilities. **Cons:** some rooms

are on the small side; very pricey. $ *Rooms from: $745* ✉ *1700 17-Mile Dr.* ☎ *831/624–3811, 800/654–9300* ⊕ *www.pebblebeach.com* ↪ *142 rooms, 19 suites* ⊙ *No meals.*

SPORTS AND THE OUTDOORS
GOLF

Links at Spanish Bay. This course, which hugs a choice stretch of shoreline, was designed by Robert Trent Jones Jr., Tom Watson, and Sandy Tatum in the rugged manner of traditional Scottish links, with sand dunes and coastal marshes interspersed among the greens. There are also chipping and putting greens, and a bagpiper signals the course's closing each day. ■ TIP→ **Nonguests of the Pebble Beach Resorts can reserve tee times up to two months in advance.** ✉ *17-Mile Dr., north end* ☎ *800/654–9300* ⊕ *www.pebblebeach.com* ⛳ *$265* ⅄ *18 holes, 6821 yards, par 72.*

Fodor's Choice **Pebble Beach Golf Links.** Pebble Beach Golf Links attracts golfers from
★   around the world. The ocean plays a major role in the 18th hole of the famed links. Each February the course is the main site of the AT&T Pebble Beach National Pro-Am, where show-business celebrities and golf pros team up for one of the nation's most glamorous tournaments. Tee times are available to guests who book a minimum two-night stay. Nonguests can reserve a tee time only one day in advance on a space-available basis (up to a year for groups); resort guests can reserve up to 18 months in advance. ✉ *17-Mile Dr., near Lodge at Pebble Beach* ☎ *800/654–9300* ⊕ *www.pebblebeach.com* ⛳ *$495* ⅄ *18 holes, 6828 yards, par 72.*

Peter Hay. A 9-hole, par-3 course, Peter Hay has attracted golfers of all skill levels since 1957. It's an ideal place for warm-ups, practicing short games, and for those who don't have time for a full 18 holes. ✉ *17-Mile Dr.* ☎ *831/622–8723* ⊕ *www.pebblebeach.com* ⛳ *$30* ⅄ *9 holes, 725 yards, par 27.*

Poppy Hills. A splendid 18-hole course designed in 1986 by Robert Trent Jones Jr., Poppy Hills reopened in 2014 after an extensive, yearlong renovation Jones also supervised. The reworked course has eco-friendly fairways—the irrigation required is substantially less than before—that meander through the Del Monte Forest. Each hole has been restored to its natural elevation along the forest floor, and all 18 greens have been rebuilt with bentgrass. Individuals may reserve up to one month in advance, groups up to a year. ✉ *3200 Lopez Rd., at 17-Mile Dr.* ☎ *831/622–8239* ⊕ *poppyhillsgolf.com* ⛳ *$210* ⅄ *18 holes, 7002 yards, par 73.5.*

Spyglass Hill. Among Pebble Beach's most challenging courses—three of the holes are rated among the toughest on the PGA tour—Spyglass Hill rewards golfers with varied terrain and glorious views. The first five holes border the Pacific, and the other 13 reach deep into the Del Monte Forest. Reservations are essential and may be made up to one month in advance (18 months for resort guests). ✉ *Stevenson Dr. and Spyglass Hill Rd.* ☎ *800/654–9300* ⊕ *www.pebblebeach.com* ⛳ *$370* ⅄ *18 holes, 6960 yards, par 72.*

PACIFIC GROVE

3 miles north of Carmel-by-the-Sea.

This picturesque town, which began as a summer retreat for church groups more than a century ago, recalls its prim and proper Victorian heritage in its host of tiny board-and-batten cottages and stately mansions. However, long before the church groups flocked here the area received thousands of annual pilgrims—in the form of bright orange-and-black monarch butterflies. They still come, migrating south from Canada and the Pacific Northwest to take residence in pine and eucalyptus groves from October through March. In Butterfly Town USA, as Pacific Grove is known, the sight of a mass of butterflies hanging from the branches like a long, fluttering veil is unforgettable.

A prime way to enjoy Pacific Grove is to walk or bicycle the 3 miles of city-owned shoreline along Ocean View Boulevard, a cliff-top area landscaped with native plants and dotted with benches meant for sitting and gazing at the sea. You can spot many types of birds here, including the web-footed cormorants that crowd the massive rocks rising out of the surf. Two Victorians of note along Ocean View are the Queen Anne–style Green Gables, at No. 301—erected in 1888, it's now a B&B—and the 1909 Pryor House, at No. 429, a massive, shingled, private residence with a leaded- and beveled-glass doorway.

GETTING HERE AND AROUND

Reach Pacific Grove via Highway 68 off Highway 1, just south of Monterey. From Cannery Row in Monterey, head north until the road merges with Ocean Boulevard and follow it along the coast. MST buses travel within Pacific Grove and surrounding towns.

EXPLORING

FAMILY **Lovers Point Park.** The coastal views are gorgeous from this waterfront park whose sheltered beach has a children's pool and a picnic area. The main lawn has a volleyball court and a snack bar. ⊠ *Ocean View Blvd. northwest of Forest Ave.* ☎ *831/648–5730.*

FAMILY **Monarch Grove Sanctuary.** The sanctuary is a fairly reliable spot for viewing monarch butterflies between October and February. ⊠ *1073 Lighthouse Ave., at Ridge Rd.* ⊕ *www.pgmuseum.org.*

Pacific Grove Museum of Natural History. The museum is a good source for the latest information about the monarch butterflies and has a well-crafted butterfly tree exhibit. ⊠ *165 Forest Ave., at Central Ave.* ☎ *831/648–5716* ⊕ *www.pgmuseum.org* ⊒ *$3, $5 per family* ☉ *Tues.–Sun. 10–5.*

FAMILY **Point Pinos Lighthouse.** At this 1855 structure, the West Coast's oldest continuously operating lighthouse, you can learn about the lighting and foghorn operations and wander through a small museum containing U.S. Coast Guard memorabilia. ⊠ *Asilomar Ave., between Lighthouse Ave. and Del Monte Blvd.* ☎ *831/648–3176* ⊕ *www.pointpinos.org* ⊒ *$2* ☉ *Thurs.–Mon. 1–4.*

7

BEACHES

Asilomar State Beach. A beautiful coastal area, Asilomar State Beach stretches between Point Pinos and the Del Monte Forest. The 100 acres of dunes, tidal pools, and pocket-size beaches form one of the region's richest areas for marine life—including surfers, who migrate here most winter mornings. Leashed dogs are allowed on the beach. **Amenities:** none. **Best for:** sunrise; sunset; surfing; walking. ✉ *Sunset Dr. and Asilomar Ave.* ☎ *831/646–6440* 🌐 *www.parks.ca.gov.*

WHERE TO EAT

$$ MODERN AMERICAN 🍴 **Beach House.** Patrons of this blufftop perch sip classic cocktails, sample California fare, and watch the otters frolic on Lovers Point Beach below. Standouts among the appetizers include the crispy shrimp—tossed in a creamy, spicy sauce—and oysters roasted in garlic-dill butter. Among the entrées worth a try are pan-seared sea scallops in a lobster-cognac bisque, bacon-wrapped meat loaf, and thyme-infused sole almandine with wild-rice pilaf. The sunset discounts between 4 and 6 (reservations recommended) are a great value. **■ TIP→ For the best views of the beach and bay, sit on the heated outdoor patio.** [$] *Average main: $21* ✉ *620 Ocean View Blvd.* ☎ *831/375–2345* 🌐 *www.beachhousepg.com* ⏲ *No lunch.*

$$$ MEDITERRANEAN 🍴 **Fandango.** The menu here is mostly Mediterranean and southern French, with such dishes as osso bucco and paella served in a skillet. The decor follows suit: stone walls and country furniture lend the restaurant the earthy feel of a European farmhouse. This is where locals come when they want to have a big dinner with friends, drink wine, have fun, and generally feel at home. [$] *Average main: $26* ✉ *223 17th St., south of Lighthouse Ave.* ☎ *831/372–3456* 🌐 *www.fandangorestaurant.com.*

$$ SEAFOOD 🍴 **Fishwife.** Fresh fish with a Latin accent makes this a favorite of locals for lunch or a casual dinner. Standards are the sea garden salads topped with your choice of fish and the fried seafood plates with fresh veggies. Diners with large appetites appreciate the fisherman's bowls—fresh fish served with rice, black beans, spicy cabbage, salsa, vegetables, and crispy tortilla strips. [$] *Average main: $22* ✉ *1996½ Sunset Dr., at Asilomar Blvd.* ☎ *831/375–7107* 🌐 *www.fishwife.com.*

$$$ ITALIAN 🍴 **Joe Rombi's La Mia Cucina.** Pasta, fish, steaks, and chops are the specialties at this modern trattoria, which is the best in town for Italian food. The look is spare and clean, with colorful antique wine posters decorating the white walls. Next door, the affiliated La Piccola Casa serves breakfast (baked goods) and lunch daily, plus early dinner from Wednesday through Sunday. [$] *Average main: $23* ✉ *208 17th St., at Lighthouse Ave.* ☎ *831/373–2416* 🌐 *www.joerombi.com* ⏲ *Closed Mon. and Tues. No lunch.*

$$$ MODERN AMERICAN 🍴 **Passionfish.** South American artwork and artifacts decorate Passionfish, and Latin and Asian flavors infuse the dishes. Chef Ted Walter shops at local farmers' markets several times a week to find the best produce, fish, and meat available, then pairs it with creative sauces. The menu might include sea scallops with tomato-truffle butter and savory rice pudding. [$] *Average main: $23* ✉ *701 Lighthouse Ave., at Congress Ave.* ☎ *831/655–3311* 🌐 *www.passionfish.net* ⏲ *No lunch.*

$ ✕ **Peppers Mexicali Cafe.** This cheerful white-walled storefront serves

MEXICAN   traditional dishes from Mexico and Latin America, with an emphasis on fresh seafood. Excellent red and green salsas are made throughout the day, and there's a large selection of beers, along with fresh lime margaritas. $ *Average main: $15* ✉ *170 Forest Ave., between Lighthouse and Central Aves.* ☎ *831/373–6892* ⊕ *www.peppersmexicalicafe.com* ⊘ *Closed Tues. No lunch Sun.*

$$ ✕ **Red House Café.** When it's nice out, sun pours through the big windows

AMERICAN   of this cozy restaurant and across tables on the porch; when fog rolls in, the fireplace is lit. The American menu changes with the seasons but typically includes grilled lamb fillets atop mashed potatoes for dinner and Dungeness crab cakes over salad for lunch. Breakfast on weekends is a local favorite. $ *Average main: $20* ✉ *662 Lighthouse Ave., at 19th St.* ☎ *831/643–1060* ⊕ *www.redhousecafe.com* ⊘ *No dinner Mon.*

$$ ✕ **Taste Café and Bistro.** Grilled marinated rabbit, roasted half chicken,

AMERICAN   filet mignon, and other meats are the focus at Taste, which serves hearty European-inspired food in a casual, open-kitchen setting. $ *Average main: $20* ✉ *1199 Forest Ave.* ☎ *831/655–0324* ⊕ *www.tastecafebistro. com* ⊘ *Closed Sun.–Mon.*

WHERE TO STAY

$$ ⌂ **Green Gables Inn.** Stained-glass windows and ornate interior details

B&B/INN   compete with spectacular ocean views at this Queen Anne–style mansion, built by a businessman for his mistress in 1888. **Pros:** exceptional views; impeccable attention to historic detail. **Cons:** some rooms are small; thin walls. $ *Rooms from: $145* ✉ *301 Ocean View Blvd.* ☎ *831/375–2095, 800/722–1774* ⊕ *www.greengablesinnpg.com* ⟿ *10 rooms, 7 with bath; 1 suite* ⦿| *Breakfast.*

$$$ ⌂ **Martine Inn.** The glassed-in parlor and many guest rooms at this 1899

B&B/INN   Mediterranean-style villa have stunning ocean views, and thoughtful details such as robes and rocking chairs create an ambience of luxury and comfort. **Pros:** romantic; fancy breakfast; ocean views. **Cons:** not child-friendly; sits on a busy thoroughfare. $ *Rooms from: $209* ✉ *255 Ocean View Blvd.* ☎ *831/373–3388, 800/852–5588* ⊕ *www. martineinn.com* ⟿ *25 rooms* ⦿| *Breakfast.*

MONTEREY

2 miles southeast of Pacific Grove; 2 miles north of Carmel.

Early in the 20th century Carmel Martin, the first mayor of the city of Monterey, saw a bright future for his town: "Monterey Bay is the one place where people can live without being disturbed by manufacturing and big factories. I am certain that the day is coming when this will be the most desirable place in the whole state of California." His Honor was not far off the mark. Monterey is a scenic city filled with early California history: adobe buildings from the 1700s, Colton Hall, where California's first constitution was drafted in 1849, and Cannery Row, made famous by author John Steinbeck. Thousands of visitors come each year to mingle with otters and other sea creatures at the world-famous Monterey Bay Aquarium and in the protected waters of the national marine sanctuary that hugs the shoreline.

GETTING HERE AND AROUND

From San Jose or San Francisco, take U.S. 101 south to Highway 156 West at Prunedale. Head west about 8 miles to Highway 1 and follow it about 15 miles south. From San Luis Obispo, take U.S. 101 north to Salinas and drive west on Highway 68 about 20 miles.

Many MST bus lines connect at the Monterey Transit Center, at Pearl Street and Munras Avenue. In summer (daily from 10 until at least 7), the free MST Monterey Trolley travels from downtown Monterey along Cannery Row to the Aquarium and back.

TOURS

Monterey Movie Tours. Board a customized motorcoach and relax while a film-savvy local takes you on a scenic tour of the Monterey Peninsula enhanced by film clips shown on overhead monitors. More than 200 movies have been shot in the area, and scenes with Marilyn Monroe, Clint Eastwood, Tom Hanks, and other stars play when the tour passes through the exact film locations. The three-hour adventure travels a 32-mile loop through Monterey, Pacific Grove, and Carmel. ✉ *Departs from Monterey Conference Center, 1 Portola Plaza* ☎ *831/372–6278, 800/343–6437* ⊕ *www.montereymovietours.com* 🖃 *$55* ☉ *Daily at 1.*

Old Monterey Walking Tour. Learn all about Monterey's storied past by joining a guided walking tour through the historic district. Tours begin at Custom House Plaza, across from Fisherman's Wharf. 🖃 *$5, includes admission to Custom House and Pacific House* ☉ *Fri.–Sun. 10:30, 12:30, and 2.*

ESSENTIALS

Visitor Information Monterey County Convention & Visitors Bureau ☎ *877/666–8373* ⊕ *www.seemonterey.com.*

EXPLORING

TOP ATTRACTIONS

Cannery Row. When John Steinbeck published the novel *Cannery Row* in 1945, he immortalized a place of rough-edged working people. The waterfront street, edging a mile of gorgeous coastline, once was crowded with sardine canneries processing, at their peak, nearly 200,000 tons of the smelly silver fish a year. During the mid-1940s, however, the sardines disappeared from the bay, causing the canneries to close. Through the years the old tin-roof canneries have been converted into restaurants, art galleries, and malls with shops selling T-shirts, fudge, and plastic sea otters. Recent tourist development along the row has been more tasteful, however, and includes several stylish inns and hotels, wine tasting rooms, and upscale specialty shops. ✉ *Cannery Row, between Reeside and David Aves.* ⊕ *www.canneryrow.com.*

Colton Hall. A convention of delegates met here in 1849 to draft the first state constitution. The stone building, which has served as a school, a courthouse, and the county seat, is a city-run museum furnished as it was during the constitutional convention. The extensive grounds outside the hall surround the Old Monterey Jail. ✉ *570 Pacific St., between*

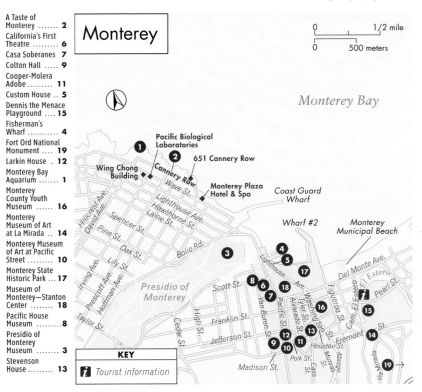

Madison and Jefferson Sts. ☎ 831/646–5640 ⊕ www.monterey.org/
museums ✉ Free ⊙ Daily 10–4 (Sun. and Tues. noon–3 in winter).

Cooper-Molera Adobe. The restored 2-acre complex includes a house dating
from the 1820s, a gift shop, and a large garden enclosed by a high adobe
wall. The mostly Victorian-era antiques and memorabilia that fill the house
provide a glimpse into the life of a prosperous sea merchant's family. If the
house is closed, you can still stop by the Cooper Store and pick up walking-
tour maps and stroll the grounds. ✉ Monterey State Historic Park, Polk
and Munras Sts. ☎ 831/649–7111 ⊕ www.parks.ca.gov/mshp ✉ $5 tour
⊙ Store, daily 10–4; gardens, daily 10–4; tours, Apr.–Aug., Fri.–Sun. and
holiday Mon. morning and afternoon (call for hrs).

Custom House. Built by the Mexican government in 1827 and now California's oldest standing public building, the Custom House was the
first stop for sea traders whose goods were subject to duties. In 1846,
Commodore John Sloat raised the American flag over this adobe structure and claimed California for the United States. The lower floor displays cargo from a 19th-century trading ship. If the house is closed,
you can visit the cactus gardens and stroll the plaza. ✉ Monterey State
Historic Park, 1 Custom House Plaza, across from Fisherman's Wharf
☎ 831/649–7118 ⊕ www.parks.ca.gov/mshp ✉ $3 (also includes
admission to Pacific House) ⊙ Fri.–Sun. and Mon. holidays 10–4.

FAMILY   **Fisherman's Wharf.** The mournful barking of sea lions provides a steady soundtrack all along Monterey's waterfront, but the best way to actually view the whiskered marine mammals is to walk along one of the two piers across from Custom House Plaza. Lined with souvenir shops, the wharf is undeniably touristy, but it's lively and entertaining. At Wharf No. 2, a working municipal pier, you can see the day's catch being unloaded from fishing boats on one side and fishermen casting their lines into the water on the other. The pier has a couple of low-key restaurants, from whose seats lucky customers might spot otters and harbor seals. ⊠ *At end of Calle Principal* ⊕ *www.montereywharf.com.*

> **JOHN STEINBECK'S CANNERY ROW**
>
> "Cannery Row in Monterey in California is a poem, a stink, a grating noise, a quality of light, a tone, a habit, a nostalgia, a dream. Cannery Row is the gathered and scattered, tin and iron and rust and splintered wood, chipped pavement and weedy lots and junk heaps, sardine canneries of corrugated iron, honky tonks, restaurants and whore houses, and little crowded groceries, and laboratories and flophouses."
> —John Steinbeck, *Cannery Row*

FAMILY
Fodor's Choice
★
Monterey Bay Aquarium. Sea creatures surround you the minute you hand over your ticket at this extraordinary facility: right at the entrance dozens of them swim in a three-story-tall, sunlit kelp-forest tank. All the exhibits here provide a sense of what it's like to be in the water with the animals—sardines swim around your head in a circular tank, and jellyfish drift in and out of view in dramatically lighted spaces that suggest the ocean depths. A petting pool puts you literally in touch with bat rays, and the million-gallon Open Seas tank illustrates the variety of creatures, from sharks to placid-looking turtles, that live in the eastern Pacific. At the Splash Zone, which has 45 interactive bilingual exhibits, kids can commune with African black-footed penguins, potbellied seahorses, and other creatures. The only drawback to the aquarium experience is that it must be shared with the throngs that congregate daily, but most visitors think it's worth it. ■TIP➔ **Through at least fall 2016, don't miss Tentacles: The Astounding Lives of Octopuses, Squid, and Cuttlefishes, a huge and fascinating exhibit of marine mollusks.** ⊠ *886 Cannery Row, at David Ave.* ☎ *831/648–4800 info, 866/963–9645 for advance tickets* ⊕ *www.montereybayaquarium.org* 🎫 *$40* 🕙 *Mar.–June daily 10–6; July–Aug./holidays weekends 9:30–6, weekends 9:30–8; Nov.–Feb. daily 10–5.*

Monterey State Historic Park. You can glimpse Monterey's early history in the well-preserved adobe buildings scattered along several city blocks. Far from being a hermetic period museum, the park facilities are an integral part of the town's day-to-day business life—within some of the buildings are a store, a theater, and government offices. The gardens at some historic structures are themselves worthy sights, and visitable even if the buildings, among them Casa Soberanes, the Cooper-Molera Adobe, and the Larkin House, are closed. ■TIP➔ **Because of state budget cuts, some buildings may be closed when you visit, but cell phone tours (☎831/998–9498) are available 24/7.** The

Trained "seals" that perform in circuses are actually California sea lions—intelligent, social animals that live (and sleep) close together in groups.

park's website has up-to-date information. ✉ *20 Custom House Plaza* ☎ *831/649–7118* ⊕ *www.parks.ca.gov/mshp* ⬜ *Free* ⊙ *Call for hrs.*

Museum of Monterey—Stanton Center. The museum displays maritime artifacts, art, photography, and costumes from Monterey's earliest days to the present. The collection's jewel is the enormous Fresnel lens from the Point Sur Light Station. ✉ *Stanton Center, 5 Custom House Plaza* ☎ *831/372–2608* ⊕ *www.museumofmonterey.org* ⬜ *$8, free 1st Wed. of month 1–5* ⊙ *May–Aug., Tues.–Sat. 10–7, Sun. noon–5; Sept.–Apr., Wed.–Sat. 11–5, Sun. noon–5.*

WORTH NOTING

A Taste of Monterey. Without driving the back roads, you can taste the wines of nearly 100 area vintners (craft beers, too) while taking in fantastic bay views. Bottles are available for purchase, and food is served from noon until closing. ✉ *700 Cannery Row, Suite KK* ☎ *831/646–5446, 888/646–5446* ⊕ *www.atasteofmonterey.com* ⬜ *Tastings $10–$20* ⊙ *Sun.–Wed. 11–7, Thurs.–Sat. 11–8.*

California's First Theatre. This adobe began its life in 1846 as a saloon and lodging house for sailors. Four years later stage curtains were fashioned from army blankets, and some U.S. officers staged plays to the light of whale oil lamps. As of this writing, the building is open only for private tours (call for times and fees), but you can stroll in the garden. ✉ *Monterey State Historic Park, Scott and Pacific Sts.* ☎ *831/649–7118* ⊕ *www.parks.ca.gov/mshp* ⬜ *Free* ⊙ *Call for hrs.*

Casa Soberanes. A classic low-ceiling adobe structure built in 1842, this was once a Custom House guard's residence. Exhibits at the house survey life in Monterey from the era of Mexican rule to the present. The building is open only for private tour requests (call for times and fees), but you can visit the peaceful rear garden and its rose-covered arbor. ⊠ *Monterey State Historic Park, 336 Pacific St., at Del Monte Ave.* ☎ *831/649–7118* ⊕ *www.parks.ca.gov/mshp* ⊡ *Free.*

FAMILY **Dennis the Menace Playground.** The late cartoonist Hank Ketcham designed this play area. Its equipment is on a grand scale and made for Dennis-like daredevils: kid favorites include the roller slide, rock-climbing area, and clanking suspension bridge. You can rent a rowboat or a paddleboat for cruising around U-shaped Lake El Estero, populated with an assortment of ducks, mud hens, and geese. ⊠ *El Estero Park, Pearl St. and Camino El Estero* ☎ *831/646–3866* ⊕ *www.monterey.org/ parks* ⊗ *Daily 10–dusk* ⊗ *Closed Tues., Sept.–May.*

Fort Ord National Monument. Scenic beauty, biodiversity, and miles of trails make this former U.S. Army training grounds a haven for nature lovers and outdoor enthusiasts. The 7,200-acre park, which stretches east over the hills between Monterey and Salinas, is also protected habitat for 35 species of rare and endangered plants and animals. There are 86 miles of single-track, dirt, and paved trails for hiking, biking, and horseback riding. The main trailheads are the Creekside, off Creekside Terrace near Portola Road, and Badger Hills. Maps are available at the various trail-access points and on the park's website. ▪ TIP→ **Dogs are permitted on trails, but should be leashed when other people are nearby.** ⊠ *Bordered by Hwy. 68 and Gen. Jim Moore and Reservation Rds.* ☎ *831/394–8314* ⊕ *www.blm.gov/pgdata/content/ca/en/fo/ hollister/fort_ord/index.html* ⊡ *Free* ⊗ *Daily ½ hr before sunrise–½ hr after sunset.*

Larkin House. A veranda encircles the second floor of this 1835 adobe, whose design bears witness to the Mexican and New England influences on the Monterey style. The building's namesake, Thomas O. Larkin, an early California statesman, brought many of the antiques inside from New Hampshire. From September through March the building is open only for special tour requests (call for times and fees), but you can peek in the windows and stroll the gardens. ⊠ *Monterey State Historic Park, 464 Calle Principal, between Jefferson and Pacific Sts.* ☎ *831/649–7118* ⊕ *www.parks.ca.gov/mshp* ⊡ *Tours $5* ⊗ *Gardens daily 10–4; tours Apr.–Aug. Fri.–Sun and Mon. holidays (call for hrs).*

FAMILY **Monterey County Youth Museum (MY Museum).** Monterey Bay comes to life from a child's perspective in this fun-filled, interactive indoor exploration center. The seven exhibit galleries showcase the science and nature of the Big Sur coast, theater arts, Pebble Beach golf, and beaches. Also here are a live performance theater, a creation station, a hospital emergency room, and an agriculture corner where kids follow artichokes, strawberries, and other fruits and veggies on their evolution from sprout to harvest to farmers' markets. ⊠ *425 Washington St., between E. Franklin St. and Bonifacio Pl.* ☎ *831/649–6444* ⊕ *www.mymuseum. org* ⊡ *$8* ⊗ *Tues.–Sat. 10–5, Sun. noon–5.*

Monterey Museum of Art at La Mirada. Asian and European antiques fill this 19th-century adobe house. A newer 10,000-square-foot gallery space, designed by Charles Moore, houses Asian and California regional art. Outside are magnificent rose and rhododendron gardens. ⊠ *720 Via Mirada, at Fremont St.* ☎ *831/372–3689* ⊕ *www.montereyart.org* ⌑ *$10, also good for admission to museum's Pacific Street facility* ⊙ *Wed.–Sun. 11–5 (Thurs. until 8).*

FORMER CAPITAL OF CALIFORNIA

In 1602 Spanish explorer Sebastián Vizcaíno stepped ashore on a remote California peninsula. He named it after the viceroy of New Spain—Count de Monte Rey. Soon the Spanish built a military outpost, and the site was the capital of California until the state came under American rule.

Monterey Museum of Art at Pacific Street. Photographs by Ansel Adams and Edward Weston, as well as works by other artists who have spent time on the peninsula, are on display here, along with international folk art, from Kentucky hearth brooms to Tibetan prayer wheels. ⊠ *559 Pacific St., across from Colton Hall* ☎ *831/372–5477* ⊕ *www.montereyart.org* ⌑ *$10, also good for admission to museum's La Mirada facility* ⊙ *Wed.–Sun. 11–5.*

Pacific House Museum. Once a hotel and saloon, this facility, also a visitor center, commemorates life in pioneer-era California with gold-rush relics and photographs of old Monterey. On the upper floor are Native American artifacts, including gorgeous baskets and pottery. ⊠ *Monterey State Historic Park, 10 Custom House Plaza* ☎ *831/649–7118* ⊕ *www.parks.ca.gov/mshp* ⌑ *$3 (includes admission to Custom House)* ⊙ *Fri.–Sun. and Mon. holidays 10–4.*

Presidio of Monterey Museum. This spot has been significant for centuries. Its first incarnation was as a Native American village for the Rumsien tribe. The Spanish explorer Sebastián Vizcaíno landed here in 1602, and Father Junípero Serra arrived in 1770. Notable battles fought here include the 1818 skirmish in which the corsair Hipólito Bruchard conquered the Spanish garrison that stood on this site and claimed part of California for Argentina. The indoor museum tells the stories; plaques mark the outdoor sites. ⊠ *Presidio of Monterey, Corporal Ewing Rd., off Lighthouse Ave.* ☎ *831/646–3456* ⊕ *www.monterey.org/museums* ⌑ *Free* ⊙ *Mon. 10–1, Thurs.–Sat. 10–4, Sun. 1–4.*

Stevenson House. This house was named in honor of author Robert Louis Stevenson, who boarded here briefly in a tiny upstairs room. Items from his family's estate furnish Stevenson's room; period-decorated chambers elsewhere in the house include a gallery of memorabilia and a children's nursery stocked with Victorian toys and games. Except on Saturday from April through August, the building is open only for special tour requests (call for times and fees), but you can stroll around the gardens. ⊠ *Monterey State Historic Park, 530 Houston St., near Pearl St.* ☎ *831/649–7118* ⊕ *www.parks.ca.gov/mshp* ⊙ *Gardens daily 9–5; house Apr.–Aug. Sat. 1–4.*

CLOSE UP

The Underwater Kingdom

Although Monterey's coastal landscapes are stunning, their beauty is more than equaled by the wonders that lie offshore. The Monterey Bay National Marine Sanctuary—which stretches 276 miles, from north of San Francisco almost down to Santa Barbara—teems with abundant life, and has topography as diverse as that aboveground.

The preserve's 5,322 square miles include vast submarine canyons, which reach down 10,663 feet at their deepest point. They also encompass dense forests of giant kelp—a kind of seaweed that can grow more than a hundred feet from its roots on the ocean floor. These kelp forests are especially robust off Monterey.

The sanctuary was established in 1992 to protect the habitat of the many species that thrive in the bay. Some animals can be seen quite easily from land. In summer and winter you might glimpse the offshore spray of gray whales as they migrate between their summer feeding grounds in Alaska and their breeding grounds in Baja. Clouds of marine birds—including white-faced ibis, three types of albatross, and more than 15 types of gull—skim the waves, or roost in the rock islands along 17-Mile Drive. Sea otters dart and gambol in the calmer waters of the bay; and of course, you can watch the sea lions—and hear their round-the-clock barking—on the wharves in Santa Cruz and Monterey.

The sanctuary supports many other creatures, however, that remain unseen by most on-land visitors. Some of these are enormous, such as the giant blue whales that arrive to feed on plankton in summer; others, like the more than 22 species of red algae in these waters, are microscopic. So whether you choose to visit the Monterey Bay Aquarium, take a whale-watch trip, or look out to sea with your binoculars, remember you're seeing just a small part of a vibrant underwater kingdom.

WHERE TO EAT

$$ MODERN AMERICAN 🍴 **Bay of Pines.** Local artists painted floor-to-ceiling murals of Monterey's natural habitats—from redwoods and sand dunes to the bay itself—and other homegrown art graces this whimsical organic restaurant. Chicken wontons on Asian slaw are among the appetizers, and the entrées might include seafood pasta puttanesca or seared ahi tuna with lemongrass rice, drizzled with apricot teriyaki sauce. The popular grass-fed beef burger comes with hummus, sautéed wild mushrooms, applewood-smoked bacon strips, and Gruyère. Musicians perform on most nights from 9 to 11:30; the bar here is a popular happy-hour hangout. [$] *Average main: $19* ✉ *150 Del Monte Ave.* ☎ *831/920–3563* 🌐 *www.bayofpinesrestaurant.com.*

$$ SEAFOOD 🍴 **Monterey Fish House.** Casual yet stylish and always packed, this seafood restaurant is removed from the hubbub of the wharf. If the dining room is full, you can wait at the bar and savor deliciously plump oysters on the half shell. The bartenders and waitstaff will gladly advise you on the perfect wine to go with your poached, blackened, or oak-grilled seafood. [$] *Average main: $21* ✉ *2114 Del Monte Ave., at Dela Vina Ave.* ☎ *831/373–4647* ✍ *Reservations essential* 🕘 *No lunch weekends.*

$$$ AMERICAN Fodor's Choice ★ 🍴 **Montrio Bistro.** This quirky, converted firehouse, with its rawhide walls and iron indoor trellises, has a wonderfully sophisticated menu. Chef Tony Baker uses organic produce and meats and sustainably sourced seafood to create imaginative dishes that reflect the area's agriculture—fire-roasted artichokes with Mediterranean relish, for instance, and pesto-rubbed sirloin prepared with brussels sprouts, dates, smoked bacon, and red wine. Monterey wineries are well represented on the California-centric wine list, and the signature cocktails are infused with local fruits, herbs, and veggies. [$] *Average main: $24* ✉ *414 Calle Principal, at W. Franklin St.* ☎ *831/648–8880* 🌐 *www.montrio.com* ✍ *Reservations essential* 🕓 *No lunch.*

$$$ SEAFOOD 🍴 **Old Fisherman's Grotto.** Otters and seals frolic in the water just below this family-run restaurant midway down Fisherman's Wharf that serves seafood, steak, and pasta. The founder's son and current owner, Chris Shake, has updated the decor while retaining the classic nautical style that prevailed when the Grotto opened in 1950. Famed for its creamy clam chowder, the restaurant serves a huge range of dishes, from seafood paella and sand dabs to filet mignon and teriyaki chicken. **■ TIP→ Reserve a windowside table for the best views.** [$] *Average main: $25* ✉ *39 Fisherman's Wharf* ☎ *831/375–4604* 🌐 *www.oldfishermansgrotto.com.*

$ AMERICAN 🍴 **Old Monterey Café.** Breakfast here gets constant local raves. The café's fame rests on familiar favorites: a dozen kinds of omelets, and pancakes from blueberry to cinnamon-raisin-pecan. For lunch are good soups, salads, and sandwiches. This is a fine place to relax with an afternoon cappuccino. [$] *Average main: $12* ✉ *489 Alvarado St., at Munras Ave.* ☎ *831/646–1021* ✍ *Reservations not accepted* 🕓 *No dinner.*

$$$$ MODERN AMERICAN Fodor's Choice ★ 🍴 **Restaurant 1833.** Housed in the historic Stokes Adobe, built in 1833, this popular restaurant and bar showcases the region's colorful history and local bounty in one of the most unusual settings anywhere. The two-story structure, a national heritage site, was once the home of the mayor of Monterey. Today it includes seven distinct dining rooms; each honors an era and characters from the adobe's storied past. Sit in a leather booth on the Founder's Balcony for a bird's-eye view of the rocking bar scene below, or outdoors by the courtyard fire pits near giant oak, redwood, palm, and magnolia trees. The casual menu changes daily and centers around seasonal local ingredients. Regular stars include bacon-cheddar biscuits with maple-chili butter and whole roasted truffle chicken, pan-roasted mahimahi, and bacon-wrapped pork loin. The cocktail menu pays tribute to the adobe's 1840s-era apothecary business with four categories: Pain Killers, Stress Relievers, Elixirs, and Aphrodisiacs, which, along with the extensive wine list, fuel a lively atmosphere indoors and out, especially on weekend nights. [$] *Average main: $32* ✉ *500 Hartnell St.* ☎ *831/643–1833* 🌐 *www.restaurant1833.com* 🕓 *No lunch.*

$$ AMERICAN 🍴 **Tarpy's Roadhouse.** Fun, dressed-up American favorites—a little something for everyone—are served in this renovated early-1900s stone farmhouse several miles east of town. The kitchen cranks out everything from Cajun-spiced prawns to meat loaf with marsala-mushroom gravy to grilled ribs and steaks. Eat indoors by a fireplace or outdoors in the courtyard. [$] *Average main: $22* ✉ *2999 Monterey–Salinas Hwy., Hwy. 68* ☎ *831/647–1444* 🌐 *www.tarpys.com.*

7

WHERE TO STAY

$$$ ⬛ **Best Western Beach Resort Monterey.** One of the area's best values, this
RESORT hotel has a great waterfront location—2 miles north of Monterey, with
views of the bay and the city skyline—and offers a surprising array of
amenities. **Pros:** on the beach; great value; family-friendly. **Cons:** several
miles from major attractions; big-box mall neighborhood. $ *Rooms
from: $189* ✉ *2600 Sand Dunes Dr.* ☎ *831/394–3321, 800/242–8627*
⊕ *www.montereybeachresort.com* ⤴ *196 rooms* ⧉ *No meals.*

$$ ⬛ **Hotel Abrego.** A half block from Monterey's transit center and a
HOTEL 15-minute walk to Fisherman's Wharf, this full-service hotel has Crafts-
man-style rooms in four mission-style buildings. **Pros:** central-Monterey
location; free parking; near public transit and highways; range of room
options. **Cons:** not on waterfront; smallish pool and exercise room;
some rooms near busy street. $ *Rooms from: $159* ✉ *755 Abrego St., at
Fremont St.* ☎ *831/372–7551, 800/982–1986 reservations* 🖷 *831/324–
4625* ⊕ *www.hotelabrego.com* ⤴ *93 rooms* ⧉ *No meals.*

$$$ ⬛ **InterContinental The Clement Monterey.** Spectacular bay views, upscale
HOTEL amenities, assiduous service, and a superb location next to the aquar-
ium propelled this luxury hotel to immediate stardom. **Pros:** a block
from the aquarium; fantastic waterfront views from some rooms; great
for families. **Cons:** a tad formal; pricey. $ *Rooms from: $199* ✉ *750
Cannery Row* ☎ *831/375–4500, 866/781–2406 toll free* ⊕ *www.
ictheclementmonterey.com* ⤴ *192 rooms, 16 suites* ⧉ *No meals.*

$$ ⬛ **Monterey Bay Lodge.** Its superior amenities and location bordering El
HOTEL Estero Park give this cheerful facility the edge over other area motels.
Pros: within walking distance of the beach and a playground; quiet at
night; good family choice. **Cons:** near a busy boulevard. $ *Rooms from:
$130* ✉ *55 Camino Aguajito* ☎ *831/372–8057, 800/558–1900* ⊕ *www.
montereybaylodge.com* ⤴ *43 rooms, 3 suites* ⧉ *No meals.*

$$$$ ⬛ **Monterey Plaza Hotel & Spa.** This hotel commands a waterfront loca-
HOTEL tion on Cannery Row, where you can see frolicking sea otters from the
wide outdoor patio and many room balconies. **Pros:** on the ocean; many
amenities; attentive service. **Cons:** touristy area; heavy traffic. $ *Rooms
from: $269* ✉ *400 Cannery Row* ☎ *831/646–1700, 800/334–3999*
⊕ *www.montereyplazahotel.com* ⤴ *280 rooms, 10 suites.*

$$$$ ⬛ **Old Monterey Inn.** This three-story manor house was the home of Mon-
B&B/INN terey's first mayor, and today it remains a private enclave within walk-
Fodor'sChoice ing distance of downtown, set off by lush gardens shaded by huge old
★ trees and bordered by a creek. **Pros:** gorgeous gardens; refined luxury;
serene. **Cons:** must drive to attractions and sights; fills quickly. $ *Rooms
from: $289* ✉ *500 Martin St.* ☎ *831/375–8284, 800/350–2344* ⊕ *www.
oldmontereyinn.com* ⤴ *6 rooms, 3 suites, 1 cottage* ⧉ *Breakfast.*

$$$ ⬛ **Spindrift Inn.** This boutique hotel on Cannery Row has beach access
HOTEL and a rooftop garden that overlooks the water. **Pros:** close to aquarium;
steps from the beach; friendly staff. **Cons:** throngs of visitors outside;
can be noisy; not good for families. $ *Rooms from: $209* ✉ *652 Can-
nery Row* ☎ *831/646–8900, 800/841–1879* ⊕ *www.spindriftinn.com*
⤴ *45 rooms* ⧉ *Breakfast.*

NIGHTLIFE

MUSIC CLUBS

Cibo. An Italian restaurant with a big bar area, Cibo brings live jazz and other music to downtown from Tuesday through Sunday. ✉ *301 Alvarado St., at Del Monte Ave.* ☎ *831/649–8151* ⊕ *www.cibo.com.*

MUSIC FESTIVALS

Jazz Bash by the Bay. Traditional jazz bands play early jazz, big band, swing, ragtime, blues, zydeco, and gypsy jazz at waterfront venues during this festival, held on the first full weekend of March. ☎ *831/675–0298, 888/349–6879* ⊕ *www.jazzbashbythebay.com.*

Monterey Jazz Festival. The world's oldest jazz festival attracts top-name performers to the Monterey Fairgrounds on the third full weekend of September. ☎ *888/248–6499 ticket office, 831/373–3366* ⊕ *www. montereyjazzfestival.org.*

THEATER

Bruce Ariss Wharf Theater (*The New Wharf Theatre*). American musicals past and present are the focus here, with dramas and comedies also in the mix. ✉ *One Fisherman's Wharf* ☎ *831/649–2332.*

SPORTS AND THE OUTDOORS

Monterey Bay waters never warm to the temperatures of their Southern California counterparts—the warmest they get is the low 60s. That's one reason why the marine life here is so diverse, which in turn brings out the fishers, kayakers, and whale-watchers. During the rainy winter, the waves grow larger, and surfers flock to the water. On land pretty much year-round, bikers find opportunities to ride, and walkers have plenty of waterfront to stroll.

BIKING

Adventures by the Sea, Inc. You can rent surreys plus tandem, standard, and electric bicycles from this outfit that also conducts bike and kayak tours and rents kayaks. ✉ *299 Cannery Row* ☎ *831/372–1807* ⊕ *www. adventuresbythesea.com* ✉ *210 Alvarado Mall* ✉ *Stillwater Cove, 17-Mile Drive, Pebble Beach* ✉ *Beach at Lovers Point, Pacific Grove.*

Bay Bikes. For bicycle and surrey rentals, visit Bay Bikes at one of its two Monterey shops. ■TIP➔ **You can rent a bike on Cannery Row and drop it off at this outfit's Carmel location.** ✉ *585 Cannery Row* ☎ *831/655–2453* ⊕ *www.baybikes.com* ✉ *486 Washington St.* ✉ *3600 The Barnyard, Carmel.*

FISHING

Randy's Fishing and Whale Watching Trips. In business since 1949, Randy's takes beginning and experienced fishers out to sea. ✉ *66 Fisherman's Wharf* ☎ *831/372–7440, 800/251–7440* ⊕ *www.randysfishingtrips.com.*

KAYAKING

Monterey Bay Kayaks. For many visitors the best way to see the bay is by kayak. This company rents equipment and conducts classes and natural-history tours. ✉ *693 Del Monte Ave.* ☎ *831/373–5357, 800/649–5357* ⊕ *www.monterey baykayaks.com.*

WALKING

Monterey Bay Coastal Trail. From Custom House Plaza, you can walk along the coast in either direction on this 29-mile-long trail for spectacular views of the sea. The trail runs from north of Monterey to Pacific Grove, with sections continuing around Pebble Beach. ☎ *831/372–3196* ⊕ *www.mtycounty.com/ pgs-parks/bike-path.html.*

WHALE-WATCHING

Thousands of gray whales pass close by the Monterey Coast on their annual migration between the Bering Sea and Baja California, and a whale-watching cruise is the best way to see these magnificent mammals close up. The migration south takes place from December through March; January is prime viewing time. The whales migrate north from March through June. Blue whales and humpbacks also pass the coast; they're most easily spotted in late summer and early fall.

Fast Raft Ocean Safaris. Naturalists lead whale-watching and sightseeing tours of Monterey Bay aboard the 33-foot *Ranger,* a six-passenger, rigid-hull inflatable boat. The speedy craft slips into coves inaccessible to larger vessels; its quiet engines enable intimate marine experiences without disturbing wildlife. Children ages 12 and older are welcome to participate. ✉ *32 Cannery Row, Suite F2* ☎ *831/324–4883 private or custom charter, 800/979-3370 reservations* ⊕ *www.fastraft.com* ✇ *$140.*

Monterey Bay Whale Watch. The marine biologists here lead three- to five-hour whale-watching tours. ✉ *84 Fisherman's Wharf* ☎ *831/375–4658* ⊕ *www.montereybaywhalewatch.com.*

Princess Monterey Whale Watching. Tours are offered daily on a 150-passenger high-speed cruiser and a large 75-foot boat. ✉ *96 Fisherman's Wharf #1* ☎ *831/372–2203, 831/205–2370 reservations, 888/223–9153 international reservations* ⊕ *www.montereywhalewatching.com.*

THE FIRST ARTICHOKE QUEEN

Castroville, a tiny town off Highway 1 between Monterey and Watsonville, produces about 95% of U.S. artichokes. Back in 1948, the town chose its first queen to preside during its Artichoke Festival—a beautiful young woman named Norma Jean Mortenson, who later changed her name to Marilyn Monroe.

AROUND MONTEREY BAY

As Highway 1 follows the curve of the bay between Monterey and Santa Cruz, it passes through a rich agricultural zone. Opening right onto the bay, where the Salinas and Pajaro rivers drain into the Pacific, a broad valley brings together fertile soil, an ideal climate, and a good water supply to create optimum growing conditions for crops such as strawberries, artichokes, brussels sprouts, and broccoli. Several beautiful beaches line this part of the coast. Salinas and Moss Landing are in Monterey County; the other cities and towns covered here are in Santa Cruz County.

GETTING HERE AND AROUND
All the towns in this area are on or just off Highway 1. MST buses serve Monterey County destinations, connecting in Watsonville with Santa Cruz METRO buses, which operate throughout Santa Cruz County.

SALINAS

17 miles east of Monterey on Hwy. 68.

Salinas, a hard-working city surrounded by vineyards and fruit and vegetable fields, honors the memory and literary legacy of John Steinbeck, its most famous native, with the National Steinbeck Center. The facility spurred the revival of Old Town Salinas, where renovated turn-of-the-20th-century stone buildings house shops and restaurants.

ESSENTIALS
Transportation Information Salinas Amtrak Station ⊠ *11 Station Pl., at W. Market St., Salinas* ☎ *800/872–7245.*

Visitor Information California Welcome Center ⊠ *1213 N. Davis Rd., west of U.S. 101, exit 330, Salinas* ☎ *831/757–8687, 831/759–8687* ⊕ *www.visitcwc.com/salinas* ☉ *Open daily 9–5.*

EXPLORING
FAMILY **Monterey Zoo.** More than a hundred exotic animals—many of them retired from film, television, and live production work, or rescued from less-than-ideal environments—find sanctuary at the Monterey Zoo at Vision Quest Ranch. Visit tigers, lions, bears, elephants, and primates on guided hour-long walking tours with professional trainers and handlers. For an in-depth experience, stay in a safari bungalow at Vision Quest Safari B&B where, in the morning, breakfast from a basket is delivered by a resident elephant. ⊠ *400 River Rd., off Hwy. 68, Salinas* ☎ *831/455–1901, 800/228–7382* ⊕ *www.montereyzoo.com* ☜ *Tours $10; optional post-tour elephant feeding $5* ☉ *Tours daily at 1, Jun.–Aug. also at 3.*

National Steinbeck Center. The center's exhibits document the life of Pulitzer- and Nobel-prize winner John Steinbeck and the history of the nearby communities that inspired novels such as *East of Eden*. Highlights include reproductions of the green pickup-camper from *Travels with Charley* and of the bunkroom from *Of Mice and Men*. **Steinbeck House**, the author's Victorian birthplace, at 132 Central Avenue, is two blocks from the center in a so-so neighborhood. Now a decent lunch spot, it displays memorabilia. ⊠ *1 Main St., at Central Ave., Salinas* ☎ *831/775–4721* ⊕ *www.steinbeck.org* ☜ *$15* ☉ *Daily 10–5.*

PINNACLES NATIONAL PARK

38 miles southeast of Salinas

Pinnacles may be the nation's newest national park, but Teddy Roosevelt recognized the uniqueness of this ancient volcano—its jagged spires and monoliths thrusting upward from chaparral-covered mountains—when he made it a national monument in 1908. Though only about two hours from the bustling Bay Area, the outside world seems to recede even before you reach the park's gates.

GETTING HERE AND AROUND

One of the first things you need to decide when visiting Pinnacles is which entrance—east or west—you'll use, because there's no road connecting the two, thanks to the rugged peaks separating them. Entering from Highway 25 on the east is straightforward. The gate is only a mile or so from the turnoff. From the west, once you head east out of Soledad on Highway 146, the road quickly becomes narrow and hilly, with many blind curves. Drive slowly and cautiously along the 11 miles or so before you reach the west entrance.

ESSENTIALS

Pinnacles Visitor Center. This is the main visitor center for the park, located at the east entrance. Here you can purchase your admission passes, get maps, browse books, and buy gifts. Because it's adjacent to the campground store, it's a good place to stock up on last-minute snacks and drinks if you're headed out to hike the trails. ⊠ *Hwy. 146, 2 miles west of Hwy. 25, Paicines* ☎ *831/389–4485* ⊕ *www.nps.gov/ pinn/planyourvisit/hours.htm.*

West Pinnacles Visitor Contact Station. This station is just past the west entrance to the park, about 14 miles east of Soledad. Here you can get maps and information, watch a 13-minute film about the park, view some displays, and browse a small gift shop. Be advised that there isn't any food or drink available at this entrance, so come prepared. ⊠ *Hwy. 146, about 14 miles east of Soledad, Soledad* ☎ *831/537–7220* ⊕ *www. nps.gov/pinn/planyourvisit/hours.htm* ☉ *Daily 9–4:30.*

EXPLORING

FAMILY **Pinnacles National Park.** This park has many unusual attractions, including talus caves, 30 miles of hiking trails, and hundreds of rock climbing routes. A mosaic of diverse habitats supports an amazing number of wildlife species: 149 birds, 49 mammals, 69 butterflies, and nearly 400 bees. The park is also home to 32 of the world's remaining few hundred condors in captivity and release areas. Fourteen of California's 34 bat species live in caves in the park. President Theodore Roosevelt declared this remarkable 26,000-acre geologic and wildlife preserve a national monument in 1908. President Barack Obama officially designated it a national park in 2013.

The pinnacles are believed to have been created when two major tectonic plates heaved and lurched at their meeting points, spawning extensive volcanic activity in what's now called the Gabilan Mountains, southeast of Salinas and Monterey. The volcano eventually dried up and began to erode, leaving a rugged landscape with rocky spires and crags, or pinnacles, at the plates' intersection. Boulders fell into canyons and valleys, creating talus caves and a paradise for modern-day rock climbers. Spring is the most popular time to visit, when color-ful wildflowers blanket the meadows; summer heat can be brutal. The park has two entrances—east and west—but they are not connected (there's no way to build a road over the spires). The Pinnacles Visitor Center, Bear Gulch Nature Center, Park Headquarters, the Pinnacles Campground, and the Bear Gulch Cave and Reservoir are on the east side. The Chaparral Ranger Station is on the west side, where you can feast on fantastic views of the Pinnacles High Peaks from the parking area. Dogs are not allowed on hiking trails. ■ TIP→ **The east entrance is 32 miles southeast of Hollister via Highway 25. The west entrance is about 12 miles east of Soledad via Highway 146.** ✉ *5000 Hwy. 146, Paicines* ☎ *831/389–4485, 831/389–4427 Westside* ⊕ *www.nps.gov/ pinn* ✑ *$5 per vehicle, $3 per visitor if biking or walking, all valid 7 days* ⊙ *West entrance, daily 7:30 am–8 pm; West Pinnacles Visitor Center, daily 9–5. East entrance, daily 24 hrs; Pinnacles Visitor Center, daily 9:30–5.*

SPORTS AND THE OUTDOORS
HIKING

Hiking is the most popular activity at Pinnacles, with more than 30 miles of trails for every interest and level of fitness. Because there isn't a road through the park, hiking is also the only way to experience the interior of the park, including the High Peaks, the talus caves, and the reservoir.

Balconies Cliffs-Cave Loop. Grab your flashlight before heading out from the Chaparral Trailhead parking lot for this 2.4-mile loop that takes you through the Balconies Caves. This trail is especially beautiful in spring when an abundance of wildflowers carpets the canyon floor. About 0.6 miles from the start of the trail, turn left to begin ascending the Balconies Cliffs Trail, where you'll be rewarded with close-up views of Machete Peak and other steep, vertical formations; you'll probably run across a few rock climbers testing their skills. *Easy.* ✉ *Pinnacles National Park* ⊕ *From West Pinnacles Visitor Contact Station, drive about 2 miles to Chaparral Trailhead parking lot. Trail picks up on west side of lot.*

FAMILY **Moses Spring-Rim Trail Loop.** This is perhaps the most popular hike at Pinnacles, as it's relatively short (2.2 miles in typically 1.5 hours) and fun for both kids and adults alike. It takes you to the Bear Gulch cave system and if your timing is right, you'll pass by several seasonal waterfalls inside the caves (if it's been raining, check with a ranger as the caves could be flooded). The caves are usually closed in spring and early summer to protect the Townsend's big-ear bats and their pups. *Easy.* ✉ *Trail can be accessed from overflow parking just past Bear Gulch Nature Center, on south side of lot.*

MOSS LANDING

17 miles north of Monterey; 12 miles north of Salinas.

Moss Landing is not much more than a couple of blocks of cafés and restaurants, art galleries, and studios, plus a busy fishing port, but therein lies its charm. It's a fine place to overnight or stop for a meal and get a dose of nature.

GETTING HERE AND AROUND

From Highway 1 north or south, exit at Moss Landing Road on the ocean side. MST buses serve Moss Landing via Watsonville.

TOURS

Elkhorn Slough Safari Nature Boat Tours. This outfit's naturalists lead two-hour tours of Elkhorn Slough aboard a 27-foot pontoon boat. Reservations are required. ✉ *Moss Landing Harbor* ☎ *831/633–5555* 🌐 *www.elkhornslough.com* 🎟 *$35.*

ESSENTIALS

Visitor Information **Moss Landing Chamber of Commerce** ☎ *831/633–4501* 🌐 *www.mosslandingchamber.com.*

EXPLORING

Elkhorn Slough National Estuarine Research Reserve. The reserve's 1,400 acres of tidal flats and salt marshes form a complex environment that supports some 300 species of birds. A walk along the meandering waterways and wetlands can reveal hawks, white-tailed kites, owls, herons, and egrets. Also living or visiting here are sea otters, sharks, rays, and many other animals. ■ **TIP→ On weekends, guided walks from the visitor center to the heron rookery begin at 10 and 1.** ✉ *1700 Elkhorn Rd., Watsonville* ☎ *831/728–2822* 🌐 *www.elkhornslough.org* 🎟 *$4 day use fee* 🕒 *Wed.–Sun. 9–5.*

WHERE TO EAT AND STAY

$$ SEAFOOD 🍴 **Phil's Fish Market & Eatery.** Exquisitely fresh, simply prepared seafood (try the cioppino) is on the menu at this warehouselike restaurant on the harbor; all kinds of glistening fish are for sale at the market in the front. ■ **TIP→ Phil's Snack Shack, a tiny sandwich-and-smoothie joint, serves quicker meals at the north end of town.** [$] *Average main: $17* ✉ *7600 Sandholdt Rd.* ☎ *831/633–2152* 🌐 *www.philsfishmarket.com.*

$$ B&B/INN 🏨 **Captain's Inn.** Commune with nature and pamper yourself with upscale creature comforts at this green-certified getaway in the heart of town. **Pros:** walk to restaurants and shops; tranquil natural setting; homey atmosphere. **Cons:** rooms in historic building don't have water views; far from urban amenities; not appropriate for young children. [$] *Rooms from: $155* ✉ *8122 Moss Landing Rd.* ☎ *831/633–5550* 🌐 *www.captainsinn.com* 🛏 *10 rooms* 🍽 *Breakfast.*

SPORTS AND THE OUTDOORS

KAYAKING

Monterey Bay Kayaks. Rent a kayak to paddle out into Elkhorn Slough for up-close wildlife encounters. ✉ *2390 Hwy. 1, at North Harbor* ☎ *831/373–5357, 800/649–5357 toll free* 🌐 *www.montereybaykayaks.com.*

WATSONVILLE

7 miles north of Moss Landing.

If ever a city was built on berries, Watsonville is it. Produce has long driven the economy here, and this is where the Santa Cruz County Fair takes place each September.

GETTING HERE AND AROUND

From Santa Cruz or Monterey, follow Highway 1 to Watsonville. From U.S. 101, take Highway 152 West from Gilroy (a curving but scenic road over the mountains) or Highway 129 West from just north of San Juan Bautista. MST and Santa Cruz METRO buses connect at the Watsonville Transit Center, at Rodriguez Street and West Lake Avenue.

EXPLORING

FAMILY **Agricultural History Project.** One feature of the Santa Cruz County Fairgrounds is the Agricultural History Project, which preserves the history of farming in the Pajaro Valley. In the Codiga Center and Museum you can examine antique tractors and milking machines, peruse an exhibit on the era when Watsonville was the "frozen food capital of the West," and watch experts restore farm implements and vehicles. ⊠ *2601 E. Lake Ave., Hwy. 152, at Carlton Rd.* ☎ *831/724–5898* ⊕ *www. aghistoryproject.org* ⊠ *$2* ☉ *Thurs.–Sun. noon–4.*

APTOS

7 miles north of Watsonville.

Backed by a redwood forest and facing the sea, downtown Aptos—known as Aptos Village—is a place of wooden walkways and false-fronted shops. Antiques dealers cluster along Trout Gulch Road, off Soquel Drive east of Highway 1.

GETTING HERE AND AROUND

Use Highway 1 to reach Aptos from Santa Cruz or Monterey. Exit at State Park Drive to reach the main shopping hub and Aptos Village. You can also exit at Freedom Boulevard or Rio del Mar. Soquel Drive is the main artery through town.

ESSENTIALS

Visitor Information Aptos Chamber of Commerce ⊠ *7605-A Old Dominion Ct.* ☎ *831/688–1467* ⊕ *www.aptoschamber.com.*

BEACHES

Seacliff State Beach. Sandstone bluffs tower above popular Seacliff State Beach. You can fish off the pier, which leads out to a sunken World War I tanker ship built of concrete. Leashed dogs are allowed on the beach. **Amenities:** food and drink; lifeguards; parking (fee); showers; toilets. **Best for:** sunset; swimming; walking. ⊠ *201 State Park Dr., off Hwy. 1* ☎ *831/685–6442* ⊕ *www.parks.ca.gov* ⊠ *$10 per vehicle* ☉ *Daily 8 am–sunset.*

SAN JUAN BAUTISTA

About as close to early-19th-century California as you can get, San Juan Bautista (15 miles east of Watsonville on Highway 156) has been protected from development since 1933, when much of it became a state park. Small antiques shops and restaurants occupy the Old West and art deco buildings that line 3rd Street.

The wide green plaza of San Juan Bautista State Historic Park is ringed by 18th- and 19th-century buildings, many of them open to the public. The cemetery of the long, low, colonnaded mission church contains the unmarked graves of more than 4,300 Native American converts. Nearby is an adobe home furnished with Spanish-colonial antiques, a hotel frozen in the 1860s, a blacksmith shop, a stable, a pioneer cabin, and a jailhouse.

The first Saturday of each month, costumed volunteers engage in quilting bees, tortilla making, and other frontier activities. 🌐 *www.san-juan-bautista.ca.us.*

WHERE TO EAT AND STAY

$$$ MEDITERRANEAN 🍴 **Bittersweet Bistro.** A large old tavern with cathedral ceilings houses this popular bistro, where chef-owner Thomas Vinolus draws culinary inspiration from the Mediterranean. The menu changes seasonally, but regular highlights include paella, seafood puttanesca, and pepper-crusted skirt steak. The decadent chocolate desserts are not to be missed. Breakfast and lunch are available in the casual Bittersweet Café. Leashed dogs are welcome on the outdoor patio, where they can order from a special menu for pooches. [$] *Average main: $25* ✉ *787 Rio Del Mar Blvd., off Hwy. 1* ☎ *831/662–9799* 🌐 *www.bittersweetbistro.com.*

$$$ HOTEL FAMILY 🏨 **Best Western Seacliff Inn.** Families and business travelers like this 6-acre property near Seacliff State Beach that's more resort than hotel. **Pros:** walking distance to the beach; family-friendly; hot breakfast buffet. **Cons:** close to freeway; occasional nighttime bar noise. [$] *Rooms from: $180* ✉ *7500 Old Dominion Ct.* ☎ *831/688–7300, 800/367–2003* 🌐 *www.seacliffinn.com* 🛏 *139 rooms, 10 suites* 🍽 *Breakfast.*

$$$ B&B/INN 🏨 **Flora Vista.** Multicolor fields of flowers, strawberries, and veggies unfold in every direction at this luxury neo-Georgian inn set on 2 acres just south of Aptos. **Pros:** private; near Sand Dollar Beach; flowers everywhere. **Cons:** no restaurants or nightlife within walking distance; not a good place for kids. [$] *Rooms from: $195* ✉ *1258 San Andreas Rd., La Selva Beach* ☎ *831/724–8663, 877/753–5672* 🌐 *www.floravistainn.com* 🛏 *5 rooms* 🍽 *Breakfast.*

$$$$ RESORT FAMILY 🏨 **Seascape Beach Resort.** It's easy to unwind at this full-fledged resort on a bluff overlooking Monterey Bay. **Pros:** time share–style apartments; access to miles of beachfront; superb views. **Cons:** far from city life; most bathrooms are small. [$] *Rooms from: $300* ✉ *1 Seascape Resort Dr.* ☎ *831/688–6800, 800/929–7727* 🌐 *www.seascaperesort.com* 🛏 *285 suites* 🍽 *No meals.*

CAPITOLA AND SOQUEL

4 miles northwest of Aptos.

On the National Register of Historic places as California's first seaside resort town, the village of Capitola has been in a holiday mood since the late 1800s. Casual eateries, surf shops, and ice-cream parlors pack its walkable downtown. Inland, across Highway 1, antiques shops line Soquel Drive in the town of Soquel. Wineries dot the Santa Cruz Mountains beyond.

GETTING HERE AND AROUND

From Santa Cruz or Monterey, follow Highway 1 to the Capitola/Soquel (Bay Avenue) exit about 7 miles south of Santa Cruz and head west to reach Capitola and east to access Soquel Village. On summer weekends, park for free in the lot behind the Crossroads Center, a block west of the freeway, and hop aboard the free Capitola Shuttle to the village.

ESSENTIALS

Visitor Information Capitola-Soquel Chamber of Commerce ✉ *716-G Capitola Ave., Capitola* ☎ *831/475–6522* 🌐 *www.capitolachamber.com.*

BEACHES

New Brighton State Beach. Once the site of a Chinese fishing village, New Brighton is now a popular surfing and camping spot. Its Pacific Migrations Visitor Center traces the history of the Chinese and other peoples who settled around Monterey Bay and documents the migratory patterns of the area's wildlife, such as monarch butterflies and gray whales. Leashed dogs are allowed in the park. New Brighton connects with Seacliff Beach, and at low tide you can walk or run along this scenic stretch of sand for nearly 16 miles south (though you might have to wade through a few creeks). **■ TIP→ The 1½-mile stroll from New Brighton to Seacliff's concrete ship is a local favorite. Amenities:** parking (fee); showers; toilets. **Best for:** sunset; swimming; walking. ✉ *1500 State Park Dr., off Hwy. 1, Capitola* ☎ *831/464–6330* 🌐 *www.parks.ca.gov* 🎟 *$10 per vehicle* 🕒 *Day use daily 8 am–sunset.*

WHERE TO EAT

$ SEAFOOD FAMILY 🍴 **Carpo's.** Locals love this casual counter where seafood predominates but you can also order burgers, salads, and steaks. Baskets of fresh battered snapper are among the favorites, along with calamari, prawns, seafood kebabs, fish and chips, and homemade olallieberry pie. Many items cost less than $10. **■ TIP→ Come early for lunch or dinner to beat the crowds.** [$] *Average main: $10* ✉ *2400 Porter St., at Hwy. 1, Capitola* ☎ *831/476–6260* 🌐 *www.carposrestaurant.com/default1.html.*

$ CAFÉ FAMILY 🍴 **Gayle's Bakery & Rosticceria.** Whether you're in the mood for an orange-olallieberry muffin, a wild rice and chicken salad, or tri-tip on garlic toast, this bakery-deli's varied menu is likely to satisfy. Munch your flourless chocolate macaroon on the shady patio, or dig into the daily blue-plate dinner—Yankee pot roast, perhaps, or white-wine coq au vin—amid the whirl of activity inside. [$] *Average main: $12* ✉ *504 Bay Ave., at Capitola Ave., Capitola* ☎ *831/462–1200* 🌐 *www.gaylesbakery.com.*

$$ AMERICAN 🍴 **Michael's on Main.** Creative variations on classic comfort food draw lively crowds to this upscale but casual creekside eatery. Chef Michael Clark's menu changes seasonally, but might include pork osso bucco in red-wine tomato-citrus sauce or pistachio-crusted salmon with mint vinaigrette. For a quiet conversation spot, ask for a table on the romantic patio overlooking the creek. The busy bar area hosts live music Tuesday through Saturday. [$] *Average main: $22* ✉ *2591 Main St., at Porter St., Capitola* ☎ *831/479–9777* 🌐 *www.michaelsonmain.net* 🕘 *Closed Mon.*

$$$$ EUROPEAN 🍴 **Shadowbrook.** To get to this romantic spot overlooking Soquel Creek, you can take a cable car or walk the stairs down a steep, fern-lined bank beside a running waterfall. Dining room options include the rooftop Redwood Room, the wood-paneled Wine Cellar, the creekside, glass-enclosed Greenhouse, the Fireplace Room, and the airy Garden Room with a cypress tree. Prime rib and grilled seafood are the stars of the simple menu. Less expensive light entrées are available in the lounge. [$] *Average main: $32* ✉ *1750 Wharf Rd., at Lincoln Ave., Capitola* ☎ *831/475–1511* 🌐 *www.shadowbrook-capitola.com* 🕘 *No lunch.*

CALIFORNIA'S OLDEST RESORT TOWN

As far as anyone knows for certain, Capitola is the oldest seaside resort town on the Pacific Coast. In 1856 a pioneer acquired Soquel Landing, the picturesque lagoon and beach where Soquel Creek empties into the bay, and built a wharf. Another man opened a campground along the shore, and his daughter named it Capitola after a heroine in a novel series. After the train came to town in the 1870s, thousands of vacationers began arriving to bask in the sun on the glorious beach.

WHERE TO STAY

$$$$ B&B/INN 🏨 **Inn at Depot Hill.** This inventively designed B&B in a former rail depot views itself as a link to the era of luxury train travel. **Pros:** short walk to beach and village; historic charm; excellent service. **Cons:** fills quickly; hot tub conversation on the patio may irk second-floor guests. [$] *Rooms from: $299* ✉ *250 Monterey Ave., Capitola* ☎ *831/462–3376, 800/572–2632* 🌐 *www.innatdepothill.com* 🛏 *12 rooms* 🍽 *Breakfast.*

SANTA CRUZ

5 miles west of Capitola; 48 miles north of Monterey.

The big city on this stretch of the California coast, Santa Cruz (pop. 57,500) is less manicured than Carmel or Monterey. Long known for its surfing and its amusement-filled beach boardwalk, the town is a mix of grand Victorian-era homes and rinky-dink motels. The opening of the University of California campus in the 1960s swung the town sharply to the left politically, and the counterculture more or less lives on here. At the same time, the revitalized downtown and an insane real-estate market reflect the city's proximity to Silicon Valley and to a growing wine country in the surrounding mountains.

GETTING HERE AND AROUND
From the San Francisco Bay Area, take Highway 17 south over the mountains to Santa Cruz, where it merges with Highway 1. Use Highway 1 to get around the area. The Santa Cruz Transit Center is at 920 Pacific Avenue, at Front Street, a short walk from the Wharf and Boardwalk, with connections to public transit throughout the Monterey Bay and San Francisco Bay areas. You can purchase day passes for Santa Cruz METRO buses (⇨ *Bus Travel, in Planner*) here.

ESSENTIALS
Visitor Information Santa Cruz County Conference and Visitors Council
✉ *303 Water St., #100* ☎ *831/425–1234, 800/833–3494* ⊕ *www.santacruz.org.*

EXPLORING

TOP ATTRACTIONS

Pacific Avenue. When you've had your fill of the city's beaches and waters, take a stroll in downtown Santa Cruz, especially on Pacific Avenue between Laurel and Water streets. Vintage boutiques and mountain sports stores, sushi bars and Mexican restaurants, day spas, and nightclubs keep the main drag and the surrounding streets hopping from midmorning until late evening.

FAMILY **Santa Cruz Beach Boardwalk.** Santa Cruz has been a seaside resort since the mid-19th century. Along one end of the broad, south-facing beach, the Boardwalk has entertained holidaymakers for more than a century. Its Looff carousel and classic wooden Giant Dipper roller coaster, both dating from the early 1900s, are surrounded by high-tech thrill rides and easygoing kiddie rides with ocean views. Video and arcade games, a mini-golf course, and a laser-tag arena pack one gigantic building, which is open daily even if the rides aren't running. You have to pay to play, but you can wander the entire boardwalk for free while sampling delicacies such as corn dogs and garlic fries. ✉ *Along Beach St.* ☎ *831/423–5590 info line* ⊕ *www.beachboardwalk.com* 💲*$32 day pass for unlimited rides, or pay per ride* ☉ *Apr.–early Sept., daily; early Sept.–Mar., weekends and holidays, weather permitting; call for hrs* ☉ *Some rides may be closed Sept.–May.*

FAMILY **Santa Cruz Municipal Wharf.** Jutting half a mile into the ocean near one end of the boardwalk, the century-old Municipal Wharf is lined with seafood restaurants, a wine bar, souvenir shops, and outfitters offering bay cruises, fishing trips, and boat rentals. A salty soundtrack drifts up from under the wharf, where barking sea lions lounge in heaps on the crossbeams. ■TIP➜ Docents from the Seymour Marine Discovery Center lead free 30-minute tours on weekends at 1 and 3; meet at the stage on the west side of the wharf between Olitas Cantina and Marini's Candies. ✉ *Beach St., at Pacific Ave.* ☎ *831/459–3800 tour information* ⊕ *www.santacruzwharf.com.*

Santa Cruz Surfing Museum. This museum inside the Mark Abbott Memorial Lighthouse chronicles local surfing history. Photographs show old-time surfers, and a display of boards includes rarities such as a heavy redwood plank predating the fiberglass era and the remains of a modern board chomped by a great white shark. Surfer docents reminisce about the good old days. ⊠ *Lighthouse Point Park, 701 W. Cliff Dr., near Pelton Ave.* ☎ *831/420–6289* ⊕ *www.santacruzsurfingmuseum.org* ⊠ *$2* ☼ *Sept.–June, Thurs.–Mon. noon–4; July–Aug., Wed.–Mon. 10–5.*

West Cliff Drive. The road that winds along an oceanfront bluff from the municipal wharf to Natural Bridges State Beach makes for a spectacular drive, but it's even more fun to walk, blade, or bike the paved path that parallels the road. Surfers bob and swoosh in Monterey Bay at several points near the foot of the bluff, especially at a break known as Steamer Lane. Named for a surfer who died here in 1965, the nearby Mark Abbott Memorial Lighthouse stands at Point Santa Cruz, the cliff's major promontory. From here you can watch pinnipeds hang out, sunbathe, and frolic on Seal Rock.

WORTH NOTING

FAMILY **Monterey Bay National Marine Sanctuary Exploration Center.** The interactive and multimedia exhibits at this fascinating interpretive center reveal and explain the treasures of the nation's largest marine sanctuary. The two-story building, across from the main beach and municipal wharf, has films and exhibits about migratory species, watersheds, underwater canyons, kelp forests, and intertidal zones. The second-floor deck has stellar ocean views and an interactive station that provides real-time weather, surf, and buoy reports. ⊠ *35 Pacific Ave.* ☎ *831/421–9993* ⊕ *montereybay.noaa.gov/vc/sec* ⊠ *Free* ☼ *Wed.–Sun. 10–5.*

Mystery Spot. Hokey tourist trap or genuine scientific enigma? Since 1940, curious throngs baffled by the Mystery Spot have made it one of the most visited attractions in Santa Cruz. The laws of gravity and physics don't appear to apply in this tiny patch of redwood forest, where balls roll uphill and people stand on a slant. ■ TIP→ Purchasing online tickets ($6) is advised for weekend and holiday visits. ⊠ *465 Mystery Spot Rd., off Branciforte Dr. (north off Hwy. 1)* ☎ *831/423–8897* ⊕ *www.mysteryspot.com* ⊠ *$5 on-site, $6 in advance, parking $5* ☼ *Late May–early Sept., daily 10–7; early Sept.–late May, weekdays 10–4, weekends 10–5.*

Santa Cruz Mountains wineries. Highway 9 heads northeast from Santa Cruz into hills densely timbered with massive coastal redwoods. The road winds through the lush San Lorenzo Valley, past hamlets consisting of a few cafés, antiques shops, and old-style tourist cabins. Residents of the hunting-and-fishing persuasion coexist with hardcore flower-power survivors, and a new generation has joined the pioneers who opened wineries decades ago. Mountain grapes produce some superb Chardonnays, Pinot Noirs, and Cabernet Sauvignons, among other wines. To sample some, you can start a **winery tour** in downtown Santa Cruz at Storrs Winery, at 303 Potrero Street—a block off River Street, which, heading north from here becomes Highway 9. Drive north to Felton to visit Hallcrest Vineyards and Organic Wine Works, just west of Highway 9 on Felton Empire Road downtown. Continue north on Highway 9 and east on Bear Creek Road to the classy Byington and David Bruce wineries, both in Los Gatos. ■ TIP→ The Santa Cruz Mountains Winegrowers Association (⊕ www.

OFF THE
BEATEN
PATH

scmwa.com) distributes a wine-touring map at member wineries and many lodgings and attractions around Santa Cruz.

Surf City Vintners. A dozen tasting rooms of limited-production wineries occupy renovated warehouse spaces west of the beach. MJA, Storrs, and Equinox are good places to start. Also here are the Santa Cruz Mountain Brewing Company and El Salchicheroa, popular for its homemade sausages, jams, and pickled and candied vegetables. ⊠ *Swift Street Courtyard, 334 Ingalls St., at Swift St., off Hwy. 1 (Mission St.)* ⊕ *www. surfcityvintners.com.*

UC Santa Cruz. The 2,000-acre University of California Santa Cruz campus nestles in the forested hills above town. Its sylvan setting, ocean vistas, and redwood architecture make the university worth a visit, as does its **arboretum** ($5, open daily from 9 to 5), whose walking path leads through areas dedicated to the plants of California, Australia, New Zealand, and South Africa. ■TIP→ Free shuttles help students and visitors get around campus, and you can join a guided tour (online reservation required). ⊠ *Main entrance at Bay and High Sts. (turn left on High for arboretum)* ☎ *831/459–0111* ⊕ *www.ucsc.edu/visit*

Vinocruz. A slick, contemporary tasting space near the Santa Cruz Museum of Art & History, Vinocruz pours samples from more than five-dozen regional wineries, including small operations without tasting rooms of their own. ⊠ *Abbott Square, 725 Front St., off Cooper St.* ☎ *831/426–8466* ⊕ *www.vinocruz.com* ☉ *Tues.–Thurs. noon–7, Fri. and Sat. noon–8, Sun. 1–6.*

BEACHES

FAMILY **Natural Bridges State Beach.** At the end of West Cliff Drive lies this stretch of soft sand edged with tide pools and sea-sculpted rock bridges. ■TIP→ From October to early March a colony of monarch butterflies roosts in a eucalyptus grove. **Amenities:** lifeguards; parking (fee); toilets. **Best for:** sunrise; sunset; surfing; swimming. ⊠ *2531 W. Cliff Dr.* ☎ *831/423–4609* ⊕ *www.parks.ca.gov* ☒ *Beach free, parking $10* ☉ *Beach: daily 8 am–sunset. Visitor center: Oct.–Feb., daily 10–4; Mar.–Sept., weekends 10–4.*

Twin Lakes State Beach. Stretching a half mile along the coast on both sides of the small-craft jetties, Twin Lakes is one of Monterey Bay's sunniest beaches. It encompasses Seabright State Beach (with access in a residential neighborhood on the upcoast side) and Black's Beach on the downcoast side. Families often come here to sunbathe, picnic, and hike the nature trail around adjacent Schwann Lake. Parking is tricky on summer weekends from April through September, but you can park all day in the harbor pay lot and walk here. Leashed dogs are allowed. **Amenities:** food and drink; lifeguards (seasonal); parking; showers; toilets; water sports (seasonal). **Best for:** sunset; surfing; swimming; walking. ⊠ *7th Ave., at East Cliff Dr.* ☎ *831/427–4868* ⊕ *www.parks.ca.gov/?page_id=547.*

WHERE TO EAT

$$
SEAFOOD
✕ **Crow's Nest.** A classic California beachside restaurant, the Crow's Nest sits right on the water in Santa Cruz Harbor. Vintage surfboards and local surf photography line the walls in the main dining room, and nearly every table overlooks sand and surf. Breakfast favorites include crab-cake eggs Benedict and olallieberry pancakes. Seafood and steaks, served with local veggies, dominate the lunch and dinner menus; favorite appetizers include fried calamari and the chilled shrimp-stuffed artichoke. For sweeping ocean views and fish tacos, burgers, and other casual fare, head upstairs to the Breakwater Bar & Grill. Ⓢ *Average main: $20* ✉ *2218 E. Cliff Dr., west of 7th Ave.* ☎ *831/476–4560* ⊕ *www.crowsnest-santacruz.com.*

$$
MEDITERRANEAN
✕ **Laili Restaurant.** Exotic Mediterranean flavors with an Afghan twist take center stage at this artsy, stylish space with soaring ceilings. Traditional dishes range from Moroccan beet salad and apricot chicken flatbread to pomegranate eggplant and *maush-awa*, a soup with lentils, split peas, and lamb, topped with yogurt. The menus also include housemade pastas and numerous vegetarian options; fresh *naan* and delectable chutneys and dips accompany every meal. Evenings are especially lively, when locals come to relax over wine and soft jazz at the blue-concrete bar, the heated patio with twinkly lights, or at a communal table near the open kitchen. Ⓢ *Average main: $18* ✉ *101–B Cooper St., near Pacific Ave.* ☎ *831/423–4545* ⊕ *lailirestaurant.com* ⊗ *Closed Mon.*

$$
ITALIAN
✕ **La Posta.** Authentic Italian fare made with fresh local produce lures diners into cozy, modern-rustic La Posta. Nearly everything is housemade, from the pizzas and breads baked in the brick oven to the pasta and the vanilla-bean gelato. The seasonal menu includes flavorful dishes such as fried artichokes, ravioli filled with crab, and sautéed fish from local waters. Ⓢ *Average main: $22* ✉ *538 Seabright Ave., at Logan St.* ☎ *831/457–2782* ⊕ *www.lapostarestaurant.com* ⊗ *Closed Mon. No lunch.*

$$$
EUROPEAN
✕ **Oswald.** Sophisticated yet unpretentious European-inspired California cooking is the order of the day at this intimate and stylish bistro. The menu changes seasonally but might include such items as sautéed abalone or roasted rack of lamb. The creative concoctions poured at the slick marble bar include whiskey mixed with apple and lemon juice, and tequila with celery juice and lime. Ⓢ *Average main: $25* ✉ *121 Soquel Ave., at Front St.* ☎ *831/423–7427* ⊕ *www.oswaldrestaurant. com* ⊗ *Closed Mon. Lunch Fri. only.*

$
AMERICAN
✕ **Seabright Brewery.** Great burgers, big salads, and stellar microbrews make this a favorite hangout in the youthful Seabright neighborhood east of downtown. Sit outside on the patio or inside at a comfortable, spacious booth; both are popular with families. Ⓢ *Average main: $13* ✉ *519 Seabright Ave., at Murray St.* ☎ *831/426–2739* ⊕ *www. seabrightbrewery.com.*

$$
MEDITERRANEAN
✕ **Soif.** Wine reigns at this sleek bistro and wineshop that takes its name from the French word for thirst. The selections come from near and far, and you can order many of them by the taste or glass. Mediterranean-inspired small plates and entrées are served at the copper-top bar, the big communal table, and private tables. A jazz combo or solo pianist plays on some evenings. Ⓢ *Average main: $22* ✉ *105 Walnut Ave., at Pacific Ave.* ☎ *831/423–2020* ⊕ *www.soifwine.com* ⊗ *No lunch.*

$ ✗**Zachary's.** This noisy café filled with students and families defines
AMERICAN   the funky essence of Santa Cruz. It also dishes up great breakfasts: stay
simple with sourdough pancakes, or go for Mike's Mess—eggs scrambled with bacon, mushrooms, and home fries, then topped with sour
cream, melted cheese, and fresh tomatoes. ■**TIP→ If you arrive after 9
am, expect a long wait for a table; lunch is a shade calmer (closing time
is 2:30 pm).** $ *Average main: $12* ⊠ *819 Pacific Ave.* ☎ *831/427–0646*
⌲ *Reservations not accepted* ⊘ *Closed Mon. No dinner.*

WHERE TO STAY

$$$ ⊞**Babbling Brook Inn.** Though it's in the middle of Santa Cruz, this B&B
B&B/INN   has lush gardens, a running stream, and tall trees that make you feel like
you're in a secluded wood. **Pros:** close to UCSC; within walking distance of downtown shops; woodsy feel. **Cons:** near a high school; some
rooms close to a busy street. $ *Rooms from: $185* ⊠ *1025 Laurel St.*
☎ *831/427–2437, 800/866–1131* ⊕ *www.babblingbrookinn.com* ⇥ *13
rooms* ⦿*| Breakfast.*

$$$$ ⊞**Chaminade Resort & Spa.** Secluded on 300 hilltop acres of redwood
RESORT   and eucalyptus forest with hiking trails, this mission-style complex commands expansive views of Monterey Bay. **Pros:** far from city life; spectacular property; ideal spot for romance and rejuvenation. **Cons:** must
drive to attractions and sights; near a major hospital. $ *Rooms from:
$269* ⊠ *1 Chaminade La.* ☎ *800/283–6569 reservations, 831/475–5600*
⊕ *www.chaminade.com* ⇥ *112 rooms, 44 suites* ⦿*| No meals.*

$ ⊞**Harbor Inn.** Family-run, friendly, and funky, this basic but sparkling-
B&B/INN   clean lodge offers exceptional value just a few blocks from Santa Cruz
Harbor and Twin Lakes Beach. **Pros:** affordable; free Wi-Fi; park
your car and walk to the beach. **Cons:** not fancy; not near downtown. $ *Rooms from: $99* ⊠ *645 7th Ave.* ☎ *831/479–9731* ⊕ *www.
harborinnsantacruz.com* ⇥ *17 rooms, 2 suites.*

$$$ ⊞**Hotel Paradox.** Less than 2 miles from the wharf and boardwalk and
HOTEL   a short walk to Pacific Avenue, this stylish, forest-theme complex is
among the few full-service hotels in town. **Pros:** close to downtown and
main beach; alternative to beach-oriented lodgings; contemporary feel.
Cons: pool area can get crowded on warm-weather days; some rooms
on the small side. $ *Rooms from: $200* ⊠ *611 Ocean St.* ☎ *831/425–
7100, 855/425–7200* ⊕ *www.thehotelparadox.com* ⇥ *164 rooms, 6
suites* ⦿*| No meals.*

$$$ ⊞**Pacific Blue Inn.** Green themes predominate in this three-story, eco-friendly
B&B/INN   B&B, built from scratch in 2009 on a sliver of prime property downtown.
Pros: free parking; free bicycles; right in downtown. **Cons:** tiny property; not
suitable for children. $ *Rooms from: $189* ⊠ *636 Pacific Ave.* ☎ *831/600–
8880* ⊕ *www.pacificblueinn.com* ⇥ *9 rooms* ⦿*| No meals.*

$$$$ ⊞**Santa Cruz Dream Inn.** A short stroll from the boardwalk and wharf, this
HOTEL   full-service luxury hotel is the only lodging in Santa Cruz directly on the
beach. **Pros:** directly on the beach; easy parking; walk to boardwalk and
downtown. **Cons:** expensive; area gets congested on summer weekends.
$ *Rooms from: $309* ⊠ *175 W. Cliff Dr.* ☎ *831/426–4330, 866/774–
7735 reservations* ⊟ *831/427–2025* ⊕ *www.dreaminnsantacruz.com*
⇥ *149 rooms, 16 suites* ⦿*| No meals.*

7

$$$
B&B/INN
West Cliff Inn. A posh nautical-theme inn with views of the boardwalk and Monterey Bay, the West Cliff perches on the bluffs across from Cowell Beach. **Pros:** killer views; walking distance of the beach; close to downtown. **Cons:** boardwalk noise; street traffic. $ *Rooms from: $185* ⊠ *174 West Cliff Dr.* ☎ *800/979–0910 toll free, 831/457–2200* ⊕ *www.westcliffinn.com* ➷ *7 rooms, 2 suites, 1 cottage* ❙❑❙ *Breakfast.*

NIGHTLIFE AND THE ARTS

NIGHTLIFE

Catalyst. Dance with the crowds at this huge, grimy, and fun club that books rock, indie rock, punk, death-metal, reggae, and other acts. ⊠ *1011 Pacific Ave.* ☎ *831/423–1338* ⊕ *www.catalystclub.com.*

Kuumbwa Jazz Center. The renowned center draws top performers such as the Brubeck Brothers Quartet, Ladysmith Black Mambazo, and Chick Corea; the café serves meals an hour before most shows. ⊠ *320–2 Cedar St.* ☎ *831/427–2227* ⊕ *kuumbwajazz.org.*

Moe's Alley. Blues, salsa, reggae, funk: delightfully casual Moe's presents it all (and more), six nights a week. ⊠ *1535 Commercial Way* ☎ *831/479–1854* ⊕ *www.moesalley.com.*

THE ARTS

Santa Cruz Baroque Festival. From February through May the festival presents classical music at various venues and holds pre- and post-season events. The focus is on 17th- and 18th-century composers such as Bach and Handel. ☎ *831/457–9693* ⊕ *www.scbaroque.org.*

SPORTS AND THE OUTDOORS

ADVENTURE TOURS

Mount Hermon Adventures. Zip-line through the redwoods, climb a giant live oak tree, and hunt for edibles or learn about sand hill habitat restoration at this adventure center in the Santa Cruz Mountains. On some summer weekends, there's an aerial adventure course with obstacles and challenges in the redwoods. ■**TIP→ To join a tour (reservations essential) you must be at least 10 years old and weigh between 75 and 250 pounds.** ⊠ *17 Conference Dr., 9 miles north of downtown Santa Cruz near Felton, Mount Hermon* ☎ *831/430–4357* ⊕ *www. mounthermonadventures.com* ➔ *From $50.*

BICYCLING

Another Bike Shop. Mountain bikers should head here for tips on the best area trails and to browse cutting-edge gear made and tested locally. ⊠ *2361 Mission St., at King St.* ☎ *831/427–2232* ⊕ *www.anotherbikeshop.com.*

BOATS AND CHARTERS

Chardonnay II Sailing Charters. The 70-foot *Chardonnay II* departs year-round from Santa Cruz yacht harbor on whale-watching, sunset, and other cruises around Monterey Bay. Most regularly scheduled excursions cost $64; food and drink are served on many of them. Reservations are essential. ⊠ *Santa Cruz West Harbor, 790 Mariner Park Way* ☎ *831/423–1213* ⊕ *www.chardonnay.com.*

CLOSE UP

O'Neill: A Santa Cruz Icon

O'Neill wet suits and beachwear weren't exactly born in Santa Cruz, but as far as most of the world is concerned, the O'Neill brand is synonymous with Santa Cruz and surfing legend.

The O'Neill wet-suit story began in 1952, when Jack O'Neill and his brother Robert opened their first Surf Shop in a garage across from San Francisco's Ocean Beach. While shaping balsa surfboards and selling accessories, the O'Neills experimented with solutions to a common surfer problem: frigid waters. Tired of being forced back to shore, blue-lipped and shivering, after just 20 or 30 minutes riding the waves, they played with

various materials and eventually designed a neoprene vest.

In 1959 Jack moved his Surf Shop 90 miles south to Cowell's Beach in Santa Cruz. It quickly became a popular surf hangout, and O'Neill's new wet suits began to sell like hotcakes. In the early 1960s, the company opened a warehouse for manufacturing on a larger scale. Santa Cruz soon became a major surf city, attracting wave riders to prime breaks at Steamer Lane, Pleasure Point, and the Hook. In 1965 O'Neill pioneered the first wet-suit boots, and in 1971 Jack's son invented the surf leash. By 1980, O'Neill stood at the top of the world wet-suit market.

Stagnaro Sport Fishing, Charters, & Whale Watching Cruises. Stagnaro operates salmon, albacore, and rock-cod fishing expeditions; the fees (from $50 to $85) include bait. The company also runs whale-watching, dolphin, and sea-life cruises ($46) year-round. ⊠ *Santa Cruz West Harbor* ☎ *831/427–2334, 800/979–3370 tickets, 212/209–3370 international tickets* ⊕ *www.stagnaros.com.*

GOLF

Pasatiempo Golf Club. Designed by famed golf architect Dr. Alister MacKenzie in 1929 this semiprivate course, set amid undulating hills just above the city, is among the nation's top championship courses. Golfers rave about the spectacular views and challenging terrain. According to the club, MacKenzie, who also designed the exclusive Cypress Point course, in Pebble Beach, and Augusta National, home of the Masters Golf Tournament, declared this his favorite layout. ⊠ *20 Clubhouse Rd.* ☎ *831/459–9155* ⊕ *www.pasatiempo.com* ▤ *From $230* ⅃ *18 holes, 6125 yards, par 72.*

KAYAKING

Kayak Connection. From March through May, participants in this outfit's tours mingle with gray whales and their calves on their northward journey to Alaska. Throughout the year, the company rents kayaks and paddleboards and conducts tours of Natural Bridges State Beach, Capitola, and Elkhorn Slough. Most regularly scheduled tours cost $55. ⊠ *Santa Cruz Harbor, 413 Lake Ave. #3* ☎ *831/479–1121* ⊕ *www. kayakconnection.com.*

Venture Quest Kayaking. Explore hidden coves and kelp forests on guided nature tours that depart from Santa Cruz Wharf. An introductory lesson and two-hour kayak tour costs $58. A three-hour kayak rental runs $30, including wet suit and gear. Venture Quest also arranges tours at other Monterey Bay destinations, including Capitola and Elkhorn Slough. ⊠ *No. 2 Santa Cruz Wharf* ☎ *831/427–2267 kayak hotline, 831/425–8445 rental office* ⊕ *www.kayaksantacruz.com.*

SURFING

Pleasure Point. Surfers gather for the spectacular waves and sunsets here. ⊠ *E. Cliff and Pleasure Point Drs.*

Steamer Lane. This area near the lighthouse on West Cliff Drive has a decent break. Steamer Lane hosts several competitions in summer.

EQUIPMENT AND LESSONS

Club-Ed Surf School and Camps. Find out what all the fun is about at Club-Ed. Your first private or group lesson ($85 and up) includes all equipment. ⊠ *Cowell's Beach, at Santa Cruz Dream Inn* ☎ *831/464–0177* ⊕ *www.club-ed.com.*

Cowell's Beach Surf Shop. This shop sells gear, clothing, and swimwear; rents surfboards, standup paddleboards, and wet suits; and offers lessons. ⊠ *30 Front St.* ☎ *831/427–2355* ⊕ *www.cowellssurfshop.com.*

SHOPPING

Annieglass. The works of famed Santa Cruz glass artist Annie Morhauser are on display at the Smithsonian and New York's MOMA—but at the gallery in Cooper Square you can collect your own luxury Annieglass tableware, decorative accessories, and jewelry, all designed and handmade in Santa Cruz County. The store also sells discounted studio seconds with barely perceptible flaws and gift items made by other artists. ⊠ *110 Cooper St.* ☎ *831/427–4260* ⊕ *www.annieglass.com.*

Bookshop Santa Cruz. The town's best and most beloved independent bookstore has been sating readers' thirst for new, used, and discount books since 1966. The children's section is especially comprehensive, and the shop's special events calendar is packed with readings, social mixers, book signings, and discussions. ⊠ *1520 Pacific Ave.* ☎ *831/423–0900* ⊕ *www.bookshopsantacruz.com.*

O'Neill Surf Shop. Local surfers get their wetties (wet suits) and other gear at this O'Neill store or the one in Capitola, at 1115 41st Ave. There's also a satellite shop on the Santa Cruz Boardwalk. ⊠ *110 Cooper St.* ☎ *831/469–4377* ⊕ *www.oneill.com.*

The True Olive Connection. Taste your way through boutique extra-virgin olive oils and balsamic vinegars from around the world at this family-run shop just off Pacific Avenue. You can also pick up gourmet food products and olive-oil-based gift items. ⊠ *106 Lincoln St.* ☎ *831/458–6457* ⊕ *www.trueoliveconnection.com.*

SAN FRANCISCO

WELCOME TO SAN FRANCISCO

TOP REASONS TO GO

★ **The bay:** It's hard not to gasp as you catch sight of sunlight dancing on the water when you crest a hill, or watch the Golden Gate Bridge vanish and reemerge in the summer fog.

★ **The food:** San Franciscans are serious about what they eat, and with good reason. Home to some of the nation's best chefs, top restaurants, and finest local produce, it's hard not to eat well here.

★ **The shopping:** Shopaholics visiting the city will not be disappointed: San Francisco is packed with browsing destinations, everything from quirky boutiques to massive malls.

★ **The good life:** A laid-back atmosphere, beautiful surroundings, and oodles of cultural, culinary, and aesthetic pleasures...if you spend too much time here, you might not leave!

★ **The great outdoors:** From Golden Gate Park to sidewalk cafés in North Beach, San Franciscans relish their outdoor spaces.

1 Union Square and Chinatown. Union Square has hotels, public transportation, and shopping; walking through Chinatown is like visiting a bustling street in Beijing.

2 SoMa and Civic Center. SoMa is anchored by SFMOMA and Yerba Buena Gardens; the city's performing arts venues are in Civic Center.

3 Nob Hill and Russian Hill. Nob Hill is old-money San Francisco; Russian Hill's steep streets have excellent eateries and shopping.

4 North Beach. This small Italian neighborhood is a great place to enjoy an espresso.

5 On the Waterfront. Head here to visit the exquisitely restored Ferry Building, Fisherman's Wharf, Pier 39, the Exploratorium and Ghirardelli Square.

6 The Marina and the Presidio. The Marina has trendy boutiques, restaurants, and cafés; the wooded Presidio offers great views of the Golden Gate Bridge.

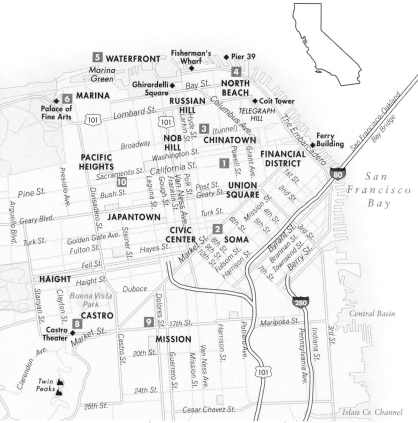

5 WATERFRONT
Marina
Green
Fisherman's
Wharf ◆ ◆ Pier 39
4
6 MARINA
Ghirardelli ◆
Square
Bay St. NORTH
BEACH
◆ Coit Tower
Palace of
Fine Arts
101
Lombard St.
RUSSIAN
HILL
TELEGRAPH
HILL
101
Broadway
NOB
HILL
(tunnel) **3**
CHINATOWN
Ferry
◆ Building
PACIFIC
HEIGHTS
Washington St.
Sacramento St.
California St.
1
FINANCIAL
DISTRICT
80
San
Francisco
Bay
Pine St.
Presidio Ave.
Bush St.
Polk St.
Van Ness Ave.
Franklin St.
Gough St.
Laguna St.
10
Post St.
Geary St.
UNION
SQUARE
1st St.
2nd St.
Geary Blvd.
Arguello Blvd.
Divisadero St.
Steiner St.
JAPANTOWN
Turk St.
Mission St.
4th St.
5th St.
3rd St.
Turk St.
Golden Gate Ave.
Fulton St.
Hayes St.
CIVIC
CENTER
Market St.
9th St.
8th St.
10th St.
Folsom St.
Harrison St.
2
SOMA
6th St.
7th St.
Bryant St.
Brannan St.
Townsend St.
Berry St.
Fell St.
HAIGHT
Haight St.
Duboce
280
Central Basin
3rd St.
Indiana St.
Pennsylvania Ave.
Stanyan St.
Clayton St.
Buena Vista
Park
CASTRO
Dolores St.
9
17th St.
Mariposa St.
8 Castro
Theater ◆
Market St.
Castro St.
MISSION
Potrero Ave.
Harrison St.
Van Ness Ave.
Guerrero St.
Mission St.
Clarendon Ave.
20th St.
101
Twin
Peaks ▲
24th St.
25th St.
Cesar Chavez St.
Islais Cr. Channel

8

7 Golden Gate Park and
the Western Shoreline.
San Francisco's 1,000-acre
backyard has sports fields,
windmills, museums, and
gardens; the windswept
Western Shoreline stretches
for miles.

8 The Haight, the Castro,
and Noe Valley. After
you've seen the blockbuster
sights, come to these neighborhoods to see where the
city's heart beats.

9 The Mission. This hip
neighborhood has destination
restaurants, bargain ethnic
eateries, and a lively bar scene.

10 Pacific Heights and
Japantown. Pacific Heights
has some of the city's
most opulent real estate;
Japantown is packed with
authentic Japanese shops
and restaurants.

GETTING ORIENTED

San Francisco is a com-
pact city; just 46.7 square
miles. Essentially a tightly
packed cluster of extremely
diverse neighborhoods, the
city dearly rewards walk-
ing. The areas that most
visitors cover are easy
(and safe) to reach on foot,
but many have steep—
make that *steep*—hills.

Updated by
Michele Bigley

On a 46½-square-mile strip of land between San Francisco Bay and the Pacific Ocean, San Francisco has charms great and small. Residents cherish their city for the same reasons visitors do: the proximity to the bay, rows of Victorian homes clinging precariously to the hillsides, the sun setting behind the Golden Gate Bridge, the world-class cuisine. Locals and visitors alike spend hours exploring downtown, Chinatown, North Beach, the northern and western waterfronts, and Golden Gate Park, along with colorful neighborhoods like the Haight, the Mission murals, and the Castro.

The city's attraction, though, goes much deeper than its alluring physical space, from the diversity of its neighborhoods to its free-spirited tolerance. Take all these things together and you'll understand why many San Franciscans—despite the dizzying cost of living and the chilly summers—can't imagine calling anyplace else home.

You won't want to miss the City by the Bay's highlights, whether it's a cable car ride over Nob Hill, a walk down the Filbert Street Steps; or gazing at the thundering Pacific from the cliffs of Lincoln Park; or cheering the San Francisco Giants to *beat L.A.* in the lively AT&T Park; or eating freshly shucked oysters at the Ferry Building. San Francisco is a beautiful metropolis packed with diverse wonders that inspire at every turn.

PLANNING

WHEN TO GO

You can visit San Francisco comfortably any time of year. Probably the best months are September and October, when the city's summer-like weather brings outdoor concerts and festivals. The climate here always feels Mediterranean and moderate—with a foggy, sometimes chilly bite. The temperature rarely drops below 40°F, and anything warmer than

80°F is considered a heat wave. Be prepared for rain in winter, especially December and January. Winds off the ocean can add to the chill factor. That old joke about summer in San Francisco feeling like winter is true at heart, but once you move inland, it gets warmer. (And some locals swear that the thermostat has inched up in recent years.)

GETTING HERE AND AROUND

AIR TRAVEL

The major gateway to San Francisco is San Francisco International Airport (SFO), 15 miles south of the city. It's off U.S. 101 near Millbrae and San Bruno. Oakland International Airport (OAK) is across the bay, not much farther away from downtown San Francisco (via I–80 east and I–880 south), but rush-hour traffic on the Bay Bridge may lengthen travel times considerably. San Jose International Airport (SJC) is about 40 miles south of San Francisco; travel time depends largely on traffic flow, but plan on an hour and a half with moderate traffic.

Airports San Francisco International Airport (SFO). ⊠ *McDonnell and Link Rds.* ☎ *800/435-9736, 650/821-8211* ⊕ *www.flysfo.com.* **Oakland International Airport** (OAK). ⊠ *1 Airport Dr., Oakland* ☎ *510/563-3300* ⊕ *www.flyoakland.com.* **San Jose International Airport** (SJC). ⊠ *1701 Airport Blvd., San Jose* ☎ *408/392-3600* ⊕ *www.flysanjose.com.*

Airport Transfers American Airporter ☎ *415/202-0733* ⊕ *www.americanairporter.com.* **BayPorter Express** ☎ *415/467-1800* ⊕ *www.bayporter.com.* **Caltrain** ☎ *800/660-4287* ⊕ *www.caltrain.com.* **East Bay Express Airporter** ☎ *877/526-0304* ⊕ *www.eastbaytransportation.com.* **GO Lorrie's Airport Shuttle** ☎ *415/334-9000* ⊕ *www.gosfovan.com.* **Marin Airporter** ☎ *415/461-4222* ⊕ *www.marinairporter.com.* **Marin Door to Door** ☎ *415/457-2717* ⊕ *www.marindoortodoor.com.* **SamTrans** ☎ *800/660-4287* ⊕ *www.samtrans.com.* **South and East Bay Airport Shuttle** ☎ *800/548-4664* ⊕ *www.southandeastbayairportshuttle.com.* **SuperShuttle** ☎ *800/258-3826* ⊕ *www.supershuttle.com.*

BART TRAVEL

BART (Bay Area Rapid Transit) trains, which run until midnight, travel under the bay via tunnel to connect San Francisco with Oakland, Berkeley, and other cities and towns beyond. Within San Francisco, stations are limited to downtown, the Mission, and a couple of outlying neighborhoods.

Trains travel frequently from early morning until evening on weekdays. After 8 pm weekdays and on weekends there's often a 20-minute wait between trains on the same line. Trains also travel south from San Francisco as far as Millbrae. BART trains connect downtown San Francisco to San Francisco International Airport; the ride costs $8.65.

Intracity San Francisco fares are $1.85; intercity fares are $3.15 to $11.65. BART bases its ticket prices on miles traveled and does not offer price breaks by zone. The easy-to-read maps posted in BART stations list fares based on destination, radiating out from your starting point of the current station.

Contact Bay Area Rapid Transit (BART). ☎ *415/989-2278* ⊕ *www.bart.gov.*

BOAT AND FERRY TRAVEL

Several ferry lines run out of San Francisco. Blue & Gold Fleet operates a number of routes, including service to Sausalito ($11 one-way) and Tiburon ($11 one-way). Tickets are sold at Pier 41 (between Fisherman's Wharf and Pier 39), where the boats depart. Alcatraz Cruises, owned by Hornblower Yachts, operates the ferries to Alcatraz Island ($30 including audio tour and National Park Service ranger-led programs) from Pier 33, about a half-mile east of Fisherman's Wharf ($3 shuttle buses serve several area hotels and other locations). Boats leave 10 times a day (14 times a day in summer), and the journey itself takes 30 minutes. Allow roughly 2½ hours for a round-trip jaunt. Golden Gate Ferry runs daily to and from Sausalito and Larkspur ($10.25 one-way), leaving from Pier 1, behind the San Francisco Ferry Building. The Alameda/Oakland Ferry operates daily between Alameda's Main Street Ferry Building, Oakland's Jack London Square, and San Francisco's Pier 41 and the Ferry Building ($6.25 one-way); some ferries go only to Pier 41 or the Ferry Building, so ask when you board. Purchase tickets on board.

Ferry Lines Alameda/Oakland Ferry ☎ 510/522–3300 ⊕ www.eastbayferry. com. **Alcatraz Cruises** ☎ 415/981–7625 ⊕ www.alcatrazcruises.com. **Blue & Gold Fleet** ☎ 415/705–8200 ⊕ www.blueandgoldfleet.com. **Golden Gate Ferry** ☎ 415/455–2000 ⊕ www.goldengateferry.org. **San Francisco Ferry Building** ✉ 1 Ferry Bldg., at foot of Market St. on Embarcadero ☎ 415/983–8030 ⊕ www.ferrybuildingmarketplace.com.

CABLE CAR TRAVEL

The fare (for one direction) is $6 (Muni Passport holders only pay a $1 supplement). You can buy tickets on board (exact change isn't necessary) or at the kiosks at the cable-car turnarounds at Hyde and Beach streets and at Powell and Market streets.

The heavily traveled Powell–Mason and Powell–Hyde lines begin at Powell and Market streets near Union Square and terminate at Fisherman's Wharf; lines for these routes can be long, especially in summer. The California Street line runs east and west from Market and California streets to Van Ness Avenue; there is often no wait to board this route.

CAR TRAVEL

Driving in San Francisco can be a challenge because of the one-way streets, snarly traffic, and steep hills. The first two elements can be frustrating enough, but those hills are tough for unfamiliar drivers. ■TIP→ **Remember to curb your wheels when parking on hills—turn wheels away from the curb when facing uphill, toward the curb when facing downhill. You can get a ticket if you don't do this.**

MUNI TRAVEL

The San Francisco Municipal Railway, or Muni, operates light-rail vehicles, the historic F-line streetcars along Fisherman's Wharf and Market Street, trolley buses, and the world-famous cable cars. Light rail travels along Market Street to the Mission District and Noe Valley (J-line), the Ingleside District (K-line), and the Sunset District (L-, M-, and N-lines); during peak hours (weekdays from 6 am to 9 am and 3 pm to 7 pm) the J-ine continues around the Embarcadero to the Caltrain station at 4th and King streets. The T-line light rail runs from the Castro, down Market Street, around the Embarcadero, and south past Hunters Point and Monster Park to Sunnydale Avenue and Bayshore Boulevard. Muni provides 24-hour service on select lines to all areas of the city.

On buses and streetcars the fare is $2. Exact change is required (coins or bills). For all Muni vehicles other than cable cars, 90-minute transfers are issued free upon request when the fare is paid. These are valid for two transfers in any direction. Cable cars cost $6 and include no transfers (⇨ *Cable-Car Travel, above*).

One-day ($15), three-day ($23), and seven-day ($29) Passports valid on the entire Muni system can be purchased at several outlets, including the cable-car ticket booth at Powell and Market streets and the visitor information center downstairs in Hallidie Plaza. A monthly ticket, called a Fast Pass, is available for $76, and can be used on all Muni lines (including cable cars) and on BART within city limits. The San Francisco CityPass, a discount ticket booklet to several major city attractions, also covers all Muni travel for seven consecutive days.

The San Francisco Municipal Transit and Street Map ($3) is a useful guide to the extensive transportation system. You can buy the map at most bookstores and at the San Francisco Visitor Information Center, on the lower level of Hallidie Plaza at Powell and Market streets. The Muni+ app provides updates and other info.

Muni Info **San Francisco Municipal Railway System** (*Muni*). ☎ *311, 415/701–3000* ⊕ *www.sfmta.com*.

TAXI TRAVEL

Hailing a cab can be frustratingly difficult in some parts of the city, especially on weekends. Popular nightspots such as the Mission, SoMa, North Beach, the Haight, and the Castro have a lot of cabs but a lot of people looking for taxis, too. Midweek, and during the day, you shouldn't have much of a problem—unless it's raining. In a pinch, hotel taxi stands are an option, as is calling for a pick-up. But be forewarned: taxi companies frequently don't answer the phone in peak periods. The absolute worst times to find a taxi are Friday afternoon and evening; plan well ahead, and if you're going to the airport, make a reservation or book a shuttle instead. Most taxi companies take reservations for airport and out-of-town runs but not in-town rides.

Alternatively, you can download the Uber or Lyft apps to participate in the city's user-generated car services. You basically join the group and pay via a credit card on your app, then order a car to pick you up from your destination and deliver you anywhere in the city. Rates vary by company, but are generally comparable to taxi rates.

Taxis in San Francisco charge $3.50 for the first 1/5 mile (one of the highest base rates in the United States), 55¢ for each additional 1/5 mile, and 55¢ per minute in stalled traffic; a $2 surcharge is added for trips to the airport. There is no charge for additional passengers; there is no surcharge for luggage. For trips outside city limits, multiply the metered rate by 1.5; tolls and tip are extra.

8

Taxi Companies **DeSoto Cab** ☎ *415/970–1300* ⊕ *www.desotosf.com.*
Luxor Cab ☎ *415/282–4141* ⊕ *www.luxorcab.com.* **Veteran's Taxicab**
☎ *415/648–1313.* **Yellow Cab** ☎ *415/626–2345* ⊕ *yellowcabsf.com.*

Complaints San Francisco Police Department Taxi Complaints
☎ *415/553–1447.*

TRAIN TRAVEL

Amtrak trains serve the Bay Area from major population centers in California and the United States. Amtrak doesn't have a train station in San Francisco, instead shuttling its passengers by bus from its Emeryville station, just across the Bay Bridge, to the Ferry Building and other points in downtown San Francisco. A California Rail Pass gives you 7 days of travel in a 21-day period for $159.

Caltrain connects San Francisco to San Jose and many smaller cities en route. The main depot in San Francisco is at 4th and Townsend streets. One-way fares cost from $3 to $13, depending on the number of zones through which you travel. A ticket from San Francisco to Palo Alto costs $7, to San Jose at least $9. A day pass (from $6 to $26) buys you unlimited travel for a 24-hour period. There are no onboard ticket sales. You must buy tickets before boarding the train or risk paying a $250 fine for fare evasion.

Train Contacts Amtrak ☎ *800/872–7245* ⊕ *www.amtrak.com.*
Caltrain ☎ *800/660–4287* ⊕ *www.caltrain.com.* **San Francisco Caltrain**
station ✉ *700 4th St., at King St.* ☎ *800/660–4287.*

VISITOR INFORMATION

The San Francisco Convention and Visitors Bureau can mail you brochures, maps, and events listings. Once in town, you can stop by the bureau's info center near Union Square.

Contacts San Francisco Visitor Information Center ✉ *Hallidie Plaza, lower level, 900 Market St., at Powell St., Union Sq.* ☎ *415/391–2000 TDD*
⊕ *www.onlyinsanfrancisco.com.*

EXPLORING SAN FRANCISCO

UNION SQUARE AND CHINATOWN

The Union Square area bristles with big-city bravado, while just a stone's throw away is a place that feels like a city unto itself, Chinatown. The two areas share a strong commercial streak, although manifested very differently. In Union Square the crowds zigzag among international brands, trailing glossy shopping bags. A few blocks north, people dash between small neighborhood stores, their arms draped with plastic totes filled with groceries or souvenirs.

UNION SQUARE

TOP ATTRACTIONS

Union Square. Ground zero for big-name shopping in the city and within walking distance of many hotels, Union Square is home base for many visitors. The Westin St. Francis Hotel and Macy's line two of the square's sides, and Saks, Neiman-Marcus, and Tiffany & Co. edge the other two. Four globular lamp sculptures by the artist R. M. Fischer preside over the landscaped, 2½-acre park, which has a café with outdoor seating, an open-air stage, and a visitor-information booth—along with a familiar kaleidoscope of characters: office workers sunning and brown-bagging, street musicians, shoppers taking a rest, kids chasing pigeons, and a fair number of homeless people. The constant clang of cable cars traveling up and down Powell Street helps maintain a festive mood.

The heart of San Francisco's downtown since 1850, the square takes its name from the violent pro-Union demonstrations staged here before the Civil War. At center stage, Robert Ingersoll Aitken's *Victory Monument* commemorates Commodore George Dewey's victory over the Spanish fleet at Manila in 1898. The 97-foot Corinthian column, topped by a bronze figure symbolizing naval conquest, was dedicated by Theodore Roosevelt in 1903 and withstood the 1906 earthquake. After the earthquake and fire of 1906, the square was dubbed "Little St. Francis" because of the temporary shelter erected for residents of the St. Francis Hotel. Actor John Barrymore (grandfather of actress Drew Barrymore and a notorious carouser) was among the guests pressed into volunteering to stack bricks in the square. His uncle, thespian John Drew, remarked, "It took an act of God to get John out of bed and the United States Army to get him to work."

The square sits atop a handy four-level garage, allegedly the world's first underground parking structure. Aboveground the convenient **TIX Bay Area** (☎ *415/433–7827* ⊕ *www.tixbayarea.com*) provides half-price, day-of-performance tickets to performing-arts events, as well as regular full-price box-office services. ■ **TIP→ Tired of shopping? Grab a coffee and pastry right in the square at Emporio Rulli, sit at a small outdoor table, and take in the action.** ⊠ *Bordered by Powell, Stockton, Post, and Geary Sts., Union Sq.*

WORTH NOTING

Maiden Lane. Known as Morton Street in the raffish Barbary Coast era, this former red-light district reported at least one murder a week during the late 19th century. Things cooled down after the 1906 fire destroyed the brothels, and these days Maiden Lane is a chic, boutique-lined pedestrian mall (favored by brides to be) stretching two blocks, between Stockton and Kearny streets. Wrought-iron gates close the street to traffic most days between 11 and 5, when the lane becomes a patchwork of umbrella-shaded tables.

At **140 Maiden Lane** you can see the only Frank Lloyd Wright building in San Francisco. Walking through the brick archway and recessed entry feels a bit like entering a glowing cave. The interior's graceful, curving ramp and skylights are said to have been his model for the Guggenheim Museum in New York. Xanadu Gallery, which showcases expensive Baltic, Latin American, and African folk art, occupies the space and welcomes Frank Lloyd Wright fans. ⊠ *Between Stockton and Kearny Sts., Union Sq.*

The epicenter of high-end shopping, Union Square is lined with department stores.

San Francisco Visitor Information Center. Head downstairs from the cable-car terminus to the visitor center, where multilingual staffers answer questions and provide maps and pamphlets. Muni Passports are sold here, and you can pick up discount coupons—the savings can be signifi-cant, especially for families. If you're planning to hit the big-ticket stops like the California Academy of Sciences and the Exploratorium and ride the cable cars, consider purchasing a CityPass (⊕ *www.citypass.com/ san-francisco*) here. ■TIP➜ The CityPass ($86, $64 ages 5–11), good for nine days, including seven days of transit, will save you more than 40%. The pass is also available at the attractions it covers, though if you choose the pass that includes Alcatraz—an excellent deal—you'll have to buy it directly from Alcatraz Cruises (⇨ *On the Waterfront, below*). ⊠ *Hallidie Plaza, lower level, 900 Market St., at Market and Powell Sts., Union Sq.* ☎ *415/391–2000* ⊕ *www.sanfrancisco.travel* ☼ *Weekdays 9–5, Sat. 9–3; also Sun. 9–3 May–Oct.*

Westin St. Francis Hotel. Architects Walter Danforth Bliss and William Baker Faville visited the great hotels of Europe seeking inspiration for the St. Francis, established in 1904 and renowned from the start for its sumptuous surroundings. After San Francisco's 1906 fire ravaged the hotel, a larger, more luxurious Italian Renaissance–style residence was opened in 1907 to attract loyal clients from among the world's rich and powerful. The hotel's checkered past includes the ill-fated 1921 bash in the suite of the silent-film superstar Fatty Arbuckle, at which a woman became ill and later died. Arbuckle endured three sensational trials for rape and murder before being acquitted, by which time his career was kaput. In 1975 Sara Jane Moore, standing among a crowd outside the hotel, attempted to shoot then-president Gerald Ford. As might be imagined, the grand lobby contains no plaques commemorating these events, though every November the hotel's pastry chef adds a new touch to his spectacular, rotating 12-foot-high gingerbread castle on display here—a fun holiday treat for families. ■TIP➡ **Some visitors make the St. Francis a stop whenever they're in town, soaking up the lobby ambience or enjoying a cocktail in Clock Bar or a meal at Michael Mina's Bourbon Steak.** ✉ *335 Powell St., at Geary St., Union Sq.* ☎ *415/397–7000* ⊕ *www.westinstfrancis.com.*

CABLE CAR TERMINUS

Two of the three cable-car lines begin and end their runs at Powell and Market streets, a couple of blocks south of Union Square. These two lines are the most scenic, and both pass near Fisherman's Wharf, so they're usually clogged with first-time sightseers. The wait to board a cable car at this terminus is longer than at any other stop in the system. To avoid the mob, board the less-touristy California line at the bottom of Market Street, at Drumm Street.

CHINATOWN
TOP ATTRACTIONS

Chinatown Gate. This is the official entrance to Chinatown. Stone lions flank the base of the pagoda-topped gate; the lions, dragons, and fish up top symbolize wealth, prosperity, and other good things. The four Chinese characters immediately beneath the pagoda represent the philosophy of Sun Yat-sen (1866–1925), the leader who unified China in the early 20th century. Sun Yat-sen, who lived in exile in San Francisco for a few years, promoted the notion of friendship and peace among all nations based on equality, justice, and goodwill. The vertical characters under the left pagoda read "peace" and "trust," the ones under the right pagoda "respect" and "love." The whole shebang telegraphs the internationally understood message of "photo op." Immediately beyond the gate, dive into souvenir shopping on Grant Avenue, Chinatown's tourist strip. ✉ *Grant Ave. at Bush St., Chinatown.*

Kong Chow Temple. This ornate temple sets a somber, spiritual tone right away with a sign warning visitors not to touch *anything.* The god to whom the members of this temple pray represents honesty and trust. Chinese stores and restaurants often display his image because he's thought to bring good luck in business. Chinese immigrants established the temple in 1851; its congregation moved to this building in 1977. Take the elevator up to the fourth floor, where incense fills the air. You can show respect by placing a dollar or two in the donation box and by leaving your camera in its case. Amid the statuary, flowers, and richly colored altars (red wards off evil spirits and signifies virility, green symbolizes longevity, and gold connotes majesty), a couple of plaques announce that "Mrs. Harry S. Truman came to this temple in June 1948 for a prediction on the outcome of the election . . . this fortune came true." ■TIP➡ **The temple's balcony has a good view of Chinatown.** ✉ *855 Stockton St., Chinatown* 🎫 *Free* ⊙ *Mon.–Sat. 9–4.*

8

Fodor's Choice ★ **Tin How Temple.** Duck into the inconspicuous doorway, climb three flights of stairs, and be assaulted by the aroma of incense in this tiny, altar-filled room. In 1852, Day Ju, one of the first three Chinese to arrive in San Francisco, dedicated this temple to the Queen of the Heavens and the Goddess of the Seven Seas, and the temple looks largely the same today as it did more than a century ago. In the entryway, elderly ladies can often be seen preparing "money" to be burned as offerings to various Buddhist gods or as funds for ancestors to use in the afterlife. Hundreds of red-and-gold lanterns cover the ceiling; the larger the lamp, the larger its donor's contribution to the temple. Gifts of oranges, dim sum, and money left by the faithful, who kneel mumbling prayers, rest on altars to different gods. Tin How presides over the middle back of the temple, flanked by one red and one green lesser god. Take a good look around, since taking photographs is not allowed. ⊠ *125 Waverly Pl., between Clay and Washington Sts., Chinatown* ⌨ *Free, donations accepted* ⊙ *Daily 9–4.*

WORTH NOTING

Chinese Historical Society of America Museum and Learning Center. The displays at this light-filled gallery document the Chinese-American experience—from 19th-century agriculture to 21st-century food and fashion trends—and include a thought-provoking collection of racist games and toys. The facility also exhibits works by contemporary Chinese-American artists. ⊠ *965 Clay St., between Stockton and Powell Sts., Chinatown* ☎ *415/391–1188* ⊕ *www.chsa.org* ⌨ *$5, free 1st Thurs. of month* ⊙ *Tues.–Fri. noon–5, Sat. 11–4.*

FAMILY **Golden Gate Fortune Cookie Factory.** Follow your nose down Ross Alley to this tiny but fragrant cookie factory. Workers sit at circular motorized griddles and wait for dollops of batter to drop onto a tiny metal plate, which rotates into an oven. A few moments later out comes a cookie that's pliable and ready for folding. It's easy to peek in for a moment, and hard to leave without a few free samples. A bagful of cookies—with mildly racy "adult" fortunes or more benign ones—costs under $5. You can also purchase the cookies "fortuneless" in their waferlike unfolded state, which makes snacking that much more efficient. ■ TIP➜ Photographing the cookie makers at work will set you back 50¢. ⊠ *56 Ross Alley, off Washington or Jackson St. west of Grant Ave., Chinatown* ☎ *415/781–3956* ⌨ *Free* ⊙ *Daily 9–8.*

Old Chinese Telephone Exchange. After the 1906 earthquake, many Chinatown buildings were rebuilt in Western style with pagoda roof and fancy balconies slapped on. This building—today EastWest Bank—is the exception, an example of top-to-bottom Chinese architecture. The intricate three-tier pagoda was built in 1909. To the Chinese, it's considered rude to refer to a person as a number, so the operators were required to memorize each subscriber's name. As the San Francisco Chamber of Commerce boasted in 1914: "These girls respond all day with hardly a mistake to calls that are given (in English or one of five Chinese dialects) by the name of the subscriber instead of by his number—a mental feat that would be practically impossible for most high-schooled American misses." ⊠ *EastWest Bank, 743 Washington St., Chinatown.*

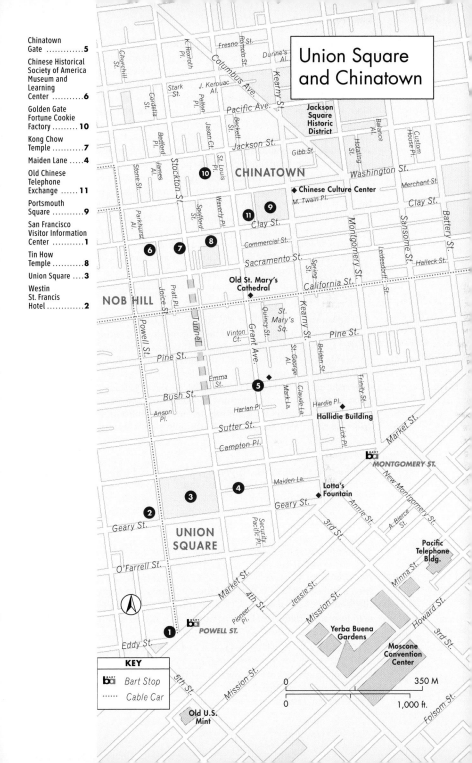

Union Square and Chinatown

CHINATOWN

Jackson Square Historic District

◆ Chinese Culture Center

Old St. Mary's Cathedral

NOB HILL

Hallidie Building

◆ Lotta's Fountain

UNION SQUARE

Pacific Telephone Bldg.

Yerba Buena Gardens

Moscone Convention Center

POWELL ST.

MONTGOMERY ST.

Old U.S. Mint

KEY

🅱 *Bart Stop*

.... *Cable Car*

0   350 M

0   1,000 ft.

Portsmouth Square. Chinatown's living room buzzes with activity. The square, with its pagoda-shape structures, is a favorite spot for morning tai chi; by noon dozens of men huddle around Chinese chess tables, engaged in not-always-legal competition. Kids scamper about the square's two grungy playgrounds (warning: the bathrooms are sketchy). Back in the late 19th century this land was near the waterfront. The square is named for the USS *Portsmouth*, the ship helmed by Captain John Montgomery, who in 1846 raised the American flag here and claimed the then-Mexican land for the United States. A couple of years later, Sam Brannan kicked off the gold rush at the square when he waved his loot and proclaimed, "Gold from the American River!" Robert Louis Stevenson, the author of *Treasure Island*, often dropped by, chatting up the sailors who hung out here. Some of the information he gleaned about life at sea found its way into his fiction. A bronze galleon sculpture, a tribute to Stevenson, anchors the square's northwest corner. A plaque marks the site of California's first public school, built in 1847. ⊠ *Bordered by Walter Lum Pl. and Kearny, Washington, and Clay Sts., Chinatown.*

SOMA, CIVIC CENTER, AND HAYES VALLEY

To a newcomer, SoMa (short for "south of Market") and the Civic Center may look like cheek-by-jowl neighbors—they're divided by Market Street. To locals, though, these areas are separate entities. Both neighborhoods have a core of cultural sights but more than their share of sketchy blocks. Locals love Hayes Valley, due west of Civic Center, for its terrific eateries and cool watering holes, the SFJAZZ Center, and the great browsing in funky clothing, home-decor, and design boutiques. Swing down the main drag, Hayes Street, between Franklin and Laguna streets and you can hit the neighborhood's highlights.

SOMA

TOP ATTRACTIONS

California Historical Society. If you're not a history buff, the CHS might seem like an obvious skip—who wants to look at fading old photographs and musty artifacts?—but these airy galleries are worth a stop. The shows here draw from the society's vast repository of Californiana—hundreds of thousands of photographs, publications, paintings, and gold-rush paraphernalia. Special exhibits have included *A Wild Flight of the Imagination: The Story of the Golden Gate Bridge* and *Hobos to Street People: Artists' Responses to Homelessness from the New Deal to the Present*. ■ TIP→ From out front, take a look across the street: this is the best view of the Museum of the African Diaspora's three-story photo mosaic. ⊠ *678 Mission St., SoMa* ☎ *415/357–1848* ⊕ *www.californiahistoricalsociety.org* ⊠ *$5* ⊗ *Tues.–Sun. noon–5; galleries close between exhibitions.*

Contemporary Jewish Museum. Daniel Liebeskind designed the postmodern CJM, whose impossible-to-ignore diagonal blue cube juts out of a painstakingly restored power substation. A physical manifestation of the Hebrew phrase *l'chaim* (to life), the cube may have obscure philosophical origins, but Liebeskind created a unique, light-filled space

Continued on page 381

CHINATOWN

Chinatown's streets flood the senses. Incense and cigarette smoke mingle with the scents of briny fish and sweet vanilla. Rooflines flare outward, pagoda-style. Loud Cantonese bargaining and honking car horns rise above the sharp clack of mah-jongg tiles and the eternally humming cables beneath the street.

Most Chinatown visitors march down Grant Avenue, buy a few trinkets, and call it a day. Do yourself a favor and dig deeper. This is one of the largest Chinese communities outside Asia, and there is far more to it than buying a back-scratcher near Chinatown Gate. To get a real feel for the neighborhood, wander off the main drag. Step into a temple or an herb shop and wander down a flag-draped alley. And don't be shy: residents welcome guests warmly, though rarely in English.

Whatever you do, don't leave without eating something. Noodle houses, bakeries, tea houses, and dim sum shops seem to occupy every other storefront. There's a feast for your eyes as well: in the market windows on Stockton and Grant, you'll see hanging whole roast ducks, fish, and shellfish swimming in tanks, and strips of shiny, pink-glazed Chinese-style barbecued pork. (For the scoop on dim sum, *see* the Union Square and Chinatown spotlight in the Where to Eat chapter.)

CHINATOWN'S HISTORY

Sam Brannan's 1848 cry of "Gold!" didn't take long to reach across the world to China. Struggling with famine, drought, and political upheaval at home, thousands of Chinese jumped at the chance to try their luck in California. Most came from the Pearl River Delta region, in the Guangdong province, and spoke Cantonese dialects. From the start, Chinese businesses circled around Portsmouth Square, which was conveniently central. Bachelor rooming houses sprang up, since the vast majority of new arrivals were men. By 1853, the area was called Chinatown.

The Street of Gamblers (Ross Alley), 1898 (top). The first Chinese telephone operator in Chinatown (bottom).

COLD WELCOME

The Chinese faced discrimination from the get-go. Harrassment became outright hostility as first the gold rush, then the work on the Transcontinental Railroad petered out. Special taxes were imposed to shoulder aside competing "coolie labor." Laws forbidding the Chinese from moving outside Chinatown kept the residents packed in like sardines,

with nowhere to go but up and down—thus the many basement establishments in the neighborhood. State and federal laws passed in the 1870s deterred Chinese women from immigrating, deeming them prostitutes. In the late 1870s, looting and arson attacks on Chinatown businesses soared.

The coup de grace, though, was the Chinese Exclusion Act, passed by the U.S.

Chinatown's Grant Avenue.

Women and children flooded into the neighborhood after the Great Quake.

Congress in 1882, which slammed the doors to America for "Asiatics." This was the country's first significant restriction on immigration. The law also prevented the existing Chinese residents, including American-born children, from becoming naturalized citizens. With a society of mostly men (forbidden, of course, from marrying white women), San Francisco hoped that Chinatown would simply die out.

OUT OF THE ASHES

When the devastating 1906 earthquake and fire hit, city fathers thought they'd seize the opportunity to kick the Chinese out of Chinatown and get their hands on that desirable piece of downtown real estate. Then Chinatown businessman Look Tin Eli had a brainstorm of Disneyesque proportions.

He proposed that Chinatown be rebuilt, but in a tourist-friendly, stylized, "Oriental" way. Anglo-American architects would design new buildings with pagoda roofs and dragon-covered columns. Chinatown would attract more tourists—the curious had been visiting on the sly

for decades—and add more tax money to the city's coffers. Ka-ching: the sales pitch worked.

PAPER SONS

For the Chinese, the 1906 earthquake turned the virtual "no entry" sign into a flashing neon "welcome!" All the city's immigration records went up in smoke, and the Chinese quickly began to apply for passports as U.S. citizens, claiming their old ones were lost in the fire. Not only did thousands of Chinese become legal overnight, but so did their sons in China, or "sons," if they weren't really related. Whole families in Chinatown had passports in names that weren't their own; these "paper sons" were not only a windfall but also an uncomfortable neighborhood conspiracy. The city caught on eventually and set up an immigration center on Angel Island in 1910. Immigrants spent weeks or months being inspected and interrogated while their papers were checked. Roughly 250,000 people made it through. With this influx, including women and children, Chinatown finally became a more complete community.

A GREAT WALK THROUGH CHINATOWN

■ Start at the Chinatown Gate and walk ahead on Grant Avenue, entering the souvenir gauntlet. (You'll also pass Old St. Mary's Cathedral.)

■ Make a right on Clay Street and walk to Portsmouth Square. Sometimes it feels like the whole neighborhood's here, playing chess and exercising.

■ Head up Washington Street to the Old Chinese Telephone Exchange building, now the EastWest Bank. Across Grant, look left for Waverly Place. Here Free Republic of China (Taiwanese) flags flap over some of the neighborhood's most striking buildings, including Tin How Temple.

■ At the Sacramento Street end of Waverly Place stands the First Chinese Baptist Church of 1908. Just across the way, the Clarion Music Center is full of unusual instruments, as well as exquisite lion-dance sets.

■ Head back to Washington Street and check out the herb shops, like the Superior Trading Company (No. 839) and the Great China Herb Co. (No. 857).

■ Follow the scent of vanilla down Ross Alley (entrance across from Superior Trading Company) to the Golden Gate Fortune Cookie Factory. Then

head across the alley to Sam Bo Trading Co., where religious items are stacked in the narrow space. Tell the owners your troubles and they'll prepare a package of joss papers, joss sticks, and candles, and tell you how and when to offer them up.

■ Turn left on Jackson Street; ahead is the real Chinatown's

main artery, Stockton Street, where most residents do their grocery shopping. Vegetarians will want to avoid Luen Fat Market (No. 1135), with tanks of live frogs, turtles, and lobster as well as chickens and ducks. Look toward the back of stores for Buddhist altars with offerings of oranges and grapefruit. From here you can loop one block east back to Grant.

ALL THE TEA IN CHINATOWN

Preparing a perfect brew at Red Blossom Tea.

San Francisco's close ties to Asia have always made it more tea-conscious than other American burgs, but these days the city is in the throes of a tea renaissance, with new tasting rooms popping up in every neighborhood. Below are our favorite spots for every tea under the sun.

Blest Tea. Chinatown's smallest tea shop is a calm, modern space with a thoughtful selection of teas by the pound. The Taiwane owners sell teas from many Asian countries, but their offerings emphasize Taiwan. Regulars rave about the service. ✉ *752 Grant Ave.* ☎ *415/951–8516.*

Red Blossom Tea. A light and modern shop—the staff really know their stuff. It's a favorite among younger tea enthusiasts, who swear by its excellent bang-for-the-buck value. While Red Blossom doesn't do formal tastings or sell tea by the cup, they'll gladly brew up perfect samples of the teas

you're interested in. ✉ *831 Grant Ave.* ☎ *415/395–0868.*

Vital Tea Leaf. Tastings here work like those for wine—one of the gregarious, knowledgeable servers chooses the teas and describes them as you sample. It's a great spot for tea newbies to get their feet wet without a hard sell, but local connoisseurs grumble about the high prices and the self-promotion. ✉ *1044 Grant Ave.* ☎ *415/981–2388.*

Imperial Tea Court. If you want to visit the most respected of traditional tea purveyors, you'll need to venture outside of Chinatown. Imperial Tea Court may have left Chinatown, but you'll find

WAITING FOR CUSTARD

As you're strolling down Grant Avenue, past the plastic Buddhas and yin/yang balls, be sure to stop at the Golden Gate Bakery (No. 1029) for some delicious eggy *dan tat* (custard tarts). These flaky-crusted treats are heaven for just a buck. There's often a line, but it's worth the wait.

DON'T-MISS SHOPS

Locals snap up flowers from an outdoor vendor.

If you're in the market for a pair of chirping metal crickets (oh you'll hear them, trust us), you can duck into any of the obvious souvenir-stuffed storefronts. But if you're looking for something special, head for these tempting sources. ■TIP➜ Fierce neighborhood competition keeps prices within reason, but for popular wares like jade, it pays to shop around before making a serious investment. Many stores accept cash only.

Chinatown Kite Shop. Family-run shop selling bright, fun-shaped kites—dragons, butterflies, sharks—since the 1960s. ✉ 717 Grant Ave. ☎ 415/989-5182.

Dragon House. A veritable museum: the store sells authentic, centuries-old antiques like ivory carvings. ✉ 455 Grant Ave. ☎ 415/421-3693.

Old Shanghai. One of the largest selections of hand-painted robes, formal dresses, and jackets in Chinatown, plus chic Asian-inspired pieces. ✉ 645 Grant Ave. ☎ 415/986-1222.

CHINATOWN WITH KIDS

It can be tough for the little ones to keep their hands to themselves, especially when all sorts of curios spill out onto the sidewalk at just the right height. To burn off some steam (in them) and relieve some stress (in you), take them to the small but spruce playground in the park in St. Mary's Square, across California from Old St. Mary's. If that setting's too tranquil, head to the more boisterous Willie Wong Playground, on Sacramento Street at Waverly Place.

that merits a stroll through the lobby even if current exhibits don't entice you into the galleries. Be sure to check out the seam where old building meets new, and check the website for fun children's activities linked to exhibits. San Francisco's best Jewish deli, Wise Sons, recently opened a counter in the museum, giving you a chance to sample the company's wildly popular smoked trout. ■TIP➔ At the StoryCorps StoryBooth, a project of the NPR oral-history series, you can listen to past interviews—or slip into the recording studio and preserve a loved one's memories right on the spot. ✉ *736 Mission St., between 3rd and 4th Sts., SoMa* ☎ *415/655–7800* ⊕ *www.thecjm.org* ⬛ *$12; $5 Thurs. after 5 pm, free 1st Tues. of month* ⊙ *Thurs. 1–8, Fri.–Tues. 11–5.*

> **LOOK UP!**
>
> When wandering around China-town, don't forget to look up! Above the chintziest souvenir shop might loom an ornate balcony or a curly pagoda roof. The best examples are on the 900 block of Grant Avenue (at Washington Street) and at Waverly Place.

Museum of the African Diaspora (MoAD). Dedicated to the influence that people of African descent have had all over the world, MoAD provokes discussion from the get-go with the question, "When did you discover you are African?" painted on the wall at the entrance. With no permanent collection, the museum is light on displays and heavy on interactive exhibits. For instance, you can sit in a darkened theater and listen to the moving life stories of slaves; hear snippets of music that helped create genres from gospel to hip-hop; and see videos about the civil rights movement or the Haitian Revolution. Some grumble that the presentations favor sweeping generalities over specifics, but almost everyone can appreciate the museum's most striking exhibit in the front window. The three-story mosaic, made from thousands of photographs, forms the image of a young girl's face. ■TIP➔ Walk up the stairs inside the museum to view the photographs up close—Malcolm X is there, Muhammad Ali, too, along with everyday folks—but the best view is from across the street. ✉ *685 Mission St., SoMa* ☎ *415/358–7200* ⊕ *www.moadsf.org* ⬛ *$10* ⊙ *Wed.–Sat. 11–6, Sun. noon–5.*

FAMILY
Fodor'sChoice
★

Yerba Buena Gardens. There's not much south of Market Street that encourages lingering outdoors—or indeed walking at all—with this notable exception. These two blocks encompass the Center for the Arts, the Metreon, Moscone Convention Center, and the convention center's rooftop Children's Creativity Museum, but the gardens themselves are the everyday draw. Office workers escape to the green swath of the East Garden, the focal point of which is the memorial to Martin Luther King Jr. Powerful streams of water surge over large, jagged stone columns, mirroring the enduring force of King's words that are carved on the stone walls and on glass blocks behind the waterfall. Moscone North is behind the memorial, and an overhead walkway leads to Moscone South and its rooftop attractions. ■TIP➔ The gardens are liveliest during the week and especially during the Yerba Buena Gardens Festival from May through October (⊕ www.ybgf.org), with free performances of everything from Latin music to Balinese dance.

8

Atop the Moscone Convention Center perch a few lures for kids. The historic Looff carousel (⊠ *$3 for two rides*) twirls daily 11 to 6. South of the carousel is the Children's Creativity Museum (☎ *415/820–3320* ⊕ *creativity.org*), a high-tech, interactive arts-and-technology center (⊠ *$11*) geared to children from age 3 to 12. Kids can make Claymation videos, work in a computer lab, check out new games and apps, and perform and record music videos. The museum is open year-round between 10 and 4 from Wednesday through Sunday, and on Tuesday during the summer. Just outside, kids adore the excellent slides, including a 25-foot tube slide, at the play circle. Also part of the rooftop complex are gardens, an ice-skating rink, and a bowling alley. ⊠ *Bordered by 3rd, 4th, Mission, and Folsom Sts., SoMa* ⊕ *www. yerbabuenagardens.com* ⊠ *Free* ⊙ *Daily sunrise–10 pm.*

WORTH NOTING

Cartoon Art Museum. Krazy Kat, Zippy the Pinhead, Batman, and other colorful cartoon icons greet you at the Cartoon Art Museum, established with an endowment from cartoonist-icon Charles M. Schulz. The museum's strength is its changing exhibits, which explore such topics as America from the perspective of international political cartoons, and the output of women and African American cartoonists. Serious fans of cartoons—especially those on the quirky underground side—will likely enjoy the exhibits; those with a casual interest may be bored. The store here carries cool titles to add to your collection. ⊠ *655 Mission St., SoMa* ☎ *415/227–8666* ⊕ *www.cartoonart.org* ⊠ *$8, pay what you wish 1st Tues. of month* ⊙ *Tues.–Sun. 11–5.*

San Francisco Museum of Modern Art. SFMOMA closed for a massive expansion project in 2013 and is scheduled to reopen in 2016. Until then, the museum will draw from its collection to create joint exhibitions with the Asian Art Museum, the Yerba Buena Center for the Arts, and other institutions. SFMOMA's store—known for its fun gadgets, artsy doodads, and superb art and kids' books—is relocating temporarily to 51 Yerba Buena Lane, off Mission and Market Streets near 4th Street. ⊠ *151 3rd St., SoMa* ☎ *415/357–4000* ⊕ *www.sfmoma.org.*

Yerba Buena Center for the Arts. You never know what's going to be on display at this facility in Yerba Buena Gardens, but whether it's an exhibit of Mexican street art (graffiti to laypeople), innovative modern dance, or a baffling video installation, it's likely to be memorable. The productions here, which lean toward the cutting edge, tend to draw a young, energetic crowd. ■TIP➜ **Present any library card to receive a $2 discount.** ⊠ *701 Mission St., SoMa* ☎ *415/978–2787* ⊕ *www.ybca. org* ⊠ *Galleries $10, free 1st Tues. of month* ⊙ *Thurs.–Sat. noon–8, Sun. noon–6, 1st Tues. of the month noon–8.*

CIVIC CENTER

TOP ATTRACTIONS

Fodor'sChoice
★
Asian Art Museum. You don't have to be a connoisseur of Asian art to appreciate a visit to this museum whose monumental exterior conceals a light, open, and welcoming space. The fraction of the Asian's collection on display (about 2,500 pieces out of 15,000-plus total) is laid out thematically and by region, making it easy to follow historical developments.

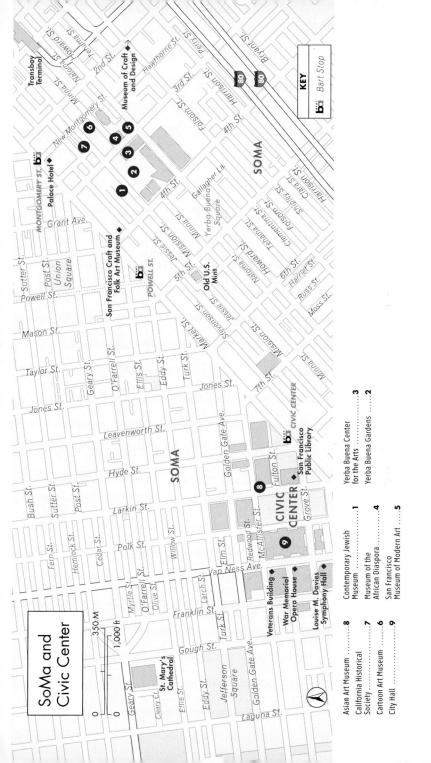

SoMa and Civic Center

0 — 350 M
0 — 1,000 ft

St. Mary's Cathedral

Veterans Building ◆
War Memorial Opera House ◆
Louise M. Davies Symphony Hall ◆

CIVIC CENTER

San Francisco Public Library ◆
🅱 CIVIC CENTER

SOMA

SOMA

Palace Hotel ◆
🅱 MONTGOMERY ST.

San Francisco Craft and Folk Art Museum ◆

🅱 POWELL ST.

Old U.S. Mint

Yerba Buena Square

Museum of Craft and Design →

Transbay Terminal

80
80

Union Square

Powell St.

KEY

🅱 Bart Stop

Asian Art Museum **8**
California Historical Society **7**
Cartoon Art Museum **6**
City Hall **9**

Contemporary Jewish Museum **1**
Museum of the African Diaspora **4**
San Francisco Museum of Modern Art **5**

Yerba Buena Center for the Arts **3**
Yerba Buena Gardens **2**

Begin on the third floor, where highlights of Buddhist art in Southeast Asia and early China include a large, jewel-encrusted, exquisitely painted 19th-century Burmese Buddha and clothed rod puppets from Java. On the second floor you can find later Chinese works, as well as pieces from Korea and Japan. The joy here is all in the details: on a whimsical Korean jar, look for a cobalt tiger jauntily smoking a pipe, or admire the delicacy of the Japanese tea implements. The ground floor is devoted to temporary exhibits, often traveling shows such as recent ones about Balinese art, and the transformation of yoga. ■TIP➜ For much of the year the museum stays open late on Thursday and hosts Matcha, an evening of cocktails, music, and activities related to current exhibitions. ✉ *200 Larkin St., between McAllister and Fulton Sts., Civic Center* ☎ *415/581–3500* ⊕ *www.asianart.org* 💲 *$12, free 1st Sun. of month; $10 Thurs. 5–9; tea ceremony $27, includes museum admission* ⊙ *Tues.–Sun. 10–5; Feb.–Oct., Thurs. until 9.*

City Hall. This imposing 1915 structure with its massive gold-leaf dome— higher than the U.S. Capitol's—is about as close to a palace as you're going to get in San Francisco. (Alas, the metal detectors detract from the grandeur.) The classic granite-and-marble behemoth was modeled after St. Peter's Basilica in Rome. Architect Arthur Brown Jr., who also designed Coit Tower and the War Memorial Opera House, designed an interior with grand columns and a sweeping central staircase. San Franciscans were thrilled, and probably a bit surprised, when his firm built City Hall in just a few years. The 1899 structure it replaced had taken 27 years to erect, as corrupt builders and politicians lined their pockets with funds earmarked for it. That building collapsed in about 27 seconds during the 1906 earthquake, revealing trash and newspapers mixed into the construction materials.

City Hall was spruced up and seismically retrofitted in the late 1990s, but the sense of history remains palpable. Some noteworthy events that have taken place here include the marriage of Marilyn Monroe and Joe DiMaggio (1954); the hosing—down the central staircase— of civil-rights and freedom-of-speech protesters (1960); the murders of Mayor George Moscone and openly gay supervisor Harvey Milk (1978); the torching of the lobby by angry members of the gay community in response to the light sentence given to the former supervisor who killed both men (1979); and the registrations of scores of gay couples in celebration of the passage of San Francisco's Domestic Partners Act (1991). February 2004 has come to be known as the Winter of Love: thousands of gay and lesbian couples responded to Mayor Gavin Newsom's decision to issue marriage licenses to same-sex partners, turning City Hall into the site of raucous celebration and joyful nuptials for a month before the state Supreme Court ordered the practice stopped. That celebratory scene replayed during 2008, when scores of couples were wed between the court's June ruling that everyone enjoys the civil right to marry and the November passage of California's ballot proposition banning same-sex marriage. In 2013, the U.S. Supreme Court resolved the issue, ruling against the proposition.

On display in the South Light Court are artifacts from the collection of the **Museum of the City of San Francisco** (⊕ *www.sfmuseum.org*), including maps, documents, and photographs. That enormous, 700-pound iron head once crowned the *Goddess of Progress* statue, which topped the old City Hall building until it crumbled during the 1906 earthquake. City Hall's centennial in 2013 kicked off three years of exhibits—the same amount of time it took to raise the building.

Across Polk Street from City Hall is **Civic Center Plaza,** with lawns, walkways, seasonal flower beds, a playground, and an underground parking garage. This sprawling space is generally clean but somewhat grim. A large part of the city's homeless population hangs out here, so the plaza can feel dodgy. ⊠ *Bordered by Van Ness Ave. and Polk, Grove, and McAllister Sts., Civic Center* ☎ *415/554–6023 recorded tour info* ⊕ *sfgsa.org/index.aspx?page=1172* ⊠ *Free* ☉ *Weekdays 8–8 except holidays; free tours weekdays at 10, noon, and 2.*

NOB HILL AND RUSSIAN HILL

In place of the quirky charm and cultural diversity that mark other San Francisco neighborhoods, Nob Hill exudes history and good breeding. Topped with some of the city's most elegant hotels, Gothic Grace Cathedral, and private blue-blood clubs, it's the pinnacle of privilege. One hill over, across Pacific Avenue, is another old-family bastion, Russian Hill. It may not be quite as wealthy as Nob Hill, but it's no slouch—and it's got jaw-dropping views.

NOB HILL

TOP ATTRACTIONS

FAMILY **Cable Car Museum.** One of the city's best free offerings, this museum is an absolute must for kids. You can even ride a cable car here—all three lines stop between Russian Hill and Nob Hill. The facility, which is inside the city's last cable-car barn, takes the top off the system to let you see how it all works. Eternally humming and squealing, the massive powerhouse cable wheels steal the show. You can also climb aboard a vintage car and take the grip, let the kids ring a cable-car bell (briefly), and check out vintage gear dating from 1873.

The gift shop sells cable-car paraphernalia, including an authentic gripman's bell for $600 (it'll sound like Powell Street in your house every day). For significantly less, you can pick up a key chain made from a piece of worn-out cable. ⊠ *1201 Mason St., at Washington St., Nob Hill* ☎ *415/474–1887* ⊕ *www.cablecarmuseum.org* ⊠ *Free* ☉ *Oct.–Mar., daily 10–5; Apr.–Sept., daily 10–6.*

Grace Cathedral. Not many churches can boast an altarpiece by Keith Haring and not one, but two labyrinths. The seat of the Episcopal Church in San Francisco, this soaring Gothic-style structure, erected on the site of the 19th-century railroad baron Charles Crocker's mansion, took 53 years to build, wrapping up in 1964. The gilded bronze doors at the east entrance were taken from casts of Lorenzo Ghiberti's incredible Gates of Paradise, which are on the Baptistery in Florence, Italy. A black-and-bronze stone sculpture of St. Francis by Beniamino Bufano greets you as you enter.

The 35-foot-wide limestone labyrinth is a replica of the 13th-century stone maze on the floor of Chartres Cathedral. All are encouraged to walk the ¼-mile-long labyrinth, a ritual based on the tradition of meditative walking. There's also a terrazzo outdoor labyrinth on the church's north side. The AIDS Interfaith Chapel, to the right as you enter Grace, contains a metal triptych by the late artist Keith Haring and panels from the AIDS Memorial Quilt. ■TIP→ **Especially dramatic times to view the cathedral are during Thursday-night evensong (5:15 pm) and during special holiday programs.** ⊠ *1100 California St., at Taylor St., Nob Hill* ☎ *415/749–6300* ⊕ *www.gracecathedral.org* ✉ *Free* ⊙ *Weekdays 7–6, Sat. 8–6, Sun. 8–7; tours weekdays at 1, Sat. at 11:30, and Sun. at 12:40.*

RUSSIAN HILL
TOP ATTRACTIONS

Fodor'sChoice
★
Ina Coolbrith Park. If you make it all the way up here, you may have the place all to yourself, or at least feel that you do. The park's terraces are carved from a hill so steep that it's difficult to see if anyone else is there or not. Locals love this park because it feels like a secret no one else knows about—one of the city's magic hidden gardens, with a meditative setting and spectacular views of the bay peeking out from among the trees. A poet, Oakland librarian, and niece of Mormon prophet Joseph Smith, Ina Coolbrith (1842–1928) introduced Jack London and Isadora Duncan to the world of books. For years she entertained literary greats in her Macondray Lane home near the park. In 1915 she was named poet laureate of California. ⊠ *Vallejo St. between Mason and Taylor Sts., Russian Hill.*

Lombard Street. The block-long "Crookedest Street in the World" makes eight switchbacks down the east face of Russian Hill between Hyde and Leavenworth streets. Residents bemoan the traffic jam outside their front doors, but the throngs continue. Join the line of cars waiting to drive down the steep hill, or avoid the whole mess and walk down the steps on either side of Lombard. You take in super views of North Beach and Coit Tower whether you walk or drive—though if you're the one behind the wheel, you'd better keep your eye on the road lest you become yet another of the many folks who ram the garden barriers. ■TIP→ **Can't stand the traffic? Thrill seekers of a different stripe may want to head two blocks south of Lombard to Filbert Street. At a gradient of 31.5%, the hair-raising descent between Hyde and Leavenworth streets is the city's steepest. Go slowly!** ⊠ *Lombard St. between Hyde and Leavenworth Sts., Russian Hill.*

Fodor'sChoice
★
Macondray Lane. San Francisco has no shortage of impressive, grand homes, but it's the tiny fairy-tale lanes that make most folks want to move here, and Macondray Lane is the quintessential hidden garden. Enter under a lovely wooden trellis and proceed down a quiet, cobbled pedestrian lane lined with Edwardian cottages and flowering plants and trees. Watch your step—the cobblestones are quite uneven in spots. A flight of steep wooden stairs at the end of the lane leads to Taylor Street—on the way down you can't miss the bay views. If you've read any of Armistead Maupin's *Tales of the City* books, you may find the lane vaguely familiar. It's the thinly disguised setting for part of the series' action. ⊠ *Between Jones and Taylor Sts., and Union and Green Sts., Russian Hill.*

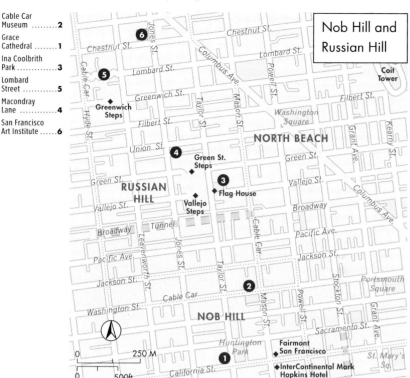

WORTH NOTING

San Francisco Art Institute. A Moorish-tile fountain in a tree-shaded court-yard draws the eye as soon as you enter the institute. The number-one reason for a visit is Mexican master Diego Rivera's *The Making of a Fresco Showing the Building of a City* (1931), in the student gallery to your immediate left inside the entrance. Rivera himself is in the fresco—his broad behind is to the viewer—and he's surrounded by his assistants. They in turn are surrounded by a construction scene, labor-ers, and city notables such as sculptor Robert Stackpole and architect Timothy Pfleuger. *Making* is one of three San Francisco murals painted by Rivera. The number-two reason to come here is the café, or more precisely the eye-popping, panoramic view from the café, which serves surprisingly decent food for a song.

The older portions of the Art Institute, including the lovely mission-style bell tower, were erected in 1926. To this day, otherwise pragmatic people claim that ghostly footsteps can be heard in the tower at night. Ansel Adams created the school's fine-arts photography department in 1946, and school directors established the country's first fine-arts film program. Notable faculty and alumni have included painter Richard Diebenkorn and photographers Dorothea Lange, Edward Weston, and Annie Leibovitz.

The **Walter & McBean Galleries** (☎ *415/749–4563* ⊙ *Open Tues. 11–7, Wed.–Sat. 11–6*) exhibit the often provocative works of established artists. ⊠ *800 Chestnut St., North Beach* ☎ *415/771–7020* ⊕ *www.sfai.edu* ⊠ *Galleries free* ⊙ *Hrs vary but building generally open Mon.–Sat. 9–7.*

NORTH BEACH

Italian bakeries appear frozen in time, homages to Jack Kerouac and Allen Ginsberg pop up everywhere, and strip joints, the modern equivalent of the Barbary Coast's "houses of ill repute," do business on Broadway. With its outdoor café tables, throngs of tourists, and holiday vibe, this is probably the part of town Europeans are thinking of when they say San Francisco is the most European city in America.

TOP ATTRACTIONS

Fodor'sChoice
★
City Lights Bookstore. Take a look at the exterior of the store: the replica of a revolutionary mural destroyed in Chiapas, Mexico, by military forces; the art banners hanging above the windows; and the sign that says "Turn your sell [sic] phone off. Be here now." This place isn't just doling out best sellers. Designated a city landmark, the hangout of Beat-era writers—Allen Ginsberg and store founder Lawrence Ferlinghetti among them—and independent publisher remains a vital part of San Francisco's literary scene. Browse the three levels of sometimes haphazardly arranged poetry, philosophy, politics, fiction, history, and local zines, to the tune of creaking wood floors. ■TIP→ Be sure to check the calendar of literary events.

Back in the day, the basement was a kind of literary living room, where writers like Ginsberg and Jack Kerouac would read and even receive mail. Ferlinghetti cemented City Lights' place in history by publishing Ginsberg's *Howl and Other Poems* in 1956. The small volume was ignored in the mainstream . . . until Ferlinghetti and the bookstore manager were arrested for obscenity and corruption of youth. In the landmark First Amendment trial that followed, the judge exonerated both men, declaring that a work that has "redeeming social significance" can't be obscene. *Howl* went on to become a classic.

Stroll Kerouac Alley, branching off Columbus Avenue next to City Lights, to read the quotes from Ferlinghetti, Maya Angelou, Confucius, John Steinbeck, and the street's namesake embedded in the pavement. ⊠ *261 Columbus Ave., North Beach* ☎ *415/362–8193* ⊕ *www. citylights.com* ⊙ *Daily 10 am–midnight.*

Coit Tower. Whether or not you agree that it resembles a fire-hose nozzle, this 210-foot tower is among San Francisco's most distinctive skyline sights. Although the monument wasn't intended as a tribute to firemen, it's often considered as such because of the donor's special attachment to the local fire company. As the story goes, a young gold rush–era girl, Lillie Hitchcock Coit (known as Miss Lil), was a fervent admirer of her local fire company—so much so that she once deserted a wedding party and chased down the street after her favorite engine, Knickerbocker No. 5, while clad in her bridesmaid finery.

Continued on page 393

CABLE CARS

The moment it dawns on you that you severely underestimated the steepness of the San Francisco hills will likely be the same moment you look down and realize those tracks aren't just for show—or just for tourists.

Sure, locals rarely use the cable cars for commuting these days. (That's partially due to the $6 fare—hear that, Muni?) So you'll likely be packed in with plenty of fellow sightseers. You may even be approaching cable-car fatigue after seeing its image on so many souvenirs. But if you fear the magic is gone, simply climb on board, and those jaded thoughts will dissolve. Grab the pole and gawk at the view as the car clanks down an insanely steep grade toward the bay. Listen to the humming cable, the clang of the bell, and the occasional quip from the gripman. It's an experience you shouldn't pass up, whether on your first trip or your fiftieth.

HOW CABLE CARS WORK

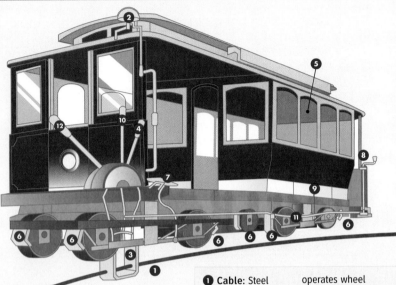

The mechanics are pretty simple: cable cars grab a moving subterranean cable with a "grip" to go. To stop, they release the grip and apply one or more types of brakes. Four cables, totaling 9 miles, power the city's three lines. If the gripman doesn't adjust the grip just right when going up a steep hill, the cable will start to slip and the car will start to back down the hill and try again. This is an extremely rare occurrence—imagine the ribbing the gripman gets back at the cable car barn!

Gripman: Stands in front and operates the grip, brakes, and bell. Favorite joke, especially at the peak of a steep hill: "This is my first day on the job folks…"

Conductor: Moves around the car, deals with tickets, alerts the grip about what's coming up, and operates the rear wheel brakes.

❶ Cable: Steel wrapped around flexible sisal core; 2 inches thick; runs at a constant 9½ mph.

❷ Bells: Used for crew communication; alerts other drivers and pedestrians.

❸ Grip: Vice-like lever extends through the center slot in the track to grab or release the cable.

❹ Grip Lever: Left-hand lever; operates grip.

❺ Car: Entire car weighs 8 tons.

❻ Wheel Brake: Steel brake pads on each wheel.

❼ Wheel Brake Lever: Foot pedal; operates wheel brakes.

❽ Rear Wheel Brake Lever: Applied for extra traction on hills.

❾ Track Brake: 2-foot-long sections of Monterey pine push down against the track to help stop the car.

❿ Track Brake Lever: Middle lever; operates track brakes.

⓫ Emergency Brake: 18-inch steel wedge, jams into street slot to bring car to an imme-diate stop.

⓬ Emergency Brake Lever: Right-hand lever, red; operates emergency brake.

ROUTES

Cars run at least every 15 minutes, from around 6 AM to about 1 AM.

Powell–Hyde line: Most scenic, with classic Bay views. Begins at Powell and Market streets, then crosses Nob Hill and Russian Hill before a white-knuckle descent down Hyde Street, ending near the Hyde Street Pier.

Powell–Mason line: Also begins at Powell and Market streets, but winds through North Beach to Bay and Taylor streets, a few blocks from Fisherman's Wharf.

California line: Runs from the foot of Market Street, at Drumm Street, up Nob Hill and back. Great views (and aromas and sounds) of Chinatown on the way up. Sit in back to catch glimpses of the Bay. ■TIP→ Take the California line if it's just the cable-car experience you're after—the lines are shorter, and the grips and conductors say it's friendlier and has a slower pace.

RULES OF THE RIDE

Tickets. A whopping $6 each way. There are ticket booths at all three turnarounds, or you can pay the conductor after you board (they can make change). Try not to grumble about the price—they're embarrassed enough as it is.

■TIP→ If you're planning to use public transit a few times, or if you'd like to ride back and forth on the cable car without worrying about the price, consider a one-day Muni passport ($14). You can get passports online, at the Powell Street turnaround, at the TIX booth on Union Square, or the Fisherman's Wharf cable-car ticket booth at Beach and Hyde streets.

All Aboard. You can board on either side of the cable car. It's legal to stand on the running boards and hang on to the pole, but keep your ears open for the gripman's warnings. ■TIP→ Grab a seat on the outside bench for the best views.

Most people wait (and wait) in line at one of the cable car turnarounds, but you can also hop on along the route. Board wherever you see a white sign showing a figure climbing aboard a brown cable car; wave to the approaching driver, and wait until the car stops.

Riding on the running boards can be part of the thrill.

CABLE CAR HISTORY

HALLIDIE FREES THE HORSES

In the 1850s and '60s, San Francisco's streetcars were drawn by horses. Legend has it that the horrible sight of a car dragging a team of horses downhill to their deaths roused Andrew Smith Hallidie to action. The English immigrant had invented the "Hallidie Ropeway," essentially a cable car for mined ore, and he was convinced that his invention could also move people. In 1873, Hallidie and his intrepid crew prepared to test the first cable car high on Russian Hill. The anxious engineer peered down into the foggy darkness, failed to see the bottom of the hill, and promptly turned the controls over to Hallidie. Needless to say, the thing worked . . . but rides were free for the first two days because people were afraid to get on.

SEE IT FOR YOURSELF

The **Cable Car Museum** is one of the city's best free offerings and an absolute must for kids. (You can even ride a cable car there, since all three lines stop between Russian Hill and Nob Hill.) The museum, which is inside the city's last cable-car barn, takes the top off the system to let you see how it all works.

Eternally humming and squealing, the massive powerhouse cable wheels steal the show. You can also climb aboard a vintage car and take the grip, let the kids ring a cable-car bell (briefly, please!), and check out vintage gear dating from 1873.

✉ *1201 Mason St., at Washington St., Nob Hill* ☎ *415/474–1887* ⊕ *www. cablecarmuseum.com* ✉ *Free* ⊙ *Oct.– Mar., daily 10–5; Apr.–Sept., daily 10–6*

■ TIP→ The gift shop sells cable car paraphernalia, including an authentic gripman's bell for $600 (it'll sound like Powell Street in your house every day). For significantly less, you can pick up a key chain made from a piece of worn-out cable.

CHAMPION OF THE CABLE CAR BELL

Each September the city's best and brightest come together to crown a bell-ringing champion at Union Square. The crowd cheers gripmen and conductors as they stomp, shake, and riff with the rope. But it's not a popularity contest; the ringers are judged by former bell-ringing champions who take each ping and gong very seriously.

CLOSE UP

The Birds

While on Telegraph Hill, you might be startled by a chorus of piercing squawks and a rushing sound of wings. No, you're not about to have a Hitchcock bird-attack moment. These small, vivid green parrots with cherry red heads number in the hundreds; they're descendants of former pets that escaped or were released by their owners. (The birds dislike cages, and they bite if bothered . . . must've been some disillusioned owners along the way.)

The parrots like to roost high in the aging cypress trees on the hill, chattering and fluttering, sometimes taking wing en masse. They're not popular with some residents, but they did find a champion in local bohemian Mark Bittner, a former street musician. Bittner began chronicling their habits, publishing a book and battling the homeowners who wanted to cut down the cypresses. A documentary, *The Wild Parrots of Telegraph Hill*, made the issue a cause célèbre. In 2007 City Hall, which recognizes a golden goose when it sees one, stepped in and brokered a solution to keep the celebrity birds in town. The city would cover the homeowners' insurance worries and plant new trees for the next generation of wild parrots.

She became the Knickerbocker Company's mascot and always signed her name "Lillie Coit 5." When Lillie died in 1929 she left the city $125,000 to "expend in an appropriate manner . . . to the beauty of San Francisco."

You can ride the elevator to the top of the tower—the only thing you have to pay for here—to enjoy the view of the Bay Bridge and the Golden Gate Bridge; due north is Alcatraz Island. Most visitors saunter right past the 19 fabulous Depression-era murals inside the tower that depict California's economic and political life, but take the time to appreciate the first New Deal art project supported by taxpayer money. The federal government commissioned the paintings from 25 local artists, and ended up funding a controversy. The radical Mexican painter Diego Rivera inspired the murals' socialist-realist style, with its biting cultural commentary, particularly about the exploitation of workers. At the time the murals were painted, clashes between management and labor along the waterfront and elsewhere in San Francisco were widespread. The elements, the thousands of visitors that pass by them every year, and the lack of climate control in the tower have taken their toll on the murals, but restoration work done on the tower in 2013 should help protect them. ■TIP→ The views from the tower's base are also expansive—and free. Parking at Coit Tower is limited; in fact, you may have to wait (and wait) for a space. Spare yourself the frustration and hike up, if you're in good shape, or take the 39 bus. ⊠ *Telegraph Hill Blvd. at Greenwich St. or Lombard St., North Beach* ☎ *415/362–0808* ⊒ *Free; elevator to top $7* ⊗ *Mar.–Sept., daily 10–5:30; Oct.–Feb., daily 9–4:30.*

Grant Avenue. Originally called Calle de la Fundación, Grant Avenue is the oldest street in the city, but it's got plenty of young blood. Here dusty bars such as the Saloon and perennial favorites like the Savoy

394 < **San Francisco**

Tivoli mix with hotshot boutiques, odd curio shops like the antique jumble that is Aria, atmospheric cafés such as the boho haven Caffè Trieste, and authentic Italian delis. While the street runs from Union Square through Chinatown, North Beach, and beyond, the fun stuff in this neighborhood is crowded into the four blocks between Columbus Avenue and Filbert Street. ⊠ *North Beach.*

Fodor'sChoice **Telegraph Hill.** Residents here have some of the city's best views, as well
★ as the most difficult ascents to their aeries. The hill rises from the east end of Lombard Street to a height of 284 feet and is capped by Coit Tower (*see above*). Imagine lugging your groceries up that! If you brave the slope, though, you can be rewarded with a "secret treasure" San Francisco moment. Filbert Street starts up the hill, then becomes the **Filbert Steps** when the going gets too steep. You can cut between the Filbert Steps and another flight, the **Greenwich Steps,** on up to the hilltop. As you climb, you can pass some of the city's oldest houses and be surrounded by beautiful, flowering private gardens. In some places the trees grow over the stairs so it feels as if you're walking through a green tunnel; elsewhere, you'll have wide-open views of the bay. And the telegraphic name? It comes from the hill's status as the first Morse code signal station back in 1853. ⊠ *Bordered by Lombard, Filbert, Kearny, and Sansome Sts., North Beach.*

Washington Square. Once the daytime social heart of Little Italy, this grassy patch has changed character numerous times over the years. The Beats hung out here in the 1950s, hippies camped out in the 1960s and early '70s, and nowadays you're more likely to see kids of Southeast Asian descent tossing a Frisbee than Italian folks reminiscing about the old country. In the morning, elderly Asians perform the motions of tai chi. Then and later you might see homeless people hanging out on the benches, and by midday young locals sunbathing or running their dogs. Lillie Hitchcock Coit, in yet another show of affection for San Francisco's firefighters, donated the statue of two firemen with a child they rescued. ■ TIP→ The North Beach Festival, the city's oldest street fair, celebrates the area's Italian culture here each June. ⊠ *Bordered by Columbus Ave. and Stockton, Filbert, and Union Sts., North Beach.*

WORTH NOTING

Beat Museum. This two-level museum is likely to see an uptick in visitors in response to the 2012 film version of *On the Road*, whose director donated the 1949 Hudson from the movie. Check out exhibits such as the *Beat Pad*, a mock-up of one of the cheap, tiny North Beach apartments the writers and artists populated in the 1950s, complete with bongos and bottle-as-candleholder. Memorabilia include the shirt Neal Cassady wore while driving Ken Kesey's Merry Prankster bus, "Further." An early photo of the legendary bus is juxtaposed with a more current picture showing it covered with moss and overgrowth, labeled "Nothing lasts." Indeed. There are also manuscripts, letters, and early editions by Jack Kerouac, Allen Ginsberg, and Lawrence Ferlinghetti. The gift store has a good selection of Beat philosophy, though it's nothing you won't find across the street at City Lights. ⊠ *540 Broadway, North Beach* ☎ *415/399–9626* ⊕ *www.thebeatmuseum.org* 🖃 *$8* ⊙ *Daily 10–7.*

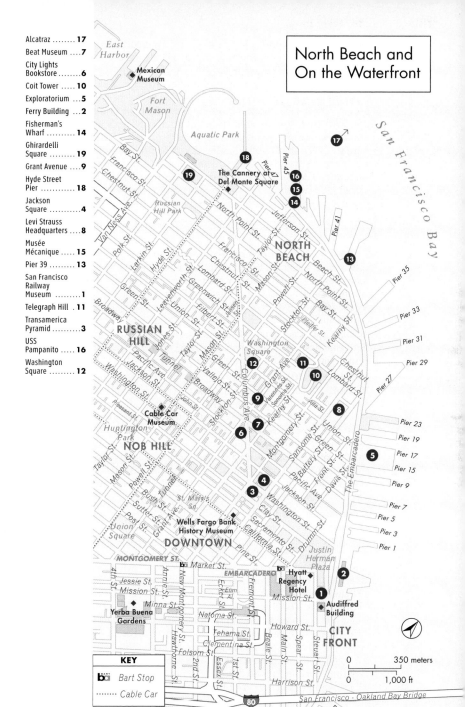

East
Harbor

Mexican
Museum

North Beach and
On the Waterfront

Fort
Mason

Aquatic Park

San Francisco Bay

Bay St.

Francisco St.

Chestnut St.

Russian
Hill Park

The Cannery at
Del Monte Square

Pier 45

Pier 41

North Point St.

**NORTH
BEACH**

Jefferson St.

Beach St.

Pier 35

Francisco St.

Chestnut St.

Lombard St.

Taylor St.

Mason St.

Powell St.

North Point St.

Bay St.

Stockton St.

Pfeiffer St.

Kearny St.

Pier 33

Pier 31

Pier 29

Van Ness Ave.

Polk St.

Larkin St.

Hyde St.

Leavenworth St.

Greenwich St.

Filbert St.

Union St.

Green St.

Broadway

**RUSSIAN
HILL**

Jones St.

Taylor St.

Mason St.

Green St.

Washington
Square

Grant Ave.

Vallejo St.

Columbus Ave.

Varennes St.

Sonoma St.

Alta St.

Chestnut St.

Lombard St.

Pier 27

Tunnel

Pacific Ave.

Jackson St.

Washington St.

Pleasant St.

Huntington
Park

Cable Car
Museum

Stockton St.

Broadway

John St.

Kearny St.

Montgomery St.

Sansome St.

Green St.

Front St.

Union St.

The Embarcadero

Pier 23

Pier 19

NOB HILL

Taylor St.

Mason St.

Powell St.

St. Mary's
Sq.

Pacific Ave.

Battery St.

Davis St.

Pier 17

Pier 15

Pier 9

Tunnel

Bush St.

Sutter St.

Grant Ave.

Wells Fargo Bank
History Museum

Jackson St.

Clay St.

Washington St.

Pier 7

Pier 5

Post St.

Union
Square

Sacramento St.

California St.

Drumm St.

Pier 3

Pier 1

DOWNTOWN

Pine St.

Justin
Herman
Plaza

MONTGOMERY ST.

Market St.

EMBARCADERO

Hyatt
Regency
Hotel

4th St.

Jessie St.

Mission St.

Annie St.

New Montgomery St.

Ecker St.

Elim
Al.

Fremont St.

Mission St.

Audiffred
Building

**CITY
FRONT**

Minna St.

Yerba Buena
Gardens

Natoma St.

Hawthorne St.

Tehama St.

Clementina St.

Folsom St.

2nd St.

1st St.

Essex St.

Beale St.

Main St.

Spear St.

Howard St.

Steuart St.

0   350 meters

0   1,000 ft

KEY	
🚇	*Bart Stop*
......	*Cable Car*

80

Taber Pl.

Bryant St.

Harrison St.

San Francisco - Oakland Bay Bridge

Pier 26

Levi Strauss headquarters. The carefully landscaped complex appears so collegiate that it's affectionately known as LSU—short for Levi Strauss University. Lawns complement the redbrick buildings, and gurgling fountains drown out the sounds of traffic, providing a perfect environment for brown-bag and picnic lunches. The Vault, the lobby exhibition space, has displays focusing on the history of the company, including jeans that saw the gold rush, videos about Levi's marketing and textile restoration, and temporary displays such as decades' worth of vintage Levi's shirts on a rotating dry-cleaner's rack. ■TIP➜ You can purchase Levi's and Dockers straight from the source at the cozy lobby boutique. The wonderful Filbert Steps to Coit Tower are across the street. ⊠ *Levi's Plaza, 1155 Battery St., North Beach* ☎ *415/501–6000* ⊕ *www.levistrauss.com* ⊙ *Weekdays 9–6, weekends noon–5.*

ON THE WATERFRONT

San Francisco's waterfront neighborhoods have fabulous views and utterly different personalities. Kitschy, overpriced Fisherman's Wharf struggles to maintain the last shreds of its existence as a working wharf, while Pier 39 is a full-fledged consumer circus. The Ferry Building draws well-heeled locals with its culinary pleasures, firmly reconnecting the Embarcadero to downtown. Between the Ferry Building and Pier 39 a former maritime no-man's-land is filling in with the recently relocated Exploratorium, a $90 million cruise-ship terminal, Alcatraz Landing, fashionable waterfront restaurants, and restored, pedestrian-friendly piers.

TOP ATTRACTIONS

Alcatraz. Thousands of visitors come every day to walk in the footsteps of Alcatraz's notorious criminals. The stories of life and death on "The Rock" may sometimes be exaggerated, but it's almost impossible to resist the chance to wander the cellblock that tamed the country's toughest gangsters and saw daring escape attempts of tremendous desperation. Fewer than 2,000 inmates ever did time on the Rock, and though they weren't the worst criminals, they were definitely the worst prisoners, include Al "Scarface" Capone, Robert "The Birdman" Stroud, and George "Machine Gun" Kelly.

Some tips for escaping to Alcatraz: 1) Buy your ticket in advance. Visit the website for Alcatraz Cruises (⊕ *www.alcatrazcruises.com*) to scout out available departure times for the ferry. Prepay by credit card and keep a receipt record; the ticket price covers the boat ride and the audio tour. Pick up your ticket at the "will call" window at Pier 33 up to an hour before sailing. 2) Dress smart. Bring a jacket to ward off the chill from the boat ride and wear comfortable shoes. 3) Go for the evening tour. You'll get even more out of your Alcatraz experience at night. The evening tour has programs not offered during the day, the bridge-to-bridge view of the city twinkles at night, and your "prison experience" will be amplified as darkness falls. 4) Be mindful of scheduled and limited-capacity talks. Some programs are only given once a day (the schedule is posted in the cell house) and have limited seating, so keep an eye out for a cell-house staffer handing out passes shortly before the start time.

Thousands of visitors take ferries to Alcatraz each day to walk in the footsteps of the notorious criminals who were held on "The Rock."

The boat ride to the island is brief (15 minutes), but affords beautiful views of the city, Marin County, and the East Bay. The audio tour, highly recommended, includes observations by guards and prisoners about life in one of America's most notorious penal colonies. Plan your schedule to allow at least three hours for the visit and boat rides combined. Not inspired by the prison? Wander around the lovely native plant gardens and (if the tide is cooperating) the tide pools on the north side of the island. ⊠ *Pier 33, Embarcadero* ☎ *415/981–7625* ⊕ *www.nps.gov/alca* 🎫 *$30, including audio tour; $37 evening tour, including audio* ⊘ *Ferry departs every 30–45 mins Sept.–late May, daily 9:30–2:15, 4:20 for evening tour Thurs.–Mon. only; late May–Aug., daily 9:30–4:15, 6:30 and 7:30 for evening tour.*

The Bay Lights. Adored by romance seekers, local families, and tourists alike, installation artist Leo Villareal's jaw-dropping LED light sculpture on the San Francisco–Oakland Bay Bridge has become an iconic San Francisco experience. As you travel west into the city along the bridge's upper deck you can view the sculpture's 25,000 lights dancing across its western span, but this installation is best seen from the Embarcadero. As of this writing, the Bay Lights was slated to end in March 2015, but locals are rallying for it to become permanent. ⊠ *Embarcadero* ⊕ *the-baylights.org.*

FAMILY
Fodor's Choice
★

Exploratorium. Walking into this fascinating "museum of science, art, and human perception" is like visiting a mad scientist's laboratory. Most of the exhibits are supersize, and you can play with everything. After moving into larger digs on the Embarcadero in 2013, the Exploratorium has even more space for its signature experiential exhibits, including a brand-new Tinkering Studio and a glass Bay Observatory building, where the exhibits inside help visitors better understand what they see outside.

Quintessential exhibits remain: Get an *Alice in Wonderland* feeling in the distortion room, where you seem to shrink and grow as you walk across the slanted, checkered floor. In the shadow room, a powerful flash freezes an image of your shadow on the wall; jumping is a favorite pose. *Pushover* demonstrates cow-tipping, but for people: stand on one foot and try to keep your balance while a friend swings a striped panel in front of you (trust us, you're going to fall).

More than 650 other exhibits focus on sea and insect life, computers, electricity, patterns and light, language, the weather, and more. "Explainers"—usually high-school students on their days off—demonstrate cool scientific tools and procedures, like DNA sample-collection and cow-eye dissection. One surefire hit is the pitch-black, touchy-feely Tactile Dome ($15 extra; reservations required). In this geodesic dome strewn with textured objects, you crawl through a course of ladders, slides, and tunnels, relying solely on your sense of touch. Lovey-dovey couples sometimes linger in the "grope dome," but be forewarned: the staff will turn on the lights if necessary. ■TIP➔ Patrons must be at least seven years old to enter the Tactile Dome, and the space is not for the claustrophobic. ⊠ *Piers 15–17, Embarcadero* ☎ *415/561–0360 general information, 415/561–0362 Tactile Dome reservations* ⊕ *www. exploratorium.edu* ▨ *$25* ☉ *Tues. and Thurs.–Sun. 10–5, Wed. 10–10; Thurs. 6 pm–10 pm ages 18 and over only.*

F-line. The city's system of vintage electric trolleys, the F-line, gives the cable cars a run for their money as a beloved mode of transportation. The beautifully restored streetcars—some dating from the 19th century—run from the Castro District down Market Street to the Embarcadero, then north to Fisherman's Wharf. Each car is unique, restored to the colors of its city of origin, from New Orleans and Philadelphia to Moscow and Milan. ■TIP➔ Purchase tickets on board; exact change is required. ⊕ *www.streetcar.org* ▨ *$2.*

Fodor'sChoice ★ **Ferry Building.** The jewel of the Embarcadero, erected in 1896, is topped by a 230-foot clock tower modeled after the campanile of the cathedral in Seville, Spain. On the morning of April 18, 1906, the tower's four clock faces, powered by the swinging of a 14-foot pendulum, stopped at 5:17—the moment the great earthquake struck—and stayed still for 12 months.

Today San Franciscans flock to the street-level marketplace, stocking up on supplies from local favorites such as Acme Bread, Scharffen Berger Chocolate, Cowgirl Creamery, and Blue Bottle Coffee. Lucky diners claim a coveted table at Slanted Door, the beloved high-end Vietnamese restaurant. The seafood bar at Hog Island Oyster Company has fantastic bay-view panoramas, including the Bay Bridge. On Saturday morning the plazas outside the building buzz with an upscale farmers' market where you can buy exotic sandwiches and other munchables. Extending south from the piers north of the building all the way to the Bay Bridge, the waterfront promenade out front is a favorite among joggers and picnickers, with a front-row view of sailboats plying the bay.

True to its name the Ferry Building still serves actual ferries: from its eastern flank they sail to Sausalito, Larkspur, Tiburon, and the East Bay. ✉ *Embarcadero at foot of Market St., Embarcadero* ☎ *415/983–8030* ⊕ *www.ferrybuildingmarketplace.com.*

QUICK BITES

Buena Vista Café. At the end of the Hyde Street cable-car line, the Buena Vista packs 'em in for its famous Irish coffee—which, according to owners, was the first served stateside (in 1952). The place oozes nostalgia, drawing devoted locals as well as out-of-towners relaxing after a day of sightseeing. It's narrow and can get crowded, but this spot provides a fine alternative to the overpriced tourist joints nearby. ✉ 2765 Hyde St., at Beach St., Fisherman's Wharf ☎ 415/474–5044 ⊕ www.thebuenavista.com.

FAMILY
Fodor'sChoice
★

Hyde Street Pier. Cotton candy and souvenirs are all well and good, but if you want to get to the heart of the Wharf—boats—there's no better place to do it than at this pier, one of the Wharf area's best bargains. Depending on the time of day, you might see boatbuilders at work or children pretending to man an early-1900s ship.

Don't pass up the centerpiece collection of historic vessels, part of the **San Francisco Maritime National Historic Park,** almost all of which can be boarded. The *Balclutha,* an 1886 full-rigged three-masted sailing vessel that's more than 250 feet long, sailed around Cape Horn 17 times. Kids especially love the *Eureka,* a side-wheel passenger and car ferry, for her onboard collection of vintage cars. The *Hercules* is a steam-powered tugboat. The *C.A. Thayer,* a three-masted schooner, recently underwent a painstaking restoration.

Across the street from the pier and almost a museum in itself is the maritime park's **Visitor Center** (✉ *499 Jefferson St.* ☎ *415/447–5000* ☉ *June–Aug., daily 9:30–5:30; Sept.–May, daily 9:30–5*), whose fun, large-scale exhibits, such as a huge First Order Fresnel lighthouse lens and a shipwrecked boat, make it an engaging quick stop. ✉ *Hyde and Jefferson Sts., Fisherman's Wharf* ☎ *415/561–7100* ⊕ *www.nps.gov/safr* 🚢 *Ships $5 (ticket good for five days)* ☉ *June–Aug., daily 9:30–5:30; Sept.–May, daily 9:30–5.*

Jackson Square Historic District. This was the heart of the Barbary Coast of the Gay Nineties—the 1890s, that is. Although most of the red-light district was destroyed in the fire that followed the 1906 earthquake, the remaining old redbrick buildings, many of them now occupied by advertising agencies, law offices, and antiques firms, retain hints of the romance and rowdiness of San Francisco's early days.

With its gentrified gold rush–era buildings, the 700 block of **Montgomery Street** just barely evokes the Barbary Coast days, but this was a colorful block in 19th century and on into the 20th. Writers Mark Twain and Bret Harte were among the contributors to the spunky *Golden Era* newspaper, which occupied No. 732 (now part of the building at No. 744). From 1959 to 1996 the late ambulance-chaser extraordinaire, lawyer Melvin Belli, had his headquarters at Nos. 722 and 728–730. There was never a dull moment in Belli's world; he represented clients from the actress Mae West to Gloria Sykes (who in 1964 claimed that a cable-car accident turned her into a nymphomaniac) to the disgraced

8

televangelists Jim and Tammy Faye Bakker. Whenever he won a case, he fired a cannon and raised the Jolly Roger. Belli was also known for receiving a letter from the never-caught Zodiac killer.

Restored 19th-century brick buildings line Hotaling Place, which connects Washington and Jackson streets. The lane is named for the head of the **A.P. Hotaling Company whiskey distillery** (⊠ *451 Jackson St., at Hotaling Pl.*), the largest liquor repository on the West Coast in its day. (Anchor Distillery still makes an occasional Hotaling whiskey in the city, by the way; look for this single malt for a sip of truly local flavor.) ■ TIP→ The exceptional City Guides (☎ 415/557–4266 ⊕ www.sfcityguides.org) Gold Rush City walking tour covers this area and brings its history to life. ⊠ *Bordered by Columbus Ave., Broadway and Pacific Ave., Washington St., and Sansome St., Jackson Square.*

FAMILY **Musée Mécanique.** A time-warped arcade with antique mechanical contrivances, including peep shows and nickelodeons, Musée Mécanique is one of the most worthwhile attractions at the Wharf. Some favorites are the giant and rather creepy Laffing Sal, an arm-wrestling machine, the world's only steam-powered motorcycle, and mechanical fortune-telling figures that speak from their curtained boxes. Note the depictions of race that betray the prejudices of the time: stoned Chinese figures in the Opium-Den and clown-faced African Americans eating watermelon in the Mechanical Farm. ■ TIP→ Admission is free, but you'll need quarters to bring the machines to life. ⊠ *Pier 45 Shed A, Fisherman's Wharf* ☎ 415/346–2000 ⊕ *www.museemechanique.org* 🎫 *Free* ☉ *Weekdays 10–7, weekends 10–8.*

FAMILY **Pier 39.** The city's most popular waterfront attraction draws millions of visitors each year who come to browse through its shops and concessions hawking every conceivable form of souvenir. The pier can be quite crowded, and the numerous street performers may leave you feeling more harassed than entertained. Arriving early in the morning ensures you a front-row view of the sea lions that bask here, but if you're here to shop—and make no mistake about it, Pier 39 wants your money—be aware that most stores don't open until 9:30 or 10 (later in winter).

Brilliant colors enliven the double-decker **San Francisco Carousel** (🎫 *$3 per ride*), decorated with images of such city landmarks as the Golden Gate Bridge and Lombard Street.

Follow the sound of barking to the northwest side of the pier to view the **sea lions** that flop about the floating docks. During the summer, orange-clad naturalists answer questions and offer fascinating facts about the playful pinnipeds—for example, that all the animals here are males.

At the **Aquarium of the Bay** (☎ *415/623–5300 or 888/732–3483* ⊕ *www.aquariumofthebay.org* 🎫 *$19.95* ☉ *Hours vary but at least 10–6 daily*) moving walkways transport you through a space surrounded on three sides by water filled with indigenous San Francisco Bay marine life, from fish and plankton to sharks. Many find the aquarium overpriced; if you can, take advantage of the family rate (🎫 *$64 for two adults and two kids under 12*).

The **California Welcome Center** (☎ *415/981–1280* ⊕ *www.visitcwc. com* ☉ *Daily 9–7*), on Pier 39's second level, can help you reserve tours and plan your time in the city.

Parking is across the street at the **Pier 39 Garage** (📖 *With validation from a Pier 39 restaurant, one hour free before 6 pm, two hours after 6 pm*), off Powell Street at the Embarcadero. ✉ *Beach St. at Embarcadero, Fisherman's Wharf* ⊕ *www.pier39.com.*

WORTH NOTING

FAMILY **Fisherman's Wharf.** It may be one of the city's best-known attractions, but the Wharf is a no-go zone for most locals, who shy away from the tourist crowds, overpriced food, and cheesy shops. If you can't resist a visit, come early to avoid the crowds and get a sense of the Wharf's functional role—it's not just an amusement park replica. Two delights amid the tackiness, both at Pier 45, are the ⇨ *Museé Mécanique*, a repository of old-fashioned but still working penny-arcade entertainments, and the World War II–era sub the ⇨ *USS Pampanito.* ✉ *Jefferson St. between Leavenworth St. and Pier 39, Fisherman's Wharf* ⊕ *www.fishermanswharf.org*

Ghirardelli Square. Most of the redbrick buildings in this early-20th-century complex were once part of the Ghirardelli factory. Now tourists come here to pick up the famous chocolate, though you can purchase it all over town and save yourself a trip to what is essentially a mall. But this is the only place to watch the cool chocolate manufactory in action. Placards throughout the square describe the factory's history. ✉ *900 North Point St., Fisherman's Wharf* 📞 *415/775–5500* ⊕ *www.ghirardellisq.com.*

USS Pampanito. Get an intriguing, if mildly claustrophobic, glimpse into life on a submarine during World War II on this sub, which sank six Japanese warships and damaged four others. ✉ *Pier 45, Fisherman's Wharf* 📞 *415/775–1943* ⊕ *www.maritime.org/pamphome.htm* 🎟 *$12 (family pass $25)* 🕐 *Oct.–late May, Sun.–Thurs. 9–6, Fri. and Sat. 9–8; late May–Sept., Thurs.–Tues. 9–8, Wed. 9–6.*

FAMILY **San Francisco Railway Museum.** A labor of love brought to you by the same vintage-transit enthusiasts responsible for the F-line's revival, this one-room museum and store celebrates the city's streetcars and cable cars with photographs, models, and artifacts. The permanent exhibit includes the replicated end of a streetcar with a working cab—complete with controls and a bell—for kids to explore; the cool, antique Wiley birdcage traffic signal; and models and display cases to view. Right on the F-line track, just across from the Ferry Building, this is a great quick stop. ✉ *77 Steuart St., Embarcadero* 📞 *415/974–1948* ⊕ *www.streetcar. org* 🎟 *Free* 🕐 *Tues.–Sun. 10–6.*

Transamerica Pyramid. It's neither owned by Transamerica nor is it a pyramid, but this 853-foot-tall obelisk *is* the most photographed of the city's high-rises. Excoriated in the design stages as "the world's largest architectural folly," the icon was quickly hailed as a masterpiece when it opened in 1972. Today it's probably the city's most recognized structure after the Golden Gate Bridge. Visit the small, street-level visitor center to see the virtual view from the top, watch videos about the building's history, and perhaps pick up a T-shirt. ■**TIP**➔ **A fragrant redwood grove along the east side of the building, replete with benches and a cheerful fountain, is a placid patch in which to unwind.** ✉ *600 Montgomery St., Financial District* ⊕ *www.thepyramidcenter.com.*

8

THE MARINA, COW HOLLOW, AND THE PRESIDIO

Yachts bob at their moorings, satisfied-looking folks jog along the Marina Green, and multimillion-dollar homes overlook the bay in the picturesque, if somewhat sterile, Marina neighborhood. Does it all seem a bit too perfect? Well, it got this way after the hard knock of Loma Prieta—the current pretty face was put on after hundreds of homes collapsed in the 1989 earthquake. Between the Marina and old-money Pacific Heights lies comfortably upscale Cow Hollow. The neighborhood's name harks back to the 19th-century dairy farms whose owners eked out a living here despite the fact that there was more sand than grass. To get a feel for this accessible bastion of affluence, stroll down Union Street. Just west of Cow Hollow and the Marina stands the Presidio. Once a military base, this sprawling beauty is mostly green space, with hills, woods, and the marshlands of Crissy Field.

THE MARINA

TOP ATTRACTIONS

Fodor's Choice **Palace of Fine Arts.** At first glance this stunning, rosy rococo palace seems
★ to be from another world, and indeed, it's the sole survivor of the many tinted-plaster structures (a temporary classical city of sorts) built for the 1915 Panama-Pacific International Exposition, the world's fair that celebrated San Francisco's recovery from the 1906 earthquake and fire. The expo buildings originally extended about a mile along the shore. Bernard Maybeck designed this faux–Roman classic beauty, which was reconstructed in concrete and reopened in 1967. A victim of the elements, the Palace required a piece-by-piece renovation that was completed in 2008.

The pseudo-Latin language adorning the Palace's exterior urns continues to stump scholars. The massive columns (each topped with four "weeping maidens"), great rotunda, and swan-filled lagoon have been used in countless fashion layouts, films, and wedding photo shoots. After admiring the lagoon, look across the street to the house at 3460 Baker Street. If the maidens out front look familiar, they should—they're original casts of the "garland ladies" you can see in the Palace's colonnade.

Inside the palace is a performance venue favored by local community groups and international musicians. ⊠ *3301 Lyon St., at Beach St., Marina* ☎ *415/561–0364 Palace history tours* ⊕ *www.palaceoffinearts. org* ⊠ *Free* ⊗ *Daily 24 hrs.*

COW HOLLOW

WORTH NOTING

Octagon House. This eight-sided home sits across the street from its original site on Gough Street; it's one of two remaining octagonal houses in the city (the other is on Russian Hill), and the only one open to the public. White quoins accent each of the eight corners of the pretty blue-gray exterior, and a colonial-style garden completes the picture. The house is full of antique American furniture, decorative arts (paintings, silver, rugs), and documents from the 18th and 19th centuries. A deck of Revolutionary-era hand-painted playing cards takes an antimonarchist position: in place of kings, queens, and jacks, the American upstarts

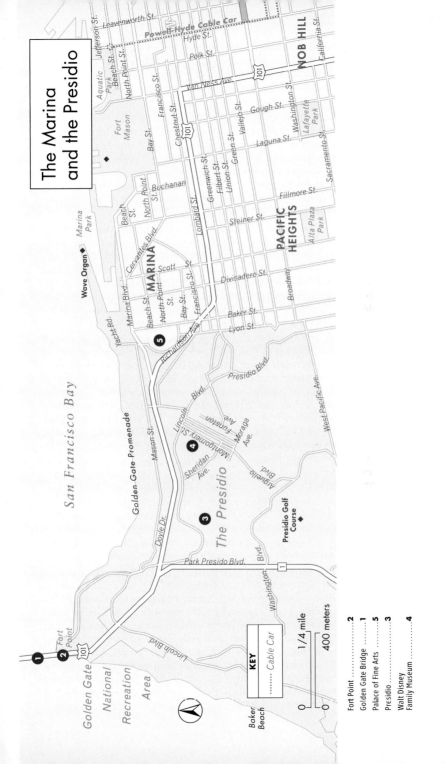

The Marina
and the Presidio

San Francisco Bay

Golden Gate
National
Recreation
Area

MARINA

**PACIFIC
HEIGHTS**

NOB HILL

The Presidio

Presidio Golf
Course

Baker
Beach

Wave Organ ◆

Marina
Park

Fort Mason

Aquatic
Park

Lafayette
Park

Alta Plaza
Park

Fort
Point

Golden Gate Promenade

Powell-Hyde Cable Car

Leavenworth St.

Jefferson St.

Hyde St.

Beach St.

North Point St.

Polk St.

Francisco St.

Van Ness Ave.

Chestnut St.

Bay St.

Gough St.

Vallejo St.

Green St.

Laguna St.

Washington St.

Sacramento St.

California St.

Buchanan

Greenwich St.

Filbert St.

Union St.

Fillmore St.

Steiner St.

Lombard St.

Cervantes Blvd.

Scott St.

Divisadero St.

Broadway

Baker St.

Lyon St.

Marina Blvd.

Beach St.

North Point St.

Bay St.

Francisco St.

Richardson Ave.

Presidio Blvd.

West Pacific Ave.

Lincoln Blvd.

Funston Ave.

Montgomery St.

Moraga Ave.

Arguello Blvd.

Sheridan Ave.

Mason St.

Doyle Dr.

Park Presido Blvd.

Blvd.

Washington

Lincoln Blvd.

Fort Point

Yacht Rd.

KEY
──── Cable Car

0 ────── 1/4 mile
0 ────── 400 meters

Fort Point **2**
Golden Gate Bridge **1**
Palace of Fine Arts **5**
Presidio **3**
Walt Disney
Family Museum **4**

substituted American statesmen, Roman goddesses, and Indian chiefs. ✉ *2645 Gough St., near Union St., Cow Hollow* ☎ *415/441–7512* 📠 *Free, donations encouraged* ☉ *Feb.–Dec., 2nd Sun. and 2nd and 4th Thurs. of month noon–3; group tours weekdays by appointment.*

THE PRESIDIO

TOP ATTRACTIONS

Fodor'sChoice
★

Golden Gate Bridge. With its simple but powerful art deco design, the 1.7-mile suspension span that connects San Francisco and Marin County was built to withstand winds of more than 100 mph. It's also not a bad place to be in an earthquake: designed to sway almost 28 feet, the Golden Gate Bridge (unlike the Bay Bridge) was undamaged by the 1989 Loma Prieta quake. If you're on the bridge when it's windy, stand still and you can feel it swaying a bit.

Crossing the Golden Gate Bridge under your own power is exhilarating—a little scary, and definitely chilly. From the bridge's eastern-side walkway, the only side pedestrians are allowed on, you can take in the San Francisco skyline and the bay islands; look west for the wild hills of the Marin Headlands, the curving coast south to Lands End, and the Pacific Ocean. On sunny days, sailboats dot the water, and brave windsurfers test the often-treacherous tides beneath the bridge. A vista point on the Marin County side provides a spectacular city panorama.

A structural engineer, dreamer, and poet named Joseph Strauss worked tirelessly for 20 years to make the bridge a reality, first promoting the idea of it and then overseeing design and construction. Though the final structure bore little resemblance to his original plan, Strauss guarded his legacy jealously, refusing to recognize the seminal contributions of engineer Charles A. Ellis. In 2007, the Golden Gate Bridge district finally recognized Ellis's role, though Strauss, who died less than a year after opening day in 1937, would doubtless be pleased with the inscription on his statue, which stands sentry in the southern parking lot: "The Man Who Built the Bridge."

You won't see it on a T-shirt, but the bridge is perhaps the world's most publicized suicide platform, with one jumper about every 10 days. Signs on the bridge refer the disconsolate to special telephones, and officers patrol the walkway and watch by security camera to spot potential jumpers. A public campaign to install a suicide barrier is under way. The unobtrusive net supported by most locals—not unlike the one that during construction saved 19 workers—completed the design phase in 2013.

While at the bridge you can grab a healthy snack at the art deco–style Bridge Café. The recently erected Bridge Pavilion sells attractive, high-quality souvenirs and has a small display of historical artifacts. At the outdoor exhibits, you can see the bridge rise before your eyes on hologram panels, learn about the features that make it art deco, and read about the personalities behind its design and construction. Head up to the Round House to join a 45-minute bridge tour, or have a photo taken ($20) of your family walking up the main cable—courtesy of a background screen, of course. ✉ *Lincoln Blvd. near Doyle Dr. and Fort Point, Presidio* ☎ *415/921–5858* ⊕ *www.goldengatebridge.org* 📠 *Bridge free, tour $12.95* ☉ *Pedestrians: Mar.–Oct., daily 5 am–9* *pm; Nov.–Feb., daily 5 am–6 pm; hrs change with daylight saving time. Bikers: daily 24 hrs. Tour: on the half hour, 10:30–3:30.*

Fodor's Choice
★

Presidio. When San Franciscans want to spend a day in the woods, they head here. The Presidio has 1,400 acres of hills and majestic woods, two small beaches, and stunning views of the bay, the Golden Gate Bridge, and Marin County. Famed environmental artist Andy Goldsworthy's sculpture greets visitors at the Arguello Gate entrance. The 100-plus-foot *Spire,* made of 37 cypress logs reclaimed from the Presidio, looks like a rough, natural version of a church spire. ■ TIP➔ The Presidio's best lookout points lie along Washington Boulevard, which meanders through the park.

Part of the **Golden Gate National Recreation Area,** the Presidio was a military post for more than 200 years. Don Juan Bautista de Anza and a band of Spanish settlers first claimed the area in 1776. It became a Mexican garrison in 1822, when Mexico gained its independence from Spain; U.S. troops forcibly occupied the Presidio in 1846. The U.S. Sixth Army was stationed here until 1994.

Presidio is now a thriving community of residential and nonresidential tenants, who help to fund the Presidio's operations by rehabilitating and leasing its more than 700 buildings. In 2005 Bay Area filmmaker George Lucas opened the **Letterman Digital Arts Center,** his 23-acre digital studio "campus," along the eastern edge of the land. Seventeen of those acres are exquisitely landscaped and open to the public. If you have kids in tow or are a *Star Wars* fan yourself, sidle over to the **Yoda Fountain** (Letterman Drive at Dewitt Road), between two of the arts-center buildings.

The Presidio Trust, created to manage the Presidio and guide its transformation from military post to national park, has now turned its focus to rolling out the welcome mat to the public. The Presidio's visitor-serving tenants, such as the Asian-theme SenSpa, the House of Air Trampoline Park, Planet Granite climbing gym, the Walt Disney museum, a fabulous lodge at the Main Post, the newly reopened Officers' Club and 12 restaurants have helped with this goal. With old military housing now repurposed as apartments and homes with rents up to $10,000 a month the Presidio is a very popular place to live and boasts a much higher rate of families with children than the rest of San Francisco (36% versus16% in the rest of the city). Still, the $6 million that Lucas Film Ltd.—since 2012 a subsidiary of the Walt Disney Company—shells out annually for rent does plant a lot of saplings.

The Presidio also has a golf course, a visitor center, and picnic sites; the views from the many overlooks are sublime.

Especially popular is **Crissy Field**, a stretch of restored marshland along the sand of the bay. Kids on bikes, folks walking dogs, and joggers share the paved path along the shore, often winding up at the Warming Hut, a combination café and fun gift store at the end of the path, for a hot chocolate in the shadow of the Golden Gate Bridge. Midway along the Golden Gate Promenade that winds along the shore is the Gulf of the Farallones National Marine Sanctuary Visitor Center, where kids can get a close-up view of small sea creatures and learn about the rich ecosystem offshore. Temporarily relocated to East Beach, just across from the Palace of Fine Arts, Crissy Field Center offers great children's programs and has cool science displays; grab lunch at the Beach Hut Café next door. West of the Golden Gate Bridge is sandy **Baker Beach,** beloved for its spectacular views and laid-back vibe (read: you'll see naked people here). This is one of those places that inspires local pride. ⊠ *Between Marina and Lincoln Park, Presidio* ⊕ *www.nps.gov/prsf and www.presidio.gov.*

Walt Disney Family Museum. This beautifully refurbished brick barracks house is a tribute to the man behind Mickey Mouse, the Disney Studios, and Disneyland. The smartly organized displays include hundreds of family photos, and well-chosen videos play throughout. Disney's legendary attention to detail becomes particularly evident in the cels and footage of *Fantasia, Sleeping Beauty,* and other animation classics. *The Toughest Period in My Whole Life* exhibit sheds light on lesser-known bits of history: the animators' strike at Disney Studios, the films Walt Disney made for the U.S. military during World War II, and his testimony before the House Un-American Activities Committee during its investigation of Communist influence in Hollywood. The glass-walled gallery showcasing Disney's wildlife films takes full advantage of the museum's location, with a lovely view of Presidio trees and the Golden Gate Bridge in the background. The liveliest exhibit and the largest gallery documents the creation of Disneyland with a fun, detailed model of what Disney imagined the park would be. Teacups spin, the Matterhorn looms, and that world-famous castle leads the way to Fantasyland. You won't be the first to leave humming "It's a Small World." In the final gallery, titled simply *December 16, 1966,* a series of sweet cartoons chronicles the world's reaction to Disney's sudden death. The one-way flow of the galleries deposits you near the attractive gift shop, which carries cool Disney-related stuff, and a café serving sandwiches, salads, and drinks. The downstairs theater shows Disney films (free with admission, $7 without) twice daily. ⊠ *Main Post, 104 Montgomery St., off Lincoln Blvd., Presidio* ☎ *415/345–6800* ⊕ *www.waltdisney.org* ⊠ *$20* ☉ *Wed.–Mon. 10–6.*

WORTH NOTING

FAMILY **Fort Point.** Dwarfed today by the Golden Gate Bridge, this brick fortress constructed between 1853 and 1861 was designed to protect San Francisco from a Civil War sea attack that never materialized. It was also used as a coastal-defense fortification post during World War II, when soldiers stood watch here. This National Historic Site is now a sprawling museum of military memorabilia. The building, which surrounds a lonely, windswept courtyard, has a gloomy air and is suitably atmospheric. It's usually chilly, too, so bring a jacket. The top floor affords a unique angle on the bay. ■TIP→ **Take care when walking along the front side of the building, as it's slippery, and the waves have a dizzying effect.**

On the days when Fort Point is staffed (on Friday and weekends), guided group tours and cannon drills take place. The popular, guided candlelight tours, available only in winter, sell out in advance, so book ahead. Living-history days take place throughout the year, when Union soldiers perform drills, a drum-and-fife band plays, and a Civil War–era doctor shows his instruments and describes his surgical technique (gulp). ⊠ *Marine Dr. off Lincoln Blvd., Presidio* ☎ *415/556–1693* ⊕ *www.nps.gov/fopo* ⊠ *Free* ☉ *Fri.–Sun. 10–5.*

Armed with only helmets, safety harnesses, and painting equipment, a full-time crew of 38 painters keeps the Golden Gate Bridge clad in International Orange.

GOLDEN GATE PARK AND THE WESTERN SHORELINE

More than 1,000 acres, stretching from the Haight all the way to the windy Pacific coast, Golden Gate Park is a vast patchwork of woods, trails, lakes, lush gardens, sports facilities, museums—even a herd of buffalo. There's more natural beauty beyond the park's borders, along San Francisco's wild Western Shoreline.

GOLDEN GATE PARK

TOP ATTRACTIONS

FAMILY

Fodor's Choice

★

California Academy of Sciences. With its native plant–covered living roof, retractable ceiling, three-story rain forest, gigantic planetarium, living coral reef, and frolicking penguins, the California Academy of Sciences is one of the city's most spectacular treasures. Dramatically designed by Renzo Piano, it's an eco-friendly, energy-efficient adventure in bio-diversity and green architecture. The roof's large mounds and hills mirror the local topography, and Piano's audacious design completes the dramatic transformation of the park's Music Concourse. Moving away from a restrictive role as a museum that catalogued natural history, the academy these days is all about sustainability and the future. The locally beloved dioramas in African Hall have survived the transition, however.

By the time you arrive, hopefully you've decided which shows and programs to attend, looked at the academy's floor plan, and designed a plan to cover it all in the time you have. And if not, here's the quick version: Head left from the entrance to the wooden walkway over otherworldly rays in the Philippine Coral Reef, then continue to the

Swamp to see Claude, the famous albino alligator. Swing through African Hall and gander at the penguins, take the elevator up to the living roof, then return to the main floor and get in line to explore the Rainforests of the World, ducking free-flying butterflies and watching for other live surprises. You'll end up below ground in the Amazonian Flooded Rainforest, where you can explore the academy's other aquarium exhibits. Phew. ■TIP→ During peak periods the museum adds a $5 surcharge to tickets purchased at the door, so buy yours online ahead of time. ✉ *55 Music Concourse Dr., Golden Gate Park* ☎ *415/379–8000* ⊕ *www.calacademy.org* ✉ *$29.95, free 1 Sun. per quarter* ⊙ *Mon.–Sat. 9:30–5, Sun. 11–5.*

Conservatory of Flowers. Whatever you do, be sure to at least drive by the Conservatory of Flowers—it's too darn pretty to miss. The gorgeous, white-framed 1878 glass structure is topped with a 14-ton glass dome. Stepping inside the giant greenhouse is like taking a quick trip to the rain forest, with its earthy smell and humid warmth. The undeniable highlight is the Aquatic Plants section, where lily pads float and carnivorous plants dine on bugs to the sounds of rushing water. On the east side of the conservatory (to the right as you face the building), cypress, pine, and redwood trees surround the Dahlia Garden, which blooms in summer and fall. Adding to the allure are temporary exhibits such as a past one devoted to prehistoric plants; an annual model-train display punctuated with mini buildings, found objects, and dwarf plants; and a butterfly garden that returns periodically. To the west is the **Rhododendron Dell,** which contains 850 varieties, more than any other garden in the country. It's a favorite local Mother's Day picnic spot. ✉ *John F. Kennedy Dr. at Conservatory Dr., Golden Gate Park* ☎ *415/666–7001* ⊕ *www.conservatoryofflowers.org* ✉ *$8, free 1st Tues. of month* ⊙ *Tues.–Sun. 10–4:30* ☞ *No strollers allowed inside.*

de Young Museum. It seems that everyone in town has a strong opinion about the de Young Museum: Some adore its striking copper facade, while others just hope that the green patina of age will mellow the effect. Most maligned is the 144-foot tower, but the view from its ninth-story observation room, ringed by floor-to-ceiling windows and free to the public, is worth a trip here by itself. The building almost overshadows the de Young's respected collection of American, African, and Oceanic art. The museum also plays host to major international exhibits, such as postimpressionist works on loan from the Musée d'Orsay and 100 works from Paris's Musée National Picasso. The annual Bouquet des Art is a fanciful tribute to the museum's collection by notable Bay Area floral designers. ■TIP→ On many Friday evenings, the museum hosts fun, free, family-centered events, with live music, art projects for children, and a wine and beer bar (the café stays open late, too). ✉ *50 Hagiwara Tea Garden Dr., Golden Gate Park* ☎ *415/750–3600* ⊕ *deyoung.famsf.org* ✉ *$10, good for same-day admittance to the Legion of Honor; free 1st Tues. of month* ⊙ *Tues.–Sun. 9:30–5:15; mid-Jan.–Nov., Fri. until 8:45.*

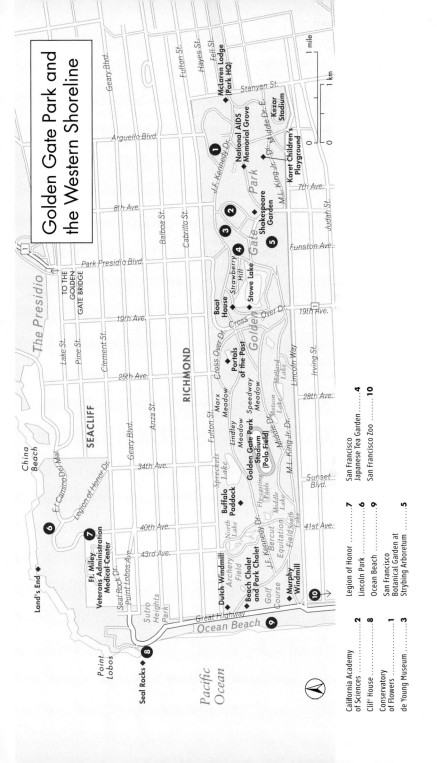

Golden Gate Park and the Western Shoreline

1 mile

1 km

McLaren Lodge
(Park HQ)

Stanyan St.

Kezar
Stadium

National AIDS
Memorial Grove

Koret Children's
Playground

M.L. King Jr. Dr.

Middle Dr. E.

7th Ave.

Judah St.

Shakespeare
Garden

Funston Ave.

Strawberry
Hill

Stowe Lake

Boat
House

Cross Over Dr.

Golden   Over Dr.

19th Ave.

Portals
of the Past

Marx
Meadow

Speedway
Meadow

Lindley
Meadow

Middle Dr.

Nancy Pelosi Dr.

Mallard
Lake

M.L. King Jr. Dr.

Lincoln Way

Irving St.

28th Ave.

Golden Gate Park
Stadium
(Polo Field)

Fulton St.

Spreckels
Lake

Buffalo
Paddock

North
Lake

Fly-casting
Pools

Middle
Lake

South
Lake

J.F. Kennedy Dr.

Golf
Course

Bercut
Equitation
Field

Sunset
Blvd.

41st Ave.

Dutch Windmill

Archery
Field

Murphy
Windmill

Beach Chalet
and Park Chalet

Ft. Miley
Veterans Administration
Medical Center

Land's End

Seal Rocks

Point
Lobos

El Camino Del Mar

Legion of Honor Dr.

China
Beach

Sutro
Heights
Park

Great Highway

Ocean Beach

Pacific
Ocean

SEACLIFF

RICHMOND

The Presidio

Geary Blvd.

Arguello Blvd.

8th Ave.

Balboa St.

Cabrillo St.

Park Presidio Blvd.

TO THE
GOLDEN
GATE BRIDGE

Lake St.

Pine St.

Clement St.

19th Ave.

25th Ave.

Anza St.

34th Ave.

40th Ave.

43rd Ave.

Seal Rock Dr.

Point Lobos Ave.

Fulton St.

Hayes St.

Fell St.

Gate   Park

Fulton St.

Geary Blvd.

1

2

3

4

5

6

7

8

9

10

San Francisco Japanese Tea Garden. As you amble through the manicured landscape, past Japanese sculptures and perfect miniature pagodas, and over ponds of carp, you may feel transported to a more peaceful plane. Or maybe the shrieks of kids clambering over the almost vertical "humpback" bridges will keep you firmly in the here and now. Either way, this garden is one of those tourist spots that's truly worth a stop (a half hour will do). And at 5 acres, it's large enough that you'll always be able to find a bit of serenity, even when the tour buses drop by. The garden is especially lovely in March and April, when the cherry blossoms are in bloom. ⊠ *Hagiwara Tea Garden Dr., off John F. Kennedy Dr., Golden Gate Park* ☎ *415/752–4227* ⊕ *www.japaneseteagardensf. com* ✏ *$7, free Mon., Wed., and Fri. if you enter by 10 am* ☉ *Mar.– Oct., daily 9–6; Nov.–Feb., daily 9–4:45.*

San Francisco Botanical Garden at Strybing Arboretum. One of the best picnic spots in a very picnic-friendly park, the 55-acre arboretum specializes in plants from areas with climates similar to that of the Bay Area. Walk the Eastern Australian garden to see tough, pokey shrubs and plants with cartoon-like names, such as the hilly-pilly tree. Kids gravitate toward the large shallow fountain and the pond with ducks, turtles, and egrets. ⊠ *Lincoln Way and 9th Ave. entrance, Golden Gate Park* ☎ *415/661–1316* ⊕ *www.sfbotanicalgarden.org* ✏ *$7, free 2nd Tues. of month* ☉ *Apr.–Oct., daily 9–6; Nov.–Mar., daily 9–5.*

THE WESTERN SHORELINE

TOP ATTRACTIONS

Cliff House. A meal at the Cliff House isn't just about the food—the spectacular ocean view is what brings folks here—but the cuisine won't leave you wanting. The vistas, which include offshore Seal Rock (the barking marine mammals who reside there are actually sea lions), can be 30 miles or more on a clear day—or less than a mile on foggy days. ■TIP➜ **Come for drinks just before sunset; then head back into town for dinner.**

Three buildings have occupied this site since 1863. The current building dates from 1909; a 2004 renovation has left a strikingly attractive restaurant and a squat concrete viewing platform out back. The complex, owned by the National Park Service, includes a gift shop.

Sitting on the observation deck is the **Giant Camera,** a camera obscura with its lens pointing skyward housed in a cute yellow-painted wooden shack. Built in the 1940s and threatened many times with demolition, it's now on the National Register of Historic Places. Step into the dark, tiny room inside (for a $3 fee); a fascinating 360-degree image of the surrounding area—which rotates as the "lens" on the roof rotates—is projected on a large, circular table. ■TIP➜ **In winter and spring you may also glimpse migrating gray whales from the observation deck.**

To the north of the Cliff House lie the ruins of the once grand glass-roof **Sutro Baths,** which you can explore on your own (they look a bit like water-storage receptacles). Adolf Sutro, eccentric onetime San Francisco mayor and Cliff House owner, built the bath complex, including a train out to the site, in 1896, so that everyday folks could enjoy the benefits of swimming. Six enormous baths (some freshwater and some seawater), more than 500 dressing rooms, and several restaurants covered 3 acres north of the Cliff House and accommodated 25,000 bathers. Likened to Roman baths in a European glass palace, the baths were for decades the favorite destination of San Franciscans in search of entertainment. The complex fell into disuse after World War II, was closed in 1952, and burned down (under questionable circumstances) during demolition in 1966. ⊠ *1090 Point Lobos Ave., Richmond* ☎ *415/386–3330* ⊕ *www.cliffhouse.com* ⊠ *Free* ☻ *Weekdays 9 am–9:30 pm, weekends 9 am–10 pm.*

Fodor's Choice ★ **Legion of Honor.** The old adage of real estate—location, location, location—is at full force here. You can't beat the site of this museum of European art atop cliffs overlooking the ocean, the Golden Gate Bridge, and the Marin Headlands. A pyramidal glass skylight in the entrance court illuminates the lower-level galleries, which exhibit prints and drawings, English and European porcelain, and ancient Assyrian, Greek, Roman, and Egyptian art. The 20-plus galleries on the upper level display the permanent collection of European art (paintings, sculpture, decorative arts, and tapestries) from the 14th century to the present day.

The noteworthy Auguste Rodin collection includes two galleries devoted to the master and a third with works by Rodin and other 19th-century sculptors. An original cast of Rodin's *The Thinker* welcomes you as you walk through the courtyard. As fine as the museum is, the setting and view outshine the collection and also make a trip here worthwhile.

The **Legion Café,** on the lower level, serves tasty light meals (soup, sandwiches, grilled chicken) inside and on a garden terrace. (Unfortunately, there's no view.) Just north of the museum's parking lot is George Segal's *The Holocaust,* a stark white installation that evokes life in concentration camps during World War II. It's haunting at night, when backlighted by lights in the Legion's parking lot. ■ TIP➜ **Admission to the Legion is also good for same-day admission to the de Young Museum in Golden Gate Park.** ⊠ *34th Ave. at Clement St., Richmond* ☎ *415/750–3600* ⊕ *legionofhonor.famsf.org* ⊠ *$10, $2 off with Muni transfer, free 1st Tues. of month* ☻ *Tues.–Sun. 9:30–5:15.*

Fodor's Choice ★ **Lincoln Park.** Although many of the city's green spaces are gentle and welcoming, Lincoln Park is a wild, 275-acre park in the Outer Richmond with windswept cliffs and panoramic views. The newly renovated Coastal Trail, the park's most dramatic one, leads out to **Lands End**; pick it up west of the Legion of Honor (at the end of El Camino del Mar) or from the parking lot at Point Lobos and El Camino del Mar. Time your hike to hit Mile Rock at low tide, and you might catch a glimpse of two wrecked ships peeking up from their watery graves. ⚠ **Be careful if you hike here; landslides are frequent, and people have fallen into the sea by standing too close to the edge of a crumbling bluff top.**

On the tamer side, large Monterey cypresses line the fairways at Lincoln Park's 18-hole golf course, near the Legion of Honor. At one time this land was the Golden Gate Cemetery, where the dead were segregated by nationality; most were indigent and interred without ceremony in the potter's field. In 1900 the Board of Supervisors voted to ban burials

8

within city limits, and all but two city cemeteries (at Mission Dolores and the Presidio) were moved to Colma, a small town just south of San Francisco. When digging has to be done in the park, bones occasionally surface again. ⊠ *Entrance at, 34th Ave. at Clement St, Richmond.*

WORTH NOTING

Ocean Beach. Stretching 3 miles along the western side of the city from the Richmond to the Sunset, this sandy swath of the Pacific coast is good for jogging or walking the dog—but not for swimming. The water is so cold that surfers wear wet suits year-round, and riptides are strong, so only brave the waves if you are a strong swimmer or surfer. As for sunbathing, it's rarely warm enough here; think meditative walking instead of sun worshipping.

Paths on both sides of the Great Highway lead from Lincoln Way to Sloat Boulevard (near the zoo); the beachside path winds through landscaped sand dunes, and the paved path across the highway is good for biking and in-line skating. (Though you have to rent bikes elsewhere.) The **Beach Chalet** restaurant and brewpub is across the Great Highway from Ocean Beach, about five blocks south of the Cliff House. ⊠ *Along Great Hwy. from Cliff House to Sloat Blvd. and beyond.*

FAMILY **San Francisco Zoo.** Occupying prime oceanfront property, the zoo is touting its metamorphosis into the "New Zoo," a wildlife-focused recreation center that inspires visitors to become conservationists. Integrated exhibits group different species of animals from the same geographic areas together in enclosures that don't look like cages. More than 250 species reside here, including endangered species such as the snow leopard, Sumatran tiger, grizzly bear, and a Siberian tiger.

The zoo's superstar exhibit is **Grizzly Gulch,** where orphaned grizzly bear sisters Kachina and Kiona enchant visitors with their frolicking and swimming. When the bears are in the water, the only thing between you and them is (thankfully thick) glass. Grizzly feedings are at 11:30 am daily.

The **Lemur Forest** has five varieties of the bug-eyed, long-tailed primates from Madagascar. You can help hoist food into the lemurs' feeding towers and watch the fuzzy creatures climb up to chow down. African Kikuyu grass carpets the circular outer area of **Gorilla Preserve,** one of the largest and most natural gorilla habitats of any zoo in the world. Trees and shrubs create communal play areas.

Ten species of rare primates—including black howler monkeys, black-and-white ruffed lemurs, and macaques—live and play at the two-tier **Primate Discovery Center,** which contains 23 interactive learning exhibits on the ground level.

Magellanic penguins waddle about the rather sad concrete **Penguin Island,** splashing and frolicking in its 200-foot pool. Feeding times are 10:30 and 3:30. Koalas peer out from among the trees in **Koala Crossing,** and kangaroos and wallabies headline the **Australian Walkabout** exhibit. The 7-acre **Puente al Sur** (Bridge to the South) re-creates habitats in South America, replete with giant anteaters and capybaras.

An **African Savanna** exhibit mixes giraffes, zebras, kudus, ostriches, and many other species, all living together in a 3-acre section with a central viewing spot accessed by a covered passageway.

The 6-acre **Children's Zoo** has about 300 mammals, birds, and reptiles, plus an insect zoo, a meerkat and prairie-dog exhibit, a nature trail, a nature theater, a huge playground, a restored 1921 Dentzel carousel, and a mini–steam train. A ride on the train costs $4, and you can hop astride one of the carousel's 52 hand-carved menagerie animals for $2. ⊠ *Sloat Blvd. and 47th Ave., Sunset* ☏ *415/753–7080* ⊕ *www.sfzoo.org* ✎ *$17, $1 off with Muni transfer (take Muni L–Taraval streetcar from downtown)* ⊗ *Mid-Mar.–Oct., daily 10–5; Nov.–mid-Mar., daily 10–4.*

THE HAIGHT, THE CASTRO, AND NOE VALLEY

These distinct neighborhoods are where the city's soul resides. They wear their personalities large and proud, and all are perfect for just strolling around. Like a slide show of San Franciscan history, you can move from the Haight's residue of 1960s counterculture to the Castro's connection to 1970s and '80s gay life to 1990s gentrification in Noe Valley. Although historic events thrust the Haight and the Castro onto the international stage, both are anything but stagnant—they're still dynamic areas well worth exploring.

THE HAIGHT
TOP ATTRACTION

Haight-Ashbury Intersection. On October 6, 1967, hippies took over the intersection of Haight and Ashbury streets to proclaim the "Death of Hip." If they thought hip was dead then, they'd find absolute confirmation of it today, what with the only tie-dye in sight on the famed corner being Ben & Jerry's storefront.

Everyone knows the Summer of Love had something to do with free love and LSD, but the drugs and other excesses of that period have tended to obscure the residents' serious attempts to create an America that was more spiritually oriented, more environmentally aware, and less caught up in commercialism. The Diggers, a radical group of actors and populist agitators, for example, operated a free shop a few blocks off Haight Street. Everything really was free at the free shop; people brought in things they didn't need and took things they did.

Among the folks who hung out in or near the Haight during the late 1960s were writers Richard Brautigan, Allen Ginsberg, Ken Kesey, and Gary Snyder; anarchist Abbie Hoffman; rock performers Marty Balin, Jerry Garcia, Janis Joplin, and Grace Slick; LSD champion Timothy Leary; and filmmaker Kenneth Anger. If you're keen to feel something resembling the hippie spirit these days, there's always Hippie Hill, just inside the Haight Street entrance of Golden Gate Park. Think drum circles, guitar players, and whiffs of pot smoke. ⊠ *Haight.*

8

THE CASTRO
TOP ATTRACTION

Castro Theatre. Here's a classic way to join in the Castro community: grab some popcorn and catch a flick at this 1,500-seat art deco theater; opened in 1922, it's the grandest of San Francisco's few remaining movie palaces. The neon marquee, which stands at the top of the Castro strip, is the neighborhood's great landmark. The Castro was the fitting host of 2008's red-carpet preview of Gus Van Sant's film *Milk*, starring Sean Penn as openly gay San Francisco supervisor Harvey Milk. The theater's elaborate Spanish baroque interior is fairly well preserved. Before many shows the theater's pipe organ rises from the orchestra pit and an organist plays pop and movie tunes, usually ending with the Jeanette McDonald standard "San Francisco" (go ahead, sing along). The crowd can be enthusiastic and vocal, talking back to the screen as loudly as it talks to them. Classics such as *Who's Afraid of Virginia Woolf?* take on a whole new life, with the assembled beating the actors to the punch and fashioning even snappier comebacks for Elizabeth Taylor. Head here to catch sing-along classics like *Mary Poppins*, a Fellini film retrospective, or the latest take on same-sex love. ⊠ *429 Castro St., Castro* ☎ *415/621–6120* ⊕ *www.castrotheatre.com.*

WORTH NOTING

✕ **Cafe Flore.** Sometimes referred to as Cafe Floorshow because it's such a see-and-be-seen place, Cafe Flore serves coffee drinks, beer, and tasty café fare. It's a good place to catch the latest Castro gossip. ⊠ *2298 Market St., at Noe St., Castro* ☎ *415/621–8579* ⊕ *cafeflore.com.*

GLBT Historical Society Museum. The one-room Gay, Lesbian, Bisexual, and Transgender (GLBT) Historical Society Museum presents multimedia exhibits from its vast holdings covering San Francisco's queer history. You might hear the audiotape Harvey Milk made for the community in the event of his assassination, view an exhibit of prominent African Americans, gays, and lesbians in the city, or flip through a memory book with pictures and thoughts on some of the more than 20,000 San Franciscans lost to AIDS. Though perhaps not for the faint of heart (those offended by sex toys and photos of lustily frolicking naked people may, well, be offended), the museum offers an inside look at these communities so integral to the fabric of San Francisco life. ⊠ *4127 18th St., near Castro St., Castro* ☎ *415/621–1107* ⊕ *www.glbthistory.org* ⊠ *$5, free 1st Wed. of the month* ☉ *Mon. and Wed.–Sat. 11–7, Sun. noon–5.*

Harvey Milk Plaza. An 18-foot-long rainbow flag, the symbol of gay pride, flies above this plaza named for the man who electrified the city in 1977 by being elected to its board of supervisors as an openly gay candidate. In the early 1970s Milk had opened a camera store on the block of Castro Street between 18th and 19th streets. The store became the center for his campaign to open San Francisco's social and political life to gays and lesbians.

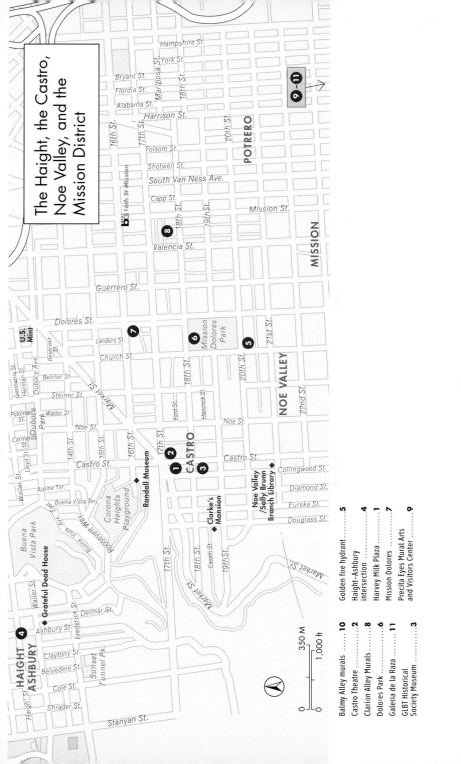

The Haight, the Castro, Noe Valley, and the Mission District

HAIGHT ASHBURY

U.S. Mint

POTRERO

MISSION

NOE VALLEY

CASTRO

Randall Museum

Clarke's Mansion

Noe Valley /Sally Brunn Branch Library

Grateful Dead House

Corona Heights Playground

Buena Vista Park

16th St Mission

Mission Dolores Park

350 M

1,000 ft

Balmy Alley murals **10**
Castro Theatre **2**
Clarion Alley Murals **8**
Dolores Park **6**
Galeria de la Raza **11**
GLBT Historical
Society Museum **3**

Golden fire hydrant **5**
Haight-Ashbury
intersection **4**
Harvey Milk Plaza **1**
Mission Dolores **7**
Precita Eyes Mural Arts
and Visitors Center **9**

The liberal Milk hadn't served a full year of his term before he and Mayor George Moscone, also a liberal, were shot in November 1978 at City Hall. The murderer was a conservative ex-supervisor named Dan White, who had recently resigned his post and then became enraged when Moscone wouldn't reinstate him. Milk and White had often been at odds on the board, and White thought Milk had been part of a cabal to keep him from returning to his post. Milk's assassination shocked the gay community, which became infuriated when the infamous "Twinkie defense"—that junk food had led to diminished mental capacity—resulted in a manslaughter verdict for White. During the so-called White Night Riot of May 21, 1979, gays and their allies stormed City Hall, torching its lobby and several police cars.

Milk, who had feared assassination, left behind a tape recording in which he urged the community to continue the work he had begun. His legacy is the high visibility of gay people throughout city government; a bust of him was unveiled at City Hall on his birthday in 2008, and the 2008 film *Milk* gives insight into his life. A plaque at the base of the flagpole lists the names of past and present openly gay and lesbian state and local officials. ⊠ *Southwest corner of Castro and Market Sts., Castro.*

NOE VALLEY
WORTH NOTING

Golden fire hydrant. When all the other fire hydrants went dry during the fire that followed the 1906 earthquake, this one kept pumping. Noe Valley and the Mission District were thus spared the devastation wrought elsewhere in the city, which explains the large number of pre-quake homes here. Every year on April 18th (the anniversary of the quake) folks gather here to share stories about the earthquake, and the famous hydrant gets a fresh coat of gold paint. ⊠ *Church and 20th Sts., southeastern corner, across from Dolores Park, Noe Valley.*

CASTRO AND NOE WALK

The Castro and Noe Valley neighborhoods beg to be walked—or ambled through, really, without time pressure or an absolute destination. Fortify yourself with a coffee, or get one to go, at the amusing **Cafe Flore**, then head west up **Market Street** to check out the shops and boutiques in the block before **Castro Street.** You're at Castro arrived when you're standing under the gigantic rainbow flag at **Harvey Milk Plaza.** Enjoy the plaza's perspective on the art deco **Castro Theatre,** then head south past the theater, popping into the shops along the way (**Cliff's Variety,** at 479 Castro Street, is a must). To tour Noe Valley, go east down 18th Street to Church (at Dolores Park), and then head south over the hill—or hop on the **J–Church** light-rail car—to 24th Street, this rambling neighborhood's center.

A colorful mosaic mural in the Castro

MISSION DISTRICT

The Mission has a number of distinct personalities: it's the Latino neighborhood, where working-class folks raise their families and where gangs occasionally clash; it's the hipster hood, where tattooed and pierced twenty- and thirtysomethings hold court in too-cool cafés and bars; it's a culinary epicenter, with destination restaurants and affordable ethnic cuisine; and it's the artists' quarter, where murals adorn literally blocks of walls. It's also the city's equivalent of the Sunshine State—this neighborhood's always the last to succumb to fog.

TOP ATTRACTIONS

Balmy Alley murals. Mission District artists have transformed the walls of their neighborhood with paintings, and Balmy Alley is one of the best-executed examples. Many murals adorn the one-block alley, with newer ones continually filling in the blank spaces. In 1971, artists began teaming with local children to create a space to promote peace in Central America, community spirit, and (later) AIDS awareness; since then dozens of artists have added their vibrant works. ■ TIP→ Be alert here: the 25th Street end of the alley adjoins a somewhat dangerous area. ✉ *24th St. between and parallel to Harrison and Treat Sts., alley runs south to 25th St., Mission.*

Fodor's Choice ★ **Dolores Park.** A two-square-block microcosm of life in the Mission, Dolores Park is one of San Francisco's liveliest green spaces: dog lovers and their pampered pups congregate, kids play at the extravagant, recently reconstructed playground, and hipsters hold court, drinking beer on sunny days. During the summer, the park hosts movie nights; performances by Shakespeare in the Park, the San Francisco Mime

Troupe, and the San Francisco Symphony; and any number of pop-up events and impromptu parties. Spend a warm day here—maybe sitting at the top of the park with a view of the city and the Bay Bridge—surrounded by locals and that laid-back San Francisco energy, and you may well find yourself plotting your move to the city. The park continues to be well visited during a major renovation expected to continue through 2015. ⊠ *Between 18th and 20th Sts. and Dolores and Church Sts., Mission.*

Mission Dolores. Two churches stand side by side at this mission, including the small adobe **Mission San Francisco de Asís,** the oldest standing structure in San Francisco. Completed in 1791, it's the sixth of the 21 California missions founded by Franciscan friars in the 18th and early 19th centuries. Its ceiling depicts original Ohlone Indian basket designs, executed in vegetable dyes. The tiny chapel includes frescoes and a hand-painted wooden altar.

There's a hidden treasure here, too. In 2004 an archaeologist and an artist crawling along the ceiling's rafters opened a trap door behind the altar and rediscovered the mission's original mural, painted with natural dyes by Native Americans in 1791. The centuries have taken their toll, so the team photographed the 20-by-22-foot mural and began digitally restoring the photographic version. Among the images is a dagger-pierced Sacred Heart of Jesus.

The small museum here covers the mission's founding and history, and the pretty little cemetery—which appears in Alfred Hitchcock's film *Vertigo*—contains the graves of mid-19th-century European immigrants. (The remains of an estimated 5,000 Native Americans lie in unmarked graves.) Services are held in both the old mission and next door in the handsome multidome basilica. ⊠ *Dolores and 16th Sts., Mission* 🕾 *415/621–8203* ⊕ *www.missiondolores.org* ⌦ *$5, audio tour $7* ۞ *Nov.–Apr., daily 9–4; May–Oct., daily 9–4:30.*

WORTH NOTING

Clarion Alley murals. A new generation of muralists is creating a fresh alley-cum-gallery here. The works by the loosely connected artists of the Clarion Alley Mural Project (CAMP) represent a broad range of styles and imagery. Carpet-draped Indonesian elephants plod calmly down the block; kung fu movie–style headlines shout slogans. The alley's murals offer a quick but dense glimpse into the Mission's contemporary art scene. ⊠ *Between Valencia and Mission Sts. and 17th and 18th Sts., Mission.*

Galería de la Raza. San Francisco's premier showcase for contemporary Latino art, the gallery exhibits the works of mostly local artists. Events include readings and spoken word by local poets and writers, screenings of Latin American and Spanish films, and theater works by local minority theater troupes. Just across the street, murals and mosaics festoon the 24th Street/York Street Minipark, a tiny urban playground. A mosaic-covered Quetzalcoatl serpent plunges into the ground and rises, creating hills for little ones to clamber over, and mural-covered walls surround the space. ⊠ *2857 24th St., at Bryant St., Mission* 🕾 *415/826–8009* ⊕ *www.galeriadelaraza.org* ۞ *Gallery Wed.–Sat. noon–6.*

Precita Eyes Mural Arts and Visitors Center. The muralists of this nonprofit arts organization design and create murals and lead guided walks of area murals. The Classic Mission Mural Walk ($20) starts with a 45-minute slide presentation before participants head outside to view murals on Balmy Alley and 24th Street. The Mission Trail Mural Walk ($15) includes some of the same murals and impressive ones at Cesar Chavez Elementary School. You can pick up a map of 24th Street's murals at the center and buy art supplies, T-shirts, postcards, and other mural-related items. ✉ *2981 24th St., Mission* ☎ *415/285–2287* 🌐 *www.precitaeyes.org* 🎟 *Center free, tours $15–$20* 🕒 *Center: weekdays 10–5, Sat. 10–4, Sun. noon–4. Walks: weekends at 11 (Mission Trail) and 1:30 (Classic).*

DOGPATCH

East of the Mission District and Potrero Hill and a short T-Third Muni Metro ride from SoMa, the Dogpatch neighborhood has been on the rise for the last decade. Artisans, designers, and craftspeople eager to protect the area's historical industrial legacy have all moved here in recent years, providing a solid customer base for shops, galleries, and boutique restaurants and artisanal food producers. The Museum of Craft and Design moved to Dogpatch in 2013 and instantly became the neighborhood's cultural anchor.

TOP ATTRACTION

Museum of Craft and Design. Right at home in this once-industrial neighborhood now bursting with creative energy, this small, four-room space mounts temporary art and design exhibitions. The focus might be sculpture, metalwork, furniture, or jewelry—or industrial design, architecture, or other topics. The MakeArt Lab gives kids the opportunity to create their own exhibit-inspired work, and the beautifully curated shop sells tempting textiles, housewares, jewelry, and other well-crafted items. ✉ *2569 3rd St. near 22nd St., Dogpatch* ☎ *415/773–0303* 🌐 *sfmcd.org* 🎟 *$8, free first Tues. of month* 🕒 *Tues.–Sat. 11–6 (Thurs. until 7), Sun. noon–5.*

8

PACIFIC HEIGHTS AND JAPANTOWN

Pacific Heights and Japantown are something of an odd couple: privileged, old-school San Francisco and the workaday commercial center of Japanese American life in the city, stacked virtually on top of each other. The extravagant mansions of Pacific Heights gradually give way to the more modest Victorians and unassuming housing tracts of Japantown. The most interesting spots in Japantown huddle in the Japan Center, the neighborhood's two-block centerpiece, and along Post Street. You can find plenty of authentic Japanese treats in the shops and restaurants. **■ TIP→ Japantown is a relatively safe area, but the Western Addition, south of Geary Boulevard, can be dangerous even during the daytime.**

PACIFIC HEIGHTS

TOP ATTRACTIONS

Haas-Lilienthal House. A small display of photographs on the bottom floor of this elaborate, gray 1886 Queen Anne house makes clear that despite its lofty stature and striking, round third-story tower, the house was modest compared with some of the giants that fell victim to the 1906 earthquake and fire. The Foundation for San Francisco's Architectural Heritage operates the home, whose carefully kept rooms provide a glimpse into late-19th-century life through period furniture, authentic details (antique dishes in the kitchen built-in), and photos of the family that occupied the house until 1972. ■ TIP➔ You can admire hundreds of gorgeous San Francisco Victorians from the outside, but this is the only one that's open to the public, and it's worth a visit. Volunteers conduct one-hour house tours three days a week, and informative two-hour walking tours of Pacific Heights on Sunday afternoon (call or check website for schedule). ✉ *2007 Franklin St., between Washington and Jackson Sts., Pacific Heights* ☎ *415/441–3004* ⊕ *www.sfheritage.org* ☑ *Tours $8* ⊙ *1-hr tour Wed. and Sat. noon–3, Sun. 11–4; 2-hr tour Sun. at 12:30.*

Spreckels Mansion. Shrouded behind tall juniper hedges at the corner of winding, redbrick Octavia Street, overlooking Lafayette Park, the estate was built for sugar heir Adolph Spreckels and his wife Alma. Mrs. Spreckels was so pleased with her house that she commissioned George Applegarth to design another building in a similar vein: the Legion of Honor. One of the city's great iconoclasts, Alma Spreckels was the model for the bronze figure atop the Victory Monument in Union Square. These days an iconoclast of another sort owns the mansion: romance novelist Danielle Steel, whose dust-up with local columnists over the size of those hedges entertained aficionados of local gossip in early 2014. ✉ *2080 Washington St., at Octavia St., Pacific Heights.*

WORTH NOTING

FAMILY **Alta Plaza Park.** Golden Gate Park's longtime superintendent, John McLaren, designed Alta Plaza in 1910, modeling its terracing on that of the Grand Casino in Monte Carlo, Monaco. From the top you can see Marin to the north, downtown to the east, Twin Peaks to the south, and Golden Gate Park to the west. ■ TIP➔ Kids love the many play structures at the large, enclosed playground at the top; everywhere else is dog territory. ✉ *Bordered by Clay, Steiner, Jackson, and Scott Sts., Pacific Heights.*

Franklin Street buildings. The three blocks south of the ➪ *Haas-Lilienthal House* contain a few curiosities of interest to architecture buffs. What at first looks like a stone facade on the **Golden Gate Church** (✉ *1901 Franklin St.*) is actually redwood painted white. A handsome Georgian-style residence built in the early 1900s for a coffee merchant sits at 1735 Franklin. On the northeast corner of Franklin and California streets is a **Christian Science church**; built in the Tuscan revival style, it's noteworthy for its terra-cotta detailing. **The Coleman House** (✉ *1701 Franklin St.*) is an impressive twin-turret Queen Anne mansion that was built for a gold-rush mining and lumber baron. Don't miss the large, brilliant-purple stained-glass window on the house's north side. ✉ *Franklin St. between Washington and California Sts., Pacific Heights.*

DID YOU KNOW?

These soft-color Victorian homes in Pacific Heights are closer to the original hues sported back in the 1900s. It wasn't until the 1960s that the bold, electric colors now seen around San Francisco gained popularity. Before that, the most typical house paint color was a standard gray.

JAPANTOWN

TOP ATTRACTIONS

Japan Center. Cool and curious trinkets, noodle houses and sushi joints, a destination bookstore, and a peek at Japanese culture high and low await at this 5-acre complex designed in 1968 by noted American architect Minoru Yamasaki. The Japan Center includes the shop- and restaurant-filled Kintetsu and Kinokuniya buildings; the excellent Kabuki Springs & Spa; the Hotel Kabuki; and the Sundance Kabuki, Robert Redford's fancy, reserved-seating cinema/restaurant complex.

The Kinokuniya Bookstores, in the Kinokuniya Building, have an extensive selection of Japanese-language books, *manga* (graphic novels), books on design, and English-language translations and books on Japanese topics. Just outside, follow the Japanese teenagers to Pika Pika, where you and your friends can step into a photo booth and then use special effects and stickers to decorate your creation. On the bridge connecting the center's two buildings, check out Shige Antiques for *yukata* (lightweight cotton kimonos) for kids and lovely silk kimonos, and Asakichi and its tiny incense shop for tinkling wind chimes and display-worthy teakettles. Continue into the Kintetsu Building for a selection of Japanese restaurants.

Between the Miyako Mall and Kintetsu Building are the five-tier, 100-foot-tall **Peace Pagoda** and the Peace Plaza, where seasonal festivals are held. The pagoda, which draws on the 1,200-year-old tradition of miniature round pagodas dedicated to eternal peace, was designed in the late 1960s by Yoshiro Taniguchi to convey the "friendship and goodwill" of the Japanese people to the people of the United States. The plaza itself is a shadeless, unwelcoming space with little seating. Continue into the Miyako Mall to Ichiban Kan, a Japanese dollar store where you can pick up fun Japanese kitchenware, tote bags decorated with hedgehogs, and erasers shaped like food. ⊠ *Bordered by Geary Blvd. and Fillmore, Post, and Laguna Sts., Japantown.*

Fodor's Choice ★ **Kabuki Springs & Spa.** This serene spa is one Japantown destination that draws locals from all over town, from hipster to grandma, Japanese-American or not. Balinese urns decorate the communal bath area of this house of tranquillity.

The massage menu has also expanded well beyond traditional shiatsu technique. The experience is no less relaxing, however, and the treatment regimen includes facials, salt scrubs, and mud and seaweed wraps. You can take your massage in a private room with a bath or in a curtained-off area.

The communal baths ($25) contain hot and cold tubs, a large Japanese-style bath, a sauna, a steam room, and showers. Bang the gong for quiet if your fellow bathers are speaking too loudly. The clothing-optional baths are open for men only on Monday, Thursday, and Saturday; women bathe on Wednesday, Friday, and Sunday. Bathing suits are required on Tuesday, when the baths are coed.

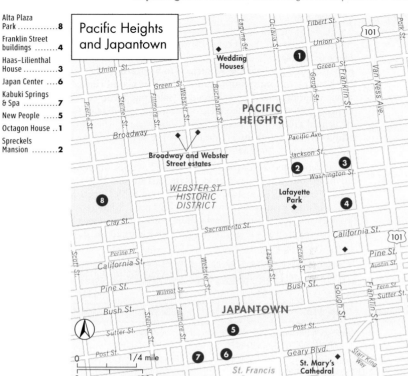

Men and women can reserve private rooms daily. An 80-minute massage-and-private-bath package costs $140 weekdays, $152 weekends; a package that includes a 50-minute massage and the use of the communal baths costs $105 weekdays, $114 weekends. ✉ *1750 Geary Blvd., Japantown* ☎ *415/922–6000* ⊕ *www.kabukisprings.com* ⏱ *Daily 10–10.*

New People. The kids' counterpart to the Japan Center, this fresh shopping center combines a cinema, a café, shops, and a gallery with a successful synergy. The basement cinema shows classic and cutting-edge Asian (largely Japanese) films and is home to the San Francisco Film Society. Grab some *onigiri* (rice balls) and a cup of Blue Bottle coffee at the café, then head upstairs and peruse Japanese pop-culture items and anime-inspired fashion. The cuteness radiating from the Rilakkuma store may overwhelm you. The tiny Superfrog Gallery upstairs exhibits cutting-edge contemporary art. ✉ *1746 Post St., Japantown* ☎ *415/525–8630 store, 415/525–8600 cinema* ⊕ *www. newpeopleworld.com* ⏱ *Mon.–Sat. noon–7, Sun. noon–6.*

WHERE TO EAT

Make no mistake, San Francisco is one of America's top food cities. Some of the biggest landmarks are restaurants; and Gary Danko is probably just as big a draw as Alcatraz. On a Saturday, the Ferry Building might attract more visitors than the Golden Gate Bridge. This temple to local eating sells cheeses, breads, "salty pig parts," homemade delicacies, and sensory-perfect vegetables and fruits that attract a rabidly dedicated group. You see, San Franciscans are a little loco about their edibles. If you ask them what their favorite season is, don't be surprised if they respond, "tomato season."

Some renowned restaurants are booked weeks or even months in advance. But you can get lucky at the last minute if you're flexible—and friendly. Most restaurants keep a few tables open for walk-ins and VIPs. Show up for dinner early (5:30 pm) or late (after 9 pm) and politely inquire about any last-minute vacancies or cancellations. *Use the coordinate (✢ A1) at the end of each listing to locate a site on the corresponding map.*

WHAT IT COSTS

	$	$$	$$$	$$$$
Restaurants	under $16	$16–$22	$23–$30	over $30

Restaurant prices are the average cost of a main course at dinner or, if dinner is not served, at lunch.

UNION SQUARE AND CHINATOWN

$ JAPANESE 🍴 **Katana-Ya.** From the moment it opens, there's a line in front of this hole-in-the-wall ramen house across from the American Conservatory Theater. Hand-drawn pictures of specials punctuate a colorful interior with too-close tables and a couple of stools around the bar. There's nothing fancy, but the ramen is among the most authentic in town. Add a couple of sushi rolls and gyozas to your order and be on your way. [$] *Average main: $8* ✉ *430 Geary St., Union Square* ☎ *415/771–1280* 🌐 *www.katanayausa.com* ✍ *Reservations not accepted* ✢ *E4.*

$$ CHINESE FAMILY 🍴 **R&G Lounge.** The name conjures up an image of a dark, smoky bar with a piano player, but this Cantonese restaurant is actually as bright as a new penny. On the lower level (entrance on Kearny Street) is a no-tablecloth dining room that's packed at lunch and dinner. The classy upstairs space (entrance on Commercial Street) is a favorite stop for special-occasion banquets and Chinese businessmen on expense accounts. The street-level room on Kearny is a comfortable spot to wait for an open table. A menu with photographs helps you pick from the many wonderful, sometimes pricey, always authentic dishes, such as the famous salt-and-pepper Dungeness crab, Peking duck, and shrimp-stuffed tofu. Much of the seafood is fresh from the tank. [$] *Average main: $16* ✉ *631 Kearny St., Chinatown* ☎ *415/982–7877* 🌐 *www.rnglounge.com* ✢ *F3.*

BEST BETS FOR SAN FRANCISCO DINING

With thousands of restaurants to choose from, how will you decide where to eat? Fodor's writers and editors have selected their favorite restaurants by price, cuisine, and experience in the Best Bets lists below. In the first column, Fodor's Choice designations represent the "best of the best" in every price category. You can also search by neighborhood for excellent eats—just peruse the following pages.

FodorsChoice★

Acquerello, $$$$, p. 434
Benu, $$$$, p. 428
Boulevard, $$$$, p. 436
Central Kitchen, $$$, p. 440
Coi, $$$$, p. 434
Coqueta, $$$, p. 436
Delfina, $$$, p. 440
Dosa on Fillmore, $$, p. 443
Dosa on Valencia, $$, p. 440
Gary Danko, $$$$, p. 436
Nopalito, $, p. 444
Rich Table, $$$, p. 429
State Bird Provisions, $$$, p. 444
Swan Oyster Depot, $$, p. 434
Zuni Café, $$$, p. 429

By Price

$

Burma Superstar, p. 445
Katana-Ya, p. 424
Nopalito, p. 444
Park Chow, p. 445
SanJalisco, p. 442
Tony's Pizza Napoletana, p. 435

$$

Bar Tartine, p. 439
Citizen's Band, p. 428
Dosa on Fillmore, p. 443
Nojo, p. 429
Zarzuela, p. 433

$$$

Cavalier, p. 428
Central Kitchen, p. 440
Coqueta, p. 436
Delfina, p. 440
Flour + Water, p. 441
Local's Corner, p. 441
Locanda, p. 441

Rich Table, p. 429
St. Vincent, p. 442
Wexler's, p. 432

$$$$

Acquerello, p. 434
Benu, $$$$, p. 428
Boulevard, p. 436
Coi, p. 434
Gary Danko, p. 436

By Cuisine

AMERICAN

Central Kitchen, $$$, p. 440
Citizen's Band, $$, p. 428
Greens, $$, p. 438
Nopa, $$$, p. 444
Park Chow, $, p. 445
Rich Table, $$$, p. 429
Verbena, $$, p. 433
Wexler's, $$$, p. 432

CHINESE

Yank Sing, $$, p. 433

ITALIAN

A16, $$$, p. 438
Delfina, $$$, p. 440
Locanda, $$$, p. 441

JAPANESE

Katana-Ya, $, p. 424
Nojo, $$, p. 429

MEDITERRANEAN

Coqueta, $$$, p. 436
Zarzuela, $$, p. 433
Zuni Café, $$$, p. 429

MEXICAN

Nopalito, $, p. 444
SanJalisco, $, p. 442

SEAFOOD

Hog Island Oyster Company, $$, p. 437
Local's Corner, $$$, p. 441
Swan Oyster Depot, $$, p. 434

By Experience

BAY VIEWS

Coqueta, $$$, p. 436
Greens, $$, p. 438
Slanted Door, $$$, p. 437

BRUNCH

Bar Tartine, $$, p. 439
Greens, $$, p. 438
Local's Corner, $$$, p. 441
Rose's Café, $$$, p. 438

8

NORCAL'S LOCAVORE FOOD MOVEMENT

FARMERS' MARKETS

Organic, local, and sustainable are buzzwords in Northern California, home to hundreds of small family farmers, sustainable ranchers, and artisan producers leading the country's back-to-the-earth food movement.

One of the best ways to taste Northern California's bounty is by stopping by the Ferry Plaza Farmers' Market, held outside the Ferry Building on the Embarcadero, at Market Street on Tuesday, Thursday, and Saturday morning. The market offers produce, meats, fish, and flowers from small regional farmers and ranchers, many of whom are certified organic producers.

When Alice Waters opened Chez Panisse in Berkeley in 1971, she sparked a culinary revolution that continues today. Initially called California cuisine, the cooking style showcased local, seasonal ingredients in fresh preparations. It also marked a new willingness by American chefs to experiment with international influences. As the movement spread, it became known as New American cooking. This "eat local, think global" ethos has led to a resurgence of artisanal producers across the country.

It is also a great place to pick up items for a picnic. Prepared foods such as tamales and pasta are available, as are jams, breads, and cheeses from local artisan producers.

The locavore (focused on sustainable, local foods) movement's epicenter is still Northern California. At the Ferry Plaza Farmers' Market in San Francisco alone, farmers bring more than 1,200 varieties of fruits and vegetables to market every year. Chefs proudly call out their purveyors on menus and websites, elevating humble vegetable growers to starring culinary roles.

Check ⊕ www.cuesa.org for hours.

FRUIT

Northern California's diverse climate makes it an ideal place to grow all types of fruit, from berries to stone fruit. Farmers' markets and restaurants abound with a staggering selection of produce: Blossom Bluff Orchards, south of San Francisco, offers more than 150 varieties of stone fruits, like apricots, nectarines, and peaches. North of the city, the Apple Farm grows 80 varieties of apples, pears, persimmons, quince, and French plums. The Bay Area is also one of the best places in the country to find rare fruit varieties such as aprium, cherimoya, cactus pear, jujube, and loquat; California's famous Meyer lemons—sweeter and less acidic than common lemons—are celebrated in restaurant desserts.

VEGETABLES

Some chefs give top billing to their produce purveyors, as in a recently observed menu touting a salad of Star Route Farm field greens with Picholine olives, sweet herbs, and goat cheese. Along with these tantalizing items, be on the lookout for locally grown artichokes, Asian vegetables, multihued beets and carrots, and heirloom varieties of tomatoes, squash, and beans.

MEAT

Family-owned ranches and farms are prominent in the region, with many raising organic or "humane certified"

beef, pork, lamb, and poultry. Upscale Bay Area restaurants are fervent about recognizing their high-quality protein producers. From recent menus at two well-known San Francisco restaurants: Wolfe Ranch quail with Murcott mandarins, smoked bacon and bok choy, and vanilla gastrique; and Prather Ranch lamb with fava greens, cranberry beans, crispy artichokes, and salsa verde.

FISH

Diners and shoppers will find myriad seafood from local waters, from farm-raised scallops to line-caught California salmon. On menus, look for Hog Island Oysters, a local producer that raises more than 3 million oysters a year in Tomales Bay. Sardines netted in Monterey Bay are popular in preparations like mesquite-grilled sardines with fava beans, French radish and fennel salad, and preserved Meyer lemon.

CHEESE

Restaurant cheese plates, often served before—or in lieu of—dessert, are a great way to experience the region's excellent local cheeses. Look for selections from Cypress Grove Chevre, popular for its artisan goat cheeses, and Cowgirl Creamery, a renowned local producer of fresh and aged cow's milk cheeses. Additionally, some shops and bakeries offer fresh local butter and cheeses.

8

SOMA

$$$$ MODERN AMERICAN Fodor's Choice ★ 🍴 **Benu.** One of the city's most high-profile establishments, chef-owner Corey Lee's contemporary American restaurant delights food-obsessed locals and travelers alike. Lee's pedigree spans 15 years in fine dining, including a position as chef de cuisine at Thomas Keller's the French Laundry, but Benu is decidedly more relaxed—no jacket required. The dining room is very minimalist, with bare-wood tables and high-backed banquettes along the walls. The pricy tasting menu ($195 per person) of 14 to 18 courses is mandatory. Each dish is a marvel, from the meticulous presentation (Lee has had pieces specifically designed for the restaurant and each course) to the sophisticated flavors and textures. Fans of Asian cuisine will be particularly thrilled to see his elegant handling of ingredients like a thousand-year-old quail egg, *xiao long bao* dumplings, and sea cucumber. He utilizes many modern techniques, but never in an alienating way. You may find dishes like Hokkaido sea cucumber stuffed with lobster, pork belly, eggplant, fermented pepper or eel, *feuille de brik* (flaky pastry), crème fraiche, lime. An extremely professional staff is behind the quick pacing and on-point wine pairings. Couples expecting an ultraromantic environment may be a bit disappointed by the stark atmosphere, but culinary adventurers will be thrilled. [$] *Average main: $195* ✉ *22 Hawthorne St., SoMa* ☎ *415/685–4860* 🌐 *www.benusf.com* ✍ *Reservations essential* 🕓 *Closed Sun. and Mon. No lunch* ✣ *G5.*

$$$ MODERN BRITISH 🍴 **Cavalier.** Occupying a hefty slice of Hotel Zetta's ground floor, Cavalier is a British pub with a Nor Cal sensibility. The celebratory space, the brainchild of restaurateur Anna Weinberg and chef Jennifer Puccio, has high ceilings, red walls, stuffed animal heads, large arched windows, and clusters of paintings imparting a decidedly British temperament. The gin-based cocktails pair well with starters such as deviled crab, rock shrimp, and duck-egg confit, and hearty mains include the Sunday chicken—bathed in a bacon-mustard *jus*—and rib-eye steak atop a bed of horseradish mashed potatoes. The service here is top-notch. [$] *Average main: $23* ✉ *Hotel Zetta, 360 Jessie St., SoMa* ☎ *415/321–6000* 🌐 *thecavaliersf.com* ✍ *Reservations essential* ✣ *E5.*

$$ DINER 🍴 **Citizen's Band.** A fresh take on the classic American diner, this busy corner spot seems to always pack in its coveted 40 seats. The draw: one of the city's tastiest versions of mac and cheese (topped with onion rings), fried chicken with red-eye gravy, and an excellent burger sandwiched inside a bun from the next-door neighbor, Pinkie's Bakery. Other "fine diner" dishes—among them seasonal salads and pan-roasted rock cod—further reveal chef-owner Chris Beerman's experience in upscale restaurants. Brunch brings eggs Benedict, while lunch has more sandwich options (try the fried chicken). The vibe is very SoMa, with an edgy and eclectic crowd that can match the rock-and-roll playing (sometimes loudly) on the stereo or at the club next door, but the well-chosen wine list keeps things elevated. Solo diners can try for a seat at the counter. The restaurant shares restrooms with the rock club next door. [$] *Average main: $22* ✉ *1198 Folsom St., at 8th St., SoMa* ☎ *415/556–4901* 🌐 *www.citizensbandsf.com* ✣ *E6 .*

HAYES VALLEY

$$ JAPANESE

🍴 **Nojo.** For a little bonhomie before the symphony, this buzzy yakitori and izakaya spot serves stellar Japanese pub food, made from Bay Area ingredients, and it encourages sharing. The menu is divided into items "on a stick" and "not on a stick." For the stick items, much of it is *yakitori* (grilled chicken), like chicken skin with matcha sea salt, neck with *tare* (a thick grilled sauce), or *tsukune* (a chicken meatball) with egg yolk sauce—all the different notes in the varied sauces are part of the taste adventure. The savory, rich custard, *chawan mushi*, has chunks of Dungeness crabmeat and shiitake mushrooms. Seating is at bamboo tables in a mod-Japanese-slash-San Franciscan setting with large windows overlooking Hayes Valley's main thoroughfare of Franklin. There are 20 sakes by the glass. **TIP→ Nojo requires a credit card number to hold a reservation.** [$] *Average main: $20* ✉ *231 Franklin St., Hayes Valley* ☎ *415/896–4587* 🌐 *www.nojosf.com* ⏲ *Closed Tues. No lunch Mon.* ✥ *C6.*

$$$ MODERN AMERICAN Fodor's Choice ★

🍴 **Rich Table.** This Hayes Valley restaurant is a brilliant example of fine dining without preciousness or formality. Beginning with the bar bites co-chefs Evan and Sarah Rich, alumni of Manhattan's Bouley restaurant and Mas (farmhouse) and San Francisco's Quince, Michael Mina, and Coi, magically transform simple ingredients such as Castelvetrano olives by marinating them in wasabi, seaweed, and lime juice. Casual doughnuts become exquisite delicacies—the dried-porcini ones are served with a raclette béchamel sauce for dipping. To this point, it's all finger food, but forks and knives are put to use for the half-dozen pastas and an equal number of appetizer and mains. Vased branches decorate the dining room, which has weathered-wood wallboards repurposed from a Northern California sawmill. There's a nice selection of wines by the glass and artisanal cocktails. There are even some original dessert cocktails, including the 1 Up (for Mario Bros. fans), with porcini-infused gin, sherry, egg, and cream. **TIP→ Ten bar seats are available for walk-ins.** [$] *Average main: $30* ✉ *199 Gough St., at Oak, Hayes Valley* ☎ *415/355–9085* 🌐 *www.richtablesf.com* ✍ *Reservations essential* ⏲ *Closed Tues. No lunch* ✥ *C6.*

$$$ MEDITERRANEAN Fodor's Choice ★

🍴 **Zuni Café.** After one bite of Zuni's succulent brick-oven-roasted whole chicken with Tuscan bread salad, you'll understand why the café is a perennial star. Food is served on two floors; the rabbit warren of rooms on the second level includes a balcony overlooking the main dining room. At the long copper bar a disparate mix of patrons reflecting the city's diversity—casual and dressy, young and old, hip and staid—communes over fresh oysters on the half shell and cocktails and wine. The southern French–Italian menu changes daily, though the signature chicken, prepared for two, is a fixture.

The simple dishes, made with excellent ingredients, include house-cured anchovies with Parmigiano-Reggiano, deep-fried squid and lemons, ricotta gnocchi with seasonal vegetables, and brick-oven squab with polenta. Nearly as famous as the chicken is the chocolatey flourless *gâteau Victoire*, served since the '80s. The most cheerful spot to sit is at the tip of the "pyramid window" near the bar, easier to score if you plan a late lunch. Zuni's world famous chef-owner, Judy Rodgers,

8

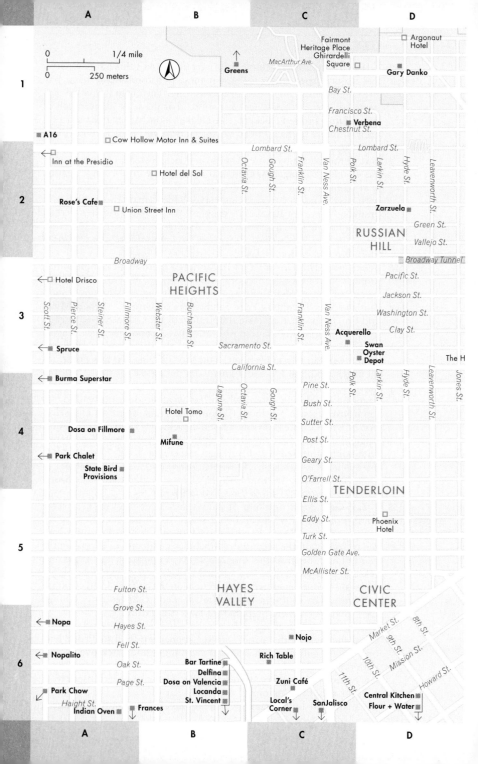

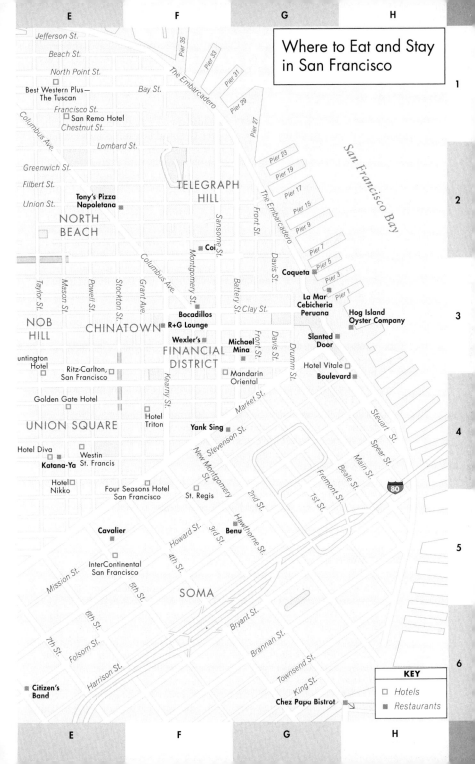

Where to Eat and Stay in San Francisco

KEY

☐ Hotels

■ Restaurants

passed away in 2013, but thanks to her strong guidance, the food remains outstanding. Ⓢ *Average main: $28* ✉ *1658 Market St., Hayes Valley* ☎ *415/552–2522* ⊕ *www.zunicafe.com* ◷ *Closed Mon.* ✛ *C6.*

FINANCIAL DISTRICT

$$
SPANISH

✕ **Bocadillos.** The name means "sandwiches," but that's only half the story here. You'll find a baker's dozen of bocadillos at lunchtime: plump rolls (pick two for $12) filled with everything from Serrano ham to Catalan sausage with arugula to a memorable lamb burger. At night chef-owner Gerald Hirigoyen, who also owns the high-profile Piperade, focuses on tapas, offering two-dozen choices, including roasted Monterey Bay squid, pig's trotters with chopped egg salad, and *patatas bravas* (potatoes) with *romesco* sauce (a thick combination of red pepper, tomato, almonds, and garlic). His wine list is well matched to the dishes. A youngish crowd typically piles into the redbrick dining space, whose aesthetic includes wire chairs and small, square light fixtures. Be prepared to wait for a seat. The large communal table is a good perch for singles. ■TIP➔ Breakfast is served here, too. The choices include house-made chorizo and eggs and a scrambled-eggs-and-cheese bocadillo. Ⓢ *Average main: $18* ✉ *710 Montgomery St., Financial District* ☎ *415/982–2622* ⊕ *www.bocasf.com* ⬁ *Reservations not accepted* ◷ *Closed Sun. No lunch Sat.* ✛ *F3.*

$$$$
ECLECTIC

✕ **Michael Mina.** Chef Michael Mina moved his eponymous restaurant and reopened in the former AQUA location on California Street, where he got his start (and worked for 13 years). In another flashback, Mina hired chef Ron Siegel, a former AQUA cook, to collaborate with him in the kitchen. The Euro-Japanese menu remains a treat, with luxurious renditions of shabu shabu, as well as classics like the lemon-poached fluke with black truffles. The most popular item, a lobster pot pie with Meyer lemons and smoked potatoes, blew up the blogosphere with raves. The space is chic and airy, highlighting natural elements like dark walnut tables and custom porcelain. The lounge area is the center of activity, drawing a busy Financial District scene after work (the cocktails and hors d'oeuvres sampler are recommended). Lunch is the time to sample the mastery of Mina at half the price, like his ahi tuna tartare with habanero-infused sesame oil, Asian pear, pine nuts, and quail egg yolk. Ⓢ *Average main: $38* ✉ *252 California St., Financial District* ☎ *415/397–9222* ⊕ *www. michaelmina.net* ◷ *No lunch Sat. and Sun.* ✛ *G3.*

$$$
BARBECUE

✕ **Wexler's.** Four words: bourbon banana cream pie. Of course, there's a slew of tempting barbecue items that threaten whether you'll have room at the end of the meal. This upscale comfort-food joint neighbors Wayfare Tavern, but for our food money Wexler's is first choice. The interior is chic, almost minimalist, with one mighty interesting ceiling sculpture and a couple of red chandeliers to liven up the place. Barbecue traditionalists should come with an open mind. The crispy Scotch eggs, fork-tender short ribs, and smoked wings (with Point Reyes blue cheese dressing) take their cues from barbecue but wander into more creative territory—chef Charlie Kleinman earned accolades while at the Hotel Palomar's late Fifth Floor restaurant. Purists might do better with Wexler's food truck parked out back on weekdays, serving pulled pork, chicken, and brisket with traditional sides such as hush puppies. **TIP→ The cocktails are fantastic here.** [$] *Average main: $24* ✉ *568 Sacramento St., Financial District* ☎ *415/983–0102* 🌐 *www.wexlerssf.com* 🕓 *Closed Sun. No dinner Mon. No lunch weekends* ✥ *F3.*

$$ CHINESE FAMILY 🍴 **Yank Sing.** The granddaddy of local dim sum teahouses opened in a plain-Jane storefront in Chinatown in 1959 but left its Cantonese neighbors behind for the high-rises of downtown in the 1970s. This brightly decorated location on quiet Stevenson Street—there's also a big, brassy branch in the Rincon Center—serves some of San Francisco's best dim sum to office workers on weekdays and boisterous families on weekends. The several dozen varieties of dim sum prepared daily include both the classic (steamed pork buns, shrimp dumplings, egg custard tartlets) and the creative (scallion-skewered prawns tied with bacon, lobster and *tobiko* roe dumplings, basil seafood dumplings). The Shanghai soup dumplings are perfection. Staffers pushing food carts whiz by tables constantly, and the tab can rise quickly, so pace yourself. The take-out counter makes a meal on the run a satisfying and penny-wise compromise when office duties—or touring—won't wait. [$] *Average main: $16* ✉ *49 Stevenson St., Financial District* ☎ *415/541–4949* 🌐 *www.yanksing.com* 🕓 *No dinner* ✥ *F4.*

RUSSIAN HILL

$$ MODERN AMERICAN 🍴 **Verbena.** Attention to detail and artistic presentations are the hallmarks of this recent venture from the creators of Berkeley's Gather restaurant. The dining room's brick walls, soft lighting, and dark-wood accents hint at chef Sean Baker's meticulous approach, and jars of pickled onions, peppers, and other vegetables—backlit and stacked high on wooden shelves—make clear the important role plant life plays in his menu. Each element seems carefully thought out, from the artisanal bread and butter to the carrots swimming in a smoky, barbecue-like sauce whose ingredients include cashews, lemon verbena, and mulberry-date molasses. The menu changes often but might include sardines with cauliflower, horseradish, trout roe, and chickweed; Koji quail served on Sonoma grains with slices of hedgehog mushroom awash in pumpkin juice; or duck meatballs in mole sauce. [$] *Average main: $22* ✉ *2323 Polk St, Russian Hill* ☎ *415/441–2323* 🌐 *www.verbenarestaurant.com* ✍ *Reservations essential* 🕓 *No lunch weekdays* ✥ *C1.*

$$ TAPAS 🍴 **Zarzuela.** Full-blooded Spaniards swear by the paella at this tiny old world–style bistro, complete with matador art on the wall, not far from the crookedest street in the world (Lombard). Also not to be missed is the homemade sangria—or the goat cheese baked in tomato sauce or poached octopus prepared by chef Lucas Gasco, who grew up in Madrid. Opened in 1994, Zarzuela was among the Bay Area's first wave of modern tapas restaurants and today offers about 30 small plates, as well as heartier dishes such as Catalan seafood stew. Arched windows overlook Hyde Street and the cable cars rolling by. Riding the Powell–Hyde line to and from dinner adds to the romance of the evening and saves you the nightmare of parking in this neighborhood where spaces are scarce. [$] *Average main: $21* ✉ *2000 Hyde St., Russian Hill* ☎ *415/346–0800* ✍ *Reservations not accepted* 🕓 *Closed Sun. and Mon. No lunch* ✥ *D2.*

VAN NESS/POLK

$$$$ ITALIAN Fodor's Choice ★

🍴 **Acquerello.** Devotees of chef-owner Suzette Gresham-Tognetti's high-end but soulful Italian cooking have swooned for years over her incomparable Parmesan *budino* (pudding) as well as the ridged pasta with foie gras and truffles. The latter dish, even with the California ban on foie gras, is still a favorite—Tognetti's chef de cuisine Mark Pensa has created a faux foie that is a dead ringer for the real item. Classics pepper the menu but there are also some cutting-edge touches, techniques, and flavors. Dinners are prix-fixe, with three ($82), four ($96), or five ($110) courses and at least six choices within each course. Tognetti also tempts with a seasonal eight-course tasting menu ($145). The cheese course is not to be missed, with rare cheeses from Piemonte, and other regions, rolled tableside. Co-owner Giancarlo Paterlini oversees the service and his son Gianpaolo presides over the roughly 1,900-bottle list of Italian wines. The room, in a former chapel, with wooden vaulted ceiling and terra-cotta and pale-ocher palette, is refined but never stuffy—and neither is the service. Every member of the dining staff is honest and welcoming, knowing that many people here are celebrating special occasions. They will make it a night to be remembered. This true San Francisco dining gem is worth every penny. [$] *Average main: $82* ✉ *1722 Sacramento St., Van Ness/Polk* ☎ *415/567–5432* 🌐 *www.acquerello.com* ✍ *Reservations essential* 🕓 *Closed Sun. and Mon. No lunch* ✥ *C3.*

$$ SEAFOOD Fodor's Choice ★

🍴 **Swan Oyster Depot.** Half fish market and half diner, this small, slim, family-run seafood operation, open since 1912, has no tables, just a narrow marble counter with about a dozen-and-a-half stools. Most people come in to buy perfectly fresh salmon, halibut, crabs, and other seafood to take home. Everyone else hops onto one of the rickety stools to enjoy a bowl of clam chowder—the only hot food served—a dozen oysters, half a cracked crab, a slice of crusty sourdough, a big shrimp salad, or a smaller shrimp cocktail. It's all served up with a side of big personality from the jovial folks behind the counter who make you feel like a regular. **■ TIP→ Come before 11 am or after 2 pm to avoid a long wait, and bring a full wallet: old-school Swan only takes cash.** [$] *Average main: $18* ✉ *1517 Polk St., Nob Hill* ☎ *415/673–1101* ✍ *Reservations not accepted* 💳 *No credit cards* 🕓 *Closed Sun. No dinner* ✥ *D3.*

NORTH BEACH

$$$$ MODERN AMERICAN Fodor's Choice ★

🍴 **Coi.** Daniel Patterson, who has made a name for himself internationally both as a chef and as a pundit on contemporary restaurant trends, has created a destination restaurant, an enchanting spot on the gritty end of Broadway. There are two dining rooms: the front room, casual with chocolate-color leather chairs and rustic wood tables, and the 30-seat formal dining room, with soft lighting, natural linens, and handcrafted pottery. The 11-course meal ($195) chef Patterson prepares fully expresses the bounty of Bay Area produce and other ingredients. The highly seasonal and obsessively sourced food—some of it foraged by Patterson himself—matches the space in sophistication. The inspired

CLOSE UP

Eating with Kids

Kids can be fussy eaters, and parents can be, too. Fortunately, there are plenty of excellent options in the city that will satisfy both.

✕ **City View Restaurant.** Over in Chinatown, City View serves a varied selection of dim sum, with tasty pork buns for kids and more exotic fare such as chicken feet and turnip cakes for adults. Though less expensive than nearby Yank Sing, this bustling restaurant is no less busy, so be prepared for epic weekend waits. $ *Average main: $1* ⊠ *662 Commercial St., near Kearny St.* ☎ *415/398–2838.*

The Ferry Building on the Embarcadero has plenty of kid-friendly options, from **Mijita Cocina Mexicana,** which has its own kids' menu, to **Gott's Roadside,** for burgers, shakes, and more. (And the outdoor access can help keep the little ones entertained.)

✕ **La Corneta.** The Mission has dozens of no-frills taco-and-burrito parlors; especially worthy is La Corneta, known for its baby burrito (which is basically just a smaller-sized

version) and the huge quesadillas. Vegetarians will be satisfied by the bean selection. $ *Average main: $1* ⊠ *2731 Mission St., between 23rd and 24th Sts.* ☎ *415/643–7001.*

Rosamunde Sausage Grill. In Lower Haight, the small Rosamunde serves a slew of different sausages, from Polish to duck to *Weisswurst* (Bavarian veal). Toppings (choose two) include grilled onions, sauerkraut, chili, and sweet and hot peppers. There are only six stools, so plan on take-out. ■ TIP➔ **Nearby Duboce Park has a cute playground.** ⊠ *545 Haight St., between Steiner and Fillmore Sts.* ☎ *415/437–6851.*

Park Chalet. Finally, both kids and adults love to be by the ocean, and the Park Chalet, hidden behind the two-story Beach Chalet, offers pizza, mac and cheese, sticky ribs, and a big banana split. On sunny days, you'll be hard-pressed to find a plot of grass to claim as families gather on blankets and folding chairs to sip the house-brewed beers and listen to live music. ⊠ *1000 Great Hwy., at Fulton St.* ☎ *415/386–8439.*

8

dishes include Dungeness crab raviolo with sheep sorrel and butter crab broth, and aged duck breast with stuffed cabbage, roasted beets, horseradish, and dill. Patterson is always tinkering and innovating, brining and curing, so the culinary experience always feels new and exciting. $ *Average main: $195* ⊠ *373 Broadway, North Beach* ☎ *415/393–9000* ⊕ *www.coirestaurant.com* ⤳ *Reservations essential* ⊗ *Closed Sun. and Mon. No lunch* ✛ *F2.*

$

PIZZA

FAMILY

✕ **Tony's Pizza Napoletana.** Locals hotly debate who makes the city's best pizza, and for many Tony Gemignani takes the prize. His reputation extends well beyond the city: at the World Pizza Cup in Naples he eclipsed the Italians for the title of World Champion Pizza Maker. The dough at his restaurant is flavorful and fired just right, with multiple wood-burning ovens in his casual, modern pizzeria turning out many different pies—the famed Neapolitan-style Margherita, but also Sicilian, Romana, and Detroit styles, and even coal-fired. Salads, antipasti, homemade pastas, and calzone, round out the menu. At the counter next door you can grab a slice quickly. ■ TIP→ If you're dining with kids, ask for some pizza dough to keep them entertained. Ⓢ *Average main: $15 ⊠ 1570 Stockton St., North Beach* ☎ *415/835–9888* ⊕ *www. tonyspizzanapoletana.com* ⌂ *Reservations not accepted* ⊙ *Closed Mon. and Tues.* ✛ *E2.*

FISHERMAN'S WHARF

$$$$
MODERN
AMERICAN
Fodor'sChoice
★

✕ **Gary Danko.** In high season plan on reserving two months ahead at Chef Danko's namesake restaurant—his legion of fans typically keep the reservation book full. The cost of a meal ($73–$107) is pegged to the number of courses, from three to five, and the menu spans a classic yet Californian style that changes seasonally. Dishes might include risotto with lobster and rock shrimp, lemon pepper duck breast with duck hash, and herb-crusted lamb loin. A diet-destroying chocolate soufflé with two sauces is usually among the desserts. The wine list is the size of a small-town phone book, and the banquette-lined rooms, with beautiful wood floors and stunning (but restrained) floral arrangements, are as memorable as the food and impeccable service. Ⓢ *Average main: $73 ⊠ 800 N. Point St., Fisherman's Wharf* ☎ *415/749–2060* ⊕ *www.garydanko.com* ⌂ *Reservations essential* 🏠 *Jacket required* ⊙ *No lunch* ✛ *D1.*

EMBARCADERO

$$$$
AMERICAN
Fodor'sChoice
★

✕ **Boulevard.** Two local restaurant celebrities—chef Nancy Oakes and designer Pat Kuleto—are behind this high-profile, high-priced eatery in the 1889 Audiffred Building, a Parisian look-alike that survived the 1906 quake. Kuleto's Belle-Époque interior and Oakes's sophisticated American food with a French accent attract well-dressed locals and flush out-of-towners. The menu changes seasonally, but count on generous portions of dishes such as Maine lobster ravioli, grilled king salmon with wild rice and vegetables that include chanterelle mushrooms, and a wood-grilled pork prime rib chop with Kabocha squash gnocchi (all the entrées come with delicious side dishes). Save room for one of the dynamite desserts, among them the dark-chocolate brioche custard. There's counter seating for folks too hungry to wait for a table, and an American Wagyu beef burger with Cowgirl Creamery cheese at lunchtime for those who want to dine here without raiding the piggy bank. The wine list and excellent service are two additional Boulevard hallmarks. Ⓢ *Average main: $36 ⊠ 1 Mission St., Embarcadero* ☎ *415/543–6084* ⊕ *www.boulevardrestaurant.com* ⌂ *Reservations essential* ⊙ *No lunch weekends* ✛ *H4.*

$$$
SPANISH
Fodor'sChoice
★

✕ **Coqueta.** With its Embarcadero perch, Bay Bridge views, and stellar Spanish tapas, celebrity chef Michael Chiarello's San Francisco debut was an instant hit. Equal parts rustic and chic, his dining room's bold decor—stained wooden beams, cowhide rugs, marble bar—sends out the visual message that Chiarello is at the top of his game, and it's fun to see him mingling with diners as they enjoy toothpicked *pintxos* (small snacks) such as quail egg with Serrano ham. The real draws, though, are the inventive cocktails, luscious paella, and dazzling variation on the cut of pork *secreto Ibérico* (Iberian secret). The desserts are also small bites, so you'll likely have room to end your experience on a sweet note. ■ **TIP→ Book well in advance for dinner.** [$] *Average main: $30* ✉ *Pier 5, on the Embarcadero, near Broadway, Embarcadero* ☎ *415/704–8866* 🌐 *coquetasf.com* ✍ *Reservations essential* ✣ *G3.*

$$ SEAFOOD 🍴 **Hog Island Oyster Company.** A thriving oyster farm north of San Francisco in Tomales Bay, Hog Island serves up its harvest at its newly expanded raw bar and restaurant in the busy Ferry Building. Devotees come here for impeccably fresh oysters (from Hog Island and elsewhere) and clams (from Hog Island) on the half shell. Other mollusk-centered options include a first-rate oyster stew, baked oysters, clam chowder, and "steamer" dishes atop a bed of local greens. The bar also turns out one of the city's best grilled-cheese sandwiches, made with three artisanal cheeses on artisanal bread. [$] *Average main: $20* ✉ *Ferry Bldg., Embarcadero at Market St., Embarcadero* ☎ *415/391–7117* 🌐 *www.hogislandoysters.com* ✍ *Reservations not accepted* ✣ *H3.*

$$$ PERUVIAN 🍴 **La Mar Cebicheria Peruana.** Right on the water's edge, the casually chic La Mar is divided into three areas: a lounge with a long ceviche bar where diners watch the chefs put plates together; the Pisco Bar facing the Embarcadero, where bartenders mix cocktails based on Peru's famed Pisco brandy; and a bright blue and whitewashed dining room overlooking an outdoor patio and the bay. Your waiter will start you out with a pile of potato and plantain chips with three dipping sauces, but after that you're on your own, choosing from a long list of ceviches, can't-miss *causas* (whipped potatoes topped with a choice of fish, shellfish, or vegetable salads), and everything from crisp, lightly deep-fried fish and shellfish to soups and stews and rice dishes, many spiked with Peruvian chilis. The original La Mar is in Lima, Peru. San Francisco was the first stop in its campaign to open a string of *cebicherías* across the United States and Latin America. The view of the water is especially enjoyable during lunch or a warm evening. [$] *Average main: $25* ✉ *Pier 1½ between Washington and Jackson Sts., Embarcadero* ☎ *415/397–8880* 🌐 *www.lamarcebicheria.com* ✣ *G3.*

8

$$$ VIETNAMESE 🍴 **Slanted Door.** If you're looking for homey Vietnamese food served in a down-to-earth dining room at a decent price, *don't* stop here. Celebrated chef-owner Charles Phan has mastered the upmarket, Western-accented Vietnamese menu. To showcase his cuisine, he built a big space with sleek wooden tables and chairs, white marble floors, a cocktail lounge, a bar, and an enviable bay view. Among his popular cult dishes are green-papaya salad, daikon rice cakes, cellophane crab noodles, chicken clay pot, and shaking beef (tender beef cubes with garlic and onion). They don't come cheap, but they're made with quality ingredients. The restaurant has also become a regular stop for those who appreciate finely made cocktails, many of them created by star bartender Erik Adkins. ■ **TIP→ To avoid the midday and evening crowds (and to save some bucks), dine at the bar, drop by for afternoon tea (2:30–4:30), or visit Out the Door, Phan's take-out counter around the corner.** [$] *Average main: $29* ✉ *Ferry Bldg., Embarcadero at Market St., Embarcadero* ☎ *415/861–8032* 🌐 *www.slanteddoor.com* ✍ *Reservations essential* ✣ *H3.*

MARINA

$$$ ✕ **A16.** Marina residents—and, judging from the crowds, everybody
ITALIAN else—gravitate to this trattoria named for the autostrada that traverses
Italy's sunny south. The kitchen serves the food of Naples and surround-
ing Campania, with the added twist of seasonal California ingredients.
Cult classics include the creamy burrata with olive oil and crostini and
crisp-crust pizzas, including a classic Neapolitan Margherita (mozza-
rella, tomato, and basil). Rustic pasta favorites such as *maccaronara*
with *ragu napoletana* and house-made salted ricotta might show up
on the menu, and for an entrée perhaps petrale sole with crispy black
trumpet mushrooms. The selection of primarily southern Italian wines,
augmented by some well-chosen California vintages, supports the food
perfectly, and there's a substantial beer list. ■TIP➜ **The animated bar
scene near the door sets the tone at A16; for a quieter time request a
table in the alcove at the far end or try for the patio.** Ⓢ *Average main:
$25* ✉ *2355 Chestnut St., Marina* ☎ *415/771–2216* ⊕ *www.a16sf.com*
⌂ *Reservations essential* ☽ *No lunch Sat.–Tues.* ✛ *A1.*

$$ ✕ **Greens.** Owned and operated by the San Francisco Zen Center, this
VEGETARIAN nonprofit vegetarian restaurant gets some of its fresh produce from
the center's organic Green Gulch Farm. Floor-to-ceiling windows give
diners a sweeping view of the Marina and the Golden Gate Bridge.
Despite the lack of meat, hearty dishes from chef Annie Somerville—
shepherd's pie with wild mushrooms, for example, or the vegetable
brochette plate—really satisfy. Other standouts include thin-crust pizza
with local cheese, potato, and grilled onions, and the salads are something special, especially the wilted spinach salad with croutons, feta, and
olives. An à la carte menu is offered on Sunday and weeknights, but on
Saturday a $56 four-course prix-fixe dinner is served. Weekend brunch
is a good time to watch boaters on the bay. A small counter just inside
the front door stocks sandwiches, soups, and sweets for easy takeout,
and it's open in the morning. Ⓢ *Average main: $19* ✉ *Bldg. A, Fort
Mason, enter across Marina Blvd. from Safeway, Marina* ☎ *415/771–
6222* ⊕ *www.greensrestaurant.com* ⌂ *Reservations essential* ☽ *No
lunch Mon.* ✛ *B1.*

COW HOLLOW

$$$ ✕ **Rose's Café.** Sleepy-headed locals turn up at Rose's for the break-
ITALIAN fast pizza of smoked ham, eggs, and fontina; house-baked pastries and
FAMILY breads; poached eggs with Yukon Gold potato and mushroom hash;
and soft polenta with mascarpone and jam. Midday is time for pizza
with wild nettles, or linguine with clams. Evening hours find customers
eating their way through more pizza and pasta if on a budget, and skirt
steak and a glorious roasted chicken if not. The ingredients are top-
notch, the service is friendly, and the seating is in comfortable booths
and at tables and a counter. Heaters above the outdoor tables keep
things toasty when the temperature dips. ■TIP➜ **Expect long lines for
Sunday brunch.** Ⓢ *Average main: $27* ✉ *2298 Union St., Cow Hollow*
☎ *415/775–2200* ⊕ *www.rosescafesf.com* ✛ *A2.*

THE HAIGHT

$ ✕ **Indian Oven.** This white-tablecloth northern Indian restaurant draws
INDIAN diners from all over the city who come for the tandoori specialties—
chicken, lamb, breads. Classics like *saag paneer* (spinach with Indian
cheese), *aloo gobhi* (potato, cauliflower, and spices), and *bengan bar-
tha* (roasted eggplant with onions and spices) are also excellent. The
chef wants to keep his clientele around for the long haul, too, and puts
a little "heart healthy" icon on the menu next to items that warrant
it. On Friday and Saturday night, famished patrons overflow onto
the sidewalk to wait for open tables; some retreat next door to the
affiliated Clay Oven. If you linger too long over a mango *lassi* or the
excellent *kheer* (rice pudding) on one of these nights, you'll likely be
hurried along by a waiter. For better service, come on a weeknight
or for lunch. $ *Average main: $13* ✉ *233 Fillmore St., Lower Haight*
☎ *415/626–1628* ✛ *A6.*

THE CASTRO

$$$ ✕ **Frances.** Still one of the hottest tickets in town, Frances is located,
FRENCH ironically, on one of the Castro's quieter streets. Chef-owner Melissa
Perello's California and French cuisine is well executed and, for the
quality, notably affordable. Bacon beignets, tender gnocchi, and a
savory bavette steak are longtime favorites on the seasonally driven
menu, with newer entries such as baked clams with bacon cream and
a duck confit and baby kale salad angling to become standbys as well.
The apple galette for dessert hits all the right notes. The small space is
simply designed, with a limited number of tables (hence the difficulty
in landing a reservation) and a small bar area with counter seating for
walk-ins desperate to dine here. Service is professional and warm. $ *Av-
erage main: $27* ✉ *3870 17th St., Castro* ☎ *415/621–3870* ⊕ *www.
frances-sf.com* ⌦ *Reservations essential* ◷ *No lunch* ✛ *A6.*

THE MISSION

$$ ✕ **Bar Tartine.** An offshoot of the cultlike Tartine Bakery, this neigh-
MODERN borhood restaurant in an artsy space provides a way to taste the bak-
AMERICAN ery's famed (and nearly always sold-out) country loaf. Chef Nicolaus
Balla's flavor-packed cuisine combines an Eastern European sensibility
with California seasonality and some Japanese influences. The menu
includes many house-pickled items, tempting *langos* (fried potato
bread), and seasonal salads such as one with persimmons, pressed
cheese, chicories, walnuts, and orange honey. Chicken *paprikas* and
fisherman's stew are among the larger, homey dishes Balla prepares.
The extensive wine-and-beer list makes this a fun place to swing by
for a glass—if you can find a seat. Weekend brunch is one of the
city's more distinct offerings in that category, with an array of *smørrebrød* (toppings like trumpet mushrooms, mizuna, and cultured butter on sprouted rye) and buckwheat blintzes, and a beef-brisket hash
with celery root, parsnip, Yukon Gold potatoes, and fried eggs. On
Wednesday, Thursday, and Friday afternoon, the restaurant operates

a shop that serves sandwiches, smørrebrød, and light snacks. [$] *Average main: $16* ✉ *561 Valencia St., Mission* ☎ *415/487–1600* 🌐 *www.bartartine.com* 🕐 *Closed Mon. No lunch Tues.* ✥ *B6.*

$$$ MODERN AMERICAN Fodor's Choice ★ 🍴 **Central Kitchen.** It's nearly impossible to score seats at chef Thomas McNaughton's highly lauded Flour + Water. That's why many had plum visions of sampling his cuisine again when the Gary Danko alumnus opened this spot in a former sausage factory. Central Kitchen is the centerpiece of a modern open space, with tea lights strung along the ceiling; also in the building are Salumeria (a deli and larder, which sells Flour + Water pastas) and Trick Dog, an energetic cocktail bar. The menu is original, with playful combos and surprising flavors: Parker House rolls baked with coffee and caraway; raw Hamachi topped with fennel (from the rooftop garden) roasted until it's ash, for a strong smokiness that combines with citruses into a vinaigrette; an inky cioppino, with burnt peppers as its base that make the broth luscious. In addition to the starters, there are about four main-dish items nightly. The seven-course tasting menu ($95) provides the ultimate food journey. [$] *Average main: $30* ✉ *3000 20th St., Mission* ☎ *415/826–7004* 🌐 *www.centralkitchensf.com* 🕐 *No lunch Mon.–Sat.* ✥ *D6.*

$$$ ITALIAN Fodor's Choice ★ 🍴 **Delfina.** "Irresistible." That's how countless die-hard fans describe Craig and Anne Stoll's Delfina. Such wild enthusiasm has made patience the critical virtue for anyone wanting a reservation here (although walk-ins can find some success at a counter and in the bar area). The urban interior is comfortable, with hardwood floors, aluminum-top tables, and a tile bar. Although the menu changes daily, among the usual offerings are grilled squid with warm white-bean salad and excellent tripe. As boring as spaghetti with tomato sauce may sound, it's been dialed to perfection here, and there would be a neighborhood revolt if it ever disappeared. If Piemontese fresh white truffles have made their way to San Francisco, you are likely to find hand-cut tagliarini dressed with butter, cream, and the pricey aromatic fungus on the menu alongside dishes built on more prosaic ingredients. The panna cotta is the best in its class. The storefront next door is home to pint-size Pizzeria Delfina. And for folks who can't get to the Mission, the Stolls have opened a second pizzeria on California Street in Lower Pacific Heights. [$] *Average main: $25* ✉ *3621 18th St., Mission* ☎ *415/552–4055* 🌐 *www.delfinasf.com* ✍ *Reservations essential* 🕐 *No lunch* ✥ *B6.*

$$ INDIAN Fodor's Choice ★ 🍴 **Dosa on Valencia.** If you like Indian food but crave more than chicken tikka masala and naan, Dosa is for you. This temple of South Indian cuisine, done in cheerful tones of tangerine and turmeric, serves not only the large, thin savory pancake for which it is named, but also curries, *uttapam* (open-face pancakes), and various starters, breads, rice dishes, and chutneys. You can select from about 10 different dosa fillings, ranging from traditional potatoes, onions, and cashews to spinach and fennel stems. Each comes with tomato and fresh coconut chutneys and *sambar* (lentil curry) for dipping. Tamil lamb curry with fennel and tomatoes and poppy seed prawns are popular, as are starters such as *Chennai* chicken (chicken marinated in yogurt and spices and lightly fried), and the new Indian street-food additions, among them *vada pav* (a vegetarian slider). The wine and beer lists are top drawer, and both

include some Indian brands; the cocktail list is also very food-friendly. Weekend brunch offers a nice change from the usual menu suspects (the flavorful *pani puri* are a must). Queues for this spot inspired the owners to open a second, splashier and much bigger, branch at the corner of Fillmore and Post streets in Japantown. [$] *Average main: $18* ✉ *995 Valencia St., at 21st St., Mission* ☎ *415/642–3672* 🌐 *www.dosasf.com* 🕒 *No lunch weekdays* ✥ *B6.*

$$$ ITALIAN 🍴 **Flour + Water.** Diners used to flood into this hot spot for the blistery thin-crust Neapolitan pizza, but these days it's the pasta that holds attention, merging beautifully with chef Thomas McNaughton's whole-animal sensibilities. The grand experience here is the seven-course pasta-tasting menu at $65 per person (plus $45 for wine pairings). The homemade mustard tagliatelle with smoked lamb's tongue is surprisingly zippy, with lemon zest lifting and extracting flavors. The perfectly chewy rigatoni comes with a braised pork–laced tomato sauce. Pizzas are still being pulled from the 900-degree wood-burning oven, but they aren't what they used to be. Paxton Gate designed the dining room, and the local firm's whimsical touches are in evidence throughout: tabletop beakers as candleholders, for instance, a moth-wing wall mural, and a cabinet of taxidermy in the bathroom. Expect a noisy, boisterous scene. Trying to get a reservation at Flour + Water is one of the longest-running jokes in town. Walk-ins are ecstatic to nab a seat at the reclaimed wood bar, made from wine-barrel staves. Your best bet is to come when the doors open. [$] *Average main: $26* ✉ *2401 Harrison St., Mission* ☎ *415/826–7000* 🌐 *www.flourandwater.com* 🕒 *No lunch* ✥ *D6.*

$$$ SEAFOOD 🍴 **Local's Corner.** Hang on, because chef Jake Des Voignes is about to take you on a seafood joyride. With no industrial ovens or high-powered burners, this 30-seat place is really about the delicate, natural flavors of California's seasonal bounty, from the fish to the fennel, Japanese yams, and sunchokes. In typical San Francisco style, the menu reads like a jumble of ingredients, making it difficult to imagine how they might taste together, but each dish works beautifully, like creamy uni with crunchy English peas and preserved Meyer lemon, or cured halibut with diced, sweet pluots. To immerse yourself in Des Voignes's genius, make a reservation for the seven-course tasting ($65) at the chef's counter. The three-course brunches are as well-crafted as dinner, with dishes that include waffles with chicory syrup, and chicken sausage and polenta. Although the food is solid, the service is too casual. [$] *Average main: $25* ✉ *2500 Bryant St., Mission* ☎ *415/800–7945* 🌐 *www.localscornersf.com* 🕒 *Closed Mon.* ✥ *C6.*

$$$ ITALIAN 🍴 **Locanda.** Annie and Craig Stoll, the owners of Delfina, have bestowed another culinary gift on the city. This time her name is Locanda, and the menu is Roman inspired. A dangerously addictive starter is *pizza bianca*: chewy, hot bread that holds mini puddles of olive oil and is sprinkled with sea salt. It's hard to decide on a pasta with so many represented. A signature one, *tonnarelli cacio e pepe*, is a creamy, peppery smack of flavor. A good strategy here is to double down on pastas and antipasti, then share a main, like the lamb *scottadito*, seasoned with anchovies and coriander. Finely made cocktails (Negroni flights even) arrive at dark-wood tables on a candlelit tray, and white Heath wall tiles pump up the sophisticated interior. This is a busy place with the bar stools constantly occupied, and the communal table filling quickly each night. $ *Average main: $28* ✉ *557 Valencia St., Mission* ☎ *415/863–6800* ⊕ *www.locandasf.com* ◷ *No lunch* ✛ *B6.*

$ ✕ **SanJalisco.** This old-time, sun-filled, colorful, family-run restaurant is
MEXICAN   a neighborhood gem—and not only because it serves breakfast all day.
FAMILY   Try the hearty *chilaquiles,* made from day-old tortillas cut into strips and cooked with cheese, eggs, chilies, and sauce. Or order eggs scrambled with cactus or with *chicharrones* (crisp pork skins) and served with freshly made tortillas. Soup offerings change daily, with Tuesday's *albondigas* (meatballs) comfort food at its best. On weekends, adventurous eaters may opt for *birria,* a spicy goat stew, or *menudo,* a tongue-searing soup made from tripe, calf's foot, and hominy. The latter is a time-honored hangover cure—but don't come expecting margaritas here (though you will find beer and sangria). Bring plenty of change for the jukebox loaded with Latin hits. $ *Average main: $11* ✉ *901 S. Van Ness Ave., Mission* ☎ *415/648–8383* ⊕ *www.sanjalisco.com* ✛ *C6.*

$$$ ✕ **St. Vincent.** Sommelier David Lynch is behind this modern-day Ameri-
MODERN   can tavern with a Bay Area spin. Previously at Babbo in New York
AMERICAN   and Quince in San Francisco, Lynch has put together a list of mostly European wines, with an innovative half-bottle program, and chef Bill Niles, formerly of Bar Tartine, creates rustic upscale food to accompany them. On the snacky side of things, we challenge you to eat just *one* curried, pickled egg. These starters are outrageously good, as is the hand-rolled pretzel, and the dry-aged sirloin for two comes with some of the best gratin potatoes known to man. This is lick-your-plate-clean food served in a welcoming, somewhat noisy place (wood surfaces, soaring ceilings) where Lynch himself will suggest a wine, or cicerone Sayre Piotrkowski will pair a beer with dinner or dessert. Winning seats are at the zinc-topped bar, where you can bend the ear of both men. They also run a retail wine business. $ *Average main: $27* ✉ *1270 Valencia St., Mission* ☎ *415/285–1200* ⊕ *www.stvincentsf.com* ◷ *Closed Sun. No lunch* ✛ *B6.*

POTRERO HILL

$$ ✕ **Chez Papa Bistrot.** France arrived on Potrero Hill with this restaurant,
FRENCH   which delivers food, waiters, and charm that would be right at home in Provence. The modest corner spot, with a Mediterranean blue awning, big windows overlooking the street, and a small heated patio, caters to a lively crowd that can make conversation difficult. Small plates include bistro classics such as beef tartare, mussels in pastis, and a leek and tomato tart. Duck confit, grilled flat-iron steak and frites, and homey lamb daube are among the big plates. The lavender crème brûlée and chocolate fondant provide sweet endings. The $36.95 prix-fixe menu is an excellent deal. To accommodate the overflow of Hill residents, who have packed this place since day one, the owners opened the tiny, more casual Chez Maman (crepes, burgers, salads) a few doors away. $ *Average main: $24* ✉ *1401 18th St., Potrero Hill* ☎ *415/824–8205* ⊕ *www.chezpapasf.com* ◷ *No lunch Sun.* ✛ *H6.*

PACIFIC HEIGHTS

$$$
MODERN
AMERICAN

✕ **Spruce.** A hot reservation from the day it opened, Spruce caters to the social set, with the older crowd sliding into oversized faux ostrich leather chairs for an early dinner and the younger set appearing after 8. There's also quite the lunch club during the week. The large space, an auto barn from the 1930s, contains a high-style dining room and a more casual bar and library lounge. Charcuterie, bavette steak with bordelaise sauce and duck-fat potatoes, and sweetbreads reflect the modern American menu's French leanings. The wine list, a star here, provides special delights for Riesling fans. If you can't wrangle a table, stop by the take-out café next door, which in addition to sandwiches, salads, and pastries (like the exquisite palmiers) will supply anything from the dining room menu. If you're watching your pocketbook, you can graze off the bar menu—which includes an excellent burger and *boudin blanc* (white sausage)—and over a well-crafted cocktail watch the swells come and go. $ *Average main: $34* ✉ *3640 Sacramento St., Pacific Heights* ☎ *415/931–5100* ⊕ *www.sprucesf.com* ⌖ *Reservations essential* ☾ *No lunch weekends* ✛ *A3.*

JAPANTOWN

$$
INDIAN
Fodor's Choice
★

✕ **Dosa on Fillmore.** As soon as the large door swings open to this happening two-level space, diners are greeted with a sexy atmosphere with bright colors, vivid artwork, upbeat music, a lively bar, and the smell of spices in the air. This is the second location of the popular Dosa on Valencia, but it's definitely the glamorous younger sister, with a full bar, an expanded menu, and much more room. The menu entices with savory fish dishes, fall-off-the-bone pepper chicken, and papery dosas stuffed with various fillings. The restaurant handles group dining often, and has a special menu you can customize. Return for lunch and indulge in the Indian street-food selections, and the famed *pani puri* (little crisp puffs you fill with mint and tamarind water and pop all at once into your mouth). $ *Average main: $17* ✉ *1700 Fillmore St., Japantown* ☎ *415/441–3672* ⊕ *www.dosasf.com* ☾ *No lunch Mon. and Tues.* ✛ *A4.*

$
JAPANESE
FAMILY

✕ **Mifune.** Thin brown soba and thick white udon are the stars at this long-popular North American outpost of an Osaka-based noodle empire. A line regularly snakes out the door, but the house-made noodles, served both hot and cold and with a score of toppings, are worth the wait (and the line moves quickly). Seating is at wooden tables, where diners of every age can be heard slurping down big bowls of such traditional Japanese combinations as *nabeyaki udon,* wheat noodles topped with tempura, chicken, and fish cake; and *tenzaru,* cold noodles and hot tempura with gingery dipping sauce served on lacquered trays. The noodle-phobic can choose from a few rice dishes and sushi. $ *Average main: $12* ✉ *Japan Center, Kintetsu Bldg., 1737 Post St., Japantown* ☎ *415/922–0337* ⊕ *www.mifune.com* ✛ *B4.*

8

WESTERN ADDITION

$$$ AMERICAN

🍴 **Nopa.** In the mid-2000s North of the Panhandle became the city's newest talked-about neighborhood in part because of big, bustling Nopa, which was cleverly named after it. The casual space, with its high ceilings, concrete floor, long bar, and sea of tables, suits the high-energy crowd of young professionals and stylish neighborhood residents. Because the kitchen doesn't close until 1 am, restaurant-industry types pack the bar late into the night. The rustic fare includes an always winning flatbread topped with fennel sausage and caramelized onions; Moroccan-style vegetable *tagine* (stew) with lemon yogurt; smoky, crisp-skin rotisserie chicken; a juicy grass-fed hamburger with thick-cut fries; one of the city's best pork chops; and, for dessert, the doughnut-like sopapillas. This place is so lively that raised voices are sometimes the only way to communicate with fellow diners. A big communal table and the friendly bar ease the way for those dining solo. The wine list is excellent, and weekend brunch is among the city's best—and most popular, so arrive a few minutes before the 11 am opening to score a table. [$] *Average main: $24* ✉ *560 Divisadero St., Western Addition* ☎ *415/864–8643* 🌐 *www.nopasf.com* ⏲ *No lunch weekdays* ✥ *A6.*

$ MEXICAN FAMILY Fodor's Choice ★

🍴 **Nopalito.** The two chefs at this unusual Mexican restaurant formerly worked in the kitchen at nearby Nopa; they made such delicious staff/family meals there that Nopa's owners developed this restaurant around their cuisine. The authentic, skillfully prepared dishes range from seasonal salads and a spicy beef empanada to succulent pork carnitas and a fulfilling posole. All the tortillas are made from organic house-ground *masa* (dough), also used in the tortilla chips layering the *chilaquiles* at weekend brunch. Mexico's flavorful peppers, among them the *guajillo*, *chile de arbol*, and *pasilla*, find their way into many of the offerings. Casual Nopalito is popular with families yet equally pleasing to adult groups lured by the well-selected tequilas. Expect a substantial wait in the evening. You must leave your name on a list, but you can call ahead to be put on it. (There's a take-out window if you're feeling truly impatient.) To avoid waiting, try weekday lunch, after 2, when the place clears out. A second location in the inner Sunset is less crowded. [$] *Average main: $15* ✉ *306 Broderick St., Western Addition* ☎ *415/437–0303* 🌐 *www.nopalitosf.com* ✥ *B6.*

$$$ MODERN AMERICAN Fodor's Choice ★

🍴 **State Bird Provisions.** Eating at this 14-table spot can be described as a festive parade of hors d'oeuvre, with bite-sized "provisions" rolled around on carts and diners picking what they want. Prices for provisions, ranging from $3 to $8, are displayed on placards and tallied up as the dinner unfolds. Those who eat with their eyes, and not their stomachs, should be cautious. This is dim-sum format, only rather than dumplings, the choices include half dollar–sized thick savory pancakes stuffed with sauerkraut; giant nori chips topped with Hamachi, radishes, and avocados; and kimchi yuba noodles with housemade egg bottarga. Each night roughly a dozen provisions are offered, along with commandables (larger dishes, including the state bird, quail, batter-dipped), and desserts. The colorful, airy dining room with pegboard walls has a high school art-room vibe, decorated as it is with string art and folksy wooden cutouts shaped like food. The staff is superfriendly. Because a reservation here is among the most sought-after in the city the wait can be onerous, but the host will take your number, recommend a nearby wine bar, and call when a table is ready. $ *Average main: $30* ✉ *1529 Fillmore St., Western Addition* ☎ *415/795–1272* ⊕ *www.statebirdsf.com* ⏵ *Reservations essential* ☽ *Closed Sun. No lunch* ✛ *A4.*

RICHMOND

$ ✕ **Burma Superstar.** Locals make the trek to the "Avenues" for the

ASIAN extraordinary tea-leaf salad, a combo of spicy, salty, crunchy, and sour that is mixed table-side, with fermented tea leaves from Burma, fried garlic, and peanuts. Another hit is the hearty vegetarian *samusa* soup. Forget having to decide between Thai, Indian, or Chinese. Burmese fuses flavors and techniques from all these (mostly) bordering countries. The modestly decorated, no-reservations restaurant is small, so lines can be long during peak times. Leave your number and wait for the call, or walk a couple of blocks east to B-Star, owned by the same people but lesser known and often less crowded. $ *Average main: $14* ✉ *309 Clement St., Richmond* ☎ *415/387–2147* ⊕ *www. burmasuperstar.com* ⏵ *Reservations not accepted* ✛ *A4.*

$ ✕ **Park Chow.** What do spaghetti and meatballs, Thai noodles with

AMERICAN chicken and shrimp, salads in three sizes, and big burgers have in com-

FAMILY mon? They're all on the eclectic comfort-food menu at Park Chow, and all are made with sustainable ingredients yet offered at unbeatable prices. This neighborhood standby is also known for its desserts: the fresh-baked pies and ginger cake with pumpkin ice cream are among the standouts. Kids get their own menu, with items such as burgers, grilled-cheese sandwiches, chicken fingers (made with organic chicken), fish, and mini pizzas. In cool weather fires roar in the dining-room fireplaces; in warm weather, the outdoor tables are the place to be—but arrive early for lunch or dinner. For either meal, call ahead to put your name on the waiting list. Breakfast is served on weekdays, brunch on weekends. There's another Chow in the Castro neighborhood at 215 Church St. $ *Average main: $13* ✉ *1240 9th Ave., Inner Sunset* ☎ *415/665–9912* ⊕ *www.chowfoodbar.com* ✛ *A6.*

8

WHERE TO STAY

Hotels here are more than hotels: they are a part of the cityscape, some as old as the city itself, beloved by visitors and locals alike. Like its neighborhoods, San Francisco's accommodations are diverse, from cozy inns and kitschy motels, to chic boutiques and true grande dames. *Hotel reviews have been shortened. For full information, visit Fodors. com. Use the coordinate (✛ A1) at the end of each listing to locate a site on the corresponding map.*

WHAT IT COSTS				
	$	$$	$$$	$$$$
Hotels	under $151	$151–$199	$200–$250	over $250

Hotel prices are the lowest cost of a standard double room in high season.

UNION SQUARE

$
B&B/INN
FAMILY
Fodor'sChoice
★

Golden Gate Hotel. Budget seekers looking for accommodations in the Union Square area will enjoy this homey, family-run B&B. **Pros:** friendly staff; free Wi-Fi; spotless rooms; comfortable bedding; good location if you're a walker. **Cons:** some rooms without private bath. $ *Rooms from: $135* ✉ *775 Bush St., Union Sq.* ☎ *415/392–3702, 800/835–1118* ⊕ *www.goldengatehotel.com* ⇨ *25 rooms, 14 with bath* ¶⊘*Breakfast* ✛ *E4.*

$$$
HOTEL
FAMILY
Fodor'sChoice
★

Hotel Diva. Entering this hotel requires stepping over footprints, hand-prints, and autographs embedded in the sidewalk by visiting stars; with two major theaters, the Curran and the American Conservatory, across the street, this hotel is a magnet for actors, musicians, writers, and artists. **Pros:** punchy design; in the heart of the theater district; accommodating service. **Cons:** few frills; tiny bathrooms. $ *Rooms from: $201* ✉ *440 Geary St., Union Sq.* ☎ *415/885–0200, 800/553–1900* ⊕ *www. hoteldiva.com* ⇨ *115 rooms, 3 suites* ¶⊘*No meals* ✛ *E4.*

$$$
HOTEL
FAMILY
Fodor'sChoice
★

Hotel Nikko, San Francisco. The vast surfaces of gray-flecked white marble that dominate the Nikko's neoclassical lobby have the starkness of an airport, but the crisply designed rooms, in muted tones and with Bluetooth-enabled headboards, flat-screen TVs, and modern bathrooms with sinks atop granite bases, please the business-traveler clientele. **Pros:** friendly multilingual staff; tastefully designed rooms; large indoor pool; very clean. **Cons:** lobby lacks color; atmosphere feels cold to some patrons; expensive parking. $ *Rooms from: $239* ✉ *222 Mason St., Union Sq.* ☎ *415/394–1111, 800/248–3308* ⊕ *www.hotelnikkosf.com* ⇨ *510 rooms, 22 suites* ¶⊘*No meals* ✛ *E4.*

$$
HOTEL
Fodor'sChoice
★

Hotel Triton. A spirit of fun has taken up full-time residence in this Kimpton property, which has a youngish, superfriendly staff, pink- and blue-neon elevators, and a colorful psychedelic lobby mural depicting the San Francisco art and music scene—think flower power mixed with Andy Warhol. **Pros:** attentive service; refreshingly funky atmosphere; hip arty environs; good location. **Cons:** rooms and baths are on the small side. $ *Rooms from: $189* ✉ *342 Grant Ave., Union*

Sq. ☎ *415/394–0500, 800/800–1299* 🌐 *www.hoteltriton.com* ⇨ *133 rooms, 7 suites* 🍴 *No meals* ✢ *F4.*

$$$$ HOTEL 🏨 **Westin St. Francis.** The survivor of two major earthquakes, some headline-grabbing scandals, and even an attempted presidential assassination, this grande dame that dates to 1904 remains ever above the fray—richly appointed, serenely elegant, and superbly located. **Pros:** fantastic beds; prime Union Square location; spacious rooms, some with great views. **Cons:** some guests comment on the long wait at check-in; rooms in original building can be small; glass elevators are not for the faint of heart. [$] *Rooms from: $325* ✉ *335 Powell St., Union Sq.* ☎ *415/397–7000, 800/917–7458* 🌐 *www.westinstfrancis.com* ⇨ *1,157 rooms, 38 suites* 🍴 *No meals* ✢ *E4.*

SOMA

$$$$ HOTEL Fodor's Choice ★ 🏨 **Four Seasons Hotel San Francisco.** Occupying floors 5 through 17 of a skyscraper, this exclusive, award-winning hotel is sandwiched between multimillion-dollar condos, elite shops, and a premier sports-and-fitness complex. **Pros:** near museums, galleries, restaurants, shopping, and clubs; terrific fitness facilities; luxurious rooms and amenities; MKT restaurant is worth the splurge. **Cons:** pricey; staff can be uppity. [$] *Rooms from: $425* ✉ *757 Market St., SoMa* ☎ *415/633–3000, 800/332–3442, 800/819–5053* 🌐 *www.fourseasons.com/sanfrancisco* ⇨ *231 rooms, 46 suites* 🍴 *No meals* ✢ *F4.*

$$$$ HOTEL 🏨 **InterContinental San Francisco.** The arctic-blue glass exterior and subdued, Zen-like lobby of this sparkling hotel may be as bland as an airport concourse, but they're merely a prelude to the spectacularly light, expansive, thoughtfully laid-out guest rooms, which have all the ultramodern conveniences. **Pros:** a stone's throw from Moscone Center; well-equipped gym; near hip clubs and restaurants. **Cons:** decor is short on character; borders a rough neighborhood; a few blocks off the major tourist path. [$] *Rooms from: $329* ✉ *888 Howard St., SoMa* ☎ *415/616–6500, 866/781–2364* 🌐 *www.intercontinentalsanfrancisco.com* ⇨ *536 rooms, 14 suites* 🍴 *No meals* ✢ *E5.*

$$$$ HOTEL Fodor's Choice ★ 🏨 **The St. Regis San Francisco.** Though this may be the most luxurious hotel in the city, guests often remark that it's hipper and more modern than other hotels in the St. Regis chain. **Pros:** tasteful, yet current; lap pool; good location; luxe spa; views. **Cons:** expensive; some guests report inconsistent service; hallway noise; long waits for room service and valet parking. [$] *Rooms from: $575* ✉ *125 3rd St., SoMa* ☎ *415/284–4000* 🌐 *www.stregis.com/sanfrancisco* ⇨ *214 rooms, 46 suites* 🍴 *No meals* ✢ *F4.*

THE TENDERLOIN

$$$$ HOTEL 🏨 **Phoenix Hotel.** A magnet for the hip at heart and ultracool—Little Richard, Elijah Wood, Sean Lennon, and members of R.E.M. and Pearl Jam have stayed here—the Phoenix isn't the best choice for those seeking peace and quiet (or anyone put off by the hotel's location, on the fringes of the sketchy Tenderloin District). **Pros:** boho atmosphere; cheeky design; popular with musicians; hip new restaurant/bar; free parking. **Cons:** somewhat seedy location; no elevators; can be

loud in the evenings. [$] *Rooms from: $409* ✉ *601 Eddy St., Tenderloin* ☎ *415/776–1380, 800/248–9466* 🌐 *www.thephoenixhotel.com* 🛏 *41 rooms, 3 suites* 🍴 *Breakfast* ✣ *D5.*

FINANCIAL DISTRICT

$$$$ HOTEL 🏨 **Mandarin Oriental, San Francisco.** Two towers connected by glass-enclosed sky bridges compose the top 11 floors of one of San Francisco's tallest buildings, offering spectacular panoramas from every room; the windows open so you can hear that trademark San Francisco sound: the "ding ding" of the cable cars some 40 floors below (and rooms even include binoculars). **Pros:** spectacular "bridge-to-bridge" views; attentive service; in the running for the most comfy beds in the city. **Cons:** in a business area that's quiet on weekends; extremely pricey. [$] *Rooms from: $695* ✉ *222 Sansome St., Financial District* ☎ *415/276–9600, 800/622–0404* 🌐 *www.mandarinoriental.com/sanfrancisco* 🛏 *151 rooms, 7 suites* 🍴 *No meals* ✣ *F3.*

NOB HILL

$$$$ HOTEL Fodor's Choice ★ 🏨 **The Huntington Hotel.** Stars from Bogart and Bacall to Picasso and Pavarotti have stayed in this ivy-covered hotel famed for its gracious personal service and spacious rooms and suites, most of which have great views of Grace Cathedral, the bay, or the city skyline. **Pros:** city icon; personalized service; spacious rooms; the aura of old San Francisco; first-rate spa with city views; cable cars pass by right out front. **Cons:** up a steep hill from downtown. [$] *Rooms from: $459* ✉ *1075 California St., Nob Hill* ☎ *415/474–5400, 800/227–4683* 🌐 *www.huntingtonhotel.com* 🛏 *96 rooms, 40 suites* 🍴 *No meals* ✣ *E3.*

$$$$ HOTEL Fodor's Choice ★ 🏨 **Ritz-Carlton, San Francisco.** A preferred destination for travel-industry honchos, movie stars, and visitors alike, this hotel—a stunning tribute to beauty and attentive, professional service—completed a $12.5-million renovation in 2012 to offer a modern twist to that classic Ritz style. **Pros:** terrific service; all-day food available on Club Level; beautiful surroundings; fantastic new restaurant and Lobby Lounge; renovated fitness center. **Cons:** expensive; hilly location; no pool. [$] *Rooms from: $495* ✉ *600 Stockton St., at California St., Nob Hill* ☎ *415/296–7465* 🌐 *www.ritzcarlton.com* 🛏 *276 rooms, 60 suites* 🍴 *No meals* ✣ *E3.*

NORTH BEACH

$ HOTEL Fodor's Choice ★ 🏨 **San Remo Hotel.** A few blocks from Fisherman's Wharf, this three-story 1906 Italianate Victorian—once home to longshoremen and Beat poets—has a narrow stairway from the street leading to the front desk and labyrinthine hallways; rooms are small but charming, with lace curtains, forest-green-painted wood floors, and brass beds and other antique furnishings. **Pros:** inexpensive; historic; cozy. **Cons:** some rooms are dark; only the penthouse suite has a private bath; spartan amenities. [$] *Rooms from: $89* ✉ *2237 Mason St., North Beach* ☎ *415/776–8688, 800/352–7366* 🌐 *www.sanremohotel.com* 🛏 *64 rooms with shared baths, 1 suite* 🍴 *No meals* ✣ *E1.*

FISHERMAN'S WHARF

$$$$ HOTEL FAMILY Fodor's Choice ★ **Argonaut Hotel.** When the four-story Haslett Warehouse was a fruit-and-vegetable canning complex, boats docked right up against the 1909 structure; a century later it contains a hotel with a nautical decor—think anchors, ropes, compasses, and a row of cruise-ship deck chairs in the lobby. **Pros:** bay views; near Hyde Street cable car; sofa beds; toys for the kids. **Cons:** nautical theme isn't for everyone; cramped public areas; service can be hit or miss; location requires a bit of a trek to many SF attractions. [$] *Rooms from: $309* ✉ *495 Jefferson St., at Hyde St., Fisherman's Wharf* ☎ *415/563–0800, 866/415–0704* 🌐 *www.argonauthotel.com* 🛏 *239 rooms, 13 suites* 🍴 *No meals* ✥ *D1.*

$$$$ HOTEL **Best Western Plus–The Tuscan.** The redbrick facade of this hotel some Fodors.com users describe as a "hidden treasure" barely hints at the Tuscan country villa that lies within. **Pros:** wine and beer hour; cozy feeling; great location near Fisherman's Wharf. **Cons:** congested touristy area; small rooms. [$] *Rooms from: $259* ✉ *425 North Point St., at Mason St., Fisherman's Wharf* ☎ *415/561–1100, 800/648–4626* 🌐 *www.tuscaninn.com* 🛏 *212 rooms, 12 suites* 🍴 *No meals* ✥ *E1.*

$$$$ RENTAL FAMILY Fodor's Choice ★ **Fairmont Heritage Place, Ghirardelli Square.** Housed in the former Ghirardelli chocolate factory, these one-to-three-bedroom serviced apartments just might be the most luxurious accommodations in San Francisco. **Pros:** luxury at its finest; gigantic apartments; many amenities; bay views from most accommodations; free car service within a 2-mile radius. **Cons:** a bit of a trek from downtown; expensive. [$] *Rooms from: $699* ✉ *950 North Point St., Fisherman's Wharf* ☎ *415/268–9900* 🌐 *www.fairmont.com/ghirardelli* 🛏 *53 rooms* 🍴 *Breakfast* ✥ *C1.*

8

EMBARCADERO

$$$$ HOTEL FAMILY Fodor's Choice ★ **Hotel Vitale.** "Luxury, naturally," the theme of this eight-story, terraced bay-front hotel, is apparent in every thoughtful detail: little vases of lavender mounted outside each room; the penthouse-level day spa with soaking tubs set in a rooftop bamboo forest; and the restaurant Americano, whose outdoor terrace is packed with hip jet-setters. **Pros:** family-friendly studios; great views; fanciful spa; luxurious amenities throughout. **Cons:** some rooms can feel cramped or be noisy; some guests report inconsistent service; rates are expensive. [$] *Rooms from: $479* ✉ *8 Mission St., Embarcadero* ☎ *415/278–3700, 888/890–8688* 🌐 *www.hotelvitale.com* 🛏 *190 rooms, 9 suites* 🍴 *No meals* ✥ *H3.*

THE MARINA, COW HOLLOW, AND THE PRESIDIO

$$ HOTEL Fodor's Choice ★ **Cow Hollow Motor Inn and Suites.** The suites at this large, family-owned, modern motel are more spacious than average, featuring one or two bedrooms, hardwood floors, sitting and dining areas, marble wood-burning fireplaces, big living rooms, and fully equipped kitchens. **Pros:** suites are the size of apartments; good for families; free covered parking in building for one vehicle. **Cons:** congested neighborhood has a

BEST BETS FOR SAN FRANCISCO LODGING

Fodor's offers a selective listing of quality lodging experiences at every price range, from the city's best budget motel to its most sophisticated luxury hotel. Here we've compiled our top recommendations by price and experience. The very best properties—in other words, those that provide a particularly remarkable experience in their price range—are designated in the listings with the Fodor's Choice logo.

Fodor's Choice ★

Argonaut Hotel, $$$$, p. 449

Cow Hollow Motor Inn and Suites, $$, p. 449

Fairmont Heritage Place, Ghirardelli Square, $$$$, p. 449

Four Seasons Hotel San Francisco, $$$$, p. 447

Golden Gate Hotel, $, p. 446

Hotel Diva, $$$, p. 446

Hotel Drisco, $$$$, p. 451

Hotel Nikko, San Francisco, $$$, p. 446

Hotel Tomo, $$, p. 451

Hotel Triton, $$, p. 446

Hotel Vitale, $$$$, p. 449

Huntington Hotel, $$$$, p. 448

Inn at the Presidio, $$$, p. 451

Ritz-Carlton, San Francisco, $$$$, p. 448

San Remo Hotel, $, p. 448

The St. Regis San Francisco, $$$$, p. 447

Union Street Inn, $$$, p. 451

By Price

$

Golden Gate Hotel, p. 446

San Remo Hotel, p. 448

$$

Cow Hollow Motor Inn and Suites, p. 449

Hotel Triton, p. 446

$$$

Hotel Diva, p. 446

Hotel Nikko, San Francisco, p. 446

Inn at the Presidio, p. 451

Union Street Inn, p. 451

$$$$

Argonaut Hotel, p. 449

Fairmont Heritage Place, Ghirardelli Square, p. 449

Four Seasons Hotel San Francisco, p. 447

Hotel Drisco, p. 451

Hotel Vitale, p. 449

Huntington Hotel, p. 448

Ritz-Carlton, San Francisco, p. 448

The St. Regis San Francisco, p. 447

By Experience

BUSINESS TRAVELERS

Four Seasons Hotel San Francisco, $$$$, p. 447

Hotel Nikko, San Francisco, $$$, p. 446

GREAT CONCIERGE

Ritz-Carlton, San Francisco, $$$$, p. 448

HISTORICAL FLAVOR

Inn at the Presidio, $$$, p. 451

Westin St. Francis, $$$$, p. 447

MOST KID-FRIENDLY

Argonaut Hotel, $$$$, p. 449

Hotel del Sol, $$$$, p. 451

Hotel Diva, $$$, p. 446

MOST ROMANTIC

Hotel Drisco, $$$$, p. 451

Huntington Hotel, $$$$, p. 448

Inn at the Presidio, $$$, p. 451

Union Street Inn, $$$, p. 451

TOP B&BS

Hotel Drisco, $$$$, p. 451

Union Street Inn, $$$, p. 451

TOP SPAS

Huntington Hotel, $$$$, p. 448

Mandarin Oriental San Francisco, $$$$, p. 448

The St. Regis San Francisco, $$$$, p. 447

college-rush-week feel; standard rooms are on a loud street. [$] *Rooms from: $155* ✉ *2190 Lombard St., Marina* ☎ *415/921–5800* 🌐 *www.cowhollowmotorinn.com* ⇨ *117 rooms, 12 suites* 🍴 *No meals* ✥ *A1.*

$$$$ HOTEL FAMILY 🏨 **Hotel Del Sol.** The proximity of this beach-themed, three-story 1950s motor lodge to Funston Playground, Fort Mason, the Walt Disney Family Museum, the Presidio, Crissy Field, and Chestnut Street's munchkin-favored shops already qualify this place as kid-friendly, but the toys, games, DVDs, outdoor saltwater heated pool with plenty of inflatable playthings, snow cones on summer weekends, and afternoon cookies and milk make it a virtual haven for little ones. **Pros:** kid-friendly; plenty of nearby places to eat and shop; recently renovated; $10 parking. **Cons:** far from downtown and the landmark attractions around Fisherman's Wharf; faces a busy thoroughfare. [$] *Rooms from: $329* ✉ *3100 Webster St., Marina* ☎ *415/921–5520, 877/433–5765* 🌐 *www.thehoteldelsol.com* ⇨ *47 rooms, 10 suites* 🍴 *Breakfast* ✥ *B2.*

$$$ B&B/INN Fodor's Choice ★ 🏨 **The Inn at the Presidio.** A brick facade, porches with rocking chairs, and an outdoor fire pit set the backdrop for this idyllic hotel at the base of numerous hiking and biking trails in the Presidio, a National Land Trust. **Pros:** playful design; outdoor fire pit; only hotel in the Presidio; spacious rooms; views of Golden Gate Bridge. **Cons:** no on-site restaurant; no elevator; challenging to get a taxi; very far from downtown attractions. [$] *Rooms from: $215* ✉ *42 Moraga Ave., Presidio* ☎ *415/800–7356* 🌐 *www.innatthepresidio.com* ⇨ *8 rooms, 18 suites* 🍴 *Breakfast* ✥ *A2.*

$$$ B&B/INN Fodor's Choice ★ 🏨 **Union Street Inn.** Precious family antiques and unique artwork helped British innkeepers Jane Bertorelli and David Coyle (former chef for the Duke and Duchess of Bedford) transform this green-and-cream 1902 Edwardian into a delightful B&B. **Pros:** personal service; Jane's excellent full breakfast; romantic setting. **Cons:** parking is difficult; no air-conditioning; no elevator. [$] *Rooms from: $249* ✉ *2229 Union St., Cow Hollow* ☎ *415/346–0424* 🌐 *www.unionstreetinn.com* ⇨ *6 rooms* 🍴 *Breakfast* ✥ *A2.*

8

PACIFIC HEIGHTS AND JAPANTOWN

$$$$ HOTEL Fodor's Choice ★ 🏨 **Hotel Drisco.** Pretend you're a resident of one of the wealthiest residential neighborhoods in San Francisco at this understated, elegant 1903 Edwardian hotel. **Pros:** great service; comfortable rooms; quiet residential retreat; 24-hour room service. **Cons:** far from downtown. [$] *Rooms from: $475* ✉ *2901 Pacific Ave., Pacific Heights* ☎ *415/346–2880, 800/634–7277* 🌐 *www.hoteldrisco.com* ⇨ *29 rooms, 19 suites* 🍴 *Breakfast* ✥ *A3.*

$$ HOTEL FAMILY Fodor's Choice ★ 🏨 **Hotel Tomo.** Inspired by the comic phenomena manga and anime, the Tomo draws hipsters and Japanophiles eager to surround themselves with Japanese pop culture, or J-Pop as it is known across the pond. **Pros:** cool J-Pop style; anime playing on the lobby TV and manga in your room; great price in a fun neighborhood. **Cons:** tight quarters; away from downtown. [$] *Rooms from: $169* ✉ *1800 Sutter St., Japantown* ☎ *415/921–4000* 🌐 *www.hoteltomo.com* ⇨ *125 rooms, 1 suite* 🍴 *No meals* ✥ *B1.*

NIGHTLIFE

After hours, business folk and the working class give way to costume-clad partygoers, hippies and hipsters, downtown divas, frat boys, and those who prefer something a little more clothing-optional.

Entertainment information is printed in the pink Sunday "Datebook" section and the more calendar-based Thursday "96 Hours" section (⊕ *www.sfgate.com/96hours*) in the *San Francisco Chronicle*. Also consult any of the free alternative weeklies, notably the *SF Weekly* (⊕ *www.sfweekly.com*), which blurbs nightclubs and music, and the *San Francisco Bay Guardian* (⊕ *www.sfbg.com*), which lists neighborhood, avant-garde, and budget events. SF Station (⊕ *www.sfstation.com*; online only) has an up-to-date calendar of entertainment goings-on.

UNION SQUARE

BARS

Cantina. Let the skull and crossbones over the entryway of this intimate Latin bar provide fair warning, because the magic the bartenders perform here is pure voodoo. The drinks are handcrafted with fresh ingredients, homemade bitters, and even homegrown citrus fruits. Because of this, the service can be slow during busy times; fortunately, many cocktails are served in pitchers. ■ TIP→ **The most popular cocktail is the vibrant Laughing Buddha—lime, ginger, and Serrano chilis.** ⊠ *580 Sutter St., at Mason St., Union Sq.* ☎ *415/398–0195* ⊕ *www.cantinasf.com.*

Redwood Room. Opened in 1933 and updated by designer Philippe Starck in 2001, the Redwood Room at the Clift Hotel is a San Francisco icon. The entire room, floor to ceiling, is paneled with the wood from a single redwood tree, giving the place a rich, monochromatic look. The gorgeous original art deco sconces and chandeliers still hang, but bizarre video installations on plasma screens also adorn the walls. It's packed on weekend evenings after 10, when young scenesters swarm in; for maximum glamour, visit on a weeknight. ⊠ *Clift Hotel, 495 Geary St., at Taylor St., Union Sq.* ☎ *415/929–2372 for table reservations, 415/775–4700 for hotel* ⊕ *www.clifthotel.com.*

SOMA

BARS

City Beer Store. Called CBS by locals, this friendly tasting room cum liquor mart has a wine bar's sensibility. Perfect for connoisseurs and the merely beer curious, CBS stocks more than 300 different bottled beers, and more than a dozen are on tap. The indecisive can mix and match six-packs to go. ■ TIP→ **Come early: The small space, which fills up quickly on event nights, closes at 10 pm except Sunday, when it closes at 6.** ⊠ *1168 Folsom St., at 8th St., SoMa* ☎ *415/503–1033* ⊕ *www.citybeerstore.com.*

GAY NIGHTLIFE

The Stud. Glam trannies, gay bears, tight-teed pretty boys, ladies and their ladies, and a handful of straight onlookers congregate here to dance to live DJ sounds and watch world-class drag performers on the small stage. The entertainment is often campy, pee-your-pants funny, and downright fantastic. Each night's music is different—from funk, soul, and hip-hop to '80s tunes and disco favorites. ■TIP➔ At Frolic, the Stud's most outrageous party (second Saturday of the month), club goers dance the night away dressed as bunnies, kittens, and even stranger creatures. ⊠ *1284 Harrison St., at 9th St., SoMa* ☎ *415/863–6623* ⊕ *www.studsf.com* ⊙ *Closed Mon.*

THE TENDERLOIN

BARS

Fodor's Choice **Bourbon & Branch.** The address and phone are unlisted, the black outer
★ door unmarked, and when you make your reservation (required), you get a password for entry. In short, Bourbon & Branch reeks of Prohibition-era speakeasy cool. It's not exclusive, though: everyone is granted a password. The place has sex appeal, with tin ceilings, bordello-red silk wallpaper, intimate booths, and low lighting; loud conversations and cell phones are not allowed. The menu of expertly mixed cocktails and quality bourbon and whiskey is substantial, though the servers aren't always authorities. ■TIP➔ Your reservation dictates your exit time, which is strictly enforced. There's also a speakeasy within the speakeasy, called Wilson & Wilson, that is more exclusive but just as funky. ⊠ *501 Jones St., at O'Farrell St., Tenderloin* ⊕ *www.bourbonandbranch.com.*

ROCK, POP, HIP-HOP, FOLK, AND BLUES CLUBS

Fodor's Choice **Great American Music Hall.** You can find top-drawer entertainment at
★ this eclectic nightclub. Acts range from the best in blues, folk, and jazz to up-and-coming college-radio and American-roots artists to indie rockers such as OK Go, Mates of State, and the Cowboy Junkies. The colorful marble-pillared emporium (built in 1907 as a bordello) also accommodates dancing at some shows. Pub grub is available on most nights. ⊠ *859 O'Farrell St., between Polk and Larkin Sts., Tenderloin* ☎ *415/885–0750* ⊕ *www.slimspresents.com.*

HAYES VALLEY

BARS

Hôtel Biron Wine Bar and Art Gallery. Sharing an alleylike block with the backs of Market Street restaurants, this tiny, cave-like (in a good way) spot displays artworks of the Mission School aesthetic on its brick walls. The well-behaved twenty- to thirtysomething clientele enjoys the off-the-beaten-path quarters, the wines from around the world, the soft lighting, and the hip music. ⊠ *45 Rose St., off Market St. near Gough St., Hayes Valley* ☎ *415/703–0403* ⊕ *www.hotelbiron.com.*

Smuggler's Cove. With the decor of a pirate ship and a slew of rum-based cocktails, you half expect Captain Jack Sparrow to sidle up next to you at this offbeat, Disney-esque hangout. But don't let the kitschy

Built as a bordello in 1907, the Great American Music Hall now pulls in top-tier performers.

ambience fool you. The folks at Smuggler's Cove take rum so seriously they even make their own, which you can sample along with more than 200 other offerings, some of them vintage and very hard to find. A punchcard is provided so you can try all 70 cocktails and remember where you left off without getting shipwrecked. The small space fills up quickly, so arrive early. ✉ *650 Gough St., at McAllister St., Hayes Valley* ☎ *415/869–1900* ⊕ *www.smugglerscovesf.com.*

EMBARCADERO

BARS

Hard Water. A waterfront restaurant and bar with stunning bay views, Hard Water pays homage to America's most iconic spirit—bourbon—with a wall of whiskeys and a lineup of specialty cocktails. The menu, crafted by Charles Phan of Slanted Door fame, includes spicy pork-belly cracklings, cornbread-crusted alligator, and other fun snacks. ✉ *Pier 3, Suite 3–102, at Embarcadero, Embarcadero* ☎ *415/392–3021* ⊕ *www.hardwaterbar.com.*

NORTH BEACH

BARS

Vesuvio Cafe. If you're only hitting one bar in North Beach, it should be this one. The low-ceiling second floor of this raucous boho hangout, little altered since its 1960s heyday (when Jack Kerouac frequented the place), is a fine vantage point for watching the colorful Broadway and Columbus Avenue intersection. Another part of Vesuvio's appeal is its diverse clientele, from older neighborhood regulars and young couples to Bacchanalian posses. ✉ *255 Columbus Ave., at Broadway, North Beach* ☎ *415/362–3370* ⊕ *www.vesuvio.com.*

ROCK, POP, HIP-HOP, FOLK, AND BLUES CLUBS

Bimbo's 365 Club. The plush main room and adjacent lounge of this club, here since 1951, retain a retro vibe perfect for the "Cocktail Nation" programming that keeps the crowds entertained. For a taste of the old-school San Francisco nightclub scene, you can't beat Bimbo's. Indie low-fi and pop bands such as Stephen Malkmus and the Jicks and Camera Obscura play here. ✉ *1025 Columbus Ave., at Chestnut St., North Beach* ☎ *415/474–0365* ⊕ *www.bimbos365club.com.*

THE WESTERN SHORELINE

BARS

Cliff House. Classier than the nearby Beach Chalet, with a more impressive view of Ocean Beach, the Cliff House is our pick if you must choose just one oceanfront restaurant/bar. Sure, it's the site of many high-school prom dates, and you could argue that the food and drinks are overpriced, and some say the sleek facade seems more suitable for a mausoleum—but the views are terrific. The best window seats are reserved for diners, but there's a small upstairs lounge where you can watch gulls sail high above the vast blue Pacific. ■ TIP➜ Come before sunset. ✉ *1090 Point Lobos, at Great Hwy., Lincoln Park* ☎ *415/386–3330* ⊕ *www.cliffhouse.com.*

THE MISSION

GAY NIGHTLIFE

Lexington Club. According to its slogan, "every night is ladies' night" at this all-girl club geared to urban alterna-dykes in their 20s and 30s—expect piercings and tattoos, not lipstick. ■ TIP➜ The women's room has awesome graffiti. ✉ *3464 19th St., at Valencia, Mission* ☎ *415/863–2052* ⊕ *www.lexingtonclub.com.*

Martuni's. A mixed crowd enjoys cocktails in the semirefined environment of this bar where the Castro, the Mission, and Hayes Valley intersect; variations on the martini are a specialty. In the intimate back room a pianist plays nightly, and patrons take turns boisterously singing show tunes. Martuni's often gets busy after symphony and opera performances—Davies Hall and the Opera House are both within walking distance. ■ TIP➜ The Godiva Chocolate Martini is a crowd favorite. ✉ *4 Valencia St., at Market St., Mission* ☎ *415/241–0205.*

POTRERO HILL

ROCK, POP, HIP-HOP, FOLK, AND BLUES CLUBS

Bottom of the Hill. This is a great live-music dive—in the best sense of the word—and truly the epicenter for Bay Area indie rock. The club has hosted some great acts over the years, including the Strokes and the Throwing Muses. Rap and hip-hop acts occasionally make it to the stage. ✉ *1233 17th St., at Texas St., Potrero Hill* ☎ *415/621–4455* ⊕ *www.bottomofthehill.com.*

8

WESTERN ADDITION

JAZZ CLUBS

Fodor's Choice **Yoshi's.** The legendary Oakland jazz venue's San Francisco location has
★ terrific acoustics, a 9-foot Steinway grand piano (broken in by Chick
Corea), and seating for 411; it's been hailed as "simply the best jazz club
in the city." Yoshi's serves Japanese food in an adjoining restaurant set
in a soaring two-story space, decorated with blond wood and hanging
paper lanterns (you can also order food at café tables in the club). And
yes, the coupling of sushi and jazz *is* as elegant as it sounds. Sightlines
are good from just about anywhere, including the back balcony. Yoshi's
is in the old Fillmore District, which was known as the "Harlem of the
West" in its 1940s and '50s heyday. ■TIP➔ **The club is on a tough block
in the even tougher Western Addition neighborhood, so take advantage
of the valet parking.** ⊠ *1330 Fillmore St., at Eddy St., Western Addition*
☎ *415/655–5600* ⊕ *www.yoshis.com.*

ROCK, POP, HIP-HOP, FOLK, AND BLUES CLUBS

The Fillmore. This is *the* club that all the big names, from Coldplay to
Clapton, want to play. San Francisco's most famous rock-music hall
presents national and local acts: rock, reggae, grunge, jazz, folk, acid
house, and more. Most tickets cost between $20 and $30, and some
shows are open to all ages. Go upstairs to view the amazing collection
of rock posters lining the walls. At the end of each show, free apples are
set near the door, and staffers hand out collectible posters. ■TIP➔ **Avoid
steep service charges by purchasing tickets at the club's box office on
Sunday from 10 to 4.** ⊠ *1805 Geary Blvd., at Fillmore St., Western
Addition* ☎ *415/346–6000* ⊕ *www.thefillmore.com.*

THE ARTS

Sophisticated, offbeat, and often ahead of the curve, San Francisco's
performing arts scene supports world-class opera, ballet, and theater
productions, along with alternative-dance events, avant-garde plays,
groundbreaking documentaries, and a slew of spoken-word and other
literary happenings.

The best guide to the arts is the Sunday "Datebook" section of the
San Francisco Chronicle. The four-day entertainment supplement "96
Hours" (⊕ *www.sfgate.com/96hours*) is in the Thursday *Chronicle.*
Also check out the city's free alternative weeklies, including *SF Weekly*
(⊕ *www.sfweekly.com*) and the *San Francisco Bay Guardian* (⊕ *www.
sfbg.com*).

Online, SF Station (⊕ *www.sfstation.com*) has a frequently updated
arts and nightlife calendar. San Francisco Arts Monthly (⊕ *www.sfarts.
org*), which is published at the end of the month, has arts features and
events listings, plus a helpful "Visiting San Francisco?" section. For
offbeat, emerging-artist performances, consult CounterPULSE (⊕ *www.
counterpulse.org*).

TICKETS

City Box Office. This charge-by-phone service, sells tickets for many performances and lectures. You can also buy tickets online, or in person on weekdays from 9:30 to 5:30. ✉ *180 Redwood St., Ste. 100, off Van Ness Ave., between Golden Gate Ave. and McAllister St., Civic Center* ☎ *415/392–4400* ⊕ *www.cityboxoffice.com.*

San Francisco Performances. SFP brings an eclectic array of top-flight global music and dance talents to various venues—mostly the Yerba Buena Center for the Arts, Davies Symphony Hall, and Herbst Theatre. Artists have included Yo-Yo Ma, Edgar Meyer, the Paul Taylor Dance Company, and Midori. Tickets can be purchased in person, online, or by phone. ✉ *500 Sutter St., Ste. 710* ☎ *415/392–2545* ⊕ *www.performances.org.*

TIX Bay Area. Half-price, same-day tickets for many local and touring shows go on sale (cash only) at the TIX booth in Union Square, which is open daily from 10 to 6. Discount purchases can also be made online. ✉ *Powell St. between Geary and Post Sts., Union Sq.* ☎ *415/433–7827* ⊕ *www.tixbayarea.com.*

DANCE

Fodor's Choice ★ **San Francisco Ballet.** For ballet lovers the nation's oldest professional company is reason alone to visit the Bay Area. SFB's performances, for the past three decades under direction of Helgi Tomasson, have won critical raves. The primary season runs from February through May. The repertoire includes full-length ballets such as *Don Quixote* and *Sleeping Beauty*; the December presentation of *The Nutcracker* is truly spectacular. The company also performs bold new dances from star choreographers such as William Forsythe and Mark Morris, alongside modern classics by George Balanchine and Jerome Robbins. Tickets are available at the **War Memorial Opera House.** ✉ *War Memorial Opera House, 301 Van Ness Ave., at Grove St., Civic Center* ☎ *415/865–2000* ⊕ *www.sfballet.org* ☉ *Weekdays 10–4.*

FILM

Fodor's Choice ★ **Castro Theatre.** A large neon sign marks the exterior of this 1,400-plus seat art deco movie palace whose exotic interior transports you back to 1922, when the theater first opened. High-profile festivals present films here, and classic revivals and foreign flicks also unfold. ■TIP→ Lines for the Castro's popular sing-along movie musicals often trail down the block. ✉ *429 Castro St., near Market St., Castro* ☎ *415/621–6120* ⊕ *www.castrotheatre.com.*

MUSIC

Fodor's Choice ★ **San Francisco Symphony.** One of America's top orchestras, the symphony performs from September through May, with additional summer performances of light classical music and show tunes. The orchestra and its charismatic music director, Michael Tilson Thomas, known for his daring programming of 20th-century American works, often perform with soloists of the caliber of Andre Watts, Gil Shaham, and Renée Fleming. The symphony's adventurous projects include its collaboration

8

with the heavy metal band Metallica. ■ TIP→ Tickets cost between $15 and $100; deep discounts are often available through Travelzoo, Groupon, and other vendors. ✉ *Davies Symphony Hall, 201 Van Ness Ave., at Grove St., Civic Center* ☎ *415/864–6000* ⊕ *www.sfsymphony.org.*

SFJAZZ Center. Jazz legends Branford Marsalis and Herbie Hancock have performed at the snazzy center, as have Rosanne Cash and world-music favorite Esperanza Spaulding. The sightlines and acoustics here impress. Shows often sell out quickly. ✉ *201 Franklin St., Hayes Valley* ☎ *866/920–5299* ⊕ *www.sfjazz.org.*

MUSIC FESTIVALS

Fodor'sChoice
★
Stern Grove Festival. The nation's oldest continual free summer music festival hosts Sunday-afternoon performances of symphony, opera, jazz, pop music, and dance. The amphitheater is in a beautiful eucalyptus grove, perfect for picnicking before the show. World-music favorites such as Ojos de Brujas, Seu Jorge, and Shuggie Otis get the massive crowds dancing. ■ TIP→ Shows generally start at 2 pm, but arrive hours earlier if you want to see the performances up close—and dress for cool weather, as the fog often rolls in. ✉ *Sloat Blvd. at 19th Ave., Sunset* ☎ *415/252–6252* ⊕ *www.sterngrove.org.*

OPERA

Fodor'sChoice
★
San Francisco Opera. Founded in 1923, this internationally recognized organization has occupied the War Memorial Opera House since the building's completion in 1932. From September through January and June through July, the company presents a dozen or so operas. SF opera frequently collaborates with European companies and presents unconventional, sometimes edgy projects designed to attract younger audiences. Translations are projected above the stage during most non-English productions. Ticket prices range from $25 to $195. ✉ *War Memorial Opera House, 301 Van Ness Ave., at Grove St., Civic Center* ☎ *415/864–3330 tickets* ⊕ *www.sfopera.com* ☞ *Box office: 199 Grove St., at Van Ness Ave.; open Mon. 10–5, Tues.–Fri. 10–6.*

THEATER

American Conservatory Theater. Among the nation's leading regional theater companies, ACT presents about eight plays a year, from classics to contemporary works, often in repertory. The season runs from early fall to late spring. In December ACT stages a beloved version of Charles Dickens's *A Christmas Carol.* ✉ *415 Geary St., Union Sq.* ☎ *415/749–2228* ⊕ *www.act-sf.org.*

Fodor'sChoice
★
Teatro ZinZanni. In a fabulous antique Belgian dance-hall tent, contortionists, chanteuses, jugglers, illusionists, and circus performers entertain audiences who dine on a surprisingly good five-course dinner. The show, which ran for 11 years on a waterfront pier, is scheduled to debut in its new permanent home in 2015. Tickets cost between $125 and $150; during summer and on most weekends, reservations are essential. ✉ *Broadway and the Embarcadero, Northern Waterfront* ☎ *415/438–2668* ⊕ *www.zinzanni.org.*

SPORTS AND THE OUTDOORS

BASEBALL

FAMILY

Fodor's Choice

★

San Francisco Giants. Two World Series titles (2010 and 2012) and the classic design of AT&T Park lead to sellouts for nearly every home game the National League team plays. ⊠ *AT&T Park, 24 Willie Mays Plaza, between 2nd and 3rd Sts., SoMa* ☎ *415/972–2000, 800/734–4268* ⊕ *sanfrancisco.giants.mlb.com.*

BIKING

San Francisco Bicycle Coalition. The San Francisco Bicycle Coalition has extensive information about the policies and politics of riding and lists local events for cyclists on its website. You can download (but not print) a PDF version of the *San Francisco Bike Map and Walking Guide.* ☎ *415/431–2453* ⊕ *www.sfbike.org.*

WHERE TO RENT

Bike and Roll. You can rent bikes at this national outfit's locations for $8 per hour or $32 per day; discounted weekly rates are available, and complimentary maps are provided. ⊠ *899 Columbus Ave., at Lombard St., North Beach* ☎ *415/229–2000* ⊕ *www.bikethegoldengate.com* ⊠ *353 Jefferson St., between Jones and Leavenworth Sts., Fisherman's Wharf* ⊠ *2800 Leavenworth St., at Beach St., Fisherman's Wharf* ⊠ *Pier 43½, Embarcadero at Taylor St., North Beach* ⊠ *Hyatt Regency, 5 Embarcadero Center, outside, ground level, North Beach.*

Blazing Saddles. This outfitter rents bikes for $8 to $9 an hour ($32 to $105 a day), depending on the type of bike, and shares tips on sights to see along the paths. ⊠ *2715 Hyde St., at Beach St., Fisherman's Wharf* ☎ *415/202–8888* ⊕ *www.blazingsaddles.com* ⊠ *433 Mason St., at Post St., Union Sq.* ⊠ *Pier 41, Fisherman's Wharf* ⊠ *465 Jefferson St., at Hyde St., Fisherman's Wharf* ⊠ *2555 Powell St., at the Embarcadero, Fisherman's Wharf* ⊠ *1095 Columbus, at Francisco St., North Beach* ⊠ *721 Beach St., at Hyde St., North Beach.*

FOOTBALL

San Francisco 49ers. The city's NFL team is set to debut its new Levi's Stadium for the 2014 season. The state-of-the-art facility, 44 miles south of San Francisco, will have complete Wi-Fi capability, IPTV, and more than 13,000 square feet of HD video boards. The 49ers may have left town, but the team hasn't forgotten SF cuisine: at time of writing restaurateur and season-ticket holder Michael Mina was planning to open Tailgate, based on his Bourbon and Steak restaurants. Home games usually sell out far in advance. **Ticketmaster** (⊕ *www.ticketmaster.com*) and **StubHub!** (⊕ *www.stubhub.com*) are sources for single-game tickets. ⊠ *Levi's Stadium, 4949 Marie P. DeBartolo Way, from San Francisco, take U.S. 101 south to the Lawrence Expressway and follow signs, Santa Clara* ☎ *800/745–3000 Ticketmaster, 866/788–2482 StubHub!, 408/579–4400 Santa Clara stadium* ⊕ *www.49ers.com*

RUNNING

The *San Francisco Bike Map and Walking Guide* (⊕ *www.sfbike.org/ maps*), which indicates hill grades on city streets by color, is a great resource. The **San Francisco Road Runners Club** (⊕ *www.sfrrc.org*) recommends routes on its website and has links to the websites of other clubs.

SHOPPING

UNION SQUARE

ART GALLERIES

Fodor'sChoice ★ **Hang Art.** A spirit of fun imbues this inviting gallery that showcases emerging artists. Prices range from a few hundred dollars to several thousand, making it an ideal place for novice collectors to get their feet wet. ✉ *567 Sutter St., 2nd fl., near Mason St., Union Sq.* ☎ *415/434– 4264* ⊕ *www.hangart.com.*

CLOTHING: MEN AND WOMEN

Fodor'sChoice ★ **Margaret O'Leary.** If you can only buy one piece of clothing in San Francisco, make it a hand-loomed, cashmere sweater by this Irish-born local legend. The perfect antidote to the city's wind and fog, the sweaters are so beloved by San Franciscans that some of them wear anything else. Pick up an airplane wrap for your trip home, or a media cozy to keep your iPod toasty. Another store is in Pacific Heights, at 2400 Fillmore St. ✉ *1 Claude La., at Sutter St., just west of Kearny St., Union Sq.* ☎ *415/391–1010* ⊕ *www.margaretoleary.com.*

DEPARTMENT STORES

Gump's. It's a San Francisco institution, dating to the 19th century, and it's a strikingly luxurious one. The airy store exudes a museumlike vibe, with its large decorative vases, sumptuous housewares, and Tahitian-pearl display. It's a great place to pick up gifts, such as the Golden Gate Bridge note cards or silver-plated butter spreaders in a signature Gump's box. ✉ *135 Post St., near Kearny St., Union Sq.* ☎ *415/982– 1616* ⊕ *www.gumps.com.*

Nordstrom. Somehow Nordstrom manages to be all things to all people, and this location, with spiral escalators circling a four-story atrium, is no exception. Whether you're an elegant lady of a certain age shopping for a new mink coat or a teen on the hunt for a Roxy hoodie, the salespeople are known for being happy to help. Nordstrom carries the best selections in town of designers such as Tory Burch, but its own brands have loyal followings, too. ■ TIP➜ **The café upstairs is a superb choice for a ladies-who-lunch shopping break.** ✉ *San Francisco Shopping Centre, 865 Market St., at 5th St., Union Sq.* ☎ *415/243–8500* ⊕ *shop.nordstrom.com.*

FURNITURE, HOUSEWARES, AND GIFTS

Fodor'sChoice ★ **Diptyque.** The original Diptyque boutique in Paris has attracted a long line of celebrities. You can find the full array of scented candles and fragrances in this chic shop that would be at home on the boulevard

The beat movement of the 1950s was born in San Francisco's most famous bookstore, City Lights.

St-Germain. Trademark black-and-white labels adorn the popular L'eau toilet water, scented with geranium and sandalwood. Candles come in traditional and esoteric scents, including lavender, basil, leather, and fig tree. Also available are French Mariage Frères teas. ⊠ *171 Maiden La., near Stockton St., Union Sq.* ☎ *415/402–0600* ⊕ *www.diptyqueparis.com.*

CHINATOWN

TOYS AND GADGETS

Chinatown Kite Shop. The kites sold here range from basic diamond shapes to box- and animal-shaped configurations. ■**TIP→** Colorful dragon kites make great souvenirs. ⊠ *717 Grant Ave., near Sacramento St., Chinatown* ☎ *415/989–5182* ⊕ *www.chinatownkite.com.*

SOMA

BOOKS

Chronicle Books. This local beacon of publishing produces inventively designed fiction, cookbooks, art books, and other titles, as well as diaries, planners, and address books—all of which you can purchase at three airy and attractive spaces. The other stores are at 680 2nd Street, near AT&T Park, and 1846 Union Street, in Cow Hollow. ⊠ *Metreon Westfield Shopping Center, 165 4th St., near Howard St., SoMa* ☎ *415/369–6271* ⊕ *www.chroniclebooks.com.*

FOOD AND DRINK

K&L Wine Merchants. More than any other wine store, this one has an ardent cult following around town. The friendly staffers promise not to sell what they don't taste themselves, and weekly events—on Thursday from 5 pm to 6:30 pm and Saturday from noon to 3 pm—open the tastings to customers. The best-seller list for varietals and regions for both the under- and over-$30 categories appeals to the wine lover in everyone. ⊠ *638 4th St., between Brannan and Townsend Sts., SoMa* ☎ *415/896–1734* ⊕ *www.klwines.com.*

HAYES VALLEY

FOOD AND DRINK

Miette Confiserie. There is truly nothing sweeter than a cellophane bag tied with blue-and-white twine and filled with malt balls or chocolate sardines from this European-style apothecary. Grab a gingerbread cupcake or a tantalizing macaron or some shortbread. The pastel-color cake stands make even window-shopping a treat. ⊠ *449 Octavia Blvd., between Hayes and Fell Sts., Hayes Valley* ☎ *415/626–6221* ⊕ *www.miette.com.*

NORTH BEACH

BOOKS

Fodor'sChoice ★ **City Lights Bookstore.** The city's most famous bookstore is where the Beat movement of the 1950s was born. Neal Cassady and Jack Kerouac hung out in the basement, and now regulars and tourists while hours away in this well-worn space. The upstairs room holds impressive poetry and Beat literature collections. Poet Lawrence Ferlinghetti, the owner, remains involved in the workings of this three-story shop. City Lights Publishers, which issued the poet Allen Ginsberg's *Howl* in 1956, publishes a dozen new titles each year. ⊠ *261 Columbus Ave., at Broadway, North Beach* ☎ *415/362–8193* ⊕ *www.citylights.com.*

FOOD AND DRINK

Fodor'sChoice ★ **Molinari Delicatessen.** This store has been making its own salami, sausages, and cold cuts since 1896. Other homemade specialties include meat and cheese ravioli, tomato sauces, and fresh pastas. ■TIP➔ Do like the locals: grab a made-to-order sandwich for lunch and eat it at one of the sidewalk tables or over at Washington Square Park. ⊠ *373 Columbus Ave., at Vallejo St., North Beach* ☎ *415/421–2337.*

EMBARCADERO

FARMERS' MARKETS

Fodor'sChoice ★ **Ferry Plaza Farmers' Market.** The partylike Saturday edition of the city's most upscale and expensive farmers' market places baked goods, gourmet cheeses, smoked fish, and fancy pots of jam alongside organic basil, specialty mushrooms, heirloom tomatoes, handcrafted jams, and juicy-ripe locally grown fruit. On Saturday about 100 vendors pack along three sides of the building, and sandwiches and other prepared foods are for sale in addition to fruit, vegetable, and other samples free for the nibbling. Smaller markets take place on Tuesday and Thursday (the Thursday one doesn't operate from about late December through March.) ⊠ *Ferry Plaza at Market St., Embarcadero* ☎ *415/291–3276* ⊕ *www.ferrybuildingmarketplace.com* ⊙ *Tues. and Thurs. 10–2, Sat. 8–2.*

THE HAIGHT

MUSIC

Fodor's Choice **Amoeba Music.** With more than 2.5 million new and used CDs, DVDs,
★ and records, this warehouselike offshoot of the Berkeley original carries titles you can't find on Amazon at bargain prices. No niche is ignored—from electronica and hip-hop to jazz and classical—and the stock changes daily. ■ TIP➔ **Weekly in-store performances attract large crowds.** ⊠ *1855 Haight St., between Stanyan and Shrader Sts., Haight* ☎ *415/831–1200* ⊕ *www.amoeba.com.*

THE MISSION

CERAMICS

Heath Ceramics. A darling of restaurateurs and local party hosts, Heath opened a 60,000-square-foot Mission District warehouse, complete with a Blue Bottle Coffee kiosk, to showcase its simple yet beautifully crafted ceramic bowls, plates, and vases. ⊠ *2900 18th St., at Alabama St., Mission* ☎ *415/361–5552* ⊕ *www.heathceramics.com.*

FURNITURE, HOUSEWARES, AND GIFTS

Fodor's Choice **Paxton Gate.** Elevating gardening to an art, this serene shop offers beau-
★ tiful earthenware pots, amaryllis and narcissus bulbs, decorative garden items, and coffee-table books such as *An Inordinate Fondness for Beetles.* The collection of taxidermy and preserved bugs provides more unusual gift ideas. A couple of storefronts away is too-cute Paxton Gate Curiosities for Kids, jam-packed with retro toys, books, and other stellar finds. ⊠ *824 Valencia St., between 19th and 20th Sts., Mission* ☎ *415/824–1872* ⊕ *www.paxtongate.com.*

PACIFIC HEIGHTS

BEAUTY

BeneFit Cosmetics. You can find this locally based line of cosmetics and skin-care products at Macy's and Sephora, but it's much more fun to come to one of the eponymous boutiques. No-pressure salespeople dab you with whimsical makeup such as Ooh La Lift concealer and Tinted Love, a stain for lips and cheeks. ⊠ *2117 Fillmore St., between California and Sacramento Sts., Pacific Heights* ☎ *415/567–0242* ⊕ *www. benefitcosmetics.com.*

JAPANTOWN

BOOKS

Kinokuniya Bookstore. The selection of English-language books about Japanese culture—everything from medieval history to origami instructions—is one of the finest in the country. Kinokuniya is the city's biggest seller of Japanese-language books. Dozens of glossy Asian fashion magazines attract the young and trendy; the manga and anime books and magazines are wildly popular, too. ⊠ *Kinokuniya Bldg., 1581 Webster St., at Geary Blvd., Japantown* ☎ *415/567–7625.*

THE BAY AREA

WELCOME TO THE BAY AREA

TOP REASONS TO GO

★ **Bite into the "Gourmet Ghetto":** Eat your way through this area of North Berkeley, starting with a slice of perfect pizza from the Cheese Board (just look for the line).

★ **Find solitude at Point Reyes National Seashore:** Hike beautifully rugged—and often deserted—beaches at one of the most beautiful places on earth, period.

★ **Sit on a dock by the bay:** Admire the beauty of the Bay Area from the rocky, picturesque shores of Sausalito or Tiburon.

★ **Go barhopping in Oakland's hippest hood:** Spend an evening swinging through the watering holes of Uptown, Oakland's artsy-hip and fast-rising corner of downtown.

★ **Walk among giants:** Walking into Muir Woods, a mere 12 miles north of the Golden Gate Bridge, is like entering a cathedral built by God.

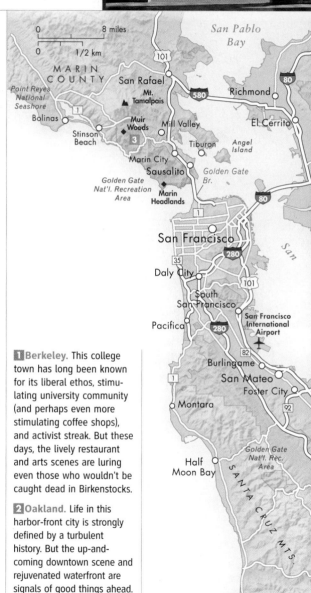

1 Berkeley. This college town has long been known for its liberal ethos, stimulating university community (and perhaps even more stimulating coffee shops), and activist streak. But these days, the lively restaurant and arts scenes are luring even those who wouldn't be caught dead in Birkenstocks.

2 Oakland. Life in this harbor-front city is strongly defined by a turbulent history. But the up-and-coming downtown scene and rejuvenated waterfront are signals of good things ahead.

3 **Marin County.** Marin is considered the prettiest of the Bay Area counties, primarily because of its wealth of open space. Anchored by water on three sides, the county is mostly parkland, including long stretches of undeveloped coastline. The picturesque small towns here—Sausalito, Tiburon, Mill Valley, and Bolinas among them—may sometimes look rustic, but they're mostly in a dizzyingly high tax bracket. There's a reason why people call BMWs "basic Marin wheels."

GETTING ORIENTED

East of the city, across the San Francisco Bay, lie Berkeley and Oakland, which most Bay Area residents refer to as the East Bay. These two towns have distinct personalities, but life here feels more relaxed than in the city—though every bit as vibrant.

Cross the Golden Gate Bridge and head north to reach Marin County's rolling hills and green expanses, where residents enjoy a haute-suburban lifestyle. Farther afield, the wild landscapes of the Muir Woods, Mt. Tamalpais, Stinson Beach, and Point Reyes National Seashore await.

9

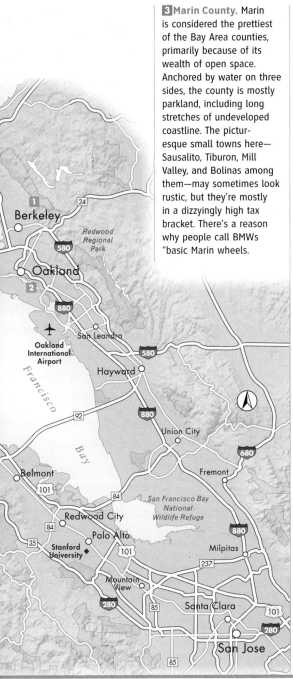

Updated by
Denise M. Leto

It's rare for a metropolis to compete with its suburbs for visitors, but the view from any of San Francisco's hilltops shows that the Bay Area's temptations extend far beyond the city limits. East of town are two energetic urban centers, Berkeley and Oakland. Famously radical Berkeley is also comfortably sophisticated, while Oakland has an art and restaurant scene so hip that it pulls San Franciscans to this side of the bay. To the north is Marin County, the beauty queen, with dramatic coastal scenery of breathtaking beauty and chic, affluent villages like Tiburon and Mill Valley.

PLANNING

WHEN TO GO

As with San Francisco, you can visit the rest of the Bay Area comfortably at any time of year, and it's especially nice in late spring and fall. Unlike in San Francisco, though, the surrounding areas are reliably sunny in summer—it gets hotter as you head inland. Even the rainy season has its charms, as hills that are golden the rest of the year turn a rich green and wildflowers become plentiful. Precipitation is usually the heaviest between November and March. Berkeley is a university town, so the rhythm of the school year might affect your visit. It's easier to navigate the streets and find parking near the university between semesters, but there's also less buzz around town.

GETTING HERE AND AROUND
BART TRAVEL
Using public transportation to reach Berkeley or Oakland is ideal. The under- and aboveground BART (Bay Area Rapid Transit) trains make stops in both towns. Trips to either take about a half hour one-way from the center of San Francisco. BART does not serve Marin County.

Contacts BART ☎ *510/465–2278* ⊕ *www.bart.gov.*

BOAT AND FERRY TRAVEL
For sheer romance, nothing beats the ferry; there's service from San Francisco to Sausalito, Tiburon, and Larkspur in Marin County, and to Alameda and Oakland in the East Bay.

The Golden Gate Ferry crosses the bay to Sausalito from San Francisco's Ferry Building (✉ *Market Street and the Embarcadero*). Blue & Gold Fleet ferries depart daily for Sausalito and Tiburon from Pier 41 at Fisherman's Wharf; weekday commuter ferries leave from the Ferry Building for Tiburon. The trip to Sausalito takes 25 minutes to an hour; to Tiburon, it takes 25 to 55 minutes.

The Angel Island–Tiburon Ferry sails to the island daily April through October and weekends the rest of the year.

The San Francisco Bay Ferry runs several times daily between San Francisco's Ferry Building or Pier 41 and Alameda and Jack London Square in Oakland; one-way tickets are $6.25. The trip lasts 20 to 45 minutes, depending on your departure point, and leads to Oakland's waterfront shopping and restaurant district. Purchase tickets on board.

Boat and Ferry Lines Angel Island–Tiburon Ferry ☎ *415/435–2131* ⊕ *www.angelislandferry.com.* **Blue & Gold Fleet** ☎ *415/705–8200* ⊕ *www.blueandgoldfleet.com.* **Golden Gate Ferry** ☎ *511* ⊕ *www.goldengateferry.org.* **San Francisco Bay Ferry** ☎ *510/522–3300* ⊕ *sanfranciscobayferry.com.*

BUS TRAVEL
Golden Gate Transit buses travel to Sausalito, Tiburon, and Mill Valley from Folsom and 8th streets and from other points in San Francisco. For Mt. Tamalpais State Park and West Marin (e.g., Stinson Beach, Bolinas, and Point Reyes Station), take one of the many routes to Marin City and transfer there to the West Marin Stagecoach (schedules vary). San Francisco Muni bus 76X runs hourly from Sutter and Sansome streets to the Marin Headlands Visitor Center on weekends and major holidays only. The trip takes about 45 minutes.

Though much less convenient than BART, AC Transit buses run between San Francisco's Transbay Temporary Terminal (on the block bordered by Main, Folsom, Beale and Howard streets) and the East Bay. AC Transit's F and FS lines stop near the university and 4th Street shopping, respectively, in Berkeley. Lines C and P travel to Piedmont in Oakland. The O bus stops at the edge of Chinatown near downtown Oakland.

Bus Lines AC Transit ☎ *511* ⊕ *www.actransit.org.* **Golden Gate Transit** ☎ *511* ⊕ *www.goldengate.org.* **San Francisco Muni** ☎ *311* ⊕ *www.sfmta.com.* **West Marin Stagecoach** ☎ *415/526–3239* ⊕ *www.marintransit.org/stage.html.*

CAR TRAVEL

To reach the East Bay from San Francisco, take Interstate 80 East across the San Francisco–Oakland Bay Bridge. Take the University Avenue exit through downtown Berkeley to reach U.C. Berkeley, or take the Ashby Avenue exit and turn left on Telegraph Avenue; there's a parking garage on Channing Way near the campus. For Oakland, take Interstate 580 off the Bay Bridge. To reach downtown and the waterfront, take Interstate 980 from Interstate 580 and exit at 12th Street. Both trips take about 30 minutes unless it's rush hour or a weekend afternoon, when you should count on an hour.

Head north on U.S.101 and cross the Golden Gate Bridge to reach all points in Marin by car, which is essential to visit the outer portions unless you want to spend all day on the bus. From San Francisco, the towns of Sausalito and Tiburon and the Marin Headlands and Point Reyes National Seashore are accessed off U.S. 101. The coastal route, Highway 1, also known as Shoreline Highway, can be accessed off U.S. 101 as well. Follow this road to Mill Valley, Muir Woods, Mt. Tamalpais State Park, Muir Beach, Stinson Beach, and Bolinas. From Bolinas, you can continue north on Highway 1 to Point Reyes. Depending on traffic, it takes from 20 to 45 minutes to get to the Marin Headlands, Sausalito, and Tiburon; driving directly to Point Reyes from San Francisco takes about 90 minutes in moderate traffic if you drive north on U.S. 101 and west on Sir Francis Drake Boulevard. Trips to Muir Woods take from 35 minutes to an hour from San Francisco. Add another 30 minutes for the drive to Stinson Beach (the curving roads make the going slower), 10 more if you continue on to Bolinas. The drive from Bolinas to Point Reyes takes an additional half hour.

RESTAURANTS

The Bay Area is home to some of the most popular and innovative restaurants in the country, including Chez Panisse in Berkeley and Commis in Oakland—for which reservations must be made well in advance. Expect an emphasis on locally grown produce, hormone-free meats, and California wine. Keep in mind that many Marin cafés don't serve dinner, and that dinner service ends on the early side.

HOTELS

Hotels in Berkeley and Oakland tend to be standard-issue, but many Marin hotels package themselves as cozy retreats. Summer is often booked well in advance, despite weather that can be downright chilly. Check for special packages during this season. *Hotel reviews have been shortened. For full information, visit Fodors.com.*

WHAT IT COSTS				
	$	$$	$$$	$$$$
Restaurants	under $16	$16–$22	$23–$30	over $30
Hotels	under $151	$151–$199	$200–$250	over $250

Restaurant prices are the average price of a main course at dinner or, if dinner is not served, at lunch. Hotel prices are the lowest cost of a standard double room in high season.

TOURS

Dylan's Tours. Spend three hours exploring San Francisco with some of the friendliest local guides around, then head to Muir Woods for an hour among giant redwoods, with a stop in Sausalito on the way back. Groups are limited to 14 people; past patrons rave about the tour's in-the-know feel. ✉ *782 Columbus Ave., North Beach, San Francisco* ☎ *415/932–6993* ⊕ *www.dylanstours.com* 🎫 *From $65.*

Extranomical Tours. Take a combination Muir Woods–Sausalito tour with Extranomical, and you can choose to ferry back to San Francisco from Sausalito. Another tour combines a Muir Woods visit with a Wine Country excursion. ☎ *866/231–3752* ⊕ *www.extranomical.com* 🎫 *From $49.*

Great Pacific Tour Co. Morning and afternoon tours to Muir Woods and Sausalito run 3½ hours, with hotel pickup, in 14-passenger vans. ☎ *415/626–4499* ⊕ *www.greatpacifictour.com* 🎫 *From $55.*

THE EAST BAY

When San Franciscans refer to it, the East Bay often means nothing more than what you can see across the bay from the city—mainly Oakland and Berkeley. There's far more here—industrial-chic Emeryville, the wooded ranchland of Walnut Creek, and sprawling, urban Richmond, to name a few other communities—but Berkeley, anchored by its world-class university, and Oakland, which struggles with violence but has booming arts, nightlife, and restaurant scenes, are the magnets that draw folks across the bay.

BERKELEY

2 miles northeast of Bay Bridge.

The birthplace of the Free Speech Movement, the radical hub of the 1960s, the home of arguably the nation's top public university, and the city whose government condemned the bombing of Afghanistan—Berkeley is all of those things. The city of 100,000 facing San Francisco across the bay is also culturally diverse, a breeding ground for social trends, a bastion of the counterculture, and an important center for writers, artists, and musicians. Berkeley residents, students, and faculty spend hours nursing various coffee concoctions while they read, discuss, and debate at any of the dozens of cafés that surround the campus. It's the quintessential university town, and many who graduated years ago still bask in daily intellectual conversation, great weather, and good food. Residents will walk out of their way to go to the perfect bread shop or consult with their favorite wine merchant.

Oakland may have Berkeley beat when it comes to cutting-edge arts, and the city may have forfeited some of its renegade 1960s spirit over the years, but unless a guy in a hot-pink satin body suit, skullcap, and cape rides a unicycle around *your* town, you'll likely find Berkeley offbeat indeed.

The epicenter of Berkeley's energy and activism: the University of California.

GETTING HERE AND AROUND

BART is the easiest way to get to Berkeley from San Francisco. Alight at the Downtown Berkeley (not North Berkeley) station, and walk a block up Center Street to get to the western edge of campus. AC Transit buses F and FS stop near the university and 4th Street shopping. By car, take Interstate 80 east across the Bay Bridge then take the University Avenue exit through downtown Berkeley to the campus or take the Ashby Avenue exit and turn left on Telegraph Avenue. Once you arrive, explore on foot. Berkeley is very pedestrian-friendly.

ESSENTIALS

Visitor Information Visit Berkeley ⊠ *2030 Addison St., Ste. 102* ☎ *510/549-7040* ⊕ *www.visitberkeley.com.*

EXPLORING

TOP ATTRACTIONS

4th Street. Several blocks centering on 4th Street north of University Avenue have evolved from light industrial uses into an upscale shopping and dining district. The compact area is busiest on bright weekend afternoons. Stained Glass Garden, Builders Booksource, and the Apple Store are among shoppers' favorites, along with a minislew of boutiques and wonderful paper stores. ■TIP→ **A walk through the East Bay Vivarium, at 1827 5th St., where turtles swim, Amazonian snakes slither, and baby mice (dinner) cower, is better than a walk through the reptile house at the zoo—and it's free.** ⊠ *4th St., between University Ave. and Delaware Sts.* ⊕ *www.fourthstreet.com.*

QUICK
BITES

✕ **Cheese Board Pizza.** With a jazz combo playing in the storefront and a long line snaking down the block, Cheese Board Pizza taps into the pulse of the Gourmet Ghetto. The cooperatively owned take-out spot and restaurant draws devoted customers with the smell of just-baked garlic, fresh vegetables, and perfect sauces: one pizza a day, always vegetarian. For just a nibble, the Cheese Board bakery–cheese shop next door sells cookies, muffins, scones, bialys, and the best sourdough baguettes in town. ✉ *1504–1512 Shattuck Ave., at Vine St.* ☎ *510/549–3055* ⊕ *cheeseboardcollective.coop/pizza* ⊙ *Tues.–Sat. 11:30–3 and 4:30–8.*

A TASTING TOUR

For an unforgettable foodie experience, take Lisa Rogovin's **Culinary Walking Tour** (☎ *415/806–5970* ⊕ *www.edible-excursions.net*). You'll taste your way through the Gourmet Ghetto, learn some culinary history, and meet the chefs behind the food. Tours ($88) run on Thursday from 11 to 2:15 and on Saturday from 10 to 1.

Fodor's Choice
★

Gourmet Ghetto. The success of Chez Panisse restaurant attracted other food-related enterprises to its stretch of Shattuck Avenue, and the area surrounding the intersection of Shattuck and Vine Street became known as the Gourmet Ghetto. Foodies will do well to spend a couple of hours here, poking around the food shops, grabbing a quick bite, or indulging in a full meal at one of the neighborhood's many excellent eateries.

The line stretches down the block in front of **Cheese Board Pizza,** at 1512 Shattuck, where live jazz bands sometimes serenade the diners that spill out onto the sidewalk and median. Next door is the **Cheese Board Collective**—worker owned since 1971—and its fabulous bakery and extensive cheese counter. Next door to Chez Panisse, César (No. 1515) wine bar and tapas house is a good place for an afternoon quaff or late-night drink.

The small food stands of **Epicurious Garden,** at 1509–1513 Shattuck, sell everything from sushi to gelato. Out back, you can find a small terraced garden—the best place to sit—that winds up four levels and ends at the **Imperial Tea Court.** Around the corner just off Vine Street is **Love at First Bite,** a cupcakery that sells scrumptious confections. Across Vine, the **Vintage Berkeley** wine shop occupies the historic former pump house at No. 2113; the offerings here are shrewdly selected and reasonably priced. Coffee lovers of the **Peet's** persuasion may want to pay respects at No. 2124, where the famed roaster got its start; the small café includes a display chronicling Peet's history.

South of Cedar Street in the next block of Shattuck is the art-filled **Guerilla Cafe** (No. 1620), a breakfast and lunch spot beloved for its waffles (the Blue Bottle Coffee doesn't hurt). Also look for the **Local Butcher Shop** (No. 1600), with locally sourced meat and hearty made-to-order sandwiches. A former Ritz-Carlton chef brings white-linen quality to his to-go counter, **Grégoire,** around the corner on Cedar Street (No. 2109). In the block north of Vine Street on Shattuck are popular **Saul's**

9

deli and restaurant and beautiful **Masse's Pastries**. On Thursday, an organic farmers' market thrives here. We could go on, but you get the idea. ✉ *Shattuck Ave. between Cedar and Rose Sts., North Berkeley* ⊕ *www.gourmetghetto.org.*

FAMILY **Tilden Regional Park.** The **Regional Parks Botanic Garden** is the star of this beautiful 2,000-acre park in the hills east of the U.C. Berkeley campus. Botanically speaking, a stroll through the garden, which focuses on native plants of California, provides a whirlwind tour of the entire state. At the garden's visitor center, you can pick up information about Tilden's other attractions, including its picnic spots, Lake Anza swimming site, golf course, and hiking trails (the paved **Nimitz Way**, at Inspiration Point, is a popular hike with wonderful views, especially at sunset). ■TIP➔ Children love Tilden Park's miniature steam trains; Little Farm, where kids can feed the animals; and the vintage carousel with wooden animals. ✉ *Regional Parks Botanic Garden, Wildcat Canyon Rd. and South Park Dr., Tilden Park* ☎ *510/544–2747* ⊕ *www. ebparks.org/parks/tilden* ☞ *Free to park and botanic garden* ☉ *Daily 8 am–10 pm.*

University of California. Known simply as "Cal," the founding campus of California's university system is one of the leading intellectual centers in the United States and a major site for scientific research. Chartered in 1868, the university sits on 178 oak-covered acres split by Strawberry Creek. Bounded by Bancroft Way to the south, Hearst Avenue to the north, Oxford Street to the west, and Gayley Road to the east, Cal has more than 30,000 students and a full-time faculty of 1,500.

Below are a few places of note on campus:

Berkeley Art Museum & Pacific Film Archive. The museum's collection spans five centuries and is strong on mid-20th-century art, particularly abstract expressionist works; admission to the downstairs galleries is free. The Pacific Film Archive, at 2575 Bancroft Way, is a major venue for foreign, independent, and avant-garde film. ✉ *2626 Bancroft Way, at Bowditch St.* ☎ *510/642–0808, film info 510/642–1124* ⊕ *www. bampfa.berkeley.edu* ☞ *$10, free 1st Thurs. of month* ☉ *Wed.–Sun. 11–5, some Fridays 11–9.*

Berkeley Visitor Information Center. You can get your bearings here and find out about campus events. Free 90-minute tours leave from here on weekdays. ✉ *101 Sproul Hall, Bancroft Way and Telegraph Ave.* ☎ *510/642–5215* ⊕ *visitors.berkeley.edu* ☉ *Weekdays 8:30–4:30, tours at 10 am.*

Sather Tower. Weekend campus tours leave from this landmark, popularly known as the Campanile, at 10 am on Saturdays and 1 pm on Sundays. The 307-foot structure, modeled on St. Mark's Tower in Venice, can be seen for miles. For a view of the campus and beyond, take the elevator up 175 feet, then walk another 38 steps to the observation deck. ☞ *Elevator $3,* ☉ *Weekdays 10–4, Sat. 10–5, Sun. 10–1:30 and 3–5.*

Sproul Plaza. The site of free-speech and civil-rights protests in the 1960s, the plaza remains a platform for political and social activists, musicians, and students. Preachers orate atop milk crates, amateur entertainers bang on makeshift drum sets, and protesters distribute

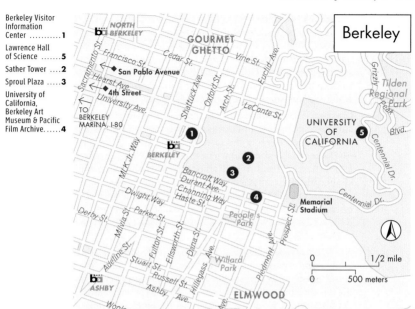

leaflets about everything from marijuana to the Middle East. Walk through at noon for the liveliest show of student spirit. ✉ *Telegraph Ave. and Bancroft Way.*

University of California Botanical Garden. Thanks to Berkeley's temperate climate, about 13,500 species of plants from all over the world flourish in this 34-acre garden. Free tours are given on Thursdays and weekends at 1:30; the views are breathtaking. ✉ *200 Centennial Dr.* ☎ *510/643–2755* ⊕ *botanicalgarden.berkeley.edu* 💲 *$10, free 1st Thurs. of month* ⊙ *Daily 9–5, closed 1st Tues. of month.* ⊕ *www. berkeley.edu.*

WORTH NOTING

Elmwood. Shops and cafés pack this pleasant neighborhood centered on College Avenue, just south of the U.C. campus. You'll know you're here when you see the logo for the beloved art-house cinema and performance space, the **Elmwood theater,** near College and Ashby avenues, though you're just as apt to see a line snaking outside nearby **Ici Ice Cream,** at 2948 College. All the treats here are made on the premises. While you're waiting, check out the architectural details of the nearby pre–World War II storefronts. Century-old shingled houses line the tree-shaded streets nearby. ✉ *College Ave. between Dwight Way and Alcatraz Ave., Elmwood.*

Indian Rock. An outcropping of nature in a sea of North Berkeley homes, this is an unbeatable spot for a sunset picnic. You know you've reached the rock when you see amateur rock climbers clinging precariously to its side. After-work walkers and cuddling couples, all watching the sun sinking beneath the Golden Gate Bridge, join you at the top. Come early to grab a spot on the rock while it's still light. ⊠ *Head east on Indian Rock Path at Solano Ave. and the Alameda.*

FAMILY **Lawrence Hall of Science.** At this dazzling hands-on science museum, kids can look at insects under microscopes, solve crimes using chemical forensics, and explore the physics of baseball. Out front they'll climb on Pheena, a life-size blue-whale model, and clamber over a giant strand of DNA. Out back, it's all about how earthquakes and water have shaped the bay, and from all vantage points sweeping views of the bay and beyond can be had. On weekends come special lectures, demonstrations, and planetarium shows. ⊠ *1 Centennial Dr.* 🕾 *510/642–5132* ⊕ *www.lawrencehallofscience.org* ✉ *$12, planetarium $4 extra* ☽ *Daily 10–5.*

San Pablo Avenue. Berkeley's diversity is front and center along this evolving north–south artery in West Berkeley, where the old and new stand side by side: sari shops and a Mexican grocery do business near a hipster dive bar, a bait-and-tackle store, a typewriter store, and a dozen cool boutiques, all cheek by jowl in a six-block microhood that doesn't have a name . . . yet.

Start at University Avenue, where you can duck into **Mi Tierra Foods** (No. 2082) for piñatas and chorizo—notice the Mission District–like mural—and **Middle East Market** (No. 2054) for rose water and rockin' baklava. **Café V** (No. 2056) has fresh, reliably good, and reasonably priced Vietnamese food, and pretty much everyone loves the thin-crust pies at **Lanesplitter Pizza & Pub** (No. 2033). The coffee at **Local 123** (No. 2049) is strong, delicious, and beautiful, and the back patio is a lovely surprise.

Old-fashioned, family-run **Country Cheese** (No. 2101) has hundreds of cheeses, of course, but it also carries great bulk foods and makes a heck of a sandwich to order. Or grab a table at industrial-cute **Gaumenkitzel** (No. 2121) and tuck in to schnitzel and other traditional German fare. The pierced-and-tattooed set loves **Acme Bar & Company** (No. 2115) for its Bloody Marys and whiskey selection.

As you move south, you'll pass lots of home-decor shops. Witness the reupholstering genius on display at **Mignonne Décor** (No. 2447). One of the Bay Area's oldest salvage shops, **Ohmega Salvage** (Nos. 2400–2407) makes for fun browsing, though its claw-foot tubs and Victorian window frames are pricey.

At the corner of Dwight Way, stop for more caffeine at **Caffè Trieste** (No. 2500), Berkeley's homey branch of North Beach's bohemian coffee bar. Arousing browsing can be had at sex-positive, woman-friendly **Good Vibrations** (No. 2504). Find wonderful gifts at **Juniper Tree Supplies** (No. 2520), with everything for the soap and candle maker, and **Kiss My Ring** (No. 2522), which stocks jewelry designed by the owner. ⊠ *San Pablo Ave., between University Ave. and Parker St.*

Telegraph Avenue. Berkeley's student-oriented thoroughfare, Telegraph Avenue is the best place to get a dose of the city's famed counterculture. On any given day, you might encounter a troop of chanting Hare Krishnas or a drumming band of Rastafarians. First and foremost, however, Telegraph is a place for socializing and shopping, the only uniquely Berkeley shopping experience in town and a definite don't-miss (though locals complain that Telegraph is heading downhill fast, with too many panhandlers, and businesses closing up shop). ■TIP➔ **Take care at night, when things get edgier. The nearby People's Park, mostly harmless by day, is best avoided after sunset.** Cafés, bookstores, poster shops, and street vendors line the avenue. T-shirt vendors and tarot-card readers come and go on a whim, but a few establishments—**Rasputin Music** (No. 2401), **Amoeba Music** (No. 2455), and **Moe's Books** (No. 2476)—are neighborhood landmarks. Allen Ginsberg wrote his acclaimed poem "Howl" at **Caffe Mediterraneum** (No. 2475), a relic of 1960s-era café culture that also lays claim to inventing the café latte.

WHERE TO EAT

Dining in Berkeley is a low-key affair; even in the finest restaurants, most folks dress casually. Late diners be forewarned: Berkeley is an "early to bed" kind of town.

$ ✕ **Angeline's Louisiana Kitchen.** There's always a line winding out the door
SOUTHERN for the delicious food at Angeline's. The brick walls, maps of Louisiana, ceiling fans, and New Orleans music create a festive atmosphere that is both welcoming and exciting. Specialties include Voo Doo shrimp with blue lake beans, crawfish étouffée, and buttermilk fried chicken. The Creole pecan pie is so good you'll be coming back for more. $ *Average main: $14 ⊠ 2261 Shattuck Ave., near Kittredge St. ☎ 510/548–6900 ⊕ www.angelineskitchen.com ⊗ No lunch Mon.*

$ ✕ **Bette's Oceanview Diner.** Buttermilk pancakes are just one of the spe-
AMERICAN cialties at this 1930s-inspired diner complete with checkered floors and burgundy booths. Huevos rancheros and lox and eggs are other breakfast options; kosher franks, generous slices of pizza, and a slew of sandwiches are available for lunch. The wait for a seat can be quite long; thankfully, 4th Street was made for strolling. ■TIP➔ **If you're starving, head to Bette's to Go, next door, for takeout.** $ *Average main: $10 ⊠ 1807 4th St., near Delaware St., 4th Street ☎ 510/644–3230 ⊕ www. bettesdiner.com ⌦ Reservations not accepted ⊗ No dinner.*

$ ✕ **César.** In true Spanish style, dinners are served late at César, whose
SPANISH kitchen closes at 11:30 pm on Friday and Saturday and at 11 pm the rest of the week. Couples spill out from its street-level windows on warm nights, or rub shoulders at the polished bar or center communal table. Founded by a trio of former Chez Panisse chefs, César is like a first cousin to that stalwart eatery right next door, each restaurant recommending the other if there's a long wait ahead. For tapas and perfectly grilled *bocadillos* (small sandwiches), there's no better choice. The bar also makes a mean martini and has an impressive wine list. ■TIP➔ **Come early to get seated quickly and to hear your tablemates; the room gets loud when the bar is in full swing.** $ *Average main: $15 ⊠ 1515 Shattuck Ave., at Vine St., North Berkeley ☎ 510/883–0222 ⊕ cesarberkeley.com ⌦ Reservations not accepted.*

9

$$$$ ✕**Chez Panisse Café & Restaurant.** At Chez Panisse even humble pizza is
AMERICAN   reincarnated, with innovative toppings of the freshest local ingredients.
Fodor'sChoice   The downstairs portion of Alice Waters's legendary eatery is noted
★   for its formality and personal service. The daily-changing multicourse
dinners are prix-fixe ($$$$), with the cost slightly lower on weekdays.
Upstairs, in the informal café, the crowd is livelier, the prices are lower
($$–$$$), and the ever-changing menu is à la carte. The food is sim-
pler, too: penne with new potatoes, arugula, and sheep's-milk cheese;
fresh figs with Parmigiano-Reggiano cheese and arugula; and grilled
tuna with savoy cabbage, for example. Legions of loyal fans insist that
Chez Panisse lives up to its reputation and delivers a dining experience
well worth the price. ■TIP➔ **It's wise to make your reservation a few
weeks ahead of your visit.** $ *Average main: $95* ✉ *1517 Shattuck Ave.,
at Vine St., North Berkeley* ☎ *510/548–5525 restaurant, 510/548–5049
café* ⊕ *www.chezpanisse.com* ⬥ *Reservations essential* ⊘ *Closed Sun.
No lunch in the restaurant.*

$$ ✕**Corso Trattoria.** On the edge of Berkeley's Gourmet Ghetto, this lively
TUSCAN   spot serves up excellent Florentine cuisine in a spare but snazzy space.
The open kitchen at the back dominates the room (which can get smoky
at times), and the closely spaced tables add to the festivity of dining
here. The seasonal menu might include pan-roasted sturgeon with brus-
sels sprouts or butter-roasted chicken breast. Side dishes are ordered
separately; the baked polenta with mascarpone and Parmesan is a
definite crowd pleaser. An extensive Italian wine list complements the
menu; save room for the memorable panna cotta. $ *Average main: $18*
✉ *1788 Shattuck Ave., at Delaware St., North Berkeley* ☎ *510/704–
8004* ⊕ *www.trattoriacorso.com* ⊘ *No lunch.*

$$ ✕**Gather.** Here organic, sustainable, and all things Berkeley reside har-
AMERICAN   moniously beneath one tasty roof. This vibrant, well-lit eatery boasts
funky lighting fixtures, a variety of shiny wood furnishings, and banquettes made of recycled leather belts. Everything feels contemporary
and local, especially the food. The vegan "charcuterie," made of root
vegetables, put the restaurant on the national map; the stinging nettles
pizza is refreshing, and the grilled chicken is oh so juicy. This is a
haven for vegetarian, vegan, and gluten-free eaters, but there's plenty
for meat eaters to choose from, too. Desserts don't get much better
than the chocolate semifreddo with Zinfandel-braised Mission figs and
pine nuts. $ *Average main: $20* ✉ *2200 Oxford St., at Allston Way*
☎ *510/809–0400* ⊕ *www.gatherrestaurant.com.*

$$ ✕**Ippuku.** More Tokyo street chic than standard sushi house, this
JAPANESE   *izakaya*—the Japanese equivalent of a bar with appetizers—with
bamboo-screen booths serves up surprising fare, from chicken tartare
to wonderful *yakitori*, skewers such as bacon-wrapped enoki, bacon-
wrapped mushrooms, and pork belly. (Anything skewered here is sure
to please.) Dinner beats lunch at Ippuku, and savvy diners make reserva-
tions and arrive early for the best selection. The bar, which opens onto
the street, pours an impressive array of sakes and *shōchū* (liquor dis-
tilled from sweet potatoes, rice, or barley). $ *Average main: $19* ✉ *2130
Center St., Downtown* ☎ *510/665–1969* ⊕ *www.ippukuberkeley.com*
⊘ *No lunch Sun.–Thurs.*

The pioneering restaurant Chez Panisse focuses on seasonal local ingredients.

$$$ MEDITERRANEAN Fodor's Choice ★

🍴 **Lalime's.** Inside a charming, flower-covered house, this restaurant serves dishes that reflect the entire Mediterranean region. The menu, constantly changing and unfailingly great, depends on the availability of fresh seasonal ingredients. Choices might include grilled ahi tuna or creamy Italian risotto. Light colors used in the dining room, which has two levels, help to create a cheerful mood. Excellent and long-lived but not flashy, the restaurant has a legion of dedicated fans, many middle-aged and up. **■ TIP→ Lalime's is a good second choice if Chez Panisse is booked up.** [$] *Average main: $27* ✉ *1329 Gilman St., at Tevlin St., North Berkeley* ☎ *510/527–9838* 🌐 *www.lalimes.com* ✍ *Reservations essential* ⏲ *Closed Mon. and Tues. No lunch.*

$ MEXICAN FAMILY

🍴 **Picante.** A barnlike space full of cheerful Mexican tiles and folk-art masks, Picante is a find for anyone seeking good, Cal-Mex food for a song. The masa is freshly ground for the tortillas and tamales (it's fun to watch the tamale maker in action), the salsas are complex, and the flavor combinations are inventive. Try tamales filled with butternut squash and chilis or a simple taco of roasted poblanos and sautéed onions; we challenge you to finish a plate of supernachos. Picante is beloved of Berkeley families with raucous children, as they fit right in to the festival-like atmosphere and are happily distracted by the fountain on the back patio. [$] *Average main: $12* ✉ *1328 6th St., near Camelia St.* ☎ *510/525–3121* 🌐 *www.picanteberkeley.com* ✍ *Reservations not accepted.*

$ AMERICAN FAMILY

🍴 **Saul's.** Well known for its homemade sodas and enormous sandwiches, the Saul's of today uses sustainably sourced seafood, grass-fed beef, and organic eggs. The restaurant is a Berkeley institution, and its loyal clientele swears by the pastrami sandwiches, stuffed-cabbage rolls, and tuna melts. For breakfast, the challah French toast is so thick it's almost too big to bite, and the deli omelets are served pancake style. The high ceilings and red-leather booths add to the friendly, retro atmosphere. ■ TIP➜ Don't overlook the glass deli case, where you can order food to go. $ *Average main: $14* ✉ *1475 Shattuck Ave., near Vine St., North Berkeley* ☎ *510/848-3354* ⊕ *www.saulsdeli.com* ⌲ *Reservations not accepted* ☉ *Closed Thanksgiving and Yom Kippur.*

WHERE TO STAY

For inexpensive lodging, investigate University Avenue, west of campus. The area can be noisy, congested, and somewhat dilapidated, but it does include a few decent motels and chain properties. All Berkeley lodgings, except for the swanky Claremont, are strictly mid-range.

$
HOTEL

The Bancroft Hotel. Lovingly remodeled in 2012, this green boutique hotel—across from the U.C. campus—is fresh, stylish, and completely eco-friendly. **Pros:** heating under the floorboards; great rooftop deck; closest hotel in Berkeley to campus. **Cons:** some rooms are small; bathrooms could be freshened up; no elevator. $ *Rooms from: $149* ✉ *2680 Bancroft Way* ☎ *510/549-1000* ⊕ *bancrofthotel.com* ⇱ *22* �’⊖❘ *Breakfast.*

$$$$
HOTEL
Fodor'sChoice
★

Claremont Resort and Spa. Straddling the Oakland–Berkeley border, this amenities-rich resort—which celebrates its centennial in 2015—beckons like a gleaming white castle in the hills. **Pros:** amazing spa; supervised child care; solid business amenities; great bay views from some rooms. **Cons:** parking is pricey; resort charge for use of spa, tennis courts, pool, gym, etc.; additional fee for breakfast. $ *Rooms from: $260* ✉ *41 Tunnel Rd., at Ashby and Domingo Aves., Claremont* ☎ *510/843-3000, 800/551-7266* ⊕ *www.claremontresort.com* ⇱ *249 rooms, 30 suites* �’⊖❘ *No meals.*

$$
HOTEL

Holiday Inn Express. Convenient to the freeway and 4th Street shopping, this peach-and-beige hotel provides good bang for the buck. **Pros:** good breakfast; short walk to restaurant options on San Pablo and University; free Internet in rooms. **Cons:** area can be noisy and congested with traffic during commute hours; neighborhood can feel sketchy after dark. $ *Rooms from: $189* ✉ *1175 University Ave., at Curtis St.* ☎ *510/548-1700, 866/548-1700* ⊕ *www.hiexberkeley.com* ⇱ *69 rooms, 3 suites* �’⊖❘ *Breakfast.*

$$
HOTEL

Hotel Durant. A mainstay of parents visiting their children at U.C. Berkeley, this boutique hotel is also a good option for those who want to be a short walk from Telegraph Avenue. **Pros:** convenient location to Cal and public transit; blackout shades; organic bathrobes. **Cons:** downstairs bar can get noisy during Cal games; parking can be pricey. $ *Rooms from: $180* ✉ *2600 Durant Ave., at Bowditch St.* ☎ *510/845-8981* ⊕ *www.hoteldurant.com* ⇱ *143 rooms* �’⊖❘ *No meals.*

$$
HOTEL
Fodor'sChoice
★

Hotel Shattuck Plaza. This historic boutique hotel sits amid Berkeley's downtown arts district, just steps from the U.C. campus and a short walk from the Gourmet Ghetto. **Pros:** central location; near public transit; modern facilities; good views; great restaurant. **Cons:** pricey parking; limited fitness center. $ *Rooms from: $195* ✉ *2086 Allston Way, at Shattuck Ave., Downtown* ☎ *510/845-7300* ⊕ *www. hotelshattuckplaza.com* ⇱ *199 rooms, 17 suites* �’⊖❘ *No meals.*

NIGHTLIFE AND THE ARTS
NIGHTLIFE

Fodor'sChoice
★
Freight & Salvage Coffeehouse. Some of the most talented practitioners of folk, blues, Cajun, and bluegrass perform in this alcohol-free space, one of the country's finest folk houses. Most tickets cost less than $25. ✉ *2020 Addison St., between Shattuck Ave. and Milvia St.* ☎ *510/644–2020* ⊕ *www.thefreight.org.*

THE ARTS

Berkeley Repertory Theatre. One of the region's highly respected resident professional companies, Berkeley Rep performs classic and contemporary plays. Well-known pieces such as *Crime and Punishment* and *The Arabian Nights* mix with edgier fare like Green Day's *American Idiot* and Lemony Snicket's *The Composer Is Dead.* The theater's complex is in the heart of downtown Berkeley's arts district, near BART's Downtown Berkeley station. ✉ *2025 Addison St., near Shattuck Ave.* ☎ *510/647–2949* ⊕ *www.berkeleyrep.org.*

Berkeley Symphony Orchestra. The works of 20th-century composers are a focus of this prominent orchestra, but traditional pieces are also performed. BSO plays a handful of concerts each year, in Zellerbach Hall and other locations. ✉ *1942 University Ave., Ste. 207* ☎ *510/841–2800* ⊕ *www.berkeleysymphony.org.*

Cal Performances. The series, running from September through May at Zellerbach Hall and various other U.C. Berkeley venues, offers the Bay Area's most varied bill of internationally acclaimed artists in all disciplines, from classical soloists to the latest jazz, world-music, theater, and dance ensembles. Look for frequent campus colloquiums or preshow talks featuring Berkeley's professors. ✉ *Zellerbach Hall, Telegraph Ave. and Bancroft Way* ☎ *510/642–9988* ⊕ *calperformances.org.*

SHOPPING

Fodor'sChoice
★
Amoeba Music. Heaven for audiophiles, this legendary Berkeley favorite is *the* place to head for new and used CDs, records, cassettes, and DVDs. The dazzling stock includes thousands of titles for all music tastes. The store even has its own record label. There are branches in San Francisco and Hollywood, but this is the original. ✉ *2455 Telegraph Ave., at Haste St.* ☎ *510/549–1125* ⊕ *www.amoeba.com.*

Body Time. Founded in Berkeley in 1970, this local chain uses premium-quality ingredients to create its natural perfumes and skin-care and aromatherapy products. Sustainably harvested essential oils that you can combine and dilute to create your own personal fragrances are the specialty. The Citrus, Lavender-Mint, and China Rain scents are all popular. ✉ *1950 Shattuck Ave., at Berkeley Way* ☎ *510/841–5818* ⊕ *www.bodytime.com.*

Kermit Lynch Wine Merchant. Lynch's newsletters describing his finds are legendary, as is his friendship with Alice Waters of Chez Panisse. Credited with taking American appreciation of French wine to another level, this shop is a great place to peruse as you educate your palate. The friendly salespeople can direct you to the latest French bargains. ✉ *1605 San Pablo Ave., at Dwight Way* ☎ *510/524–1524* ⊕ *kermitlynch.com.*

9

Moe's Books. The spirit of Moe—the cantankerous, cigar-smoking late proprietor—lives on in this four-story house of books. Students and professors come here to browse the large selection of used books, including literary and cultural criticism, art titles, and literature in foreign languages. ⊠ *2476 Telegraph Ave., near Haste St.* ☎ *510/849–2087* ⊕ *moesbooks.com.*

Rasputin Music. A huge selection of new music for every taste draws crowds. In any other town, Rasputin's stock of used CDs and vinyl would likely be unsurpassed. ⊠ *2403 Telegraph Ave., at Channing Way* ☎ *510/848–9004* ⊕ *www.rasputinmusic.com.*

OAKLAND

Directly east of Bay Bridge.

Often overshadowed by San Francisco's beauty and Berkeley's storied counterculture, Oakland's allure lies in its amazing diversity. Here you can find a Nigerian clothing store, a beautifully renovated Victorian home, a Buddhist meditation center, and a lively salsa club, all within the same block.

Oakland's multifaceted nature reflects its colorful and often tumultuous history. Once a cluster of Mediterranean-style homes and gardens that served as a bedroom community for San Francisco, the city became a hub of shipbuilding and industry almost overnight when the United States entered World War II. New jobs in the city's shipyards and factories attracted thousands of workers, including some of the first female welders, and the city's neighborhoods were imbued with a proud but gritty spirit. In the 1960s and '70s this intense community pride gave rise to such militant groups as the Black Panther Party and the Symbionese Liberation Army, but they were little match for the economic hardships and racial tensions that plagued Oakland. In many neighborhoods the reality was widespread poverty and gang violence—subjects that dominated the songs of such Oakland-bred rappers as the late Tupac Shakur. The highly publicized protests of the Occupy Oakland movement in 2011 and 2012 illustrated just how much Oakland remains a mosaic of its past.

The affluent reside in the city's hillside homes, wooded enclaves like Claremont and Montclair, which provide a warmer, more spacious, and more affordable alternative to San Francisco, while a constant flow of newcomers—many from Central America and Asia—ensures continued diversity, vitality, and growing pains. Many neighborhoods to the west and south of the city center remain run-down and unsafe, but a renovated downtown area—sparking a vibrant arts scene—and the waterfront around Jack London Square on the edge of finding its footing have injected new energy into the city. Even San Franciscans, often loathe to cross the Bay Bridge—why should they?—come to Uptown and Temescal for the crackling arts and restaurant scenes there.

Everyday life here revolves around the neighborhood, with a main business strip attracting both shoppers and strollers. In some areas, such as high-end Piedmont and Rockridge, you'd swear you were in Berkeley

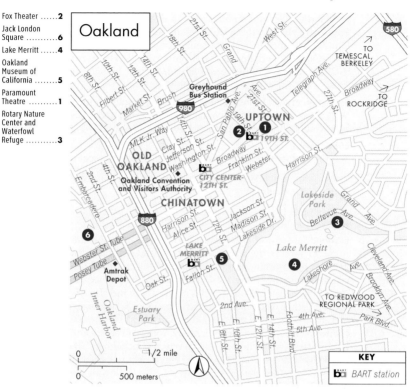

or San Francisco's Noe Valley or Cow Hollow. Along Telegraph Avenue just south of 51st Street, Temescal is pulsing with creative culinary and design energy. These are perfect places for browsing, eating, or just relaxing between sightseeing trips to Oakland's architectural gems, rejuvenated waterfront, and numerous green spaces.

GETTING HERE AND AROUND

Driving from San Francisco, take Interstate 80 East across the Bay Bridge, then take Interstate 580 to the Grand Avenue exit for Lake Merritt. To reach downtown and the waterfront, take Interstate 980 from Interstate 580 and exit at 12th Street; exit at 18th Street for Uptown. For Temescal, take Interstate 580 to Highway 24 and exit at 51st Street.

By BART, use the Lake Merritt Station for the Oakland Museum and southern Lake Merritt; the Oakland City Center–12th Street Station for downtown, Chinatown, and Old Oakland; and the 19th Street Station for Uptown, the Paramount Theatre, and the north side of Lake Merritt.

By bus, take the AC Transit's C and P lines to get to Piedmont in Oakland. The O bus stops at the edge of Chinatown near downtown Oakland.

Oakland's Jack London Square is an easy hop on the ferry from San Francisco. Those without cars can take advantage of the free Broadway Shuttle, which runs from the square down Broadway through Chinatown/Old Oakland, downtown, Uptown, and Lake Merritt, all the way to 27th Street. The shuttle runs late on Friday and Saturday nights; its website has full schedule information.

Once you arrive, be aware of how quickly neighborhoods can change. Walking is safe downtown and in the Piedmont and Rockridge areas, but avoid walking west and south of downtown.

ESSENTIALS

Shuttle Contact Broadway Shuttle ⊕ *www.meetdowntownoak.com.*

Visitor Information Visit Oakland ✉ *481 Water St.* ☎ *510/839–9000* ⊕ *www.visitoakland.org.*

EXPLORING

TOP ATTRACTIONS

FAMILY

Fodor'sChoice

★

Oakland Museum of California. One of Oakland's top attractions, the museum surveys the state's art, history, and natural wonders in three galleries of absorbing, detailed exhibits. You can travel through myriad ecosystems in the Gallery of California Natural Sciences, from the sand dunes of the Pacific to the coyotes and brush of the Nevada border. Kids love the lifelike wild-animal exhibits, especially the snarling wolverine, big-eyed harbor seal, and trove of hidden creatures. The rambling Gallery of California History includes everything from Spanish-era armor to a small but impressive collection of vintage vehicles, including a candy-apple-red "Mystery" car from the 1960s and a gleaming red, gold, and silver fire engine that battled the flames in San Francisco following the 1906 earthquake. The Gallery of California Art holds an eclectic collection of modern works and early landscapes. Of particular interest are paintings by Richard Diebenkorn, Joan Brown, Elmer Bischoff, and David Park, all members of the Bay Area figurative school, which flourished here after World War II. Fans of Dorothea Lange won't want to miss the gallery's comprehensive collection of her work. The museum also has a sculpture garden with a view of the Oakland and Berkeley hills in the distance. ✉ *1000 Oak St., at 10th St., Downtown* ☎ *510/238–2200* ⊕ *www.museumca.org* ☞ *$15, free 1st Sun. of month* ☽ *Wed.–Sun. 11–5, Fri. until 9.*

Fodor'sChoice

★

Paramount Theatre. Perhaps the most glorious art deco specimen in the city, if not the entire Bay Area, the Paramount operates as a venue for concerts and performances of all kinds, from the Oakland East Bay Symphony to Tom Waits and Elvis Costello. The popular monthly movie nights start off with a 30-minute Wurlitzer concert preceding classic films such as *Casablanca.* ■TIP➔ **At 10 am on the first and third Saturday of each month, you can take a marvelous two-hour tour of the building.** ✉ *2025 Broadway, at 20th St., Uptown* ☎ *510/465–6400* ⊕ *www.paramounttheatre.com* ☞ *Tour $5.*

Rockridge. This upscale neighborhood is one of Oakland's most desirable places to live. Explore the tree-lined streets that radiate out from **College Avenue** just north and south of the Rockridge BART station for a look at California bungalow architecture at its finest. By day

College Avenue between Broadway and Alcatraz Avenue is crowded with shoppers buying fresh flowers, used books, and clothing; by night the same folks are back for dinner and locally brewed ales in the numerous restaurants and pubs. With its pricey specialty-food shops, **Market Hall,** an airy European-style marketplace at Shafter Avenue, is a hub of culinary activity. ⊕ *www.rockridgedistrict.com.*

Fodor's Choice ★ **Temescal.** Centering on Telegraph Avenue between Piedmont and South Berkeley, up-and-coming Temescal ("sweat house" in the language of the Aztec) is a low-pretension, moneyed-hipster hood with a lot of young families and—gasp—middle-aged folks thrown into the mix. A critical mass of excellent eateries, from veteran Doña Tomás and favorites Pizzaiola and Aunt Mary's to **Bakesale Betty** (✉ *5098 Telegraph Ave.*), where folks line up for the fried-chicken sandwich on the one-item menu, and **Doughnut Dolly** (✉ *482B 49th St.*), who fills her fried treats to order, draws folks from around the Bay Area. Old-time dive bars and check-cashing places share space with newer arrivals like crafty, local children's clothing shop **Ruby's Garden** (✉ *5026 Telegraph Ave.*); **Article Pract** (✉ *5010 Telegraph Ave.*), purveyor of gorgeous yarn; and the **East Bay Depot for Creative Reuse** (✉ *4695 Telegraph Ave.*), where you might find a bucket of buttons or 1,000 muffin wrappers for $1 among bird cages, furniture, lunch boxes, and ribbon.

Around the corner, **Temescal Alley** (✉ *49th St.*), a tucked-away lane of tiny storefronts, crackles with the creative energy of the craftspeople who have set up shop there, among them fashion designer Ali Golden and jewelry designer Marisa Haskell. You can make some surprising finds at Crimson Horticultural Rarities and the fresh home-decor shop Bounty and Feast.

This neighborhood is *the* place to go to put your finger on the pulse of Oakland right now. ✉ *Telegraph Ave., between 45th and 51st Sts.* ⊕ *www.temescaldistrict.org.*

Uptown. This is where nightlife and cutting-edge art happens in Oakland, along the formerly gritty, currently crazy-cool Telegraph Avenue/Broadway corridor north of downtown. Dozens of galleries cluster around Telegraph, showing everything from photography and video installations to glasswork and textile arts. On the first Friday of the month, thousands descend for the neighborhood's biggest happening, the gallery walk **Art Murmur** (⊕ *oaklandartmurmur.org*). In addition to galleries open late, Art Murmur has expanded into **First Friday,** a veritable festival featuring food trucks, street vendors, and live music along Telegraph Avenue. Less raucous and more intimate is the **Saturday Stroll,** with 17 galleries and eight mixed-use venues open on Saturday from 1 to 5, often with special events.

Lively restaurants with a distinctly urban vibe make the neighborhood a dining destination; favorites include friendly **Luka's Taproom and Lounge** (✉ *2221 Broadway*); beautiful art deco **Flora** (✉ *1900 Telegraph Ave.*), one of the best brunch places in town; trendy, graffiti-walled **Hawker Fare** (✉ *2300 Webster St.*), serving Asian street food; elegant **Picán** (✉ *2295 Broadway*), for upscale Southern comfort food; and the sophisticated **Plum** (✉ *2214 Broadway*) and its attached bar, just to name a few.

9

Toss in the bevy of bars, and there's plenty within walking distance to keep you busy for an entire evening: **Cafe Van Kleef** (⊠ *1621 Telegraph Ave.*), the friendly jumble that started it all Uptown; **Bar Three Fifty-Five** (⊠ *355 19th St.*), a house of great cocktails; strikingly beautiful but low-key **Dogwood** (⊠ *1644 Telegraph Ave.*), which has tasty nibbles; and **Somar** (⊠ *1727 Telegraph Ave.*), a bar, music lounge, and gallery in one. Uptown's shopping element hasn't yet gelled, making this more of an evening destination. The Paramount Theatre, the Fox Theater, and other late-art deco architectural gems distinguish this neighborhood. ⊠ *Telegraph Ave. and Broadway from 16th to 26th Sts.*

WORTH NOTING

Chinatown. Across Broadway from Old Oakland but worlds apart, Chinatown is a densely packed, bustling neighborhood. Unlike its San Francisco counterpart, Oakland's Chinatown makes no concessions to tourists; you won't find baskets of trinkets lining the sidewalk and souvenir displays in the shop windows. But supermarkets such as **Yuen Hop Noodle Company** and **Asian Food Products** (⊠ *824 Webster St.*), open since 1931, overflow with goodies. And the line for sweets, breads, and towering cakes snakes out the door of **Napoleon Super Bakery** (⊠ *810 Franklin St.*). ⊠ *Between Broadway and Lakeside Dr. and between 6th and 12th Sts.*

Fox Theater. An art deco movie palace built in 1928, the Fox sat decaying and mostly unused for decades until the last of several redevelopment schemes culminated in a stunning renovation. The Mediterranean Moorish–style theater and its attached buildings contain the main theater, these days used for music concerts; the Oakland School for the Arts; and the Den, a gorgeous lounge. The theater's restoration helped revive what's now known as the Uptown neighborhood. ⊠ *1807 Telegraph Ave., at 18th St., Uptown* ☎ *510/302–2250* ⊕ *www.thefoxoakland.com.*

Jack London Square. A few shops, some minor historic sites, and a growing number of noteworthy restaurants (along with the well-estabished Yoshi's Jazz Club) line Jack London Square, which is named after the author of *The Call of the Wild, The Sea Wolf,* and other books. London, who was born in San Francisco, also lived in Oakland, where he spent many a day boozing and brawling in the waterfront area, most notably at the tiny, wonderful **Heinold's First and Last Chance Saloon** (⊠ *48 Webster St., at Embarcadero W.*). The saloon has been serving since 1883, although it's a little worse for the wear since the 1906 earthquake. Next door is the Klondike cabin in which London spent a summer in the late 1890s. The cabin was moved from Alaska and reassembled here in 1970.

During the week, the square can feel desolate, albeit with great views. Weekends are much livelier, with diners filling the many outdoor patios, and shoppers perusing Sunday's farmers' market, which takes place from 9 am to 2 pm. ■ TIP➜ **The square is an obvious spot for tourists to visit, and it's worth a peek if you've arrived on the ferry that docks here; but to get a real feel for Oakland, you'll do better to check out downtown, Temescal, or at least Rockridge.** ⊠ *Embarcadero W. at Broadway* ☎ *510/645–9292* ⊕ *www.jacklondonsquare.com.*

A fun place to wet your whistle, Heinold's First and Last Chance Saloon

Lake Merritt. Joggers and power walkers charge along the 3-mile path that encircles this 155-acre natural saltwater lake in downtown Oakland. Crew teams often glide across the water, and boatmen guide snuggling couples in authentic Venetian gondolas (✉ *Fares start at $40 per couple for 30 minutes* ☎ *510/663–6603* ⊕ *gondolaservizio.com*). **Lakeside Park,** which surrounds the north side of Lake Merritt, has several outdoor attractions, including a small children's park and a waterfowl refuge. The lake is less an attraction than a pleasant backdrop to Oaklanders' everyday life. ✉ *Lakeside Park, Bellevue and Grand Aves.* ⊕ *www.lakemerritt.org.*

Old Oakland. In the shadow of the convention center and towering downtown hotels, Old Oakland was once a booming business district. Today the restored Victorian storefronts lining four historic blocks house restaurants, cafés, shops, galleries, and a lively three-block farmers' market, which takes place on Friday morning. Architectural consistency distinguishes the area from surrounding streets and lends it a distinct neighborhood feel. The Italian grocery **Ratto's International Market** (✉ *827 Washington St.*) has been in business for more than a century. Stop in for a deli sandwich, or head over to the genial **Pacific Coast Brewing Company** (✉ *902 Washington St.*) for a microbrew on the patio. One of the best beer bars in California, the **Trappist** (✉ *460 8th St.*) wins loyalty for its exhaustive selection of Belgian ales. Various pop-up boutiques throughout the neighborhood are reinvigorating the storefront scene. ✉ *Bordered by 7th, 10th, Clay, and Washington Sts.* ⊕ *old-oakland.com.*

WHERE TO EAT

$$
MEDITERRANEAN

✕ **À Côté.** This place for Mediterranean food is all about small plates, cozy tables, family-style eating—and truly excellent food. The butternut-squash ravioli, wild-boar chestnut sausage, and duck confit flatbread with apples and cantelet cheese are all fine choices, and you won't find a better plate of *pommes frites* (french fries) anywhere. The restaurant pours more than 40 wines by the glass. Among the tempting desserts here are the lemon pudding cake with lemon cream, huckleberries, and candied pistachios, and the tangy pomegranate sorbet. Heavy wooden tables, cool tiles, and natural light make this a destination for students, families, couples, and the after-work crowd; the heated back patio is warm and welcoming in any weather. $ *Average main: $20* ✉ *5478 College Ave., at Taft Ave., Rockridge* ☎ *510/655–6469* ⊕ *www. acoterestaurant.com* ⊘ *No lunch.*

$
AMERICAN
Fodor's Choice
★

✕ **Brown Sugar Kitchen.** Chef and owner Tanya Holland, named chef of 2012 by the California Travel Association, has turned an isolated corner in West Oakland into a breakfast and lunch destination. Influenced by her African American heritage and her culinary education in France—and using local, organic, and seasonal products—she blends sweet and savory flavors like no one else and pairs her dishes with well-chosen wines. The dining room is fresh and bright, with a long, sleek counter, red-leather stools, and spacious booths and tables. ■ TIP➜ This is the place to come for chicken and waffles. $ *Average main: $13* ✉ *2534 Mandela Pkwy., at 26th St., West Oakland* ☎ *510/839–7685* ⊕ *www. brownsugarkitchen.com* ⊘ *Closed Mon. No dinner.*

$$$
AMERICAN

✕ **Camino.** Chef-owner Russell Moore cooked at Chez Panisse for two decades before opening this restaurant with co-owner Allison Hopelain that focuses on simple, seasonal, straightforward dishes cooked in an enormous, crackling *camino* (Italian for "fireplace"). Everything is made with top-notch ingredients, including local sardines and smelts, grilled lamb and sausage, and Dungeness crab (cooked in the fireplace with rutabagas). The menu changes nightly and includes vegetarian options such as eggplant gratin. Camino is decorated in a Craftsman-meets-refectory style, with brick walls and two long redwood communal tables. ■ TIP➜ The small bar here turns out delicious, seasonally inspired cocktails, among them a gin-based one with house-made cherry and hibiscus bitters. $ *Average main: $26* ✉ *3917 Grand Ave., at Boulevard Way, Grand Lake* ☎ *510/547–5035* ⊕ *www.caminorestaurant. com* ⊘ *Closed Tues. No lunch (weekend brunch 10–2).*

$$
MODERN
AMERICAN

✕ **Chop Bar.** The walls and tables are made of reclaimed wood at this small, stylish space whose knowing, tattooed bartenders serve potent cocktails to a crowd of hipsters and area residents and workers. A great neighborhood joint for every meal of the day (and brunch on weekends), Chop Bar serves upmarket gastro-pub grub, including favorites such as oxtail poutine, pork confit with polenta and kale, and burgers that rank among the Bay Area's best. On sunny days when the glass garage door is raised, extending the outdoor seating area out front, you'll feel like an insider who's stumbled upon an industrial neighborhood's cool secret. $ *Average main: $18* ✉ *247 4th St., at Alice St., Jack London Square* ☎ *510/834–2467* ⊕ *www.oaklandchopbar.com.*

$$$$ MODERN AMERICAN

🍴 **Commis.** Blink and you'll miss the only East Bay restaurant with a Michelin star. No sign announces Commis, a slender, unassuming storefront in Oakland's Piedmont neighborhood, and the room is simple and polished: nothing distracts from the artistry of the food served here. Chef James Syhabout creates a fixed, multicourse menu ($95, wine pairing $55 additional) based on the season and his distinctive vision. Dishes might include poached egg yolk with smoked dates and alliums (members of the onion/garlic family) in malt vinegar, or duck roasted on the bone over charcoal with renderings, walnut, and persimmon. Diners don't see the menu until after the meal, the chef's way of ensuring that everyone comes to the table with an open mind. This isn't a place to grab a quick bite: meals last about three hours. The service is excellent. [$] *Average main: $95* ✉ *3859 Piedmont Ave., at Rio Vista Ave., Piedmont* ☎ *510/653–3902* 🌐 *www.commisrestaurant.com* ✍ *Reservations essential* 🕓 *Closed Mon.–Tues. No lunch.*

$$ MEXICAN

🍴 **Doña Tomás.** A neighborhood favorite, this spot in Oakland's hot Temescal District serves seasonal Mexican fare to a hip but low-key crowd. Mexican textiles and art adorn walls in two long rooms; there's also a vine-covered patio. Banish all images of taqueria grub and tuck into starters such as quesadillas filled with butternut squash and goat cheese and entrées such as *albondigas en sopa zanahoria* (pork-and-beef meatballs in carrot purée). Some mighty fine tequilas complement the offerings. Brunch is served on weekends. [$] *Average main: $19* ✉ *5004 Telegraph Ave., near 51st St., Temescal* ☎ *510/450–0522* 🌐 *www.donatomas.com* 🕓 *Closed Mon. No lunch weekdays. No dinner Sun.*

$$$ MODERN AMERICAN

🍴 **Haven.** Daniel Patterson of San Francisco's revered Coi opened this waterfront space in 2011, focusing on vegetables, whole-animal preparations, dishes to share, and great cocktails. Floor-to-ceiling windows overlook the yachts of Jack London Square, and warm lighting casts a glow over the wood-and-brick dining room. Look for anything smoked or with marrow on executive chef Kim Alter's menu and you can't miss; smoked black rice with citrus and uni is striking and flavorful, and the shepherd's pie—pig belly, rutabaga, and potato purée—is earthy and delicious. The family menu ($35 per person), three courses served family-style and based on what's fresh at the market, is a fun way to experience this restaurant's inventive approach. Sunday brunch is served from 10:30 am to 1:30 pm. [$] *Average main: $26* ✉ *44 Webster St., at 1st St. and Embarcadero W, Jack London Square* ☎ *510/663–4440* 🌐 *www.havenoakland.com* 🕓 *No lunch Mon.–Sat.*

$ VIETNAMESE

🍴 **Le Cheval Restaurant.** This cavernous restaurant, a lunchtime favorite, is a good place to sample *pho,* Hanoi-style beef noodle soup fragrant with star anise. Other entrées include lemon chicken, cubed beefsteak, and clay-pot snapper. It's hard to spend more than $20 for an entire meal unless you order the seven courses of beef ($28). The complimentary minibowls of soup that are placed on the table as soon as you sit down are a great balm to hungry diners, though the service is lightning-quick anyway. [$] *Average main: $12* ✉ *1019 Clay St., at 11th St., Old Oakland* ☎ *510/763–8495* 🌐 *www.lecheval.com* 🕓 *No lunch Sun.*

9

$$ BELGIAN 🍴 **Luka's Taproom & Lounge.** Hip and urban, with an unpretentious vibe, Luka's is a real taste of Uptown. Diners nibble on *frites* (fries) any Belgian would embrace and entrées such as crispy-skin salmon or gratinéed mac and cheese. The brews draw them in, too—a nice selection of Trappist ales complements plentiful beers on tap and international bottles—and the DJs in the adjacent lounge keep the scene going late. **■ TIP→ Hungry night owls appreciate the late-night menu, served daily until midnight.** [$] *Average main: $17* ✉ *2221 Broadway, at West Grand Ave., Uptown* ☎ *510/451–4677* 🌐 *www.lukasoakland.com* ⏲ *No lunch Sat.*

$$ PIZZA 🍴 **Pizzaiolo.** Apparently no length of a wait can discourage locals who persevere to enjoy the legendary thin-crust, wood-fired pizza served up by Chez Panisse alum Charlie Hallowell in this rustic-chic dining room. Diners—mostly neighborhood hipsters but also young families and foodies of all ages—perch in wooden chairs with red-leather backs; weathered wood floors and brick walls peeking through the plaster create an always-been-here feel. Seasonal pizza options might include wild nettles and pecorino, or rapini and house-made sausage; don't overlook non-pizza dishes such as wild steelhead salmon with fava greens, English peas, and Meyer-lemon butter. Except on Sunday, early risers get to skip the crowds and enjoy Blue Bottle Coffee and pastries from 8 until noon. [$] *Average main: $17* ✉ *5008 Telegraph Ave., at 51st St., Temescal* ☎ *510/652–4888* 🌐 *www.pizzaiolooakland.com* ⏲ *Closed Sun. No lunch.*

WHERE TO STAY

$$ HOTEL 🏨 **Best Western Plus Bayside Hotel.** Sandwiched between the serene and scenic Oakland Estuary on one side and train tracks and an eight-lane freeway on the other, this all-suites property has handsome accommodations with balconies or patios, many overlooking the water. **Pros:** attractive, budget-conscious choice; free parking; recently renovated; water views make city bustle seem far away. **Cons:** not near anything of interest; city-side rooms can be loud. [$] *Rooms from: $179* ✉ *1717 Embarcadero, off I–880, at 16th St. exit* ☎ *510/356–2450* 🌐 *www.baysidehoteloakland.com* 🛏 *81 suites* 🍴 *Breakfast.*

$$ HOTEL 🏨 **Waterfront Hotel.** The only bayfront hotel in town, this thoroughly modern, pleasantly appointed Joie de Vivre property sits among the appealing restaurants (including the hotel's own) of Jack London Square. **Pros:** great location; lovely views; dog-friendly. **Cons:** passing trains can be noisy; parking is pricey; hotel is beginning to show its age. [$] *Rooms from: $159* ✉ *10 Washington St., Jack London Square* ☎ *510/836–3800, 800/729–3638* 🌐 *www.waterfrontplaza.com* 🛏 *143 rooms* 🍴 *No meals.*

NIGHTLIFE AND THE ARTS

Artists have found cheap rent and loft spaces in Oakland, giving rise to an underground cultural scene—visual arts, indie music, spoken word, film—that's definitely buzzing, especially in Uptown (which is pretty much downtown). Trendy bars and clubs seem to pop up by the week—everything from artisan breweries to all-out retro dives. The nightlife scene here is less crowded and more intimate than what you'll find in San Francisco. Music is just about everywhere, though the most popular venues are downtown.

NIGHTLIFE

Fodor'sChoice **Café Van Kleef.** Dutch artist Peter Van Kleef's candle-strewn, funky café-
★ bar crackles with creative energy. Van Kleef has a lot to do with the
convivial atmosphere; the garrulous owner loves sharing tales about
his quirky, floor-to-ceiling collection of mementos, including what he
claims are Cassius Clay's boxing gloves and Dorothy's ruby slippers
from *The Wizard of Oz*. The café also has a consistently solid calendar
of live music, heavy on the jazz side. The drinks are among the stiffest
in town. ✉ *1621 Telegraph Ave., between 16th and 17th Sts., Uptown*
☎ *510/763–7711* ⊕ *www.cafevankleef.com* ☺ *No lunch Sat.–Mon.*

Fox Theater. Willie Nelson, Counting Crows, Rebelution, and B.B. King
have all played at this renovated art deco stunner that has good sight
lines, a state-of-the-art sound system and acoustics, and bars and other
amenities. ✉ *1807 Telegraph Ave., at 18th St., Uptown* ☎ *510/548–
3010* ⊕ *www.thefoxoakland.com.*

The Layover Music Bar and Lounge. Bright, bold, and very hip, this hangout
filled with recycled furniture is constantly evolving because everything is
for sale, from the artwork to the pillows, rugs, and lamps. The busy bar
serves up organic cocktails, and depending on the night, the entertainment might include comedy or live or DJ music. ✉ *1517 Franklin St.,
near 15th St., Uptown* ☎ *510/834–1517* ⊕ *www.oaklandlayover.com.*

Mua. Cuisine, cocktails, and culture—Mua puts it all together in a bright
and airy former garage. The chefs serve up beautifully crafted meals like
softshell crab and duck confit; the bartenders shake up elegant cocktails;
and the rich cultural offerings include poetry readings, art shows, DJ
music, and more. ✉ *2442a Webster St., between 16th and 17th Sts.,
Uptown* ☎ *510/238–1100* ⊕ *www.muaoakland.com.*

The Trappist. Grand pillars, brick walls, soft lighting, and the buzz of
conversation set a warm and mellow tone inside this Victorian space
that's been renovated to resemble a traditional Belgian pub. The setting is definitely a draw, but the real stars are the artisan beers: more
than a hundred Belgian, Dutch, and North American ones. The light
fare includes panini made with organic ingredients. ✉ *460 8th St., at
Broadway, Old Oakland* ☎ *510/238–8900* ⊕ *www.thetrappist.com.*

THE ARTS

Paramount Theatre. The art deco movie palace is home to the Oakland
East Bay Symphony and also presents ballet, comedy (Cedric, Sinbad,
Bill Cosby), well-known rock and other musical acts, and monthly
classic films. ✉ *2025 Broadway, at 20th St., Uptown* ☎ *510/465–6400*
⊕ *www.paramounttheatre.com.*

Fodor'sChoice **Yoshi's.** Omar Sosa and Charlie Hunter are among the musicians who
★ play at Yoshi's, one of the area's best jazz venues. Shows start at 8 pm
and 10 pm except on Sunday, when they're usually at 6 and 8. The
cover runs from $16 to $50. ✉ *510 Embarcadero St., between Washington and Clay Sts., Jack London Square* ☎ *510/238–9200* ⊕ *www.
yoshis.com.*

9

SPORTS AND THE OUTDOORS
BASEBALL
Oakland A's. Billy Beane of *Moneyball* fame is the general manager of the American League baseball team. Same-day tickets can usually be purchased at the **O.co Coliseum** box office (Gate D). To get to the game, take a BART train to the Coliseum/Oakland Airport Station. ✉ *O.co Coliseum, 7000 Coliseum Way, off I–880, north of Hegenberger Rd.* ☎ *510/638–4900* ⊕ *oakland.athletics.mlb.com.*

BASKETBALL
Golden State Warriors. The NBA team plays basketball at **Oracle Arena** from late October into April. BART trains serve the arena; get off at the Coliseum/Oakland Airport Station. Purchase single tickets through Ticketmaster (☎ *800/653–8000* ⊕ *www.ticketmaster.com*). ✉ *Oracle Arena, 7000 Coliseum Way, off I–880, north of Hegenberger Rd.* ☎ *888/479–4667 tickets* ⊕ *www.nba.com/warriors.*

FOOTBALL
Oakland Raiders. The National Football League's brawling Oakland Raiders play at **O.co Coliseum.** Tickets are available through Ticketmaster. ✉ *O.co Coliseum, 7000 Coliseum Way, off I–880, north of Hegenberger Rd.* ☎ *510/864–5000* ⊕ *www.raiders.com*

SHOPPING
College Avenue and Piedmont Avenue are great for upscale strolling, shopping, and people-watching. Temescal—especially Temescal Alley—is another shopping hot spot, with bespoke clothing and artisan jewelry in tiny storefronts. The more casual streets around Lake Merritt and Grand Lake have smaller, less fancy boutiques.

Diesel. Wandering bibliophiles collect armfuls of the latest fiction and nonfiction here. The loftlike space, with its high ceilings and spare design, encourages contemplation, and on chilly days a fire burns in the hearth. Past participants in the excellent authors' events have included Ian Rankin, Annie Leibovitz, Kareem Abdul-Jabbar, and Michael Moore. ✉ *5433 College Ave., at Kales Ave., Rockridge* ☎ *510/653–9965* ⊕ *www.dieselbookstore.com.*

Maison d'Etre. Close to the Rockridge BART station, this store epitomizes the Rockridge neighborhood's funky-chic shopping scene. Look for impulse buys like whimsical watches, imported fruit-tea blends, and funky slippers. ✉ *5640 College Ave., at Keith Ave., Rockridge* ☎ *510/658–2801* ⊕ *maisondetre.com.*

MARIN COUNTY

Marin is quite simply a knockout—some go so far as to call it spectacular and wild. This isn't an extravagant claim, since more than 40% of the county (180,000 acres), including the majority of the coastline, is parkland. The territory ranges from chaparral, grassland, and coastal scrub to broadleaf and evergreen forest, redwood, salt marsh, and rocky shoreline. It's well worth the drive over the Golden Gate Bridge to explore the Headlands and the stunning beauty of sprawling Point Reyes National Seashore, with more than 80 miles of shoreline.

Regardless of its natural beauty, what gave the county its reputation was Cyra McFadden's 1977 book *The Serial*, a literary soap opera that depicted the county as a bastion of hot-tubbing and "open" marriages. Indeed old-time bohemian, but also increasingly jet-set, Marinites still spend a lot of time outdoors, and surfing, cycling, and hiking are common after-work and weekend activities. Adrenaline junkies mountain bike down Mt. Tamalpais, and those who want solitude take a walk on one of Point Reyes's many empty beaches. The hot tub remains a popular destination, but things have changed since the boho days. Artists and musicians who arrived in the 1960s have set the tone for mellow country towns, but Marin is now undeniably chic, with BMWs supplanting VW buses as the cars of choice.

After exploring Marin's natural beauty, consider a stop in one of its lovely villages. Most cosmopolitan is Sausalito, the town just over the Golden Gate Bridge from San Francisco. Across the inlet from Sausalito, Tiburon and Belvedere are lined with grand homes that regularly appear on fund-raising circuits, and to the north, landlocked Mill Valley is a hub of wining and dining and tony boutiques.

In general, the farther west of U.S. 101 you go the more country things become, and West Marin is about as far as you can get from the big city, both physically and ideologically. Separated from the inland county by the slopes and ridges of giant Mt. Tamalpais, this territory beckons to mavericks, artists, ocean lovers, and other free spirits. Stinson Beach has tempered its isolationist attitude to accommodate out-of-towners, as have Inverness and Point Reyes Station. Bolinas, on the other hand, would prefer you not know its location.

VISITOR INFORMATION
Contact Marin Convention & Visitors Bureau ✉ *1 Mitchell Blvd., Suite B, San Rafael* ☎ *415/925–2060* ⊕ *www.visitmarin.org.*

THE MARIN HEADLANDS

Due west of the Golden Gate Bridge's northern end.

The term *Golden Gate* may now be synonymous with the world-famous bridge, but it originally referred to the grassy, poppy-strewn hills flanking the passageway into San Francisco Bay. To the north of the gate lie the Marin Headlands, part of the Golden Gate National Recreation Area (GGNRA) and among the most dramatic scenery in these parts. Windswept hills plunge down to the ocean, and creek-fed thickets shelter swaying wildflowers.

GETTING HERE AND AROUND
Driving from San Francisco, head north on U.S. 101. Just after you cross the Golden Gate Bridge, take the Alexander Avenue exit. From there take the first left (signs read "San Francisco/U.S. 101 South"), go through the tunnel under the freeway, and turn right up the hill where the sign reads "Forts Barry and Cronkhite." Muni bus 76X runs hourly from Sutter and Sansome streets to the Marin Headlands Visitor Center on weekends and major holidays only. Once here, you can explore this beautiful countryside on foot.

EXPLORING

TOP ATTRACTIONS

FAMILY

Fodor's Choice

★

Marin Headlands. The headlands stretch from the Golden Gate Bridge to Muir Beach. Photographers perch on the southern headlands for shots of the city, with the bridge in the foreground and the skyline on the horizon. Equally remarkable are the views north along the coast and out to sea, where the Farallon Islands are visible on clear days. ■TIP→ **Nearly all the roads, all of them windy and winding, offer great coastal views.**

The headlands' strategic position at the mouth of San Francisco Bay made them a logical site for World War II military installations. Today you can explore the crumbling concrete batteries where naval guns protected the approaches from the sea. The headlands' main attractions are centered on Forts Barry and Cronkhite, which lie just across Rodeo Lagoon from each other. Fronting the lagoon is Rodeo Beach, a dark stretch of sand that attracts sand-castle builders and dog owners. The beaches at the Marin Headlands are not safe for swimming. The giant cliffs are steep and unstable, so hiking down them can be dangerous. Stay on trails.

The visitor center is a worthwhile stop for its exhibits on the area's history and ecology, and kids enjoy the "please touch" educational sites and small play area inside. You can pick up guides to historic sites and wildlife at the center, as well as the park's newspaper, which has a schedule of guided walks. ⊠ *Visitor Center, Fort Barry Chapel, Fort Barry, Bldg. 948, Field and Bunker Rds., Sausalito* 🕾 *415/331–1540* ⊕ *www.nps.gov/goga/marin-headlands.htm* ☯ *Park: sunrise–sunset. Visitor center: daily 9:30–4.*

FAMILY

Point Bonita Lighthouse. At the end of Conzelman Road, in the southern headlands, is the Point Bonita Lighthouse, a restored beauty that still guides ships to safety with its original 1855 refractory lens. Half the fun of a visit is the steep ½-mile walk from the parking area down to the lighthouse, which takes you through a rock tunnel and across a suspension bridge. Signposts along the way detail the bravado of surfmen, as the early lifeguards were called, and the tenacity of the "wickies," the first keepers of the light. ⊠ *End of Conzelman Rd.* ⊕ *www.nps.gov/ goga/pobo.htm* 🕮 *Free* ☯ *Sat.–Mon. 12:30–3:30.*

WORTH NOTING

Hawk Hill. Craggy Hawk Hill is the best place on the West Coast to watch the migration of eagles, hawks, and falcons as they fly south for winter. The main migration period is from September through November. As many as 1,000 birds have been sighted in a single day. The viewing area is about 2 miles up Conzelman Road from U.S. 101; look for a Hawk Hill sign and parking, right before the road becomes one way. In September and October, on rain- and fog-free weekends at noon, enthusiastic docents from the Golden Gate Raptor Observatory give free lectures on Hawk Hill, and a raptor-banding demonstration follows at 1 pm. ⊠ *Sausalito* ⊕ *www.ggro.org.*

Headlands Center for the Arts. The center's main building, formerly the army barracks, exhibits contemporary art in a rustic natural setting; the downstairs "archive room" contains objects found and created by residents, such as natural rocks, interesting glass bottles filled with

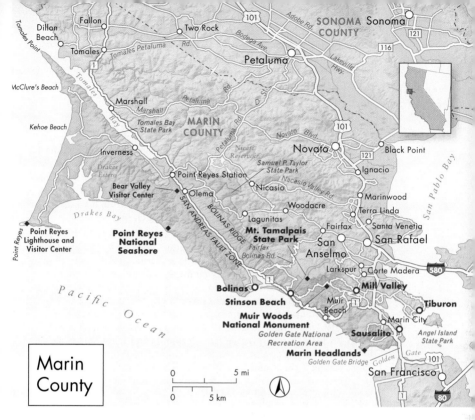

Marin
County

0   5 mi

0   5 km

collected items, and unusual masks. Stop by the industrial gallery space, two flights up, to see what the resident visual artists are up to—most of the work is quite contemporary. ✉ *Fort Barry, 944 Simmonds Rd., Sausalito* ☎ *415/331–2787* ⊕ *www.headlands.org* ☉ *Sun.–Thurs. noon–5.*

FAMILY **Marine Mammal Center.** If you're curious about the rehabilitation of sea mammals from the Pacific—and the human practices that endanger them—stop by this amazing facility for rescued seals, sea lions, dolphins, and otters. An observation area overlooks the pools where the animals convalesce, and nearby plaques describe what you're seeing. ■**TIP→** **You'll learn even more—and get closer to the animals—on a worthwhile, docent-led tour.** ✉ *Fort Cronkhite, 2000 Bunker Rd., off U.S. 101's Alexander Ave. exit, Sausalito* ☎ *415/289–7325* ⊕ *www. marinemammalcenter.org* 🎟 *Center free, tour $9* ☉ *Daily 10–5.*

Nike Missile Site SF-88-L. For a look at a relatively recent episode in the area's military history, head to the now defunct Nike missile site, above Fort Barry, which is the only accessible site of its kind in the United States. It gives you a firsthand view of menacing Hercules missiles and missile-tracking radar. Free, guided tours take place at 12:45, 1:45, and 2:30 pm. ■**TIP→** **On the first Saturday of the month the site holds an open house at which some of the docents leading walking tours are Nike veterans who describe their experiences.** The site is closed to the public during inclement weather, so call ahead to confirm open hours. ✉ *Field Rd., off Bunker Hill Rd.* ☎ *415/331–1453* ⊕ *www.nps.gov/ goga/nike-missile-site.htm* 🎟 *Free* 🕙 *Thurs.–Sat. 12:30–3:30.*

SAUSALITO

2 miles north of Golden Gate Bridge.

Bougainvillea-covered hillsides and an expansive yacht harbor give Sausalito the feel of an Adriatic resort. The town sits on the northwestern edge of San Francisco Bay, where it's sheltered from the ocean by the Marin Headlands; the mostly mild weather here is perfect for strolling and outdoor dining. Nevertheless, morning fog and afternoon winds can roll over the hills without warning, funneling through the central part of Sausalito once known as Hurricane Gulch.

South on Bridgeway (toward San Francisco), which snakes between the bay and the hills, a waterside esplanade is lined with restaurants on piers that lure diners with good seafood and even better views. Stairs along the west side of Bridgeway climb the hill to wooded neighborhoods filled with both rustic and opulent homes. As you amble along Bridgeway past shops and galleries, you'll notice the absence of basic services. If you need an aspirin or some groceries (or if you want to see the locals), you'll have to head to Caledonia Street, which runs parallel to Bridgeway, north of the ferry terminus and inland a couple of blocks. The streets closest to the ferry landing flaunt their fair share of shops selling T-shirts and kitschy souvenirs. Venture into some of the side streets or narrow alleyways to catch a bit more of the town's taste for eccentric jewelry and handmade crafts.

■ TIP→ **The ferry is the best way to get to Sausalito from San Francisco; you get more romance (and less traffic) and disembark in the heart of downtown.**

Sausalito developed its bohemian flair in the 1950s and '60s, when creative types, led by a charismatic Greek portraitist named Varda, established an artists' colony and a houseboat community here. Today more than 450 houseboats are docked in Sausalito, which has since also become a major yachting center. Some of these floating homes are ragged, others deluxe, but all are quirky (one, a miniature replica of a Persian castle, even has an elevator inside). For a close-up view of the community, head north on Bridgeway—Sausalito's main thoroughfare—from downtown, turn right on Gate Six Road, park where it dead-ends at the public shore, and enter through the unlocked gates. Keep a respectful distance; these are homes, after all, and the residents become a bit prickly from too much ogling.

GETTING HERE AND AROUND

From San Francisco by car or bike, follow U.S. 101 north across the Golden Gate Bridge and take the first exit, Alexander Avenue, just past Vista Point; continue down the winding hill to the water to where the road becomes Bridgeway. Golden Gate Transit buses 10 and 2 will drop you off in downtown Sausalito, and the ferries dock downtown as well.

The crowded piers and rolling hillside of the Sausalito waterfront

The center of town is flat, with plenty of sidewalks and bay views. It's a pleasure and a must to explore on foot.

ESSENTIALS

Visitor Information Sausalito Chamber of Commerce ✉ *780 Bridgeway* ☎ *415/332–0505* ⊕ *www.sausalito.org.*

EXPLORING

FAMILY **Bay Area Discovery Museum.** Sitting at the base of the Golden Gate Bridge, this indoor-outdoor museum offers entertaining and enlightening hands-on exhibits for children under eight. Kids can fish from a boat at the indoor wharf, imagine themselves as marine biologists in the Wave Workshop, and play outdoors at Lookout Cove (made up of scaled-down sea caves, tidal pools, and even a re-created shipwreck). At Tot Spot, toddlers and preschoolers dress up in animal costumes and crawl through miniature tunnels. ■**TIP→ From San Francisco, take U.S. 101's Alexander Avenue exit and follow signs to East Fort Baker.** ✉ *557 McReynolds Rd., at East Rd. off Alexander Ave.* ☎ *415/339–3900* ⊕ *www.baykidsmuseum. org* ✍ *$11, free 1st Wed. of the month* ⊗ *Tues.–Sun. 9–5.*

FAMILY **Bay Model.** An anonymous-looking World War II shipyard building holds a great treasure: the sprawling (more than 1½ acres) Bay Model of the entire San Francisco Bay and the San Joaquin–Sacramento River delta, complete with flowing water. The U.S. Army Corps of Engineers uses the model to reproduce the rise and fall of tides, the flow of currents, and the other physical forces at work on the bay. ✉ *2100 Bridgeway, at Marinship Way* ☎ *415/332–3870 recorded information, 415/332–3871 operator assistance* ⊕ *www.spn.usace.army.mil* ✍ *Free* ⊗ *Late May–early Sept., Tues.–Fri. 9–4, weekends 10–5; early Sept.–late May, Tues.–Sat. 9–4.*

Drinking Fountain. On the waterfront between the Hotel Sausalito and the Sausalito Yacht Club is an unusual historic landmark—a drinking fountain. It's inscribed with "Have a drink on Sally" in remembrance of Sally Stanford, the former San Francisco madam who became the town's mayor in the 1970s. Sassy Sally, as they called her, would have appreciated the fountain's eccentric custom attachment: a knee-level basin that reads "Have a drink on Leland," in memory of her beloved dog.

QUICK BITES

🍴 Hamburgers. Patrons queue up daily for a sandwich made from the juicy, hand-formed beef patties sizzling on the grill here. Brave the line (it moves fast), get your food to go, and head to the esplanade to enjoy the sweeping views. [$] ***Average main: $25* ✉ *737 Bridgeway, at Humboldt Ave.* ☎ *415/332–9471* 🕒 *Daily 11–5.***

Plaza Viña del Mar. The landmark Plaza Viña del Mar, named for Sausalito's sister city in Chile, marks the center of town. Flanked by two 14-foot-tall elephant statues (created in 1915 for the Panama-Pacific International Exposition), the fountain is a great setting for snapshots and people-watching. ✉ *Bridgeway and Park St.*

Sausalito Visitors Center and Historical Exhibit. The local historical society operates the center, where you can get your bearings, learn some history, and find out what's happening in town. ✉ *780 Bridgeway, at Bay St.* ☎ *415/332–0505* 🌐 *www.sausalitohistoricalsociety.com* 🕒 *Closed Mon.*

WHERE TO EAT

$$ SEAFOOD FAMILY Fodor's Choice ★

🍴 **Fish.** When locals want fresh seafood, they head to this gleaming dockside fish house a mile north of downtown. Order at the counter and then grab a seat by the floor-to-ceiling windows or at a picnic table on the pier, overlooking the yachts and fishing boats. Most of the sustainably caught fish is hauled in from the owner's boats, docked right outside. Try the ceviche, crab Louis, cioppino, barbecue oysters, or anything fresh that's being grilled over the oak-wood fire. Outside, kids can doodle with sidewalk chalk on the pier. [$] *Average main: $20* ✉ *350 Harbor Dr., off Bridgeway* ☎ *415/331–3474* 🌐 *www.331fish.com* ✍ *Reservations not accepted* 💳 *No credit cards.*

$$$ FRENCH

🍴 **Le Garage.** Brittany-born Olivier Souvestre serves traditional French bistro fare in a relaxed, sidewalk café–style bayside setting. The menu is small, but the dishes are substantial in flavor and presentation. Standouts include frisée salad with poached egg, bacon, croutons, and pancetta vinaigrette; steak frites with a shallot confit and crispy fries; and a chef's selection of cheese or charcuterie with soup and mixed greens. The restaurant only seats 35 inside and 15 outside, so to avoid a long wait for lunch, arrive before 11:30 or after 1:30. [$] *Average main: $23* ✉ *85 Liberty Ship Way, off Marinship Way* ☎ *415/332–5625* 🌐 *www.legaragebistrosausalito.com* ✍ *Reservations essential* 🕒 *No dinner Sun.*

$$ ITALIAN

🍴 **Poggio.** One of the few restaurants in Sausalito to attract both food-savvy locals and tourists, Poggio serves modern Tuscan cuisine in a handsome, open-wall space that spills onto the street. Expect dishes such as grilled chicken with roasted beets and sunchokes, braised artichokes with polenta, featherlight gnocchi, and pizzas from the open kitchen's wood-fired oven. [$] *Average main: $22* ✉ *777 Bridgeway, at Bay St.* ☎ *415/332–7771* 🌐 *www.poggiotrattoria.com* ✍ *Reservations essential.*

$$ JAPANESE Fodor's Choice ★ 🍴 **Sushi Ran.** Sushi aficionados swear that this is the Bay Area's best option for raw fish, but don't overlook the excellent Pacific Rim fusions, a melding of Japanese ingredients and French cooking techniques, served up in unusual presentations. Because Sushi Ran is so highly ranked among area foodies, book two to seven days in advance for dinner. Otherwise, expect a long wait, which you can soften by sipping one of the 45 by-the-glass sakes from the outstanding wine-and-sake bar. **■ TIP→ If you arrive without a reservation and can't get a table, you can sometimes dine in the noisy bar.** [$] *Average main: $18* ✉ *107 Caledonia St., at Pine St.* ☎ *415/332–3620* 🌐 *www.sushiran.com* ✍ *Reservations essential* ⏲ *No lunch weekends.*

$ WINE BAR 🍴 **Wellingtons Wine Bar.** British memorabilia decorates the walls of this establishment that celebrates English and Californian liquid culture. The space is bright, warm, and welcoming, and when the weather is nice, you can sit on the boat dock and drink your pint of lager or sip a glass of wine while scooping up hummus with garlic pita chips. The menu is as big as a book. **■ TIP→ Wellingtons opens at 3 pm on Fridays and weekends, and at 4 the rest of the week.** [$] *Average main: $12* ✉ *300 Turney St., at Bridgeway* ☎ *415/331–9463* 🌐 *www.wellingtonswinebar.com* ✍ *Reservations not accepted* ⏲ *No lunch.*

WHERE TO STAY

$$$$ HOTEL 🏨 **Cavallo Point.** Set in the Golden Gate National Recreation Area, this luxury hotel and resort's location is truly one of a kind, featuring turn-of-the-20th-century buildings converted into well-appointed yet eco-friendly rooms. **Pros:** stunning views and numerous activities: a cooking school, yoga classes, and nature walks; spa with a tea bar; art gallery. **Cons:** landscaping feels incomplete; isolated from urban amenities. [$] *Rooms from: $375* ✉ *601 Murray Circle, Fort Baker* ☎ *415/339–4700* 🌐 *www.cavallopoint.com* 🛏 *68 historic and 74 contemporary guest rooms* 🍽 *No meals.*

$$ B&B/INN 🏨 **Hotel Sausalito.** Handmade furniture and tasteful original art and reproductions give this well-run inn the feel of a small European hotel. **Pros:** great staff; excellent central location; feels like home away from home. **Cons:** no room service; some rooms feel cramped. [$] *Rooms from: $180* ✉ *16 El Portal* ☎ *415/332–0700, 888/442–0700* 🌐 *www.hotelsausalito.com* 🛏 *14 rooms, 2 suites* 🍽 *No meals.*

$$$$ B&B/INN 🏨 **The Inn Above Tide.** This is the only hotel in the Bay Area with balconies literally hanging over the water, and each of its rooms has a perfect-10 view that takes in wild Angel Island as well as the city lights across the bay. **Pros:** great complimentary breakfast; minutes from restaurants/attractions; in-room binoculars let you indulge in the incredible views. **Cons:** costly parking; some rooms are on the small side. [$] *Rooms from: $360* ✉ *30 El Portal* ☎ *415/332–9535, 800/893–8433* 🌐 *www.innabovetide.com* 🛏 *29 rooms, 3 suites* 🍽 *Breakfast.*

9

THE ARTS

Sausalito Art Festival. The annual event, held over Labor Day weekend, attracts more than 30,000 people to the northern waterfront; Blue & Gold Fleet ferries from San Francisco dock at the pier adjacent to the festival. ☎ *415/332–3555* ⊕ *www.sausalitoartfestival.org* ⊠ *$25.*

SPORTS AND THE OUTDOORS

Sea Trek Ocean Kayaking and SUP Center. The center (SUP stands for stand-up paddleboarding) offers guided half-day sea-kayaking trips underneath the Golden Gate Bridge and full- and half-day trips to Angel Island, both for beginners. Trips for experienced kayakers, classes, and rentals are also available. ■ TIP→ **Starlight and full-moon paddles are particularly popular.** ⊠ *Schoonmaker Point Marina, off Libertyship Way* ☎ *415/332–8494* ⊕ *www.seatrek.com* ⊠ *From $20 per hr for rentals, $65 for 3-hr guided trip.*

SF Bay Adventures. This outfit's expert skippers conduct sunset and full-moon sails around the bay, as well as fascinating eco and whale-watching tours with the possibility of viewing great white sharks. If you're interested, they can arrange for you to barbecue on Angel Island or even spend the night in a lighthouse. ⊠ *60 Liberty Ship Way, Ste. 4* ☎ *415/331–0444* ⊕ *www.sfbayadventures.com.*

SHOPPING

FAMILY **Sausalito Ferry Co.** Eccentric and fun, this shop is a great place to buy trendy T-shirts, wallets, and clocks—not to mention solar-powered bobbleheads, outrageous cocktail napkins, and one-of-a-kind key chains. ⊠ *688 Bridgeway, near Princess St.* ☎ *415/332–9590* ⊕ *www. sausalitoferry.com.*

Something/Anything Gallery. Where Bridgeway ends and curves toward the dock, this gallery with a friendly staff carries jewelry and gifts, from unique watches to humorous pendants. ■ TIP→ **This a good spot to pick up your Sausalito memento.** ⊠ *20 Princess St., at Broadway* ☎ *415/339–8831* ⊕ *www.somethinganythinggallery.com.*

TIBURON

2 miles north of Sausalito, 7 miles north of Golden Gate Bridge.

On a peninsula that was called Punta de Tiburon (Shark Point) by the Spanish explorers, this beautiful Marin County community retains the feel of a village—it's more low-key than Sausalito—despite the encroachment of commercial establishments from the downtown area. The harbor faces Angel Island across Raccoon Strait, and San Francisco is directly south across the bay—which makes the views from the decks of harbor restaurants a major attraction. Since its incarnation, in 1884, when ferries from San Francisco connected the point with a railroad to San Rafael, the town has centered on the waterfront. ■ TIP→ **The ferry is the most relaxing (and fastest) way to get here, particularly in summer, allowing you to skip traffic and parking problems. If visiting midweek, keep in mind that many shops close either Tuesday or Wednesday, or both.**

ESSENTIALS

Visitor Information Tiburon ☒ *Town Hall, 1505 Tiburon Blvd.* ☎ *415/435–7373* ⊕ *www.townoftiburon.org.*

GETTING HERE AND AROUND

Blue & Gold Fleet ferries travel between San Francisco and Tiburon daily. By car, head north from San Francisco on U.S. 101 and get off at CA 131/Tiburon Boulevard/East Blithedale Avenue (Exit 447). Turn right onto Tiburon Boulevard and drive just over 4 miles to downtown. Golden Gate Transit bus 8 serves downtown Tiburon from San Francisco on weekdays. Tiburon's Main Street is made for wandering, as are the footpaths that frame the water's edge.

EXPLORING

Ark Row. Past the pink-brick bank building, Main Street is known as Ark Row, and has a tree-shaded walk lined with antiques and specialty stores. Some of the buildings are actually old houseboats that floated in Belvedere Cove before being beached and transformed into stores. ■ TIP→ If you're curious about architectural history, the Tiburon Heritage & Arts Commission has a self-guided walking-tour map, available online and at local businesses. ☒ *Ark Row, parallel to Main St.* ⊕ *tiburonheritageandarts.org.*

Old St. Hilary's Landmark and Wildflower Preserve. The architectural centerpiece of the Old St. Hilary's Landmark and Wildflower Preserve is a stark-white 1886 Carpenter Gothic church that overlooks the town and the bay from its hillside perch. Surrounding the church, which was barged over from Strawberry Point in 1957, is a wildflower preserve that's spectacular in May and June, when the rare black jewelflower blooms. Expect a steep walk uphill to reach the preserve. ■ TIP→ The hiking trails behind the landmark wind up to a peak that has 360-degree views of the entire Bay Area (great photo op). ☒ *201 Esperanza St., off Mar West St. or Beach Rd.* ☎ *415/435–1853* ⊕ *landmarkssociety.com* 🖼 *$3 suggested donation* ☉ *Apr.–Oct., Sun. 1–4 and by appointment.*

WHERE TO EAT

$$$$
AMERICAN
✕ **The Caprice.** For more than 50 years this Tiburon landmark that overlooks the bay has been the place to come to mark special occasions. The views are spectacular, and soft-yellow walls and starched white tablecloths help to make the space bright and light. Elegant comfort food is the premise, with choices like seared day-boat scallops or pan-roasted filet mignon. Polishing off the warm chocolate cake with almond ice cream while gazing out at the sunset and porpoises bobbing in the waves below is a near perfect end to the evening. $ *Average main: $31* ☒ *2000 Paradise Dr.* ☎ *415/435–3400* ⊕ *www.thecaprice.com* ☉ *No lunch.*

$
AMERICAN
✕ **New Morning Cafe.** Omelets and scrambles are served all day long at this homey café. If you're past morning treats, choose from the many soups, salads, and sandwiches. The café is open from 6:30 until 2:30 on weekdays, until 4 on weekends. $ *Average main: $13* ☒ *1696 Tiburon Blvd., near Main St.* ☎ *415/435–4315* ☉ *No dinner.*

$$$
AMERICAN
✕ **Sam's Anchor Cafe.** Open since 1921, this casual dockside restaurant with mahogany wainscoting is the town's most famous eatery. Today most people flock here for the deck, where out-of-towners and old

salts sit shoulder to shoulder for bay views, beer, seafood, and Ramos fizzes. The lunch menu has the usual suspects—burgers, sandwiches, salads, fried fish with tartar sauce—and you'll sit on plastic chairs at tables covered with blue-and-white-checked oilcloths. At night you can find standard seafood dishes with vegetarian and meat options. Mind the seagulls; they know no restraint. ■ TIP→ Expect a wait for outside tables on sunny summer days or weekends; there are no reservations for deck seating or weekend lunch. $ *Average main: $23* ✉ *27 Main St.* ☎ *415/435–4527* ⊕ *www.samscafe.com.*

WHERE TO STAY

$$$

B&B/INN

Waters Edge Hotel. Checking into this elegant hotel feels like tucking away into an inviting retreat by the water—the views are stunning and the lighting is perfect. **Pros:** complimentary wine and cheese for guests every evening; restaurants/sights are minutes away; free bike rentals for guests. **Cons:** downstairs rooms lack privacy and views; except for breakfast delivery, no room service; fitness center is off-site; not a great place to bring small children. $ *Rooms from: $250* ✉ *25 Main St., off Tiburon Blvd.* ☎ *415/789–5999, 877/789–5999* ⊕ *www.marinhotels. com* ⤳ *23 rooms* ⦿| *Breakfast.*

MILL VALLEY

2 miles north of Sausalito, 4 miles north of Golden Gate Bridge.

Chic and woodsy Mill Valley has a dual personality. Here, as elsewhere in the county, the foundation is a superb natural setting. Virtually surrounded by parkland, the town lies at the base of Mt. Tamalpais and contains dense redwood groves traversed by countless creeks. But this is no lumber camp. Smart restaurants and chichi boutiques line the streets, and more rock stars than one might suspect live here.

The rustic village flavor isn't a modern conceit but a holdover from the town's early days as a logging camp. In 1896 the Mill Valley and Mt. Tamalpais Scenic Railroad—called "the crookedest railroad in the world" because of its curvy tracks—began transporting visitors from Mill Valley to the top of Mt. Tam and down to Muir Woods, and the town soon became a vacation retreat for city slickers. The trains stopped running in the 1940s, but the old railway depot still serves as the center of town: the 1924 building has been transformed into the popular Depot Bookstore & Cafe, at 87 Throckmorton Avenue.

The small downtown area has the constant bustle of a leisure community; even at noon on a Tuesday, people are out shopping for fancy cookware and lacy pajamas.

ESSENTIALS

Visitor Information Mill Valley Chamber of Commerce ✉ *85 Throckmorton Ave.* ☎ *415/388–9700* ⊕ *www.millvalley.org.*

GETTING HERE AND AROUND

By car from San Francisco, head north on U.S. 101 and get off at CA 131/Tiburon Boulevard/East Blithedale Avenue (Exit 447). Turn left onto East Blithedale and continue west to Throckmorton Avenue; turn left to reach Lytton Square, then park. Golden Gate Transit bus

4 leaves for Mill Valley from San Francisco every 30 minutes during afternoon commute hours. Once here, explore the town on foot; it's great for strolling.

EXPLORING

FAMILY **Lytton Square.** Mill Valley locals congregate on weekends to socialize in the many coffeehouses near the town's central square (which is unmarked), but it bustles most any time of day. Shops, restaurants, and cultural venues line the nearby streets. ⊠ *Miller and Throckmorton Aves.*

OFF THE BEATEN PATH

Marin County Civic Center. A wonder of arches, circles, and skylights about 8 miles north of Mill Valley, the civic center was Frank Lloyd Wright's last major architectural undertaking. Docent-led tours ($5) leave from the gift shop, on the second floor, on Wednesday mornings at 10:30. You can also wander about on your own; pick up a self-guided tour map at the gift shop (50¢) or access one on the center's website. ■ TIP→ Don't miss the photographs on the first floor, which show Marin County homes designed by Wright. ⊠ *3501 Civic Center Dr., off N. San Pedro Rd., San Rafael* ☎ *415/473–3762 for docent tour* ⊕ *www. marincounty.org/depts/cu/visitor-services* ⊡ *Free* ☉ *Weekdays 8–5.*

WHERE TO EAT

$$$
AMERICAN

✕ **Buckeye Roadhouse.** This is Mill Valley's secret den of decadence, where house-smoked meats and fish, grilled steaks, and old-fashioned dishes such as brisket bring the locals coming back for more. The restaurant also serves beautiful organic salads and desserts so heavenly—like the s'more pie—you'll just about melt into the floor. The look of the 1937 roadhouse is decidedly hunting-lodge chic, with a river-rock fireplace, topped by a trophy fish, dominating one wall. The busy but cozy bar with elegant mahogany paneling and soft lighting is a good place to quench your thirst for a Marin martini or Napa Valley Merlot. Ⓢ *Average main: $23* ⊠ *15 Shoreline Hwy., off U.S. 101* ☎ *415/331–2600* ⊕ *buckeyeroadhouse.com* ⊛ *Reservations essential.*

$$$
CONTEMPORARY
Fodor's Choice
★

✕ **El Paseo House of Chops.** Chef Tyler Florence and rocker Sammy Hagar teamed up to restore El Paseo, which was established in 1947 and remains *the* place for a romantic and culinary night out. You'll feel as if you're on one of Spain's tiny cobbled lanes as you enter the secluded brick walkway that wraps around a candlelit dining room. If you reserve well in advance you can sit in the bougainvillea-framed courtyard, but the dining room casts its own atmospheric charms, with soft leather chairs, white tablecloths, and dark wooden walls. And then there's Tyler Florence's famous seasonal Californian cuisine. Favorites include pan-roasted duck breast and the traditional steak frites. Don't overlook the decadent desserts. Ⓢ *Average main: $27* ⊠ *17 Throckmorton Ave., at E. Blithedale Ave.* ☎ *415/388–0741* ⊕ *www.elpaseomillvalley.com* ⊛ *Reservations essential* ☉ *No lunch.*

$
BURGER
FAMILY

✕ **Pearl's Phat Burgers.** Families, couples, and teenagers flock to Pearl's for juicy, grass-fed organic burgers stacked high with tomatoes, lettuce, bacon, and cheese; sweet-potato fries that are not too crispy and not too soft; and thick, creamy milk shakes. The food here is among the freshest, biggest, and fastest in town. No wonder there's always a line out the door. Ⓢ *Average main: $14* ⊠ *8 E. Blithedale Ave., at Sunnyside Ave.* ☎ *415/381–6010.*

9

WHERE TO STAY

$$$ B&B/INN **Mill Valley Inn.** The only hotel in downtown Mill Valley has smart-looking rooms done up in Tuscan colors of ocher and olive, with handcrafted beds, armoires, and lamps by local artisans. **Pros:** minutes from local shops and restaurants; great complimentary Continental breakfast; free parking; free mountain bikes. **Cons:** some rooms are noisy; dark in winter because of surrounding trees; some rooms are not accessible via elevator; no in-room coffeemakers. [$] *Rooms from: $239* ✉ *165 Throckmorton Ave., near Miller Ave.* ☎ *415/389–6608, 800/595–2100* 🌐 *www.marinhotels.com* 🛏 *22 rooms, 1 suite, 2 cottages* 🍴 *Breakfast.*

$$$$ B&B/INN Fodor's Choice ★ **Mountain Home Inn.** Abutting 40,000 acres of state and national parks, the inn sits on the skirt of Mt. Tamalpais, where you can follow hiking trails all the way to Stinson Beach. **Pros:** amazing deck and views; peaceful, remote setting. **Cons:** nearest town is a 20-minute drive away; restaurant can get crowded on sunny weekend days; too rustic for some. [$] *Rooms from: $279* ✉ *810 Panoramic Hwy., at Edgewood Ave.* ☎ *415/381–9000* 🌐 *www.mtnhomeinn.com* 🛏 *10 rooms* 🍴 *Breakfast.*

NIGHTLIFE AND THE ARTS

NIGHTLIFE

Mill Valley Beerworks. A place to rest your feet after shopping or hiking, Beerworks serves more than 100 local, national, and international beers, from ale to port to lager. For food, you'll find cheese plates, olives, homemade pretzels, and sandwiches. ✉ *173 Throckmorton Ave., at Madrona St.* ☎ *415/888–8218* 🌐 *millvalleybeerworks.com.*

THE ARTS

Sweetwater Music Hall. With the help of part-owner Bob Weir of the Grateful Dead, this renowned club reopened in an old Masonic Hall. The location may be new, but the Sweetwater's reputation as the best music club and bar in Marin remains. In its former life, it hosted the likes of John Lee Hooker and Jerry Garcia. Today, famous as well as up-and-coming bands play nightly, and local stars such as Bonnie Raitt and Huey Lewis have been known to stop in for a pickup session. ✉ *19 Corte Madera Ave., between Throckmorton and Lovell Aves.* ☎ *415/388–3850* 🌐 *www.sweetwatermusichall.com.*

MUIR WOODS NATIONAL MONUMENT

12 miles northwest of the Golden Gate Bridge.

Climbing hundreds of feet into the sky, *Sequoia sempervirens* are the tallest living things on Earth. One of the last remaining old-growth stands of these redwood behemoths, Muir Woods is nature's cathedral: imposing, awe-inspiring, reverence-inducing, and not to be missed.

GETTING HERE AND AROUND

Driving to Muir Woods, especially in summer and early fall, causes epic traffic jams around the tiny parking areas and miles-long walks to reach the entrance. Do yourself (and everyone else) a favor and take a shuttle instead, if you can. On weekends and holidays, from Memorial Day through Labor Day, Marin Transit's Route 66 shuttle (🎫 *$5 round-trip* 🌐 *www.marintransit.org*) is timed to meet boats at Sausalito's ferry

landing four times daily en route to Muir Woods. The shuttle also runs every half hour from the Manzanita Park-and-Ride three miles north of the ferry. To get there, take the Highway 1 exit off U.S. 101 (look for the lot under the elevated freeway), or take connecting bus service from San Francisco with Golden Gate Transit. To drive directly from San Francisco by car, take U.S. 101 north across the Golden Gate Bridge to the Mill Valley/Stinson Beach exit, then follow signs to Highway 1 north. Once here, you can wander by foot through this pristine patch of nature.

EXPLORING

Fodor's Choice   **Muir Woods National Monument.** Walking among some of the last old-growth redwoods on the planet, trees hundreds of feet tall and a millennium or more old, is magical, an experience like few others to clearly illustrate our tiny place in a bigger world. Ancestors of redwood and sequoia trees grew throughout what is now the United States 150,000,000 years ago. Today the *Sequoia sempervirens* can be found only in a narrow, cool coastal belt from Monterey to Oregon. The 550 acres of Muir Woods National Monument contain some of the most majestic redwoods in the world—some more than 250 feet tall. (To see the real giants, though, you'll have to head north to Humboldt County, where the tallest redwood, in Redwood National Park, has been measured at 380 feet.) The Marin stand was saved from destruction in 1905, when it was purchased by a couple who donated it to the federal government. Three years later it was named after naturalist John Muir, whose environmental campaigns helped to establish the national park system. His response: "Saving these woods from the ax and saw is in many ways the most notable service to God and man I have heard of since my forest wandering began."

Muir Woods, part of the Golden Gate National Recreation Area, is a pedestrian's park. Old paved trails have been replaced by wooden walkways, and the trails vary in difficulty and length. Beginning from the park headquarters, an easy 2-mile, wheelchair-accessible **loop trail** crosses streams and passes ferns and azaleas, as well as magnificent redwood groves. Among the most famous are **Bohemian Grove** and the circular formation called **Cathedral Grove.** On summer weekends visitors oohing and aahing in a dozen languages line the trail. If you prefer a little serenity, consider the challenging **Dipsea Trail,** which climbs west from the forest floor to soothing views of the ocean and the Golden Gate Bridge. For a complete list of trails, check with rangers, who can also help you pick the best one for your ability level.

■ TIP➡ The weather in Muir Woods is usually cool and often wet, so wear warm clothes and shoes appropriate for damp trails. Picnicking and camping aren't allowed, and pets aren't permitted. Crowds can be large, especially from May through October, so try to come early in the morning or late in the afternoon. The **Muir Woods Visitor Center** has books and exhibits about redwood trees and the woods' history; the café here serves locally sourced, organic food, and the gift shop has plenty of souvenirs. ✉ *1 Muir Woods Trail, off Panoramic Hwy., Mill Valley* ☎ *415/388–2595 park information, 415/526–3239 shuttle information* ⊕ *www.nps.gov/muwo* ☜ *$7* ☉ *Daily 8 am–sunset.*

MT. TAMALPAIS STATE PARK

16 miles northwest of Golden Gate Bridge.

The view of Mt. Tamalpais from all around the bay can be a beauty, but that's nothing compared to the views *from* the mountain, which range from jaw-dropping to spectacular and take in San Francisco, the East Bay, the coast, and beyond—on a clear day, all the way to the Farallon Islands, 26 miles away.

GETTING HERE AND AROUND

By car, take the Highway 1–Stinson Beach exit off U.S. 101 and follow the road west and then north. From San Francisco, the trip can take from 30 minutes up to an hour, depending on traffic. By bus, take the 10, 70 or 80 (on weekdays also the 92) to Marin City; in Marin City transfer to the West Marin Stagecoach (☎ *415/226–0855* ⊕ *www.marintransit. org/stage.html*). Once here, the only way to explore is on foot or by bike.

EXPLORING

Mt. Tamalpais State Park. Although the summit of Mt. Tamalpais is only 2,571 feet high, the mountain rises practically from sea level, dominating the topography of Marin County. Adjacent to Muir Woods National Monument, Mt. Tamalpais State Park affords views of the entire Bay Area and the Pacific Ocean to the west. The mountain was sacred to Native Americans, who saw in its profile—as you can see today—the silhouette of a sleeping Indian maiden. Locals fondly refer to it as the "Sleeping Lady." For years the 6,300-acre park has been a favorite destination for hikers. There are more than 200 miles of trails, some rugged but many developed for easy walking through meadows, grasslands, and forests and along creeks. Mt. Tam, as it's called by locals, is also the birthplace (in the 1970s) of mountain biking, and today many spandex-clad bikers whiz down the park's winding roads.

The park's major thoroughfare, Panoramic Highway, snakes its way up from U.S. 101 to the **Pantoll Ranger Station.** The office is staffed sporadically, depending on funding. From the ranger station, Panoramic Highway drops down to the town of Stinson Beach. Pantoll Road branches off the highway at the station, connecting up with Ridgecrest Boulevard. Along these roads are numerous parking areas, picnic spots, scenic overlooks, and trailheads. Parking is free along the roadside, but there's a fee at the ranger station and at some of the other parking lots ($8).

The **Mountain Theater,** also known as the Cushing Memorial Amphitheatre, is a natural amphitheater with terraced stone seats (for nearly 4,000 people) constructed in its current form by the Civilian Conservation Corps in the 1930s. The theater celebrated its 100th year of performances in 2013.

The **Rock Spring Trail** starts at the Mountain Theater and gently climbs about 1¾ miles to the **West Point Inn,** once a stop on the Mt. Tam railroad route. Relax at a picnic table and stock up on water before forging ahead, via Old Railroad Grade Fire Road and the Miller Trail, to Mt. Tam's Middle Peak, about 2 miles uphill.

Starting from the Pantoll Ranger Station, the precipitous **Steep Ravine Trail** brings you past stands of coastal redwoods and, in the springtime, numerous small waterfalls. Take the connecting **Dipsea Trail** to reach the town of Stinson Beach and its swath of golden sand. ■TIP→ If you're too weary to make the 3½-mile trek back up, Marin Transit Bus 61 takes you from Stinson Beach back to the ranger station. ⊠ *Pantoll Ranger Station, 3801 Panoramic Hwy., at Pantoll Rd.* ☎ *415/388–2070* ⊕ *www.parks.ca.gov.*

NIGHTLIFE AND THE ARTS

FAMILY **Mountain Play.** Every May and June, locals tote overstuffed picnic baskets to the Mountain Theater to see the Mountain Play, popular musicals such as *The Music Man* and *My Fair Lady*. Depending on the play, this can be a great family activity. Summer 2013 marked the 100th anniversary of this Bay Area tradition. ⊠ *Mt. Tamalpais, Richardson Blvd. off Panoramic Hwy.* ☎ *415/383–1100* ⊕ *www.mountainplay.org* ⊠ *$40.*

BEACH TOWNS

The winds whip wildly around Marin County's miles of coastline. If you've never heard sand "sing" as the wind rustles through it you're in for a treat— though when it lands in your sandwich you might not rejoice. But when the weather's calm and sunny as you stroll Stinson Beach—or you're communing with nature at rocky Muir Beach—you'll realize this landscape is ever so choice.

GETTING HERE AND AROUND

If you're driving, take the Highway 1–Stinson Beach exit off U.S. 101 and follow Highway 1, also signed as Shoreline Highway, west and then north. Public transit serves Stinson Beach and Bolinas but not Muir Beach.

MUIR BEACH

12 miles northwest of Golden Gate Bridge; 6 miles southwest of Mill Valley.

Except on the sunniest of weekends Muir Beach is relatively quiet. But this craggy cove has seen its share of history. Sir Francis Drake disembarked here five centuries ago, rock star Janis Joplin's ashes were scattered here among the sands, and this is where author Ken Kesey hosted the second of his famed Acid Tests.

GETTING HERE AND AROUND

A car is the best way to reach Muir Beach. From Highway 1, follow Pacific Way southwest ¼ mile.

EXPLORING

Green Gulch Farm Zen Center. Giant eucalyptus trees frame the long and winding road that leads to this tranquil retreat. Meditation programs, workshops, and various events take place here, and there's an extensive organic garden. Visitors are welcome to roam the acres of gardens that reach down toward Muir Beach. ■TIP→ Follow the main dirt road to a peaceful path (birds, trees, ocean breezes) that meanders to the beach. ⊠ *1601 Shoreline Hwy., at Green Gulch Rd.* ☎ *415/383–3134* ⊕ *www. sfzc.org* ⊠ *Free* ☺ *Tues.–Sat. 9–noon and 2–4, Sun. 9–10 am.*

Shutterbugs rejoice in catching a scenic Muir Beach sunset.

BEACHES

FAMILY **Muir Beach.** Small but scenic, this beach—a rocky patch of shoreline off Highway 1 in the northern Marin Headlands—is a good place to stretch your legs and gaze out at the Pacific. Locals often walk their dogs here; families and cuddling couples come for picnicking and sunbathing. At one end of the sand are waterfront homes (and where nude sunbathers lay their towels), and at the other are the bluffs of Golden Gate National Recreation Area. **Amenities:** parking (free); toilets. **Best for:** solitude; nudists; walking. ✉ *190 Pacific Way, off Shoreline Highway* 🌐 *www.nps.gov/goga/planyourvisit/muirbeach.htm.*

WHERE TO STAY

$$$ B&B/INN 🏨 **Pelican Inn.** From its slate roof to its whitewashed plaster walls, this inn looks so Tudor that it's hard to believe it was built in the 1970s, but the Pelican is English to the core, with its smallish guest rooms upstairs (no elevator), high half-tester beds draped in heavy fabrics, and bangers and grilled tomatoes for breakfast. **Pros:** five-minute walk to beach; great bar and restaurant; peaceful setting. **Cons:** 20-minute drive to nearby attractions; some rooms are quite small. [$] *Rooms from: $220* ✉ *10 Pacific Way, off Hwy. 1* ☎ *415/383–6000* 🌐 *www.pelicaninn.com* 🛏 *7 rooms* 🍴 *Breakfast.*

STINSON BEACH

20 miles northwest of Golden Gate Bridge; 5½ miles north of Muir Beach.

This laid-back hamlet is all about the beach, and folks come from all over the Bay Area to walk its sandy, often windswept shore. Ideal day trip: a morning Mt. Tam hike followed by lunch at one of Stinson's unassuming eateries and leisurely beach stroll.

GETTING HERE AND AROUND

By car from U.S. 101, take the Highway 1–Stinson Beach exit off U.S. 101 and head west on Highway 1, also signed as Shoreline Highway. Follow signs to 12½ miles to Stinson Beach. Or take Golden Gate Transit bus 10, 70, or 80 to Marin City; in Marin City transfer to the West Marin Stagecoach. Intimate Stinson is perfect for casual walking.

BEACHES

FAMILY **Stinson Beach.** When the fog hasn't rolled in, this expansive stretch of sand is about as close as you can get in Marin to the stereotypical feel of a Southern California beach. There are several clothing-optional areas, among them a section called Red Rock Beach. ⚠ **Swimming at Stinson Beach is recommended only from early May through September, when lifeguards are on duty, because the undertow can be strong and shark sightings, although infrequent, aren't unheard of.** On any hot summer weekend, every road to Stinson is jam-packed, so factor this into your plans. The down-to-earth town itself—population 600, give or take—has a surfer vibe, with a few good eating options and pleasant hippie-craftsy browsing. **Amenities:** food and drink; lifeguards; parking (free); showers; toilets. **Best for:** nudists; sunset; surfing; swimming; walking. ✉ *Hwy. 1* 🌐 *www.stinsonbeachonline.com.*

WHERE TO EAT AND STAY

$$ AMERICAN FAMILY 🍴 **Parkside Cafe.** The Parkside is popular for its beachfront snack bar (cash only), but inside is tiny Stinson's best restaurant, with classic Cal-cuisine offerings such as the day-boat-scallop and ceviche appetizers, and mains like the lamb with goat-cheese-stuffed red peppers. Breakfast is served until 2 pm. Creeping vines on the sunny patio shelter diners from the wind; for a cozier ambience eat by the fire in the dining room. [$] *Average main: $20* ✉ *43 Arenal Ave., off Shoreline Hwy. 1* ☎ *415/868–1272* 🌐 *www.parksidecafe.com.*

$$ AMERICAN 🍴 **Sand Dollar.** The town's oldest restaurant still attracts all the old salts from Muir Beach to Bolinas, but these days they sip whiskey over an up-to-date bar or beneath market umbrellas on the spiffy deck. The food is good—try the panfried sand dabs (small flatfish) and pear salad with blue cheese—but the big draw is the lively atmosphere. Musicians play on Sundays in summer, and on sunny afternoons the deck gets so packed that people sit on the fence rails sipping beer. From Monday through Thursday the restaurant opens at 3. [$] *Average main: $20* ✉ *3458 Shoreline Hwy.* ☎ *415/868–0434* 🌐 *www.stinsonbeachrestaurant.com* 🕒 *No lunch Mon.–Thurs.*

$$ B&B/INN FAMILY 🏨 **Sandpiper Lodging.** Recharge, rest, and enjoy the local scenery at this ultra-popular lodging that books up months, even years, in advance. **Pros:** bright rooms; lush gardens; minutes from the beach. **Cons:** walls

are thin; some guests say motel rooms are overpriced. $ *Rooms from:*
$145 ✉ *1 Marine Way, at Arenal Ave.* ☎ *415/868–1632* ⊕ *www.*
sandpiperstinsonbeach.com ⇆ *6 rooms, 4 cabins* ⊘ *No meals.*

$$
B&B/INN
⬚ **Stinson Beach Motel.** Built in the 1930s, this motel surrounds three
courtyards that burst with flowering greenery, and rooms are clean,
simple, and summery; the two cottages have kitchenettes. **Pros:** minutes
from the beach; cozy, unpretentious rooms. **Cons:** smaller rooms are
cramped; some linens need replacing. $ *Rooms from: $130* ✉ *3416*
Shoreline Hwy. ☎ *415/868–1712* ⊕ *www.stinsonbeachmotel.com* ⇆ *6*
rooms, 2 cottages ⊘ *No meals.*

EN ROUTE
Martin Griffin Preserve. A 1,000-acre wildlife sanctuary along the
Bolinas Lagoon, this Audubon Canyon Ranch preserve gets the most
traffic during late spring, when great blue herons and egrets nest in the
evergreens covering the hillside. It's spectacular to see these large birds
in white and gray, dotting the tops of the trees. Quiet trails through the
rest of the preserve offer tremendous vistas of the Bolinas Lagoon and
Stinson Beach—and fabulous birding. On weekends, "Ranch Guides" are
posted throughout to point out nests—scopes are provided—and answer
questions. During the week, check in at the small bookstore and take a self-
guided tour. ✉ *4900 Shoreline Hwy. 1, between Stinson Beach and Bolinas*
☎ *415/868–9244* ⊕ *www.egret.org* ⬚ *Free* ⊘ *Mid-Dec.–mid-Mar.*

BOLINAS

7 miles north of Stinson Beach.

The tiny town of Bolinas wears its 1960s idealism on its sleeve, attract-
ing potters, poets, and peace lovers to its quiet streets. With a funky
gallery, a general store selling organic produce, a café, and an offbeat
saloon, the main thoroughfare, Wharf Road, looks like a hippie-fied
version of Main Street, USA.

9

GETTING HERE AND AROUND

Bolinas isn't difficult to find, though locals notoriously remove the street
sign for their town from the highway: heading north from Stinson
Beach, follow Highway 1 west and then north. Make a left at the first
road just past the Bolinas Lagoon (✉ *Olema–Bolinas Road*), and then
turn left at the stop sign. The road dead-ends smack-dab in the middle
of town. By bus, take the 10, 70, or 80 to Marin City; in Marin City,
transfer to the West Marin Stagecoach. Walking is the only way to see
this small town.

WHERE TO EAT

$$
AMERICAN
✕ **Coast Cafe.** Decked out in a nautical theme with surfboards and
buoys, the dining room at the Coast serves dependably good American
fare, including specials such as shepherd's pie, pot roast, local fresh
fish, grass-fed steaks, and gorgeous salads. Live music accompanies
dinner on Thursday and Sunday. On weekends, the café is open for
brunch. $ *Average main: $19* ✉ *46 Wharf Rd., off Olema–Bolinas*
Rd. ☎ *415/868–2298.*

POINT REYES NATIONAL SEASHORE

Bear Valley Visitor Center is 12 miles north of Bolinas.

With sandy beaches stretching for miles, a dramatic rocky coastline, a gem of a lighthouse, and idyllic, century-old dairy farms, Point Reyes National Seashore is one of the most varied and strikingly beautiful corners of the Bay Area.

GETTING HERE AND AROUND

From San Francisco, take U.S. 101 north, head west at Sir Francis Drake Boulevard (Exit 450B), and follow the road just under 20 miles to Bear Valley Road. From Stinson Beach or Bolinas, drive north on Highway 1 and turn left on Bear Valley Road. If you're going by bus, take Golden Gate Transit bus 70 to the San Rafael Transit Center and transfer to the West Marin Stagecoach, which stops at the Bear Valley Visitor Center. Allow two and a half hours for the trip.

EXPLORING

FAMILY   **Bear Valley Visitor Center.** A life-size orca model hovers over the center's engaging exhibits about the wildlife and history of the Point Reyes National Seashore. The rangers at the barnlike facility are fonts of information about beaches, whale-watching, hiking trails, and camping. Winter hours may be shorter; call or check the website for details. ⊠ *Bear Valley Visitor Center Access Rd., west of Hwy. 1* ☎ *415/464–5100* ⊕ *www.nps.gov/pore/planyourvisit* ☉ *Weekdays 9–5; weekends 8–5.*

FAMILY   **Duxbury Reef.** Excellent tide pooling can be had along mile-long Duxbury Reef, the largest shale intertidal reef in North America. Look for sea stars, barnacles, sea anemones, purple urchins, limpets, sea mussels, and the occasional abalone. But check a tide table (⊕ *www.wrh. noaa.gov/mtr/marine.php*) or the local papers if you plan to explore the reef—it's accessible only at low tide. The reef is a 30-minute drive from the Bear Valley Visitor Center. Take Highway 1 south from the center, turn right at Olema-Bolinas Road (keep an eye peeled; the road is easy to miss), left on Horsehoe Hill Road, right on Mesa Road, left on Overlook Drive, and then right on Elm Road, which dead-ends at the Agate Beach County Park parking lot.

FAMILY   **Point Blue Conservation Science.** Birders adore Point Blue (formerly the Point Reyes Bird Observatory), which lies in the southernmost part of Point Reyes National Seashore and is accessed through Bolinas. (Those not interested in birds might find it ho-hum.) The unstaffed Palomarin Field Station, open daily from sunrise to sunset, has excellent interpretive exhibits, including a comparative display of real birds' talons. The surrounding woods harbor more than 200 bird species. As you hike the quiet trails through forest and along ocean cliffs, you're likely to see biologists banding birds to aid in the study of their life cycles. ■ TIP→ Visit Point Blue's website to find out when banding will occur; it's a fun time to come here. ⊠ *Mesa Rd., Bolinas* ☎ *415/868–0655* ⊕ *www.pointblue.org* 🎫 *Free* ☉ *Daily sunrise–sunset.*

FAMILY
Fodor's Choice
★
Point Reyes Lighthouse. In operation since December 1, 1870, this lighthouse is one of the premier attractions of the Point Reyes National Seashore. It occupies the tip of Point Reyes, 22 miles from the Bear Valley Visitor Center, a scenic 45-minute drive over hills scattered with longtime dairy farms. The lighthouse originally cast a rotating beam lighted by four wicks that burned lard oil. Keeping the wicks lighted and the 6,000-pound Fresnel lens soot-free in Point Reyes's perpetually foggy climate was a constant struggle that reputedly drove the early attendants to alcoholism and insanity. ■TIP➜ The lighthouse is one of the best spots on the coast for watching gray whales: on both legs of their annual migration, the magnificent animals pass close enough to see with the naked eye. Southern migration peaks in mid-January, and the whales head back north in March; see the slower mothers and calves in late April and early May.

On busy whale-watching weekends (from late December through mid-April), buses shuttle visitors from the Drakes Beach parking lot to the top of the stairs leading down to the lighthouse (🚌 *Bus $5, admission free*) and the road is closed to private vehicles. However you've arrived, consider whether you have it in you to walk down—and up—the 308 steps to the lighthouse. The view from the bottom is worth the effort, but the whales are visible from the cliffs above the lighthouse. ✉ *Visitor Center, Western end of Sir Francis Drake Blvd., Inverness* ☎ *415/669–1534* ⊙ *Fri.–Mon. 10–4:30; weather lens room 2:30–4, except during very windy weather.*

Fodor's Choice
★
Point Reyes National Seashore. One of the Bay Area's most spectacular treasures and the only national seashore on the West Coast, the 66,500-acre Point Reyes National Seashore encompasses hiking trails, secluded beaches, and rugged grasslands as well as Point Reyes itself, a triangular peninsula that juts into the Pacific. The town of **Point Reyes Station** is a quaint, one-main-drag affair, with a charming bakery, some good gift shops with locally made and imported goods, and a few places to eat. It's nothing fancy, but that's part of its relaxed charm.

When explorer Sir Francis Drake sailed along the California coast in 1579, he missed the Golden Gate and San Francisco Bay, but he did land at what he described as a convenient harbor. In 2012 the federal government finally officially recognized Drake's Bay, which flanks the point on the east, as that harbor, designating the spot a National Historic Landmark and silencing competing claims in the 433-year-old controversy. Today Point Reyes's hills and dramatic cliffs attract other kinds of explorers: hikers, whale-watchers, and solitude seekers.

The infamous San Andreas Fault runs along the eastern edge of the park and up the center of Tomales Bay; take the short **Earthquake Trail** from the visitor center to see the impact near the epicenter of the 1906 earthquake that devastated San Francisco. A ½-mile path from the visitor center leads to **Kule Loklo**, a brilliantly reconstructed Miwok village that sheds light on the daily lives of the region's first inhabitants. From here, trails also lead to the park's free, hike-in campgrounds (camping permits are required).

■ TIP→ In late winter and spring, take the short walk at Chimney Rock, just before the lighthouse, to the Elephant Seal Overlook. Even from the cliff, the male seals look enormous as they spar, growling and bloodied, for resident females.

You can experience the diversity of Point Reyes's ecosystems on the scenic **Coast Trail**, which starts at the Palomarin Trailhead, just outside Bolinas. From here, it's a 3-mile trek through eucalyptus groves and pine forests and along seaside cliffs to beautiful and tiny Bass Lake. To reach the Palomarin Trailhead, take Olema–Bolinas Road toward Bolinas, follow signs to Point Blue Conservation Science, and then continue until the road dead-ends.

The 4.7-mile-long (one-way) **Tomales Point Trail** follows the spine of the park's northernmost finger of land through a Tule Elk Preserve, providing spectacular ocean views from the high bluffs. Expect to see elk, but keep your distance from the animals. To reach the fairly easy hiking trail, look for the Pierce Point Road turnoff on the right, just north of the town of Inverness; park at the end of the road by the old ranch buildings. ✉ *Bear Valley Visitor Center, Bear Valley Visitor Center Access Rd., off Hwy. 1, Point Reyes Station* ☎ *415/464–5100* 🌐 *www.nps.gov/pore.*

WHERE TO EAT

$$ ITALIAN Fodor's Choice ★ 🍴 **Osteria Stellina.** The vaguely industrial-chic overtones of this West Marin star's otherwise rustic-contemporary decor hint at the panache that enlivens chef-owner Christian Caiazzo's "Point Reyes Italian" cuisine. The emphasis on locally sourced ingredients makes for ingenious combinations—oysters harvested just a few miles away, for instance, anchor a pizza with leeks braised in cream from Marin and Sonoma cows and garnished with parsley and lemon thyme. Pastas and pizzas dominate the menu, which might contain as few as two entrées for lunch and a handful for dinner. The hit at lunch, tomato minestra, is a lightly spiced seafood concoction reminiscent of gumbo; dinner might include osso buco that pairs Niman Ranch veal with Marin-grown kale, or braised goat with greens from Stellina's own farm. [$] *Average main: $19* ✉ *11285 Hwy. 1, at 3rd St., Point Reyes Station* ☎ *415/663–9988* 🌐 *www.osteriastellina.com* 🕓 *Closed Thurs.*

$$$ AMERICAN 🍴 **Station House Cafe.** In good weather, hikers fresh from the park fill the Station House's garden to enjoy alfresco dining, and on weekends there's not a spare seat on the banquettes in the dining room, so prepare for a wait. The focus is on local, seasonal, and sustainable food: oyster shooters, Niman Ranch braised lamb, Californian white sea bass, and sweet bread pudding are the standbys. The place is also open for breakfast, and there's a full bar. [$] *Average main: $30* ✉ *11180 Hwy. 1, Point Reyes Station* ☎ *415/663–1515* 🌐 *www.stationhousecafe.com* 🕓 *Closed Wed.*

$$$ AMERICAN FAMILY 🍴 **Tomales Bay Foods.** A renovated hay barn off the main drag houses this collection of food shops, a favorite stopover among Bay Area foodies. Watch workers making Cowgirl Creamery cheese; then buy some at a counter that sells exquisite artisanal cheeses from around the world. Tomales Bay Foods showcases local organic fruits and vegetables and

premium packaged foods, and the kitchen turns the best ingredients into creative sandwiches, salads, and soups. You can eat at a small café table or the picnic areas outside. [$] *Average main: $23* ✉ *80 4th St., at B St., Point Reyes Station* ☎ *415/663–9335 cheese shop* 🌐 *No dinner* ⏲ *Closed Mon. and Tues.*

WHERE TO STAY

$$ B&B/INN FAMILY 🏨 **Cottages at Point Reyes Seashore.** Amid a 15-acre valley on the north end of town, this secluded getaway offers spacious one- and two-bedroom cabins with fireplaces and patios perfect for sunset barbecues and leisurely breakfasts. **Pros:** spacious accommodations; great place to bring kids. **Cons:** 3-plus miles from downtown Inverness; small pool. [$] *Rooms from: $160* ✉ *13275 Sir Francis Drake Blvd., Inverness* ☎ *415/669–7250, 800/406–0405* 🌐 *www.cottagespointreyes.com* 🛏 *20 cabins* 🍴 *No meals.*

$$$$ B&B/INN 🏨 **Manka's Inverness Lodge.** Chef-owner Margaret Grade takes rustic fantasy to extravagant heights in her 1917 hunting lodge and cabins, where mica-shaded lamps cast an amber glow, and bearskin rugs warm wide-planked floors. **Pros:** extremely romantic, remote and quiet. **Cons:** no on-site restaurant; sounds from neighboring rooms are easily heard; some question the value for the price. [$] *Rooms from: $365* ✉ *30 Callendar Way, at Argyle Way, Inverness* ☎ *415/669–1034* 🌐 *www.mankas.com* 🛏 *5 rooms, 2 suites, 1 boathouse, 2 cabins.*

$$ B&B/INN 🏨 **Ten Inverness Way.** This is the kind of down-to-earth place where you sit around after breakfast and share tips for hiking Point Reyes or linger around the living room and its stone fireplace and library. **Pros:** great base for exploring the nearby wilderness; peaceful garden and friendly staff. **Cons:** overly folksy decor; some rooms are on the small side; poor cell-phone reception. [$] *Rooms from: $170* ✉ *10 Inverness Way, Inverness* ☎ *415/669–1648* 🌐 *www.teninvernessway.com* 🛏 *5 rooms* 🍴 *Breakfast.*

SPORTS AND THE OUTDOORS

Blue Waters Kayaking. This outfit rents kayaks ($50 for two hours), stand-up paddleboards ($25 for one hour), and electric bikes ($30 for one hour, $10 for each additional hour) and offers tours and lessons. ✉ *12944 Sir Francis Drake Blvd., Inverness* ☎ *415/669–2600* 🌐 *www.bwkayak.com.*

Five Brooks Stable. Tour guides here lead private and group horse rides lasting from one to six hours; trails from the stable wind through Point Reyes National Seashore and along the beaches. ✉ *8001 Hwy. 1, north of town, Olema* ☎ *415/663–1570* 🌐 *www.fivebrooks.com* 🎟 *From $40.*

THE WINE
COUNTRY

WELCOME TO WINE COUNTRY

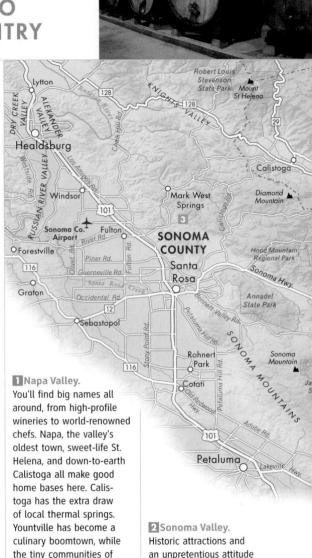

TOP REASONS TO GO

★ **Biking:** Cycling is one of the best ways to see the Wine Country—the Russian River and Dry Creek valleys, in Sonoma County, are particularly beautiful.

★ **Browsing the farmers' markets:** Many towns in Napa and Sonoma have seasonal farmers' markets, each rounding up an amazing variety of local produce.

★ **Wandering di Rosa:** Though this art and nature preserve is just off the busy Carneros Highway, it's a relatively unknown treasure. The galleries and gardens are filled with hundreds of artworks.

★ **Canoeing on the Russian River:** Trade in your car keys for a paddle and glide down the Russian River in Sonoma County. From May through October is the best time to be on the water.

★ **Touring Wineries:** Let's face it: this is the reason you're here, and the range of excellent sips to sample would make any oeno-phile (or novice drinker, for that matter) giddy.

1 Napa Valley.
You'll find big names all around, from high-profile wineries to world-renowned chefs. Napa, the valley's oldest town, sweet-life St. Helena, and down-to-earth Calistoga all make good home bases here. Calistoga has the extra draw of local thermal springs. Yountville has become a culinary boomtown, while the tiny communities of Oakville and Rutherford are home to major wineries such as Robert Mondavi and Beaulieu. Rutherford in particular is the source for outstanding Cabernet Sauvignon.

2 Sonoma Valley.
Historic attractions and an unpretentious attitude prevail here. The town of Sonoma, with its picture-perfect central plaza, is rich with 19th-century buildings. Glen Ellen, meanwhile, has a special connection with author Jack London.

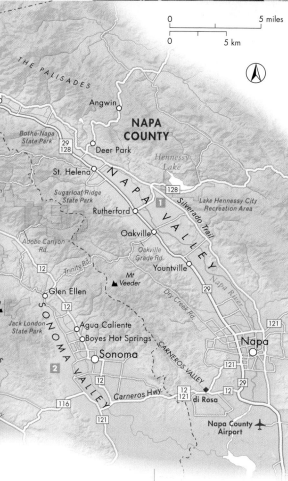

THE PALISADES

Angwin

NAPA COUNTY

Botha-Napa State Park

29 128

Deer Park

St. Helena

Hennessy Lake

Sugarloaf Ridge State Park

128

Rutherford

Lake Hennessy City Recreation Area

Oakville

Adobe Canyon Rd.

12

Trinity Rd.

Mt Veeder

Oakville Grade Rd.

Yountville

Glen Ellen

12

Dry Creek Rd.

29

Napa River

Jack London State Park

Agua Caliente

Boyes Hot Springs

Sonoma

2

CARNEROS VALLEY

Napa

121

12

116

121

Carneros Hwy.

12 121

12

29

di Rosa

121

Napa County Airport

0 ___ 5 miles
0 ___ 5 km

GETTING ORIENTED

The Napa and Sonoma valleys run roughly parallel, northwest to southeast, and are separated by the Mayacamas Mountains. Northwest of the Sonoma Valley are several more important viticultural areas in Sonoma County, including the Dry Creek, Alexander, and Russian River valleys. The Carneros region, which spans southern Sonoma and Napa counties, is just north of San Pablo Bay.

10

3 Elsewhere in Sonoma. The winding, rural roads here feel a world away from Napa's main drag. The Russian River, Dry Creek, and Alexander valleys are all excellent places to seek out Pinot Noir, Zinfandel, and Sauvignon Blanc. The small town of Healdsburg gets lots of attention, thanks to its terrific restaurants, bed-and-breakfasts, and chic boutiques.

Updated by
Daniel Mangin

Life is lived well in California's premiere wine-making region, where eating and drinking are cultivated as high arts. Prestigious wineries can be found in the Napa Valley and in Sonoma County's Russian River, Dry Creek, and Sonoma valleys, and boutique operations flourish throughout. Marquee chefs preside over restaurants everywhere, though the largest concentrations are in the Napa Valley's Yountville and St. Helena and the Sonoma County towns of Sonoma and Healdsburg. The food fest continues at shops and farmers' markets selling artisanal produce, olive oils, cheeses, charcuterie, and baked goods.

The Wine Country is also rich in history. In Sonoma you can explore California's Spanish and Mexican pasts at the Sonoma Mission, and the origins of modern California wine making at Buena Vista Winery. Well before the mission or the wineries existed, Native Americans bathed in the hot mineral waters on the site now occupied by the Fairmont Sonoma Mission Inn & Spa. Some wineries, among them St. Helena's Beringer and Rutherford's Inglenook, have cellars or tasting rooms dating to the late 1800s. Calistoga is a flurry of late-19th-century Steamboat Gothic architecture, though the town's oldest-looking building, the medieval-style Castello di Amorosa, is a 21st-century creation.

Tours at the Napa Valley's Beringer, Mondavi, and Inglenook—and at Buena Vista in the Sonoma Valley—provide an entertaining overview of Wine Country history. The tour at the splashy visitor center at St. Helena's Hall winery will introduce you to 21st-century wine-making technology, and over in Glen Ellen's Benziger Family Winery you can see how its vineyard managers apply biodynamic farming principles to grape growing. At numerous facilities you can play winemaker for a day at seminars in the fine art of blending wines.

If blending strikes you as too much work, fear not. Sit-down tastings that pair food and wine—all the rage these days—provide an elegant way to experience the lifestyle that attracted so many vintners and chefs here in the first place. If even that sounds too much effort, you can always pamper yourself at a luxury spa. To delve further into the fine art of Wine Country living, grab a copy of *Fodor's InFocus Napa & Sonoma.*

PLANNING

WHEN TO GO

"Crush," the term used to indicate the time when grapes are picked and crushed, usually takes place in September or October, depending on the weather. From September until November the Wine Country celebrates its bounty with street fairs and festivals. The Sonoma County Harvest Fair, with its famous grape stomp, is held on the first weekend in October. Wine auctions and art and food fairs occur from spring through fall.

The Wine Country is usually hot and dry all summer and into autumn, so dress appropriately if you visit during these seasons. From May through November the Napa Valley draws crowds of tourists, and traffic along Highway 29 from St. Helena to Calistoga often backs up on weekends. The Sonoma Valley and northern Sonoma County are less crowded, though even that's changing. To avoid crowds, visit during the week. Because many wineries close as early as 4 or 4:30—and few are open past 5—you'll need to get a reasonably early start if you want to fit in more than one or two, especially if you're going to enjoy the leisurely lunch customary in these parts. Keep in mind that many wineries require appointments for tastings and most do so for tours.

GETTING HERE AND AROUND

AIR TRAVEL

Wine Country regulars often bypass San Francisco and Oakland and fly into Santa Rosa's Charles M. Schulz Sonoma County Airport (STS) on Alaska Airlines, which has nonstop flights from San Diego, Los Angeles, Portland, and Seattle. Avis, Budget, Enterprise, Hertz, and National rent cars here. ■ TIP➔ Alaska allows passengers flying out of STS to check up to one case of wine for free.

BUS TRAVEL

Bus travel is an inconvenient way to explore the Wine Country. Greyhound and Golden Gate Transit travel from San Francisco to Petaluma and Santa Rosa, where you can transfer to Sonoma County Transit buses, but connections aren't always smooth. VINE provides service in the Napa Valley; the San Francisco Bay Ferry *(see Ferry Travel, below)* is the easiest way to connect with the VINE network from San Francisco.

Bus Lines Golden Gate Transit 🕾 *415/455–2000* ⊕ *www.goldengatetransit.org.* **Greyhound** 🕾 *800/231–2222* ⊕ *www.greyhound.com.* **Sonoma County Transit** 🕾 *707/576–7433, 800/345–7433* ⊕ *www.sctransit.com.* **VINE** 🕾 *707/251–2800, 800/696–6443* ⊕ *www.ridethevine.com.*

10

CAR TRAVEL

Driving your own car is by far the most convenient way to explore the Wine Country. Distances between towns are fairly short, and in normal traffic you can drive from one end of the Napa or Sonoma valley to the other in less than an hour. Although this is a mostly rural area, the usual rush hours still apply, and high-season weekend traffic can often be slow.

Five major roads serve the region. U.S. 101 and Highways 12 and 121 travel through Sonoma County. Highway 29 and the parallel, more scenic, and often less crowded Silverado Trail travel north–south between Napa and Calistoga.

The easiest way to travel from Napa Valley to Sonoma County is along Highway 12/121 to the south, or Highway 128 to the north. Travel between the middle sections of either area requires taking the slow, winding drive over the Mayacamas Mountains on the Oakville Grade, which links Oakville, in Napa, and Glen Ellen, in Sonoma.

■ TIP➔ If you're wine tasting, either select a designated driver or be careful of your wine intake—the police keep an eye out for tipsy drivers.

From San Francisco to Napa: Cross the Golden Gate Bridge, then go north on U.S. 101. Head east on Highway 37 toward Vallejo, then north on Highway 121, aka the Carneros Highway. Turn left (north) when Highway 121 runs into Highway 29. This should take about an hour in light traffic.

From San Francisco to Sonoma: Cross the Golden Gate Bridge, then go north on U.S. 101, east on Highway 37 toward Vallejo, and north on Highway 121. When you reach Highway 12, take it north to the town of Sonoma. This trip takes about an hour in light traffic. For Sonoma County destinations north of Sonoma Valley stay on U.S. 101, which passes through Santa Rosa and Healdsburg.

From Berkeley and Oakland: Take Interstate 80 north to Highway 37 west, then on to Highway 29 north. For the Napa Valley, continue on Highway 29; to reach Sonoma County, head west on Highway 121. The trip from Berkeley or Oakland to Napa takes about 50 minutes in normal traffic, to Sonoma about an hour.

FERRY TRAVEL

The San Francisco Bay Ferry sails from the Ferry Building and Pier 41 in San Francisco to Vallejo, where you can board a VINE bus to Napa. Buses sometimes fill in for the ferries.

Contact San Francisco Bay Ferry ☎ *510/522-3300*
⊕ *sanfranciscobayferry.com.*

RESTAURANTS

Excellent meals can be found in all the major Wine Country towns, but tiny Yountville has become a culinary crossroads under the influence of chef Thomas Keller. In St. Helena the elegant Restaurant at Meadowood has achieved almost as much critical acclaim as Keller's French Laundry, yet is easier to get into. And the buzzed-about restaurants in Sonoma County, including Glen Ellen Star and the Farmhouse Inn, offer plenty of mouthwatering options.

If you're on a budget, many high-end delis prepare superb picnic fare. Stopping for lunch or brunch can be a cost-effective strategy at pricey restaurants, as can sitting at the bar and ordering appetizers instead of having a full meal.

Except as noted in individual restaurant listings, dress is informal. Where reservations are indicated as essential, book a week or more ahead in summer and early fall.

HOTELS

Wine Country inns and hotels range from low-key to sumptuous, and generally maintain high standards. Many inns are in historic Victorian buildings, and when rates include breakfast the preparations often involve fresh local produce. The newer hotels tend to have a more modern, streamlined aesthetic and elaborate, spa-like bathrooms, and many have excellent restaurants on-site.

Accommodations generally have lower rates on weeknights, and prices are about 20% lower in winter. The towns of Napa and Santa Rosa have the widest selection of moderately priced rooms. On weekends, two- or even three-night minimum stays are commonly required at smaller lodgings. Book well ahead for stays at such places during the busy summer or fall season. If your party will include travelers under age 16, inquire about policies regarding younger guests; some smaller lodgings discourage (or discreetly forbid) children.

The Napa Valley Hotels & Resorts page on the Visit Napa Valley website lists hotels, inns, and other accommodations throughout Napa County. The members of the Sonoma Valley Bed & Breakfast Association operate noteworthy small inns and vacation-rental properties throughout the valley; Wine Country Inns represents small lodgings throughout Sonoma County. *Hotel reviews have been shortened. For full information, visit Fodors.com.*

Contacts Napa Valley Hotels & Resorts ☎ *707/251–9188, 855/333–6272* ⊕ *www.visitnapavalley.com/napa_valley_hotels.htm.* **Wine Country Inns** ✉ *Cloverdale* ☎ *800/946–3268* ⊕ *www.winecountryinns.com.*

WHAT IT COSTS				
	$	$$	$$$	$$$$
Restaurants	under $16	$16–$22	$23–$30	over $30
Hotels	under $121	$121–$300	$301–$400	over $400

Restaurant prices are the average cost of a main course at dinner or, if dinner is not served, at lunch. Hotel prices are for the lowest cost of a standard double room in high season.

10

TOURS

Whether you want to tour wineries in a van or bus along with other passengers or spring for a private limo, there are plenty of operators who can accommodate you. Tours generally last from five to seven hours and stop at four or five wineries. Rates vary—from $80 to $100 per person to $250 or more, depending on the vehicle and whether the tour includes other guests. Some include lunch and tasting and other fees, but not all do, so ask. On most tours, at least one of the day's stops includes a behind-the-scenes look at wine-production facilities and the chance to meet winemakers or others involved in the wine-making process. Most tour operators will pick you up at Wine Country hotels or a specified meeting place.

Perata Luxury Tours & Car Services. Perata's customized private tours, led by well-trained, knowledgeable drivers, are tailored to its patrons' interests—you can create your own itinerary or have your guide craft one for you. Tours, in luxury SUVs, cover Napa and Sonoma. The options include exclusive, appointment-only boutique wineries. ☎ 707/227–8271 ⊕ www.perataluxurycarservices.com ✉ From $325 per day, plus fuel surcharge ($25–$35), tasting fees, and 18% gratuity charge.

Platypus Wine Tours. The emphasis at Platypus is on "fun" experiences at off-the-beaten-path wineries. Expect intimate winery experiences with jolly, well-informed guides. You can join an existing tour with other guests or book a private one. ☎ 707/253–2723 ⊕ www.platypustours. com ✉ From $99, excluding tasting fees.

Valley Wine Tours. Historic, family-owned wineries are the specialty of this Sonoma-based company that provides a gourmet picnic lunch—on china with cloth napkins, no less. The Valley Wine tour rate includes tasting fees. ☎ 707/975–6462 ⊕ www.valleywinetours.com ✉ From $135.

Woody's Wine Tours. The amiable, well-informed Woody Guderian favors small wineries but will customize a tour to suit your taste and budget. In addition to winery tours in both Napa and Sonoma, Woody also conducts tours of local craft breweries. ☎ 707/396–8235 ⊕ www. woodyswinetours.com ✉ From $80 per hr, excluding tasting fees.

VISITOR INFORMATION

Pre-Trip Planning Visit Napa Valley ☎ 707/251–5895 ⊕ www.visitnapavalley. com. **Visit Sonoma** ☎ 707/522–5800, 800/576–6662 ⊕ www.sonomacounty.com.

Visitor Centers California Welcome Center ✉ 9 4th St., at Wilson St., Santa Rosa ☎ 800/404–7673 ⊕ www.visitcalifornia.com/california-welcome-centers/ santa-rosa. **Napa Valley Welcome Center** ✉ 600 Main St., at 5th St., Napa ☎ 707/251–5895 ⊕ www.visitnapavalley.com/welcome_centers.htm. **Sonoma Valley Visitors Center** ✉ 453 1st St. E, east side of Sonoma Plaza, Sonoma ☎ 707/996–1090, 866/996–1090 ⊕ www.sonomavalley.com.

THE NAPA VALLEY

With more than 450 wineries and many of the biggest brands in the business, the Napa Valley is the Wine Country's star. But what's the area like beyond the glossy advertising and boldface names? The small towns strung along Highway 29 are where many wine-industry workers live, and they're where most of the lodging is. Napa—population 78,340 and the valley's largest town—lures with its cultural attractions and (relatively) reasonably priced accommodations. A few miles farther north, compact Yountville is densely packed with top-notch restaurants and hotels, and Rutherford and Oakville are renowned for their Cabernet Sauvignon–friendly soils (Merlot, too). Beyond them, St. Helena teems

Continued on page 534

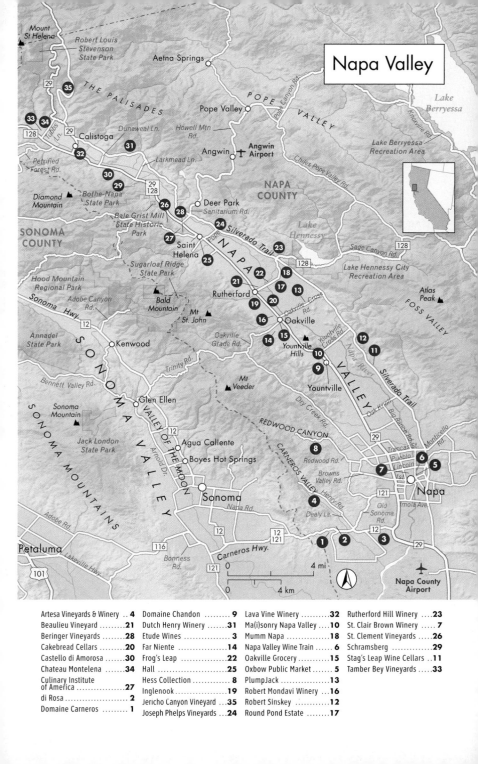

Napa Valley

WINE
TASTING *in*
NAPA *and*
SONOMA

VISITING WINERIES

Napa and Sonoma are outstanding destinations for both wine newcomers and serious wine buffs. Tasting rooms range from modest to swanky, offering everything from a casual conversation over a few sips of wine to in-depth tours of wine-making facilities and vineyards. And there's a tremendous variety of wines to taste. The one constant is a deep, shared pleasure in the experience of wine tasting.

Wineries in Napa and Sonoma range from faux châteaus with vast gift shops to rustic converted barns where you might have to step over the vintner's dog in the doorway. Many are regularly open to the public, usually daily from around 10 am to 5 pm. Others require reservations to visit, and still others are closed to the public entirely. When in doubt, call ahead.

There are many, many more wineries in Napa and Sonoma than we could possibly include here. Free maps pinpointing most of them are widely available, though; ask the staff at the tasting rooms you visit or look for the ubiquitous free tourist magazines.

Pick a designated driver before setting out for the day. Although wineries rarely advertise it, many will provide a free non-alcoholic drink for the designated driver; it never hurts to ask.

Fees. In the past few years, tasting fees have skyrocketed. Most Napa wineries charge $20 or $25 to taste four or so wines, though $35, $45 or even $65 fees aren't unheard of. Sonoma wineries are often a bit cheaper, in the $10 to $25 range, and you'll still find the occasional freebie.

Some winery tours are free, in which case you're usually required to pay a separate fee if you want to taste the wine. If you've paid a fee for the tour—often $20 to $40—your wine tasting is usually included in that price.

The tantalizing pop of a cork. Roads unspooling through hypnotically even rows of vines. Sun glinting through a glass of sparkling wine or ruby colored cabernet. If these are your daydreams, you won't be disappointed when you get to Napa and Sonoma. The vineyard-blanketed hills, shady town squares, and ivy-draped wineries—not to mention the luxurious restaurants, hotels, and spas—really *are* that captivating.

(opposite page) Carneros vineyards in autumn, Napa Valley. (top) Pinot Gris grapes (bottom) Bottles from Far Niente winery.

MAKING THE MOST OF YOUR TIME

■**Call ahead.** Some wineries require reservations to visit or tour and others are closed to the public entirely. It's wise to check before visiting.

■**Come on weekdays,** especially if you're visiting during high season (May to November), to avoid traffic-clogged roads and crowded tasting rooms. For more info on the best times of year to visit, see this chapter's Planner.

■**Get an early start.** Tasting rooms are often deserted before 11 am or so, when most visitors are still lingering over a second cup of coffee. If you come early, you'll have the staff's undivided attention. You'll usually encounter the largest crowds between 3 and 5 pm.

(top) Sipping and swirling in the De Loach tasting room. (bottom) Learning about barrel aging at Robert Mondavi Winery.

■**Consider skipping Napa.** If you've got less than two days to spend in the Wine Country, dip into the Carneros area or the Sonoma Valley rather than Napa Valley or northern Sonoma County. Though you might find fewer big-name wineries and critically acclaimed restaurants, these regions are only about an hour away from San Francisco . . . if you don't hit traffic.

■**Divide your attention.** If you're lucky enough to have three nights or more here, split your overnights between Napa and Sonoma to easily see the best that both counties have to offer.

Domaine Carneros.

AT THE BAR

In most tasting rooms, you'll be handed a list of the wines available that day. The wines will be listed in a suggested tasting order, starting with the lightest-bodied whites, progressing to the most intense reds, and ending with dessert wines. If you can't decide which wines to choose, tell the server what types of wines you usually like and ask for a recommendation.

The server will pour you an ounce or so of each wine you select. As you taste it, feel free to take notes or ask questions. Don't be shy—the staff are there to educate you about the wine. If you don't like a wine, or you've simply tasted enough, feel free to pour the rest into one of the dump buckets on the bar.

TOURS

Tours tend to be the most exciting (and the most crowded) in September and October, when the harvest and crushing are underway. Tours typically last from 30 minutes to an hour and give you a brief overview of the wine-making process. At some of the older wineries, the tour guide might focus on the history of the property.

■ TIP→ If you plan to take any tours, wear comfortable shoes, since you might be walking on wet floors or dirt or gravel pathways or stepping over hoses or other equipment.

MONEY-SAVING TIPS

■ Many hotels and B&Bs distribute coupons for free or discounted tastings to their guests—don't forget to ask.

■ If you and your travel partner don't mind sharing a glass, servers are happy to let you split a tasting.

■ Some wineries will refund all or part of the tasting fee if you buy a bottle. Usually one fee is waived per bottle purchased, though sometimes you must buy two or more.

■ Most wineries will waive the fee if you join their wine club program. This typically commits you to buying a certain number of bottles on a regular basis, so be sure you really like the wines before signing up.

Preston Vineyards bottles only estate-grown grapes.

TOP 2-DAY ITINERARIES

First-Timer's Napa Tour

Start: Oxbow Public market, Napa. Get underway by browsing the shops selling wines, spices, locally grown produce, and other fine foods, for a taste of what the Wine Country has to offer.

Inglenook, Rutherford. The tour here is a particularly fun way to learn about the history

of Napa winemaking—and you can see the old, atmospheric, ivy-covered château.

Frog's Leap, Rutherford. Its friendly, unpretentious, and knowledgeable staff makes this place great for wine newbies. (Make sure you get that reservation lined up.)

Dinner and Overnight: St. Helena. Splurge at Meadowood Napa Valley and you won't need to leave the property for

Domaine Carneros

di Rosa Preserve

121

12

Old Sonoma Rd.

Oxbow Public Market

Napa

29

NAPA COUNTY

Robert Mondavi

Far Niente

Yountville

Oakville

KEY

First-Timer's Napa Tour

Wine Buff's Tour

Silverado Trail

Stag's Leap Wine Cellars

Wine Buff's Tour

Start: Stag's Leap Wine Cellars, Yountville. Famed for its Cabernet Sauvignon and Bordeaux blends.

Beaulieu Vineyard, Rutherford. Pony up the extra fee to visit the reserve tasting room to try the flagship Cabernet Sauvignon.

Mumm Napa, Rutherford. Come for the bubbly—which is available in a variety of tastings—stay for the photography exhibits.

Dinner and Overnight: Yountville. Have dinner at one of the Thomas Keller restaurants. Splurge at Bardessono; save at

Maison Fleurie.

Next Day: Robert Mondavi, Oakville. Spring for the reserve room tasting so you can sip the top-of-the-line wines, especially the Cabernet Sauvignon. Head across Highway 29 to the Oakville Grocery to pick up a picnic lunch.

10

an extravagant dinner at its restaurant. Save at El Bonita Motel with dinner at Gott's.

Next Day: Poke around St. Helena's shops, then drive to Yountville for lunch.

di Rosa, Napa. Call ahead to book a one- or two-hour tour of the acres of gardens and galleries here

showcasing about 2,000 artworks.

Domaine Carneros, Napa. Toast your trip with a glass of outstanding bubbly.

Sonoma Backroads

0 ____ 4 miles
0 ____ 4 km

0 ____ 3 miles
0 ____ 3 km

Start: Iron Horse Vineyards, Russian River Valley.
Soak up a view of vine-covered hills and Mount St. Helena while sipping a sparkling wine or Pinot Noir at this beautifully rustic spot.

Hartford Family Winery, Russian River Valley.
A terrific source for Pinot Noir and Chardonnay, the stars of this valley.

Dinner and Overnight: Forestville. Go all out with a stay at the Farmhouse Inn, whose award-winning restaurant is one of the best in all of Sonoma.

Next Day: Westside Road, Russian River Valley.
This scenic route, which follows the river, is crowded with worthwhile wineries like Gary Farrell and Rochioli—but it's not crowded with visitors. Pinot fans will find a lot to love.

Matanzas Creek Winery, near Santa Rosa.
End on an especially relaxed note with a walk through the lavender fields (best in June).

Far Niente, Oakville. You have to make a reservation and the fee for the tasting and tour is steep, but the

payoff is an especially intimate winery experience. You'll taste excellent Cabernet and Chardonnay, then end your trip on a sweet note with a dessert wine.

WINE TASTING 101

TAKE A GOOD LOOK.

Hold your glass by the stem, raise it to the light, and take a close look at the wine. Check for clarity and color. (This is easiest to do if you can hold the glass in front of a white background.) Any tinge of brown usually means that the wine is over the hill or has gone bad.

BREATHE DEEP.

1. Sniff the wine once or twice to see if you can identify any smells.

2. Swirl the wine gently in the glass. Aerating the wine this way releases more of its aromas. (It's called "volatilizing the esters," if you're trying to impress someone.)

3. Take another long sniff. You might notice that experienced wine tasters spend more time sniffing the wine than drinking it. This is because this step is where the magic happens. The number of scents you might detect is almost endless, from berries, apricots, honey, and wildflowers to leather, cedar, or even tar. Does the wine smell good to you? Do you detect any "off" flavors, like wet dog or sulfur?

Sniff

AT LAST! TAKE A SIP.

1. Swirl the wine around your mouth so that it makes contact with all your taste buds and releases more of its aromas. Think about the way the wine feels in your mouth. Is it watery or rich? Is it crisp or silky? Does it have a bold flavor, or is it subtle? The weight and intensity of a wine are called its body.

2. Hold the wine in your mouth for a few seconds and see if you can identify any developing flavors. More complex wines will reveal many different flavors as you drink them.

SPIT OR SWALLOW.

The pros typically spit, since they want to preserve their palate (and sobriety!) for the wines to come, but you'll find that swallowers far outnumber the spitters in the winery tasting rooms. Whether you spit or swallow, notice the flavor that remains after the wine is gone (the finish).

Sip

DODGE THE CROWDS

To avoid bumping elbows in the tasting rooms, look for wineries off the main drags of Highway 29 in Napa and Highway 12 in Sonoma. The back roads of the Russian River, Dry Creek, and Alexander valleys, all in Sonoma, are excellent places to explore. In Napa, try the northern end. Also look for wineries that are open by appointment only; they tend to schedule visitors carefully to avoid a big crush at any one time.

HOW WINE IS MADE

1. CRUSHING
Harvested grapes go into a stemmer-crusher, which separates stems from fruit and crushes the grapes to release "free-run" juice.

2. PRESSING
Remaining juice is gently extracted from grapes. Usually done by pressing grapes against the walls of a tank with an inflatable bladder.

3. FERMENTING
Extracted juice (and also grape skins and pulp, when making red wine) goes into stainless-steel tanks or oak barrels to ferment. During fermentation, sugars convert to alcohol.

4. AGING
Wine is stored in stainless-steel or oak casks or barrels to develop flavors.

5. RACKING
Wine is transferred to clean barrels; sediment is removed. Wine may be filtered and fined (clarified) to improve its clarity, color, and sometimes flavor.

6. BOTTLING
Wine is bottled either at the winery or at a special facility, then stored again for bottle-aging.

WHAT'S AN APPELLATION?

A specific region with a particular set of grape-growing conditions, such as soil type, climate, and elevation, is called an appellation. What makes things a little confusing is that appellations, which are defined by the Alcohol and Tobacco Tax and Trade Bureau, often overlap. California is an appellation, for example, but so is the Napa Valley. Napa and Sonoma counties are each county appellations, but they, too, are divided into even smaller regions, usually called subappellations or AVAs (American Viticultural Areas). You'll hear a lot about these AVAs from the staff in the tasting rooms; they might explain, for example, why the Russian River Valley AVA is such an excellent place to grow Pinot Noir grapes.

By law, if the label on a bottle of wine lists the name of an appellation, then at least 85% of the grapes in that wine must come from that appellation.

with elegant boutiques and restaurants, and casual Calistoga, known for spas and hot springs, has the feel of an Old West frontier town.

NAPA

46 miles northeast of San Francisco

Visitors who glimpse Napa's malls and big-box stores from Highway 29 often speed past the town on the way to the more seductive Yountville or St. Helena. But Napa is changing. After many years as a blue-collar burg detached from the Wine Country scene, Napa has spent the past decade reshaping its image.

A recently completed walkway that follows the Napa River has made downtown more pedestrian-friendly, and each year high-profile new restaurants pop up. The shopping has become more chic and varied, and the Oxbow Public Market, a klatch of high-end food purveyors, is popular with locals and tourists. If you establish your base in Napa, you'll undoubtedly want to explore the wineries amid the surrounding countryside, but plan on spending at least a half a day strolling the downtown district of the valley's least pretentious town.

GETTING HERE AND AROUND

Downtown Napa lies a mile east of Highway 29—take the 1st Street exit and follow the signs. Ample parking, much of it free for the first three hours and some for the entire day, is available on or near Main Street. Several VINE buses serve downtown and beyond.

EXPLORING
TOP ATTRACTIONS

Fodor'sChoice
★
Artesa Vineyards & Winery. From a distance the modern, minimalist architecture of Artesa blends harmoniously with the surrounding Carneros landscape, but up close its pools, fountains, and outdoor sculptures make a vivid impression. So, too, do the wines crafted by Mark Beringer—a great-great-grandson of the 19th-century Napa winemaking pioneer Jacob Beringer—who focuses on Chardonnay and Pinot Noir but also produces Cabernet Sauvignon and other limited-release wines such as Albariño and Tempranillo. You can taste wines by themselves or paired with chocolate ($50), cheese ($60), tapas ($60), and gourmet small bites ($80). ⊠ *1345 Henry Rd., off Old Sonoma Rd. and Dealy La.* ☎ *707/224-1668* ⊕ *www.artesawinery.com* ⊡ *Tastings $15–$80, tours $20–$45* ⊙ *Daily 10–5, winery tour daily at 11 and 2.*

Fodor'sChoice
★
di Rosa. About 2,000 works from the 1960s to the present by Northern California artists are displayed on this 217-acre art property. They can be found not only in galleries and in the former residence of its late founder, Rene di Rosa, but also on every lawn, in every courtyard, and even on the lake. Some works were commissioned especially for di Rosa, among them Paul Kos's meditative *Chartres Bleu*, a video installation in a chapel-like setting that replicates a stained-glass window from the cathedral in Chartres, France. ■TIP→ You can view the current temporary exhibition and a few permanent works at the Gatehouse Gallery, but to experience the breadth of this incomparable collection you'll need to book a tour. ⊠ *5200 Sonoma Hwy./Hwy. 121*

Wine and contemporary art find a home at di Rosa.

☎ 707/226–5991 ⊕ www.dirosaart.org ✉ Gatehouse Gallery $5, tours $12–$15 ⊘ Wed.–Sun. 10–4.

Fodor's Choice
★
Domaine Carneros. A visit to this majestic château is an opulent way to enjoy the Carneros District—especially in fine weather, when the vineyard views are spectacular. The château was modeled after an 18th-century French mansion owned by the Taittinger family. Carved into the hillside beneath the winery, the cellars produce delicate sparkling wines reminiscent of those made by Taittinger, using only Los Carneros AVA grapes. The winery sells full glasses, flights, and bottles of its wines, which also include Chardonnay, Pinot Noir, and other still wines. Enjoy them all with cheese and charcuterie plates, caviar, or smoked salmon. Seating is in the Louis XV–inspired salon or on the terrace overlooking the vines. The tour here covers traditional methods of making sparkling wines. ✉ 1240 Duhig Rd., at Hwy. 121 ☎ 707/257–0101, 800/716–2788 ⊕ www.domainecarneros.com ✉ Tastings $7–$30, tour $30 ⊘ Daily 10–5:45; tour daily at 11, 1, and 3.

10

Fodor's Choice
★
The Hess Collection. About 9 miles northwest of Napa, up a winding road ascending Mt. Veeder, this winery is a delightful discovery. The limestone structure, rustic from the outside but modern and airy within, contains Swiss owner Donald Hess's art collection, including large-scale works by contemporary artists such as Andy Goldsworthy, Anselm Kiefer, and Robert Rauschenberg. Cabernet Sauvignon is a major strength, and the 19 Block Cuvée, Mt. Veeder, a Cabernet blend, shows off the Malbec and other estate varietals. ■TIP➜ Food-wine pairings include one with chocolates that go well with the Mount Veeder Cabernet Sauvignon. ✉ 4411 Redwood Rd., west off Hwy. 29 at Trancas St./Redwood Rd.

exit ☎ *707/255–1144* ⊕ *www.hesscollection.com* ✉ *Art gallery free, tasting $15–$85* ⊙ *Daily 10–5:30; guided tours daily 10:30–3:30.*

Fodor's Choice ★ **Oxbow Public Market.** The market's two-dozen shops, wine bars, and artisanal food producers provide an introduction to Napa Valley's wealth of foods and wines. Swoon over decadent charcuterie at the Fatted Calf, slurp bivalves at Hog Island Oyster Company, or chow down on tacos with homemade tortillas at C Casa. Afterward, sip wine at Ca' Momi Enoteca or sample the barrel-aged cocktails and handcrafted vodka of the Napa Valley Distillery. The owner of C Casa also runs Cate & Co., a bakeshop that makes going gluten-free an absolute delight. ■ TIP➜ Locals head to Model Bakery around 3 pm for hot-from-the-oven "late bake" bread. ✉ *610 and 644 1st St., at McKinstry St.* ⊕ *www. oxbowpublicmarket.com* ✉ *Free* ⊙ *Weekdays 9–9, weekends 10–9; merchants hrs vary.*

WORTH NOTING

Etude Wines. Wine and food seminars are a big draw at Etude, but the most seductive part of a visit here is tasting the suave Pinot Noirs. Though the handsome, modern winery is in Napa County, its flagship Carneros Estate Pinot Noir comes from grapes grown in the Sonoma portion of Los Carneros, as does the rarer Heirloom Carneros Pinot Noir. Both are sophisticated wines whose smooth tannins linger on the palate. These or other Pinots—along with Pinot Gris, Chardonnay, Cabernet Sauvignon, and other wine—are paired with small bites of food at informative tasting seminars ($35). ■ TIP➜ Don't leave without stopping to survey the landscape. You're apt to see (or hear) geese, hawks, egrets, and other wildlife. ✉ *1250 Cuttings Wharf Rd., 1 mile south of Hwy. 121* ☎ *877/586–9361* ⊕ *www.etudewines.com* ✉ *Tastings $15–$35* ⊙ *Daily 10–4:30.*

Napa Valley Wine Train. Several restored Pullman railroad cars travel a scenic route between Napa and St. Helena. Although the Wine Train is no bargain and can feel hokey, the staffers are pleasant and the meals served are generally good. ■ TIP➜ It's best to make this trip during the day, when you can enjoy the vineyard views. ✉ *1275 McKinstry St., off 1st St.* ☎ *707/253–2111, 800/427–4124* ⊕ *www.winetrain.com* ✉ *Lunch and dinner $119* ⊙ *Lunch: Jan. and Feb., Fri.–Sun. 11:30; Mar.– Dec. daily 11:30. Dinner: Jan.–Mar., Sat. 6:30; Apr. and Nov.–Dec., Fri. and Sat. 6:30; May, Fri.–Sun. 6:30; June–Oct., Thurs.–Mon. 6:30.*

St. Clair Brown Winery. Tastings at this women-run "urban winery" a few blocks north of downtown take place in an intimate, light-filled greenhouse. Winemaker Elaine St. Clair, well regarded for her stints at Domaine Carneros and Black Stallion, produces elegant vintages—crisp yet complex whites and smooth, French-style reds whose star is Syrah from grapes grown in the Coombsville appellation. The wines are paired with addictive appetizers that include almonds roasted with rosemary, cumin, and Meyer lemon juice. ■ TIP➜ You can sip single wines by the glass or half glass, or opt for the four-wine sampler. ✉ *850 Vallejo St., off Soscol Ave.* ☎ *707/255–5591* ⊕ *www.stclairbrownwinery.com* ✉ *Tasting $4–$20* ⊙ *Daily 11–8.*

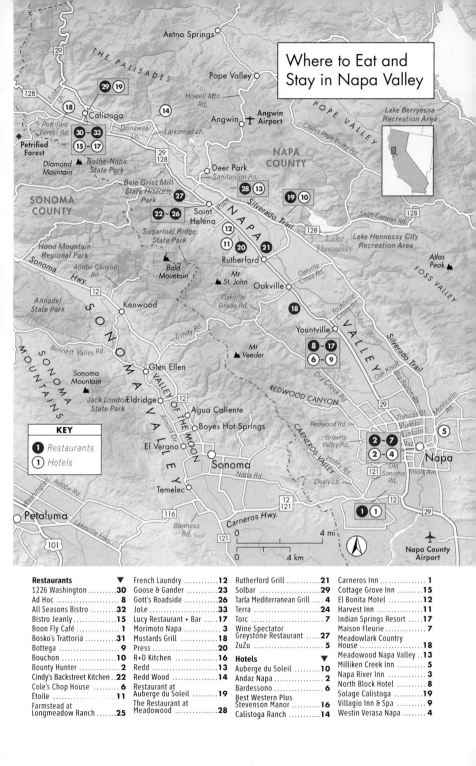

Where to Eat and Stay in Napa Valley

Restaurants ▼

Restaurant	No.
1226 Washington	30
Ad Hoc	8
All Seasons Bistro	32
Bistro Jeanly	15
Boon Fly Café	1
Bosko's Trattoria	31
Bottega	9
Bouchon	10
Bounty Hunter	2
Cindy's Backstreet Kitchen	22
Cole's Chop House	6
Étoile	11
Farmstead at Longmeadow Ranch	25
French Laundry	12
Goose & Gander	23
Gott's Roadside	26
JoLe	33
Lucy Restaurant + Bar	17
Morimoto Napa	3
Mustards Grill	18
Press	20
R+D Kitchen	16
Redd	13
Redd Wood	14
Restaurant at Auberge du Soleil	19
The Restaurant at Meadowood	28
Rutherford Grill	21
Solbar	29
Tarla Mediterranean Grill	4
Terra	24
Torc	7
Wine Spectator Greystone Restaurant	27
ZuZu	5

Hotels ▼

Hotel	No.
Auberge du Soleil	10
Andaz Napa	2
Bardessono	6
Best Western Plus Stevenson Manor	16
Calistoga Ranch	14
Carneros Inn	1
Cottage Grove Inn	15
El Bonita Motel	12
Harvest Inn	11
Indian Springs Resort	17
Maison Fleurie	7
Meadowlark Country House	18
Meadowood Napa Valley	13
Milliken Creek Inn	5
Napa River Inn	3
North Block Hotel	8
Solage Calistoga	19
Villagio Inn & Spa	9
Westin Verasa Napa	4

KEY
❶ Restaurants
① Hotels

Climbing ivy and lily pads decorate the Hess Collection's rustic exterior.

WHERE TO EAT

$$
MODERN
AMERICAN
Fodor's Choice
★

✕ **Boon Fly Café.** This small spot melds rural charm with industrial chic. Outside, swings occupy the porch of a modern red barn; inside, things get sleek with high ceilings and galvanized-steel tabletops. The menu of three squares a day updates American classics such as roasted pork chop, served here with sweet potatoes, and chicken and waffles. The flatbread topped with bacon, Point Reyes blue cheese, and portobello mushrooms is a local favorite. There's a good selection of wines by the glass. ■TIP→ One of the rare Wine Country restaurants open all day, Boon Fly makes a convenient midmorning or late-afternoon stop. $ *Average main: $20* ✉ *Carneros Inn, 4048 Sonoma Hwy.* ☎ *707/299–4870* ⊕ *www.theboonflycafe.com.*

$$$
AMERICAN
Fodor's Choice
★

✕ **Bounty Hunter.** A triple threat, Bounty Hunter is a wine store, wine bar, and restaurant in one. You can stop by for just a glass—about 40 choices are available in both 2- and 5-ounce pours—or a bottle, but it's best to come with an appetite. Every dish on the small menu is a standout, including the pulled-pork and beef brisket sandwiches served with three types of barbecue sauce, the signature beer-can chicken, and meltingly tender St. Louis–style ribs. The space is whimsically rustic, with stuffed game trophies mounted on the wall and leather saddles standing in for seats at a couple of tables. $ *Average main: $26* ✉ *975 1st St., near Main St.* ☎ *707/226–3976* ⊕ *www.bountyhunterwinebar. com* ♦ *Reservations not accepted.*

$$$$
STEAKHOUSE
Fodor's Choice
★

✕ **Cole's Chop House.** When only a fat slab of steak will do, popular Cole's is the best choice in town. The prime steaks—New York, porterhouse, and filet mignon among them—are dry-aged by Allen Brothers of Chicago, purveyors to America's top steak houses. New Zealand lamb chops are the house's non-beef favorite, and seasonal additions might include pork tenderloin. Inside a handsome 1886 stone building, Chops hews to tradition with the starters and sides. Expect oysters Rockefeller, creamed spinach, grilled asparagus with hollandaise, and other standbys, all prepared with finesse. The wine list is borderline epic, with the best of the Napa Valley amply represented. $ *Average main: $38* ✉ *1122 Main St., at Pearl St.* ☎ *707/224–6328* ⊕ *www.coleschophouse. com* 🖚 *Reservations essential* ⊗ *No lunch.*

$$$$
JAPANESE
✕ **Morimoto Napa.** *Iron Chef* star Masuharu Morimoto is the big name behind this downtown Napa hot spot. Organic materials such as twisting grapevines above the bar and rough-hewn wooden tables seem simultaneously earthy and modern, creating a fitting setting for the gorgeously plated Japanese fare, from sashimi served with grated fresh wasabi to elaborate concoctions that include sea-urchin *carbonara*, made with udon noodles. Everything's delightfully overdone, right down to desserts. ■TIP➡ For the full experience, leave the choice up to the chef and opt for the omakase menu ($120–$160). $ *Average main: $44* ✉ *610 Main St., at 5th St.* ☎ *707/252–1600* ⊕ *www. morimotonapa.com.*

$$
MEDITERRANEAN
✕ **Tarla Mediterranean Grill.** The menu at Tarla challenges the Napa Valley's notoriously Italo-centric diners to venture deeper into the Mediterranean. You can build a meal by combining such traditional *mezes* (tapas) as stuffed grape leaves with fresh *tzatziki* (a thick yogurt sauce with cucumber, dill, and mint) and *spanakopita* (phyllo dough stuffed with spinach and feta cheese) with more contemporary, seasonally offered creations—perhaps a crab, spinach, and hearts of palm fondue. The entrées include updates of moussaka and other Mediterranean mainstays, along with fancifully modern items such as beef short ribs braised with a pomegranate-wine sauce and accompanying them with a corn-and-white-truffle risotto. A sister restaurant, Napkins Bar + Grill, at Main and 2nd streets, serves high-style comfort food and stays open late. $ *Average main: $19* ✉ *Andaz Napa, 1480 1st St., at School St.* ☎ *707/255–5599* ⊕ *www.tarlagrill.com.*

$$$
MODERN
AMERICAN
✕ **Torc.** *Torc* means "wild boar" in an early Celtic dialect, and chef Sean O'Toole occasionally incorporates his restaurant's namesake beast into dishes at his eclectic downtown restaurant. Bolognese sauce, for example, might include ground wild boar, tomato, lime, and cocoa. O'Toole has helmed kitchens at top New York City, San Francisco, and Yountville establishments. Torc is the first restaurant he's owned, and he crafts meals with style and precision that are reflected in the gracious service and classy, contemporary decor. ■TIP➡ The Bengali sweet potato–pakora appetizer, which comes with a dreamy-creamy yogurt-truffle dip, has been a hit since day one. $ *Average main: $25* ✉ *1140 Main St., at Pearl St.* ☎ *707/252–3292* ⊕ *www.torcnapa.com* ⊗ *No lunch weekdays.*

$$$
SPANISH
Fodor'sChoice
★
✕ **ZuZu.** A recent seismic retrofitting changed ZuZu's look but not its festive vibe or the sharp focus on Spanish favorites like tapas and paella. Diners down *Cava* (Spanish sparkling wine) or sangria with such dishes as white anchovies with boiled egg and remoulade on grilled bread. Locals revere the paella, made with Spanish Bomba rice. Latin jazz

10

on the stereo helps make this place a popular spot for get-togethers. **■ TIP→ Reservations aren't accepted, so expect a wait on weekends, when a young crowd floods the zone.** [$] *Average main: $29* ✉ *829 Main St., near 3rd St.* ☎ *707/224–8555* 🌐 *www.zuzunapa.com* ✍ *Reservations not accepted* ⏲ *No lunch weekends.*

WHERE TO STAY

$$$ HOTEL Fodor's Choice ★ 🏨 **Andaz Napa.** By far Napa's hippest place to stay, this boutique hotel has luxurious rooms, many of them suites. **Pros:** proximity to downtown restaurants, theaters, and tasting rooms; access to modern fitness center; complimentary snacks and nonalcoholic beverages. **Cons:** parking can be a challenge on weekends; unremarkable views from some rooms. [$] *Rooms from: $309* ✉ *1450 1st St.* ☎ *707/224–3900* 🌐 *www.napa.andaz.hyatt.com* 🛏 *50 rooms, 91 suites* 🍴 *No meals.*

$$$$ RESORT Fodor's Choice ★ 🏨 **Carneros Inn.** Freestanding board-and-batten cottages with rocking chairs on each porch are simultaneously rustic and chic at this luxurious property. **Pros:** cottages have lots of privacy; beautiful views from hilltop pool and hot tub; heaters on private patios; excellent Boon Fly Café is open all day. **Cons:** a long drive from destinations up-valley; smallish rooms with limited seating options. [$] *Rooms from: $600* ✉ *4048 Sonoma Hwy./Hwy. 121* ☎ *707/299–4900, 888/400–9000* 🌐 *www.thecarnerosinn.com* 🛏 *76 cottages, 10 suites.*

$$$ B&B/INN 🏨 **Milliken Creek Inn.** Wine-and-cheese receptions at sunset set a romantic mood in this hotel's intimate lobby, with its terrace overlooking a lush lawn and the Napa River. **Pros:** soft-as-clouds beds; serene spa; breakfast delivered to your room (or elsewhere on the beautiful grounds). **Cons:** expensive; road noise audible in outdoor areas. [$] *Rooms from: $379* ✉ *1815 Silverado Trail* ☎ *707/255–1197* 🌐 *www.millikencreekinn.com* 🛏 *12 rooms.*

$$ B&B/INN 🏨 **Napa River Inn.** Part of a complex of restaurants, shops, a nightclub, and a spa, this waterfront inn is within easy walking distance of downtown hot spots. **Pros:** wide range of room sizes and prices; near downtown action; pet-friendly. **Cons:** river views could be more scenic; some rooms get noise from nearby restaurants. [$] *Rooms from: $249* ✉ *500 Main St.* ☎ *707/251–8500, 877/251–8500* 🌐 *www.napariverinn.com* 🛏 *65 rooms, 1 suite* 🍴 *Breakfast.*

$$ HOTEL 🏨 **Westin Verasa Napa.** Near the Napa Valley Wine Train depot and the Oxbow market, this spacious resort is sophisticated and soothing. **Pros:** two heated saline pools; most rooms have well-equipped kitchenettes (some have full kitchens); spacious double-headed showers; good value for the price. **Cons:** "amenities fee" added to room rate. [$] *Rooms from: $259* ✉ *1314 McKinstry St.* ☎ *707/257–1800, 800/937–8461* 🌐 *www.westinnapa.com* 🛏 *160 suites, 20 rooms* 🍴 *No meals.*

NIGHTLIFE AND THE ARTS

Fodor's Choice ★ **1313 Main.** Cool, sexy 1313 Main attracts a youngish crowd for top-drawer spirits and sparkling and still wines. The on-site **LuLu's Kitchen** serves comfort food ranging from the classic (mini lobster rolls) to the intricate (shaved black truffle with ricotta) to the highly whimsical (s'mores *semifreddo*). ✉ *1313 Main St., at Clinton St.* ☎ *707/258–1313* 🌐 *www.1313main.com.*

City Winery Napa. A recent makeover transformed the 1879 Napa Valley Opera House into a combination wine bar, restaurant, and live-music venue that features top singer-songwriters and small acts. Many of the three-dozen wines on tap are exclusive to the club from prestigious area wineries. ⊠ *1030 Main St., near 1st St.* ☎ *707/260–1600* ⊕ *www. citywinery.com/napa.*

Empire. This groovy nightclub attached to the Andaz Napa hotel draws locals and tourists for cocktails, gourmet bites, and, on some nights, dancing to DJ music. If the beautiful people in motion don't mesmerize you, perhaps the jellyfishes undulating in their tubular tanks will. ⊠ *1400 1st St., at Franklin St.* ☎ *707/254–8888* ⊕ *empirenapa.com.*

Uptown Theatre. This top-notch live-music venue, a former movie house, attracts B.B. King, Ani DiFranco, Napa Valley resident and winery owner Boz Scaggs, and other performers. ⊠ *1350 3rd St., at Franklin St.* ☎ *707/259–0123* ⊕ *www.uptowntheatrenapa.com.*

YOUNTVILLE

9 miles north of the town of Napa.

These days Yountville is something like Disneyland for food lovers. You could stay here for a week and not exhaust all the options—several of them owned by the French Laundry's Thomas Keller—and the tiny town is full of small inns and high-end hotels that cater to those who prefer to walk (not drive) after an extravagant meal. It's also well located for excursions to many big-name Napa wineries, especially those in the Stags Leap District, from which big, bold Cabernet Sauvignons helped make the Napa Valley's wine-making reputation.

GETTING HERE AND AROUND

Downtown Yountville sits just off Highway 29. Approaching from the south take the Yountville exit—from the north take Madison—and proceed to Washington Street, home to the major shops and restaurants. Yountville Cross Road connects downtown to the Silverado Trail, along which many noted wineries do business. The free Yountville Trolley serves the town daily from 10 am to 7 pm (on-call service until 11 except on Sunday).

Contact Yountville Trolley ☎ *707/944–1234 10 am–7 pm, 707/312–1509 7–11 pm.*

EXPLORING
TOP ATTRACTIONS

Domaine Chandon. On a knoll shaded by ancient oak trees, this French-owned maker of sparkling wines claims one of Yountville's prime pieces of real estate. Chandon is best known for bubblies, but the still wines—Cabernet Sauvignon, Chardonnay, Pinot Meunier, and Pinot Noir—are also worth a try. Tours of the production facility, which focus on how the winemakers adapt traditional Champagne-making methods to 21st-century wine science and technology, end with a seated tasting. For the complete experience, order hors d'oeuvres to accompany the wines in the tasting room. ⊠ *1 California Dr., at Solano Ave., west of Hwy. 29* ☎ *707/204–7530, 888/242–6366* ⊕ *www.chandon.com* ⊠ *Tastings $18–$30, tours $40–$45* ⊙ *Daily 10–5; tours daily at 10:30, 11:30, and 3.*

10

Ma(i)sonry Napa Valley. An art-and-design gallery that also pours the wines of two-dozen limited-production wineries, Ma(i)sonry occupies an atmospheric stone manor house constructed in 1904. Tasting flights can be sampled in fair weather in the beautiful garden, in a private nook, or at the communal redwood table, and in any weather indoors among the contemporary artworks and some well-chosen *objets*—which might include 17th-century furnishings, industrial lamps, or slabs of petrified wood. ■TIP➜ Walk-ins are welcome space permitting, but during summer, at harvest time, and on weekends and holidays it's best to book in advance. ✉ *6711 Washington St., at Pedroni St.* ☎ *707/944–0889* ⊕ *www.maisonry.com* ✆ *Tasting $15–$35* ☾ *Sun.–Thurs. daily 10–6, Fri. and Sat. daily 10–7; check for later hrs in summer and early fall.*

Stag's Leap Wine Cellars. A 1973 Stag's Leap Cabernet Sauvignon put this winery and the Napa Valley on the oenological map by placing first in the famous Paris tasting of 1976. The grapes for that wine came from a vineyard visible from a new stone-and-glass tasting room that is scheduled to open in fall 2014. The room will have views of a second fabled Cabernet vineyard and the promontory that gives both the winery and the Stags Leap District AVA their names. ■TIP➜ A $30 tasting includes the top-of-the-line estate-grown Cabernets, which sell for more than $100; a $15 tasting of more modestly priced wines is also available. ✉ *5766 Silverado Trail, at Wappo Hill Rd., Napa* ☎ *707/944–2020, 866/422–7523* ⊕ *www.cask23.com* ✆ *Tastings $15–$30, tour $40* ☾ *Daily 10–4:30; tours by appointment.*

WORTH NOTING

Robert Sinskey Vineyards. Although the winery produces a well-regarded Stags Leap Cabernet Sauvignon, two supple red blends called Marcien and POV, and white wines, Sinskey is best known for its intense, brambly Carneros District Pinot Noirs. All the grapes are grown in organic, certified biodynamic vineyards. The influence of Robert's wife, Maria Helm Sinskey—a chef and cookbook author and the winery's culinary director—is evident during the tastings, which are accompanied by a few bites of food with each wine. ■TIP➜ The Farm to Table Tour ($75) takes in the winery's gardens and ends with a seated pairing of food and wine. ✉ *6320 Silverado Trail, at Yountville Cross Rd., Napa* ☎ *707/944–9090* ⊕ *www.robertsinskey.com* ✆ *Tasting $25, tour $75* ☾ *Daily 10–4:30; tours daily at 11 by appointment.*

WHERE TO EAT

$$$$
MODERN
AMERICAN
✕ **Ad Hoc.** At this casual spot, superstar chef Thomas Keller offers a single, fixed-price menu ($52) nightly, with a small lineup of decadent brunch items served on Sunday. The dinner selection might include a juicy pork loin and buttery polenta, served family style, or a delicate *panna cotta* with a citrus glaze. The dining room is warmly low-key, with zinc-top tables, wine served in tumblers, and rock and jazz on the stereo. Call a day ahead to find out the next day's menu. ■TIP➜ From Thursday through Saturday, except in winter, you can pick up a boxed lunch to go—the buttermilk fried chicken one is delicious—at the on-site and aptly named Addendum. Ⓢ *Average main: $52* ✉ *6476 Washington St., at Oak Circle* ☎ *707/944–2487* ⊕ *www.adhocrestaurant.com* ☾ *No lunch Mon.–Sat. No dinner Tues. and Wed.*

$$$ FRENCH 🍴 **Bistro Jeanty.** French classics and obscure delicacies tickle patrons' palates at chef Philippe Jeanty's genteel country bistro. Jeanty prepares the greatest hits—escargots, cassoulet, *daube de boeuf* (beef stewed in red wine)—with the utmost precision and turns out pike dumplings and lamb tongue with equal élan. Regulars often start with the extraordinary, rich tomato soup in a flaky puff pastry before proceeding to sole *meunière*, slow-roasted pork shoulder, or coq au vin (always choosing the simple, suggested side: thin egg noodles cooked with just the right amount of butter and salt). Chocolate pot de crème, warm apple tart tartin, and other authentic desserts complete the French sojourn. [$] *Average main: $26* ✉ *6510 Washington St., at Mulberry St.* ☎ *707/944–0103* 🌐 *www.bistrojeanty.com.*

$$$ ITALIAN 🍴 **Bottega.** The food at chef Michael Chiarello's trattoria is simultaneously soulful and inventive, transforming local ingredients into regional Italian dishes with a twist. The antipasti shine: you can order grilled short-rib meatballs, house-made charcuterie, or incredibly fresh fish. Potato gnocchi might be served with pumpkin *fonduta* (Italian-style fondue) and roasted root vegetables, and hearty main courses such as twice-cooked pork chops with peck seasoning might be accompanied by cinnamon stewed plums and crispy black kale. The vibe is festive, with exposed-brick walls and an open kitchen, but service is spot-on, and the wine list includes interesting choices from Italy and California. [$] *Average main: $27* ✉ *V Marketplace, 6525 Washington St., near Mulberry St.* ☎ *707/945–1050* 🌐 *www.botteganapavalley.com* ⏲ *No lunch Mon.*

$$$ FRENCH 🍴 **Bouchon.** The team that created the French Laundry is also behind this place, where everything—the lively and crowded zinc-topped bar, the elbow-to-elbow seating, the traditional French onion soup—could have come straight from a Parisian bistro. Roast chicken with sautéed chicken livers and button mushrooms, and steamed mussels served with crispy, addictive *frites* (french fries) are among the dishes served. ■ **TIP→ The adjacent Bouchon Bakery sells marvelous macarons (meringue cookies) in many flavors, along with brownies, pastries, and other baked goods.** [$] *Average main: $27* ✉ *6534 Washington St., near Humboldt St.* ☎ *707/944–8037* 🌐 *www.bouchonbistro.com.*

10

$$$$ AMERICAN Fodor's Choice ★ 🍴 **Étoile.** Domaine Chandon's quietly elegant restaurant seems built for romance, with delicate orchids on each table and views of the wooded grounds from the large windows. Chef Perry Hoffman has racked up numerous awards for his sophisticated California cuisine. The menu might include a salad of tender Spanish octopus and heirloom melon or a slow-poached egg and caviar on a blini as preludes to entrées such as roulade of rabbit prepared with applewood bacon and chanterelles. Four- and six-course tasting menus can be ordered with or without wine pairings. The wine list features Domaine Chandon sparklers but is strong in wines from throughout California as well. [$] *Average main: $34* ✉ *1 California Dr., at Solano Ave., west of Hwy. 29* ☎ *888/242–6366* 🌐 *www.chandon.com/etoile-restaurant* ⏲ *Closed Jan. and Tues. and Wed.*

$$$$ AMERICAN Fodor's Choice ★ 🍴 **French Laundry.** An old stone building laced with ivy houses the most acclaimed restaurant in the Napa Valley—and, indeed, one of the most highly regarded in the country. The two nine-course prix-fixe menus (both $270), one of which highlights vegetables, vary, but

"oysters and pearls," a silky dish of pearl tapioca with oysters and white sturgeon caviar, is a signature starter. Some courses rely on luxe ingredients like *calotte* (cap of the rib eye), while others take humble foods such as fava beans and elevate them to art. Many courses also offer the option of "supplements"—sea urchin, for instance, or black truffles. ■TIP➜ Reservations are hard-won here; to get one call two months ahead to the day at 10 am, on the dot. $ *Average main: $270* ✉ *6640 Washington St., at Creek St.* ☎ *707/944–2380* ⊕ *www.frenchlaundry.com* 🍴 *Reservations essential* 🏛 *Jacket required* 🌙 *No lunch Mon.–Thurs.*

$$$$ ✕ **Lucy Restaurant & Bar.** In a sleek modern space radiating offhand elegance, Lucy seduces with sophisticated flavors and suave service. Chef Victor Scargle builds his menu around produce from an on-site garden. Being one of its farmers he's intimately acquainted with its bounty, which includes the components of the (truly) freshly dug carrot salad. Sunchoke soup and ahi tuna ceviche also make excellent starters, and you can stay small even with the entrées, which come in full and half portions. A modern take on duck à l'orange is a consistent pleaser, but game diners can opt for a chop—in this case antelope—served with wild rice and tangy huckleberry jus. The sommelier, formerly of the French Laundry and New York City's Per Se, graciously guides diners through the well-conceived wine list. $ *Average main: $33* ✉ *Bardessono, 6526 Yount St., at Finnell St.* ☎ *707/204–6030* ⊕ *www.bardessono.com/restaurant_bar.*

MODERN
AMERICAN

$$$ ✕ **Mustards Grill.** Cindy Pawlcyn's Mustards fills day and night with fans of her hearty cuisine. The menu mixes updated renditions of traditional American dishes (what Pawlcyn dubs "deluxe truck stop classics")— among them barbecued baby back pork ribs and a lemon-lime tart piled high with browned meringue—with more fanciful choices such as sweet corn tamales with tomatillo-avocado salsa and wild mushrooms. A black-and-white marble tile floor and upbeat artworks keep the mood jolly. $ *Average main: $27* ✉ *7399 St. Helena Hwy./Hwy. 29, 1 mile north of Yountville, Napa* ☎ *707/944–2424* ⊕ *www.mustardsgrill.com.*

AMERICAN

$$$ ✕ **Redd.** The minimalist dining room here seems a fitting setting for chef Richard Reddington's up-to-date menu. The culinary influences include California, Mexico, Europe, and Asia, but the food always feels modern and never fussy. The glazed pork belly with apple purée, set amid a pool of soy caramel, is a prime example of the East-meets-West style. The seafood preparations—among them petrale sole, clams, and chorizo poached in a saffron-curry broth—are deft variations on the original dishes. For the full experience, consider the five-course tasting menu ($80 per person, $125 with wine pairing). ■TIP➜ For a quick bite, order small plates and a cocktail and sit at the bar. $ *Average main: $30* ✉ *6480 Washington St., at Oak Circle* ☎ *707/944–2222* ⊕ *www.reddnapavalley.com* 🍴 *Reservations essential.*

MODERN
AMERICAN
Fodor's Choice
★

$$ ✕ **Redd Wood.** Chef Richard Reddington's casual restaurant specializes in thin-crust wood-fired pizzas and contemporary variations on rustic Italian classics. The cool nonchalance of the industrial decor mirrors the service, which is less officious than elsewhere in town, and the cuisine itself. The glazed beef short ribs, for instance, seem like yet another fancy take on a down-home favorite until you realize how cleverly the sweetness

ITALIAN

of the glaze plays off the creamy polenta and the piquant splash of salsa verde. Redd Wood does for Italian comfort food what nearby Mustards Grill does for the American version: it spruces it up but retains its innate pleasures. [$] *Average main: $22* ✉ *North Block Hotel, 6755 Washington St., at Madison St.* ☎ *707/299–5030* 🌐 *www.redd-wood.com.*

WHERE TO STAY

$$$$ RESORT Fodor's Choice ★ 🏨 **Bardessono.** Although Bardessono bills itself as the "greenest luxury hotel in America," there's nothing spartan about its accommodations; arranged around four landscaped courtyards, the rooms have luxurious organic bedding, gas fireplaces, and huge bathrooms with walnut floors. **Pros:** large rooftop lap pool; exciting restaurant; excellent spa, with in-room treatments available; polished service. **Cons:** expensive; limited view from some rooms. [$] *Rooms from: $550* ✉ *6526 Yount St.* ☎ *707/204–6000* 🌐 *www.bardessono.com* 🛏 *56 rooms, 6 suites* 🍴 *No meals.*

$ B&B/INN 🏨 **Maison Fleurie.** A stay at this comfortable inn places you within easy walking distance of Yountville's fine restaurants. **Pros:** smallest rooms a bargain; outdoor hot tub; pool (open in season); free bike rental. **Cons:** breakfast room can be crowded at peak times. [$] *Rooms from: $160* ✉ *6529 Yount St.* ☎ *707/944–2056, 800/788–0369* 🌐 *www.maisonfleurienapa.com* 🛏 *13 rooms* 🍴 *Breakfast.*

$$$$ HOTEL 🏨 **North Block Hotel.** With a chic Tuscan style, this 20-room hotel has dark-wood furniture and soothing decor in brown and sage. **Pros:** extremely comfortable beds; attentive service; room service by Redd Wood restaurant. **Cons:** outdoor areas get some traffic noise. [$] *Rooms from: $420* ✉ *6757 Washington St.* ☎ *707/944–8080* 🌐 *northblockhotel.com* 🛏 *20 rooms* 🍴 *Breakfast.*

$$$ RESORT 🏨 **Villagio Inn & Spa.** With a layout that resembles a Tuscan village, this relaxing haven has streamlined furnishings, subdued color schemes, and high ceilings that create a sense of spaciousness in the guest rooms, each of which has a wood-burning fireplace and, beyond louvered doors, a balcony or a patio. **Pros:** amazing buffet breakfast; no extra charge for the spa facilities; steps from many dining options. **Cons:** can be bustling with large groups; highway noise audible from many balconies or patios. [$] *Rooms from: $375* ✉ *6481 Washington St.* ☎ *707/944–8877, 800/351–1133* 🌐 *www.villagio.com* 🛏 *86 rooms, 26 suites* 🍴 *Breakfast.*

10

SPORTS AND THE OUTDOORS

BALLOONING

Napa Valley Aloft. Between 8 and 12 passengers soar over the Napa Valley in balloons that launch from downtown Yountville. The rates include preflight refreshments and a huge breakfast. ✉ *V Marketplace, 6525 Washington St., near Mulberry St.* ☎ *707/944–4400, 855/944–4408* 🌐 *www.nvaloft.com* 🎟 *From $220 per person.*

Napa Valley Balloons. The valley's oldest balloon company offers trips that are elegant from start to finish. Satisfied customers include Chelsea Clinton and *Today* show host Matt Lauer. ✉ *Domaine Chandon, 1 California Dr., at Solano Ave., west of Hwy. 29* ☎ *707/944–0228, 800/253–2224* 🌐 *www.napavalleyballoons.com* 🎟 *$215 per person.*

BIKING

Napa Valley Bike Tours. With dozens of wineries within 5 miles, this shop makes a fine starting point for vineyard and wine-tasting excursions. The outfit also rents bikes. ⊠ *6500 Washington St., at Mulberry St.* ☎ *707/944–2953* ⊕ *www.napavalleybiketours.com* ☒ *From $89.*

SPAS

Spa Villagio. The perks abound at this 13,000-square-foot Mediterranean-style facility equipped with huge spa suites—complete with flat-screen TVs and wet bars—that are perfect for couples and groups. The pièce de résistance among the treatments, the Suite Sensations experience ($575), draws on Asian, Mediterranean, and Middle-Eastern traditions and includes matching wine-and-food pairings. Body peels, facials, manicures, and massages are among the à la carte services. ⊠ *6481 Washington St., at Oak Circle* ☎ *707/948–5050, 800/351–1133* ⊕ *www.villagio.com/spavillagio* ☒ *Treatments $75–$575.*

SHOPPING

V Marketplace. The clothing boutiques, art galleries, and gift stores amid this vine-covered market include NapaStyle, which sells cookbooks, kitchenware, and prepared foods that are perfect for picnics. ⊠ *6525 Washington St., near Mulberry St.* ☎ *707/944–2451* ⊕ *www.vmarketplace.com.*

OAKVILLE

2 miles northwest of Yountville.

A large butte that runs east–west just north of Yountville blocks the cooling fogs from the south, facilitating the myriad microclimates of the Oakville AVA, home to several high-profile wineries.

GETTING HERE AND AROUND

Driving along Highway 29, you'll know you've reached Oakville when you see the Oakville Grocery on the east side of the road. You can reach Oakville from the Sonoma County town of Glen Ellen by heading east on Trinity Road from Highway 12. The twisting route, along the mountain range that divides Napa and Sonoma, eventually becomes the Oakville Grade. The views on this drive are breathtaking, though the continual curves make it unsuitable for those who suffer from motion sickness.

EXPLORING

TOP ATTRACTIONS

Far Niente. Though the fee for the combined tour and tasting is high, guests at Far Niente are welcomed by name and treated to a glimpse of one of the Napa Valley's most beautiful properties. Small groups are escorted through the historic 1885 stone winery, including some of the 40,000 square feet of caves, for a lesson on the labor-intensive method of making Far Niente's two wines: a Cabernet Sauvignon blend and a Chardonnay. The next stop is the Carriage House, which holds a gleaming collection of classic cars. The tour concludes with a seated tasting of wines and cheeses. ⊠ *1350 Acacia Dr., off Oakville Grade Rd.* ☎ *707/944–2861* ⊕ *www.farniente.com* ☒ *Tasting and tour $65* ☉ *Daily 10–3 by appointment.*

Far Niente's wine cellars have a touch of ballroom elegance.

PlumpJack. With its metal chandelier and wall hangings, the tasting room at this casual winery looks like a stage set for a modern Shakespearean production. (The name "PlumpJack" is a nod to Shakespeare's Falstaff.) A youngish crowd assembles here to sample vintages that include the citrusy reserve Chardonnay and a Merlot that's blended like a Cab, providing the wine sufficient tannins to ensure it can age at least another five years. The luscious Syrah, from Atlas Peak and Carneros grapes, is available only through the winery. ■**TIP→ The Hilltop Tasting and Tour takes in the cellar and grounds and ends with a seated tasting overlooking the vineyards. Limited to six guests, it books up quickly in summer.** ⊠ *620 Oakville Cross Rd., off Silverado Trail* ☎ *707/945–1220* ⊕ *www. plumpjack.com* 🖃 *Tastings $20–$30; tour $30* ⊘ *Daily 10–4; hilltop tour spring and summer Tues.–Fri. at 11 by appointment.*

Oakville Grocery. Built in 1881 as a general store, Oakville Grocery carries unusual and high-end groceries and prepared foods. On busy summer weekends the grocery is often packed with customers stocking up on picnic provisions: meats, cheeses, breads, and hearty sandwiches. ■**TIP→ This is a fine place to sit on a bench and sip an espresso between winery visits.** ⊠ *7856 St. Helena Hwy./Hwy. 29, at Oakville Rd.* ☎ *707/944–8802* ⊕ *www.oakvillegrocery.com.*

WORTH NOTING

Robert Mondavi Winery. The arch at the center of the sprawling mission-style building frames the lawn and the vineyard behind, inviting a stroll under the lovely arcades. You can head for one of the two tasting rooms, but if you've not toured a winery before, the Signature Tour and Tasting ($30) is a good way to learn about oenology, as well as the late Robert Mondavi's role in California wine making. Those new to tasting and mystified by all that swirling and sniffing should consider the 45-minute Wine Tasting Basics experience ($20). Serious wine lovers should opt for the one-hour $55 Exclusive Cellar tasting, during which a server pours and explains limited-production, reserve, and older-vintage wines. ■TIP➔ Concerts, mostly jazz and R&B, take place in summer on the lawn; call ahead for tickets. ✉ *7801 St. Helena Hwy./ Hwy. 29* ☎ *888/766–6328* ⊕ *www.robertmondaviwinery.com* 🍷 *Tastings and tours $15–$55* ⊙ *Daily 10–5; tour times vary.*

RUTHERFORD

2 miles northwest of Oakville.

With its singular microclimate and soil, Rutherford is an important viticultural center, with more big-name wineries than you can shake a corkscrew at. Cabernet Sauvignon is king here. The well-drained, loamy soil is ideal for those vines, and since this part of the valley gets plenty of sun, the grapes develop exceptionally intense flavors.

GETTING HERE AND AROUND
Wineries around Rutherford are dotted along Highway 29 and the parallel Silverado Trail north and south of Rutherford Road/Conn Creek Road, on which wineries can also be found.

EXPLORING
TOP ATTRACTIONS

FAMILY
Fodor's Choice
★

Frog's Leap. John Williams, owner of Frog's Leap, maintains a goofy sense of humor about wine that translates into an entertaining yet informative experience—if you're a novice, the tour here is a fine way to begin your education. You'll taste wines that might include Zinfandel, Cabernet Sauvignon, Merlot, Chardonnay, Sauvignon Blanc, and Frögenbeerenauslese, a variation on the German dessert wine Trockenbeerenauslese. The winery includes a barn built in 1884, 5 acres of organic gardens, an eco-friendly visitor center, and a frog pond topped with lily pads. ■TIP➔ The tour is highly recommended, but you can also just sample wines either inside or on a porch overlooking the garden. ✉ *8815 Conn Creek Rd.* ☎ *707/963–4704, 800/959–4704* ⊕ *www. frogsleap.com* 🍷 *Tasting $20, tour $20* ⊙ *Tastings daily 10–4 by appointment only; tours weekdays at 10:30 and 2:30 by appointment.*

Inglenook. Filmmaker Francis Ford Coppola began his wine-making career in 1975, when he bought part of the historic Inglenook estate. Over the next few decades he reunited the original property acquired by Inglenook founder Gustave Niebaum, purchased Niebaum's ivy-covered 1880s château, and purchased the rights to the Inglenook name. Various tours cover the estate's history, the local climate and geology, the sensory evaluation of wine, and the evolution of Coppola's signature wine, Rubicon, a Cabernet Sauvignon–based blend. Some tastings are held in an opulent, high-ceilinged room, others in a wine-aging cave. ■TIP➔ You can taste wines by the glass (or the bottle) at The Bistro, an on-site wine bar with a picturesque courtyard. ✉ *1991 St. Helena Hwy./Hwy. 29* ☎ *707/968–1100, 800/782–4266* ⊕ *www.inglenook.com* 🍷 *Tastings $45–$60, tours $50–$85* ⊙ *Daily 10–5; call for tour times.*

Frog's Leap's picturesque country charm extends all the way to the white picket fence.

Mumm Napa. Although this is one of California's best-known sparkling-wine producers, enjoying the bubbly from the light-filled tasting room—available in either single flutes or by the flight—isn't the only reason to visit Mumm. An excellent gallery displays 30 Ansel Adams prints and presents temporary exhibits by local photographers. You can even take that glass of crisp Brut Rosé with you as you wander. ■ TIP→ **For a leisurely tasting of library wines while seated on the Oak Terrace ($40), reserve in advance.** ⊠ *8445 Silverado Trail* ☎ *707/967–7700, 800/686–6272* ⊕ *www.mummnapa.com* ⊠ *Tastings $8–$40, tour $25 (includes tasting)* ⊙ *Daily 10–4:45; tours daily at 10, 11, 1, and 3.*

Fodor's Choice

★

Round Pond Estate. Sophisticated wines come from Round Pond, but the estate also produces premium olive oils, most from olives grown and crushed on the property. Informative olive-related seminars begin with a look at some trees and a tour of the high-tech mill, followed by tastings of the aromatic oils, both alone and with house-made red-wine vinegars. You'll also sip wines, but for a full tasting, head across the street to the winery. The basic tasting includes a suave Sauvignon Blanc and Round Pond's supple, well-rounded reds. The flagship Estate Cabernet Sauvignon has the structure and heft of the classic 1970s Rutherford Cabs, but gracefully acknowledges 21st-century palates with smoother, if still sturdy, tannins. The Estate Tasting ($45) pairs small morsels with the wines. ⊠ *875 Rutherford Rd., near Conn Creek Rd.* ☎ *707/302–2575, 888/302–2575* ⊕ *www.roundpond.com* ⊠ *Wine tasting $25, tour and tasting $55; olive mill tour and tasting $45* ⊙ *All tastings and tours by appointment 24–48 hrs in advance.*

WORTH NOTING

Beaulieu Vineyard. The influential André Tchelistcheff (1901–1994), who helped define the California style of wine making, worked his magic here for many years. BV, founded in 1900 by Georges de Latour and his wife, Fernande, is known for its widely distributed Chardonnay, Pinot Noir, and Cabernet Sauvignon wines, but many others are produced in small lots and are available only at the winery. The most famous of the small-lot wines is the flagship Georges De Latour Cabernet Sauvignon, first crafted by Tchelistcheff himself in the late 1930s. ■ TIP→ The historic tour ($35) includes a peek at Prohibition-era artifacts and tastes of finished wines and ones still aging in their barrels. ✉ *1960 St. Helena Hwy./Hwy. 29* ☎ *707/967–5233, 800/264–6918 Ext. 5233* ⊕ *www.bvwines.com* 🍷 *Tasting $15–$50, tours $20* ☉ *Daily 10–5.*

Cakebread Cellars. The Cakebreads, at first Jack and Dolores and these days also their children, have been making luscious, complex Chardonnays, Cabernet Sauvignons, and Sauvignon Blancs since the 1970s. With a portfolio that now includes Merlot, Pinot Noir, and other varietals, Cakebread has built its reputation on crafting food-friendly wines. Case in point: winemaker Julianne Laks's Sauvignon Blanc. Blended with Sèmillon and Sauvignon Musqué grapes and aged lightly in neutral French oak, it's both accessible and sophisticated and the ideal accompaniment to seafood and pasta dishes. A basic tasting includes six current releases; the all-reds option is popular with Cab and Merlot fans. ✉ *8300 St. Helena Hwy./Hwy. 29* ☎ *707/963–5222, 800/588–0298* ⊕ *www.cakebread.com* 🍷 *Tastings $15–$45, tour $25* ☉ *Daily 10–4; tastings and tour by appointment.*

Rutherford Hill Winery. This place is a Merlot lover's paradise in a Cabernet Sauvignon world. When the winery's founders were deciding what grapes to plant, they discovered that the climate and soil conditions resembled those of Pomerol, a region of Bordeaux where Merlot is king. Now owned by the Terlato family, Rutherford Hill has extensive wine caves—nearly a mile of tunnels and passageways. You can glimpse them and the barrels inside on the tours, and you can make your own Merlot at entertaining Saturday blending sessions ($95). The winery's hillside picnic area, amid oak and olive trees, is a magical spot. ■ TIP→ The $35 picnic-reservation fee includes a $20 voucher toward the purchase of wine and two glasses. ✉ *200 Rutherford Hill Rd., east of Silverado Trail* ☎ *707/963–1871* ⊕ *www.rutherfordhill.com* 🍷 *Tastings $20–$75; tour $30 (includes tasting)* ☉ *Daily 10–5; tours daily at 11:30, 1:30, and 3:30.*

WHERE TO EAT

$$$$
MODERN
AMERICAN
Fodor's Choice
★

✗ **Restaurant at Auberge du Soleil.** Possibly the most romantic roost for a dinner in all the Wine Country is a terrace seat at the Auberge du Soleil's illustrious restaurant, and the Mediterranean-inflected cuisine more than matches the dramatic vineyards views. The prix-fixe dinner menu ($105 for three courses, $125 for four; $150 for six-course tasting menu), which relies largely on local produce, might include veal sweetbreads with slow-cooked egg yolk, frisée, fried capers, and salsa verde or prime beef pavé with hand-foraged wild rice and chanterelles. The service is polished, and the wine list is comprehensive. $ *Average* *main: $105* ✉ *Auberge du Soleil, 180 Rutherford Hill Rd., off Silverado Trail* ☎ *707/963–1211, 800/348–5406* 🌐 *www.aubergedusoleil.com* ✍ *Reservations essential.*

$$$ AMERICAN Fodor's Choice ★ 🍴 **Rutherford Grill.** Dark-wood walls, subdued lighting, and red-leather banquettes make for a perpetually clubby mood at this trusty Rutherford hangout. Many of the entrées—steaks, burgers, fish, succulent rotisserie chicken, and barbecued pork ribs—emerge from an oak-fired grill operated by master technicians. So, too, do alluring starters such as the grilled jumbo artichokes and the iron-skillet cornbread, a ton of butter being the secret of success with both. The French dip sandwich is a local legend, and the wine list includes rare selections from Caymus and other celebrated producers at (for Napa) reasonable prices. **TIP→ Between or after wine tastings, the margaritas and other clever cocktails the bartenders shake, stir, and pour are superb palate cleansers.** [$] *Average main: $25* ✉ *1180 Rutherford Rd., at Hwy. 29* ☎ *707/963–1792* 🌐 *www.rutherfordgrill.com* ✍ *Reservations essential.*

WHERE TO STAY

$$$$ RESORT Fodor's Choice ★ 🏨 **Auberge du Soleil.** Taking a cue from the olive-tree-studded landscape, this hotel with a renowned restaurant and spa cultivates a luxurious Mediterranean look—earth-tone tile floors, heavy wood furniture, and terra-cotta colors. **Pros:** stunning views over the valley; spectacular pool and spa areas; the most expensive suites are fit for a superstar. **Cons:** stratospheric prices; least expensive rooms get some noise from the bar and restaurant. [$] *Rooms from: $850* ✉ *180 Rutherford Hill Rd.* ☎ *707/963–1211, 800/348–5406* 🌐 *www.aubergedusoleil.com* 🛏 *31 rooms, 21 suites* 🍽 *Breakfast.*

ST. HELENA

2 miles northwest of Oakville.

Downtown St. Helena is a symbol of how well life can be lived in the Wine Country. Sycamore trees arch over Main Street (Highway 29), a funnel of outstanding restaurants and tempting boutiques. At the north end of town looms the hulking stone building of the Culinary Institute of America. Weathered stone and brick buildings from the late 1800s give off that gratifying whiff of history.

By the time pioneering winemaker Charles Krug planted grapes in St. Helena around 1860, vineyards already existed in the area. Today the town is hemmed in by wineries, and you could easily spend days visiting vintners within a few miles.

GETTING HERE AND AROUND

Downtown St. Helena stretches along Highway 29, which is called Main Street here. Many wineries lie north and south of downtown along Highway 29. More can be found off Silverado Trail, and some of the most scenic spots are on Spring Mountain, which rises southwest of town.

EXPLORING
TOP ATTRACTIONS

Beringer Vineyards. Arguably the Napa Valley's most beautiful winery, the 1876 Beringer Vineyards is also the oldest continuously operating property. In 1884 Frederick and Jacob Beringer built the Rhine House Mansion to serve as Frederick's family home. Today it serves as the reserve tasting room, where you can sample wines surrounded by Belgian art nouveau hand-carved oak and walnut furniture and stained-glass windows. The assortment includes a limited-release Chardonnay, a few big Cabernets, and a luscious white dessert wine named Nightingale. A less expensive tasting takes place in the original stone winery. ■TIP➔ First-time visitors to the valley will learn a lot about the region's wine-making history on the introductory tour. Longer tours, which might pass through a demonstration vineyard or end with a seated tasting in the Rhine House, are also offered. ⊠ *2000 Main St./ Hwy. 29, near Pratt Ave.* ☎ *707/963–8989, 866/708–9463* ⊕ *www. beringer.com* ✉ *Tastings $20–$50, tours $25–$40* ☯ *June–mid-Oct. daily 10–6; mid-Oct.–May daily 10–5; many tours daily, call for times.*

Culinary Institute of America. The West Coast headquarters of the country's leading school for chefs are in the 1889 Greystone Winery, an imposing building that once was the world's largest stone winery. On the ground floor you can check out the quirky Corkscrew Museum and browse a shop stocked with gleaming gadgets and many cookbooks. At the adjacent Flavor Bar you can sample various ingredients (for example, chocolate or olive oil). Plaques upstairs at the Vintners Hall of Fame commemorate winemakers past and present. Beguiling one-hour cooking demonstrations (reservations required) take place on weekends. The student-run Bakery Café by Illy serves soups, salads, sandwiches, and baked goods; the Institute also operates a full restaurant. ⊠ *2555 Main St./ Hwy. 29* ☎ *707/967–1100* ⊕ *www.ciachef.edu* ✉ *Museum and store free, cooking demonstrations $20, tastings $10–$15, tour $10* ☯ *Museum and store: daily 10:30–6 (Mon.–Thurs. 11–5 in winter). Tour: 11:45, 2:45, 5.*

Fodor'sChoice
★

Hall. The award-winning Cabs, Merlots, and an impeccable Syrah produced here are works of art—and of up-to-the-minute organic-farming science and high technology. A new glass-wall tasting center allows you to see in action some of the technology winemaker Steve Leveque employs to craft wines that also include a Cabernet Franc and late-harvest Sauvignon Blanc dessert wines. The Production Tour and Barrel Tasting provides an even more in-depth look. For an understatedly elegant experience, book an Artisan Tasting at Hall's Rutherford winery, where the hilltop vistas enthrall and even the stainless-steel aging tanks are dazzlingly ornate. Tastings take place deep inside a dramatic brick-lined cave. ⊠ *401 St. Helena Hwy./Hwy. 29, near White La.* ☎ *707/967–2626, 800/688–4255* ⊕ *www.hallwines.com* ✉ *Tastings $35–$60; tours (with tastings) $40–$75* ☯ *St. Helena daily: 10–5:30. Rutherford: by appointment only.*

Fodor'sChoice
★

Joseph Phelps Vineyards. An appointment is required for tastings at the winery started by the legendary Joseph Phelps—his son Bill now runs the operation—but it's well worth the effort. Phelps makes fine whites, but the blockbuster wines are reds, particularly the Cabernet

Sauvignon and the flagship Bordeaux-style blend called Insignia. The luscious-yet-subtle Insignia sells for more than $200 a bottle. Luckily, all tastings include the current vintage. The 90-minute seminars include one on wine-and-cheese pairing and another focusing on blending. In the latter you mix the various varietals that go into the Insignia blend. ■TIP→ Through early 2015, a visit to the winery will take place in a temporary tasting pavilion among the vines while the main guest center undergoes renovation. ⊠ *200 Taplin Rd., off Silverado Trail* ☎ *707/963–2745, 800/707–5789* ⊕ *www.josephphelps.com* ⬒ *Tastings $35–$150, seminars $75* ⊗ *Weekdays 9–5, weekends 10–4; tastings by appointment.*

WORTH NOTING

St. Clement Vineyards. A winery steeped in history, St. Clement is blessed with such splendid views that you might drift into reverie even before tasting the signature Bordeaux-style blend, Oroppas. (That's Sapporo spelled backward—the famous Japanese brewery once owned this place.) The tasting room is inside the 1878 Rosenbaum House, named for the wealthy merchant who built it on land purchased from his neighbor, the winemaker Charles Krug. You can also sip wine at café tables on the front porch while taking in views of nearby vineyards and beyond them Howell Mountain. Wines of note include three single-vineyard Cabernet Sauvignons made from grapes grown on Mt. Veeder and Howell and Diamond mountains. ⊠ *2867 St. Helena Hwy. N/Hwy. 29, near Deer Park Rd.* ☎ *707/967–3030* ⊕ *www.stclement. com* ⬒ *Tastings $20–$30* ⊗ *Daily 11–5.*

WHERE TO EAT

$$
MODERN
AMERICAN
Fodor'sChoice
★

✕**Cindy's Backstreet Kitchen.** At her upscale-casual St. Helena outpost, Cindy Pawlcyn serves variations on the comfort food she made popular at Mustards Grill, but spices things up with dishes influenced by Mexican, Central American, and occasionally Asian cuisines. Along with mainstays such as herb-marinated hanger steak, meat loaf with garlic mashed potatoes, and beef and duck burgers served with flawless fries, the menu might include a rabbit tostada or chicken served with avocado salsa and a two-cheese stuffed green chili. Two dessert favorites are the high-style yet homey warm pineapple upside-down cake and the nearly ethereal parfait. Ⓢ *Average main: $21* ⊠ *1327 Railroad Ave., at Hunt St., 1 block east of Main St.* ☎ *707/963–1200* ⊕ *www. cindysbackstreetkitchen.com.*

$$$
MODERN
AMERICAN

✕**Farmstead at Long Meadow Ranch.** Housed in a former barn, Farmstead revolves around an open kitchen where chef Stephen Barber cooks with as many local and organic ingredients as possible. Many of them—including grass-fed beef, fruits and vegetables, eggs, extra-virgin olive oil, wine, and honey—come from the property of parent company Long Meadow Ranch. Entrées might include grilled rainbow trout with wild mushrooms, or potato gnocchi with beef *ragù*, herbs, and Parmesan. Tuesday is the popular pan-fried chicken night—$35 for a three-course meal. ■TIP→ In warm weather, you can dine on an open-air patio among apple trees. Ⓢ *Average main: $23* ⊠ *738 Main St., at Charter Oak Ave.* ☎ *707/963–4555* ⊕ *www.longmeadowranch. com/Farmstead-Restaurant.*

10

$$$ MODERN AMERICAN Fodor's Choice ★ 🍴 **Goose & Gander.** The pairing of food and drink at clubby Goose & Gander is as likely to involve cocktails as it is wine. Main courses such as Scottish salmon with shaved brussels sprouts, chanterelles, and crispy prosciutto work well with starters that include an heirloom chicory salad with smoked trout and cream of mushroom soup made from both wild and cultivated varieties. You might enjoy your meal with a top-notch Chardonnay or Pinot Noir—or a Manhattan made with three kinds of bitters and poured over a hand-carved block of ice. On cold days a fireplace warms the main dining room, and in good weather the outdoor patio is a splendid spot for dining alfresco. **■ TIP→ Year-round the basement bar is a good stop for a drink.** [$] *Average main: $25* ✉ *1245 Spring St., at Oak St.* ☎ *707/967–8779* 🌐 *www.gooseganders.com.*

$ AMERICAN 🍴 **Gott's Roadside.** A 1950s-style outdoor hamburger stand goes upscale at this spot whose customers brave long lines to order breakfast sandwiches, juicy burgers, root-beer floats, and garlic fries. Choices not available a half century ago include the ahi tuna burger and the chili spice–marinated chicken breast served with Mexican slaw. **■ TIP→ Arrive early or late for lunch, or all of the shaded picnic tables on the lawn might be filled.** A second branch does business at Napa's Oxbow Public Market. [$] *Average main: $12* ✉ *933 Main St./Hwy. 29* ☎ *707/963–3486* 🌐 *www.gotts.com* ✍ *Reservations not accepted* [$] *Average main: $12* ✉ *Oxbow Public Market, 644 1st St., at McKinstry St., Napa* ☎ *707/224–6900* ✍ *Reservations not accepted.*

$$$$ MODERN AMERICAN Fodor's Choice ★ 🍴 **Press.** Few taste sensations surpass the combination of a sizzling steak and a Napa Valley red, a union that the chef and sommeliers here celebrate with a reverence bordering on obsession. Beef from carefully selected local and international purveyors is the star—especially the rib eye for two—but chef Stephen Rogers also prepares pork chops and free-range chicken and veal on his cherry-and-almond-wood-fired grill and rotisserie. The cellar holds thousands of wines; if you recall having a great steak with a 1985 Mayacamas Mt. Veeder Cab, you'll be able to re-create, and perhaps exceed, the original event. The kitchen's attention to detail is matched by the efforts at the bar, whose tenders know their way around both rad and trad cocktails. [$] *Average main: $36* ✉ *587 St. Helena Hwy./Hwy. 29, at White La.* ☎ *707/967–0550* 🌐 *www.pressstelena.com* ✍ *Reservations essential* ⏲ *Closed Tues. No lunch.*

$$$$ MODERN AMERICAN Fodor's Choice ★ 🍴 **The Restaurant at Meadowood.** Chef Christopher Kostow has garnered rave reviews—and three Michelin stars for several years running—for creating a unique dining experience. After you reserve your table, your party will be interviewed about food likes and dislikes, allergies, and desired level of culinary adventure. Inspired by these conversations, Kostow will transform seasonal local ingredients, some grown on or near the property, into an elaborate, multi-course experience. If you choose the Tasting Menu option ($225, $450 with wine pairings), you'll enjoy your meal in the romantic dining room, its beautiful finishes aglow with warm lighting. Choose the Counter Menu ($500, $850 with wine pairings), and you and up to three guests can sit inside the kitchen and watch Kostow's team prepare your meal. **■ TIP→ The restaurant also offers a limited, three-course menu ($90) at its bar.** [$] *Average main: $225* ✉ *900 Meadowood La., off Silverado Trail N*

☎ 707/967–1205, 800/458–8080 🌐 www.meadowood.com ⏲ Closed Sun. No lunch.

$$$$ MEDITERRANEAN Fodor's Choice ★ 🍴 **Terra.** For old-school romance and service, many diners return year after year to this quiet favorite in an 1884 fieldstone building. Beloved chef Hiro Sone gives an unexpected twist to Italian and southern French cuisine in such dishes as porcini mushroom soup with grilled Berkshire pork jowl. A few standouts, like the signature sake-marinated black cod in a *shiso* broth, draw on Sone's Japanese background. Homey yet elegant desserts, courtesy of Sone's wife, Lissa Doumani, might include a chocolate brownie parfait with vanilla bean ice cream, caramelized bananas, and fudge sauce. Next door, the lively Bar Terra serves cocktails, local wines, and a menu of smaller, lighter dishes, among them succulent fried rock shrimp served with a chive-mustard sauce. [$] *Average main: $36 ✉ 1345 Railroad Ave., off Hunt Ave. ☎ 707/963–8931 🌐 www.terrarestaurant.com ⏲ Closed Tues. No lunch.*

$$$ MEDITERRANEAN 🍴 **Wine Spectator Greystone Restaurant.** On busy nights at the Culinary Institute's stone-walled restaurant you may find the student chefs toiling in their open stations more entertaining than your dining companions. The dishes prepared are Mediterranean in spirit and emphasize locally grown produce. Typical main courses include seared breast of Sonoma duck with a celery-root purée and house-made pasta with trumpet mushrooms and a sherry cream sauce. **■ TIP→ The terrace, with broad vineyard views and tables shaded by red umbrellas, is a delightful place to dine in fine weather.** [$] *Average main: $26 ✉ 2555 Main St./Hwy. 29 ☎ 707/967–1010 🌐 www.ciachef.edu ⏲ Closed Sun. and Mon. late Dec.–Apr.*

WHERE TO STAY

$ HOTEL 🏨 **El Bonita Motel.** For budget-minded travelers the tidy rooms at this roadside motel are pleasant enough, and the landscaped grounds and picnic tables elevate this property over similar places. **Pros:** cheerful rooms; hot tub; microwaves and mini-refrigerators. **Cons:** road noise is a problem in some rooms. [$] *Rooms from: $149 ✉ 195 Main St./Hwy. 29 ☎ 707/963–3216, 800/541–3284 🌐 www.elbonita.com 🛏 38 rooms, 4 suites 🍴 Breakfast.*

$$$$ HOTEL 🏨 **Harvest Inn.** Although this inn sits just off Highway 29, its patrons remain mostly above the fray, strolling 8 acres of landscaped gardens with views of adjoining vineyards, partaking in spa services, and drifting off to sleep in beds adorned with fancy linens and down pillows. **Pros:** garden setting; spacious rooms; professional staff; off-season packages a good value. **Cons:** some lower-priced rooms lack elegance; high weekend rates; ho-hum breakfast. [$] *Rooms from: $439 ✉ 1 Main St. ☎ 707/963–9463, 800/950–8466 🌐 www.harvestinn.com 🛏 69 rooms, 5 suites 🍴 Breakfast.*

$$$$ RESORT Fodor's Choice ★ 🏨 **Meadowood Napa Valley.** Founded in 1964 as a country club, Meadowood has evolved into a five-star resort, a gathering place for Napa's wine-making community, and a celebrated dining destination. **Pros:** superb restaurant; pleasant hiking trails; gracious service. **Cons:** very expensive; far from downtown St. Helena. [$] *Rooms from: $700 ✉ 900 Meadowood La. ☎ 707/963–3646, 800/458–8080 🌐 www.meadowood.com 🛏 85 rooms, suites, and cottages.*

CALISTOGA

3 miles northwest of St. Helena.

With false-fronted, Old West–style shops and 19th-century inns and hotels lining its main drag, Lincoln Avenue, Calistoga comes across as more down-to-earth than its more polished neighbors. Don't be fooled, though. On its outskirts lie some of the Wine Country's swankest (and priciest) resorts and its most fanciful piece of architecture, the medieval-style Castello di Amorosa.

Calistoga was developed as a tourist-oriented getaway from the start. In 1859 entrepreneur Sam Brannan snapped up 2,000 acres of prime property, intending to use the area's natural hot springs as the centerpiece of a resort complex. Brannan's gamble didn't pay off as he'd hoped, but some of his era's hotels and bathhouses still operate. You can come for an old-school mud bath or a dip in a spring-fed pool at one of them, or go completely 21st century and experience lavish treatments based on the latest innovations in skin and body care.

GETTING HERE AND AROUND

Highway 29 heads east (turn right) at Calistoga, where in town it is signed as Lincoln Avenue. If arriving via the Silverado Trail, head west at Highway 29/Lincoln Avenue.

EXPLORING

TOP ATTRACTIONS

Castello di Amorosa. An astounding medieval structure complete with drawbridge and moat, chapel, stables, and secret passageways, the Castello commands Diamond Mountain's lower eastern slope. Some of the 107 rooms contain replicas of 13th-century frescoes (cheekily signed [the-artist's-name].com), and the dungeon has an actual iron maiden from Nuremberg, Germany. You must pay for a tour to see most of Dario Sattui's extensive eight-level property, though basic tastings include access to part of the complex. Wines of note include several Italian-style wines, including La Castellana, a robust "super Tuscan" blend of Cabernet Sauvignon, Sangiovese, and Merlot; and Il Barone, a praiseworthy cab made largely from Diamond Mountain grapes. ■ TIP→ The two-hour food-and-wine pairing ($72) by sommelier Mary Davidek is among the Wine Country's best. ⊠ *4045 N. St. Helena Hwy./ Hwy. 29* ☎ *707/967–6272* ⊕ *www.castellodiamorosa.com* ☜ *Tastings $19–$29, tours $34–$44* ☯ *Mar.–Oct., daily 9:30–6; Nov.–Feb., daily 9:30–5; tours and food-wine pairing by appointment.*

Chateau Montelena. Set amid a bucolic northern Calistoga landscape, this winery helped establish the Napa Valley's reputation for high-quality wine making. At the legendary Paris tasting of 1976, the Chateau Montelena 1973 Chardonnay took first place, beating out four white Burgundies from France and five other California Chardonnays. The 2008 movie *Bottle Shock* immortalized the event, and the winery honors its four decades of classic wine making with a special Beyond Paris & Hollywood tasting of the winery's Napa Valley Chardonnays ($40). You can also opt for a Current Release Tasting ($20) or a Limited Release Tasting ($50) that includes some stellar Cabernet Sauvignons.

Floor-to-ceiling stacked bottles are no exaggeration in Schramsberg's cellars.

✉ *1429 Tubbs La., off Hwy. 29* ☎ *707/942–5105* ⊕ *www.montelena. com* 🖃 *Tastings $20–$50, tours $30–$40; appointment required for some tastings and tours* ☉ *Daily 9:30–4, tour times vary.*

Fodor's Choice
★

Schramsberg. Founded in 1865, Schramsberg produces bubblies made using the traditional *méthode champenoise*. To taste, you first must tour, but what a tour: in addition to glimpsing the winery's historic architecture, you see the underground cellars dug in the late 19th century by Chinese laborers. A mind-boggling 2 million–plus bottles are stacked in gravity-defying configurations. The tour includes generous pours of very different sparkling wines. To learn more about them, consider the three-day **Camp Schramsberg.** Fall participants harvest grapes and explore food-and-wine pairing, riddling (the process of turning the bottles every few days to nudge the sediment into the neck of the bottle), and other topics. In spring the focus is on blending sparklers. ✉ *1400 Schramsberg Rd., off Hwy. 29* ☎ *707/942–4558, 800/877– 3623* ⊕ *www.schramsberg.com* 🖃 *Tasting and tour $50* ☉ *Tours at 10, 11:30, 12:30, 1:30, and 2:30 by appointment.*

WORTH NOTING

Dutch Henry Winery. The casual style and lack of crowds at this pet-friendly winery make it a welcome change of pace from some of its overly serious neighbors. Towering oak barrels hold excellent Cabernet Sauvignon, Pinot Noir, Zinfandel, Syrah, and other single-varietal wines, along with a well-regarded Bordeaux blend called Argos. Dutch Henry also sells a Sauvignon Blanc and a charming Rosé. ✉ *4310 Silverado Trail, near Dutch Henry Canyon Rd., Calistoga* ☎ *707/942–5771, 888/224–5879* ⊕ *www.dutchhenry.com* 🖃 *Tasting $25* ☉ *Daily 10–4:30.*

Jericho Canyon Vineyard. It takes a Polaris all-terrain vehicle to tour the vineyards at this family-owned winery whose grapes grow on hillsides that slope as much as 45 degrees. The rocky, volcanic soils of this former cattle ranch yield intensely flavored grapes that winemaker Aaron Potts fashions into old world–style Cabernet Sauvignons, some 100%, others blended with Cabernet Franc, Merlot, Petit Verdot, and other estate-grown varietals. Tastings, which might also include a Sauvignon Blanc or a Chardonnay, are held in an underground barrel cave dug into the canyon and redolent of French oak and red wine. Topics covered on the Polaris tour include the nuances of sustainable farming in this challenging environment. ✉ *3322 Old Lawley Toll Rd., off Hwy. 29* ☎ *707/942–9665* 🌐 *jerichocanyonvineyard.com* 🎟 *Winery tour and tasting $40, Polaris tour and tasting $80* 🕒 *Tastings and tours: daily at 10, 11:30, 1, and 2:30 by appointment only.*

Lava Vine Winery. The owners and staff of this jolly spot pride themselves on creating a family- and dog-friendly environment, and you're apt to hear rock, pop, and other tunes as you taste small-lot wines that include Cabernet Sauvignon, Chenin Blanc, Syrah, and Port. The wry Pete might even start playing the banjo. If they're available, be sure to taste the Suisun Valley Petite Sirah and the Knights Valley Reserve Cabernet. ✉ *965 Silverado Trail N.* ☎ *707/942–9500* 🌐 *www.lavavine.com* 🎟 *Tasting $10* 🕒 *Daily 10–5.*

Tamber Bey Vineyards. Endurance riders Barry and Jennifer Waitte share their passion for horses and wine at their glam-rustic winery north of Calistoga. Their 22-acre Sundance Ranch remains a working equestrian facility, but the site has been revamped to include a state-of-the-art winery with separate fermenting tanks for grapes from Tamber Bey's vineyards in Yountville, Oakville, and elsewhere. The winemakers produce two Chardonnays and a Sauvignon Blanc, but the winery's stars are several subtly powerful reds, including a flagship Cabernet Sauvignon, a Merlot, and blends dominated by Cabernet Franc, Cabernet Sauvignon, and Petit Verdot. **■ TIP→ Appointments are required, but even on a few minutes' notice they're generally easy to get.** ✉ *1251 Tubbs La., at Myrtledale Rd.* ☎ *707/942–2100* 🌐 *www.tamberbey.com* 🎟 *Tastings $25–$35, tour and tasting $45* 🕒 *Daily 10–5, by appointment only.*

WHERE TO EAT

$$ MODERN AMERICAN

🍴 **1226 Washington.** At this appealing homage to comfort foods worldwide you can take your meal in the boisterous but classy tavern, in a placid outdoor garden, or in the pine-walled, high-ceilinged dining room. Fried pickles, the egg-topped bubble and squeak (a Yankee's take on a Brit version of hash), pulled-chicken sliders with caramelized bacon slaw, and similar starters shake up the palate for less frolicsome mains, which might include the day's fresh fish rubbed in green tea or stuffed breast of pheasant with a parsnip purée. The cuisine here is satisfying and often tantalizing. [$] *Average main: $21* ✉ *1226 Washington St., near Lincoln Ave.* ☎ *707/942–4268* 🌐 *www.1226washington.com* 🕒 *Closed Mon. and Tues.*

$$ AMERICAN

🍴 **All Seasons Bistro.** Flowers top the tables at this Calistoga mainstay, a delightful stop for lunch or dinner. The seasonal menu might include braised lamb shank with creamy polenta or seared salmon fillet with chive-scallion mashed potatoes, and year-round the grilled Angus-beef burger comes with super-crispy fries and a smoked-onion aioli. Among the homey desserts are a well-executed vanilla-bean crème brûlée and a warm dark-chocolate torte. ■ TIP➡ **You can order reasonably priced wines from the extensive list, or buy a bottle at the attached shop and have it poured at your table.** $ *Average main: $21* ✉ *1400 Lincoln Ave., at Washington St.* ☎ *707/942–9111* ⊕ *www. allseasonsnapavalley.net* ⊗ *Closed Mon.*

$$ ✕ **Bosko's Trattoria.** Affable Bosko's provides tasty Italian cuisine at a
ITALIAN fair price. The specialties include house-made pastas and thin-crust pizzas cooked in a wood-fired oven. Two of the hefty sandwiches worth trying are the free-range chicken breast sandwich on garlicky focaccia (also made in-house) and the Italian sausage on a sourdough roll. Both come with a salad or a bowl of minestrone or other soup. Nothing super-fancy here, just good value in a pleasant setting. $ *Average main: $17* ✉ *1364 Lincoln Ave., at Washington St.* ☎ *707/942– 9088* ⊕ *www.boskos.com* ⊜ *Reservations not accepted.*

$$$ ✕ **Jolē.** Local produce plays a starring role at this modern American
MODERN restaurant, not surprising as chef Matt Spector is one of the area's big-
AMERICAN gest proponents of farm-to-table dining. Depending on when you visit, you might enjoy roasted cauliflower served with almonds, dates, capers, and balsamic; kale stew with Tasso ham, kabocha squash, and finger-ling potatoes; and molasses-glazed quail with farro risotto, roasted pumpkin, and a maple-bourbon demi-glace. The menu is available à la carte, and there are four-, five-, and six-course prix-fixe options. With about four-dozen wines by the glass, it's easy to find something to pair with each course. $ *Average main: $25* ✉ *Mount View Hotel, 1457 Lincoln Ave., near Fair Way* ☎ *707/942–9538* ⊕ *jolerestaurant. com* ⊗ *No lunch.*

$$$$ ✕ **Solbar.** Chef Brandon Sharp is known around the region for his subtle
MODERN and sophisticated take on Wine Country cooking. As befits a restaurant
AMERICAN at a spa resort, the menu here is divided into "healthy, lighter dishes"
Fodor's Choice and "hearty cuisine." On the lighter side, the lemongrass-poached
★ petrale sole comes with jasmine rice and hearts of palm. On the heartier side you might find a New York strip steak served with Yukon gold potatoes, sautéed rapini, oxtail marmalade, and sauce bordelaise. The service at Solbar is uniformly excellent, and in good weather the patio is a festive spot for breakfast, lunch, or dinner. $ *Average main: $31* ✉ *So-lage Calistoga, 755 Silverado Trail, at Rosedale Rd.* ☎ *707/226–0850* ⊕ *www.solagecalistoga.com/solbar.*

WHERE TO STAY

$ 🛏 **Best Western Plus Stevenson Manor.** Budget travelers get what they
HOTEL pay for—and a little bit more—at this clean, well-run motel a few blocks from Calistoga's downtown. **Pros:** great price for region; friendly staff; nice pool area; complimentary full breakfast. **Cons:** decidedly lacking in glamour. $ *Rooms from: $159* ✉ *1830 Lincoln Ave.* ☎ *707/942–1112, 800/780–7234* ⊕ *www.bestwestern.com* ⤴ *34 rooms* ⦿❘ *Breakfast.*

10

$$$$ ⬚ **Calistoga Ranch.** Spacious cedar-shingle lodges throughout this posh,
RESORT   wooded property have outdoor living areas, and even the restaurant,
Fodor'sChoice   spa, and reception space have outdoor seating and fireplaces. **Pros:**
★   almost half the lodges have private hot tubs on the deck; lovely hiking
trails on the property; guests have reciprocal privileges at Auberge du
Soleil and Solage Calistoga. **Cons:** innovative indoor-outdoor organization works better in fair weather than in rain or cold. ⓢ *Rooms from:*
$750 ✉ *580 Lommel Rd.* ☎ *707/254–2800, 800/942–4220* ⊕ *www.*
calistogaranch.com ⤴ *50 rooms* ⏀ *No meals.*

$$$ ⬚ **Cottage Grove Inn.** A long driveway lined with freestanding cottages,
B&B/INN   each shaded by elm trees and with rocking chairs on the porch, looks
a bit like Main Street, USA, but inside the skylighted buildings include
all the perks necessary for a romantic weekend getaway. **Pros:** loaner
bicycles available; plenty of privacy; huge bathtubs. **Cons:** no pool;
some may find the decor too old school. ⓢ *Rooms from: $375* ✉ *1711*
Lincoln Ave. ☎ *707/942–8400, 800/799–2284* ⊕ *www.cottagegrove.*
com ⤴ *16 cottages* ⏀ *Breakfast.*

$$ ⬚ **Indian Springs Resort and Spa.** Stylish Indian Springs—operating as a
RESORT   spa since 1862—ably splits the difference between laid-back style and
ultrachic touches. **Pros:** lovely grounds with outdoor seating areas; stylish for the price; enormous mineral pool; free touring bikes. **Cons:** lodge
rooms are small; service could be more polished. ⓢ *Rooms from: $262*
✉ *1712 Lincoln Ave.* ☎ *707/942–4913* ⊕ *www.indianspringscalistoga.*
com ⤴ *24 rooms, 17 suites* ⏀ *No meals.*

$$ ⬚ **Meadowlark Country House.** Two charming European gents run this
B&B/INN   laid-back but sophisticated inn on 20 wooded acres just north of down-
Fodor'sChoice   town. **Pros:** charming innkeepers; tasty sit-down breakfasts; welcoming
★   vibe that attracts diverse guests. **Cons:** clothing-optional pool policy
isn't for everyone. ⓢ *Rooms from: $210* ✉ *601 Petrified Forest Rd.*
☎ *707/942–5651, 800/942–5651* ⊕ *www.meadowlarkinn.com* ⤴ *5*
rooms, 3 suites, 1 cottage, 1 guesthouse ⏀ *Breakfast.*

$$$$ ⬚ **Solage Calistoga.** The aesthetic at this 22-acre property is Napa Val-
RESORT   ley barn meets San Francisco loft, so the rooms have high ceilings, pol-
ished concrete floors, recycled walnut furniture, and all-natural fabrics
in soothingly muted colors. **Pros:** great service; complimentary bikes;
separate pools for kids and adults. **Cons:** the vibe may not suit every-
one. ⓢ *Rooms from: $465* ✉ *755 Silverado Trail* ☎ *855/942–7442,*
707/226–0800 ⊕ *www.solagecalistoga.com* ⤴ *83 rooms, 6 suites*
⏀ *No meals.*

SPAS

Fodor'sChoice   **Spa Solage.** This eco-conscious spa has reinvented the traditional Cal-
★   istoga mud and mineral water therapies. Case in point: the hour-long
"Mudslide," a three-part treatment that includes a mud body mask
(in a heated lounge), a soak in a thermal bath, and a power nap in
a comfy sound/vibration chair. The mud here is a mix of clay, volca-
nic ash, and essential oils. Traditional spa services—combination Shi-
atsu-Swedish and other massages, full-body exfoliations, facials, and
waxes—are available, as are fitness and yoga classes. ✉ *755 Silverado*
Trail, at Rosedale Rd. ☎ *707/226–0825* ⊕ *www.solagecalistoga.com/*
spa ✎ *Treatments $35–$335* ⊙ *Daily 8–8.*

All it needs is a fair maiden: Castello di Amorosa's re-created castle.

SPORTS AND THE OUTDOORS

Calistoga Bikeshop. Options here include regular and fancy bikes that rent for $12 an hour and up, and there's a self-guided wine tour ($90) that includes tastings at three or four small wineries. ⊠ *1318 Lincoln Ave., near Washington St.* ☎ *707/942–9687* ⊕ *www.calistogabikeshop.net.*

THE SONOMA VALLEY

Although the Sonoma Valley may not have the cachet of the neighboring Napa Valley, wineries here entice with an unpretentious attitude and, for the most part, smaller crowds. Sonoma's landscape seduces, too, its roads gently climbing and descending on their way to wineries hidden from the road by trees.

The scenic valley, bounded by the Mayacamas Mountains on the east and Sonoma Mountain on the west, extends north from San Pablo Bay nearly 20 miles to the eastern outskirts of Santa Rosa. The varied terrain, soils, and climate (cooler in the south because of the bay influence and hotter toward the north) allow grape growers to raise cool-weather varietals such as Chardonnay and Pinot Noir as well as Merlot, Cabernet Sauvignon, and other heat-seeking vines. The valley is home to dozens of wineries, many of them on or near Highway 12, which runs the length of the valley.

ESSENTIALS

Contact Sonoma Valley Visitors Bureau ☎ *707/996–1090, 866/996–1090* ⊕ *www.sonomavalley.com.*

10

SONOMA

14 miles west of Napa, 45 miles northeast of San Francisco.

Founded in the early 1800s, Sonoma is the oldest town in the Wine Country. The central Sonoma Plaza dates from the mission era; surrounding it are 19th-century adobes, atmospheric hotels, and the swooping marquee of the 1930s Sebastiani Theatre. On summer days the plaza is a hive of activity, with children blowing off steam in the playground while their folks stock up on picnic supplies and browse the boutiques surrounding the square. On your way into town from the south, you pass through the vineyards of the Carneros District, which straddles the southern sections of Sonoma and Napa counties.

GETTING HERE AND AROUND

Highway 12 (signed as Broadway as it approaches Sonoma Plaza) heads north into Sonoma from Highway 121 and south from Santa Rosa into downtown Sonoma, where (signed as West Spain Street) it travels east to the plaza. Parking is relatively easy to find on or near the plaza, and you can walk to many restaurants, shops, and tasting rooms. You'll likely want to drive to the several wineries a mile or more east of the plaza. Signs on East Spain Street or East Napa Street point the way.

EXPLORING

TOP ATTRACTIONS

Fodor'sChoice
★
Bartholomew Park Winery. Although this winery was founded in 1994, grapes were grown in some of its vineyards as early as the 1830s. The emphasis here is on handcrafted, single-varietal wines—Cabernet Sauvignon, Chardonnay, Sauvignon Blanc, Syrah, and Zinfandel—made from organically farmed grapes. A small museum off the tasting room contains vivid exhibits about the history of the winery and the Sonoma region. Another plus is the beautiful, slightly off-the-beaten-path location amid a 375-acre private park about 2 miles from downtown Sonoma. Gather a lunch to enjoy on the woodsy grounds, one of Sonoma's prettier picnic spots, or hike 3 miles on the property's marked trails. ■TIP➔ To get here from Sonoma Plaza, head east on East Napa Street and follow the signs. ⊠ *1000 Vineyard La., off Castle Rd.* ☎ *707/935–9511* ⊕ *www.bartpark.com* ⊠ *Tasting $10, tour $20* ☉ *Daily 11–4:30; tours Fri. and Sat. at 11:30 and 2, Sun. at 2, by reservation.*

Fodor'sChoice
★
Gundlach Bundschu. Visitors may mispronounce this winery's name ("gun lock bun shoe" gets you close), but still they flock here to sample polished wines served by some of Sonoma's friendliest pourers. Most of the winery's land has been in the Bundschu family since 1858. Fine Cabernet Franc, Cabernet Sauvignon, Chardonnay, Merlot, and Tempranillo wines all are available in the standard $10 tasting. Add $5 to taste the signature Vintage Reserve red blend. For a more comprehensive experience, tour the cave ($20) or head into the vineyard ($50; available only between May and October). ■TIP➔ In fine weather you can taste outdoors at tables that have splendid vineyard views. ⊠ *2000 Denmark St., at Bundschu Rd., off 8th St. E.* ☎ *707/938–5277* ⊕ *www. gunbun.com* ⊠ *Tastings $10–$15, tours $20–$50* ☉ *June–mid.-Oct., daily 11–5:30; mid.-Oct.–May, daily 11–4:30.*

Fodor'sChoice **Ram's Gate Winery.** Stunning views, ultrachic architecture, and wines
★ made from grapes grown by acclaimed producers make a visit to
Ram's Gate an event. The welcoming interior spaces—think Restoration Hardware with a dash of high-style whimsy—open up to the
entire western Carneros. During fine weather you'll experience (in
comfort) the cooling breezes that sweep through the area while sipping
sophisticated wines, mostly Pinot Noirs and Chardonnays, but also
Sauvignon Blanc, Cabernet Sauvignon, Syrah, late-harvest Zinfandel, and even a sparkler. With grapes sourced from the Sangiacomo,
Lee Hudson, and other illustrious vineyards, winemaker Jeff Gaffner
focuses on creating balanced vintages that express what occurred in
nature that year. One food-wine pairing ($60) includes tapas, wine
tasting, and a winery tour; the other ($125) focuses on food and wine
education. ✉ *28700 Arnold Dr./Hwy. 121* ☎ *707/721–8700* ⊕ *www.*
ramsgatewinery.com ✉ *Tasting $7–$125* ⊙ *Thurs.–Mon. 10–6; tours*
(times vary) by appointment.

Sonoma Mission. The northernmost of the 21 missions established
by Franciscan friars in California, Sonoma Mission was founded in
1823 as Mission San Francisco Solano. It serves as the centerpiece
of **Sonoma State Historic Park,** which includes several other sites in
Sonoma and nearby Petaluma. Some early structures were destroyed,
but all or part of several remaining buildings date to the days of
Mexican rule over California. These include the **Sonoma Barracks,** a
block west of the mission at 20 East Spain Street, which housed troops
under the command of General Mariano Guadalupe Vallejo, who con-
trolled vast tracks of land in the region. The modest museum contains
displays about the missions and information about the other historic
sites. ✉ *114 E. Spain St., at 1st St. E.* ☎ *707/938–9560* ⊕ *www.parks.*
ca.gov/?page_id=479 ✉ *$3, includes same-day admission to other his-*
toric sites ⊙ *Daily 10–5.*

Fodor'sChoice **Walt Wines.** You could spend a full day sampling wines in the tasting
★ rooms bordering Sonoma Plaza, but one not to miss is Walt, which
specializes in Pinot Noir. Fruit-forward yet subtle, these wines win over
even the purists who pine for the genre's days of lighter, more perfume-
y vintages. Walt is a good place to compare the Pinots one winemaker
crafts from local grapes with others from grapes grown in Mendocino
County (just north of Sonoma County), California's Central Coast, and
even Oregon's Willamette Valley. Critics routinely bestow high ratings
on all these wines. ✉ *380 1st St. W, at W. Spain St.* ☎ *707/933–4440*
⊕ *www.waltwines.com* ✉ *Tastings $10–$20.*

WORTH NOTING

Buena Vista Winery. The site where modern California wine making
got its start has been transformed into an entertaining homage to the
accomplishments of the 19th-century wine pioneer Count Agoston
Haraszthy. Tours, sometimes conducted by the count himself—as chan-
neled by actor George Webber and others—pass through the original
aging caves dug deep into the hillside by Chinese laborers. Reserve tastings ($50) include library and current wines, plus ones still aging in bar-
rels. The stylish former press house (used for pressing grapes into wine),
which dates to 1862, hosts the standard tastings. The barrel tour and

10

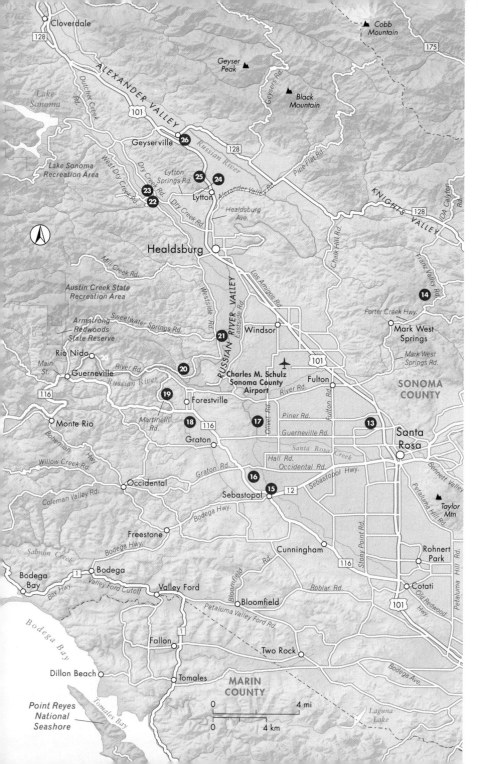

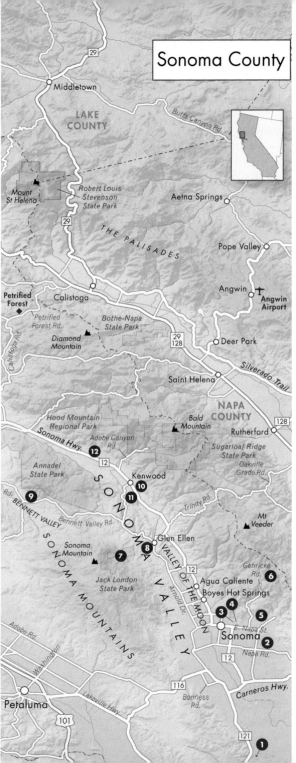

Sonoma County

tasting ($30) includes finished and barrel wines. ■TIP➔ **Chardonnays and Pinot Noirs from Los Carneros AVA are this winery's strong suits.** ✉ *18000 Old Winery Rd., off Napa Rd.* ☎ *800/926–1266* ⊕ *www. buenavistawinery.com* ✉ *Tastings $15–$50; tours $10–$30* ☉ *Daily 10–5; tours by appointment 1–2 days in advance.*

WHERE TO EAT

$$
AMERICAN
Fodor'sChoice
★
✕ **Cafe La Haye.** In a postage-stamp-size open kitchen, the skillful chef turns out main courses that star on a small but worthwhile seasonal menu emphasizing local ingredients. Chicken, beef, pasta, and fish get deluxe treatment without fuss or fanfare. The daily roasted chicken and the risotto specials are always good. Butterscotch pudding is a homey signature dessert. The dining room is compact, but the friendly owner, always there to greet diners, maintains a particularly welcoming vibe. $ *Average main: $22* ✉ *140 E. Napa St., at 1st. St. E.* ☎ *707/935–5994* ⊕ *www.cafelahaye.com* ☉ *Closed Sun. and Mon. No lunch.*

$$$
MODERN
AMERICAN
Fodor'sChoice
★
✕ **El Dorado Kitchen.** The visual delights at this winning restaurant include its clean lines and handsome decor, but the eye inevitably drifts westward to the open kitchen, where chef Armando Navarro and his diligent crew craft flavorful dishes full of subtle surprises. Pumpkin seeds and spiced marshmallows top the popular butternut squash soup, for instance, adding a crunchy-sweet piquancy that plays well off the dish's predominantly savory sentiments. Focusing on locally sourced ingredients, the menu might include Petaluma duck breast enlivened by the tangy flavors of parsnip purée, braised endive, roasted turnips, persimmons, and huckleberries. Even a simple dish, like truffle-oil fries liberally sprinkled with Parmesan cheese, charms with its combination of tastes and textures. The noteworthy desserts include an apple tart tatin, banana crisp with lime curd, and molten chocolate cake. $ *Average main: $26* ✉ *El Dorado Hotel, 405 1st St. W., at W. Spain St.* ☎ *707/996–3030* ⊕ *www.eldoradosonoma.com/restaurant.*

$$$
FRENCH
✕ **The Girl & the Fig.** Chef Sondra Bernstein transformed the historic bar room of the Sonoma Hotel into a hot spot for inventive French cooking. You can always find a dish with the signature figs on the menu, whether it's a fig-and-arugula salad or an aperitif blending sparkling wine with fig liqueur. Also look for duck confit, a burger with matchstick fries, or wild flounder *meunière*. The wine list is notable for its emphasis on Rhône varietals, and a counter in the bar area sells artisanal cheese platters for eating here as well as cheese by the pound to go. The indulgent Sunday brunch includes potato pancakes with smoked salmon, dill crème fraîche, and caviar. $ *Average main: $24* ✉ *Sonoma Hotel, 110 W. Spain St., at 1st St. W.* ☎ *707/938–3634* ⊕ *www.thegirlandthefig.com.*

$$
AMERICAN
Fodor'sChoice
★
✕ **Harvest Moon Cafe.** It's easy to feel like one of the family at this little restaurant with an odd, zigzagging layout. Diners seated at one of the two tiny bars chat with the servers like old friends, but the husband-and-wife team in the kitchen is serious about the food, much of which relies on local produce. The ever-changing menu might include homey dishes such as grilled pork loin with crispy polenta and artichokes, Niman Ranch rib-eye steak with a red-wine sauce, or seared ahi tuna au poivre. Everything is so perfectly executed and the vibe is so

genuinely warm that a visit here is deeply satisfying. **■ TIP→ A spacious back patio with tables arranged around a fountain more than doubles the seating; a heated tent keeps this area warm in winter.** [$] *Average main: $22* ✉ *487 1st St. W., at W. Napa St.* ☎ *707/933–8160* 🌐 *www.harvestmooncafesonoma.com* 🕒 *Closed Tues. No lunch.*

$$$ MODERN AMERICAN 🍴 **Hot Box Grill.** Comfort foods aren't often described as *nuanced*, but the term aptly describes the locally sourced preparations chef Norm Owens conjures up at his modest roadside restaurant. Take the fries (but not too many): long and not at all lean, they're cooked in duck fat and served with malt-vinegar aioli, lending them a richness that lingers pleasingly in your memory. There's lots of frying going on—even Cornish game hen gets the treatment. Up against these dishes, the pasta offerings almost seem light, and the appetizers—among them spicy ahi tuna with a ponzu sauce, avocado mousse, and crispy wontons—downright dainty. [$] *Average main: $24* ✉ *18350 Sonoma Hwy./Hwy. 12* ☎ *707/939–8383* 🌐 *www.hotboxgrill.com* 🕒 *Closed Mon. and Tues. No lunch.*

$$$ PORTUGUESE 🍴 **LaSalette.** Born in the Azores and raised in Sonoma, chef-owner Manuel Azevedo serves dishes inspired by his native Portugal in this warmly decorated spot. The best seats are on a patio along an alleyway off Sonoma Plaza. Such boldly flavored dishes as pork tenderloin *recheado*, stuffed with olives and almonds and topped with a Port sauce, might be followed by a dish of rice pudding with Madeira-braised figs or a Port from the varied list. The daily seafood specials are also well worth a try. [$] *Average main: $24* ✉ *452 1st St. E., near E. Spain St.* ☎ *707/938–1927* 🌐 *www.lasalette-restaurant.com.*

$$$$ AMERICAN Fodor's Choice ★ 🍴 **Santé.** This elegant dining room has evolved into a destination restaurant through its focus on seasonal and locally sourced ingredients. The room is understated, with dark walls and soft lighting, but the food is anything but. Dishes such as the Sonoma Liberty duck breast and confit leg, served with wild rice, gray shallots, and quince mustard, are sophisticated without being fussy. Others, like the sampler of Niman Ranch beef that includes a petite filet mignon, a skirt steak, and braised *pavé beef à la bourguignonne*, are pure decadence. The restaurant offers a seasonal tasting menu ($135). [$] *Average main: $43* ✉ *Fairmont Sonoma Mission Inn & Spa, 100 Boyes Blvd./Hwy. 12, 2½ miles north of Sonoma Plaza, Boyes Hot Springs* ☎ *707/938–9000* 🌐 *www.santediningroom.com* 🕒 *No lunch.*

$ AMERICAN 🍴 **Sunflower Caffé.** The food at this casual eatery, mostly salads and sandwiches, is simple but satisfying. Highlights include the smoked duck breast sandwich, served on a baguette and slathered with caramelized onions. A meal of soup and local cheeses is a good option if you just want to nibble. Both the pretty patio, which is in the back, and the sidewalk seating area facing Sonoma Plaza are equipped with heating lamps and get plenty of shade, so they're comfortable in all but the most inclement weather. Cheerful artwork brightens up the interior, where locals hunker over their computers and take advantage of the free Wi-Fi. Omelets and waffles are the stars at breakfast. [$] *Average main: $13* ✉ *421 1st St. W, at W. Spain St.* ☎ *707/996–6645* 🌐 *www.sonomasunflower.com* 🕒 *No dinner.*

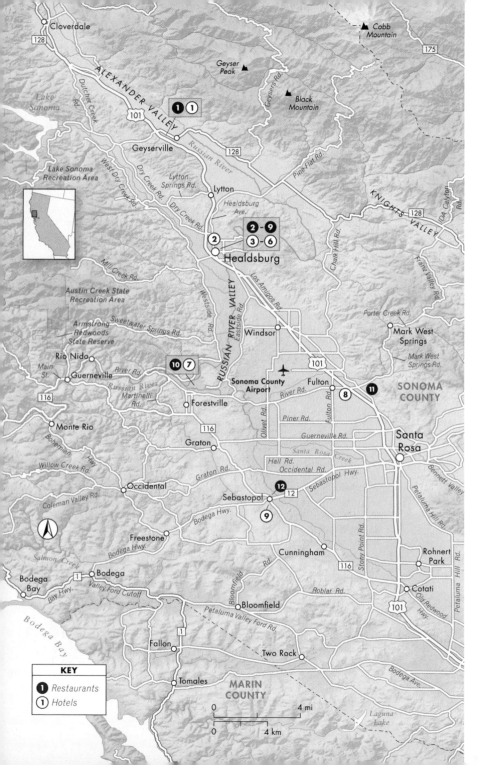

Where to Eat and Stay in Sonoma County

WHERE TO STAY

$$
B&B/INN
El Dorado Hotel. Rooms in this remodeled 1843 building strike a spare, modern pose with their pristine white bedding, but the Mexican-tile floors hint at Sonoma's mission-era past. **Pros:** stylish for the price; hip on-site restaurant; good café for breakfast; central location. **Cons:** rooms are small; lighting could be better; noisy. $ *Rooms from: $200* ⊠ *405 1st St. W.* ☎ *707/996–3030* ⊕ *www.eldoradosonoma.com/hotel* ⌁ *27 rooms* ❘○❘ *No meals.*

$$$$
RESORT
Fairmont Sonoma Mission Inn & Spa. The real draw at this mission-style resort is the extensive, swank spa with its array of massages and treatments, some designed for couples. **Pros:** enormous spa; excellent restaurant; free shuttle to downtown. **Cons:** standard rooms on the smaller side; lacks intimacy of similarly priced options. $ *Rooms from: $439* ⊠ *100 Boyes Blvd./Hwy. 12, 2½ miles north of Sonoma Plaza, Boyes Hot Springs* ☎ *707/938–9000* ⊕ *www.fairmont.com/sonoma* ⌁ *166 rooms, 60 suites* ❘○❘ *No meals.*

$
B&B/INN
FAMILY
Sonoma Creek Inn. The small but cheerful rooms at this motel-style inn are individually decorated with painted wooden armoires, cozy quilts, and brightly colored contemporary artwork. **Pros:** clean, well-lighted bathrooms; lots of charm for the price; popular with bicyclists. **Cons:** office not staffed 24 hours a day; a 10-minute drive from Sonoma Plaza. $ *Rooms from: $145* ⊠ *239 Boyes Blvd., off Hwy. 12* ☎ *707/939–9463, 888/712–1289* ⊕ *www.sonomacreekinn.com* ⌁ *16 rooms.*

SPAS

Willow Stream Spa at Fairmont Sonoma Mission Inn & Spa. With 40,000 square feet and 30 treatment rooms, the Wine Country's largest spa provides every amenity you could possibly want, including pools and hot tubs fed by local thermal springs. Although the place bustles with patrons in summer and on some weekends, the vibe is always soothing. The signature bathing ritual includes an exfoliating shower, dips in two mineral-water soaking pools, an herbal steam, a dry sauna, and cool-down showers. Other popular treatments include the warm ginger-oil float, which involves relaxation in a weightless environment, and the perennially popular caviar facial. The most requested room among couples is outfitted with a two-person copper bathtub. ⊠ *100 Boyes Blvd./Hwy. 12, 2½ miles north of Sonoma Plaza, Boyes Hot Springs* ☎ *707/938–9000* ⊕ *www.fairmont.com/sonoma/willow-stream* ◲ *Treatments $65–$485.*

SHOPPING

Sonoma Plaza is the town's main shopping magnet, with tempting boutiques and specialty food purveyors facing the square or just a block or two away.

Fodor'sChoice
★
Chateau Sonoma. The fancy furniture, lighting fixtures, and objets d'art at this upscale shop make it a dangerous place to enter: after just a few minutes you may find yourself reconsidering your entire home's aesthetic. The owner's keen eye for style and sense of whimsy make a visit here a delight. ⊠ *153 W. Napa St., near 2nd St. W* ☎ *707/935–8553* ⊕ *www.chateausonoma.com.*

Horseback riding tours loop around Jack London State Historic Park.

The Epicurean Connection. In addition to selling Délice de La Vallée, her award-winning cheese made from triple-cream cow and goat milk, Sheana Davis offers jams, sauces, tapenades, and other toppings from local producers. She also sells sandwiches and sweets, and stages good live music from Thursday through Saturday evening and on Sunday afternoon. ✉ *122 W. Napa St., at 1st St.* ☎ *707/935–7960* ⊕ *www.the epicureanconnection.com.*

GLEN ELLEN

10

7 miles north of Sonoma.

Unlike its flashier Napa Valley counterparts, Glen Ellen eschews well-groomed sidewalks lined with upscale boutiques and restaurants, preferring instead its crooked streets, some with no sidewalks at all, shaded with stands of old oak trees. Jack London, who represents Glen Ellen's rugged spirit, lived in the area for many years; the town commemorates him with place names and nostalgic establishments. Hidden among sometimes-ramshackle buildings abutting Sonoma and Calabasas creeks are low-key shops and galleries worth poking through, and several fine dining establishments.

GETTING HERE AND AROUND

Glen Ellen sits just off Highway 12. From the north or south, take Arnold Drive west and follow it south less than a mile. The walkable downtown straddles a half-mile stretch of Arnold Drive.

EXPLORING

Fodor's Choice ★ **Benziger Family Winery.** One of the best-known Sonoma County wineries sits on a sprawling estate in a bowl with 360-degree sun exposure, the benefits of which are explored on popular tram tours that depart several times daily. Guides explain Benziger's biodynamic farming practices and give you a glimpse of the extensive cave system. The regular tram tour costs $20; another tour costing $40 concludes with a seated tasting. Noted for its Chardonnay, Cabernet Sauvignon, Merlot, Pinot Noir, and Sauvignon Blanc wines, the winery is a beautiful spot for a picnic. **■ TIP→ Reserve a seat on the tram tour through the winery's website or arrive early in the day on summer weekends and during harvest season.** ✉ *1883 London Ranch Rd., off Arnold Dr.* ☎ *707/935–3000, 888/490–2739* 🌐 *www.benziger.com* 🎟 *Tastings $10–$20, tours $20–$40* 🕓 *Daily 10–5; tours daily at 11:15, 12:45, 2:15.*

Fodor's Choice ★ **Jack London State Historic Park.** The pleasures are both pastoral and intellectual at the beloved former ranch of the late Jack London. You could easily spend the afternoon hiking along the edge of vineyards and through stands of oaks. Several manuscripts and a handful of personal effects are on view at the House of Happy Walls Museum, which provides a tantalizing overview of the author's life and literary passions. A short hike away lie the ruins of Wolf House, which mysteriously burned down just before the writer was to move in. Also open to the public are a few restored farm outbuildings and the Cottage, a wood-framed building where he penned many of his later works. London is buried on the property. ✉ *2400 London Ranch Rd., off Arnold Dr.* ☎ *707/938–5216* 🌐 *www.jacklondonpark.com* 🎟 *Parking $10 ($5 walk-in or bike), includes admission to museum; cottage $4* 🕓 *Mar.–Nov. park daily 9:30–5, museum 10–5, cottage noon–4; Dec.–Feb., Thurs.–Mon. park 9:30–5, museum 10–5, cottage noon–4.*

WHERE TO EAT

$$ FRENCH Fodor's Choice ★ 🍴 **The Fig Cafe.** Pale sage walls, a sloping ceiling, and casual but warm service set a sunny mood in this little bistro. The compact menu focuses on California and French comfort food—pot roast and duck confit, for instance, as well as thin-crust pizza. Steamed mussels are served with terrific crispy fries, which also accompany the sirloin burger. Weekend brunch brings out locals and tourists for French toast, pizza with applewood-smoked bacon and poached eggs, corned-beef hash, and other delights. **■ TIP→ The unusual no-corkage-fee policy makes this a great place to drink the wine you discovered down the road.** [$] *Average main: $18* ✉ *13690 Arnold Dr., at O'Donnell La.* ☎ *707/938–2130* 🌐 *www.thefigcafe.com* ✍ *Reservations not accepted* 🕓 *No lunch weekdays.*

$$ ECLECTIC 🍴 **Glen Ellen Inn Oyster Grill & Martini Bar.** Tucked inside a creekside 1940s cottage, this cozy restaurant exudes romance, especially if you sit in the shady garden or on the patio strung with tiny lights. After taking the edge off your hunger with some oysters on the half shell and an ice-cold martini, order from a menu that plucks elements from California, French, and other cuisines. You might find ginger tempura calamari with grilled pineapple salsa, or hanger steak with chimichurri sauce

and a side of garlic fries. Desserts tend toward the indulgent; witness the warm cinnamon-pecan bread pudding with a chocolate center that sits in a puddle of brandy sauce. [$] *Average main: $20* ✉ *13670 Arnold Dr., at O'Donnell La.* ☎ *707/996–6409* 🌐 *www.glenelleninn.com* ⏲ *No lunch Wed.*

$$ ECLECTIC Fodor's Choice ★ 🍴 **Glen Ellen Star.** Chef Ari Weiswasser honed his craft at the French Laundry, Daniel, and other bastions of culinary finesse, but the goal at his hot-ticket Wine Country boîte is haute-rustic cuisine, much of which emerges from a wood-fired oven that burns a steady 600°F. Pizzas such as the crisp-crusted, richly sauced Margherita thrive in the torrid heat, as do root and other vegetables roasted in small iron skillets. Ditto for entrées that include juicy, tender roasted whole fish. Weiswasser signs each dish with a sauce, emulsion, or sly blend of spices that jazzes things up without upstaging the primary ingredient. The restaurant's decor is equally restrained, with an open-beam ceiling, exposed hardwood floors, and utilitarian seating. **■ TIP→ Many regulars perch on a stool at the kitchen-view counter to watch the chefs at work.** [$] *Average main: $21* ✉ *13648 Arnold Dr., at Warm Springs Rd.* ☎ *707/343–1384* 🌐 *glenellenstar.com* ✍ *Reservations essential* ⏲ *No lunch.*

WHERE TO STAY

$ B&B/INN Fodor's Choice ★ 🏨 **Beltane Ranch.** On a slope of the Mayacamas range a few miles from Glen Ellen, this 1892 ranch house, shaded by magnificent oak trees, contains charmingly old-fashioned rooms, each individually decorated with antiques and original artwork by noted artists. **Pros:** casual, friendly atmosphere; reasonable prices; beautiful grounds with ancient oak trees. **Cons:** downstairs rooms get some noise from upstairs rooms; ceiling fans instead of air-conditioning. [$] *Rooms from: $185* ✉ *11775 Sonoma Hwy./Hwy. 12* ☎ *707/996–6501* 🌐 *www.beltaneranch.com* 🛏 *3 rooms, 2 suites, 1 cottage* 🍽 *Breakfast.*

$$ B&B/INN Fodor's Choice ★ 🏨 **Gaige House.** Asian objets d'art and leather club chairs cozied up to the lobby fireplace are just a few of the graceful touches in this luxurious but understated bed-and-breakfast. **Pros:** beautiful lounge areas; lots of privacy; excellent service; full breakfasts, afternoon wine and appetizers. **Cons:** sound carries in the main house; the least expensive rooms are on the small side. [$] *Rooms from: $275* ✉ *13540 Arnold Dr.* ☎ *707/935–0237, 800/935–0237* 🌐 *www.gaige.com* 🛏 *10 rooms, 13 suites* 🍽 *Breakfast.*

$$ B&B/INN Fodor's Choice ★ 🏨 **Olea Hotel.** The husband-and-wife team of Ashish and Sia Patel gave an extreme makeover to a run-down former B&B, and after a year's labor unveiled a boutique lodging that's at once sophisticated and down-home country casual. **Pros:** beautiful style; welcoming staff; chef-prepared breakfasts; complimentary wine throughout stay. **Cons:** fills up quickly on weekends; minor road noise in some rooms. [$] *Rooms from: $257* ✉ *5131 Warm Springs Rd., west off Arnold Dr.* ☎ *707/996–5131* 🌐 *www.oleahotel.com* 🛏 *10 rooms, 2 cottages* 🍽 *Breakfast.*

Hitching a ride on the Benziger Family Winery tram tour

KENWOOD

3 miles north of Glen Ellen.

Tiny Kenwood consists of little more than a few restaurants and shops and a historic train depot. But hidden in this pretty landscape of meadows and woods at the north end of Sonoma Valley are several good wineries, most just off the Sonoma Highway (Highway 12).

GETTING HERE AND AROUND
To get to Kenwood from Glen Ellen, drive north on Highway 12.

EXPLORING
Deerfield Ranch Winery. The focus at Deerfield is on producing "clean wines"—ones low in histamines and sulfites—the better to eliminate the headaches and allergic reactions some red-wine drinkers experience. Winemaker Robert Rex accomplishes this goal with no loss of flavor or complexity. Deerfield wines are bold, fruit-forward wines with a long finish. The lush DRX and Meritage Bordeaux-style red blends invite contemplation about the vineyards, weather, and winemaking skills involved in their creation. To taste these and other wines, including a finely tuned blend of four white grapes, you walk deep into a 23,000-square-foot cave. ■**TIP→** Standard tastings ($15) include five wines; for an additional $5, you can sample more, including at least one older, library wine. ✉ *10200 Sonoma Hwy./Hwy. 12* ☎ *707/833–5215* ⊕ *www.deerfieldranch.com* ✉ *Tastings $15–$20* ☺ *Daily 10:30–4:30.*

and a side of garlic fries. Desserts tend toward the indulgent; witness the warm cinnamon-pecan bread pudding with a chocolate center that sits in a puddle of brandy sauce. $ *Average main: $20* ✉ *13670 Arnold Dr., at O'Donnell La.* ☎ *707/996–6409* ⊕ *www.glenelleninn. com* ⊗ *No lunch Wed.*

$$
ECLECTIC
Fodor'sChoice
★

✕ **Glen Ellen Star.** Chef Ari Weiswasser honed his craft at the French Laundry, Daniel, and other bastions of culinary finesse, but the goal at his hot-ticket Wine Country boîte is haute-rustic cuisine, much of which emerges from a wood-fired oven that burns a steady 600°F. Pizzas such as the crisp-crusted, richly sauced Margherita thrive in the torrid heat, as do root and other vegetables roasted in small iron skillets. Ditto for entrées that include juicy, tender roasted whole fish. Weiswasser signs each dish with a sauce, emulsion, or sly blend of spices that jazzes things up without upstaging the primary ingredient. The restaurant's decor is equally restrained, with an open-beam ceiling, exposed hardwood floors, and utilitarian seating. ■**TIP➜ Many regulars perch on a stool at the kitchen-view counter to watch the chefs at work.** $ *Average main: $21* ✉ *13648 Arnold Dr., at Warm Springs Rd.* ☎ *707/343–1384* ⊕ *glenellenstar.com* ⬛ *Reservations essential* ⊗ *No lunch.*

WHERE TO STAY

$
B&B/INN
Fodor'sChoice
★

🏨 **Beltane Ranch.** On a slope of the Mayacamas range a few miles from Glen Ellen, this 1892 ranch house, shaded by magnificent oak trees, contains charmingly old-fashioned rooms, each individually decorated with antiques and original artwork by noted artists. **Pros:** casual, friendly atmosphere; reasonable prices; beautiful grounds with ancient oak trees. **Cons:** downstairs rooms get some noise from upstairs rooms; ceiling fans instead of air-conditioning. $ *Rooms from: $185* ✉ *11775 Sonoma Hwy./Hwy. 12* ☎ *707/996–6501* ⊕ *www.beltaneranch.com* ⬆ *3 rooms, 2 suites, 1 cottage* ❤❤ *Breakfast.*

$$
B&B/INN
Fodor'sChoice
★

🏨 **Gaige House.** Asian objets d'art and leather club chairs cozied up to the lobby fireplace are just a few of the graceful touches in this luxurious but understated bed-and-breakfast. **Pros:** beautiful lounge areas; lots of privacy; excellent service; full breakfasts, afternoon wine and appetizers. **Cons:** sound carries in the main house; the least expensive rooms are on the small side. $ *Rooms from: $275* ✉ *13540 Arnold Dr.* ☎ *707/935–0237, 800/935–0237* ⊕ *www.gaige.com* ⬆ *10 rooms, 13 suites* ❤❤ *Breakfast.*

$$
B&B/INN
Fodor'sChoice
★

🏨 **Olea Hotel.** The husband-and-wife team of Ashish and Sia Patel gave an extreme makeover to a run-down former B&B, and after a year's labor unveiled a boutique lodging that's at once sophisticated and down-home country casual. **Pros:** beautiful style; welcoming staff; chef-prepared breakfasts; complimentary wine throughout stay. **Cons:** fills up quickly on weekends; minor road noise in some rooms. $ *Rooms from: $257* ✉ *5131 Warm Springs Rd., west off Arnold Dr.* ☎ *707/996–5131* ⊕ *www.oleahotel.com* ⬆ *10 rooms, 2 cottages* ❤❤ *Breakfast.*

10

Hitching a ride on the Benziger Family Winery tram tour

KENWOOD

3 miles north of Glen Ellen.

Tiny Kenwood consists of little more than a few restaurants and shops and a historic train depot. But hidden in this pretty landscape of meadows and woods at the north end of Sonoma Valley are several good wineries, most just off the Sonoma Highway (Highway 12).

GETTING HERE AND AROUND

To get to Kenwood from Glen Ellen, drive north on Highway 12.

EXPLORING

Deerfield Ranch Winery. The focus at Deerfield is on producing "clean wines"—ones low in histamines and sulfites—the better to eliminate the headaches and allergic reactions some red-wine drinkers experience. Winemaker Robert Rex accomplishes this goal with no loss of flavor or complexity. Deerfield wines are bold, fruit-forward wines with a long finish. The lush DRX and Meritage Bordeaux-style red blends invite contemplation about the vineyards, weather, and winemaking skills involved in their creation. To taste these and other wines, including a finely tuned blend of four white grapes, you walk deep into a 23,000-square-foot cave. ■ **TIP→ Standard tastings ($15) include five wines; for an additional $5, you can sample more, including at least one older, library wine.** ✉ *10200 Sonoma Hwy./Hwy. 12* ☎ *707/833–5215* ⊕ *www.deerfieldranch.com* 🍷 *Tastings $15–$20* ⏱ *Daily 10:30–4:30.*

Kunde Estate Winery & Vineyards. On your way into Kunde you pass a terrace flanked by fountains, virtually coaxing you to stay for a picnic with views over the vineyard. Best known for its toasty Chardonnays, the winery also makes well-regarded Sauvignon Blanc, Cabernet Sauvignon, Merlot, and Zinfandel wines. Among the Destination wines available only through the winery, the Dunfillan Cuvée, an astute blend of Cabernet and Syrah grapes, is worth checking out. The free basic tour of the grounds includes the caves, some of which stretch 175 feet below a vineyard. **TIP→ Reserve ahead for the Mountain Top Tasting, a popular tour that ends with a sampling of reserve wines ($40).** ✉ *9825 Sonoma Hwy./Hwy. 12* ☎ *707/833–5501* 🌐 *www.kunde.com* 🎫 *Tastings $10–$40, tours free–$50* 🕘 *Daily 10:30–5, tours daily at various times.*

St. Francis Winery. Nestled at the foot of Mt. Hood, St. Francis has earned national acclaim for its food-and-wine pairings. With its red-tile roof and dramatic bell tower, the winery's California mission–style visitor center occupies one of Sonoma's most scenic locations. The charm of the surroundings is matched by the wines, most of them red, including rich, earthy Zinfandels from the Dry Creek, Russian River, and Sonoma valleys. Chef David Bush's five-to-seven-course small bites and wine pairings ($50)—bouillabaisse with a mellifluous Cabernet Franc, for example—are offered from Thursday through Monday; pairings with cheeses and charcuterie ($30) are available daily. ✉ *100 Pythian Rd., off Hwy. 12* ☎ *888/675–9463, 707/833–6146* 🌐 *www.stfranciswinery.com* 🎫 *Tastings $10–$50* 🕘 *Daily 10–5.*

WHERE TO EAT AND STAY

$ ITALIAN

🍴 **Café Citti.** Classical music in the background, a friendly staff, and a roaring fire when it's cold outside keep this roadside café from feeling too spartan. Order dishes such as roast chicken and slabs of tiramisu from the counter and they're delivered to your table, indoors or on an outdoor patio. The array of prepared salads and sandwiches means the café does a brisk business in takeout for picnic packers, but you can also choose pasta made to order. [$] *Average main: $13* ✉ *9049 Sonoma Hwy./Hwy. 12* ☎ *707/833–2690* 🌐 *www.cafecitti.com* ✍ *Reservations not accepted.*

$$$$ B&B/INN Fodor's Choice ★

🏨 **Kenwood Inn and Spa.** French doors opening onto terraces or balconies, fluffy featherbeds, and wood-burning fireplaces give the uncommonly spacious guest rooms, many with tile floors, at this inn a particularly romantic air. **Pros:** large rooms; lavish furnishings; excellent restaurant; romantic. **Cons:** road or lobby noise in some rooms; expensive. [$] *Rooms from: $475* ✉ *10400 Sonoma Hwy./Hwy. 12* ☎ *707/833–1293, 800/353–6966* 🌐 *www.kenwoodinn.com* 🛏 *25 rooms, 4 suites* 🍽 *Breakfast.*

SPAS

Spa at Kenwood Inn. A pretty setting, expert practitioners, and rejuvenating French therapies make a visit to the Spa at Kenwood Inn a marvelously ethereal experience. The wine-based Vinothérapie treatments and beauty products from the French line Caudalíe combine in the delicious-sounding Honey Wine Wrap, which involves a warming, full-body slathering of wine yeast and honey, the better to rehydrate your parched and neglected skin. The Crushed Cabernet Scrub, designed to stimulate and soften your skin, raises the sweetness ante by adding brown sugar to the honey, along with crushed grape seeds and grape-seed oil. The spa's other services include massages and facials using the products and treatments by iS Clinical and Intraceuticals. ✉ *10400 Sonoma Hwy./Hwy. 12* ☎ *707/833–1293, 800/353–6966* ⊕ *www.kenwoodinn.com/spa.php* 💳 *Treatments $125–$390.*

ELSEWHERE IN SONOMA COUNTY

At nearly 1,598 square miles, there's more to Sonoma County than the day-tripper favorites of Sonoma, Glen Ellen, and Kenwood. To the north is Healdsburg, a small town that receives national media attention for its swank hotels and remarkable restaurants. An ideal base for wine tasting in northern Sonoma County, it's within easy striking distance of the scenic vineyards of the Alexander, Dry Creek, and Russian River valleys, home to some of the country's best Pinot Noir, Cabernet Sauvignon, Zinfandel, and Sauvignon Blanc vineyards. Though hardly unknown regions, the quiet roads that pass by them feel a world away from Highway 29 in Napa. The western stretches of Sonoma County are sparsely populated in comparison to the rest of Sonoma and have fewer wineries.

ESSENTIALS

Sonoma County Tourism Bureau ✉ *3637 Westwind Blvd., Santa Rosa* ☎ *707/522–5800, 800/576–6662* ⊕ *www.sonomacounty.com.*

SANTA ROSA

8 miles northwest of Kenwood; 55 miles north of San Francisco.

With more than 170,000 people, Santa Rosa, the Wine Country's largest city, isn't likely to charm you with its malls, office buildings, and frequent traffic snarls. Its moderately priced lodgings, however, can come in handy, especially since Santa Rosa is roughly equidistant from Sonoma, Healdsburg, and notable Russian River wineries.

GETTING HERE AND AROUND

Santa Rosa straddles U.S. 101, the route to take (north) from San Francisco. From the Sonoma Valley, take Highway 12 north. Factor in extra time when driving around sprawling Santa Rosa, especially during morning and evening commute hours.

EXPLORING

TOP ATTRACTIONS

Fodor'sChoice ★ **Matanzas Creek Winery.** The visitor center at Matanzas Creek sets itself apart with an understated Japanese aesthetic, extending to a tranquil fountain, a koi pond, and a vast field of lavender. The winery specializes in Sauvignon Blanc, Chardonnay, and Merlot wines, although it also produces Pinot Noirs and a rich Bordeaux blend called Journey. All tours take in the beautiful estate and include tastings. The Signature tour concludes with tastings of limited-production and library wines paired with artisanal cheeses. ■TIP→ **The ideal time to visit is in May and June, when lavender perfumes the air.** ✉ *6097 Bennett Valley Rd.* ☎ *707/528–6464, 800/590–6464* ⊕ *www.matanzascreek.com* ☕ *Tastings $10–$20, tours $10–$35* ☉ *Daily 10–4:30; estate tour ($10) daily at 10:30, others by appointment.*

FAMILY **Safari West.** An unexpected bit of wilderness in the Wine Country, this African wildlife preserve covers 400 acres. A visit begins with a stroll around enclosures housing lemurs, cheetahs, giraffes, and rare birds such as the brightly colored scarlet ibis. Next, climb with your guide onto open-air vehicles that spend about two hours combing the expansive property, where more than 80 species—including gazelles, wildebeests, and zebras—inhabit the hillsides. ✉ *3115 Porter Creek Rd., off Mark West Springs Rd.* ☎ *707/579–2551, 800/616–2695* ⊕ *www.safariwest.com* ☕ *$78–$80* ☉ *Safaris: mid-Mar.–early Sept. at 9, 10, 1, 2, and 4; hrs vary rest of year.*

WORTH NOTING

FAMILY **Charles M. Schulz Museum.** Fans of Snoopy and Charlie Brown will love this museum dedicated to the late Charles M. Schulz, who lived his last three decades in Santa Rosa. Permanent installations include a re-creation of the cartoonist's studio, and temporary exhibits often focus on a particular theme in his work. ■TIP→ **Children and adults can take a stab at creating cartoons in the Education Room.** ✉ *2301 Hardies La., at W. Steele La.* ☎ *707/579–4452* ⊕ *www.schulzmuseum.org* ☕ *$10* ☉ *Labor Day–Memorial Day, Mon. and Wed.–Fri. 11–5, weekends 10–5; Memorial Day–Labor Day, weekdays 11–5, weekends 10–5.*

DeLoach Vineyards. Slightly off the beaten track in western Santa Rosa, DeLoach is best known for its Russian River Valley Pinot Noirs, among them the much-lauded Pennacchio Vineyard edition and the Estate Collection Pinot Noir. The winery also produces old-vine Zinfandels, Chardonnays, and a handful of other varietals. Some of the reds are made using open-top wood fermentation vats that are uncommon in Sonoma but have been used in France for centuries to intensify a wine's flavor. The history-rich tour focuses on the estate vineyards outside the tasting-room door, where you can learn about the winery's labor-intensive biodynamic and organic farming methods. ✉ *1791 Olivet Rd., off Guerneville Rd.* ☎ *707/526–9111* ⊕ *www.deloachvineyards.com* ☕ *Tastings $10–$50, tour and tasting $15* ☉ *Daily 10–5; tour at 11.*

WHERE TO EAT

$$$
ECLECTIC
Fodor's Choice
★

✕ **Willi's Wine Bar.** Don't let the name fool you: instead of a sedate spot serving wine and delicate nibbles, you'll find a cozy warren of rooms where boisterous crowds snap up small plates from the globe-trotting menu. Dishes such as the pork-belly pot stickers represent Asia, and Moroccan-style lamb chops and balsamic roasted fig and Serrano-ham flatbread are some of the Mediterranean-inspired foods. The plate of crispy-skin Mt. Lassen trout is among the many using California-sourced ingredients. Wines are available in 2-ounce pours, making it easier to pair each of your little plates with a different glass. ■TIP→ It

10

can get noisy inside on busy nights, so consider a table on the covered patio. [$] *Average main: $28* ✉ *4404 Old Redwood Hwy., at Ursuline Rd.* ☎ *707/526–3096* 🌐 *williswinebar.net* 🕒 *No lunch Sun. and Mon.*

WHERE TO STAY

$$ HOTEL **Vintners Inn.** The owners of Ferrari-Carano Vineyards operate this oasis set amid 80 acres of vineyards that's known for its comfortable lodgings. **Pros:** spacious rooms with comfortable beds; jogging path through the vineyards; online deals pop up year-round. **Cons:** occasional noise from adjacent events center; some decor seems dated. [$] *Rooms from: $265* ✉ *4350 Barnes Rd.* ☎ *707/575–7350, 800/421–2584* 🌐 *www.vintnersinn.com* 🛏 *38 rooms, 6 suites* 🍴 *No meals.*

RUSSIAN RIVER VALLEY

10 miles northwest of Santa Rosa.

The Russian River flows from Mendocino to the Pacific, but Russian River Valley wine making centers on a triangle with points at Healdsburg, Guerneville, and Sebastopol. Tall redwoods shade the two-lane roads of this scenic area, where, thanks to the cooling marine influence, Pinot Noir and Chardonnay are the king and queen of grapes.

GETTING HERE AND AROUND

Many Russian River Valley visitors base themselves in Healdsburg. You can find noteworthy purveyors of Pinots and Chards by heading west from downtown on Mill Street, which eventually becomes Westside Road. For Forestville and Sebastopol wineries, continue south and west along Westside until it intersects River Road and turn west. Turn south at Mirabel Road and follow it to Highway 116. Turn west for Forestville and east for Sebastopol. Follow Highway 12 west 6 miles from Sebastopol to visit Freestone; Occidental is 4 miles north on the Bohemian Highway.

ESSENTIALS

Contacts Russian River Wine Road ☎ *707/433–4335, 800/723–6336* 🌐 *www.wineroad.com.*

EXPLORING

TOP ATTRACTIONS

Fodor's Choice ★ **Hartford Family Winery.** Pinot Noir lovers appreciate the subtle differences in the wines Hartford's Jeff Stewart crafts from grapes grown in Sonoma County's three top AVAs for the varietal—Los Carneros, Russian River Valley, and the Sonoma Coast—along with one from the Anderson Valley, just north in Mendocino County. The Pinot Noirs win praise from major wine critics, and Stewart also makes highly rated Chardonnays and old-vine Zinfandels. A reserve tasting ($15) includes a flight of six wines; a tour of the winery is part of the seated private library tasting ($35). ■ **TIP→ If the weather's good and you've made a reservation, your reserve tasting can take place on the patio outside the opulent main winery building.** ✉ *8075 Martinelli Rd., off Hwy. 116 or River Rd., Forestville* ☎ *707/887–8030, 800/588–0234* 🌐 *www.hartfordwines.com* 🎫 *Tastings $15–$35* 🕒 *Daily 10–4:30, tours by appointment.*

Fodor'sChoice **Iron Horse Vineyards.** A meandering one-lane road leads to this winery
★ known for its sparkling wines and estate Chardonnays and Pinot
Noirs. The sparklers have made history: Ronald Reagan served them
at his summit meetings with Mikhail Gorbachev; George Herbert
Walker Bush took some along to Moscow for treaty talks; and Barack
Obama has included them at official state dinners. Despite Iron Horse's
brushes with fame, a casual rusticity prevails at its outdoor tasting
area (large heaters keep things comfortable on chilly days), which
gazes out on acres of rolling, vine-covered hills. Tours take place on
weekdays at 10 am. ■TIP➔ **Winemaker David Munksgard leads the
Friday tour when his schedule permits.** ⊠ *9786 Ross Station Rd., off
Hwy. 116, Sebastopol* ☎ *707/887–1507* ⊕ *www.ironhorsevineyards.
com* ▭ *Tasting $20, tour $25* ⊙ *Daily 10–4:30, tour (by appointment) weekdays at 10.*

Fodor'sChoice **Merry Edwards Winery.** Winemaker Merry Edwards describes the Rus-
★ sian River Valley as "the epicenter of great Pinot Noir," and she
produces wines that express the unique characteristics of the soils,
climates, and Pinot Noir clones from which they derive. (Edwards's
research into Pinot Noir clones is so extensive that there's even one
named after her.) The valley's advantages, says Edwards, are warmer-
than-average daytime temperatures that encourage more intense fruit,
and evening fogs mitigate the extra heat's potential negative effects.
Group tastings of the well-composed single-vineyard and blended
Pinots take place throughout the day, and there are five sit-down
appointment slots available except on Sunday. Edwards also makes a
fine Sauvignon Blanc that's lightly aged in old oak. Tastings end, rather
than begin, with this singular white wine so as not to distract guests'
palates from the Pinot Noirs. ⊠ *2959 Gravenstein Hwy. N/Hwy. 116,
near Oak Grove Ave., Sebastopol* ☎ *707/823–7466, 888/388–9050*
⊕ *www.merryedwards.com* ▭ *Tasting free* ⊙ *Daily 9:30–4:30; call for
appointment or drop in and join next available tasting.*

Fodor'sChoice **Rochioli Vineyards and Winery.** Claiming one of the prettiest picnic sites
★ in the area, with tables overlooking the vineyards, this winery has an
airy little tasting room with an equally romantic view. Production is
small and fans on the winery's mailing list snap up most of the bottles,
but the winery is still worth a stop. Because of the cool growing conditions in the Russian River Valley, the flavors of the Chardonnay and
Sauvignon Blanc are intense and complex, and the Pinot Noir, which
helped cement the Russian River's status as a Pinot powerhouse, is consistently excellent. ⊠ *6192 Westside Rd., Healdsburg* ☎ *707/433–2305*
⊕ *www.rochioliwinery.com* ▭ *Tasting $10* ⊙ *Early Jan.–mid-Dec.,
Thurs.–Mon. 11–4, Tues. and Wed. by appointment.*

WORTH NOTING

The Barlow. On the site of a former apple cannery, this cluster of buildings celebrates Sonoma County's "maker" culture with an inspired
combination production space and marketplace. The complex contains
breweries and wine-making facilities, along with areas where people
create or sell crafts, large-scale artwork, and artisanal food, herbs, and
beverages. There's even a studio where artists using traditional methods
are creating the world's largest *thangka* (Tibetan painting). Only club

10

DID YOU KNOW?

People often refer to the
Wine Country as having a
Mediterranean climate. The
temperature year-around and
precipitation patterns are
very similar to those found
in Italy and Greece. But there
are also a number of microclimates that provide the
prime conditions for a variety
of wines.

members can visit the anchor wine tenant, Kosta Browne, but La Follette (sublimely aromatic Pinot Noirs and velvety Chardonnays) and other small producers have tasting rooms open to the public. Warped Brewing Company and Woodfour Brewing Company make and sell ales on-site, and you can have a nip of gin at Spirit Works Distillery. ✉ *6770 McKinley St., at Morris St., north off Hwy. 12, Sebastopol* ☎ *707/824–5600* 🌐 *www.thebarlow.net* 🎟 *Free to complex; tasting fees at wineries, breweries, distillery* 🕒 *Daily, hrs vary.*

Gary Farrell Winery. Pass through an impressive metal gate and wind your way up a steep hill to reach Gary Farrell, a spot with knockout views over the rolling hills and vineyards below. Though its Zinfandels and Chardonnays often excel, the winery built its reputation on Pinot Noirs, crafted these days by winemaker Theresa Heredia. **■ TIP→ Worth seeking out are the wines in the Inspiration Series, made from small lots of grapes—perhaps from certain vineyard blocks or a particular clone—that Heredia finds of special merit.** ✉ *10701 Westside Rd., Healdsburg* ☎ *707/473–2909* 🌐 *www.garyfarrellwines.com* 🎟 *Tastings $15–$25, tour $35* 🕒 *Daily 10:30–4:30, tour by appointment.*

WHERE TO EAT

$$$$ FRENCH Fodor's Choice ★

🍴 **The Farmhouse Inn.** From the sommelier who assists you with wine choices to the servers who describe the provenance of the black truffles shaved over the intricate pasta dishes, the staff matches the quality of this restaurant's French-inspired cuisine. The signature dish, "Rabbit Rabbit Rabbit," a trio of confit of leg, rabbit loin wrapped in applewood-smoked bacon, and roasted rack of rabbit with a whole-grain mustard sauce, is typical of preparations that are both rustic and refined. The menu is prix-fixe (three courses $69, four $84). **■ TIP→ The inn is a favorite of wine-industry foodies, so reserve well in advance; if it's full, you might be able to dine in the small lounge.** [$] *Average main: $69* ✉ *7871 River Rd., at Wohler Rd., Forestville* ☎ *707/887–3300, 800/464–6642* 🌐 *www.farmhouseinn.com* ✍ *Reservations essential* 🕒 *Closed Tues. and Wed. No lunch.*

$$$ MODERN AMERICAN

🍴 **Zazu Kitchen + Farm.** "Serve food from people you know" is the motto at Zazu, and some of the local ingredients in dishes here come from the owners themselves: executive chef Duskie Estes and her husband, John Stewart, the house *salumist* (specialist in all things pig). Small plates such as *chicharrones* (fried pork rinds), tamarind Petaluma chicken wings, and baby back ribs can add up to a meal, or you can sample a few appetizers before moving on to a bacon burger, duck-leg cassoulet, pasta, or steak and fries. In good weather the industrial-looking space's huge doors lift up to admit the breeze that often graces the open-air patio, which is surrounded by raised garden beds that supply produce and spices for diners' meals. Service can be chaotic. [$] *Average main: $26* ✉ *The Barlow, 6770 McKinley St., No. 150, Sebastopol* ☎ *707/523–4814* 🌐 *www.zazukitchen.com* 🕒 *Closed Tues. No lunch Mon.*

WHERE TO STAY

$$$
B&B/INN
Fodor's Choice
★

⊡ **The Farmhouse Inn.** With a rustic-farmhouse-meets-modern-loft aesthetic, the spacious rooms in this pale yellow farmhouse dating from 1873 are filled with king-size four-poster beds, whirlpool tubs, and terraces overlooking the hillside. **Pros:** fantastic restaurant; luxury bath products; full-service spa. **Cons:** road noise audible in rooms closest to the street. $ *Rooms from: $350* ✉ *7871 River Rd., Forestville* ☎ *707/887–3300, 800/464–6642* ⊕ *www.farmhouseinn.com* ⥱ *12 rooms, 6 suites* †○| *Breakfast.*

$
HOTEL
FAMILY

⊡ **Sebastopol Inn.** The cheerful rooms clustered around a pleasant courtyard at this reasonably priced inn are steps away from the Barlow, a hip collection of restaurants, wine-tasting rooms, brewpubs, galleries, and other spaces occupied by artisans and entrepreneurs. **Pros:** good rates; friendly staff; across from the Barlow complex; near noteworthy wineries. **Cons:** no frills; bland decor; beds too firm for some guests. $ *Rooms from: $139* ✉ *6751 Sebastopol Ave., Sebastopol* ☎ *707/829– 2500* ⊕ *www.sebastopolinn.com* ⥱ *29 rooms, 2 suites* †○| *No meals.*

SPORTS AND THE OUTDOORS

CANOE TRIPS

Burke's Canoe Trips. You get a real feel for the Russian River's flora and fauna on a leisurely 10-mile paddle from Burke's downstream to Guerneville. A shuttle bus returns you to your car at the end of the journey, which is best taken from late May through mid-October. The cost is $65 per canoe. ✉ *8600 River Rd., at Mirabel Rd., Forestville* ☎ *707/887–1222* ⊕ *www.burkescanoetrips.com.*

HEALDSBURG

17 miles north of Santa Rosa.

Just when it seems that the buzz about Healdsburg couldn't get any more intense, another glossy food or wine magazine will publish an article about the chic hotels and restaurants that keep popping up here. Despite all the hype, you needn't be a tycoon to enjoy this town. For every ritzy restaurant or hotel there's a great bakery, modest B&B, or swell motel. The tin-roof bandstand on Healdsburg Plaza hosts free concerts, at which you might hear anything from bluegrass to Sousa marches. Add to that the plaza's fragrant magnolia trees and bright flower beds, and the whole ensemble seems right out of a Norman Rockwell painting.

The setting is no less idyllic in the adjacent countryside, where food stands along relatively untrafficked roads sell just-plucked fruits and vine-ripened tomatoes. Tucked behind groves of eucalyptus or hidden high on fog-shrouded hills, the winery buildings here are barely visible.

GETTING HERE AND AROUND

Healdsburg sits just off U.S. 101. Heading north, take the Central Healdsburg exit to reach Healdsburg Plaza; heading south, take the Westside Road exit and pass east under the freeway. From the plaza you can walk to many restaurants, shops, and tasting rooms.

10

Annual barrel tasting along Russian River's wine road

WHERE TO EAT

$$$$
AMERICAN

✕ **Barndiva.** This hip joint abandons the homey vibe of many Wine Country spots for a more urban feel. Electronic music plays quietly in the background while servers ferry inventive seasonal cocktails. The food is as stylish as the couples cozying up next to each other on the banquette seats. Make a light meal out of starters like "The Artisan," a bountiful plate of cheeses and charcuterie, or settle in for the evening with such dishes as bacon-wrapped pork tenderloin with stone-ground polenta or crispy young chicken served with roasted brussels sprouts, and egg-yolk ravioli. ■ TIP→ **During warm weather the open-air patio is the place to be.** $ *Average main: $31* ✉ *231 Center St., at Matheson St.* ☎ *707/431–0100* ⊕ *www.barndiva.com* ⊗ *Closed Mon. and Tues.*

$$
MODERN
AMERICAN
Fodor's Choice
★

✕ **Chalkboard.** Unvarnished oak flooring, wrought-iron accents, and a vaulted white ceiling create a polished yet rustic ambience for the playfully ambitious cuisine of chef Shane McAnelly. Starters such as pork-belly biscuits might at first glance seem frivolous, but the silky flavor blend—maple glaze, pickled onions, and chipotle mayo playing off feathery biscuit halves—signals a supremely capable tactician at work. Likewise with vegetable sides such as fried brussels sprouts perched upon a perky kimchi purée, or moist and crispy buttermilk-fried quail. House-made pasta dishes favor rich country flavors—the robust Sonoma lamb *sugo* (sauce) with Pecorino-Romano tickles the entire palate—while desserts named The Candy Bar and Donuts O' the Day aim to please (and do). The canny wine selections ably support McAnelly's cuisine. $ *Average main: $19* ✉ *Hotel Les Mars, 29 North St., west of Healdsburg Ave.* ☎ *707/473–8030* ⊕ *chalkboard healdsburg.com.*

$ ✕ **Costeaux.** This French-style bakery and café has won numerous
FRENCH awards for its bread, and the croissants are among Sonoma County's
best. Breakfast, served all day, includes homemade quiche, the signature omelet (sun-dried tomatoes, applewood-smoked bacon, and Brie),
and French toast made from thick slabs of cinnamon-walnut bread.
Among the lunch items are two au courant variations on classic sandwiches: a French dip made from house-roasted rib eye and a Monte
Cristo (turkey, ham, and Jarlsberg cheese) on that addictive cinnamon-
walnut bread. ■ TIP➔ **Arrive early on weekends to grab a seat on the
open-air patio.** Ⓢ *Average main: $13* ✉ *417 Healdsburg Ave., at North
St.* ☎ *707/433–1913* ⊕ *www.costeaux.com* ☾ *No dinner.*

$ ✕ **Downtown Bakery & Creamery.** To catch the Healdsburg spirit, hit the
BAKERY plaza in the early morning to down a cup of coffee and a fragrant sticky
Fodor'sChoice bun or a too-darlin' *canelé,* a French-style pastry with a soft custard
★ center surrounded by a dense caramel crust. Until 2 pm you can also
go the full breakfast route: pancakes, granola, poached farm eggs on
polenta, or perhaps the dandy bacon-and-egg pizza. For lunch there are
sandwiches and focaccia. Ⓢ *Average main: $8* ✉ *308A Center St., at
North St.* ☎ *707/431–2719* ⊕ *www.downtownbakery.net* ⊿ *Reservations not accepted* ☾ *No dinner.*

$$ ✕ **Scopa.** At his tiny, deservedly popular eatery, chef Ari Rosen prepares
ITALIAN rustic Italian specialties such as *sugo Calabrese* (tomato-braised beef
Fodor'sChoice and pork rib served with smoked mozzarella in a tomato sauce) and
★ house-made ravioli stuffed with braised rabbit, leeks, and black trum-
pets. Simple thin-crust pizzas make fine meals, too. Locals love the res-
taurant for its lack of pretension: wine is served in juice glasses, and the
friendly hostess makes the rounds to ensure everyone is satisfied. You'll
be packed in elbow-to-elbow with your fellow diners, but for a convivial
evening over a bottle of Nebbiolo, there's no better choice. Ⓢ *Average
main: $20* ✉ *109A Plaza St., near Healdsburg Ave.* ☎ *707/433–5282*
⊕ *www.scopahealdsburg.com* ☾ *No lunch.*

$$$ ✕ **Spoonbar.** Cantina doors that open onto Healdsburg Avenue make
MODERN this trendy eatery especially appealing in summer, when a warm breeze
AMERICAN wafts into the stylish space. Midcentury modern furnishings, concrete
Fodor'sChoice walls, and a long communal table fashioned from rough-hewn acacia
★ wood create an urbane setting for chef Louis Maldonado's contemporary American fare. Divided into five sections, the menu lets you mix
and match to create a memorable meal. The mains might include Cornish game hen roulade with artichokes or loin of beef in red wine *jus,*
served with quinoa and cider-braised root vegetables. The perpetually
packed bar, known for inventive seasonal and historic cocktails, is the
real draw for many locals. Ⓢ *Average main: $23* ✉ *h2hotel, 219 Healds-
burg Ave., at Vine St.* ☎ *707/433–7222* ⊕ *www.h2hotel.com/spoonbar*
☾ *No lunch Mon.–Thurs. in winter.*

$$$ ✕ **Willi's Seafood & Raw Bar.** The perpetually packed Willi's draws a
SEAFOOD festive crowd that likes to enjoy specialty cocktails at the full bar
Fodor'sChoice before sitting down to a dinner of small, mostly seafood-oriented
★ plates. The warm Maine lobster roll with garlic butter and fennel
conjures up a New England fish shack, while the ceviches and the
scallops served with a cilantro-and-pumpkin-seed pesto suggest Latin

10

America. [$] *Average main: $25* ✉ *403 Healdsburg Ave., at North St.* ☎ *707/433–9191* 🌐 *www.willisseafood.net* ☞ *Reservations not accepted Fri.–Sun.*

$$$ AMERICAN 🍴 **Zin Restaurant and Wine Bar.** Concrete floors and large canvases on the walls lend this restaurant a casual, industrial, and slightly artsy feel. The American cuisine—such as the roasted pork belly with pickled apples or the free-range chicken braised in red wine—is hearty and highly seasoned. Portions are large, so consider sharing if you hope to save room for such desserts as the brownie sundae with house-made ice cream. As you might have guessed from the name, Zinfandel is the drink of choice here, though Sonoma County's other major varietals show up on the 100-bottle wine list. ■ **TIP→ From Sunday through Thursday, blue-plate specials featuring homey fare (think pot roast and chicken and dumplings) make this place a bargain.** [$] *Average main: $25* ✉ *344 Center St., at North St.* ☎ *707/473–0946* 🌐 *zinrestaurant.com* ⏲ *No lunch weekends.*

WHERE TO STAY

$$ HOTEL 🏨 **Best Western Plus Dry Creek Inn.** Spotless rooms and easy access both to downtown and outlying hot spots make this Spanish mission–style motel near U.S. 101 Healdsburg's best low-budget option. **Pros:** laundry facilities; frequent Internet discounts. **Cons:** thin walls; highway noise audible in many rooms; bland furnishings in standard rooms. [$] *Rooms from: $172* ✉ *198 Dry Creek Rd.* ☎ *707/433–0300, 800/222–5784* 🌐 *www.drycreekinn.com* 🛏 *163 rooms* 🍽 *Breakfast.*

$$ B&B/INN Fodor's Choice ★ 🏨 **h2hotel.** Eco-friendly touches abound at this hotel, from the plant-covered "green" roof to wooden decks made from salvaged lumber. **Pros:** stylish modern design; popular bar; complimentary bikes. **Cons:** least expensive rooms lack bathtubs; no fitness facilities. [$] *Rooms from: $275* ✉ *219 Healdsburg Ave.* ☎ *707/922–5251* 🌐 *www.h2hotel.com* 🛏 *34 rooms, 2 suites* 🍽 *Breakfast.*

$$$ B&B/INN Fodor's Choice ★ 🏨 **The Honor Mansion.** An 1883 Italianate Victorian houses this photogenic hotel; rooms in the main house preserve a sense of the building's heritage, whereas the larger suites are comparatively understated. **Pros:** homemade sweets available at all hours; spa pavilions by pool available for massages in fair weather. **Cons:** almost a mile from Healdsburg's plaza; walls can seem thin. [$] *Rooms from: $325* ✉ *891 Grove St.* ☎ *707/433–4277, 800/554–4667* 🌐 *www.honormansion.com* 🛏 *5 rooms, 7 suites, 1 cottage* ⏲ *Closed 2 wks around Christmas* 🍽 *Breakfast.*

$$$ RESORT 🏨 **Hotel Healdsburg.** Across the street from the tidy town plaza, this spare, sophisticated hotel caters to travelers with an urban sensibility. **Pros:** several rooms overlook the town plaza; comfortable lobby with a small attached bar; extremely comfortable beds. **Cons:** exterior rooms get some street noise; rooms could use better lighting. [$] *Rooms from: $375* ✉ *25 Matheson St.* ☎ *707/431–2800, 800/889–7188* 🌐 *www.hotelhealdsburg.com* 🛏 *49 rooms, 6 suites* 🍽 *Breakfast.*

$$$$ HOTEL Fodor's Choice ★ 🏨 **Hôtel Les Mars.** This Relais & Châteaux property takes the prize for opulence with guest rooms spacious and elegant enough for French nobility, 18th- and 19th-century antiques and reproductions, canopy beds dressed in luxe linens, and gas-burning fireplaces. **Pros:** large

rooms; just off Healdsburg's plaza; fancy bath products. **Cons:** very expensive. $ *Rooms from: $625* ✉ *27 North St.* ☎ *707/433–4211* ⊕ *www.hotellesmars.com* ↪ *16 rooms* ⦿ *Breakfast.*

SPAS

Fodor'sChoice **Spa Dolce.** Owner Ines von Majthenyi Scherrer has a good local rep, ★ having run a popular nearby spa before opening this stylish facility just off Healdsburg Plaza. Spa Dolce specializes in skin and body care for men and women, and makeup, waxing, and nail care for women. Curved white walls and fresh-cut floral arrangements set a subdued tone for such treatments as the exfoliating Hauschka body scrub, which combines organic brown sugar with scented oil. There's a romantic room for couples to enjoy massages for two. Many guests come just for the facials, which range from a straightforward cleansing to an anti-aging peel. ✉ *250 Center St., at Matheson St.* ☎ *707/433–0177* ⊕ *www.spadolce.com* ✂ *Treatments $20–$210* ☉ *Tues.–Sun. 10–7.*

SPORTS AND THE OUTDOORS

Wine Country Bikes. This shop in downtown Healdsburg is perfectly located for single or multi-day treks into the Dry Creek and Russian River valleys. Bikes, including tandems, rent for $39 to $145 a day. One-day tours start at $149. ✉ *61 Front St., at Hudson St.* ☎ *707/473–0610, 866/922–4537* ⊕ *www.winecountrybikes.com.*

SHOPPING

Fodor'sChoice **Saint Dizier Home.** With its selection of furniture and contemporary items ★ for the home, this shop reminds mere mortals why the universe provides us with decorators and designers—they really do know best. ✉ *259 Center St., at Matheson St.* ☎ *707/473–0980* ⊕ *www.saintdhome.com.*

Fodor'sChoice **The Shed.** Inside a glass-front, steel-clad variation on a traditional ★ grange hall, this shop-cum-eatery celebrates local agriculture with specialty foods. It also stocks seeds and plants, gardening and farming implements, cookware, and everything a smart pantry should hold. ✉ *25 North St., west of Healdsburg Ave.* ☎ *707/431–7433* ⊕ *healdsburgshed.com.*

10

DRY CREEK AND ALEXANDER VALLEYS

With its diverse terrain and microclimates, the Dry Creek Valley supports an impressive range of varietals. Zinfandel grapes flourish on the benchlands, whereas the gravelly, well-drained soil of the valley floor is better known for Chardonnay and, in the north, Sauvignon Blanc. Pinot Noir, Syrah, and other cool-climate grapes thrive on eastern-facing slopes that receive less afternoon sun than elsewhere in the valley.

Dry Creek wineries tend to be smaller, which make them a good bet on summer weekends, when tourists flood more easily accessible locales. The Alexander Valley, which lies northeast of Healdsburg, is similarly rustic. The largely family-owned wineries are known for Zinfandels, Chardonnays, and Cabernet Sauvignons, though Cabernet Franc and other less high-profile wines are also made here.

GETTING HERE AND AROUND

To reach the Dry Creek Valley from Healdsburg, drive north on Healdsburg Avenue and turn left on Dry Creek Road. West of U.S. 101, you'll see signs pointing the way to wineries on that road and West Dry Creek Road, which runs roughly parallel about a mile to the west. To get to the Alexander Valley from the plaza, drive north on Healdsburg Avenue and veer right onto Alexander Valley Road. Follow it to Highway 128, where many of this appellation's best wineries lie.

EXPLORING

TOP ATTRACTIONS

Dry Creek Vineyard. Fumé Blanc is king at Dry Creek, where the refreshing white wine is made in the style of those in Sancerre, France. The winery also makes well-regarded Zinfandels, a zesty dry Chenin Blanc, a Pinot Noir, and a handful of Cabernet Sauvignon blends. Since many wines are priced below $30 a bottle (some less than $20), it's a popular stop for wine lovers looking to stock their cellars for a reasonable price. You can picnic on the lawn next to a flowering magnolia tree. Conveniently, a general store and deli is close by. ⊠ *3770 Lambert Bridge Rd., off Dry Creek Rd., Healdsburg* ☎ *707/433–1000, 800/864–9463* ⊕ *www.drycreekvineyard.com* ᗌ *Tastings $5–$45, tour $15* ⊙ *Daily 10:30–4:30, tour 11 and 1 by appointment.*

FAMILY   **Francis Ford Coppola Winery.** The film director's over-the-top fantasyland is the sort of place the midlevel Mafiosi in his *The Godfather* saga might declare had real class—the "everyday wines" poured here are pretty much beside the point. The fun here is all in the excess, and you may find it hard to resist having your photo snapped standing next to Don Corleone's desk from *The Godfather* or beside memorabilia from other Coppola films, including some directed by his daughter, Sofia. A bandstand reminiscent of one in *The Godfather Part II* is the centerpiece of a large pool area where you can rent a changing room, complete with shower, and spend the afternoon lounging poolside, perhaps ordering food from the adjacent café. A more elaborate restaurant, Rustic, overlooks the vineyards. ⊠ *300 Via Archimedes, off U.S. 101, Geyserville* ☎ *707/857–1400* ⊕ *www.franciscoppolawinery.com* ᗌ *Tastings free–$15, tours $20–$75, pool pass $30* ⊙ *Tasting room daily 11–6, restaurant daily 11–9; pool hrs vary seasonally.*

Fodor's Choice   **Locals Tasting Room.** Though trending upscale, downtown Geyserville
★   remains little more than a crossroads with a few shops and restaurants. But if you're serious about wine, Carolyn Lewis's tasting room is alone worth a trek. Connoisseurs come to sample the output of a dozen or so small wineries, most without tasting rooms of their own. There's no fee for tasting—a bargain for wines of this quality—and the extremely knowledgeable staff is happy to pour you a flight of several wines so you can compare, say, different Cabernet Sauvignons. ⊠ *21023A Geyserville Ave., at Hwy. 128, Geyserville* ☎ *707/857–4900* ⊕ *www. tastelocalwines.com* ᗌ *Tasting free* ⊙ *Daily 11–6.*

Quivira Vineyards and Winery. An unassuming winery in a modern wooden barn topped by solar panels, Quivira produces some of Dry Creek's most interesting wines. Hugh Chappelle, the winemaker since

2010, crafts well-balanced reds, among them a lush Syrah, several hearty Zinfandels, and a Petite Sirah that showcases this unheralded varietal's noblest attributes. He also makes a zesty yet refined Sauvignon Blanc. The excellent tour provides information about the winery's biodynamic and organic farming practices and offers a glimpse of the beautiful garden and the property's pigs, chickens, and beehives. **■ TIP→ You can take a free self-guided tour through the garden, some of whose bounty—including estate-grown honey and olive oil—is available for sale.** ✉ *4900 W. Dry Creek Rd., near Wine Creek Rd., Healdsburg* ☎ *707/431–8333, 800/292–8339* 🌐 *www.quivirawine.com* 🎟 *Tasting $10, tours $20–$30* 🕓 *Daily 11–5; tours by appointment.*

Fodor's Choice ★ **Ridge Vineyards.** Ridge stands tall among California wineries, and not merely because one of its 1971 Cabernet Sauvignons placed first in a 2006 re-creation of the 1976 Judgment of Paris tasting. The winery built its reputation on Cabernet Sauvignons, Zinfandels, and Chardonnays of unusual depth and complexity, but you'll also find blends of Rhône varietals. Ridge makes wines using grapes from several California locales—including the Dry Creek Valley, Sonoma Valley, Napa Valley, and Paso Robles—but the focus is on single-vineyard estate wines such as the exquisitely textured Lytton Springs Zinfandel blend from grapes grown near the tasting room. In good weather you can taste outside, taking in views of rolling vineyard hills while you sip. **■ TIP→ The $20 tasting option includes a pour of the top-of-the-line Monte Bello Cabernet Sauvignon blend from grapes grown in the Santa Cruz Mountains.** ✉ *650 Lytton Springs Rd., off U.S. 101, Healdsburg* ☎ *707/433–7721* 🌐 *www.ridgewine.com* 🎟 *Tastings $5–$20, tours $30–$40* 🕓 *Daily 11–4.*

WHERE TO EAT AND STAY

$$ ITALIAN Fodor's Choice ★ 🍴 **Diavola Pizzeria & Salumeria.** A cozy dining room with hardwood floors, a pressed-tin ceiling, and exposed-brick walls provide a fitting setting for the rustic cuisine at this Geyserville charmer. Chef Dino Bugica studied with several artisans in Italy before opening this restaurant that specializes in pizzas pulled from a wood-burning oven and several types of house-cured meats. A few salads and meaty main courses round out the menu. **■ TIP→ If you're impressed by the antipasto plate, you can pick up some smoked pork belly, pancetta, or spicy Calabrese sausage to take home.** [$] *Average main: $19* ✉ *21021 Geyserville Ave., at Hwy. 128, Geyserville* ☎ *707/814–0111* 🌐 *www.diavolapizzeria.com* ✍ *Reservations not accepted.*

$$ HOTEL 🏨 **Geyserville Inn.** Clever travelers give the Healdsburg hubbub and prices the heave-ho but still have easy access to outstanding Dry Creek and Alexander Valley wineries from this modest, well-run inn. **Pros:** pool; second-floor rooms in back have vineyard views; picnic area. **Cons:** occasional noise bleed-through from corporate and other events. [$] *Rooms from: $155* ✉ *21714 Geyserville Ave., Geyserville* ☎ *707/857–4343, 877/857–4343* 🌐 *www.geyservilleinn.com* 🛏 *41 rooms* 🍽 *No meals.*

THE NORTH COAST

From the Sonoma Coast to
Redwood National Park

WELCOME TO THE NORTH COAST

TOP REASONS TO GO

★ **Scenic coastal drives:** There's hardly a road here that *isn't* scenic.

★ **Wild beaches:** This stretch of California is one of nature's masterpieces. Revel in the unbridled, rugged coastline, without a building in sight.

★ **Dinnertime:** When you're done hiking the beach, refuel with delectable food; you'll find everything from burritos to bouillabaisse.

★ **Romance:** Here you can end almost every day with a perfect sunset.

★ **Wildlife:** Watch for migrating whales, sunbathing sea lions and huge Roosevelt elk with majestic antlers.

1 The Sonoma Coast. As you enter Sonoma County from the south on Highway 1, you pass first through gently rolling pastureland. North of Bodega Bay dramatic shoreline scenery takes over. The road snakes up, down, and around sheer cliffs and steep inclines—some without guardrails—where cows seem to cling precariously. Stunning vistas (or cottony fog) and hairpin turns make for an exhilarating drive.

2 The Mendocino Coast. The timber industry gave birth to most of the small towns along this stretch of coastline. Although tourism now drives the economy, the region has retained much of its old-fashioned charm. The beauty of the landscape, of course, has not changed.

3 Redwood Country. There's a different state of mind in Humboldt County. Here, instead of spas, there are old-time hotels. Instead of wineries, there are breweries. The landscape is primarily thick redwood forest; the interior mountains get snow in winter and sizzle in summer while the coast sits covered in fog. Until as late as 1924, there was no road north of Willits; the coastal towns were reachable only by sea. That legacy is apparent in the communities of today: Eureka and Arcata, both former ports, are sizeable, but otherwise towns are tiny and nestled in the woods, and people have an independent spirit that recalls the original homesteaders. Coming from the south, Garberville is a good place to stop for picnic provisions and stretch your legs.

4 Redwood National and State Parks. For a pristine encounter with giant redwoods, make the trek to these coastal parks where even casual visitors have easy access to the trees. *(See Chapter 12, Redwood National and State Parks.)*

11

Smith River
Point St. George
Crescent City
199
SISKIYOU MOUNTAINS
101
96
Klamath
Redwoods National
& State Parks **4**
Orick
Patrick's Point
State Park
Trinidad
McKinleyville
96
Willow Creek
Arcata Bay **3** Arcata
Humboldt Bay Eureka
Fortuna
299
Ferndale Hydesville
Cape
Mendocino Rio
Point Dell
Gorda Humboldt
Redwoods
State Park
Hayfork
36
KLAMATH MOUNTAINS
COAST
KING MTN RANGE
Garberville
Richardson Grove
State Park
Leggett
Laytonville
RANGES
Fort Bragg 101
Mendocino Willits
Little River 20
Albion
2 Elk 128 Ukiah
Point Arena
Lighthouse
Lucerne
ANDERSON VALLEY
Point Arena Kelseyville
Gualala Cloverdale
Clearlake
Lower Lake
Pacific Coast Hwy
Stewarts
Point **1**
Healdsburg
Jenner 101
Occidental Sebastopol
Bodega Bay
Petaluma
Inverness Novato
Point Reyes
National Seashore
Bolinas
Marin Headlands
San Francisco Oakland
Daly City
Calistoga
Saint Helena
Santa Rosa
29
Napa
Sonoma
Vallejo
80 Concord
Richmond
Berkeley

PACIFIC OCEAN

0   30 mi
0   30 km

GETTING ORIENTED

It's all but impossible to explore the Northern California coast without a car. Indeed, you wouldn't want to—driving here is half the fun. The main road is Highway 1, two lanes that twist and turn (sometimes 180 degrees) up cliffs and down through valleys. Towns appear every so often, but this is mostly a land of green pasture, dense forest, and natural, undeveloped coastline. ■TIP➔ Pace yourself: Most drivers stop frequently to appreciate the views (and you can't drive faster than 20–40 mph on many portions of the highway), so don't plan to drive too far in one day.

Updated by Christine Vovakes

The spectacular coastline between Marin County and the Oregon border defies expectations. The landscape is defined by the Pacific Ocean, but instead of boardwalks and bikinis there are ragged cliffs and pounding waves—and the sunbathers are mostly sea lions. Instead of strip malls and freeways, you'll find a single-lane road that follows a fickle shoreline. Although the towns along the way vary from deluxe spa retreat to hippie hideaway, all are reliably sleepy—and that's exactly why many Californians, especially those from the Bay Area, escape here to enjoy nature unspoiled by the agitations of daily life.

This stretch of Highway 1 is made up of numerous little worlds, each different from the next. From Point Reyes toward Bodega Bay, the land spreads out into green, rolling pastures and sandy beaches. The road climbs higher and higher as it heads north through Sonoma County, and in Mendocino County the coastline follows the ins and outs of lush valleys where rivers pour down from the forests and into the ocean. At Humboldt County the highway heads inland to the redwoods, and then returns to the shoreline at the tidal flats surrounding the ports of Eureka and Arcata. Heading north to the Oregon border, the coast is increasingly wild and lined with giant redwood trees.

PLANNING

WHEN TO GO
The North Coast is a year-round destination, though when you go determines what you will see. The migration of the Pacific gray whales is a wintertime phenomenon, which lasts roughly from mid-December to early April. Wildflowers follow the winter rain, as early as January in southern areas through June and July farther north. Summer is the

high season for tourists, but spring, fall, and even winter are arguably better times to visit when the pace is slower, towns are quieter, and lodging is cheaper.

The coastal climate is similar to San Francisco's, although winter nights are colder than in the city. In July and August thick fog can drop temperatures to the high 50s, but fear not! You need only drive inland to find temperatures that are often 20 degrees higher.

GETTING HERE AND AROUND

AIR TRAVEL

The only North Coast airport with commercial air service, Arcata/ Eureka Airport (ACV) receives United Express flights. The airport is in McKinleyville, which is 16 miles from Eureka. A taxi to Eureka costs about $50 and takes roughly 25 minutes. Door-to-door airport shuttles cost $20 to Arcata and Trinidad, $24 to Eureka, and $50 to Ferndale. All prices are for the first person, and go up $5 for each additional person.

Airport Contact Arcata/Eureka Airport ⌧ *3561 Boeing Ave., McKinleyville* ☎ *707/839–5401.*

Shuttle Contact Door to Door Airport Shuttle ☎ *888/338–5497, 707/839–4186* ⊕ *www.doortodoorairporter.com.*

BUS TRAVEL

Greyhound buses travel along U.S. 101 from San Francisco to Garberville, Eureka, and Arcata. Humboldt Transit Authority connects Eureka, Arcata, and Trinidad.

Bus Contacts Greyhound ☎ *800/231–2222* ⊕ *www.greyhound.com.*
Humboldt Transit Authority ☎ *707/443–0826* ⊕ *www.hta.org.*

CAR TRAVEL

Although U.S. 101 has excellent services, long stretches separate towns along Highway 1, and services are even fewer and farther between on the smaller roads. ■TIP➜ **If you're running low on fuel and see a gas station, stop for a refill.** Twisting Highway 1 is the scenic route to Mendocino from San Francisco, but the fastest one is U.S. 101 north to Highway 128 west (from Cloverdale) to Highway 1 north. The quickest route to the far North Coast is a straight shot up U.S. 101, which runs inland until Eureka. Weather sometimes forces closure of parts of Highway 1, but it's rare.

Road Conditions Caltrans ☎ *800/427–7623* ⊕ *www.dot.ca.gov.*

RESTAURANTS

A few restaurants with national reputations, plus several more of regional note, entice palates on the North Coast. Even the smallest cafés take advantage of the abundant fresh seafood and locally grown vegetables and herbs. Attire is usually informal, though at pricier establishments dressy casual is the norm. Most kitchens close at 8 or 8:30 and few places serve past 9:30. Many restaurants close for a winter break in January or early February.

HOTELS

Restored Victorians, rustic lodges, country inns, and vintage motels are among the accommodations available here. Few have air-conditioning (the ocean breezes make it unnecessary), and many have no phones or TVs in the rooms. Although several towns have only one or two places to spend the night, some of these lodgings are destinations in themselves. Budget accommodations are rare, but in winter you're likely to find reduced rates and nearly empty inns and B&Bs. In summer and on the weekends, though, make bed-and-breakfast reservations as far ahead as possible—rooms at the best inns often sell out months in advance. *Hotel reviews have been shortened. For full information, visit Fodors.com.*

WHAT IT COSTS				
	$	**$$**	**$$$**	**$$$$**
Restaurants	under $16	$16–$22	$23–$30	over $30
Hotels	under $121	$121–$175	$176–$250	over $250

Restaurant prices are the average cost of a main course at dinner or, if dinner is not served, at lunch, excluding sales tax of 7.5–9%. Hotel prices are the lowest cost of a standard double room in high season, excluding service charges and 8%–11% tax.

VISITOR INFORMATION

Contacts Humboldt County Convention and Visitors Bureau ✉ *1034 2nd St., Eureka* ☎ *707/443–5097, 800/346–3482* ⊕ *www.redwoods.info.* **Mendocino Coast Chamber of Commerce** ✉ *217 S. Main St., Fort Bragg* ☎ *707/961–6300* ⊕ *www.mendocinocoast.com.* **Redwood Coast Chamber: Sonoma to Mendocino** ☎ *707/884–1080, 800/778–5252* ⊕ *www.redwoodcoastchamber.com.* **Sonoma County Tourism** ☎ *707/522–5800, 800/576–6662* ⊕ *www.sonomacounty.com.* **Visit Mendocino County** ✉ *345 N. Franklin St., Ft. Bragg* ☎ *707/964–9010, 866/466–3636* ⊕ *www.visitmendocino.com.*

THE SONOMA COAST

BODEGA BAY

23 miles west of Santa Rosa.

From the busy harbor here, commercial boats pursue fish and Dungeness crab. There's nothing quaint about this working town without a center—it's just a string of businesses along several miles of Highway 1. But some tourists still come to see where Alfred Hitchcock shot *The Birds* in 1962. The Tides Wharf complex, an important location used for the movie, has been expanded and remodeled several times and is no longer recognizable. But a few miles inland, in Bodega, you can find Potter Schoolhouse, which is now a private residence.

GETTING HERE AND AROUND

To reach Bodega Bay, exit U.S. 101 at Santa Rosa and take Highway 12 west (it's called Bodega Highway west of Sebastopol) 23 miles to the coast. A scenic alternative is to take U.S. 101's East Washington Street/Central Petaluma exit and follow signs west to Bodega Bay; just after you merge onto Highway 1, you'll pass through down-home Valley Ford. Mendocino Transit Authority (🌐 *www.mendocinotransit.org*) Route 95 buses connect Bodega Bay with coastal towns and Santa Rosa.

BEACHES

Fodor's Choice ★ **Sonoma Coast State Park.** The park's gorgeous sandy coves stretch for 17 miles from Bodega Head to 4 miles north of Jenner. **Bodega Head** is an especially popular perch for whale-watchers, though if you're lucky you'll catch sight of migrating whales from any of the beaches. **Rock Point, Duncan's Landing,** and **Wright's Beach,** clustered at about the halfway mark, have picnic areas, as do several other spots. Rogue waves have swept people off the rocks at Duncan's Landing, so don't stray past signs warning you away. Relatively calmer **Shell Beach,** about 2 miles north, is known for beachcombing, tide pooling, and fishing. About 2½ miles north of Shell Beach, near the mouth of the Russian River at Jenner, a long road leads from the highway to **Goat Rock.** Harbor seals lounge at the long beach here; pupping season is from March through August. Bring binoculars and walk north from the parking lot to view the seals. During summer lifeguards are on duty at some beaches, but strong rip currents and heavy surf keep most would-be swimmers on shore. Wright's Beach and Bodega Dunes have developed campsites. **Amenities:** parking; toilets. **Best for:** solitude; sunset; walking. ✉ *Park Headquarters/Salmon Creek Ranger Station, 3095 Hwy. 1, 2 miles north of Bodega Bay* ☎ *707/865–2391* 🌐 *www.parks.gov* 🎫 *$8 per vehicle* 🕒 *Daily 8 am–sunset (some beach hrs may be curtailed because of budget cuts).*

WHERE TO EAT AND STAY

$$ SEAFOOD 🍴 **Sandpiper Restaurant.** A local favorite, this friendly café on the marina does a good job for a fair price. Peruse the board for the day's fresh catch or order a menu regular such as crab stew or steak and prawns; clam chowder is the house specialty. Breakfast is served on summer weekends. [$] *Average main: $22* ✉ *1400 N. Hwy. 1* ☎ *707/875–2278.*

$$$ HOTEL 🏨 **Bodega Bay Lodge.** Looking out to the ocean across a wetland, a group of shingle-and-river-rock buildings houses Bodega Bay's finest accommodations. **Pros:** most rooms have fireplaces and patios; variety of pampering treatments; ocean views. **Cons:** on the highway. [$] *Rooms from: $239* ✉ *103 Coast Hwy. 1* ☎ *707/875–3525, 888/875–2250* 🌐 *www.bodegabaylodge.com* 🛏 *78 rooms, 5 suites* 🍽 *No meals.*

$ HOTEL 🏨 **Bodega Harbor Inn.** As humble as can be, this is one of the few places on this stretch of the coast with rooms for less than $100 a night. **Pros:** budget choice; rooms for larger groups. **Cons:** an older facility. [$] *Rooms from: $85* ✉ *1345 Bodega Ave.* ☎ *707/875–3594* 🌐 *www.bodegaharborinn.com* 🛏 *14 rooms, 2 suites* 🍽 *No meals.*

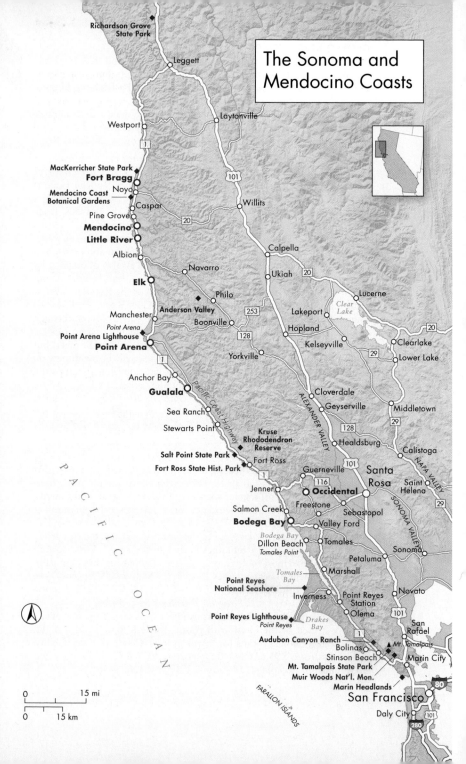

The Sonoma and Mendocino Coasts

Richardson Grove State Park

Leggett

Laytonville

Westport

MacKerricher State Park
Fort Bragg
Noyo
Mendocino Coast Botanical Gardens
Caspar
Pine Grove
Mendocino
Little River
Albion

Willits

101

20

Navarro

Calpella

Ukiah

20

Elk

Philo

Lucerne

Clear Lake

Manchester
Point Arena
Point Arena Lighthouse
Point Arena

Anderson Valley
Boonville

253

Lakeport

Hopland

Kelseyville

Clearlake

Lower Lake

29

20

Yorkville

128

Anchor Bay
Gualala

Pacific Coast Highway

Sea Ranch
Stewarts Point
Kruse Rhododendron Reserve
Salt Point State Park
Fort Ross State Hist. Park

Fort Ross

Cloverdale

Geyserville

ALEXANDER VALLEY

128

Healdsburg

Middletown

29

Calistoga

NAPA VALLEY

Jenner

Salmon Creek
Bodega Bay

Guerneville

116

Occidental

Freestone

Sebastopol

Santa Rosa

Saint Helena

101

SONOMA VALLEY

29

Valley Ford

Bodega Bay
Dillon Beach
Tomales Point

Tomales

Petaluma

Sonoma

Tomales Bay

Marshall

Point Reyes National Seashore

Inverness

Point Reyes Lighthouse
Point Reyes

Drakes Bay

Point Reyes Station
Olema

Novato

101

San Rafael

Audubon Canyon Ranch
Bolinas
Stinson Beach
Mt. Tamalpais State Park
Muir Woods Nat'l. Mon.
Marin Headlands

Mt. Tamalpais

Marin City

80

San Francisco

PACIFIC OCEAN

FARALLON ISLANDS

Daly City

280

101

0   15 mi

0   15 km

SPORTS AND THE OUTDOORS

11

GOLF

The Links at Bodega Harbour. Robert Trent Jones II designed this Scottish-style, incredibly scenic, and fairly challenging 18-hole oceanfront course. Rates include a golf cart. ⊠ *21301 Heron Dr.* ☎ *707/875–3538, 866/905–4657* ⊕ *www.bodegaharbourgolf.com* ⊡ *$60 for weekdays; $90 for weekends* ⚑. *18 holes, 6290 yards, par 70.*

HORSEBACK RIDING

Horse N Around Trail Rides. Saddle up at this ranch for guided horseback trail rides, some along the beach. Reservations are required. ⊠ *2660 N. Hwy. 1* ☎ *707/875–8849* ⊕ *www.horsenaroundtrailrides.com.*

WHALE-WATCHING

Bodega Bay Sportfishing. This outfitter charters ocean-fishing boats, rents equipment, and conducts whale-watching trips from mid-winter through spring. ⊠ *1410 B Bay Flat Rd.* ☎ *707/875–3344* ⊕ *www. bodegabaysportfishing.com.*

OCCIDENTAL

14 miles northeast of Bodega Bay.

A village surrounded by redwood forests, orchards, and vineyards, Occidental is a former logging hub with a bohemian vibe. The 19th-century downtown offers a top-notch B&B, good food, and a handful of art galleries and boutiques. On your way, you'll pass through the neighboring town of Freestone, which has a popular bakery and an excellent winery.

GETTING HERE AND AROUND

To reach Occidental, take Highway 12 (Bodega Highway) east 5 miles from Highway 1. Take a left onto Bohemian Highway, where you'll find Freestone; after another 3½ miles you'll be in Occidental. From U.S. 101 north or south take Highway 12 west from Santa Rosa about 13 miles, then head north on Bohemian Highway about 3½ miles to the village.

EXPLORING

Fodor's Choice ★

Joseph Phelps Freestone Vineyards Guest Center. The renowned Napa Valley winery's western Sonoma outpost is a good place to learn about biodynamic growing techniques while tasting crisp Chardonnays and earthy Pinot Noirs. Phelps wines have always garnered praise for their expression of *terroir* (the land), and the ones made here have a composed, ascetic quality that perfectly mirrors the rugged Sonoma Coast. You can almost taste the vines sending out long roots to find nutrients in the rocky, mineral-laden soil. If prompted, your pourer may regale you with descriptions of biodynamic strategies that involve timing vineyard activities to the waxing or waning moon and compost preparations that incorporate yarrow, stinging nettle, and other herbs. Sonoma Coast wines predominate on the tasting list—the estate-grown Pinot Noir is a standout—but there's nearly always a Napa Valley selection also. ⊠ *12747 El Camino Bodega, at Bohemian Hwy.* ☎ *707/874–1010* ⊕ *www.josephphelps.com* ⊡ *Tastings $10–$15* ☉ *Daily 11–5.*

WHERE TO EAT AND STAY

$ BAKERY 🍴 **Wild Flour Bread.** The sticky buns at Wild Flour are legendary in western Sonoma, as are the mouthwatering rye bread and sock-it-to-me scones in flavors like double chocolate, espresso, and hazelnut. There's a long table inside, but most people enjoy their baked goods on the benches outside. **■TIP→ On weekends after 1 pm, the most popular items start running out.** [$] *Average main: $5* ✉ *140 Bohemian Hwy., at El Camino Bodega, Freestone* ☎ *707/874–2938* 🌐 *www.wildflourbread.com* 💳 *No credit cards* 🕒 *Closed Tues.–Thurs. No dinner.*

$$$ B&B/INN 🏨 **The Inn at Occidental.** Quilts, folk art, and original paintings and photographs fill this colorful and friendly inn. **Pros:** whimsical decor; most rooms have private decks and jetted tubs; friendly. **Cons:** not for those with minimalist tastes; not for kids. [$] *Rooms from: $249* ✉ *3657 Church St.* ☎ *707/874–1047, 800/522–6324* 🌐 *www.innatoccidental.com* 🛏 *13 rooms, 3 suites, 1 cottage* 🍽 *Breakfast.*

SHOPPING

SPA

Osmosis Day Spa Sanctuary. The signature treatment at this locally popular spa is a traditional Japanese detoxifying bath. You'll slip into a deep redwood tub filled with damp cedar shavings and rice bran that are naturally heated to 140°F by the action of enzymes. Attendants bury you up to the neck and throughout the 20-minute bath session bring sips of water and place cool cloths on your forehead. After a shower, you can lie down and listen to brain-balancing music through headphones or have a massage, perhaps in one of the creek-side pagodas. Facials and other treatments are also available. Reservations are recommended. ✉ *209 Bohemian Hwy., Freestone* ☎ *707/823–8231* 🌐 *www.osmosis.com* 🎫 *Treatments $99–$299* 🕒 *Daily 9–9* ☞ *$99 90-min Signature Cedar Enzyme Bath & Wrap; $219 2½-hr Rejuvenation package; $299 2½-hr Bath as Medicine package; $139 75-min massage. Services: Aromatherapy, body wraps, facials, massage.*

FORT ROSS STATE HISTORIC PARK

22 miles north of Bodega Bay.

With its reconstructed Russian Orthodox chapel, stockade, and officers' barracks, Fort Ross looks much the way it did after the Russians made it their major California coastal outpost in 1812. An excellent museum documents the fort's history.

GETTING HERE AND AROUND

From Santa Rosa, head west on Highway 116 about 31 miles to Jenner, then north 12 miles on Highway 1 to the park entrance. The Mendocino Transit Authority (🌐 *www.mendocinotransit.org*) Route 95 bus provides service between Fort Ross and other coastal towns.

EXPLORING

FAMILY **Fort Ross State Historic Park.** Established in 1812, Fort Ross became Russia's major outpost in California, meant to produce crops and other supplies for northerly fur-trading operations. The Russians brought Aleut sea-otter hunters down from Alaska. By 1841 the area was depleted of

Surfers check out the waves near Bodega Bay on the Sonoma Coast.

seals and otters, and the Russians sold their post to John Sutter, later of gold-rush fame. After a local Anglo rebellion against the Mexicans, the land fell under U.S. domain, becoming part of California in 1850. The state park service has reconstructed Fort Ross, including its Russian Orthodox chapel, a redwood stockade, the officers' barracks, and a blockhouse. The excellent museum here documents the history of the fort and this part of the North Coast. ⊠ *19005 Hwy. 1* ☎ *707/847–3286* ⊕ *www.parks.ca.gov* ⌷ *$8 per vehicle* ☉ *Weekends 10–4:30* ☞ *No dogs allowed past parking lot and picnic area.*

SALT POINT STATE PARK

6 miles north of Fort Ross.

Enjoy dramatic views, forested acres, and a rocky, rugged shoreline along Highway 1's 5-mile route through this park. With 20 miles of hiking trails and a variety of picnicking, horseback riding, scuba diving, and fishing opportunities, you'll want to stay a while. At Fisk Mill Cove you'll see where centuries of wind and rain erosion have carved unusual honeycomb patterns in the sandstone called "tafonis."

GETTING HERE AND AROUND

Exit U.S. 101 in Santa Rosa and travel west on Highway 116 about 31 miles to Jenner, then north 18 miles on Highway 1 to reach the park. Mendocino Transit Authority (⊕ *www.mendocinotransit.org*) Route 95 buses stop at Salt Point and connect with other North Coast towns.

EXPLORING

Salt Point State Park. For 5 miles, Highway 1 winds through this park, 6,000 acres of forest, meadows, and rocky shoreline. Heading north, the first park entrance (on the right) leads to forest hiking trails and several campgrounds. The next entrance—the park's main road—winds through meadows and along the wave-splashed coastline. This is also the route to the visitor center and Gerstle Cove, a favorite spot for abalone divers and sunbathing seals. Next along the highway is Stump Beach Cove, with picnic tables, toilets, and a ¼-mile walk to the sandy beach. The park's final entrance is at Fisk Mill Cove, where centuries of wind and rain erosion have carved unusual honeycomb patterns in the sandstone called "tafonis." A five-minute walk uphill from the parking lot leads to a dramatic view of Sentinel Rock, an excellent spot for sunsets.

Just up the highway, narrow, unpaved Kruse Ranch Road leads to the **Kruse Rhododendron State Reserve**, where each May thousands of rhododendrons bloom within a quiet forest of redwoods and tan oaks. ✉ *25050 Hwy. 1* ☎ *707/847–3221, 707/865–2391* ⊕ *www.parks.ca.gov* 🎟 *$8 per vehicle* ☉ *Daily sunrise–sunset; some sections closed in winter, call ahead.*

THE MENDOCINO COAST

GUALALA

16 miles north of Salt Point State Park.

This former lumber port on the Gualala River has become a headquarters for exploring the coast. The busiest town on Highway 1 between Bodega Bay and Mendocino, it has all the basic services plus some galleries and gift shops.

GETTING HERE AND AROUND

From San Francisco, take U.S. 101 to the East Washington Street/Central Petaluma exit and follow signs west through Valley Ford (you're on Highway 1 by this point) to Bodega Bay. From there, continue north on Highway 1. From Ukiah, exit U.S. 101 at Highway 253, driving southwest to Boonville/Highway 128. From Boonville, turn west on Mountain View Road, which winds 24 miles to Highway 1; from there, drive south 18½ miles. Mendocino Transit Authority (⊕ *www. mendocinotransit.org*) Routes 75 and 95 buses connect Gualala with coastal and inland towns.

EXPLORING

Gualala Point Regional Park. This 195-acre park has a long, sandy beach and picnic areas, and is an excellent whale-watching spot from December through April. Opposite the beach, along the Gualala River estuary, two-dozen campsites are shaded by redwoods. Dogs must be on a leash at all times throughout the park. ■ TIP→ **Watch out for unpredictable sleeper waves which are common along the North Coast.** ✉ *42401 Hwy. 1, 1 mile south of Gualala* ☎ *707/785–2377* ⊕ *www.sonomacounty.org/parks/pk_glala.htm* 🎟 *$7 per vehicle (day use)* ☉ *Daily 8 am–sunset.*

WHERE TO EAT AND STAY

$$$$ AMERICAN

🍴 **St. Orres.** Resembling a traditional Russian dacha with two onion-dome towers, this intriguing lodge stands on 42 acres of redwood forest and meadow. In one of the towers is a spectacular atrium dining room. Here, locally farmed and foraged ingredients appear in dishes such as garlic flan with black chanterelles and rack of venison medallions with wild huckleberries. The prix-fixe menu ($45) includes soup and salad but no appetizer or dessert (available à la carte). A fine brunch is served on weekends. [$] *Average main: $48* ✉ *36601 Hwy. 1, 3 miles north of Gualala* ☎ *707/884–3303* 🌐 *www.saintorres.com* ✍ *Reservations essential* ⏲ *Closed Tues. and Wed Dec.–May. No lunch weekdays.*

$$$ HOTEL Fodor's Choice ★

🏨 **Mar Vista Cottages.** Escape to nature and retro-charm at these refurbished, gadget-free 1930s cottages, where your daily activities will include snipping flowers for a bouquet, harvesting a bounty of vegetables for dinner from the organic garden and greenhouse, finding a basket of freshly-laid eggs at your door every morning, roaming open meadows with resident goats and chickens, and soaking in views of the blustery coastline. **Pros:** commune-with-nature solitude, peaceful retreat. **Cons:** no other businesses within walking distance. [$] *Rooms from: $185* ✉ *35101 S. Hwy 1, 5 miles north of Gualala* ☎ *707/884–3522, 877/855–3522* 🌐 *www.marvistamendocino.com* 🛏 *8 1-bedroom cottages, 4 2-bedroom cottages* 🍽 *No meals.*

$$ HOTEL

🏨 **Seacliff on the Bluff.** Wedged in front of a small shopping center, this motel is not much to look at—the interiors are motel standard—but you'll spend your time here staring at the Pacific panorama since all rooms have ocean views. **Pros:** budget choice; great views. **Cons:** limited dining options nearby. [$] *Rooms from: $140* ✉ *39140 S. Hwy. 1* ☎ *707/884–1213, 800/400–5053* 🌐 *www.seacliffmotel.com* 🛏 *16 rooms* 🍽 *No meals.*

POINT ARENA

14 miles north of Gualala.

Occupied by an eclectic mix of long-time locals and long-haired surfers, this former timber town on Highway 1 is part New Age, part rowdy—and always laid-back. The one road going west out of downtown will lead you to the harbor, where fishing boats unload sea urchins and salmon and there's almost always someone riding the waves.

GETTING HERE AND AROUND

To reach Point Arena from Santa Rosa, drive north on U.S. 101, exit at Cloverdale, and follow Highway 128 northwest 28 miles to Boonville. From Boonville take winding Mountain View Road west 25 miles to Highway 1. Point Arena is 4 miles south. From points north, exit U.S. 101 at Ukiah, take Highway 253 southwest to Boonville and follow Mountain View Road west to Highway 1 south. Mendocino Transit Authority (🌐 *www.mendocinotransit.org*) Routes 75 and 95 buses stop in Point Arena.

EXPLORING

Point Arena Lighthouse. For an outstanding view of the ocean and, in winter, migrating whales, take the marked road off Highway 1 north of town to the 115-foot lighthouse. It's possible to stay out here, in one of four rental units ($$), all of which have full kitchens. (On weekends there's a two-night minimum.) ✉ *45500 Lighthouse Rd., off Hwy. 1* ☎ *707/882–2809, 877/725–4448* ⊕ *www.pointarenalighthouse.com* 🎫 *Tour $7.50* ⊙ *Late May–early Sept. daily 10–4:30, early Sept.–late May daily 10–3:30.*

BEACHES

Manchester State Park. Before slipping into the sea, the northernmost segment of the San Andreas Fault cuts through this park beloved by locals for its 5 miles of sandy, usually empty shoreline and trails that wind through dunes and wetlands. Hiking, bird-watching, and beach strolling are the popular activities here. There's steelhead fishing most of the year at Brush and Alder creeks, and beautiful coastal wildflowers bloom in early spring. Tundra swans winter in this area, and migrating whales are often spotted close to shore. Swimming and water sports are too dangerous because of the strong undertow. Dogs are not allowed on the beach. **Amenities:** parking. **Best for:** solitude; sunset; walking. ✉ *Park entrance, 44500 Kinney La., off Hwy. 1, ½ mile north of Manchester* ☎ *707/937–5804* ⊕ *www.parks.ca.gov* ⊙ *Some reduced services and hrs due to budget cutbacks; call ahead.*

WHERE TO EAT

$ ✕ **Arena Market and Café.** The simple café at this all-organic grocery store
CAFÉ   serves up hot soups, fine sandwiches and has an ample salad bar. The market, which specializes in food from local farms, sells cheese, bread, and other picnic items. $ *Average main: $8* ✉ *185 Main St.* ☎ *707/882–3663* ⊕ *www.arenaorganics.org* ⊙ *Mon.–Sat. 7–7; Sun. 8–6.*

$ ✕ **Franny's Cup and Saucer.** Aided by her mother, Barbara, a former
CAFÉ   pastry chef at Chez Panisse, Franny turns out baked goods that are sophisticated and inventive. Morning favorites include scones and sweet pastries as well as savory twists. Specialty cakes are dazzling concoctions such as Champagne cake layered with raspberries and lemon curd, or rich chocolate almond tortes spread with marzipan and berry preserves and iced with dark chocolate ganache. More familiar options at this delightful spot include fruit tarts and strawberry-apricot crisps, plus a mouth-watering assortment of cookies, candy, jams, and jellies. $ *Average main: $5* ✉ *213 Main St.* ☎ *707/882–2500* ⊕ *www.frannyscupandsaucer.com* ▭ *No credit cards* ⊙ *Closed Sun.–Tues. No dinner.*

ANDERSON VALLEY

28 miles east of Elk.

At the town of Albion, Highway 128 leads southeast into the Anderson Valley, where warm summer weather lures those weary of the persistent coastal fog. Most of the first 13 miles wind through redwood forest along the Navarro River, then the road opens up to reveal farms and vineyards. While the community here is anchored in ranching, in the past few decades a progressive, gourmet-minded counterculture has taken root and that is what defines most visitors' experiences. In the towns of Philo and Boonville, you'll find B&Bs with classic Victorian style as well as small eateries.

Anderson Valley is best known to outsiders for its wineries. Tasting rooms here are more low-key than their counterparts in Napa; most are in farmhouses, and you're as likely to hear reggae as classical music as you sip. That said, Anderson Valley wineries produce world-class wines, particularly Pinot Noirs and Gewürztraminers, whose grapes thrive in the moderate coastal climate. Many wineries straddle Highway 128, mostly in Navarro and Philo with a few east of Boonville.

GETTING HERE AND AROUND

From the coast, pick up Highway 128 at Albion. From inland points south, take Highway 128 northwest from U.S. 101 at Cloverdale. From inland points north, exit U.S. 101 in Ukiah and take Highway 253 southwest 17 miles to Boonville. Mendocino Transit Authority (⊕ *www.mendocinotransit.org*) Route 75 buses serve the Anderson Valley between the coast and Ukiah.

EXPLORING

TOP ATTRACTIONS

Navarro River Redwoods State Park. Described by locals as the "11-mile-long redwood tunnel to the sea," this park that straddles Highway 128 is great for walks amid second-growth redwoods and for summer swimming in the gentle Navarro River. There's also fishing, canoeing, and kayaking in the late winter and spring, when the river is higher. The two campgrounds (one on the river "beach") are quiet and clean. ⊠ *Hwy. 128, 2 miles east of Hwy. 1, Navarro* ☎ *707/937–5804* ⊕ *www.parks.ca.gov.*

Navarro Vineyards. A visit to this family-run winery is a classic Anderson Valley experience. Make time if you can for a vineyard tour—the guides draw from years of hands-on experience to explain every aspect of production, from sustainable farming techniques to the choices made in aging and blending. Best known for Alsatian varietals such as Gewürztraminer and Riesling, Navarro also makes Chardonnay, Pinot Noir, and other wines. The tasting room sells cheese and charcuterie for picnickers. ⊠ *5601 Hwy. 128, Philo* ☎ *707/895–3686* ⊕ *www.navarrowine.com* ☜ *Tasting free* ⊗ *Apr.–Oct. daily 9–6; Nov.–Mar. daily 9–5; tour daily at 10:30 and 3 by appointment.*

Roederer Estate. The Anderson Valley is particularly hospitable to Pinot Noir and Chardonnay grapes, the two varietals used to create Roederer's well-regarded sparkling wines. The view from the patio here is splendid. ⊠ *4501 Hwy. 128, Philo* ☎ *707/895–2288* ⊕ *www.roedererestate.com* ☜ *Tasting $6* ⊗ *Tasting room daily 11–5.*

WORTH NOTING

Greenwood Ridge Vineyards. White Riesling is the specialty of this winery that also makes Pinot Noir, Syrah, and other wines. You can picnic here at tables on an island in the middle of a pond. ⊠ *5501 Hwy. 128, Philo* ☎ *707/895–2002* ⊕ *www.greenwoodridge.com* ☜ *Tasting $5* ⊗ *Daily 10–5.*

Husch Vineyards. Anderson Valley's oldest winery, known for white wines and its reasonably priced Pinot Noir, has a cozy tasting room next to sheep pastures and picnic tables under a grapevine-covered arbor. ✉ *4400 Hwy. 128, Philo* ☎ *800/554–8724* 🌐 *www.huschvineyards.com* 🎟 *Tasting free* 🕒 *Daily 10–5.*

WHERE TO EAT AND STAY

$ CAFÉ 🍴 **The Boonville General Store.** The café menu here is nothing surprising, but the exacting attention paid to ingredients elevates each dish above the ordinary. Sandwiches are served on fresh-baked bread, and the beet salad comes with roasted pecans and local blue cheese. Breakfast options include granola and pastries, made in-house. [$] *Average main: $11* ✉ *14077A Hwy. 128, Boonville* ☎ *707/895–9477* 🕒 *No dinner.*

$$$$ AMERICAN Fodor'sChoice ★ 🍴 **Table 128.** The restaurant at the Boonville Hotel takes small-town dining into the 21st century. Proprietor Johnny Schmitt and his kitchen staff prepare one prix-fixe meal per night ($40 for three courses, $50 for four) and serve it family-style, with platters of food brought to the table to be shared. Expect an expertly grilled or roasted entrée (such as prosciutto wrapped halibut, flank steak, or slow roasted lamb), a sophisticated side dish (radicchio with polenta; curried cauliflower soup), and don't forget dessert (linzer torte with Chantilly cream; local blackberry tart). This is essentially home cooking done at a high level, and despite the limited menu—posted a few days in advance on the restaurant's website—most diners will leave satisfied. [$] *Average main: $45* ✉ *14050 Hwy. 128, Boonville* ☎ *707/895–2210* 🌐 *www.boonvillehotel.com* 🕒 *No lunch; closed Mon.–Thurs. Nov.–Apr; closed Tues. and Wed. May–mid-June; closed Tues. mid-June–Oct.*

$$$ HOTEL 🏨 **Boonville Hotel.** From the street this looks like a standard small-town hotel, but once you cross the threshold you start picking up on the laid-back sophistication that makes the entire Anderson Valley so appealing. **Pros:** stylish but homey; beautiful gardens and grounds. **Cons:** friendly but straightforward service—don't expect to be pampered; two-night stay required most weekends. [$] *Rooms from: $185* ✉ *14050 Hwy. 128, Boonville* ☎ *707/895–2210* 🌐 *www.boonvillehotel.com* 🛏 *8 rooms, 7 cottages* 🍽 *Breakfast.*

$$$ HOTEL Fodor'sChoice ★ 🏨 **The Philo Apple Farm.** Set in an orchard of organic, heirloom apples, the three cottages and one guest room here are tasteful, inviting, and inspired by the surrounding landscape. **Pros:** country charm; a unique back-to-nature, off-the-grid experience. **Cons:** occasionally hot in summer. [$] *Rooms from: $200* ✉ *18501 Greenwood Rd., Philo* ☎ *707/895–2333* 🌐 *www.philoapplefarm.com* 🛏 *1 room, 3 cottages* 🍽 *Breakfast.*

LITTLE RIVER

14 miles north of Elk.

The town of Little River is not much more than a post office and a convenience store; Albion, its neighbor to the south, is even smaller. Along this winding portion of Highway 1 though, you'll find numerous inns and restaurants, all of them quiet and situated to take advantage of the breathtaking ocean views.

You'll find excellent vintages and great places to taste wine in the Anderson Valley—but it's much more laid-back than Napa.

GETTING HERE AND AROUND

From inland points south, exit U.S. 101 at Cloverdale and follow Highway 128 northwest about 56 miles to Highway 1, then head north 7 miles. From points north, exit U.S. 101 in Ukiah at Highway 253 and follow it west 17 miles to Boonville, where you'll pick up Highway 128 and drive northwest to Highway 1. Mendocino Transit Authority (⊕ *www.mendocinotransit.org*) Route 60 buses serve the area.

EXPLORING

Van Damme State Park. Best known for its beach, this park is a prime abalone diving spot. Upland trails lead through lush riparian habitat and the bizarre **Pygmy Forest**, where acidic soil and poor drainage have produced mature cypress and pine trees that are no taller than a person. The visitor center has displays on ocean life and the historical significance of the redwood lumber industry along the coast. ⊠ *Little River Park Rd., off Hwy. 1* ☎ *707/937–5804* ⊕ *www.parks.ca.gov.*

WHERE TO EAT AND STAY

$$$
FRENCH
Fodor'sChoice
★

⨉ **Ledford House.** The only thing separating this bluff-top wood-and-glass restaurant from the Pacific Ocean is a great view. Entrées evoke the flavors of southern France and include hearty bistro dishes—stews, cassoulets, and pastas—and large portions of grilled meats and freshly caught fish (though the restaurant also is vegetarian friendly). The long bar, with its unobstructed water view, is a scenic spot for a sunset aperitif. $ *Average main: $24* ⊠ *3000 N. Hwy. 1, Albion* ☎ *707/937–0282* ⊕ *www.ledfordhouse.com* ⊙ *Closed Mon. and Tues. and mid-Feb.–mid-Mar. No lunch.*

$$$ B&B/INN **Albion River Inn.** Contemporary New England–style cottages at this inn overlook the dramatic bridge and seascape where the Albion River empties into the Pacific. **Pros:** great views; great bathtubs. **Cons:** newer buildings aren't as quaint as they could be. [$] *Rooms from: $195* ✉ *3790 N. Hwy. 1, Albion* ☎ *707/937–1919, 800/479–7944* 🌐 *www.albionriverinn.com* 🛏 *18 rooms, 4 cottages* 🍴 *Breakfast.*

MENDOCINO

3 miles north of Little River.

Many of Mendocino's original settlers came from the Northeast and built houses in the New England style. Thanks to the logging boom, the town flourished for most of the second half of the 19th century. As the timber industry declined, many residents left, but the town's setting was too beautiful to be ignored. Artists and craftspeople began flocking here in the 1950s, and Elia Kazan chose Mendocino as the backdrop for his 1955 film adaptation of John Steinbeck's *East of Eden*, starring James Dean. As the arts community thrived, restaurants, cafés, and inns sprang up. Today, the small downtown area consists almost entirely of places to eat and shop.

GETTING HERE AND AROUND

From U.S. 101, exit at Cloverdale and follow Highway 128 northwest about 56 miles and Highway 1 north 10 miles. You can also exit at Willits and drive west on Highway 20 about 33 miles to Highway 1, then south 8 miles. Mendocino Transit Authority (🌐 *www.mendocinotransit.org*) Route 60 buses serve the area.

EXPLORING

Ford House. The restored Ford House, built in 1854, serves as the visitor center for Mendocino Headlands State Park and the town. The house has a scale model of Mendocino as it looked in 1890, when it had 34 water towers and a 12-seat public outhouse. From the museum, you can head out on a 3-mile trail across the spectacular seaside cliffs that border the town. ✉ *735 Main St., west of Lansing St.* ☎ *707/937–5397* 🌐 *mendoparks.org/mendocino-headlands-state-park-ford-house-museum* 🎟 *$2* 🕓 *Daily 11–4.*

Kelley House Museum. An 1861 structure holds this museum, whose artifacts include Victorian-era furniture and historical photographs of Mendocino coast's logging days. ✉ *45007 Albion St.* ☎ *707/937–5791* 🌐 *www.kelleyhousemuseum.org* 🎟 *$2* 🕓 *Late May–early Sept., Thurs.–Tues. 11–3; early Sept.–late May, Fri.–Mon. 11–3.*

Mendocino Art Center. The center has an extensive program of workshops, mounts exhibits in its galleries, and is the home of the Mendocino Theatre Company. Artists from several states paint and sell their work during the center's plein air festival the second week of September. ✉ *45200 Little Lake St.* ☎ *707/937–5818, 800/653–3328* 🌐 *www.mendocinoartcenter.org.*

The North Coast is famous for its locally caught Dungeness crab; be sure to try some during your visit.

WHERE TO EAT AND STAY

$$$ AMERICAN 🍴 **Cafe Beaujolais.** The yellow Victorian cottage that houses this popular restaurant is surrounded by a garden of heirloom and exotic plantings. A commitment to the freshest possible organic and local ingredients guides the chef here. The menu is eclectic and ever-evolving, but often includes free-range fowl, line-caught fish, and Niman Ranch beef. The bakery turns out several delicious varieties of bread from a wood-fired oven. [$] *Average main: $29* ✉ *961 Ukiah St.* ☎ *707/937–5614* 🌐 *www.cafebeaujolais.com* 🕒 *No lunch Mon. and Tues.*

$$$$ B&B/INN Fodor's Choice ★ 🏨 **Brewery Gulch Inn.** The feel is modern yet tasteful at this smallish inn—furnishings are redwood and leather, beds are plush, and two rooms have whirlpool tubs with views. **Pros:** stylish; peaceful with ocean views; wine hour and buffet included in room rate. **Cons:** must drive to town. [$] *Rooms from: $295* ✉ *9401 N. Hwy. 1, 1 mile south of Mendocino* ☎ *707/937–4752, 800/578–4454* 🌐 *www.brewerygulchinn.com* 🛏 *10 rooms, 1 suite* 🍽 *Breakfast.*

$$ B&B/INN Fodor's Choice ★ 🏨 **Glendeven Inn Medocino.** If Mendocino is the New England village of the West Coast, then Glendeven is the local country manor with sea views. **Pros:** great ocean views; elegant; romantic. **Cons:** not within walking distance of town; on the main drag. [$] *Rooms from: $165* ✉ *8205 N. Hwy. 1* ☎ *707/937–0083, 800/822–4536* 🌐 *www.glendeven.com* 🛏 *6 rooms, 4 suites* 🍽 *Breakfast.*

$$ B&B/INN 🏨 **MacCallum House.** Set on two flower-filled acres in the middle of town, this inn is a perfect mix of Victorian charm and modern luxury. **Pros:** excellent breakfast; great central location. **Cons:** new luxury suites on a separate property are less charming. [$] *Rooms from: $159* ✉ *45020*

Albion St. ☎ *707/937–0289, 800/609–0492* ⊕ *www.maccallumhouse. com* ⤴ *19 rooms, 9 suites, 7 cottages* ⦿| *Breakfast.*

THE ARTS

THEATER

Mendocino Theatre Company. Dedicated to producing plays of substance and excitement, this well-established company mounts a repertoire that ranges all over the contemporary map, including works by Pulitzer Prize winners and local playwrights. ⊠ *Mendocino Art Center, 45200 Little Lake St.* ☎ *707/937–4477* ⊕ *www.mendocinotheatre.org.*

SPORTS AND THE OUTDOORS

Catch-A-Canoe and Bicycles Too. Rent kayaks and regular and outrigger canoes here, as well as mountain and suspension bicycles. Book a variety of tours that explore Big River and its estuary, some by moonlight. ⊠ *Stanford Inn by the Sea, Comptche-Ukiah Rd., east of Hwy. 1* ☎ *707/937–0273* ⊕ *www.catchacanoe.com* ⊠ *From $65.*

FORT BRAGG

10 miles north of Mendocino.

Fort Bragg is a working-class town that many feel is the most authentic place on the coast; it's certainly less expensive than its neighbors to the south. The declining timber industry has been steadily replaced by booming tourism, but the city maintains a local feel since most people who work at the area hotels and restaurants also live here, as do many artists. A stroll down Franklin Street (one block east of Highway 1) takes you past numerous bookstores, antiques shops, and boutiques.

GETTING HERE AND AROUND

From U.S. 101 at Willits follow Highway 20 west about 33 miles to Highway 1 and drive north 2 miles. Mendocino Transit Authority (⊕ *www. mendocinotransit.org*) Route 60 buses serve the town and region.

EXPLORING

Fodor'sChoice ★ **Mendocino Coast Botanical Gardens.** Something beautiful is always abloom in these marvelous gardens. Along 3½ miles of trails, including pathways with ocean views and observation points for whale-watching, lie a splendid profusion of flowers. The rhododendrons are at their peak from April through June; the dahlias begin their spectacular show in August and last until October. Even in winter, the heather and camellias add more than a splash of color. The main trails are wheelchair accessible. ⊠ *18220 N. Hwy. 1, 2 miles south of Fort Bragg* ☎ *707/964–4352* ⊕ *www.gardenbythesea.org* ⊠ *$14* ☉ *Mar.–Oct., daily 9–5; Nov.–Feb., daily 9–4.*

Museum in the Triangle Tattoo Parlor. At the top of a steep staircase, this two-room museum pays homage to Fort Bragg's rough-and-tumble past with memorabilia that includes early 20th-century Burmese tattooing instruments, pictures of astonishing tattoos from around the world, and a small shrine to sword-swallowing sideshow king Captain Don Leslie. ⊠ *356-B N. Main St.* ☎ *707/964–8814* ⊕ *www.triangletattoo. com* ⊠ *Free* ☉ *Daily noon–6.*

FAMILY **The Skunk Train.** In the 1920s, a fume-spewing gas-powered train car shuttled passengers along a rail line dating from the logging days of the 1880s. Nicknamed the Skunk Train, it traversed redwood forests inaccessible to automobiles. A reproduction train now travels the same route, making a 3½–4 hour round-trip trek between Fort Bragg and the town of Northspur, 21 miles inland. The schedule varies depending on the season and in summer includes evening barbecue excursions and wine parties. ✉ *Foot of Laurel St., west of Main St.* ☎ *707/964–6371, 866/457–5865* 🌐 *www.skunktrain.com* 🎟 *$54–$74.*

BEACHES

Glass Beach. The ocean isn't visible from most of Fort Bragg, but a gravel path on Elm Street three blocks west of Main Street leads to wild coastline where you can walk for miles along the bluffs. The sandy coves nearest the road are called Glass Beach because here lies more sea glass than you've likely ever seen in one place (this area formerly served as the city dump, and the surf pulverized the trash into beautiful treasures). You can gaze at the dazzling colors, but don't take any glass with you; it's now against the law. No swimming at this beach either, for safety's sake. **Amenities:** parking; toilets. **Best for:** sunset; walking. ✉ *Elm St. and Old Haul Rd.* 🌐 *www.parks.ca.gov.*

MacKerricher State Park. This park begins at Glass Beach and stretches north for 9 miles, beginning with rocky headlands that taper into dunes and sandy beaches. The headland is a good place for whale-watching from December to mid-April. Fishing at Lake Cleone (a freshwater lake stocked with trout), canoeing, hiking, tidepooling, jogging, bicycling, beachcombing, camping, and harbor seal watching at Laguna Point are among the popular activities, many of which are accessible to the mobility-impaired. Rangers, who lead nature hikes in summer, discourage swimming in the treacherous surf and remind those on shore to be vigilant for rogue waves and to never turn their backs on the sea. Dogs must be leashed. **Amenities:** parking; toilets. **Best for:** solitude; sunset; walking. ✉ *Hwy. 1, 3 miles north of Fort Bragg* ☎ *707/937–5804* 🌐 *www.parks.ca.gov* 🎟 *$8 per vehicle.*

WHERE TO EAT AND STAY

$$ AMERICAN FAMILY 🍴 **Mendo Bistro.** Everything on this menu is made from scratch, including the bread, pastas, and charcuterie. Though the chef doesn't tout it, his ingredients are nearly all organic, many of them local. In season, the roasted whole crab with three dipping sauces is sensational. A wide selection of pastas includes something for everyone—or, if not, there's the DIY menu: select your protein (beef, chicken, tofu), method of cooking, and sauce. This is a good place for upscale family dining. [$] *Average main: $22* ✉ *301 N. Main St.* ☎ *707/964–4974* 🌐 *www.mendobistro.com* 🕒 *No lunch.*

$ ITALIAN 🍴 **Piaci Pub and Pizzeria.** The seats are stools and your elbows might bang a neighbor's, but nobody seems to mind at this cozy spot that's hands down the area's most popular casual restaurant. The food is simple, mostly pizza and calzones, but everything is carefully prepared and comes out tasty. The well-chosen beers served here receive the same respect the wines do: the chalkboard list notes the origin, brewmaster, and alcohol content. Dogs and their owners are welcome at the tables outside. Cash only. $ *Average main: $14* ✉ *120 W. Redwood Ave.* ☎ *707/961–1133* ⊕ *www.piacipizza.com* ▬ *No credit cards* ⊘ *No lunch Sun.*

$ ⌂ **Surf and Sand Lodge.** As its name implies, this hotel sits practically

HOTEL   on the beach; pathways lead from the property down to the rock-strewn beach. **Pros:** beach location; gorgeous sunsets. **Cons:** motel style; no restaurants close by. $ *Rooms from: $119* ✉ *1131 N. Main St.* ☎ *707/964–9383, 800/964–0184* ⊕ *www.surfsandlodge.com* ⬥ *30 rooms* ⦿ *No meals.*

$$$ ⌂ **Weller House Inn.** It's hard to believe that this house was abandoned

B&B/INN   and slated for demolition when it was purchased in 1994 and then carefully restored into the loveliest Victorian in Fort Bragg. **Pros:** handcrafted details; radiant heat in the wood floors; friendly innkeepers. **Cons:** some may find it too old-fashioned. $ *Rooms from: $210* ✉ *524 Stewart St.* ☎ *707/964–4415* ⊕ *www.wellerhouse.com* ⬥ *9 rooms* ⦿ *Breakfast.*

SPORTS AND THE OUTDOORS

HORSEBACK RIDING

Ricochet Ridge Ranch. Come here for private and group trail rides through redwood forest and on the beach. ✉ *24201 N. Hwy. 1* ☎ *707/964–7669, 888/873–5777* ⊕ *www.horse-vacation.com* ⬥ *From $50.*

WHALE-WATCHING

All Aboard Adventures. Captain Tim of All Aboard operates fishing excursions year-round and whale-watching trips from late December through April. ✉ *Noyo Harbor, 32410 N. Harbor Dr.* ☎ *707/964–1881* ⊕ *www. allaboardadventures.com* ⬥ *From $35.*

REDWOOD COUNTRY

HUMBOLDT REDWOODS STATE PARK

20 miles north of Garberville, 43 miles south of Eureka.

Conservationists banded together a century ago as the Save the Redwoods League and scored a key victory when a memorial grove was dedicated in 1921. That grove is now part of Humboldt Redwoods State Park, which these days has grown to nearly 53,000 acres, about a third of which are filled with untouched old-growth coast redwoods.

GETTING HERE AND AROUND

Access the park right off U.S. 101. *(See Bus Travel, at the beginning of this chapter, for Humboldt County public transportation information.)*

EXPLORING

FAMILY   **Avenue of the Giants.** Some of the tallest trees on Earth tower over this

Fodor's Choice   magnificent 32-mile stretch of two-lane blacktop, also known as High-

★   way 254, that follows the south fork of the Eel River through Humboldt Redwoods State Park. The highway runs more or less parallel to U.S. 101 from Phillipsville in the south to the town of Pepperwood in the north. A brochure available at either end of the highway or

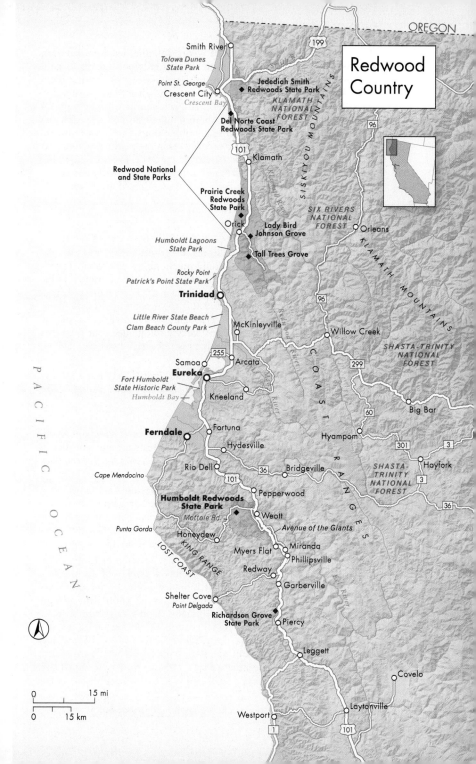

OREGON

199

Redwood Country

Smith River

Tolowa Dunes State Park

Point St. George
Crescent City
Crescent Bay

Jedediah Smith
Redwoods State Park

KLAMATH
NATIONAL
FOREST

SISKIYOU MOUNTAINS

96

Del Norte Coast
Redwoods State Park

101

Klamath

Redwood National
and State Parks

Prairie Creek
Redwoods
State Park

Orick

Lady Bird
Johnson Grove

SIX RIVERS
NATIONAL
FOREST

Orleans

*Humboldt Lagoons
State Park*

Tall Trees Grove

Rocky Point
Patrick's Point State Park

KLAMATH MOUNTAINS

Trinidad

Little River State Beach
Clam Beach County Park

McKinleyville

Willow Creek

96

SHASTA-TRINITY
NATIONAL
FOREST

255

Samoa
Eureka

*Fort Humboldt
State Historic Park*
Humboldt Bay

Arcata

299

Kneeland

COAST

60

Big Bar

Cape Mendocino

Ferndale

Fortuna

Hydesville

Rio Dell

36

Bridgeville

Hyampom

301

Hayfork

3

RANGES

SHASTA-
TRINITY
NATIONAL
FOREST

3

101

Pepperwood

**Humboldt Redwoods
State Park**

Mottole Rd.

Weott

Avenue of the Giants

36

Punta Gorda

Honeydew

KING RANGE

Myers Flat

Miranda
Phillipsville

Redway

LOST COAST

Garberville

Shelter Cove
Point Delgada

**Richardson Grove
State Park**

Piercy

Eel River

Leggett

Covelo

Westport

1

Laytonville

101

P A C I F I C   O C E A N

0   15 mi

0   15 km

the **visitor center**, 2 miles south of Weott, contains a self-guided tour, with short and long hikes through various redwood groves. A trail at **Founders Grove** passes by several impressive trees, among them the fallen 362-foot-long Dyerville Giant, whose root base points skyward 35 feet. The tree can be reached via a short trail that begins 4 miles north of the visitor center. About 6 miles north of the center lies **Rockefeller Forest**. The largest remaining old-growth coast redwood forest, it contains 40 of the 100 tallest trees in the world. ✉ *Humboldt Redwoods State Park Visitor Center, Hwy. 254, Weott* ☏ *707/946–2263* ⊕ *www.parks.ca.gov* 🖃 *Free; $8 day-use fee for Williams Grove* ⊙ *Visitor center: Apr.–Sept., daily 9–5; Oct.–Mar., daily 10–4.*

FERNDALE

35 miles northwest of Weott; 57 miles northwest of Garberville.

Though gift shops and ice-cream stores comprise a fair share of the businesses here, Ferndale remains a fully functioning small town. There's a butcher, a small grocery, and a local saloon (the westernmost in the contiguous United States), and descendants of the Portuguese and Scandinavian dairy farmers who settled this town continue to raise dairy cows in the surrounding pastures. Ferndale is best known for its colorful Victorian architecture; many shops carry a self-guided tour map that highlights the town's most interesting historical buildings.

GETTING HERE AND AROUND

Ferndale is about 19 miles south of Eureka. Exit U.S. 101 at Highway 211 and follow it southwest 5 miles. There is no public transit service to Ferndale.

EXPLORING

Eel River Delta Tours. Bruce Slocum's engaging two-hour boat trips examine the wildlife and history of the Eel River's estuary and salt marsh. ✉ *285 Morgan Slough Rd.* ☏ *707/786–4902 leave message for call back* 🖃 *From $25.*

Ferndale Historic Cemetery. The worn, lovely gravestones at this cemetery on Ferndale's east side provide insight into the hard, often short lives of the European immigrants who cultivated this area in the mid-18th century. From the top of the hill here you can view the town, the surrounding farms, and the ocean. ✉ *Bluff St. and Craig St.*

Ferndale Museum. The main building of this museum exhibits Victoriana and historical photographs and has a display of an old-style barbershop and another of Wiyot Indian baskets. In the annex are a horse-drawn buggy, a re-created blacksmith's shop, and antique farming, fishing, and dairy equipment. Don't miss the historic Bosch-Omori seismograph, installed in 1933 in Ferndale; it's still checked daily for recordings of earthquake activity. ✉ *515 Shaw Ave.* ☏ *707/786–4466* ⊕ *www.ferndale-museum.org* 🖃 *$1* ⊙ *June–Sept., Tues.–Sat. 11–4, Sun. 1–4; Oct.–Dec. and Feb.–May, Wed.–Sat. 11–4, Sun. 1–4; closed Jan.*

WHERE TO STAY

$$ B&B/INN 🏨 **Gingerbread Mansion.** A dazzler that rivals San Francisco's "painted ladies," this Victorian mansion has detailed exterior spindle work, turrets, and gables. **Pros:** elegant; relaxing; friendly. **Cons:** some may find it gaudy. [$] *Rooms from: $150* ✉ *400 Berding St.* ☎ *707/786–4000, 855/786–4001* 🌐 *www.thegingerbreadmansion.com* 🛏 *7 rooms, 4 suites* 🍴 *Breakfast.*

EUREKA

19 miles north of Ferndale; 67 miles north of Garberville.

With a population of 27,191, Eureka is the North Coast's largest city. Over the past century, it has cycled through several periods of boom and bust—first with mining and later with timber and fishing—but these days tourism helps keep the local economy afloat. The town's nearly 100 Victorian buildings have inspired some to dub it "the Williamsburg of the West." Shops draw people to the renovated downtown, and a walking pier extends into the harbor.

GETTING HERE AND AROUND

U.S. 101 travels through Eureka. From Redding and Interstate 5, travel west along Highway 299 about 138 miles to U.S. 101; Eureka is 9 miles south. Eureka Transit (🌐 *www.eurekatransit.org*) buses serve the town and connect with regional transit.

EXPLORING

Blue Ox Millworks. This woodshop is among a handful in the country specializing in Victorian-era architecture, but what makes it truly unique is that its craftspeople use antique tools to do the work. The most modern tool here is a 1948 band saw. Lucky for curious craftspeople and history buffs, the shop doubles as a dusty historical park. Visitors can watch craftsmen use printing presses, lathes, and even a mill that pares down whole redwood logs into the ornate fixtures for Victorians like those around town. The museum is less interesting on Saturday, when most craftspeople take the day off. ✉ *1 X St.* ☎ *707/444–3437, 800/248–4259* 🌐 *www.blueoxmill.com* 🎟 *$10* 🕒 *Weekdays 9–5, Sat. 9–4; Dec.–Mar., closed Sat.*

Clarke Historical Museum. The Native American Wing of this museum contains a beautiful collection of northwestern California basketry. Artifacts from Eureka's Victorian, logging, and maritime eras fill the rest of the space. ✉ *240 E St.* ☎ *707/443–1947* 🌐 *www.clarkemuseum.org* 🎟 *$3* 🕒 *Wed.–Sat. 11–4.*

Eureka Chamber of Commerce Visitor Center. The center has maps of self-guided driving tours of Eureka's Victorian architecture, and you can learn about organized tours. ✉ *2112 Broadway* ☎ *707/442–3738* 🌐 *www.eurekachamber.com* 🕒 *Mon.–Fri. 8:30–5, Sat. 10–3; Sept.–May, closed Sat.*

FAMILY **Fort Humboldt State Historic Park.** The structure that gives this park its name was built in response to conflicts between white settlers and Native Americans. It no longer stands, but on its grounds are some reconstructed buildings, fort and logging museums, and old logging locomotives. ⊠ *3431 Fort Ave.* ☎ *707/445–6547* ⊕ *www.parks.ca.gov* ⊠ *Free* ☺ *Daily 8–5.*

QUICK BITES

Lost Coast Brewery & Cafe. This bustling microbrewery is the best place in town to relax with a pint of ale or porter. Soups, salads, and light meals are served for lunch and dinner. ⊠ *617 4th St.* ☎ *707/445–4480* ⊕ *www.lostcoast.com.*

WHERE TO EAT AND STAY

$$$
AMERICAN
Fodor'sChoice
★

✕ **Restaurant 301.** Eureka's most elegant restaurant, situated in the Carter House, uses ingredients selected from the farmers' market, local cheese makers and ranchers, and the on-site gardens. Dishes are prepared with a delicate hand and a sensuous imagination. There's always a fresh seafood offering, and you can dine à la carte or choose from two prix-fixe menus (five courses, $62; eight courses, $92). The restaurant has earned high praise for its comprehensive wine selection. $ *Average main: $28* ⊠ *301 L St.* ☎ *707/444–8062, 800/404–1390* ⊕ *carterhouse.com* ☺ *No lunch.*

$$
AMERICAN
FAMILY

✕ **Samoa Cookhouse.** Waiters at this former cafeteria for local mill workers deliver family-style bowls—whatever is being served at the meal you've arrived for—to long, communal tables. For breakfast that means eggs, sausage, biscuits and gravy, and the like. Lunch and dinner usually feature soup, potatoes, salad, and pie, plus daily-changing entrées such as pot roast and pork loin. A museum in the back pays homage to logging culture, but the entire place is a tribute to the rough-and-tumble life and hard work that tamed this wild land. Dieters and vegetarians should look elsewhere for sustenance. $ *Average main: $16* ⊠ *908 Vance Ave., near Cookhouse Rd., Samoa* ☎ *707/442–1659* ⊕ *www.samoacookhouse.net.*

$
HOTEL
Fodor'sChoice
★

🏨 **Abigail's Elegant Victorian Mansion.** Innkeepers Doug and Lily Vieyra have devoted themselves to honoring this National Historic Landmark by decorating it with authentic, Victorian-era opulence; and indeed, it seems that every square inch of the home—once owned by the town's millionaire real-estate sultan—is covered in brocade, antique wallpaper, or redwood paneling, and from every possible surface hangs a painting with gilt frame, or a historical costume. **Pros:** unique; lots of character; delightful innkeepers. **Cons:** downtown is not within walking distance. $ *Rooms from: $115* ⊠ *1406 C St.* ☎ *707/444–3144* ⊕ *www.eureka-california.com* ⇆ *4 rooms, 2 with shared bath* ⦿ *No meals.*

$$$
HOTEL
Fodor'sChoice
★

🏨 **Carter House.** Owner Mark Carter says he trains his staff always to say yes; whether it's breakfast in bed or an in-room massage, someone here will get you what you want. **Pros:** elegant; every detail in place; excellent dining at Restaurant 301; bar off lobby. **Cons:** kids are allowed, but it's best suited for grown-ups. $ *Rooms from: $179* ⊠ *301 L St.* ☎ *707/444–8062, 800/404–1390* ⊕ *carterhouse.com* ⇆ *22 rooms, 8 suites, 2 cottages* ⦿ *Breakfast.*

11

SHOPPING

Eureka has several art galleries and numerous antiques stores in the district running from C to I streets between 2nd and 3rd streets.

ART GALLERY

First Street Gallery. Run by Humboldt State University, this is the best spot for contemporary art by local and regional artists, with some national and international representation. ⊠ *422 1st St.* ☎ *707/443–6363* ⊕ *www.humboldt.edu/first.*

BOOKS

Eureka Books. Along with classics and bestsellers, this bibliophile's haven has an exceptional collection of used books on all topics. ⊠ *426 2nd St.* ☎ *707/444–9593* ⊕ *www.eurekabooksellers.com.*

SPORTS AND THE OUTDOORS

WHALE-WATCHING

Humboats Kayak Adventures. Kayak rentals and lessons are available here, along with group kayaking tours, including whale-watching trips ($75, December–June) that get you close enough for good photos of migrating gray whales and resident humpback whales. ⊠ *Dock A, Woodley Island Marina* ☎ *707/443–5157* ⊕ *www.humboats.com* ⊠ *From $50.*

TRINIDAD

21 miles north of Eureka.

Trinidad got its name from the Spanish mariners who entered the bay on Trinity Sunday, June 9, 1775. The town became a principal trading post for the mining camps along the Klamath and Trinity rivers. Mining and whaling have faded from the scene, and now Trinidad is a quiet and genuinely charming community with ample sights and activities to entertain low-key visitors.

GETTING HERE AND AROUND

Trinidad sits right off U.S. 101. To reach the town from Interstate 5, head west from Redding on Highway 299 and turn north on U.S. 101 north of Arcata. Redwood Transit System (⊕ *www.redwoodtransit. org*) provides bus service between Trinidad, Eureka, and nearby towns.

EXPLORING

Patrick's Point State Park. On a forested plateau almost 200 feet above the surf, the park has stunning views of the Pacific, great whale- and sea lion–watching, picnic areas, bike paths, and hiking trails through old-growth spruce forest. There are also tidal pools at Agate Beach, a re-created Yurok Indian village, and a small museum with natural-history exhibits. Because the park is far from major tourist hubs, there are few visitors (most are local surfers)—it's sublimely quiet here. Three campgrounds amid spruce and alder trees have all amenities except RV hookups. Reservations are recommended in summer. Dogs are not allowed on trails or the beach. ⊠ *U.S. 101, 5 miles north of Trinidad* ☎ *707/677–3570* ⊕ *www.parks.ca.gov* ⊠ *$8 per vehicle.*

BEACHES

FAMILY **Clam Beach County Park and Little River State Beach.** Together these make a park that stretches for several miles south of Trinidad. The sandy beach here is exceptionally wide, perfect for kids who need to get out of the car and burn off some energy. Beachcombing and clamming are favored activities, as well as savoring fabulous sunsets. The two parks share day-use facilities. **Amenities:** parking; toilets. **Best for:** solitude; sunset; walking. ⊠ *Clam Beach Dr. & U.S. 101, 6 miles south of Trinidad* ☎ *707/445–7651* ⊕ *www.parks.ca.gov* ☉ *5 am–midnight.*

WHERE TO EAT AND STAY

$ ╳ **Katy's Smokehouse.** This tiny operation has been doing things the
SEAFOOD same way since the 1940s, curing day-boat, line-caught fish with its original smokers. Albacore jerky, smoked scallops, and salmon cured with brown sugar are popular. Buy bread and drinks in town and walk to the waterside for fine alfresco snacking. $ *Average main: $10* ⊠ *740 Edwards St.* ☎ *707/677–0151* ⊕ *www.katyssmokehouse. com* ☉ *No dinner.*

$$$ ╳ **Larrupin' Cafe.** Set in a two-story house on a quiet country road north
AMERICAN of town, this restaurant—locally considered one of the best places to eat on the North Coast—is often thronged with people enjoying fresh seafood, Cornish game hen, or mesquite-grilled ribs. The garden setting and candlelight stir thoughts of romance. $ *Average main: $29* ⊠ *1658 Patrick's Point Dr.* ☎ *707/677–0230* ⊕ *www.larrupin.com* ☉ *No lunch.*

$$$$ ⊡ **Trinidad Bay Bed and Breakfast Inn.** Staying at this small Cape Cod–
B&B/INN style inn perched above Trinidad Bay is like spending the weekend at a friend's vacation house. **Pros:** great location above bay; lots of light. **Cons:** if all rooms are full, the main house can feel a bit crowded. $ *Rooms from: $260* ⊠ *560 Edwards St., Box 849* ☎ *707/677–0840* ⊕ *www.trinidadbaybnb.com* ⊟ *4 rooms* ⫿◯⫿ *Breakfast.*

$$$$ ⊡ **Turtle Rocks Oceanfront Inn.** This comfortable inn has the best view in
B&B/INN Trinidad, and the builders have made the most of it, adding private, glassed-in decks to each room so that guests can fully enjoy the ocean and sunning sea lions. **Pros:** great ocean views; comfy king beds. **Cons:** no businesses within walking distance. $ *Rooms from: $295* ⊠ *3392 Patrick's Point Dr., 4½ miles north of town* ☎ *707/677–3707* ⊕ *www. turtlerocksinn.com* ⊟ *5 rooms, 1 suite* ⫿◯⫿ *Breakfast.*

REDWOOD
NATIONAL PARK

WELCOME TO REDWOOD NATIONAL PARK

TOP REASONS TO GO

★ **Giant trees:** These mature coastal red- woods are the tallest trees in the world.

★ **Hiking to the sea:** The park's trails wind through majestic redwood groves, and many con- nect to the Coastal Trail running along the west- ern edge of the park.

★ **Rare wildlife:** Mighty Roosevelt elk favor the park's flat prairie and open lands; seldom-seen black bears roam the back- country; trout and salmon leap through streams; and Pacific gray whales swim along the coast during their biannual migrations.

★ **Stepping back in time:** Hike Fern Canyon Trail and explore a prehistoric scene of lush vegeta- tion and giant ferns.

★ **Cheeps, not beeps:** Amid the majestic redwoods you're out of range for cell-phone service—and in range for the sooth- ing sounds of warblers and burbling creeks.

1 Del Norte Coast Redwoods State Park. The rugged terrain of this far northwest corner of California combines stretches of treacher- ous surf, steep cliffs, and forested ridges. On a clear day it's postcard-perfect; with fog, it's mysteriously mesmerizing.

2 Jedediah Smith Redwoods State Park. Gargantuan old-growth redwoods dominate the scenery here. The Smith River cuts through canyons and splits across boulders, carrying salmon to the inland creeks where they spawn.

3 Prairie Creek Redwoods State Park. The forests here give way to spacious, grassy plains where abundant wildlife thrives. Roosevelt elk are a common sight in the meadows and down to Gold Bluffs Beach.

4 Orick Area. The highlight of the southern portion of Redwood National and State Parks is the Tall Trees Grove. It's difficult to reach and requires a special pass, but it's worth the hassle—this section has the tallest coast redwood trees, with a new record holder discovered in 2006.

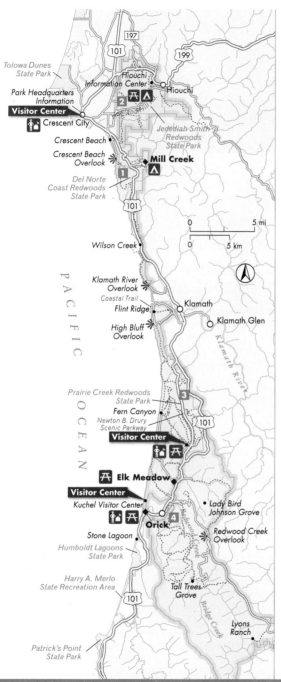

CALIFORNIA

12

GETTING ORIENTED

U.S. 101 weaves through the southern portion of the park, skirts around the center, and then slips back through redwoods in the north and on to Crescent City. Kuchel Visitor Center, Prairie Creek Redwoods State Park and Visitor Center, Tall Trees Grove, Fern Canyon, and Lady Bird Johnson Grove are all in the park's southern section. In the park's central section, where the Klamath River Overlook is the dominant feature, the narrow, mostly graveled Coastal Drive loop yields ocean vistas. To the north you'll find Mill Creek Trail, Enderts Beach, and Crescent Beach Overlook in Del Norte Coast Redwoods State Park as well as Jedediah Smith Redwoods State Park, Stout Grove, Little Bald Hills, and Simpson-Reed Grove.

Updated
by Christine
Vovakes

Soaring to more than 300 feet, the coastal redwoods that give this park its name are miracles of efficiency— some have survived hundreds of years (a few live for more than 2,000 years). These massive trees glean nutrients from the rich alluvial flats at their feet and from the moisture and nitrogen trapped in their uneven canopy. Their huge, thick-barked trunks can hold thousands of gallons of water, reservoirs that have helped them withstand centuries of firestorms.

REDWOOD PLANNER

WHEN TO GO

Campers and hikers flock to the park from mid-June to early September. Crowds disappear in winter, but you'll have to contend with frequent rains and nasty potholes on side roads. Temperatures fluctuate widely throughout the park: the foggy coastal lowland is much cooler than the higher-altitude interior.

The average annual rainfall here is 90 to 100 inches, and during dry summer months thick fog rolling in from the Pacific veils the forests.

GETTING HERE AND AROUND

CAR TRAVEL

U.S. 101 runs north–south along the park, and Highway 199 cuts east–west through its northern portion. Access routes off 101 include Bald Hills Road, Davison Road, Newton B. Drury Scenic Parkway, Coastal Drive loop, Requa Road, and Enderts Beach Road. From 199 take South Fork Road to Howland Hill Road. Many of the park's roads aren't paved, and winter rains can turn them into obstacle courses or close them completely. Motorhomes/RVs and trailers aren't permitted on some routes. ■ TIP→ **Park rangers say don't rely solely on GPS; closely consult park maps, available at the visitor information centers.**

PARK ESSENTIALS
PARK FEES AND PERMITS

Admission to Redwood National Park is free. There's an $8 day-use fee to enter one or all of Redwood's state parks; for camping at these state parks it's an additional $35. To visit Tall Trees Grove, you must get a free permit at the Kuchel Information Center in Orick. Permits also are needed to camp in all designated backcountry camps.

PARK HOURS

The park is open year-round, 24 hours a day.

VISITOR INFORMATION
PARK CONTACT INFORMATION

Redwood National and State Parks ⊠ *1111 2nd St., Crescent City* ☎ *707/465–7335* ⊕ *www.nps.gov/redw.*

VISITOR CENTERS

Crescent City Information Center. As the park's headquarters, this center is the main information stop if you're approaching the redwoods from the north. A gift shop and picnic area are here. ⊠ *1111 Second St., near K St., off U.S. 101, Crescent City* ☎ *707/465–7335* ⊕ *www.nps.gov/ redw* ☉ *Mid-May–mid-Oct., daily 9–6; mid-Oct.–mid-May, daily 9–4.*

Hiouchi Information Center. Located in Jedediah Smith Redwoods State Park, 2 miles west of Hiouchi and 9 miles east of Crescent City off Highway 199, this center has a bookstore, film, and exhibits about the flora and fauna in the park. It's also a starting point for seasonal ranger programs. ⊠ *Hwy. 199* ☎ *707/458–3294, 707/465–7335* ⊕ *www.nps. gov/redw* ☉ *Late May–early Sept., daily 9–6.*

Jedediah Smith Visitor Center. Located off Highway 199, this center has information about ranger-led walks and evening campfire programs in the summer in Jedediah Smith Redwoods State Park. Also here are nature and history exhibits, a gift shop, and a picnic area. ⊠ *Off Hwy. 199, Hiouchi* ☎ *707/458–3496, 707/465-7335* ⊕ *www.parks.ca.gov* ☉ *Late May–early-Sept., daily 10–6; closed early Sept.–late-May.*

Fodor's Choice **Prairie Creek Visitor Center.** Housed in a redwood lodge, this center has
★ wildlife displays and a massive stone fireplace that was built in 1933. Several trailheads begin here. Stretch your legs with an easy stroll along Revelation Trail, a short loop behind the lodge. Pick up information about summer programs in Prairie Creek Redwoods State Park. There's a nature museum, gift shop, picnic area, and exhibits on flora and fauna. ■TIP➜ **Roosevelt elk often roam in the vast field adjacent to the center.** ⊠ *Off southern end of Newton B. Drury Scenic Pkwy., Orick* ☎ *707/488–2039* ⊕ *www.parks.ca.gov* ☉ *Mid-May–mid-Oct., daily 9–5; mid-Oct.–mid-May, daily 9–4.*

Thomas H. Kuchel Visitor Center. If you're approaching the park from the south end, stop here to get brochures, advice, and a free permit to drive up the access road to Tall Trees Grove. Whale-watchers find the deck of the visitor center an excellent observation point, and bird-watchers enjoy the nearby Freshwater Lagoon, a popular layover for migrating waterfowl. Many of the exhibits here are hands-on and kid-friendly. ⊠ *Off U.S. 101, Orick* ☎ *707/465–7765* ⊕ *www.nps.gov/redw* ☉ *Mid-May–mid-Oct., daily 9–5; mid-Oct.–mid-May, daily 9–4.*

12

Plants and Wildlife in Redwood

Coast redwoods, the world's tallest trees (a new record holder, topping out at 379 feet, was found within the park in 2006) grow in the moist, temperate climate of California's North Coast. These ancient giants thrive in an environment that exists in only a few hundred coastal miles along the Pacific Ocean. They commonly live 600 years—though some have been around for 2,000 years.

A healthy redwood forest is diverse and includes Douglas firs, western hemlocks, tan oaks, and madrone trees. The complex soils of the forest floor support a verdant profusion of ferns, mosses, and fungi, along with numerous shrubs and berry bushes. In spring, California rhododendron bloom throughout the forest, providing a dazzling purple and pink contrast to the dense greenery.

Redwood National and State Parks hold 45% of all California's old-growth redwood forests. Of the original 3,125 square miles (2 million acres) in the Redwoods Historic Range, only 4% remain following the logging that began in 1850; 1% is privately owned and managed, and 3% is on public land.

In the park's backcountry, you might spot mountain lions, black bears, black-tailed deer, river otters, beavers, and minks. Roosevelt elk roam the flatlands, and the rivers and streams teem with salmon and trout. Gray whales, seals, and sea lions cavort near the coastline. And thanks to the area's location along the Pacific Flyway, more than 400 species of birds have been recorded in the park.

EXPLORING

SCENIC DRIVES

Coastal Drive. This 8-mile, narrow and mostly unpaved road is closed to trailers and RVs and takes about one hour to drive. The slow pace alongside stands of redwoods offers close-up views of the Klamath River and expansive panoramas of the Pacific. From here you'll find access to the Flint Ridge section of the Coastal Trail. Recurring landslides have closed sections of the original road; this loop is all that remains. ⊠ *On U.S. 101, 1 mile south of Klamath* ✛ *Take the Klamath Beach Rd. exit and follow signs to Coastal Dr.*

SCENIC STOPS

Crescent Beach Overlook. The scenery here includes ocean views and, in the distance, Crescent City and its working harbor; in balmy weather this is a great place for a picnic. From the overlook you can spot migrating gray whales going south November through December and returning north February through April. ⊠ *Off Enderts Beach Rd., 2 miles south of Crescent City.*

Fodor's Choice **Fern Canyon.** Enter another world and be surrounded by 30-foot can-
★ yon walls covered with sword, maidenhair, and five-finger ferns. Allow

an hour to explore the ¼-mile-long vertical garden along a 0.7-mile loop. From the north end of Gold Bluffs Beach it's an easy walk, although you'll have to wade across a small stream several times (in addition to driving across streams on the way to the parking area). But the lush surroundings are otherwise worldly, and worth a visit when creeks aren't running too high. Be aware that motorhomes/RVs and all trailers are prohibited here. ⊠ *Davison Rd., off U.S. 101, 10 miles northwest of Prairie Creek Visitor Center, Orick ⊕ www.nps.gov/redw.*

Lady Bird Johnson Grove. This section of the park was dedicated by, and named for, the former first lady. A 1-mile nature loop follows an old logging road through a mature redwood forest. Allow 45 minutes to complete the trail. ⊠ *1 mile north of Orick off U.S. 101 onto Bald Hills Rd., Orick ✛ Turn onto Bald Hills Rd. for 2½ miles to trailhead ⊕ www.nps.gov/redw.*

Tall Trees Grove. From the Kuchel Visitor Center, you can get a free permit to make the steep 14-mile drive (the last 6½ miles, on Tall Trees Access Road, are unpaved) to the grove's trailhead (trailers and RVs not allowed). Access to the popular grove is first-come, first-served, and a maximum of 50 permits are handed out each day. ⊠ *On U.S. 101, 1 mile north of Orick ✛ Turn right at Bald Hills Rd. and follow signs about 6½ miles to access road, then 6½ miles, unpaved, to trailhead.*

SPORTS AND THE OUTDOORS

HIKING

MODERATE

Coastal Trail. Although this easy-to-difficult trail runs along most of the park's length, smaller sections—of varying degrees of difficulty—are accessible via frequent, well-marked trailheads. The moderate-to-difficult DeMartin section leads past 6 miles of old growth redwoods and through prairie. If you're up for a real workout, you'll be well rewarded with the brutally difficult but stunning Flint Ridge section, a 4.5-mile stretch of steep grades and numerous switchbacks that leads past redwoods and Marshall Pond. The moderate 5.5-mile-long Klamath section, which connects the Wilson Creek picnic area with Hidden Beach tidepools and up to the Klamath Overlook, provides coastal views and whale-watching opportunities. *Moderate.* ⊠ *Shares Flint Ridge trailhead, at Douglas Bridge parking area, north end of Coastal Dr., Klamath.*

KAYAKING

With many miles of often-shallow rivers and streams in the area, kayaking is a popular pastime in the park.

OUTFITTERS

Humboats Kayak Adventures. Kayak rental and lessons are available here, along with a variety of group kayak tours, including full-moon and sunset tours and popular whale-watching trips (October–June) that

Best Campgrounds in Redwood

Within a 30-minute drive of Redwood National and State Parks there are nearly 60 public and private camping facilities. None of the four primitive areas in Redwood—DeMartin, Flint Ridge, Little Bald Hills, and Nickel Creek—is a drive-in site. You will need to get a free permit from any visitor center except Prairie Creek before camping in these campgrounds, and along Redwood Creek in the backcountry. Bring your own water, since drinking water isn't available in any of these sites. These campgrounds, plus Gold Bluffs Beach, are first-come, first-served.

If you'd rather drive than hike in, Redwood has four developed campgrounds—Elk Prairie, Gold Bluffs Beach, Jedediah Smith, and Mill Creek—that are within the state-park boundaries. None has RV hookups, and some length restrictions apply. Fees are $35 in state park campgrounds. For details and reservations, call ☎ 800/444-7275 or check ⊕ www.reserveamerica.com.

Elk Prairie Campground. Roosevelt elk frequent this popular campground adjacent to a prairie and old-growth redwoods. ⊠ On Newton B. Drury Scenic Pkwy., 6 miles north of Orick in Prairie Creek Redwoods State Park ☎ 800/444-7275.

Gold Bluffs Beach Campground. You can camp in tents or RVs right on the beach at this Prairie Creek Redwoods State Park campground near Fern Canyon. ⊠ At end of Davison Rd., 5 miles south of Prairie Creek Visitor Center off U.S. 101 ☎ 707/465-7335.

Jedediah Smith Campground. This is one of the few places to camp—in tents or RVs—within groves of old-growth redwood forest. ⊠ 8 miles east of Crescent City on Hwy. 199 ☎ 800/444-7275.

Mill Creek Campground. Mill Creek is the largest of the state-park campgrounds. ⊠ East of U.S. 101, 7 miles southeast of Crescent City ☎ 800/444-7275.

Nickel Creek Campground. An easy hike gets you to this primitive site, which is near tide pools and has great ocean views. ⊠ On Coastal Trail ½ mile from end of Enderts Beach Rd. ☎ 707/465-7335.

get you close enough for photos of migrating gray whales and resident humpback whales. ⊠ Dock A, Woodley Island Marina, Eureka ☎ 707/443-5157 ⊕ www.humboats.com.

WHALE-WATCHING

Good vantage points for whale-watching include Crescent Beach Overlook, the Kuchel Visitor Center in Orick, points along the Coastal Trail, and the Klamath River Overlook. Late November through January are the best months to see their southward migrations; February through April they return and generally pass closer to shore.

THE INLAND EMPIRE

East of Los Angeles to the
San Jacinto Mountains

WELCOME TO THE INLAND EMPIRE

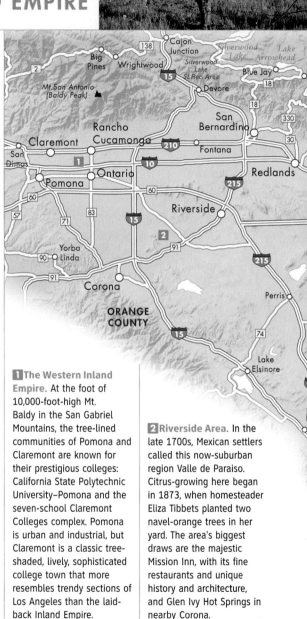

TOP REASONS TO GO

★ **Wine Country:** The Temecula Valley is a mélange of rolling hills, faint ocean breezes, beautiful and funky wineries, lovely lodging options, and gourmet restaurants.

★ **The Mission Inn:** One of the most unique hotels in America, Riverside's rambling, eclectic Mission Inn feels like an urban Hearst Castle.

★ **Apple country:** Oak Glen is one of Southern California's largest apple-growing regions. Attend an old-fashioned hoedown, take a wagon ride, and sample Mile High apple pies and homemade ciders.

★ **Soothing spas:** The lushly landscaped grounds, bubbling hot springs, and playful mud baths of Glen Ivy are ideal spots to unwind, while Kelly's Spa at the historic Mission Inn provides a cozy Tuscan-style retreat.

★ **Alpine escapes:** Breathe in the clean mountain air or cozy up in a rustic cabin at one of the Inland Empire's great mountain hideaways: Lake Arrowhead, Big Bear, and Idyllwild.

1 **The Western Inland Empire.** At the foot of 10,000-foot-high Mt. Baldy in the San Gabriel Mountains, the tree-lined communities of Pomona and Claremont are known for their prestigious colleges: California State Polytechnic University–Pomona and the seven-school Claremont Colleges complex. Pomona is urban and industrial, but Claremont is a classic tree-shaded, lively, sophisticated college town that more resembles trendy sections of Los Angeles than the laid-back Inland Empire.

2 **Riverside Area.** In the late 1700s, Mexican settlers called this now-suburban region Valle de Paraiso. Citrus-growing here began in 1873, when homesteader Eliza Tibbets planted two navel-orange trees in her yard. The area's biggest draws are the majestic Mission Inn, with its fine restaurants and unique history and architecture, and Glen Ivy Hot Springs in nearby Corona.

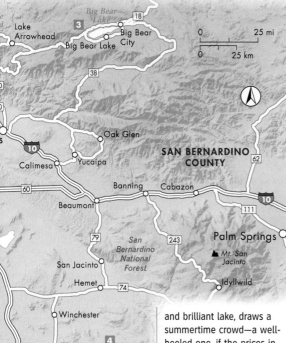

GETTING ORIENTED

Several freeways provide access to the Inland Empire from Los Angeles and San Diego. Ontario and Temecula line up along Interstates 10 and 215; and Corona, Riverside, and San Bernardino lie along Highway 91. As a Los Angeles bedroom community, the area sees nasty freeway congestion on Highway 60 and Interstates 10 and 15, so try to avoid driving during rush hour, usually from 6 to 9 am and 4 to 7 pm.

3 San Bernardino Mountains. Lake Arrowhead and always-sunny Big Bear are the recreational centers of this area. Though the two are geographically close, they're distinct in appeal. Lake Arrowhead, with its cool mountain air, trail-threaded woods, and brilliant lake, draws a summertime crowd—a well-heeled one, if the prices in its shops and restaurants are any indication. Big Bear's ski and snowboarding slopes, cross-country trails, and cheerful lodges come alive in winter and provide a quiet retreat in summer. Even if you're not interested in visiting the resorts themselves, the Rim of the World Scenic Byway (Highway 18), which connects Big Bear Lake and Lake Arrowhead at an elevation up to 8,000 feet, is a magnificent drive. On a clear day, you'll feel that you can see forever.

4 The Southern Inland Empire. Life is quieter in the southern portion of the Inland Empire than it is to the north. In this corner of Riverside County, towns such as Idyllwild and Temecula are oases of the good life for locals and visitors alike.

Updated by
Bobbi Zane

The Inland Empire, an area often overlooked by visitors because of its tangled freeways and suburban sprawl, has more than its share of charms. Just a couple of hours' drive from metropolitan Los Angeles or San Diego, you can ski a 7,000-foot mountain overlooking a crystal blue lake, savor SoCal's excellent wines in a vineyard cooled by ocean breezes, or hide out in a cozy cottage deep in the forest. As well as the rolling wine country of the Temecula Valley, you'll find apple country in Oak Glen, and orange country—and the tree that started California's multimillion-dollar navel-orange industry—in Riverside.

The San Bernardino Mountains offer Big Bear Lake, Lake Arrowhead, and plentiful recreational opportunities, while Idyllwild in the San Jacinto Mountains is a year-round getaway with romantic cottages, impressive art galleries, and cozy restaurants.

PLANNING

WHEN TO GO

The climate varies greatly depending on what part of the Inland Empire you're visiting. Summer temperatures in the mountains and in Temecula, 20 miles from the coast, usually hover around 80°F, though it's not uncommon for Riverside to reach temperatures of 100°F or higher. From September to March this area is subject to increasingly high Santa Ana winds, sometimes strong enough to overturn trucks on the freeway. In winter, temperatures in the mountains and in Temecula usually range from 30°F to 55°F, and in the Riverside area from 40°F to 60°F. Most of the ski areas open when the first natural snow falls (usually in November) and close in mid-March.

GETTING HERE AND AROUND

AIR TRAVEL

LA/Ontario International Airport (ONT) is the local airport. Aeromexico, Alaska, American, Delta, Southwest, and United fly here.

Airport Contacts LA/Ontario International Airport ✉ *2500 East Airport Dr., Archibald Ave. exit off I–10, Ontario* ☎ *909/937–2700* ⊕ *www.lawa.org.*

CAR TRAVEL

Avoid Highway 91 if possible; it's almost always backed up from Corona through Orange County. Check with Caltrans for information about highway conditions, or dial 511 or log on to the IE511 website, which also has bus-train trip planners.

Contacts Caltrans ☎ *800/427–7623* ⊕ *www.dot.ca.gov.*
IE511 ⊕ *www.ie511.org.*

TRAIN TRAVEL

■ TIP➔ **Many locals get around on Metrolink, which is clean and quick, and generally a much nicer way to travel than by bus.** Metrolink trains stop at several stations on the Inter-County, San Bernardino, and Riverside lines. You can buy tickets and passes at station vending machines, or by telephone. The IE511 website *(⇨ Car Travel, above)* has bus-train trip planners; dial 511 for recorded train-schedule information.

Train Contact Metrolink ☎ *800/371–5465* ⊕ *www.metrolinktrains.com.*

RESTAURANTS

Downtown Riverside is home to a few ambitious restaurants, along with the familiar chains. The college towns of Claremont and Redlands have creative contemporary and ethnic fare. Innovative cuisine has become the norm in Temecula, especially at the wineries, many of which showcase their products alongside fine dining. The options are more limited in the smaller mountain communities; typically each town supports a single upscale restaurant, along with fast-food outlets, steak-and-potatoes family spots, and perhaps an Italian or Mexican eatery. Universally, dining out is casual.

HOTELS

In the San Bernardino Mountains, many accommodations are bed-and-breakfasts or rustic cabins, though Lake Arrowhead and Big Bear offer more luxurious resort lodging. Rates for Big Bear lodgings fluctuate widely, depending on the season. When winter snow brings droves of Angelenos to the mountains for skiing, expect to pay sky-high prices for any kind of room. Most establishments require a two-night stay on weekends. In Riverside, the landmark Mission Inn is the marquee accommodation. In the Wine Country, lodgings can be found at wineries, golf resorts, and chain hotels. *Hotel reviews have been shortened. For full information, visit Fodors.com.*

13

WHAT IT COSTS

	$	$$	$$$	$$$$
Restaurants	under $16	$16–$22	$23–$30	over $30
Hotels	under $121	$121–$175	$176–$250	over $250

Restaurant prices are the average cost of a main course at dinner or, if dinner is not served, at lunch, excluding sales tax of 8%–9%. Hotel prices are the lowest cost of a standard double room in high season, excluding service charges and 8%–13% tax.

THE WESTERN INLAND EMPIRE

Straddling the line between Los Angeles and San Bernardino counties, the western section of the Inland Empire is home to some of California's oldest vineyards and original citrus orchards. Now a busy suburban community, it holds the closest ski slopes to metro Los Angeles. Fairplex, where the L.A. County Fair is held each year, is here, as is Claremont, home to a collection of high-ranking colleges.

GETTING HERE AND AROUND

To reach this area from Los Angeles, take Interstate 10, which bisects the Western Inland Empire west to east; from Pasadena, take Interstate 210, which runs parallel to the north. Take Highway 57 from Anaheim. Some areas are quite walkable, especially the Claremont Colleges, where you can stroll through parks from one school building to another.

The Foothill Transit Bus Line serves Pomona, Claremont, and Montclair, with stops at Cal Poly and the Fairplex. Metrolink serves the area from Los Angeles and elsewhere.

Bus Contact Foothill Transit ☎ *800/743-3463* ⊕ *www.foothilltransit.org.*

POMONA

23 miles north of Anaheim, 27 miles east of Pasadena.

The green hills of Pomona, dotted with horses and houses, are perhaps best known as the site of the Los Angeles County Fair and of California State Polytechnic University–Pomona. Named for the Roman goddess of fruit, the city has a rich citrus-growing heritage.

GETTING HERE AND AROUND

The most direct routes from Los Angeles to Pomona are the Pomona Freeway (Highway 60) and Interstate 10. It pays to check traffic reports before starting out. Mission Boulevard (west–east) and Garey Avenue (north–south) are the main surface streets through downtown.

ESSENTIALS

Visitor Information Pomona Chamber of Commerce ✉ *101 W. Mission Blvd.* ☎ *909/622-8484* ⊕ *www.pomonachamber.org* ▬ *No credit cards.*

EXPLORING

California Polytechnic University at Pomona. The university occupies 1,438 rolling acres of the Kellogg Ranch, originally the winter home of cereal magnate W.K. Kellogg. Cal Poly specializes in teaching agriculture, and you can find rose gardens, avocado groves, many farm animals, and a working Arabian horse ranch. The Farm Store (✉ *4102 University Dr. S.* ☎ *909/869–4906* ⊗ *Daily 10–6*) sells locally grown meat, produce, and cheeses, along with plants grown in the university nursery. ✉ *3801 W. Temple Ave.* ☎ *909/869–7659* ⊕ *www. csupomona.edu.*

Fairplex. The site of the Los Angeles County Fair (North America's largest county fair), the Fairplex exposition center hosts open-air markets, antiques shows, roadster shows, historical train and model train exhibits, horse shows and racing, dog shows, and the annual International Wine and Spirits competition. Also here is the **Wally Parks NHRA Motorsports Museum** (⊕ *www.museum.nhra.com*), which pays tribute to the rich history of American motor sports with exhibits of vintage racing vehicles and has an amusing collection of tricked-out drag-racing cars. ✉ *1101 W. McKinley Ave.* ☎ *909/623–3111, 909/622–2133 museum* ⊕ *www.fairplex.com* ✉ *Museum $10* ⊗ *Museum Wed.–Sun. 10–5.*

W.K. Kellogg Arabian Horse Shows. The classic shows, started by cereal maker Kellogg in 1926, remain a tradition on the CSU–Pomona campus. Many purebreds live at the ranch, and the university presents exhibitions of the equines in English and Western tack the first Sunday of the month at 2 pm from October through May. Stable visits and pony rides ($5) take place after the show. ✉ *3801 W. Temple Ave.* ☎ *909/869–2224* ⊕ *www.csupomona.edu/~equine* ✉ *$4.*

WHERE TO EAT AND STAY

$$$ ✕ **Pomona Valley Mining Company.** Atop a hill near an old mining site, this AMERICAN rustic steak-and-seafood restaurant provides great city views at night. Though somewhat dated, the decor reflects the regional mining heritage. Authentic gold-rush pieces and 1800s memorabilia hang on the walls, and old lanterns adorn the tables. The food—heavy on steak and prime rib—is well prepared; save space for dessert that includes mud pie or bourbon bread pudding. $ *Average main: $26* ✉ *1777 Gillette Rd.* ☎ *909/623–3515* ⊕ *www.pomonavalleyminingco.com* ⌨ *Reservations essential* ⊗ *Closed Mon. No lunch Tues.–Sat.*

$$ 🏨 **Sheraton Fairplex Hotel & Conference Center.** County-fair murals and HOTEL whimsical carousel animals welcome you to this all-suites hotel at the entrance to Pomona's Fairplex. **Pros:** adjacent to convention center; clean rooms; most rooms have balconies. **Cons:** parts feel dated; not close to many restaurants. $ *Rooms from: $149* ✉ *601 W. McKinley Ave.* ☎ *800/325–3535, 909/622–2220* ⊕ *www.sheratonfairplex.com* ⊶ *247 suites* ⌾ *No meals.*

CLAREMONT

4 miles north of Pomona.

The seven Claremont Colleges are among the most prestigious in the nation. The campuses are all laid out cheek-by-jowl; as you wander from one leafy street to the next, you won't be able to tell where one college ends and the next begins.

Claremont was originally the home of the Sunkist citrus growers cooperative movement. Today, Claremont Village, home to descendants of those early farmers, is bright and lively. The business district village, with streets named for prestigious eastern colleges, is walkable and appealing with a collection of boutiques, fancy food emporiums, cafés, and lounges. The downtown district is a beautiful place to visit, with Victorian, Craftsman, and Spanish-colonial buildings.

GETTING HERE AND AROUND

If you're driving, exit Interstate 10 at Indian Hill Boulevard, and drive north to Claremont. Parking can be difficult, although there are metered spots. Overnight parking is prohibited within the village; however there is a parking structure adjacent to the College Heights Packing House that is also north of the freeway; exit Garey and drive toward the mountains. You can reach this area by public transportation, but you'll need a car to get around unless you plan to spend all your time in the Claremont Village.

ESSENTIALS

Visitor Information Claremont Chamber of Commerce ⊠ *205 Yale Ave.* ☎ *909/624–1681* ⊕ *www.claremontchamber.org.*

EXPLORING

Claremont Heritage. College walking tours, a downtown tour, and historic home tours are conducted throughout the year by Claremont Heritage. On the first Saturday of each month the organization gives guided walking tours ($5) of the village. The website has self-guided tour maps. ⊠ *840 N. Indian Hill Blvd.* ☎ *909/621–0848* ⊕ *www. claremontheritage.org* ☞ *$5.*

Pomona College Museum of Art. This small museum on the campus of Pomona College exhibits significant contemporary art, works by old masters, and examples of Native American arts and artifacts. Highlights include the first mural painted by the Mexican artist Jose Clemente Orozco in North America, first-edition etchings by Goya, and the Kress collection of 15th- and 16th-century Italian panel paintings. The fun Art After Hours events on Thursday nights often include local bands and music. ⊠ *333 N. College Ave.* ☎ *909/621–8283* ⊕ *www.pomona. edu/museum* ☞ *Free* ⊗ *Tues.–Sun. 12–5, Thurs. until 11.*

QUICK BITES

Bert & Rocky's Cream Company. The sinfully innovative concoctions at this popular ice-cream store include the Elvis special with bananas and peanut butter and the Tuscany marble, chocolate-raspberry swirl, and blueberry-cheesecake ice creams. The vanilla's delightful, too. ⊠ *242 Yale Ave.* ☎ *909/625–1852.*

Fodor's Choice
★

Rancho Santa Ana Botanic Garden. Founded in 1927 by Susanna Bixby Bryant, a wealthy landowner and conservationist, the garden is a living museum and research center dedicated to the conservation of native-California plant species. You can meander here for hours enjoying the shade of an oak tree canopy

CLAREMONT WEATHER

Be prepared for hot and smoggy conditions in summer; the town is not gifted with SoCal's best climate.

13

or take a guided tour of the grounds, whose 86 acres of ponds and greenery shelter such specimens as California wild lilacs (*ceanothus*), big berry manzanita, and four-needled pinyon. Countless birds also make their homes here. Guided tram tours ($5) are offered the third Sunday of every month; seats are limited and tickets are first come, first served. ✉ *1500 N. College Ave.* ☎ *909/625–8767* ⊕ *www.rsabg. org* 💲 *$8* ⊗ *Daily 8–5.*

WHERE TO EAT

$$
ITALIAN

✕ **La Parolaccia.** Locals line up on weekends to get a table at this busy spot where waiters zip through a series of small rooms delivering fresh and beautifully seasoned items from an extensive Italian menu. Popular dishes include pasta with fresh salmon and capers, and risotto with seafood, white wine, and tomato sauce. Topping the dessert list is bread pudding made with ciabatta bread and crème anglaise. 💲 *Average main: $19* ✉ *201 N. Indian Hill Blvd.* ☎ *909/624–1516* ⊕ *www. laparolacciausa.com.*

$$$$
ITALIAN

✕ **Tutti Mangia Italian Grill.** A popular spot for college students and their visiting parents, this storefront dining room has a warm and cozy feel and top menu choices that include Meyer Farm's beef, roasted double pork chops, osso buco, and pan-roasted salmon with blood-orange sauce. The small plates always entice. 💲 *Average main: $40* ✉ *102 Harvard Ave.* ☎ *909/625–4669* ⊕ *www.tuttimangia.com* 🍴 *Reservations essential* ⊗ *No lunch weekends.*

$$
ECLECTIC

✕ **Walter's Restaurant.** With a menu that roams the globe from France to Italy to Afghanistan, Walter's is where locals gather to dine, sip wine, and chat. You can eat outside on the sidewalk, on the lively patio, or in a cozy setting inside. Wherever you sit, the owner, Nangy, will stroll by to make sure you're happy with your meal. He'll urge you to try the puffy Afghan fries with hot sauce, tabouleh salad, or lamb stew. Breakfast possibilities include omelets, sausage and eggs, and burritos; for lunch are salads, soups, pastas, kebabs, and vegetarian items. 💲 *Average main: $21* ✉ *310 N. Yale Ave.* ☎ *909/624–4914* ⊕ *www.waltersrestaurant. com* 🍴 *Reservations essential.*

WHERE TO STAY

$$$
B&B/INN
Fodor's Choice
★

🛏 **Casa 425.** This boutique inn on a corner opposite the College Heights Lemon Packing House entertainment and shopping complex is the most attractive lodging option in Claremont Village. **Pros:** walking distance to attractions and restaurants; bicycles available; most rooms have fireplaces and soaking tubs. **Cons:** occasional noise. 💲 *Rooms from: $195* ✉ *425 W. 1st St.* ☎ *866/450–0425* ⊕ *www.foursisters.com* 🛏 *28 rooms* 🍽 *Some meals.*

$$ HOTEL FAMILY **DoubleTree by Hilton Hotel Claremont.** The hotel of choice for parents visiting children attending local colleges has spacious rooms clustered in three Spanish-style buildings that surround a flower-decked central courtyard. **Pros:** convenient to colleges; swimming pool; chocolate chip cookies. **Cons:** small bathrooms. [$] *Rooms from: $169* ✉ *555 W. Foothill Blvd.* ☎ *909/626–2411* 🌐 *www.doubletreeclaremont.com* 🛏 *190 rooms* 🍴 *No meals.*

NIGHTLIFE

Being a college town, Claremont has many bars and cafés, some of which showcase bands.

Flappers Comedy Club. A typical stand-up venue, Flappers is a branch of a Burbank club. Headliners such as Hal Sparks and Titus perform, as do up-and-coming comedians. Snacks, wine and beverages are available. ✉ *532 W. 1st St.* ☎ *818/845–9721* 🌐 *www.flapperscomedy.com* 🎟 *$10–$20, some shows free* 🕒 *Closed Mon.–Wed.*

SPORTS AND THE OUTDOORS

SKIING

Mt. Baldy Ski Resort. The 10,064-foot mountain's real name is Mt. San Antonio, but Mt. Baldy Ski Resort—the oldest ski area in Southern California—takes its name from the treeless slopes. The Mt. Baldy base lies at 6,500 feet, and four chairlifts ascend to 8,600 feet. The resort is known for its steep triple-diamond runs; the longest of the 26 runs here is 2,100 vertical feet. Backcountry skiing is available via shuttle in the spring, and there's a school on weekends for kids ages 5 to 12. Winter or summer, you can take a scenic chairlift ride ($25) to the Top of the Notch restaurant and hiking and mountain-biking trails. ✉ *8401 Mt. Baldy Rd., Mt. Baldy* ☎ *909/982–0800* 🌐 *www.mtbaldyskilifts.com* 🎟 *Full day $69, half day $49* 🕒 *Snow season: Nov.–Apr., weekdays 8–4:30, weekends 7:30–4:30. Summer season May–Oct., weekends 7–sunset.*

ONTARIO

6 miles east of Pomona.

Ontario has a rich agricultural and industrial heritage. The valley's warm climate once supported vineyards that produced grape varietals such as Grenache, Mourvèdre, and Zinfandel. Today, housing tracts and shopping malls have replaced most of the vineyards. But the airport is here, so you may well find yourself passing through.

GETTING HERE AND AROUND

Ontario lies between Interstate 10 to the north and Highway 60 (Pomona Freeway) to the south. Metrolink connects the L.A. area to the airport and other destinations, but driving is the best way to get around the area.

ESSENTIALS

Visitor Information **Ontario Convention Center** ✉ *2000 E. Convention Center Way* ☎ *909/937–3000* 🌐 *www.ontariocc.com.*

EXPLORING

Graber Olive House. Ontario's oldest business opened in 1894, when C.C. Graber bottled his meaty, tree-ripened olives and started selling them. They're still sold throughout the United States. Stop by the gourmet shop for a jar, then have a picnic on the shaded grounds. Tours are conducted year-round; in fall you can watch workers grade, cure, and can the olives. ⊠ *315 E. 4th St.* ☎ *800/996–5483* ⊕ *www.graberolives. com* ⊠ *Free* ⊙ *Daily 9–5:30.*

WHERE TO STAY

$ ☷ **DoubleTree by Hilton Ontario Airport.** A beautifully landscaped court-
HOTEL yard greets you at Ontario's only full-service hotel. **Pros:** clean, large
FAMILY rooms; free shuttle to airport and Ontario Mills Mall; chocolate chip cookies. **Cons:** airport and freeway noise; Internet charge; dated rooms. $ *Rooms from: $99* ⊠ *222 N. Vineyard Ave.* ☎ *909/937–0900, 800/222–8733* ⊕ *www.doubletree.com* ⇱ *482 rooms.*

SHOPPING

FAMILY **Ontario Mills Mall.** The gargantuan mall packs in more than 200 outlet stores including Nordstrom Rack and Sax Fifth Avenue Off 5th. Also here are Carleton Day Spa, a 30-screen movie theater, the Improv Comedy Club and Dinner Theater, and two entertainment complexes. Dining options include a food court, Chipotle Mexican Grill, and the kid-friendly Rainforest Cafe. ⊠ *1 Mills Circle, off 4th St. and I–15* ☎ *909/484–8300* ⊕ *www.ontariomills.com* ⊙ *Mon.–Sat. 10–9, Sun. 11–8.*

RANCHO CUCAMONGA

5 miles north of Ontario.

Once a thriving wine-making area with more than 50,000 acres of wine grapes, Rancho Cucamonga—the oldest wine district in California— lost most of its pastoral charm after real-estate developers bought up the land for a megamall and affordable housing. Most of it is now a squeaky-clean planned community, but the wine-making tradition still thrives at the Joseph Filippi Winery.

GETTING HERE AND AROUND

Historic Route 66 (Foothill Boulevard) cuts east–west across Rancho Cucamonga. The community is best reached via Interstate 10.

EXPLORING

Joseph Filippi Winery. J.P. and Jared Filippi continue the family tradition that was started in 1922 at Joseph Filippi, crafting wines from Caber-net, Sangiovese, and Zinfandel grapes, among other varietals. A small museum chronicles the history of Rancho Cucamonga wine making. ⊠ *12467 Base Line Rd.* ☎ *909/899–5755* ⊕ *www.josephfilippiwinery. com* ⊠ *Tasting $5* ⊙ *Tues.–Thurs. and Sun., 12–6, Fri. and Sat. 11–7; tour Wed.–Sun. at 1* ⊙ *Closed Mon.*

FAMILY **Victoria Gardens.** With its vintage signs, antique lampposts, and relax-ing 1920s-style Town Square—complete with old-fashioned trolley— this family-oriented shopping, dining, and entertainment complex feels a lot like Disneyland. Amid 12 blocks you'll find Macy's, A&F,

13

Williams-Sonoma, an AMC movie multiplex, and a Ben & Jerry's ice-cream shop. Restaurants include The Cheesecake Factory and Fleming's Prime Steak House & Wine Bar. Carriage and trolley rides are available on weekends. The Victoria Gardens Cultural Center houses a 540-seat performing-arts center. ⊠ *12505 N. Mainstreet* ☎ *909/463–2830 info, 909/477–2775 Cultural Center* ⊕ *www.victoriagardensie.com* ▧ *Free* ☉ *Mon.–Thurs. 10–9, Fri. and Sat. 10–10, Sun. 11–7.*

WHERE TO EAT

$$$$
STEAKHOUSE

✕ **The Sycamore Inn.** Flickering gas lamps and a glowing fireplace greet you at this rustic restaurant. Built in 1921, the Sycamore Inn occupies the site of a stagecoach stop on Historic Route 66. The specialty here is USDA dry-aged prime steak—portion sizes range from 8 to 22 ounces—but also on the menu are ahi tuna, Australian lobster tail, and Colorado rack of lamb. The impressive wine list includes selections from the best Napa and Sonoma wineries, and France, New Zealand, Australia, and South America are also well represented. Ⓢ *Average main: $34* ⊠ *8318 Foothill Blvd.* ☎ *909/982–1104* ⊕ *www.thesycamoreinn.com* ⌖ *Reservations essential* ☉ *No lunch.*

RIVERSIDE AREA

Historic Riverside lies at the heart of the Inland Empire. Major highways linking it to other regional destinations spoke out from this city to the north, south, and east.

GETTING HERE AND AROUND

The most direct route from Los Angeles to Riverside is by Highway 60 (Pomona Freeway). From San Diego take Interstate 15 northeast to the junction with Highway 60. From North Orange County, Highway 91 is the best route.

Bus Contacts Omnitrans ☎ *800/966–6428* ⊕ *www.omnitrans.org.*
Riverside Transit Authority ☎ *951/562–5002* ⊕ *www.riversidetransit.com.*

CORONA

13 miles south of Ontario.

Corona's Temescal Canyon is named for the dome-shaped mud saunas that the Luiseño Indians built around the area's artesian hot springs in the early 19th century. Starting in 1860, weary Butterfield Overland Stage Company passengers stopped here to relax in the soothing mineral springs. In 1890 Mr. and Mrs. W.G. Steers turned the springs into Glen Ivy Hot Springs, whose popularity has yet to fade.

GETTING HERE AND AROUND

Primarily a bedroom community, Corona lies at the intersection of Interstate 15 and Highway 91. The many roadside malls make it a convenient stop for food or gas.

It's okay to get a little dirty at Glen Ivy Hot Springs, which offers a wide variety of treatments at its famous spa—including the red clay pool at Club Mud.

EXPLORING

FAMILY **Tom's Farms.** Opened as a produce stand along I–15 in 1974, Tom's Farms has grown to include a locally popular hamburger stand, a furniture showroom, and a sweets shop. You can still buy produce here, but the big draw is various weekend attractions for the kiddies: tractor driving, Tom's mining company, a petting zoo, a children's train, a pony ride, free magic shows, face painting, and an old-style carousel. Most cost a modest fee. Of interest for adults is the wine-and-cheese shop, which has more than 600 varieties of wine, including some from the nearby Temecula Valley. ✉ *23900 Temescal Canyon Rd.* ☎ *951/277–4422* ⊕ *www.tomsfarms.com* ✉ *Free, attraction fees vary; wine tasting $5* ☉ *Daily 8 am–8 pm; wine tasting 11–5.*

SHOPPING

SPAS

Glen Ivy Hot Springs Spa. Presidents Herbert Hoover and Ronald Reagan are among the guests who have soaked their toes at this beautiful, relaxing spa. Colorful bougainvillea and birds-of-paradise surround the secluded Glen Ivy, which offers a full range of facials, manicures, pedicures, body wraps, and massages. Some treatments are performed in underground granite chambers (highly recommended by readers) known collectively as the Grotto. The Under the Oaks treatment center holds eight open-air massage rooms surrounded by waterfalls and ancient oak trees. Don't bring your best bikini if you plan to dive into the red clay (brought in daily from a local mine) of Club Mud. Paying the admission fee entitles you to lounge here all day. Make reservations for treatments, which cost extra. ✉ *25000 Glen Ivy Rd.*

☎ 888/453–6489 ⊕ *www.glenivy.com* ✉ *Admission Mon.–Thurs. $46, Fri.–Sun. $64; treatments $25–$183* ☉ *Daily 9–5, closes later in warm weather.*

RIVERSIDE

14 miles northeast of Corona, 34 miles northeast of Anaheim.

By 1882 Riverside was home to more than half of California's citrus groves, making it the state's wealthiest city per capita in 1895. The prosperity produced a downtown area of opulent architecture, which is well preserved today. Main Street's pedestrian strip is lined with antiques and gift stores, art galleries, salons, and the UCR/California Museum of Photography.

GETTING HERE AND AROUND

Downtown Riverside lies north of Highway 91 at the University Avenue exit. The Mission Inn is at the corner of Mission Inn Avenue and Orange Street, and key museums, shops, and restaurants are near by. You can park around here and walk to them.

EXPLORING

Mission Inn Museum. The crown jewel of Riverside is the Mission Inn, a Spanish-revival hotel whose elaborate turrets, clock tower, mission bells, and flying buttresses rise above downtown. Docent-led tours of the hotel are offered by the Mission Inn Foundation, which also operates an expansive museum with displays depicting the building's illustrious history. The inn was designed in 1902 by Arthur B. Benton and Myron Hunt; the team took its cues from the Spanish missions in San Gabriel and Carmel. You can climb to the top of the Rotunda Wing's five-story spiral stairway, or linger a while in the Courtyard of the Birds, where a tinkling fountain and shady trees invite meditation. You can also peek inside the St. Francis Chapel, where celebrities such as Bette Davis, Humphrey Bogart, and Richard and Pat Nixon tied the knot before the Mexican cedar altar. The Presidential Lounge, a bright, wood-panel bar, has been patronized by eight U.S. presidents. ✉ *3696 Main St.* ☎ *951/788–9556* ⊕ *www.missioninnmuseum.com* ✉ *Admission $2, tour $13* ☉ *Daily 9:30–4:30.*

Riverside Art Museum. Hearst Castle architect Julia Morgan designed this museum that houses a fine collection of paintings by Southern California landscape artists, including William Keith, Robert Wood, and Ralph Love. Major temporary exhibitions are mounted year-round. ✉ *3425 Mission Inn Ave.* ☎ *951/684–7111* ⊕ *www.riversideartmuseum.org* ✉ *$5; free 1st Thurs. of month 6–9* ☉ *Tues.–Sat. 10–4, Sun. 1–4.*

Fodor's Choice ★ **UCR/California Museum of Photography.** With an impressive collection that includes thousands of Kodak Brownie and Zeiss Ikon cameras, this museum—the centerpiece of UCR ARTSblock—surveys the history of photography *and* the devices that produced it. Exhibitions—some of contemporary images, others historically oriented—are always top-notch and often incorporate photographs from the permanent collection. When not on display, works by Ansel Adams, Olindo Ceccarini, and other greats can be viewed by appointment.

CLOSE UP

Navel Oranges in California: Good as Gold

In 1873 a woman named Eliza Tibbets changed the course of California history when she planted two Brazilian navel-orange trees in her Riverside garden.

The trees (which were called Washington Navels in honor of America's first president) flourished in the area's warm climate and rich soil—and before long, Tibbett's garden was producing the sweetest seedless oranges anyone had ever tasted. After winning awards at several major exhibitions, Tibbets realized she could make a profit from her trees. She sold buds to the increasing droves of citrus farmers flocking to the Inland Empire, and by 1882, almost 250,000 citrus trees had been planted in Riverside alone. California's citrus industry had been born.

Today, Riverside still celebrates its citrus-growing heritage. The downtown Marketplace district contains several restored packing houses, and the Riverside Metropolitan Museum is home to a permanent exhibit of historic tools and machinery once used in the industry. The University of California at Riverside still remains at the forefront of citrus research; its Citrus Variety Collection includes specimens of 1,000 different fruit trees from around the world.

✉ *3824 Main St.* ☎ *951/827–4787* 🌐 *artsblock.ucr.edu/exhibitions* 🎟 *$3* 🕒 *Tues.–Sat. 12–5.*

WHERE TO EAT AND STAY

$$$$ ITALIAN 🍴 **Mario's Place.** The clientele is as beautiful as the food at this intimate jazz and supper club across the street from the Mission Inn. The northern Italian cuisine is first-rate, as are the jazz bands that perform Friday and Saturday at 10 pm. Try the pear-and-Gorgonzola wood-fired pizza, followed by the star anise panna cotta for dessert. Jazz groups play weekend nights in the Lounge. [$] *Average main: $36* ✉ *3646 Mission Inn Ave.* ☎ *951/684–7755* 🌐 *www.mariosplace.com* ✍ *Reservations essential* 🕒 *Closed Sun.*

$ AMERICAN 🍴 **Simple Simon's.** Expect to wait in line at this popular little sandwich shop on the pedestrian-only shopping strip outside the Mission Inn. It's a good place to grab a breakfast sandwich or some french toast. At lunchtime, salads, soups, and sandwiches on house-baked breads are served; standouts include the chicken-apple sausage sandwich and the roast lamb sandwich topped with grilled eggplant, red peppers, and tomato-fennel-olive sauce. [$] *Average main: $10* ✉ *3636 Main St.* ☎ *951/369–6030* ✍ *Reservations not accepted* 🕒 *Closed Sun. No dinner.*

$ HOTEL FAMILY Fodor's Choice ★ 🏨 **Mission Inn and Spa.** One of California's most historic hotels, the inn grew from a modest adobe lodge in 1876 to the grand Spanish-revival hotel it is today. **Pros:** fascinating historical site; luxurious rooms; great restaurants; family-friendly. **Cons:** train noise can be deafening at night. [$] *Rooms from: $119* ✉ *3649 Mission Inn Ave.* ☎ *951/784–0300, 800/843–7755* 🌐 *www.missioninn.com* 🛏 *238 rooms, 29 suites* 🍽 *No meals.*

NIGHTLIFE

Sevilla Nightclub. Patrons dance to live music on most nights at this nightclub that serves tapas in both small-plate and entrée-size portions. Expect Salsa with lessons on Wednesday nights, Latin-Euro Top 40 dancing on weekends. ✉ *3252 Mission Inn Ave.* ☎ *949/648– 0246* ⊕ *www.sevillanightclub.com* ▤ *Cover charge varies* ⊙ *Closed Tues.*

BEFORE YOU GO PICKING

Be sure to call before visiting the farms, most of which are family run. Unpasteurized cider— sold at some farms—should not be consumed by children, the elderly, or those with weakened immune systems.

REDLANDS

15 miles northeast of Riverside.

Redlands lies at the center of what once was the largest navel-orange-producing region in the world. Orange groves are still plentiful throughout the area. Populated in the late 1800s by wealthy citrus farmers, the town holds a colorful collection of Victorian homes.

GETTING HERE AND AROUND

Redlands straddles Interstate 10 north and south of the freeway at its intersection with Highway 210, one of the main roads into the San Bernardino Mountains.

ESSENTIALS

Visitor Information Redlands Chamber of Commerce ✉ *1 E. Redlands Blvd.* ☎ *909/793–2546* ⊕ *www.redlandschamber.org.*

EXPLORING

Asistencia Mission de San Gabriel. Franciscan Fathers built the mission in 1819, but it functioned as one for only a few years. In 1834 it became part of a rancho and later served as a school and a factory. The current mission is a replica. The landscaped courtyard contains an old Spanish mission bell, and one building holds a small museum. ✉ *26930 Barton Rd.* ☎ *909/793–5402* ⊕ *www.sbcounty.gov/museum/branches/asist.htm* ▤ *$5* ⊙ *Tues.–Sat. 10–3.*

Kimberly Crest House and Gardens. In 1897 Cornelia A. Hill built what's now Kimberly Crest House and Gardens to mimic the châteaux of France's Loire Valley. Surrounded by orange groves, lily ponds, and terraced Italian gardens, the mansion has a French-revival parlor, a mahogany staircase, a glass-mosaic fireplace, and a bubbling fountain in the form of Venus rising from the sea. Alfred and Helen Kimberly, founders of the Kimberly-Clark Paper Company, purchased the estate in 1905, and their daughter, Mary, lived here until 1979. Most of the 22 rooms are in original condition. ✉ *1325 Prospect Dr.* ☎ *909/792– 2111* ⊕ *www.kimberlycrest.org* ▤ *$10* ⊙ *Thurs., Fri., and Sun. 1–3:30* ⊙ *Closed Aug. and major holidays.*

Lincoln Memorial Shrine. The shrine houses the largest collection of Abraham Lincoln artifacts on the West Coast. You can view a marble bust of Lincoln by sculptor George Grey Barnard, along with more than a dozen letters and rare pamphlets. The gift shop sells many books, toys, and reproductions pertaining to the Civil War. ⊠ *125 W. Vine St.* ☎ *909/798–7636, 909/798–7632* ⊕ *www.lincolnshrine.org* ✉ *Free* ⊙ *Tues.–Sun. 1–5.*

OAK GLEN

17 miles east of Redlands.

More than 60 varieties of apples are grown in Oak Glen. This rustic village, tucked in the foothills above Yucaipa, is home to acres of farms, produce stands, country shops, and homey cafés. The town really comes alive during the fall harvest (from September through December), which is celebrated with piglet races, live entertainment, and other events. Many farms also grow berries and stone fruit, which are available in summer. Most of the apple farms lie along Oak Glen Road.

13

GETTING HERE AND AROUND

Oak Glen is tucked into a mountainside about halfway up the San Bernardinos. Exit Interstate 10 at Yucaipa Boulevard, heading east to the intersection with Oak Glen Road, a 5-mile loop along which you'll find most of the shops, cafés, and apple orchards.

ESSENTIALS

Visitor Information Oak Glen Apple Growers Association ⊠ *39600 Oak Glen Rd., Yucaipa* ⊕ *www.oakglen.net.*

EXPLORING

Mom's Country Orchards. Oak Glen's informal information center is at Mom's, where you can belly up to the bar and learn about the nuances of apple tasting, or warm up with a hot cider heated on an antique stove. Organic produce, local honey, apple butter, and salsa are also specialties here. ⊠ *38695 Oak Glen Rd.* ☎ *909/797–4249* ⊙ *Mon.–Fri. 10–5, Sat.–Sun. 10–6.*

FAMILY **Oak Tree Village.** This 14-acre children's park has miniature train rides, trout fishing, gold panning, exotic animal exhibits, shops, and a petting zoo and several eateries. ⊠ *38480 Oak Glen Rd.* ☎ *909/797–4420* ⊕ *www.oaktreevillageoakglen.net* ✉ *$5* ⊙ *Daily 10–5.*

FAMILY **Riley's Farm.** Employees dress in period costumes at Riley's Farm, one of the most interactive and kid-friendly ranches in apple country. The farm hosts school groups from September to June. Individuals can join the groups by reservation. You can hop on a hayride, take part in a barn dance, pick your own apples, press some cider, or throw a tomahawk while enjoying living-history performances throughout the orchard. The farm is also home to Colonial Chesterfield, a replica New England–style estate where costumed 18th-century reenactors offer lessons in cider pressing, candle dipping, and colonial games, and etiquette. The four-hour Revolutionary War Adventures are especially popular. Afterward, head to the Public House for a bite of colonial specialties. The warm apple pies are unforgettable. ⊠ *12261 S. Oak Glen Rd.* ☎ *909/797–7534* ⊕ *www.rileysfarm.com* ✉ *Free to visit ranch, fees vary for activities* ⊙ *Mon.–Sat. 9–4.*

Rileys at Los Rios Rancho. This farm, with 50 acres of apple trees, has a fantastic country store where you can stock up on jams, cookbooks, syrups, and candied apples. Head into the bakery for a hot tri-tip sandwich before going outside to the picnic grounds for lunch. During the fall, you can pick your own apples and pumpkins, take a hayride, or enjoy live bluegrass music. On the rancho grounds, the **Wildlands Conservancy** preserves 400 acres of nature trails, open weekends from 8:30 to 4:30. From April through December, guided night walks take place on the third Saturday of the month. ✉ *39611 Oak Glen Rd.* ☎ *909/797–1005* 🌐 *www.losriosrancho.com* 🕒 *Oct.–Nov., daily 9–5; Dec.–Sept., Wed.–Sun. 10–5.*

WHERE TO EAT

$ AMERICAN 🍴 **Apple Annie's Restaurant and Bakery.** You won't leave hungry from this country-western diner, known for its 5-pound apple pies and family-style seven-course dinners. The decor is comfortable and rustic; old guns and handcuffs hang on the walls alongside pictures of cowboys, trail wagons, and outlaws. Standout dishes include the tuna melt and the Annie deluxe burger. [$] *Average main: $12* ✉ *38480 Oak Glen Rd.* ☎ *909/797–7311* 🕒 *Daily 8–8.*

$ AMERICAN 🍴 **Law's Oak Glen Coffee Shop.** Since 1953, this old-fashioned coffee shop has been serving up hot java, hearty breakfasts and lunches, and famous apple pies. Menu stalwarts include meat loaf, country-fried steak, and Reuben sandwiches. Law's stays open until 7 pm on Fridays and weekends and closes at 3 the rest of the week. [$] *Average main: $8* ✉ *38392 Oak Glen Rd.* ☎ *909/797–1642* 🌐 *www.lawsoakglen.com* 🕒 *No dinner Mon.–Thurs.*

SAN BERNARDINO MOUNTAINS

One of three transverse mountain ranges that lie in the Inland Empire, the San Bernardino range holds the tallest peak in Southern California, San Gorgonio Mountain, at 11,503 feet. It's frequently snowcapped in winter, providing the region's only challenging ski slopes. In summer the forested hillsides and lakes provide a cool retreat from the city for many locals.

LAKE ARROWHEAD

37 miles northeast of Riverside.

Lake Arrowhead Village is an alpine community with lodgings, shops, outlet stores, and eateries that descend a hill to the lake. Outside the village, access to the lake and its beaches is limited to area residents and their guests.

GETTING HERE AND AROUND

Access Lake Arrowhead by driving north from Interstate 10 at Redlands on Highway 210 and continuing north on Highway 330 to the town of Running Springs, where you'll turn west onto Highway 18. Also called the Rim of the World, Highway 18 straddles a mountainside ledge at elevation 5,000 feet, revealing fabulous views. At the Lake Arrowhead turnoff, you'll descend into a wooded bowl surrounding the lake. The village itself is walkable, but hilly. Scenic Highway 173 winding along the east side of the lake offers scenic blue water views through the forest. In winter, check for chain control along this route.

ESSENTIALS

Visitor Information Lake Arrowhead Communities Chamber of Commerce ✉ *28200 Hwy. 189, Lake Arrowhead* ☎ *909/337–3715* 🌐 *lakearrowhead.net.*

13

EXPLORING

Lake Arrowhead Queen. One of the few ways visitors can access Lake Arrowhead is on a 50-minute *Lake Arrowhead Queen* cruise, operated daily from the Lake Arrowhead Village marina. ✉ *28200 Hwy. 189, Building C-100, Lake Arrowhead* ☎ *909/336–6992* 🌐 *lakearrowhead-queen.com* 🎟 *$16.*

WHERE TO EAT AND STAY

$ CAFÉ FAMILY 🍴 **Belgian Waffle Works.** This dockside eatery, just steps from the *Lake Arrowhead Queen*, is quaint and homey, with country decor and beautiful lake views. Dive into a mud-pie Belgian waffle with chocolate fudge sauce or try a Belgian S'more with a marshmallow-and-chocolate sauce. For lunch there are delicious burgers, tuna melts, chili, meat loaf, chicken dishes, and salads. Dinner is served in the summer months only. Weekends at lunchtime can get crowded. [$] *Average main: $9* ✉ *28200 Hwy. 189, Suite 150* ☎ *909/337–5222* 🌐 *belgianwaffle.com* ✍ *Reservations not accepted* 🕒 *No dinner.*

$$$$ AMERICAN 🍴 **Casual Elegance.** Owner-chef Kathleen Kirk charms diners with her inventive cuisine at this upscale restaurant. The specialties include rack of lamb prepared with an herb crust, crispy breast of duck, and Alaskan halibut. Dine by the fireplace for a particularly cozy experience. [$] *Average main: $38* ✉ *26848 Hwy. 189, Blue Jay* ☎ *909/337–8932* 🌐 *www.casualelegancerestaurant.com* ✍ *Reservations essential* 🕒 *Closed Mon. and Tues. No lunch.*

$$$ RESORT FAMILY Fodor's Choice ★ 🏨 **Lake Arrowhead Resort and Spa.** This lakeside lodge offers water or forest views from private patios or balconies, an on-site spa, and a warm and comfy atmosphere thanks to the roaring fireplaces everywhere. **Pros:** most rooms offer beautiful views; spa; delicious on-site dining. **Cons:** some rooms have thin walls; resort amenity fee $20 per night. [$] *Rooms from: $215* ✉ *27984 Hwy. 189* ☎ *909/336–1511* 🌐 *www.lakearrowheadresort.com* 🛏 *162 rooms, 11 suites* 🍽 *No meals.*

SPORTS AND THE OUTDOORS

WATERSKIING

McKenzie Waterski School. Summer ski-boat rides and waterskiing and wakeboarding lessons are available through this school in summer. ✉ *28200 Hwy. 189* ☎ *909/337–3814* 🌐 *www.mckenziewaterskischool.com.*

BIG BEAR LAKE

24 miles east of Lake Arrowhead.

When Angelenos say they're going to the mountains, they usually mean Big Bear, where alpine-style villages surround the 7-mile-long lake. The south shore has ski slopes, the Big Bear Alpine Zoo, water-sports opportunities, restaurants, and lodgings that include Apples Bed & Breakfast Inn. The more serene north shore offers easy to moderate hiking and biking trails, splendid alpine scenery, a fascinating nature center, and the gorgeous Windy Point Inn.

GETTING HERE AND AROUND

Driving is the best way to get to and explore the Big Bear area. But there are alternatives. The Mountain Area Regional Transit Authority (MARTA) provides bus service to and in San Bernardino Mountain communities and connects with Metrolink and Omnitrans.

ESSENTIALS

Bus Contact MARTA ☎ *909/878-5200* ⊕ *www.marta.cc.*

Visitor Information Big Bear Lake Visitors Bureau ⊠ *630 Bartlett Rd.* ☎ *800/424-4232* ⊕ *www.bigbearinfo.com.*

EXPLORING

FAMILY **Alpine Slide at Magic Mountain.** Take a ride down a twisting Olympic-style bobsled course in winter, or beat the summer heat on a dual waterslide at Alpine Slide, which also has an 18-hole miniature golf course and go-carts. ⊠ *800 Wildrose La.* ☎ *909/866-4626* ⊕ *www.alpineslidebigbear. com* ⊠ *$5 single rides, $20 5-ride pass, $25 all-day snow-play pass* ☉ *Daily 10-6.*

FAMILY **Big Bear Discovery Center.** At this nature center you can sign up for a
Fodor'sChoice canoe ride through Grout Bay or a naturalist-led tour of the Baldwin
★ Lake Ecological Reserve or the Holcomb Valley, where a small gold rush took place more than a century ago. Exhibits here explain the area's flora and fauna, and staffers provide maps and camping and hiking information. ⊠ *40971 North Shore Dr. (Hwy. 38), 2½ miles east of Fawnskin, Fawnskin* ☎ *909/382-2790* ⊕ *www.bigbeardiscoverycenter. com* ⊠ *Free* ☉ *Thurs.–Mon. 8:30–4:30.*

Big Bear Marina. The paddle wheeler *Big Bear Queen* departs from the marina for 90-minute lake tours. The marina also rents fishing boats, Jet Skis, kayaks, and canoes. ⊠ *500 Paine Ct.* ☎ *909/866-3218* ⊕ *www. bigbearmarina.com* ⊠ *$19* ☉ *Tours: May–early Sept., daily noon, 2, and 4; call to confirm.*

FAMILY **Big Bear Alpine Zoo.** This rescue and rehabilitation center specializes in animals native to the San Bernardino Mountains. Among its residents are black and (nonnative) grizzly bears, bald eagles, coyotes, beavers, mountain lions, grey wolves, and bobcats. An animal presentation takes place daily at noon and a feeding tour daily (except Wednesday) at 3. ⊠ *43285 Goldmine Dr.* ☎ *909/584-1299* ⊕ *www.bigbearzoo.com* ⊠ *$12* ☉ *June–early Sept., daily 10–5; early Sept.–May, weekdays 10–4, weekends 10–5.*

FAMILY **Time Bandit Pirate Ship.** Featured in the 1981 movie *Time Bandits,* this small-scale replica of a 17th-century English galleon cruises Big Bear Lake daily from roughly April through October. The ship travels along the southern lakeshore to 6743-foot-high Big Bear Dam; along the way you'll pass big bayfront mansions, some owned by celebrities. A sightseeing excursion with the crew dressed up like pirates, the cruise is popular with kids and adults. There's a bar, but no dining on board. ✉ *Holloway's Marina and RV Park, 398 Edgemoor Rd.* ☎ *909/878–4040* 🌐 *www.bigbearboating.com/pirateship* 🎫 *$19* 🕒 *Confirmed tours daily at 2 in warm weather; call for additional times.*

WHERE TO EAT

$ NEPALESE FAMILY 🍴 **Himalayan Restaurant.** It's best to order family style at this no-frills storefront restaurant so that everyone gets a taste of the many Nepalese and Indian delicacies offered. Customer favorites include the spicy *mo-mo* (potstickers), *daal* (green lentils), lamb and shrimp-curry vindaloo, fish and chicken masala, and clay-oven-roasted tandoori meats and seafood. The aromatic teas and lemonades provide a perky contrast to your meal's savory flavors. [$] *Average main: $15* ✉ *672 Pine Knot Ave., Ste. 2* ☎ *909/866–2907* 🌐 *www.himalayanbigbear.com* ✍ *Reservations essential* 🕒 *Closed Wed.*

$$$$ FRENCH 🍴 **Madlon's Restaurant.** A triple threat that also serves breakfast (many types of waffles) and lunch (burgers and other standards), this restaurant in a cozy, gingerbread-style cottage shines brightest at dinner with sophisticated French-inspired dishes. As might be expected, escargots, rack of lamb, and dry-aged filet mignon are on the menu, along with diversions like the chicken breast served with dried cherries and a Gorgonzola-sherry sauce or the 18-ounce porterhouse steak. Midweek prix-fixe three-course specials include wine. ■ **TIP→ Advance reservations are needed here.** [$] *Average main: $42* ✉ *829 W. Big Bear Blvd., Big Bear City* ☎ *909/585–3762* 🌐 *www.madlonsrestaurant.com* ✍ *Reservations essential* 🕒 *Closed Tues. and Wed.*

WHERE TO STAY

$$$ B&B/INN 🏨 **Apples Bed & Breakfast Inn.** Despite its location on a busy road to the ski lifts, the inn feels remote and peaceful, thanks to the surrounding pines. **Pros:** large rooms; clean; free snacks and movies; delicious big breakfast. **Cons:** some traffic noise; fussy decor; sometimes feels busy. [$] *Rooms from: $198* ✉ *42430 Moonridge Rd.* ☎ *909/866–0903* 🌐 *www.applesbigbear.com* 🛏 *19 rooms* 🍽 *Some meals.*

$$ B&B/INN Fodor's Choice ★ 🏨 **Gold Mountain Manor.** Each room at this restored 1928 log mansion has its own theme based on a rich Hollywood history: the Clark Gable room, for example, contains the Franklin stove that once warmed the honeymoon suite Gable and actress Carole Lombard shared. **Pros:** gracious hosts; snowshoes and kayaks available; congenial ambience. **Cons:** somewhat thin walls; 10-minute drive to the village; many stairs; narrow corridors. [$] *Rooms from: $149* ✉ *1117 Anita Ave., Big Bear City* ☎ *909/585–6997, 800/509–2604* 🌐 *www.goldmountainmanor.com* 🛏 *4 rooms, 3 suites* 🍽 *Multiple meal plans.*

$ HOTEL 🏨 **Northwoods Resort.** A giant log cabin with the amenities of a resort, Northwoods has a lobby that resembles a 1930s hunting lodge: canoes, antlers, and fishing poles decorate the walls, and there's a grand stone fireplace. **Pros:** pool heated in winter; ski packages available; beautiful grounds. **Cons:** parts of hotel showing their age; noise at night in some rooms; rate increases when it snows. $ *Rooms from: $89* ✉ *40650 Village Dr.* ☎ *909/866–3121, 800/866–3121* ⊕ *www. northwoodsresort.com* ⤳ *140 rooms, 7 suites* ⭘ *No meals.*

$$
B&B/INN
⛺ **Windy Point Inn.** Surrounded on three sides by water, Windy Point offers the best views and the most luxurious accommodations in the Big Bear area. **Pros:** secure parking; gracious hosts; privacy; views. **Cons:** remote from lake activities; windy at times. $ *Rooms from: $145* ✉ *31094 North Shore Dr., Fawnskin* ☎ *909/866–2746* ⊕ *windypointinn.com* ⤳ *5 rooms* ⭘ *Breakfast.*

SPORTS AND THE OUTDOORS

BOATS AND CHARTERS

Pine Knot Landing Marina. This full-service marina rents fishing boats, pontoon boats, and kayaks and sells bait, ice, and snacks. You can take water ski lessons here or pick up some Jet Skis and parasailing equipment. On weekends, the paddle wheeler *Miss Liberty* leaves from the landing for a 90-minute tour ($20; times vary) of Big Bear Lake from late April through September. Refreshments are available on board. ✉ *439 Pine Knot Blvd.* ☎ *909/866–7766* ⊕ *pineknotmarina.com.*

HORSEBACK RIDING

Baldwin Lake Stables. Explore the forested mountain on horseback on a group or private guided trail ride (one hour to a half day) arranged by this outfit. The facility has a petting zoo for kids and offers pony rides. Reservations are required for private rides and suggested for all. ✉ *46475 Pioneertown Rd., Big Bear City* ☎ *909/585–6482* ⊕ *www. baldwinlakestables.com* ✉ *$40 and up per person per hr.*

SKIING

Big Bear Mountain Resorts. Two distinct resorts, Bear Mountain and Snow Summit, comprise Southern California's largest winter playground, one of the few that challenge skilled skiers. The complex offers 438 skiable acres, 55 runs, and 26 chairlifts, including four high-speed quads. The vibe is youthful at Bear, which has beginner slopes (training available) and the after-ski hangout The Scene. Snow Summit holds challenging runs and is open for night skiing. On weekends and holidays it's best to reserve tickets for either mountain. Bear rents skis and boards.

The resorts are open in summer for mountain biking, hiking, golfing, and some special events. The Snow Summit Scenic Sky Chair zips to the mountain's 8,200-foot peak, where View Haus ($), a casual outdoor restaurant, has breathtaking views of the lake and San Gorgonio Mountain. ✉ *Big Bear, 880 Summit Blvd., off Moonridge Rd.* ☎ *909/866–5766* ⊕ *www.bigbearmountainresorts.com* ✉ *$60–$75.*

THE SOUTHERN INLAND EMPIRE

The southern end of the Inland Empire is devoted to the good life. Mile-high Idyllwild atop Mt. San Jacinto holds a renowned arts academy, charming restaurants, and galleries. It's also a good place to hike, mountain climb, and test high-altitude biking skills. Temecula, lying at the base of the mountain, is a popular wine region where you'll find vineyards, tasting rooms, fine dining, and cozy lodgings.

13

IDYLLWILD

44 miles east of Riverside.

Set in a valley halfway up Mt. San Jacinto, Idyllwild has been a serene forested getaway for San Diegans and Angelenos for nearly a century. The town's simple, quiet lifestyle attracts artists and performers as well as outdoor types who enjoy hiking, biking, and serious rock climbing.

GETTING HERE AND AROUND

Two routes from the interstates lead to Idyllwild; both are slow and winding but provide memorable mountain views. From Interstate 10 in Banning, take scenic Highway 243 south to Idyllwild. From Interstate 15 near Lake Elsinore, drive east on Highway 74 to Highway 243 and turn north. Once in Idyllwild, you can walk nearly everywhere in the village, though you'll need to drive to trailheads, fishing holes, and rock-climbing locations.

ESSENTIALS

Visitor Information Idyllwild Town Crier and Visitor Center. When the Idyllwild Chamber of Commerce disbanded, the *Town Crier* newspaper (at the same location) picked up the responsibility of distributing tourism information. ✉ *54325 N. Circle Dr.* ⊕ *www.idyllwildchamber.com* ☉ *Mon.–Fri. 9–5, weekends 10–4.*

EXPLORING

FAMILY **Idyllwild Nature Center.** At the center, you can learn about the area's Native American history and listen to traditional storytellers. Outside are 3 miles of hiking trails, plus biking and equestrian trails and picnic areas. The park is pet-friendly. ✉ *25225 Hwy. 243* ☎ *951/659–3850* ⊕ *www. rivcoparks.org/parks* 🎫 *$3* ☉ *Tues.–Sun. 9–4:30* ☉ *Closed Mon.*

WHERE TO EAT

$$$$ ✕ **Restaurant Gastrognome.** Elegant and dimly lighted, with wood panel-
FRENCH ing, lace curtains, and an oft-glowing fireplace, "The Gnome" is where locals go for a romantic dinner. The overall feel is French, but the menu goes beyond the Gallic, with entrées such as calamari almandine, sausage pasta, and lobster tacos. The French onion soup always satisfies, and the roast duck with orange sauce and the Southwest-style grilled pork are excellent entrées. The crème brûlée makes for a sweet finale. For lighter dinner fare, check out the cafe menu. $ *Average main: $39* ✉ *54381 Ridgeview Dr.* ☎ *951/659–5055* ⊕ *www.gastrognome.com* 🍴 *Reservations essential.*

DID YOU KNOW?

Many water-sport options—
including waterskiing, jet
skiing, fishing, parasailing,
and boating—are available at
Big Bear Lake.

THE ARTS

Idyllwild Arts Academy. The Idyllwild Arts Academy provides professional training for gifted arts students and more than 95 summer workshops in dance, music, Native American arts, theater, visual arts, and writing. There are free summer concerts and theater productions featuring students and professional performers. ⊠ *52500 Temecula Rd.* ☎ *951/659–2171* ⊕ *www.idyllwildarts.org.*

SPORTS AND THE OUTDOORS

FISHING

Lake Fulmor. The lake is stocked with rainbow trout, largemouth bass, catfish, and bluegill. To fish, you'll need a California fishing license and a National Forest Adventure Pass ($5 per vehicle per day). ⊠ *Hwy. 243, 10 miles north of Idyllwild* ☎ *951/659–2117* ⊕ *www.fs.usda.gov/sbnf.*

HIKING

Humber Park Trailhead. Two great hikes begin at this site, the 2.5-mile Devils Slide Trail and the 2.6-mile Ernie Maxwell Scenic Trail. Adventure permits ($5) are needed for both; wilderness permits needed for Devils Slide. ⊠ *At top of Fern Valley Rd.* ☎ *951/659–2117* ⊕ *www.fs.usda.gov/recarea/sbnf/recarea/?recid=26483.*

Pacific Crest Trail. Access the trail at Highway 74, 1 mile east of Highway 371; or via the Fuller Ridge Trail at Black Mountain Road, 15 miles north of Idyllwild. Permits ($5 per day), required for camping and day hikes in the San Jacinto Wilderness, are available online or at the Idyllwild Ranger Station (⊠ *Pine Crest Ave., off Hwy. 243* ☎ *951/659–2117* ⊕ *www.fs.usda.gov/sbnf.*

TEMECULA

43 miles south of Riverside, 60 miles north of San Diego, 90 miles southeast of Los Angeles.

Fodor's Choice ★ Temecula, with its rolling green vineyards, country inns, and first-rate restaurants, bills itself as "Southern California Wine Country." The region is home to three-dozen wineries, several of which offer spas, fine dining, or luxury lodging and shopping. The name Temecula comes from a Luiseño Indian word meaning "where the sun shines through the mist"—ideal conditions for growing wine grapes. Intense afternoon sun and cool nighttime temperatures, complemented by ocean breezes that flow through the Rainbow and Santa Margarita gaps in the coastal range, help grapevines flourish in the area's granite soil. Once best known for Chardonnay, Temecula Valley winemakers are moving in new directions, producing Viognier, Syrah, and other Rhône-style blended reds and whites. Most wineries charge a small fee ($10 to $15) for a tasting that includes several wines.

The oldest wineries are strung out along Rancho California Road, east of Interstate 15; a few newer ones lie along the eastern portion of De Portola Road. On its website the Temecula Valley Winegrowers Association offers suggestions for self-guided winery tours and has coupons good for tasting discounts.

GETTING HERE AND AROUND

Interstate 15 cuts right through Temecula. The wineries lie on the east side of the freeway along Rancho California Road. Old Town Temecula lies west of the freeway along Front Street.

TOURS

Destination Temecula runs full-day winery tours, with pickups in Old Town Temecula (starting at $89 round-trip) and at San Diego hotels ($97). Tours include stops at three wineries, a picnic lunch, and time to explore Old Town.

ESSENTIALS

Tour Contacts Destination Temecula ☎ *951/695–1232* ⊕ *www.destem.com.* **Grapeline Wine Country Shuttle** ☎ *951/693–5755, 888/894–6379* ⊕ *www.gogrape.com.*

Visitor Information Temecula Valley Convention and Visitors Bureau ✉ *28690 Mercedes St.* ☎ *951/491–6085, 888/363–2852* ⊕ *www.temeculacvb. com.* **Temecula Valley Winegrowers Association** ✉ *34567 Rancho California Rd.* ☎ *951/699–3626* ⊕ *www.temeculawines.org.*

EXPLORING

TOP ATTRACTIONS

Fodor'sChoice
★

Hart Family Winery. A perennial crowd pleaser, this winery specializes in well-crafted red wines made by father-son winemakers Joe and Jim Hart. Joe, who started the winery in the 1970s with his wife, Nancy, focuses on growing grapes suited to the Temecula region's singular climate and soils—Zinfandel, Cabernet Sauvignon, and Sangiovese as might be expected, but also little known varietals such as Aleatico, used in the winery's marvelous dessert wine. The reds are the stars, though, along with the amiable Hart family members themselves. ✉ *41300 Avenida Biona* ☎ *951/676–6300* ⊕ *www.hartfamilywinery.com* 🍷 *Tasting $10* ⊗ *Daily 9–4:30.*

Old Town Temecula. Temecula is more than just vineyards and tasting rooms. For a bit of old-fashioned fun, head to Old Town Temecula, a turn-of-the-20th-century-style cluster of storefronts and boardwalks that holds more than 640 antiques stores, boutiques, a performing-arts center and jazz club, restaurants, and art galleries. ✉ *Front St., between Rancho California Rd. and Hwy. 79* ☎ *888/363–2852* ⊕ *www.temeculacvb.com.*

FAMILY

Pennypickle's Workshop—Temecula Children's Museum. If you have the kids along, check out the fictional 7,500-square-foot workshop of Professor Phineas T. Pennypickle, PhD. This elaborately decorated children's museum is filled with secret passageways, machines, wacky contraptions, and time-travel inventions. ■TIP→ **Take one of the two-hour tours offered daily to get the most out of your visit.** ✉ *42081 Main St.* ☎ *951/308–6376* ⊕ *www.pennypickles.org* 🍷 *$5* ⊗ *Tues.–Sat. 10–5, Sun. 12:30–5.*

Ponte Family Estates. Lush gardens and more than 300 acres of vineyards provide a rustic, elegant setting at Ponte, whose small-lot wines range from sparklers and light whites to potent super Tuscan–style offerings. In the airy, light-filled tasting room you can sample the aptly named Super T, a blend of Cabernet Sauvignon and Sangiovese grapes, and other vintages crafted by winemaker Mark Schabel; ceramics, specialty foods, and gift baskets are for sale at the adjacent marketplace. The shaded, outdoor Restaurant at Ponte serves salads, sandwiches, wood-fired pizzas, and seafood daily for lunch and on weekends for dinner. ✉ *35053 Rancho California Rd.* ☎ *951/694–8855* ⊕ *www.pontewinery.com* ✉ *Tasting $15 weekdays, $20 weekends* ☽ *Winery: daily 10–5. Restaurant: Mon.– Thurs. 11–4, Fri. and Sat. 11–8, Sun. 11–5.*

Thornton Winery. In a French Mediterranean–style stone building, you can taste winemaker David Vergari's Blanc de Noirs or Cuvée Rouge sparkling wines at a table in the lounge, or over lunch or dinner at Café Champagne. The Syrah and Barbera (grapes grown on the property) stand out among the reds here. On weekends, take a free 20-minute tour of the grounds and the wine cave. The winemaker dinners ($80) and the summer Champagne Jazz Series concerts ($55–$95), featuring performers such as George Benson and David Benoit, make this a fun place to spend an afternoon or evening. ✉ *32575 Rancho California Rd.* ☎ *951/699–0099* ⊕ *www.thorntonwine.com* ✉ *Tastings $12–$17* ☽ *Daily 10–5; tours Sat. 11–4 on the hr, Sun. 11, 12:30, 2, and 4.*

WORTH NOTING

Callaway Vineyard and Winery. One of the oldest wineries in Temecula is centered on a stunning steel-and-glass cube with vineyard views all around. You can draw your own wine from tap stations placed around the room. Callaway made its reputation with Chardonnay but has moved on to Spanish- and Italian-style varietals such as Sangiovese, Mourverde, and Dolcetto. The Meritage Restaurant, open for lunch daily and dinner on weekends, specializes in tapas, salads, and sandwiches. ✉ *32720 Rancho California Rd.* ☎ *951/676–4001* ⊕ *www. callawaywinery.com* ✉ *Tasting $10–$15; tour $5* ☽ *Daily 10–5; tour weekdays at 11, 1, and 3, Sat.–Sun. 11, 12, 1, 2.*

Europa Village. Though all of this luxury wine resort's dining, lodging, winery, and other components won't be completed for a few years, a pleasant tasting room here serves wines made from French, Spanish, and Italian varietals. The selections range from light whites like Sauvignon Blanc and Albariño to heavy reds like a complex Syrah and a powerful Primitivo. Winemaker dinners take place in the village, which also presents live music on some weekend nights. ✉ *33475 La Serena Way* ☎ *888/383–8767* ⊕ *www.europavillage.com* ✉ *Tasting $15* ☽ *Daily 10–5.*

Leoness Cellars. Rhone- and Tuscan-style blends—along with killer views— are the specialties of this mountaintop facility. Winemaker Tim Kramer and his staff produce about a dozen and a half wines each year, of which you can select six. If you like reds, be sure to try the Syrahs, which are almost always winners. Winery tours take in the vineyards and the wine-making areas. The tours require a reservation, as do wine-and-food pairing sessions that might include fruits and cheeses or, in the case of dessert wines, some chocolates. ✉ *38311 DePortola Rd.* ☎ *951/302–7601* ⊕ *www. leonesscellars.com* ✉ *Tasting $15–$18, tours $18–$85* ☽ *Daily 11–5.*

Miramonte Winery. At Temecula's hippest winery, perched on a hilltop, listen to Spanish-guitar recordings while sampling the slightly pricey Opulente Meritage, a supple Roussanne, or the sultry Syrah. Owner Cane Vanderhoof's wines have earned dozens of awards. While you're enjoying your wine on the deck, order an artisan cheese plate. On Friday and Saturday nights from 7 to 10, the winery turns into a local hot spot with tastings of signature wines ($17) and beer, live music, and dancing that spills out into the vineyards. ✉ *33410 Rancho California Rd.* ☎ *951/506–5500* 🌐 *www.miramontewinery.com* 🎟 *Tastings $15–17, tours $75 (reservations required Sat.–Sun.)* 🕒 *Sun.–Thurs. 11–6, Fri. and Sat. 11–10.*

Mount Palomar Winery. One of the original Temecula Valley wineries, opened in 1969, Mount Palomar introduced Sangiovese grapes, a varietal that has proven perfectly suited to the region's soil and climate. New owners have transformed the homey winery into a grand Mediterranean villa with acres of gardens and trees. Some of the wines are made from grapes brought from Italy nearly 50 years ago. Try the dry Sangiovese or Bordeaux-style Meritage. Shorty's Bistro, open for lunch daily and for dinner on Fridays and weekends, presents live entertainment on Friday nights. ✉ *33820 Rancho California Rd.* ☎ *951/676–5047* 🌐 *www.mountpalomar.com* 🎟 *Winery free, tasting $12 Mon.–Thurs., $16 Fri.– Sun.* 🕒 *Daily 10:30–6.*

Fodor's Choice ★ **Wiens Family Cellars.** Up-and-coming Wiens promotes its "Big Reds"—among them the Reserve Primitivo and an intriguing Tempranillo–Petite Sirah blend—but many visitors often wind up taking home a bottle of the perky-fruity Amour De L'Orange sparkling wine. Other wines of note include the Ruby Port and the Dulce Maria, made from Chardonnay and Muscat Canelli grapes. The ambiance at Wiens is informal, but the cordial tasting-room staffers are well informed about the wines they enthusiastically pour. ✉ *35055 Via Del Ponte* ☎ *951/694–9892* 🌐 *www.wienscellars.com* 🎟 *Tasting $15* 🕒 *Daily 10:30–6.*

Wilson Creek Winery & Vineyards. One of Temecula's busiest tasting rooms sits amid inviting, parklike grounds. Wilson is known for its Almond Champagne, but the winery also produces appealing still wines. The Viognier, Reserve Syrah, Reserve Zinfandel, and late-harvest Zinfandel all merit a taste. The on-site Creekside Grill Restaurant serves sandwiches, salads, and entrées such as Mexican white sea bass and gluten-free vegetable potpie. Dine inside or select a picnic spot and the servers will deliver your meal to you. ✉ *35960 Rancho California Rd.* ☎ *951/699–9463* 🌐 *www.wilsoncreekwinery.com* 🎟 *Tasting $15 weekdays, $20 weekends* 🕒 *Daily 10–5, restaurant Mon.–Fri. 11–4, Sat. 11–5, Sun. 10–3.*

WHERE TO EAT AND STAY

$$$ AMERICAN FAMILY 🍴 **Baily's Fine Dining and Front Street Bar & Grill.** Locals swoon over the cuisine served upstairs (dinner only) at Baily's Fine Dining. The menu varies according to the chef's creative whims and might include chicken schnitzel drizzled with lemon-caper-wine sauce or salmon Wellington. Temecula Valley wines are well represented on the extensive list here. Downstairs at Front Street the fare is more casual—fish prepared several ways, burgers, pastas, soups, and salads. On weekend evenings, Front Street turns into a locally popular nightclub. [$] *Average main: $26* ✉ *28699 Old Town Front St.* ☎ *951/676–9567* 🌐 *www.oldtowndining.com* ✍ *Reservations essential.*

$$$$ CONTEMPORARY 🍴 **Café Champagne.** The spacious patio, with its bubbling fountain, flowering trellises, and vineyard views, is the perfect place to lunch on a

There's no more relaxing way to enjoy Temecula's Wine Country than by taking a peaceful hot-air balloon ride over the vineyards.

sunny day. Inside, the dining room is decked out in French country style, and the open kitchen turns out such dishes as braised beef short ribs and cioppino. The reasonably priced wines served here include the signature Thornton Winery sparklers. $ *Average main: $34* ✉ *Thornton Winery, 32575 Rancho California Rd.* ☎ *951/699–0099* ⊕ *www.thorntonwine. com* ⬧ *Reservations essential.*

$$$
HOTEL
Ponte Vineyard Inn. Slow down in Old California–rancho style at this delightful hotel that opened in 2012 on the grounds of the Ponte Family Estate winery. **Pros:** huge rooms; lounges everywhere; excellent winery on-site; gracious service. **Cons:** weddings; very, very quiet. $ *Rooms from: $200* ✉ *35001 Rancho California Rd.* ☎ *951/587–6688* ⊕ *www. pontevineyardinn.com* ⬧ *60 rooms* ⦿ *No meals.*

$$
RESORT
Temecula Creek Inn. Each room at this inn has a private patio or balcony overlooking the championship golf course and is decorated in soothing earth tones with a Southwestern theme. **Pros:** beautiful grounds; top golf course; spacious; great views. **Cons:** simple furnishings; shows its age; location away from Old Town and wineries. $ *Rooms from: $129* ✉ *44501 Rainbow Canyon Rd.* ☎ *951/694–1000, 888/976–3404* ⊕ *www.temeculacreekinn.com* ⬧ *130 rooms, 1 guesthouse* ⦿ *No meals.*

NIGHTLIFE

Pechanga Resort and Casino. Casino gambling is the main attraction here, and there are several entertainment venues. Headliners such as Paul Anka, B.B. King, and Jerry Seinfeld have appeared at the Showroom Theater, while the intimate Comedy Club books up-and-coming talent. HBO and Fox Sports championship boxing matches draw thousands of fans. The largest Native American casino in California, Pechanga holds a 517-room hotel, golf course, spa, and RV park. ✉ *45000 Pechanga Pkwy.* ☎ *877/711–2946, 951/770–1819* ⊕ *www.pechanga.com.*

SPORTS AND THE OUTDOORS

GOLF

Temecula has several championship golf courses cooled by the valley's ocean breezes.

Redhawk Golf Club. Considered one of the best 18-hole public golf courses in California, the Ron Fream–designed championship golf course is designed to take advantage of Temecula's tree-studded rolling hills set against craggy mountains. The course holds a bunch of traps to challenge your swing or putt. Watch out for wind, doglegs, skinny sand traps, and tiered greens. Rico's Cantina here offers Mexican and Italian items, served up buffet style for breakfast or lunch. ✉ *45100 Redhawk Pkwy.* ☎ *951/302–3850* ⊕ *www.redhawkgolfcourse.com* ✑ *$60 on weekdays; $80 on weekends* ⚑ *18 holes, 7110 yards, par 72.*

Temecula Creek Inn Golf Resort. For a special treat, head to the Temecula Creek Inn Golf Resort, designed by Ted Robinson and Dick Rossen. The Inn's 27 holes offer golfers three distinct course options in picturesque Southern California wine country. The most challenging of the Temecula Creek golf courses is the Stonehouse nine, which demands precise tee shots in order to get lower scores. ✉ *44501 Rainbow Canyon Rd.* ☎ *951/676–2405* ⊕ *www.temeculacreekinn.com* ✑ *$80 on weekdays; $95 on weekends* ⚑ *Creek: 9 holes, 3348 yards, par 36; Oaks: 9 holes, 3436 yards, par 36; Stonehouse: 9 holes, 3257 yards, par 36.*

Temeku Hills Golf Club. The tiered greens, five lakes, and many blind spots make for challenging rounds at this club's Ted Robinson-designed championship course. ✉ *41687 Temeku Dr.* ☎ *951/694–9998* ⊕ *www.temekuhillsgolfcourse.com* ✑ *$40 on weekdays; $65 on weekends* ⚑ *18 holes, 6636 yards, par 72.*

HOT-AIR BALLOONING

California Dreamin'. Float serenely above Temecula's vineyards and country estates on an early-morning balloon adventure. The ride includes Champagne, coffee, a pastry breakfast, and a souvenir photo. ✉ *Flights depart from La Vindemia Vineyard, 33133 Vista Del Monte Rd.* ☎ *800/373–3359* ⊕ *www.californiadreamin.com* ✑ *$148.*

SHOPPING

Temecula Lavender Co. Owner Jan Schneider offers an inspiring collection of the herb that fosters peace, purification, sleep, and longevity. Bath salts, hand soaps, essential oil—she's got it all, even dryer bags to freshen up the laundry. ✉ *28561 Old Town Front St.* ☎ *951/676–1931* ⊕ *www.temeculalavenderco.com* ☺ *Mon.–Thurs. 10-6, Fri.–Sat. 10-8.*

Temecula Olive Oil Company. While you're shopping in Old Town, stop by the cool tasting room here for a sample of extra-virgin olive oils, flavored balsamic vinegars and sea salts, bath products, and Mission, Ascalano, and Italian olives. Guided tours of the ranch where the olives are grown are available. ✉ *28653 Old Town Front St., Suite H* ☎ *951/693–0607* ⊕ *www.temeculaoliveoil.com* ☺ *Daily 9:30–6.*

PALM SPRINGS

And the Desert Resorts

WELCOME TO PALM SPRINGS

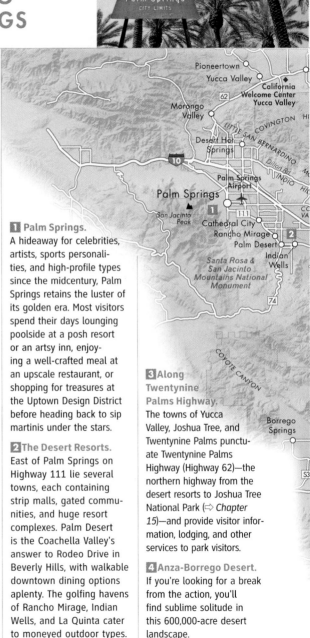

TOP REASONS TO GO

★ **Fun in the sun:** The Palm Springs area has 350 days of sun each year, and the weather's usually perfect for playing one of the area's more than 100 golf courses.

★ **Spa under the stars:** Many resorts and small hotels now offer after-dark spa services, including outdoor soaks and treatments you can savor while sipping wine under the clear, starry sky.

★ **Personal pampering:** The resorts here have it all: beautifully appointed rooms packed with amenities, professional staffs, sublime spas, and delicious dining options.

★ **Divine desert scenery:** You'll probably spend a lot of time taking in the gorgeous 360-degree natural panorama, a flat desert floor surrounded by 10,000-foot mountains rising into a brilliant blue sky.

★ **The Hollywood connection:** The Palm Springs area has more celebrity ties than any other resort community. So keep your eyes open for your favorite star.

1 Palm Springs.
A hideaway for celebrities, artists, sports personalities, and high-profile types since the midcentury, Palm Springs retains the luster of its golden era. Most visitors spend their days lounging poolside at a posh resort or an artsy inn, enjoying a well-crafted meal at an upscale restaurant, or shopping for treasures at the Uptown Design District before heading back to sip martinis under the stars.

2 The Desert Resorts.
East of Palm Springs on Highway 111 lie several towns, each containing strip malls, gated communities, and huge resort complexes. Palm Desert is the Coachella Valley's answer to Rodeo Drive in Beverly Hills, with walkable downtown dining options aplenty. The golfing havens of Rancho Mirage, Indian Wells, and La Quinta cater to moneyed outdoor types.

3 Along Twentynine Palms Highway.
The towns of Yucca Valley, Joshua Tree, and Twentynine Palms punctuate Twentynine Palms Highway (Highway 62)—the northern highway from the desert resorts to Joshua Tree National Park (⇨ *Chapter 15*)—and provide visitor information, lodging, and other services to park visitors.

4 Anza-Borrego Desert.
If you're looking for a break from the action, you'll find sublime solitude in this 600,000-acre desert landscape.

GETTING ORIENTED

14

The Palm Springs resort area lies within the Colorado Desert, on the western edge of the Coachella Valley. The area holds seven cities that are strung out along Highway 111, with Palm Springs at the northwestern end of this strip and Indio at the southeastern end. North of Palm Springs, between Interstate 10 and Highway 62, is Desert Hot Springs. Northeast of Palm Springs, the towns of the Morongo Valley lie along Twentynine Palms Highway (Highway 62), which leads to Joshua Tree National Park (⇨ *Chapter 15*). Head south on Highway 86 from Indio to reach Anza-Borrego Desert State Park and the Salton Sea. All of the area's attractions are easy day trips from Palm Springs.

Updated by
Michele Bigley

With the Palm Springs area's year-round sunshine, luxurious spas, chef-driven restaurants, and see-and-be-seen pool parties, it's no wonder that Hollywood A-listers and weekend warriors make the desert a getaway. Stretching south and east of the city along Highway 111, the Desert Resort towns—Cathedral City, Rancho Mirage, Palm Desert, Indian Wells, La Quinta, and Indio, along with Desert Hot Springs to the north—teem with resorts, golf courses, and shopping centers. Yucca Valley, Joshua Tree, and other artistic communities lie farther north and northeast. To the south, the wildflowers of Anza-Borrego Desert State Park herald the arrival of spring.

Well before it became the darling of the current crop of überhip Angelenos, the Palm Springs area was the playground of the celebrity elite. In the 1920s Al Capone opened the Two Bunch Palms Hotel in Desert Hot Springs (with multiple tunnels to help him avoid the police); Marilyn Monroe was discovered poolside in the late 1940s at a downtown Palm Springs tennis club; Elvis and Priscilla Presley honeymooned here—and the list goes on.

In recent years the desert arts scene has blossomed as spectacularly as the wildflowers of Anza-Borrego. For urban-chic contemporary artwork, stop by downtown Palm Springs' Backstreet Arts District, but try to slip away to the rural areas—the aforementioned Yucca Valley but also Joshua Tree, Pioneertown, and Twentynine Palms. Each April, attention centers on Indio, where the Coachella Valley Music and Arts Festival, California's largest outdoor concert, generates a frenzy of cultural activity.

PLANNING

WHEN TO GO

Desert weather is best between January and April, the height of the visitor season. The fall months are nearly as lovely, but less crowded and less expensive (although autumn draws many conventions and business travelers). In summer, a popular time with European visitors, daytime temperatures may rise above 110°F (though evenings cool to the mid-70s); some attractions and restaurants close or reduce their hours during this time.

GETTING HERE AND AROUND

AIR TRAVEL

Palm Springs International Airport serves California's desert communities. Alaska, Allegiant, American, Delta, Frontier, Sun Country, United, Virgin America, and WestJet all fly to Palm Springs, some only seasonally. Yellow Cab of the Desert serves the airport, which is about 3 miles from downtown. The fare is $2.50 to enter the cab and about $3.12 per mile.

Airport Information Palm Springs International Airport ✉ *3200 E. Tahquitz Canyon Way, Palm Springs* ☏ *760/323–8299* ⊕ *www.palmspringsairport.com.*

Airport Transfers Yellow Cab of the Desert ✉ *75150 St. Charles Pl., Palm Desert* ☏ *760/340–8294* ⊕ *www.yellowcabofthedesert.com.*

BUS TRAVEL

Greyhound provides service to Palm Springs from many cities. SunBus, operated by the SunLine Transit Agency, serves the entire Coachella Valley, from Desert Hot Springs to Mecca.

Bus Contacts Greyhound ✉ *3700 Vista Chino Rd., Suite D, Palm Desert* ☏ *800/231–2222* ⊕ *www.greyhound.com.* **SunLine Transit Agency** ✉ *32-505 Harry Oliver Tr., Thousand Palms* ☏ *800/347–8628* ⊕ *www.sunline.org.*

CAR TRAVEL

The desert resort communities occupy a 20-mile stretch between Interstate 10, to the east, and Palm Canyon Drive (Highway 111), to the west. The region is about a two-hour drive east of the Los Angeles area and a three-hour drive northeast of San Diego. It can take twice as long to make the trip from Los Angeles to the desert on winter and spring weekends because of heavy traffic. From Los Angeles take the San Bernardino Freeway (Interstate 10) east to Highway 111. From San Diego, Interstate 15 heading north connects with the Pomona Freeway (Highway 60), leading to the San Bernardino Freeway east.

To reach Borrego Springs from Los Angeles, take Interstate 10 east past the desert resorts area to Highway 86 south to the Borrego Salton Seaway (Highway S22) west. You can reach the Borrego area from San Diego via Interstate 8 to Highway 79 through Cuyamaca State Park. This will take you to Highway 78 in Julian, which you follow east to Yaqui Pass Road (S3) into Borrego Springs.

TAXI TRAVEL

Yellow Cab of the Desert serves the entire Coachella Valley. The fare is $2.50 to enter a cab and about $3 per mile.

TRAIN TRAVEL

The Amtrak Sunset Limited, which runs between Florida and Los Angeles, stops in Palm Springs.

Train Contact Amtrak ☎ *800/872-7245* ⊕ *www.amtrakcalifornia.com.*

HEALTH AND SAFETY

Never travel alone in the desert. Let someone know your trip route, destination, and estimated time and date of return. Before setting out, make sure your vehicle is in good condition. Stay on main roads, and watch out for horses and range cattle.

Drink at least a gallon of water a day (three gallons if you're hiking or otherwise exerting yourself). Dress in layered clothing and wear comfortable, sturdy shoes and a hat. Keep snacks, sunscreen, and a first-aid kit on hand. If you suddenly have a headache or feel dizzy or nauseous, you could be suffering from dehydration. Get out of the sun immediately and drink plenty of water. Dampen your clothing to lower your body temperature.

Do not enter mine tunnels or shafts. Avoid canyons during rainstorms. Never place your hands or feet where you can't see them: Rattlesnakes, scorpions, and black widow spiders may be hiding there.

TOUR OPTIONS

Art in Public Places. Several self-guided tours cover the works in Palm Desert's 150-piece Art in Public Places collection. Each tour is walkable or drivable. Maps and information about guided tours (one Saturday each month) are available at the city's visitor center and online. ⊠ *Palm Desert Visitor Center, 73-470 El Paseo, Suite F-7, Palm Desert* ☎ *760/568–1441* ⊕ *www.palm-desert.org/arts-culture/public-art* ☞ *Free.*

Best of the Best Tours. One of the valley's largest outfits leads tours into Andreas Canyon, along the celebrity circuit, or to view windmills up close. ☎ *760/320–1365* ⊕ *www.thebestofthebesttours.com* ☞ *From $45.*

Desert Adventures. This outfit's two- to four- hour jeep tours cover topics such as the San Andreas Fault, local craft breweries, celebrity homes, and gay history. Tours also head off-road through Joshua Tree National Park. The groups are small and the guides are knowledgeable. Departures are from Palm Springs and La Quinta; hotel pickups are available. ☎ *760/324–5337* ⊕ *www.red-jeep.com* ☞ *From $55.*

Trail Discovery Hiking Guides. For more than two decades, this outfit has been guiding hikers of all abilities through the desert canyons of the Palm Springs area. ☎ *760/413–1575* ⊕ *www.palmspringshiking.com* ☞ *From $65.*

Palm Springs Tours. You can explore celebrity history or the inner reaches of Joshua Tree with this longtime local operator. ☎ *800/409–3174* ⊕ *www.palmspringstours.net* ☞ *From $100.*

RESTAURANTS

During the season, restaurants can be busy, as many locals and visitors dine out every night, and some for every meal. An influx of talented chefs has expanded the dining possibilities of a formerly staid scene. The meat-and-potatoes crowd still has plenty of options, but you'll also find fresh seafood superbly prepared and contemporary Californian, Asian, Indian, and vegetarian cuisine, and Mexican food abounds. Most restaurants have early-evening happy hours, with discounted drinks and small-plate menus. Restaurants that remain open in July and August frequently discount deeply; others close in July and August or offer limited service.

HOTELS

In general you can find the widest choice of lodgings in Palm Springs, from tiny bed-and-breakfasts and chain motels to business and resort hotels. Massive resort properties predominate in down-valley communities, such as Palm Desert and Rancho Mirage. You can stay in the desert for as little as $80 or spend more than $1,000 a night. Rates vary widely by season and expected occupancy—a $200 room midweek can jump in price to $450 on Saturday.

Hotel and resort prices are frequently 50% cheaper in summer and fall than in winter and early spring. From January through May prices soar, and lodgings book up far in advance. You should book well ahead for stays during events such as Modernism Week or the Coachella and Stagecoach music festivals.

Most resort hotels charge a daily fee of up to $35 that is not included in the room rate; be sure to ask about extra fees when you book. Many hotels are pet-friendly and offer special services, though these also come with additional fees. Small boutique hotels and B&Bs have plenty of character and are popular with hipsters and artsy types; discounts are sometimes given for extended stays. Casino hotels often offer good deals on lodging. Take care, though, when considering budget lodgings; other than reliable chains, they may not be up to par. *Hotel reviews have been shortened. For full information, visit Fodors.com.*

WHAT IT COSTS			
	$	$$	$$$	$$$$
Restaurants	under $16	$16–$22	$23–$30	over $30
Hotels	under $121	$121–$175	$176–$250	over $250

Restaurant prices are the average cost of a main course at dinner or, if dinner is not served, at lunch. Hotel prices are the lowest cost of a standard double room in high season.

NIGHTLIFE

Desert nightlife is concentrated and abundant in Palm Springs, where there are many straight and gay bars and clubs, as well as hotel bars and lively pool parties. Arts festivals occur on a regular basis, especially in winter and spring. *Palm Springs Life* magazine (⊕ *www.palmspringslife. com*), available at hotels and visitor centers, has nightlife listings, as does the *Desert Sun* newspaper (⊕ *www.mydesert.com*). The *Gay Guide to Palm Springs* (⊕ *palmspringsgayinfo.com*) covers the lesbian and gay scenes.

PALM SPRINGS

A tourist destination since the late 19th century, Palm Springs evolved into an ideal hideaway for early Hollywood celebrities who slipped into town to play tennis, lounge poolside, attend a party or two, and, unless things got out of hand, remain beyond the reach of gossip columnists. But the place really blossomed in the 1930s after actors Charlie Farrell and Ralph Bellamy bought 200 acres of land for $30 an acre and opened the Palm Springs Racquet Club, which soon listed Ginger Rogers, Humphrey Bogart, and Clark Gable among its members.

Today's Palm Springs is embracing its glory days. Owners of resorts, B&Bs, and galleries have renovated midcentury modern buildings, luring a new crop of celebs and high-powered executives. LGBT travelers, twentysomethings, and even families also sojourn here now. Pleasantly touristy Palm Canyon Drive is jam-packed with alfresco restaurants, many with views of the bustling sidewalk, along with indoor cafés and semi-chic shops. Farther west is the Uptown Design District, the area's exclusive shopping and dining destination. Continuing east on Palm Canyon Drive just outside downtown lie resorts and boutique hotels that host lively pool parties and house exclusive dining establishments and trendy bars.

GETTING HERE AND AROUND

Palm Springs is 90 miles southeast of Los Angeles on Interstate 10. Most visitors arrive in the Palm Springs area by car from the Los Angeles or San Diego area via this freeway, which intersects with Highway 111 north of Palm Springs. Tahquitz Canyon Way marks the division between north and south on major streets (e.g., North and South Palm Canyon Drive).

ESSENTIALS

Visitor Information Greater Palm Springs Convention and Visitors Bureau ✉ *Visitor Center, 70-100 Hwy. 111, at Via Florencia, Rancho Mirage* ☎ *760/770–9000, 800/967-3767* ⊕ *www.palmspringsoasis.com* ☽ *Weekdays 8:30–5.* **Palm Springs Visitor Information Center** ✉ *2901 N. Palm Canyon Dr., Palm Springs* ☎ *760/778-8418, 800/347-7746* ⊕ *www.palm-springs.org* ☽ *Daily 9–5.*

EXPLORING

TOP ATTRACTIONS

Elvis's Honeymoon Hideaway. The hideaway where the King of rock 'n' roll and his young bride, Priscilla, lived during the first year of their marriage perches on a hilltop abutting the San Jacinto Mountains. A stunning example of local midcentury modern architecture, the house is rich in Elvis lore, photos, and furnishings. Docents describe the fabulous parties that took place here and the celebrities and local legends who attended them. Built in 1962 by one of Palm Spring's largest developers, Robert Alexander, the house consists of four perfect circles, each set on a different level. At the time, *Look* magazine described the structure as the "house of tomorrow," and indeed many of its features are standard in the homes of today. ✉ *1350 Ladera Circle, Palm Springs* ☎ *760/322–1192* ⊕ *www.elvishoneymoon.com* 💲 *$30 weekdays, $35 weekends and holidays* ☽ *Tours daily at 1 and 3:30 by appointment only.*

The green revolution is proudly on display in many parts of the Palm Springs area.

FAMILY **Indian Canyons.** The Indian Canyons are the ancestral home of the Agua
Fodor's Choice Caliente, part of the Cahuilla people. You can see remnants of their
★ ancient life, including rock art, house pits and foundations, irrigation
ditches, bedrock mortars, pictographs, and stone houses and shelters
atop cliff walls. Short, easy walks through the canyons reveal palm
oases, waterfalls, and spring wildflowers. Tree-shaded picnic areas are
abundant. The attraction includes three canyons open for touring:
Palm Canyon, noted for its stand of Washingtonia palms; Murray
Canyon, home of Peninsula bighorn sheep and a herd of wild ponies;
and Andreas Canyon, where a stand of fan palms contrast with sharp
rock formations. Ranger-led hikes to Palm and Andreas canyons are
offered daily for an additional charge. The trading post at the entrance
to Palm Canyon has hiking maps and refreshments, as well as Native
American art, jewelry, and weavings. ⊠ *38520 S. Palm Canyon Dr.,
south of Acanto Dr., Palm Springs* ☎ *760/323–6018* ⊕ *www.indian-
canyons.com* ☜ *$9, ranger hikes $3* ☉ *Oct.–June, daily 8–5; July–
Sept., Fri.–Sun. 8–5.*

FAMILY **Palm Springs Aerial Tramway.** A trip on the Palm Springs Aerial Tramway
Fodor's Choice provides a 360-degree view of the desert through the picture windows
★ of rotating tramcars. The 2½-mile ascent through Chino Canyon, the
steepest vertical cable ride in the United States, brings you to an elevation of 8,516 feet in less than 20 minutes. On clear days, which are common, the view stretches 75 miles—from the peak of Mt. San Gorgonio
in the north, to the Salton Sea in the southeast. Stepping out into the
snow at the summit is a winter treat. At the top, a bit below the summit of Mt. San Jacinto, are several diversions. Mountain Station has an

observation deck, two restaurants, a cocktail lounge, apparel and gift shops, picnic facilities, a small wildlife exhibit, and a theater that screens movies on the history of the tramway and the state park. Take advantage of free guided and self-guided nature walks through the adjacent Mount San Jacinto State Park and Wilderness, or if there's snow on the ground, rent skis, snowshoes, or snow tubes (inner tubes or similar contraptions for sliding down hills). The tramway generally closes for maintenance in mid-September. ■TIP➔ Ride-and-dine packages are available in late afternoon. The tram is a popular attraction; to avoid a two-hour or longer wait, arrive before the first car leaves in the morning. ✉ *1 Tramway Rd., off N. Palm Canyon Dr. (Hwy. 111), Palm Springs* ☎ *888/515–8726* ⊕ *www.pstramway.com* ✆ *$23.95, ride-and-dine package $36* ✆ *Tramcars depart at least every 30 mins. from 10 am weekdays and 8 am weekends; last car up leaves at 8 pm, last car down leaves Mountain Station at 9:45 pm.*

FAMILY
Fodor'sChoice
★

Palm Springs Air Museum. This museum's impressive collection of World War II aircraft includes a B-17 Flying Fortress bomber, a P-51 Mustang, a Lockheed P-38, and a Grumman TBF Avenger. Among the cool exhibits are model warships, a Pearl Harbor diorama, and a Grumman Goose into which kids can crawl. Photos, artifacts, memorabilia, and uniforms are also on display, and educational programs take place on Saturday. Flight demonstrations are scheduled regularly. Biplane rides are offered on Saturday. ✉ *745 N. Gene Autry Trail, Palm Springs* ☎ *760/778–6262* ⊕ *palmspringsairmuseum.org* ✆ *$15* ✆ *Daily 10–5.*

Palm Springs Art Museum. This world-class art museum focuses on photography, modern architecture, and the traditional arts of the Americas. Galleries are bright and open. The permanent collection includes a shimmering exhibition of contemporary studio glass, highlighted by works by Dale Chihuly, Ginny Ruffner, and William Morris. You'll also find handcrafted furniture by the late actor George Montgomery, a collection of midcentury modern architectural photos by Julius Shulman, an array of enormous Native American baskets, and works by artists like Allen Houser, Arlo Namingha, and Fritz Scholder. The museum also displays significant works of 20th-century sculpture by Henry Moore, Marino Marina, Deborah Butterfield, and Mark Di Suvero. The Annenberg Theater presents plays, concerts, lectures, operas, and other cultural events. ✉ *101 Museum Dr., off W. Tahquitz Canyon Dr., Palm Springs* ☎ *760/322–4800* ⊕ *www.psmuseum.org* ✆ *$12.50, free Thurs. 4–8 during Villagefest* ✆ *Tues.–Sun. 10–5* ✆ *Closed Mon.*

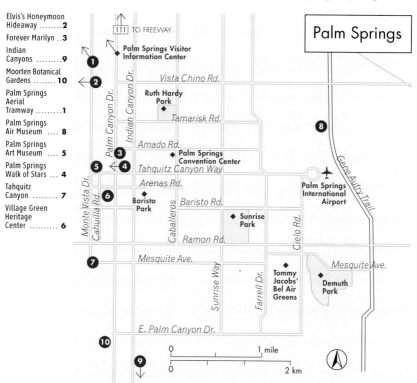

14

Tahquitz Canyon. On ranger-led tours of this secluded canyon on the Agua Caliente Reservation, you can view a spectacular 60-foot waterfall, rock art, ancient irrigation systems, and native wildlife and plants. Tours are conducted several times daily; participants must be able to navigate 100 steep rock steps. (You can also take a self-guided tour of the 1.8-mile trail.) A visitor center at the canyon entrance screens a video, displays artifacts, and sells maps. ⊠ *500 W. Mesquite Ave., west of S. Palm Canyon Dr., Palm Springs* ☎ *760/416–7044* ⊕ *www. tahquitzcanyon.com* ✉ *$12.50* ☉ *Oct.–June, daily 7:30–5; July–Sept., Fri.–Sun. 7:30–5.*

WORTH NOTING

Backstreet Art District. Galleries and live-work studios just off East Canyon Drive showcase the works of highly acclaimed artists. Joseph and Leena Pilcher—he's a marvelous wood sculptor and she's a renowned mixed-media painter—and sculptor Bill Anson are among stars here. The gallery of the Russian-born painter Elena Bulatova displays her modernistic desert landscape paintings. ■ TIP→ **On the first Wednesday evening of the month, the galleries remain open until 9.** ⊠ *2600 S. Cherokee Way, Palm Springs* ⊕ *www.backstreetartdistrict.com* ✉ *Free* ☉ *Hrs vary; check Galleries page on website* ☉ *Most galleries closed Mon. and Tues.*

Forever Marilyn. In the heart of downtown Palm Springs you can embrace, stand in awe of, or look up the skirt of the 26-foot statue of Marilyn Monroe in a pose from her movie *The Seven Year Itch*. This 34,000-pound Norma Jeane tribute, designed by Seward Johnson, holds sway a few miles south of the Racquet Club, where pin-up photographer Bruno Bernard discovered her in 1947. ✉ *245 S. Palm Canyon Dr., Palm Springs.*

Moorten Botanical Garden. In the 1920s, Chester "Cactus Slim" Moorten and his wife, Patricia, opened this showpiece for desert plants—now numbering in the thousands—that includes an ocotillo, a massive elephant tree, a boojum tree, and vine cacti. Their son, Clark, now operates the garden. ■ **TIP→ Take a stroll through the Cactarium to spot rare finds such as the welwitschia, which originated in the Namib Desert in southwestern Africa.** ✉ *1701 S. Palm Canyon Dr., Palm Springs* ☎ *760/327–6555* 🌐 *www.moortengarden.com* 🎟 *$4* 🕒 *Sept.–June, Thurs.–Tues. 10–4; July and Aug., Thurs.–Tues. 9–1.*

Palm Springs Walk of Stars. Along the walk, more than 300 bronze stars are embedded in the sidewalk (à la Hollywood Walk of Fame) to honor celebrities with a Palm Springs connection. Frank, Elvis, Marilyn, Dinah, Lucy, Ginger, Liz, and Liberace have all received their due. Those still around to walk the Walk and see their stars include Nancy Sinatra, Kathy Griffin, and Adam West. ✉ *Palm Canyon Dr., around Tahquitz Canyon Way, and Tahquitz Canyon Way, between Palm Canyon and Indian Canyon Drs., Palm Springs* ☎ *760/320–3129* 🌐 *www.palmsprings.com/stars.*

Village Green Heritage Center. Three small museums at the Village Green Heritage Center illustrate early life in Palm Springs. The **Agua Caliente Cultural Museum,** the centerpiece, traces the culture and history of the Cahuilla tribe with several exhibits. The **McCallum Adobe** holds the collection of the Palm Springs Historical Society. **Rudy's General Store Museum** is a re-creation of a 1930s general store. ✉ *219–221 S. Palm Canyon Dr., Palm Springs* ☎ *760/323–8297* 🎟 *Agua Caliente free, McCallum $2, Rudy's $1* 🕒 *Agua Caliente Sept.–May, Wed.–Sat. 10–5; Sun. noon–5, call for others.*

WHERE TO EAT

$$ MEDITERRANEAN

🍴 **Alicante.** This sidewalk café near the Plaza Theatre is one of the best people-watching spots in Palm Springs. Pasta, pizza, *pollo alla diavolo* (macadamia-crusted chicken breast), and veal scaloppini are among the hearty items on the lunch and dinner menus. A separate tapas menu contains tasty surprises: spicy chickpeas with Mediterranean chicken sausage, chorizo-stuffed calamari, pine nuts with honey topped with blue cheese, or spicy lime-drizzled shrimp. [$] *Average main: $20* ✉ *140 S. Palm Canyon Dr., at La Plaza, Palm Springs* ☎ *760/325–9464* 🌐 *www.alicanteps.com* ✍ *Reservations essential.*

$ AMERICAN Fodor's Choice ★

🍴 **Cheeky's.** The artisanal bacon bar and hangover-curing mimosas attract legions to this breakfast and lunch spot, but traditional eats such as the brioche French toast also contribute to the epic wait on weekends. Huevos rancheros, the goat-cheese scramble, and other farm-centric

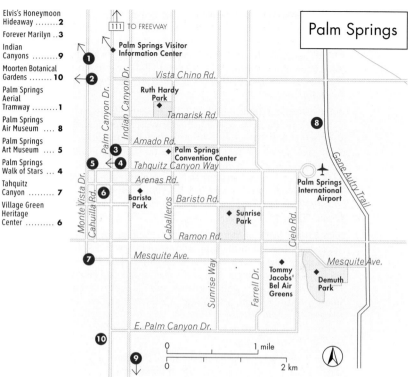

Palm Springs

14

Tahquitz Canyon. On ranger-led tours of this secluded canyon on the Agua Caliente Reservation, you can view a spectacular 60-foot waterfall, rock art, ancient irrigation systems, and native wildlife and plants. Tours are conducted several times daily; participants must be able to navigate 100 steep rock steps. (You can also take a self-guided tour of the 1.8-mile trail.) A visitor center at the canyon entrance screens a video, displays artifacts, and sells maps. ⊠ *500 W. Mesquite Ave., west of S. Palm Canyon Dr., Palm Springs* ☎ *760/416–7044* ⊕ *www. tahquitzcanyon.com* ✑ *$12.50* ⊙ *Oct.–June, daily 7:30–5; July–Sept., Fri.–Sun. 7:30–5.*

WORTH NOTING

Backstreet Art District. Galleries and live-work studios just off East Canyon Drive showcase the works of highly acclaimed artists. Joseph and Leena Pilcher—he's a marvelous wood sculptor and she's a renowned mixed-media painter—and sculptor Bill Anson are among stars here. The gallery of the Russian-born painter Elena Bulatova displays her modernistic desert landscape paintings. ■ **TIP→ On the first Wednesday evening of the month, the galleries remain open until 9.** ⊠ *2600 S. Cherokee Way, Palm Springs* ⊕ *www.backstreetartdistrict.com* ✑ *Free* ⊙ *Hrs vary; check Galleries page on website* ⊙ *Most galleries closed Mon. and Tues.*

Forever Marilyn. In the heart of downtown Palm Springs you can embrace, stand in awe of, or look up the skirt of the 26-foot statue of Marilyn Monroe in a pose from her movie *The Seven Year Itch*. This 34,000-pound Norma Jeane tribute, designed by Seward Johnson, holds sway a few miles south of the Racquet Club, where pin-up photographer Bruno Bernard discovered her in 1947. ✉ *245 S. Palm Canyon Dr., Palm Springs.*

Moorten Botanical Garden. In the 1920s, Chester "Cactus Slim" Moorten and his wife, Patricia, opened this showpiece for desert plants—now numbering in the thousands—that includes an ocotillo, a massive elephant tree, a boojum tree, and vine cacti. Their son, Clark, now operates the garden. **■ TIP→ Take a stroll through the Cactarium to spot rare finds such as the welwitschia, which originated in the Namib Desert in southwestern Africa.** ✉ *1701 S. Palm Canyon Dr., Palm Springs* ☎ *760/327–6555* 🌐 *www.moortengarden.com* 🎟 *$4* ⏲ *Sept.–June, Thurs.–Tues. 10–4; July and Aug., Thurs.–Tues. 9–1.*

Palm Springs Walk of Stars. Along the walk, more than 300 bronze stars are embedded in the sidewalk (à la Hollywood Walk of Fame) to honor celebrities with a Palm Springs connection. Frank, Elvis, Marilyn, Dinah, Lucy, Ginger, Liz, and Liberace have all received their due. Those still around to walk the Walk and see their stars include Nancy Sinatra, Kathy Griffin, and Adam West. ✉ *Palm Canyon Dr., around Tahquitz Canyon Way, and Tahquitz Canyon Way, between Palm Canyon and Indian Canyon Drs., Palm Springs* ☎ *760/320–3129* 🌐 *www.palmsprings.com/stars.*

Village Green Heritage Center. Three small museums at the Village Green Heritage Center illustrate early life in Palm Springs. The **Agua Caliente Cultural Museum,** the centerpiece, traces the culture and history of the Cahuilla tribe with several exhibits. The **McCallum Adobe** holds the collection of the Palm Springs Historical Society. **Rudy's General Store Museum** is a re-creation of a 1930s general store. ✉ *219–221 S. Palm Canyon Dr., Palm Springs* ☎ *760/323–8297* 🎟 *Agua Caliente free, McCallum $2, Rudy's $1* ⏲ *Agua Caliente Sept.–May, Wed.–Sat. 10–5; Sun. noon–5, call for others.*

WHERE TO EAT

$$ MEDITERRANEAN

🍴 **Alicante.** This sidewalk café near the Plaza Theatre is one of the best people-watching spots in Palm Springs. Pasta, pizza, *pollo alla diavolo* (macadamia-crusted chicken breast), and veal scaloppini are among the hearty items on the lunch and dinner menus. A separate tapas menu contains tasty surprises: spicy chickpeas with Mediterranean chicken sausage, chorizo-stuffed calamari, pine nuts with honey topped with blue cheese, or spicy lime-drizzled shrimp. [$] *Average main: $20* ✉ *140 S. Palm Canyon Dr., at La Plaza, Palm Springs* ☎ *760/325–9464* 🌐 *www.alicanteps.com* ✍ *Reservations essential.*

$ AMERICAN Fodor's Choice ★

🍴 **Cheeky's.** The artisanal bacon bar and hangover-curing mimosas attract legions to this breakfast and lunch spot, but traditional eats such as the brioche French toast also contribute to the epic wait on weekends. Huevos rancheros, the goat-cheese scramble, and other farm-centric dishes entice the foodie crowd. Lunch options include a tantalizing gem salad with green goddess dressing, and there's a burger from grass-fed cows that's stupendous when topped with the famous house bacon. The spacious outdoor patio is a fine perch when the weather's not too hot. ⑤ *Average main: $10* ⊠ *622 N. Palm Canyon Dr., at E. Granvia Valmonte, Palm Springs* ☎ *760/327-7595* ⊕ *www.cheekysps.com* ⊗ *Closed Tues. No dinner.*

$$$ ✕ **Copley's on Palm Canyon.** Chef Manion Copley prepares innovative
MODERN cuisine in a setting that's straight out of Hollywood—a hacienda once
AMERICAN owned by Cary Grant. Dine in the clubby house or under the stars in the garden. Start with appetizers such as roasted beet and warm goat cheese salad or one of the Hawaiian ahi tacos. Tandoori-spiced salmon is a hit among entrées that also include sesame-seared tofu and lavender-and-parsley-crusted rack of lamb. ■ **TIP→ Save room for Copley's sweet and savory herb ice creams.** ⑤ *Average main: $29* ⊠ *621 N. Palm Canyon Dr., at E. Granvia Valmonte, Palm Springs* ☎ *760/327-9555* ⊕ *www.copleyspalmsprings.com* ⌂ *Reservations essential* ⊗ *No lunch.*

$$ ✕ **El Mirasol at Los Arboles.** Chef Felipe Castañeda owns two Mexican
MODERN restaurants in Palm Springs—this one, part of the Los Arboles Hotel, is
MEXICAN outside on a charming patio set amid flower gardens and shaded by red umbrellas. Castañeda prepares classic combinations of tacos, tamales, and enchiladas, along with specialties such as double-cooked pork and *pollo en pipián* (chicken with a pre-Columbian sauce made of ground roasted pumpkin seeds and dry chilis). Vegetarian offerings include delicate spinach enchiladas and fine chiles rellenos. ■ **TIP→ Castañeda's more casual café, also called El Mirasol, is 2 miles south at 140 East Palm Canyon Drive.** ⑤ *Average main: $18* ⊠ *266 Via Altamira, off N. Indian Canyon Dr., Palm Springs* ☎ *760/459-3136* ⊕ *www.elmirasolrestaurants.com.*

$$$$ ✕ **The Falls.** A mile-long martini menu lures a chic, moneyed crowd to
STEAKHOUSE this hot spot overlooking Palm Canyon Drive. Reserve well in advance for one of the outdoor balcony tables to get the best view. The restaurant specializes in dry aged beef, but you can also get seafood and chops, and there are vegetarian choices. Steaks and chops are prepared your way with a selection of sides that includes mac and cheese, roasted potatoes, and steamed asparagus with hollandaise sauce. Go early for the nightly happy hour (between 4 and 6:30), when items on the bar menu are half price—or hang around late to catch the action at the Martini Dome bar. ⑤ *Average main: $38* ⊠ *155 S. Palm Canyon Dr., near W. Arenas Rd., Palm Springs* ☎ *760/416-8664* ⊕ *thefallsprimesteakhouse.com* ⌂ *Reservations essential* ⊗ *No lunch.*

$$$$ ✕ **Le Vallauris.** A longtime favorite that occupies the historic Roberson
FRENCH House, Le Vallauris is popular with ladies who lunch, all of whom get a hug from the maître d'. The menu changes daily, and each day it's hand-written on a white board. Lunch entrées might include perfectly rare tuna niçoise salad, or grilled whitefish with Dijon mustard sauce. Dinner might bring a sublime smoked salmon, sautéed calf's liver, roasted quail with orange sauce, or rack of lamb. There are also weekly prix-fixe menus, with and without wine, for lunch and dinner. The restaurant has a lovely tree-shaded garden. On cool winter evenings, request a

14

table by the fireplace. [$] *Average main: $35* ✉ *385 W. Tahquitz Canyon Way, west of Palm Canyon Dr., Palm Springs* ☎ *760/325–5059* 🌐 *www.levallauris.com* ✍ *Reservations essential* ⏲ *Closed July and Aug.*

$$ ITALIAN FAMILY 🍴 **Matchbox Vintage Pizza Bistro.** The name says pizza, but this bistro also serves interesting salads topped with grilled tuna, and a selection of sandwiches like crab cakes on a toasted brioche. Main courses include bacon-wrapped scallops, macaroni and cheese, a hearty pork chop, and fish-and-chips. The pizzas are made just about any way you'd like, including vegetarian, and are topped with everything from figs to pepperoni. On the second-floor overlooking the action on Palm Canyon Drive, this is a great place to go for cocktails and small plates. ■ **TIP→ Kids love the balls of pizza dough the servers dole out.** [$] *Average main: $18* ✉ *155 S. Palm Canyon Dr., near W. Arenas Rd., Palm Springs* ☎ *760/778–6000* 🌐 *www.matchboxpalmsprings.com* ⏲ *No lunch Mon. and Tues.*

$$$$ MODERN AMERICAN 🍴 **Purple Palm.** The hottest tables in Palm Springs are those that surround the pool at the Colony Palms Hotel, where the hip and elite pay homage to Purple Gang mobster Al Wertheimer, who reportedly built the hotel in the mid-1930s. Now it's a casual, convivial place where you can dine alfresco surrounded by a tropical garden. The dinner menu is heavy on seafood, such as bouillabaisse and roasted barrammundi; you can also shuck oysters, crab legs, and prawns. The impressive wine list roams the globe. The restaurant is also open for breakfast, lunch, and dinner. ■ **TIP→ The ladies room features a fabulous black-and-white image of a very young Paul Newman.** [$] *Average main: $31* ✉ *572 N. Indian Canyon Dr., at E. Granvia Valmonte, Palm Springs* ☎ *800/557–2187* 🌐 *www.colonypalmshotel.com* ✍ *Reservations essential.*

$$$$ MODERN AMERICAN 🍴 **Spencer's Restaurant.** The swank dining space inside the Palm Springs Tennis Club Resort occupies a historic midcentury modern structure, but the cuisine of chef Eric Wadlund, a local star with a national reputation, is the main attraction. Crab cakes, kung pao calamari, and crispy flash-fried oysters are favorite starters. Filet mignon topped with a Gorgonzola-sage sauce, rack of lamb, and crispy-skin Lake Superior whitefish, are among the crowd-pleasing entrées. Desserts can be hit or miss, though the banana-cream pie in a martini glass is a delightful way to end a meal. Spencer's serves breakfast, lunch, and dinner. You can dine inside or on the pet-friendly patio under a massive ficus tree that's strung with lights. [$] *Average main: $35* ✉ *701 W. Baristo Rd., Palm Springs* ☎ *760/327–3446* 🌐 *www.spencersrestaurant.com* ✍ *Reservations essential.*

$$$$ BASQUE Fodor's Choice ★ 🍴 **Tinto.** Jose Garces, a winner on the Food Network's *Iron Chef America* show and the recipient of a James Beard Foundation Award, concocts delightfully exotic tapas at his Basque-inpsired wine bar in the Saguaro Hotel. The inventive small plates include bacon-wrapped Coachella dates with almonds and pearl onions in a Valdeón cheese fondue, *jamón ibérico de bellota* (cured Spanish ham made from acorn-fed pigs), and Spanish octopus with potato confit, smoked paprika, and lemon. The chef's tasting menu (from $55 to $65 per person) is available with wine pairing ($30). Tinto is a fun place with closely spaced tables; dinner becomes a party as the Spanish guitarist plays to the crowd. [$] *Average*

dishes entice the foodie crowd. Lunch options include a tantalizing gem salad with green goddess dressing, and there's a burger from grass-fed cows that's stupendous when topped with the famous house bacon. The spacious outdoor patio is a fine perch when the weather's not too hot. $ *Average main: $10* ⊠ *622 N. Palm Canyon Dr., at E. Granvia Valmonte, Palm Springs* ☎ *760/327–7595* ⊕ *www.cheekysps.com* ⊘ *Closed Tues. No dinner.*

$$$
MODERN
AMERICAN

✕ **Copley's on Palm Canyon.** Chef Manion Copley prepares innovative cuisine in a setting that's straight out of Hollywood—a hacienda once owned by Cary Grant. Dine in the clubby house or under the stars in the garden. Start with appetizers such as roasted beet and warm goat cheese salad or one of the Hawaiian ahi tacos. Tandoori-spiced salmon is a hit among entrées that also include sesame-seared tofu and lavender-and-parsley-crusted rack of lamb. ■**TIP➔** Save room for Copley's sweet and savory herb ice creams. $ *Average main: $29* ⊠ *621 N. Palm Canyon Dr., at E. Granvia Valmonte, Palm Springs* ☎ *760/327–9555* ⊕ *www. copleyspalmsprings.com* ⌑ *Reservations essential* ⊘ *No lunch.*

$$
MODERN
MEXICAN

✕ **El Mirasol at Los Arboles.** Chef Felipe Castañeda owns two Mexican restaurants in Palm Springs—this one, part of the Los Arboles Hotel, is outside on a charming patio set amid flower gardens and shaded by red umbrellas. Castañeda prepares classic combinations of tacos, tamales, and enchiladas, along with specialties such as double-cooked pork and *pollo en pipián* (chicken with a pre-Columbian sauce made of ground roasted pumpkin seeds and dry chilis). Vegetarian offerings include delicate spinach enchiladas and fine chiles rellenos. ■**TIP➔** Castañeda's more casual café, also called El Mirasol, is 2 miles south at 140 East Palm Canyon Drive. $ *Average main: $18* ⊠ *266 Via Altamira, off N. Indian Canyon Dr., Palm Springs* ☎ *760/459–3136* ⊕ *www. elmirasolrestaurants.com.*

$$$$
STEAKHOUSE

✕ **The Falls.** A mile-long martini menu lures a chic, moneyed crowd to this hot spot overlooking Palm Canyon Drive. Reserve well in advance for one of the outdoor balcony tables to get the best view. The restaurant specializes in dry aged beef, but you can also get seafood and chops, and there are vegetarian choices. Steaks and chops are prepared your way with a selection of sides that includes mac and cheese, roasted potatoes, and steamed asparagus with hollandaise sauce. Go early for the nightly happy hour (between 4 and 6:30), when items on the bar menu are half price—or hang around late to catch the action at the Martini Dome bar. $ *Average main: $38* ⊠ *155 S. Palm Canyon Dr., near W. Arenas Rd., Palm Springs* ☎ *760/416–8664* ⊕ *thefallsprimesteakhouse. com* ⌑ *Reservations essential* ⊘ *No lunch.*

$$$$
FRENCH

✕ **Le Vallauris.** A longtime favorite that occupies the historic Roberson House, Le Vallauris is popular with ladies who lunch, all of whom get a hug from the maître d'. The menu changes daily, and each day it's handwritten on a white board. Lunch entrées might include perfectly rare tuna niçoise salad, or grilled whitefish with Dijon mustard sauce. Dinner might bring a sublime smoked salmon, sautéed calf's liver, roasted quail with orange sauce, or rack of lamb. There are also weekly prix-fixe menus, with and without wine, for lunch and dinner. The restaurant has a lovely tree-shaded garden. On cool winter evenings, request a

14

table by the fireplace. $[\$]$ *Average main: $35* $\boxtimes$ *385 W. Tahquitz Canyon Way, west of Palm Canyon Dr., Palm Springs* $\boxtimes$ *760/325–5059* $\oplus$ *www. levallauris.com* $\triangle$ *Reservations essential* $\odot$ *Closed July and Aug.*

$$ $ $ \quad \times$ **Matchbox Vintage Pizza Bistro.** The name says pizza, but this bistro

ITALIAN   also serves interesting salads topped with grilled tuna, and a selec-

FAMILY   tion of sandwiches like crab cakes on a toasted brioche. Main courses include bacon-wrapped scallops, macaroni and cheese, a hearty pork chop, and fish-and-chips. The pizzas are made just about any way you'd like, including vegetarian, and are topped with everything from figs to pepperoni. On the second-floor overlooking the action on Palm Canyon Drive, this is a great place to go for cocktails and small plates. ■ TIP→ **Kids love the balls of pizza dough the servers dole out.** $[\$]$ *Average main: $18* $\boxtimes$ *155 S. Palm Canyon Dr., near W. Arenas Rd., Palm Springs* $\boxtimes$ *760/778–6000* $\oplus$ *www.matchboxpalmsprings.com* $\odot$ *No lunch Mon. and Tues.*

$$ $ $ $ \quad \times$ **Purple Palm.** The hottest tables in Palm Springs are those that surround

MODERN   the pool at the Colony Palms Hotel, where the hip and elite pay homage

AMERICAN   to Purple Gang mobster Al Wertheimer, who reportedly built the hotel in the mid-1930s. Now it's a casual, convivial place where you can dine alfresco surrounded by a tropical garden. The dinner menu is heavy on seafood, such as bouillabaisse and roasted barrammundi; you can also shuck oysters, crab legs, and prawns. The impressive wine list roams the globe. The restaurant is also open for breakfast, lunch, and dinner. ■ TIP→ **The ladies room features a fabulous black-and-white image of a very young Paul Newman.** $[\$]$ *Average main: $31* $\boxtimes$ *572 N. Indian Canyon Dr., at E. Granvia Valmonte, Palm Springs* $\boxtimes$ *800/557–2187* $\oplus$ *www.colonypalmshotel.com* $\triangle$ *Reservations essential.*

$$ $ $ $ \quad \times$ **Spencer's Restaurant.** The swank dining space inside the Palm Springs

MODERN   Tennis Club Resort occupies a historic midcentury modern structure,

AMERICAN   but the cuisine of chef Eric Wadlund, a local star with a national rep- utation, is the main attraction. Crab cakes, kung pao calamari, and crispy flash-fried oysters are favorite starters. Filet mignon topped with a Gorgonzola-sage sauce, rack of lamb, and crispy-skin Lake Superior whitefish, are among the crowd-pleasing entrées. Desserts can be hit or miss, though the banana-cream pie in a martini glass is a delight- ful way to end a meal. Spencer's serves breakfast, lunch, and dinner. You can dine inside or on the pet-friendly patio under a massive ficus tree that's strung with lights. $[\$]$ *Average main: $35* $\boxtimes$ *701 W. Baristo Rd., Palm Springs* $\boxtimes$ *760/327–3446* $\oplus$ *www.spencersrestaurant.com* $\triangle$ *Reservations essential.*

$$ $ $ $ \quad \times$ **Tinto.** Jose Garces, a winner on the Food Network's *Iron Chef America*

BASQUE   show and the recipient of a James Beard Foundation Award, concocts

Fodor's Choice   delightfully exotic tapas at his Basque-inpsired wine bar in the Saguaro

★   Hotel. The inventive small plates include bacon-wrapped Coachella dates with almonds and pearl onions in a Valdeón cheese fondue, *jamón ibérico de bellota* (cured Spanish ham made from acorn-fed pigs), and Spanish octopus with potato confit, smoked paprika, and lemon. The chef's tasting menu (from $55 to $65 per person) is available with wine pairing ($30). Tinto is a fun place with closely spaced tables; dinner becomes a party as the Spanish guitarist plays to the crowd. $[\$]$ *Average* *main: $55 ✉ 1800 E. Palm Canyon Dr., at S. Sunshine Way, Palm Springs ☎ 760/323–1711 🌐 palmsprings.tintorestaurant.com ✍ Reservations essential.*

$$ MODERN AMERICAN
🍴 **Trio.** The owners of this high-energy Uptown Design District restaurant claim that it's "where Palm Springs eats," and it certainly seems so on nights when the lines run deep near the front door. The menu includes home-style staples such as Yankee pot roast along with crawfish pie and other trendy dishes. Vegetarian and gluten-free items are available. You can dine outside or inside, where works by local artists hang on the walls. [$] *Average main: $18 ✉ 707 N. Palm Canyon Dr., Palm Springs ☎ 760/864–8746 🌐 www.triopalmsprings.com ✍ Reservations essential.*

$$$ INTERNATIONAL
🍴 **The Tropicale.** Tucked onto a side-street corner, the Tropicale is a mid-century–style watering hole with a contemporary vibe. The bar and main dining room hold cozy leather booths, and flowers and water features brighten the outdoor area. The menu spans the globe with small and large plates, from the miso-glazed salmon rice bowl, to the grilled Idaho trout with aioli sauce, to filet mignon with Zinfandel sauce. [$] *Average main: $28 ✉ 330 E. Amado Rd., at N. Calle Encilia, Palm Springs ☎ 760/866–1952 🌐 www.thetropicale.com ✍ Reservations essential ⏲ No lunch.*

$ AMERICAN FAMILY
Fodor's Choice ★
🍴 **Tyler's Burgers.** Families, singles, and couples head to Tyler's for simple, casual lunch fare that appeals to carnivores and vegetarians alike. Expect mid-20th-century America's greatest hits: heaping burgers, stacks of fries, root beer floats, milk shakes. The sandwiches lure the first-time customers, but everyone comes back for the cole slaw, made in-house and well worth a try. On weekends, be prepared to wait with the masses. [$] *Average main: $6 ✉ 149 S. Indian Canyon Dr., at La Plaza, Palm Springs ☎ 760/325–2990 🌐 tylersburgers.com 💳 No credit cards ⏲ Closed Sun. late May–mid-Feb.*

$$$$ AMERICAN
🍴 **Workshop Kitchen + Bar.** Chef Michael Beckman's Uptown Design District hot spot pairs high-quality California cuisine with creative cocktails in a sleek, almost utilitarian, setting. The outdoor patio lures the oversize-sunglasses Sunday-brunch crowd who slurp Cava mimosas and artisanal cocktails. Inside, the sleek concrete booths are topped with black leather cushions. The dinner menu changes with the seasons but might feature a brussels sprouts salad, whole chicken (ideal for sharing), or pan-roasted scallops atop squash slaw. Deep-pocketed diners will appreciate Beckman's artistry, though be advised that portions are small—three scallops for $36? [$] *Average main: $30 ✉ 800 N. Palm Canyon Dr., at E. Tamarisk Rd., Palm Springs ☎ 760/459–3451 🌐 workshoppalmsprings.com ✍ Reservations essential ⏲ No lunch Mon.–Sat.*

WHERE TO STAY

$$ RESORT
🏨 **Ace Hotel and Swim Club.** Take a trip back to the 1960s at the Ace: With the hotel's vintage feel and hippie-chic decor, it would be no surprise to find the Grateful Dead playing in the bar. **Pros:** Amigo Room has late-night dining; poolside stargazing deck; Sunday DJ scene at the pool. **Cons:** party atmosphere not for everyone; limited amenities; casual staff and service. [$] *Rooms from: $129 ✉ 701 E. Palm Canyon*

Dr., Palm Springs ☎ 760/325–9900 🌐 www.acehotel.com/palmsprings 🛏 180 rooms, 8 suites 🍴 No meals.

$$ HOTEL 🏨 **Alcazar Palm Springs.** Amid an area known as the Movie Colony, Alcazar embodies the desert's popular midcentury modern design style; the ample, blazing-white guestrooms here wrap around a sparkling pool. **Pros:** walking distance of downtown; parking on-site; bikes available. **Cons:** limited service; wall air-conditioners; resort fee ($9). [$] *Rooms from: $129 ✉ 622 N. Indian Canyon Dr., Palm Springs ☎ 760/318–9850 🌐 www.alcazarpalmsprings.com 🛏 34 rooms 🍴 No meals.*

$ B&B/INN 🏨 **Casa Cody.** The service is personal and gracious at this historic B&B near the Palm Springs Art Museum; spacious studios and one- and two-bedroom suites hold Santa Fe–style rustic furnishings. **Pros:** family-size digs; friendly ambience; good value. **Cons:** old buildings; limited amenities. [$] *Rooms from: $99 ✉ 175 S. Cahuilla Rd., Palm Springs ☎ 760/320–9346, 800/231–2639 🌐 www.casacody.com 🛏 18 rooms, 8 suites, 1 cottage 🍴 Breakfast.*

$$ HOTEL 🏨 **Colony Palms Hotel.** This hotel has been a hip place to stay since the 1930s, when gangster Al Wertheimer built it to front his casino, bar, and brothel. **Pros:** glam with a swagger; attentive staff; all that history. **Cons:** high noise level outside; not for families with young children. [$] *Rooms from: $159 ✉ 572 N. Indian Canyon Dr., Palm Springs ☎ 760/969–1800, 800/577–2187 🌐 www.colonypalmshotel.com 🛏 43 rooms, 3 suites, 8 casitas 🍴 No meals.*

$$ HOTEL Fodor's Choice ★ 🏨 **Hotel California.** Expect homey accommodations for all budgets at this delightful hotel whose guest rooms are decked out in rustic Mexican furniture. **Pros:** comfortable design; friendly hosts; free limo service in the evenings. **Cons:** away from downtown. [$] *Rooms from: $159 ✉ 424 E. Palm Canyon Dr., Palm Springs ☎ 760/322–8855 🌐 www.palmspringshotelcalifornia.com 🛏 7 rooms, 7 suites 🍴 No meals.*

$$ B&B/INN Fodor's Choice ★ 🏨 **Korakia Pensione.** The painter Gordon Coutts, best known for desert landscapes, constructed this Moroccan villa in 1924 as an artist's studio, and these days creative types gather in the main house and the adjacent Mediterranean-style villa to soak up the spirit of that era. **Pros:** design-minded decor; international vibe; complimentary breakfast; yoga on weekends. **Cons:** might not appeal to those who prefer standard resorts; no TVs or phones in rooms. [$] *Rooms from: $169 ✉ 257 S. Patencio Rd., Palm Springs ☎ 760/864–6411 🌐 www.korakia.com 🛏 11 rooms, 9 suites, 8 rental units 🍴 No meals.*

$$ B&B/INN 🏨 **La Maison.** Offering all the comforts of home, this small bed-and-breakfast contains large guest rooms that surround the pool area, where you can spend quiet time soaking up the sun or taking a dip. **Pros:** restaurants nearby; quiet; genial hosts. **Cons:** on busy Highway 111; rooms open directly onto pool deck. [$] *Rooms from: $169 ✉ 1600 E. Palm Canyon Dr., Palm Springs ☎ 760/325–1600 🌐 www.lamaisonpalmsprings.com 🛏 13 rooms 🍴 Breakfast.*

$ B&B/INN 🏨 **Movie Colony Hotel.** Designed in 1935 by Albert Frey, this intimate hotel evokes midcentury minimalist ambience; its gleaming white, two-story buildings, flanked with balconies and porthole windows, bring to mind a luxury yacht. **Pros:** architectural icon; happy hour; cruiser bikes. **Cons:** close quarters; off the beaten path; staff not available 24 hours.

$ Rooms from: $89 ⊠ 726 N. Indian Canyon Dr., Palm Springs ☎ 760/320–6340, 888/953–5700 ⊕ www.moviecolonyhotel.com ⤣ 13 rooms, 3 suites ⦿ Breakfast.

$$
B&B/INN
Fodor'sChoice
★

⊡ Orbit In Hotel. The architectural style of this hip inn on a quiet back-street dates back to the late 1940s and '50s—nearly flat roofs, wide overhangs, glass everywhere—and the period feel continues inside. **Pros:** saltwater pool; in-room spa services; Orbitini cocktail hour. **Cons:** best for couples; style not to everyone's taste; staff not available 24 hours. $ Rooms from: $149 ⊠ 562 W. Arenas Rd., Palm Springs ☎ 760/323–3585, 877/996–7248 ⊕ www.orbitin.com ⤣ 9 rooms ⦿ Breakfast.

$$$$
RESORT
Fodor'sChoice
★

⊡ The Parker Palm Springs. A cacophony of color and over-the-top contemporary art assembled by New York City–based designer Jonathan Adler mixes well with the brilliant desert garden, two pools, fire pits, and expansive spa of this hip hotel that attracts a stylish, worldly clientele. **Pros:** fun in the sun; celebrity clientele; high jinks at the Palm Springs Yacht Club Spa; design-centric. **Cons:** pricey drinks and wine; a bit of a drive from downtown; resort fee ($30). $ Rooms from: $325 ⊠ 4200 E. Palm Canyon Dr., Palm Springs ☎ 760/770–5000, 800/543–4300 ⊕ www.theparkerpalmsprings.com ⤣ 131 rooms, 13 suites ⦿ No meals.

$$$$
RESORT

⊡ Riviera Resort & Spa. A party place built in 1958 and renovated in 2008, the Riviera attracts young, well-heeled, bikini-clad guests who hang out around the pool by day and the Bikini Bar by night. **Pros:** personal beachy fire pits throughout the property; hip vibe; excellent spa. **Cons:** high noise level outdoors; party atmosphere; location at north end of Palm Springs. $ Rooms from: $299 ⊠ 1600 N. Indian Canyon Dr., Palm Springs ☎ 760/327–8311 ⊕ www.psriviera.com ⤣ 406 rooms, 43 suites ⦿ No meals.

$
HOTEL
Fodor'sChoice
★

⊡ The Saguaro. A startling, rainbow-hued oasis—the brainchild of Manhattan-based architects Peter Stamberg and Paul Aferiat—the Saguaro caters to pet-toting partygoers who appreciate its lively pool and casual- and fine-dining options. **Pros:** fun atmosphere; excellent on-site dining; daily yoga; shuttle service to downtown. **Cons:** a few miles from downtown. $ Rooms from: $99 ⊠ 1800 E. Palm Canyon Dr., Palm Springs ☎ 760/323–1711 ⊕ thesaguaro.com ⤣ 230 rooms, 14 suites ⦿ No meals.

$$$$
RESORT
FAMILY

⊡ Smoke Tree Ranch. A world apart from Palm Springs' pulsating urban village, the area's most under-the-radar resort complex occupies 400 pristine desert acres, surrounded by mountains and unspoiled vistas.

TRIBAL WEALTH

The Agua Caliente Band of Cahuilla Indians owns nearly half the land in the Palm Springs area. Wanting to encourage the railroad to bring their trains through the desert, Congress granted half the land to the railroad and the other half to the Native Americans. The Cahuilla were granted all the even-numbered one-square-mile sections—but they were unable to develop the land for years due to litigation. The resulting patchwork of developed and vacant land can still be seen today, though the Cahuilla are making up for lost time by opening new hotels and casinos.

14

Pros: priceless privacy; simple luxury; recreational choices include horseback riding, lawn bowling, hiking, golfing, a playground, and jogging. **Cons:** no glitz; limited entertainment options; family atmosphere not for everyone. $ *Rooms from: $330* ✉ *1850 Smoke Tree La., Palm Springs* ☎ *760/327–1221, 800/787–3922* ⊕ *www.smoketreeranch.com* ⌁ *49 cottages, includes 18 suites* ☻ *Closed Apr.– late Oct.* ⦿ *Multiple meal plans.*

$$
B&B/INN
⊡ **Sparrows.** Rustic earthiness meets haute design at the adult-centered Sparrows, just off Palm Springs' main drag. **Pros:** unique design that draws an urban clientele; intimate property; private patios; relaxed ambience. **Cons:** rooms feel a little dark; some guests might deem them charmless. $ *Rooms from: $150* ✉ *1330 E. Palm Canyon Dr., Palm Springs* ☎ *760/327–2300* ⊕ *www.sparrowshotel.com* ⌁ *18 rooms, 2 suites* ⦿ *Breakfast.*

$$$$
RESORT
⊡ **The Viceroy Palm Springs.** A visit to the Viceroy is like entering a tableau of bright white and yellow, reminiscent of a sun-filled desert day. **Pros:** poolside cabanas; complimentary fitness classes; celebrity clientele. **Cons:** uneven service; popular wedding site. $ *Rooms from: $300* ✉ *415 S. Belardo Rd., Palm Springs* ☎ *760/320–4117, 800/327–3687* ⊕ *www.viceroypalmsprings.com* ⌁ *67 rooms, 12 villas* ⦿ *No meals.*

$$$$
B&B/INN
⊡ **Willows Historic Palm Springs Inn.** An opulent Mediterranean-style mansion built in the 1920s to host the rich and famous, this luxurious hillside B&B has gleaming hardwood and slate floors, stone fireplaces, frescoed ceilings, hand-painted tiles, iron balconies, antiques throughout, and a 50-foot waterfall that splashes into a pool outside the dining room. **Pros:** luxurious; sublime service; expansive breakfast. **Cons:** closed from June to September; pricey. $ *Rooms from: $375* ✉ *412 W. Tahquitz Canyon Way, Palm Springs* ☎ *760/320–0771, 800/966–9597* ⊕ *www.thewillowspalmsprings.com* ⌁ *8 rooms* ⦿ *Breakfast.*

NIGHTLIFE AND THE ARTS

NIGHTLIFE

BARS AND PUBS

Bar. The mural-covered exterior of Bar makes it clear that this hot spot caters to the L.A. crowd. Pulled-pork sandwiches and flatbreads pair well with whiskey drinks and artisan-beer cocktails such as gin, lemon, honey, and pale ale. DJs spin music throughout the week. ■**TIP**→ **On most nights there's no cover charge.** ✉ *340 N. Palm Canyon Dr., Palm Springs* ☎ *760/537–7337* ⊕ *barwastaken.com.*

Hair of the Dog English Pub. Drawing a young crowd that likes to tip back English ales and ciders, this bar is lively and popular. ✉ *238 N. Palm Canyon Dr., near E. Amado Rd., Palm Springs* ☎ *760/323–9890* ⊕ *www.thehairofthedog.net.*

Fodor'sChoice
★
Village Pub. With live entertainment, DJs, and friendly service, this popular bar caters to a young crowd. Happy hour is fantastic. On weekend days there is live music as well. ✉ *266 S. Palm Canyon Dr., at Baristo Rd., Palm Springs* ☎ *760/323–3265* ⊕ *www.palmspringsvillagepub.com.*

CASINOS

Casino Morongo. A 20-minute drive west of Palm Springs, this casino has 2,000 slot machines, video games, the Vibe nightclub, plus Vegas-style shows. ✉ *49500 Seminole Dr., off I–10, Cabazon* ☎ *800/252–4499, 951/849–3080* ⊕ *www.morongocasinoresort.com.*

Spa Resort Casino. This resort holds 1,000 slot machines, blackjack tables, a high-limit room, four restaurants, two bars, and the Cascade Lounge for entertainment. ✉ *401 E. Amado Rd., at N. Calle Encilia, Palm Springs* ☎ *888/999–1995* ⊕ *www.sparesortcasino.com.*

DANCE CLUBS

Zelda's Nightclub. At this Palm Springs institution the high-energy DJs, dancing, and drinking are still going strong and the dance floor is still thumping with Latin, hip-hop, and sounds from the '60s, '70s, and '80s. Zelda's offers bottle service in the VIP Sky Box. ✉ *611 S. Palm Canyon Dr., at E. Camino Parocela, Palm Springs* ☎ *760/325–2375* ⊕ *www. zeldasnightclub.com* ☾ *Closed Mon.*

THEMED ENTERTAINMENT

Fodor'sChoice
★
Ace Hotel and Swim Club. Events are held here nearly every night, including film screenings, full moon parties, live concerts, and DJ music with dancing. Many are free, and some are family-friendly. The poolside venue makes most events fun and casual. ✉ *701 E. Palm Canyon Dr., at Calle Palo Fierro, Palm Springs* ☎ *760/325–9900* ⊕ *www.acehotel.com.*

GAY AND LESBIAN

Hunter's Video Bar. Drawing a young gay and straight crowd, Hunter's is a club-scene mainstay. ✉ *302 E. Arenas Rd., at Calle Encilia, Palm Springs* ☎ *760/323–0700* ⊕ *huntersnightclubs.com.*

Fodor'sChoice
★
Toucans Tiki Lounge. A friendly place with a tropical–rain forest setting, Toucans serves festive drinks and hosts live entertainment and theme nights. On Sunday it seems as though all of Palm Springs has turned out for drag night. ✉ *2100 N. Palm Canyon Dr., at W. Via Escuela, Palm Springs* ☎ *760/416–7584* ⊕ *www.toucanstikilounge.com.*

White Party Palm Springs. Held during spring break, the White Party draws tens of thousands of gay men from around the world for four days of parties and events. ✉ *Palm Springs* ⊕ *jeffreysanker.com.*

THE ARTS

ARTS CENTERS

Annenberg Theater. Broadway shows, operas, lectures, Sunday-afternoon chamber concerts, and other events take place at the Palm Springs Art Museum's handsome theater. ✉ *101 N. Museum Dr., at W. Tahquitz Canyon Way, Palm Springs* ☎ *760/325–4490* ⊕ *www. psmuseum.org.*

FESTIVALS

Modernism Week. Each February, the desert communities celebrate the work of the architects and designers who created the Palm Springs "look" in the 1940s, 1950s, and 1960s. Described these days as midcentury modern (you'll also see the term "desert modernism" used), these structures were created by Albert Frey, Richard Neutra, William

Palm Springs is a golfer's paradise: the area is home to more than 125 courses.

F. Cody, John Lautner, and other notables. The 11-day event features lectures, a modernism show, films, vintage car and trailer shows, galas, and home and garden tours. ✉ *Palm Springs* ☎ *760/322–2502* ⊕ *www.modernismweek.com.*

FILM

Palm Springs International Film Festival. In mid-January this 12-day festival brings stars and nearly 200 feature films from several dozen countries, plus panel discussions, short films, and documentaries, to various venues. ✉ *Palm Springs* ☎ *760/322–2930, 800/898–7256* ⊕ *www.psfilmfest.org.*

SPORTS AND THE OUTDOORS

BIKING

Many hotels and resorts have bicycles available for guest use.

Big Wheel Tours. Rent cruisers, performance road bikes, and mountain bikes from this agency that also offers road tours to La Quinta Loop, Joshua Tree National Park, and the San Andreas Fault. Off-road tours are available, too. The company will pick up and deliver bikes to your hotel and supply you with maps. ✉ *Palm Springs* ☎ *760/779–1837* ⊕ *www.bwbtours.com.*

Palm Springs Recreation Division. This organization can provide you with maps of city bike trails. Printable versions of several routes are available on the website. ✉ *401 S. Pavilion Way, Palm Springs* ☎ *760/323–8272* ⊕ *www.palmspringsca.gov/index.aspx?page=752* ☽ *Weekdays 7:30–6.*

GOLF

Indian Canyons Golf Resort. Operated by the Aqua Caliente tribe, this spot at the base of the mountains includes two 18-hole courses open to the public. In the 1960s this was *the* place to play for celebrities visiting the desert, including presidents Dwight Eisenhower, Lyndon Johnson, and Ronald Reagan. The North Course, designed by William F. Bell, is adjacent to property once owned by Walt Disney and has six water hazards. The South Course, redesigned in 2004 by Casey O'Callaghan with input from the LPGA player Amy Alcott, has four ponds, hundreds of palm trees, and five par-5 holes. ⊠ *1097 E. Murray Canyon Dr., at Kings Rd. E, Palm Springs* ☎ *760/833–8700* ⊕ *www. indiancanyonsgolf.com* ✉ *North Course, $40–$99; South Course, $40–$115* ⚹ *North Course: 18 holes, 6943 yards, par 72; South Course: 18 holes, 6582 yards, par 72.*

Palm Springs Desert Resorts Convention and Visitors Bureau. Palm Springs hosts more than 100 golf tournaments annually; the bureau's website posts listings. ⊕ *www.palmspringsusa.com.*

Tahquitz Creek Golf Resort. Conveniently located in Palm Springs near Cathedral City, the resort has two popular courses open to the public. Golfers have been walking the Legend course for more than 50 years—the back nine here are challenging, particularly the greens. The newer Resort course, designed by Ted Robinson, offers sweeping mountain views and scenic waterscapes. ⊠ *1885 Golf Club Dr., at 34th Ave., Palm Springs* ☎ *760/328–1005* ⊕ *www.tahquitzgolfresort.com* ✉ *Both courses $25–$90* ⚹ *Legend Course: 18 holes, 6815 yards, par 71; Resort Course: 18 holes, 6705 yards, par 72.*

HORSEBACK RIDING

Smoke Tree Stables. At Smoke Tree you can explore desert canyons on horseback like the earliest pioneers. One-hour tours depart on the hour and take riders along the base of the Santa Rosa Mountains. Two-hour tours depart four times daily for trips that take in the Aqua Caliente Indian Reservation. ⊠ *2500 Toledo Ave., Palm Springs* ☎ *760/327–1372* ⊕ *www.smoketreestables.com* ✉ *$50 for 1 hr, $100 for 2 hrs* ☉ *Daily 8–4.*

SHOPPING

BOUTIQUES

Fodor's Choice ★ **Raymond | Lawrence.** This colorful concept gallery showcases paintings and sculptures, clothing and accessories, and home decor and other items by contemporary artists. You can also shop for hand creams from The Body Deli, underwear from Chelsea Lane, and photo prints by William Dey. ⊠ *830 N. Palm Canyon Dr., Palm Springs* ☎ *760/322–3344* ⊕ *www.raymond-lawrence.com.*

Trina Turk Boutique. Celebrity designer Trina Turk's empire takes up a city block in the Uptown Design District. Turk, famous for men's and women's outdoor wear, reached out to another celebrity, interior designer Kelly Wearstler, to create adjoining clothing and residential boutiques. Lively fabrics brighten up the many chairs and couches for sale at the

14

residential store, which also carries bowls, paintings, and other fun pieces to spiff up your home. ✉ *891 N. Palm Canyon Dr., Palm Springs* ☎ *760/416–2856* ⊕ *www.trinaturk.com.*

OUTLET MALL

Fodor'sChoice
★

Desert Hills Premium Outlets. About 20 miles west of Palm Springs lies one of California's largest outlet centers. The 180 brand-name discount fashion shops include Jimmy Choo, Neiman Marcus, Versace, Saint Laurent Paris, J. Crew, Armani, Gucci, and Prada. ✉ *48400 Seminole Rd., off I–10, Cabazon* ☎ *951/849–6641* ⊕ *www.premiumoutlets.com.*

SHOPPING DISTRICT

Fodor'sChoice
★

Uptown Heritage Galleries & Antiques District. A loose-knit collection of consignment and secondhand shops, galleries, and lively restaurants extends north of Palm Springs' main shopping area. The theme here is decidedly retro. Many businesses sell midcentury modern furniture and decorator items, and others carry clothing and estate jewelry. One spot definitely worth a peek is **Shag, the Store,** the gallery of fine-art painter Josh Agle. For antique costume jewelry check out **Dazzles.** If you dig the mid-mod aesthetic, breeze through the furnishings at **Towne Palm Springs.** ✉ *N. Palm Canyon Dr., between Amado Rd. and Vista Chino, Palm Springs* ⊕ *www.palmcanyondrive.org.*

SPAS

Fodor'sChoice
★

Estrella Spa at the Viceroy Palm Springs. This spa earns top honors each year for the indoor/outdoor experience it offers with a touch of Old Hollywood ambience. You can enjoy your massage in one of four outdoor treatment canopies in a garden, experience a Vichy shower massage, get a facial or pedicure fireside, or receive a full-body treatment with lemon crystals in the spa's Ice Haus. Whatever the treatment, you can use the spa's private pool, take a break for lunch, and order a drink from the hotel's bar. ✉ *415 S. Belardo Rd., Palm Springs* ☎ *760/320– 4117* ⊕ *www.viceroypalmsprings.com* ☞ *Services: body wrap, facials, specialty massages, prenatal massages, outdoor treatments, salon, wellness classes. $135 60-min massage, $370 spa package.*

Feel Good Spa at the Ace Hotel. Despite its funkiness, this 21st-century indie hangout takes its services very seriously. The estheticians use local clay, mud, and sea algae, and you can make your own scrub from organic botanicals such as lotions and essential oils. There are a variety of settings where you can get a rubdown, but the most relaxing is poolside. ✉ *701 E. Palm Canyon Dr., Palm Springs* ☎ *760/866–6188* ⊕ *www.acehotel.com/ palmsprings* ☞ *Services: wraps and scrubs, massage, facials, paraffin, manicures, pedicures, in-room treatments, fully equipped gym, wellness classes, yoga, water aerobics. $95 60-min massage.*

Palm Springs Yacht Club. It's all about fun at the Palm Springs Yacht Club in the Parker Palm Springs hotel. Guests receive a complimentary shot of whiskey, vodka, or the Commodore Special while lounging in a poolside tent. Before your treatments, you can play video games, use an iPod Touch, or select a book from the spa's library. When you're ready to crash, wander over to the outdoor café for a burger and Pimm's. Treatments might feature local clay or stones. There's a fine Thai massage as well. ✉ *4200 E. Palm Canyon Dr., Palm Springs* ☎ *760/321–4606*

⊕ *www.theparkerpalmsprings.com/spa* ⚲ *Sauna, steam room, indoor pool, library. Services: scrubs and wraps, massage, facials, manicures, pedicures, waxing, salon, fitness center with Cybex equipment, dining and cocktails. $150 60-min massage.*

Spa Resort Casino. Taking the waters at this resort is an indulgent pleasure. You can spend a full day enjoying a five-step, wet-and-dry treatment that includes a mineral bath with water from the original spring, steam, sauna, and eucalyptus inhalation. The program allows you to take fitness classes and use the gym and, for an extra charge, add massage or body treatments. Bring a swimsuit for sunbathing and swimming in the pool. ✉ *100 N. Indian Canyon Dr., at E. Tahquitz Canyon Way, Palm Springs* ☎ *760/778–1772* ⊕ *www.sparesortcasino.com* ⚲ *Hair and nail salon, sauna, steam room, hot tubs, relaxation room, lounge. Gym with: cardiovascular equipment, free weights, circuit machines. Services: body wraps and scrubs, facials, massage, waxing, salon services. $115 50-min massage, $285 spa package.*

THE DESERT RESORTS

The term *desert resorts* refers to the communities along or just off Highway 111—Cathedral City, Rancho Mirage, Palm Desert, Indian Wells, Indio, and La Quinta—along with Desert Hot Springs, which is north of Palm Springs off Highway 62 and Interstate 10.

CATHEDRAL CITY

2 miles southeast of Palm Springs.

Cathedral City is more residential than tourist-oriented, with large and small malls everywhere, but the city has several good restaurants and entertainment venues with moderate prices.

GETTING HERE AND AROUND

Cathedral City lies due east of the Palm Springs International Airport. Main streets north and south are Landau and Date Palm; west to east are Ramon Road, Dinah Shore, and Highway 111.

EXPLORING

FAMILY **Boomers Palm Springs.** At this theme park you can play mini golf, drive bumper boats, climb a rock wall, drive a go-kart, swing in the batting cages, test your skills in an arcade, and play video games. ✉ *67-700 E. Palm Canyon Dr., at Cree Rd.* ☎ *760/770–7522* ⊕ *www.boomersparks. com/site/PalmSprings* ⚐ *$7–$9 per activity, $27 day passes* ☉ *Mon.– Thurs. 12–9, Fri. 12–11, Sat. 11–11, Sun. 11–8.*

Pickford Salon at the Mary Pickford Theater. This small museum inside a multiplex celebrates silent film star Mary Pickford. Items on display include her 1976 Oscar for contributions to the film industry, a gown she wore in the 1927 film *Dorothy Vernon of Haddon Hall,* and dinnerware from Pickfair, the Beverly Hills mansion she shared with actor Douglas Fairbanks. Pickford herself produced one of the film bios the Salon screens. ✉ *Mary Pickford Theatre, 36-850 Pickfair St., at Buddy Rogers Ave.* ☎ *760/328–7100* ⚐ *Free* ☉ *Daily 10:30 am–midnight.*

14

WHERE TO EAT

$$$ ✕ **Cello's.** A favorite of locals and critics, this art-laden café in a strip
BISTRO mall serves modern twists on classics such as the crab Napoleon and
onion soup fondue, as starters, and liver and onions, chicken *Caprese*,
and eggplant Parmesan as main courses. The owner, Bonnie Barley, is as
friendly as they come. $ *Average main: $23* ✉ *35-943 Date Palm Dr.,
at Gerald Ford Dr.* ☎ *760/328–5353* ⊕ *www.cellosbistro.com* ⌂ *Reservations essential.*

$$$ ✕ **Trilussa.** Locals gather here for delicious food, big drinks, and a
ITALIAN friendly welcome. The bar is busy during happy hour, after which diners drift to their nicely spaced tables indoors and out. The long menu
changes daily, but staples include antipasti, homemade pasta, pizza,
risotto, veal, and fish. All come with an Italian accent. $ *Average main:
$27* ✉ *68718 E. Palm Canyon Dr., at Monty Hall Dr.* ☎ *760/328–2300*
⌂ *Reservations essential.*

DESERT HOT SPRINGS

9 miles north of Palm Springs.

Desert Hot Springs's famous hot mineral waters, thought by some to
have curative powers, bubble up at temperatures of 90°F to 148°F and
flow into the wells of more than 40 hotel spas.

GETTING HERE AND AROUND
Desert Hot Springs lies due north of Palm Springs. Take Gene Autry
Trail north to Interstate 10, where the street name changes to Palm.
Continue north to Pierson Boulevard, the town's center.

EXPLORING
Cabot's Pueblo Museum. Cabot Yerxa, the man who found the spring that
made Desert Hot Springs famous, built a quirky four-story, 35-room
pueblo between 1939 and his death in 1965. Now a museum run by
the city of Desert Hot Springs—Yerxa was the town's first mayor—the
Hopi-inspired adobe structure is filled with memorabilia of his time as
a homesteader; his encounters with Hollywood celebrities at the nearby
Bar-H Ranch; his expedition to the Alaskan gold rush; and many other
events. The home, much of it crafted out of materials Yerxa recycled
from the desert, can only be seen on hour-long tours. Outside, you can
walk the beautiful grounds to a lookout with amazing desert views.
✉ *67-616 E. Desert View Ave., at Eliseo Rd.* ☎ *760/329–7610* ⊕ *www.
cabotsmuseum.org* ⌂ *$11* ⊙ *Tues.–Sun. 9–4, tours 9:30, 10:30, 11:30,
1:30, 2:30.*

WHERE TO STAY
$$$ ⛺ **The Spring.** Designed for those who want to detox, lose weight, or
HOTEL chill out in the mineral pools, The Spring delivers quiet and personal
service atop a Desert Hot Springs hill. **Pros:** access to mineral pools 24
hours a day; complimentary Continental breakfast; spa and lodging
packages available. **Cons:** rooms lack character. $ *Rooms from: $179*
✉ *12699 Reposo Way* ☎ *760/251–6700, 877/200–2110* ⊕ *www.the-
spring.com* ⇲ *12 rooms* ❙❀❙ *Breakfast.*

The Desert
Resorts

SHOPPING

SPAS

 Fodor's Choice ★ **Two Bunch Palms.** This iconic retreat has long been a favorite with Los Angeles yogis for its peaceful, palm-shaded grounds and hot springs pools. With 2014 came big changes, with new rooms added and a fresh look for the existing ones. Guests can still purchase a day pass to soak in the grotto, attend yoga classes, and lounge on the grounds, and of course enjoy a spa treatment or two. ■**TIP→ This is an adults-only, whispers-only destination.** ✉ *67-425 Two Bunch Palms Tr.* ☎ *760/329–8791* ⊕ *www.twobunchpalms.com* 🖃 *Day pass $25 weekdays, $40 weekends* ⊙ *Day use daily 10–6* ☞ *Services: facials, nail care, solo and couple's massages, breath work, water, and other therapies. $130 60-min massage.*

RANCHO MIRAGE

4 miles southeast of Cathedral City.

The rich and famous of Rancho Mirage live in beautiful estates and patronize elegant resorts and expensive restaurants. Although many mansions here are concealed behind the walls of gated communities and country clubs, the grandest of them all, Sunnylands, the Annenberg residence, is open to the public as a museum and public garden.

The city's golf courses host many high-profile tournaments. You'll find some of the desert's fanciest resorts in Rancho Mirage, and plenty of peace and quiet. For those truly needing to take things down a notch further, the Betty Ford Center, the famous drug-and-alcohol rehab center, is also here.

GETTING HERE AND AROUND

Due east of Cathedral City, Rancho Mirage stretches from Ramon Road on the north to the hills south of Highway 111. The western border is Da Vall Drive, the eastern one Monterey Avenue. Major east–west cross streets are Frank Sinatra Drive and Country Club Drive. Most shopping and dining spots are on Highway 111.

EXPLORING

The Annenberg Retreat at Sunnylands. The stunning 25,000-square-foot winter home and retreat of the late Ambassador Walter H. and Leonore Annenberg opened to the public in 2012. You can spend a whole day enjoying the 9 glorious acres of gardens, or take a guided 90-minute tour of the residence (reservations essential), a striking midcentury modern edifice designed by A. Quincy Jones. Floor-to-ceiling windows frame views of the gardens and Mount San Jacinto, and the expansive rooms hold furnishings from the 1960s and later, along with impressionist art (some original, some replicas). The history made here is as captivating as the surroundings. Eight U.S. presidents—from Dwight Eisenhower to Barack Obama—and their First Ladies have visited Sunnylands; Ronald and Nancy Reagan were frequent guests. Britain's Queen Elizabeth and Prince Philip also relaxed here, as did Princess Grace of Monaco and Japanese Prime Minister Toshiki Kaifu. Photos, art, letters, journals, and mementos provide insights into some of the history that unfolded here. ⌂ *37-977 Bob Hope Dr., south of Gerald Ford Dr.* ☎ *760/202–2260* ⊕ *www.sunnylands.org* ☑ *Tours $35, tickets available online 2 wks in advance; visitor center and gardens free* ⊙ *Thurs.–Sun. 9-4* ⊙ *Closed July–Aug. and during retreats.*

FAMILY **Children's Discovery Museum of the Desert.** With instructive hands-on exhibits, this museum contains a miniature rock-climbing area, a magnetic sculpture wall, make-it-and-take-it-apart projects, a rope maze, and an area for toddlers. Kids can paint a VW Bug, work as chefs in the museum's pizza parlor, and build pies out of arts and crafts supplies. There's also a racetrack for which kids can assemble their own cars. ⌂ *71-701 Gerald Ford Dr., at Bob Hope Dr.* ☎ *760/321–0602* ⊕ *www. cdmod.org* ☑ *$8* ⊙ *Jan.–Apr., daily 10–5; May–Dec., Tues.–Sun. 10–5.*

WHERE TO EAT AND STAY

$$ ✕ **Acqua Pazza.** At this hoppin' spot in The River complex, you can dine
AMERICAN outside along the titular man-made waterway or indoors in the colorful dining room. Acqua Pazza serves well-made salads, pizzas, burgers, and steaks, along with more adventurous fare such as the half a duck entrée and wild Corvina sea bass, both served on rice pilaf. The plentiful desserts include a fanciful selection of Italian-style ice creams. The same people operate the equally lively and popular Lulu's California Bistro, in downtown Palm Springs. $ *Average main: $22* ⌂ *The River, 71-800 Hwy. 111* ☎ *760/862–9800* ⊕ *www.acquapazzabistro.com.*

$$$ MEDITERRANEAN 🍴 **Catalan.** Beautifully prepared and presented Mediterranean cuisine stands out in this inventive restaurant, where you can dine inside or under the stars in the atrium. The service is attentive, and the menu roams the Riviera and beyond. Entrées include fabulous seared scallops with wild mushrooms, pan-roasted rainbow trout, and paella with clams, calamari chorizo, and Laughing Bird shrimp. [$] *Average main: $30* ✉ *70026 Hwy. 111* ☎ *760/770–9508* 🌐 *www.catalanrestaurant.com* ✍ *Reservations essential.*

$ RESORT 🏨 **Agua Caliente Casino, Resort & Spa.** As in Las Vegas, the Agua Caliente casino is in the lobby, but once you get into the spacious, beautifully appointed rooms of the resort, all the cacophony at the entrance is forgotten. **Pros:** gorgeous; access to high-rollers room offered for $25; value priced. **Cons:** casino ambience; not appropriate for kids. [$] *Rooms from: $111* ✉ *32-250 Bob Hope Dr.* ☎ *888/999–1995* 🌐 *www.hotwatercasino.com* 🛏 *340 rooms, 26 suites* 🍽 *No meals.*

14

$$$$ RESORT FAMILY 🏨 **Rancho Las Palmas Resort & Spa.** The desert's most family-friendly resort, this large venue holds Splashtopia, a huge water play-zone. **Pros:** family-friendly; trails for hiking and jogging; nightly entertainment. **Cons:** second-floor rooms accessed by very steep stairs; golf course surrounds rooms; resort hosts conventions. [$] *Rooms from: $279* ✉ *41-000 Bob Hope Dr.* ☎ *760/568–2727, 866/423–1195* 🌐 *www.rancholaspalmas.com* 🛏 *422 rooms, 22 suites* 🍽 *No meals.*

$$$ RESORT FAMILY 🏨 **Westin Mission Hills Resort and Spa.** A sprawling resort on 360 acres, the Westin is surrounded by fairways, putting greens, and time-share accommodations; rooms, in two-story buildings amid patios and fountains, have a stylish Arts and Crafts look with sleek mahogany furnishings accented with sand-color upholstery and crisp white linens. **Pros:** gorgeous grounds; first-class golf facilities; daily activity program for kids. **Cons:** rooms are spread out. [$] *Rooms from: $239* ✉ *71333 Dinah Shore Dr.* ☎ *760/328–5955, 800/937–8461* 🌐 *www.westinmissionhills.com* 🛏 *512 rooms, 40 suites* 🍽 *No meals.*

NIGHTLIFE

Agua Caliente Casino. This elegant and surprisingly quiet casino contains 1,400 slot machines, 39 table games, an 18-table poker room, a high-limit room, a no-smoking area, and six restaurants. The Show, the resort's concert theater, presents acts such as Liza Minnelli, ZZ Top, and Ray Romano, as well as live sporting events. ✉ *32-250 Bob Hope Dr., at E. Ramon Rd.* ☎ *760/321–2000* 🌐 *www.hotwatercasino.com.*

SPORTS AND THE OUTDOORS

GOLF

Kraft Nabisco Championship. The best female golfers in the world compete in this championship held in late March or early April. ✉ *Mission Hills Country Club* ☎ *760/324–4546* 🌐 *www.kncgolf.com.*

Fodor's Choice ★ **Westin Mission Hills Resort Golf Club.** Golfers at the Westin Mission Hills Resort have two courses to choose from, the Pete Dye and the Gary Player Signature. They're both great, with amazing mountain views and wide fairways, but if you've only got time to play one, choose the Dye. The club is a member of the Troon Golf Institute, and has several teaching facilities, including the Westin Mission Hills Resort Golf Academy and the *Golf Digest* Golf School. ■TIP➜ The resort's Best Available Rate program guarantees golfers (with a few conditions) the best Internet rate possible. ✉ *71333 Dinah Shore Dr.* ☎ *760/328–3198* ⊕ *www. playmissionhills.com* ✉ *$99–$109* ⛳. *Pete Dye Resort: 18 holes, 5525 yards, par 72; Gary Player Signature: 18 holes, 5327 yards, par 70.*

SHOPPING

MALL

The River at Rancho Mirage. This shopping-dining-entertainment complex holds 20 high-end shops, including the So-Cal darling Diane's Beachwear, all fronting a faux river with cascading waterfalls. Also here are a 12-screen cinema, an outdoor amphitheater, and eight restaurants including Acqua Pazza, Fleming's Prime Steakhouse, and Babe's Bar-B-Que and Brewery. ✉ *71-800 Hwy. 111, at Bob Hope Dr.* ☎ *760/341– 2711* ⊕ *www.theriveratranchomirage.com.*

SPAS

The Spa at Mission Hills. The emphasis at this spa tucked into a quiet corner of the Weston Mission Hills Resort is on comfort rather than glitz and glamour. The treatments the attentive therapists administer incorporate coconut milk, lemon balm, mint, thyme, red algae, hydrating honey, and other botanicals. Yoga and other wellness classes are also available. ✉ *71333 Dinah Shore Dr.* ☎ *760/770–2134* ⊕ *www.spaatmissionhills. com* ⌇ *Steam room. Gym with: machines, cardio, pool. Services: rubs and scrubs, massage, facials, nail services. $145 50-min massage.*

PALM DESERT

2 miles southeast of Rancho Mirage.

Palm Desert is a thriving retail and business community with popular restaurants, private and public golf courses, and premium shopping along the main commercial drag, El Paseo. Each October, the Palm Desert Golf Cart Parade launches "the season" with a procession of 80 golf carts decked out as floats buzzing up and down El Paseo. The town's stellar sight to see is the Living Desert complex.

GETTING HERE AND AROUND

Palm Desert stretches from north of Interstate 10 to the hills south of Highway 111. West–east cross streets north to south are Frank Sinatra Drive, Country Club Drive (lined on both sides with gated golfing communities), and Fred Waring Drive. Monterey Avenue marks the western boundary, and Washington Street forms the eastern edge.

EXPLORING

Fodor'sChoice
★

El Paseo. West of and parallel to Highway 111, this mile-long Mediterranean-style shopper's paradise is lined with fountains, courtyards, and upscale boutiques. You'll find shoe salons, jewelry stores, children's shops, two-dozen restaurants, and nearly as many art galleries. The strip is a pleasant place to stroll, window-shop, people-watch, and exercise your credit cards. ■TIP➜ In winter and spring a free bright-yellow shuttle ferries shoppers from store to store and back to their cars. ✉ *Between Monterey and Portola Aves.* ☎ *877/735–7273* ⊕ *www. elpaseo.com*

FAMILY Fodor's Choice ★ **Living Desert.** Come eyeball-to-eyeball with wolves, coyotes, mountain lions, cheetahs, bighorn sheep, golden eagles, warthogs, and owls at the 1,800-acre Living Desert. Easy-to-challenging scenic trails traverse desert terrain populated with plants of the Mojave, Colorado, and Sonoran deserts in numerous habitats. In recent years, the park has expanded its vision to include Africa. At the 3-acre African WaTuTu village, you'll find a traditional marketplace as well as camels, leopards, hyenas, and other African animals. Children can pet African domesticated animals, including goats and guinea fowl, in a "petting kraal." Gecko Gulch is a children's playground with crawl-through underground tunnels, climb-on snake sculptures, a carousel, and a Discovery Center that holds ancient Pleistocene animal bones. Elsewhere, a small enclosure contains butterflies and hummingbirds, and a cool model train travels through miniatures of historic California towns. ■ **TIP→ A garden center sells native desert flora, much of which is unavailable elsewhere.** ✉ *47900 Portola Ave., south from Hwy. 111* ☎ *760/346–5694* 🌐 *www.livingdesert.org* 🎟 *$17.25* 🕓 *June–Sept., daily 8–1:30; Oct.–May, daily 9–5.*

Palm Springs Art Museum in Palm Desert. A satellite branch of the Palm Springs Art Museum, this gallery space tucked into a desert garden at the west entrance to El Paseo exhibits cutting-edge works by contemporary sculptors and painters. ■ **TIP→ The on-site restaurant Cuistot (☎ 760/340–1000 🌐 www.cuistotrestaurant.com) is a splendid, if pricey, place to enjoy French cuisine.** ✉ *72-567 Hwy. 111* ☎ *760/346–5600* 🌐 *www.psmuseum.org* 🎟 *$5, free Thurs. 4–8* 🕓 *Tues., Wed., and Fri.–Sun. 10–5, Thurs. noon–8.*

Santa Rosa and San Jacinto Mountains National Monument. Administered by the U.S. Bureau of Land Management, this monument protects Peninsula bighorn sheep and other wildlife on 280,000 acres of desert habitat. Stop by the visitor center for an introduction to the site and information about the natural history of the desert. A landscaped garden displays native plants and frames a sweeping view. The well-informed staffers can recommend hiking trails that show off the beauties of the desert. ■ **TIP→ Free guided hikes are offered on Thursday and Saturday.** ✉ *51-500 Hwy. 74* ☎ *760/862–9984* 🌐 *www.ca.blm.gov/palmsprings* 🎟 *Free* 🕓 *Daily 9–4.*

WHERE TO EAT AND STAY

$ AMERICAN Fodor's Choice ★ 🍴 **Bouchee.** This La Quinta favorite disappeared abruptly, leaving devotees perplexed until it reemerged in a sparkling new space in a Palm Desert strip mall. Order the salads or gorgeous sandwiches—the salmon-salad one is to die for—at the counter and then repair to the French-inspired dining area. There's some shaded outdoor seating as well. ■ **TIP→ Bouchee closes at 6:30 on weekdays and 5 on weekends; arrive before then to buy wines, cheeses, and premade foods for dinner to go.** [$] *Average main: $8* ✉ *72-785 Hwy. 111* ☎ *442/666–3296* 🕓 *No dinner.*

$ ECLECTIC Fodor's Choice ★ 🍴 **Clementine's Gourmet Marketplace and Cafe.** A favorite of families, lunching ladies, and couples enjoying an afternoon tryst, Clementine's presents an artful mix of Mediterranean flavors. Diners at the café perch at long wooden communal tables to tuck into baked egg Ficelle, lamb burgers, and other specialties, but this space's nerve center is the take-out counter and kitchen that brims with pre-made salads, boulangerie-style meats and cheeses, and decadent French-inspired pastries and desserts. A small retail area sells aprons, glassware, and wines. Check the website to learn about evening events such as Italian-tapas dinners or the tastes of Greece. [$] *Average main: $12* ✉ *72990 El Paseo* ☎ *760/834–8814* 🌐 *www.clementineshop.com* ⏲ *No dinner.*

> **GREEN PALM DESERT**
>
> The City of Palm Desert's ambitious plan to reduce energy consumption includes incentives to install efficient pool pumps, air-conditioners, refrigeration, and lighting. The city has banned drive-through restaurants and made golf carts legal on city streets.

$$$$ SEAFOOD 🍴 **Pacifica Seafood.** Sublime seafood, rooftop dining, and reduced prices at sunset draw locals to this busy restaurant on the second floor of the Gardens of El Paseo. Seafood that shines in dishes such as butter-poached Maine lobster tail, grilled Pacific swordfish, and barbecued sugar-spiced salmon arrives daily from San Diego; the menu also includes chicken, steaks, and meal-size salads. Preparations feature sauces such as orange-cumin glaze, Szechuan peppercorn butter, and green curry-coconut. The restaurant bar boasts a 130-bottle vodka collection. **■ TIP→ Arrive between 3 and 5:30 to select from the lower-price sunset menu.** [$] *Average main: $36* ✉ *73505 El Paseo* ☎ *760/674–8666* 🌐 *www.pacificaseafoodrestaurant.com* ✍ *Reservations essential* ⏲ *No lunch June–Aug.*

$$$$ RESORT FAMILY 🏨 **Desert Springs J. W. Marriott Resort and Spa.** With a dramatic U-shape design, this sprawling convention-oriented hotel is set on 450 landscaped acres and wraps around the desert's largest private lake. **Pros:** gondola rides on the lake to restaurants; Kids Club daily activities; popular lobby bar; wonderful spa. **Cons:** crowded in season; high resort fee; extra charges; business-traveler vibe. [$] *Rooms from: $279* ✉ *74-855 Country Club Dr.* ☎ *760/341–2211, 888/538–9459* 🌐 *www.desertspringsresort.com* 🛏 *833 rooms, 51 suites* 🍽 *No meals.*

THE ARTS

McCallum Theatre. The principal cultural venue in the desert, this theater hosts productions from fall through spring. *Fiddler on the Roof* has played here; Lily Tomlin and Michael Feinstein have performed, and Joffrey Ballet dancers have pirouetted across the stage. ✉ *73-000 Fred Waring Dr.* ☎ *760/340–2787* 🌐 *www.mccallumtheatre.com.*

SPORTS AND THE OUTDOORS

BALLOONING

Fantasy Balloon Flights. Sunrise excursions ($195 per person) over the southern end of the Coachella Valley lift off at 6 am and take from 60 to 90 minutes; a traditional Champagne toast follows the landing. Afternoon excursions are timed to touch down at sunset. ☎ *760/568–0997* 🌐 *www.fantasyballoonflight.com.*

BIKING

Big Wheel Bike Tours. This outfit delivers rental mountain, three-speed, and tandem bikes to area hotels. The company also conducts full- and half-day escorted on- and off-road bike tours throughout the area, starting at about $95 per person. ☎ *760/779–1837* 🌐 *www.bwbtours.com.*

GOLF

Desert Willow Golf Resort. Praised for its environmentally smart design, this golf resort features pesticide-free and water-thrifty turf grasses. A public facility, this is one of the top-rated golf courses in the country. Mountain View has four configurations; Firecliff is tournament quality with five configurations. ✉ *38-995 Desert Willow Dr.* ☎ *760/346–0015* 🌐 *www.desertwillow.com* 🎫 *Mountain View from $99, Firecliff from $65* ⛳ *Mountain View: 18 holes, 7079 yards, par 72; Firecliff: 18 holes, 7056 yards, par 72.*

INDIAN WELLS

5 miles east of Palm Desert.

For the most part a quiet and exclusive residential enclave, Indian Wells hosts major golf and tennis tournaments throughout the year, including the BNP Paribus Open tennis tournament. Three hotels share access to championship golf and tennis facilities, and there are several noteworthy resort spas and restaurants.

GETTING HERE AND AROUND

Indian Wells lies between Palm Desert and La Quinta, with most resorts, restaurants, and shopping set back from Highway 111.

WHERE TO EAT AND STAY

$$$ AMERICAN — 🍴 **Vue Grille and Bar at the Indian Wells Golf Resort.** This not-so-private restaurant at the Indian Wells Golf Resort offers a glimpse of how the country club set lives. The service is impeccable, and the outdoor tables provide views of mountain peaks that seem close enough to touch. The focus is on farm-to-table cuisine, with kale and quinoa salads, diver scallops atop a yuzu purée, and a Jidori chicken breast hugged by cheesy polenta among the offerings. [$] *Average main: $29* ✉ *44-500 Indian Wells La.* ☎ *760/834–3800* 🌐 *www.iwclub.com* ✍ *Reservations essential.*

$$$ RESORT FAMILY Fodor's Choice ★ — 🏨 **Hyatt Grand Regency Indian Wells Resort.** This stark-white resort, set adjacent to the Golf Resort at Indian Wells, is one of the grandest in the desert. **Pros:** spacious rooms; excellent business services; butler service in some rooms; very pet-friendly. **Cons:** big and impersonal; spread out over 45 acres; noisy public areas. [$] *Rooms from: $239* ✉ *44-600 Indian Wells La.* ☎ *760/341–1000, 800/552–4386* 🌐 *www.grandchampions.hyatt.com* 🛏 *454 rooms, 26 suites, 40 villas* 🍽 *No meals.*

$$$$ RESORT — 🏨 **Miramonte Resort & Spa.** A warm bit of Tuscany against a backdrop of the Santa Rosa Mountains characterizes the smallest, most intimate, and most opulent of the Indian Wells hotels. **Pros:** romantic intimacy; gorgeous gardens; daily wellness classes; one of the desert's best spas. **Cons:** adult-oriented; limited resort facilities on-site; rooms could use some refreshing. [$] *Rooms from: $259* ✉ *45000 Indian Wells Lane* ☎ *760/341–2200* 🌐 *www.miramonteresort.com* 🛏 *215 rooms* 🍽 *Some meals.*

$$$$ RESORT FAMILY [hotel] **Renaissance Esmeralda Resort and Spa.** The centerpiece of this luxurious resort, adjacent to the Golf Resort at Indian Wells, is an eight-story atrium lobby, onto which most rooms open. **Pros:** balcony views; adjacent to golf-tennis complex; kids club; bicycles available. **Cons:** higher noise level in rooms surrounding pool; somewhat impersonal ambience. [$] *Rooms from: $259* ✉ *44-400 Indian Wells La.* ☎ *760/773–4444* 🌐 *www.renaissanceesmeralda.com* 🛏 *538 rooms, 22 suites* 🍴 *No meals.*

SPORTS AND THE OUTDOORS

GOLF

Fodor's Choice ★ **Golf Resort at Indian Wells.** Adjacent to the Hyatt Regency Indian Wells, this complex includes the Celebrity Course, designed by Clive Clark and twice a host to the PGA's Skins game (lots of water here), and the Players Course, designed by John Fought to incorporate views of the surrounding mountain ranges. Both courses consistently rank among the best public courses in California. **TIP→ It's a good idea to book tee times well in advance, up to 60 days.** ✉ *44-500 Indian Wells La.* ☎ *760/346–4653* 🌐 *www.indianwellsgolfresort.com* 🎫 *Celebrity, $59–$199; Players, $79–$239* ⛳ *Celebrity Course: 18 holes, 7050 yards, par 72; Players Course: 18 holes, 7376 yards, par 72.*

TENNIS

BNP Paribas Open. Drawing 200 of the world's top players, this tennis tournament takes place at Indian Wells Tennis Garden for two weeks in March. Various ticket plans are available, with some packages including stays at the adjoining Hyatt Regency Indian Wells or Renaissance Esmeralda resorts. ✉ *78200 Miles Ave.* ☎ *800/999–1585* 🌐 *www.bnpparibasopen.com.*

SHOPPING

SPAS

Fodor's Choice ★ **The Well.** The desert's most innovative spa, a luxurious 12,000-square-foot facility, draws on international treatments and ingredients to indulge the senses and relax the body. Treatments such as wine baths, water massages, table yoga, and the ancient Ayurvedic Shirodhara experience, which involves liquids poured over the forehead, are well worth the splurge. Diamond facials and precious-stone exfoliating scrubs may well restore the soul in addition to the skin. ✉ *Miramonte Resort, 45-000 Indian Wells La.* ☎ *866/843–9355* 🌐 *www.miramonteresort.com* 🕘 *Daily 9–8* ☞ *Services: facials, nail care, solo and couple's massages, and scrubs, water, and other body therapies; massage treatments begin at $100 for 60 mins.*

LA QUINTA

4 miles south of Indian Wells.

The desert became a Hollywood hideout in the 1920s, when La Quinta Hotel (now La Quinta Resort and Club) opened, introducing the Coachella Valley's first golf course. Old Town La Quinta is a popular attraction; the area holds dining spots, shops, and galleries.

GETTING HERE AND AROUND

Most of La Quinta lies south of Highway 111. The main drag through town is Washington Street.

WHERE TO EAT AND STAY

$$$ AMERICAN 🍴 **Arnold Palmer's.** From the photos on the walls to the trophy-filled display cases to the putting green for diners awaiting a table, Arnie's essence infuses this restaurant. It's a big, clubby place where families gather for birthdays and Sunday dinners, and the service is always attentive. Among the well-crafted main courses are Arnie's homemade meat loaf, double-cut pork chops, and the popular mac and cheese. The wine list is top-notch, and there's entertainment most nights. At Arnie's Pub, the more limited menu focuses on comfort food. [$] *Average main: $28* ✉ *78164 Ave. 52* ☎ *760/771–4653* 🌐 *www.arnoldpalmersrestaurant.com* ✍ *Reservations essential.*

$$$$ BISTRO Fodor's Choice ★ 🍴 **Lavender Bistro.** This romantic bistro gives diners the impression that they've been transported to southern France. The spacious outdoor atrium is decked out with flowers, fountains, and twinkling lights. Choices on the large menu include a take-home portion of steamed mussels, rack of lamb with olive tapenade, and crispy roasted duck with orange sauce. For dessert you can't go wrong with the baked apple tart with frangipane or the banana walnut brioche bread pudding. Dessert wines and cognacs are also available. [$] *Average main: $34* ✉ *78073 Calle Barcelona* ☎ *760/327–8311* 🌐 *www.lavenderbistro.com* ✍ *Reservations essential.*

$$$ AMERICAN Fodor's Choice ★ 🍴 **Hog's Breath Inn La Quinta–The Desert Hog.** Clint Eastwood watches over this replica of his Hog's Breath restaurant in Carmel, aptly nicknamed the "Desert Hog"; his presence is felt in the larger-than-life photos that fill the walls of the bright dining room. The large selection of American comfort food ranges from Guinness-braised short ribs to sole stuffed with crab. The signature dish is the Dirty Harry dinner: chopped sirloin with capers, garlic mashed potatoes, and red cabbage, served with horseradish mushroom sauce. **TIP→ The three-course Sunset Dinner ($19.95) is served between 4:30 and 6 except on holidays and holiday weekends.** [$] *Average main: $27* ✉ *78-065 Main St., 2nd floor* ☎ *760/564–5556, 866/464–7888* 🌐 *hogsbreathlaquinta.com* ✍ *Reservations essential.*

$$$ RESORT FAMILY 🏨 **La Quinta Resort and Club.** Opened in 1926 and now a member of the Waldorf-Astoria Collection, the desert's oldest resort is a lush green oasis set on 45 acres. **Pros:** individual swimming pools; gorgeous gardens; pet- and family-friendly. **Cons:** a party atmosphere sometimes prevails; spotty housekeeping/maintenance. [$] *Rooms from: $179* ✉ *49499 Eisenhower Dr.* ☎ *760/564–4111, 800/598–3828* 🌐 *www.laquintaresort.com* 🛏 *562 rooms, 24 suites, 210 villas* 🍽 *No meals.*

THE ARTS

La Quinta Arts Festival. More than 200 artists participate each March in a four-day juried show that's considered one of the best in the West. The event, held at La Quinta Civic Center, includes sculptures, paintings, watercolors, fiber art, and ceramics. ✉ *78495 Calle Tampico* ☎ *760/564–1244* 🌐 *www.lqaf.com* 🎟 *$12; multiday tickets $15.*

SPORTS AND THE OUTDOORS

GOLF

Fodor'sChoice   **PGA West.** A world-class golf destination where Phil Mickelson and Jack
★   Nicklaus play, this private/public facility includes five resort courses and
four private ones. Courses meander through indigenous desert landscapes, water features, and bunkers. The Norman, Nick Tournament
and TPC Stadium courses are "shot-makers" courses made for pros.
TPC highlights include its two lakes, "San Andreas Fault" bunker, and
island green called "Alcatraz." The Norman course has tight fairways
and small greens. ⊠ *49-499 Eisenhower Dr.* ☎ *760/564-5729 for tee
times* ⊕ *www.pgawest.com* ✉ *Mountain Course, $69–$230; Dunes,
$49–$185; Greg Norman, $69–$225; TPC Stadium, $79–$230; Jack
Nicklaus Tournament, $69–$230* ⚑ *Mountain Course: 18 holes, 6732
yards, par 72; Dunes: 18 holes, 6712 yards, par 72; Greg Norman: 18
holes, 7156 yards, par 72; TPC Stadium: 18 holes, 7300 yards, par 72;
Jack Nicklaus Tournament: 18 holes, 7204 yards, par 72.*

SHOPPING

SPAS

Spa La Quinta. The gorgeous Spa La Quinta may be the grandest spa in
the entire desert. At this huge stand-alone facility you'll find everything
from massages to facials to salon services, plus a beautiful garden setting
with a large fountain, flowers galore, and plenty of nooks where you
can hide out and enjoy the sanctuary. There are four outdoor treatment
spaces, showers, secluded soaking tubs, and a Jacuzzi with a waterfall.
The spa uses organic products including SpaRitual and Davines hair-
care line. ■TIP➔ **Spa La Quinta has a Canine Suite where your dog
can enjoy a massage. The canine services are also offered in-room.**
⊠ *49499 Eisenhower Dr.* ☎ *760/777–4800* ⊕ *www.laquintaresort.com*
↻ *Fitness center with: cardio and weight training machines. Services:
aromatherapy, body wraps and scrubs, massage, skin care, waxing,
salon services, water therapies. $150 50-min massage; $250 30-min
HydraFacial; $105 45-min junior spa; $36 10-min celestial shower;
$50 20-min garden bath.*

INDIO

5 miles east of Indian Wells.

Indio is the home of the date shake, which is exactly what it sounds
like: an extremely thick milk shake made with dates. The city and surrounding countryside generate 95% of the dates grown and harvested
in the United States. If you take a hot-air balloon ride, you will likely
drift over the tops of date palm trees.

GETTING HERE AND AROUND

Indio is east of Indian Wells and north of La Quinta. Highway 111 runs
right through Indio, and Interstate 10 skirts it to the north.

EXPLORING

FAMILY   **Coachella Valley History Museum.** Make a date to learn about dates at
this museum inside a former farmhouse. The exhibits here provide an
intriguing glimpse into irrigation, harvesting, and other farming practices;

a timeline and other displays chronicle how the industry emerged in the desert a century ago. ✉ *82616 Miles Ave.* ☎ *760/342–6651* 🌐 *www.cvhm.org* 🎫 *$10* 🕘 *Oct.–May, Thurs.–Sat. 10–4, Sun. 1–4.*

FAMILY **National Date Festival and Riverside County Fair.** Indio celebrates its raison d'être each February at this festival and county fair. The mid-month festivities include an Arabian Nights pageant, camel and ostrich races, and exhibits of local dates, plus monster truck shows, a demolition derby, a nightly musical pageant, and a rodeo. Admission includes camel rides. ✉ *Riverside County Fairgrounds, 82-503 Hwy. 111* ☎ *800/811–3247, 760/863–8247* 🌐 *www.datefest.org* 🎫 *$8.*

Shields Date Garden and Café. Sample, select, and take home some of Shields's locally grown dates. Ten varieties are available, including the giant super-sweet royal medjools, along with specialty date products such as date crystals, stuffed dates, confections, and local honey. At the Shields Date Garden Café, you can try an iconic date shake, dig into date pancakes, or go exotic with a date tamale. Breakfast and lunch are served daily. ✉ *80-225 Hwy. 111* ☎ *760/347–0996* 🌐 *www.shieldsdategarden.com* 🕘 *Store 9–5, café 7–2:30* 🕘 *No dinner.*

14

WHERE TO EAT AND STAY

$$ SICILIAN 🍴 **Ciro's Ristorante and Pizzeria.** Serving pizza and pasta since the 1960s, this popular casual restaurant has a few unusual pies on the menu, including cashew with three cheeses. The decor is classic pizza joint, with checkered tablecloths and bentwood chairs. Daily pasta specials vary but might include red- or white-clam sauce or scallops with parsley and red wine. [$] *Average main: $17* ✉ *81-963 Hwy. 111* ☎ *760/347–6503* 🌐 *www.cirospasta.com* 🕘 *No lunch Sun.*

$$$ AMERICAN 🍴 **Jackalope Ranch.** It's worth the drive to Indio to sample flavors of the Old West here, 21st-century style. Inside a rambling 21,000 foot building, holding a clutch of indoor/outdoor dining spaces, you may be seated near an open kitchen, a bar, fountains, fireplaces, or waterworks (both inside and out). Jackalope can be a busy, noisy place; ask for a quiet corner if that's your pleasure. The large menu roams the West, featuring grilled and barbecued items of all sorts, spicy and savory sauces, flavorful vegetables, and sumptuous desserts. Locals like the place, especially the bar; but some urbanites complain that the quality of the food doesn't match the setting. [$] *Average main: $24* ✉ *80-400 Hwy. 111* ☎ *760/342–1999* 🌐 *www.thejackaloperanch.com* ✍ *Reservations essential.*

$$ HOTEL FAMILY 🏨 **Fantasy Springs Resort Casino.** Operated by the Cabazon Band of Mission Indians, this family-oriented resort casino stands out in the Coachella Valley, affording mountain views from most rooms and the rooftop wine bar. **Pros:** headliner entertainment; great views from the rooftop bar; bowling alley; golf course. **Cons:** in the middle of nowhere; average staff service. [$] *Rooms from: $139* ✉ *84-245 Indio Springs Pkwy.* ☎ *760/342–5000, 800/827–2946* 🌐 *www.fantasyspringsresort.com* 🛏 *240 rooms, 11 suites* 🍽 *No meals.*

NIGHTLIFE AND THE ARTS
MUSIC FESTIVALS

Fodor'sChoice ★ **Coachella Valley Music and Arts Festival.** Among Southern California's biggest parties, the festival draws hundreds of thousands of rock music fans to Indio each April for two weekends of live concerts. Headliners include acts such as Arcade Fire, Jack Johnson, Beck, Lorde, Portishead, Roger Waters, and Radiohead. Many attendees camp on-site, but to give your ears a rest post-concert you might want to stay at a nearby hotel. ■TIP→ The festival sells out within hours in January, when the lineup is announced, so expect to pay big bucks if you haven't purchased tickets by then. ✉ *Empire Polo Club, 81-800 Ave. 51* ⊕ *www. coachella.com.*

EN ROUTE **Coachella Valley Preserve.** For a glimpse of how the desert appeared before development, head northeast from Palm Springs to this preserve. It has a system of sand dunes and several palm oases that were formed because the San Andreas Fault lines here allow water flowing underground to rise to the surface. A mile-long walk along Thousand Palms Oasis reveals pools supporting the tiny endangered desert pupfish and more than 183 bird species. Families like the relatively flat trail that is mostly shaded. The preserve has a visitor center, nature and equestrian trails, restrooms, and picnic facilities. Guided hikes are offered. ■TIP→ Be aware that it's exceptionally hot in summer here. ✉ *29200 Thousand Palms Canyon Rd., Thousand Palms* ☎ *760/343–2733* ⊕ *www.coachellavalleypreserve.org* ✑ *Free* ☉ *Visitor Center: Sept. 1–Oct. 14, daily 8–noon; Oct. 15–Apr. 14, daily 8–4; Apr. 15–May 31, daily 8–noon* ☉ *Closed June–Aug.*

ALONG TWENTYNINE PALMS HIGHWAY

Designated a California Scenic Highway, the Twentynine Palms Highway connects two of the three entrances to Joshua Tree National Park and provides gorgeous high-desert views, especially in winter and spring when you might find yourself driving beneath snowcapped peaks or through a field of wildflowers. Park entrances are located at Joshua Tree and Twentynine Palms. Yucca Valley and Twentynine Palms have lodging and dining options, and other services. If you see any strange artwork along the way, they might be created by artists associated with the avant-garde High Desert Test Sites (⊕ *www.highdeserttestsites.com).*

YUCCA VALLEY

30 miles northeast of Palm Springs.

One of the high desert's fastest-growing cities, Yucca Valley is emerging as a bedroom community for people who work as far away as Ontario, 85 miles to the west. In this suburb you can shop for necessities, get your car serviced, grab coffee or purchase vintage furnishings, and chow down at fast-food outlets. Just up Pioneertown Road you'll find the most-talked-about dining establishment in the desert, Pappy and Harriet's, the famed performance venue that hosts big-name talent.

GETTING HERE AND AROUND

The drive to Yucca Valley on Highway 62/Twentynine Palms Highway passes through the Painted Hills and drops down into a valley. Take Pioneertown Road north to the Old West outpost.

EXPLORING

FAMILY **Hi-Desert Nature Museum.** Creatures that make their homes in Joshua Tree National Park are the focus here. A small live-animal display includes scorpions, snakes, ground squirrels, and chuckwallas (a type of lizard). You'll also find rocks, minerals, and fossils from the Paleozoic era and Native American artifacts, and there's a children's room. ✉ *Yucca Valley Community Center, 57116 Twentynine Palms Hwy.* ☎ *760/369–7212* 🌐 *hidesertnaturemuseum.org* 🎟 *Free* 🕒 *Tues.–Sat. 10–5.*

Pioneertown. In 1946 Roy Rogers, Gene Autry, the Sons of the Pioneers (the music group for whom the town is named), and Russ Hayden built Pioneertown, an 1880s-style Wild West movie set complete with hitching posts, saloon, and an OK Corral. You can stroll past wooden and adobe storefronts and feel like you're back in the Old West. Or not: Pappy and Harriet's Pioneertown Palace, now the town's top draw, has evolved into a hip venue for indie and other bands. ✉ *53688 Pioneertown Rd., 4 miles north of Yucca Valley, Pioneertown* 🌐 *pappyandharriets.com.*

WHERE TO EAT AND STAY

$$$ AMERICAN FAMILY Fodor's Choice ★ 🍴 **Pappy & Harriet's Pioneertown Palace.** Smack in the middle of a Western-movie-set town is this Western-movie-set saloon where you can have dinner, relax over a drink at the bar, or check out some great indie and other bands—Leon Russell, Sonic Youth, the Get Up Kids, and Robert Plant have all played here, as have many Cali groups. The food ranges from Tex-Mex to Santa Maria–style barbecue to steak and burgers. No surprises but plenty of fun. **■ TIP→ Pappy & Harriet's may be in the middle of nowhere, but you'll need reservations for dinner on weekends, especially on Sunday night.** [$] *Average main: $24* ✉ *53688 Pioneertown Rd., Pioneertown* ☎ *760/365–5956* 🌐 *www.pappyandharriets.com* ✍ *Reservations essential* 🕒 *Closed Tues. and Wed.*

$ HOTEL 🏨 **Best Western Joshua Tree Hotel & Suites.** This hotel has spacious, nicely appointed rooms decorated in soft desert colors. **Pros:** convenient to Joshua Tree National Park; pleasant lounge. **Cons:** location on busy highway; limited service. [$] *Rooms from: $99* ✉ *56525 Twentynine Palms Hwy.* ☎ *760/365–3555* 🌐 *www.bestwestern.com* 🛏 *95 rooms* 🍽 *Breakfast.*

JOSHUA TREE

12 miles east of Yucca Valley.

Artists and renegades have long found solace in the small upcountry desert town of Joshua Tree, home to artsy vintage shops, cafés, and B&Bs and a gateway to Joshua Tree National Park. Those who zip through town might wonder what all the hype is about, but if you slow down and spend time chatting with the folks in this funky community, you'll find much to love.

14

GETTING HERE AND AROUND

Highway 62 is the main route to and through Joshua Tree. Most businesses are here or along Park Boulevard as it heads toward the park.

ESSENTIALS

Visitor Information **Joshua Tree Visitor Center** ✉ *6554 Park Blvd.* ☎ *760/366–1855* 🕒 *Daily 8–5.*

WHERE TO EAT AND STAY

$ AMERICAN 🍴 **Crossroads Cafe.** Mexican breakfasts, chicken-cilantro soup, and hearty sandwiches are among the draws at this Joshua Tree institution for pre-hike breakfasts, birthday lunches, and early dinners. With its stained-wood bar and black-and-white photos of the national park, the remodeled wooden interior still feels like it's been around for ages. Taxidermied animals and beer-can lights hint at the community's consciousness, while the tattooed waitresses and slew of veggie options make it clear the Crossroads is unlike anywhere else in San Bernardino County. [$] *Average main: $10* ✉ *61715 29 Palms Hwy.* ☎ *760/366–5414* 🌐 *www.crossroadscafejtree.com.*

$$$$ B&B/INN Fodor's Choice ★ 🏨 **Sacred Sands.** The dramatic exterior of this strawbale house, atop a mountain near Joshua Tree National Park's western entrance, hints at the design-forward intentions of the friendly owners, Scott and Steve. **Pros:** gorgeous design; extravagant breakfasts; convenient to Joshua Tree. **Cons:** expensive for the area; few nearby dining options. [$] *Rooms from: $329* ✉ *63155 Quail Springs Rd.* ☎ *760/424–6407* 🌐 *www.sacredsands.com* 🛏 *2 rooms* 🍽 *Breakfast.*

TWENTYNINE PALMS

12 miles east of Joshua Tree.

The main gateway town to Joshua Tree National Park (⇨ *see Chapter 15*), Twentynine Palms is also the location of the U.S. Marine Air Ground Task Force Training Center. You can find services, supplies, and lodging in town.

GETTING HERE AND AROUND

Highway 62 is the main route to and through Twentynine Palms. Most businesses here center around Highway 62 and Utah Trail, 3 miles north of Joshua Tree's entrance.

ESSENTIALS

Visitor Information **Twentynine Palms Chamber of Commerce and Visitor Center** ✉ *73484 Twentynine Palms Hwy.* ☎ *760/367–6197* 🌐 *www.visit29.org* 🕒 *Visitor Center Mon.–Fri. 9–5, Sat.–Sun. 10–4.*

EXPLORING

Oasis of Murals. The history and current life of Twentynine Palms is depicted in this collection of 20 murals painted on the sides of buildings. If you drive around town, you can't miss the murals, but you can also pick up a free map from the Twentynine Palms Chamber of Commerce.

29 Palms Art Gallery. This gallery features work by local painters, sculptors, and jewelry makers who find inspiration in the desert landscape. ✉ *74055 Cottonwood Dr.* ☎ *760/367–7819* 🌐 *www.29palmsartgallery.com* 🕒 *Wed.–Sun. noon–3.*

WHERE TO STAY

$ B&B/INN FAMILY Fodor'sChoice ★ 🏨 **29 Palms Inn.** The closest lodging to the entrance to Joshua Tree National Park, the funky 29 Palms Inn scatters a collection of adobe and wood-frame cottages, some dating back to the 1920s and 1930s, over 70 acres of grounds that include the ancient Oasis of Mara, a popular destination for birds and bird-watchers year-round. **Pros:** gracious hospitality; exceptional bird-watching; popular with artists. **Cons:** rustic accommodations; limited amenities. [$] *Rooms from: $70* ✉ *73950 Inn Ave.* ☎ *760/367–3505* 🌐 *www.29palmsinn.com* 🛏 *18 rooms, 5 suites* 🍴 *Breakfast.*

$$ B&B/INN 🏨 **Roughley Manor.** To the wealthy pioneer who erected the stone mansion now occupied by this B&B, expense was no object, which is evident in the 50-foot-long planked maple floor in the great room, the intricate carpentry on the walls, and the huge stone fireplaces that warm the house on the rare cold night. **Pros:** elegant rooms and public spaces; good stargazing in the gazebo; great horned owls on property. **Cons:** somewhat isolated location; three-story main building doesn't have an elevator. [$] *Rooms from: $135* ✉ *74744 Joe Davis Dr.* ☎ *760/367–3238* 🌐 *www.roughleymanor.com* 🛏 *2 suites, 7 cottages* 🍴 *Breakfast.*

ANZA-BORREGO DESERT

Largely uninhabited, the Anza-Borrego Desert is popular with those who love solitude, silence, space, starry nights, light, and sweeping mountain vistas. This desert lies south of the Palm Springs area, stretching along the western shore of the Salton Sea down toward Interstate 8 along the Mexican border. Isolated from the rest of California by mile-high mountains to the north and west, most of this desert falls within the borders of Anza-Borrego Desert State Park, which at more than 600,000 acres is the largest state park in the contiguous United States.

For thousands of years Native Americans of the Cahuilla and Kumeyaay people inhabited this area, spending their winters on the warm desert floor and their summers in the mountains. The first Europeans—a party led by the Spanish explorer Juan Baptiste de Anza—crossed this desert in 1776. Anza, for whom the desert is named, made the trip through here twice. Roadside signs along Highways 86, 78, and S2 mark the route of the Anza expedition, which spent Christmas Eve 1776 in what is now Anza-Borrego Desert State Park. Seventy-five years later thousands of immigrants on their way to the goldfields up north crossed the desert on the Southern Immigrant Trail, remnants of which remain along Highway S2. Permanent settlers arrived early in the 20th century, and by the 1930s the first adobe resort cottage had been built.

BORREGO SPRINGS

59 miles south of Indio.

The permanent population of Borrego Springs, set squarely in the middle of Anza-Borrego Desert State Park, hovers around 2,500. From September through June, when temperatures stay in the 80s and 90s, you can engage in outdoor activities such as hiking, nature study, golfing, tennis, horseback riding, and mountain biking. If winter rains cooperate, Borrego Springs puts on some of the best wildflower displays in the low desert. In some years the desert floor is carpeted with color: yellow dandelions and sunflowers, pink primrose, purple sand verbena, and blue wild heliotrope. The bloom generally lasts from late February through April. For current information on wildflowers around Borrego Springs, call Anza-Borrego Desert State Park's wildflower hotline (☎ 760/767–4684).

GETTING HERE AND AROUND

You can access Anza Borrego by taking the Highway 86 exit from Interstate 10, south of Indio. Highway 86 passes through Coachella and along the western shore of the Salton Sea. Turn west on Highway S22 at Salton City and follow it to Peg Leg Road, where you turn south until you reach Palm Canyon Drive. Turn west and the road leads to the center of Borrego Springs, Christmas Circle, where most major roads come together. Well-marked roads radiating from the circle will take you to the most popular sites in the state park. If coming from the San Diego area, drive east on Interstate 8 to the Cuyamaca Mountains, exit at Highway 79, and enjoy the lovely 23-mile drive through the mountains until you reach Julian; head east on Highway 78 and follow signs to Borrego Springs.

ESSENTIALS

Visitor Information Borrego Springs Chamber of Commerce ✉ *786 Palm Canyon Dr.* ☎ *760/767–5555, 800/559–5524* ⊕ *www.borregospringschamber.com.*

EXPLORING

Fodor's Choice   **Anza-Borrego Desert State Park.** One of the richest living natural-history
★   museums in the nation, this state park is a vast, nearly uninhabited wilderness where you can step through a field of wildflowers, cool off in a palm-shaded oasis, count zillions of stars in the black night sky, and listen to coyotes howl at dusk. The landscape, largely undisturbed by humans, reveals a rich natural history. There's evidence of a vast inland sea in the piles of oyster beds near Split Mountain and of the power of natural forces such as earthquakes and flash floods. In addition, recent scientific work has confirmed that the Borrego Badlands, with more than 6,000 meters of exposed fossil-bearing sediments, is likely the richest such deposit in North America, telling the story of 7 million years of climate change, upheaval, and prehistoric animals. They've found evidence of sabertooth cats, flamingos, zebras, and the largest flying bird in the Northern Hemisphere beneath the now-parched sand. Today the desert's most treasured inhabitants are the herds of elusive and endangered native bighorn sheep, or *borrego*, for which the park is named. Among the strange desert plants you may observe are the

If you think the desert is just a sandy wasteland, the colorful beauty of the Anza-Borrego Desert will be a pleasant surprise.

gnarly elephant trees. As these are endangered, rangers don't encourage visitors to seek out the secluded grove at Fish Creek, but there are a few examples at the visitor center garden. After a wet winter you can see a short-lived but stunning display of cacti, succulents, and desert wildflowers in bloom.

The park is unusually accessible to visitors. Admission to the park is free, and few areas are off-limits. There are two developed campgrounds, but you can camp anywhere; just follow the trails and pitch a tent wherever you like. There are more than 500 miles of dirt roads, two huge wilderness areas, and 110 miles of riding and hiking trails. Many sites can be seen from paved roads, but some require driving on dirt roads, for which rangers recommend you use a four-wheel-drive vehicle. When you do leave the pavement, carry the appropriate supplies: a cell phone (which may be unreliable in some areas), a shovel and other tools, flares, blankets, and plenty of water. The canyons are susceptible to flash flooding, so inquire about weather conditions (even on sunny days) before entering. ■ TIP➔ **Borrego resorts, restaurants, and the state park have Wi-Fi, but the service is spotty at best. If you need to talk to someone in the area, it's best to find a phone with a landline.**

The sites and hikes listed below are arranged by region of the park and distance from the visitor center: in the valley and hills surrounding Borrego Springs, near Tamarisk Campground, along Highway S2, south of Scissors Crossing, and south of Ocotillo Wells.

Stop by the **visitor center** to get oriented, to pick up a park map, and to learn about weather, road, and wildlife conditions. Designed to keep cool during the desert's blazing hot summers, the center is built underground, beneath a demonstration desert garden containing examples of most of the native flora and a little pupfish pond. Displays inside the center illustrate the natural history of the area. Picnic tables are scattered throughout, making this a good place to linger and enjoy the view. A 1½-mile trail leads to **Borrego Palm Canyon,** one of the few native palm groves in North America. The canyon, about 1 mile west of the visitor center, holds a grove of more than 1,000 native fan palms, a stream, and a waterfall. Wildlife is abundant along this route. This moderate hike is the most popular in the park.

With a year-round stream and lush plant life, **Coyote Canyon,** approximately 4½ miles north of Borrego Springs, is one of the best places to see and photograph spring wildflowers. Portions of the canyon road follow a section of the old Anza Trail. This area is closed between June 15 and September 15 to allow native bighorn sheep undisturbed use of the water. The dirt road that gives access to the canyon may be sandy enough to require a four-wheel-drive vehicle.

The late-afternoon vista of the Borrego badlands from **Font's Point,** 13 miles east of Borrego Springs, is one of the most breathtaking views in the desert, especially when the setting sun casts a golden glow in high relief on the eroded mountain slopes. The road from the Font's Point turnoff can be rough enough to make using a four-wheel-drive vehicle advisable; inquire about road conditions at the visitor center before starting out. Even if you can't make it out on the paved road, you can see some of the view from the highway.

East of Tamarisk Grove campground (13 miles south of Borrego Springs), the **Narrows Earth Trail** is a short walk off the road. Along the way you can see evidence of the many geologic processes involved in forming the canyons of the desert, such as a contact zone between two earthquake faults, and sedimentary layers of metamorphic and igneous rock.

The 1.6-mile round trip **Yaqui Well Nature Trail** takes you along a path to a desert water hole where birds and wildlife are abundant. It's also a good place to look for wildflowers in spring. At the trailhead across from Tamarisk Campground, you can pick up a brochure describing what can be seen along the trail.

Traversing a boulder-strewn trail is the easy, mostly flat **Pictograph/Smuggler's Canyon Trail.** At the end is a collection of rocks covered with muted red and yellow pictographs painted within the last hundred years or so by Native Americans. Walk about ½ mile beyond the pictures to reach Smuggler's Canyon, where an overlook provides views of the Vallecito Valley. The hike, from 2 to 3 miles round-trip, begins in Blair Valley, 6 miles southeast of Highway 78, off Highway S2, at the Scissors Crossing intersection.

Just a few steps off the paved road, **Carrizo Badlands Overlook** offers a view of eroded and twisted sedimentary rock that obscures the fossils of the mastodons, saber-tooths, zebras, and camels that roamed this region a million years ago. The route to the overlook through Earthquake Valley and Blair Valley parallels the Southern Emigrant Trail. It's off Highway S2, 40 miles south of Scissors Crossing.

Geology students from all over the world visit the Fish Creek area of Anza-Borrego to explore the canyon through Split Mountain. The narrow gorge with 600-foot walls was formed by an ancient stream. Fossils in this area indicate that a sea once covered the desert floor. From Highway 78 at Ocotillo Wells, take Split Mountain Road south 9 miles. ⊠ *Visitor Center, 200 Palm Canyon Dr., Hwy. S22* ☎ *760/767–5311, 800/444–7275 campground reservations only, 760/767–4684 wildflower hotline* ⊕ *www.parks.ca.gov* ⊠ *Free* ☼ *Park: daily dawn–dusk. Visitor Center: Oct.–May 1, daily 9–5.*

Galleta Meadows. Flowers aren't the only things popping up from the earth in Borrego Springs. At Galleta Meadows camels, llamas, saber-toothed tigers, tortoises, and monumental gomphotherium (a sort of ancient elephant) appear to roam the earth again. These life-size bronze figures are of prehistoric animals whose fossils can be found in the Borrego Badlands. The collection, more than 130 sculptures created by Ricardo Breceda, was commissioned by the late Dennis Avery, who installed the works of art on property he owned for the entertainment of locals and visitors. Maps are available from Borrego Springs Chamber of Commerce. ⊠ *Borrego Springs Rd. from Christmas Circle to Henderson Canyon* ☎ *760/767–5555* ⊕ *www. galletameadows.com* ⊠ *Free.*

WHERE TO EAT

$$
MODERN
AMERICAN
✕ **The Arches.** On the edge of the Borrego Springs Resort & Spa's golf course, set beneath a canopy of grapefruit trees, The Arches is a pleasant place to eat. For breakfast you'll find burritos alongside standard fare such as pancakes and biscuits and gravy. For lunch, best enjoyed on the patio, or dinner the options include sandwiches, salads, and entrées such as molasses-sriracha smothered ribs, fish-and-chips, and Cuban-style roasted pork. Ⓢ *Average main: $19* ⊠ *1112 Tilting T Dr.* ☎ *760/767–5700* ⊕ *www.borregospringsresort.com/dining.asp* ☼ *Summer hrs vary; call ahead.*

$$$
AMERICAN
✕ **Carlee's Place.** Sooner or later most visitors to Borrego Springs wind up at Carlee's Place for a drink and a bite to eat. It's an all-American type of establishment, where your server might call you "honey" while setting a huge steak in front of you. The extra-large menu has everything: burgers, salads, seafood, sandwiches, and prime rib. At the bar ask for a lemon-drop martini. Ⓢ *Average main: $23* ⊠ *660 Palm Canyon Dr.* ☎ *760/767–3262.*

$
MEXICAN
✕ **Carmelita's Mexican Grill and Cantina.** A friendly, family-run eatery tucked into a back corner of what is called "The Mall," Carmelita's draws locals and visitors all day, whether it's for a hearty breakfast, a cooked-to-order enchilada or burrito, or to tip back a brew at the bar. The menu lists typical combination plates (enchiladas, burritos, tamales, and tacos). Salsas have a bit of zing, and the *masas* (corn dough used to make tortillas and tamales) are tasty and tender. Ⓢ *Average main: $12* ⊠ *575 Palm Canyon Dr.* ☎ *760/767–5666.*

$
MEXICAN
✕ **Jilberto's Taco Shop.** A casual local favorite for affordable Mexican dishes, Jilberto's serves up big burritos and meaty enchiladas. Ⓢ *Average main: $5* ⊠ *655 Palm Canyon Dr.* ☎ *760/767–1008* ▬ *No credit cards.*

14

$$$ MODERN AMERICAN

🍴 **Krazy Coyote/Red Ocotillo.** The owners of the Palms at Indian Head operate these two restaurants together. Red Ocotillo serves breakfast (all the usual suspects) and lunch—burgers, Caesar salads, fish-and-chips, and the like. The more upscale Krazy Coyote serves rack of lamb, filet mignon, and other hearty standbys for dinner. What you eat is less important than the 1950s-modern setting and the casual atmosphere. Dog lovers will appreciate the canine menu, whose treats include house-made peanut-butter dog cookies. [$] *Average main: $23* ✉ *2220 Hoberg Rd.* ☎ *760/767–7400* 🌐 *www.thepalmsatindianhead.com* ✍ *Reservations essential* ⏲ *Krazy Coyote, no breakfast or lunch; Red Ocotillo, no breakfast or lunch July and Aug.*

WHERE TO STAY

$$ RESORT

🏨 **Borrego Springs Resort & Spa.** The large, smart-looking rooms at this quiet resort surround a swimming pool and come with either a shaded balcony or a patio with desert views. **Pros:** golf and tennis; good desert views from most rooms. **Cons:** limited amenities; average service. [$] *Rooms from: $129* ✉ *1112 Tilting T Dr.* ☎ *760/767–5700, 888/826–7734* 🌐 *www.borregospringsresort.com* 🛏 *66 rooms, 34 suites* 🍽 *No meals.*

$$$ B&B/INN Fodor's Choice ★

🏨 **Borrego Valley Inn.** Desert gardens of mesquite, ocotillo, and creosote surround the adobe Southwestern-style buildings here that house spacious rooms with plenty of natural light, original art, pine beds, and double futons facing corner fireplaces. **Pros:** swimming under the stars in the clothing-optional pool; exquisite desert gardens. **Cons:** potential street noise in season; not a good choice for families with young children or pets. [$] *Rooms from: $235* ✉ *405 Palm Canyon Dr.* ☎ *760/767–0311, 800/333–5810* 🌐 *www.borregovalleyinn.com* 🛏 *15 rooms, 1 suite* 🍽 *Breakfast.*

$$$ RESORT FAMILY Fodor's Choice ★

🏨 **La Casa Del Zorro.** The draws at this desert hideaway a short drive from Anza Borrego State Park include five public pools, a hot tub, six night-lit tennis courts, a spa, a restaurant, and the lively Fox Den Bar. **Pros:** upscale accommodations that aren't stuffy or overpriced; outdoor activities; on-site spa, bar, and restaurant. **Cons:** service can be spotty. [$] *Rooms from: $209* ✉ *3845 Yaqui Pass Rd.* ☎ *760/767–0100* 🌐 *www.lacasadelzorro.com* 🛏 *48 rooms, 19 casitas* 🍽 *No meals.*

SPORTS AND THE OUTDOORS

GOLF

Borrego Springs Resort & Spa Country Club. The 18 holes of golf at this resort and country club are open to the public. Formerly part of a trio of three 9-hole courses (one has since closed), the remaining two, Mesquite and Desert Willow, are generally played as an 18-hole round by most golfers, starting with Mesquite. Both courses have natural desert landscaping and mature date palms. ✉ *1112 Tilting T Dr.* ☎ *760/767–5700* 🌐 *www.borregospringsresort.com* 🎫 *From $30* ⛳ *18 holes, 6760 yards, par 71.*

RoadRunner Golf and Country Club. Adjacent to the Springs at Borrego course and with some shared facilities, this club has an 18-hole par-3 golf course. Though the course has views of the Santa Rosa, San Ysidro, and Vallecito Mountains and Indian Head Mountain, the terrain is relatively flat. Another bonus: there's rarely a wait for a tee time. ⊠ *1010 Palm Canyon Dr.* ☎ *760/767–5373* ⊕ *www.roadrunnerclub. com* ⊠ *$35* 🏌 *18 holes, 2451 yards, par 54.*

The Springs at Borrego. Part of a luxurious RV-park complex, this public golf course has 9 holes that can be configured to play as 18. The tight course, designed by David Pfaff, has narrow fairways and a series of challenging traps and bunkers. With views of Indian Head Mountain and birds of numerous species passing through, the setting is gorgeous. The course closes for the summer. ⊠ *2255 DiGiorgio Rd.* ☎ *760/767– 0004* ⊕ *www.springsatborrego.com* ⊠ *$45 for 18 holes* 🏌 *9 holes, 3084 yards, par 36.*

TENNIS

Anza Borrego Tennis Center. A busy tennis club that's also open for public play, this center has four hard-surface courts, a swimming pool, and clubhouse. ⊠ *286 Palm Canyon Dr.* ☎ *760/767–0577* ⊠ *$5 (all day) for tennis; $10 for all facilities* ⊗ *Closed May–Sept.*

SHOPPING

Anza-Borrego State Park Store. You can find guidebooks and maps, clothing, desert art, and gifts for kids here, and the staffers organize hikes, naturalist talks, classes, research programs, and nature walks. ⊠ *587 Palm Canyon Dr., No. 110* ☎ *760/767–4063* ⊕ *shop.theabf.org/main. sc* ⊗ *Oct.–mid-May, daily 10–4; mid-May–Sept., weekdays 11–3.*

Borrego Outfitters. This contemporary general store stocks high-end outdoor gear from Kelty and Columbia, personal care items from Burt's Bees, footwear from Teva and Acorn, Speedo and Fresh Produce swimsuits, and tabletop and home-decor items. You can browse through racks of clothing and piles of hats, all suited to the desert climate. The off season brings some great bargains. ⊠ *579 Palm Canyon Dr.* ☎ *760/767–3502* ⊕ *www.borregooutfitters.com.*

SALTON SEA

30 miles southeast of Indio, 29 miles east of Borrego Springs.

The Salton Sea, one of the largest inland seas on Earth, is the product of both natural and artificial forces. The sea occupies the Salton Basin, a remnant of prehistoric Lake Cahuilla. Over the centuries the Colorado River flooded the basin and the water drained into the Gulf of California. In 1905 a flood once again filled the Salton Basin, but the exit to the gulf was blocked by sediment. The floodwaters remained in the basin, creating a saline lake 228 feet below sea level, about 35 miles long and 15 miles wide, with a surface area of nearly 380 square miles. The sea, which lies along the Pacific Flyway, supports 400 species of birds. Fishing for tilapia, boating, camping, and bird-watching are popular activities year-round.

GETTING HERE AND AROUND

Salton Sea State Recreation Area includes about 14 miles of coastline on the northeastern shore of the sea, about 30 miles south of Indio via Highway 111. The Sonny Bono Salton Sea National Wildlife Refuge fills the southernmost tip of the sea's shore. To reach it from the recreation area, continue south about 60 miles to Niland; continue south to Sinclair Road, and turn west following the road to the Refuge Headquarters.

EXPLORING

FAMILY **Salton Sea State Recreation Area.** This huge recreation area on the sea's north shore draws thousands each year to its playgrounds, hiking trails, fishing spots, and boat launches. Ranger-guided bird walks take place on Saturday; you'll see migrating and native birds including Canada geese, pelicans, and shorebirds. On Sunday there are free kayak tours. ⊠ *100-225 State Park Rd., North Shore* ☎ *760/393–3052* ⊕ *www. parks.ca.gov* ⊒ *$5* ⊙ *Park daily 8–sunset.*

Sonny Bono Salton Sea National Wildlife Refuge. The 2,200-acre wildlife refuge here, on the Pacific Flyway, is a wonderful spot for viewing migratory birds. There's an observation deck where you can watch Canada geese, and along the trails you might view eared grebes, burrowing owls, great blue herons, ospreys, and yellow-footed gulls. ⊠ *906 W. Sinclair Rd., Calipatria* ☎ *760/348–5278* ⊕ *www.fws.gov/ saltonsea* ⊒ *Free* ⊙ *Park: Oct.–Feb., daily sunrise–sunset. Visitor center: Oct.–Feb., weekdays 7–3:, weekends 8–4:15* ⊙ *Closed weekends Mar.–Sept.*

JOSHUA TREE
NATIONAL PARK

WELCOME TO JOSHUA TREE NATIONAL PARK

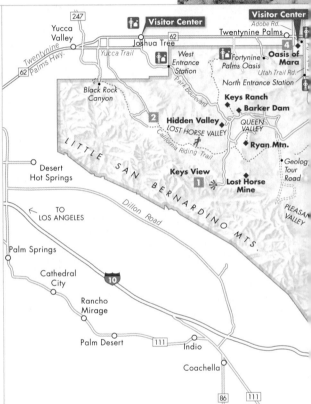

TOP REASONS TO GO

★ **Rock climbing:** Joshua Tree is a world-class site with challenges for climbers of just about every skill level.

★ **Peace and quiet:** Savor the solitude of one of the last great wildernesses in America.

★ **Stargazing:** You'll be mesmerized by the Milky Way flowing across the summer sky. For spectacular natural fireworks, visit in mid-August during the Perseid meteor shower and watch shooting stars streak overhead.

★ **Wildflowers:** In spring, the hillsides explode in a patchwork of yellow, blue, pink, and white.

★ **Sunsets:** Twilight is a magical time here, especially during the winter, when the setting sun casts a golden glow on the mountains.

1 Keys View. This is the most dramatic overlook in the park—on clear days you can see Signal Mountain in Mexico.

2 Hidden Valley. Crawl between the big rocks and you'll understand why this boulder-strewn area was once a cattle rustlers' hideout.

3 Cholla Cactus Garden. Come here in the late afternoon, when the spiky stalks of the Bigelow (jumping) cholla cactus are backlit against an intense blue sky.

4 Oasis of Mara. Walk the nature trail around this desert oasis, which the first settlers, the Serrano, dubbed "the place of little springs and much grass."

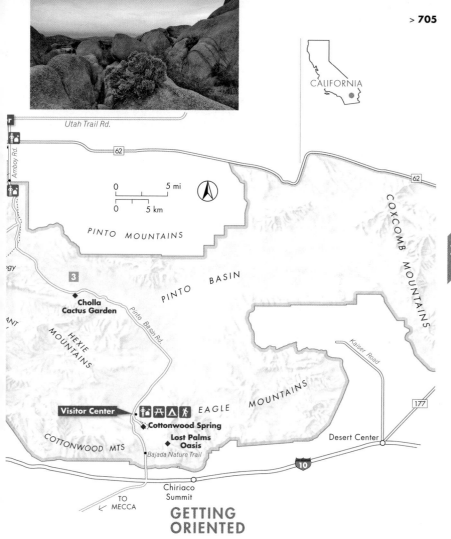

CALIFORNIA

0   5 mi

0   5 km

15

Utah Trail Rd.

62

Amboy Rd.

PINTO MOUNTAINS

COXCOMB MOUNTAINS

62

PINTO BASIN

3

Cholla Cactus Garden

Pinto Basin Rd.

HEXIE MOUNTAINS

EAGLE MOUNTAINS

Kaiser Road

177

Visitor Center

Cottonwood Spring

Lost Palms Oasis

Desert Center

COTTONWOOD MTS

Bajada Nature Trail

10

Chiriaco Summit

TO
MECCA

GETTING
ORIENTED

Daggerlike tufts grace the branches of the namesake of Joshua Tree National Park in southeastern California, where the arid Mojave Desert meets the sparsely vegetated Colorado Desert (part of the Sonoran Desert, which lies across California, Arizona, and northern Mexico). Passenger cars are fine for paved areas, but you'll need four-wheel drive for many of the rugged backcountry roadways. At the park's most popular sites, parking is limited. Joshua Tree does not have public transportation.

Updated by
John Blodgett

Ruggedly beautiful desert scenery attracts more than a million visitors each year to Joshua Tree National Park, one of the last great wildernesses in the continental United States. Its mountains support mounds of enormous boulders and jagged rock; natural cactus gardens and lush oases shaded by tall fan palms mark the meeting place of the Mojave (high) and Sonora (low) deserts. Extensive stands of Joshua trees gave the park its name; the plants (members of the yucca family of shrubs) reminded Mormon pioneers of the biblical Joshua, with their thick, stubby branches representing the prophet raising his arms toward heaven.

JOSHUA TREE PLANNER

WHEN TO GO

October through May, when the desert is cooler, is when most visitors arrive. Daytime temperatures range from the mid-70s in December and January to mid-90s in October and May. Lows can dip to near freezing in midwinter, and you may even encounter snow at the higher elevations. Summers can be torrid, with daytime temperatures reaching 110°F.

PLANNING YOUR TIME

JOSHUA TREE IN ONE DAY

After stocking up on water, snacks, and lunch in Yucca Valley or Joshua Tree (you won't find any supplies inside the park), begin your visit at the **Joshua Tree Visitor Center,** where you can pick up maps and peruse exhibits to get acquainted with what awaits you. Enter the park itself at the nearby **West Entrance Station** and continue driving along the highly scenic and well-maintained **Park Boulevard.** Stop first at **Hidden Valley,** where you can relax at the picnic area or hike the easy 1-mile loop trail. After a few more miles turn left onto the spur road that takes you to the trailhead for the **Barker Dam Nature Trail.** Walk the easy 1.3-mile loop to view a water tank ranchers built to quench their cattle's thirst; along the way you'll spot birds and a handful of cactus varieties. Return to Park Boulevard and head south; you'll soon leave the main road again for the drive to **Keys View.** The easy loop trail here is only 0.25 miles, but the views extend for miles in every direction—look for the San Andreas Fault, the Salton Sea, and nearby mountains. Return to Park Boulevard, where you'll find **Cap Rock,** another short loop trail winding amid rock formations and Joshua trees.

Continuing along Park Boulevard, the start of the 18-mile self-guided **Geology Tour Road** will soon appear on your right. A brochure outlining its 16 stops is available here; note that the round trip will take about two hours, and high-clearance vehicles are recommended after stop 9. ⚠ Do not attempt if it has recently rained. Back on Park Boulevard, you'll soon arrive at the aptly named **Skull Rock.** This downright spooky formation is next to the parking lot; a nearby trailhead marks the beginning of a 1.7-mile nature trail. End your day with a stop at the **Oasis Visitor Center** in Twentynine Palms, where you can stroll through the historic **Oasis of Mara,** popular with area settlers.

GETTING HERE AND AROUND
CAR TRAVEL
An isolated island of pristine wilderness—a rarity these days—Joshua Tree National Park is within a short drive of 11 million Southern California residents. Most visitors, in fact, make the two-hour drive from the Los Angeles area to enjoy a weekend of solitude in 792,726 acres of untouched desert. The urban sprawl of Palm Springs (home to the nearest airport) is 45 miles away, but gateway towns Joshua Tree, Yucca Valley, and Twentynine Palms are just north of the park. If you're staying in the Palm Springs area, you can enjoy the highlights of the park in one day, including a stop for a picnic at a scenic spot.

■ TIP➜ If you'd prefer not to drive, most Palm Springs area hotels can arrange a half- or full-day tour that hits the highlights of Joshua Tree National Park. But you'll need to spend two or three days camping here to truly experience the quiet beauty of the desert.

PARK ESSENTIALS
PARK FEES AND PERMITS
Park admission is $15 per car, $5 per person on foot, bicycle, motorcycle, or horse. The Joshua Tree Pass, good for one year, is $30. Free permits—available at all visitor centers—are required for rock climbing.

PARK HOURS
The park is open every day, around the clock. The park is in the Pacific time zone.

VISITOR INFORMATION
PARK CONTACT INFORMATION
Joshua Tree National Park ✉ *74485 National Park Dr., Twentynine Palms* ☏ *760/367–5500* ⊕ *www.nps.gov/jotr.*

VISITOR CENTERS

Joshua Tree Visitor Center. This visitor center has interesting exhibits illustrating park geology, cultural and historic sites, and hiking and rock-climbing activities. There's also a small bookstore. Restrooms with flush toilets are on the premises, and showers are nearby. ⊠ *6554 Park Blvd., Joshua Tree* ☎ *760/366–1855* ⊕ *www.nps.gov/jotr* ☼ *Daily 8–5.*

Oasis Visitor Center. Exhibits here illustrate how Joshua Tree was formed, reveal the differences between the park's two types of desert, and demonstrate how plants and animals eke out an existence in this arid climate. Take the 0.5-mile nature walk through the nearby Oasis of Mara, which is alive with cottonwood trees, palm trees, and mesquite shrubs. Facililities include picnic tables, restrooms, and a bookstore. ⊠ *74485 National Park Dr., Twentynine Palms* ☎ *760/367–5500* ⊕ *www.nps.gov/jotr* ☼ *Daily 8–5.*

PLANTS AND WILDLIFE IN JOSHUA TREE

Joshua Tree will shatter your notions of the desert as a wasteland. Life flourishes here, as flora and fauna have adapted to heat and drought. In most areas you'll be walking among native Joshua trees, ocotillos, and yuccas. One of the best spring desert wildflower displays in Southern California blooms here. You'll see plenty of animals—reptiles such as nocturnal sidewinders, birds like golden eagles or burrowing owls, and occasionally mammals like coyotes and bobcats.

EXPLORING

SCENIC DRIVES

Park Boulevard. If you have time only for a short visit, driving Park Boulevard is your best choice. Traversing the most scenic portions of Joshua Tree, this well-paved road connects the north and west entrances in the park's high-desert section. Along with some sweeping desert views, you'll see jumbles of splendid boulder formations, stands of Joshua trees, and Hidden Valley and Barker Dam, remnants of the area's wild and woolly past. From the Oasis Visitor Center, drive south. After about 5 miles, the road forks; turn right and head west toward Jumbo Rocks (clearly marked with a road sign).

Pinto Basin Road. This paved road takes you from high Mojave desert to low Colorado desert. A long, slow drive, the route runs from the main part of the park to I–10; it can add as much as an hour to and from Palm Springs (round-trip), but the views and roadside exhibits make it worth the extra time. From the Oasis Visitor Center, drive south. After about 5 miles, the road forks; take a left and continue another 9 miles to the Cholla Cactus Garden, where the sun fills the cactus needles with light. Past that is the Ocotillo Patch, filled with spindly plants bearing razor-sharp thorns and brilliant red flowers. Side trips from this route require a 4X4.

HISTORIC SITES

FAMILY **Hidden Valley.** This legendary cattle-rustlers hideout is set among big boulders, which kids love to scramble over and around. There are shaded picnic tables here. ☒ *Park Blvd., 14 miles south of West Entrance.*

Fodor'sChoice **Keys Ranch.** This 150-acre ranch, which once belonged to William and
★ Frances Keys and is now on the National Historic Register, illustrates one of the area's most successful attempts at homesteading. The couple raised five children under extreme desert conditions. Most of the original buildings, including the house, school, store, and workshop, have been restored to the way they were when William died in 1969. The only way to see the ranch is on one of the 90-minute walking tours usually offered daily October to May; call ahead to confirm. ☒ *2 miles north of Barker Dam Rd.* ☎ *760/367–5555* ⊕ *www.nps.gov* ☒ *Tour $5, available at visitor centers* ☾ *Oct.–May, daily at 10 and 1.*

SCENIC STOPS

15

Barker Dam. Built in 1905 by ranchers and miners to hold water for cattle and mining operations, the dam now collects rainwater and is a good place to spot wildlife such as the elusive bighorn sheep. ☒ *Barker Dam Rd., off Park Blvd., 14 miles south of West Entrance.*

Cholla Cactus Garden. This stand of Bigelow cholla (sometimes called jumping cholla, since its hooked spines seem to jump at you) is best seen and photographed in late afternoon, when the backlit spiky stalks stand out against a colorful sky. ☒ *Pinto Basin Rd., 20 miles north of Cottonwood Visitor Center.*

Cottonwood Spring. Home to the native Cahuilla people for centuries, this spring provided water for travelers and early prospectors. The area, which supports a large stand of fan palms, is a stop for migrating birds and a winter water source for bighorn sheep. A number of gold mines were located here, and the area still has some remains, including an *arrastra* (a gold ore–grinding tool) and concrete pillars. ☒ *Cottonwood Visitor Center.*

Fortynine Palms Oasis. A short drive off Highway 62, this site is a bit of a preview of what the park's interior has to offer: stands of fan palms, interesting petroglyphs, and evidence of fires built by early American Indians. Since animals frequent this area, you may spot a coyote, bobcat, or roadrunner. ☒ *End of Canyon Rd., 4 miles west of Twentynine Palms.*

Fodor'sChoice **Keys View.** At 5,185 feet, this point affords a sweeping view of the Santa
★ Rosa Mountains and Coachella Valley, the San Andreas Fault, the peak of 11,500-foot Mount San Gorgonio, the shimmering surface of Salton Sea, and—on a rare clear day—Signal Mountain in Mexico. Sunrise and sunset are magical times, when the light throws rocks and trees into high relief before bathing the hills in brilliant shades of red, orange, and gold. ☒ *Keys View Rd., 21 miles south of park's west entrance.*

Lost Palms Oasis. More than 100 fan palms make up the largest group of the exotic plants in the park. A spring bubbles from between the rocks, but disappears into the sandy, boulder-strewn canyon. If you hike along the 4-mile trail, you might spot bighorn sheep. ☒ *Cottonwood Visitor Center.*

SPORTS AND THE OUTDOORS

HIKING

There are more than 190 miles of hiking trails in Joshua Tree, ranging from quarter-mile nature trails to 35-mile treks. Some connect with each other, so you can design your own desert maze. Remember that drinking water is hard to come by—you won't find water in the park except at the entrances. Bring along at least a gallon per person for all but the shortest hikes, more if the weather is hot. Before striking out on a hike or apparent nature trail, check out the signage. Roadside signage identifies hiking- and rock-climbing routes.

EASY

Cap Rock. This 0.5-mile wheelchair-accessible loop—named after a boulder that sits atop a huge rock formation like a cap—winds through fascinating rock formations and has signs that explain the geology of the Mojave Desert. *Easy.* ⊠ *Trailhead at junction of Park Blvd. and Keys View Rd.*

MODERATE

Fodor'sChoice **Ryan Mountain Trail.** The payoff for hiking to the top of 5,461-foot Ryan
★ Mountain is one of the best panoramic views of Joshua Tree. From here you can see Mt. San Jacinto, Mt. San Gorgonio, Lost Horse Valley, and the Pinto Basin. You'll need two to three hours to complete the 3-mile round trip. *Moderate.* ⊠ *Trailhead at Ryan Mountain parking area, 16 miles southeast of park's west entrance, or at Sheep Pass, 16 miles southwest of Oasis Visitor Center.*

DIFFICULT

Mastodon Peak Trail. Some boulder scrambling is required on this 3-mile hike up 3,371-foot Mastodon Peak, but the journey rewards you with stunning views of the Salton Sea. The trail passes through a region where gold was mined from 1919 to 1932, so be on the lookout for open mines. The peak draws its name from a large rock formation that early miners believed looked like the head of a prehistoric behemoth. *Difficult.* ⊠ *Trailhead at Cottonwood Spring Oasis.*

ROCK CLIMBING

Fodor'sChoice With an abundance of weathered igneous boulder outcroppings, Joshua
★ Tree is one of the nation's top winter-climbing destinations. There are more than 4,500 established routes offering a full menu of climbing experiences—from bouldering for beginners in the Wonderland of Rocks to multiple-pitch climbs at Echo Rock and Saddle Rock. The best-known climb in the park is Hidden Valley's Sports Challenge Rock. A map inside the *Joshua Tree Guide* shows locations of selected wilderness and nonwilderness climbs.

THE MOJAVE DESERT

With Owens Valley

WELCOME TO THE MOJAVE DESERT

TOP REASONS TO GO

★ **Nostalgia:** Old neon signs, historic motels, and restored (or neglected but still striking) rail stations abound across this desert landscape. Don't miss the classic eateries along the way, including Summit Inn in Oak Hills and Emma Jean's Holland Burger Cafe in Victorville.

★ **Death Valley wonders:** Visit this distinctive landscape to tour some of the most varied desert terrain in the world.

★ **Great ghost towns:** California's gold rush brought miners to the Mojave, and the towns they left behind have their own unique charms.

★ **Cool down in Sierra country:** Head up U.S. 395 toward Bishop to visit the High Sierra, home to majestic Mt. Whitney.

★ **Explore ancient history:** The Mojave Desert is replete with rare petroglyphs, some dating back almost 16,000 years.

1 The Western Mojave. Stretching from the town of Ridgecrest to the base of the San Gabriel Mountains, the western Mojave is a varied landscape of ancient Native American petroglyphs, tufa towers, and hillsides covered in bright orange poppies.

2 The Eastern Mojave. Joshua trees and cacti dot a predominantly flat landscape that is interrupted by dramatic, rock-strewn mountains. The area is largely uninhabited, so be cautious when driving the back roads, where towns and services are scarce.

3 Owens Valley. Lying in the shadow of the Eastern Sierra Nevada, the Owens Valley stretches along U.S. 395 from the Mono–Inyo county line, in the north, to the town of Olancha, in the south. Tiny towns punctuate the highway, and the scenery is quietly powerful. If you're traveling between Yosemite National Park and Death Valley National Park or are headed from Lake Tahoe or Mammoth to the desert, U.S. 395 is your north–south corridor.

4 Death Valley National Park. This arid desert landscape is one of the hottest, lowest, and driest places in North America. From the surrounding mountains, you look down on its vast beauty. Among the beautiful canyons and wide-open spaces, you'll find quirky bits of Americana, including the elaborate Scotty's Castle inside the park and eclectic Amargosa Opera House outside.

GETTING ORIENTED

The Mojave Desert, once part of an ancient inland sea, is one of the largest swaths of open land in Southern California. Its boundaries include the San Gabriel and San Bernardino mountain ranges to the south; the areas of Palmdale and Ridgecrest to the west; Death Valley to the north; and Needles and Lake Havasu in Arizona, to the east. The area is distinguishable by its wide-open sandy spaces, peppered with creosote bushes, Joshua trees, cacti, and abandoned homesteads. You can access the Mojave via interstates 40 and 15, highways 14 and 95, and U.S. 395.

16

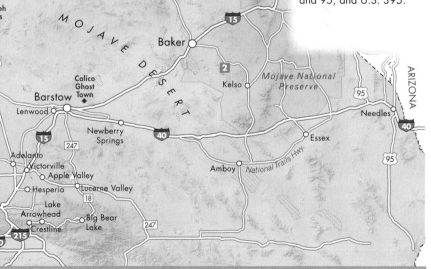

0   20 mi
0   20 km

NEVADA
CALIFORNIA

Stovepipe Wells

190   190

DEATH VALLEY

178

127

15

MOJAVE DESERT

Baker

2

Calico Ghost Town

Kelso

Mojave National Preserve

95

Barstow

Lenwood

Newberry Springs

15   247   40

Adelanto
Victorville
Apple Valley

Hesperia   Lucerne Valley

18

Lake Arrowhead
Crestline   Big Bear Lake

215   247

Amboy   National Trails Hwy.

Essex

ARIZONA

Needles   40

95

Updated by
John Blodgett

Dust and desolation, tumbleweeds and rattlesnakes, barren landscapes and failed dreams—these are the bleak images that come to mind when most people hear the word *desert*. Yet the remote regions east of the Sierra Nevada possess a singular beauty, the vast open spaces populated with spiky Joshua trees, undulating sand dunes, faulted mountains, and dramatic rock formations. With a few exceptions the area is not heavily peopled, providing expanses in which visitors can both lose and find themselves.

The topography is extreme; while Death Valley drops to almost 300 feet below sea level and contains the lowest (and hottest) spot in North America, the Mojave Desert, which lies to the south, has elevations ranging from 3,000 to 5,000 feet. Owens Valley is where the desert meets the mountains; its 80-mile width separates the depths of Death Valley from Mt. Whitney, the highest mountain in the contiguous United States.

PLANNING

WHEN TO GO
Spring and fall are the best seasons to tour the desert and Owens Valley. Winters are generally mild, but summers can be cruel. If you're on a budget, be aware that room rates drop as the temperatures rise.

GETTING HERE AND AROUND
AIR TRAVEL
Inyokern Airport, near Ridgecrest, is served by SkyWest from Los Angeles. McCarran International Airport in Las Vegas is the nearest airport to many eastern Mojave destinations. Needles Airport serves small, private planes.

Contacts **Inyokern Airport** ✉ *1669 Airport Rd., off Hwy. 178, 9 miles west of Ridgecrest, Inyokern* ☎ *760/377–5844* ⊕ *www.inyokernairport.com.* **McCarran International Airport** ✉ *5757 Wayne Newton Blvd., Las Vegas, Nevada* ☎ *702/261–5211* ⊕ *www.mccarran.com.* **Needles Airport** ✉ *711 Airport Rd., Needles* ☎ *760/247–2371* ⊕ *cms.sbcounty.gov/airports.*

BUS TRAVEL

Greyhound provides bus service to Barstow, Victorville, and Palmdale; check with the chambers of commerce about local bus service, which is generally more useful to residents than to tourists.

Contact **Greyhound** ☎ *800/231–2222* ⊕ *www.greyhound.com.*

CAR TRAVEL

The major north–south route through the western Mojave is U.S. 395, which intersects with Interstate 15 between Cajon Pass and Victorville. U.S. 395 travels north into the Owens Valley, passing such relatively remote outposts as Lone Pine, Independence, Big Pine, and Bishop. Farther west, Highway 14 runs north–south between Inyokern (near Ridgecrest) and Palmdale. Two major east–west routes travel through the Mojave: to the north, Interstate 15 to Las Vegas, Nevada; to the south, Interstate 40 to Needles. At the intersection of the two interstates, in Barstow, Interstate 15 veers south toward Victorville and Los Angeles, and Interstate 40 gives way to Highway 58 west toward Bakersfield.

■ TIP→ For the latest Mojave traffic and weather, tune in to the Highway Stations (98.1 FM near Barstow, 98.9 FM near Essex, and 99.7 FM near Baker). Traffic can be especially troublesome Friday through Sunday, when thousands of Angelenos head to Las Vegas for a bit of R&R.

Contacts **Caltrans Current Highway Conditions** ☎ *800/427–7623* ⊕ *www.dot.ca.gov.*

TRAIN TRAVEL

Amtrak trains traveling east and west stop in Victorville, Barstow, and Needles, but the stations aren't staffed, so you'll have to purchase tickets in advance and handle your own baggage. The Barstow station is served daily by Amtrak California motor coaches that stop in Los Angeles, Bakersfield, Las Vegas, and elsewhere.

Contact **Amtrak** ☎ *800/872–7245* ⊕ *www.amtrak.com.*

HEALTH AND SAFETY

Let someone know your trip route, destination, and estimated time of return. Before setting out, make sure your vehicle is in good condition. Carry water, a jack, tools, and towrope or chain. Keep an eye on your gas gauge and try to keep the needle above half. Stay on main roads, and watch out for wildlife, horses, and cattle.

Drink at least a gallon of water a day (more if you're hiking or otherwise exerting yourself). Dress in layered clothing and wear comfortable, sturdy shoes and a hat. Keep snacks, sunscreen, and a first-aid kit on hand. If you have a headache or feel dizzy or nauseous, you could be suffering from dehydration. Get out of the sun immediately and drink plenty of water. Dampen your clothing to lower your body temperature. Do not enter abandoned mine tunnels or shafts, of which there are hundreds in the Mojave Desert. The structures may be unstable, and there may be hidden dangers such as pockets of bad air. Avoid canyons during rainstorms. Floodwaters can quickly fill up dry riverbeds and cover or wash away roads. Never place your hands or feet where you can't see them: rattlesnakes, scorpions, and black widow spiders may be hiding there.

Contacts Barstow Community Hospital ⊠ *820 E. Mountain View St., Barstow* ☎ *760/256–1761* ⊕ *www.barstowhospital.com.* **BLM Rangers** ☎ *916/978–4400* ⊕ *www.blm.gov/ca.* **San Bernardino County Sheriff** ☎ *760/256–4838 in Barstow, 760/733–4448 in Baker* ⊕ *cms.sbcounty.gov/sheriff.*

RESTAURANTS
Throughout the desert and the Eastern Sierra, dining is a fairly simple affair. Owens Valley is home to many mom-and-pop eateries, as well as a few fast-food chains. There are chain establishments in Ridgecrest, Victorville, and Barstow, as well as some ethnic eateries.

HOTELS
Chain hotel properties and roadside motels are the desert's primary lodging options. The tourist season runs from late May through September. Reservations are rarely a problem, but it's still wise to make them. *Hotel reviews have been shortened. For full information, please visit Fodors.com.*

WHAT IT COSTS			
	$	**$$**	**$$$**	**$$$$**
Restaurants	under $16	$16–$22	$23–$30	over $30
Hotels	under $121	$121–$175	$176–$250	over $250

Restaurant prices are the average cost of a main course at dinner or, if dinner is not served, at lunch, excluding sales tax of 7.75%. Hotel prices are the lowest cost of a standard double room in high season, excluding service charges and 7.25% tax.

TOURS
Sierra Club. The San Gorgonio Chapter of the Sierra Club and the chapter's Mojave Group conduct interesting field trips and desert excursions. Activities are often volunteer-run and free, but participants are sometimes required to cover parking and other expenses. ☎ *951/684–6203* ⊕ *content.sierraclub.org/outings/local-outdoors* ▨ *Some free; fee tour prices vary.*

VISITOR INFORMATION
Contacts Barstow Welcome Center ⊠ *2796 Tanger Way, Barstow* ☎ *760/253–4782* ⊕ *www.visitcwc.com/Barstow.* **Bureau of Land Management** ⊠ *California Desert District Office, 22835 Calle San Juan De Los Lagos, Moreno Valley* ☎ *909/697–5200* ⊕ *www.blm.gov/ca.* **Death Valley Chamber of Commerce** ⊠ *860 Tecopa Hot Springs Rd., Tecopa* ☎ *760/852–4420* ⊕ *www.deathvalleychamber.com.*

THE WESTERN MOJAVE

This vast area is especially beautiful along U.S. 395. From January through March, wildflowers are in bloom and temperatures are manageable. Year-round, snowcapped mountain peaks are irresistible sights.

PALMDALE

60 miles north of Los Angeles.

Before proclaiming itself the aerospace capital of the world, the town of Palmdale was an agricultural community. Settlers of Swiss and German descent, moving west from Illinois and Nebraska, populated the area in 1886, and most residents made their living as farmers, growing alfalfa, pears, and apples. After World War II, with the creation of Edwards Air Force Base and U.S. Air Force Plant 42, the region evolved into a center for aerospace and defense activities, with contractors such as McDonnell Douglas, Rockwell, Northrop, and Lockheed establishing factories here. Until the housing crisis and recent recession struck, Palmdale was one of Southern California's fastest-growing cities.

16

GETTING HERE AND AROUND

From the Los Angeles basin take Highway 14 to get to Palmdale. From the east, arrive via the Pearblossom Highway (Highway 18/138). Regional Metrolink trains serve the area from Los Angeles. Palmdale attractions are most easily seen by car, but you can see some of the town via local transit.

ESSENTIALS

Antelope Valley Transit Authority ☎ *661/945–9445* ⊕ *www.avta.com.*

Metrolink ☎ *800/371–5465* ⊕ *www.metrolinktrains.com.*

Visitor Information Palmdale Chamber of Commerce ✉ *817 East Ave., Ste. Q-9* ☎ *661/273-3232* ⊕ *www.palmdalechamber.org.*

EXPLORING

Devil's Punchbowl Natural Area. A mile from the San Andreas Fault, the namesake of this attraction is a natural bowl-shaped depression in the earth, framed by 300-foot rock walls. At the bottom is a stream, which you can reach via a moderately strenuous 1-mile hike. You also can detour on a short nature trail; at the top an interpretive center has displays of native flora and fauna, including live animals such as snakes, lizards, and birds of prey. ✉ *28000 Devil's Punchbowl Rd., south of Hwy. 138, Pearblossom* ☎ *661/944–2743* 🎫 *Free* ☉ *Park daily sunrise–sunset; center daily 8–4.*

St. Andrew's Abbey. This Benedictine monastery occupies 760 acres made lush by natural springs. The Abbey Ceramics studio, established here in 1969, sells handmade tile saints, angels, and plaques designed by Father Maur van Doorslaer, a Belgian monk whose work U.S. and Canadian collectors favor. ✉ *31101 N. Valyermo Rd., south of Hwy. 138, Valyermo* ☎ *888/454–5411, 661/944–1047 ceramics studio* ⊕ *www.saintsandangels.org* 🎫 *Free* ☉ *Weekdays 9–12:30 and 1:30–4:30, weekends 9–11:45 and 12:30–4:30.*

WHERE TO STAY

$ HOTEL 🏨 **Best Western John Jay Inn & Suites.** All rooms at this modern hotel have large desks and ergonomic chairs; suites have balconies, fireplaces, wet bars, and Jacuzzis. **Pros:** clean; good rates; spacious rooms. **Cons:** no on-site restaurant; ambulance noise from the hospital next door. [$] *Rooms from: $89* ✉ *600 W. Palmdale Blvd.* ☎ *661/575–9322* 🌐 *www.bestwestern.com* 🛏 *66 rooms, 13 suites* 🍴 *Breakfast.*

$$ HOTEL 🏨 **Residence Inn Palmdale.** Accommodations here range from studios to one-bedroom suites, all with full kitchens, sitting areas, and sleeper sofas. **Pros:** spacious rooms; close to town. **Cons:** no room service. [$] *Rooms from: $149* ✉ *514 W. Ave. P* ☎ *661/947–4204, 800/331–3131* 🌐 *www.marriott.com* 🛏 *90 suites* 🍴 *Breakfast.*

SPORTS AND THE OUTDOORS

AERIAL TOURS

Brian Ranch Airport. The airport's school offers introductory flights that allow you to pilot (with an instructor) two-seater ultralight aircraft across the Mojave. The annual World's Smallest Air Show, held on Memorial Day weekend, draws many aviation enthusiasts. ✉ *34180 Largo Vista Rd., off Hwy. 138, Llano* ☎ *661/261–3216* 🌐 *www.brianranch.com* 🎟 *$40, 15-min flight; $75, 30 min; $130, 1 hr.*

SKYDIVING

Southern California Soaring Academy. The academy operates sailplane rides (no engines!) over the scenic San Gabriel mountain pines, across the jagged San Andreas Fault, and over the sandy soil of El Mirage Dry Lake. Accompanied by a certified instructor, you'll learn the basics before handling the craft on your own. Reservations are required. ✉ *32810 165th St. E, off Hwy. 138, Llano* ☎ *661/944–1090* 🌐 *www.soaringacademy.org* 🎟 *$109–$250* ⏲ *Fri.–Mon. 9–5.*

LANCASTER

8 miles north of Palmdale.

Lancaster was founded in 1876, when the Southern Pacific Railroad arrived. Before that, several Native American tribes, some of whose descendants still live in the surrounding mountains, inhabited it. Points of interest around Lancaster are far from the downtown area, and some are in neighboring communities.

GETTING HERE AND AROUND

From the Los Angeles basin take Highway 14, which proceeds north to Mojave and Highway 58, a link between Bakersfield and Barstow. Regional Metrolink trains serve Lancaster from the Los Angeles area. Local transit exists, but a car is the best way to experience this area.

ESSENTIALS

Visitor Information Destination Lancaster ✉ *44933 Fern Ave., at W. Lancaster Blvd.* ☎ *661/723–6110* 🌐 *www.destinationlancasterca.org.*

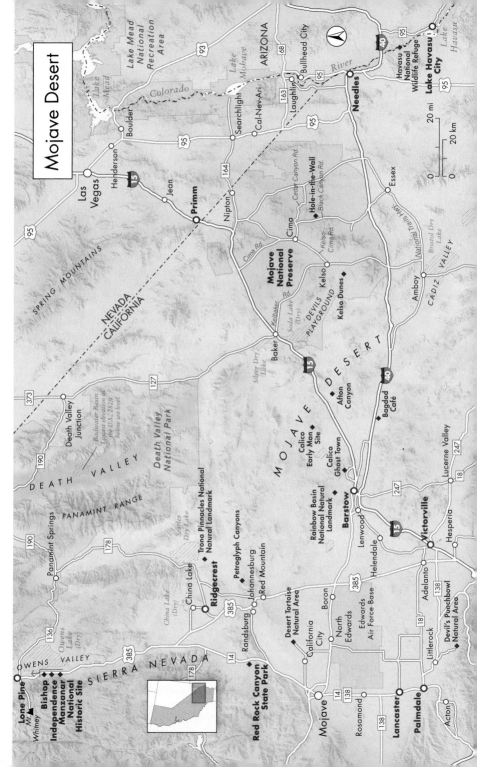

Mojave Desert

EXPLORING
TOP ATTRACTIONS

Antelope Valley Indian Museum. Notable for its one-of-a-kind artifacts from California, Southwest, and Great Basin native tribes, the museum occupies an unusual Swiss chalet–style building that clings to the rocky hillside of Piute Butte. To get here, exit north off Highway 138 at 165th Street East and follow the signs. ⊠ *15701 E. Ave. M* 🕾 *661/946–3055* ⊕ *www. avim.parks.ca.gov* 🖾 *$3* ⊘ *Weekends 11–4.*

Antelope Valley Poppy Reserve. The California poppy, the state flower, can be spotted throughout the state, but this quiet park holds the densest concentration. Seven miles of trails—parts of which are paved, though inclines are too steep for wheelchairs—wind through 1,745 acres of hills carpeted with poppies and other wildflowers. ■TIP→ **Peak blooming time is usually March through May.** On a clear day at any time of year, you'll be treated to sweeping views of Antelope Valley. ⊠ *15101 Lancaster Rd., west off Hwy. 14, Ave. I Exit* 🕾 *661/724–1180, 661/942–0662* ⊕ *www.parks. ca.gov/?page_id=627* 🖾 *$8 per vehicle* ⊘ *Visitor center mid-Mar.–mid-May daily 9–5.*

OFF THE
BEATEN
PATH

Exotic Feline Breeding Compound's Feline Conservation Center. About a dozen species of wild cats, from the weasel-size jaguarundi to leopards, tigers, and jaguars, inhabit this small, orderly facility. You can see the cats (behind barrier fences) in the parklike public zoo and research center. ⊠ *Rhyolite Ave. off Mojave-Tropico Rd., Rosamond* 🕾 *661/256–3793* ⊕ *www.cathouse-fcc.org* 🖾 *$7* ⊘ *Thurs.–Tues. 10–4.*

WORTH NOTING

Air Flight Test Center Museum at Edwards Air Force Base. The museum at what many consider to be the birthplace of supersonic flight chronicles the rich history of flight testing. Numerous airplanes are on exhibit, from the first F-16B to the giant B-52D bomber. The 3½-hour walking and driving tour is open to the public once a month. ■TIP→ **To take the tour you must pass a security screening at least a week in advance (a month for non-U.S. residents). On the base's website, click Tours for details.** ⊠ *405 S. Rosamond Blvd., off Yeager Blvd., Edwards* 🕾 *661/277–3517* ⊕ *www.edwards.af.mil* 🖾 *Free* ⊘ *1 day a month, 9–12:30.*

Antelope Valley Winery/Donato Family Vineyard. Desert vineyards? Industry scoffing didn't deter Cecil W. McLester, a graduate of UC Davis's renowned wine-making and viticulture program, from crafting decent wines—yes, from grapes grown on-site—including an award-winning

---

HIKING IN THE MOJAVE DESERT

Hiking trails are abundant throughout the desert and along the eastern base of the Sierra, meandering toward sights that you can't see from the road. Some of the best trails are unmarked; ask locals for directions. Among the prime hiking spots is the John Muir Trail, which starts near Mt. Whitney. Whether you're exploring the high or low desert, wear sunscreen, protective clothing, and a hat. Watch for tarantulas, black widows, scorpions, snakes, and other creatures.

Tempranillo and Paloma Blanca, a Riesling-style blend. Cecil has since retired, but the winery is still going strong. It also hosts a Saturday farmers' market (from May through November between 9 and noon) and sells grass-fed buffalo and other game and exotic meats such as venison, pheasant, and wild boar. ✉ *42041 20th St. W, at Ave. M* ☎ *661/722–0145, 888/282–8332* ⊕ *www.avwinery.com* ✉ *Winery free, tasting $6* ⊙ *Wed.–Sun. 11–6.*

RED ROCK CANYON STATE PARK

48 miles north of Lancaster.

On the stretch of Highway 14 that slices through Red Rock Canyon State Park, it's easy to become caught up in the momentum of rushing to your "real" destination. But it would be a shame not to stop for this deeply beautiful canyon, with its rich, layered colors and Native American heritage.

GETTING HERE AND AROUND

The only practical way to get here is by car, taking Highway 14 north from the Palmdale-Lancaster area or south from Ridgecrest.

Red Rock Canyon State Park. A geological feast for the eyes with its layers of pink, white, red, and brown rock, this remote canyon is also a region of fascinating biological diversity—the ecosystems of the Sierra Nevada, the Mojave Desert, and the Basin Range all converge here. Entering the park from the south just beyond Red Rock–Randsburg Road, you pass through a steep-walled gorge to a wide bowl tinted pink by volcanic ash. Native Americans known as the Kawaiisu lived here some 20,000 years ago; later, Mojave Indians roamed the land for centuries. Gold-rush fever hit the region in the mid-1800s, and you can still see remains of mining operations in the park. In the 20th century, Hollywood invaded the canyon, shooting westerns, TV shows, commercials, music videos, and movies such as *Jurassic Park* here. Be sure to check out the Red Cliffs Preserve on Highway 14, across from the entrance to the Ricardo Campground. ✉ *Visitor Center, 37749 Abbott Dr., off Hwy. 14, Cantil* ☎ *661/946–6092* ⊕ *www.parks.ca.gov* ✉ *$6 per vehicle* ⊙ *Daily sunrise–sunset visitor center open mid-March–early June and early Sept.–Nov., Fri.–Sun.*

RIDGECREST

28 miles northeast of Red Rock Canyon State Park; 77 miles south of Lone Pine.

A military town that serves the U.S. Naval Weapons Center to its north, Ridgecrest has scores of stores, restaurants, and hotels. With about 25,000 residents, it's the last city of any significant size you'll encounter as you head northeast toward Death Valley National Park. It's a good base for visiting regional attractions such as the Trona Pinnacles and Petroglyph Canyons.

GETTING HERE AND AROUND

Arrive here by car via U.S. 395 or, from the Los Angeles area, Highway 14. The local bus service is of limited use to tourists.

ESSENTIALS

Transportation Contacts **Ridgerunner Transit** ☎ *760/499–5040* ⊕ *ridgecrest-ca.gov/transit/transit.*

Visitor Information **Ridgecrest Area Convention and Visitors Bureau** ✉ *139 Balsam St., at Panamint Ave.* ☎ *760/375–8202, 800/847–4830* ⊕ *www.visitdeserts.com.*

EXPLORING

TOP ATTRACTIONS

Fodor's Choice
★

Petroglyph Canyons. Two canyons in the Coso Mountain range, commonly called Big Petroglyph and Little Petroglyph, hold a superlative concentration of ancient rock art, the largest of its kind in the Northern Hemisphere. Thousands of well-preserved images of animals and humans are scratched or pecked into dark basaltic rocks. The canyons lie within the million-acre U.S. Naval Weapons Center at China Lake. Only the drawings of Little Petroglyph can be visited, and only on a guided tour arranged in advance through the ⇨ *Maturango Museum.* ■TIP➜ Tour participants must be U.S. citizens over 10 years of age and must supply birthdate, birthplace, and Social Security information before visiting. Upon arrival, valid ID must be presented, along with vehicle registration and proof of insurance. ☎ *760/375–6900* ⊕ *www. maturango.org* 🖃 *$40* ⊙ *Feb.–June, and Sept. or Oct.–early Dec.; call or check website for times.*

Trona Pinnacles National Natural Landmark. Fantastic-looking formations of calcium carbonate, known as tufa, were formed underwater along fault lines in the bed of what is now Searles Dry Lake. Some of the more than 500 spires stand as tall as 140 feet, creating a landscape so surreal that it doubled for outer-space terrain in the film *Star Trek V.*

An easy-to-walk ½-mile trail allows you to see the tufa up close, but wear sturdy shoes—tufa cuts like coral. The best road to the area can be impassable after a rainstorm. ✉ *Pinnacle Rd., 5 miles south of Hwy. 178, 18 miles east of Ridgecrest* ☎ *760/384–5400 Ridgecrest BLM office* ⊕ *www.blm.gov/ca/st/en/fo/ridgecrest/trona.3.html.*

WORTH NOTING

OFF THE
BEATEN
PATH

Indian Wells Brewing Company. After driving through the hot desert, you'll surely appreciate a cold one at Indian Wells Brewing Company, where master brewer Rick Lovett lovingly crafts his Lobotomy Bock, Amnesia I.P.A., and Death Valley Pale Ale, among others. If you have the kids along, grab a six-pack of his specialty root beer, black cherry, orange, or cream soda. ✉ *2565 N. Hwy. 14, 2 miles west of U.S. 395, Inyokern* ☎ *760/377–5989* ⊕ *www.mojavered.com* 🖃 *$5 beer tasting* ⊙ *Daily 9:30–5.*

Maturango Museum. The museum contains interesting exhibits that survey the Upper Mojave Desert area's art, history, and geology and sponsors tours of the amazing rock drawings in ⇨ *Petroglph Canyons.* ✉ *100 E. Las Flores Ave., at Hwy. 178* ☎ *760/375–6900* ⊕ *www.maturango. org* 🖃 *$5* ⊙ *Daily 10–5.*

16

WHERE TO STAY

$$ HOTEL 🏨 **Hampton Inn & Suites Ridgecrest.** Clean and reliable, the Hampton has a well-equipped exercise room, spotless Internet service, and a welcoming breakfast area that help keep guests in shape, in touch, and invigorated. **Pros:** attentive, friendly service; good breakfast; big rooms. **Cons:** a rather strong chain vibe. [$] *Rooms from: $129* ✉ *104 East Sydnor Ave., Ridgecrest* ☎ *760/446–1968* 🛏 *93 rooms* 🍴 *Breakfast.*

$ HOTEL 🏨 **SpringHill Suites Ridgecrest.** The bar might not be set that high, but this is the best hotel in Ridgecrest. **Pros:** clean; good breakfast; helpful staff. **Cons:** some guests complain of a bleach smell. [$] *Rooms from: $119* ✉ *113 E. Sydnor Ave.* ☎ *888/236–2427, 760/446–1630* 🌐 *www.marriott.com/hotels/travel/iyksh-springhill-suites-ridgecrest* 🍴 *Breakfast.*

RANDSBURG

21 miles south of Ridgecrest; 26 miles east of Red Rock Canyon State Park.

Randsburg and nearby Red Mountain and Johannesburg make up the Rand Mining District, which first boomed with the discovery of gold in the Rand Mountains in 1895. Rich tungsten ore, used in World War I to make steel alloy, was discovered in 1907, and silver was found in 1919. The boom has gone bust, but the area still has some residents, a few antiques shops, and plenty of character. Butte Avenue is the main drag in Randsburg, whose tiny city jail, just off Butte, is among the original buildings still standing. An archetypal Old West cemetery perched on a hillside looms over Johannesburg.

GETTING HERE AND AROUND

Arriving by car is the best transportation option. From Red Rock Canyon, drive east on Redrock Randsburg Road. From Ridgecrest, drive south on South China Lake Road and U.S. 395.

EXPLORING

Rand Desert Museum. The small museum celebrates the Rand Mining District's heyday with historic photographs and mining paraphernalia and other artifacts. ✉ *161 Butte Ave.* ☎ *760/371–0965* 🌐 *www.randdesertmuseum.com* 🎟 *Free* 🕒 *Weekends 10–4, or by appointment.*

OFF THE BEATEN PATH

Desert Tortoise Natural Area. Between mid-March and mid-June, this natural habitat of the elusive desert tortoise blazes with desert candles, primroses, lupine, and other wildflowers. Arrive bright and early to spot the state reptile, while it grazes on fresh flowers and grass shoots. The area is also a great spot to see desert kit fox, red-tailed hawks, cactus wrens, and Mojave rattlesnakes. ✉ *8 miles northeast of California City via Randsburg Mojave Rd.* ☎ *951/683–3872* 🌐 *www.tortoise-tracks.org* 🎟 *Free* 🕒 *Daily.*

General Store. Built as Randsburg's Drug Store in 1896, the General Store is one of the area's few surviving ghost-town buildings with an original tin ceiling, light fixtures, and 1906-era marble-and-stained-glass soda fountain. You can still enjoy a phosphate soda from that same fountain, or lunch on chili dogs, burgers, and barbecue-beef sandwiches.

✉ *35 Butte Ave.* ☎ *760/374–2143* ⊕ *www.randsburggeneralstore.com* ⊙ *Mon. and Fri. 10–4; Tues. and Thurs. 11-4; weekends 10–5.*

White House Saloon. One of the Wild West's few surviving saloons, swinging wooden doors and all, the White House is an atmospheric stop. Step in for a drink and, if you're feeling adventurous and aren't too picky, order some food (burgers, hot dogs, fries, chili). ■TIP→ **Across the street and also worth a peek is another joint—The Joint.** ✉ *168 Butte Ave.* ☎ *760/374–2464.*

THE EASTERN MOJAVE

Majestic, wide-open spaces define this region, with the Mojave National Preserve being one of the state's most remote but rewarding destinations.

VICTORVILLE

87 miles south of Ridgecrest.

At the southwest corner of the Mojave is the sprawling town of Victorville, a town with a rich Route 66 heritage. Victorville was named for Santa Fe Railroad pioneer Jacob Nash Victor, who drove the first locomotive through the Cajon Pass here in 1885. Once home to Native Americans, the town later became a rest stop for Mormons and missionaries. In 1941, George Air Force Base, now an airport and storage area, brought scores of military families to the area, many of which have stayed on to raise families of their own.

GETTING HERE AND AROUND

Drive here on Interstate 15 from Los Angeles or Las Vegas, or from the north via U.S. 395. Amtrak and Greyhound also serve the town. There are local buses, but touring by car is more practical.

ESSENTIALS

Transportation Information The Victor Valley Transit Authority ☎ *760/948-3030* ⊕ *www.vvta.org.*

Visitor Information Victor Valley Chamber of Commerce ✉ *14174 Green Tree Blvd., at St. Andrews Dr.* ☎ *760/245-6506* ⊕ *www.vvchamber.com.*

EXPLORING

TOP ATTRACTIONS

California Route 66 Museum. Fans of the Mother Road (as John Steinbeck dubbed Route 66) will love this museum whose exhibits chronicle the famous highway's history. A book sold here contains a self-guided tour of 11 miles of the old Sagebrush Route from just north of Victorville in Oro Grande to Helendale. The tour passes by icons such as Potapov's Gas and Service Station and the once-rowdy Sagebrush Inn, now a private residence. ✉ *16825 D St., between 5th and 6th Sts.* ☎ *760/951-0436* ⊕ *www.califrt66museum.org* ▭ *Free* ⊙ *Mon. and Thurs.–Sat. 10-4, Sun. 11–3.*

16

WORTH NOTING

FAMILY **Mojave Narrows Regional Park.** In one of the few spots where the Mojave River flows aboveground, this park has two lakes surrounded by cottonwoods and cattails. You'll find fishing, rowboat rentals, a bait shop, equestrian paths, and a wheelchair-accessible trail. ✉ *18000 Yates Rd., north on Ridgecrest Rd. off Bear Valley Rd.* ☎ *760/245–2226* 🌐 *cms.sbcounty.gov/parks* 🎟 *$8 weekdays, $10 weekends and holidays.*

WHERE TO EAT AND STAY

$ AMERICAN 🍴 **Emma Jean's Holland Burger Cafe.** This circa-1940s diner sits right on U.S. Historic Route 66 and is favored by locals for its generous portions and old-fashioned home cooking. Try the biscuits and gravy, chicken-fried steak, or the famous Trucker's Sandwich, stuffed with roast beef, bacon, chilis, and cheese. The Brian Burger also elicits consistent praise. [$] *Average main: $10* ✉ *17143 N. D St., at Water Power Housing Dr.* ☎ *760/243–9938* ⏲ *Closed Sun. No dinner.*

$ AMERICAN 🍴 **Summit Inn.** Elvis Presley and Pearl Bailey are two of many famous customers who passed through this kitschy diner perched atop the Cajon Pass. Open since 1952, the restaurant is filled with Route 66 novelty items, a gift shop, and a vintage jukebox that plays oldies from the 1950s to 1980s. All-day breakfast, including omelets made with ostrich or emu eggs, and the funky decor and historic significance make it worth a stop. [$] *Average main: $10* ✉ *5970 Mariposa Rd., exit I–15 at Oak Hills, Oak Hills* ☎ *760/949–8688.*

$ HOTEL 🏨 **La Quinta Inn and Suites Victorville.** If you're looking for a clean, comfortable, and non-smoking hotel with reasonable prices, this is a good choice. **Pros:** near shopping mall; clean rooms; hot breakfast. **Cons:** near a busy freeway. [$] *Rooms from: $94* ✉ *12000 Mariposa Rd., Hesperia* ☎ *760/949–9900* 🌐 *www.lq.com* 🛏 *53 rooms, 22 suites* 🍽 *Breakfast.*

BARSTOW

32 miles northeast of Victorville.

Barstow was born in 1886, when a subsidiary of the Atchison, Topeka, and Santa Fe Railway began construction of a depot and hotel here. Outlet stores, chain restaurants, and motels define today's landscape, though old-time neon signs light up the town's main street.

GETTING HERE AND AROUND

Driving here on Interstate 15 from Los Angeles or Las Vegas is the best option, although you can reach Barstow via Amtrak or Greyhound. The local bus service is helpful for sights downtown.

ESSENTIALS

Transportation Information **Barstow Area Transit** ☎ *760/256–0311* 🌐 *www.barstowca.org.*

Visitor Information **Barstow Area Chamber of Commerce and Visitors Bureau** ✉ *681 N. 1st Ave., near Riverside Dr.* ☎ *760/256–8617* 🌐 *www.barstowchamber.com.* **California Welcome Center** ✉ *2796 Tanger Way, off Lenwood Rd.* ☎ *760/253–4782* 🌐 *www.visitcwc.com* ⏲ *Daily 9–8.*

Many of the buildings in the popular Calico Ghost Town are authentic.

EXPLORING
TOP ATTRACTIONS

FAMILY **Calico Early Man Site.** The earliest-known Americans fashioned the arti-facts buried in the walls and floors of the pits here. Nearly 12,000 stone tools—used for scraping, cutting, and gouging—have been excavated here. The apparent age of some of these items (said to be as much as 50,000 years old) contradicts the dominant archaeological theory that humans populated North America only 13,000 years ago. Noted archaeologist Louis Leakey was so impressed with the Calico site that he became its director in 1963 and served in that capacity until his death in 1972. His old camp is now a visitor center and museum. Self-guided tours can be accompanied by a lecture from a volunteer if desired; guided tours are available on request. ■TIP➡ **Volunteers host an open-to-the-public dig the first full weekend of every month from October through May. Digging tools and instructions are pro-vided. Any items found cannot be removed from the site.** ⊠ *Off I–15, Minneola Rd. exit, 15 miles northeast of Barstow* ☎ *760/218–6931* ⊕ *www.calicoarchaeology.com* ⊠ *$5* ☉ *Visitor center: Wed. 12:30–4:30, Thurs.–Sun. 9–4:30.*

FAMILY **Calico Ghost Town.** Once a wild and wealthy mining town, Calico took off in 1881 when prospectors found a rich deposit of silver in the area, and by 1886 more than $85 million worth of silver, gold, and other precious metals had been harvested from the surrounding hills. Many buildings here are authentic, but the restoration has created a sanitized version of the 1880s. You can stroll the wooden sidewalks of Main Street, browse shops filled with Western goods, roam the tunnels of

Maggie's Mine ($2), and take an enjoyable ride on the Calico-Odessa Railroad ($4). Calico, 12 miles northeast of Barstow, is a fun and mildly educational place for families to stretch their legs on the drive between Los Angeles and Las Vegas. Festivals throughout the year celebrate Calico's Wild West theme. ⊠ *36600 Ghost Town Rd., off I–15, Yermo* ☎ *760/254–2122* ⊕ *www.calicotown.com* ✉ *$8* ⊙ *Daily 9–5.*

Casa Del Desierto Harvey House. This distinctive two-story structure—its Spanish name means "house of the desert"—was one of many hotel and restaurant depots opened by Santa Fe Railroad guru Fred Harvey in the early 20th century. In its heyday the building starred in Judy Garland's film *The Harvey Girls;* now, it houses the Route 66 Mother Road Museum and the Western Railroad Museum. ⊠ *681 N. 1st Ave., near Riverside Dr.* ☎ *760/255–1890* ⊕ *www.route66museum.org* ✉ *Free* ⊙ *Fri.–Sat. 10–4; Sun. 11–4; guided tours by appointment.*

FAMILY
Fodor's Choice
★

Goldstone Deep Space Communications Complex. Friendly and enthusiastic staffers conduct guided tours of this 53-square-mile complex. Tours start at the Goldstone Museum, where exhibits detail past and present space missions and Deep Space Network history. From there, you'll drive out to see the massive concave antennas, starting with those used for early manned space flights and culminating with the 24-story-tall "listening" device and its always-staffed mission control room used to track spacecraft that have drifted beyond our solar system. ■TIP➜ Appointments are required; contact the complex to reserve a slot. ⊠ *Ft. Irwin Military Base, Ft. Irwin Rd. off I–15, 35 miles north of Barstow* ☎ *760/255–8688* ⊕ *www.gdscc.nasa.gov* ✉ *Free* ⊙ *Guided tours by appointment only.*

Rainbow Basin National Natural Landmark. Many science-fiction movies set on Mars have been filmed at this landmark 8 miles north of Barstow. Huge slabs of red, orange, white, and green stone tilt at crazy angles like ships about to capsize. Hike the washes, and you might see the fossilized remains of mastodons and bear-dogs, which roamed the basin up to 16 million years ago. At times, only 4-wheel-drive vehicles are permitted. If you have the time, park and hike. ⊠ *Fossil Bed Rd., 3 miles west of Fort Irwin Rd. (head north from (I–15)* ☎ *760/252–6000* ⊕ *www.blm. gov/ca/barstow/basin.html.*

Skyline Drive-In Theatre. Check out a bit of surviving Americana at this dusty drive-in, where you can watch the latest Hollywood flicks among the Joshua trees and starry night sky. ⊠ *31175 Old Hwy. 58* ☎ *760/256–3333* ⊕ *www.barstowtheaters.com* ✉ *$7 per person ($10 per carload Tues.)* ⊙ *Showtime 7:30 pm.*

FAMILY
Western American Rail Museum. For a truly nostalgic experience, check out the old locomotives and cabooses at this museum that houses memorabilia from Barstow's early railroad days, as well as interactive and historic displays on railroad history. ⊠ *Casa Del Desierto, 685 N. 1st St., near Riverside Dr.* ☎ *760/256–9276* ⊕ *www.barstowrailmuseum. org* ✉ *Free* ⊙ *Fri.–Sun. 11–4.*

WORTH NOTING

Afton Canyon. Because of its colorful, steep walls, Afton Canyon is often called the Grand Canyon of the Mojave. It was carved over thousands of years by the rushing waters of the Mojave River, which makes one of its few aboveground appearances here. The dirt road that leads to the canyon is ungraded in spots, so it is best to explore it in an all-terrain vehicle. ✉ *Off Afton Rd., 36 miles northeast of Barstow via I–15* ⊕ *www.blm.gov/ca/st/en/fo/barstow/afton.html.*

FAMILY **Desert Discovery Center.** The center's main attraction is Old Woman Meteorite, the second-largest such celestial object ever found in the United States. It was discovered in 1976 about 50 miles from Barstow. The center also has exhibits of fossils, plants, and local animals. Environmental education, history, and the arts are among the topics of workshops and presentations the center hosts. ✉ *831 Barstow Rd., at E. Virginia Way* ☎ *760/252–6060* ⊕ *www.desertdiscoverycenter.com* 🖭 *Free* ☉ *Tues.–Sat. 11–4.*

Inscription Canyon. With nearly 10,000 petroglyphs and pictographs of bighorn sheep and other Mojave wildlife, Inscription is one of the world's largest natural Native American art galleries. The canyon lies 42 miles northwest of Barstow in the Black Mountains. ✉ *EF373, off Copper City Rd., 10 miles west of Fort Irwin Rd.* ☎ *760/252–6000* ⊕ *www.blm.gov/ca/st/en/fo/barstow/petroglyph1.html.*

16

FAMILY **Mojave River Valley Museum.** Two blocks from the the intersection of I–15 and Barstow Road, this museum is crowded with exhibits that include American Indian pottery, mammoth bones, and elephant tracks. Worth a look outside are the iron-strap jail, a rare Santa Fe Railroad drover's car, and a 130-year-old log cabin. ✉ *270 E. Virginia Way, at Belinda St.* ☎ *760/256–5452* ⊕ *www.mojaverivervalleymuseum.org* 🖭 *Free* ☉ *Daily 11–4.*

WHERE TO EAT AND STAY

$ ✕ **Bagdad Café.** Tourists from all over the world flock to the Route 66 AMERICAN eatery where the 1987 film of the same name was shot. Built in the 1940s, the divey Bagdad Café's walls are crammed with memorabilia donated by visitors famous and otherwise. The menu includes standards such as burgers and chicken-fried steak; the quality of both food and service can be inconsistent. 💲*Average main: $12* ✉ *46548 National Trails Hwy., at Nopal La., Newberry Springs* ☎ *760/257–3101.*

$$$ ✕ **Idle Spurs Steakhouse.** Since the 1950s this roadside ranch has been a AMERICAN Barstow dining staple, and it's still beloved by locals. Covered in cacti outside and Christmas lights inside, it's a colorful, cheerful place with a big wooden bar. The menu features prime cuts of meat, ribs, and lobster, and there's a great microbrew list. 💲*Average main: $24* ✉ *690 Old Hwy. 58, at Camarillo Ave.* ☎ *760/256–8888* ⊕ *thespurs.us* ☉ *Closed Mon.; no lunch weekends.*

$ ✕ **Peggy Sue's 50s Diner.** Checkerboard floors and life-size versions of AMERICAN Elvis and Marilyn Monroe greet you at this funky little coffee shop FAMILY and pizza parlor in the middle of the Mojave. Outside, kids can play by the duck pond before heading in to spin a tune on the jukebox or order from the soda fountain. The fare is basic American—fries, onion rings, burgers, pork chops. Ⓢ *Average main: $10* ✉ *35654 W. Yermo Rd., at Daggett-Yermo Rd., Yermo* ☎ *760/254–3370* ⊕ *www. peggysuesdiner.com.*

Ⓢ ✕ **Slash X Ranch Cafe.** Burgers, cold beer, and chili-cheese fries in hearty

SOUTHERN portions lure visitors and locals to this rowdy Wild West-esque watering hole named for the cattle ranch that preceded it. Shuffleboard tables and horseshoe pits add to the fun, provided it's not too sizzling hot outside. Ⓢ *Average main: $13* ✉ *28040 Barstow Rd., at Powerline Rd.* ☎ *760/252–1197* ⊕ *slashxranch.com* ⊗ *Closed Mon.–Thurs.*

Ⓢ ⏨ **Country Inn & Suites By Carlson.** A friendly and attentive staff makes

HOTEL this chain hotel stand out in a town that has a sea of them. **Pros:** clean rooms, engaged management; entirely nonsmoking. **Cons:** pricey for Barstow. Ⓢ *Rooms from: $99* ✉ *2812 Lenwood Rd.* ☎ *760/307–3121* ⊕ *www.countryinns.com* ⇖ *92 rooms and suites* ❐ *Breakfast.*

MOJAVE NATIONAL PRESERVE

Visitor center 118 miles east of Barstow, 58 miles west of Needles.

The 1.6 million acres of the Mojave National Preserve hold a surprising abundance of plant and animal life—especially considering their elevation (nearly 8,000 feet in some areas). There are traces of human history here as well, including abandoned army posts and vestiges of mining and ranching towns.

GETTING HERE AND AROUND

A car is the best way to access the preserve, which lies between interstates 15 and 40. Kelbaker Road bisects the park from north to south; northbound from I–40, Essex Road gets you to Hole-in-the-Wall on pavement but is graveled beyond there.

EXPLORING

TOP ATTRACTIONS

Hole-in-the-Wall. Created millions of years ago by volcanic activity, Hole-in-the-Wall formed when gases were trapped between layers of deposited ash, rock, and lava; the gas bubbles left holes in the solidified material.

According to some tale spinners, a member of the Butch Cassidy gang gave the area its name because it reminded him of his former hideout in Wyoming. You will encounter one of California's most distinctive hiking experiences here. Proceeding clockwise from a small visitor center, you walk gently down and around a craggy hill, past cacti and fading petroglyphs to Banshee Canyon, whose pockmarked walls resemble Swiss cheese. From there you head back out of the canyon, supporting yourself with widely spaced iron rings (some of which wiggle precariously from their rock moorings) as you ascend a 200-foot incline that deposits you back near the visitor center. The 90-minute adventure is mildly dangerous but wholly entertaining. ✉ *From I–40, take Essex Rd. exit, drive north 10 miles to Black Canyon Rd., and continue north another 10 miles* ☎ *760/928–2572* ⊕ *www.nps.gov/moja* ⛶ *Free* ⊗ *Hole-in-the-Wall, 24 hrs; visitor center, Fri.–Sun. 9–4.*

Fodor'sChoice **Kelso Dunes.** As you enter the preserve from the south, you'll pass miles
★ of open scrub brush, Joshua trees, and beautiful red-black cinder cones
before encountering the Kelso Dunes. These golden, fine-sand slopes
cover 70 square miles, reaching heights of 600 feet. You can reach them
via a ½-mile walk from the main parking area, but be prepared for a
serious workout. When you reach the top of a dune, kick a little bit
of sand down the lee side and listen to the sand "sing." North of the
dunes, in the town of Kelso, is the mission revival–style **Kelso Depot
Visitor Center.** The striking building, which dates to 1923, contains
several rooms of desert- and train-themed exhibits. ✉ *For Kelso Depot
Visitor Center, take Kelbaker Rd. exit from I–15 (head south 34 miles)
or I–40 (head north 22 miles)* ☎ *760/252–6100* ⊕ *www.nps.gov/moja*
🎫 *Free* ☉ *Dunes 24 hrs; visitor center Fri.–Tues. 9–5.*

NEEDLES

150 miles east of Barstow.

Along Route 66 and the Colorado River, Needles is a decent base
for exploring Mojave National Preserve and other desert attractions.
Founded in 1883, the town, named for the jagged mountain peaks
that overlook the city, served as a stop along the Santa Fe railroad line.

16

GETTING HERE AND AROUND
Greyhound and Amtrak both pass through town daily, though most
travelers arrive by car, either via Interstate 40 (east–west) or Highway
95 (north–south). Needles Area Transit is the local bus service.

ESSENTIALS
Bus Information Needles Area Transit ☎ *866/669–6309*
⊕ *www.cityofneedles.com.*

Visitor Information Needles Chamber of Commerce ✉ *100 G St.,
at Front St.* ☎ *760/326–2050* ⊕ *www.needleschamber.com.*

EXPLORING
TOP ATTRACTIONS
FAMILY **Havasu National Wildlife Refuge.** In 1941, after the construction of Parker
Fodor'sChoice Dam, President Franklin D. Roosevelt set aside Havasu National Wild-
★ life Refuge, a 24-mile stretch of land along the Colorado River between
Needles and Lake Havasu City. Best seen by boat, this beautiful water-
way is punctuated with isolated coves, sandy beaches, and Topock
Marsh, a favorite nesting site of herons, egrets, and other waterbirds.
You can see wonderful petroglyphs on the rocky red canyon cliffs of
Topock Gorge. The refuge has three points that provide boat access to
Topock Marsh, though not to the lower Colorado River. ■ TIP➜ **Spring
is by far the best time to visit, as the river is more likely to be robust
and wildflowers in bloom.** ✉ *Off I–40, 13 miles southeast of Needles*
☎ *760/326–3853* ⊕ *www.fws.gov/refuge/havasu.*

WHERE TO EAT AND STAY

$ PIZZA 🍴 **River City Pizza.** This inexpensive pizza place off Interstate 40 is a local favorite. Try the Vegetarian Deluxe pizza with a mug of cold lager, or a glass of wine out on the small patio. [$] *Average main: $10* ✉ *1901 Needles Hwy., at P St.* ☎ *760/326–9191* 🌐 *www.rivercitypizzaco.com.*

$ HOTEL 🏨 **Best Western Colorado River Inn.** The spartan rooms at the best lodging in town are decorated in rich colors; expect the standard Best Western amenities. **Pros:** good rates; clean rooms; nice pool. **Cons:** town's dead at night (and not much livelier during the day); occasional train noise. [$] *Rooms from: $80* ✉ *2371 Needles Hwy.* ☎ *760/326–4552, 800/780–7234* 🌐 *www.bestwestern.com* 🛏 *63 rooms* 🍽 *Breakfast.*

$ RESORT FAMILY 🏨 **Fender's River Road Resort.** On a calm section of the Colorado River, this funky little 1960s-era motel-resort—off the beaten path in a town that's in the proverbial middle of nowhere—caters to families. **Pros:** on the river; clean rooms; peaceful. **Cons:** several minutes from the freeway; rooms could use refreshing. [$] *Rooms from: $69* ✉ *3396 Needles Hwy.* ☎ *760/326–3423* 🛏 *10 rooms, 27 campsites with full hookups.*

LAKE HAVASU CITY, AZ

43 miles southeast of Needles.

This wide spot in the Colorado River, created in the 1930s by Parker Dam, is accessed from its eastern shore in Arizona. Here you can swim; zip around on a Jet Ski; paddle a kayak; fish for trout, bass, or bluegill; or boat beneath the London Bridge, one of the desert's oddest sights. During sunset the views are breathtaking. Just be wary of coming here during March, when spring-breaking students definitely change the vibe.

GETTING HERE AND AROUND

Shuttles operate between here and Las Vegas, but as with other desert sites, traveling by car is the only practical way to go. Havasu Area Transit is the local bus service.

ESSENTIALS

Transportation Contacts Havasu Area Transit ☎ *928/453–7600* 🌐 *www.lhcaz.gov/operations/transit.html.*

EXPLORING

London Bridge. The piece-by-piece reconstruction in 1971 of London Bridge put Lake Havasu City on the map. Today, the circa-1831 bridge connects the city to a small island. Riverbanks on both sides have numerous restaurants, hotels, and RV parks. ☎ *928/855–4115* 🌐 *www.havasuchamber.com* 🎟 *Free* 🕒 *Daily 24 hrs.*

WHERE TO EAT

$$$ AMERICAN 🍴 **Shugrue's.** This lakefront restaurant serves up beautiful views of London Bridge and the English Village, along with fresh seafood, steak, and specialties such as Bombay chicken and shrimp, served with spicy yogurt sauce and mango chutney. [$] *Average main: $24* ✉ *1425 N. McCulloch Blvd.* ☎ *928/453–1400* 🌐 *shugrueslakehavasu.com.*

SPORTS AND THE OUTDOORS
TOURS

London Bridge Watercraft Tours & Rentals. Right on the beach, this outfitter rents personal watercraft such as Jet Skis and Sea-Doos. ⊠ *Crazy Horse Campground, 1534 Beachcomber Blvd.* ☎ *928/453–8883* ⊕ *www. londonbridgewatercraft.com.*

OWENS VALLEY

Along U.S. 395 east of the Sierra Nevada.

In this undervisited region, the snowcapped Sierra Nevada range abruptly and majestically rises to the west, and the high desert whistles to the east. In between are a series of roadside towns full of character, history, and outfits that cater to adventurers and other visitors. The best dining and lodging options can be found along U.S. 395 in Lone Pine and Bishop.

LONE PINE

30 miles west of Panamint Valley.

Mt. Whitney towers majestically over this tiny community, which supplied nearby gold- and silver-mining outposts in the 1860s, and for the past century the town has been touched by Hollywood glamour: several hundred movies, TV episodes, and commercials have been filmed here.

GETTING HERE AND AROUND

Arrive by car via U.S. 395 from the north or south, or Highway 190 from Death Valley National Park. No train or regularly scheduled bus service is available.

ESSENTIALS

Visitor Information Lone Pine Chamber of Commerce ⊠ *120 S. Main St., at Whitney Portal Rd.* ☎ *760/876–4444* ⊕ *www.lonepinechamber.org.*

EXPLORING
TOP ATTRACTIONS

Alabama Hills. Drop by the Lone Pine Visitor Center for a map of the Alabama Hills and take a drive up Whitney Portal Road (turn west at the light) to this wonderland of granite boulders. Erosion has worn the rocks smooth; some have been chiseled to leave arches and other formations. The hills have become a popular location for rock climbing. Tuttle Creek campground sits among the rocks, with a nearby stream for fishing. ⊠ *Whitney Portal Rd., 4½ miles west of Lone Pine.*

Mt. Whitney. Straddling the border of Sequoia National Park and Inyo National Forest–John Muir Wilderness, Mt. Whitney (14,496 feet) is the highest mountain in the contiguous United States. A favorite game for travelers passing through Lone Pine is trying to guess which peak is Mt. Whitney. Almost no one gets it right because Mt. Whitney is hidden behind other mountains. There is no road that ascends the peak, but you can catch a glimpse of the mountain by driving curvy Whitney Portal Road west from Lone Pine into the mountains. The pavement ends at the trailhead to the top of the mountain, which is also the start of

16

the 211-mile John Muir Trail from Mt. Whitney to Yosemite National Park. Day and overnight permits are required to ascend Mt. Whitney. The highly competitive lottery for these permits opens on February 1st. At the portal, a restaurant (known for its pancakes) and a small store cater to hikers and campers staying at Whitney Portal Campground. You can see a waterfall from the parking lot and go fishing in a small trout pond. The portal area is closed from mid-October to early May; the road closes when snow conditions require. ⊠ *Whitney Portal Rd., west of Lone Pine* ⊕ *www.fs.usda.gov/attmain/inyo.*

WORTH NOTING

Beverly and Jim Rogers Museum of Lone Pine Film History. Hopalong Cassidy, Barbara Stanwyck, Roy Rogers, John Wayne—even Robert Downey Jr.—are among the stars who have starred in westerns and other films shot in the Alabama Hills and surrounding dusty terrain. The marquee-embellished museum relates this Hollywood-in-the-desert tale via exhibits and a rollicking 20-minute documentary. ⊠ *701 S. Main St., U.S. 395* ☎ *760/876–9909* ⊕ *www.lonepinefilmhistorymuseum.org* ⊠ *$5* ⊙ *Mon.–Sat. 10–5, Sun. 10–4.*

WHERE TO EAT AND STAY

$ ✕ **Alabama Hills Café & Bakery.** The extensive breakfast and lunch menus
AMERICAN   at this eatery just off the main drag include many vegetarian items. Portions are huge. Sandwiches are served on homemade bread; choose from up to six varieties baked fresh daily. Get a homemade pie, cake, or loaf to go. Ⓢ *Average main: $11* ⊠ *111 W. Post St., at S. Main St.* ☎ *760/876–4675.*

$ Ⓣ **Dow Villa Motel and Dow Hotel.** The Dow Villa Motel and the his-
HOTEL   toric Dow Hotel sit in the center of Lone Pine. **Pros:** clean rooms; great mountain views; in-room whirlpool tubs in motel. **Cons:** some rooms share bathrooms. Ⓢ *Rooms from: $110* ⊠ *310 S. Main St.* ☎ *760/876–5521, 800/824–9317* ⊕ *www.dowvillamotel.com* ⟿ *187 rooms* ⦙⊙⦙ *No meals.*

INDEPENDENCE

17 miles north of Lone Pine.

Named for a military outpost that was established near here in 1862, sleepy Independence has some wonderful historic buildings and is worth a stop for two other reasons. The Eastern California Museum provides a marvelous overview of regional history, and 6 miles south of the small downtown lies the Manzanar National Historic Site, one of 10 camps in the West where people of Japanese descent were confined during the Second World War.

GETTING HERE AND AROUND

Greyhound passes through town, but most travelers arrive by car on U.S. 395.

ESSENTIALS

Visitor Information Independence Chamber of Commerce ⊠ *139 N. Edwards. St.* ☎ *760/878–0084.*

A memorial honors the 11,000 Japanese-Americans who were held at the Manzanar War Relocation Center during World War II.

EXPLORING
TOP ATTRACTIONS

FAMILY **Eastern California Museum.** The highlights of this museum dedicated to Inyo County and the Eastern Sierra's history include Paiute and Shoshone baskets, photos and artifacts from Manzanar War Relocation Center, and a yard full of equipment used by early miners and ranchers. ⊠ *155 N. Grant St., at W. Center St.* ☎ *760/878–0258* ⊕ *www. inyocounty.us/ecmsite* ⊠ *Free* ⊙ *Daily 10–5.*

Fodor's Choice **Manzanar National Historic Site.** A reminder of an ugly episode in U.S.
★ history, the former Manzanar War Relocation Center is where more than 11,000 Japanese-Americans were confined behind barbed-wire fences between 1942 and 1945. A visit here is both deeply moving and inspiring—the former because it's hard to comprehend the United States was capable of confining its citizens in such a way, the latter because those imprisoned here showed great pluck and perseverance in making the best of a bad situation. Most of the buildings from 1940s are gone, but two sentry posts, the auditorium, and numerous Japanese rock gardens remain. One of eight guard towers and two barracks have been reconstructed, and a mess hall has been restored. You can drive the one-way dirt road on a self-guided tour past various ruins to a small cemetery, where a monument stands. Signs mark where the barracks, a hospital, a school, and the fire station once stood. ■ TIP→ An outstanding 8,000-square-foot interpretive center has exhibits and documentary photographs and screens a short film. ⊠ *West side of U.S. 395 between Independence and Lone Pine* ☎ *760/878–2194* ⊕ *www.nps.gov/manz* ⊠ *Free* ⊙ *Park daily dawn–dusk; center daily 9–4:30.*

WORTH NOTING

FAMILY **Mt. Whitney Fish Hatchery.** A delightful place for a family picnic, the hatchery was one of California's first trout farms. The Tudor revival–style structure, completed in 1917, is an architectural stunner, its walls nearly 3-feet thick with locally quarried granite. Fish production ceased in 2007 after a fire and subsequent mudslide, but dedicated volunteers staff the facility and raise trout for display purposes in a large pond out front. ■ TIP→ Bring change for the fish-food machines. ⊠ *Fish Hatchery Rd., 2 miles north of town* ☎ *760/876–4128* ⊕ *mtwhitneyfishhatchery.org* ▣ *Free* ☉ *Thurs.–Mon. 10–3:30* ☉ *Closed mid-Dec.–mid-Apr.*

EN ROUTE **Ancient Bristlecone Pine Forest.** About an hour's drive from Independence or Bishop you can view some of the oldest living trees on earth, some of which date back more than 40 centuries. The world's largest bristlecone pine can be found in Patriarch Grove. ⊠ *Schulman Grove Visitor Center, White Mountain Rd.* ✛ *From U.S. 395, turn east onto Hwy. 168 and follow signs for 23 miles* ⊕ *www.fs.usda.gov/main/inyo/home* ▣ *$3* ☉ *Mid-May–Nov., weather permitting.*

BISHOP

43 miles north of Independence.

One of the biggest towns along U.S. 395, bustling Bishop has views of the Sierra Nevada and the White and Inyo mountains. First settled by the Northern Paiute Indians, the area was named in 1861 for cattle rancher Samuel Bishop, who established a camp here. Paiute and Shoshone people reside on four reservations in the area. Bishop's kicks off the summer season with its Mule Days Celebration. Held over Memorial Day weekend, the five-day event includes mule races, a rodeo, an arts-and-crafts show, and country-music concerts.

GETTING HERE AND AROUND

To fully enjoy the many surrounding attractions, you must get here by car. Arrive and depart via U.S. 395 or, from Nevada, U.S. 6. Local transit provides limited service to nearby tourist sites.

ESSENTIALS

Bus Information Eastern Sierra Transit Authority ☎ *760/872–1901* ⊕ *estransit.com.*

Visitor Information Bishop Chamber of Commerce ⊠ *690 N. Main St., at Park St.* ☎ *760/873–8405, 888/395–3952* ⊕ *www.bishopvisitor.com.*

EXPLORING

FAMILY **Laws Railroad Museum.** The laid-back and wholly nostalgic railroad museum celebrates the Carson and Colorado Railroad Company, which set up a narrow-gauge railroad yard here in 1883. Among the exhibits are a self-propelled car from the Death Valley Railroad, a stamp mill from an area mine, and a full village of rescued buildings, including a post office, the original 1883 train depot, and a restored 1900 ranch house. Many of the buildings are full of "modern amenities" of days gone by. ⊠ *200 Silver Canyon Rd., off U.S. 6, 4.5 miles north of town* ☎ *760/873–5950* ⊕ *www.lawsmuseum.org* ▣ *$5 suggested donation* ☉ *Daily 10–4.*

WHERE TO EAT AND STAY

$ ✕ **Erick Schat's Bakkerÿ.** A bustling stop for motorists traveling to and BAKERY from Mammoth Lakes, this shop is crammed with delicious pastries, cookies, rolls, and other baked goods. The biggest draw, though, is the sheepherder bread, a hand-shaped and stone hearth–baked sourdough that was introduced during the gold rush by immigrant Basque sheepherders in 1907. That bread and others baked here are sliced to make the mammoth sandwiches the shop is also famous for. $ *Average main: $8* ⊠ *763 N. Main St., near Park St.* ☎ *760/873–7156* ⊕ *www. erickschatsbakery.com.*

$$ 🛏 **Bishop Creekside Inn.** The nicest spot to stay in Bishop, this clean B&B/INN and comfortable mountain-style hotel is a good base from which to explore the town or go skiing and trout fishing nearby. **Pros:** nice pool; spacious and modern rooms. **Cons:** pets not allowed. $ *Rooms from: $150* ⊠ *725 N. Main St.* ☎ *760/872–3044, 800/273–3550* ⊕ *www. bishopcreeksideinn.com* ⤴ *89 rooms* ⍝ *Breakfast.*

SPORTS AND THE OUTDOORS

The Owens Valley is trout country; its glistening alpine lakes and streams are brimming with feisty rainbow, brown, brook, and golden trout. Good spots include Owens River, the Owens River gorge, and Pleasant Valley Reservoir. Although you can fish year-round here, some fishing is catch-and-release. Bishop is the site of fishing derbies throughout the year, including the Blake Jones Blind Bogey Trout Derby, in March. Rock-climbing, mountain biking, and hiking are also popular Owens Valley outdoor activities.

FISHING

Brock's Flyfishing Specialists and Tackle Experts. Whether you want to take a fly-fishing class or a guided wade trip, Brock's is a valuable resource. Its website has up-to-date fish reports. ⊠ *100 N. Main St.* ☎ *760/872–3581* ⊕ *www.brocksflyfish.com.*

TOURS

Sierra Mountain Center. The guided experiences Sierra Mountain offers include hiking, skiing, snowshoeing, rock-climbing, and mountain-biking trips for all levels of expertise. ⊠ *200 S. Main St.* ☎ *760/873–8526* ⊕ *www.sierramountaincenter.com.*

16

DEATH VALLEY
NATIONAL PARK

WELCOME TO DEATH VALLEY NATIONAL PARK

TOP REASONS TO GO

★ **Roving rocks:** Death Valley's Racetrack is home to moving boulders, an unexplained phenomenon that has scientists baffled.

★ **Lowest spot on the continent:** Stand on the lowest spot on the continent at Badwater, 282 feet below sea level.

★ **Wildflower explosion:** During the spring, this desert landscape is ablaze with greenery and colorful flowers, especially between Badwater and Ashford Mill.

★ **Ghost towns:** Death Valley is renowned for its Wild West heritage and is home to dozens of crumbling settlements including Ballarat, Cerro Gordo, Keeler, Panamint City, and Rhyolite.

★ **Naturally amazing:** From canyons to sand dunes to salt flats and dry lake beds, Death Valley serves up plenty of geological treasures.

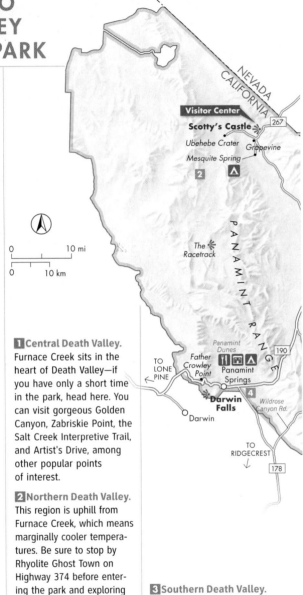

1 Central Death Valley. Furnace Creek sits in the heart of Death Valley—if you have only a short time in the park, head here. You can visit gorgeous Golden Canyon, Zabriskie Point, the Salt Creek Interpretive Trail, and Artist's Drive, among other popular points of interest.

2 Northern Death Valley. This region is uphill from Furnace Creek, which means marginally cooler temperatures. Be sure to stop by Rhyolite Ghost Town on Highway 374 before entering the park and exploring Moorish Scotty's Castle, colorful Titus Canyon, and jaw-dropping Ubehebe Crater.

3 Southern Death Valley. This is a desolate area, but there are plenty of sights that help convey Death Valley's rich history.

4 Western Death Valley.
Panamint Springs Resort
is a nice place to grab a
meal and get your bearings
before moving on to quaint
Darwin Falls, smooth rolling
sand dunes, beehive-
shaped Wildrose Charcoal
Kilns, and historic Stovepipe
Wells Village.

CALIFORNIA

GETTING ORIENTED

Death Valley National Park
covers 5,235 square miles,
ranges up to 60 miles wide,
and measures 160 miles
north to south. Within the
park, the Panamint Range
parallels Death Valley to the
west, the Amargosa Range is
outside the park to the east.
Nearly the entire park lies
in southeastern California,
with a small eastern portion
crossing over into Nevada.

17

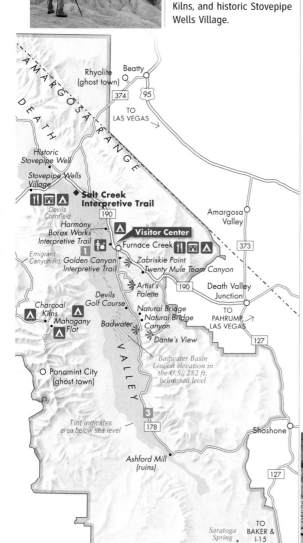

Rhyolite
(ghost town)
Beatty
374
95
TO
LAS VEGAS

AMARGOSA RANGE
DEATH

Historic
Stovepipe Well
Stovepipe Wells
Village

**Salt Creek
Interpretive Trail**

Devils
Cornfield
190

Amargosa
Valley

Harmony
Borax Works
Interpretive Trail

Visitor Center

Furnace Creek
373

Emigrant
Canyon Rd.
Golden Canyon
Interpretive Trail

Zabriskie Point
Twenty Mule Team Canyon

Artist's
Palette
190

Death Valley
Junction

Devils
Golf Course

Charcoal
Kilns

Mahogany
Flat

Natural Bridge
Natural Bridge
Canyon

Badwater

Dante's View

TO
PAHRUMP
LAS VEGAS

127

VALLEY

*Badwater Basin
Lowest elevation in
the U.S., 282 ft.
below sea level*

Panamint City
(ghost town)

*Tint indicates
area below sea level*

3

178

Shoshone

Ashford Mill
(ruins)

127

*Saratoga
Spring*

TO
BAKER &
I-15

Updated by
John Blodgett

The desert is no Disneyland. With its scorching summer heat and vast, sparsely populated tracts of land, it's not often at the top of the list when most people plan their California vacations. But the natural riches of Death Valley—the largest national park outside Alaska—are overwhelming: rolling waves of sand dunes, black cinder cones thrusting up hundreds of feet from a blistered desert floor, riotous sheets of wildflowers, bizarrely shaped Joshua trees basking in the orange glow of a sunset, tiny pupfish that enthrall youngsters, and a silence that is both dramatic and startling.

DEATH VALLEY PLANNER

WHEN TO GO
Most of the park's 1 million annual visitors still come between late fall and early spring, taking advantage of moderate temperatures and the lack of rainfall. During these cooler months you will need to book a room in advance, but don't worry: the park never feels crowded. If you visit during summer, believe everything you've ever heard about desert heat—it can be brutal, with temperatures often topping 120°F. The dry air wicks moisture from the body without causing a sweat, so drink plenty of water. Bring sunglasses, a hat, and sufficient clothing to block the sun's rays and the wind. Flash floods are fairly common; sections of roadway can be flooded or washed away. The wettest month is February, when the park receives an average of 0.5 inch of rain.

GETTING HERE AND AROUND
CAR TRAVEL
It can take more than three hours to cross from one side of the park to another, so it's important to choose an entrance point that makes sense for what you want to see. If you're driving from Los Angeles,

enter through the western portion along Highway 395; if you're coming from Las Vegas, enter from the north at Beatty, Nevada, or via the central entrance at Death Valley Junction. Travelers from Orange County, San Diego, and the Inland Empire should access the park via Interstate 15 North at Baker.

When driving in Death Valley, reliable maps are important, as signage is often limited or, in a few places, nonexistent. Other important accessories include a compass, a mobile phone (though these don't always work in remote areas), and extra food and water (at least 1 gallon per person per day is recommended, plus additional radiator water). If you're able to take a four-wheel-drive vehicle, bring it: many of Death Valley's most spectacular canyons are otherwise inaccessible. Be aware of possible winter closures or driving restrictions due to snow.

Driving Information California Highway Patrol. The California Highway Patrol offers the latest traffic incident information. ☎ 800/427-7623 recorded info, 760/872-5900 live dispatcher ⊕ www.chp.ca.gov.

PARK ESSENTIALS

PARK FEES AND PERMITS
The entrance fee is $20 per vehicle and $10 for those entering on foot, bus, bike, or motorcycle. The payment, valid for seven consecutive days, is collected at the park's entrance stations and at the visitor center at Furnace Creek. (If you enter the park on Highway 190, you won't find an entrance station; remember to pay at a self-service fee station or stop by the visitor center to pay the fee.) Annual park passes, valid only at Death Valley, are $40.

A permit is not required for groups of 19 or fewer, but if you're planning an overnight visit to the backcountry, complete a registration form at the Furnace Creek Visitor Center. Backcountry camping is allowed in areas that are at least 2 miles from maintained campgrounds and the main paved or unpaved roads and ¼ mile from water sources. Most abandoned mining areas are restricted to day use.

PARK HOURS
Most facilities within the park remain open year-round, daily 8–6. Call ahead to see if seasonal changes are in effect.

WHAT IT COSTS			
$	$$	$$$	$$$$
Restaurants	under $12	$13–$20	$21–$30	over $30
Hotels	under $100	$101–$150	$151–$200	over $200

Restaurant prices are the average cost of a main course at dinner or, if dinner is not served, at lunch. Hotel prices are the lowest cost of a standard double room in high season.

TOURS
Death Valley Tours. Choose from a variety of roughly 10-hour tours via all manner of vehicles: luxury motor-coach, SUV, even a Hummer. Tours of the park pass through its most famous landmarks, and include lunch

17

and hotel pickup from designated Las Vegas–area hotels. ☎ *800/719–3768 Death Valley Tours ⊕ www.deathvalleytours.net ✉ From $204.*

Farabee's Jeep Rentals. At Farebbe's Jeep Rentals, you can make a reservation for a guided tour into Titus Canyon (4 hours, $145) or Badwater Basin (2 hours, $65), or rent a two- or four-door Jeep for a do-it-yourself tour. All Jeeps come equipped with air-conditioning, automatic transmission, and an ice chest filled with water. ✉ *Across from Inn at Furnace Creek, Hwy. 190, Furnace Creek* ☎ *760/786–9872, 877/970–5337 ⊕ www.farabeesjeeprentals.com ✉ From $65.*

Furnace Creek Visitor Center tours. This center has many tour options, including a weekly 2-mile Harmony Borax Walk and guided hikes to Mosaic Canyon and Golden Canyon. Less strenuous options include wildflower, birding, and geology walks, and a Furnace Creek Inn historical tour. Visit the website for a complete list. The visitor center also shows a movie about the park every half hour daily from 8 to 5. ✉ *Furnace Creek Visitor Center, Rte. 190, 30 miles northwest of Death Valley Junction* ☎ *760/786–2331 ⊕ www.nps.gov/deva/planyourvisit/tours.htm.*

Pink Jeep Tours Las Vegas. Hop aboard a distinctive, pink four-wheel-drive vehicle with Pink Jeep Tours Las Vegas to visit places—the Charcola Kilns, the Racetrack, and Titus Canyon among them—that your own vehicle might not be able to handle. Pink Jeep tours are professionally narrated, and last 9 to 10 hours from Las Vegas (you also can board at Furnace Creek). ✉ *3629 West Hacienda Ave., Las Vegas, Nevada* ☎ *888/900–4480 ⊕ pinkjeeptours.com ✉ From $244.*

VISITOR INFORMATION

PARK CONTACT INFORMATION
Death Valley National Park ☎ *760/786–3200 ⊕ www.nps.gov/deva.*

VISITOR CENTERS
Furnace Creek Visitor Center and Museum. The exhibits and artifacts here provide a broad overview of how Death Valley formed; you can pick up maps at the bookstore run by the Death Valley Natural History Association. This is also the place to learn about or sign up for ranger-led walks (available November through April) or check out a live presentation about the valley's cultural and natural history. The helpful center offers a 20-minute movie about the park every 30 minutes. Your children are likely to receive plenty of individual attention from the enthusiastic rangers. ✉ *Hwy. 190, 30 miles northwest of Death Valley Junction* ☎ *760/786–3200 ⊕ www.nps.gov/deva ⊙ Daily 8–5.*

Scotty's Castle Visitor Center and Museum. During your visit to Death Valley, make sure you make the hour's drive north from Furnace Creek to Scotty's Castle. In addition to living-history tours, you'll find a nice display of exhibits, books, self-guided tour pamphlets, and displays about the castle's creators, Death Valley Scotty and Albert M. Johnson. Fuel up with sandwiches or souvenirs (there's no gasoline sold here anymore) before heading back out to the park. ✉ *Rte. 267, 53 miles northwest of Furnace Creek and 45 miles northwest of Stovepipe Wells Village* ☎ *760/786–2392 ⊕ www.nps.gov/deva ⊙ Daily 9–4:15 (hours vary seasonally).*

EXPLORING

SCENIC DRIVE

Artist's Drive. This 9-mile, one-way route skirts the foothills of the Black Mountains and provides intimate views of the changing landscape. Once inside the "palette," the huge expanses of the valley are replaced by the small-scale natural beauty of pigments created by volcanic deposits or sedimentary layers. It's a quiet, lonely drive, and shouldn't be rushed. Reach Artist's Palette by heading south on Badwater Road from its intersection with Rte. 190. ⊠ *Death Valley National Park.*

HISTORIC SITES

FAMILY **Scotty's Castle.** This Moorish-style mansion, begun in 1924 and never completed, takes its name from Walter Scott, better known as Death Valley Scotty. An ex-cowboy, prospector, and performer in Buffalo Bill's Wild West Show, Scotty always told people the castle was his, financed by gold from a secret mine. In reality, there was no mine, and the house belonged to a Chicago millionaire named Albert Johnson, whom Scott had finagled into investing in the fictitious mine. Despite the con, Johnson and Scott became great friends. The house functioned for a while as a hotel and still contains works of art, imported carpets, handmade European furniture, and a tremendous pipe organ. Costumed rangers, with varying degrees of enthusiasm, re-create life at the castle circa 1939. Check out the Underground Tour, which takes you through a ¼-mile tunnel in the castle basement. ⊠ *Scotty's Castle Rd. (Hwy. 267), 53 miles north of Salt Creek Interpretive Trail* ☎ *760/786–2392* ⊕ *www.nps.gov/deva* ⊠ *$15* ⊙ *Daily 8:30–4:15, tours daily 9–4 (hours vary seasonally).*

SCENIC STOPS

Artist's Palette. So called for the contrasting colors of its volcanic deposits and sedimentary layers, this is one of signature sights of Death Valley. Artist's Drive, the approach to the area, is one way heading north off Badwater Road, so if you're visiting Badwater from Furnace Creek, come here on the way back. The drive winds through foothills of sedimentary and volcanic rocks. About 4 miles into the drive, a short side road veers right to a parking lot that's a few hundred feet before the "palette," whose natural colors include shades of green, gold, and pink. ⊠ *off Badwater Rd., 11 miles south of Furnace Creek.*

Badwater. At 282 feet below sea level, Badwater is the lowest spot on land in North America—and also one of the hottest. Stairs and wheelchair ramps descend from the parking lot to a wooden platform that overlooks a sodium chloride pool, a small but remarkably persistent reminder that the valley floor used to contain a lake. You can continue past the platform on a broad, white path that peters out after a half-mile or so. Badwater is one of the most popular and easily accessible sites within the park. From this lowest point, be sure to look across to Telescope Peak, which towers more than 2 miles above the valley floor. ⊠ *Badwater Rd., 19 miles south of Furnace Creek.*

17

DID YOU KNOW?

One of the best ways to experience Artist's Palette—a beautiful landscape of colorful mineral deposits—is by following Artist's Drive, a 9-mile one-way road through the area.

CLOSE UP

Plants and Wildlife in Death Valley

There's a general misconception that Death Valley National Park consists of mile upon endless mile of flat desert sands, scattered cacti, and an occasional cow skull. Many people don't realize that across the valley floor from Badwater—the lowest point in North America—Telescope Peak towers at 11,049 feet above sea level. The extreme topography of Death Valley is a lesson in geology. Two hundred million years ago seas covered the area, depositing layers of sediment and fossils. Between 3.5 million and 5 million years ago faults in the Earth's crust and volcanic activity pushed and folded the ground, causing mountain ranges to rise and the valley floor to drop. The valley was then filled periodically by lakes, which eroded the surrounding rocks into fantastic formations and deposited the salts that now cover the floor of the basin.

Most animal life in Death Valley (51 mammal, 36 reptile, 307 bird, and 3 amphibian species) is found near the limited sources of water. The bighorn sheep spend most of their time in the secluded upper reaches of the park's rugged canyons and ridges. Coyotes often can be seen lazing in the shade next to the golf course and have been known to run onto the fairways to steal a golf ball. The only native fish in the park is the pupfish, which grows to slightly longer than 1 inch. In winter, when the water is cold, the fish lie dormant in the bottom mud, becoming active again in spring. Because they are wary of large moving shapes, you must stand quietly over a pool at Salt Creek to see them.

Botanists say there are more than 1,000 species of plants here (21 exist nowhere else in the world), though many annual plants lie dormant as seeds for all but a few months in spring, when rains trigger a bloom. The rest congregate around the few water sources. Most of the low-elevation vegetation grows around the oases at Furnace Creek and Scotty's Castle, where oleanders, palms, and salt cedar grow. At higher elevations you will find pinyon, juniper, and bristlecone pine.

Fodor's Choice **Dante's View.** This lookout is more than 5,000 feet up in the Black Mountains. In the dry desert air you can see across most of 160-mile-long Death Valley. The view is astounding. Take a 10-minute, mildly strenuous walk from the parking lot toward a series of rocky overlooks, where with binoculars you can spot some of Death Valley's signature sites. A few interpretive signs point out the highlights below in the valley and across, in the Sierra. Getting here from Furnace Creek takes about an hour—time well invested. ⊠ *Dante's View Rd., off Hwy. 190, 35 miles from Badwater, 20 miles south of Twenty Mule Team Canyon.*

Devil's Golf Course. Thousands of miniature salt pinnacles carved into surreal shapes by the desert wind dot this wildly varied landscape. The salt was pushed up to the earth's surface by pressure created as underground salt- and water-bearing gravel crystallized. Get out of your vehicle and take a closer look; you'll see perfectly round holes descending into the ground. ⊠ *Badwater Rd., 13 miles south of Furnace Creek. Turn right onto dirt road and drive 1 mile.*

Racetrack. Getting here involves a 28-mile journey over a rough dirt road, but the reward is well worth the trip. Where else in the world do rocks move on their own? This phenomenon has baffled scientists for years and is perhaps one of the last great natural mysteries. No one has actually seen the rocks in motion, but theory has it that when it rains, the hard-packed lake bed becomes slippery enough that gusty winds push the rocks along—sometimes for several hundred yards. When the mud dries, a telltale trail remains. The trek to the Racetrack can be made in a sedan, but beware—sharp rocks can slash tires; a truck or SUV with thick tires, high clearance, and a spare tire are suggested. ⊠ *27 miles west of Ubehebe Crater via dirt road.*

Sand Dunes at Mesquite Flat. These dunes, made up of minute pieces of quartz and other rock, are ever-changing products of the wind-rippled hills, with curving crests and a sun-bleached hue. The dunes are the most photographed destination in the park, and you can see them at their best at sunrise and sunset. Keep your eyes open for animal tracks—you may even spot a coyote or fox. Bring plenty of water, and note where you parked your car: it's easy to become disoriented in this ocean of sand. If you lose your bearings, climb to the top of a dune and scan the horizon for the parking lot. ⊠ *19 miles north of Hwy. 190, northeast of Stovepipe Wells Village.*

Titus Canyon. This popular one-way, 27-mile drive starts at Nevada Hwy. 374 (Daylight Pass Road), 2 miles from the park's boundary. Along the way you'll see Leadville Ghost Town and spectacular limestone and dolomite narrows at the end of the canyon. Toward the end, a two-way-section of gravel road leads you into the mouth of the canyon from Scotty's Castle Road. High-clearance vehicles are strongly recommended. ⊠ *Access road off Nevada Hwy. 374, 6 miles west of Beatty, NV.*

Zabriskie Point. Although only about 710 feet in elevation, this is one of Death Valley National Park's most scenic spots, overlooking a striking panorama of wrinkled, multicolor hills. It's a great place to watch the sunrise, but it can be bustling any time of day. Pair it with a drive out to magnificent Dante's View. ⊠ *Hwy. 190, 5 miles south of Furnace Creek.*

SPORTS AND THE OUTDOORS

BIRD-WATCHING

Approximately 307 bird species have been identified in Death Valley. The best place to see the park's birds is along the Salt Creek Interpretive Trail, where you can spot ravens, common snipes, killdeer, spotted sandpipers, and great blue herons. Along the fairways at Furnace Creek Golf Club, you can see kingfishers, peregrine falcons, hawks, Canada geese, yellow warblers, and the occasional golden eagle. Scotty's Castle attracts wintering birds from around the globe that are attracted to its running water, shady trees, and shrubs. Other good spots to find birds are at Saratoga Springs, Mesquite Springs, Travertine Springs, and Grimshaw Lake near Tecopa. You can download a complete park bird checklist, divided by season, at ⊕ *www.nps.gov/deva/naturescience/birds.htm.* Rangers at Furnace Creek Visitor Center often lead birding walks nearby between November and March.

FOUR-WHEELING

Maps and SUV guidebooks for four-wheel-drive and other backcountry roads (including the popular Cottonwood/Marble canyons, Racetrack, Eureka Dunes, Saratoga Springs, and Warm Springs Canyon) are offered at the Furnace Creek Visitor Center. Remember: Never travel alone and be sure to pack plenty of water and snacks. Driving off established roads is strictly prohibited in the park.

HIKING

Plan to hike before or after midday in the spring, summer, or fall; note that park rangers strongly discourage hiking during these seasons because of the heat. Carry plenty of water, wear protective clothing, and keep an eye out for black widows, scorpions, snakes, and other potentially dangerous creatures. Some of the best trails are unmarked; if the opportunity arises, ask for directions.

EASY

FAMILY Fodor's Choice ★ **Darwin Falls.** This lovely 2-mile round-trip hike rewards you with a refreshing waterfall surrounded by thick vegetation and a rocky gorge. No swimming or bathing is allowed, but it's a beautiful place for a picnic. Adventurous hikers can scramble higher toward more rewarding views of the falls. *Easy.* ⊠ *Access the 2-mile graded dirt road and parking area off Hwy. 190, 1 mile west of Panamint Springs Resort.*

FAMILY **Salt Creek Interpretive Trail.** This trail, a ½-mile boardwalk circuit, loops through a spring-fed wash. The nearby hills are brown and gray, but the floor of the wash is alive with aquatic plants such as pickleweed and salt grass. The stream and ponds here are among the few places in the park to see the rare pupfish, the only native fish species in Death Valley. Animals such as bobcats, fox, coyotes, and snakes visit the spring, and you may also see ravens, common snipes, killdeer, and great blue herons. *Easy.* ⊠ *Off Hwy. 190, 14 miles north of Furnace Creek.*

MODERATE

Fall Canyon. This is a 3-mile, one-way hike from the Titus canyon parking area. First, walk ½ miles north along the base of the mountains to a large wash, then go 2½ miles up the canyon to a 35-foot dry fall. You can continue by climbing around to the falls on the south side. *Moderate.* ⊠ *Access road off Scotty's Castle Rd., 33 miles northwest of Furnace Creek.*

FAMILY **Mosaic Canyon.** A gradual uphill trail (4 miles round-trip) winds through the smoothly polished walls of this narrow canyon. There are dry falls to climb at the upper end. *Moderate.* ⊠ *Access road off Hwy. 190, ½ mile west of Stovepipe Wells Village.*

"I'd always wanted to photograph this remote location, and on my drive into Death Valley I was rewarded at Zabriskie Point with this amazing view." —photo by Rodney Ee, Fodors.com member

DIFFICULT

Fodor's Choice
★ **Telescope Peak Trail.** The 14-mile round-trip begins at Mahogany Flat Campground, which is accessible by a rough dirt road. The steep and at some points treacherous trail winds through pinyon, juniper, and bristlecone pines, with excellent views of Death Valley and Panamint Valley. Ice axes and crampons may be necessary in winter—check at the Furnace Creek Visitor Center. It takes a minimum of six grueling hours to hike to the top of the 11,049-foot peak and then return. Getting to the peak is a strenuous endeavor; take plenty of water and only attempt it in fall unless you're an experienced hiker. *Difficult.* ⊠ *Off Wildrose Rd., south of Charcoal Kilns.*

HORSEBACK AND CARRIAGE RIDES

TOURS AND OUTFITTERS

Furnace Creek Stables. Set off on a one- or two-hour guided horseback or carriage ride from Furnace Creek Stables. The rides traverse trails with views of the surrounding mountains, where multicolor volcanic rock and alluvial fans form a background for date palms and other vegetation. Evening carriage rides take passengers around the golf course and Furnace Creek Ranch. The stables are open October–May only. ⊠ *Hwy. 190, Furnace Creek* ☎ *760/614–1018* ⊕ *www.furnacecreekstables.net* ⊡ *From $45.*

WHERE TO EAT

$$ CAFÉ FAMILY 🍴 **Forty-Niner Cafe.** This casual coffee shop serves basic American fare for breakfast (except in the summer), lunch, and dinner. It's done up in a rustic mining style with whitewashed pine walls, vintage map-covered tables, and prospector-branded chairs. Past menus and old photographs decorate the walls. [$] *Average main: $20* ✉ *Ranch at Furnace Creek, Hwy. 190, Furnace Creek* ☎ *760/786–2345* 🌐 *www.furnacecreekresort.com.*

$$$$ AMERICAN Fodor's Choice ★ 🍴 **Inn at Furnace Creek Dining Room.** Fireplaces, beamed ceilings, and spectacular views provide a visual feast to match the inn's ambitious menu. Dishes may include such desert-theme items as High Sierra Nevada pasta, and simpler fare such as salmon and free-range chicken and filet mignon pair well with the signature prickly-pear margarita. There's a seasonal menu of vegetarian dishes, too. There's a minimal evening dress code (no T-shirts or shorts). Lunch is served, too, and you can always have afternoon tea in the lobby, an inn tradition since 1927. Breakfast and Sunday brunch are also served. Reservations are essential for dinner only. [$] *Average main: $35* ✉ *Inn at Furnace Creek, Hwy. 190, Furnace Creek* ☎ *760/786–3385* 🌐 *www.furnacecreekresort.com* ✍ *Reservations essential* ⏲ *Closed Mother's Day–mid-Oct.*

WHERE TO STAY

During the busy season (November through March) you should make reservations for lodgings within the park several months in advance.

$$$$ HOTEL Fodor's Choice ★ 🏨 **The Inn at Furnace Creek.** Built in 1927, this adobe-brick-and-stone lodge nestled in one of the park's greenest oases is Death Valley's most luxurious accommodation, going so far as to have valet parking. **Pros:** refined; comfortable; great views. **Cons:** a far cry from roughing it; expensive. [$] *Rooms from: $375* ✉ *Furnace Creek Village, near intersection of Hwy. 190 and Badwater Rd.* ☎ *760/786–2345* 🌐 *www.furnacecreekresort.com* 🛏 *66 rooms* ⏲ *Closed Mother's Day–mid-Oct.* 🍽 *Breakfast.*

$ B&B/INN 🏨 **Panamint Springs Resort.** Ten miles inside the west entrance of the park, this low-key resort overlooks the sand dunes and peculiar geological formations of the Panamint Valley. **Pros:** slow-paced; friendly; there's a glorious amount of peace and quiet after sundown. **Cons:** far from the park's main attractions. [$] *Rooms from: $79* ✉ *Hwy. 190, 28 miles west of Stovepipe Wells* ☎ *775/482–7680* 🌐 *www.deathvalley.com/psr* 🛏 *14 rooms, 1 cabin* 🍽 *No meals.*

$ HOTEL 🏨 **Stovepipe Wells Village.** If you prefer quiet nights and an unfettered view of the night sky and nearby sand dunes and Mosaic Canyon, this property is for you. **Pros:** intimate, relaxed; no big-time partying; authentic desert-community ambience. **Cons:** isolated; a bit dated. [$] *Rooms from: $118* ✉ *Hwy. 190, Stovepipe Wells* ☎ *760/786–2387* 🌐 *www.escapetodeathvalley.com* 🛏 *83 rooms* 🍽 *No meals.*

THE CENTRAL VALLEY

Highway 99 from Bakersfield to Lodi

WELCOME TO THE CENTRAL VALLEY

TOP REASONS TO GO

★ **Down under:** Forestiere Underground Gardens is not the flashiest tourist attraction in California, but it is one of the strangest—and oddly inspirational.

★ **Grape escape:** In the past two decades, Lodi's wineries have grown sufficiently in stature for the charming little town to become a must-sip destination.

★ **Utopian spirit:** A century ago, a small but resourceful group of citizens established the state's first all–African American town. Colonel Allensworth State Historic Park celebrates their utopian spirit.

★ **Go with the flow:** White-water rafting will get your blood pumping, and maybe your clothes wet, on the Stanislaus River near Oakdale.

★ **Hee haw!:** Kick up your heels and break out your drawl at Buck Owens' Crystal Palace in Bakersfield, a city some believe is the heart of country music.

1 Southern Central Valley. When gold was discovered in Kern County in the 1860s, settlers flocked to the southern end of the Central Valley. Black gold—oil—is now the area's most valuable commodity; the county provides two-thirds of California's oil production. Kern is also among the country's five most productive agricultural counties. From the flat plains around Bakersfield, the landscape grows gently hilly and then graduates to mountains as it nears Kernville, which lies in the Kern River valley.

2 Mid-Central Valley. The Mid-Central Valley extends over three counties—Tulare, Kings, and Fresno. Historic Hanford and bustling Visalia are off the tourist-traffic radar but have their charms. From Visalia, Highway 198 winds east 35 miles to Generals Highway, which passes through Sequoia and Kings Canyon national parks (⇨ Chapter 21). Highway 180 snakes east 55 miles to Sequoia and Kings Canyon. From Fresno, Highway 41 leads north 95 miles to Yosemite National Park (⇨ Chapter 20).

3 North Central Valley. The northern section of the valley cuts through Merced, Madera, Stanislaus, and San Joaquin counties, from the flat, abundantly fertile terrain between Merced and Modesto north to the edges of the Sacramento River delta and the fringes of the Gold Country. If you're heading to Yosemite National Park (⇨ Chapter 20) from Northern California, chances are you'll travel through (or near) one or more small gateway communities such as Oakdale.

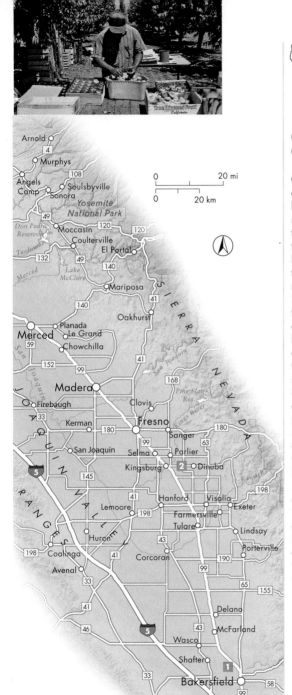

GETTING ORIENTED

California has a diversity of delicious vacation possibilities. Among its many outstanding regions, however, the Central Valley is arguably the least inviting. This flat landscape, sometimes blistery hot and smelly, contains no famous attractions beyond its bountiful farmland, which few would regard as scenic except perhaps just before harvest. For many vacationers, it is a region to drive through as quickly as possible on the way to fabulous Sequoia, Kings Canyon, and Yosemite national parks (⇨ *Chapters 20 and 21*). For those who have an extra day or two, whose tourism tastes don't demand Disneyland-level excitement, it can represent a pleasant diversion and provide insights into an enormous agricultural region. The valley is the vast geographical center of California and, from a breadbasket perspective, its proverbial heart.

18

Updated
by Cheryl
Crabtree

In California's family of diverse regions, the 225-mile-long Central Valley is literally and figuratively a middle sibling. Cradled between the popular coastal communities to the west and the national parks in the mighty Sierra Nevada to the east, the "Big Valley" is among the world's most fertile working lands, filled with orchards, vineyards, and farms. The area also supports myriad bird and other animal species.

The Central Valley encompasses all or part of eight counties. Vineyards, especially in the northern valley around Lodi, and almond orchards, whose white blossoms make February a brighter month, are pleasant sights out motorists' windows. In the towns, historical societies display artifacts of the region's eccentric past, concert halls and restored theaters showcase samplings of contemporary culture, and museums provide a blend of both. Country-music enthusiasts will find a lot to appreciate on the radio and on stages, especially in the Bakersfield area. Summer nights spent at a minor-league baseball park—Bakersfield, Fresno, Modesto, and Visalia have teams—can be a relaxing, affordable experience. Whether you're on back roads or main streets, you'll find the locals proud to help outsiders explore the area.

PLANNING

WHEN TO GO

Spring, when wildflowers are in bloom and the scent of fruit blossoms is in the air, and fall, when the air is brisk and leaves turn red and gold, are the best times to visit. Many of the valley's biggest festivals take place during these seasons. (If you suffer from allergies, though, beware of spring, when stone-fruit trees blossom.) Summer, when temperatures often top 100°F, can be oppressive, though area water parks and lakes provide much-needed respite. Many attractions close in winter, when thick, ground-hugging tule fog is a common driving hazard.

GETTING HERE AND AROUND

AIR TRAVEL

The area's main airport is Fresno Yosemite International Airport (FAT), served by AeroMexico, Alaska/Horizon, Allegiant, American, Delta, Frontier, United/United Express, US Airways, and Volaris. Bakersfield's Kern County Airport at Meadows Field (BFL), served by Frontier, United Express, and US Airways, is the southern air gateway to the Central Valley. United Express serves Modesto's airport (⇨ *Modesto, below)*.

Airport Contacts Fresno Yosemite International Airport *(FAT).* ✉ *5175 E. Clinton Way, Fresno* ☎ *559/621–4500, 800/244–2359 automated information* ⊕ *www.flyfresno.com.* **Meadows Field Airport** *(BFL).* ✉ *1401 Skyway Dr., Bakersfield* ☎ *661/391–1800* ⊕ *www.meadowsfield.com.*

BUS TRAVEL

Greyhound provides bus service to several major cities, and Orange Belt Stages provides coach service (and some Amtrak connections) to Bakersfield, Visalia, and other large towns. KART (Kings Area Rural Transit) provides service throughout Kings County.

Bus Contact Greyhound ☎ *800/231–2222* ⊕ *www.greyhound.com.* **KART** ☎ *559/584–0101* ⊕ *www.mykartbus.com.* **Orange Belt Stages** ☎ *800/266–7433, 559/730–4408* ⊕ *www.orangebelt.com.*

CAR TRAVEL

Highway 99 is the main route between the valley's major cities and towns. Interstate 5 runs roughly parallel to it to the west but misses the major population centers; its main use is for quick access to San Francisco or Los Angeles. Major roads that connect the interstate with Highway 99 are highways 58 (to Bakersfield), 198 (to Visalia), 152 (to Chowchilla, via Los Banos), 140 (to Merced), 132 (to Modesto), and 120 (to Manteca).

Road Conditions Caltrans ☎ *800/427–7623* ⊕ *www.dot.ca.gov.*

TRAIN TRAVEL

Amtrak's daily *San Joaquin* stops in Bakersfield, Fresno, Merced, Modesto, and Stockton.

Train Contact Amtrak ☎ *800/872–7245* ⊕ *www.amtrakcalifornia.com.*

RESTAURANTS

Fast-food places and chain restaurants dominate valley highways, but away from the main drag, homegrown bistros and fine restaurants take advantage of the local produce and meats that are the cornerstone of California cuisine. Superb Mexican restaurants can be found here, and Chinese, Italian, Armenian, and Basque cuisines are amply represented.

HOTELS

Chain motels and hotels—utilitarian but clean and comfortable—predominate, but there are also upscale lodgings, small inns, and Victorian-style B&Bs. *Hotel reviews have been shortened. For full information, visit Fodors.com.*

18

WHAT IT COSTS				
	$	$$	$$$	$$$$
Restaurants	under $16	$16–$22	$23–$30	over $30
Hotels	under $121	$121–$175	$176–$250	over $250

Restaurant prices are the average cost of a main course at dinner, excluding sales tax of 7%–10% (depending on location). Hotel prices are in the lowest cost of a standard double room in high season, excluding service charges and 8%–13% tax.

SOUTH CENTRAL VALLEY

BAKERSFIELD

110 miles north of Los Angeles; 110 miles west of Ridgecrest.

Bakersfield's founder, Colonel Thomas Baker, arrived with the discovery of gold in the nearby Kern River valley in 1851. With 355,000 residents, including the country's largest Basque community, his namesake town is Kern County's biggest city. A country-music haven nicknamed Nashville West, Bakersfield is closely affiliated with performers Buck Owens (who died here in 2006) and Merle Haggard (who was born here in 1937). It also has some fine museums.

GETTING HERE AND AROUND
Arrive here by car via Highway 99 from the north or south, or via Highway 58 from the east or west. Amtrak and Greyhound provide train and bus service. GETbus operates local buses.

ESSENTIALS
Bus Contact GETbus ☎ *661/869-2438* ⊕ *www.getbus.org.*

Visitor Information Bakersfield Convention & Visitors Bureau
✉ *515 Truxtun Ave.* ☎ *661/852-7282, 866/425-7353* ⊕ *www.visitbakersfield. com* ⊗ *Weekdays 8–5.* **VisitKern** ✉ *2101 Oak St.* ☎ *661/868-5376, 661/861-2017* ⊕ *www.visitkern.com.*

EXPLORING
FAMILY   **California Living Museum.** At this combination zoo, botanical garden, and
Fodor'sChoice   natural-history museum, the emphasis is on the zoo. All animal and
★   plant species displayed are native to the state. Within the reptile house lives every species of rattlesnake found in California. The landscaped grounds—in the hills about a 20-minute drive northeast of Bakersfield— also shelter captive bald eagles, tortoises, coyotes, black bears, and foxes. ✉ *10500 Alfred Harrell Hwy., Hwy. 178 east to Harrell Hwy. north* ☎ *661/872-2256* ⊕ *calmzoo.org* 🎫 *$9* ⊗ *Mar.–Oct., daily 9–5; Nov.–Feb., daily 9–4.*

FAMILY   **Kern County Museum and Lori Brock Children's Discovery Center.** This 16-acre
Fodor'sChoice   site is one of the Central Valley's top museum complexes. The indoor-
★   outdoor Kern County Museum is an open-air, walk-through historic village with more than 55 restored or re-created buildings dating from the 1860s to the 1940s. *Black Gold: The Oil Experience*, a permanent

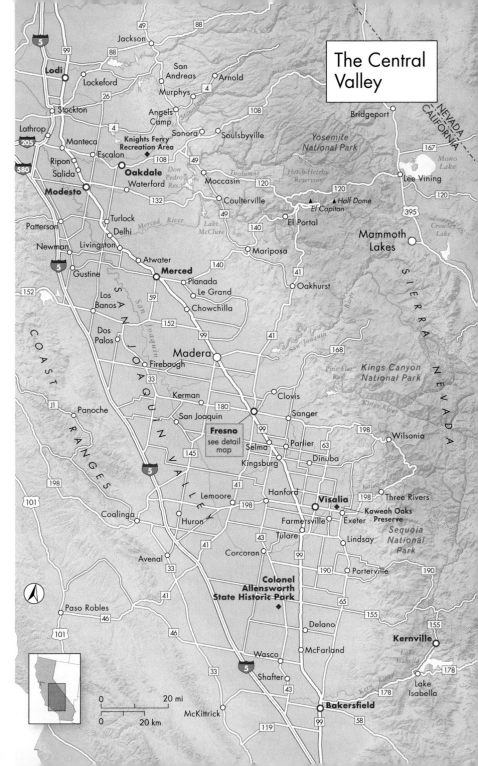

The Central Valley

exhibit, shows how oil is created, discovered, extracted, and transformed for various uses. The Lori Brock Children's Discovery Center, for ages eight and younger, has hands-on displays and an indoor playground. ✉ *3801 Chester Ave., at 38th St.* ☎ *661/437–3330* 🌐 *www.kcmuseum.org* 🎟 *$10* 🕘 *Tue.–Sat. 10–5, Sun. noon–5.*

FAMILY **Murray Family Farms.** You can partake of the southern Central Valley's agricultural bounty at the farm's popular Big Red Barn location—owners Steve and Vickie Murray promise more free samples than Costco, and they deliver. You'll find whatever's in season, including peaches, plums, and apricots that are all the more juicy because they're picked as late as possible. ■ **TIP→ If it's cherry-pickin' time, don't fail to drop by—the farm grows a dozen and a half varieties.** There are plenty of prepared foods, too, and fun activities for kids (jumping pillow, petting zoo, hay rides). The Cal-Okie Kitchen sells tasty fry pies filled with eggs and other ingredients for breakfast and pulled chicken and other meats for lunch and dinner. ✉ *6700 General Beale Rd., off Hwy. 58, 18 miles south of downtown* ☎ *661/330–0100* 🌐 *www.murrayfamilyfarms.com* 🎟 *Free to store; $4 weekdays, $6 weekends for farm tours (includes petting zoo)* 🕘 *Daily 8–7.*

WHERE TO EAT

$$ ITALIAN Fodor's Choice ★ 🍴 **Luigi's.** The same family has operated the wildly popular Luigi's restaurant, bar, and delicatessen at the same site since 1910. Feast on generous portions of homemade pastas and sauces, made from family recipes handed down over the decades. The extensive menu also includes beans, sandwiches, steaks, salads, and daily specials such as prime rib and lasagna. Plates are served family style in several casual rooms, reminiscent of a Tuscan trattoria and decorated with local sports photos. ■ **TIP→ Luigi's isn't open for dinner, but you can order to-go items, or pick up meal fixings at the adjacent deli and wine shop.** [$] *Average main: $16* ✉ *725 E. 19th St.* ☎ *661/322–0926* 🌐 *www.shopluigis.com* ✍ *Reservations not accepted* 🕘 *Closed Sun. and Mon. No dinner.*

$$ MODERN AMERICAN 🍴 **The Mark.** An upscale restaurant and bar in the downtown arts district, The Mark specializes in fresh seafood, hand-cut steaks, pastas, homemade soups, and comfort foods such as chicken potpie and bacon-wrapped meat loaf. Though the dishes are straightforward, they're skillfully executed. The wine list favors California but includes representatives from France, Italy, and elsewhere abroad. At the bar, which hosts live music, you can sink into leather high-back chairs and booths and order creative cocktails. [$] *Average main: $19* ✉ *1623 19th St.* ☎ *661/322–7665* 🕘 *Closed Sun. No lunch Sat.*

WHERE TO STAY

$$ HOTEL 🏨 **Bakersfield Marriott Convention Center.** A safe choice, the full-service Marriott caters to the business and convention crowd with spacious, tech-updated rooms that also serve vacationing families well. **Pros:** clean; large pool; good fitness center; convenient to convention center; business services; discounted weekend rates often available online. **Cons:** not much character; service can be spotty. [$] *Rooms from: $144* ✉ *801 Truxtun Ave.* ☎ *661/323–1900, 800/267–3983* 🌐 *www.bakersfieldmarriott.com* 🛏 *250 rooms , 9 suites* 🍽 *No meals.*

$$ HOTEL Fodor's Choice ★ [hotel icon] **Padre Hotel.** Erected in 1928 during the oil rush era, the eight-story Padre Hotel reopened in 2010 after an $18-million renovation transformed it into a sophisticated contemporary haven. **Pros:** in the heart of historic downtown; hip urban vibe. **Cons:** noise from the bars and lounges travels to some rooms; service sometimes inconsistent. [$] *Rooms from: $149* ✉ *1702 18th St.* ☎ *661/427–4900* 🌐 *www.thepadrehotel.com* 🛏 *108 rooms, 2 suites* 🍴 *No meals.*

NIGHTLIFE AND THE ARTS

Buck Owens' Crystal Palace and Museum. Buck Owens is Bakersfield's local boy made good, and this venue is a combination nightclub, restaurant, souvenir store, and showcase of country-music memorabilia. Country-and-western singers perform here, as Owens did countless times before his death in 2006. A dance floor beckons patrons who can still twirl after sampling the menu of steaks, burgers, nachos, and gooey desserts. **■ TIP→ Expect a cover charge some weeknights and most weekends.** ✉ *2800 Buck Owens Blvd., off Hwy. 178* ☎ *661/328–7560* 🌐 *www.buckowens.com* 🕒 *Closed Mon.*

KERNVILLE

50 miles northeast of Bakersfield.

The wild Kern River, which flows through Kernville en route from Mt. Whitney to Bakersfield, delivers some of the most exciting white-water rafting in the state. Kernville (population 1,700) rests in a mountain valley on both banks of the river and at the northern tip of Lake Isabella, a dammed portion of the river used as a reservoir and for recreation.

By far the most scenic town in this region, Kernville has lodgings, restaurants, and antiques shops. Old West–style buildings line the main streets, reflecting Kernville's heritage as a rough-and-tumble gold-mining town once known as Whiskey Flat. Present-day Kernville dates from the 1950s, when it was moved upriver to make room for Lake Isabella. The road from Bakersfield includes stretches where the rushing river is on one side and granite cliffs are on the other.

GETTING HERE AND AROUND

Highway 178 connects Kernville and Bakersfield; take Highway 155 if coming from Delano. There's no train line or scheduled bus service.

ESSENTIALS

Visitor Information VisitKern.com ☎ *661/868–5376, 661/868–2017* 🌐 *www.visitkern.com.*

EXPLORING

Fodor's Choice ★ **Kern Valley Museum.** A cadre of sweet, well-informed volunteers runs this jam-packed throwback of a museum that's bigger than it looks from the outside. With exhibits about Lake Isabella, minerals and gems, old tools and farming implements, pioneer and native life, and Hollywood Westerns shot in the area, you'll likely find something to intrigue you. ✉ *49 Big Blue Rd., off Kernville Rd.* ☎ *760/376–6683* 🌐 *www.kernvalleymuseum.org* 🎟 *Free* 🕒 *Thurs.–Sun 10–4.*

WHERE TO EAT AND STAY

$ ✕ **That's Italian.** For northern Italian cuisine in a no-frills trattoria, this is
ITALIAN the spot. Try the braised lamb shanks in a Chianti wine sauce, grilled rib
eye with chef's seasonal sauce, or the filet mignon with shrimp, roasted
pepper, and onions in a demi-glace sauce. To drift back to Old Italy—or
1950s Kernville, perhaps—sample the spaghetti and meatballs. $ *Average main: $14 ⊠ 9 Big Blue Rd., at Kernville Rd.* ☎ *760/376–6020*
⊙ *Closed Mon. year-round, Tues. mid-Sept.–Mar. No lunch.*

$$$ ⛺ **Whispering Pines Lodge.** On the banks of the Kern River, this 8-acre
B&B/INN property has units that are motel-style or in duplex bungalows; all have
fireplaces, coffeemakers, and king-size beds. **Pros:** rustic setting; big
breakfasts; great views; very clean. **Cons:** bungalows are pricey; town
is remote. $ *Rooms from: $189 ⊠ 13745 Sierra Way* ☎ *760/376–3733,
877/241–4100* ⊕ *pineskernville.com* ⤴ *17 rooms* ⦿ *Breakfast.*

SPORTS AND THE OUTDOORS

BOATING AND WINDSURFING

The Lower Kern River, which extends from Lake Isabella to Bakersfield
and beyond, is open for fishing year-round. Catches include rainbow
trout, catfish, smallmouth bass, crappie, and bluegill. Lake Isabella is
popular with anglers, water-skiers, sailors, and windsurfers. Its shore-
line marinas have boats for rent, bait and tackle, and moorings.

French Gulch Marina. This marina is near the dam on Lake Isabella's west
shore. ☎ *760/379–8774* ⊕ *www.frenchgulchmarina.com.*

North Fork Marina. The original marina erected on Lake Isabella, North
Fork has been around since the 1950s. ⊠ *100 Tuttle Rd., Wofford
Heights* ☎ *760/376–1812* ⊕ *www.northforkmarina.com.*

WHITE-WATER RAFTING

The three sections of the Kern River—known as the Lower Kern, Upper
Kern, and the Forks—add up to nearly 50 miles of white water, ranging
from Class I (easy) to Class V (expert). The Lower and Upper Kern are
the most popular and accessible sections. Organized trips can last from
one hour to more than two days. Rafting season usually runs from late
spring until the end of summer.

Kern River Tours. This outfit leads rafting tours—from half a day or
less on Class II or III rapids to three-day excursions on Class V ones.
The company also arranges mountain-bike trips. ⊠ *2712 Mayfair, Lake
Isabella* ☎ *800/844–7238, 760/379–4616* ⊕ *www.kernrivertours.com*
⤴ *From $35.*

Mountain & River Adventures. The lineup at this outfit includes calm-water
kayaking and stand-up paddleboard tours, white-water rafting trips,
and mountain-bike excursions. The company also has a campground, a
climbing wall, and a ropes course. ⊠ *11113 Kernville Rd.* ☎ *760/376–
6553, 800/861–6553* ⊕ *www.mtnriver.com* ⤴ *From $40.*

Sierra South. Half-day Class II and III white-water rafting trips are
emphasized at Sierra South, which also offers kayaking classes and
calm-water excursions. ⊠ *11300 Kernville Rd.* ☎ *760/376–3745,
800/457–2082* ⊕ *www.sierrasouth.com* ⤴ *From $45.*

MID-CENTRAL VALLEY

COLONEL ALLENSWORTH STATE HISTORIC PARK

45 miles north of Bakersfield.

GETTING HERE AND AROUND

The easiest way to get here is by car. The park is off Highway 43, a 15-minute drive west of Highway 99.

Fodor'sChoice

★

Colonel Allensworth State Historic Park. It's worth the slight detour off Highway 99 to learn about and pay homage to the dream of Allen Allensworth and other black pioneers who in 1908 founded Allensworth, the only California town settled, governed, and financed by African Americans. At its height, the town prospered as a key railroad transfer point, but after cars and trucks reduced railroad traffic and water was diverted for Central Valley agriculture, the town declined and was eventually deserted. Today, the restored and rebuilt schoolhouse, library, and other structures commemorate Allensworth's heyday, as do festivities that take place each October. ■TIP→ The parking lot is open only on Thursday, Friday, and weekends, but daily you can park nearby, walk over to the buildings, and peek in. ⊠ *4129 Palmer Ave., off Hwy. 43; from Hwy. 99 at Delano, take Garces Hwy. west to Hwy. 43 north; from Earlimart, take County Rd. J22 west to Hwy. 43 south* ☎ *661/849–3433* ⊕ *www.parks.ca.gov* ⬛ *$6 per car* ☉ *Daily sunrise–sunset; visitor center Thurs.–Sun. 10–4; buildings open by appointment.*

VISALIA

18

75 miles north of Bakersfield.

Visalia's combination of a reliable agricultural economy and civic pride has yielded the Central Valley's most vibrant downtown. If you're into Victorian and other old houses, drop by the city's visitor center and pick up a free map of them. A clear day's view of the Sierra from Main Street is spectacular, if sadly rare due to smog and dust, and even Sunday night can find the streets bustling with pedestrians. In addition to providing easy access to Sequoia National Park, Visalia is a good base from which to make three disparate detours: to kitschy Bravo Farms Traver, mural-filled Exeter, and the serene Kaweah Oaks Preserve.

GETTING HERE AND AROUND

Highway 198, just east of its exit from Highway 99, cuts through town (and proceeds up the hill to Sequoia National Park). Greyhound stops here, but not Amtrak. KART buses serve the locals.

ESSENTIALS

Visitor Information Visalia Convention & Visitors Bureau ⊠ *Kiosk, 303 E. Acequia Ave., at S. Bridge St.* ☎ *559/334–0141, 800/524–0303* ⊕ *www.visitvisalia.org* ☉ *Weekdays 8–5.*

EXPLORING

TOP ATTRACTIONS

Kaweah Oaks Preserve. Trails at this 322-acre wildlife sanctuary off the main road to Sequoia National Park *(⇨ Chapter 21)* lead past majestic valley oak, sycamore, cottonwood, and willow trees. Among the 134 bird species you might spot are hawks, hummingbirds, and great blue herons. Lizards, coyotes, and cottontails also live here. ✉ *Follow Hwy. 198 for 7 miles east of Visalia, turn north on Rd. 182, and proceed ½ mile to gate on left side* ☎ *559/738–0211* 🌐 *www.sequoiariverlands.org* 🎟 *Free* 🕒 *Daily sunrise–sunset.*

WORTH NOTING

FAMILY **Bravo Farms Traver.** For one-stop truck-stop entertainment, pull off the highway in Traver, where at Bravo Farms you can try your luck at an arcade shooting gallery, watch cheese being made, munch on barbecue and ice cream, play a round of mini golf, peruse funky antiques, buy produce at a fruit stand, and climb a multistory tree house. If you've got kids in tow or just love critters, there's a petting zoo, too. Taste a few "squeekers" (fresh cheese curds, so named because chewing them makes your teeth squeak), and then be on your way. May the rest of your vacation be this diverting. ✉ *36005 Hwy. 99, 9 miles north of Hwy. 198 and Visalia, Traver* ☎ *559/897–5762* 🌐 *www.bravofarmstraver.com* 🎟 *Free* 🕒 *Daily 7–7.*

FAMILY **Mooney Grove Park.** Amid shady oaks you can picnic alongside duck ponds, rent a boat for a ride around the lagoon, and view a replica of the famous *End of the Trail* statue. The original, designed by James Earl Fraser for San Francisco's 1915 Panama-Pacific International Exposition, is now in the Cowboy Hall of Fame in Oklahoma. ✉ *27000 S. Mooney Blvd., Hwy. 63, 5 miles south of downtown* 🎟 *$7 per car, free in winter (dates vary)* 🕒 *Daily 8–sunset; sometimes closed Tues. and Wed.*

Tulare County Museum. This indoor-outdoor museum contains several re-created environments from the pioneer era. Also on display are Yokuts tribal artifacts (basketry, arrowheads, clamshell-necklace currency) as well as saddles, guns, dolls, quilts, and gowns. A separate wing chronicles farm history and labor. ✉ *Mooney Grove Park, 27000 S. Mooney Blvd., Hwy. 63, 5 miles south of downtown* ☎ *559/733–6616* 🌐 *www.tularecountyhistoricalsociety.org* 🎟 *Free with park entrance fee of $7* 🕒 *Mon., Thurs., and Fri. 10–4, weekends 12–4.*

WHERE TO EAT

$ MEXICAN 🍴 **Henry Salazar's Fresh Mex Grill.** Traditional Mexican food with a contemporary twist is served at this restaurant that uses fresh ingredients from local farms. Two signature dishes are the Burrito Fantastico—a large flour tortilla stuffed with your choice of meat, beans, and chili sauce, and smothered with melted Monterey Jack cheese—and grilled salmon with lemon-butter sauce. Colorfully painted walls, soft reflections from candles in wall niches, and color-coordinated tablecloths and napkins make the atmosphere cozy and restful. [$] *Average main: $12* ✉ *123 W. Main St.* ☎ *559/741–7060* 🌐 *www.henrysalazars.com.*

Each spring the fruit orchards along the Blossom Trail, near Fresno, burst into bloom.

$$$ EUROPEAN Fodor's Choice ★ 🍴 **The Vintage Press.** Built in 1966, this is the best restaurant in the Central Valley. Cut-glass doors and bar fixtures decorate the artfully designed rooms. The California–Continental cuisine includes dishes such as crispy veal sweetbreads with a Port-wine sauce, and a bacon-wrapped filet mignon stuffed with mushrooms. The chocolate Grand Marnier cake is a standout among the homemade desserts and ice creams. The wine list has more than 900 selections. [$] *Average main: $30* ✉ *216 N. Willis St.* ☎ *559/733–3033* 🌐 *www.thevintagepress.com.*

18

WHERE TO STAY

$ HOTEL 🏨 **Hampton Inn Visalia.** In a town with a fair share of outmoded properties the Hampton stands out as a clean, well-run facility with a friendly staff. **Pros:** clean; friendly staff; complimentary breakfast; 24-hour business center; free trolley to downtown; less than an hour's drive from Sequoia National Park. **Cons:** on a service road and hard to find; some guests may find rooms facing freeway too noisy. [$] *Rooms from: $101* ✉ *4747 W. Noble Ave., off Hwy. 198 Akers exit* ☎ *559/732–3900, 800/426–7866* 🌐 *hamptoninn.hilton.com* 🛏 *88 rooms* 🍴 *Breakfast.*

FRESNO

44 miles north of Visalia.

Sprawling Fresno, with half a million people, is the center of the richest agricultural county in the United States. Cotton, grapes, and tomatoes are among the major crops; poultry and milk are also important. About 75 ethnic groups, including Armenians, Laotians, and Indians, live here. The city has a relatively vibrant arts scene, several public parks, and

Fresno Area

KEY

🚹 *Tourist information*

0   4 miles
0   6 km

many low-price restaurants. The Tower District—with its chic restaurants, coffeehouses, and boutiques—is the trendy spot, though like the rest of Fresno it can look drab on a cloudy day.

GETTING HERE AND AROUND
Highway 99 is the biggest road through Fresno. Highways 41 and 180 also bisect the city. Amtrak trains stop here daily (and often). Fresno Area Express (FAX) provides comprehensive local bus service.

ESSENTIALS
Transportation Contacts FAX ☎ 559/621–7433 ⊕ www.fresno.gov/ discoverfresno.

Visitor Information Fresno/Clovis Convention & Visitors Bureau ✉ 1550 E. Shaw Ave. ☎ 559/981–5500, 800/788–0836 ⊕ playfresno.org.

EXPLORING
TOP ATTRACTIONS
FAMILY **Forestiere Underground Gardens.** Sicilian immigrant Baldasare Forestiere
Fodor'sChoice spent four decades (1906–46) carving out an odd, subterranean realm
★ of rooms, tunnels, grottoes, alcoves, and arched passageways that once extended for more than 10 acres between Highway 99 and busy, mall-pocked Shaw Avenue. Though not an engineer, Forestiere called on his memories of the ancient Roman structures he saw as a youth and

ESSENTIALS

Bus Contact The Bus ☎ 209/725–3813 ⊕ www.mercedthebus.com.

Visitor Information Merced Visitor Services ✉ 710 W. 16th St. ☎ 209/724–8104, 800/446–5353 ⊕ www.yosemite-gateway.org.

EXPLORING

Merced County Courthouse Museum. Even if you don't go inside, be sure to swing by this three-story former courthouse. Built in 1875, it's a striking example of Victorian Italianate style. The upper two floors contain a museum of early Merced history. Highlights include ornate restored courtrooms and an 1870 Chinese temple with carved redwood altars. ✉ 621 W. 21st St., at N St. ☎ 209/723–2401 ⊕ www.mercedmuseum.org ✑ Free ⊙ Wed.–Sun. 1–4.

Merced Multicultural Arts Center. The center displays paintings, sculpture, and photography. The Big Valley Arts & Culture Festival, which celebrates the area's ethnic diversity and children's creativity, takes place here in the fall. ✉ 645 W. Main St., at N St. ☎ 209/388–1090 ⊕ www.artsmerced.org ✑ Free ⊙ Wed. and Thur. 11–6, Fri. and Sat. 10–2.

WHERE TO EAT AND STAY

$$ **✕ The Branding Iron.** Beef is what this restaurant is all about. It's the
STEAKHOUSE place where farmers and ranchers come to refuel as they travel through cattle country. Try the juicy cut of prime rib paired with potato and Parmesan-cheese bread. California cattle brands decorate the walls, and when the weather is nice, cooling breezes refresh diners on the outdoor patio. $ Average main: $21 ✉ 640 W. 16th St., between M and N Sts. ☎ 209/722–1822 ⊕ www.thebrandingiron-merced.com ⊙ No lunch weekends.

$$ **✕ DeAngelo's.** This restaurant, about 2 miles east of downtown, is one
ITALIAN of the Central Valley's best. Chef Vincent DeAngelo, a graduate of the Culinary Institute of America, brings his considerable skill to everything from crab ravioli to calamari steak. Half the restaurant is occupied by Bellini's, a bar-bistro with its own menu, which includes brick-oven pizza. $ Average main: $20 ✉ 2000 E. Childs Ave., at Parsons Ave. ☎ 209/383–3020 ⊕ www.deangelosrestaurant.com.

$$ **Hooper House Bear Creek Inn.** This 1931 neocolonial home stands
B&B/INN regally at the corner of M Street; rooms are appointed with well-chosen antiques and big, soft beds. **Pros:** historic charm; friendly staff; good breakfast. **Cons:** front rooms can be noisy. $ Rooms from: $129 ✉ 575 W. N. Bear Creek Dr., at M St. ☎ 209/723–3991 ⊕ www.hooperhouse.com ⇌ 4 rooms, 1 cottage ⊙ Breakfast.

EN ROUTE
Castle Air Museum. You can stroll among dozens of restored military aircraft at this outdoor facility. The vintage war birds include the B-25 Mitchell medium-range bomber—best known for the Jimmy Doolittle raid on Tokyo after the attack on Pearl Harbor—and the speedy SR-71 Blackbird, used for reconnaissance over Vietnam and Libya. ✉ Castle Airport, 5050 Santa Fe Dr., 6 miles north of Merced, Buhach Rd. exit off Hwy. 99, Atwater ☎ 209/723–2178 ⊕ www.castleairmuseum.org ✑ $10 ⊙ Apr.–Sept., daily 9–5; Oct.–Mar., daily 10–4.

on techniques he learned digging subways in New York and Boston. Only a fraction of his prodigious output is on view, but you can tour his underground living quarters, including bedrooms (one with a fireplace), the kitchen, living room, and bath, as well as a fishpond and auto tunnel. Skylights allow exotic full-grown fruit trees to flourish more than 20 feet belowground. ✉ 5021 W. Shaw Ave., 2 blocks east of Hwy. 99 ☎ 559/271–0734 ⊕ www.undergroundgardens.com ✑ $15 ⊙ Tours June–Aug., Wed.–Sun. 10–4; call or check website for other tour times ⊙ Closed Dec.–Feb.

Fresno Art Museum. The museum's key permanent collections include pre-Columbian Mesoamerican art, Andean pre-Columbian textiles and artifacts, Japanese prints, Berkeley School abstract expressionist paintings, and contemporary sculpture. Temporary exhibits include important traveling shows. ✉ Radio Park, 2233 N. 1st St., at E. Yale Ave. ☎ 559/441–4221 ⊕ www.fresnoartmuseum.org ✑ $5 ⊙ Thur.–Sun. 11–5.

Meux Home Museum. A restored 1889 Victorian, "the Meux" contains furnishings typical of an upper-class household in early Fresno. The house's namesake, Thomas Richard Meux, was a Confederate army doctor during the Civil War who became a family practitioner after moving to Fresno. The Meux can be viewed on guided tours only. ✉ 1007 R St., at Tulare St. ☎ 559/233–8007 ⊕ www.meux.mus.ca.us ✑ $5 ⊙ Fri.–Sun. noon–3.

WORTH NOTING

Blossom Trail. The 62-mile self-guided Blossom Trail driving tour takes in Fresno-area orchards, citrus groves, and vineyards during spring blossom season. The trail passes through small towns and past rivers, lakes, and canals. The most colorful and aromatic time to go is from late February to mid-March, when almond, plum, apple, apricot, and peach blossoms shower the landscape with shades of white, pink, and red. ☎ 559/600–4271 ⊕ www.goblossomtrail.com.

Kearney Mansion Museum. The drive along palm-lined Kearney Boulevard is one of the best reasons to visit the museum, which stands in shaded 225-acre **Kearney Park**. The century-old home of M. Theo Kearney, Fresno's onetime "raisin king," is accessible only on guided 45-minute tours. ✉ 7160 W. Kearney Blvd., 6 miles west of Fresno off Hwy. 180 ☎ 559/441–0862 ⊕ www.valleyhistory.org ✑ Museum $5; park entry $5 ⊙ Park: 7 am–10 pm. Museum tours: Fri.–Sun. at 1, 2, and 3.

FAMILY **Roeding Park.** Tree-shaded Roeding Park is a place of respite on hot summer days; it has picnic areas, playgrounds, tennis courts, horseshoe pits, and a zoo (⇨ Fresno Chaffee Zoo). A train, little race cars, paddleboats, a carousel, and other rides for kids are among the amusements at **Playland.** Children can explore attractions with fairy-tale themes at **Rotary Storyland.** ✉ 890 W Belmont Ave., at Olive Ave. ☎ 559/486–2124 ⊕ storylandplayland.com ✑ Roeding Park $5 per vehicle; Playland free (rides $1.50–$3, day pass $16); Storyland $5 ⊙ park: daily Apr.–Oct. 6 am–10 pm, Nov.–Mar. 6 am–7 pm. Playland: June–Aug. Weds. eve 5–8, Thurs.–Sun. 10–6; Sept.–mid-June weekends 10–4. Storyland: weekends 10–4, plus some holidays.

18

Fresno Chaffee Zoo. The zoo's most striking exhibit is its tropical rain forest, where you'll encounter exotic birds along paths and bridges. Elsewhere at the zoo live tigers, sloth bears, sea lions, tule elk, camels, elephants, and siamang apes. The facility has a high-tech reptile house and there's a petting zoo. ⊠ *Roeding Park, 894 W. Belmont Ave., east of Hwy. 99* ☏ *559/498–5910* ⊕ *www.fresnochaffeezoo.org* 🖃 *$7* ☉ *Apr.– Oct., daily 9–6; Sept.–Oct., closes at 4 weekdays; Nov.–Mar., daily 9–4.*

Old Town Clovis. The restored brick buildings of a former lumber-industry district now hold antiques shops, art galleries, restaurants, and saloons. At the visitor center (or online) you can access a walking-tour map. To get here from Fresno, head east on Herndon Avenue for about 10 miles to Clovis Avenue and drive south. Note that not much is open on Sunday. ⊠ *Visitor Center, 399 Clovis Ave., at 4th St., Clovis* ⊕ *www. visitclovis.com.*

Veterans Memorial Museum. Military-history buffs enjoy this museum whose collection includes German bayonets and daggers, a Japanese Namby pistol, a Gatling gun, Japanese, German, and American uniforms, and nearly 20,000 other memorabilia items. The staff is extremely enthusiastic. ⊠ *2425 Fresno St., between N and O Sts.* ☏ *559/498–0510* ⊕ *www.fresnovetsmuseum.com* 🖃 *Free* ☉ *Mon.–Sat. 10–3.*

Woodward Park. The Central Valley's largest urban park, with 300 acres of jogging trails, picnic areas, and playgrounds in the city's northern reaches, is especially pretty in spring, when plum and cherry trees, magnolias, and camellias bloom. Outdoor concerts take place in summer. The **Shinzen Friendship Garden** has a teahouse, a koi pond, arched bridges, a waterfall, and Japanese art. ⊠ *Audubon Dr. and Friant Rd.* ☏ *559/621–2900, 559/227–8940 Shinzen garden* ⊕ *www.fresno.gov* 🖃 *$5 per car; additional $3 for Shinzen garden* ☉ *Apr.–Oct., daily 7 am–10 pm; Nov.–Mar., daily 7–7.*

WHERE TO EAT AND STAY

$ ✕ **Irene's Cafe Dining.** Downtown workers pack this Tower District restaurant at lunchtime. Handmade, half-pound burgers are the most popular, and most filling, items on the menu. Other favorites include the smoked ham and melted Swiss cheese sandwich served on a hard roll, and fresh salads. For breakfast, homemade granola, huge buttermilk pancakes, and the Denver omelet (with ham, onions, and green peppers) will fill up even those with the heartiest of appetites. $ *Average main: $12* ⊠ *747 E. Olive Ave.* ☏ *559/237–9919* ⊕ *irenescafe.com.*

AMERICAN

$$ ✕ **Tahoe Joe's.** This restaurant is known for its steaks—rib eye, strip, or filet mignon. Other selections include the slow-roasted prime rib, center-cut pork chops, and chicken breast in a whiskey-peppercorn sauce. The baked potato that accompanies almost every dish is loaded tableside with your choice of butter, sour cream, chives, and bacon bits. Tahoe Joe's has two Fresno locations. $ *Average main: $18* ⊠ *7006 N. Cedar Ave., at E. Herndon Ave.* ☏ *559/299–9740* ⊕ *www. tahoejoes.com* 🖈 *Reservations not accepted* $ *Average main: $18* ⊠ *2700 W. Shaw Ave., at N. Marks Ave.* ☏ *559/277–8028* ⊕ *www. tahoejoes.com.*

STEAKHOUSE

$ 🏨 **Piccadilly Inn Shaw.** This two-story property has 7½ attractively landscaped acres and a big swimming pool. **Pros:** big rooms; nice pool; town's best lodging option. **Cons:** some rooms show mild wear; neighborhood is somewhat sketchy. $ *Rooms from: $99* ⊠ *2305 W. Shaw Ave.* ☏ *559/348–5520* ⊕ *www.piccadillyinn.com* 🛏 *183 rooms, 5 suites* ¶○ *Breakfast.*

HOTEL

NIGHTLIFE AND THE ARTS

Roger Rocka's Dinner Theater. This Tower District venue stages Broadway-style musicals. ⊠ *1226 N. Wishon Ave., at E. Olive Ave.* ☏ *559/266–9494, 800/371–4747* ⊕ *www.rogerrockas.com.*

Tower Theatre for the Performing Arts. The restored 1930s art deco movie house, the anchor and namesake of the trendy Tower District of theaters, clubs, restaurants, and cafés, presents theater, ballet, concerts, and other cultural events. ⊠ *815 E. Olive Ave., at N. Wishon Ave.* ☏ *559/485–9050* ⊕ *www.towertheatrefresno.com.*

SPORTS AND THE OUTDOORS

WATER PARKS

Wild Water Adventures. This 52-acre water park about 10 miles east of Fresno is open from late May to early September. ⊠ *11413 E. Shaw Ave., off Hwy. 168, Clovis* ☏ *559/299–9453* ⊕ *www.wildwater.net* 🖃 *$30, $17 after 4 pm.*

WHITE-WATER RAFTING

Kings River Expeditions. This outfit arranges one- and two-day white-water rafting trips on the Kings River. ⊠ *1840 W. Shaw Ave., Clovis* ☏ *559/233–4881, 800/846–3674* ⊕ *www.kingsriver.com.*

> **LOCAL LITERARY LEGENDS**
>
> The Central Valley's cultural diversity and agricultural roots have woven a textured social fabric that has been chronicled by some of the country's finest writers, including Fresno native William Saroyan, Stockton native Maxine Hong Kingston, and *The Grapes of Wrath* author John Steinbeck.

NORTH CENTRAL VALLEY

MERCED

50 miles north of Fresno.

The 2005 debut of a branch of the University of California helped spur redevelopment in Merced County's namesake seat of government. Though not yet complete, the transformation has resulted in a brewpub, several boutiques, a multiplex, the restoration of historic buildings, and foot traffic won back from outlying strip malls.

GETTING HERE AND AROUND

Most people arrive in Merced by car via Highway 99, but Amtrak also stops several times daily. The Bus provides local transit service except on Sunday.

18

MODESTO

38 miles north of Merced.

Modesto, a gateway to Yosemite (⇨ *Chapter 20*) and the southern reaches of the Gold Country, was founded in 1870 to serve the Central Pacific Railroad. The frontier town was originally to be named Ralston, after a railroad baron, but as the story goes, he modestly declined—thus the name Modesto. The Stanislaus County seat, a tree-lined city of 203,000, is perhaps best known as the site of the annual Modesto Invitational Track Meet and Relays and the birthplace of producer-director George Lucas, creator of the *Star Wars* film series.

GETTING HERE AND AROUND

Highway 99 is the major traffic artery; Highway 132 heads east from here toward Yosemite National Park. United serves the airport here, and several Amtrak trains arrive daily. Modesto Area Express (MAX) is the local bus service.

ESSENTIALS

Airport Contacts Modesto City-County Airport ⊠ *617 Airport Way, of Mitchell Rd., south from Yosemite Blvd./Hwy. 132* ☎ *209/577–5200* ⊕ *www.modairport.com.*

Bus Contact MAX ☎ *209/521–1274* ⊕ *www.modestoareaexpress.com.*

Visitor Information Modesto Convention and Visitors Bureau ⊠ *1150 9th St., Suite C* ☎ *209/526–5588, 888/640–8467* ⊕ *www.visitmodesto.com.*

EXPLORING

Blue Diamond Growers Store. You can witness the everyday abundance of the Modesto area with a visit here; on offer are tasty samples, a film about almond growing, and many roasts and flavors of almonds, as well as other nuts. ⊠ *4800 Sisk Rd., at Kiernan Ave., off Hwy. 99* ☎ *209/545–6230* ⊕ *www.bluediamond.com.*

McHenry Mansion. A rancher and banker built the 1883 McHenry Mansion, the city's sole surviving original Victorian home. The Italianate mansion has been decorated to reflect Modesto life in the late 19th century. Its period-appropriate wallpaper is especially impressive. ⊠ *15th and I Sts.* ☎ *209/577–5341, 209/549–0428 gift shop* ⊕ *www.mchenrymansion.org* ⌦ *Free* ☉ *Tours Sun.–Thurs. 1–4, Fri. noon–3.*

McHenry Museum. The best exhibits at this repository of early Modesto and Stanislaus County memorabilia include the re-creations of an old-time dentist's office, a blacksmith's shop, and a schoolroom. Also worth a peek are the extensive doll collection and a general store stocked with period goods such as hair crimpers and corsets. ⊠ *1402 I St., at 14th St.* ☎ *209/577–5235* ⊕ *www.mchenrymuseum.org* ⌦ *Free* ☉ *Tues.–Sun. noon–4.*

Modesto Arch. One of the broadest and most striking "welcome to downtown" signs you'll see, the Modesto Arch bears the city's motto: "Water, Wealth, Contentment, Health." ⊠ *9th and I Sts.* ⊕ *www.historicmodesto.com/thearch.html.*

18

WHERE TO EAT

$

AMERICAN

✕ **A&W Root Beer Drive-in.** Only two reasons to come here, but they're both delightful: frosty-glassed root-beer floats and drive-in service that transports patrons (by the view of carhops on roller skates alone) back to the 1950s of Modesto native and *American Graffiti* director George Lucas. It's a kick. The cheese curds and onion rings aren't bad either. $ *Average main: $5* ⊠ *1404 G St.* ☎ *209/522–7700* ⊕ *www. awrestaurants.com* ⌂ *Reservations not accepted.*

$$$$

MODERN AMERICAN

Fodor'sChoice

★

✕ **Dewz.** Modestans hankering for a fine-dining experience—especially one involving prime rib or filet mignon—invariably head to Dewz and its handsome, if sometimes high-decibel, dining room. Chef Vincent Alvarado introduces French influences (by way of the sauces) and Asian ones (by way of the spices) to beef, chicken, and seafood standards. Beef predominates on the menu, but the sea bass is a good alternative, as is the pan-roasted pork tenderloin, served with a sweet and spicy plum sauce. The sauces accompanying the filet mignon change daily and might involve wine and butter reductions or bleu cheese. For a decadent finish, order the crème brûlée, the Napoleon, or any of the chocolate desserts. The wine list, noteworthy for the Central Valley, would impress anywhere, and the waitstaff is always solicitous, if sometimes slow of foot. $ *Average main: $31* ⊠ *1505 J St.* ☎ *209/549–1101* ⌂ *Reservations essential.*

$$$

AMERICAN

✕ **Tresetti's World Caffé.** An intimate setting with white tablecloths and contemporary art draws diners to this establishment—part wineshop, part restaurant—with a seasonally changing menu. The Cajun-style crab cakes, served for lunch year-round, are outstanding. ■ **TIP→ For a small fee, your waiter will uncork any wine you select from the shop.** $ *Average main: $26* ⊠ *927 11th St., at J St.* ☎ *209/572–2990* ⊕ *tresetti.com* ⊘ *No lunch Sun.*

OAKDALE

15 miles northeast of Modesto.

Oakdale was founded as an orchard community and, in a real stretch, calls itself the Cowboy Capital of the World. Formerly the home of a Hershey's chocolate factory, the city still holds the Oakdale Chocolate Festival, on the third weekend in May. The main attraction of this sweet event, which attracts more than 50,000 people, is Chocolate Avenue, where vendors proffer cakes, cookies, ice cream, fudge, and cheesecake.

GETTING HERE AND AROUND

Reach Oakdale via Highway 108 from Modesto. Local transit is of little use to tourists.

ESSENTIALS

Visitor Information Oakdale Chamber of Commerce ⊠ *590 N. Yosemite Ave., at E. A St.* ☎ *209/847–2244* ⊕ *www.oakdalechamber.com.*

EXPLORING

FAMILY

Knights Ferry Recreation Area. The featured attraction is the 355-foot-long Knights Ferry covered bridge. The beautiful and haunting structure, built in 1863, crosses the Stanislaus River near the ruins of an old gristmill. The park has camping, picnic, and barbecue areas along

The Central Valley is California's agricultural powerhouse.

the riverbanks, as well as campgrounds accessible only by boat. You can hike, fish, canoe, and raft on miles of rapids. ✉ *Corps of Engineers Park, 17968 Covered Bridge Rd., Knights Ferry, 12 miles east of Oakdale via Hwy. 108* ☎ *209/881–3517* 🎫 *Free* ☉ *Daily dawn–dusk.*

FAMILY **Oakdale Cheese & Specialties.** You can sample the wares at this homey factory complex, which has tastings (try the aged Gouda) and cheese-making tours, a store, and a bakery. Outside are a picnic area and a petting zoo. ✉ *10040 Valley Home Rd., at River Rd.* ☎ *209/848–3139* 🌐 *www.oakdalecheese.com.*

SPORTS AND THE OUTDOORS
WHITE-WATER RAFTING
River Journey. Rafting on the Stanislaus River is a popular activity near Oakdale. River Journey will take you out for a few hours of fun. ✉ *14842 Orange Blossom Rd., off Hwy. 120/108, 4 miles* ☎ *209/847–4671, 800/292–2938* 🌐 *www.riverjourney.com.*

LODI

34 miles south of Sacramento.

Founded on agriculture, Lodi was once the watermelon capital of the country. Today it's surrounded by fields of asparagus, pumpkins, beans, safflowers, sunflowers, kiwis, melons, squashes, peaches, and cherries. It's also emerged as a wine-grape hub, particularly for Zinfandel, Merlot, Cabernet Sauvignon, Chardonnay, and Sauvignon Blanc grapes. Seven-dozen wineries, many offering tours and tastings, do business in Lodi and neighboring Acampo, Lockeford, and Woodbridge. Lodi itself retains an old rural charm. You can stroll downtown or visit a wildlife refuge, all the while benefiting from a Sacramento River delta breeze that keeps this microclimate cooler in summer than anyplace else in the area.

GETTING HERE AND AROUND

Most of Lodi lies to the west of Highway 99, several miles east of Interstate 5. Buses and Amtrak trains stop here frequently. Although the GrapeLine bus (☎ 209/333–6806) can get you around town and to many of the wineries, you are better off with your own vehicle.

ESSENTIALS

Visitor Information Lodi Conference & Visitors Bureau ⊠ 25 N. School St. ☎ 209/365–1195, 800/798–1810 ⊕ www.visitlodi.com.

EXPLORING

TOP ATTRACTIONS

Berghold Vineyards & Winery. The tasting room at Berghold recalls an earlier wine era with its vintage Victorian interior, including restored, salvaged mantlepieces, leaded glass, and a 26-foot-long bar. The wines—among them Viognier, Cabernet Sauvignon, Merlot, Syrah, and Zinfandel—pay homage to French wine-making styles. ⊠ 17343 N. Cherry Rd., off E. Victor Rd./Hwy. 12 ☎ 209/333–9291 ⊕ bergholdvineyards.com ☞ Tasting $7 ⊙ Thurs.–Sun. 11–5.

Fodor'sChoice ★ **Lucas Winery.** David Lucas was one of the first local producers to start making serious wine, and today his Zinfandels and other vintages are among Lodi's most sought-after vintages. In addition to fruity Zins, Lucas makes a light Chardonnay with subtle oaky flavors. The 90-minute tour and tasting ($20) will get you up to speed on the Lodi wine appellation. ⊠ 18196 N. Davis Rd., at W. Turner Rd. ☎ 209/368–2006 ⊕ www.lucaswinery.com ☞ Tastings $10–$50, tour (includes tasting) $20 ⊙ Thurs.–Sun. noon–4:30.

FAMILY **Micke Grove Regional Park.** This 258-acre, oak-shaded park, about 5 miles south of downtown, has a Japanese tea garden, picnic areas, children's play areas, softball fields, an agricultural museum, a golf course, and a water-play feature. Most rides and attractions at **Fun Town at Micke Grove,** a family-oriented amusement park, are geared toward children. Geckos and frogs, black-and-white ruffed lemurs, and hissing cockroaches found only on Madagascar inhabit *An Island Lost in Time,* an exhibit at the **Micke Grove Zoo.** California sea lions, Chinese alligators and a walk-through Mediterranean aviary are among the other highlights. **Micke Grove Golf Links,** an 18-hole course, is next to the park. ⊠ 11793 N. Micke Grove Rd., off Hwy. 99 Armstrong Rd. exit ☎ 209/953–8800 park info, 209/369–7330 Fun Town, 209/331–2010 zoo ☞ Parking $5 weekdays, $6 weekends and holidays; pets $1 (leash required); Fun Town ride prices vary; zoo $5 ⊙ Park: daily 8–sunset. Fun Town: daily 11–5, weekends and holidays Apr.–Sept. 11–6. Zoo: May–Sept. 10–6, Oct.–Apr. 10–5.

Fodor'sChoice ★ **Phillips Farms Fruit Stand/Michael David Winery.** Fifth-generation farmers turned winery owners, Michael and David Phillips operate their tasting room at a rustic roadside fruit stand where they also sell their family's gorgeous produce. Michael David is well known for its Zinfandels,

Lodi Lake Park is a great place to escape the Central Valley heat in summer.

including the widely distributed 7 Deadly Zins, but the Rhône-style wines labeled Incognito are especially worth a try. ■TIP→ Breakfast or lunch at the café here is a treat. ⊠ 4580 W. Hwy. 12, at N. Ray Rd. ☎ 209/368–7384 ⊕ www.michaeldavidwinery.com ✉ Tastings $5–$10 ⊙ Daily 10–5, reserve tasting Fri.–Sun. only.

Van Ruiten Family Vineyards. For an affordable experience of what Lodi's hardworking old Zinfandel vines can produce, head to this winery's convivial tasting room and sample the Van Ruiten Old Vine Zin and the Reserve Sideways Lot 69 Old Vine Zin. Other wines of note include the Chardonnays and the Cabernet-Shiraz blend. ⊠ 340 W. Hwy. 12 ☎ 209/334–5722 ⊕ www.vrwinery.com ✉ Tastings $5–$10 ⊙ Daily 11–5.

WORTH NOTING

Jessie's Grove Winery. Shaded by ancient oak trees, a ramshackle 1870s farm building houses the tasting room of this winery whose vineyards and horse ranch have been in the same family since 1863. In addition to producing old-vine Zinfandels, it presents blues concerts on various Saturdays from June through October. Jessie's also has a downtown tasting room, open on Friday and weekends, at 27 East Locust St. ⊠ 1973 W. Turner Rd., west of Davis Rd. ☎ 209/368–0880 ⊕ www.jessiesgrovewinery.com ✉ Tasting $5 ⊙ Daily noon–5.

Lodi Wine & Visitor Center. A fine place to sample Lodi wines (there's a tasting bar), the center has exhibits that chronicle Lodi's viticultural history. You can also buy wine here and pick up a map of area wineries to explore. ⊠ 2545 W. Turner Rd., at Woodhaven La. ☎ 209/365–0621 ⊕ www.lodiwine.com ✉ Tasting $5 ⊙ Daily 10–5.

Woodbridge Winery. At huge Woodbridge, you can take a 30-minute tour of the vineyard and barrel room and learn about the label's legendary founder, the late Robert Mondavi. In the tasting room, look for hard-to-find and exclusive offerings such as the Lodi Old Vine Zinfandel and the well-aged Port. ✉ *5950 E. Woodbridge Rd., east of N. Hildebrand Rd., Acampo* ☎ *209/365–8139* 🌐 *www.woodbridgewines.com* 🎟 *Tasting $5, tour $5* 🕒 *Daily 10:30–4:30, tour 9:30 and 1:30.*

WHERE TO EAT

$ MEXICAN 🍴 **Habañero Hots.** If your mouth can handle the heat promised by the restaurant's name, try the tamales. If you want to take it easy on your taste buds, stick with the rest of the menu. [$] *Average main: $10* ✉ *1024 E. Victor Rd., at N. Cluff Ave.* ☎ *209/369–3791* 🌐 *www.habanerohots.com.*

$$$ AMERICAN 🍴 **Rosewood Bar & Grill.** Operated by the folks at Wine & Roses Hotel and Restaurant, this low-key downtown spot serves American fare with a twist, such as meat loaf wrapped in bacon, and daily seafood specials. The bar has a full-service menu, and live music on Friday and Saturday. [$] *Average main: $29* ✉ *28 S. School St., at W. Oak St.* ☎ *209/369–0470* 🌐 *rosewoodbarandgrill.com* 🕒 *No lunch Mon.–Thurs.*

WHERE TO STAY

$$ B&B/INN 🏨 **The Inn at Locke House.** Built between 1862 and 1882, this B&B occupies a pioneer doctor's family home that rates a listing on the National Register of Historic Places. **Pros:** friendly; quiet; lovely. **Cons:** remote; can be hard to find. [$] *Rooms from: $150* ✉ *19960 Elliott Rd., Lockeford* ☎ *209/727–5715* 🌐 *www.theinnatlockehouse.com* 🛏 *4 rooms, 1 suite* 🍽 *Breakfast.*

$$$ HOTEL 🏨 **Wine & Roses Hotel and Restaurant.** Set on 7 acres amid a tapestry of informal gardens, this hotel has cultivated a sense of refinement typically associated with Napa or Carmel. **Pros:** luxurious; relaxing; quiet. **Cons:** expensive; isolated; some guests mention that walls are thin. [$] *Rooms from: $249* ✉ *2505 W. Turner Rd.* ☎ *209/334–6988* 🌐 *www.winerose.com* 🛏 *60 rooms, 6 suites* 🍽 *No meals.*

SPORTS AND THE OUTDOORS

Lodi Lake Park. Even locals need respite from the heat of Central Valley summers, and Lodi Lake Park is where they find it. The banks, shaded by grand old elms and oaks, are much cooler than other spots in town. Swimming, bird-watching, and picnicking are possibilities, as is renting a kayak, canoe, or pedal boat. ✉ *1101 W. Turner Rd., at Mills Ave.* ☎ *209/333–6742* 🎟 *$5.*

THE SOUTHERN SIERRA

Around Sequoia, Kings Canyon,
and Yosemite National Parks

WELCOME TO
THE SOUTHERN SIERRA

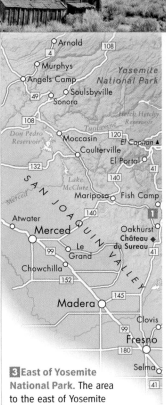

TOP REASONS
TO GO

★ **Strap 'em on:** Whether you walk the paved loops in the national parks (⇨ Chapter 20, Yosemite National Park, and Chapter 21, Sequoia and Kings Canyon National Parks) or head off the beaten path into the backcountry, a hike through groves and meadows or alongside streams and waterfalls will allow you to see, smell, and feel nature up close.

★ **Down you go:** Famous for its incredible snow-pack—some of the deepest in the North American continent—the Sierra Nevada has something for every winter-sports fan.

★ **Live it up:** Mammoth Lakes is eastern California's most exciting resort area.

★ **Pamper yourself:** Tucked in the hills south of Oakhurst, the elegant Château du Sureau will make you feel as if you've stepped into a fairy tale.

★ **Go with the flow:** Three Rivers, the gateway to Sequoia National Park, is the launching pad for white-water trips down the Kaweah River.

1 South of Yosemite National Park. Several gateway towns to the south and west of Yosemite National Park (⇨ Chapter 20), most within an hour's drive of Yosemite Valley, have food, lodging, and other services.

2 Mammoth Lakes. A jewel in the vast Eastern Sierra Nevada, the Mammoth Lakes area lies just east of the Sierra crest, on the backside of Yosemite and the Ansel Adams Wilderness. It's a place of rugged beauty, where giant sawtooth mountains drop into the vast deserts of the Great Basin. In winter, 11,053-foot-high Mammoth Mountain offers the finest skiing and snowboarding in California—sometimes as late as June or even July. Once the snows melt, Mammoth transforms itself into a warm-weather playground, with fishing, mountain biking, golfing, hiking, and horseback riding. Nine deep-blue lakes are spread throughout the Mammoth Lakes Basin, and another 100 lakes dot the surrounding countryside.

3 East of Yosemite National Park. The area to the east of Yosemite National Park (⇨ Chapter 20) includes some ruggedly handsome, albeit desolate, terrain, most notably around Mono Lake. The area is best visited by car, as distances are great and public transportation is negligible. U.S. 395 is the main north–south road on the eastern side of the Sierra Nevada, at the western edge of the Great Basin. It's one of California's most beautiful highways; plan to snap pictures at roadside pullouts.

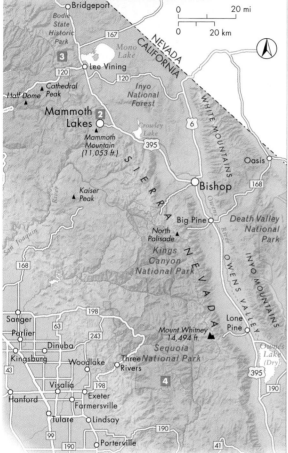

GETTING ORIENTED

The transition between the Central Valley and the rugged Southern Sierra may be the most dramatic in California sightseeing; as you head into the mountains, your temptation to stop the car and gawk will increase with every foot gained in elevation. Although you should spend most of your time here in the national parks (⇨ Chapter 20, Yosemite National Park, and Chapter 21, Sequoia and Kings Canyon National Parks), be sure to check out some of the mountain towns on the parks' fringes—in addition to being great places to stock up on supplies, they have worthy attractions, restaurants, and lodging options.

19

4 **South of Sequoia and Kings Canyon: Three Rivers.** Scenic Three Rivers is the main gateway for Sequoia and Kings Canyon National Parks (⇨ Chapter 21).

Updated
by Cheryl
Crabtree

The Southern Sierra's granite peaks and giant sequoias bedazzle heart and soul so completely that for many visitors the experience surpasses that at more famous urban attractions. Most of the Sierra's wonders lie within national parks accessed most easily via the gateway towns surrounding them—Oakhurst, Fish Camp, and Lee Vining for Yosemite, and Three Rivers for Sequoia and Kings Canyon. Lee Vining also provides entrée to deep-blue Mono Lake, a much-photographed attraction. The megaresort Mammoth Lakes, meanwhile, lures skiers and snowboarders in winter and hikers and mountain bikers in summer.

Outside the national parks (⇨ *Chapter 20, Yosemite National Park, and Chapter 21, Sequoia and Kings Canyon National Parks)*, the Southern Sierra's pristine lakes and rolling hills—not to mention the region's laid-back small towns—offer year-round opportunities for rest and relaxation. Or not. In winter, the thrill of the slopes (and their relative isolation, especially compared to busy Lake Tahoe) draws a hearty breed of outdoor enthusiast. In summer, a hike through groves and meadows or alongside streams and waterfalls allows you to see, smell, and feel nature up close. Whether you're taking it easy, though, or braving the elements, you're in for a treat.

PLANNING

GETTING HERE AND AROUND

AIR TRAVEL

Three main airports provide access to the Southern Sierra: Fresno Yosemite International (FAT), on the western side, and, on the eastern side, Mammoth-Yosemite (MMH), 6 miles east of Mammoth Lakes, and Reno–Tahoe (RNO), 130 miles north of Mammoth Lakes via U.S.

395. Alaska, Alaska, Allegiant, American, Delta, Frontier, United, and a few other carriers serve Fresno and Reno. Alaska and United serve Mammoth Lakes.

Airports Fresno Yosemite International Airport ✉ *5175 E. Clinton Ave., Fresno* ☎ *559/621–4500, 800/244–2359* ⊕ *www.flyfresno.org.* **Mammoth Yosemite Airport** ✉ *1200 Airport Rd., Mammoth Lakes* ☎ *760/934–2712, 888/466–2666* ⊕ *www.visitmammoth.com.* **Reno–Tahoe International Airport** ✉ *2001 E. Plumb La., Reno, Nevada* ☎ *775/328–6400* ⊕ *www.renoairport.com.*

BUS TRAVEL

Greyhound serves Fresno, Madera, and other Central Valley towns west of the Sierra. Madera County Connection buses travel between Madera and Oakhurst. Eastern Sierra Transit Authority buses serve Mammoth Lakes and other eastern Sierra towns. YARTS (Yosemite Area Regional Transportation System) *connects Yosemite National Park with surrounding towns; this is a good option during summer, when parking there is difficult.*

Bus Contacts Eastern Sierra Transit Authority ☎ *760/872–1901* ⊕ *www.estransit.com.* **Greyhound** ☎ *800/231–2222* ⊕ *www.greyhound.com.* **Madera County Connection** ✉ *Madera* ☎ *559/661–7433* ⊕ *www.maderactc. com/pubtrans.html.* **YARTS** *(Yosemite Area Regional Transportation System).* ☎ *877/989–2787* ⊕ *www.yarts.com.*

CAR TRAVEL

From San Francisco, heading east on Interstate 80 to 580 to 205E is the most efficient connecting route to Interstate 5 and Highway 99, which straddle the western side of the Sierra Nevada. From Los Angeles, head north on Interstate 5 and Highway 99. To best reach the eastern side from the Bay Area, take Interstate 80 to U.S. 395, then head south. To get to Mammoth Lakes in summer and early fall you can travel via Highway 120 (to U.S. 395 south) through the Yosemite high country (Tioga Pass is closed from November to April). In winter, the quickest route from the San Francisco Bay Area is Interstate 80 to U.S. 50 to Highway 207 (also known as the Kingsbury Grade, just east of South Lake Tahoe) to U.S. 395 south. From Los Angeles, take Interstate 5 to Highway 14 to U.S. 395 and head north. All routes take about seven hours. ■TIP➔ Watch your gas gauge. Gas stations are few and far between in the Sierra, so fill your tank when you can. If you're traveling between October and May, heavy snow may cover mountain roads. Carry tire chains, know how to put them on (on Interstate 80 and U.S. 50 you can pay a chain installer $35 to do it for you, but on other routes you'll have to do it yourself), and always check road conditions before you leave.

Travel Reports Caltrans Current Highway Conditions ☎ *800/427–7623* ⊕ *www.dot.ca.gov.*

TRAIN TRAVEL

Amtrak San Joaquin trains stop daily in Bakersfield, Hanford, Fresno, and Merced, where you can connect with local transit.

Amtrak ☎ *800/872–7245* ⊕ *www.amtrak.com.*

19

TOUR OPERATORS

Mammoth All Weather Shuttle. In summer, multilingual guides drive vans and SUVs on regular tours from Mammoth Lakes to Yosemite; north to June Lake, Mono Lake, and Bodie Ghost Town; and around the Mammoth Lakes region. MAW also provides charter shuttles to Los Angeles, Reno, and Las Vegas airports—very useful when flights at Mammoth Yosemite Airport are cancelled due to inclement weather. Custom itineraries are possible as well. ⊠ *Mammoth Lakes* ☎ *760/709–2927* ⊕ *www.mawshuttle.com.*

VISITOR INFORMATION

Mammoth Lakes Tourism ⊠ *Mammoth Lakes* ☎ *760/934–2712, 888/466–2666* ⊕ *www.visitmammoth.com.* **Mono County Tourism** ⊠ *Mammoth Lakes* ☎ *800/845–7922* ⊕ *monocounty.org.*

RESTAURANTS

Most small towns in the Sierra Nevada have at least one restaurant; with few exceptions, dress is casual. You'll most likely be spending a lot of time in the car while you're exploring the area, so pick up snacks and drinks to keep with you. With picnic supplies on hand, you'll be able to enjoy an impromptu meal under giant trees or in one of the eastern Sierra towns' municipal parks.

HOTELS

For visits to the Sierra Nevada's western side, book your hotel in advance—especially in summer—or you may wind up in the Central Valley, far from the action. Booking in advance is less crucial for travel to the Eastern Sierra, except in Mammoth Lakes. In either area, keep in mind that rural and rustic does not always mean inexpensive. *Hotel reviews have been shortened. For full information, visit Fodors.com.*

Hotel Contacts Mammoth Reservations ⊠ *Mammoth Lakes* ☎ *800/223–3032* ⊕ *www.mammothreservations.com.*

WHAT IT COSTS			
	$	$$	$$$	$$$$
Restaurants	under $16	$16–$22	$23–$30	over $30
Hotels	under $121	$121–$175	$176–$250	over $250

Restaurant prices are the average cost of a main course at dinner or, if dinner is not served, at lunch. Hotel prices are the lowest cost of a standard double room in high season.

SOUTH OF YOSEMITE NATIONAL PARK

People heading to Yosemite National Park, especially those interested in seeing the giant redwoods on the park's south side, pass through Oakhurst and Fish Camp on Highway 41.

OAKHURST

40 miles north of Fresno on Hwy. 41.

Motels, restaurants, gas stations, and small businesses line Highway 41 in Oakhurst, the last sizeable community before Yosemite (⇨ *Chapter 20)*—the southern entrance is 23 miles north of town—and a good spot to find provisions. Continue north on Highway 41 to get to Yosemite. Three miles north of town on Highway 41, then 6 miles east, lies honky-tonk Bass Lake, a popular spot in summer with motorboaters, Jet Skiers, and families looking to cool off in the reservoir.

GETTING HERE AND AROUND

At the junction of highways 41 and 49, Oakhurst is about an hour's drive north of Fresno. It's the southern gateway to Yosemite, so many people fly into Fresno and rent a car to get here and beyond. The town has no public transportation of consequence.

ESSENTIALS

Visitor Information Yosemite Sierra Visitors Bureau ☎ *559/683–4636* ⊕ *www.yosemitethisyear.com.*

WHERE TO EAT

$$$$ ✕ **Erna's Elderberry House.** Erna Kubin-Clanin, the grande dame of Châ-
EUROPEAN teau du Sureau, created this culinary oasis, stunning for its understated
Fodor'sChoice elegance, gorgeous setting, and impeccable service. Red walls and wood
★ beams accent the dining room's high ceilings, and arched windows reflect the glow of candles. The seasonal six-course prix-fixe dinner ($95) can be paired with superb wines, with every course delivered in perfect synchronicity by the elite waitstaff. ■ TIP➜ **Diners can also order à la carte, and a short bar menu is served in the former wine cellar.** Ⓢ *Average main: $38* ⊠ *Château du Sureau, 48688 Victoria La., off Hwy. 41* ☎ *559/683–6800* ⊕ *www.elderberryhouse.com* ⚑ *Reservations essential* ☺ *No lunch Mon.–Sat.*

WHERE TO STAY

$$ ⊞ **Best Western Yosemite Gateway Inn.** Oakhurst's best motel has care-
HOTEL fully tended landscaping and rooms with attractive colonial-style fur-
FAMILY niture and slightly kitschy hand-painted wall murals of Yosemite. **Pros:** close to Yosemite's southern entrance and Wawona area; clean; indoor and outdoor swimming pools; comfortable. **Cons:** some rooms on the small side; Internet connection can be slow. Ⓢ *Rooms from: $150* ⊠ *40530 Hwy. 41, Oakhurst* ☎ *888/256–8042, 559/683–2378* ⊕ *www. yosemitegatewayinn.com* ⥱ *133 rooms, 16 suites.*

$$$$ ⊞ **Château du Sureau.** You'll feel pampered from the moment you drive
RESORT through the wrought-iron gates of this fairy-tale castle. **Pros:** luxu-
Fodor'sChoice rious; great views. **Cons:** expensive; if you're not really into spas,
★ it might not be worth your while. Ⓢ *Rooms from: $385* ⊠ *48688*

19

Victoria La., Oakhurst ☎ *559/683–6860* 🌐 *www.chateausureau.com* 🛏 *10 rooms, 1 villa* 🍴 *Breakfast.*

$$ B&B/INN 🏨 **Homestead Cottages.** Set on 160 acres of rolling hills that once held a Miwok village, these cottages (the largest sleeps six) have gas fireplaces, fully equipped kitchens, and queen-size beds. **Pros:** remote location; quiet setting; friendly owners. **Cons:** might be too quiet for some. [$] *Rooms from: $169* ✉ *41110 Rd. 600, 2½ miles off Hwy. 49, Ahwahnee* ☎ *559/683–0495* 🌐 *www.homesteadcottages.com* 🛏 *6 cottages.*

FISH CAMP

57 miles north of Fresno and 4 miles south of Yosemite National Park's south entrance.

As you climb in elevation along Highway 41 northbound, you see nothing but trees until you get to the small settlement of Fish Camp, where there's a post office and general store, but no gasoline (for gas, head 10 miles north to Wawona, in the park, or 17 miles south to Oakhurst).

GETTING HERE AND AROUND

Arrive here by car via Highway 41, from Yosemite National Park a few miles to the north, or from Oakhurst (and, farther down the road, Fresno) to the south. Unless you're on foot or a bicycle, a car is your only option.

EXPLORING

FAMILY **Yosemite Mountain Sugar Pine Railroad.** Travel back to a time when powerful steam locomotives hauled massive log trains through the Sierra. This 4-mile, narrow-gauge railroad excursion takes you near Yosemite's south gate; there's also a moonlight special, with dinner and entertainment ($55). Take Highway 41 south from Yosemite about 8 miles to the departure point. ✉ *56001 Hwy. 41, Fish Camp* ☎ *559/683–7273* 🌐 *www.ymsprr.com* 🎟 *$21* 🕒 *May–Sept., daily; Apr. and Oct., weekends and selected weekdays.*

WHERE TO STAY

$$$ B&B/INN 🏨 **Narrow Gauge Inn.** The well-tended rooms at this family-owned property have balconies with great views of the surrounding woods and mountains. **Pros:** close to Yosemite's south entrance; nicely appointed rooms; wonderful balconies. **Cons:** rooms can be a bit dark; dining options are limited, especially for vegetarians. [$] *Rooms from: $209* ✉ *48571 Hwy. 41, Fish Camp* ☎ *559/683–7720, 888/644–9050* 🌐 *www.narrowgaugeinn.com* 🛏 *26 rooms* 🍴 *Breakfast.*

$$$$ HOTEL 🏨 **Tenaya Lodge.** One of the region's largest hotels, Tenaya Lodge is ideal for people who enjoy wilderness treks by day but prefer creature comforts at night. **Pros:** rustic setting with modern comforts; good off-season deals; very close to Yosemite National Park. **Cons:** so big it can seem impersonal; pricey during summer. [$] *Rooms from: $295* ✉ *1122 Hwy. 41, Fish Camp* ☎ *559/683–6555, 888/514–2167* 🌐 *www.tenayalodge.com* 🛏 *244 rooms, 6 suites* 🍴 *No meals.*

MAMMOTH LAKES

30 miles south of the eastern edge of Yosemite National Park.

International real-estate developers joined forces with Mammoth Mountain Ski Area to transform the once sleepy town of Mammoth Lakes (elevation 7,800 feet) into an upscale ski destination. The Village at Mammoth has been a focus of recent attention—relatively sophisticated dining and lodging options have been added, and there is a busy schedule of concerts and events. The "downtown" area of Old Mammoth Road is experiencing a renaissance, as tired motels and restaurants have undergone multimillion-dollar transformations under new owners. It's also the home of the hoppin' Mammoth Rock 'n' Bowl, a two-story activity, dining, and entertainment complex. Winter is high season at Mammoth; in summer, the room rates drop.

GETTING HERE AND AROUND

The best way to get to Mammoth Lakes is by car. The town is a couple of miles west of U.S. 395. Highway 203 heads west from U.S. 395, becoming Main Street as it passes through the town of Mammoth Lakes, and later Minaret Road (which makes a right turn) as it continues westward to the Mammoth Mountain Ski Area and Devils Postpile National Monument. In summer, YARTS (Yosemite Area Regional Transportation System ⊕ *www.yarts.com*) provides once-a-day public-transit service between Mammoth Lakes and Yosemite Valley. The shuttle buses of Eastern Sierra Transit Authority (☎ *800/922–1930* ⊕ *www.estransit.com*) serve Mammoth Lakes and nearby tourist sites.

ESSENTIALS

Visitor Information Mammoth Lakes Visitor Center ⊠ *Welcome Center, 2510 Main St., near Sawmill Cutoff Rd.* ☎ *760/934–2712, 888/466–2666* ⊕ *www.visitmammoth.com.*

19

EXPLORING

TOP ATTRACTIONS

Fodor's Choice ★ **Devils Postpile National Monument.** West of Mammoth Lakes lies this formation of smooth, vertical basalt columns sculpted by volcanic and glacial forces. A short, steep trail winds to the top of the 60-foot cliff for a bird's-eye view of the columns. A 2-mile hike past Devils Postpile leads to the monument's second scenic wonder, **Rainbow Falls**, where a branch of the San Joaquin River plunges more than 100 feet over a lava ledge. When the water hits the pool below, sunlight turns the resulting mist into a spray of color. Scenic picnic spots dot the banks of the river. ■TIP→ Follow Highway 203 west to Mammoth Mountain Ski Area to board the shuttle bus to the monument, which day-use visitors must take from mid-June to early September. ⊠ *13 miles southwest of Mammoth Lakes off Minaret Rd. (Hwy. 203)* ☎ *760/934–2289, 760/872–1901 shuttle* ⊕ *www.nps.gov/depo* ⊠ *$7 per person* ☉ *Shuttle daily mid-June–early Oct.*

Mammoth Lakes Basin. Mammoth's seven main lakes are popular for fishing and boating in summer, and a network of multi-use paths connects them to the North Village. First comes Twin Lakes, at the far end of which is Twin Falls, where water cascades 300 feet over a shelf of volcanic rock. Also popular are Lake Mary, the largest lake in the basin; Lake Mamie; and Lake George. ■TIP→ **Horseshoe Lake is the only lake in which you can swim.** ⊠ *Lake Mary Rd., off Hwy. 203, southwest of town.*

Mammoth Rock 'n' Bowl. The biggest attraction in town apart from the ski slopes, Mammoth Rock 'n' Bowl offers one-stop recreation, entertainment, and dining for all ages along with sweeping views of the Sherwin Mountains. The sprawling, two-story complex opened in spring 2014. Downstairs are 12 bowling lanes, a band stage and dance floor, Ping-Pong and foosball tables, dartboards, and a casual bar-restaurant ($$) serving burgers, pizzas, and small plates. The upstairs floor has three golf simulators, a pro shop, and Mammoth Rock Brasserie ($$$), an upscale dining room and lounge. ■TIP→ **If the weather's nice, sit on the outdoor patio or the upstairs deck and soak in the unobstructed vistas.** ⊠ *3029 Chateau Rd.* ☎ *760/934–4200* ⊕ *mammothrocknbowl. com* ⊠ *Bowling: weekends and evenings $7 per game per person + $3 shoe rental, weekdays $5 per game per person + $3 shoe rental* ◷ *Daily 9–midnight.*

Panorama Gondola. Even if you don't ski, ride the gondola to see Mammoth Mountain, the aptly named dormant volcano that gives Mammoth Lakes its name. Gondolas serve skiers in winter and mountain bikers and sightseers in summer. The high-speed, eight-passenger gondolas whisk you from the chalet to the summit, where you can read about the area's volcanic history and take in top-of-the-world views. Standing high above the tree line, you can look west 150 miles across the state to the Coast Range; to the east are the highest peaks of Nevada and the Great Basin beyond. You won't find a better view of the Sierra High Country without climbing. Remember, though, that the air is thin at the 11,053-foot summit; carry water, and don't overexert yourself. The boarding area is at the Main Lodge. ⊠ *Off Minaret Rd. (Hwy. 203), west of village center* ☎ *760/934–2571* ⊠ *$25* ◷ *July 4–Oct., daily 9–4:30; Nov.–July 3, daily 8:30–4.*

WORTH NOTING

Minaret Vista. The glacier-carved sawtooth spires of the Minarets, the remains of an ancient lava flow, are best viewed from the Minaret Vista. ⊠ *Off Hwy. 203, 1¼ mile west of Mammoth Mountain Ski Area.*

Village at Mammoth. This huge complex of shops, restaurants, and luxury accommodations is the town's tourist center and the venue for many special events—check the website for the weekly schedule. The complex is also the transfer hub for the free public transit system, with fixed routes throughout the Mammoth Lakes area. The free village gondola starts here and travels up the mountain to Canyon Lodge and back. Unless you're staying in the village and have access to the on-site lots, parking can be very difficult here, if not impossible. ■TIP→ **If you must drive, try your luck getting a space in the public lot across the street**

Twin Lakes, in the Mammoth Lakes region, is a great place to unwind.

on Minaret Road; as a compromise, you could drive to the park-and-ride lot at Old Mammoth and Tavern roads and ride a free shuttle bus to and from the Village. ✉ *100 Canyon Blvd.* ☎ *760/924–1575* 🌐 *villageatmammoth.com.*

WHERE TO EAT

$ 🍴 **Bleu Handcrafted Foods.** Handcrafted artisanal cheeses and meats, wine and beer tastings, bread baked on-site, and specialty meats and seafood draw patrons to Bleu, a combination market and wine bar. Chef-owner Brandon Brocia and his wife, Theresa, cure their own salumi and prepare daily specials such as duck confit, pastas, and tapenades. Bleu, open daily from 11 to 8, also sells fine foods from California, the U.S., and Europe. Tastings can include cheeses, charcuterie, pâté, and olives, along with flights of beer, wine, or Port. **■ TIP→ You can order a gourmet box lunch to take hiking or skiing.** [$] *Average main: $11* ✉ *3325 Main St., Unit C* ☎ *760/914–2538* 🌐 *www.bleufoods.com.*

WINE BAR

$$$ 🍴 **The Mogul.** A local longtime favorite, the Mogul is the place to go for straightforward steaks—top sirloin, New York, filet mignon, and porterhouse. The only catch is that the waiters cook them, and the results vary depending on their experience. But generally you can't go wrong, and kids love the experience. The knotty-pine walls lend a woodsy touch and suggest Mammoth Mountain before all the development. **■ TIP→ For vegetarians and other lettuce lovers, there's an extensive salad bar—all you can eat, with hot bread included.** [$] *Average main: $24* ✉ *1528 Tavern Rd., off Old Mammoth Rd., Mammoth Lakes* ☎ *760/934–3039* 🌐 *www.themogul.com* ⏲ *No lunch.*

STEAKHOUSE
FAMILY

$$$ AMERICAN 🍴 **Petra's Bistro & Wine Bar.** The ambience at Petra's—quiet, dark, and warm (there's a great fireplace)—complements its seductive meat and seafood entrées and smart selection of mostly California-made wines. The service is top-notch. With its pub grub, whiskies, and craft beers and ales, the downstairs Clocktower Cellar bar provides a lively, if sometimes rowdy, alternative. [$] *Average main: $28* ✉ *Alpenhof Lodge, 6080 Minaret Rd.* ☎ *760/934–3500* 🌐 *www.petrasbistro.com* ✍ *Reservations essential* 🕒 *Closed Mon. No lunch.*

$$$$ AMERICAN 🍴 **Restaurant at Convict Lake.** The lake, named for an 1871 gunfight between local vigilantes and six escaped prisoners, is one of the most spectacular spots in the eastern Sierra, and the food here lives up to the view. The chef's specialties include beef Wellington, rack of lamb, and pan-seared local trout, all beautifully prepared. The woodsy room has a vaulted knotty-pine ceiling and a copper-chimney fireplace that roars on cold nights. Natural light abounds in the daytime, but if it's summer opt for a table outdoors under the white-barked aspens. Service is exceptional, as is the wine list, with reasonably priced European and California varietals. [$] *Average main: $32* ✉ *Convict Lake Rd. off U.S. 395, 4 miles south of Mammoth Lakes* ☎ *760/934–3803* 🌐 *www.convictlake.com* ✍ *Reservations essential* 🕒 *No lunch early Sept.–mid-June.*

$$ WINE BAR 🍴 **Side Door Café.** Half wine bar, half café, this is a laid-back spot for an easy lunch or a long afternoon. The Side Door serves grilled panini, sweet and savory crepes, and espresso. At the wine bar, order cheese plates and charcuterie platters, designed to pair with the 25 wines (fewer in summertime) available by the glass. If you're lucky, a winemaker will show up and hold court at the bar. [$] *Average main: $18* ✉ *Village at Mammoth, 100 Canyon Blvd., Unit 229* ☎ *760/934–5200* 🌐 *www.sidedoormammoth.com.*

$$ AMERICAN 🍴 **The Stove.** Down-to-earth, folksy cooking is the hallmark of this casual place—the kind to chow down at before or after a long car ride. New owners have freshened up the menu but have kept the comfort-food tradition alive with prime-rib hash and strawberry waffles, fried chicken, meat loaf, and other items. Breakfast is served all day; chicken and waffles are among the mainstays. Save room for the house-made pie, baked daily. The dining room here is cozy, with gingham curtains and dark-wood booths, and the service is friendly. Reservations are accepted for dinner only. [$] *Average main: $16* ✉ *644 Old Mammoth Rd.* ☎ *760/934–2821* 🌐 *www.thestoverestaurantmammoth.com* ✍ *Reservations not accepted* 🕒 *No dinner occasionally during off-season months; call for hrs.*

$$ MODERN AMERICAN FAMILY 🍴 **Toomey's.** After 16 years at the helm of Lee Vining's popular Whoa Nellie Deli, chef Matt Toomey started this restaurant just steps from the Village Gondola. A passionate baseball fan, Toomey designed the casual space to resemble a dugout and decorated it with baseball memorabilia. At breakfast, don't miss the coconut mascarpone pancakes. After a day on the slopes you can relax over lobster taquitos, giant chicken wings with homemade ranch dressing, fish tacos, and Angus beef sliders. Favorite lunch and dinner entrées include buffalo meat loaf, seafood jambalaya, a New Zealand elk rack chop, and

Caesar salad topped with grilled steak. Save room for homemade, organic, gluten-free pie and other desserts. **TIP→ If you're in a real hurry, place your order by phone, and someone will deliver your meal curbside to your car.** [$] *Average main: $20* ✉ *6085 Minaret Rd., at the Village* ☎ *760/924–4408* 🌐 *www.toomeyscatering.com.*

WHERE TO STAY

$ B&B/INN **Alpenhof Lodge.** The owners of Alpenhof lucked out when developers built the Village at Mammoth across the street from their mom-and-pop motel, which remains a simple lodging offering basic comforts and a few niceties such as the attractive pine furniture. **Pros:** convenient for skiers; reasonable rates. **Cons:** some bathrooms on the small side; rooms above the pub can be noisy. [$] *Rooms from: $109* ✉ *6080 Minaret Rd., Box 1157* ☎ *760/934–6330, 800/828–0371* 🌐 *www.alpenhof-lodge.com* 🛏 *54 rooms, 3 cabins* 🍴 *Breakfast.*

$$ B&B/INN **Cinnamon Bear Inn Bed and Breakfast.** In a business district off Main Street, this bed-and-breakfast feels more like a small motel, with nicely decorated rooms, many with four-poster beds. **Pros:** comparatively quiet; affordable; friendly. **Cons:** a bit tricky to find; limited parking. [$] *Rooms from: $129* ✉ *113 Center St.* ☎ *760/934–2873, 800/845–2873* 🌐 *www.cinnamonbearinn.com* 🛏 *22 rooms* 🍴 *Breakfast.*

$$$ RESORT **Double Eagle Resort and Spa.** You won't find a better spa retreat in the eastern Sierra than this one under lofty pine peaks on the June Lake Loop. **Pros:** pretty setting; generous breakfast; spectacular indoor pool; 1½ mile from June Mountain Ski Area. **Cons:** expensive; remote. [$] *Rooms from: $229* ✉ *5587 Hwy. 158, Box 736, June Lake* 🌐 *www.doubleeagle.com* 🛏 *17 2-bedroom cabins, 16 rooms, 1 3-bedroom house* 🍴 *No meals.*

$$ RESORT **Juniper Springs Resort.** Tops for slope-side comfort, these condominium-style units have full kitchens and ski-in ski-out access to the mountain. **Pros:** bargain during summer; direct access to the slopes; good views. **Cons:** no nightlife within walking distance; no air-conditioning. [$] *Rooms from: $159* ✉ *4000 Meridian Blvd.* ☎ *760/924–1102, 800/626–6684* 🌐 *www.mammothmountain.com* 🛏 *10 studios, 99 1-bedrooms, 92 2-bedrooms, 3 3-bedrooms* 🍴 *No meals.*

$$ RESORT **Mammoth Mountain Inn.** If you want to be within walking distance of the Mammoth Mountain Main Lodge, this is the place. **Pros:** great location; big rooms; a traditional place to stay. **Cons:** can be crowded in ski season. [$] *Rooms from: $134* ✉ *1 Minaret Rd.* ☎ *760/934–2581, 800/626–6684* 🌐 *www.mammothmountain.com* 🛏 *124 rooms, 91 condos.*

$$ RESORT **Sierra Nevada Resort.** A full-service resort in the heart of Old Mammoth, the Sierra Nevada has it all: three restaurants, four bars, a dedicated spa facility, on-site ski and snowboard rentals, a pool and Jacuzzi, miniature golf, and room and suite options in three buildings. **Pros:** many on-site amenities; walk to restaurants on property or downtown area. **Cons:** must drive or ride a bus to the slopes; thin walls in some rooms. [$] *Rooms from: $149* ✉ *164 Old Mammoth Rd.* ☎ *760/934–2515, 800/824–5132* 📠 *760/934–7319* 🌐 *thesierranevadaresort.com* 🛏 *143 rooms, 6 townhomes* 🍴 *No meals.*

19

$$$ RESORT Fodor's Choice ★ **Tamarack Lodge Resort & Lakefront Restaurant.** On the edge of the John Muir Wilderness Area, where cross-country ski trails loop through the woods, this 1924 lodge looks like something out of a snow globe. **Pros:** rustic; eco-sensitive; many nearby outdoor activities. **Cons:** pricey; shared bathrooms for some main lodge rooms. [$] *Rooms from: $218* ✉ *Lake Mary Rd., off Hwy. 203* ☎ *760/934–2442, 800/626–6684* 🌐 *www.tamaracklodge.com* 🛏 *11 rooms, 35 cabins* 🍴 *No meals.*

$$$ RESORT **The Village Lodge.** With their exposed timbers and peaked roofs, these four-story condo buildings at the epicenter of Mammoth's dining and nightlife scene pay homage to alpine style. **Pros:** central location; clean; big rooms; good restaurants nearby. **Cons:** pricey; can be noisy outside. [$] *Rooms from: $239* ✉ *1111 Forest Trail* ☎ *760/934–1982, 800/626–6684* 🌐 *www.mammothmountain.com* 🛏 *277 units* 🍴 *No meals.*

$$$$ RESORT **Westin Monache Resort.** On a hill just steps from the Village at Mammoth, the Westin provides full-service comfort and amenities close to restaurants, entertainment, and free public transportation to all Mammoth Lakes destinations. **Pros:** upscale amenities; prime location; free gondola across the street to the slopes. **Cons:** long, steep stairway down to village; added resort fee. [$] *Rooms from: $349* ✉ *50 Hillside Dr.* ☎ *760/934–0400, 888/627–8154 reservations* 📠 *760/934–4686* 🌐 *www.westinmammoth.com* 🛏 *109 rooms, 121 suites* 🍴 *No meals.*

SPORTS AND THE OUTDOORS

BIKING

Mammoth Mountain Bike Park. The park opens when the snow melts, usually by July, and has 100-plus miles of single-track trails—from mellow to super-challenging. Chairlifts and shuttles provide trail access, and rentals are available. ✉ *Mammoth Mountain Ski Area* ☎ *760/934–0677, 800/626-6684* 🌐 *www.mammothmountain.com* 🎟 *$47 day pass.*

FISHING

The fishing season runs from the last Saturday in April until the end of October. Crowley Lake is the top trout-fishing spot in the area; Convict Lake, June Lake, and the lakes of the Mammoth Basin are other prime spots. One of the best trout rivers is the San Joaquin, near Devils Postpile. Hot Creek, a designated Wild Trout Stream, is renowned for fly-fishing (catch-and-release only).

Kittredge Sports. This outfit rents rods and reels and also conducts guided trips. ✉ *3218 Main St., at Forest Trail* ☎ *760/934–7566* 🌐 *www.kittredgesports.com.*

Sierra Drifters Guide Service. To maximize your time on the water, get tips from local anglers, or better yet, book a guided fishing trip, contact Sierra Drifters. ☎ *760/935–4250* 🌐 *www.sierradrifters.com.*

HIKING

Hiking in Mammoth is stellar, especially along the trails that wind through alpine scenery around the Lakes Basin. Carry lots of water; and remember, the air is thin at 8,000-plus feet.

U.S. Forest Service Ranger Station. Stop at the ranger station, just east of the town of Mammoth Lakes, for an area trail map and permits for backpacking in wilderness areas. ⊠ *2510 Main St., Hwy. 203* ☎ *760/924–5500* ⊕ *www.fs.usda.gov/main/inyo.*

HORSEBACK RIDING

Stables around Mammoth are typically open from June through September.

Mammoth Lakes Pack Outfit. This company runs day and overnight horseback trips and will shuttle you to the high country. ⊠ *Lake Mary Rd., between Twin Lakes and Lake Mary* ☎ *888/475–8747* ⊕ *www. mammothpack.com.*

McGee Creek Pack Station. These folks customize pack trips or will shuttle you to camp alone. ⊠ *2990 McGee Creek Rd., Crowley Lake* ☎ *760/935–4324 summer, 760/878–2207, 800/854–7407* ⊕ *www. mcgeecreekpackstation.com.*

SKIING

In winter, check the On the Snow website or call the Snow Report for information about Mammoth weather conditions.

FAMILY **June Mountain Ski Area.** In their rush to Mammoth Mountain, most people overlook June Mountain, a compact, low-key resort 20 miles to the north. Snowboarders especially dig it. Three beginner-to-intermediate terrain areas—the Silverado Fun Zone, Mambo Playground, and Bucky's Adventure—are for both skiers and boarders. There's rarely a line for the lifts here: if you must ski on a weekend and want to avoid the crowds, this is the place to come. In a storm, June is better protected from wind and blowing snow than Mammoth is. (If it starts to storm, you can use your Mammoth ticket at June.) Expect all the usual services, including a rental-and-repair shop, a ski school, and a sports shop. There's food, too, but the options are better at Mammoth. Lift tickets cost $72, with discounts for multiple days. ■ TIP➔ **Kids 12 and under ski and ride free, making this is a great choice for families.** ⊠ *3819 Hwy. 158, off June Lake Loop, June Lake* ☎ *760/648–7733, 888/586–3686* ⊕ *www.junemountain.com* ⌕ *35 trails on 1,400 acres, rated 35% beginner, 45% intermediate, 20% advanced. Longest run 2 miles, base 7,545 feet, summit 10,190 feet. Lifts: 7.*

Fodor's Choice **Mammoth Mountain Ski Area.** One of the West's largest and best ski areas, ★ Mammoth has more than 3,500 acres of skiable terrain and a 3,100-foot vertical drop. The views from the 11,053-foot summit are some of the most stunning in the Sierra. Below, you'll find a 6½-mile-wide swath of groomed boulevards and canyons, as well as pockets of tree-skiing and a dozen vast bowls. Snowboarders are everywhere on the slopes; there are three outstanding freestyle terrain parks of varying technical difficulty, with jumps, rails, tabletops, and giant super pipes—this is the location of several international snowboarding competitions, and, in summer, mountain-bike ones. Mammoth's season begins in November and often lingers into May. Lift tickets start at $79. Lessons and equipment are available, and there's a children's ski and snowboard school. Mammoth runs free shuttle-bus routes around town and to the ski area, and the Village Gondola runs from the Village complex

19

to Canyon Lodge. But only overnight guests are allowed to park at the Village for more than a few hours. ⚠ **The main lodge is dark and dated, unsuited in almost every way for the crush of ski season. Within a decade, it's likely to be replaced.** ✉ *Minaret Rd., west of Mammoth Lakes* ☎ *760/934–2571, 800/626–6684, 760/934–0687 shuttle* ⊕ *www. mammothmountain.com* ☞ *150 trails on 3,500 acres, rated 25% beginner, 40% intermediate, 20% advanced, 15% expert. Longest run 3 miles, base 7,953 feet, summit 11,053 feet. Lifts: 28, including 11 highspeed and 3 gondolas.*

Tamarack Cross Country Ski Center. Trails at the center, adjacent to Tamarack Lodge, meander around several lakes. Rentals are available. The all-day inclusive rate is $55. ✉ *Lake Mary Rd., off Hwy. 203* ☎ *760/934–5293, 760/934–2442* ⊕ *tamaracklodge.com.*

SKI RENTALS AND RESOURCES

Fodor'sChoice
★
Black Tie Ski Rentals. Skiers and snowboarders love this rental outfit whose staffers will deliver and custom-fit equipment for free. They also offer slope-side assistance. ☎ *760/934–7009* ⊕ *mammoth.black tieskis.com.*

Footloose. When the U.S. Ski Team visits Mammoth and needs boot adjustments, everyone heads to Footloose, the best place in town—and possibly all California—for ski-boot rentals and sales, as well as custom insoles. ✉ *3043 Main St., at Mammoth Rd.* ☎ *760/934–2400* ⊕ *www. footloosesports.com.*

Kittredge Sports. Advanced skiers should consider this outfit, which has been around since the 1960s. ✉ *3218 Main St.* ☎ *760/934–7566* ⊕ *www.kittredgesports.com.*

Mammoth Sporting Goods. This company rents good skis for intermediates and sells equipment, clothing, and accessories. ✉ *452 Old Mammoth Rd.* ☎ *760/934–3239* ⊕ *www.mammothoutdoorsports.com.*

OntheSnow.com. This website provides ski and weather reports. ⊕ *www. onthesnow.com/california/mammoth-mountain-ski-area/skireport.html.*

Snow Report. For information on winter conditions around Mammoth, call the Snow Report. ☎ *760/934–7669, 888/766–9778.*

EAST OF YOSEMITE NATIONAL PARK

Most people enter Yosemite National Park from the west, having driven out from the Bay Area or Los Angeles. The eastern entrance on Tioga Pass Road (Highway 120), however, provides stunning, sweeping views of the High Sierra. Gray rocks shine in the bright sun, with scattered, small vegetation sprinkled about the mountainside. To drive from Lee Vining to Tuolumne Meadows is an unforgettable experience, but keep in mind the road tends to be closed for at least seven months of the year.

LEE VINING

20 miles east of Tuolumne Meadows via Hwy. 120 to U.S. 395; 30 miles north of Mammoth Lakes on U.S. 395.

Tiny Lee Vining is known primarily as the eastern gateway to Yosemite National Park (summer only; ⇨ *Chapter 20*) and the location of vast and desolate Mono Lake. Pick up supplies at the general store year-round, or stop here for lunch or dinner before or after a drive through the high country. In winter the town is all but deserted, except for the ice climbers who come to scale frozen waterfalls. To try your hand at ice climbing, contact Doug Nidever (☎ *760/937–6922* ⊕ *www. themountainguide.com*), aka the Mountain Guide.

GETTING HERE AND AROUND

Lee Vining is on U.S. 395, just north of the road's intersection with Highway 120 and on the south side of Mono Lake. In summer, Yosemite Area Regional Transportation System (YARTS ⊕ *www.yarts.com*) can get you here from Yosemite Valley, but you'll need a car to explore the area.

ESSENTIALS

Visitor Information Lee Vining Chamber of Commerce ☎ *760/647–6629* ⊕ *www.leevining.com.* **Mono Basin National Forest Scenic Area Visitor Center** ✉ *Visitor Center Dr., off U.S. 395, 1 mile north of Hwy. 120* ☎ *760/647– 3044* ⊕ *www.monolake.org/visit/vc* ⊗ *Mid-May–mid-Oct., daily 8–5; early Apr.– mid-May and mid-Oct.–Nov., Thurs.–Mon. 9–4:30.*

EXPLORING

Fodor'sChoice
★

Mono Lake. Since the 1940s Los Angeles has diverted water from this lake, exposing striking towers of tufa, or calcium carbonate. Court victories by environmentalists have meant fewer diversions, and the lake is rising again. Although to see the lake from U.S. 395 is stunning, make time to walk about South Tufa, whose parking lot is 5 miles east of U.S. 395 off Highway 120. There in summer you can join the naturalist-guided **South Tufa Walk**, which lasts about 1½ hours. The sensational **Scenic Area Visitor Center,** off U.S. 395, is open daily (8–5) from mid-May through mid-October; hours vary at other times, and it's closed in winter. The center's hilltop and sweeping views of Mono Lake, along with its interactive exhibits inside, make this one of California's best visitor centers. Rangers and naturalists lead walking tours of the tufa daily in summer and on weekends (sometimes on cross-country skis) in winter. In town at U.S. 395 and 3rd Street, the **Mono Lake Committee Information Center & Bookstore,** open 9 to 5 daily, has more information about this beautiful area. ✉ *Hwy. 120, east of Lee Vining, Lee Vining* ☎ *760/647–3044 visitor center, 760/647–6595 Mono Lake Committee Information Center* ⊕ *www.monolake.org*

EN
ROUTE

June Lake Loop. Heading south from Lee Vining, U.S. 395 intersects the June Lake Loop. This gorgeous 17-mile drive follows an old glacial canyon past Grant, June, Gull, and other lakes before reconnecting with U.S. 395 on its way to Mammoth Lakes. ■ **TIP→ The loop is especially colorful in fall.** ✉ *Hwy. 158 W.*

19

WHERE TO EAT AND STAY

$ ✕ **Tioga Gas Mart & Whoa Nelli Deli.** This might be the only gas station
AMERICAN in the United States that serves craft beers and lobster taquitos, but its
appeal goes way beyond novelty. Everything on the inventive menu
is well executed, from the succulent fish tacos with mango salsa to a
generous portion of barbecued ribs served with a slightly sweet huckleberry glaze.■ TIP→ **Order at the counter and grab a seat inside, or,
better yet, sit at one of the picnic tables on the lawn outside, which
have a distant view of Mono Lake.** Ⓢ *Average main: $15* ⊠ *Hwy. 120
and U.S. 395* ☎ *760/647–1088* ⊕ *www.whoanelliedeli.com* ☉ *Closed
early Nov.–late Apr.*

$ ▥ **Lake View Lodge.** Enormous rooms and lovely landscaping, which
B&B/INN includes several shaded sitting areas, set this motel apart from its competitors in town. **Pros:** attractive; clean; friendly staff. **Cons:** could use
updating. Ⓢ *Rooms from: $89* ⊠ *51285 U.S. 395* ☎ *760/647–6543,
800/990–6614* ⊕ *www.lakeviewlodgeyosemite.com* ⤳ *76 rooms,
12 cottages.*

BODIE STATE HISTORIC PARK

23 miles northeast of Lee Vining via U.S. 395 to Hwy. 270.

The historic town of Bridgeport is the gateway to Bodie State Historic
Park, and the only supply center for miles around. The scenery is spectacular, with craggy, snowcapped peaks looming over vast prairies. Tiny
and for tourist purposes worth nothing more than a place to sleep and
eat, Bridgeport's claim to fame is that most of the 1947 film-noir classic *Out of the Past,* starring Robert Mitchum in his prime as a private
eye whose past catches up with him, was filmed here. In winter, much
of Bridgeport shuts down.

GETTING HERE AND AROUND

A car is the best way to reach this area. About 15 miles north of Lee
Vining (7 miles south of Bridgeport), look for signs for the ghost town,
another 13 miles east via Highway 270. The last 3 miles are unpaved.
A snowmobile might be necessary to reach Bodie in winter.

EXPLORING

Fodor'sChoice **Bodie Ghost Town.** The mining village of Rattlesnake Gulch, abandoned
★ mine shafts, and the remains of a small Chinatown are among the sights
at this fascinating ghost town. The town boomed from about 1878 to
1881, but by the late 1940s all its residents had departed. A state park
was established here in 1962, with a mandate to preserve everything
in a state of "arrested decay." Evidence of Bodie's wild past survives
at an excellent museum, and you can tour an old stamp mill where ore
was crushed into fine powder to extract gold and silver. The town is
23 miles from Lee Vining, north on U.S. 395, then east on Highway
270; the last 3 miles are unpaved. Snow may close Highway 270 from
late fall through early spring. No food, drink, or lodging is available in
Bodie. ⊠ *Main and Green Sts.* ☎ *760/647–6445* ⊕ *www.parks.ca.gov/
bodie* ◪ *$5* ☉ *Mid-May–Oct., daily 9–6; Nov.–mid-May, daily 9–3.*

19

SOUTH OF SEQUOIA AND KINGS CANYON: THREE RIVERS

Numerous towns and cities tout themselves as "gateways" to Sequoia and Kings Canyon national parks, but one that merits the distinction is frisky Three Rivers, a foothills hamlet along the Kaweah River. Close to Sequoia National Park's Ash Mountain and Lookout Point entrances, Three Rivers is a good spot to find a room when park lodgings are full. Either because Three Rivers residents appreciate their idyllic setting or because they know that tourists are their bread and butter, you'll find them almost uniformly pleasant and eager to share tips about the best spots for "Sierra surfing" the Kaweah's smooth, moss-covered rocks or where to find the best cell phone reception (it's off to the cemetery for Verizon customers).

GETTING HERE AND AROUND

Driving is the easiest way to get to and around long and slender Three Rivers, which straddles a long stretch of Highway 198. From late May to early September, the Sequoia Shuttle (☎ 877/404–6473 ⊕ www.ci.visalia. ca.us) connects Three Rivers to Visalia and Sequoia National Park.

WHERE TO EAT AND STAY

$$$ ✕ **Gateway Restaurant and Lodge.** The view's the main draw at this rau-
AMERICAN cous roadhouse that overlooks the roaring Kaweah River as it plunges out of the high country. Taking seriously its role as its town's only true fine-dining establishment, the Gateway serves everything from panfried trout to osso buco to shrimp in Thai chili sauce. Some menu items are pricey, but you can also order a pizza or a Kobe beef or salmon burger. In general, the simpler the preparation is, the better the result. Dinner reservations are essential on summer weekends. $ *Average main: $29* ✉ *45978 Sierra Dr., Three Rivers* ☎ *559/561–4133* ⊕ *www.gateway-sequoia.com* ☽ *No breakfast weekdays Nov.–March.*

$$ ⓣ **Buckeye Tree Lodge.** Every room at this two-story motel has a patio
B&B/INN facing a sun-dappled grassy lawn, right on the banks of the Kaweah River. **Pros:** near the park entrance; fantastic river views; friendly staff; kitchenette in some rooms. **Cons:** can fill up quickly in the summer; could use a little updating. $ *Rooms from: $134* ✉ *46000 Sierra Dr., Hwy. 198, Three Rivers* ☎ *559/561–5900* ⊕ *www.buckeyetree.com* ☞ *11 rooms* ⓘⓞⓘ *Breakfast* ☞ *2-night minimum on summer weekends.*

SPORTS AND THE OUTDOORS

RAFTING

Kaweah White Water Adventures. Owner Frank Root's outfit offers three Kaweah River trips: a two-hour excursion (good for families) through Class III rapids, a longer paddle through Class IV rapids, and an extended trip (typically Class IV and V rapids). ✉ *40443 Sierra Dr.* ☎ *559/740–8251, 800/229–8658* ⊕ *www.kaweah-whitewater.com* ⓐ *$50–$140 per person.*

YOSEMITE
NATIONAL PARK

WELCOME TO YOSEMITE NATIONAL PARK

TOP REASONS TO GO

★ **Wet and wild:** An easy stroll brings you to the base of Lower Yosemite Falls, where roaring springtime waters make for misty lens caps and lasting memories.

★ **Tunnel vision:** Approaching Yosemite Valley, Wawona Road passes through a mountainside and emerges before one of the park's most heart-stopping vistas.

★ **Inhale the beauty:** Pause to smell the light, pristine air as you travel about the High Sierra's Tioga Pass and Tuolumne Meadows, where 10,000-foot granite peaks just might take your breath away.

★ **Walk away:** Leave the crowds behind—but do bring along a buddy—and take a hike somewhere along Yosemite's 800 miles of trails.

★ **Powder your nose:** Winter's hush floats into Yosemite on snowflakes. Lift your face to the sky and listen to the trees.

1 Yosemite Valley. At an elevation of 4,000 feet, in roughly the center of the park, beats Yosemite's heart. This is where you'll find the park's most famous sights and biggest crowds.

2 Wawona and Mariposa Grove. The park's southern tip holds Wawona, with its grand old hotel and pioneer history center, and the Mariposa Grove of Big Trees, filled with giant sequoias. These are closest to the South Entrance, 35 miles (a one-hour drive) south of Yosemite Village.

3 Tuolumne Meadows. The highlight of east-central Yosemite is this wildflower-strewn valley with hiking trails, nestled among sharp, rocky peaks. It's a 1½-hour drive northeast of Yosemite Valley along Tioga Road (closed mid-October–late May).

4 Hetch Hetchy. The most remote, least visited part of Yosemite accessible by automobile, this glacial valley is dominated by a reservoir and veined with wilderness trails. It's near the park's western boundary, about a half-hour drive north of the Big Oak Flat Entrance.

CALIFORNIA

GETTING ORIENTED

Yosemite is so large that you can think of it as five parks. Yosemite Valley, famous for waterfalls and cliffs, and Wawona, where the giant sequoias stand, are open all year. Hetch Hetchy, home of less-used backcountry trails, is most accessible from late spring through early fall. The subalpine high country, Tuolumne Meadows, is open for summer hiking and camping; in winter it's accessible via cross-country skis or snowshoes. Badger Pass Ski Area is open in winter only. Most visitors spend their time along the park's southwestern border, between Wawona and Big Oak Flat Entrance; a bit farther east in Yosemite Valley and Badger Pass Ski Area; and along the east–west corridor of Tioga Road, which spans the park north of Yosemite Valley and bisects Tuolumne Meadows.

20

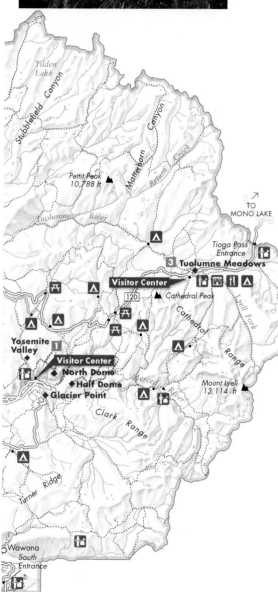

Tilden Lake

Stubblefield Canyon

Matterhorn Canyon

Return Creek

Pettit Peak 10,788 ft

Tuolumne River

TO MONO LAKE

Tioga Pass Entrance

3 **Tuolumne Meadows**

Visitor Center

120

Cathedral Peak

Cathedral Range

Lyell Fork

Yosemite Valley

1

Visitor Center

◆ **North Dome**

◆ **Half Dome**

◆ **Glacier Point**

Merced River

Mount Lyell 13,114 ft

Clark Range

Turner Ridge

Wawona South Entrance

41

Updated by
Sharron Wood

By merely standing in Yosemite Valley and turning in a circle, you can see more natural wonders in a minute than you could in a full day pretty much anywhere else. Half Dome, Yosemite Falls, El Capitan, Bridalveil Fall, Sentinel Dome, the Merced River, white-flowering dogwood trees, maybe even bears ripping into the bark of fallen trees or sticking their snouts into beehives—it's all in Yosemite Valley.

In the mid-1800s, when tourists were arriving to the area, the valley's special geologic qualities and the giant sequoias of Mariposa Grove 30 miles to the south so impressed a group of influential Californians that they persuaded President Abraham Lincoln to grant those two areas to the state for protection. On October 1, 1890—thanks largely to lobbying efforts by naturalist John Muir and Robert Underwood Johnson, the editor of *Century Magazine*—Congress set aside 1,500 square miles for Yosemite National Park.

YOSEMITE PLANNER

WHEN TO GO
During extremely busy periods—such as July 4—you will experience delays at the entrance gates. For smaller crowds, visit midweek. Or come mid-April through Memorial Day or mid-September through October, when the park is a bit less busy and the days usually are sunny and clear.

Summer rainfall is rare. In winter, heavy snows occasionally cause road closures, and tire chains or four-wheel drive may be required on the roads that remain open. The road to Glacier Point beyond the turnoff for Badger Pass is closed after the first major snowfall; Tioga Road is closed from late October through May or mid-June. Mariposa Grove Road is typically closed for a shorter period in winter.

GETTING HERE AND AROUND

BUS TRAVEL

Once you're in Yosemite you can take advantage of the free shuttle buses, which operate on low emissions, have 21 stops, and run from 7 am to 10 pm year-round. Buses run about every 10 minutes in summer, a bit less frequently in winter. A separate (but also free) summer-only shuttle runs out to El Capitan. Also in summer, you can pay to take the morning "hikers' bus" from Yosemite Valley to Tuolumne or the bus up to Glacier Point. Bus service from Wawona is geared for people who are staying there and want to spend the day in Yosemite Valley. Free and frequent shuttles transport people between the Wawona Hotel and Mariposa Grove. During the snow season, buses run regularly between Yosemite Valley and Badger Pass Ski Area.

CAR TRAVEL

Roughly 200 miles from San Francisco, 300 miles from Los Angeles, and 500 miles from Las Vegas, Yosemite takes a while to reach—and its many sites and attractions merit much more time than what rangers say is the average visit: four hours. Most people arrive via automobile or tour bus, but public transportation (courtesy of Amtrak and the regional YARTS bus system) also can get you to the valley efficiently.

Of the park's four entrances, Arch Rock is the closest to Yosemite Valley. The road that goes through it, Route 140 from Merced and Mariposa, is a scenic western approach that snakes alongside the boulder-packed Merced River. Route 41, through Wawona, is the way to come from Los Angeles (or Fresno, if you've flown in and rented a car). Route 120, through Crane Flat, is the most direct route from San Francisco. The only way in from the east is Tioga Road, which may be the best route in terms of scenery—though due to snow accumulation it's open for a frustratingly short amount of time each year (typically early June through mid-October).

There are few gas stations within Yosemite (Crane Flat, Tuolumne Meadows, and Wawona; none in the valley), so fuel up before you reach the park. From late fall until early spring, the weather is especially unpredictable, and driving can be treacherous. You should carry chains.

PARK ESSENTIALS

PARK FEES AND PERMITS

The admission fee, valid for seven days, is $20 per vehicle or $10 per individual.

If you plan to camp in the backcountry or climb Half Dome, you must have a wilderness permit. Availability of permits depends upon trailhead quotas. It's best to make a reservation, especially if you will be visiting May through September. You can reserve two days to 24 weeks in advance by phone, mail, or fax (✉ *Box 545, Yosemite, CA 95389* ☎ *209/372–0740* 🖷 *209/372–0739*); you'll pay $5 per person plus $5 per reservation if and when your reservations are confirmed. Requests must include your name, address, daytime phone, the number of people in your party, trip date, alternative dates, starting and ending trailheads, and a brief itinerary. Without a reservation, you may still get a free permit on a first-come, first-served basis at wilderness permit offices at Big

20

CLOSE UP

Plants and Wildlife in Yosemite

Dense stands of incense cedar and Douglas fir—as well as ponderosa, Jeffrey, lodgepole, and sugar pines—cover much of the park, but the stellar standout, quite literally, is the *Sequoiadendron giganteum*, the giant sequoia. Sequoias grow only along the west slope of the Sierra Nevada between 4,500 and 7,000 feet in elevation. Starting from a seed the size of a rolled-oat flake, each of these ancient monuments assumes remarkable proportions in adulthood; you can see them in the Mariposa Grove of Big Trees. In late May the valley's dogwood trees bloom with white, starlike flowers. Wildflowers, such as black-eyed Susan, bull thistle, cow parsnip, lupine, and meadow goldenrod, peak in June in the valley and in July at higher elevations.

The most visible animals in the park—aside from the omnipresent western gray squirrel, which fearlessly attempt to steal your food at every campground and picnic site—are the mule deer. Though sightings of bighorn sheep are infrequent in the park itself, you can sometimes see them on the eastern side of the Sierra Crest, just off Route 120 in Lee Vining Canyon. You may also see the American black bear, which often has a brown, cinnamon, or blond coat. The Sierra Nevada is home to thousands of bears, and you should take all necessary precautions to keep yourself—and the bears—safe. Bears that acquire a taste for human food can become very aggressive and destructive and often must be destroyed by rangers, so store all your food and even scented toiletries in the bear lockers located at many campgrounds and trailheads, or use bear-resistant canisters if you'll be hiking in the backcountry.

Watch for the blue Steller's jay along trails, near public buildings, and in campgrounds, and look for golden eagles soaring over Tioga Road.

Oak Flat, Hetch Hetchy, Tuolumne Meadows, Wawona, the Wilderness Center in Yosemite Village, and Yosemite Valley in summer. From fall to spring, visit the Valley Visitor Center.

PARK HOURS

The park is open 24/7 year-round. All entrances are open at all hours, except for Hetch Hetchy Entrance, which is open roughly dawn to dusk. Yosemite is in the Pacific time zone.

TOURS

Fodor's Choice **Ansel Adams Photo Walks.** Photography enthusiasts shouldn't miss these
★ 90-minute guided camera walks offered four mornings (Mon., Tues., Thurs., and Sat.) each week by professional photographers. All are free, but participation is limited to 15 people. Meeting points vary, and advance reservations are essential. ☎ *209/372–4413* ⊕ *www.anseladams.com* 🎦 *Free.*

FAMILY **Wee Wild Ones.** Designed for kids under 7, this 45-minute program includes animal-theme games, songs, stories, and crafts. The event is held outdoors before the regular Yosemite Lodge or Curry Village evening programs in summer and fall; it moves to the Ahwahnee's big fireplace in winter and spring. All children must be accompanied by an adult. ☎ *209/372–1240* ⊕ *www.yosemitepark.com* 🎦 *Free.*

VISITOR INFORMATION

PARK CONTACT INFORMATION

Yosemite National Park ☎ *209/372–0200* ⊕ *www.nps.gov/yose.*

VISITOR CENTERS

Le Conte Memorial Lodge. This small but striking National Historic Landmark, with its granite walls and steeply pitched shingle roof, is Yosemite's first permanent public information center. Step inside to see the cathedral-like interior, which contains a library and environmental exhibits. To find out about evening programs, check the kiosk out front. ✉ *Southside Dr., about ½ mile west of Curry Village* ⊕ *www.nps.gov/yose* ⊙ *May–Sept., Wed.–Sun. 10–4.*

Valley Visitor Center. Learn about Yosemite Valley's geology, vegetation, and human inhabitants at this visitor center, which is also staffed with helpful rangers and contains a bookstore with a wide selection of books and maps. Don't leave without watching *Spirit of Yosemite,* a 23-minute introductory film that runs every half hour in the theater behind the visitor center. ✉ *Yosemite Village* ☎ *209/372–0299* ⊕ *www.nps.gov/yose* ⊙ *Late May–early Sept., daily 9–7:30; early Sept.–late May, daily 9–5.*

EXPLORING

HISTORIC SITES

Ahwahneechee Village. This solemn smattering of structures, accessed by a short loop trail behind the Yosemite Valley Visitor Center, is a look at what American Indian life might have been like in the 1870s. One interpretive sign points out that the Miwok people referred to the 19th-century newcomers as "Yohemite" or "Yohometuk," which have been translated as meaning, "some of them are killers." ✉ *Northside Dr., Yosemite Village* ✉ *Free* ⊙ *Daily sunrise–sunset.*

Pioneer Yosemite History Center. Some of Yosemite's first structures—those not occupied by American Indians, that is—were relocated here in the 1950s and 1960s. You can spend a pleasurable and informative half-hour walking about them and reading the signs, perhaps springing for a self-guided-tour pamphlet (50¢) to further enhance the history lesson. Weekends and some weekdays in the summer, costumed docents conduct free blacksmithing and "wet-plate" photography demonstrations, and for a small fee you can take a stagecoach ride. ✉ *Rte. 41, Wawona* ☎ *209/375–9531, 209/379–2646* ✉ *Free* ⊙ *Building interiors: mid-June–Labor Day, Wed. 2–5, Thurs.–Sun. 10–1 and 2–5.*

SCENIC STOPS

El Capitan. Rising 3,593 feet—more than 350 stories—above the valley, El Capitan is the largest exposed-granite monolith in the world. Since 1958, people have been climbing its entire face, including the famous "nose." You can spot adventurers with your binoculars by scanning the smooth and nearly vertical cliff for specks of color. ✉ *Off Northside Dr., about 4 miles west of the Valley Visitor Center.*

20

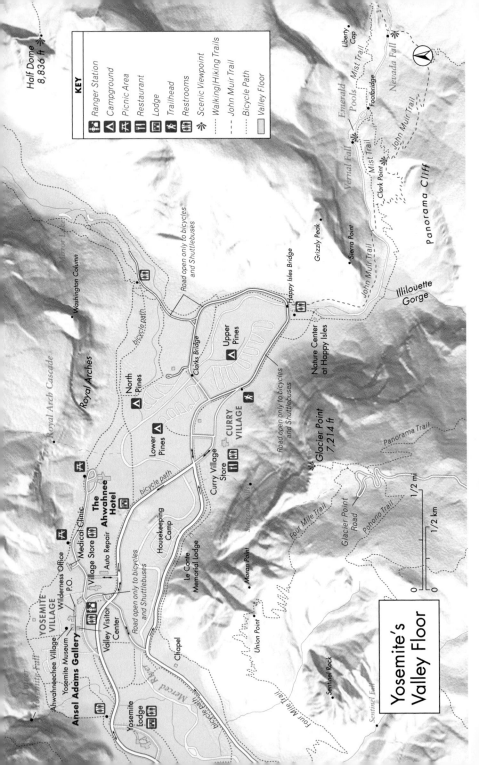

Yosemite's Valley Floor

Half Dome
8,836 ft

Liberty Cap

Emerald Pools
Mist Trail
Footbridge
Nevada Fall
Vernal Fall
Mist Trail
John Muir Trail
Clark Point
John Muir Trail
Panorama Cliff

Mirror L.

Washington Column

Royal Arch Cascade

Royal Arches

Grizzly Peak
Sierra Point
John Muir Trail
Illilouette Gorge

Road open only to bicycles and Shuttlebuses

bicycle path

Happy Isles Bridge

Upper Pines

Clarks Bridge

North Pines

Nature Center at Happy Isles

Road open only to bicycles and Shuttlebuses

Lower Pines

CURRY VILLAGE

Curry Village Store

Glacier Point
7,214 ft

Panorama Trail

bicycle path

The Ahwahnee Hotel

Medical Clinic
Auto Repair
Village Store
Housekeeping Camp

Le Conte Memorial Lodge

Moran Point

Four Mile Trail

Glacier Point Road

Pohono Trail

1/2 mi

1/2 km

YOSEMITE VILLAGE
Yosemite Museum
Ahwahneechee Village
Wilderness Office
P.O.
Ansel Adams Gallery
Valley Visitor Center

Road open only to bicycles and Shuttlebuses

Chapel

Union Point

Yosemite Falls

Merced River

bicycle path

Yosemite Lodge

Sentinel Rock

Sentinel Fall

Four Mile Trail

KEY

🏛	Ranger Station
⛺	Campground
🏕	Picnic Area
🍴	Restaurant
🏨	Lodge
🥾	Trailhead
🚻	Restrooms
🌲	Scenic Viewpoint
⋯⋯	Walking/Hiking Trails
– – –	John Muir Trail
⋯⋯⋯	Bicycle Path
▢	Valley Floor

Glacier Point. If you lack the time, desire, or stamina to hike more than 3,200 feet up to Glacier Point from the Yosemite Valley floor, you can drive here—or take a bus from the valley—for a bird's-eye view. You are likely to encounter a lot of day-trippers on the short, paved trail that leads from the parking lot to the main overlook. Take a moment to veer off a few yards to the Geology Hut, which succinctly explains and illustrates what the valley looked like 10 million, 3 million, and 20,000 years ago. ⊠ *Glacier Point Rd., 16 miles northeast of Rte. 41* ☏ *209/372–1240.*

Half Dome. Visitors' eyes are continually drawn to this remarkable granite formation that tops out at more than 4,700 feet above the valley floor. Despite its name, the dome is actually about three-quarters intact. You can hike to the top of Half Dome on an 8.5-mile (one-way) trail whose last 400 feet must be ascended while holding onto a steel cable. Permits are required (and checked on the trail), and available only by lottery. Visit ⊕ *www.recreation.gov* well in advance of your trip for details. Back down in the valley, see Half Dome reflected in the Merced River by heading to Sentinel Bridge just before sundown. The brilliant orange light on Half Dome is a stunning sight.

Hetch Hetchy Reservoir. When Congress approved the O'Shaughnessy Dam in 1913, pragmatism triumphed over aestheticism. Some 2.5 million residents of the San Francisco Bay Area continue to get their water from this 117-billion-gallon reservoir. Although spirited efforts are being made to restore the Hetch Hetchy Valley to its former, pristine glory, three-quarters of San Francisco voters in 2012 ultimately opposed a measure to even consider draining the reservoir. Eight miles long, the reservoir is Yosemite's largest body of water, and one that can be seen up close from several trails. ⊠ *Hetch Hetchy Rd., about 15 miles north of the Big Oak Flat entrance station.*

Mariposa Grove of Big Trees. Of Yosemite's three sequoia groves—the others being Merced and Tuolumne, both near Crane Flat well to the north—Mariposa is by far the largest and easiest to walk around. Grizzly Giant, whose base measures 96 feet around, has been estimated to be one of the largest in the world. Perhaps more astoundingly, it's about 2,700 years old. Up the hill, you'll find many more sequoias, a small museum, and fewer people. Summer weekends are especially crowded here. Consider taking the free shuttle from Wawona. ⊠ *Rte. 41, 2 miles north of the South Entrance station.*

Tuolumne Meadows. The largest subalpine meadow in the Sierra (at 8,600 feet) is a popular way station for backpack trips along the Pacific Crest and John Muir trails. The setting is not as dramatic as Yosemite Valley, 56 miles away, but the almost perfectly flat basin, about 2½ miles long, is intriguing, and in July it's resplendent with wildflowers. The most popular day hike is up Lembert Dome, atop which you'll have breathtaking views of the basin below. Keep in mind that Tioga Road rarely opens before June and usually closes by mid-October. ⊠ *Tioga Rd. (Rte. 120), about 8 miles west of the Tioga Pass entrance station.*

20

"This is us taking a break before conquering the top of Lembert Dome, while enjoying the beautiful view over Yosemite's high country." —photo by Rebalyn, Fodors.com member

WATERFALLS

Yosemite's waterfalls are at their most spectacular in May and June. When the snow starts to melt (usually peaking in May), streaming snow-melt spills down to meet the Merced River. By summer's end, some falls, including the mighty Yosemite Falls, trickle or dry up. Their flow increases in late fall, and in winter they may be hung dramatically with ice. Even in drier months, the waterfalls can be breathtaking. If you choose to hike any of the trails to or up the falls, be sure to wear shoes with no-slip soles; the rocks can be extremely slick. Stay on trails at all times.

■TIP→ Visit the park during a full moon and you can stroll without a flashlight and still make out the ribbons of falling water, as well as silhouettes of the giant granite monoliths.

Bridalveil Fall. This 620-foot waterfall is often diverted dozens of feet one way or the other by the breeze. It is the first marvelous site you will see up close when you drive into Yosemite Valley. ✉ *Yosemite Valley, access from parking area off Wawona Rd.*

Nevada Fall. Climb Mist Trail from Happy Isles for an up close view of this 594-foot cascading beauty. If you don't want to hike (the trail's final approach is quite taxing), you can see it—albeit distantly—from Glacier Point. ⚠ Stay safely on the trail, as people sometimes die when they climb over the railing and onto the slippery rocks. ✉ *Yosemite Valley, access via Mist Trail from Nature Center at Happy Isles.*

Ribbon Fall. At 1,612 feet, this is the highest single fall in North America. It's also the first waterfall to dry up in summer; the rainwater and melted snow that create the slender fall evaporate quickly at this height. Look just west of El Capitan for the best view of the fall from the base of Bridalveil Fall. ⊠ *Yosemite Valley, west of El Capitan Meadow.*

Vernal Fall. Fern-covered black rocks frame this 317-foot fall, and rainbows play in the spray at its base. You can get a distant view from Glacier Point, or hike to see it close up. You'll get wet, but the view is worth it. ⊠ *Yosemite Valley, access via Mist Trail from Nature Center at Happy Isles.*

Fodor's Choice ★ **Yosemite Falls.** Actually three falls, they together constitute the highest waterfall in North America and the fifth highest in the world. The water from the top descends a total of 2,425 feet, and when the falls run hard, you can hear them thunder across the valley. If they dry up—that sometimes happens in late summer—the valley seems naked without the wavering tower of spray. ■TIP→ If you hike the mile-long loop trail (partially paved) to the base of the Lower Falls in May, prepare to get wet. You can get a good full-length view of the falls from the lawn of Yosemite Chapel, off Southside Drive. ⊠ *Yosemite Valley, access from Yosemite Lodge or trail parking area.*

EDUCATIONAL OFFERINGS

CLASSES AND SEMINARS

Art Classes. Professional artists conduct workshops in watercolor, etching, drawing, and other mediums. Bring your own materials or purchase the basics at the Art Activity Center, next to the Village Store. Children under 13 must be accompanied by an adult. ⊠ *Art Activity Center, Yosemite Village* ☎ *209/372–1442* ⊕ *www.yosemitepark.com* ⊠ *Free* ⊙ *Early Apr.–early Oct., Mon.–Sat. 10–2.*

Yosemite Outdoor Adventures. Naturalists, scientists, and park rangers lead multihour to multiday educational outings on topics from woodpeckers to fire management to pastel painting. Most sessions take place spring through fall, but a few focus on winter phenomena. ⊠ *Various locations* ☎ *209/379–2321* ⊕ *www.yosemitepark.com* ⊠ *$82–$465.*

RANGER PROGRAMS

Junior Ranger Program. Children ages 7 to 13 can participate in the informal, self-guided Junior Ranger program. A park activity handbook ($4) is available at the Valley Visitor Center or the Nature Center at Happy Isles. Once kids complete the book, rangers present them with a certificate and a badge. ⊠ *Yosemite Valley Visitor Center or the Nature Center at Happy Isles* ☎ *209/372–0299.*

Ranger-Led Programs. Rangers lead entertaining walks and give informative talks several times a day from spring to fall. The schedule is more limited in winter, but most days you can find a program somewhere in the park. In the evenings at Yosemite Lodge and Curry Village, lectures, slide shows, and documentary films present unique perspectives on Yosemite. On summer weekends, Camp Curry and Tuolumne Meadows Campground host sing-along campfire programs. Schedules and locations are posted on bulletin boards throughout the park as well as in the indispensable *Yosemite Guide,* which is distributed to visitors as they arrive at the park. ⊕ *www.yosemitepark.com.*

20

SPORTS AND THE OUTDOORS

BIKING

One enjoyable way to see Yosemite Valley is to ride a bike beneath its lofty granite monoliths. The eastern valley has 12 miles of paved, flat bicycle paths across meadows and through woods, with bike racks at convenient stopping points. For a greater challenge but at no small risk, you can ride on 196 miles of paved park roads—but bicycles are not allowed on hiking trails or in the backcountry. Kids under 18 must wear a helmet.

TOURS AND OUTFITTERS

Yosemite bike rentals. You can arrange for rentals from Yosemite Lodge and Curry Village bike stands. Bikes with child trailers, baby-jogger strollers, and wheelchairs are also available. The cost for bikes is $11.50 per hour, or $31.50 per day. ⊠ *Yosemite Lodge or Curry Village* ☎ *209/372–1208* ⊕ *www.yosemitepark.com* ۞ *Apr.–Oct.*

BIRD-WATCHING

More than 250 bird species have been spotted in the park, including the sage sparrow, pygmy owl, blue grouse, and mountain bluebird. Park rangers lead free bird-watching walks in Yosemite Valley a few days each week in summer; check at a visitor center or information station for times and locations. Binoculars sometimes are available for loan.

HIKING

TOURS AND OUTFITTERS

Wilderness Center. This facility provides free wilderness permits, which are required for overnight camping (advance reservations are available for $5 per person plus $5 per reservation and are highly recommended for popular trailheads in summer and on weekends). The staff here also provide maps and advice to hikers heading into the backcountry, as well as rent bear-resistant canisters, which are required if you don't have your own. ☎ *209/372–0308.*

Yosemite Mountaineering School and Guide Service. From April to November, Yosemite Mountaineering School and Guide Service leads two-hour to full-day treks, as well as backpacking and overnight excursions. Reservations are recommended. ⊠ *Yosemite Mountain Shop, Curry Village* ☎ *209/372–8344.*

EASY

Yosemite Falls Trail. This is the highest waterfall in North America. The upper fall (1,430 feet), the middle cascades (675 feet), and the lower fall (320 feet) combine for a total of 2,425 feet and, when viewed from the valley, appear as a single waterfall. The 0.25-mile trail leads from the parking lot to the base of the falls. Upper Yosemite Fall Trail, a strenuous 3½-mile climb rising 2,700 feet, takes you above the top of the falls. Lower trail: *Easy.* Upper trail: *Difficult.* ⊠ *Trailhead off Camp 4, north of Northside Dr.*

GOOD READS

■ *The Photographer's Guide to Yosemite*, by Michael Frye, is an insider's guide to the park, with maps for shutterbugs looking to capture perfect images.

■ John Muir penned his observations of the park he long advocated for in *The Yosemite*.

■ *Yosemite and the High Sierra*, edited by Andrea G. Stillman and John Szarkowski, features beautiful reproductions of landmark photographs by Ansel Adams, accompanied by excerpts from the photographer's journals written when Adams traveled in Yosemite National Park in the early 20th century.

■ An insightful collection of essays accompanies the museum-quality artworks in *Yosemite: Art of an American Icon*, by Amy Scott.

■ Perfect for budding botanists, *Sierra Nevada Wildflowers*, by Karen Wiese, identifies more than 230 kinds of flora growing in the Sierra Nevada region.

MODERATE

Mist Trail. Except for Lower Yosemite Falls, more visitors take this trail (or portions of it) than any other in the park. The trek up to and back from Vernal Fall is 3 miles. Add another 4 miles total by continuing up to 594-foot Nevada Fall; the trail becomes quite steep and slippery in its final stages. The elevation gain to Vernal Fall is 1,000 feet, and to Nevada Fall an additional 1,000 feet. Merced River tumbles down both falls on its way to a tranquil flow through the Valley. *Moderate.* ⊠ *Trailhead at Happy Isles.*

Fodor'sChoice **Panorama Trail.** Few hikes come with the visual punch that this 8.5-mile
★ trail provides. The star attraction is Half Dome, visible from many intriguing angles, but you also see three waterfalls up close and walk through a manzanita grove. Before you begin, look down on Yosemite Valley from Glacier Point, a special experience in itself. ⚠ **If you start after taking the last bus from the valley floor to Glacier Point, you might run out of daylight before you finish.** *Moderate.* ⊠ *Trailhead at Glacier Point.*

DIFFICULT

Fodor'sChoice **John Muir Trail to Half Dome.** Ardent and courageous trekkers continue
★ on from Nevada Fall to the top of Half Dome. Some hikers attempt this entire 10- to 12-hour, 16.75-mile round-trip trek in one day; if you're planning to do this, remember that the 4,800-foot elevation gain and the 8,842-foot altitude will cause shortness of breath. Another option is to hike to a campground in Little Yosemite Valley near the top of Nevada Fall the first day, then climb to the top of Half Dome and hike out the next day. Get your wilderness permit (required for a one-day hike to Half Dome, too) at least a month in advance. Be sure to wear hiking boots and bring gloves. The last pitch up the back of Half Dome is very steep—the only way to climb this sheer rock face is to pull yourself up using the steel cable handrails, which are in place only from late spring to early fall. Those who brave the ascent will be rewarded with an unbeatable view of Yosemite Valley below and the high country beyond. ⚠ **Only 300 hikers per day are allowed atop Half Dome, and they all must have permits,**

20

which are distributed by lottery, one in the spring before the season starts and another two days before the climb. Contact ⊕ www.recreation.gov for details. *Difficult.* ⊠ *Trailhead at Happy Isles.*

HORSEBACK RIDING

Reservations for guided trail rides must be made in advance at the hotel tour desks or by phone. Scenic trail rides range from two hours to a half day; four- and six-day High Sierra saddle trips are also available.

TOURS AND OUTFITTERS

Tuolumne Meadows Stables. Tuolumne Meadows Stables runs two- and four-hour trips that start at $64, as well as four- to six-day camping treks on mules that start at $1,018. Reservations are mandatory. ⊠ *Off Tioga Rd., 2 miles east of Tuolumne Meadows Visitor Center* ☎ *209/372–8427* ⊕ *www.yosemitepark.com.*

Wawona Stables. Two- and five-hour rides start at $64. Reservations are recommended. ⊠ *Rte. 41, Wawona* ☎ *209/375–6502.*

Yosemite Valley Stables. You can tour the valley on two-hour and four-hour rides starting from the Yosemite Valley Stables. Reservations are strongly recommended for the trips, which start at $64. ⊠ *At entrance to North Pines Campground, 100 yards northeast of Curry Village* ☎ *209/372–8348* ⊕ *www.yosemitepark.com.*

RAFTING

Rafting is permitted only on designated areas of the Middle and South Forks of the Merced River. Check with the Valley Visitor Center for closures and other restrictions.

OUTFITTERS

Curry Village raft stand. The per-person rental fee ($30) at Curry Village raft stand covers the four- to six-person raft, two paddles, and life jackets, plus a return shuttle at the end of your trip. ⊠ *South side of Southside Dr., Curry Village* ☎ *209/372–4386* ⊕ *www.yosemitepark. com* 🖃 *$30* ☉ *Late May–July.*

ROCK CLIMBING

Fodor's Choice The granite canyon walls of Yosemite Valley are world-renowned for
★   rock climbing. El Capitan, with its 3,593-foot vertical face, is the most famous, but there are many other options here for all skill levels.

TOURS AND OUTFITTERS

Yosemite Mountaineering School and Guide Service. The one-day basic lesson at Yosemite Mountaineering School and Guide Service includes some bouldering and rappelling, and three or four 60-foot climbs. Climbers must be at least 10 years old and in reasonably good physical condition. Intermediate and advanced classes include instruction in first aid, anchor building, multipitch climbing, summer snow climbing, and big-wall climbing. There's a Nordic program in the winter. ⊠ *Yosemite Mountain Shop, Curry Village* ☎ *209/372–8344* ⊕ *www.yosemitepark. com* 🖃 *Starting at $148* ☉ *Apr.–Nov.*

WINTER SPORTS

ICE-SKATING

Curry Village Ice Rink. Winter visitors have skated at this outdoor rink for decades, and there's no mystery why: it's a kick to glide across the ice while soaking up views of Half Dome and Glacier Point. ⊠ *South side of Southside Dr., Curry Village* ☎ *209/372–8319* ⊠ *$9.75 per session, $4 skate rental* ☉ *Mid-Nov.–mid-Mar. afternoons and evenings daily, morning sessions weekends (hrs vary).*

SKIING AND SNOWSHOEING

Badger Pass Ski Area. California's first ski resort has five lifts and 10 downhill runs, as well as 90 miles of groomed cross-country trails. Free shuttle buses from Yosemite Valley operate between December and the end of March, weather permitting. Lift tickets are $47, downhill equipment rents for $36, and snowboard rental with boots is $37.50. ⊠ *Badger Pass Rd., off Glacier Point Rd., 18 miles from Yosemite Valley* ☎ *209/372–8430.*

Yosemite Ski School. The gentle slopes of Badger Pass make Yosemite Ski School an ideal spot for children and beginners to learn downhill skiing or snowboarding for as little as $45.50 for a group lesson. ☎ *209/372–8430* ⊕ *www.yosemitepark.com.*

Yosemite Cross-Country Ski School. The highlight of Yosemite's cross-country skiing center is a 21-mile loop from Badger Pass to Glacier Point. You can rent cross-country skis for $25 per day at the Cross-Country Ski School, which also rents snowshoes ($24 per day) and telemarking equipment ($29.50). ☎ *209/372–8444* ⊕ *www.yosemitepark.com.*

Yosemite Mountaineering School. This branch of the Yosemite Mountaineering School, open at the Badger Pass Ski Area during ski season only, conducts snowshoeing, cross-country skiing, telemarking, and skate-skiing classes starting at $35.50. ⊠ *Badger Pass Ski Area* ☎ *209/372–8344* ⊕ *www.yosemitepark.com.*

WHERE TO EAT

In addition to the dining options listed here, you'll find fast-food grills and cafeterias, plus temporary snack bars, hamburger stands, and pizza joints lining park roads in summer. Many dining facilities in the park are open summer only.

WHAT IT COSTS			
$	**$$**	**$$$**	**$$$$**
Restaurants	under 12	$13–$20	$21–$30	over $30
Hotels	under $100	$101–$150	$151–$200	over $200

Restaurant prices are the average cost of a main course at dinner or, if dinner is not served, at lunch. Hotel prices are the lowest cost of a standard double room in high season, excluding taxes and service charges.

$$$$ EUROPEAN Fodor's Choice ★ 🍴 **Ahwahnee Hotel Dining Room.** Rave reviews about the dining room's appearance are fully justified—it features towering windows, a 34-foot-high ceiling with interlaced sugar-pine beams, and massive chandeliers. Although many continue to applaud the food, others have reported that they sense a dip in the quality of both the service and what is being served. Diners must spend a lot of money here, so perhaps that inflates the expectations and amplifies the disappointments. In any event, the lavish $43 Sunday brunch is a popular way to experience the grand room. Reservations are always advised, and the attire is "resort casual." [$] *Average main: $35* ✉ *Ahwahnee Hotel, Ahwahnee Rd., about ¾ mile east of Yosemite Valley Visitor Center, Yosemite Village* ☎ *209/372–1489* 🌐 *www.yosemitepark.com* ✍ *Reservations essential.*

$$$ AMERICAN Fodor's Choice ★ 🍴 **Mountain Room.** Though good, the food becomes secondary when you see Yosemite Falls through this dining room's wall of windows—almost every table has a view. The chef makes a point of using locally sourced, organic ingredients whenever possible, so you can be assured of fresh vegetables to accompany the hearty main courses, such as steaks and seafood, as well as vegetarian and even vegan options. The Mountain Room Lounge, a few steps away in the Yosemite Lodge complex, has about 10 beers on tap. Weather permitting, take your drink out onto the small back patio. [$] *Average main: $23* ✉ *Yosemite Lodge, Northside Dr. about ¾ mile west of the visitor center, Yosemite Village* ☎ *209/372–1281* 🌐 *www.yosemitepark.com* 🕒 *No lunch.*

$ FAST FOOD 🍴 **Tuolumne Meadows Grill.** Serving continuously throughout the day until 5 or 6, this fast-food eatery cooks up basic breakfast, lunch, and snacks. It's possible that ice cream tastes better at this altitude. Stop in for a quick meal before exploring the meadows. [$] *Average main: $8* ✉ *Tioga Rd. (Rte. 120), 1½ miles east of Tuolumne Meadows Visitor Center* ☎ *209/372–8426* 🕒 *Closed Oct.–Memorial Day.*

$$ AMERICAN 🍴 **Tuolumne Meadows Lodge.** At the back of a small building that contains the lodge's front desk and small gift shop, this restaurant serves a menu of hearty American fare at breakfast and dinner. The decor is ultrawoodsy, with dark-wood walls, red-and-white-checkered tablecloths, and a handful of communal tables, which give it the feeling of an old-fashioned summer camp. The menu is small, often featuring a few meat and seafood dishes and one pasta or other special, including a vegetarian choice. If you have any dietary restrictions, let the front desk know in advance and the cooks will not let you down. Order box lunches from here for before hikes. [$] *Average main: $20* ✉ *Tioga Rd. (Rte. 120)* ☎ *209/372–8413* 🌐 *www.yosemitepark.com* ✍ *Reservations essential* 🕒 *Closed late Sept.–mid-June. No lunch.*

$$$ AMERICAN 🍴 **Wawona Hotel Dining Room.** Watch deer graze on the meadow while you dine in the romantic, candlelit dining room of the whitewashed Wawona Hotel, which dates from the late 1800s. The American-style cuisine favors fresh ingredients and flavors; trout and flatiron steaks are menu staples. There's also a brunch on some Sunday holidays, like Mother's Day and Easter, and a barbecue on the lawn Saturday evenings in summer. [$] *Average main: $27* ✉ *Wawona Hotel, Rte. 41, Wawona* ☎ *209/559–4935* ✍ *Reservations essential* 🕒 *Closed Dec.–Mar.*

PICNIC AREAS

Considering how large the park is and how many visitors come here—some 4 million people every year, most of them just for the day—it is somewhat surprising that Yosemite has so few formal picnic areas, though in many places you can find a smooth rock to sit on and enjoy breathtaking views along with your lunch. The convenience stores all sell picnic supplies, and prepackaged sandwiches and salads are widely available. Those options can come in especially handy during the middle of the day, when you might not want to spend precious daylight hours in such a spectacular setting sitting in a restaurant for a formal meal.

> **LODGING TIP**
>
> Reserve your room or cabin in Yosemite as far in advance as possible. You can make a reservation up to a year before your arrival (within minutes after the reservation office makes a date available, the Ahwahnee, Yosemite Lodge, and Wawona Hotel often sell out their weekends, holiday periods, and all days between May and September).

WHERE TO STAY

Hotel reviews have been shortened. For full information, visit Fodors.com.

$$$$ HOTEL Fodor's Choice ★ **Ahwahnee Hotel.** A National Historic Landmark, the hotel is constructed of sugar-pine logs and features American Indian design motifs; public spaces are enlivened with art deco flourishes, oriental rugs, and elaborate iron- and woodwork. **Pros:** best lodge in Yosemite; helpful concierge. **Cons:** expensive rates; some reports that service has slipped in recent years. [$] *Rooms from: $471* ✉ *Ahwahnee Rd., about ¾ miles east of Yosemite Valley Visitor Center, Yosemite Village* ☎ *801/559–4884* 🌐 *www.yosemitepark.com* ⇨ *99 lodge rooms, 4 suites, 24 cottage rooms* 🍴 *No meals.*

$$ HOTEL **Curry Village.** Opened in 1899 as a place for budget-conscious travelers, Curry Village has plain accommodations: standard motel rooms, simple cabins with either private or shared baths, and tent cabins with shared baths. **Pros:** close to many activities; family-friendly atmosphere. **Cons:** not that economical after a recent price surge; can be crowded; sometimes a bit noisy. [$] *Rooms from: $124* ✉ *South side of Southside Dr.* ☎ *801/559–4884* 🌐 *www.yosemitepark.com* ⇨ *18 rooms, 389 cabins* 🍴 *No meals.*

$$ HOTEL **Wawona Hotel.** This 1879 National Historic Landmark at Yosemite's southern end is an old-fashioned New England–style estate, with whitewashed buildings, wraparound verandahs, and pleasant, no-frills rooms decorated with period pieces. **Pros:** lovely building; peaceful atmosphere. **Cons:** few modern amenities, such as phones and TVs; an hour's drive from Yosemite Valley. [$] *Rooms from: $159* ✉ *Rte. 41, Wawona* ☎ *801/559–4884* 🌐 *www.yosemitepark.com* ⇨ *104 rooms, 50 with bath* ⏲ *Closed Dec.–Mar., except Dec. 20–Jan. 2* 🍴 *No meals.*

CLOSE UP

Best Campgrounds in Yosemite

If you are going to concentrate solely on valley sites and activities, you should endeavor to stay in one of the "Pines" campgrounds, which are clustered near Curry Village and within an easy stroll from that busy complex's many facilities. For a more primitive and quiet experience, and to be near many backcountry hikes, try one of the Tioga Road campgrounds.

National Park Service Reservations Office. Reservations are required at many of Yosemite's campgrounds, especially in summer; you can book a site up to five months in advance, starting on the 15th of the month. Unless otherwise noted, book your site through the central National Park Service Reservations Office. If you don't have reservations when you arrive, many sites, especially those outside Yosemite Valley, are available on a first-come, first-served basis. ☎ *877/436–7275* ⊕ *www.recreation. gov* ☉ *Daily 7–7.*

Bridalveil Creek. This campground sits among lodgepole pines at 7,200 feet, above the valley on Glacier Point Road. From here, you can easily drive to Glacier Point's magnificent valley views. ✉ *From Rte. 41 in Wawona, go north to Glacier Point Rd. and turn right; entrance to campground is 25 miles ahead on right side.*

Camp 4. Formerly known as Sunnyside Walk-In, and extremely popular with rock climbers, who don't mind that a total of six are assigned to each campsite, no matter how many are in your group, this is the only valley campground available on a first-come, first-served basis. ✉ *Base of Yosemite Falls Trail, just west of Yosemite Lodge on Northside Dr., Yosemite Village.*

Housekeeping Camp. Composed of three concrete walls and covered with two layers of canvas, each unit has an open-ended fourth side that can be closed off with a heavy white canvas curtain. You can rent "bedpacks," consisting of blankets, sheets, and other comforts. ✉ *Southside Dr., ½ mile west of Curry Village.*

Porcupine Flat. Sixteen miles west of Tuolumne Meadows, this campground sits at 8,100 feet. If you want to be in the high country, this is a good bet. ✉ *Rte. 120, 16 miles west of Tuolumne Meadows.*

Tuolumne Meadows. In a wooded area at 8,600 feet, just south of its namesake meadow, this is one of the most spectacular and sought-after campgrounds in Yosemite. ✉ *Rte. 120, 46 miles east of Big Oak Flat entrance station.*

Upper Pines. This is one of the valley's largest campgrounds and the closest one to the trailheads. Expect large crowds in the summer—and little privacy. ✉ *At east end of valley, near Curry Village.*

Wawona. Near the Mariposa Grove, just downstream from a popular fishing spot, this year-round campground has larger, less densely packed sites than campgrounds in the valley. ✉ *Rte. 41, 1 mile north of Wawona.*

White Wolf. Set in the beautiful high country at 8,000 feet, this is a prime spot for hikers from early July to mid-September. ✉ *Tioga Rd., 15 miles east of Big Oak Flat entrance.*

20

$$ HOTEL 🏨 **White Wolf Lodge.** Set in a subalpine meadow, the rustic accommodations at White Wolf Lodge make it an excellent base camp for hiking the backcountry. **Pros:** quiet location; near some of Yosemite's most beautiful, less crowded hikes; good restaurant. **Cons:** far from the valley. [$] *Rooms from: $124* ✉ *Off Tioga Rd. (Rte. 120), 25 miles west of Tuolumne Meadows and 15 miles east of Crane Flat* ☎ *801/559–4884* 🛏 *24 tent cabins, 4 cabins* 🕒 *Closed mid-Sept.–mid-June* 🍴 *No meals.*

$$$ HOTEL 🏨 **Yosemite Lodge at the Falls.** This 1915 lodge near Yosemite Falls more closely resembles a 1960s resort with its numerous two-story structures tucked beneath the trees, and it doesn't help that the brown buildings are surrounded by large parking lots. **Pros:** centrally located; dependably clean rooms; lots of tours leave from out front. **Cons:** can feel impersonal; appearance is a little dated; prices recently skyrocketed. [$] *Rooms from: $199* ✉ *Northside Dr., about ¾ mile west of the visitor center, Yosemite Village* ☎ *801/559–4884* 🌐 *www.yosemitepark.com* 🛏 *245 rooms* 🍴 *No meals.*

SEQUOIA AND KINGS CANYON NATIONAL PARKS

WELCOME TO SEQUOIA AND KINGS CANYON NATIONAL PARKS

TOP REASONS TO GO

★ **Gentle giants:** You'll feel small—in a good way—walking among some of the world's largest living things in Sequoia's Giant Forest and Kings Canyon's Grant Grove.

★ **Because it's there:** You can't even glimpse it from the main part of Sequoia, but the sight of majestic Mt. Whitney is worth the trek to the eastern face of the High Sierra.

★ **Underground exploration:** Far older even than the giant sequoias, the gleaming limestone formations in Crystal Cave will draw you along dark, marble passages.

★ **A grander-than-Grand Canyon:** Drive the twisting Kings Canyon Scenic Byway down into the jagged, granite Kings River Canyon, deeper in parts than the Grand Canyon.

★ **Regal solitude:** To spend a day or two hiking in a subalpine world of your own, pick one of the 11 trailheads at Mineral King.

1 **Giant Forest–Lodgepole Village.** The most heavily visited area of Sequoia lies at the base of the "thumb" portion of Kings Canyon National Park and contains major sights such as Giant Forest, General Sherman Tree, Crystal Cave, and Moro Rock.

2 **Grant Grove Village–Redwood Canyon.** The "thumb" of Kings Canyon National Park is its busiest section, where Grant Grove, General Grant Tree, Panoramic Point, and Big Stump are the main attractions.

3 **Cedar Grove.** The drive through the high-country portion of Kings Canyon National Park to Cedar Grove Village, on the canyon floor, reveals magnificent granite formations of varied hues. Rock meets river in breathtaking fashion a few miles beyond Cedar Grove in Zumwalt Meadow.

4 **Mineral King.** In the southeast section of Sequoia, the highest road-accessible part of the park is a good place to hike, camp, and soak up the unspoiled grandeur of the Sierra Nevada.

5 **Mount Whitney.** The highest peak in the Lower 48 stands on the eastern edge of Sequoia; to get there from Giant Forest you must either backpack eight days through the mountains or drive nearly 400 miles around the park to its other side.

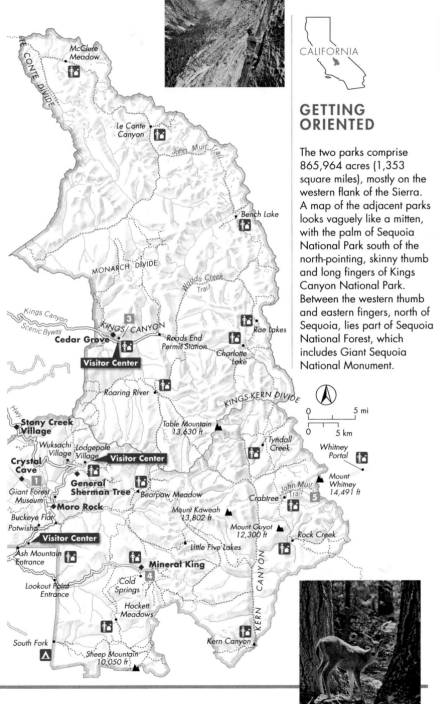

CALIFORNIA

GETTING ORIENTED

The two parks comprise 865,964 acres (1,353 square miles), mostly on the western flank of the Sierra. A map of the adjacent parks looks vaguely like a mitten, with the palm of Sequoia National Park south of the north-pointing, skinny thumb and long fingers of Kings Canyon National Park. Between the western thumb and eastern fingers, north of Sequoia, lies part of Sequoia National Forest, which includes Giant Sequoia National Monument.

McClure Meadow

LE CONTE DIVIDE

Le Conte Canyon

John Muir Trail

Bench Lake

MONARCH DIVIDE

Woods Creek Trail

Kings Canyon Scenic Byway

KINGS CANYON

3

Cedar Grove

Rae Lakes

Roads End Permit Station

Charlotte Lake

Visitor Center

Roaring River

KINGS-KERN DIVIDE

0   5 mi
0   5 km

Hwy

Stony Creek Village

Table Mountain 13,630 ft

Tyndall Creek

Whitney Portal

Wuksachi Village

Lodgepole Village

Visitor Center

Mount Whitney 14,491 ft

Crystal Cave

John Muir Trail

Giant Forest Museum

1

General Sherman Tree

Bearpaw Meadow

Crabtree

5

Moro Rock

Mount Kaweah 13,802 ft

Buckeye Flat

Potwisha

Mount Guyot 12,300 ft

Rock Creek

Visitor Center

Little Five Lakes

Ash Mountain Entrance

Mineral King

4

KERN CANYON

Cold Springs

Lookout Point Entrance

Hockett Meadows

South Fork

Kern Canyon

Sheep Mountain 10,050 ft

Updated by
Daniel Mangin

Although *Sequoiadendron giganteum* is the formal name for the redwoods that grow here, everyone outside the classroom calls them sequoias, big trees, or Sierra redwoods. Their monstrously thick trunks and branches, remarkably shallow root systems, and neck-craning heights are almost impossible to believe, as is the fact they can live for more than 2,500 years. Many of these towering marvels are in the Giant Forest stretch of Generals Highway, which connects Sequoia and Kings Canyon national parks.

Next to or a few miles off the 43-mile Generals Highway are most of Sequoia National Park's main attractions and Grant Grove Village, the orientation hub for Kings Canyon National Park. The two parks share a boundary that runs from the Central Valley in the west, where the Sierra Nevada foothills begin, to the range's dramatic eastern ridges. Kings Canyon has two portions: the smaller is shaped like a bent finger and encompasses Grant Grove Village and Redwood Mountain Grove (the two parks' largest concentration of sequoias), and the larger is home to stunning Kings River Canyon, whose vast, unspoiled peaks and valleys are a backpacker's dream. Sequoia is in one piece and includes Mt. Whitney, the highest point in the Lower 48 states (although it is impossible to see from the western part of the park and is a chore to ascend from either side).

SEQUOIA AND KINGS CANYON PLANNER

WHEN TO GO

The best times to visit are late spring and early fall, when temperatures are moderate and crowds thin. Summertime can draw hordes of tourists to see the giant sequoias, and the few, narrow roads mean congestion at peak holiday times. If you must visit in summer, go during the week. By contrast, in wintertime you may feel as though you have the parks all to yourself. But because of heavy snows, sections of the main park roads can be closed without warning, and low-hanging clouds can move in and obscure mountains and valleys for days. From mid-November to late April, check road and weather conditions before venturing out.

GETTING HERE AND AROUND

CAR TRAVEL

Sequoia is 36 miles east of Visalia on Route 198; Grant Grove Village in Kings Canyon is 56 miles east of Fresno on Route 180. There is no automobile entrance on the eastern side of the Sierra. Routes 180 and 198 are connected by Generals Highway, a paved two-lane road that sometimes sees delays at peak times due to ongoing improvements. The road is extremely narrow and steep from Route 198 to Giant Forest, so keep an eye on your engine temperature gauge, as the incline and congestion can cause vehicles to overheat; to avoid overheated brakes, use low gears on downgrades.

If you are traveling in an RV or with a trailer, study the restrictions on these vehicles. Do not travel beyond Potwisha Campground on Route 198 with an RV longer than 22 feet; take straighter, easier Route 180 instead. Maximum vehicle length on Generals Highway is 40 feet, or 50 feet combined length for vehicles with trailers.

Generals Highway between Lodgepole and Grant Grove is sometimes closed by snow. The Mineral King Road from Route 198 into southern Sequoia National Park is closed 2 miles below Atwell Mill either on November 1 or after the first heavy snow. The Buckeye Flat–Middle Fork Trailhead Road is closed from mid-October to mid-April when the Buckeye Flat Campground closes. The lower Crystal Cave Road is closed when the cave closes in November. Its upper 2 miles, as well as the Panoramic Point and Moro Rock–Crescent Meadow roads, close with the first heavy snow. Because of the danger of rockfall, the portion of Kings Canyon Scenic Byway east of Grant Grove closes in winter. For current road and weather conditions, call ☎ *559/565–3341.*

■ TIP➜ **Snowstorms are common from late October through April. Unless you have a four-wheel-drive vehicle with snow tires, you should carry chains and know how to install them.**

PARK ESSENTIALS

PARK FEES AND PERMITS

The admission fee is $20 per vehicle and $10 for those who enter by bus, on foot, bicycle, motorcycle, or horse; it is valid for seven days in both parks. U.S. residents over the age of 62 pay $10 for a lifetime pass, and permanently disabled U.S. residents are admitted free.

If you plan to camp in the backcountry, you need a permit, which costs $15 for hikers or $30 for stock users (e.g., horseback riders). One permit covers the group. Availability of permits depends upon trailhead quotas. Reservations are accepted by mail or fax for a $15 processing fee, beginning March 1, and must be made at least 14 days in advance (☎ *559/565–3766*). Without a reservation, you may still get a permit on a first-come, first-served basis starting at 1 pm the day before you plan to hike. For more information on backcountry camping or travel with pack animals (horses, mules, burros, or llamas), contact the Wilderness Permit Office (☎ *530/565–3761*).

PARK HOURS

The parks are open 24/7 year-round. They are in the Pacific time zone.

VISITOR INFORMATION

NATIONAL PARK SERVICE

Sequoia and Kings Canyon National Parks ⊠ *47050 Generals Hwy. (Rte. 198), Three Rivers* ☎ *559/565–3341* ⊕ *www.nps.gov/seki/planyourvisit/ things2know.htm.*

SEQUOIA VISITOR CENTERS

Foothills Visitor Center. Exhibits here focus on the foothills and resource issues facing the parks. You can pick up books, maps, and a list of ranger-led walks, and get wilderness permits. ⊠ *47050 Generals Hwy. (Rte. 198), 1 mile north of Ash Mountain entrance* ☎ *559/565–4212* ⊙ *Daily 8–4:30.*

Lodgepole Visitor Center. Along with exhibits on the area's history, geology, and wildlife, the center screens an outstanding 22-minute film about bears. You can buy books, maps, and tickets to cave tours and the Wolverton barbecue here. ⊠ *Generals Hwy. (Rte. 198), 21 miles north of Ash Mountain entrance* ☎ *559/565–4436* ⊙ *Late May–early Sept., daily 7–7; days and hrs vary Apr.–late May and early Sept.–Dec. Closed Jan.–Mar.* ⌨ *Shuttle: Giant Forest or Wuksachi-Lodgepole-Dorst.*

KINGS CANYON VISITOR CENTERS

Cedar Grove Visitor Center. Off the main road and behind the Sentinel Campground, this small ranger station has books and maps, plus information about hikes and other activities. ⊠ *Kings Canyon Scenic Byway, 30 miles east of Rte. 180/198 junction* ☎ *559/565–3793* ⊙ *Late May–early Sept., Tues.–Sun. 9–5.*

Kings Canyon Park Visitor Center. The center's 15-minute film and various exhibits provide an overview of the park's canyon, sequoias, and human history. Books, maps, and weather advice are dispensed here, as are (if available) free wilderness permits. ⊠ *Grant Grove Village, Generals Hwy. (Rte. 198), 3 miles northeast of Rte. 180, Big Stump entrance* ☎ *559/565–4307* ⊙ *Mid-May–early Sept., daily 8–5; hrs vary rest of year.*

WHAT IT COSTS				
	$	**$$**	**$$$**	**$$$$**
Restaurants	under 12	$13–$20	$21–$30	over $30
Hotels	under $100	$101–$150	$151–$200	over $200

Restaurant prices are the average cost of a main course at dinner or, if dinner is not served, at lunch. Hotel prices are the lowest cost of a standard double room in high season, excluding taxes and service charges.

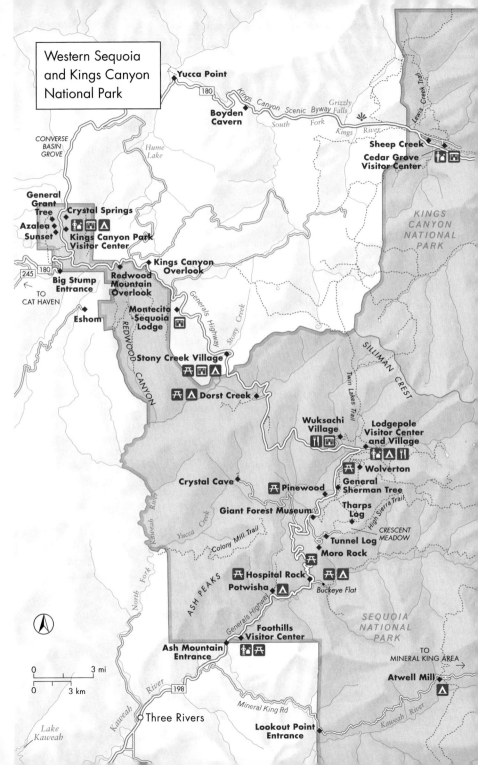

Western Sequoia and Kings Canyon National Park

Yucca Point

180

Kings Canyon Scenic Byway

Grizzly Falls

Lewis Creek Trail

Boyden Cavern

South Fork

Kings River

Sheep Creek

Cedar Grove Visitor Center

CONVERSE BASIN GROVE

Hume Lake

KINGS CANYON NATIONAL PARK

General Grant Tree

Crystal Springs

Azalea
Sunset

Kings Canyon Park Visitor Center

180

245

← TO CAT HAVEN

Big Stump Entrance

Redwood Mountain Overlook

Kings Canyon Overlook

Eshom

Montecito Sequoia Lodge

REDWOOD CANYON

Generals Highway

Stony Creek

Stony Creek Village

Dorst Creek

SILLIMAN CREST

Twin Lakes Trail

Wuksachi Village

Lodgepole Visitor Center and Village

Wolverton

Crystal Cave

Pinewood

Giant Forest Museum

General Sherman Tree

Tharps Log

High Sierra Trail

CRESCENT MEADOW

Kaweah River

Yucca Creek

Colony Mill Trail

Tunnel Log

Moro Rock

North Fork

ASH PEAKS

Hospital Rock

Potwisha

Buckeye Flat

SEQUOIA NATIONAL PARK

Generals Highway

Foothills Visitor Center

TO MINERAL KING AREA →

Ash Mountain Entrance

Atwell Mill

0   3 mi

0   3 km

Kaweah River

198

Mineral King Rd

Three Rivers

Lookout Point Entrance

Lake Kaweah

SEQUOIA NATIONAL PARK

EXPLORING

SCENIC DRIVES

Fodor's Choice ★ **Generals Highway.** One of California's most scenic drives, this 43-mile road is the main asphalt artery between Sequoia and Kings Canyon national parks. Some portions are also signed as Route 180, others as Route 198. Named after the landmark Grant and Sherman trees that leave so many visitors awestruck, Generals Highway runs from Sequoia's Foothills Visitor Center north to Kings Canyon's Grant Grove Village. Along the way, it passes the turnoff to Crystal Cave, the Giant Forest Museum, Lodgepole Village, and other popular attractions. The lower portion, from Hospital Rock to the Giant Forest, is especially steep and winding. If your vehicle is 22 feet or longer, avoid that stretch by entering the parks via Route 180 (from Fresno) rather than Route 198 (from Visalia or Three Rivers). ■TIP➔ Take your time on this road—there's a lot to see, and wildlife can scamper across at any time.

SCENIC STOPS

Sequoia National Park is all about the trees, and to understand the scale of these giants you must walk among them. But there is much more to the park than the trees. Try to access one of the vista points that provide a panoramic view over the forested mountains. Generals Highway (on Routes 198 and 180) will be your route to most of the park's sights. A few short spur roads lead from the highway to some sights, and Mineral King Road branches off Route 198 to enter the park at Lookout Point, winding east from there to park's the southernmost section.

Crescent Meadow. A sea of ferns signals your arrival at what John Muir called the "gem of the Sierra." Walk around for an hour or two and you might decide that the Scotland-born naturalist was exaggerating a wee bit, but the verdant meadow is quite pleasant and you just might see a bear. ■TIP➔ Wildflowers bloom here throughout the summer. ⊠ *End of Moro Rock–Crescent Meadow Rd., 2.6 miles east off Generals Hwy.* ⌧ *Shuttle: Moro Rock–Crescent Meadow.*

Fodor's Choice ★ **Crystal Cave.** One of more than 200 caves in Sequoia and Kings Canyon, Crystal Cave is composed largely of marble, the result of limestone being hardened under heat and pressure. It contains several eye-popping formations. There used to be more, but some were damaged or obliterated by early-20th-century dynamite blasting. You can only see the cave on a tour. The Daily Tour ($15), a great overview, takes about 50 minutes. To immerse yourself in the cave experience—at times you'll be crawling on your belly—book the exhilarating Wild Cave Tour ($130). ■TIP➔ Purchase Daily Tour tickets at either the Foothills or Lodgepole visitor center; they're not sold at the cave itself. ⊠ *Crystal Cave Rd., off Generals Hwy.* ☎ *559/565-3759* ⊕ *www.sequoiahistory.org* ⌧ *$15* ☺ *Mid-May–Nov., daily 10–4.*

Fodor's Choice ★ **General Sherman Tree.** The 274.9-foot-tall General Sherman is one of the world's tallest and oldest sequoias, and it ranks no. 1 in volume, adding the equivalent of a 60-foot-tall tree every year to its approximately

CLOSE UP

Plants and Wildlife in Sequoia and Kings Canyon   21

The parks can be divided into three distinct zones. In the west (1,500–4,500 feet) are the rolling, lower elevation foothills, covered with shrubby chaparral vegetation or golden grasslands dotted with oaks. Chamise, red-barked manzanita, and the occasional yucca plant grow here. Fields of white popcorn flower cover the hillsides in spring, and the yellow fiddleneck flourishes. In summer, intense heat and absence of rain cause the hills to turn golden brown. Wildlife includes the California ground squirrel, noisy blue-and-gray scrub jay, black bears, coyotes, skunks, and gray fox.

At middle elevation (5,000–9,000 feet), where the giant sequoia belt resides, rock formations mix with meadows and huge stands of evergreens—red and white fir,

incense cedar, and ponderosa pines, to name a few. Wildflowers like yellow blazing star and red Indian paintbrush bloom in spring and summer. Mule deer, golden-mantled ground squirrels, Steller's jays, mule deer, and black bears (most active in fall) inhabit the area, as does the chickaree.

The high alpine section of the parks is extremely rugged, with a string of rocky peaks reaching above 13,000 feet to Mt. Whitney's 14,494 feet. Fierce weather and scarcity of soil make vegetation and wildlife sparse. Foxtail and whitebark pines have gnarled and twisted trunks, the result of high wind, heavy snowfall, and freezing temperatures. In summer you can see yellow-bellied marmots, pikas, weasels, mountain chickadees, and Clark's nutcrackers.

52,500 cubic feet of mass. The tree doesn't grow taller, though—it's dead at the top. A short, wheelchair-accessible trail leads to the tree from Generals Highway, but the main trail (0.5 mile) winds down from a parking lot off Wolverton Road. ■TIP➜ The walk back up the main trail is steep, but benches along the way provide rest for the short of breath. ⊠ *Wolverton Rd., off Generals Hwy. (Rte. 198)* ⚓ *Shuttle: Giant Forest or Wolverton–Sherman Tree.*

Mineral King Area. A subalpine valley of fir, pine, and sequoia trees, Mineral King sits at 7,800 feet at the end of a steep, winding road *(⇨ Scenic Drives, above).* This is the highest point to which you can drive in the park. ⊠ *Mineral King Rd., 25 miles east of Generals Hwy. (Rte. 198).*

Fodor's Choice **Moro Rock.** Sequoia National Park's best non-tree attraction offers pan-
★ oramic views to those fit and determined enough to mount its 350 or so steps. In a case where the journey rivals the destination, Moro's stone stairway is so impressive in its twisty inventiveness that it's on the National Register of Historic Places. The rock's 6,725-foot summit overlooks the Middle Fork Canyon, sculpted by the Kaweah River and approaching the depth of Arizona's Grand Canyon, although smoggy, hazy air often compromises the view. ⊠ *Moro Rock–Crescent Meadow Rd., 2 miles east off Generals Hwy. (Rte. 198) to parking area* ⚓ *Shuttle: Moro Rock–Crescent Meadow.*

Tunnel Log. This 275-foot tree fell in 1937, and soon a 17-foot-wide, 8-foot-high hole was cut through it for vehicular passage (not to mention the irresistible photograph) that continues today. Large vehicles take the nearby bypass. ✉ *Moro Rock–Crescent Meadow Rd., 2 miles east of Generals Hwy. (Rte. 198)* ☞ *Shuttle: Moro Rock–Crescent Meadow.*

EDUCATIONAL OFFERINGS

PROGRAMS AND SEMINARS

Evening Programs. Film and slide shows and evening campfire lectures about Sequoia and Kings Canyon take place often during the summer. The Wonders of the Night Sky programs celebrate the often-stunning views of the heavens experienced at both parks. ☎ *559/565–3341* ⊕ *www.sequoiahistory.org/snhacalendar.asp* ☼ *Locations and hrs vary.*

Free Nature Programs. Almost any summer day, half-hour to 1½-hour ranger talks and walks explore subjects such as the life of the sequoia, the geology of the park, and the habits of bears. Giant Forest, Lodgepole Visitor Center, Wuksachi Village, and Dorst Creek Campground are frequent starting points. Check bulletin boards throughout the park for the week's offerings.

Seminars. Expert naturalists lead seminars on a range of topics, including birds, wildflowers, geology, botany, photography, park history, backpacking, and pathfinding. Reservations are recommended. Information about times and prices is available at the visitor centers or through the Sequoia Natural History Association. ☎ *559/565–3759* ⊕ *www.sequoiahistory.org.*

TOURS

Fodor'sChoice **Sequoia Field Institute.** The Sequoia Natural History Association's ★ highly regarded educational division conducts single-day and multi-day "EdVenture" tours that include backpacking hikes, natural-history walks, and kayaking excursions. ✉ *47050 Generals Hwy., Unit 10, Three Rivers* ☎ *559/565–4251* ⊕ *www.sequoiahistory.org.*

Sequoia Sightseeing Tours. This operator's friendly, knowledgeable guides conduct interpretive sightseeing tours in a 10-passenger van. Reservations are essential. The company also offers private tours of Kings Canyon. ✉ *Three Rivers* ☎ *559/561–4489* ⊕ *www.sequoiatours.com* 🎫 *$65 half-day tour, $88 full-day tour.*

SPORTS AND THE OUTDOORS

The best way to see Sequoia is to take a hike. Unless you do so, you'll miss out on the up-close grandeur of mist wafting between deeply scored, red-orange tree trunks bigger than you've ever seen. If it's winter, put on some snowshoes or cross-country skis and plunge into the snow-swaddled woodland. There are not too many other outdoor options: no off-road driving is allowed in the parks, and no special provisions have been made for bicycles. Boating, rafting, and snowmobiling are also prohibited.

BIRD-WATCHING

More than 200 species of birds inhabit Sequoia and Kings Canyon national parks. Not seen in most parts of the United States, the white-headed woodpecker and the pileated woodpecker are common in most

Mt. Whitney

At 14,494 feet, Mt. Whitney is the highest point in the contiguous United States and the crown jewel of Sequoia National Park's wild eastern side. The peak looms high above the tiny, high-mountain desert community of Lone Pine, where numerous Hollywood Westerns have been filmed. The high mountain ranges, arid landscape, and scrubby brush of the eastern Sierra are beautiful in their vastness and austerity.

Despite the mountain's scale, you can't see it from the more traveled west side of the park because it is hidden behind the Great Western Divide. The only way to access Mt. Whitney from the main part of the park is to circumnavigate the Sierra Nevada via a 10-hour, nearly 400-mile drive outside the park. No road ascends the peak; the best vantage point from which to catch a glimpse of the mountain is at the end of Whitney Portal Road. The 13 miles of winding road leads from U.S. 395 at Lone Pine to the trailhead for the hiking route to the top of the mountain. Whitney Portal Road is closed in winter.

mid-elevation areas here. There are also many hawks and owls, including the renowned spotted owl. Species are diverse in both parks due to the changes in elevation, and range from warblers, kingbirds, thrushes, and sparrows in the foothills to goshawk, blue grouse, red-breasted nuthatch, and brown creeper at the highest elevations. Ranger-led bird-watching tours are held on a sporadic basis. Call the park's main information number to find out more about these tours. The Sequoia Natural History Association (📞 559/565–3759 ⊕ www.sequoiahistory.org) also has information about bird-watching in the southern Sierra.

CROSS-COUNTRY SKIING

Wuksachi Lodge. Rent skis here. Depending on snowfall amounts, instruction may also be available. Reservations are recommended. Marked trails cut through Giant Forest, about 5 miles south of the lodge. ⊠ Off Generals Hwy. (Rte. 198), 2 miles north of Lodgepole 📞 559/565–4070 ☉ Nov.–May (unless no snow), daily 9–4 ☞ Shuttle: Wuksachi-Lodgepole-Dorst.

HIKING

The best way to see the park is to hike it. Carry a hiking map and plenty of water. Visitor center gift shops sell maps and trail books and pamphlets. Check with rangers for current trail conditions, and be aware of rapidly changing weather. As a rule of thumb, plan on covering about a mile per hour.

EASY

Fodor'sChoice
★

Congress Trail. This 2-mile trail, arguably the best hike in the parks in terms of natural beauty, is a paved loop that begins near General Sherman Tree. You'll get close-up views of more big trees here than on any other Sequoia hike. Watch for the clusters known as the House and Senate. The President Tree, also on the trail, supplanted the General Grant Tree in 2012 as the world's second largest in volume (behind the General Sherman). ■TIP→ An offshoot of the Congress Trail leads to

Crescent Meadow, where in summer you can catch a free shuttle back to the Sherman parking lot. *Easy.* ⊠ *Trailhead off Generals Hwy. (Rte. 198), 2 miles north of Giant Forest* ⟿ *Shuttle: Giant Forest.*

Crescent Meadow Trails. A 1.8-mile trail loops around lush Crescent Meadow past Tharp's Log, a cabin built from a fire-hollowed sequoia. ■ TIP→ Brilliant wildflowers bloom here in midsummer. *Easy.* ⊠ *Trailhead at the end of Moro Rock–Crescent Meadow Rd., 2.6 miles east off Generals Hwy. (Rte. 198)* ⟿ *Shuttle: Moro Rock–Crescent Meadow.*

MODERATE

Tokopah Falls Trail. This trail with a 500-foot elevation gain follows the Marble Fork of the Kaweah River for 1.75 miles one way and dead-ends below the impressive granite cliffs and cascading waterfall of Tokopah Canyon. The trail passes through a mixed-conifer forest. It takes 2½ to 4 hours to make the round-trip journey. *Moderate.* ⊠ *Trailhead off Generals Hwy. (Rte. 198), ¼ mile north of Lodgepole Campground* ⟿ *Shuttle: Lodgepole-Wuksachi-Dorst.*

DIFFICULT

Mineral King Trails. Many trails to the high country begin at Mineral King. Two popular day hikes are Eagle Lake (6.8 miles round-trip) and Timber Gap. (4.4 miles round-trip) ■ TIP→ At the Mineral King Ranger Station (☎ 559/565–3768) you can pick up maps and check about conditions. *Difficult.* ⊠ *Trailheads at end of Mineral King Rd., 25 miles east of Generals Hwy. (Rte. 198).*

HORSEBACK RIDING

TOURS AND OUTFITTERS

Grant Grove Stables. Grant Grove Stables (⇨ *Horseback Riding in Kings Canyon National Park)* isn't too far from parts of Sequoia National Park and is perfect for short rides. ⊕ *www.visitsequoia.com/grant-grove-stables.aspx.*

Horse Corral Pack Station. One- and two-hour trips through Sequoia are available for beginning and advanced riders. ⊠ *Big Meadow Rd., 12 miles east of Generals Hwy. (Rte. 198) between Sequoia and Kings Canyon national parks* ☎ *559/565–3404 in summer, 559/564–6429 year-round* ⊠ *$40–$75* ☉ *May–Sept.*

KINGS CANYON NATIONAL PARK

EXPLORING

SCENIC DRIVES

Fodor's Choice ★ **Kings Canyon Scenic Byway.** The 30-mile stretch of Route 180 between Grant Grove Village and Zumwalt Meadow delivers eye-popping scenery—granite cliffs, a roaring river, waterfalls, and Kings River Canyon itself—much of which you can experience at vista points or on easy walks. The canyon comes into view about 10 miles east of the village at **Junction View.** Five miles beyond at **Yucca Point,** the canyon is thousands of feet deeper than the more famous Grand Canyon. **Canyon View,** a special spot 1 mile east of the Cedar Grove Village turnoff, showcases evidence of the area's glacial history. Here, perhaps more than anywhere else, you'll understand why John Muir compared Kings Canyon vistas with those in Yosemite. ■TIP➜ Driving the byway takes about an hour each way without stops.

HISTORIC SITES

Fallen Monarch. This toppled sequoia's hollow base was used in the second half of the 19th century as a home for settlers, a saloon, and even to stable U.S. Cavalry horses. As you walk through it (assuming entry is permitted, which is not always possible), notice how little the wood has decayed, and imagine yourself tucked safely inside, sheltered from a storm or protected from the searing heat. ⊠ *Grant Grove Trail, 1 mile north of Kings Canyon Park Visitor Center.*

SCENIC STOPS

General Grant Tree. President Coolidge proclaimed this to be "the nation's Christmas tree," and 30 years later President Eisenhower designated it as a living shrine to all Americans who have died in wars. Bigger at its base than the General Sherman Tree, it tapers more quickly. It's estimated to be the world's third-largest sequoia by volume. ■TIP➜ A spur trail winds behind the tree, where scars from a long-ago fire remain visible. ⊠ *Trailhead 1 mile north of Grant Grove Visitor Center.*

Redwood Mountain Sequoia Grove. One of the world's largest sequoia groves, Redwood contains within its 2,078 acres nearly 2,200 sequoias whose diameters exceed 10 feet. Your can view the grove from afar at an overlook or hike 6 to 10 miles down into the richest regions, which include two of the world's 25 heaviest trees. ⊠ *Drive 5 miles south of Grant Grove on Generals Hwy. (Rte. 198), then turn right at Quail Flat; follow it 1½ miles to the Redwood Canyon trailhead ✛ From Grant Grove, drive south on Generals Hwy. (Rte. 198) 5 miles, turn right (west) at sign for Redwood Canyon, and follow road 2 miles to Redwood Canyon trailhead.*

SPORTS AND THE OUTDOORS

The siren song of beauty, challenge, and relative solitude (by national parks standards) draws hard-core outdoors enthusiasts to the Kings River Canyon and the backcountry of the park's eastern section. Backpacking, rock-climbing, and extreme-kayaking opportunities abound, but the park also has day hikes for all ability levels. Winter brings sledding, skiing, and snowshoeing fun. No off-road driving or biking is allowed in the park, and snowmobiling is also prohibited.

CROSS-COUNTRY SKIING

Roads to Grant Grove are accessible even during heavy snowfall, making the trails here a good choice over Sequoia's Giant Forest when harsh weather hits.

HIKING

You can enjoy many of Kings Canyon's sights from your car, but the giant gorge of the Kings River Canyon and the sweeping vistas of some of the highest mountains in the United States are best seen on foot. Carry a hiking map—available at any visitor center—and plenty of

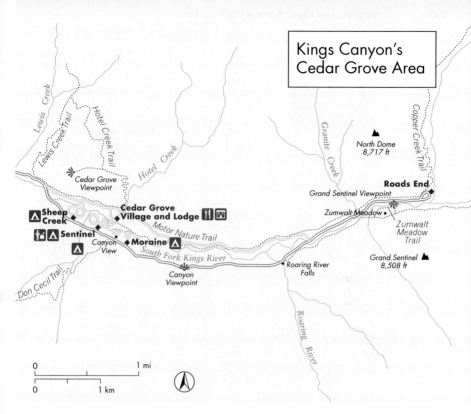

North Dome
8,717 ft

Roads End

Grand Sentinel Viewpoint

Zumwalt Meadow

Zumwalt
Meadow
Trail

Grand Sentinel
8,508 ft

Roaring River
Falls

Canyon
Viewpoint

Cedar Grove
Viewpoint

Sheep
Creek

Cedar Grove
Village and Lodge

Sentinel

Canyon
View

Moraine

Motor Nature Trail

South Fork Kings River

0   1 mi

0   1 km

water. Check with rangers for current trail conditions, and be aware of rapidly changing weather. Except for one trail to Mt. Whitney, permits are not required for day hikes.

Roads End Permit Station. You can obtain wilderness permits, maps, and information about the backcountry at this station, where bear canisters, a must for campers, can be rented or purchased. When the station is closed, complete a self-service permit form. ⊠ *Eastern end of Kings Canyon Scenic Byway, 6 miles east of Cedar Grove Visitor Center* ☉ *Mid-May–Sept., daily 7–4.*

EASY

FodorsChoice **Zumwalt Meadow Trail.** Rangers say this is the best (and most popular) day hike in the Cedar Grove area. Just 1.5 miles long, it offers three visual treats: the South Fork of the Kings River, the lush meadow, and the high granite walls above, including those of Grand Sentinel and North Dome. *Easy.* ⊠ *Trailhead 4½ miles east of Cedar Grove Village turnoff from Kings Canyon Scenic Byway.*

MODERATE

Big Baldy. This hike climbs 600 feet and 2 miles up to the 8,209-feet summit of Big Baldy. Your reward is the view of Redwood Canyon. Round-trip the hike is 4 miles. *Moderate.* ⊠ *Trailhead 8 miles south of Grant Grove on Generals Hwy. (Rte. 198).*

Redwood Canyon Trails. Two main trails lead into Redwood Canyon Grove, the world's largest sequoia grove. The 6.5-mile **Hart Tree and Fallen Goliath Loop** passes by a 19th-century logging site, pristine Hart Meadow, and the hollowed-out Tunnel Tree before accessing a side trail to the grove's largest sequoia, the 277.9-foot-tall Hart Tree. The 6.4-mile **Sugar Bowl Loop** provides views of Redwood Mountain and Big Baldy before winding down into its namesake, a thick grove of mature and young sequoias. *Moderate.* ⊠ *Trail begins off Quail Flat. Drive 5 miles south of Grant Grove on Generals Hwy. (Rte. 198), then turn right at Quail Flat; follow it 1½ miles to the Redwood Canyon trailhead.*

DIFFICULT

Hotel Creek Trail. For gorgeous canyon views, take this trail from Cedar Grove up a series of switchbacks until it splits. Follow the route left through chaparral to the forested ridge and rocky outcrop known as Cedar Grove Overlook, where you can see the Kings River Canyon stretching below. This strenuous 5-mile round-trip hike gains 1,200 feet and takes three to four hours to complete. *Difficult.* ⊠ *Trailhead at Cedar Grove Pack Station, 1 mile east of Cedar Grove Village.*

HORSEBACK RIDING

One-day destinations by horseback out of Cedar Grove include Mist Falls and Upper Bubb's Creek. In the backcountry, many equestrians head for Volcanic Lakes or Granite Basin, ascending trails that reach elevations of 10,000 feet. Costs per person range from $35 for a one-hour guided ride to around $250 per day for fully guided trips for which the packers do all the cooking and camp chores.

TOURS AND OUTFITTERS

Cedar Grove Pack Station. Take a day or overnight trip along the Kings River Canyon with Cedar Grove Pack Station. Popular routes include the Rae Lakes Loop and Monarch Divide. ⊠ *Kings Canyon Scenic Byway, 1 mile east of Cedar Grove Village* ☎ *559/565–3464* ☜ *Call for prices* ☽ *Late May–early Sept.*

Grant Grove Stables. A one- or two-hour trip through Grant Grove leaving from the stables provides a taste of horseback riding in Kings Canyon. ⊠ *Rte. 180, ½ mile north of Grant Grove Visitor Center* ☎ *559/335–9292 mid-June–Sept.* ☜ *$45–$70* ☽ *June–Labor Day, daily 8–6.*

SLEDDING AND SNOWSHOEING

In winter, Kings Canyon has a few great places to play in the snow. Sleds, inner tubes, and platters are allowed at both the Azalea Campground area on Grant Tree Road, ¼ mile north of Grant Grove Visitor Center, and at the Big Stump picnic area, 2 miles north of the lower Route 180 entrance to the park.

Snowshoeing is good around Grant Grove, where you can take naturalist-guided snowshoe walks on Saturdays and holidays from mid-December through mid-March as conditions permit. For a small donation, you can rent snowshoes at the Grant Grove Visitor Center for the guided walks. Grant Grove Market rents sleds and snowshoes.

Hiking in the Sierra Mountains is a thrilling experience, putting you amid some of the world's highest trees.

WHERE TO EAT

SEQUOIA

$ CAFÉ 🍴 **Lodgepole Market and Snack Bar.** The choices here run the gamut from simple to very simple, with the three counters only a few strides apart in a central eating complex. For hot food, venture into the snack bar. The deli sells prepackaged salads, sandwiches, and wraps along with ice cream scooped from tubs. You'll find other prepackaged foods in the market. [$] *Average main: $6* ✉ *Next to Lodgepole Visitor Center* ☎ *559/565–3301* ⏲ *Closed late Sept.–mid-Apr.*

$$$ MODERN AMERICAN 🍴 **The Peaks.** Huge windows run the length of the Wuksachi Lodge's high-ceilinged dining room, and a large fireplace on the far wall warms both body and soul. The diverse dinner menu—by far the best at both parks—includes items such as venison medallions, grilled pork tenderloin, and pan-seared mountain trout. The menu might also include pastas, a vegan burger or other vegan dish, and ratatouille. The wine selection is serviceable but lacks imagination. Breakfast and lunch are also served. [$] *Average main: $24* ✉ *Wuksachi Village* ☎ *559/565–4070* 🌐 *www.visitsequoia.com/the-peaks-restaurant.aspx* ✍ *Reservations essential.*

$$$ BARBECUE 🍴 **Wolverton Barbecue.** Weather permitting, diners congregate nightly on a wooden porch that looks directly out onto a small but strikingly verdant meadow. In addition to the predictable meats such as ribs and chicken, the all-you-can-eat buffet has sides that include baked beans, corn on the cob, and potato salad. Following the meal, listen to a ranger talk and clear your throat for a campfire sing-along. Purchase

tickets at Lodgepole Market, Wuksachi Lodge, or Wolverton Recreation Area's office. ⓢ *Average main: $24* ✉ *Wolverton Rd., 1½ miles northeast off Generals Hwy. (Rte. 198)* ☎ *559/565–4070* ☽ *Closed early Sept.–mid-June. No lunch.*

KINGS CANYON

$ ✕ **Cedar Grove Restaurant.** The menu here is surprisingly extensive,
AMERICAN   with dinner entrées such as pasta, pork chops, trout, and steak. For breakfast, try the biscuits and gravy, French toast, pancakes, or cold cereal. Burgers (including vegetarian patties) and hot dogs dominate the lunch choices. Outside, a patio dining area overlooks the Kings River. ⓢ *Average main: $14* ✉ *Cedar Grove Village* ☎ *559/565–0100* ☽ *Closed Oct.–May.*

$$ ✕ **Grant Grove Restaurant.** In a no-frills, open room, this restaurant offers
AMERICAN   utterly standard American fare such as pancakes for breakfast or hot sandwiches and chicken for later meals. Take-out service is available year-round, and during the summer, there's also a pizza parlor. ⓢ *Average main: $17* ✉ *Grant Grove Village* ☎ *559/335–5500.*

WHERE TO STAY

Hotel reviews have been shortened. For full information, visit Fodors.com.

SEQUOIA

$$$ ☷ **Wuksachi Lodge.** The striking cedar-and-stone main building here is
HOTEL   a fine example of how a structure can blend effectively with lovely
Fodor'sChoice   mountain scenery. **Pros:** best place to stay in the parks; lots of wildlife.
★   **Cons:** rooms can be small; main lodge is a few-minutes' walk from guest rooms. ⓢ *Rooms from: $185* ✉ *64740 Wuksachi Way, Wuksachi Village* ☎ *559/565–4070, 888/252–5757* ⊕ *www.visitsequoia.com* ⤴ *102 rooms* ❡❍❘ *No meals.*

KINGS CANYON

$$$ ☷ **John Muir Lodge.** This modern, timber-sided lodge occupies a wooded
HOTEL   area in the hills above Grant Grove Village. **Pros:** open year-round; common room stays warm; lodge is far enough from the main road to be quiet. **Cons:** check-in is down in the village. ⓢ *Rooms from: $184* ✉ *Kings Canyon Scenic Byway, ¼ mile north of Grant Grove Village* ☎ *877/522–6966* ⊕ *www.visitsequoia.com/kings-canyon.aspx* ⤴ *36 rooms* ❡❍❘ *No meals.*

SACRAMENTO AND THE GOLD COUNTRY

WELCOME TO SACRAMENTO AND THE GOLD COUNTRY

TOP REASONS TO GO

★ **Gold Rush:** Marshall Gold Discovery State Park and Hangtown's Gold Bug & Mine conjure up California's mid-19th century boom.

★ **State Capital:** Easygoing Sacramento offers sights like the Capitol and historic Old Sacramento along with a sophisticated dining scene.

★ **Bon appetit:** Sacramento is home to the California state fair in July and several ethnic food festivals. Nevada City and environs are known for summer mountain-music festivals and Victorian and Cornish winter-holiday celebrations.

★ **Wine Tasting:** With bucolic scenery and friendly tasting rooms, the Gold Country's Shenandoah Valley has become an acclaimed wine-making region, specializing in Zinfandel.

★ **Sequoias and Caverns:** Calaveras Big Trees State Park is filled with giant sequoias, and Moaning Cavern's main chamber is big enough to hold the Statue of Liberty.

1 Sacramento and Nearby. The gateway to the Gold Country, the seat of state government, and an agricultural hub, Sacramento plays many important contemporary roles. About 2.5 million people live in the metropolitan area, which offers up more sunshine and lower prices than coastal California.

2 The Gold Country— South. South of its junction with U.S. 50, Highway 49 traces in asphalt the famed Mother Lode. The peppy former gold-rush towns strung along the road have for the most part been restored and made presentable to visitors with an interest in one of the most frenzied episodes of American history.

3 The Gold Country— North. Highway 49 north of Placerville links the towns of Coloma, Auburn, Grass Valley, and Nevada City. Most are gentrified versions of once-rowdy mining camps, vestiges of which remain in roadside museums, old mining structures, and restored homes now serving as inns.

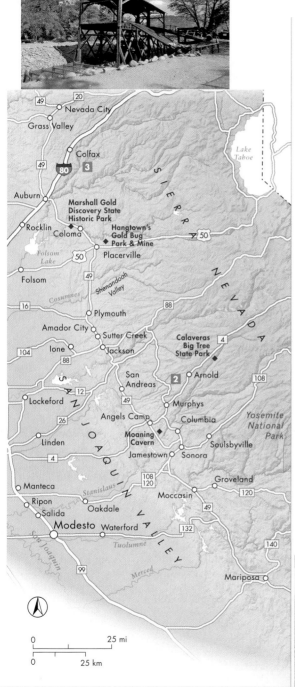

22

GETTING ORIENTED

The Gold Country is a largely laid-back destination popular with those seeking a reasonably priced escape from Southern California and the Bay Area. Sacramento, Davis, and Woodland are in an enormous valley just east of the Sierra Nevada range. Foothill communities Nevada City, Placerville, and Sutter Creek were products of the gold rush and remain popular stopovers with travelers en route to Lake Tahoe.

Updated by
Jenie Skoy

The Gold Country is one of California's less expensive destinations, a region of the Sierra Nevada foothills that's filled with natural and cultural pleasures. Visitors come to Nevada City, Auburn, Coloma, Sutter Creek, and Columbia not only to relive the past but also to explore art galleries, shop for antiques, and stay at friendly, atmospheric inns. Spring brings wildflowers, and in fall the hills are colored by bright red berries and changing leaves. Because it offers plenty of outdoor diversions, the Gold Country is a great place to take kids.

Old Sacramento's museums provide a good introduction to the region's considerable history, but the Gold Country's heart lies along Highway 49, which winds the approximately 300-mile north–south length of the historic mining area. The highway—often a twisting, hilly—two-lane road, begs for a convertible with the top down.

A new era dawned for California when James Marshall turned up a gold nugget in the tailrace of a sawmill he was constructing along the American River. On January 24, 1848, Mexico and the United States were still wrestling for ownership of what would become the Golden State. Marshall's discovery helped compel the United States to tighten its grip on the region, and prospectors from all over the world soon came to seek their fortunes in the Mother Lode.

As gold fever seized the nation, California's population of 15,000 swelled to 265,000 within three years. The mostly young, male adventurers who arrived in search of gold—the forty-niners—became part of a culture that discarded many of the button-down conventions of the eastern states. It was also a violent time. Yankee prospectors chased Mexican miners off their claims, and California's leaders initiated a plan to exterminate the local Native American population. Bounties were paid and private militias were hired to wipe out the Native Americans or sell them into slavery. California was to be dominated by the Anglo.

22

The gold-rush boom lasted scarcely 20 years, but it changed California forever, producing 546 mining towns, of which fewer than 250 remain. The hills of the Gold Country were alive, not only with prospecting and mining but also with business, the arts, gambling, and a fair share of crime. Opera houses went up alongside brothels, and the California State Capitol, in Sacramento, was built partly with the gold dug out of the hills.

The mild climate and rich soil in and around Sacramento Valley are responsible for the region's current riches: fresh and bountiful food and high-quality wines. Gold Country restaurants and wineries continue to earn national acclaim, and they're without the high prices of the Bay Area and Sonoma and Napa wine regions. There's a growing local craft beer scene, too.

PLANNING

WHEN TO GO
The Gold Country is most pleasant in spring, when the wildflowers are in bloom, and in fall. Summers can be hot: temperatures of 100°F are fairly common. Sacramento winters tend to be cool with occasionally foggy or rainy days; many Sacramentans drive to the foothills (or the coast) for a dose of winter sunshine. Throughout the year Gold Country towns stage community and ethnic celebrations. In December many towns are decked out for Christmas.

GETTING HERE AND AROUND
AIR TRAVEL
Sacramento International Airport (SMF) is served by Aeromexico, Alaska/Horizon, American, Delta, Hawaiian, JetBlue, Southwest, United, and Volaris. A private taxi from the airport to Downtown Sacramento costs about $40; the Super Shuttle fare is $25. Public buses (⇨ *Bus and Light-Rail Travel)* are also an option.

Contacts Sacramento International Airport ✉ *6900 Airport Blvd., 12 miles northwest of downtown off I–5, Sacramento* ☎ *916/929–5411* ⊕ *www. sacramento.aero/smf.* **Super Shuttle** ☎ *800/258–3826* ⊕ *www.supershuttle.com.*

BUS AND LIGHT-RAIL TRAVEL
Greyhound serves Sacramento from San Francisco and Los Angeles. Sacramento Regional Transit serves the capital area with buses and light-rail vehicles. Yolobus public buses Nos. 42A and 42B connect SMF airport and Downtown Sacramento, West Sacramento, Davis, and Woodland.

Contacts Greyhound ☎ *800/231–2222* ⊕ *www.greyhound.com.* **Sacramento Regional Transit** ☎ *916/321–2877* ⊕ *www.sacrt.com.* **Yolobus** ☎ *530/666– 2837, 916/371–2877* ⊕ *www.yolobus.com.*

CAR TRAVEL
Interstate 5 (north–south) and Interstate 80 (east–west) are the two main routes into and out of Sacramento. From Sacramento, three highways fan out toward the east, all intersecting with historic Highway 49: Interstate 80 heads northeast 34 miles to Auburn; U.S. 50 goes east

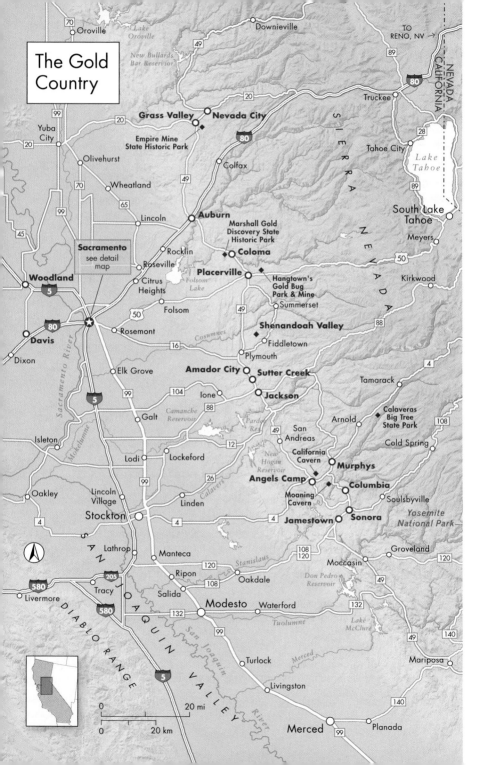

The Gold Country

Oroville
70
Lake
Oroville
Downieville
TO
RENO, NV →
49
New Bullards
Bar Reservoir
89
80
NEVADA
CALIFORNIA
Truckee
20

Grass Valley • Nevada City
Empire Mine
State Historic Park
80
Colfax
28
Tahoe City
Lake
Tahoe

Yuba
City
99
20
Olivehurst
49
SIERRA
South Lake
Tahoe

Wheatland
70
65
Auburn
Marshall Gold
Discovery State
Historic Park
Coloma
50
Kirkwood
Meyers

45
Lincoln
99
Rocklin
Roseville
Citrus
Heights
Placerville
Hangtown's
Gold Bug
Park & Mine
Summerset
49
88

Woodland
5
Folsom
Lake
Folsom
Shenandoah Valley
Fiddletown
Plymouth
NEVADA

Davis
80
50
Rosemont
Cosumnes River
16
Elk Grove
Amador City • Sutter Creek
Jackson
Tamarack
4

Dixon
99
104
Ione
88
Galt
Camanche
Reservoir
Pardee
Res.
San
Andreas
49
Arnold
Calaveras
Big Tree
State Park
Cold Spring
108

Isleton
Mokelumne River
Lodi
Lockeford
12
New
Hogan
Reservoir
California
Cavern
Murphys
Columbia
Soulsbyville

Oakley
Lincoln
Village
Stockton
99
Linden
26
Calaveras River
Angels Camp
Moaning
Cavern
Jamestown • Sonora
Yosemite
National Park

4
5
Lathrop
205
Manteca
120
Ripon
108
Salida
Oakdale
Stanislaus River
108
120
Moccasin
Don Pedro
Reservoir
49
Groveland
120

580
Livermore
580
Tracy
132
Modesto
Waterford
132
Lake
McClure

DIABLO RANGE
5
Salida
99
Tuolumne
River
49
140

SAN JOAQUIN VALLEY
Turlock
Merced River
Mariposa

20 mi
0
20 km
Livingston
Merced
99
Planada
140

40 miles to Placerville; and Highway 16 angles southeast 45 miles to Plymouth. Highway 49 is an excellent two-lane road that winds and climbs through the foothills and valleys, linking the principal Gold Country towns. Traveling by car is the only practical way to explore the Gold Country.

22

TRAIN TRAVEL

One of the most authentic ways to relive the Old West is traveling via train. On the Amtrak California Zephyr, you can ride the same route traveled by prospectors in the late 1800s. Docents from the Sacramento Railroad Museum ride the route from Sacramento to Reno daily, and are available to answer questions. The route into the Sierra Nevadas is memorable, especially if you book a sleeper car. Amtrak trains serves Sacramento and Davis from San Jose, Oakland, and Emeryville (Amtrak buses transport passengers from San Francisco's Ferry Building to Emeryville). The trip takes 2½ hours. Amtrak also runs trains and connecting motor coaches from the Central Valley.

Contacts Amtrak ☎ *800/872-7245* ⊕ *www.amtrak.com.*

RESTAURANTS

American, Italian, and Mexican are common Gold Country fare, but chefs also prepare ambitious European, French, and contemporary regional cuisine that mixes California ingredients with international preparations. Grass Valley's meat- and vegetable-stuffed *pasties,* introduced by 19th-century gold miners from Cornwall, are one of the region's more unusual treats.

HOTELS

Sacramento has plenty of full-service hotels, budget motels, and small inns. Larger towns along Highway 49—among them Auburn, Grass Valley, and Jackson—have chain motels and inns. Many Gold Country bed-and-breakfasts occupy former mansions, miners' cabins, and other historic buildings. *Hotel reviews have been shortened. For full information, visit Fodors.com.*

Contacts Amador Council of Tourism ✉ *115 Valley View Way, Sutter Creek* ☎ *209/267-9249, 877/868-7262* ⊕ *www.touramador.com.* **California Association of Bed & Breakfast Inns** ☎ *800/373-9251* ⊕ *www.cabbi.com/region/ Sierra-Foothills.* **Gold Country Inns of Tuolumne County** ⊕ *www.goldbnbs.com.*

VISITOR INFORMATION

Contacts Amador County Chamber of Commerce & Visitors Bureau ✉ *115 Main St., Jackson* ☎ *209/223-0350* ⊕ *www.amadorcountychamber.com.* **El Dorado County Visitors Authority** ✉ *542 Main St., Placerville* ☎ *530/621-5885, 800/457-6279* ⊕ *visit-eldorado.com.* **Grass Valley/Nevada County Chamber of Commerce** ✉ *128 E. Main St., Grass Valley* ☎ *530/273-4667, 800/655-4667* ⊕ *www.grassvalleychamber.com.* **Yosemite/Mariposa County Tourism Bureau** ✉ *5158 Hwy. 140, Mariposa* ☎ *209/742-4567* ⊕ *www. mariposachamber.org.* **Tuolumne County Visitors Bureau** ✉ *542 W. Stockton Rd., Sonora* ☎ *209/533-4420, 800/446-1333* ⊕ *www.yosemitegoldcountry.com.*

WHAT IT COSTS				
	$	**$$**	**$$$**	**$$$$**
Restaurants	under $16	$16–$22	$23–$30	over $30
Hotels	under $121	$121–$175	$176–$250	over $250

Restaurant prices are the average cost of a main course at dinner or, if dinner is not served, at lunch, excluding sales tax. Hotel prices are the lowest cost of a standard double room in high season, excluding taxes.

SACRAMENTO AND NEARBY

California's capital is an ethnically diverse city, with sizable Mexican, Hmong, and Ukrainian populations, among many others.

SACRAMENTO

87 miles northeast of San Francisco; 384 miles north of Los Angeles.

All around the Golden State's seat of government you'll experience echoes of the gold-rush days, most notably in Old Sacramento, whose wooden sidewalks and horse-drawn carriages on cobblestone streets lend the waterfront district a 19th-century feel. The California State Railroad Museum and other venues hold artifacts of state and national significance, and historic buildings house shops and restaurants. River cruises and train rides are fun family diversions for an hour or two.

Due east of Old Sacramento is Downtown, where landmarks include the Capitol building and the surrounding Capitol Park. The convention center is also here. The area is a little uneven economically, but some of the boarded-up storefronts have begun to enjoy some revitalization in recent years.

Farther east, starting at about 15th Street, lies the city's most interesting neighborhood, Midtown, a mix of genteel Victorian edifices, ultramodern lofts, and innovative restaurants and cozy wine bars. The neighborhood springs to life on the second Saturday evening of the month, when art galleries hold open houses and the sidewalks are packed. A few intersections are jumping most evenings when the weather's good; they include the corner of 20th and L streets in what's known as Lavender Heights, the center of the city's gay and lesbian community.

GETTING HERE AND AROUND

Most people drive to Sacramento and get around by car. Yellow Cab is a reliable company.

Bus Travel Sacramento Regional Transit buses and light-rail vehicles serve the area. The No. 30 DASH shuttle bus links Old Sacramento, Midtown, and Sutter's Fort.

Car Travel Assuming that traffic is not a factor (though it often is), Sacramento is a 90-minute drive from San Francisco and a seven-hour drive from Los Angeles. Parking garages serve Old Sacramento and other tourist spots; on-street parking Downtown can be difficult to find.

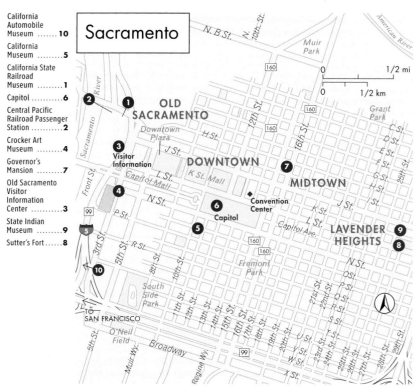

ESSENTIALS

Transportation Contacts Sacramento Regional Transit ☎ *916/321–2877*
⊕ *www.sacrt.com.* **Yellow Cab Co. of Sacramento** ☎ *916/444–2222*
⊕ *www.yellowcabsacramento.com.*

Visitor Information Old Sacramento Visitor Information Center
✉ *1002 2nd St.* ☎ *916/442–7644* ⊕ *www.discovergold.org* ☉ *Daily 10–5.*
Sacramento Convention and Visitors Bureau ✉ *1608 I St.* ☎ *916/808–7777*
⊕ *www.visitsacramento.com.*

EXPLORING

TOP ATTRACTIONS

American River Bicycle Trail. The Jedediah Smith Memorial Trail, as it's
formally called, runs for 32 miles from Old Sacramento to Beals Point in
Folsom. Walk or ride a bit of it and you'll see why local cyclists and pedestrians adore its scenic lanes, if not always each other: confrontations do
occur between humorless speeders and meandering gawkers. Enjoy great
views of the American River and the bluffs overlooking it. ■**TIP→** Bring
lunch or a snack. Pretty parks and picnic areas dot the trail.

California Automobile Museum. More than 150 vintage automobiles—
including Model Ts, Hudsons, Studebakers, Pontiacs, and other bygone
makes and models—are on display at this museum that pays tribute to

automotive history and car culture. Check out a replica of Henry Ford's 1896 Quadracycle and a 1920s roadside café and garage exhibit. The docents are ready to explain everything you see. The museum is near Downtown and Old Sacramento, with ample free parking. ⊠ *2200 Front St., Downtown* ☎ *916/442–6802* ⊕ *www.calautomuseum.org* 🖾 *$8* ☉ *Daily 10–6.*

FAMILY **California State Railroad Museum.** Near what was the terminus of the transcontinental and Sacramento Valley railroads, this 100,000-square-foot museum is a recreation of the original train station and roundhouse. There are 21 locomotives and railroad cars on display along with dozens of other exhibits. You can walk through a post-office car and peer into cubbyholes and canvas mailbags, enter a sleeping car that simulates the swaying on the roadbed and the flashing lights of a passing town at night, or glimpse inside the first-class dining car. The room containing the gold "Last Spike," one of two cast in 1869 to commemorate the completion of the transcontinental railroad, is quietly compelling. Kids have lots of fun at this museum, especially in the play area upstairs. ■TIP➜ You can visit an original roundhouse, not just a replica, at Railtown 1897 in Jamestown, near Sonora. ⊠ *125 I St., at 2nd St., Old Sacramento* ☎ *916/445–6645* ⊕ *www.csrmf.org* 🖾 *$10* ☉ *Daily 10–5.*

Capitol. The lacy plasterwork of the Capitol's 120-foot-high rotunda has the complexity and colors of a Fabergé egg. Underneath the gilded dome are marble floors, glittering chandeliers, monumental staircases, reproductions of century-old state offices, and legislative chambers decorated in the style of the 1890s (the Capitol was built in 1869). Guides conduct tours of the building and the 40-acre Capitol Park, which contains a rose garden, a fragrant display of camellias (Sacramento's city flower), and the California Vietnam Veterans Memorial. ■TIP➜ Wander the Capitol's botanical grounds to glimpse the diverse collection of trees, shrubs, and flowers, including some 1,200 trees from around the world. The original Deodar Cedars on the west side date back to 1872. ⊠ *Capitol Mall and 10th St., Downtown* ☎ *916/324–0333* ⊕ *www. statecapitolmuseum.com* 🖾 *Free* ☉ *Daily 9–5; tours hourly 9–4.*

Fodor's Choice **Crocker Art Museum.** Established in 1885, this esteemed art museum con-
★ tains one of the finest collections of Californian art in the nation—two highlights include *Sunday Morning in the Mines* (1872), a large canvas by Charles Christian Nahl depicting the original mining industry, and the magnificent *Great Canyon of the Sierra, Yosemite* (1871), by Thomas Hill. The Crocker has exceptional holdings of master drawings as well as an impressive collection of international ceramics and works from Europe, Asia, and Africa. A huge contemporary wing was added in 2010 and regularly hosts outstanding traveling exhibitions. On view in 2015 are works by Toulouse-Lautrec, William S. Rice, David Ligare, and Armin Hansen. ⊠ *216 O St., at 3rd St., Downtown* ☎ *916/808–7000* ⊕ *www.crockerartmuseum.org* 🖾 *$10* ☉ *Tues., Wed., and Fri.–Sun. 10–5; Thurs. 10–9.*

Governor's Mansion. This 15-room Italianate mansion was built in 1877 and used by the state's chief executives from the early 1900s until 1967, when Ronald Reagan vacated it in favor of an upscale modern

22

residence. Many of the interior decorations were ordered from the Huntington, Hopkins & Co. Hardware Store, one of whose partners, Albert Gallatin, was the original occupant. Each of the seven marble fireplaces has a petticoat mirror that ladies strolled past to see if their slips were showing. ⊠ *1526 H St., at 16th St., Midtown* ☎ *916/323–3047* ⊕ *www. parks.ca.gov* ◫ *$5* ⊗ *Wed.–Sun.10–5; tours hourly until 4.*

WORTH NOTING

FAMILY **California Museum.** Some of the exhibits at this celebration of all things California are high-tech and interactive, but there are also scores of archival drawers that you can pull out to see the real artifacts of history and culture—from the California State Constitution to surfing magazines. Board a 1949 cross-country bus to view a video on immigration, visit a Chinese herb shop maintained by a holographic proprietor, or find familiar names inducted into the annually expanded California Hall of Fame. The museum's café is open on weekdays until 2:30 pm. ⊠ *1020 O St., at 11th St., Downtown* ☎ *916/653–7524* ⊕ *www. californiamuseum.org* ◫ *$9* ⊗ *Tues–Sat. 10–5, Sun. noon–5.*

FAMILY **Central Pacific Railroad Passenger Station.** At this reconstructed 1876 depot there's rolling stock to admire, a typical waiting room, and a small restaurant. Part of the year a train departs from the freight depot, south of the passenger station, making a 40-minute out-and-back trip between the Sacramento River and, less interestingly, Interstate 5. ⊠ *930 Front St., at J St., Old Sacramento* ☎ *916/445–6645* ◫ *Station $4 (free with same-day ticket from state railroad museum); train rides $10* ⊗ *Train rides: Apr.–Sept., weekends 11–5, Oct.–Dec., call for hrs.*

State Indian Museum. Among the interesting displays at this museum near Sutter's Fort is one about Ishi, the last Yahi Indian to emerge from the mountains, in 1911. Ishi provided anthropologists with insight into his people's traditions and culture. Arts-and-crafts exhibits, a demonstration village, and an evocative 10-minute video also explore the lives and history of California's native peoples. ⊠ *2618 K St., at 27th St.* ☎ *916/324–0971* ⊕ *www.parks.ca.gov* ◫ *$3* ⊗ *Daily 10–5.*

FAMILY **Sutter's Fort.** German-born Swiss immigrant John Augustus Sutter founded Sacramento's earliest Euro-American settlement in 1839. Audio speakers give information at each stop along a self-guided tour that includes a blacksmith's shop, bakery, prison, living quarters, and livestock areas. Costumed docents sometimes reenact fort life, demonstrating crafts, food preparation, and firearms maintenance. ⊠ *2701 L St., at 27th St., Midtown* ☎ *916/445–4422* ⊕ *www.parks.ca.gov* ◫ *$5 most days, $7 on interpretive program days* ⊗ *Mon.–Sun. 10–5.*

WHERE TO EAT

$$$
ITALIAN
Fodor'sChoice
★

✕ **Biba.** Owner Biba Caggiano is a nationally recognized authority on Italian cuisine, having written numerous cookbooks, several of which are sold here in her inviting restaurant. The Capitol crowd flocks here for exceptional renditions of lasagna with Bolognese sauce, classic Milanese-style veal osso buco with saffron-risotto cakes, and pan-roasted halibut topped with a light caper-lemon-butter sauce. For dessert, try delicious *zuccotto Florentino* (a layer of rum-soaked cake with chocolate ganache crowned with a mountain of whipped cream, and bites

The California State Railroad Museum is North America's most popular railroad museum.

of hazelnuts, almonds, and chocolate. A pianist adds to the upscale ambience nightly. [$] *Average main: $28* ✉ *2801 Capitol Ave., at 28th St., Midtown* ☎ *916/455–2422* 🌐 *www.biba-restaurant.com* ✍ *Reservations essential* 🕒 *Closed Sun. No lunch Mon. or Sat.*

$$$ MODERN AMERICAN

🍴 **Ella.** With fresh white calla lilies on the tables, ivory linen curtains, and distressed-wood shutters installed across the ceiling, this swank restaurant and bar near the Capitol building is artfully designed and thoroughly modern—a nice fit for the stellar California-French farm-to-table cuisine served within. The menu changes seasonally, but typical are the steak tartare with garlic popovers and a farm egg, seared local sturgeon with caul fat, grilled endive, and romanesco sauce, and wood-fired pork chop with root vegetables. The impeccable waitstaff works with Ninja-like precision, paying close attention to every detail. [$] *Average main: $30* ✉ *1131 K St., Downtown* ☎ *916/443–3772* 🌐 *www.elladiningroomandbar.com.*

$$$$ AMERICAN Fodor's Choice ★

🍴 **The Firehouse.** Long celebrated by locals and foodies as one of the city's top restaurants, this historic eatery has a full bar, breezy courtyard seating, and creative American cooking, such as char-grilled spring rack of lamb served with roasted French fingerling potatoes and baby artichoke and fava bean succotash. Visitors who can afford to treat themselves to a fine and leisurely meal can do no better in Old Sacramento—although they might also opt for the less-pricey **Ten 22.** Located a block away and under the same ownership as the Firehouse, it serves pizza and other fancified comfort food. [$] *Average main: $36* ✉ *1112 2nd St., at L St., Old Sacramento* ☎ *916/442–4772* 🌐 *www.firehouseoldsac.com* 🕒 *No lunch Sat.*

$$ ✕ **Hook & Ladder Manufacturing Company.** Youthful and hip, with found-
MODERN   art decorative elements and exposed vents, this historic former fire sta-
AMERICAN   tion is a favorite stop for creative cocktails, craft beers, and creative
gastropub fare. Lighter dishes include pizza with gooey burrata cheese
and fresh tomatoes, house-made sausages with assorted chutneys and
mustards, and and seared-ahi *bahn mi* sliders. There's more complex
fare, too, such as bacon-wrapped pork tenderloin with gnocchi and
smoked tomato, and roasted-pumpkin risotto with mascarpone. A
refined drink list includes rotating local wine and beers on tap. ⓈAv-
erage main: $18 ✉ *1630 S. St., Midtown* ☎ *916/442–4885* ⊕ *www.*
hookandladder916.com.

$$ ✕ **Magpie Cafe.** This hip Midtown eatery with a casual vibe takes its food
AMERICAN   quite seriously: nearly all the produce is sourced locally, and menus are
Fodor's Choice   printed each day reflecting availability from local farms. The array of
★   small-batch farmstead cheeses, all from California, is mouthwatering
(especially the Point Reyes Blue, drizzled with honey).
Recent offerings have included roasted chicken for two with a chervil-
ginger green sauce, and—at lunch—a smoked-trout and Meyer lemon
sandwich with dill, capers, and cream cheese. Be sure to choose a couple
of the perfectly braised or roasted side vegetable dishes, perhaps asparagus with green-garlic oil, or pan-seared creamy polenta with sage. If you
make it here for brunch, consider the savory bread pudding with bacon,
chipotle-cheddar, and chives. The pub next door can get loud after 9,
so arrive before if aiming for a relaxed dinner. Ⓢ*Average main: $21*
✉ *1409 R St., No.102, Midtown* ☎ *916/452–7594* ⊕ *www.magpiecafe.*
com ☾ *No dinner Sun.*

$$ ✕ **Rio City Café.** Contemporary and seasonal Mediterranean and Califor-
AMERICAN   nian cuisine, and huge floor-to-ceiling windows and an outdoor deck
overlooking the river are the attractions of this popular restaurant that's
designed to resemble a vintage steamship warehouse. Consider din-
ing here for lunch or brunch, when you can enjoy the beautiful water
views. The food is unfussy and consistently good—burgers with rose-
mary fries, Baja-style fish tacos with pineapple-papaya salsa, Dungeness
crab and shrimp Louie salad. The big draw here, however, is the ambi-
ence. Ⓢ*Average main: $18* ✉ *1110 Front St., at L St., Old Sacramento*
☎ *916/442–8226* ⊕ *www.riocitycafe.com.*

$$$ ✕ **The Waterboy.** Rural French cooking with locally sourced, high-
ECLECTIC   quality (often organic) ingredients are the hallmark of this upscale
Fodor's Choice   but refreshingly unfussy Midtown restaurant that's as appealing for
★   a casual meal with friends as it is for a drawn-out romantic dinner
for two. The artisan cheese and antipasto plates are appealing starters
for sharing, as is a standout chicken-liver crostini with fennel, frisée,
apple, and caramelized shallots. Among the mains, try the braised
Niman Ranch pork cheeks with green garlic *jus*, or pan-seared day-
boat scallops with a celery root–sunchoke–bacon hash and a Meyer
lemon–brown butter sauce. Ⓢ*Average main: $27* ✉ *2000 Capitol Ave.,*
at 20th St., Midtown ☎ *916/498–9891* ⊕ *www.waterboyrestaurant.*
com ☾ *No lunch weekends.*

22

WHERE TO STAY

$$$ B&B/INN 🏨 **Amber House Bed & Breakfast Inn.** About a mile from the Capitol, this B&B has rooms in a 1905 Craftsman-style home and an 1895 Dutch colonial–revival home. **Pros:** Midtown location; attentive service. **Cons:** freeway access isn't easy. [$] *Rooms from: $179* ✉ *1315 22nd St., Midtown* ☎ *916/444–8085, 800/755–6526* 🌐 *www.amberhouse.com* 🛏 *10 rooms* 🍴 *Breakfast.*

$$$ HOTEL Fodor's Choice ★ 🏨 **Citizen Hotel.** This boutique hotel built within the historic 1926 Cal Western Life building is dapper and refined, with marble stairs, striped wallpaper, and plush velvet chairs, lending the place a Roaring Twenties charm. **Pros:** hip, sophisticated decor; smooth and solicitous service; terrific restaurant and bar. **Cons:** rooms near elevator can be noisy. [$] *Rooms from: $189* ✉ *926 J St., Downtown* ☎ *916/447–2700* 🌐 *www.jdvhotels.com* 🛏 *175 rooms, 23 suites* 🍴 *Breakfast.*

$$ HOTEL 🏨 **Delta King.** For the opportunity to sleep in one of Sacramento's most unusual and historic relics, book a stay in this riverboat that's been gloriously restored. **Pros:** exudes old-world charm; steps from historic Old Town shopping and dining. **Cons:** slanted floors can feel a bit jarring; rooms are a bit cramped. [$] *Rooms from: $165* ✉ *1000 Front St., Old Sacramento* ☎ *916/444–5464, 800/825–5464* 🌐 *www.deltaking.com* 🛏 *44 rooms* 🍴 *Breakfast.*

$$$ HOTEL 🏨 **Hyatt Regency Sacramento.** With a marble-and-glass lobby and luxurious rooms, this hotel across from the Capitol and adjacent to the convention center is arguably Sacramento's finest. **Pros:** beautiful Capitol Park is across the street; some rooms have small balconies. **Cons:** nearby streets can feel a little dodgy at night; somewhat impersonal. [$] *Rooms from: $195* ✉ *1209 L St., Downtown* ☎ *916/443–1234, 800/633–7313* 🌐 *www.hyatt.com* 🛏 *500 rooms, 24 suites* 🍴 *No meals.*

NIGHTLIFE AND THE ARTS

NIGHTLIFE

Blue Cue. A billiard lounge known for its selection of single-malt scotches, the Blue Cue is upstairs from the popular Mexican restaurant Centro. Wednesday night's trivia contest is a spirited event. ✉ *1004 28th St., at J St., Midtown* ☎ *916/441–6810* 🌐 *www.bluecue.com.*

Dive Bar. Live "mermaids" and "mermen" swim in a massive tank above the bar at this lively Downtown nightspot known for its extensive list of craft cocktails and local beers. ✉ *1016 K St, Downtown* ☎ *916/737–5999* 🌐 *divebarsacramento.com.*

Fox and Goose. This casual pub with live music serves fish-and-chips, Cornish pasties, and other traditional items—plus vegetarian/vegan fare—on weekdays until 9:30. ✉ *1001 R St., at 10th St., Downtown* ☎ *916/443–8825* 🌐 *www.foxandgoose.com.*

Harlow's. This sceney restaurant draws a young-ish crowd to its art deco bar-nightclub for live music after 9 pm. ✉ *2708 J St., at 27th St., Midtown* ☎ *916/441–4693* 🌐 *www.harlows.com.*

Streets of London Pub. A favorite among Anglophiles, Streets is open after midnight every night. Darts and TV soccer, anyone? ✉ *1804 J St., at 18th St., Midtown* ☎ *916/498–1388* 🌐 *streetsoflondon.net.*

THE ARTS

California Musical Theatre. This group presents Broadway shows at the Sacramento Community Center Theater and the summer Music Circus offerings (think *Oklahoma, Annie*) at the theater-in-the-round Wells Fargo Pavilion. ⊠ *1419 H St., at 14th St., Downtown* ☎ *916/557–1999* ⊕ *www.calmt.com.*

Crest Theatre. It's worth peeking inside the Crest even if you don't catch a show there, just to see the swirling and flambouyant art deco design in the foyer. It's a beloved venue for classic and art-house films, along with concerts and other cultural events. ⊠ *1013 K St., at 10th St., Downtown* ☎ *916/442–7378* ⊕ *www.thecrest.com.*

Sacramento Box Office. Tickets to major comedy, music, theater, and other cultural and sports events are sold through this online vendor. ☎ *888/583–6046* ⊕ *sacramentoboxoffice.com.*

SHOPPING

Greater Sacramento is filled with familiar shops. To try something new, wander through Midtown, especially J, K, and L streets between 16th and 26th streets.

Westfield Galleria at Roseville. The Sacramento region's largest shopping complex is a sprawling, heavily trafficked collection of chain stores and restaurants. It's always jumping. ⊠ *1151 Galleria Blvd., north of Sacramento off I–80 Exit 105A, Roseville* ⊕ *www.westfield.com/galleriaatroseville.*

WOODLAND

20 miles northwest of Sacramento.

In its heyday, Woodland was among California's wealthiest cities. Established by gold seekers and entrepreneurs, it later became an agricultural gold mine. The legacy of the old land barons lives on in the restored Victorian and Craftsman architecture downtown; the best examples are south of Main Street on College, Elm, 1st, and 2nd streets. The town's top attraction is the splendid Heidrick Ag History Center.

GETTING HERE AND AROUND

Yolobus (⊕ *www.yolobus.com*) serves downtown Woodland from Sacramento, but it's far more practical to drive here via Interstate 5.

ESSENTIALS

Visitor Information Woodland Chamber of Commerce ⊠ *307 1st St., at Dead Cat Alley* ☎ *530/662–7327* ⊕ *www.woodlandchamber.org.*

EXPLORING

FAMILY **Heidrick Ag History Center Tractor & Truck Museum.** This gigantic space provides a marvelous overview of the entire history of motorized agricultural vehicles. Souped-up and shiny, the antique threshers, harvesters, combines, tractors, and proto-tractors on display here look ready to service the farms of their eras all over again. And there's more. A separate wing surveys the evolution of the truck, with an emphasis on ones used for farm work. ⊠ *1962 Hays La., off County Rd. 102* ☎ *530/666–9700* ⊕ *www.aghistory.org* 🏷 *$8* ☾ *Mid-Mar.–early Nov. Wed.–Sun. 10–5; early Nov.–mid-Mar. 10–4.*

Woodland Opera House. This 1896 structure hosted minstrel shows, John Philip Sousa's marching band, and early vaudeville acts before closing for six decades (a sad saga that involved a penny-pinching Hershey's chocolate heir). Now restored, it hosts plays, musicals, and concerts. If the box office is open, ask for a backstage tour or a peek at the auditorium. ✉ *340 2nd St.* ☎ *530/666–9617* 🌐 *www.woodlandoperahouse.org* 🕓 *Tours: Tues. 1–4 or by appointment.*

WHERE TO EAT

$$ AMERICAN 🍴 **Mojo's Kitchen428.** Woodland's dining scene turned a shade greener when Mojo's opened with restored furnishings reportedly rescued from other businesses. The steaks, lamb shanks, and turkey potpies all have their adherents, but if you're not into meat you'll find salmon and other seafood on the menu, along with vegetarian and even a few vegan items. There's a popular brunch on weekends. A friendly, stylish place, Mojo's rewards customers for also adopting green practices: ride a bike here, and you'll receive 10% off your bill. [$] *Average main: $20* ✉ *428 1st St., off Main St.* ☎ *530/661–0428* 🌐 *www.mojoskitchen428.com.*

DAVIS

10 miles west of Sacramento.

Davis began as a rich agricultural area and remains one, but it doesn't feel like a cow town. It's home to the University of California at Davis, whose students hang at downtown cafés, galleries, and bookstores (most of the action takes place between 1st and 4th and C and G streets), lending the city a vaguely cosmopolitan feel.

GETTING HERE AND AROUND

Most people arrive here by car via Interstate 80. In a pinch, you can get here via Yolobus (🌐 *www.yolobus.com*) from Sacramento. Downtown is walkable. Touring by bicycle is also a popular option—Davis is mostly flat.

ESSENTIALS

Visitor Information Davis Chamber of Commerce ✉ *640 3rd St.* ☎ *530/756–5160* 🌐 *www.davischamber.com.*

EXPLORING

University of California, Davis. A top research university, UC Davis educates many of the Wine Country's vintners and grape growers. Campus tours depart from Buehler Alumni and Visitors Center. On a tour or not, worthy stops include the **Arboretum** (🌐 *arboretum.ucdavis.edu*)—this is a major agricultural school, and it shows—and the **Mondavi Center for the Performing Arts** (🌐 *www.mondaviarts.org*), a striking modern glass structure that presents top-tier artists. ✉ *Visitor Center, Alumni La.* ☎ *530/752–8111* 🌐 *visit.ucdavis.edu* 🕓 *Visitor Center, weekdays 8–5, Sat. 10–2; campus tours, Sat. at 11:30.*

THE GOLD COUNTRY—SOUTH

This hilly region has an old-timey vibe. It's rich with antiques shops, quaint coffee shops, and delightfully appointed Victorian B&Bs.

PLACERVILLE

44 miles east of Sacramento.

It's hard to imagine now, but in 1849 about 4,000 miners staked out every gully and hillside in Placerville, turning the town into a rip-roaring camp of log cabins, tents, and clapboard houses. The area was then known as Hangtown, a graphic allusion to the nature of frontier justice. It took on the name Placerville in 1854 and became an important supply center for the miners. (*Placer* is defined roughly as valuable minerals found in riverbeds or lakes.) Mark Hopkins, Philip Armour, and John Studebaker were among the industrialists who got their starts here. Today, Placerville ranks among the hippest towns in the region, its Main Street abuzz with indie shops, coffeehouses, and wine bars, many of them inside rehabbed historic buildings.

GETTING HERE AND AROUND
You'll need a car to get to and around Placerville; it's a 45-minute drive from Sacramento via U.S. 50.

EXPLORING

FAMILY **Apple Hill.** During the fall harvest season (September through December), the members of the Apple Hill Growers Association open their orchards and vineyards for apple and berry picking, picnicking, and wine and cider tasting. Start your tour at High Hill Ranch, where there are fishing ponds for kids (they'll clean and pack the fish for you). Nibble on apple doughnuts or buy jewelry from local crafters. Stop at Larsen Apple Barn, a legacy farm. Family-favored Kid's Inc. serves apples pie and empanadas, and you can sample Cabernet and Bordeaux-style blends at Grace Patriot Wines, and fresh-pressed juices at Barsotti. Stop at Wofford Acres Vineyard just to see a dramatic view of the American River canyon below. ⚠ Traffic on weekends is often backed up, so take the Camino exit or go during the week to avoid the crowds (although kid-centric events are on weekends). ⊠ *About 5 miles east of Hwy. 49; take Camino exit from U.S. 50* ☎ *530/644–7692* ⊕ *www.applehill.com.*

FAMILY **Hangtown's Gold Bug Park & Mine.** Take a self-guided tour of this fully lighted mine shaft owned by the City of Placerville. The worthwhile audio tour (included) makes clear what you're seeing. ■TIP➔ A shaded stream runs through the park, and there are picnic facilities. ⊠ *2635 Goldbug La., off Bedford Ave., 1 mile off U.S. 50* ☎ *530/642–5207* ⊕ *www.goldbugpark.org* ☜ *$5* ⊙ *Apr.–Oct., daily 10–4; Nov.–Mar., weekends noon–4.*

WHERE TO EAT AND STAY

$ ✕ **The Cozmic Cafe.** Crowds come for healthful wraps, burritos, sand-
VEGETARIAN wiches, salads, and the like, plus breakfast (served anytime), smoothies, and espresso drinks. Portions are big, prices are low, and the ambience is distinctive. The eatery is in the 1859 Pearson's Soda Works

Building and extends back into the side of a mountain, into what used to be a mineshaft. The live music here is among the best in the foothills, and an upstairs pub beckons with local wines and microbrews. [$] *Average main: $9* ✉ *594 Main St.* ☎ *530/642–8481* 🌐 *www.ourcoz.com* ⏲ *Closed Mon.*

> **WORD OF MOUTH**
>
> "The Shenandoah Valley is what Napa was 30 years ago. Beautiful scenery, free tasting (for the most part), no appointments required (for the most part), really good wines, and a chance to talk to the actual winemakers."
>
> —janisj

$$$ B&B/INN Fodor's Choice ★ 🏨 **Eden Vale Inn.** Hand-crafted by the owners, this lavish but rustic B&B occupies a converted turn-of-the-20th-century hay barn, the centerpiece of which is a 27-foot slate fireplace that rises to a sloping roof of timber beams. **Pros:** rooms are exceptionally plush; the patio and grounds are stunning; plenty of places outside for kids to run. **Cons:** fairly expensive for the area. [$] *Rooms from: $200* ✉ *1780 Springvale Rd* ☎ *530/621-0901* 🌐 *www.edenvaleinn.com* 🛏 *5 rooms, 2 suites* 🍴 *Breakfast.*

$$ B&B/INN 🏨 **Seasons Bed & Breakfast.** One of Placerville's oldest homes has been transformed into a lovely and relaxing oasis. **Pros:** quiet setting; short walk to downtown; attentive hosts; great breakfasts. **Cons:** B&B environment not for everyone. [$] *Rooms from: $135* ✉ *2934 Bedford Ave.* ☎ *530/626–4420* 🌐 *www.theseasons.net* 🛏 *1 room, 2 suites, 1 cottage* 🍴 *Breakfast.*

SHENANDOAH VALLEY

20 miles south of Placerville.

The most concentrated Gold Country wine-touring area lies in the hills of the Shenandoah Valley, east of Plymouth. Robust Zinfandel is the primary grape grown here, but vineyards here produce plenty of other varietals, from Rhône blends to Italian Barberas and Sangioveses. Most wineries are open for tastings at least on weekend afternoons, and some of the top ones are open daily; several have shaded picnic areas. **■ TIP→ This region is gaining steam as a less-congested alternative to the Napa Valley.**

GETTING HERE AND AROUND

Reach the Shenandoah Valley by turning east on Fiddletown Road in Plymouth, between Placerville and Sutter Creek, and then north on Plymouth-Shenandoah Road. You will need a car to explore the valley and its vineyards.

EXPLORING

Shenandoah Vineyards. A plummy Barbera and an almost chocolaty Zinfandel top this winery's repertoire, but for a contrast you can also try a startlingly crisp Sauvignon Blanc. The Tempranillo is also good. An adjacent gallery sells contemporary art, pottery, photographs, and souvenirs. **■ TIP→ Shenandoah is affiliated with the nearby Sobon Estate Winery, which has an engaging on-site museum about the area.** ✉ *12300 Steiner Rd.* ☎ *209/245–4455* 🌐 *www.sobonwine.com* 🎟 *Tasting $5* ⏲ *Daily 10–5.*

Terre Rouge and Easton Wines. The winery of Bill and Jane Easton has two labels with two different wine-making styles: Terre Rouge focuses on Rhône-style wines, while Easton covers old-vine Zinfandel and Barbera. The winery has had good results with inky, soft Syrahs and Enigma, a Rhône-style white blend of Marsanne, Viognier, and Roussane. **■TIP→ You can picnic on the shaded patio here and there's a pétanque court nearby.** ✉ *10801 Dickson Rd.* ☎ *209/245–4277* 🌐 *www.terrerougewines.com* 🎫 *Tasting $5* 🕓 *Nov.–Aug., Thurs.–Mon. 11–4; Sept.–Oct., daily 11–4.*

Vino Noceto. This winery is an example of the benefits of focusing mostly on one varietal—in this case Sangiovese—and doing it well. Owners Suzy and Jim Gullett produce their Sangioveses in several different styles, from light and fruity to rich and heavy. They also produce small lots of wines from other varietals. ✉ *11011 Shenandoah Rd., at Dickson Rd.* ☎ *209/245–6556* 🌐 *www.noceto.com* 🎫 *Tasting free* 🕓 *Weekdays 11–4, weekends 11–5.*

WHERE TO EAT

$$$$ MODERN AMERICAN Fodor's Choice ★

🍴 **Taste.** A serendipitous find on the dusty streets of tiny Plymouth, Taste serves eclectic modern dishes made from fresh local fare. Phyllo-wrapped mushroom "cigars" or pan-seared scallops served with golden-beet risotto, kumquat, mint, fennel, and orange butter. Toss in tahini-grilled cauliflower with red wine–braised carrots and turnip greens, and even the vegetarians leave happy. **■TIP→ Gold Country wine making can be hit or miss, but with several sommeliers on staff, this is a terrific place to find out which producers are worth seeking out. There's also a great beer list.** [$] *Average main: $32* ✉ *9402 Main St.* ☎ *209/245–3463* 🌐 *www.restauranttaste.com* 🕓 *Closed Tues. and Wed. No lunch weekdays.*

AMADOR CITY

6 miles south of Plymouth.

The history of tiny Amador City mirrors the boom-bust-boom cycle of many Gold Country towns. With an output of $42 million in gold, its Keystone Mine was one of the most productive in the Mother Lode. After all the gold was extracted, the miners cleared out, and the area suffered. Amador City now derives its wealth from tourists, who come to browse through its antiques and specialty shops, most of them on or just off Highway 49.

GETTING HERE AND AROUND

Park where you can along Old Highway 49 (a bypass diverts Highway 49 traffic around Sutter Creek and Amador City), and walk around.

WHERE TO STAY

$$ B&B/INN

🏨 **Imperial Hotel.** The whimsically decorated mock-Victorian rooms at this 1879 hotel give a modern twist to the excesses of the era. **Pros:** comfortable; good restaurant and bar; tiny-town charm. **Cons:** no nightlife. [$] *Rooms from: $135* ✉ *14202 Old Hwy. 49* ☎ *209/267–9172* 🌐 *www.imperialamador.com* 🛏 *6 rooms, 3 suites* 🍽 *Breakfast.*

SUTTER CREEK

2 miles south of Amador City.

Sutter Creek is a charming conglomeration of balconied buildings, Victorian homes, and neo–New England structures. The stores on Main Street (formerly part of Highway 49, which was rerouted) are worth visiting for works by the many local artists and craftspeople.

GETTING HERE AND AROUND

Arrive here by car on Highway 49. There's no public transit, but downtown is walkable. The visitor center organizes walking tours.

ESSENTIALS

Information Sutter Creek Visitor Center ✉ *71A Main St.* ☎ *209/267–1344* 🌐 *www.suttercreek.org.*

EXPLORING

Monteverde Store Museum. This store, opened 1896, is a relic from the past: its final owner walked out more than four decades ago and never returned. These days you can peruse what he left behind, including typical wares from a century ago, an elaborate antique scale, and a chair-encircled potbellied stove. ✉ *3 Randolph St.* ☎ *209/267–0493* 🕒 *Thurs.–Mon. if volunteers available, hrs vary.*

WHERE TO EAT AND STAY

$$ AMERICAN 🍴 **Susan's Place.** Fresh produce, prompt and attentive service, and a lovely patio (especially so on warm summer evenings) distinguish this local favorite a half-block off the main drag. The serving of wine is a big deal here; there's even a "mystery wine" option that leaves the bottle (or glass) choice up to the owner. Try the eggplant and Portobello mushrooms on grilled panini bread. [$] *Average main: $20* ✉ *15 Eureka St.* ☎ *209/267–0945* 🌐 *www.susansplace.com* 🕒 *Closed Mon.–Wed.*

$$ B&B/INN 🏨 **Eureka Street Inn.** The lead- and stained-glass windows and the original redwood paneling, wainscoting, and beams—and, oh yes, those gas-log fireplaces in most rooms—lend the Eureka Street Inn a cozy feel. **Pros:** quiet location; lovely porch; engaging owners. **Cons:** only four rooms. [$] *Rooms from: $145* ✉ *55 Eureka St.* ☎ *209/267–5500, 800/399–2389* 🌐 *www.eurekastreetinn.com* 🛏 *4 rooms* 🍽 *Breakfast.*

$$$ B&B/INN 🏨 **The Foxes Inn of Sutter Creek.** The rooms in this 1857 white-clapboard house are handsome, with high ceilings, antique beds, and armoires; five have gas fireplaces. **Pros:** lovely inside and out; friendly owners. **Cons:** pricey. [$] *Rooms from: $200* ✉ *77 Main St.* ☎ *209/267–5882, 800/987–3344* 🌐 *www.foxesinn.com* 🛏 *5 rooms, 2 suites* 🍽 *Breakfast.*

$$ B&B/INN 🏨 **Grey Gables Inn.** Charming yet modern, this inn brings a touch of the English countryside to the Gold Country; the rooms, named after British poets, have gas-log fireplaces. **Pros:** English feel; tasteful interiors. **Cons:** hovers over main road; not much to do in town after dark. [$] *Rooms from: $163* ✉ *161 Hanford St.* ☎ *209/267–1039, 800/473–9422* 🌐 *www.greygables.com* 🛏 *8 rooms* 🍽 *Breakfast.*

$ HOTEL 🏨 **Sutter Creek Days Inn.** If you're on a budget, this hotel is a good choice; the rooms have coffeemakers, and most have queen-size beds. **Pros:** affordable; convenient; clean. **Cons:** can feel a bit impersonal. [$] *Rooms from: $84* ✉ *271 Hanford St.* ☎ *209/267–9177* 🌐 *www.daysinn.com/suttercreek* 🛏 *52 rooms* 🍽 *Breakfast.*

Continued on page 860

EUREKA! CALIFORNIA'S GOLD RUSH

When James W. Marshall burst into John Sutter's Mill on January 24, 1848, carrying flecks of gold in his hat, the millwright unleashed the glittering California gold rush with these immortal words:

"Boys, I believe I've found a gold mine!"

Before it was over, drowsy San Francisco had become the boomtown of the Golden West, Columbia's mines alone yielded $87,000,000, and California's Mother Lode—a vein of gold-bearing quartz that stretched 150 miles across the Sierra Nevada foothills—had been nearly tapped dry. Even though the gold rush soon became the gold bust, today you can still strike it rich by visiting the historic sites where it all happened.

Journey down the Gold Country Highway—a serpentine, nearly 300-mi-long two-lane route appropriately numbered 49—to find pure vacation treasure: fascinating mother lode towns, rip-roaring mining camps, and historic strike sites. In fact, in Placerville—as the former Hangtown, this spot saw so much new money and crime that outlaws were hanged in pairs—you can still pan the streams. And after you've seen the sights, the prospects remain just as golden: the entire region is a trove of gorgeous wineries, fun eateries, and Victorian-era hotels.

by: Reed Parsell and Robert I.C. Fisher

ALL THAT GLITTERED: '49ER FEVER

From imagination springs adventure, and perhaps no event in the 19th century provoked more wild adventures than the California gold rush of 1848 to 1855.

| James Marshall | 1856 U.S. quarter | John Sutter |

GOLD IN THEM THAR HILLS California's golden lava was discovered purely by accident. Upon finding his cattle ranch had gone to ruin while he was away fighting in the Mexican-American War, New Jersey native James W. Marshall decided to build a sawmill, with John Sutter, outside the town of Coloma, 40 miles upstream of Sutter's Fort on the American River. To better power the mill, he had a wider siphon created to divert the river water and, one morning, spotted golden flakes in the trench. Rich fur magnate Sutter tried to keep the mother strike quiet, but his own staff soon decamped to pan the streams and the secret was out. The gold rush's impact was so profound that, practically overnight, it catapulted San Francisco into one of the nation's—and the world's—wealthiest cities.

BROTHER, CAN YOU SPARE AN INGOT? After Marshall, 37 at the time, saw his fledgling mill abandoned by workers who went to pan the streams, he left Coloma for almost a decade. During the 1860s he made some money as a vintner there—a dicey profession for a reported alcoholic. Eventually Marshall's wine business dried up, and he returned to prospecting in the 1870s. But without success. For six years starting in 1872, the state Legislature gave him a small pension as an acknowledgment of his gold rush importance, but for the last years of his life he was practically penniless. He died on Aug. 10, 1885, at age 74.w

THE GOLD CRUSH Before the gold rush ended, in 1855, it is estimated that it drew 300,000 people—Americans, Europeans, and Chinese—to the Sierra Nevada foothills to seek their fortune. Sadly, accidents, disease, and skirmishes with Native Americans took their toll on both the prospectors and the environment. In addition, the gold lust of '49er fever left more than a thousand murders in its wake (not counting the infamous "suspended" sentences meted out at Hangtown).

BOOM TO BUST

Jan. 24, 1848: James W. Marshall spies specks of bright rock in the streambed at his sawmill's site; Sutter certifies they are gold.
May, 1848: California's coastal communities empty out as prospectors flock to the hills to join the "forty-eighters."
Aug. 19, 1848: The *New York Herald* is the first East Coast newspaper to report a gold rush in California.
Oct. 13, 1849: California's state constitution is approved in Monterey. The state's new motto becomes "Eureka!"
1855: The California gold rush effectively ends, as digging for the precious mineral becomes increasingly difficult, and large corporations monopolize mining operations.

DID YOU KNOW?

You can still pan the streams, but any shiny stuff will usually be worthless iron pyrite. Here a young prospector tries his hand at Marshall Gold Discovery State Park.

GOING FOR THE GOLD

Marshall Gold Discovery State Park

If you want to go prospecting for the best sightseeing treasures in Gold Country, just follow this map.

Coloma

Empire Mine State Historic Park, Grass Valley: During the century that it was operating, Empire Mine produced some 5.6 million ounces of gold. More than 350 miles of tunnels were dug, most under water. Operations ceased in 1956, but today visitors to the 800-acre park can go on 50-minute guided tours of the mines and enjoy great hiking trails and picnic spots.

Marshall Gold Discovery State Historic Park, Coloma: Here's where it all began—a can't-miss gold rush site. See the stone cairn that marks the spot of James Marshall's discovery, the huge statue of him that rests on his grave site, and visit—together with crowds of schoolchildren—the updated museum, and more.

Hangtown's Gold Bug Park & Mine, Placerville: Put on a hardhat and step into the 19th century at Gold Bug, located a few miles south of Marshall's jackpot site. Take a self-guided audio tour of a mine that opened in 1888, or a special tour of a mine opened in the 1850s, and do some "placering" (panning for gold) yourself, outside the gift shop. "Fool's gold" (used for billiard tables and chalkboards) was mostly found here before digging stopped in 1942.

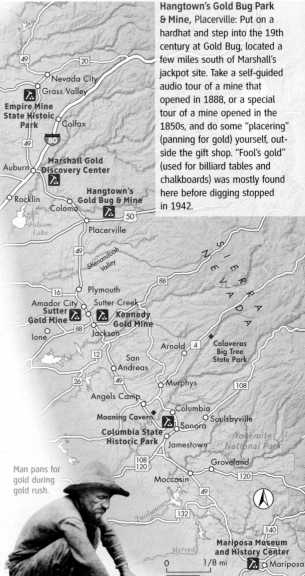

Man pans for gold during gold rush.

Empire Mine State Historic Park   Gold sifting pan   Columbia State Historic Park

Sutter Gold Mine: Between Amador City and Sutter Creek off Highway 49, this is the place to see how the so-called "Forty-Niner" individual prospectors were succeeded by large, deep-pocket mining companies. One-hour tours, offered daily April through most of October, take visitors deep into a hard-rock mine, where they can see ore veins that contain gold and learn the basics of hydraulic extraction.

Kennedy Gold Mine, Jackson: At 5,912 feet below ground, this is one of the world's deepest mines. Its head frame is one of the most dominant man-made sights along Highway 49's 295 miles. In operation from 1880 until World War II, the mine produced tens of millions of dollars of gold. One-hour tours, offered weekends and holidays from March through October, include a look inside the stately Mine Office.

Columbia State Historic Park

Columbia State Historic Park. Just north of Sonora, this is the best extant example of a gold rush-era town as it appeared in the mid-19th century. During its "golden" years, Columbia yielded more than $85 million in gold. Since World War II, the town has been restored. Fandango halls, Wells Fargo stage coaches, and a costumed staff bring a working 1850's mining town to life again.

Gold dollars

Mariposa Museum and History Center, Mariposa: Find all sorts of mining equipment, including a five-stamp ore mill, at this modest museum in the gold rush region's southernmost area. Also here is the fascinating California State Mining and Mineral Museum, home to a famous 13-pound golden nugget.

A PROSPECTING PRIMER

Grab any non-Teflon-coated pan with sloping sides and head up to "them thar hills." Find a stream—preferably one containing black sand—you can stoop beside, and then:

■ Scoop out sediment to fill your pan.

■ Add water, then gently shake the pan sideways, back and forth. This allows any gold to settle at the bottom.

■ Pick out and toss away any larger rocks.

■ Keep adding water, keep shaking the pan, and slowly pour the loosened waste gravel over the rim of the pan, making sure not to upend the pan while doing so.

■ If you're left with gold, yell "Eureka!" then put it in a glass container. Your findings may not make you rich, but will entitle you to bragging rights for as long as you keep the gold handy to show friends.

■ TIP→ If you'd rather not pan on your own, plenty of attractions and museums in the Gold Country will let you try your hand at prospecting. See listings in this chapter for more details on these historic sites.

JACKSON

8 miles south of Sutter Creek.

Jackson wasn't the Gold Country's rowdiest town, but the party lasted longer here than most anywhere else: "girls' dormitories" (aka brothels) and nickel slot machines flourished until the mid-1950s. Jackson also had the world's deepest and richest gold mines, the Kennedy and the Argonaut, which together produced $70 million in gold. Most of the miners who worked the lode were of Serbian or Italian origin, and they gave the town a European character that persists to this day. Jackson has pioneer cemeteries whose headstones tell the stories of local Serbian and Italian families. The city's official website (🌐 *ci.jackson.ca.us*; click on "Visitor Center") has great cemetery and walking-tour maps; there are some interesting shops downtown.

GETTING HERE AND AROUND

Arrive by car on Highway 49. You can walk to downtown sights but otherwise will need a car.

EXPLORING

Fodor's Choice ★ **Preston Castle.** History buffs and ghost hunters regularly make the trip to this fantastically creepy building that was built to house troubled youth in 1894. Having fallen into a state of disrepair, the building is slowly undergoing a full renovation, and tours are available by appointment and on certain Saturdays throughout the year (it's best to call ahead to confirm schedule). The dramatic Romanesque-revival structure has appeared on TV's *Ghost Hunters*, and during tours of this 156-room building you'll learn all sorts of spine-tingling tales, including one about a student murdering a housekeeper and then rolling her up in a carpet. ✉ *909 Palm Dr., 12 miles west of Jackson via Hwys. 88 and 104, Ione* ☎ *209/256–3623* 🌐 *www.prestoncastle.com* 🎟 *$10* 🕒 *1st, 2nd, and 3rd Sat. of month, 10–1; or by appointment.*

St. Sava Serbian Orthodox Church. The terraced cemetery on the grounds of the handsome church is an impressive sight. ✉ *724 N. Main St.*

WHERE TO EAT AND STAY

$ AMERICAN 🍴 **Mel and Faye's Diner.** A local hangout famous for its "Moo Burger"—so big it still makes cow sounds, presumably—the diner is run by its namesakes' son, who has added slightly more sophisticated fare for breakfast, lunch, and dinner. [$] *Average main: $10* ✉ *31 Main St.* ☎ *209/223–0853* 🌐 *melandfayesdiner.com* 🕒 *Closed Tues.*

$ HOTEL 🏨 **Hotel Leger.** Home to a still convivial old saloon that was one of the rowdiest miners' haunts back in the day, this atmospheric 1851 inn, which is about 8 miles south of Jackson, is inhabited today by friendly ghosts. **Pros:** friendly and accomodating proprietors; rich in history; reasonably priced. **Con:** bathrooms are private but some are located across the hall; thin walls and creaky floorboards. [$] *Rooms from: $95* ✉ *8304 Main St., Mokelumme Hill* ☎ *209/286–1401* 🌐 *www.hotelleger.com* 🛏 *7 rooms, 6 suites* 🍽 *No meals.*

ANGELS CAMP

20 miles south of Jackson.

Angels Camp is famous chiefly for its May jumping-frog contest, based on Mark Twain's short story "The Celebrated Jumping Frog of Calaveras County." The writer reputedly heard the story of the jumping frog from Ross Coon, proprietor of Angels Hotel, which has been in operation since 1856. It's a favorite destination these days among outdoor adventurers, who love exploring the subterranean caverns, and fishing for salmon, trout, and bass in the area's crystal clear rivers and lakes.

22

GETTING HERE AND AROUND

Angels Camp is at the intersection of Highway 49 and Highway 4. You'll need a car to get here and around.

EXPLORING

Angels Camp Museum. Gold-rush relics are on display here: photos, rocks, petrified wood, blacksmith and mining equipment, even a horse-drawn hearse. The carriage house out back holds 31 carriages and impressive mineral specimens. ⊠ *753 S. Main St.* ☎ *209/736–2963* ⊕ *www. angelscampmuseumfoundation.org* ✏ *$5* ⊙ *Thurs.–Mon. 10–4.*

FAMILY **California Cavern.** A ½-mile subterranean trail winds through large chambers and past underground streams and lakes. There aren't many steps to climb, but it's a strenuous walk with some narrow passageways and steep spots. The caverns, at a constant 55°F, contain crystalline formations not found elsewhere, and the 80-minute guided tour explains local history and geology. ⊠ *Cave City Rd., 9 miles east of San Andreas on Mountain Ranch Rd., then about 3 miles on Cave City Rd.* ☎ *209/736–2708* ⊕ *www.caverntours.com* ✏ *$14.95* ⊙ *Mar. and Apr., daily 10–4; May–Oct., daily 10–5; Nov.–Feb. weekends 10–4; hrs can vary, call to confirm.*

FAMILY **Moaning Cavern.** There's no better way than to see what life was like
Fodor's Choice underground for prospectors than to descend into the belly of the
★ land. This fascinating tour let's you wander down a chasm into the wonder of an ancient limestone cave. Take the 235-step spiral staircase built in 1922 into this vast cavern. More intrepid explorers can rappel into the chamber—ropes and instruction are provided. Otherwise, the only way inside is via the 45-minute tour, during which you'll see giant (and still growing) stalactites and stalagmites and an archaeological site that holds some of the oldest human remains yet found in America. Outside there are three zip lines, starting at $44 per person. ⊠ *5350 Moaning Cave Rd., off Parrots Ferry Rd., about 2 miles south of Vallecito* ☎ *209/736–2708* ⊕ *www.caverntours.com* ✏ *$14.95* ⊙ *May–Oct., daily 9–6; Nov.–Apr., weekdays 10–5, weekends 9–5; hrs can vary, call to confirm.*

22

MURPHYS

10 miles northeast of Angels Camp.

Murphys is the Gold Country's most compact, orderly town, with enough shops and restaurants to keep families busy for at least a half-day, and more than 20 tasting rooms within walking distance. A well-preserved town of white-picket fences, Victorian houses, and interesting shops, it exhibits an upscale vibe. Horatio Alger and Ulysses S. Grant came through here, staying at what's now called the Murphys Historic Hotel & Lodge when they, along with many other 19th-century tourists, came to investigate the giant sequoia groves in nearby Calaveras Big Trees State Park.

GETTING HERE AND AROUND

Murphys is 10 miles northeast of Highway 49 on Highway 4. You'll need to drive here. Parking can be difficult on summer weekends.

EXPLORING

Calaveras Big Tree State Park. The park protects hundreds of the largest and rarest living things on the planet—magnificent giant sequoia redwood trees. Some are 3,000 years old, 90 feet around at the base, and 250 feet tall. There are campgrounds and picnic areas; swimming, wading, fishing, and sunbathing on the Stanislaus River are popular in summer. Enjoy the "three senses" trail, designated for the blind, with interpretive signs in Braille that guide visitors to touch the bark and encourage children to slow down and enjoy the forest in a more sensory way. ✉ *Off Hwy. 4, 15 miles northeast of Murphys, 4 miles northeast of Arnold, Angels Camp* ☎ *209/795–2334* 🌐 *www.parks.ca.gov* 🎟 *$10 per vehicle* 🕒 *Park: daily sunrise–sunset. Visitor center: May–Oct., daily 10–4; Nov.–Apr., weekends 9–5.*

Ironstone Vineyards. Tours here take in spectacular gardens and underground tunnels cooled by a waterfall, and include the automated performance of a restored silent-movie-era pipe organ. On display near the tasting room is a 44-pound specimen of crystalline gold. The winery, known for Merlot, Cabernet Sauvignon, and Cabernet Franc, hosts concerts and other events. Its deli has picnic items. ■ **TIP→ Ironstone is worth a visit even if you don't drink wine.** ✉ *1894 6 Mile Rd.* ✥ *From Jones St. in town, head south on Scott St.* ☎ *209/728–1251* 🌐 *www.ironstonevineyards.com* 🎟 *Tastings $3–$6* 🕒 *Daily 10–5; open until 6 in summer.*

WHERE TO EAT AND STAY

$$ AMERICAN 🍴 **Grounds.** Light entrées, grilled vegetables, chicken, seafood, and steak are the specialties at this bustling bistro and coffee shop with a good wine list. Sandwiches, salads, and homemade soups are served for lunch. The crowd is friendly and the service attentive. [$] *Average main: $20* ✉ *402 Main St.* ☎ *209/728–8663* 🌐 *www.groundsrestaurant.com.*

$ HOTEL 🏨 **Murphys Historic Hotel & Lodge.** This 1855 stone hotel, whose register has seen the signatures of Mark Twain and the bandit Black Bart, figured in a Bret Harte short story. **Pros:** historical ambience; great bar; downtown location. **Cons:** dated; creaky. [$] *Rooms from: $109* ✉ *457 Main St.* ☎ *209/728–3444, 800/532–7684* 🌐 *www.murphyshotel.com* 🛏 *29 rooms, 20 with bath* 🍽 *No meals.*

COLUMBIA

14 miles south of Angels Camp.

Columbia is the gateway for Columbia State Historic Park, one of the Gold Country's most visited sites. The historic Fallon House Theater is a great place for families to participate in living history activities like candle dipping and soap making on weekends. There are several inviting spots for a picnic in the area.

GETTING HERE AND AROUND

The only way to get here is by car, via either Highway 4 (the northern route) or Highway 49 (the southern) from Angels Camp.

EXPLORING

FAMILY

Fodor's Choice

★

Columbia State Historic Park. Columbia comes as close to a gold-rush town in its heyday as any site in the Gold Country. Usually, you can ride a stagecoach, pan for gold, and watch a blacksmith working at an anvil. Street musicians perform in summer. Restored or reconstructed buildings include a Wells Fargo Express office, a Masonic temple, an old-fashioned candy store, saloons, a firehouse, churches, a school, and a newspaper office. At times, all are staffed to simulate a working 1850s town. The park also includes the must-stop, **Historic Fallon House Theater,** where Broadway-quality shows are performed Wednesday through Sunday—Mark Twain once performed in this gorgeous Victorian structure. The town's two 19th-century historic lodgings, the Fallon Hotel ($) and City Hotel ($–$$) perch you in the past; to reserve a hotel or cottage go to ⊕ *www.reserveamerica.com.* ✉ *11255 Jackson St.* ☎ *209/588-9128* ⊕ *www.parks.ca.gov/columbia* 🎟 *Free* ☉ *Daily 9–5.*

SONORA

4 miles south of Columbia.

Miners from Mexico founded Sonora and made it the biggest town in the Mother Lode. Following a period of racial and ethnic strife, the Mexican settlers moved on, and Yankees built the commercial city visible today. Sonora's historic downtown section sits atop the Big Bonanza Mine, one of the richest in the state. Another mine, on the site of nearby Sonora High School, yielded 990 pounds of gold in a single week in 1879. Reminders of the gold rush are everywhere in Sonora, in prim Victorian houses, typical Sierra-stone storefronts, and awning-shaded sidewalks. Reality intrudes beyond the town's historic heart, with strip malls, shopping centers, and modern motels.

GETTING HERE AND AROUND

Arrive in Sonora by car via Highway 49 (if coming from Columbia, drive south on Parrots Ferry Road). Parking can be difficult on the busy main drag, Washington Street (Highway 49).

EXPLORING

Tuolumne County Museum and History Center. The small museum occupies a historic gold rush–era building that served as a jail until 1960. Vintage firearms and paraphernalia, gold specimens, and MiWuk

baskets are among the many artifacts on display. ✉ *158 W. Bradford St.* ☎ *209/532–1317* 🌐 *www.tchistory.org* 🎫 *Free* 🕐 *Weekdays 10–4, Sat. 10–3:30* 🕐 *Closed Sun.*

WHERE TO EAT AND STAY

$ AMERICAN 🍴 **Diamondback Grill and Wine Bar.** The bright decor and refined atmosphere suggest more ambitious fare, but burgers are what this place is about. Locals crowd the tables, especially after 6 pm, for the ground-meat patties, beer-battered onion rings, veggie burger, and fine wines. [$] *Average main: $11* ✉ *93 S. Washington St.* ☎ *209/532–6661* 🌐 *www.thediamondbackgrill.com* 🕐 *Closed Sun.*

$$ B&B/INN 🏨 **Barretta Gardens Bed and Breakfast Inn.** This inn is perfect for a romantic getaway, with elegant Victorian rooms varying in size, all furnished with period pieces. **Pros:** lovely grounds; yummy breakfasts; romantic. **Cons:** only seven rooms. [$] *Rooms from: $159* ✉ *700 S. Barretta St.* ☎ *209/532–6039, 800/206–3333* 🌐 *www.barrettagardens.com* 🔑 *7 rooms* 🍽 *Breakfast.*

JAMESTOWN

4 miles south of Sonora.

Compact Jamestown supplies a touristy view of gold rush–era life. Shops in brightly colored buildings along Main Street sell antiques and gift items. You can try your hand at panning for gold here or explore a bit of railroad history.

GETTING HERE AND AROUND

Jamestown lies at the intersection of north–south Highway 49 and east–west Highway 108. You'll need a car to tour here.

EXPLORING

FAMILY **Gold Prospecting Adventures.** You'll get a real feel (sort of) for the life of a prospector on the three-hour gold-panning excursions led by this outfit's congenial, steeped-in-history tour guides. You might even strike gold at the Jimtown Mine. ✉ *18170 Main St.* ☎ *209/984–4653, 800/596–0009* 🌐 *www.goldprospecting.com* ☞ *Call for hrs and fees.*

Fodor's Choice ★ **Railtown 1897.** A must for rail enthusiasts and families with kids, this is one of the most intact early roundhouses (maintenance facilities) in North America. You can hop aboard a steam train for a 40-minute journey—bring along the family dog if you'd like. The docents entertain guests with tales about the history of locomotion. Listen to the original rotor and pulleys in the engine house and take in the smell of axle grease. Walk through a genteel passenger car with dusty-green velvet seats and ornate metalwork, where Grace Kelly and Gary Cooper filmed a scene in the epic Western *High Noon*. You can also climb onto a historic train to see where the fireman once shoveled coal into the tender. ✉ *5th Ave. and Reservoir Rd.* ☎ *209/984–3953* 🌐 *www.railtown1897.org* 🎫 *Roundhouse tour $5; train ride $15* 🕐 *Apr.–Oct., daily 9:30–4:30; Nov.–Mar., daily 10–3; train ride, weekends Apr.–Oct. (additional holiday rides are offered some weekends in late Nov. and Dec.).*

WHERE TO STAY

$ RESORT FAMILY
🏨 **Black Oak Casino Resort.** About 12 miles east of Jamestown off Highway 108, this flashy, contemporary property appeals heavily to casino gamers, but it's also just a nice place to stay with well-outfitted rooms (comfy bedding, down pillows, and alarm clocks with MP3 players) and a central Gold Country location. **Pros:** clean and spacious rooms; plenty of diversions on hand for both kids and adults. **Cons:** must go through smokey casino to reach bowling alley and restaurants; there's nothing quaint or historic about this place. [$] *Rooms from: $109* ✉ *19400 Tuolumne Rd. N, Tuolumne* ☎ *209/928–9300* 🌐 *www.blackoakcasino.com* 🛏 *148 rooms* 🍴 *No meals.*

$$ B&B/INN
🏨 **McCaffrey House Bed and Breakfast Inn.** Remoteness is one of McCaffrey's appeals—it's about 20 miles east of Jamestown on Highway 108 in the mountain community of Twain Harte. **Pros:** large rooms; wonderful nearby hiking; romantically remote. **Cons:** remote. [$] *Rooms from: $169* ✉ *23251 Hwy. 108* ☎ *209/586–0757, 888/586–0757* 🌐 *www.mccaffreyhouse.com* 🛏 *8 rooms* 🍴 *Breakfast.*

$$ HOTEL
🏨 **National Hotel.** The National has been in business since 1859, and its furnishings—brass beds, regal comforters, and lace curtains—are authentic but not overly embellished. **Pros:** historic feel; great brunches. **Cons:** not much happens in town after dark. [$] *Rooms from: $140* ✉ *18183 Main St.* ☎ *209/984–3446, 800/894–3446 in CA* 🌐 *www.national-hotel.com* 🛏 *9 rooms* 🍴 *Breakfast.*

THE GOLD COUNTRY—NORTH

Gold has had a significant presence along this northern stretch of Highway 49, whose highlights include the bucolic Empire State Historic Park and Coloma, where the discovery of a few nuggets triggered the gold rush.

COLOMA

8 miles northwest of Placerville.

The California gold rush started in Coloma. "My eye was caught with the glimpse of something shining in the bottom of the ditch," James Marshall recalled. Marshall himself never found any more "color," as gold came to be called.

GETTING HERE AND AROUND

A car is the only practical way to get to Coloma, via Highway 49. Once parked, you can walk to all the worthwhile sights.

EXPLORING

FAMILY
Marshall Gold Discovery State Historic Park. Most of Coloma lies within the historic park. Though crowded with tourists in summer, Coloma hardly resembles the mob scene it was in 1849, when 2,000 prospectors staked out claims along the streambed. The town's population grew to 4,000, supporting seven hotels, three banks, and many stores and businesses. But when reserves of the precious metal dwindled, prospectors left as quickly as they had come. A working reproduction of an 1840s mill lies near the spot where James Marshall first saw gold. A trail

leads to a modest sign (considering the impact) marking his discovery. ■ **TIP→ Take a stroll up the surrounding hills for sublime views.** ✉ *310 Back St., off Hwy. 49* ☎ *530/622–3470* 🌐 *www.parks.ca.gov* 🎟 *$8 per vehicle* ⏲ *Park: daily 8–sunset. Museum: Mar.–Oct., Tues.–Sat. 10–4; Nov.–Feb., daily 10–3.*

WHERE TO STAY

$$ B&B/INN 🏨 **Coloma Country Inn.** Four of the rooms at this B&B on 2½ acres in the state historic park are inside an 1850s farmhouse, and two suites with kitchenettes occupy the carriage house. **Pros:** convenient to the park; quiet; leisurely ambience. **Cons:** no nightlife. [$] *Rooms from: $135* ✉ *345 High St.* ☎ *530/622–6919* 🌐 *www.colomacountryinn.com* 🛏 *4 rooms, 2 suites* 🍴 *Breakfast.*

AUBURN

18 miles northwest of Coloma; 34 miles northeast of Sacramento.

Auburn is the Gold Country town most accessible to travelers on Interstate 80. An important transportation center during the gold rush, downtown Auburn has a small Old Town district with narrow climbing streets, cobblestone lanes, wooden sidewalks, and many original buildings. ■ **TIP→ Fresh produce, flowers, baked goods, and gifts are for sale at the farmers' market, held on Saturday morning year-round.**

GETTING HERE AND AROUND

Amtrak serves Auburn, though most visitors arrive by car on Highway 49 or Interstate 80. Once downtown, you can tour on foot.

EXPLORING

Bernhard Museum Complex. Party like it's 1889 at this space whose main structure opened in 1851 as the Traveler's Rest Hotel and for 100 years was the residence of the Bernhard family. The congenial docents, dressed in Victorian garb, describe the family's history and 19th-century life in Auburn. ✉ *291 Auburn–Folsom Rd.* ☎ *530/889–6500* 🎟 *Free* ⏲ *Tues.–Sun. 11–4.*

FAMILY **Gold Country Museum.** You'll get a feel for life in the mines at this museum whose highlights include a re-created mine tunnel, a gold-panning stream, and a reproduction saloon. ✉ *1273 High St.* ☎ *530/889–6500* 🎟 *Free to museum, $3 to pan for gold* ⏲ *Tues.–Sun. 11–4.*

Placer County Courthouse. Auburn's standout structure is the Placer County Courthouse. The classic gold-dome building houses the Placer County Museum, which documents the area's history—Native American, railroad, agricultural, and mining—from the early 1700s to 1900. ✉ *101 Maple St.* ☎ *530/889–6500* 🎟 *Free* ⏲ *Daily 10–4.*

WHERE TO EAT AND STAY

$ AMERICAN 🍴 **Awful Annie's.** Big patio umbrellas (and outdoor heaters when necessary) allow patrons to take in the Old Town view from this popular spot for lunch or breakfast—one specialty is a chili omelet. A second Annie's is at 490 G Street in nearby Lincoln. [$] *Average main: $10* ✉ *160 Sacramento St.* ☎ *530/888–9857* 🌐 *www.awfulannies.com* ⏲ *No dinner.*

$$$

MODERN

AMERICAN

Fodor's Choice

★

✕ **Carpe Vino.** Chef Eric Alexander is known for his hearty and imaginative French-inspired dishes—sophisticated fare presented in a nonchalant, almost effortless way, as if ingredients rolled right from the farm basket onto your plate. Consider purple and yellow beets in olive oil with fans of sliced fennel stalks and creamy panna cotta, roasted bone marrow, duck-fat fries, and brothy mussels steamed with lemon and chilis. This gem is tucked into an old downtown saloon and mine with a handsome old bar. Note the extensive and varied wine list. $ *Average main: $28* ✉ *1568 Lincoln Way* ☎ *530/823–0320* ⊕ *www. carpevinoauburn.com* ☾ *Closed Mon.*

$$

HOTEL

⛆ **Holiday Inn Auburn Hotel.** Above the freeway across from Old Town, this hotel has a welcoming lobby and chain-standard but nice rooms. **Pros:** convenient; clean; books available on loan. **Cons:** noise in rooms near parking lot. $ *Rooms from: $127* ✉ *120 Grass Valley Hwy.* ☎ *530/887–8787, 800/814–8787* ⊕ *www.auburnhi.com* ⇗ *96 rooms, 6 suites* ⊚ *Breakfast.*

GRASS VALLEY

24 miles north of Auburn.

More than half of California's total gold production was extracted from mines around Grass Valley, including the Empire Mine, which, along with the North Star Mining Museum, is among the Gold Country's most fascinating attractions.

GETTING HERE AND AROUND

You'll need a car to get here. Take Highway 20 east from Interstate 5 or west from Interstate 80. Highway 49 is the north–south route into town. Gold Country Stage vehicles (☎ *530/477–0103* ☾ *Weekdays 7–6*) serve some attractions. Expect to wait, though.

EXPLORING

FAMILY

Empire Mine State Historic Park. Relive the days of gold, grit, and glory, when this mine was one of the biggest and most prosperous hard-rock gold mines in North America. Visit Bourn Cottage with its exquisite woodwork, lovely fountains, and stunning gardens. On a tour, you can walk into a mineshaft and peer into into dark, deep recesses—you can almost imagine what it felt like to work this vast operation. An estimated 5.8 million ounces of gold were extracted from the mine's 367 miles of underground passages during its lifetime. Dressed-up docents portraying colorful characters who shaped Northern California's history share stories about the period. The grounds have picnic tables and gentle trails—perfect for a family outing. ✉ *10791 E. Empire St.* ☎ *530/273–8522* ⊕ *www.parks.ca.gov* 🎫 *$7* ☾ *Daily 10–5.*

Holbrooke Hotel. The recently refurnished landmark hotel ($$), built in 1851, hosted entertainer Lola Montez and writer Mark Twain as well as Ulysses S. Grant and other U.S. presidents. The restaurant-saloon ($$) is one of the oldest operating west of the Mississippi. ✉ *212 W. Main St.* ☎ *530/273–1353, 800/933–7077* ⊕ *www.holbrooke.com.*

FAMILY

North Star Mining Museum. Housed in a former powerhouse, the museum displays the 32-foot-high Pelton Water Wheel, said to be the largest ever

Almost 6 million ounces of gold were extracted from the Empire Mine.

built. It was used to power mining operations and was a forerunner of the modern turbines that generate hydroelectricity. Hands-on displays are geared to children. You can picnic nearby. ✉ *10933 Allison Ranch Rd.* ☎ *530/273–4255* 🌐 *www.nevadacountyhistory.org* 🎫 *Donation requested* 🕑 *May–mid-Oct., Tues.–Sun. 11–5.*

WHERE TO EAT AND STAY

$ BRITISH 🍴 **Cousin Jack Pasties.** Meat- and vegetable-stuffed pasties are a taste of the region's history, having come across the Atlantic with Cornish miners and their families in the mid-19th century. The flaky crusts practically melt in your mouth. A simple food stand, Jack's is nonetheless a local landmark. [$] *Average main: $8* ✉ *100 S. Auburn St.* ☎ *530/272–9230* 💳 *No credit cards.*

$$ ITALIAN 🍴 **Villa Venezia Restaurant.** Pasta and seafood are the specialties served up in a cozy, warm Victorian building with an intimate patio area. The appetizers and salads very nearly outshine the outstanding main dishes. [$] *Average main: $22* ✉ *124 Bank St.* ☎ *530/273–3555* 🌐 *www.villavenezia.info* 🕑 *No lunch Sat.–Thurs.*

NEVADA CITY

4 miles north of Grass Valley.

Nevada City, once known as the Queen City of the Northern Mines, is the most appealing of the northern Mother Lode towns. The iron-shutter brick buildings that line the narrow downtown streets contain antiques shops, galleries, boutiques, B&Bs, restaurants, and a winery. Horse-drawn carriage tours add to the romance, as do gas street lamps.

At one point in the 1850s, Nevada City had a population of nearly 10,000—enough to support much cultural activity. Today, about 3,100 people live here.

GETTING HERE AND AROUND

You'll need a car to get here. Take Highway 20 east from Interstate 5 or west from Interstate 80. Highway 49 is the north–south route into town. Gold Country Stage vehicles (☎ *530/477–0103* 🕓 *Weekdays 7–6*) serve some attractions.

ESSENTIALS

Visitor Information Nevada City Chamber of Commerce ✉ *132 Main St.* ☎ *530/265–2692* 🌐 *www.nevadacitychamber.com.*

EXPLORING

Firehouse No. 1. With its gingerbread-trim bell tower, Firehouse No. 1 is one of the Gold Country's most distinctive buildings. A museum, it houses gold-rush artifacts and the altar from a Chinese joss house (temple). ✉ *214 Main St.* ☎ *530/265–5468* 🎟 *Donation suggested* 🕓 *May–Nov., Tue.–Sun. 1–4.*

Nevada City Winery. Watch wine being created while you sip at this winery whose tasting room overlooks the production area. Syrah and Zinfandel are among the strengths here. ✉ *Miners Foundry Garage, 321 Spring St., at Bridge St.* ☎ *530/265–9463, 800/203–9463* 🌐 *www.ncwinery.com* 🎟 *Tasting and tour free* 🕓 *Sun.–Thurs. noon–5, Fri. and Sat. noon–6; tour on Sat. at 1:30.*

WHERE TO EAT AND STAY

$$$ ECLECTIC 🍴 **Friar Tuck's.** Popular Friar Tuck's specializes in creative, interactive fondues and has an extensive menu of seafood, steaks, and pasta dishes, too. The sparkling interior has a late-19th century ambience—it's one of Nevada City's best indoor spaces. [$] *Average main: $25* ✉ *111 N. Pine St.* ☎ *530/265–9093* 🌐 *friartucks.com* 🕓 *No lunch.*

$ AMERICAN 🍴 **South Pine Cafe.** Locals flock here, especially for brunch. Lobster and beef are on the menu, but the real attention-grabbers are vegetarian entrées and side dishes, such as breakfast potatoes and apple-ginger muffins. There's a branch in Grass Valley at 102 North Richardson Street. [$] *Average main: $11* ✉ *110 S. Pine St.* ☎ *530/265–0260* 🌐 *www.southpinecafe.com* 🕓 *No dinner.*

$$ B&B/INN Fodor's Choice ★ 🏨 **Red Castle Historic Lodgings.** Antique furnishings and Oriental rugs decorate the rooms of this 1857 Gothic-revival mansion, a fine option for those who appreciate the finer points of Victorian design. **Pros:** friendly owners; spectacular food; fascinating architecture. **Cons:** the walk uphill from downtown is a workout. [$] *Rooms from: $155* ✉ *109 Prospect St.* ☎ *530/265–5135, 800/761–4766* 🌐 *www.redcastleinn.com* 🛏 *4 rooms, 3 suites* 🍽 *Breakfast.*

LAKE TAHOE

With Reno, Nevada

WELCOME TO LAKE TAHOE

TOP REASONS TO GO

★ **The lake:** Blue, deep, and alpine pure, Lake Tahoe is far and away the main reason to visit this high Sierra paradise.

★ **Skiing:** Daring black-diamond runs or baby-bunny bumps—whether you're an expert, a beginner, or somewhere in between, there are many slopes to suit your skills at the numerous Tahoe-area ski parks.

★ **The great outdoors:** A ring of national forests and recreation areas linked by miles of trails makes Tahoe excellent for nature lovers.

★ **Dinner with a view:** You can picnic lakeside at state parks or dine in restaurants perched along the shore.

★ **A date with lady luck:** Whether you want to roll dice, play the slots, or hope the blackjack dealer goes bust before you do, you'll find round-the-clock gambling at the casinos on the Nevada side of the lake and in Reno.

1 California Side. With the exception of Stateline, Nevada—which, aside from its casino-hotel towers, seems almost indistinguishable from South Lake Tahoe, California—the California side is more developed than the Nevada side. Here you can find both commercial enterprises—restaurants, motels, lodges, resorts, residential subdivisions—and public-access facilities, such as historic sites, parks, campgrounds, marinas, and beaches.

2 Nevada Side. You don't need a highway sign to know when you've crossed from California into Nevada: the flashing lights and elaborate marquees of casinos announce legal gambling in garish hues. But you'll find more here than tables and slot machines. Reno, the Biggest Little City in the World, has a vibrant art scene and a serene downtown RiverWalk. And when you really need to get away from the chip-toting crowds, you can hike through pristine wilderness at Lake Tahoe–Nevada State Park, or hit the slopes near Incline Village.

GETTING ORIENTED

In the northern section of the Sierra Nevada mountain range, the Lake Tahoe area covers portions of four national forests, several state parks, and rugged wilderness areas with names like Desolation and Granite Chief. Lake Tahoe, the star attraction, straddles California and Nevada and is one of the world's largest, clearest, and deepest alpine lakes. The region's proximity to the Bay Area and Sacramento to the west and Reno to the east draws thrill seekers during ski season and again in summer when water sports, camping, and hiking are the dominant activities.

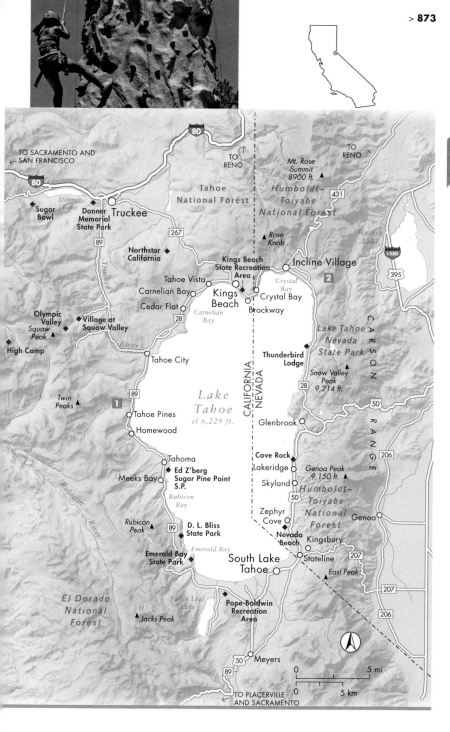

TO SACRAMENTO AND
SAN FRANCISCO

80

TO
RENO

TO
RENO

Mt. Rose
Summit
8900 ft.

*Tahoe
National Forest*

431

*Humboldt–
Toiyabe
National Forest*

*Washoe
Lake*

I-580

Donner
Lake

Sugar
Bowl

Donner
Memorial
State Park

Truckee

267

89

*Rose
Knob*

Incline Village

2

395

Northstar
California

Kings Beach
State Recreation
Area

**Kings
Beach**

*Crystal
Bay*

Tahoe Vista

Crystal Bay

Carnelian Bay

Cedar Flat

Brockway

28

*Carnelian
Bay*

Olympic
Valley
*Squaw
Peak*

Village at
Squaw Valley

High Camp

89

River

Tahoe City

**Thunderbird
Lodge**

*Lake Tahoe
Nevada
State Park*

*C
A
R
S
O
N*

*Snow Valley
Peak
9,214 ft.*

28

50

206

Twin
Peaks

89

1

Tahoe Pines

Homewood

*Lake
Tahoe*
el 6,229 ft.

C
A
L
I
F
O
R
N
I
A

N
E
V
A
D
A

Glenbrook

Cave Rock

Lakeridge

*Genoa Peak
9,150 ft.*

*R
A
N
G
E*

Tahoma

Ed Z'berg
Sugar Pine Point
S.P.

Meeks Bay

*Rubicon
Bay*

Skyland

50

Zephyr
Cove

*Humboldt–
Toiyabe
National
Forest*

Genoa

*Rubicon
River*

*Rubicon
Peak*

89

D. L. Bliss
State Park

Emerald Bay
State Park

Emerald Bay

**Nevada
Beach**

Kingsbury

Stateline

207

**South Lake
Tahoe**

East Peak

207

206

*El Dorado
National
Forest*

*Fallen Leaf
Lake*

Jacks Peak

Pope-Baldwin
Recreation
Area

N

0   5 mi

0   5 km

50

Meyers

89

TO PLACERVILLE
AND SACRAMENTO

Updated
by Christine
Vovakes

Whether you swim, fish, sail, or simply rest on its shores, you'll be wowed by the overwhelming beauty of Lake Tahoe, the largest alpine lake in North America. Famous for its cobalt-blue water and surrounding snowcapped peaks, Lake Tahoe straddles the state line between California and Nevada. The border gives this popular Sierra Nevada resort region a split personality. About half its visitors are intent on low-key sightseeing, hiking, camping, and boating. The rest head directly to the Nevada side, where bargain dining, big-name entertainment, and the lure of a jackpot draw them into the glittering casinos.

To explore the lake area and get a feel for its many differing communities drive the 72-mile road that follows the shore through wooded flatlands and past beaches, climbing to vistas on the rugged southwest side of the lake and passing through busy commercial developments and casinos on its northeastern and southeastern edges. Another option is to actually go out *on* the 22-mile-long, 12-mile-wide lake on a sightseeing cruise or kayaking trip.

The lake, the communities around it, the state parks, national forests, and protected tracts of wilderness are the region's main draws, but other nearby destinations are gaining in popularity. Truckee, with an Old West feel and innovative restaurants, entices visitors looking for a relaxed pace and easy access to Tahoe's north shore and Olympic Valley ski parks. And today Reno, once known only for its casinos, attracts tourists with its buzzing arts scene, revitalized downtown riverfront, and campus events at the University of Nevada.

PLANNING

WHEN TO GO

A sapphire blue lake shimmering deep in the center of an ice white wonderland—that's Tahoe in winter. But those blankets of snow mean lots of storms that often close roads and force chain requirements on the interstate. In summer the roads are open, but the lake and lodgings are clogged with visitors seeking respite from valley heat. If you don't ski, the best times to visit are early fall—September and October—and late spring. The crowds thin, prices dip, and you can count on Tahoe being beautiful.

Most Lake Tahoe accommodations, restaurants, and even a handful of parks are open year-round, but many visitor centers, mansions, state parks, and beaches are closed from October through May. During those months, winter-sports enthusiasts swamp Tahoe's downhill resorts and cross-country centers, North America's largest concentration of skiing facilities. In summer it's cooler here than in the scorched Sierra Nevada foothills, the clean mountain air is bracingly crisp, and the surface temperature of Lake Tahoe is an invigorating 65°F to 70°F (compared with 40°F to 50°F in winter). This is also the time, however, when it may seem as if every tourist at the lake—100,000 on peak weekends—is in a car on the main road circling the shoreline (especially on Highway 89, just south of Tahoe City; on Highway 28, east of Tahoe City; and on U.S. 50 in South Lake Tahoe). Christmas week and July 4th are the busiest times, and prices go through the roof; plan accordingly.

GETTING HERE AND AROUND

AIR TRAVEL

The nearest airport to Lake Tahoe is Reno–Tahoe International Airport (RNO), in Reno, 50 miles northeast of the closest point on the lake. Airlines serving RNO include Alaska, Allegiant Air, American, Delta, Southwest, and United. Except for Allegiant Air, these airlines plus Aeromexico, Hawaiian, and JetBlue serve Sacramento International Airport (SMF), 112 miles from South Lake Tahoe. North Lake Tahoe Express runs buses ($45 one-way, $85 round-trip) between RNO and towns on the lake's western and northern shores, plus Incline Village, Truckee, Squaw Valley, and Northstar. South Tahoe Express runs buses ($29.75 one-way, $53 round-trip) between Reno–Tahoe Airport and resort hotels in the South Lake Tahoe area.

Airport Contacts Reno–Tahoe International Airport ✉ *2001 E. Plumb La., off U.S. 395/I-580, at Reno-Tahoe International Airport Exit, Reno, Nevada* ☎ *775/328-6400* ⊕ *www.renoairport.com.* **Sacramento International Airport** ✉ *6900 Airport Blvd., 12 miles northwest of downtown off I-5, Sacramento* ☎ *916/929-5411* ⊕ *www.sacramento.aero/smf.*

Transfer Contacts North Lake Tahoe Express ☎ *866/216-5222* ⊕ *www.northlaketahoeexpress.com.* **South Tahoe Express** ☎ *775/325-8944, 866/898-2463* ⊕ *www.southtahoeexpress.com.*

23

BUS TRAVEL

Greyhound stops in San Francisco, Sacramento, Truckee, and Reno. BlueGO ($2 per ride) provides year-round local service in South Lake Tahoe. On the north shore, Tahoe Area Regional Transit (TART; $1.75) operates buses between Tahoma and Incline Village and runs shuttles to Truckee. RTC RIDE buses ($2) serve the Reno area. All local rides require exact change.

In winter, BlueGO provides free ski shuttle service from South Lake Tahoe hotels and resorts to various Heavenly Mountain ski lodge locations. Most of the major ski resorts offer shuttle service to nearby lodging.

Bus Contacts Greyhound ☏ *800/231–2222* ⊕ *www.greyhound.com.* **BlueGO** ☏ *530/541–7149* ⊕ *www.tahoetransportation.org/southtahoe.* **RTC RIDE** ☏ *775/348–7433* ⊕ *www.rtcwashoe.com.* **Tahoe Area Regional Transit (TART)** ☏ *530/550–1212, 800/736–6365* ⊕ *www.placer.ca.gov/ departments/works/transit/tart.*

CAR TRAVEL

Lake Tahoe is 198 miles northeast of San Francisco, a drive of less than four hours in good weather and light traffic—if possible avoid heavy weekend traffic, particularly leaving the San Francisco area for Tahoe on Friday afternoon and returning on Sunday afternoon. The major route is Interstate 80, which cuts through the Sierra Nevada about 14 miles north of the lake. From there Highway 89 and Highway 267 reach the west and north shores, respectively.

U.S. 50 is the more direct route to the south shore, a two-hour drive from Sacramento. From Reno you can get to the north shore by heading south on U.S. 395/Interstate 580 for 10 miles, then west on Highway 431 for 25 miles. For the south shore, head south on U.S. 395/ Interstate 580 through Carson City, and then turn west on U.S. 50 (56 miles total).

The scenic 72-mile highway around the lake is marked Highway 89 on the southwest and west shores, Highway 28 on the north and northeast shores, and U.S. 50 on the east and southeast. Sections of Highway 89 sometimes close during snowy periods, usually at Emerald Bay because of avalanche danger, which makes it impossible to complete the circular drive around the lake. Interstate 80, U.S. 50, and U.S. 395/Interstate 580 are all-weather highways, but there may be delays while snow is cleared during major storms.

Interstate 80 is a four-lane freeway; much of U.S. 50 is only two lanes with no center divider. Carry tire chains from October through May, or rent a four-wheel-drive vehicle. Most rental agencies do not allow tire chains to be used on their vehicles; ask when you book.

Contacts California Highway Patrol ☏ *530/577–1001 South Lake Tahoe* ⊕ *www.chp.ca.gov.* **Caltrans Current Highway Conditions** ☏ *800/427–7623* ⊕ *www.dot.ca.gov.* **Nevada Department of Transportation Road Information** ☏ *877/687–6237* ⊕ *nvroads.com.* **Nevada Highway Patrol** ☏ *775/687–5300* ⊕ *nhp.nv.gov.*

TRAIN TRAVEL

Amtrak's cross-country rail service makes stops in Truckee and Reno. Amtrak also operates several buses daily between Reno and Sacramento to connect with coastal train routes.

Train Contact Amtrak ☎ *800/872-7245* ⊕ *www.amtrak.com.*

OUTDOORS AND BACKCOUNTRY TIPS

If you're planning to spend any time outdoors around Lake Tahoe, whether hiking, climbing, skiing, or camping, be aware that weather conditions can change quickly in the Sierra. To avoid hypothermia, always bring a pocket-size, fold-up rain poncho (available in all sporting-goods stores) to keep you dry. Wear long pants and a hat. Carry plenty of water. Because you'll likely be walking on granite, wear sturdy, closed-toe hiking boots, with soles that grip rock. If you're going into the backcountry, bring a signaling device (such as a mirror), emergency whistle, compass, map, energy bars, and water purifier. When heading out alone, tell someone where you're going and when you plan to return.

If you plan to ski, be aware of resort elevations. In the event of a winter storm, determine the snow level before you choose the resort you'll ski. Often the level can be as high as 7,000 feet, which means rain at some resorts' base areas but snow at others.

BackCountry, in Truckee, operates an excellent website with current information about how and where to (and where not to) ski, mountain bike, and hike in the backcountry around Tahoe. The store also stocks everything from crampons to transceivers. For storm information, check the National Weather Service's website; for ski conditions, visit ⊕ *onthesnow.com.* For reservations at campgrounds in California state parks, contact Reserve America. If you plan to camp in the backcountry of the national forests, you'll need to purchase a wilderness permit, which you can pick up at the forest service office or at a ranger station at any forest entrance. If you plan to ski the backcountry, check the U.S. Forest Service's recorded information for conditions.

Contacts and Information BackCountry ✉ *11400 Donner Pass Rd., at Meadow Way, Truckee* ☎ *530/582-0909 Truckee* ⊕ *www.thebackcountry. net.* **National Weather Service** ⊕ *www.wrh.noaa.gov/rev.* **OntheSnow. com** ⊕ *www.onthesnow.com/california/skireport.html.* **Reserve America** ☎ *800/444-7275* ⊕ *www.reserveamerica.com.* **U.S. Forest Service** ✉ *Office, 35 College Dr., South Lake Tahoe* ☎ *530/543-2600 general information, 530/587-3558 backcountry recording* ⊕ *www.fs.usda.gov/ltbmu.*

TOURS

Lake Tahoe Balloons. Take a hot-air balloon flight over the lake from mid-may through mid-October with this experienced company. The experience begins shortly after sunrise and takes four hours total, including a traditional champagne toast at journey's end. ✉ *Tahoe Keys Marina, South Lake Tahoe* ☎ *530/544–1221, 800/872-9294* ⊕ *www. laketahoeballoons.com* 🎫 *From $295.*

MS Dixie II. The 520-passenger *MS Dixie II*, a stern-wheeler, sails year-round from Zephyr Cove to Emerald Bay on sightseeing and dinner cruises. ✉ *Zephyr Cove Marina, 760 U.S. Hwy. 50, near Church*

St., Zephyr Cove, Nevada ☎ *775/589–4906, 800/238–2463* ⊕ *www. zephyrcove.com/cruises* ✉ *From $49.*

Sierra Cloud. From May to September, the *Sierra Cloud*, a 41-passenger catamaran, departs from the Hyatt Regency beach at Incline Village and cruises the north shore area. ✉ *Hyatt Regency Lake Tahoe, 111 Country Club Dr., Incline Village* ☎ *775/831–4386* ⊕ *www.awsincline. com* ✉ *From $65.*

Tahoe Queen. The 312-passenger *Tahoe Queen*, a partially glass-bottomed paddle wheeler, departs from South Lake Tahoe daily for 2½-hour sightseeing cruises year-round by reservation and 3-hour dinner-dance cruises daily from late spring to early fall (weekly the rest of the year). Fares range from $49 to $75. ✉ *Ski Run Marina, 900 Ski Run Blvd., off U.S. 50, South Lake Tahoe* ☎ *530/543–6191, 800/238–2463* ⊕ *www.zephyrcove.com/cruises* ✉ *From $47.*

Tahoe Boat Cruises. From April to October, this company offers various boating experiences. The *Woodwind II*, a 50-passenger catamaran, sails from Zephyr Cove on regular and Champagne cruises. The company's *Safari Rose*, an 80-foot-long wooden motor yacht, departs from Tahoe Keys Marina for half-day cruises around the lake. From late May to mid-October, their classic wooden boat, the *Tahoe*, takes passengers on an east shore cruise with a walking tour of Thunderbird Lodge historic site. ✉ *Zephyr Cove Resort, 760 U.S. Hwy. 50, near Church St., Zephyr Cove* ☎ *775/588–1881, 888/867–6394* ⊕ *www.tahoecruises. com* ✉ *From $34.*

RESTAURANTS

On weekends and in high season, expect a long wait at the more popular restaurants. And expect to pay resort prices almost everywhere. Some restaurants are only open six out of 12 months a year; during the "shoulder seasons" (from April to May and September to November), some places may close temporarily or limit their hours, so call ahead. Also, check local papers for deals and discounts during this time, especially two-for-one coupons. Many casinos use their restaurants to attract gamblers. Marquees often tout "$8.99 prime rib dinners" or "$2.99 breakfast specials." Some of these meals are downright lousy and they are usually available only in the coffee shops and buffets, but at those prices, it's hard to complain. The finer restaurants in casinos deliver pricier food, as well as reasonable service and a bit of atmosphere. Unless otherwise noted, even the most expensive area restaurants welcome customers in casual clothes.

HOTELS

Quiet inns on the water, suburban-style strip motels, casino hotels, slope-side ski lodges, and house and condo rentals throughout the area constitute the lodging choices at Tahoe. The crowds come in summer and during ski season; reserve as far in advance as possible, especially for holiday periods when prices skyrocket. Spring and fall give you a little more leeway and lower—sometimes significantly lower, especially at casino hotels—rates. Check hotel websites for the best deals.

Head to South Lake Tahoe for the most activities and the widest range of lodging options. Heavenly Village in the heart of town has an ice rink, cinema, shops, fine-dining restaurants, and simple cafés, plus a gondola that will whisk you up to the ski park. Walk two blocks south from downtown, and you can hit the casinos.

Tahoe City, on the west shore, has a small-town atmosphere and is accessible to several nearby ski resorts. A few miles northwest of the lake, Squaw Valley USA has its own self-contained upscale village, an aerial tram to the slopes, and numerous outdoor activities once the snow melts.

Looking for a taste of old Tahoe? The north shore with its woodsy backdrop is your best bet, with Carnelian Bay and Tahoe Vista on the California side. And across the Nevada border are casino resorts where Hollywood's glamour-stars once romped. *Hotel reviews have been shortened. For full information, visit Fodors.com.*

23

WHAT IT COSTS				
	$	$$	$$$	$$$$
Restaurants	under $16	$16–$22	$23–$30	over $30
Hotels	under $121	$121–$175	$176–$250	over $250

Restaurant prices are the average cost of a main course at dinner or, if dinner is not served, at lunch. Hotel prices are the lowest cost of a standard double room in high season.

SKIING AND SNOWBOARDING

The mountains around Lake Tahoe are bombarded by blizzards throughout most winters and sometimes in fall and spring; 10- to 12-foot bases are common. Indeed, the Sierras often have the deepest snowpack on the continent, but because of the relatively mild temperatures over the Pacific, falling snow can be very heavy and wet—it's nicknamed "Sierra Cement" for a reason. The upside is that you can sometimes ski and board as late as May (snowboarding is permitted at all Tahoe ski areas). The major resorts get extremely crowded on weekends. If you're going to ski on a Saturday, arrive early and quit early. Avoid moving with the masses: eat at 11 am or 1:30 pm, not noon. Also consider visiting the ski areas with few high-speed lifts or limited lodging and real estate at their bases: Alpine Meadows, Sugar Bowl, Homewood, Mt. Rose, Sierra-at-Tahoe, Diamond Peak, and Kirkwood. And to find out the true ski conditions, talk to waiters and bartenders—most of them are ski bums.

The Lake Tahoe area is also a great destination for Nordic skiers. "Skinny" (i.e., cross-country) skiing at the resorts can be costly, but you get the benefits of machine grooming and trail preparation. If it's bargain Nordic you're after, take advantage of thousands of acres of public forest and parkland trails.

VISITOR INFORMATION

Contacts Lake Tahoe Visitors Authority ✉ *169 U.S. Hwy. 50, Stateline, Nevada* ☎ *775/588–5900, 800/288–2463* ⊕ *tahoesouth.com.* **U.S. Forest Service** ☎ *530/587–3558 backcountry recording* ⊕ *www.fs.usda.gov/tahoe.*

THE CALIFORNIA SIDE

The most hotels, restaurants, ski resorts, and state parks are on the California side of the lake, but you'll also encounter the most congestion and developed areas.

SOUTH LAKE TAHOE

50 miles south of Reno, 198 miles northeast of San Francisco.

The city of South Lake Tahoe's raison d'être is tourism: the casinos of adjacent Stateline, Nevada; the ski slopes at Heavenly Mountain; the beaches, docks, bike trails, and campgrounds all around the south shore; and the backcountry of Eldorado National Forest and Desolation Wilderness. The main road into town, however, shows less attractive features: older motels, strip malls, and low-rise prefab-looking buildings that line both sides of U.S. 50. Though there are plenty of places to stay, we haven't recommended many because they're not top choices. The small city's saving grace is its convenient location and bevy of services, as well as its gorgeous lake views.

GETTING HERE AND AROUND

The main route into and through South Lake Tahoe is U.S. 50; signs say "Lake Tahoe Boulevard" in town. Arrive by car or, if coming from Reno Airport, take the South Tahoe Express bus. BlueGO operates daily bus service in the south shore area year-round, plus a ski shuttle from the large hotels to Heavenly Ski Resort in the winter.

ESSENTIALS

Visitor Information Lake Tahoe Visitors Authority ⊠ *Visitor Center, 169 U.S. Hwy. 50, at Kingsbury Grade, Stateline, Nevada* ☎ *775/588–5900, 800/288–2463* ⊕ *tahoesouth.com* ⊠ *Visitor Center, 3066 Lake Tahoe Blvd., at San Francisco Ave.* ☎ *530/541–5255* ⊕ *tahoesouth.com.*

EXPLORING

FAMILY

Fodor'sChoice

★

Heavenly Gondola. Whether you ski or not, you'll appreciate the impressive view of Lake Tahoe from the Heavenly Gondola. Its eight-passenger cars travel from the middle of town 2.4 miles up the mountain in 15 minutes. When the weather's fine, you can take one of three hikes around the mountaintop and then have lunch at Tamarack Lodge. Heavenly also offers day care for children. ⊠ *4080 Lake Tahoe Blvd.* ☎ *775/586–7000, 800/432–8365* ⊕ *www.skiheavenly.com* ☜ *$45* ☉ *Summer, daily 10–5; winter, weekdays 9–4, weekends 8:30–4.*

Heavenly Village. The centerpiece of South Lake Tahoe's efforts to reinvent itself and provide a focal point for tourism, this complex at the base of the gondola has restaurants, some good shopping, a cinema, an arcade for kids, and the Heavenly Village Outdoor Ice Rink. ⊠ *1001 Heavenly Village Way, at U.S. 50* ⊕ *www.theshopsatheavenly.com.*

WHERE TO EAT

$

ECLECTIC

✕ **Blue Angel Café.** A favorite of locals, who fill the dozen or so wooden tables, this cozy spot with Wi-Fi serves basic sandwiches and salads along with internationally inspired dishes like chipotle shrimp tacos and Thai curry. On cold days warm up with wine or an espresso in front of the fireplace. [$] *Average main: $13* ✉ *1132 Ski Run Blvd., at Larch Ave.* ☎ *530/544–6544* 🌐 *www.theblueangelcafe.com.*

$ MEXICAN 🍴 **The Cantina.** A casual Tahoe favorite, the Cantina serves traditional Mexican dishes—huge burritos, enchiladas, and rellenos—as well as stylized Southwestern fare such as smoked-chicken polenta with grilled vegetables, and crab cakes in jalapeño cream sauce. The bartenders make great margaritas and serve 30 different kinds of beer. [$] *Average main: $13* ✉ *765 Emerald Bay Rd., Hwy. 89, at 10th St.* ☎ *530/544–1233* 🌐 *www.cantinatahoe.com* ✍ *Reservations not accepted.*

$$$$ ECLECTIC Fodor's Choice ★ 🍴 **Evan's American Gourmet Cafe.** Its excellent service, world-class food, and superb wine list make this the top choice for high-end dining in South Lake. Inside a converted cabin, the restaurant serves creative American cuisine that includes catch-of-the-day seafood offerings and meat dishes such as rack of lamb marinated with rosemary and garlic and served with raspberry demi-glace. Some diners find the table spacing a tad close. Evan's is intimate, to be sure, but the food always pleases. [$] *Average main: $32* ✉ *536 Emerald Bay Rd., Hwy. 89, at 15th St.* ☎ *530/542–1990* 🌐 *evanstahoe.com* 🕓 *No lunch.*

$$$ SEAFOOD 🍴 **Fresh Ketch.** Fish is the specialty at this dockside restaurant, where you can look out at the yachts in the Tahoe Keys marina. The upstairs dining room serves full dinners (no lunch) that feature fresh seafood and meats. The menu downstairs in the lively fireside seafood bar, beginning with lunch, is lighter and more eclectic, with reasonably priced hot and cold appetizers, salads, and sandwiches served through dinner. Have a hankering for something sweet? Stop by for dessert only and enjoy the view. There's live entertainment on Tuesday, Thursday, and Friday nights year-round, and on Saturday in summer. [$] *Average main: $23* ✉ *2435 Venice Dr., off Tahoe Keys Blvd.* ☎ *530/541–5683* 🌐 *thefreshketch.com.*

$$ ECLECTIC 🍴 **Freshies.** When you've had your fill of junk food, come here for delicious, healthful meals prepared with an "earth-friendly" attitude and commitment. Specialties include seafood and vegetarian dishes, but good grilled meats are always available, such as teriyaki steak and Hawaiian spare ribs with grilled pineapple. Freshies is in a minimall, and can be loud and crowded—try to snag a spot on the upstairs lake-view deck. [$] *Average main: $16* ✉ *Lakeview Plaza, 3330 Lake Tahoe Blvd., at Fremont Ave.* ☎ *530/542–3630* 🌐 *www.freshiestahoe.com* ✍ *Reservations not accepted* 🕓 *Closed Nov. until weekend after Thanksgiving.*

$$$$ ASIAN 🍴 **Kalani's.** Fresh-off-the-plane seafood gets delivered from the Honolulu fish market to Heavenly Village's sexiest (and priciest) restaurant. The sleek, white-tablecloth dining room is decked out with carved bamboo, a burnt-orange color palette, and a modern-glass sculpture, all of which complement contemporary Pacific Rim specialties such as melt-from-the-bone baby back pork ribs with sesame-garlic soy sauce. Sushi selections with inventive rolls and sashimi combos, plus less expensive vegetarian dishes, add depth to the menu. [$] *Average main: $34* ✉ *1001 Heavenly Village Way, #26, at U.S. 50* ☎ *530/544–6100* 🌐 *www.kalanis.com* 🕓 *No lunch weekdays in winter.*

$ THAI 🍴 **Orchid's Thai.** If you're hungry for Thai, stop here for good food at reasonable prices served in an attractive dining room. Tucked into a tiny mall, the restaurant isn't fantastic, but it's reliably good, and when every place in town is booked, this is a great backup. Carry outs are welcome. $ *Average main: $12* ⊠ *2180 Lake Tahoe Blvd., at 3rd St.* ☎ *530/544–5541* ⊘ *No lunch Sun.*

$ ✕ **Red Hut Café.** A vintage-1959 Tahoe diner, all chrome and red plastic,
AMERICAN the Red Hut is a tiny place with a wildly popular breakfast menu: huge omelets; banana, pecan, and coconut waffles; and other tasty vittles. A second South Lake branch has a soda fountain and is the only one that serves dinner. There's a third location in Stateline. $ *Average main: $9* ⊠ *2723 Lake Tahoe Blvd., near Blue Lake Ave.* ☎ *530/541–9024* ⊕ *www.redhutcafe.com* ⚭ *Reservations not accepted* ⊘ *No dinner* $ *Average main: $9* ⊠ *3660 Lake Tahoe Blvd., at Ski Run Blvd.* ☎ *530/544–1595* ⊕ *www.redhutcafe.com* $ *Average main: $9* ⊠ *229 Kingsbury Grade, off U.S. 50, Stateline, Nevada* ☎ *775/588–7488* ⊕ *www.redhutcafe.com* ⊘ *No dinner.*

$$ ✕ **Scusa! Italian Ristorante.** This longtime favorite turns out big plates
ITALIAN of veal scallopine, chicken piccata, and garlicky linguine with clams— straightforward Italian-American food (and lots of it), served in an intimate dining room warmed by a crackling fire on many nights. There's an outdoor patio that's open in warm weather. $ *Average main: $20* ⊠ *2543 Lake Tahoe Blvd., at Sierra Blvd.* ☎ *530/542–0100* ⊕ *www. scusalaketahoe.com* ⊘ *No lunch.*

WHERE TO STAY

$$$ 🛏 **Black Bear Inn Bed and Breakfast.** The rooms and cabins at South Lake
B&B/INN Tahoe's most luxurious inn feature 19th-century American antiques,
Fodor's Choice fine art, and fireplaces; cabins also have kitchenettes. **Pros:** intimate;
★ serene, woodsy grounds; within walking distance of good restaurants. **Cons:** not appropriate for children under 16; pricey. $ *Rooms from: $225* ⊠ *1202 Ski Run Blvd.* ☎ *530/544–4451, 877/232–7466* ⊕ *www. tahoeblackbear.com* ⤹ *5 rooms, 4 cabins* ⦿| *Breakfast.*

$$ 🛏 **Forest Suites Resort.** The location of this resort is excellent—5½ acres
HOTEL bordering a forest, right behind the Heavenly Village, a half block from the casinos, and adjacent to a supermarket, cinema, and shops. **Pros:** as close to the city center as pricier hotels; good bet for families. **Cons:** an older facility with some rooms still being updated. $ *Rooms from: $147* ⊠ *1 Lake Pkwy.* ☎ *530/541–6655, 800/822–5950* ⊕ *www.forestsuites. com* ⤹ *17 rooms, 102 suites* ⦿| *Breakfast.*

$$$ 🛏 **Inn by the Lake.** Across the road from a beach, this "inn" is essen-
HOTEL tially a high-end motel, with spacious, spotless rooms and suites. **Pros:** great value; stellar service; short drive from Heavenly Mountain. **Cons:** on busy Lake Tahoe Boulevard. $ *Rooms from: $180* ⊠ *3300 Lake Tahoe Blvd., at Fremont Ave.* ☎ *530/542–0330, 800/877–1466* ⊕ *www.innbythelake.com* ⤹ *90 rooms, 10 suites* ⦿| *No meals.*

$$ 🛏 **Marriott's Grand Residence and Timber Lodge.** You can't beat the loca-
RESORT tion of these two gigantic, modern condominium complexes right at the base of Heavenly Gondola, smack in the center of town. **Pros:** central location; great for families; near excellent restaurants. **Cons:** can be jam-packed on weekends. $ *Rooms from: $175* ⊠ *1001 Heavenly Village Way* ☎ *530/542–8400 Marriott's Grand Residence, 800/845–5279, 530/542–6600 Marriott's Timber Lodge* ⊕ *www.marriott.com* ⤹ *431 condos* ⦿| *No meals.*

Continued on page 890

TAHOE A LAKE FOR ALL SEASONS

by Christine Vovakes

Best known for its excellent skiing, Lake Tahoe is a year-round resort and outdoor sports destination. All kinds of activities are available, from snowboarding some of the best runs in North America and gliding silently along the lakeshore on cross-country skis in winter, to mountain biking through lush forests and puttering around the alpine lake in a classic yacht in summer. Whatever you do—and whenever you visit—the sapphire lake is at the center of it all, pulling you out of your posh resort or rustic cabin rental like a giant blue magnet. There are many ways to enjoy and experience Lake Tahoe, but here are some of our favorites.

(top) Heavenly Mountain Resort, (bottom) Sand Harbor Beach.

WINTER WONDERLAND

Home to a host of world-famous Sierra resorts, Tahoe is a premier ski destination. Add sledding, ice skating, cross-country skiing, and jingly sleigh rides under the stars to the mix, and you begin to get a glimpse of Tahoe's cold-weather potential.

DOWNHILL SKIING AND SNOWBOARDING

Even if you've never made it off the bunny hill before, you should definitely hit the slopes here at least once. The Lake Tahoe region has the deepest snowpack in North America, and you can ski from Thanksgiving until it melts—which is sometimes July.

One of the top-rated resorts in the country, Olympic Valley's **Squaw Valley USA** hosted the 1960 Winter Olympics that put Tahoe on the map. A great classic resort is **Sugar Bowl,** where you can revel in a bit of Disney nostalgia while you swoop down the slopes. Walt helped start the resort, which opened in 1939 and had Tahoe's first chair lift.

Even if you're not hitting the slopes at South Lake Tahoe's **Heavenly Mountain,** be sure to take a ride on their **Heavenly Gondola** so you can take in awe-inspiring views of the frozen circle of white ice that rings the brilliant lake.

(top) Skiing in Lake Tahoe,. (above left) Cross-country skiing, (above right) Snow boarding at Heavenly Mountain.

SKI RESORT	LOCATION	TRAILS	ACRES	BEGIN.	INTER.	ADV./ EXP.
CALIFORNIA						
Alpine Meadows	Tahoe City	100	2,400	25%	40%	35%
Heavenly Mountain	South Lake Tahoe	97	4,800	20%	45%	35%
Homewood Mountain	Homewood	64	1,260	15%	50%	35%
Kirkwood	Kirkwood	81	2,300	15%	50%	35%
Northstar California	Truckee	97	3,170	13%	60%	27%
Sierra-at-Tahoe	South Lake Tahoe	46	2,000	25%	50%	25%
Squaw Valley USA	Olympic Valley	170	3,600	25%	45%	30%
Sugar Bowl	Truckee	102	1,650	17%	45%	38%
NEVADA						
Diamond Peak	Incline Village	30	655	18%	46%	36%
Mt. Rose Ski Tahoe	Incline Village	61	1,200	20%	30%	50%

CROSS-COUNTRY SKIING

Downhill skiing may get all the glory here, but Lake Tahoe is also a premier cross-country (or Nordic) skiing destination. "Skinny" skiers basically have two options: pony up the cash to ski the groomed trails at a resort, or hit the more rugged (but cheaper—or free) public forest and parkland trails.

Beautiful **Royal Gorge** is the country's largest cross-country ski resort. Other resorts with good skinny skiing include **Kirkwood, Squaw Valley USA, Tahoe Donner,** and **Northstar California.** Private operators **Spooner Lake Cross Country** and **Hope Valley Cross Country** will also have you shushing through pristine powder in no time.

For bargain Nordic on public trails, head to **Sugar Pine Point State Park.** Other good low-cost cross-country skiing locations include **Donner Memorial State Park, Lake Tahoe—Nevada State Park,** and **Tahoe Meadows** near Incline Village.

CAUTION⚠ Cross-country skiing is relaxing and provides a great cardiovascular workout—but it's also quite strenuous. If it's your first time out or you're not in great shape, start out slow.

SLEDDING AND TUBING

Kirkwood, Squaw Valley USA, Boreal, Soda Springs, and many other Tahoe resorts have areas where you can barrel down hills on inflatable tubes. Some good non-resort sledding spots are **Tahoe National Forest** and **Tahoe Meadows,** near Incline Village.

ICE SKATING

Want to work on your triple lutz? You can skate seasonally at **Heavenly Village Outdoor Ice Rink,** or year-round at the **South Tahoe Ice Arena.** Other great gliding spots include **Squaw Valley USA's Olympic Ice Pavilion.**

WARMING UP

To defrost your ski-stiff limbs, take a dip in a resort's heated pool, de-stress in a hotel spa...or enjoy a brandy by the fire at a cozy restaurant. Our favorite places to warm up and imbibe include Graham's of Squaw Valley and Soule Domain, near Crystal Bay.

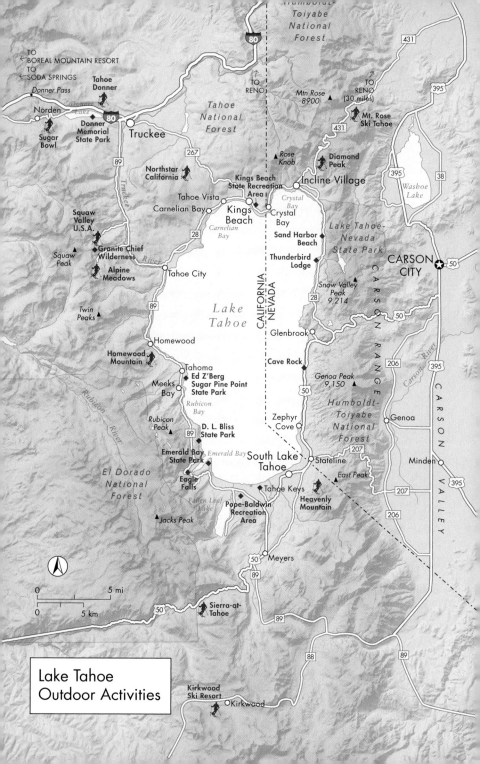

Lake Tahoe
Outdoor Activities

FROSTY CATCH

Too cold to fish? Nonsense. South Lake's Tahoe Sport Fishing runs charters year-round with crews that will clean and package your catch.

IN THE WARM CALIFORNIA SUN

Summer in Tahoe means diving into pure alpine waters, hiking a mountain trail with stunning lake views, or kayaking on glorious Emerald Bay. From tennis to golf to fishing, you can fill every waking moment with outdoor activity—or just stretch out on a sunny lakeside beach with a good book and a cool drink.

HIKING

The lake is surrounded by protected parkland, offering countless opportunities to take jaunts through the woods or rambles along lakeside trails.

One of the most unique hiking experiences in Tahoe is at Heavenly Mountain Resorts, where the **Heavenly Gondola** runs up to three nice trails. When you're done enjoying sky-high views of the lake, grab lunch at the nearby Tamarack Lodge.

Another out-of-the-ordinary option is a romantic moonlit trek. **Camp Richardson** has lots of trails and a long curve of lake to catch the moonlight.

In **Eldorado National Forest and Desolation Wilderness,** you can hike a small portion of the famous Pacific Crest Trail and branch off to discover beautiful backcountry lakes. Nearby **Eagle Falls** has stunning views of Emerald Bay.

One of Tahoe's best hikes is a 4½-mi trail at **D.L. Bliss State Park;** it has lovely views of the lake and leads to bizarre **Vikingsholm** (*see box on next page*).

Other great places to hike in Lake Tahoe include **Sugar Pines Point State Park, Olympic Valley's Granite Chief Wilderness, Squaw Valley USA's High Camp, Donner Memorial State Park,** and **Lake Tahoe—Nevada State Park.**

You can pick up hiking maps at the **U.S. Forest Service** office at the **Lake Tahoe Visitor Center.**

HIT THE BEACH

Lake Tahoe has some gorgeous lakeside sunbathing terrain; get to perennial favorite **Kings Beach State Recreation Area** early to snag a choice spot. Or, if you never want to be far from the water, reserve one of the prime beachside spots at **D.L. Bliss State Park Campground.**

(left) Fannette Island in Emerald Bay. (right) A young man leaps off a cliff into Lake Tahoe.

MOUNTAIN BIKING AND CYCLING

You don't need to be preparing for the Tour de France to join the biking fun. While there are myriad rugged mountain biking trails to choose from, the region is also blessed with many flat trails.

Truly intrepid cyclists take the lift up **Northstar California** and hit the resort's 100 mi of trails. Another good option is **Sugar Pine Point State Park,** where you can hop on a 10-mi trail to Tahoe City.

Tahoe Sports in South Lake Tahoe is a good place for bike rentals and tips for planning your trip. **Cyclepaths Mountain Bikes Adventures** in Truckee leads guided mountain biking tours, and **Flume Trail Bikes** on the Nevada side of the lake, near Glenbrook, rents bikes and operates a bike shuttle to popular trails.

LAKE TOURS AND KAYAKING

One of the best ways to experience the lake is by getting out on the water.

The *Tahoe Queen* is a huge glass-bottomed paddle-wheel boat that offers sightseeing cruises and dinner-dance cruises. The *Sierra Cloud, MS Dixie II,* and

Woodwind II also ply the lake, offering a variety of enjoyable cruises. *(See Tour Options in the Planner section of this chapter for contact info.)*

Another enjoyable option is taking a throwback wooden cruiser from Tahoe Keys Marina in South Lake Tahoe to tour **Thunderbird Lodge,** the meticulously crafted stone mansion built in 1936 by socialite George Whittell.

For a more personal experience, rent a kayak and glide across **Emerald Bay. Kayak Tahoe** in South Lake Tahoe will have you paddling in no time.

VIKINGS?

As you kayak around Tahoe, you'll see many natural wonders...and a few manmade ones as well. One of the most impressive and strangest is **Vikingsholm**, a grand 1929 estate that looks like an ancient Viking castle. You can see it from **Emerald Bay** (which, appropriately, resembles a fjord), or hike to it via a steep one-mile trail.

(left top) Biking along the shore. (left bottom) Kayaking. (right) Steamboat cruise.

$$ **Sorensen's Resort.** Escape civili-
RESORT zation by staying in a log cabin at
this woodsy 165-acre resort within
the Eldorado National Forest, 20
minutes south of town. **Pros:** gor-
geous, rustic setting. **Cons:** nearest
nightlife is 20 miles away. $ *Rooms
from: $135* ✉ *14255 Hwy. 88,
Hope Valley* ☎ *530/694–2203,
800/423–9949* ⊕ *www.sorensens
resort.com* ⇄ *2 rooms with shared
bath, 29 cabins, 5 houses* ⍟ *No meals.*

NIGHTLIFE

Most of the area's nightlife is concentrated in the casinos over the bor-
der in Stateline. To avoid slot machines and blinking lights, try the
California-side nightspots in and near Heavenly Village. The Marriott
Timber Lodge bars are always dependable.

BARS

Mc P's Irish Pub & Grill. You can hear live bands—rock, jazz, blues, alter-
native—on most nights at Mc P's, across the street from the Heavenly
Gondola. ✉ *4093 Lake Tahoe Blvd., near Friday Ave.* ☎ *530/542–4435*
⊕ *www.mcpspubtahoe.com.*

SPORTS AND THE OUTDOORS

FISHING

Tahoe Sport Fishing. One of the area's largest and oldest fishing-charter
services offers morning and afternoon trips. Outings include all neces-
sary gear and bait, and the crew cleans and packages your catch. ✉ *900
Ski Run Blvd., off U.S. 50* ☎ *530/541–5448, 800/696–7797 in CA*
⊕ *www.tahoesportfishing.com* ⍟ *From $90.*

GOLF

Lake Tahoe Golf Course. Set in a meadow with mountain views, this public
championship course was designed by William Bell. The Upper Truckee
River comes into play on several holes. The twilight rate ($29) starts
at 4 pm. ✉ *2500 Emerald Bay Rd, Hwy. 89/U.S. 50* ☎ *530/577–0788*
⊕ *www.laketahoegc.com* ⍟ *$65 for weekdays, $85 for weekends; $20
for golf cart* ⚑ *18 holes, 6741 yards, par 71.*

HIKING

The south shore is a great jumping-off point for day treks into nearby
Eldorado National Forest and Desolation Wilderness.

Desolation Wilderness. Trails within the 63,960-acre wilderness lead to
gorgeous backcountry lakes and mountain peaks. It's called Desolation
Wilderness for a reason, so bring a topographic map and compass, and
carry water and food. In summer, you can access this area by boarding a
boat taxi (⍟ *$12 one-way*) at **Echo Chalet** (✉ *9900 Echo Lakes Rd., off
U.S. 50* ☎ *530/659–7207* ⊕ *www.echochalet.com*) and crossing Echo
Lake. The Pacific Crest Trail also traverses Desolation Wilderness. ✉ *El
Dorado National Forest Information Center* ☎ *530/644–6048* ⊕ *www.
fs.usda.gov/eldorado.*

Pacific Crest Trail. Hike a couple of miles on this famous mountain trail that stretches from Mexico to Canada. ✉ *Echo Summit, about 12 miles southwest of South Lake Tahoe off U.S. 50* ☎ *916/285–1846, 888/728–7245* ⊕ *www.pcta.org.*

ICE-SKATING

FAMILY **Heavenly Village Outdoor Ice Rink.** If you're here in winter, practice your jumps and turns at this rink between the gondola and the cinema. ✉ *1001 Heavenly Village Way* ☎ *530/542–4230* ⊕ *www.theshopsatheavenly. com* 🖃 *$20; skate rental available* ☉ *Nov.–Mar., Mon.–Fri, noon–8; Sat.–Sun.10–8, weather permitting.*

South Tahoe Ice Arena. For year-round fun, head to this city-operated, NHL regulation–size indoor rink where you can rent equipment and sign up for lessons. In the evening the lights are turned low and a disco ball lights up the ice. ✉ *1176 Rufus Allen Blvd.* ☎ *530/542–6056* ⊕ *tahoearena.com* 🖃 *$15; includes skate rental* ☉ *Daily, hrs vary.*

KAYAKING

Kayak Tahoe. Sign up for lessons and excursions (to the south shore, Emerald Bay, and Sand Harbor), offered from May through September. You can also rent a kayak and paddle solo on the lake. ✉ *Timber Cove Marina, 3411 Lake Tahoe Blvd., at Balbijou Rd.* ☎ *530/544–2011* ⊕ *www.kayaktahoe.com* 🖃 *From $40.*

MOUNTAIN BIKING

Tahoe Sports Ltd. You can rent road and mountain bikes and get tips on where to ride from the friendly staff at this full-service sports store. ✉ *Tahoe Crescent V Shopping Center, 4000 Lake Tahoe Blvd.* ☎ *530/542–4000* ⊕ *www.tahoesportsltd.com.*

SKIING

If you don't want to pay the high cost of rental equipment at the resorts, you'll find reasonable prices and expert advice at Tahoe Sports Ltd. (⇨ *Mountain Biking, above*).

Fodor's Choice **Heavenly Mountain Resort.** Straddling two states, vast Heavenly Moun-
★ tain Resort—composed of nine peaks, two valleys, and four base-lodge areas, along with the largest snowmaking system in the western United States—has terrain for every skier. Beginners can choose wide, well-groomed trails, accessed from the California Lodge or the gondola from downtown South Lake Tahoe; kids have short and gentle runs in the Enchanted Forest area all to themselves. The Sky Express high-speed quad chair whisks intermediate and advanced skiers to the summit for wide cruisers or steep tree-skiing. Mott and Killebrew canyons draw experts to the Nevada side for steep chutes and thick-timber slopes. For snowboarders and tricksters, there are five different terrain parks.

The ski school is big and offers everything from learn-to-ski packages to canyon-adventure tours. Call about ski and boarding camps. Skiing lessons are available for children ages four and up; there's day care for infants older than six weeks. ✉ *Ski Run Blvd., off U.S. 50* ☎ *775/586–7000, 800/432–8365* ⊕ *www.skiheavenly.com* ⌁ *97 trails on 4,800 acres, rated 20% beginner, 45% intermediate, 35% expert. Longest run 5½ miles, base 6,540 feet, summit 10,067 feet. Lifts: 30, including 1 aerial tram, 1 gondola, 2 high-speed 6-passenger lifts, and 8 high-speed quads.*

23

Hope Valley Cross Country. Operating from a yurt at Pickett's Junction, Hope Valley provides lessons and equipment rentals to prepare you for cross-country skiing and snowshoeing. The outfit has 60 miles of trails through Humboldt–Toiyabe National Forest, 10 of which are groomed. ✉ *Hwy. 88, at Hwy. 89, Hope Valley* ☎ *530/721–2015* ⊕ *www.hopevalleyoutdoors.com.*

Kirkwood Ski Resort. Thirty-six miles south of Lake Tahoe, Kirkwood is the hard-core skiers' and boarders' favorite south-shore mountain, known for its craggy gulp-and-go chutes, sweeping cornices, steep-aspect glade skiing, and high base elevation. But there's also fantastic terrain for newbies and intermediates down wide-open bowls, through wooded gullies, and along rolling tree-lined trails. Tricksters can show off in two terrain parks on jumps, wall rides, rails, and a half-pipe, all visible from the base area. The mountain gets hammered with more than 600 inches of snow annually, and often has the most in all of North America. If you're into out-of-bounds skiing, check out Expedition Kirkwood, a backcountry-skills program that teaches basic safety awareness. Kirkwood is also the only Tahoe resort to offer Cat-skiing. If you're into cross-country, the resort has 80 km (50 miles) of superb groomed-track skiing, with skating lanes, instruction, and rentals. Nonskiers can snowshoe, snow-skate, and go dogsledding or snow-tubing. The children's ski school has programs for ages three to 12. ✉ *1501 Kirkwood Meadows Dr., off Hwy. 88, 14 miles west of Hwy. 89, Kirkwood, Kirkwood* ☎ *800/967–7500 information, 209/258–7248 cross-country, 209/258–7293 lodging information, 877/547–5966 snow phone* ⊕ *www.kirkwood.com* ☞ *81 trails on 2,300 acres, rated 15% beginner, 50% intermediate, 20% advanced, 15% expert. Longest run 2½ miles, base 7,800 feet, summit 9,800 feet. Lifts: 15, including 2 high-speed quads.*

Sierra-at-Tahoe. Often overlooked by skiers and boarders rushing to Heavenly or Kirkwood, Sierra-at-Tahoe has meticulously groomed intermediate slopes, some of the best tree-skiing in California, and gated backcountry access. Extremely popular with snowboarders, Sierra also has six terrain parks, including a super-pipe with 17-foot walls. For nonskiers there's a snow-tubing hill. Sierra has a low-key atmosphere that's great for families. Kids and beginners take the slow routes in the Mellow Yellow Zone. ✉ *1111 Sierra-at-Tahoe Rd., 12 miles from South Lake Tahoe off U.S. 50, past Echo Summit, Twin Bridges* ☎ *530/659–7453 information, 530/659–7475 snow phone* ⊕ *www.sierraattahoe.com* ☞ *46 trails on 2,000 acres, rated 25% beginner, 50% intermediate, 25% advanced. Longest run 2½ miles, base 6,640 feet, summit 8,852 feet. Lifts: 14, including 3 high-speed quads.*

POPE-BALDWIN RECREATION AREA

5 miles west of South Lake Tahoe.

To the west of downtown South Lake Tahoe, U.S. 50 and Highway 89 come together, forming an intersection nicknamed "the Y." If you head northwest on Highway 89, also called Emerald Bay Road, and follow the lakefront, commercial development gives way to national forests and state parks. One of these is Pope-Baldwin Recreation Area.

GETTING HERE AND AROUND

The entrance to the Pope-Baldwin Recreation Area is on the east side of Emerald Bay Road. The area is closed to vehicles in winter, but you can cross-country ski here.

EXPLORING

Tallac Historic Site. At this site, you can stroll or picnic lakeside, and then explore three historic estates. The **Pope House** is the magnificently restored 1894 mansion of George S. Pope, who made his money in shipping and lumber and played host to the business and cultural elite of 1920s America. The **Baldwin Museum** is in the estate that once belonged to entrepreneur "Lucky" Baldwin; today it houses a collection of family memorabilia and Washoe Indian artifacts. The **Valhalla** (⊕ *valhallatahoe.com*), with a spectacular floor-to-ceiling stone fireplace, belonged to Walter Heller. Its Grand Hall and a lakeside boathouse, refurbished as a theater, host summertime concerts, plays, and cultural activities. Docents conduct tours of the Pope House in summer; call for tour times. In winter you can cross-country ski around the site. ⊠ *Hwy. 89* ☎ *530/541–5227 late May–Oct., 530/543–2600 year-round* ⊕ *tahoeheritage.org* ☜ *Free, Pope House tour $8* ⊙ *Grounds: daily sunrise–sunset. Pope House and Baldwin Museum: late May–late Sept., call for hrs.*

FAMILY **Taylor Creek Visitor Center.** At this center operated by the U.S. Forest Service, you can visit the site of a Washoe Indian settlement; walk self-guided trails through meadow, marsh, and forest; and inspect the Stream Profile Chamber, an underground display with windows right into Taylor Creek. In fall you may see spawning kokanee salmon digging their nests. In summer Forest Service naturalists organize discovery walks and evening programs. ⊠ *Hwy. 89, 3 miles north of junction with U.S. 50* ☎ *530/543–2674 late May–Oct., 530/543–2600 year-round* ⊕ *www.fs.usda.gov/recarea/ltbmu/recarea/?recid=11785* ☜ *Free* ⊙ *Late May–late Sept., 10–4; call for Oct. hrs.*

23

Fjord-like Emerald Bay is quite possibly the prettiest part of Lake Tahoe.

EMERALD BAY STATE PARK

4 miles west of Pope-Baldwin Recreation Area.

You can hike, bike, swim, camp, scuba dive, kayak, or tour a lookalike Viking castle at this state park. Or you can simply enjoy the most popular tourist stop on Lake Tahoe's circular drive: the high cliff overlooking Emerald Bay, famed for its jewel-like shape and color.

GETTING HERE AND AROUND

The entrance to Emerald Bay State Park is on the east side of a narrow, twisting section of Highway 89. Caution is the keyword for both drivers and pedestrians. The park is closed to vehicles in winter.

EXPLORING

Fodor's Choice
★
Emerald Bay. A massive glacier millions of years ago carved this 3-mile-long and 1-mile-wide fjordlike inlet. Famed for its jewel-like shape and colors, the bay surrounds Fannette, Tahoe's only island. Highway 89 curves high above the lake through Emerald Bay State Park; from the Emerald Bay lookout, the centerpiece of the park, you can survey the whole scene. This is one of the don't-miss views of Lake Tahoe. The light is best in mid- to late morning, when the bay's colors really pop. ⊠ *Hwy. 89, 20 miles south of Tahoe City* ☎ *530/525–7232* ⊕ *www.parks.ca.gov* ⊠ *$10 parking fee.*

Vikingsholm. This 38-room estate was completed in 1929. The original owner, Lora Knight, had this precise copy of a 1,200-year-old Viking castle built out of materials native to the area. She furnished it with Scandinavian antiques and hired artisans to build period reproductions. The sod roof sprouts wildflowers each spring. There are picnic tables nearby and a gray-sand beach for strolling. A steep 1-mile-long trail from the Emerald Bay lookout leads down to Vikingsholm, and the hike back up is hard (especially if you're not yet acclimated to the elevation), although there are benches and stone culverts to rest on. At the 150-foot peak of Fannette Island are the ruins of a stone structure known as the Tea House, built in 1928 so that Knight's guests could have a place to enjoy afternoon refreshments after a motorboat ride. The island is off-limits from February through mid-June to protect nesting Canada geese. The rest of the year it's open for day use. ⊠ *Hwy. 89* ☎ *530/541–6498 summer, 530/525–7232 year-round* ⊕ *www.vikingsholm.com* ✉ *Day-use parking fee $10; mansion tour $10* ☼ *Late May–Sept., daily 10:30–4.*

SPORTS AND THE OUTDOORS
HIKING
Eagle Falls. To reach these falls, leave your car in the parking lot of the Eagle Falls picnic area (near Vikingsholm; arrive early for a good spot), and walk up the short but fairly steep canyon nearby. You'll have a brilliant panorama of Emerald Bay from this spot near the boundary of Desolation Wilderness. For a strenuous full-day hike, continue 5 miles, past Eagle Lake, to Upper and Middle Velma Lakes. Pick up trail maps at Taylor Creek Visitor Center in summer, or year-round at the main U.S. Forest Service Office in South Lake Tahoe, at 35 College Drive. ⊠ *Hwy. 89, South Lake Tahoe.*

D.L. BLISS STATE PARK

3 miles north of Emerald Bay State Park, 17 miles south of Tahoe City.

This park shares six miles of shoreline with adjacent Emerald Bay State Park and has two white-sand beaches. Hike the Rubicon Trail for stunning views of the lake.

GETTING HERE AND AROUND
The entrance to D.L. Bliss State Park is on the east side of Highway 89 just north of Emerald Bay. No vehicles are allowed in when the park is closed for the season.

EXPLORING
D.L. Bliss State Park. This park takes its name from Duane LeRoy Bliss, a 19th-century lumber magnate. At one time Bliss owned nearly 75% of Tahoe's lakefront, along with local steamboats, railroads, and banks. The park shares 6 miles of shoreline with Emerald Bay State Park; combined the two parks cover 1,830 acres, 744 of which the Bliss family donated to the state. At the north end of Bliss is Rubicon Point, which overlooks one of the lake's deepest spots. Short trails lead to an old lighthouse and Balancing Rock, which weighs 250,000 pounds and balances on a fist of granite. The 4.5-mile Rubicon Trail—one of Tahoe's premier hikes—leads to Vikingsholm and provides stunning lake views. Two white-sand beaches front some of Tahoe's warmest water. ⊠ *Hwy. 89* ☎ *530/525–3345, 800/777–0369* ⊕ *www.parks.ca.gov* ✉ *$8 per vehicle, day use* ☼ *Late May–Sept., daily sunrise–sunset.*

ED Z'BERG SUGAR PINE POINT STATE PARK

8 miles north of D. L. Bliss State Park, 10 miles south of Tahoe City.

Visitors love to hike, swim, and fish here in the summer, but this park is also popular in winter, when a small campground remains open. Eleven miles of cross-country ski and snowshoe trails allow beginners and experienced enthusiasts alike to whoosh through pine forests and glide past the lake.

GETTING HERE AND AROUND

The entrance to Sugar Pine Point is on the east side of Highway 89, about a mile south of Tahoma. A bike trail links Tahoe City to the park.

EXPLORING

Hellman-Ehrman Mansion. The main attraction at Sugar Pine Point State Park is Ehrman Mansion, a 1903 stone-and-shingle summer home furnished in period style. In its day it was the height of modernity, with a refrigerator, an elevator, and an electric stove. Also in the park are a trapper's log cabin from the mid-19th century, a nature preserve with wildlife exhibits, a lighthouse, the start of the 10-mile biking trail to Tahoe City, and an extensive system of hiking and cross-country skiing trails. If you're feeling less ambitious, you can relax on the sun-dappled lawn behind the mansion and gaze out at the lake. ⊠ *Hwy. 89* ☎ *530/525–7982 mansion in season, 530/525–7232 year-round* ⊕ *www.parks.ca.gov* 🎟 *$10 per vehicle, day use; mansion tour $10* ☉ *Mansion: late May–Aug., daily 10–3; call for Sept. hrs.*

Ed Z'Berg Sugar Pine Point State Park. Named for a state lawmaker who sponsored key conservation legislation, Lake Tahoe's largest state park has 2,000 acres of dense forests and nearly 2 miles of shore frontage. A popular spot during snow season, Sugar Pine provides 11 miles of cross-country trails and winter camping on a first-come, first-served basis. Rangers lead full-moon snowshoe tours from January to March. ⊠ *Hwy. 89, 1 mile south of Tahoma* ☎ *530/525–7982* ⊕ *www.parks. ca.gov.*

TAHOMA

1 mile north of Ed Z'berg Sugar Pine Point State Park, 23 miles south of Truckee.

With its rustic waterfront vacation cottages, Tahoma exemplifies life on the lake in its quiet early days before bright-lights casinos and huge crowds proliferated. In 1960 Tahoma was host of the Olympic Nordic-skiing competitions. Today there's little to do here except stroll by the lake and listen to the wind in the trees, making it a favorite home base for mellow families and nature buffs.

GETTING HERE AND AROUND

Approach Tahoma by car on Highway 89, called West Lake Boulevard in this section. From the northern and western communities, take a TART bus to Tahoma. A bike trail links Tahoe City to Tahoma.

WHERE TO STAY

$$ B&B/INN 🏠 **Tahoma Meadows B&B Cottages.** It's hard to beat this serene property for atmosphere and woodsy charm; it's a great retreat for families and couples. **Pros:** lovely setting; good choice for families; close to Homewood ski resort. **Cons:** far from the casinos. [$] *Rooms from: $159* ✉ *6821 W. Lake Blvd.* ☎ *530/525–1553, 866/525–1553* 🌐 *www.tahomameadows.com* 🛏 *16 cabins* 🍴 *Breakfast.*

SPORTS AND THE OUTDOORS

SKIING

Homewood Mountain Resort. Schuss down these slopes for fantastic views—the mountain rises across the road from the Tahoe shoreline. This small, usually uncrowded resort is the favorite area of locals on a snowy day, because you can find lots of untracked powder. It's also the most protected and least windy Tahoe ski area during a storm; when every other resort's lifts are on wind hold, you can almost always count on Homewood's to be open. There's only one high-speed chairlift, but there are rarely any lines, and the ticket prices are some of the cheapest around—kids 5 to 12 ski for $24, and those four and under are free. The resort may look small as you drive by, but most of it isn't visible from the road. ✉ *5145 W. Lake Blvd., Hwy. 89, 6 miles south of Tahoe City, Homewood* ☎ *530/525–2992 information, 530/525–2900 snow phone* 🌐 *www.skihomewood.com* ☞ *64 trails on 1,260 acres, rated 15% beginner, 50% intermediate, and 35% advanced. Longest run 2 miles, base 6,230 feet, summit 7,880 feet. Lifts: 4 chairlifts, 4 surface lifts.*

TAHOE CITY

9 miles north of Tahoma, 14 miles south of Truckee.

Tahoe City is the only lakeside town with a charming downtown area good for strolling and window-shopping. Stores and restaurants are all within walking distance of the Outlet Gates, where water is spilled into the Truckee River to control the surface level of the lake. You can spot giant trout in the river from Fanny Bridge, so-called for the views of the backsides of sightseers leaning over the railing.

GETTING HERE AND AROUND

Tahoe City is at the junction of Highway 28, also called North Lake Boulevard, and Highway 89 where it turns northwest toward Squaw Valley and Truckee. TART buses serve the communities along the north and west shores, and connects them to Truckee.

ESSENTIALS

Visitor Information North Lake Tahoe Resort Association ☎ *530/583–3494, 888/434–1262* 🌐 *www.gotahoenorth.com.*

EXPLORING

Gatekeeper's Museum. This museum preserves a little-known part of the region's history. Between 1910 and 1968 the gatekeeper who lived on this site was responsible for monitoring the level of the lake, using a hand-turned winch system (still used today) to keep the water at the correct level. Also on this site, the fantastic Marion Steinbach Indian

Basket Museum displays 800 baskets from 85 tribes. ✉ *130 W. Lake Blvd.* ☎ *530/583–1762* 🌐 *www.northtahoemuseums.org* 🎟 *$5* 🕒 *Late June–Sept., Wed.–Mon. 10–5; Oct.–late June., Fri. and Sat. 10–4.*

Watson Cabin Living Museum. In the middle of Tahoe City sits a 1909 log cabin built by Robert M. Watson and his son. Now a museum, it's filled with century-old furnishings and many reproductions. Docents are available to answer questions and will lead tours if you call ahead. ✉ *560 N. Lake Blvd.* ☎ *530/583–8717, 530/583–1762* 🌐 *www.northtahoemuseums.org* 🎟 *$2* 🕒 *Late May–early Sept., Thurs.–Mon. 10–5.*

WHERE TO EAT

$$$ AMERICAN 🍴 **Christy Hill.** Huge windows give diners here some of the best lake views in Tahoe. The menu features solid Euro–Cal preparations of fresh seafood, filet of beef, or vegetarian dishes. The extensive wine list and exceptionally good desserts earn accolades, as do the gracious service and casual vibe. If the weather is balmy, have dinner on the deck. In any season, this is a romantic choice for lake gazing and wine sipping. [$] *Average main: $27* ✉ *115 Grove St., at N. Lake Blvd.* ☎ *530/583–8551* 🌐 *www.christyhill.com* 🕒 *No lunch.*

$ AMERICAN 🍴 **Fire Sign Café.** Watch the road carefully or you'll miss this great little diner two miles south of Tahoe City on Highway 89. There's often a wait for breakfast and lunch, but it's worth it. The pastries are made from scratch, the salmon is smoked in-house, the salsa is hand cut, and there's real maple syrup for the many types of pancakes and waffles. Leave room for dessert; a fruit cobbler is almost always on the menu. [$] *Average main: $10* ✉ *1785 W. Lake Blvd., at Fountain Ave.* ☎ *530/583–0871* 🌐 *www.firesigncafe.com* ✍ *Reservations not accepted* 🕒 *No dinner.*

$ AMERICAN 🍴 **Syd's Bagelry & Espresso.** For breakfast bagels and pastries and lunchtime salads and sandwiches, locals head to Syd's, which brews good coffee and provides free Wi-Fi, too. Want the skinny on Tahoe City? Talk to Dean, the affable owner. [$] *Average main: $8* ✉ *550 N. Lake Tahoe Blvd., at Grove St.* ☎ *530/583–2666* 🕒 *No dinner.*

$$$ ECLECTIC Fodor's Choice ★ 🍴 **Wolfdale's.** Consistent, inspired cuisine makes Wolfdale's one of the top restaurants on the lake. Seafood is the specialty on the changing menu; the imaginative entrées merge Asian and European cooking (drawing on the chef-owner's training in Japan) and lean toward the light and healthful, rather than the heavy and overdone. Everything from teriyaki glaze to smoked fish is made in-house. Request a window table, and book early enough to see the lake view from the elegantly simple dining room. [$] *Average main: $28* ✉ *640 N. Lake Blvd., near Grove St.* ☎ *530/583–5700* 🌐 *www.wolfdales.com* 🕒 *Closed Tues. No lunch.*

WHERE TO STAY

$$ B&B/INN 🏨 **Cottage Inn.** Avoid the crowds by staying in one of these charming circa-1938 log cottages under the towering pines on the lake's west shore. **Pros:** romantic, woodsy setting; each room has a fireplace; full breakfast. **Cons:** no kids under 12. [$] *Rooms from: $160* ✉ *1690 W. Lake Blvd., Box 66* ☎ *530/581–4073, 800/581–4073* 🌐 *www.thecottageinn.com* 🛏 *22 rooms* 🍽 *Breakfast.*

$$$$ HOTEL Fodor's Choice ★ **Sunnyside Steakhouse and Lodge.** The views are superb at this pretty little lodge right on the lake, three miles south of Tahoe City. **Pros:** complimentary Continental breakfast and afternoon tea; most rooms have balconies overlooking the lake. **Cons:** can be pricey for families. [$] *Rooms from: $265* ✉ *1850 W. Lake Blvd., Box 5969* ☎ *530/583–7200, 800/822–2754* 🌐 *www.sunnysideresort.com* *18 rooms, 5 suites* 🍴 *Breakfast.*

SPORTS AND THE OUTDOORS

GOLF

Tahoe City Golf Course. This 9-hole course, which opened in 1917, gives golfers views of Lake Tahoe. Rent a cart for $10. **TIP→ All greens break toward the lake.** ✉ *251 N. Lake Blvd.* ☎ *530/583–1516* *$30 for 9 holes; $50 for 18* *18 holes, 5261 yards, par 66.*

RAFTING

FAMILY **Truckee River Rafting.** In summer you can take a self-guided raft trip down a gentle 5-mile stretch of the Truckee River. This outfitter will shuttle you back to Tahoe City at the end of your two- to three-hour trip. On a warm day, this makes a great family outing. ✉ *175 River Rd., near W. Lake Blvd.* ☎ *530/583–1111* 🌐 *www.truckeeriverrafting.com* *From $28.*

SKIING

Fodor's Choice ★ **Alpine Meadows Ski Area.** With 450 inches of snow annually, Alpine has some of Tahoe's most reliable conditions. It's usually one of the first areas to open in November and one of the last to close in May or June. Alpine isn't the place for show-offs; instead, you'll find down-to-earth alpine fetishists. The two peaks here are well suited to intermediate skiers, with a number of runs for experts only. Snowboarders and hot-dog skiers will find a terrain park with a super-pipe, rails, and tabletops, as well as a boarder-cross course. Alpine is a great place to learn to ski and has a ski school that coaches those with physical and mental disabilities. On Saturday, because of the limited parking, there's more acreage per person than at other resorts. Lift tickets are good at neighboring Squaw Valley; a free shuttle runs all day between the two ski parks. ✉ *2600 Alpine Meadows Rd., off Hwy. 89, 6 miles northwest of Tahoe City and 13 miles south of Truckee* ☎ *530/583–4232, 800/403–0206, 530/452–4356 snow phone* 🌐 *www.skialpine.com* ☞ *100 trails on 2,400 acres, rated 25% beginner, 40% intermediate, 35% advanced. Longest run 2½ miles, base 6,835 feet, summit 8,637 feet. Lifts: 13, including 1 high-speed 6-passenger lift and 2 high-speed quads.*

Tahoe Dave's Skis and Boards. You can rent skis, boards, and snowshoes at this shop, which has the area's best selection of downhill rental equipment. ✉ *590 N. Lake Blvd.* ☎ *530/583–6415* 🌐 *www.tahoedaves.com.*

OLYMPIC VALLEY

7 miles north of Tahoe City to Squaw Valley Road; 8½ miles south of Truckee.

Olympic Valley got its name in 1960, when Squaw Valley USA, the ski resort here, hosted the Winter Olympics. Snow sports remain the primary activity, but once summer comes, you can hike into the adjacent Granite Chief Wilderness, explore wildflower-studded alpine meadows, or lie by a swimming pool in one of the Sierra's prettiest valleys.

GETTING HERE AND AROUND

Squaw Valley Road, the only way into Olympic Valley, branches west off Highway 89 about 8 miles south of Truckee. TART connects the Squaw Valley ski area with the communities along the north and west shores, and Truckee, with year-round public transportation. Squaw Valley Ski Resort provides a free shuttle to many stops in those same areas.

EXPLORING

High Camp. You can ride the Squaw Valley Aerial Tram to this activity hub, which at 8,200 feet commands superb views of Lake Tahoe and the surrounding mountains. In summer, go for a sunset hike, sit by the pool, or have a cocktail and watch the sunset. In winter, you can ski, ice-skate, snow-tube or go for a full-moon hike. There's also a restaurant, a lounge, and a small Olympic museum. Pick up trail maps at the tram building. ✉ *Aerial Tram Bldg., Squaw Valley* ☎ *800/403–0206* 🌐 *squaw.com/the-village* 🎟 *Aerial Tram, $29* 🕒 *Daily; call for hrs.*

FAMILY **Village at Squaw Valley.** The centerpiece of Olympic Valley is a pedestrian mall at the base of several four-story ersatz Bavarian stone-and-timber buildings, where you'll find restaurants, high-end condo rentals, boutiques, and cafés. ✉ *1750 Village East Rd.* ☎ *530/584–1000, 800/403–0206 information, 800/731–8021 condo reservations* 🌐 *squaw.com/the-village.*

WHERE TO EAT

$$ PIZZA FAMILY 🍴 **Fireside Pizza Company.** Adults might opt for the signature pear and Gorgonzola pizza at this modern Italian restaurant, but most kids clamor for the house favorite: an Italian-sausage-and-pepperoni combo with a bubbly blend of four cheeses. Salads and pasta dishes round out the menu at this family-friendly spot. [$] *Average main: $16* ✉ *The Village at Squaw Valley, 1985 Squaw Valley Rd., #25* ☎ *530/584–6150* 🌐 *firesidepizza.com.*

$$$ ECLECTIC 🍴 **Graham's of Squaw Valley.** Sit by a floor-to-ceiling river-rock hearth under a knotty-pine peaked ceiling in the intimate dining room in the Christy Inn Lodge. The southern European–inspired menu changes often, but expect hearty entrées such as grilled beef tenderloin with wild mushroom sauce, along with lighter-fare small plates like quail with fig demi-glace. You can also stop in at the fireside bar for appetizers and wine from Graham's highly regarded wine list. [$] *Average main: $30* ✉ *1650 Squaw Valley Rd.* ☎ *530/581–0454* 🕒 *Closed Mon. No lunch.*

$$ JAPANESE 🍴 **Mamasake.** The hip sushi spot at Squaw serves stylized presentations. On some evenings you can sit at the bar and watch extreme-skiing movies, many of them filmed right outside the window. From 3 to 5 enjoy the afternoon special: a spicy-tuna or salmon hand roll and a can of Bud

Squaw Valley USA has runs for skiers of all ability levels—from beginner trails to cliff drops for experts.

for five bucks. $ *Average main: $16* ⊠ *1850 Village South Rd., No. 52, off Squaw Valley Rd.* ☎ *530/584–0110* ⊕ *mamasake.com.*

$$$$ ✕ **PlumpJack Café.** The best restaurant in the entire Tahoe Basin is the
AMERICAN epitome of discreet chic for serious foodies. The menu changes season-
Fodor's Choice ally, but look for filet mignon "Oscar" with Dungeness crab, crispy
★ sweetbreads, and inventive vegetarian dishes. Rather than complicated, heavy sauces, the chef uses simple reductions to complement a dish. The result: clean, dynamic flavors. The wine list is exceptional for its variety and reasonable prices. A less expensive but equally adventurous menu, including lunch, is served at the bar. $ *Average main: $34* ⊠ *1920 Squaw Valley Rd.* ☎ *530/583–1578, 800/323–7666* ⊕ *www. plumpjackcafe.com* ⌕ *Reservations essential.*

WHERE TO STAY

$$$$ ⊡ **PlumpJack Squaw Valley Inn.** Stylish and luxurious, this two-story,
HOTEL cedar-sided inn has a snappy, sophisticated look and laid-back sensi-
Fodor's Choice bility, perfect for the Bay Area cognoscenti who flock here on week-
★ ends. **Pros:** small; intimate; lots of attention to details. **Cons:** not the best choice for families with small children. $ *Rooms from: $255* ⊠ *1920 Squaw Valley Rd.* ☎ *530/583–1576, 800/323–7666* ⊕ *www. plumpjacksquawvalleyinn.com* ⌕ *56 rooms, 8 suites* ⦿ *Breakfast.*

$$$$ ⊡ **Resort at Squaw Creek.** This multi-facility Squaw Valley resort offers a
RESORT plethora of year-round activities. **Pros:** every conceivable amenity; private chairlift to Squaw Valley USA for ski-in, ski-out. **Cons:** large and pricey. $ *Rooms from: $259* ⊠ *400 Squaw Creek Rd.* ☎ *530/583–6300, 800/327–3353* ⊕ *www.squawcreek.com* ⌕ *205 rooms, 200 suites* ⦿ *No meals.*

$$$ HOTEL **The Village at Squaw Valley USA.** Right at the base of the slopes, at the center point of Olympic Valley, the Village's condominiums (from studio to three bedrooms) come complete with gas fireplaces, daily maid service, and heated slate-tile bathroom and kitchen floors. **Pros:** family-friendly; near Village restaurants and shops. **Cons:** claustrophobia-inducing crowds on weekends. [$] *Rooms from: $199* ✉ *1750 Village East Rd.* ☎ *530/584–1000, 888/259–1428* 🌐 *www.squaw.com/the-village/lodging* 🛏 *198 suites* 🍴 *No meals.*

SPORTS AND THE OUTDOORS

GOLF

Resort at Squaw Creek Golf Course. For beautiful views of Squaw Valley's surrounding peaks, play this narrow, challenging championship course designed by Robert Trent Jones Jr. Rates start at $98 with midrange twilight fees beginning at noon for $78; the lowest rate, $60, starts at 3 pm. All fees include a golf cart plus valet parking. ✉ *400 Squaw Creek Rd.* ☎ *530/583–6300, 530/581–6637 pro shop* 🌐 *www.squawcreek.com* 🎫 *$98* ⛳ *18 holes, 6931 yards, par 71.*

ICE-SKATING

FAMILY **Olympic Ice Pavilion.** Ice-skate here from late November to early March. A ride up the mountain in the Aerial Tram costs $29, plus $12 for skate rental and one hour of skate time. End your outing in the hot tub ($14). In summer, the pavilion converts into a roller-skating rink. Year-round, you get fabulous views of the lake and the Sierra Nevada. ✉ *1960 Squaw Valley Rd., High Camp, Squaw Valley* ☎ *800/403–0206* 🌐 *squaw.com/things-to-do/high-camp/ice-skating.*

MINIATURE GOLF

FAMILY **Squaw Valley Adventure Center.** Next to the Olympic Village Lodge, on the far side of the creek, this seasonal activities center has an 18-hole miniature golf course, a ropes course, and sometimes a bungee trampoline, a blast for kids. ✉ *1960 Squaw Valley Rd.* ☎ *530/581–7563* 🌐 *www.squawadventure.com.*

ROCK CLIMBING

Headwall Climbing Wall. Before you rappel down a granite monolith, hone your skills at this challenging wall at the base of the Aerial Tram. ✉ *Squaw Valley Adventure Center, 1960 Squaw Valley Rd.* ☎ *530/581–7563* 🌐 *www.squawadventure.com.*

SKIING

Resort at Squaw Creek. Cross-country skiers enjoy looping through the valley's giant alpine meadow. The resort rents ski equipment and provides trail maps. ✉ *400 Squaw Creek Rd.* ☎ *530/583–6300, 530/581–6637 pro shop* 🌐 *www.squawcreek.com.*

Fodor's Choice ★ **Squaw Valley USA.** Known for some of the toughest skiing in the Tahoe area, this park was the centerpiece of the 1960 Winter Olympics. Today it's the definitive North Tahoe ski resort and among the top-three megaresorts in California (the other two are Heavenly and Mammoth). Although Squaw has changed significantly since the Olympics, the skiing is still world-class and extends across vast bowls stretched between six peaks. Experts often head directly to the untamed terrain of the infamous KT-22 face, which has bumps, cliffs, and gulp-and-go chutes, or to the nearly vertical Palisades, where many famous extreme-skiing films have been shot. Fret not, beginners and intermediates: you have plenty of wide-open, groomed trails at High Camp (which sits at the *top* of the mountain) and around the more challenging Snow King Peak. Snowboarders and show-off skiers can tear up the six fantastic terrain parks, which include a giant super-pipe. Ski passes are good at neighboring Alpine Meadows; free shuttles run all day between the two ski parks. ⊠ *1960 Squaw Valley Rd., off Hwy. 89, 7 miles northwest of Tahoe City* ☎ *800/731–8021 lodging reservations, 530/452–4355 snow phone, 800/403–0206 information* ⊕ *squaw.com* ☞ *170 trails on 3,600 acres, rated 25% beginner, 45% intermediate, 30% advanced. Longest run 3.2 miles, base 6,200 feet, summit 9,050 feet. Lifts: 29, including a gondola-style funitel, a tram, 7 high-speed chairs, and 15 fixed-grip chairs and 5 surface lifts.*

Tahoe Dave's Skis and Boards. If you don't want to pay resort prices, you can rent and tune downhill skis and snowboards at this shop. ⊠ *3039 Hwy. 89, at Squaw Valley Rd.* ☎ *530/583–5665* ⊕ *www.tahoedaves.com.*

TRUCKEE

13 miles northwest of Kings Beach, 14 miles north of Tahoe City.

Formerly a decrepit railroad town in the mountains, Truckee is now the trendy first stop for many Tahoe visitors. The town was officially established around 1863, and by 1868 it had gone from a stagecoach station to a major stopover for trains bound for the Pacific via the new transcontinental railroad. Freight trains and Amtrak's California Zephyr still stop every day at the depot right in the middle of town. Stop inside the depot for a walking-tour map of historic Truckee. Across from the station, where Old West facades line the main drag, you'll find galleries, gift shops, boutiques, old-fashioned diners, and several remarkably good restaurants. Look for outlet stores, strip malls, and discount skiwear shops along Donner Pass Road, north of the freeway. Because of its location on Interstate 80, Truckee is a favorite stopover for people traveling from the San Francisco Bay Area to the north shore of Lake Tahoe, Reno, and points east.

GETTING HERE AND AROUND

Truckee is just off Interstate 80 between highways 89 and 267. Greyhound and Amtrak stop here, Enterprise and Hertz provide car rentals, and TART buses serve Truckee and north shore communities.

ESSENTIALS

Visitor Information Truckee Donner Chamber of Commerce and the California Welcome Center ⊠ *Amtrak depot, 10065 Donner Pass Rd., near Spring St.* ☎ *530/587–8808 chamber of commerce, 866/443–2027 welcome center* ⊕ *www.truckee.com.*

EXPLORING

Donner Memorial State Park and Emigrant Trail Museum. The park and museum commemorate the Donner Party, westward-bound pioneers—about 90; historians debate the exact number—who became trapped in the Sierra in the winter of 1846–47 in snow 22 feet deep. Barely more than half the pioneers survived, some by resorting to cannibalism. The Emigrant Trail Museum details the Donner Party's plight, and other displays explain railroad development through the Sierra. In the park, you can picnic, hike, camp, and go boating, fishing, and waterskiing in summer; winter brings cross-country skiing and snowshoeing on groomed trails. Slated for a 2015 debut, a new High Sierra Crossing Museum will contain exhibits about the Donner Party, regional Native Americans, and railroad and transportation development through Donner Pass. ✉ *12593 Donner Pass Rd., off I–80, 2 miles west of Truckee* ☎ *530/582–7892 museum, 800/444–7275 camping reservations* 🌐 *www.parks.ca.gov* 🎟 *$8 parking, day use* 🕒 *Museum daily 10–5.*

OFF THE BEATEN PATH

Tahoe National Forest. Draped along the Sierra Nevada Crest north of Lake Tahoe, the national forest offers abundant outdoor recreation: hiking, picnicking, and camping in summer, and snowshoeing, skiing, and sledding over some of the deepest snowpack in the West in winter. ✉ *Truckee ranger station, 10811 Stockrest Springs Rd.* ☎ *530/587–3558 Truckee ranger station, 530/265–4531 forest headquarters* 🌐 *www.fs.usda.gov/tahoe.*

WHERE TO EAT

$$$ ECLECTIC Fodor's Choice ★

🍴 **Cottonwood Restaurant & Bar.** Perched above town on the site of North America's first chairlift, this restaurant is an institution. The bar is decked out with old wooden skis, sleds, skates, and photos of Truckee's early days. The ambitious menu includes everything from grilled steak to baby back ribs with Cajun spices to butternut-squash enchiladas—plus fresh-baked breads and desserts. But people come here mainly for the atmosphere and hilltop views. [$] *Average main: $24* ✉ *10142 Rue Hilltop Rd., off Brockway Rd., ¼ mile south of downtown* ☎ *530/587–5711* 🌐 *www.cottonwoodrestaurant.com* 🕒 *No lunch.*

$$$ ASIAN

🍴 **Dragonfly.** Flavors are bold and zingy at this Cal-Asian spot, where every dish is well executed and stylishly presented. Southeast Asian cooking inspires most dishes, which you can savor in the bright, contemporary dining rooms—one for sushi—or, when the weather's nice, an outdoor terrace overlooking the busy street scene and the train depot. Lunch is a bargain, and there are many choices for vegetarians. Look for the staircase: the restaurant is on the second floor. [$] *Average main: $26* ✉ *10118 Donner Pass Rd., near Spring St.* ☎ *530/587–0557* 🌐 *www.dragonflycuisine.com.*

$$ AMERICAN

🍴 **FiftyFifty Brewing Company.** In this Truckee brewpub, warm red tones and comfy booths, plus a pint of the Donner Party porter, will take the nip out of a cold day on the slopes. The menu includes salads, burgers, and the house specialty, a pulled-pork sandwich, plus barbecued ribs and pan-seared salmon. Their inventive pizzas are popular anytime. There's a full bar along with the brews, and lots of après-ski action. [$] *Average main: $21* ✉ *11197 Brockway Rd.* ☎ *530/587–2337* 🌐 *www.fiftyfiftybrewing.com.*

$$$ ECLECTIC

🍴 **Moody's Bistro Bar & Beats.** Head here for contemporary-Cal cuisine in a sexy dining room with pumpkin-color walls, burgundy velvet banquettes, and art deco fixtures. The earthy, sure-handed cooking features organically grown ingredients: look for ahi *poke*, snazzy pizzas bubbling-hot from a brick oven, braised lamb shanks, pan-roasted wild game, fresh seafood, and organic beef. Lunch fare is lighter. In summer dine alfresco surrounded by flowers. From Thursday through Saturday there's music in the borderline-raucous bar that gets packed with Truckee's bon vivants. $ *Average main: $23* ✉ *10007 Bridge St., at Donner Pass Rd.* ☎ *530/587–8688* ⊕ *moodysbistro.com.*

WHERE TO STAY

$$$
HOTEL

⊡ **Cedar House Sport Hotel.** The clean, spare lines of the Cedar House's wooden exterior evoke a modern European feel, while energy-saving heating, cooling, and lighting systems emphasize the owners' commitment to sustainability. **Pros:** environmentally friendly; comfortable; hip. **Cons:** some bathrooms on the small side. $ *Rooms from: $190* ✉ *10918 Brockway Rd.* ☎ *530/582–5655, 866/582–5655* ⊕ *www. cedarhousesporthotel.com* ⤴ *40 rooms* ⦿ *Breakfast.*

$$$
RESORT

⊡ **Northstar California Resort.** The area's most complete destination resort entices families with its sports activities and concentration of restaurants, shops, and accommodations. **Pros:** array of lodging types; on-site shuttle; several dining options in Northstar Village. **Cons:** family accommodations are very pricey. $ *Rooms from: $249* ✉ *100 Northstar Dr., off Hwy. 267, 6 miles southeast of Truckee* ☎ *530/562–1010, 800/466–6784* ⊕ *www.northstarcalifornia.com* ⤴ *250 units* ⦿ *No meals.*

$$$$
RESORT

⊡ **Ritz-Carlton Highlands Court, Lake Tahoe.** Nestled midmountain on the Northstar ski resort, the plush accommodations of the Ritz-Carlton have floor-to-ceiling windows for maximum views, along with fireplaces, cozy robes, and down comforters. **Pros:** superb service; gorgeous setting. **Cons:** prices as breathtaking as the views; must go off-site for golf and tennis. $ *Rooms from: $569* ✉ *13031 Ritz-Carlton Highlands Court* ☎ *530/562–3000, 800/241–3333* ⊕ *www.ritzcarlton.com/ laketahoe* ⤴ *153 rooms, 17 suites* ⦿ *No meals.*

$$
B&B/INN

⊡ **River Street Inn.** On the banks of the Truckee River, this 1885 wood-and-stone inn has uncluttered, comfortable rooms that are simply decorated, with attractive, country-style wooden furniture and extras like flat-screen TVs. **Pros:** nice rooms; good value. **Cons:** parking is a half-block from inn. $ *Rooms from: $145* ✉ *10009 E. River St.* ☎ *530/550–9290* ⊕ *www.riverstreetinntruckee.com* ⤴ *11 rooms* ⦿ *Breakfast.*

SPORTS AND THE OUTDOORS

GOLF

Coyote Moon Golf Course. With towering pine trees lining the fairways and no houses to spoil the view, this course is as beautiful as it is challenging. Fees include a shared cart; the greens fee drops at 1 pm and dips again at 3. ✉ *10685 Northwoods Blvd., off Donner Pass Rd.* ☎ *530/587–0886* ⊕ *www.coyotemoongolf.com* 💳 *$155* ⛳ *18 holes, 7177 yards, par 72* ☼ *Closed late fall–late spring.*

Northstar. The front nine holes here are open-links style, while the challenging back nine move through tight, tree-lined fairways. Fees include a shared cart. Twilight rates begin at 1 pm. You can play nine holes for $45; special teen rates encourage family outings. The restaurant serves breakfast and lunch only. ✉ *168 Basque Dr., off Northstar Dr., west off Hwy. 267* ☎ *530/562–3290 pro-shop* ⊕ *www.northstarcalifornia.com/ info/summer/golf.asp* 💳 *$70* ⛳ *18 holes, 6781 yards, par 72.*

23

Old Greenwood. Beautiful mountain and forest views add to the pleasure of a round played at north Lake Tahoe's only Jack Nicklaus Signature Golf Course. The regular fees are high, but there's a $75 twilight rate beginning at 4 pm. ⊠ *12915 Fairway Dr., off Overland Trail Rd., off I–80, Exit 190* ☎ *530/550–7010* ⊕ *www.golfintahoe.com/old_greenwood* ⊠ *$200* ⚑ *18 holes, 7518 yards, par 72.*

MOUNTAIN BIKING

Northstar California. In summer you can rent a bike and ride the lifts ($46, ages 13 and up) to the mountain-biking park for 100 miles of challenging terrain. The season extends from mid-June through September with varying hours. ⊠ *Northstar Dr., off Hwy. 267* ☎ *530/562–1010* ⊕ *www.northstarcalifornia.com/info/summer/biking.asp.*

Cyclepaths Mountain Bike Adventures. This combination full-service bike shop and bike-adventure outfitter offers instruction in mountain biking, guided tours, tips for self-guided bike touring, bike repairs, and books and maps on the area. ⊠ *10095 W. River St., by Bridge St.* ☎ *530/582–1890* ⊕ *www.cyclepaths.net.*

SKIING

Several smaller resorts around Truckee offer access to the Sierra's slopes for less than half the price of the big resorts. Though you'll sacrifice vertical rise, acreage, and high-speed lifts, you can ski or ride and still have money left over for room and board. These are great places for first-timers and families with kids learning to ski.

Boreal Mountain Resort. These slopes have 480 skiable acres and 500 vertical feet of terrain visible from the freeway. Lift-served snow-tubing and night skiing go until 9. ⊠ *19749 Boreal Ridge Rd., at I–80, Boreal/Castle Peak exit, Soda Springs* ☎ *530/426–3666* ⊕ *www.rideboreal.com.*

Donner Ski Ranch. This ski park has 505 acres and 750 vertical feet. A popular area with kids in this small, family-friendly park is the Tubing Hill. Riders whisk down the slope in a huge inflated inner tube and then go back to the top on a moving carpet. ⊠ *19320 Donner Pass Rd., Norden* ☎ *530/426–3635* ⊕ *www.donnerskiranch.com.*

Fodor's Choice **Northstar California.** With two tree-lined, northeast-facing, wind-protected bowls, this park is the ideal place in a storm, and just may be the best all-around family ski resort at Tahoe. Hotshot experts unfairly call the mountain "Flatstar," but the meticulous grooming and long cruisers make it an intermediate skier's paradise. Boarders are especially welcome, with awesome terrain parks, including a 420-foot-long superpipe, a half-pipe, rails and boxes, and lots of kickers. Experts can ski the steeps and bumps off Lookout Mountain, where there's rarely a line for the high-speed quad. Northstar-at-Tahoe's cross-country center has 35 km (22 miles) of groomed trails, including double-set tracks and skating lanes. The school has programs for skiers ages three and up, and day care is available for tots two and older. The mountain gets packed on busy weekends, but when there's room on the slopes, Northstar is loads of fun. ⊠ *5001 Northstar Dr.* ☎ *530/562–1010 information, 800/466–6784 lodging, 530/562–1330 snow phone* ⊕ *www.northstarcalifornia.com* ⚐ *97 trails on 3,170 acres, rated 13% beginner, 60% intermediate,*

27% advanced. *Longest run 1.4 miles, base 6,330 feet, summit 8,610 feet. Lifts: 20, including 2 gondolas and 7 high-speed quads.*

Royal Gorge. If you love to cross-country, don't miss Royal Gorge, which serves up 200 km (124 miles) of track for all abilities, 75 trails on a whopping 6,000 acres, a ski school, and eight warming huts. Two trailside cafés and two lodges round out the facilities. Because the complex sits right on the Sierra Crest, the views are drop-dead gorgeous. ✉ *9411 Pahatsi Dr., off I–80, Soda Springs/Norden exit, Soda Springs* ☎ *530/426–3871* ⊕ *www.royalgorge.com.*

23

Soda Springs. Along with 200 acres and 652 vertical feet, this ski park also has lift-served snow-tubing. ✉ *10244 Soda Springs Rd., I–80 Soda Springs exit, Soda Springs* ☎ *530/426–3901* ⊕ *www.skisodasprings.com.*

Fodor'sChoice
★

Sugar Bowl Ski Resort. Opened in 1939 by Walt Disney, this is the oldest—and one of the best—resorts at Tahoe. Atop Donner Summit, it receives an incredible 500 inches of snowfall annually. Four peaks are connected by 1,650 acres of skiable terrain, with everything from gentle groomed corduroy to wide-open bowls to vertical rocky chutes and outstanding tree skiing. Snowboarders can hit two terrain parks with numerous boxes, rails, and jumps. Because it's more compact than some of the area's megaresorts, there's a gentility here that distinguishes Sugar Bowl from its competitors, making this a great place for families and a low-pressure, low-key place to learn to ski. It's not huge, but there's some very challenging terrain (experts: head to the Palisades). There's limited lodging at the base area. ✉ *629 Sugar Bowl Rd., off Donner Pass Rd., 3 miles east of I–80 Soda Springs/Norden exit, 10 miles west of Truckee, Norden* ☎ *530/426–9000 information and lodging reservations, 530/426–1111 snow phone, 866/843–2695 lodging referral* ⊕ *www.sugarbowl.com* ⚲ *102 trails on 1,650 acres, rated 17% beginner, 45% intermediate, 38% advanced. Longest run 3 miles, base 6,883 feet, summit 8,383 feet. Lifts: 13, including 5 high-speed quads.*

Tahoe Dave's. You can save money by renting skis and boards at this shop, which has the area's best selection and also repairs and tunes equipment. ✉ *10200 Donner Pass Rd., near Spring St.* ☎ *530/582–0900* ⊕ *www.tahoedaves.com.*

Tahoe Donner. Just north of Truckee, this park covers 120 acres and 600 vertical feet; the cross-country center includes 51 trails on 100 km (62 miles) of groomed tracks on 4,800 acres, with night skiing on Wednesday in January and February. ✉ *11603 Snowpeak Way* ☎ *530/587–9444* ⊕ *www.tahoedonner.com.*

CARNELIAN BAY TO KINGS BEACH

5–10 miles northeast of Tahoe City.

The small lakeside commercial districts of Carnelian Bay and Tahoe Vista service the thousand or so locals who live in the area year-round and the thousands more who have summer residences or launch their boats here. Kings Beach, the last town heading east on Highway 28 before the Nevada border, is to Crystal Bay what South Lake Tahoe is to Stateline: a bustling town full of basic motels and rental condos, restaurants, and shops, used by the hordes of hopefuls who pass through on their way to the casinos.

GETTING HERE AND AROUND

To reach Kings Beach and Carnelian Bay from the California side, take Highway 89 north to Highway 28 north and then east. From the Nevada side, follow Highway 28 north and then west. TART provides public transportation in this area.

BEACHES

FAMILY **Kings Beach State Recreation Area.** The 28-acre Kings Beach State Recreation Area, one of the largest such areas on the lake, is open year-round. The 700-foot-long sandy beach gets crowded in summer with people swimming, sunbathing, Jet Skiing, riding in paddleboats, spiking volleyballs, and tossing Frisbees. If you're going to spend the day, come early enough to snag a table in the picnic area; there's also a good playground. **Amenities:** food and drink; parking (fee); toilets; water sports. **Best for:** sunrise; swimming; windsurfing. ⊠ *8318 N. Lake Blvd., Hwy. 28, Kings Beach* ☎ *530/546–7248* ⊕ *www.parks.ca.gov* ⊠ *$8 parking fee.*

WHERE TO EAT AND STAY

$$$ ✕ **Gar Woods Grill and Pier.** The view's the thing at this lakeside stalwart, ECLECTIC where you can watch the sun shimmer on the water through the dining room's plate-glass windows or from the heated outdoor deck. Grilled steak and fish are menu mainstays, but be sure to try specialties like crab chilis rellenos and chipotle chicken salad. At all hours in season, the bar gets packed with boaters who pull up to the restaurant's private pier. Ⓢ *Average main: $29* ⊠ *5000 N. Lake Blvd., Hwy. 28, Carnelian Bay* ☎ *530/546–3366* ⊕ *www.garwoods.com.*

$$$ ✕ **Spindleshanks American Bistro and Wine Bar.** This restaurant, which relo-AMERICAN cated in 2014 to the Old Brockway Golf Course, serves mostly classic American cooking—ribs, steaks, and seafood updated with adventurous sauces—as well as house-made ravioli. Savor a drink from the full bar or choose a wine from the extensive list while you enjoy views of Lake Tahoe or the historic greens, where Bing Crosby hosted his first golf tournament in 1934. Ⓢ *Average main: $23* ⊠ *400 Brassie Ave., at Hwy. 267 & N. Lake Tahoe Blvd., Tahoe Vista* ☎ *530/546–2191* ⊕ *www. spindleshankstahoe.com* ⊘ *No lunch except in summer.*

$ 🛏 **Ferrari's Crown Resort.** Great for families with kids, the family-HOTEL owned and-operated Ferrari's has straightforward motel rooms in FAMILY a resort setting. **Pros:** family-friendly; lakeside location. **Cons:** older facility. Ⓢ *Rooms from: $105* ⊠ *8200 N. Lake Blvd., Kings Beach* ☎ *530/546–3388, 800/645–2260* ⊕ *www.tahoecrown.com* ⤢ *72 rooms* ⦾ *Breakfast.*

$$$$ 🛏 **Shore House.** The lovingly tended, knotty-pine-paneled guest rooms B&B/INN at this lakefront B&B in Tahoe Vista beautifully and simply capture the woodsy spirit of Tahoe, but without overdoing the pinecone motif. **Pros:** waterfront honeymoon cottage; massage appointments available. **Cons:** not a good choice for children. Ⓢ *Rooms from: $276* ⊠ *7170 N. Lake Blvd., Tahoe Vista* ☎ *530/546–7270, 800/207–5160* ⊕ *www. shorehouselaketahoe.com* ⤢ *8 rooms, 1 cottage* ⦾ *Breakfast.*

THE NEVADA SIDE

The difference on the Nevada side of the lake is, of course, gambling, with all its repercussions.

CRYSTAL BAY

1 mile east of Kings Beach, 30 miles north of South Lake Tahoe.

Right at the Nevada border, Crystal Bay features a cluster of casinos, a few spunky ones with personality and some smaller ones that locals tend to favor. There's not much lodging; the largest property, the Cal-Neva Resort, Spa and Casino that Frank Sinatra owned, is, as of this writing, undergoing a multimillion-dollar remodel. Look for it to reopen with great hoopla in 2015. For now, one of Tahoe's best restaurants, Soule Domain, is reason enough for a stop in Crystal Bay.

GETTING HERE AND AROUND

From the California side, reach Crystal Bay via Highway 89 or 267 to Highway 28. TART serves the communities along the north and west shores.

WHERE TO EAT

$$$ ECLECTIC

🍴 **Soule Domain.** Rough-hewn wood beams, a vaulted wood ceiling, and, in winter, a roaring fireplace lend high romance to this cozy 1927 pine-log cabin next to the Tahoe Biltmore. Chef-owner Charlie Soule's specialties include curried almond chicken, fresh sea scallops poached in Champagne with a kiwi and mango cream sauce, and a vegan sauté with ginger, jalapeños, and tofu. If you're looking for a place with a sterling menu where you can hold hands by candlelight, this is it. [$] *Average main: $27* ✉ *9983 Cove St., ½ block up Stateline Rd. off Hwy. 28, Kings Beach* ☎ *530/546–7529* 🌐 *www.souledomain.com* 🕓 *No lunch.*

NIGHTLIFE

CASINOS

Crystal Bay Club. Known for its classic steak and lobster dinner, the restaurant in this casino has a distinctive open-truss ceiling. With entertainment in two venues, and accomodations in its historic 10-room Border House ($$$) next to the club, this refurbished casino tempts tourists to linger on Tahoe's north shore. ✉ *14 Hwy. 28, near Stateline Rd.* ☎ *775/833–6333* 🌐 *www.crystalbaycasino.com.*

Tahoe Biltmore. A daily happy hour keeps this old favorite hopping, along with dinner specials in Bilty's Brew & Q restaurant, and inexpensive breakfasts in their café. Expect simple accommodations ($–$$) in the casino's hotel. The circular Tahoe Biltmore sign is a 1962 "Googie-style" architectural riff off the Seattle Space Neeedle, which debuted the same year. ✉ *5 Hwy. 28, at Stateline Rd.* ☎ *800/245–8667* 🌐 *www.tahoebiltmore.com.*

INCLINE VILLAGE

3 miles east of Crystal Bay.

Incline Village dates to the early 1960s when an Oklahoma developer bought 10,000 acres north of Lake Tahoe. His idea was to sketch out a plan for a town without a central commercial district, hoping to prevent congestion and to preserve the area's natural beauty. One-acre lakeshore lots originally fetched $12,000 to $15,000; today you couldn't buy the same land for less than several million.

GETTING HERE AND AROUND

From the California side, reach Incline Village via Highway 89 or 267 to Highway 28. From South Lake Tahoe, take U.S. 50 north to Highway 28 north. TART serves the communities along Lake Tahoe's north and west shores from Incline Village to Tahoma.

ESSENTIALS

Visitor Information Lake Tahoe Incline Village/Crystal Bay Visitors Bureau ✉ *969 Tahoe Blvd.* ☎ *775/832–1606, 800/468–2463* ⊕ *www.gotahoenorth.com.*

EXPLORING

Lakeshore Drive. Take this beautiful drive to see some of the most expensive real estate in Nevada. The route is discreetly marked: to find it, start at the Hyatt hotel and drive westward along the lake.

Fodor's Choice **Thunderbird Lodge.** George Whittell, a San Francisco socialite who once
★ owned 40,000 acres of property along the lake, built this lodge in 1936. You can tour the mansion and the grounds by reservation only, and though it's pricey to do so, you'll be rewarded with a rare glimpse of a time when only the very wealthy had homes at Tahoe. The lodge is accessible via a bus from the Incline Village Visitors Bureau, a catamaran from the Hyatt in Incline Village ($110), or a 1950 wooden cruiser from Tahoe Keys Marina in South Lake Tahoe, which includes Continental breakfast and lunch ($135). ✉ *5000 Nevada 28* ☎ *775/832–8750 lodge info, 800/468–2463 reservations, 775/588–1881, 888/867–6394 Tahoe Keys boat, 775/831–4386 Hyatt Incline catamaran* ⊕ *thunderbirdtahoe.org/tours* 🚤 *$39 bus tour, $110 & 135 for boat tours* 🕙 *May–Oct., Tues.–Sat., call for tour times.*

BEACHES

Lake Tahoe–Nevada State Park and Sand Harbor Beach. Protecting much of the lake's eastern shore from development, this park comprises several sections that stretch from Incline Village to Zephyr Cove. Beaches and trails provide access to a wilder side of the lake, whether you're into cross-country skiing, hiking, or just relaxing at a picnic. With a gently sloping beach for lounging, crystal clear water for swimming and snorkeling, and a picnic area shaded by cedars and pines, **Sand Harbor Beach** is so popular that it sometimes fills to capacity by 11 am on summer weekends. Boaters have two launch ramps. A handicap-accessible nature trail has interpretive signs and beautiful lake views. Pets are not allowed. **Amenities:** food and drink; parking ($12 mid-Apr.–mid-Oct., $7 rest of the year); toilets; water sports. **Best for:** snorkeling; sunset; swimming; walking. ✉ *Sand Harbor Beach, Hwy. 28, 3 miles south of Incline Village* ☎ *775/831–0494* ⊕ *parks.nv.gov/parks/sand-harbor.*

WHERE TO EAT AND STAY

$$$
ECLECTIC
✕ **Fredrick's Fusion Bistro.** Copper-top tables lend a chic look to the dining room at this intimate bistro. The menu consists of a mélange of European and Asian dishes, most of them prepared with organic produce and free-range meats. Try the braised short ribs, roasted duck with caramel-pecan glaze, or the deliciously fresh sushi rolls. ■TIP➜ **On cold nights ask for a table by the fire.** Ⓢ *Average main: $24* ✉ *907 Tahoe Blvd., at Village Blvd.* ☎ *775/832–3007* ⊕ *fredricksbistro.com* ☉ *Closed Sun. and Mon. No lunch.*

$$$
FRENCH
Fodor's Choice
★
✕ **Le Bistro.** Incline Village's hidden gem serves expertly prepared French-country cuisine in a relaxed, romantic dining room. The chef-owner makes everything himself, using organically grown ingredients. Expect such dishes as pâté de campagne, escargot, herb-crusted roast lamb and fresh fish. Try the five-course prix-fixe menu ($54), which can be paired with award-winning wines. Service is gracious and attentive. ■TIP➜ **This restaurant is hard to find, so ask for directions when you book.** Ⓢ *Average main: $30* ✉ *120 Country Club Dr., No. 29, off Lakeshore Blvd.* ☎ *775/831–0800* ⊕ *www.lebistrorestaurant.net* ☉ *Closed Sun. and Mon. No lunch.*

$
SOUTHERN
✕ **T's Rotisserie.** There's nothing fancy about T's (it looks like a small snack bar), but the mesquite-grilled chicken and tri-tip steaks are delicious and inexpensive—a rare combination in pricey Incline Village. It's mainly a take-out spot; seating is limited. Ⓢ *Average main: $9* ✉ *901 Tahoe Blvd., at Village Blvd.* ☎ *775/831–2832* ▭ *No credit cards.*

$$$$
RESORT
🏨 **Hyatt Regency Lake Tahoe.** A full-service destination resort on 26 acres of prime lakefront property, the Hyatt has a range of luxurious accommodations, from tower-hotel rooms to lakeside cottages. **Pros:** incredible views; low-key casino. **Cons:** pricey (especially for families). Ⓢ *Rooms from: $359* ✉ *111 Country Club Dr.* ☎ *775/832–1234, 888/899–5019* ⊕ *www.laketahoe.hyatt.com* ⇥ *386 rooms, 36 suites* ⦿ *No meals.*

SPORTS AND THE OUTDOORS

GOLF

Incline Championship. Robert Trent Jones Sr. designed this challenging course of tightly cut, tree-lined fairways laced with water hazards that demand accuracy as well as distance skills. Greens fee includes a cart, except the 4:30 pm Super Twilight rate of $3 per hole (cart $25). ✉ *955 Fairway Blvd., at Northwood Blvd., north off Hwy. 28* ☎ *866/925–4653 reservations, 775/832–1146 pro shop* ⊕ *www.inclinegolf.com* ⛳ *$179* ⛳ *18 holes, 7106 yards, par 72.*

Incline Mountain. Robert Trent Jones Jr. designed this executive (shorter) course that requires accuracy more than distance skills. The greens fee includes a cart. ✉ *690 Wilson Way, at Golfer's Pass, south off Hwy. 431* ☎ *866/925–4653 reservations, 775/832–1150 pro shop* ⊕ *www. inclinegolf.com* ⛳ *$65 for weekdays, $75 for weekends* ⛳ *18 holes, 3519 yards, par 58.*

23

Get to Sand Harbor Beach in Lake Tahoe–Nevada State Park early; the park sometimes fills to capacity before lunchtime in summer.

MOUNTAIN BIKING

Flume Trail Bikes. You can rent bikes and get helpful tips from this company, which also operates a bike shuttle to popular trailheads. Ask about the secluded backcountry rental cabins for overnight rides. ⊠ *1115 Tunnel Creek Rd., at Ponderosa Ranch Rd., off Hwy. 28* ☎ *775/298–2501* ⊕ *www.flumetrailtahoe.com.*

SKIING

Diamond Peak. A fun family mood prevails at Diamond Peak, which has affordable rates and many special programs. Snowmaking covers 75% of the mountain, and runs are groomed nightly. The ride up the 1-mile Crystal Express rewards you with fantastic views. Diamond Peak is less crowded than Tahoe's larger ski parks and provides free shuttles to nearby lodgings. A great place for beginners and intermediates, it's appropriately priced for families. Though there are some steep-aspect black-diamond runs, advanced skiers may find the acreage too limited. For snowboarders there's a small terrain park. ⊠ *1210 Ski Way, off Country Club Dr.* ☎ *775/832–1177* ⊕ *www.diamondpeak.com* ☞ *30 trails on 655 acres, rated 18% beginner, 46% intermediate, 36% advanced. Longest run 2½ miles, base 6,700 feet, summit 8,540 feet. Lifts: 7, including 1 high-speed quad and a surface lift.*

Mt. Rose Ski Tahoe. At this park, ski some of Tahoe's highest slopes and take in bird's-eye views of Reno, the lake, and Carson Valley. Though more compact than the bigger Tahoe resorts, Mt. Rose has the area's highest base elevation and consequently the driest snow. The mountain has a wide variety of terrain. The most challenging is the Chutes, 200 acres of gulp-and-go advanced-to-expert vertical. Intermediates can choose steep groomers or mellow, wide-open boulevards. Beginners have their own corner of the mountain, with gentle, wide slopes. Boarders and tricksters have three terrain parks to choose from, on opposite sides of the mountain, allowing them to follow the sun as it tracks across the resort. The mountain gets hit hard in storms; check conditions before heading up during inclement weather or on a windy day. ✉ *22222 Mt. Rose Hwy., Hwy. 431, 11 miles north of Incline Village, Reno* ☎ *775/849–0704, 800/754–7673* 🌐 *www.skirose.com* ☞ *61 trails on 1,200 acres, rated 20% beginner, 30% intermediate, 40% advanced, 10% expert. Longest run 2½ miles, base 8,260 feet, summit 9,700 feet. Lifts: 8, including 2 high-speed 6-passenger lifts.*

> **TAHOE TESSIE**
>
> Local lore claims this huge sea monster slithers around Lake Tahoe. Skeptics laugh, but true believers keep their eyes peeled for surprise sightings.

Tahoe Meadows Snowplay Area. This is the most popular area near the north shore for noncommercial cross-country skiing, sledding, tubing, snowshoeing, and snowmobiling. ✉ *Off Hwy. 431, between Incline Village and Mt. Rose.*

ZEPHYR COVE

22 miles south of Incline Village.

The largest settlement between Incline Village and the Stateline area is Zephyr Cove, a tiny resort. It has a beach, marina, campground, picnic area, coffee shop in a log lodge, rustic cabins, and nearby riding stables.

GETTING HERE AND AROUND

From the north shore communities, reach Zephyr Cove by following Highway 28 along the eastern side of the lake. From South Lake Tahoe, take U.S. 50 north and then west. Public transportation isn't available in Zephyr Cove.

EXPLORING

Cave Rock. Near Zephyr Cove, this 75 feet of solid stone at the southern end of Lake Tahoe–Nevada State Park is the throat of an extinct volcano. Tahoe Tessie, the lake's version of the Loch Ness monster, is reputed to live in a cavern below the impressive outcropping. Cave Rock towers over a parking lot, a lakefront picnic ground, and a boat launch. The views are some of the best on the lake; this is a good spot to stop and take a picture. But this area is a sacred burial site for the Washoe Indians, and climbing up to the cave, or through it, is prohibited. ✉ *U.S. 50, 4 miles north of Zephyr Cove* ☎ *775/831–0494.*

WHERE TO STAY

$$$ RENTAL FAMILY 🏠 **Zephyr Cove Resort.** Beneath towering pines at the lake's edge stand 28 cozy, modern vacation cabins with peaked knotty-pine ceilings. **Pros:** family-friendly. **Cons:** lodge rooms are basic; can be noisy. [$] *Rooms from: $199* ✉ *760 U.S. 50, 4 miles north of Stateline* ☎ *775/589–4907, 800/238–2463* 🌐 *www.zephyrcove.com* 🛏 *28 cabins; 4 lodge rooms* 🍴 *No meals.*

STATELINE

5 miles south of Zephyr Cove.

Stateline is the archetypal Nevada border town. Its four high-rise casinos are as vertical and contained as the commercial district of South Lake Tahoe, on the California side, is horizontal and sprawling. And Stateline is as relentlessly indoors-oriented as the rest of the lake is focused on the outdoors. This strip is where you'll find the most concentrated action at Lake Tahoe: restaurants (including typical casino buffets), showrooms with famous headliners and razzle-dazzle revues, tower-hotel rooms and suites, and 24-hour casinos.

GETTING HERE AND AROUND

From South Lake Tahoe take U.S. 50 north across the Nevada border to reach Stateline and its casinos. If coming from Reno's airport, take U.S. 395/Interstate 580 south to Carson City, and then head west on U.S. 50 to the lake and head south. Or take the South Tahoe Express bus. BlueGO operates daily bus service in the south shore area year-round, plus a ski shuttle from the large hotels to Heavenly in the winter.

BEACHES

Nevada Beach. Although less than a mile long, this is the widest beach on the lake and especially good for swimming (many Tahoe beaches are rocky). You can boat and fish here, and there are picnic tables, barbecue grills, and a campground beneath the pines. This is the best place to watch the July 4th or Labor Day fireworks, but most of the summer the subdued atmosphere attracts families and those seeking a less-touristy spot. **Amenities:** parking ($7 fee), water sports, toilets. **Best for:** sunrise, swimming, walking. ✉ *Elk Point Rd., off U.S. 50, 3 miles north of Stateline* ☎ *530/543–2600* 🌐 *www.fs.usda.gov/ltbmu* ⏲ *Open daily late May–Oct.* ☞ *No pets.*

WHERE TO EAT AND STAY

$$$ FRENCH Fodor's Choice ★ 🍴 **Mirabelle.** Don't be put off by this restaurant's nondescript exterior. Inside there's an airy dining room with creamy yellow walls and white tablecloths. Enticing scents drift from the kitchen, where the Alsatian-born chef-owner, Camille Schwartz, prepares everything from puff pastry to meringues to homemade bread. Specialties include sautéed veal sweetbreads, garlicky escargot, and rack of lamb with fresh thyme. There's always a fresh fish entrée, plus a $31.50 prix-fixe "epicurean menu." [$] *Average main: $27* ✉ *290 Kingsbury Grade, off U.S. 50* ☎ *775/586–1007* 🌐 *www.mirabelletahoe.com* ⏲ *Closed Mon. No lunch.*

$ HOTEL 🏨 **Harrah's Tahoe Hotel/Casino.** The hotel's major selling point is that every room has two full bathrooms, a boon if you're traveling with family. **Pros:** central location; great midweek values. **Cons:** can get noisy. [$] *Rooms from: $109* ✉ *15 U.S. 50, at Stateline Ave.* ☎ *775/588–6611, 800/427–7247* 🌐 *www.harrahslaketahoe.com* 🛏 *470 rooms, 62 suites* 🍽 *No meals.*

$ HOTEL 🏨 **Harveys Resort Hotel/Casino.** This resort began as a cabin in 1944, and now it's Tahoe's largest casino-hotel; premium rooms have custom furnishings, oversize marble baths, minibars, and good lake views. **Pros:** hip entertainment; just a few blocks north of the Heavenly Gondola.

Cons: can get loud at night. [$] *Rooms from: $79* ✉ *18 U.S. 50, at Stateline Ave.* ☎ *775/588–2411, 800/648–3361* 🌐 *www.harveystahoe.com* 🛏 *742 rooms, 36 suites* 🍴 *No meals.*

NIGHTLIFE

Each of the major casinos has its own showroom, featuring everything from comedy to magic acts to sexy floor shows to Broadway musicals.

DANCE CLUBS

Peek. You can dance the night away with top-notch DJs, and often hear live performances, at this club that emulates a Vegas vibe. ✉ *Harrah's Lake Tahoe, 15 U.S. 50* ☎ *775/588–6611 information, 775/586–6705 Peek reservations* 🌐 *www.caesars.com/peek.*

LIVE MUSIC

Harveys Outdoor Summer Concert Series. Harveys Lake Tahoe books outdoor concerts on weekends in summer with headliners such as the Zac Brown Band, Journey, and Bruno Mars. ✉ *18 U.S. 50* ☎ *775/588–2411* 🌐 *www.harveystahoe.com/shows.html.*

South Shore Room. Classic acts like the Temptations and legendary reggae band the Wailers play Harrah's big showroom, along with tribute shows for groups such as the Beatles and Bruce Springsteen and the E Street Band. ✉ *Harrah's Lake Tahoe, 15 U.S. 50* ☎ *775/586–6244 tickets, 775/588–6611* 🌐 *www.harrahslaketahoe.com/shows.html.*

SPORTS AND THE OUTDOORS

GOLF

Edgewood Tahoe. Golfers of all skill levels enjoy this scenic lakeside course that has four sets of tees, offering a variety of course lengths. The greens fee includes an optional cart. ✉ *100 Lake Pkwy., at U.S. 50* ☎ *775/588–3566, 866/761–4653* 🌐 *www.edgewood-tahoe.com* 🎟 *$220 for weekdays, $240 for weekends* ⛳ *18 holes, 7543 yards, par 72.*

RENO

32 miles east of Truckee, 38 miles northeast of Incline Village.

Established in 1859 as a trading station at a bridge over the Truckee River, Reno grew along with the silver mines of nearby Virginia City and the transcontinental railroad that chugged through town. Train officials named it in 1868, but gambling—legalized in 1931—put Reno on the map. This is still a gambling town, with most of the casinos crowded into five square blocks downtown, but a thriving university scene and outdoor activities also attract tourists.

Parts of downtown are sketchy, but things are changing. Several defunct casinos are being converted into condominiums, and the riverfront is being reconceived. The town now touts family-friendly activities like kayaking on the Truckee, and new shops and excellent restaurants have sprung up outside the hotels. Temperatures year-round in this high-mountain-desert climate are warmer than at Tahoe, though it rarely gets as hot here as in Sacramento and the Central Valley, making strolling around town a pleasure.

GETTING HERE AND AROUND

Interstate 80 bisects Reno east–west, U.S. 395 north–south (south of town the road is signed U.S. 395/Interstate 580). Greyhound and Amtrak stop here, and several airlines fly into Reno-Tahoe International Airport. RTC Ride provides bus service in the greater Reno area.

ESSENTIALS

Bus Contact RTC Ride ⌧ *Transit Center, E. 4th and Lake Sts.* ☎ *775/348–7433* ⊕ *rtcwashoe.com.*

Visitor Information Reno-Sparks Convention and Visitors Authority ⌧ *4001 S. Virginia St.* ☎ *775/827–7650, 800/367–7366* ⊕ *www.visitrenotahoe.com.*

EXPLORING

TOP ATTRACTIONS

FAMILY **National Automobile Museum.** Antique and classic automobiles, including an Elvis Presley Cadillac, a Mercury coupe driven by James Dean in the movie *Rebel Without a Cause*, and the experimental and still futuristic-looking 1938 Phantom Corsair, are all on display at this museum. ⌧ *10 S. Lake St., at Mill St.* ☎ *775/333–9300* ⊕ *www.automuseum.org* ⌧ *$10* ☉ *Mon.–Sat. 9:30–5:30, Sun. 10–4.*

Nevada Museum of Art. A dramatic four-level structure designed by Will Bruder houses this splendid museum's collection, which focuses on themes such as the Sierra Nevada/Great Basin and altered-landcape photography. The building's exterior torqued walls are sided with a black zinc-based material that has been fabricated to resemble textures found in the Black Rock Desert. Inside the building, a staircase installed within the central atrium is lit by skylights and suspended by a single beam attached to the atrium ceiling; visitors can climb 55 feet to the fourth-floor, rooftop landing. ⌧ *160 W. Liberty St., and Hill St.* ☎ *775/329–3333* ⊕ *www.nevadaart.org* ⌧ *$10* ☉ *Wed. and Fri.–Sun. 10–6, Thurs. 10–8.*

Fodor's Choice ★ **Riverwalk District.** The makeover of Reno's waterfront has transformed this formerly dilapidated area into the toast of the town. The Riverwalk itself is a half-mile promenade on the north side of the Truckee River, which flows around lovely Wingfield Park, where outdoor festivals and other events take place. On the third Saturday of each month, local merchants host a **Wine Walk** between 2 and 5. For $20, you receive a wine glass and can sample fine wines at participating shops, bars, restaurants, and galleries. In July look for stellar outdoor art, opera, dance, and kids' performances as part of the month-long **Artown festival** (⊕ *renoisartown.com*), presented mostly in Wingfield Park. Also at Wingfield is the **Truckee River Whitewater Park.** With activities for all skill levels, it's become a major attraction for water-sports enthusiasts. ⌧ *Riverwalk, north side of Truckee River between Lake and Ralston Sts.* ⊕ *renoriver.org.*

WORTH NOTING

FAMILY **Fleischmann Planetarium.** Digital star shows provide the glittering lights inside this facility. The shows aim to make learning about astronomy entertaining for kids and adults. ✉ *University of Nevada, 1664 N. Virginia St., near E. 15th St.* ☎ *775/784–4811 recorded information, 775/784–4812 office* 🌐 *www.planetarium.unr.nevada.edu* 🎟 *Exhibits free, films and star shows $7* 🕒 *Mon.–Thurs. noon–7; Fri. noon–9; Sat. 10–9; Sun. 10–7.*

WHERE TO EAT

$$$ AMERICAN Fodor's Choice ★ 🍴 **4th St. Bistro.** For deliciously simple, smart cooking, head to this charming little bistro on the edge of town. The chef-owner uses organic produce and meats in her soulful preparation of dishes like Cabernet-braised lamb shanks with white beans, spinach, and black olive gremolata. Ochre-color sponge-painted walls, tablecloths from Provence, and a roaring fireplace in winter warm the dining room. [$] *Average main: $30* ✉ *3065 W. 4th St.* ☎ *775/323–3200* 🌐 *www.4thstbistro.com* 🕒 *Closed Sun. and Mon. No lunch.*

$ THAI 🍴 **Bangkok Cuisine.** To eat well but not break the bank, come to this busy Thai restaurant and sample the delicious soups, salads, stir-fries, and curries. [$] *Average main: $12* ✉ *55 Mt. Rose St., at S. Virginia St.* ☎ *775/322–0299* 🌐 *thaifoodreno.com* 🕒 *No lunch Sun.*

$$$ FRENCH Fodor's Choice ★ 🍴 **Beaujolais Bistro.** Across from the Truckee River, this Reno favorite serves earthy, country-style French food with zero pretension—classics like beef bourguignon, escargots, steak frites béarnaise, and braised lamb shoulder. Wood floors, large windows, and brick walls with a fireplace create a welcoming and intimate atmosphere. Diners who want a more casual experience can dine at the long bar. Less expensive small plates as well as an inventive cocktail menu are also offered. [$] *Average main: $28* ✉ *753 Riverside Dr.* ☎ *775/323–2227* 🌐 *www.beaujolaisbistro.com* 🕒 *No lunch. Closed Mon.*

$ CAFÉ 🍴 **Chocolate Bar.** Part café, part cocktail bar, this hip little spot close to the river makes truffles, chocolate fondue, fabulous fruity cocktails, hot chocolate, gourmet small plates, and entrees, all served at a long wooden bar or at several tables and leather banquettes. Chocolate Bar is open late each night for those craving dessert, a chocolate cocktail, or a simple, unadorned cognac. [$] *Average main: $15* ✉ *95 N. Sierra St., at W. 1st St.* ☎ *775/337–1122* 🌐 *thechocbar.com.*

WHERE TO STAY

$ HOTEL 🏨 **Harrah's Reno.** Of the big-name casino hotels in downtown Reno, double-towered Harrah's is still the best, with no surprises. **Pros:** sets the standard for downtown Reno; great online midweek rates. **Cons:** huge property. [$] *Rooms from: $67* ✉ *219 N. Center St., at E. 2nd St.* ☎ *775/786–3232, 800/427–7247* 🌐 *www.harrahsreno.com* 🛏 *876 rooms, 52 suites* 🍽 *No meals.*

$ HOTEL 🏨 **Peppermill Reno.** A few miles removed from downtown's flashy main drag, this property sets a new standard for luxury in Reno; its 600 baroque suites in the Tuscan Tower have plush king-size beds, marble bathrooms, and European soaking tubs. **Pros:** luxurious rooms; casino decor; good coffee shop. **Cons:** deluge of neon may be off-putting to some. [$] *Rooms from: $99* ✉ *2707 S. Virginia St., at Peppermill La.*

☎ *775/826–2121, 866/821–9996* ⊕ *www.peppermillreno.com* ⤳ *915 rooms, 720 suites* ⊙ *No meals.*

NIGHTLIFE

CASINOS

FAMILY **Circus Circus.** Families with kids head to this casino, where a midway above the floor has clowns, games, fun-house mirrors, and circus acts. ✉ *500 N. Sierra St., at W. 5th St.* ☎ *775/329–0711, 800/648–5010* ⊕ *www.circusreno.com.*

Eldorado. Action-packed, with lots of slots and popular bar-top video poker, this casino also has good coffee-shop and food-court fare. Don't miss the Fountain of Fortune with its massive Florentine-inspired sculptures. ✉ *345 N. Virginia St., at W. 4th St.* ☎ *775/786–5700, 800/879–8879* ⊕ *www.eldoradoreno.com.*

Harrah's Reno. Occupying two city blocks, this landmark property has a sprawling casino and an outdoor promenade. ✉ *219 N. Center St., at E. 2nd St.* ☎ *775/786–3232, 800/427–7247* ⊕ *www.harrahsreno.com.*

Peppermill. A few miles from downtown, this casino is known for its excellent restaurants and neon-bright gambling areas. The Fireside cocktail lounge is a blast. ✉ *2707 S. Virginia St., at Peppermill La.* ☎ *775/826–2121, 866/821–9996* ⊕ *www.peppermillreno.com.*

Silver Legacy. A 120-foot-tall mining rig and video poker games draw gamblers to this razzle-dazzle casino. ✉ *407 N. Virginia St., at W. 4th St.* ☎ *775/329–4777, 800/687–8733* ⊕ *www.silverlegacyreno.com.*

THE FAR NORTH

With Lake Shasta, Mt. Shasta, and
Lassen Volcanic National Park

WELCOME TO THE FAR NORTH

TOP REASONS TO GO

★ **Mother Nature's wonders:** California's Far North has more rivers, streams, lakes, forests, and mountains than you'll ever have time to explore.

★ **Rock and roll:** With two volcanoes to entice you—Lassen and Shasta—you can learn firsthand what happens when a mountain blows its top.

★ **Fantastic fishing:** Whether you like casting from a riverbank or letting your line bob beside a boat, you'll find fabulous fishing in all the northern counties.

★ **Cool hops:** On a hot day there's nothing quite as inviting as a visit to Chico's world-famous Sierra Nevada Brewery. Take the tour and then savor a chilled glass on tap at the adjacent brewpub.

★ **Shasta:** Wonderful in all its forms: lake, dam, river, mountain, forest, and town.

1 From Chico to Mt Shasta. The Far North is bisected, south to north, by Interstate 5, which passes through several historic towns and state parks, as well as miles of mountainous terrain. Halfway to the Oregon border is Lake Shasta, a favorite recreation destination, and farther north stands the spectacular snowy peak of Mt. Shasta.

2 The Backcountry. East of Interstate 5, the Far North's main corridor, dozens of scenic two-lane roads crisscross the wilderness, leading to dramatic mountain peaks and fascinating natural wonders. Small towns settled in the second half of the 19th century seem frozen in time, except that they are well equipped with tourist amenities.

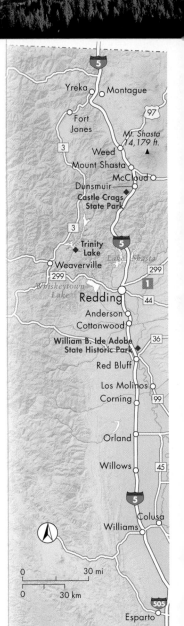

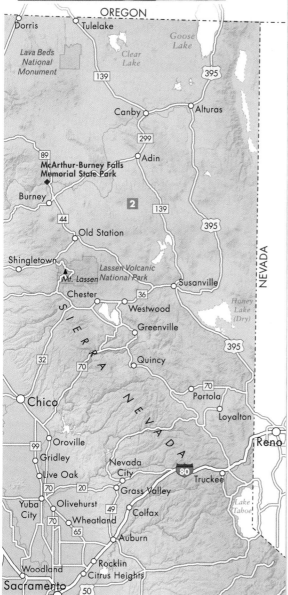

GETTING ORIENTED

24

The Far North is a vast area that stretches from the upper reaches of the Sacramento Valley north to the Oregon border and east to Nevada. The region includes all or part of eight counties with sparsely populated rural farming and mountain communities, as well as thriving small cities in the valley. Much of the landscape was shaped by two volcanoes—Mt. Shasta and Mt. Lassen—that draw amateur geologists, weekend hikers, and avid mountain climbers to their rugged terrain. An intricate network of high mountain watersheds feeds lakes large and small, plus streams and rivers that course through several forests.

Updated by Christine Vovakes

The Far North's soaring mountain peaks, trail-filled national forests, alpine lakes, and wild rivers teeming with trout make it the perfect destination for outdoor enthusiasts, including hikers, cyclists, kayakers, and bird-watchers. You won't find many hot nightspots or cultural enclaves in this region, but you will find crowd-free national and state parks, crystal clear mountain streams, superlative hiking and fishing, plus small towns worth exploring. And the spectacular landscapes of Lassen Volcanic National Park and Mt. Shasta are sure to impress.

The wondrous landscape of California's northeastern corner, relatively unmarred by development, congestion, and traffic, is the product of volcanic activity. At the southern end of the Cascade Range, Lassen Volcanic National Park is the best place to witness the Far North's fascinating geology. Beyond the sulfur vents and bubbling mud pots, the park owes much of its beauty to 10,457-foot Mt. Lassen and 50 wilderness lakes.

The most enduring image of the region, though, is Mt. Shasta, whose 14,179-foot snowcapped peak beckons outdoor adventurers of all kinds. There are many versions of Shasta to enjoy—the mountain, the lake, the river, the town, the dam, and the forest—all named after the Native Americans known as the Shatasla, or Sastise, who once inhabited the region.

PLANNING

WHEN TO GO

Heat scorches the valley in summer. Temperatures above 110°F are common, but the mountains provide cool respite. Fall throughout the Far North is beautiful, rivaled only by spring, when wildflowers and almond orchards bloom and mountain creeks fed by the snowmelt splash through the forests. Winter is usually temperate in the valley, but cold and snowy in high country. A few favorite tourist attractions are closed in winter.

GETTING HERE AND AROUND

AIR TRAVEL

For the cheapest fares, fly into Sacramento *(⇨ Chapter 22, Sacramento and the Gold Country)* and then rent a car—you'll need one anyway—and drive north. Chico and Redding, both served by United Express, have small airports. Neither has shuttle service, but you can take a taxi for about $32 to downtown Redding or $21 to downtown Chico.

Air Contacts Redding Municipal Airport ⊠ *6751 Woodrum Circle, off Airport Rd., Redding* ☎ *530/224–4320* ⊕ *www.ci.redding.ca.us/transeng/airports/rma.htm.*

Ground Transportation Taxi Service, Chico ☎ *530/893–4444, 530/898–1776.* **Taxi Service, Redding** ☎ *530/246–0577, 530/222–1234.*

BUS TRAVEL

Greyhound buses stop in Chico, Red Bluff, Redding, and Weed. Various transit authorities provide local bus transportation *(see individual town listings for details)*, though few tourists avail themselves of it.

Bus Contact Greyhound ☎ *800/231–2222* ⊕ *www.greyhound.com.*

CAR TRAVEL

Interstate 5 runs up the center of California through Red Bluff and Redding. Chico is east of Interstate 5 on Highway 32. Lassen Volcanic National Park can be reached by Highway 36 from Red Bluff or (except in winter) Highway 44 from Redding. Highway 299 connects Weaverville, Redding and Alturas. U.S. 395 leads from Susanville to Alturas. Highway 89 will take you from Mt. Shasta to Quincy. Highway 36 links Chester and Susanville. Check weather reports and carry detailed maps, warm clothing, and tire chains whenever you head into mountainous terrain in winter.

Road Conditions Caltrans Current Highway Conditions ☎ *800/427–7623* ⊕ *www.dot.ca.gov.*

TRAIN TRAVEL

Amtrak serves Chico, Redding, and Dunsmuir.

Train Contacts Amtrak ☎ *800/872–7245* ⊕ *www.amtrak.com.*

RESTAURANTS

Redding, the urban center of the Far North, and college-town Chico have the greatest selection of restaurants. Cafés and simple eateries are the rule in the smaller towns, though trendy, innovative restaurants have been popping up. Dress is always informal.

HOTELS

Aside from the large chain hotels and motels in Redding and Chico, most accommodations in the Far North blend rustic appeal, simplicity, and coziness. Rooms in Redding, Chico, and Red Bluff usually are booked solid only during popular local events. Wilderness resorts close in fall and reopen after the snow season ends in May. For

24

summer holiday weekends in towns such as Mt. Shasta, Dunsmuir, and Chester, and at camping sites within state or national parks, make lodging reservations well in advance. *Hotel reviews have been shortened. For full information, visit Fodors.com.*

B&B Info California Association of Boutique & Breakfast Inns ☎ 800/373-9251 ⊕ *www.cabbi.com/region/Mount-Shasta.*

WHAT IT COSTS				
	$	**$$**	**$$$**	**$$$$**
Restaurants	under $16	$16–$22	$23–$30	over $30
Hotels	under $121	$121–$175	$176–$250	over $250

Restaurant prices are the average cost of a main course at dinner or, if dinner is not served, at lunch. Hotel prices are the lowest cost of a standard double room in high season.

VISITOR INFORMATION

Contacts Lassen County Chamber of Commerce ✉ *75 N. Weatherlow St., Susanville* ☎ *530/257-4323* ⊕ *lassencountychamber.com.* **Shasta Cascade Wonderland Association** ✉ *1699 Hwy. 273, Anderson* ☎ *530/365-7500, 800/474-2782* ⊕ *www.shastacascade.com.* **Visit Siskiyou** ☎ *800/926-4865 Mt. Shasta Chamber of Commerce* ⊕ *visitsiskiyou.org.*

FROM CHICO TO MT. SHASTA

From the blooming almond orchards of the fertile Sacramento River valley, through the forested mountains and to the dominating peak of a dormant volcano, this section of the Far North entices tourists in all seasons.

CHICO

180 miles from San Francisco, east on I–80, north on I–505 to I–5, and east on Hwy. 32; 86 miles north of Sacramento on Hwy. 99.

Chico (which is Spanish for "small") lies in the Sacramento Valley and offers a welcome break from the monotony of Interstate 5. The Chico campus of California State University, the scores of local artisans, and the area's agriculture (primarily almond orchards) all influence the culture here. Chico's true claim to fame, however, is the popular Sierra Nevada Brewery, which keeps beer drinkers across the country happy with its distinctive brews.

GETTING HERE AND AROUND

Both Highway 99, coming north from Sacramento or south off Interstate 5 at Red Bluff, and Highway 32, going east off Interstate 5 at Orland, intersect Chico. Amtrak and Greyhound stop here, and United Express flies into the Chico airport. Butte Regional Transit's B-Line buses serve Chico and nearby towns. Anchored by a robust university scene, the downtown neighborhoods are great for walking.

24

ESSENTIALS

Bus Contact B-Line ☎ 530/342–0221, 800/822–8145 ⊕ www.blinetransit.com.

Visitor Information Chico Chamber of Commerce ✉ 441 Main St., Ste. 150, near E. 5th St. ☎ 530/891–5556, 800/852–8570 ⊕ www.chicochamber.com.

EXPLORING

Bidwell Mansion State Historic Park. Built between 1865 and 1868 by General John Bidwell, the founder of Chico, this mansion was designed by Henry W. Cleaveland, a San Francisco architect. Bidwell and his wife welcomed many distinguished guests to their distinctive pink Italianate home, including President Rutherford B. Hayes, naturalist John Muir, suffragist Susan B. Anthony, and General William T. Sherman. A one-hour tour takes you through most of the mansion's 26 rooms. Credit cards are not accepted. ✉ 525 The Esplanade, at Memorial Way ☎ 530/895–6144 ⊕ www.parks.ca.gov/parkindex 🎫 $6 ⊙ Mon. noon–5, weekends 11–5; last tour at 4 ⊙ Closed Tues.–Fri.

Bidwell Park. The sprawling 3,670-acre Bidwell Park is a community green space straddling Big Chico Creek, where scenes from Gone With the Wind and the 1938 version of Robin Hood (starring Errol Flynn) were filmed. The region's recreational hub, it includes a golf course, swimming areas, and biking, hiking, horseback riding, and in-line skating trails. One of the largest city-run parks in the country, Bidwell starts as a slender strip downtown and expands eastward 11 miles toward the Sierra foothills. Chico Creek Nature Center serves as the official information site for Bidwell Park. ✉ 1968 E. 8th St., off Hwy. 99 ☎ 530/896–7800 Chico Public Works Dept., 530/891–4671 Chico Creek Nature Center ⊕ www.bidwellpark.org.

Sierra Nevada Brewing Company. This pioneer of the microbrewery movement still has a hands-on approach to beer making. Tour the brew house and see how the beer is produced—from the sorting of hops through fermentation and bottling. You can also visit the gift shop and enjoy a hearty lunch or dinner in the brewpub where tastings are available (for a fee). ✉ 1075 E. 20th St., at Sierra Nevada St. ☎ 530/345–2739 Brew Pub, 530/899-4776 Tours ⊕ www.sierranevada.com 🎫 Free ⊙ Tours daily, call for times.

WHERE TO EAT AND STAY

$$$
STEAKHOUSE
✕ **5th Street Steakhouse.** Hand-cut steak is the star in this refurbished early 1900s building, the place to come when you're craving red meat and a huge baked potato. Exposed redbrick walls warm the small dining area. A long mahogany bar catches the overflow crowds that jam the place on weekends. Lunch is served on Fridays only. No reservations for parties smaller than six persons are accepted on Fridays and Saturdays. 💲 Average main: $29 ✉ 345 W. 5th St., at Normal Ave. ☎ 530/891–6328 ⊕ www.5thstreetsteakhouse.com ⊙ No lunch Sat.–Thurs.

$
AMERICAN
✕ **Madison Bear Garden.** This downtown favorite two blocks south of the Chico State campus is a great spot for checking out the vibrant college scene while enjoying a burger and a brew. 💲 Average main: $8 ✉ 316 W. 2nd St., at Salem St. ☎ 530/891–1639 ⊕ www.madisonbeargarden.com.

$$$
MEDITERRANEAN

✗ **Red Tavern.** With its burgundy carpet, white linen tablecloths, and mellow lighting, this is one of Chico's coziest restaurants. The Mediterranean-influenced menu, inspired by fresh local produce, changes seasonally. There's a great California wine list, and a full bar. $ *Average main: $23* ✉ *1250 The Esplanade, at E. 3rd Ave.* ☎ *530/894–3463* ⊕ *www.redtavern.com* ☉ *No dinner Sun., no lunch Mon.–Sat.*

$$
HOTEL

⊓ **Hotel Diamond.** Crystal chandeliers and gleaming wood floors and banisters elegantly welcome guests into the foyer of this restored gem in downtown Chico near the university. **Pros:** refined; great location; breakfast voucher included in room rate. **Cons:** not a good choice for families. $ *Rooms from: $139* ✉ *220 W. 4th St., near Broadway* ☎ *530/893–3100, 866/993–3100* ⊕ *hoteldiamondchico.com* ⟳ *39 rooms, 4 suites* ¶◎¶ *Breakfast.*

SHOPPING

Made in Chico. This establishment sells locally made goods, including pottery, olives, almonds, and Woof and Poof creations—whimsical home-decor items, such as stuffed Santas, elves, animals, and pillows. ✉ *127 W. 3rd St., between Main St. and Broadway* ☎ *530/894–7009* ⊕ *www.madeinchicostore.com.*

Needham Studios. Beautiful custom-made etched, stained, and beveled glass is created at Needham Studios. ✉ *237 Broadway, at 3rd St.* ☎ *530/345–4718* ⊕ *www.needhamstudios.com.*

RED BLUFF

41 miles north of Chico on Hwy 99.

Historic Red Bluff is a gateway to Lassen Volcanic National Park. Established in the mid-19th century as a shipping center on the Sacramento River, and named for the color of its soil, the town is filled with dozens of restored Victorians. It's a great home base for outdoor adventures in the area.

GETTING HERE AND AROUND

Access Red Bluff via exits off Interstate 5, or by driving north on Highway 99. Highway 36 is a long, twisting road that begins near the Pacific Coast and goes to Red Bluff, then east to the towns near Lassen Volcanic National Park. Greyhound buses stop here and also provide connecting service to Amtrak. TRAX (Tehama Rural Area Express) serves Red Bluff and neighboring towns.

ESSENTIALS

Bus Information TRAX ☎ *530/385–2877* ⊕ *www.taketrax.com.*

Visitor Information Red Bluff–Tehama County Chamber of Commerce ✉ *100 Main St., at Rio St.* ☎ *530/527–6220* ⊕ *www.redbluffchamber.com.*

EXPLORING

William B. Ide Adobe State Historic Park. Named for the first and only president of the short-lived California Republic of 1846, William B. Ide Adobe State Historic Park is on an oak-lined bank of the Sacramento River. The Bear Flag Party proclaimed California a sovereign nation, separate from Mexican rule, and the republic existed for 22 days before it was taken over by the United States. The republic's flag has survived, with minor refinements, as California's state flag. The park's main attraction is an adobe home built in the 1850s and outfitted with period furnishings. ✉ *21659 Adobe Rd., at Park Pl.* ☎ *530/529–8599* ⊕ *www.parks.ca.gov/?page_id=458* 💲 *$6 per vehicle* ⏱ *Park and picnic facilities, adobe home, and historic sites Fri.–Sun. 10–4.*

RED BLUFF ROUND-UP

Check out old-time rodeo at its best during the Red Bluff Round-Up. Held the third weekend of April, this annual event attracts some of the best cowboys in the country. For more information, visit ⊕ *redbluffroundup.com.*

WHERE TO EAT AND STAY

$$
STEAKHOUSE

✗ **Green Barn Steakhouse.** You're likely to find cowboys sporting Stetsons and spurs feasting on sizzling porterhouse, baby back ribs, and prime rib at Red Bluff's premier steak house. For lighter fare, there's rainbow trout or clam fettuccine. Don't miss the bread pudding with rum sauce. The lounge is usually hopping, especially when there's an event at the nearby rodeo grounds. 💲 *Average main: $19* ✉ *5 Chestnut Ave., at Antelope Blvd.* ☎ *530/527–3161* 🗫 *Reservations not accepted* ⏱ *Closed Sun.*

$
HOTEL

🏨 **Sportsman Lodge.** On-site owners keep this small motel neat and inviting, with practical amenities like refrigerators, microwaves, cable TV, and free Wi-Fi. **Pros:** spacious rooms; helpful owners; pet-friendly. **Cons:** an older facility. 💲 *Rooms from: $62* ✉ *768 Antelope Blvd., near Trinity Ave.* ☎ *530/527-2888* ⊕ *www.redbluffsportsmanlodge.com* 🛏 *19* ⏱❙ *No meals.*

REDDING

32 miles north of Red Bluff on I–5.

As the largest city in the Far North, Redding is an ideal headquarters for exploring the surrounding countryside.

GETTING HERE AND AROUND

Reach Redding from exits off Interstate 5 or via Highway 299, which originates near coastal Eureka and crosses Weaverville and Redding before heading northeast to Burney and Alturas. Highway 44 stretches from Susanville past Lassen Park's north entrance before ending in Redding. United Express serves the Redding airport. Amtrak and Greyhound make stops here.

ESSENTIALS

Bus Information Redding Area Bus Authority ☎ *530/241–2877* ⊕ *www.rabaride.com.*

Visitor Information Redding Convention and Visitors Bureau ✉ *2334 Washington Ave., Ste. B* ☎ *530/225–4100, 800/874–7562* ⊕ *www.visitredding.com.*

24

Anglers fish under Santiago Calatrava's striking Sundial Bridge next to Turtle Bay Exploration Park.

EXPLORING

FAMILY
Fodor's Choice ★
Turtle Bay Exploration Park. This park features walking trails, an arboretum and botanical gardens, and lots of interactive exhibits for kids, including a gold-panning area and the seasonal butterfly exhibit. The main draw is the stunning **Sundial Bridge,** which links the Sacramento River Trail and the park's arboretum and gardens. Access to the bridge and arboretum is free, but there's a fee for the museum. ✉ *844 Sundial Bridge Dr., off Hwy. 44* ☎ *530/243–8850, 800/887–8532* 🌐 *www.turtlebay.org* 🎟 *Museum $14* 🕒 *May–early Sept., Mon.–Sat. 9–5, Sun. 10–5; early Sept.–Apr., Wed.–Sat. 9–4, Sun. 10–4.*

WHERE TO EAT AND STAY

$$$ STEAKHOUSE
🍴 **Jack's Grill.** Famous for its 16-ounce steaks, this popular bar and steak house also serves shrimp and chicken. A town favorite, the place is usually jam-packed and noisy. The bar serves great martinis. [$] *Average main: $26* ✉ *1743 California St., near Sacramento St.* ☎ *530/241–9705* 🌐 *www.jacksgrillredding.com* 🕒 *Closed Sun. No lunch.*

$ AMERICAN
🍴 **Klassique Kafe.** Two sisters run this small, bustling restaurant that caters to locals looking for simple but hearty breakfast and lunch fare. The hot luncheon specials served daily might include butter beans and ham with corn bread, or chicken and dumplings. [$] *Average main: $9* ✉ *2427 Athens Ave., at Locust St.* ☎ *530/244–4939* 🕒 *Closed Sat. & Sun. No dinner.*

$$$ ITALIAN
🍴 **Nello's Place.** Fine Italian dining and romantic ambience go hand-in-hand at Nello's Place, one of Redding's best restaurants. You'll find a varied selection of veal, chicken, beef, and pasta dishes mixed with lighter fish and vegetarian fare. For special presentations, order a

Caesar salad prepared tableside for two, and bananas flambé for dessert. There's a full bar in addition to an extensinve wine list. $ *Average main: $24* ✉ *3055 Bechelli Ln., near Hartnell Ave.* ☎ *530/223-1636* ⊕ *nellosrestaurant.net* ⊘ *No lunch. Closed Mon.*

$ 🍴 **The Red Lion.** Close to Redding's convention center and regional rec-
HOTEL reation sites, this hotel is a top choice for both business and vacation travelers. **Pros:** family-friendly; close to a major shopping and dining area. **Cons:** on a noisy street. $ *Rooms from: $119* ✉ *1830 Hilltop Dr., Hwy. 44/299 exit off I–5* ☎ *530/221–8700, 800/733–5466* ⊕ *www. redlion.com* ➥ *192 rooms, 2 suites* ❌ *No meals.*

SPORTS AND THE OUTDOORS
FISHING
Fly Shop. This store sells fishing licenses and has information about guides, conditions, and fishing packages. ✉ *4140 Churn Creek Rd., at Denton Way* ☎ *530/222-3555* ⊕ *www.flyshop.com.*

24

WEAVERVILLE

46 miles west of Redding on Hwy. 299.

A man known only as Weaver struck gold here in 1849, and the fledgling community that developed at the base of the Trinity Alps was named after him. With its impressive downtown historic district, today Weaverville is a popular headquarters for family vacations and biking, hiking, fishing, and gold-panning excursions.

GETTING HERE AND AROUND
Highway 299 becomes Main Street down the center of Weaverville. Take the highway either east from the Pacific Coast or west from Redding. Highway 36 from Red Bluff to Highway 3 heading north leads to Weaverville. Trinity Transit provides minimal local bus service plus a line that links Weaverville to Interstate 5 at Redding.

EXPLORING
Trinity County Courthouse. Built in 1856 as a store, office building, and hotel, Trinity County Courthouse was converted to county use in 1865. The Apollo Saloon, in the basement, became the county jail. It's the oldest courthouse still in use in California. ✉ *Court and Main Sts.*

Trinity County Hal Goodyear Historical Park. For a vivid sense of Weaverville's past, visit the Trinity County Hal Goodyear Historical Park, especially its **Jake Jackson Memorial Museum,** which has a blacksmith shop and a stamp mill (where ore is crushed) from the 1890s that is still in use. Also here are the original jail cells of the Trinity County Courthouse. ✉ *780 Main St., at Bartlett La.* ☎ *530/623-5211* ⊕ *trinity museum.org* ⊘ *Jan.–Mar., Wed. and Sat. 11–4; Apr. and Oct., daily 11–4; May–Sept., daily 10–5; Nov. and Dec., Wed.–Sat. 11–4.*

Fodor'sChoice **Weaverville Joss House.** Weaverville's main attraction is the Joss House,
★ a Taoist temple built in 1874 and called Won Lim Miao ("the temple of the forest beneath the clouds") by Chinese miners. The oldest continuously used Chinese temple in California, it attracts worshippers from around the world. With its golden altar, antique weaponry, and carved wooden canopies, the Joss House is a piece of California history

that can best be appreciated on a guided 30-minute tour. The original temple building and many of its furnishings—some of which came from China—were lost to fire in 1873, but members of the local Chinese community soon rebuilt it. ✉ *630 Main St., at Oregon St.* ☎ *530/623–5284* 🌐 *www.parks.ca.gov/parkindex* 🎟 *Museum free; guided tour $4* 🕒 *Thurs., Sat.–Sun. 10–5; last tour at 4.*

WHERE TO EAT AND STAY

$ MEXICAN 🍴 **La Casita.** A traditional selection of Mexican food is on the menu here, including quesadillas (try the version with roasted chili peppers), tostadas, enchiladas, tacos, and tamales. Many dishes are available without meat. Open from late morning through dinner, this casual spot is great for a midafternoon snack. [$] *Average main: $9* ✉ *570 Main St.* ☎ *530/623–5797* 🕒 *Closed Sun.*

$$ AMERICAN 🍴 **La Grange Café.** In two brick buildings dating from the 1850s (they're among the oldest edifices in town), this eatery serves beef, buffalo, and other game meats, pasta, fresh fish, and farmers' market vegetables when they're available. There's a full premium bar, and the wine list is extensive. [$] *Average main: $20* ✉ *520 Main St.* ☎ *530/623–5325* 🕒 *Hours vary in winter.*

$ HOTEL 🏨 **Red Hill Motel.** This 1940s-era property is popular with anglers, who appreciate the outdoor fish-cleaning area on the premises. **Pros:** close to popular bass fishing sites; inexpensive. **Cons:** older facility; some rooms need sprucing up. [$] *Rooms from: $53* ✉ *50 Red Hill Rd., off Main St./Hwy. 299* ☎ *530/623–4331* 🌐 *www.redhillresorts.com* 🛏 *4 rooms, 6 cabins, 2 duplexes* 🍽 *No meals.*

SPORTS AND THE OUTDOORS

Fly Stretch. Below the Lewiston Dam, east of Weaverville on Highway 299, is the Fly Stretch of the Trinity River, an excellent fly-fishing area.

Pine Cove Boat Ramp. This ramp on Lewiston Lake provides fishing access for those with disabilities—decks here are built over prime trout-fishing waters.

Weaverville Ranger Station. Check here for maps and information about hiking trails in the Trinity Alps Wilderness. ✉ *360 Main St.* ☎ *530/623–2121.*

LAKE SHASTA AREA

12 miles north of Redding on I–5.

When you think of the Lake Shasta Area, picture water, wilderness, dazzling stalagmites—and a fabulous man-made project in the midst of it all.

GETTING HERE AND AROUND

Interstate 5 north of Redding is the main link to the entire Lake Shasta area. Get to the dam by passing through the tiny city of Shasta Lake. There is no local bus service.

ESSENTIALS

Shasta Cascade Wonderland Association. Stop in the association's visitor center in the Anderson outlet mall off I-5 between Red Bluff and Redding, or check the website for special events taking place during your visit to California's northernmost counties. A weekly fishing report informs anglers about stream closures and which spots are yielding the best catches. ✉ *1699 Hwy. 273, Anderson* ☎ *530/365–7500, 800/474–2782* 🌐 *www.shastacascade.com.*

EXPLORING

Lake Shasta. Numerous types of fish inhabit the lake, including rainbow trout, salmon, bass, brown trout, and the humble catfish. The lake region also has the largest nesting population of bald eagles in California. You can rent fishing boats, ski boats, sailboats, canoes, paddleboats, Jet Skis, and windsurfing boards at one of the many marinas and resorts along the 370-mile shoreline. ✉ *Shasta Lake.*

Fodor's Choice ★ **Lake Shasta Caverns.** Stalagmites, stalactites, flowstone deposits, and crystals entice visitors to the Lake Shasta Caverns. To see this impressive spectacle, you must take the two-hour tour, which includes a catamaran ride across the McCloud arm of Lake Shasta and a bus ride up North Grey Rocks Mountain to the cavern entrance. The caverns are 58°F year-round, making them a cool retreat on a hot summer day. The most awe-inspiring of the limestone rock formations is the glistening Cathedral Room, which appears to be gilded. A gift shop is open from 8 to 4:30. ✉ *20359 Shasta Caverns Rd., off I–5, 17 miles north of Redding, Lakehead* ☎ *530/238–2341, 800/795–2283* 🌐 *lakeshastacaverns.com* 🎟 *$24* 🕒 *June–Aug., tours on the half hour, daily 9–4; Apr., May, and Sept., tours on the hour, daily 9–3; Oct.–Mar., tours at 10, noon, and 2.*

Shasta Dam. This is the second-largest concrete dam in the United States (only Grand Coulee in Washington is bigger). The visitor center has computerized photographic tours of the dam construction, video presentations, fact sheets, and historical displays. Hour-long guided tours inside the dam and its powerhouse leave from the center. ✉ *16349 Shasta Dam Blvd., off Lake Blvd., Shasta Lake* ☎ *530/275–4463* 🌐 *www.usbr.gov/mp/ncao* 🎟 *Free* 🕒 *Visitor center, daily 8–5; call for tour times.*

WHERE TO EAT

$$ SEAFOOD 🍴 **Tail o' the Whale.** As its name suggests, this restaurant has a nautical theme. You can enjoy a panoramic view of Lake Shasta here while you savor house specials like charbroiled salmon, prime rib with prawns, and pasta dishes. This is a favorite spot for boaters, who anchor at a courtesy dock while they're dining. [$] *Average main: $20* ✉ *10300 Bridge Bay Rd., Bridge Bay exit off I–5, Redding* ☎ *530/275–3021* 🕒 *No dinner Mon.–Wed. in winter.*

SPORTS AND THE OUTDOORS

FISHING

The Fishen Hole. A couple of miles from the lake, this bait-and-tackle shop sells fishing licenses and provides information about conditions. ✉ *3844 Shasta Dam Blvd., at Red Bluff Ave., Shasta Lake* ☎ *530/275–4123.*

HOUSEBOATING

Houseboats here come in all sizes except small. As a rule, rentals are outfitted with cooking utensils, dishes, and most of the equipment you'll need—you supply the food and the linens. When you rent a houseboat, you receive a short course in how to maneuver your launch before you set out. You can fish, swim, sunbathe on the flat roof, or sit on the deck and watch the world go by. The shoreline of Lake Shasta is beautifully ragged, with countless inlets; it's not hard to find privacy. Expect to spend a minimum of $350 a day for a craft that sleeps six. A three-day, two-night minimum is customary. Prices are often lower during the off-season (September through May). Bridge Bay Resort rents houseboats, fishing boats, ski boats, and patio boats. Shasta Cascade offers general information.

Bridge Bay Resort. This resort offers modest lakeside lodging, a restaurant, boat and Jet Ski rentals, and a full service marina. If you want to sleep on the lake rather than beside it, rent one of the houseboats that come in sizes large enough to accomodate up to a dozen people. ⊠ *10300 Bridge Bay Rd., Redding* 📞 *800/752–9669, 530/275–3021* ⊕ *www.sevencrown.com/lakes/lake_shasta/bridge_bay/index.htm.*

DUNSMUIR

10 miles south of Mt. Shasta on I–5.

Surrounded by towering forests and boasting world-class fly-fishing in the Upper Sacramento River, tiny Dunsmuir was named for a 19th-century Scottish coal baron who offered to build a fountain if the town was renamed in his honor. Another major attraction is the Railroad Park Resort, where you can spend the night in restored cabooses.

GETTING HERE AND AROUND

Reach Dunsmuir via exits off Interstate 5 at the north and south ends of town. When snow hasn't closed the route, you can take Highway 89 from the Lassen Park area toward Burney then northeast to Interstate 5 at Mt. Shasta. From there it's a 10-mile drive south to Dunsmuir. Amtrak stops here; Greyhound stops in Weed, 20 miles north. On weekdays, STAGE buses serve Dunsmuir.

ESSENTIALS

Bus Information STAGE 📞 *530/842–8295* ⊕ *www.co.siskiyou.ca.us/GS/ stageschedule.aspx.*

Visitor Information Dunsmuir Chamber of Commerce ⊠ *5915 Dunsmuir Ave., Ste. 100* 📞 *530/235–2177* ⊕ *dunsmuir.com.*

EXPLORING

Fodor'sChoice ★ **Castle Crags State Park.** Named for its 6,000-foot glacier-polished crags, which were formed by volcanic activity centuries ago, this park offers fishing in Castle Creek, hiking in the backcountry, and a view of Mt. Shasta. The crags draw climbers and hikers from around the world. The 4,350-acre park has 28 miles of hiking trails, including a 2.75-mile access trail to **Castle Crags Wilderness,** part of the **Shasta-Trinity National Forest.** There are excellent trails at lower altitudes. Camping is allowed in winter on a first-come, first-served basis. ⊠ *6 miles* *south of Dunsmuir, Castella/Castle Crags exit off I–5* ☎ *530/235–2684* 🌐 *www.parks.ca.gov/parkindex* 🎟 *$8 per vehicle, day use.*

FINE FISHING

The upper Sacramento River near Dunsmuir is consistently rated one of the best fishing spots in the country. Check with the chamber of commerce for local fishing guides.

WHERE TO EAT AND STAY

$$ MEDITERRANEAN 🍴 **Café Maddalena.** The chef here gained experience working in top San Francisco restaurants before moving north to prepare adventurous Mediterranean fare with a French influence. Selections change seasonally but always feature a vegetarian dish, along with entrées such as Genovese seafood stew, and lamb shoulder with cassoulet. Wines from Spain, Italy, and France complement the meals. Ask about the daily prix fixe menu. [$] *Average main: $21* ✉ *5801 Sacramento Ave.* ☎ *530/235–2725* 🌐 *www.cafemaddalena.com* ⏰ *Closed Mon.–Wed. and Jan.–mid-Feb. No lunch.*

$ HOTEL FAMILY 🏨 **Railroad Park Resort.** The antique cabooses here were collected over more than three decades and have been converted into cozy motel rooms in honor of Dunsmuir's railroad legacy. **Pros:** gorgeous setting; kitschy fun. **Cons:** cabooses can feel cramped. [$] *Rooms from: $115* ✉ *100 Railroad Park Rd.* ☎ *530/235–4440* 🌐 *www.rrpark.com* 🛏 *23 cabooses, 4 cabins* 🍽 *No meals.*

24

MT. SHASTA

34 miles north of Lake Shasta on I–5.

While a snow-covered dormant volcano is the area's dazzling draw, the town of Mt. Shasta charms visitors with its small shops, friendly residents and beautiful scenery in all seasons.

GETTING HERE AND AROUND

Three exits off Interstate 5 lead to the town of Mt. Shasta. When snow hasn't closed the route, you can take Highway 89 from the Lassen Park area toward Burney then northeast to Mt. Shasta. The ski park is off Highway 89. Greyhound stops at Weed, 10 miles north; Amtrak stops at Dunsmuir, 10 miles south. There's no local bus system.

ESSENTIALS

Visitor Information Mt. Shasta Chamber of Commerce and Visitors Bureau ✉ *300 Pine St., at W. Lake St., Mt. Shasta* ☎ *530/926–4865, 800/926–4865* 🌐 *mtshastachamber.com.*

EXPLORING

Fodor's Choice ★ **Mt. Shasta.** The crown jewel of the 2.5-million-acre Shasta-Trinity National Forest, Mt. Shasta, a 14,179-foot-high dormant volcano, is a mecca for day hikers. It's especially enticing in spring, when fragrant Shasta lilies and other flowers adorn the rocky slopes. A paved road, the Everitt Memorial Highway, reaches only as far as the timberline; the final 6,000 feet are a tough climb of rubble, ice, and snow (the summit is perpetually ice packed). Only a hardy few are qualified to make the trek to the top.

The town of Mt. Shasta has real character and some fine restaurants. Lovers of the outdoors and backcountry skiers abound, and they are more than willing to offer advice on the most beautiful spots in the region, which include out-of-the-way swimming holes, dozens of high mountain lakes, and a challenging 18-hole golf course with 360 degrees of spectacular views. 🌐 *mtshastachamber.com.*

WHERE TO EAT AND STAY

$ CAFÉ 🍴 **Seven Suns Coffee and Cafe.** A favorite gathering spot for locals, this small coffee shop serves specialty wraps for breakfast and lunch, plus soup and salad selections. Pastries, made daily, include muffins and scones, and blackberry fruit bars in season. If the weather's nice, grab a seat on the patio. [$] *Average main: $9* ✉ *1011 S. Mt. Shasta Blvd., at Holly St.* ☎ *530/926–9701* 🌐 *www.mtshastacoffee.com.*

$$ HOTEL 🏨 **Best Western Tree House Motor Inn.** The clean, standard rooms at this motel less than a mile from downtown Mt. Shasta are decorated with natural-wood furnishings. **Pros:** close to ski park; lobby's roaring fireplace is a big plus on winter days. **Cons:** not all lodging buildings have elevators. [$] *Rooms from: $170* ✉ *111 Morgan Way* ☎ *530/926–3101, 800/545–7164* 🌐 *www.bestwestern.com* 🛏 *98 rooms, 7 suites* 🍽 *Breakfast.*

$$ RENTAL 🏨 **Mount Shasta Resort.** Private chalets are nestled among tall pine trees along the shore of Lake Siskiyou, all with gas-log fireplaces and full kitchens. **Pros:** incredible views; romantic woodsy setting; some pet-friendly rooms for extra fee. **Cons:** kids may get bored. [$] *Rooms from: $159* ✉ *1000 Siskiyou Lake Blvd.* ☎ *530/926–3030, 800/958–3363* 🌐 *www.mountshastaresort.com* 🛏 *65 units* 🍽 *No meals.*

SPORTS AND THE OUTDOORS

GOLF

Mount Shasta Resort. At a bit under 6,100 yards, the Mount Shasta Resort golf course isn't long, but it's beautiful and challenging, with narrow, tree-lined fairways and natural alpine terrain. Carts rent for $15; fabulous views are free. ✉ *1000 Siskiyou Lake Blvd.* ☎ *530/926–3052* 🌐 *www.mountshastaresort.com* 🎫 *$45 weekdays, $60 weekends* ⛳ *18 holes, 6035 yards, par 70.*

HIKING

Mt. Shasta Forest Service Ranger Station. Check in here for current trail conditions and avalanche reports. ✉ *204 W. Alma St., at Pine St.* ☎ *530/926–4511, 530/926–9613 avalanche conditions.*

MOUNTAIN CLIMBING

Fifth Season Mountaineering Shop. This shop rents bicycles and skiing and climbing equipment, and operates a recorded 24-hour climber-skier report. ✉ *300 N. Mt. Shasta Blvd.* ☎ *530/926–3606, 530/926–5555 ski phone* 🌐 *www.thefifthseason.com.*

Shasta Mountain Guides. These guides lead hiking, climbing, and ski-touring groups to the summit of Mt. Shasta. ☎ *530/926–3117* 🌐 *shastaguides.com.*

SKIING

FAMILY **Mt. Shasta Board & Ski Park.** On the southeast flank of Mt. Shasta, this ski park has three triple-chair lifts and two surface lifts on 425 skiable acres. Three-quarters of the trails are for beginning or intermediate skiers. The area's vertical drop is 1,435 feet, with a top elevation of 6,890 feet. The longest of the 32 trails is 1.75 miles. A package for beginners, available through the ski school, includes a lift ticket, ski rental, and a lesson. The school also runs ski and snowboard programs for children. There's night skiing for those who want to see the moon rise as they schuss. The base lodge has a simple café, a ski shop, and a ski-snowboard rental shop. ⊠ *Hwy. 89 exit east from I–5, south of Mt. Shasta* ☎ *530/926–8610, 800/754–7427* ⊕ *www.skipark.com* ☉ *Winter ski season schedule: Sun.–Wed. 9–4, Thurs.–Sat. 9–9.*

Mt. Shasta Nordic Center. This center, run by a nonprofit, maintains 15 miles of groomed cross-country ski trails. ⊠ *Ski Park Hwy., off Hwy. 89 (take I–5's McCloud exit)* ☎ *530/926–2142* ⊕ *mtshastanordic.org.*

THE BACKCOUNTRY

The Far North's primitive, rugged backcountry is arguably full of more natural wonders than any other region in California.

MCARTHUR–BURNEY FALLS MEMORIAL STATE PARK

Hwy. 89, 52 miles southeast of Mt. Shasta and 41 miles north of Lassen Volcanic National Park.

One of the most spectacular sights in the Far North is Burney Falls, where countless ribbon-like streams pour from moss-covered crevices. You have to travel forested back roads to reach this gem, but the park's beauty is well worth the trek.

GETTING HERE AND AROUND

To see some stunning falls, head east off Interstate 5 on Highway 89 at Mt. Shasta. The drive is 52 miles. From Interstate 5 in Redding, head east 55 miles on Highway 299 to connect with Highway 89; follow signs 6 miles to the park. From Alturas, head west on Highway 299 for about 86 miles and hook up with Highway 89.

EXPLORING

FAMILY **McArthur–Burney Falls Memorial State Park.** Just inside the park's southern
Fodor's Choice boundary, Burney Creek wells up from the ground and divides into
★ two falls that cascade over a 129-foot cliff into a pool below. Countless ribbonlike streams pour from hidden moss-covered crevices; resident bald eagles are frequently seen soaring overhead. You can walk a self-guided nature trail that descends to the foot of the falls, which Theodore Roosevelt—according to legend—called "the eighth wonder of the world." On warm days, swim at Lake Britton; lounge on the beach; rent motorboats, paddleboats, and canoes; or relax at one of the campsites or picnic areas. The camp store is open from late April to the end of October. ⊠ *24898 Hwy. 89, 6 miles north of Hwy. 299, Burney* ☎ *530/335–2777* ⊕ *www.parks.ca.gov/parkindex* 🖘 *$8 per vehicle, day use.*

ALTURAS

86 miles northeast of McArthur–Burney Falls Memorial State Park on Hwy. 299.

Alturas is the county seat and largest town in Modoc County. The Dorris family arrived in the area in 1874, built Dorris Bridge over the Pit River, and later opened a small wayside stop for travelers. As in the past, travelers today come to see eagles and other wildlife, the Modoc National Forest, and active geothermal areas.

GETTING HERE AND AROUND

To get to Alturas from Susanville take Main Street/Highway 36 south for about 4 miles; turn left at U.S. 395 and stay on that highway for 99 miles. From Redding, take the Lake Blvd./299E exit off Interstate 5, head east and stay on Highway 299 for 140 miles. Sage Stage buses serve Alturas from Redding and Susanville.

ESSENTIALS

Bus Information Modoc County Sage Stage ☎ *530/233–6410* 🌐 *www.sagestage.com.*

Visitor Information Alturas Chamber of Commerce ✉ *600 S. Main St.* ☎ *530/233–4434* 🌐 *www.alturaschamber.org.*

EXPLORING

Modoc National Forest. Encompassing 1.6 million acres, Modoc National Forest protects 300 species of wildlife, including Rocky Mountain elk, wild horses, mule deer, and pronghorn antelope. In spring and fall, watch for migratory waterfowl as they make their way along the Pacific Flyway above the forest. Hiking trails lead to Petroglyph Point, one of the largest panels of rock art in the United States. ✉ *Park Headquarters, 225 W. 8th St.* ☎ *530/233–5811* 🌐 *www.fs.usda.gov/modoc.*

Modoc National Wildlife Refuge. The 7,021-acre Modoc National Wildlife Refuge was established in 1961 to protect migratory waterfowl. You might see Canada geese, sandhill cranes, mallards, teal, wigeon, pintail, white pelicans, cormorants, and snowy egrets. The refuge is open for hiking, bird-watching, and photography, but one area is set aside for hunters. Regulations vary according to season. ✉ *5364 County Rd. 115, U.S. 395, 1½ miles south of Alturas, left on Rd. 56, then right on Rd. 115* ☎ *530/233–3572* 🌐 *www.fws.gov/refuge/modoc* 🎟 *Free* ⏲ *Daily dawn–dusk.*

WHERE TO EAT

$$ SPANISH 🍴 **Brass Rail.** Prix-fixe dinners at this authentic Basque restaurant include wine, homemade bread, soup, salad, side dishes, coffee, and ice cream. Steak, lamb chops, fried chicken, shrimp, and scallops are among the best entrée selections. A lounge with a full bar adjoins the dining area. [$] *Average main: $21* ✉ *395 Lake View Dr.* ☎ *530/233–2906* ⏲ *Closed Mon.*

SUSANVILLE

104 miles south of Alturas via U.S. 395; 65 miles east of Lassen Volcanic National Park via Highway 36.

Susanville, established as a trading post in 1854, tells the tale of its rich history through murals painted on buildings in the historic uptown area. You can take a self-guided tour around the original buildings and stop for a bite at one of the restaurants now housed within them. If you'd rather work up a sweat, you can hit the Bizz Johnson Trail and Eagle Lake recreation areas just outside town.

GETTING HERE AND AROUND

U.S. 395 connects Susanville and Alturas, about a 100-mile trip. From Red Bluff, take Interstate 5's Highway 36E/Fairgrounds exit and drive east for about 3 miles; turn left at Highway 36E and continue through the mountains for 103 miles. Lassen Rural Bus serves Susanville Monday through Saturday, and surrounding areas on weekdays only.

ESSENTIALS

Bus Information **Lassen Rural Bus** ☎ *530/252–7433* 🌐 *www.lassentransportation.com/a/Lassen-Rural-Bus-LRB.php.*

Visitor Information **Lassen County Chamber of Commerce** ✉ *75 N. Weatherlow St., off Main St.* ☎ *530/257–4323* 🌐 *lassencountychamber.com.*

EXPLORING

Bizz Johnson Trail. This trail follows a defunct line of the Southern Pacific Railroad for 25 miles. Known to locals as the Bizz, the trail is open for hikers, walkers, mountain bikers, horseback riders, and cross-country skiers. It skirts the Susan River through a scenic landscape of canyons, bridges, and forests abundant with wildlife. ✉ *Trailhead, old railroad depot, 601 Richmond Rd., near N. Railroad Ave.* ☎ *530/257–0456* 🌐 *www.blm.gov/ca/st/en/fo/eaglelake/bizztrail.html* 🎫 *Free.*

Eagle Lake. Anglers travel great distances to fish the waters of this large lake where the trout is prized for its size and fighting ability. Surrounded by high desert to the north and alpine forests to the south, Eagle Lake is also popular for picnicking, hiking, boating, waterskiing and windsurfing, and bird-watching—ospreys, pelicans, and many other waterfowl visit the lake. On land you might see mule deer, small mammals, and even pronghorn antelope—and be sure to watch for bald-eagle nesting sites. ✉ *16 miles north of Susanville, Eagle Lake Rd. off Hwy. 139* ☎ *530/257–0456 for Eagle Lake Recreation Area, 530/825–3454 for Eagle Lake Marina* 🌐 *www.blm.gov/ca/st/en/fo/eaglelake.html.*

WHERE TO EAT AND STAY

$ MEXICAN 🍴 **Mazatlan Grill.** The sauces are prepared on-site in this friendly, family-run restaurant and lounge, which serves lunch and dinner daily. The dining room is simple and tidy, with comfortable upholstered booths. The extensive menu offers authentic, inexpensive Mexican fare ranging from fajitas and enchiladas to a vegetarian burrito. [$] *Average main: $10* ✉ *1535 Main St., at Park St.* ☎ *530/257–1800.*

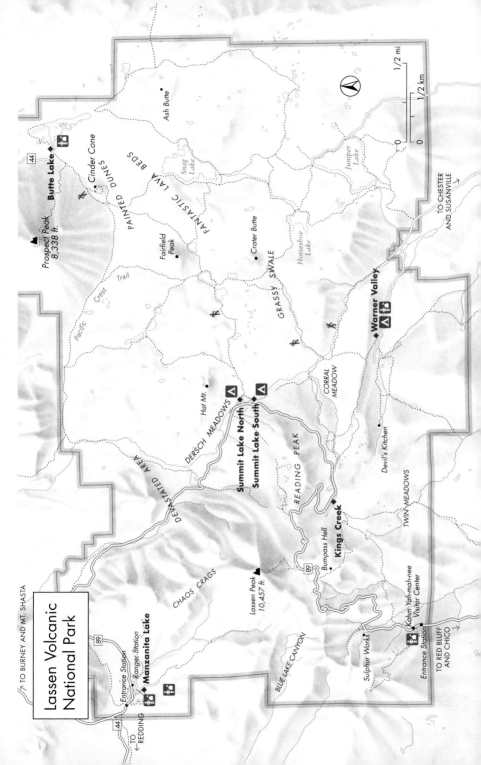

Lassen Volcanic National Park

TO BURNEY AND MT. SHASTA

TO REDDING

Entrance Station

Ranger Station

Manzanita Lake

89

44

CHAOS CRAGS

DEVASTATED AREA

Lassen Peak
10,457 ft.

BLUE LAKE CANYON

Sulphur Works

Kohm Yah-mah-nee
Visitor Center

Entrance Station

TO RED BLUFF
AND CHICO

89

Bumpass Hell

Kings Creek

READING PEAK

TWIN MEADOWS

Devil's Kitchen

CORAL MEADOW

Summit Lake North

Summit Lake South

DERSCH MEADOWS

Hat Mt.

Pacific Crest Trail

Prospect Peak
8,338 ft.

Butte Lake

44

Cinder Cone

PAINTED DUNES

FANTASTIC LAVA BEDS

Snag Lake

Ash Butte

Fairfield Peak

Crater Butte

GRASSY SWALE

Horseshoe Lake

Juniper Lake

Warner Valley

TO CHESTER
AND SUSANVILLE

0   1/2 km   1/2 mi

$ HOTEL **High Country Inn.** Rooms are spacious in this colonial-style motel on the eastern edge of town. **Pros:** great mountain views; heated pool. **Cons:** lots of traffic in the area. [$] *Rooms from: $87* ✉ *3015 Riverside Dr., at Main St.* ☎ *530/257–3450, 866/454–4566* 🌐 *www.high-country-inn.com* 🛏 *66 rooms* 🍴 *Breakfast.*

LASSEN VOLCANIC NATIONAL PARK

45 miles east of Redding on Hwy. 44; 48 miles east of Red Bluff on Hwy. 36.

Fissures and fumaroles burble and belch as reminders of Lassen Peak's dramatic eruption a century ago. Four different types of volcanoes form part of this park's fascinating geothermal landscape.

GETTING HERE AND AROUND

Whether coming from the west or the east, reach the park's southern entrance via Highway 36E, and turn onto Highway 89 for a short drive to the park. The northwest entrance is reached via Highway 44 from Redding and Susanville. No buses serve the area.

EXPLORING

Fodor's Choice ★ **Lassen Scenic Byway.** This 185-mile scenic drive begins in Chester and loops through the forests, volcanic peaks, geothermal springs, and lava fields of Lassen National Forest and Lassen Volcanic National Park, providing for an all-day excursion into dramatic wilderness. From Chester, take Route 36 west to Route 89 north through the park, then Route 44 east to Route 36 west back to Chester. Parts of the road are inaccessible in winter. ✉ *Lassen Volcanic National Park* ☎ *800/427–7623 CA Highway info service, 530/595-4480 Lassen Park visitor center* 🌐 *www.nps.gov/lavo.*

Fodor's Choice ★ **Lassen Volcanic National Park.** A dormant plug dome, Lassen Peak is the focus of Lassen Volcanic National Park's 165.6 square miles of distinctive landscape. The peak began erupting in May 1914, sending pumice, rock, and snow thundering down the mountain and gas and hot ash billowing into the atmosphere. Lassen's most spectacular outburst occurred in 1915 when it blew a cloud of ash some 7 miles into the stratosphere. The resulting mudflow destroyed vegetation for miles in some directions; the evidence is still visible today, especially in the Devastated Area. The volcano finally came to rest in 1921. Today, fumaroles, mud pots, lakes, and bubbling hot springs create a fascinating but dangerous landscape that can be viewed throughout the park, especially via a hiked descent into Bumpass Hell. Because of its significance as a volcanic landscape, Lassen became a national park in 1916. Several volcanoes—the largest of which is now Lassen Peak—have been active in the area for roughly 600,000 years. The four types of volcanoes found in the world are represented in the park, including shield (Prospect Peak), plug dome (Lassen Peak), cinder cone (Cinder Cone), and composite (Brokeoff Volcano). Lassen Park Road (the continuation of Highway 89 within the park) and 150 miles of hiking trails provide access to many of these volcanic wonders. **■ TIP→ Caution is key here: heed signs that warn visitors to**

stay on the trails and railed boardwalks to avoid falling into boiling water or through dangerous thin-crusted areas of the park. Although the park is closed to cars in winter, it's usually open to intrepid cross-country skiers and snowshoers. 🌐 *www.nps.gov/lavo* 🎫 *$10 per car, $5 per person if not in a car.*

> **WORD OF MOUTH**
>
> "Lassen is one of those best-kept-secret spots. It has a little bit of everything: peaks, waterfalls, snow, trees, awesome flowers, a mini Yellowstone, and not tons of folks everywhere."
>
> —spirobulldog

FAMILY **Sulphur Works Thermal Area.** Proof of Lassen Peak's volatility becomes evident shortly after you enter the park at the southwest entrance. Sidewalks skirt boiling springs and sulphur-emitting steam vents. This area is usually the last site to close because of snow. ✉ *Lassen Park Rd., 1 mile from the southwest entrance ranger station, Lassen Volcanic National Park* 🌐 *www.nps.gov/lavo.*

24

WHERE TO STAY

$$$$ B&B/INN 🏨 **Drakesbad Guest Ranch.** With propane furnaces and kerosene lamps, everything about this century-old property harkens back to a simpler time. **Pros:** a true back-to-nature experience; great for family adventures. **Cons:** accessible only via a partially paved road leading out of Chester. [$] *Rooms from: $338* ✉ *End of Warner Valley Rd., Chester* ☎ *866/999–0914* 🌐 *www.drakesbad.com* 🛏 *19 rooms* 🕒 *Closed mid Oct.–early June* 🍴 *All meals.*

SPORTS AND THE OUTDOORS

HIKING

Fodor's Choice ★ **Bumpass Hell Trail.** Boiling springs, steam vents, and mud pots highlight this 3-mile round-trip hike. Expect the loop to take about two hours. During the first mile of the hike there's a gradual climb of 500 feet before a steep 300-foot descent to the basin. You'll encounter rocky patches, so wear hiking boots. ⚠ **Stay on trails and boardwalks near the thermal areas, as what appears to be firm ground may be only a thin crust over scalding mud.** *Moderate.* ✉ *Trailhead at end of paved parking area off Lassen Park Rd., 6 miles from the southwest entrance ranger station, Lassen Volcanic National Park* 🌐 *www.nps.gov/lavo.*

Fodor's Choice ★ **Lassen Peak Hike.** This trail winds 2½ miles to the mountaintop. It's a tough climb—2,000 feet uphill on a steady, steep grade—but the reward is a spectacular view. At the peak you can see into the rim and view the entire park (and much of California's far north). Bring sunscreen, water, and a jacket since it's often windy and much cooler at the summit. **■ TIP→ A multiyear restoration project means that all or part of the trail will be open only a few times during the year, so call ahead. Depending on funding, trail work is expected to be completed by the end of 2015.** ✉ *Trailhead past a paved parking area off Lassen Park Rd., 7 miles north of the southwest entrance ranger station, Lassen Volcanic National Park* ☎ *530/595–4480* 🌐 *www.nps.gov/lavo.*

CHESTER

36 miles west of Susanville on Hwy 36.

The population of this small town on Lake Almanor swells from 2,500 to nearly 5,000 in summer as tourists come to visit. Chester serves as a gateway to Lassen Volcanic National Park.

GETTING HERE AND AROUND

Chester is on Highway 36E. When snow doesn't close Highway 89, the main road through Lassen Park, visitors can take Highway 44 from Redding to Highway 89 through the park and to Highway 36E and onto Chester and Lake Almanor. Plumas County Transit connects Chester to the Quincy area.

ESSENTIALS

Bus Information Plumas County Transit ☎ *530/283–2538* 🌐 *www.plumastransit.com.*

Visitor Information Lake Almanor Area Chamber of Commerce and Visitors Bureau ✉ *289 #7 Main St., near Stone Ave.* ☎ *530/258–2426* 🌐 *www.lakealmanorarea.com.*

EXPLORING

Lake Almanor. This lake's 52 miles of forested shoreline are popular with campers, swimmers, water-skiers, and anglers. At an elevation of 4,500 feet, the lake warms to above 70°F for about eight weeks in summer. ✉ *Off Hwys. 89 and 36* ☎ *530/258–2426* 🌐 *www.lakealmanorarea.com.*

WHERE TO EAT AND STAY

$ AMERICAN 🍴 **Kopper Kettle Cafe.** Locals return again and again to this tidy restaurant that serves home-cooked lunches and dinners. Head here for breakfast whenever you've got a hankering for scrambled eggs or biscuits and gravy. [$] *Average main: $14* ✉ *243 Main St., at Myrtle St.* ☎ *530/258–2698.*

$$ HOTEL 🏨 **Best Western Rose Quartz Inn.** Down the road from Lake Almanor and close to Lassen Volcanic National Park, this small-town inn balances traditional decor and up-to-the-minute amenities like Wi-Fi. **Pros:** near national park; within easy walking distance of town's restaurants. **Cons:** standard rooms on the pricey side. [$] *Rooms from: $130* ✉ *306 Main St.* ☎ *530/258–2002, 888/571–4885* 🌐 *bestwesterncalifornia.com/chester-hotels* 🛏 *51 rooms* 🍽 *Breakfast.*

$$ B&B/INN Fodor's Choice ★ 🏨 **Bidwell House.** Some guest rooms at this 1901 ranch house have wood-burning stoves, claw-foot tubs, and antique furnishings; a separate cottage with a kitchen sleeps six. **Pros:** unique decor in each room; beautiful wooded setting; near Lake Almanor. **Cons:** not ideal for kids. [$] *Rooms from: $125* ✉ *1 Main St.* ☎ *530/258–3338* 🌐 *www.bidwellhouse.com* 🛏 *14 rooms, 2 with shared bath* 🍽 *Breakfast.*

QUINCY

67 miles southwest of Susanville via Hwys. 36 and 89.

A center for mining and logging in the 1850s, Quincy is nestled against the western slope of the Sierra Nevada. The county seat and largest community in Plumas County, the town is rich in historic buildings that have been the focus of preservation and restoration efforts. The

Lassen Volcanic National Park's King Creek Falls Hike, which takes you through forests and meadows dotted with wildflowers, is a good hike for nature photographers.

four-story courthouse on Main Street, one of several stops on a self-guided tour, was built in 1921 with marble posts and staircases. The arts are thriving in Quincy, too: catch a play or a bluegrass performance at the Town Hall Theatre.

GETTING HERE AND AROUND

Quincy is on Highway 70 and is accessible from all directions via mountain roads. Highway 70 goes through the Feather River Canyon to Highway 149, then Highway 99 to Chico and Red Bluff, a 198-mile trip. From Quincy, Highway 70 connects to Highway 89 and then to Highway 36E toward Susanville in the east, or westward toward Chester and Lassen Park. Plumas County Transit serves Chester and Quincy. Lassen Rural Bus connects Quincy and Susanville.

ESSENTIALS

Bus Information Lassen Rural Bus ☎ *530/252–7433*
⊕ *www.lassentransportation.com/a/Lassen-Rural-Bus-LRB.php.*
Plumas County Transit ☎ *530/283–2538* ⊕ *www.plumastransit.com.*

Visitor Information Quincy Chamber of Commerce ⊠ *336 W. Main St., inside Plumas Bank* ☎ *530/283–0188* ⊕ *www.quincychamber.com.*

EXPLORING

Bucks Lake Recreation Area. The main recreational attraction in central Plumas County is 17 miles southwest of Quincy at elevation 5,200 feet. During warm months the lake's 17-mile shoreline, two marinas, and eight campgrounds attract anglers and water-sports enthusiasts. Trails through the tall pines beckon hikers and horseback riders. In winter much of the area remains open for snowmobiling and cross-country skiing. ⊠ *Bucks Lake Rd.* ☎ *530/283–0188* ⊕ *www. plumascounty.org/Communities/BucksLake.htm.*

Plumas County Museum. The cultural, home arts, and industrial history displays at the Plumas County Museum contain artifacts dating to the 1850s. Highlights include collections of Maidu Indian basketry, pioneer weapons, and rooms depicting life in the early logging and mining days of Plumas County. Out in the Exhibit Yard are a working blacksmith shop, a restored goldminer's cabin, and a railroad exhibit. ⊠ *500 Jackson St., at Coburn St.* ☎ *530/283–6320* ⊕ *www.plumasmuseum.org* 🔼 *$2* ⊗ *Tues.–Sat. 10–4.*

Plumas National Forest. Plumas County is known for its wide-open spaces, and the 1.2-million-acre Plumas National Forest, with its high alpine lakes and crystal clear woodland streams, is a beautiful example. Hundreds of campsites are maintained in the forest, and picnic areas and hiking trails abound. You can enter the forest along highways 70 and 89. ⊠ *U.S. Forest Service, 159 Lawrence St., near W. Main St.* ☎ *530/283–2050* ⊕ *www.fs.usda.gov/plumas* ⊗ *Office weekdays 8–4:30.*

WHERE TO EAT AND STAY

$$ ✕ **Sweet Lorraine's.** Hearty fare served in this casual, bustling restau-
AMERICAN   rant in Quincy's historic downtown area includes meaty dishes like St. Louis–style ribs as well as vegetarian options and lighter items; there's also a good selection of wines. If the weather is mild, dine alfresco on the patio. Counter seating is fast and friendly. $ *Average main: $17* ⊠ *384 Main St., at Harbison Ave.* ☎ *530/283–5300* ⊗ *Closed Sun. and Mon.*

$ ⛨ **Ada's Place.** This place is actually four uniquely beautiful cottages,
RENTAL   secluded on a quiet street one block from the county courthouse and
Fodor's Choice   downtown Quincy. **Pros:** on-site owners' meticulous upkeep. **Cons:** not
★   a good choice for children. $ *Rooms from: $100* ⊠ *562 Jackson St., near Court St.* ☎ *530/283–1954, 877/234–2327* ⊕ *www.adasplace.com* 🛏 *4 cottages* ⊗ *No meals.*

$ ⛨ **Lariat Lodge.** This small, single-story motel two miles east of down-
HOTEL   town is a quiet haven surrounded by views of the Plumas National Forest. **Pros:** inexpensive rooms; lovely setting. **Cons:** older facility. $ *Rooms from: $70* ⊠ *2370 E. Main St.* ☎ *530/283–1000, 800/999– 7199* 🖶 *530/283–2164* 🛏 *19 rooms* ⊗ *No meals.*

TRAVEL SMART CALIFORNIA

GETTING HERE AND AROUND

Wherever you plan to go in California, getting there will likely involve driving, even if you fly. With the exception of San Diego, major airports are usually far from main attractions. For example, four airports serve the Los Angeles area—but three of them are outside the city limits. You'll find a similar situation in San Francisco, where it's a 30-minute-plus trip between any Bay Area airport and Downtown. California's major airport hubs are LAX in Los Angeles and SFO in San Francisco, but you can find satellite airports around most major cities. When booking flights, it pays to check these options for more convenient times and a better location in relation to your hotel. Most small cities have their own commercial airports, with connecting flights to larger cities—but service may be extremely limited, and it may be cheaper to rent a car and drive from L.A. or San Francisco.

FROM LOS ANGELES TO:	BY AIR	BY CAR
San Diego	55 mins	2 hours
Death Valley		5 hours
San Francisco	1 hr 30 mins	5 hrs 40 mins
Monterey	1 hr 10 mins	5 hrs
Santa Barbara	45 mins	1 hr 40 mins
Big Sur		5 hrs 30 mins
Sacramento	1 hr 30 mins	5 hrs 30 mins

FROM SAN FRANCISCO TO:	BY AIR	BY CAR
San Jose		1 hr
Monterey	45 mins	2 hrs
Los Angeles	1 hr 30 mins	5 hrs 40 mins
Portland, OR	1 hr 50 mins	10 hrs
Mendocino		3 hrs
Yosemite NP/ Fresno	1 hr	3 hrs 30 mins
Lake Tahoe/ Reno	1 hr	3 hrs 30 mins

▌ AIR TRAVEL

Flying time to California is about 5½ hours from New York and 4 hours from Chicago. Travel from London to either Los Angeles or San Francisco is 11 hours and from Sydney approximately 15½. Flying between San Francisco and Los Angeles takes about 90 minutes.

AIRPORTS

California's gateways are Los Angeles International Airport (LAX), San Francisco International Airport (SFO), San Diego International Airport (SAN), Sacramento International Airport (SMF), and San Jose International Airport (SJC). Oakland International Airport (OAK) is another option in the Bay Area, and other Los Angeles airports include Long Beach (LGB), Bob Hope Airport (BUR), LA/Ontario (ONT), and John Wayne Airport (SNA).

Airport Information Bob Hope Airport ✉ Burbank ☎ 818/840–8840 ⊕ www. burbankairport.com. **John Wayne Airport** ☎ 949/252–5200 ⊕ www.ocair.com. **LA/ Ontario International Airport** ☎ 909/937–2700 ⊕ www.flyontario.com. **Long Beach Airport** ☎ 562/570–2600 ⊕ www.lgb.org. **Los Angeles International Airport** ☎ 310/646–5252 ⊕ www.lawa.org/lax. **Oakland International Airport** ☎ 510/563–3300 ⊕ www.

flyoakland.com. **Sacramento International Airport** ☎ *916/929-5411* ⊕ *www.sacramento. aero/smf.* **San Diego International Airport** ☎ *619/400-2404* ⊕ *www.san.org.* **San Francisco International Airport** ☎ *650/821-8211, 800/435-9736* ⊕ *www.flysfo.com.* **San Jose International Airport** ☎ *408/392-3600* ⊕ *www.flysanjose.com.*

FLIGHTS

United, with hubs in San Francisco and Los Angeles, has the greatest number of flights into and within California. But most national and many international airlines fly to the state. Southwest Airlines and United Airlines connect smaller cities within California, often from satellite airports near major cities.

Airline Contacts Air Canada ☎ *888/247-2262* ⊕ *www.aircanada.com.* **Alaska Airlines/Horizon Air** ☎ *800/252-7522* ⊕ *www.alaskaair.com.* **American Airlines** ☎ *800/433-7300* ⊕ *www.aa.com.* **British Airways** ☎ *800/247-9297* ⊕ *www. britishairways.com.* **Cathay Pacific** ☎ *800/233-2742* ⊕ *www.cathaypacific.com.* **Delta Airlines** ☎ *800/221-1212 for U.S. reservations, 800/241-4141 for international reservations* ⊕ *www.delta.com.* **Frontier Airlines** ☎ *800/432-1359* ⊕ *www.flyfrontier. com.* **Japan Air Lines** ☎ *800/525-3663* ⊕ *www.jal.com.* **JetBlue** ☎ *800/538-2583* ⊕ *www.jetblue.com.* **Qantas** ☎ *800/227-4500* ⊕ *www.qantas.com.au.* **Southwest Airlines** ☎ *800/435-9792* ⊕ *www.southwest.com.* **Spirit Airlines** ☎ *801/401-2200* ⊕ *www. spirit.com.* **United Airlines** ☎ *800/864-8331 for U.S. reservations, 800/538-2929 for international reservations* ⊕ *www.united.com.* **US Airways** ☎ *800/428-4322 for U.S. and Canada reservations, 800/622-1015 for international reservations* ⊕ *www.usairways.com.*

▌ BOAT TRAVEL

CRUISES

A number of major cruise lines offer trips that begin or end in California. Most voyages sail north along the Pacific coast to Alaska or south to Mexico. California cruise ports include Los Angeles, San Diego, and San Francisco.

Cruise Lines Carnival Cruise Line ☎ *305/599-2600, 800/227-6482* ⊕ *www. carnival.com.* **Celebrity Cruises** ☎ *800/647-2251, 800/437-3111* ⊕ *www.celebritycruises. com.* **Crystal Cruises** ☎ *310/785-9300, 888/722-0021* ⊕ *www.crystalcruises.com.* **Disney Cruise Line** ☎ *800/951-3532* ⊕ *disneycruiseline.com.* **Holland America Line** ☎ *206/281-3535, 877/932-4259* ⊕ *www.hollandamerica.com.* **Norwegian Cruise Line** ☎ *305/436-4000, 866/234-7350* ⊕ *www.ncl.com.* **Princess Cruises** ☎ *661/753-0000, 800/774-6237* ⊕ *www. princess.com.* **Regent Seven Seas Cruises** ☎ *954/776-6123, 877/505-5370* ⊕ *www. rssc.com.* **Royal Caribbean International** ☎ *305/539-6000, 866/562-7625* ⊕ *www. royalcaribbean.com.* **Silversea Cruises** ☎ *954/522-4477, 877/276-6816* ⊕ *www. silversea.com.*

▌ BUS TRAVEL

Greyhound is the major bus carrier in California. Regional bus service is available in metropolitan areas.

Bus Information Greyhound ☎ *800/231-2222* ⊕ *www.greyhound.com.*

▌ CAR TRAVEL

There are two basic north–south routes in California: Interstate 5 runs inland most of the way from the Oregon border to the Mexican border; and U.S. 101 hugs the coast for part of the route from Oregon to Mexico. A slower but much more scenic option is to take California State Route 1, also referred to as Highway 1 and the Pacific Coast Highway, which winds along much of the California coast and provides an occasionally hair-raising, but breathtaking, ride.

From north to south, the state's east–west interstates are Interstate 80, Interstate 15, Interstate 10, and Interstate 8. Much of California is mountainous, and you may encounter winding roads, frequently cliff-side, and steep mountain grades. In winter, roads crossing the Sierra from east to west may close at any time due to weather. Also in winter, Interstate 5 north of Los Angeles closes during snowstorms.

The flying and driving times in the accompanying charts represent best-case scenario estimates, but know that the infamous California traffic jam can occur at any time.

FROM LOS ANGELES TO:	ROUTE	DISTANCE
San Diego	I–5 or I–405	127 miles
Las Vegas	I–10 to I–15	265 miles
Death Valley	I–10 to I–15 to Hwy. 127 to Hwy. 190	290 miles
San Francisco	I–5 to I–580 to I–80	382 miles
Monterey	U.S. 101 to Salinas, Hwy. 68 to Hwy. 1	320 miles
Santa Barbara	U.S. 101	95 miles
Big Sur	U.S. 101 to Hwy. 1	297 miles
Sacramento	I–5	386 miles

GASOLINE
Gasoline prices in California vary widely, depending on location, oil company, and whether you buy it at a full-service or self-serve pump. It's less expensive to buy fuel in the southern part of the state than in the north. If you're planning to travel near Nevada, you can sometimes save a bit by purchasing gas over the border. Gas stations are plentiful throughout the state. Most stay open late (24 hours along major highways and in big cities), except in rural areas, where Sunday hours are limited and where you may drive long stretches without a chance to refuel.

FROM SAN FRANCISCO TO:	ROUTE	DISTANCE
San Jose	U.S. 101	50 miles
Monterey	U.S. 101 to Hwy. 156 to Hwy. 1	120 miles
Los Angeles	U.S. 101 to Hwy. 156 to I–5	382 miles
Portland, OR	I–80 to I–505 to I–5	635 miles
Mendocino	Hwy. 1	174 miles
Yosemite NP	I–80 to I–580 to I–205 to Hwy. 120 east	184 miles
Lake Tahoe/ Reno	I–80	220 miles

ROAD CONDITIONS
Rainy weather can make driving along the coast or in the mountains treacherous. Some of the smaller routes over mountain ranges and in the deserts are prone to flash flooding. When the rains are severe, coastal Highway 1 can quickly become a slippery nightmare, buffeted by strong winds and obstructed by falling debris from the cliffs above. When the weather is particularly bad, Highway 1 may be closed due to mud and rock slides.

Many smaller roads over the Sierra Nevada are closed in winter, and if it's snowing, tire chains may be required on routes that are open, most notably those to Yosemite and Lake Tahoe. From October through April, if it's raining along the coast, it's usually snowing at higher elevations. Consider renting a four-wheel-drive vehicle, or purchase chains before you get to the mountains. (Chains or cables generally cost $30 to $70, depending on tire size; cables are easier to attach than chains, but chains are more durable.) If you delay and purchase them in the vicinity of the chain-control area, the cost may double. Be aware that most rental-car companies prohibit chain installation on their vehicles. If you choose to risk it and do not tighten them properly, they may snap—your insurance likely will not cover any resulting damage. Uniformed chain installers on Interstate 80 and U.S. 50 will apply them at the checkpoint for about $40 or take them off for less than that. Chain installers are independent business people, not highway employees, and set their own fees. They are not allowed to sell or rent chains. On smaller roads, you're on your own. Always carry extra clothing, blankets, water, and food when driving to the mountains in the winter, and keep your gas tank full to prevent the fuel line from freezing.

Road Conditions Caltrans Current Highway Conditions ☎ *800/427–7623* ⊕ *www.dot. ca.gov.*

Weather Conditions National Weather Service ☎ *707/443–6484 northernmost California, 831/656–1725 San Francisco Bay area and central California, 775/673–8100 Reno, Lake Tahoe, and northern Sierra, 805/988–6610 Los Angeles area, 858/675– 8700 San Diego area, 916/979–3051 Sacramento area* ⊕ *www.weather.gov.*

ROADSIDE EMERGENCIES

Dial 911 to report accidents and to reach the police, the California Highway Patrol (CHP), or the fire department. On some rural highways and on most interstates, look for emergency phones on the side of the road. In Los Angeles, the Metro Freeway Service Patrol provides assistance to stranded motorists under nonemergency conditions. Dial 511 from a cell phone and choose the "motorist aid" option to reach them 24 hours a day.

RULES OF THE ROAD

All passengers must wear seat belts at all times. It is illegal to leave a child six years of age or younger unattended in a motor vehicle. A child must be secured in a federally approved child passenger restraint system and ride in the back seat until at least eight years of age or until the child is at least 4 feet 9 inches tall. Children who are eight but don't meet the height requirement must ride in a booster seat or a car seat. Unless indicated, right turns are allowed at red lights after you've come to a full stop. Left turns between two one-way streets are allowed at red lights after you've come to a full stop.

Drivers with a blood-alcohol level higher than 0.08 who are stopped by police are subject to arrest, and those under 21 convicted of driving with a level of 0.01 or more can have their driving privileges revoked for a year. California's drunk-driving laws are extremely tough—violators may have their licenses immediately suspended, pay hefty fines, and spend the night in jail.

The speed limit on many interstate highways is 70 mph; unlimited-access roads are usually 55 mph. In cities, freeway speed limits are between 55 mph and 65 mph. Many city routes have commuter lanes during rush hour.

You must turn on your headlights whenever weather conditions require the use of windshield wipers.

Those 18 and older must use a hands-free device for their mobile phones while driving; those under 18 may not use mobile phones or wireless devices while driving. Texting on a wireless device is illegal for all drivers. Smoking in a vehicle where a minor is present is an infraction. For more information, refer to the Department of Motor Vehicles driver's handbook at ⊕ *www.dmv.ca.gov.*

CAR RENTAL

When you reserve a car, ask about cancellation penalties, taxes, drop-off charges (if you're planning to pick up the car in one city and leave it in another), and surcharges (for being under or over a certain age, for additional drivers, or for driving across state or country borders or beyond a specific distance from your point of rental). All these things can add substantially to your costs. Request car seats and extras such as GPS when you book.

Rates are sometimes—but not always—better if you book in advance or reserve through a rental agency's website. There are other reasons to book ahead, though: for popular destinations, during busy times of the year, or to ensure that you get certain types of cars (vans, SUVs, exotic sports cars).

■TIP➔ Make sure that a confirmed reservation guarantees you a car. Agencies sometimes overbook, particularly for busy weekends and holiday periods.

A car is essential in most parts of California, though in compact San Francisco it's better to use public transportation to avoid parking headaches. In sprawling cities such as Los Angeles and San Diego, however, you'll have to take the freeways to get just about anywhere.

Rates statewide for the least expensive vehicle begin as low as $30 a day, usually on weekends, and less than $200 a week (though they increase rapidly from here, especially in some of the larger metropolitan areas). This does not include additional fees or the tax on car rentals, which is 9.00% in Los Angeles, 8.75% in San Francisco, and 8.00% in San Diego. Be sure to shop around—you can get a decent deal by shopping the major car rental companies' websites. Also, rates are sometimes lower in San Diego; compare prices by city before you book, and ask about "drop charges" if you plan to return the vehicle in a city other than the one where you rented it. If you pick up at an airport, there may also be a facility charge of as much as $12 per rental, plus higher tax rates; ask when you book.

In California, you must have a valid driver's license and be 21 to rent a car; rates may be higher if you're under 25. Some agencies will not rent to those under 25; check when you book. Non-U.S. residents must have a license with text that is in the Roman alphabet that is valid for the entire rental period. Though it need not be entirely written in English, it must have English letters that clearly identify it as a driver's license. In addition, most companies also require an international license; check in advance.

If you dream of driving down the coast with the top down, or you want to explore the desert landscape not visible from the road, consider renting a specialty vehicle. Agencies that specialize in convertibles and sport-utility vehicles will often arrange airport delivery in larger cities. Unlike most of the major agencies, the following companies guarantee the car class that you book.

Specialty Car Agencies Enterprise Exotic Car Rentals ☎ 800/400-8412, 866/458-9227 *locations in San Francisco, Los Angeles, and other Southern California locations* ⊕ *exotic cars.enterprise.com.* **Beverly Hills Rent a Car** ☎ 800/479-5996 *San Francisco and several locations in Los Angeles,* 310/274-6969 ⊕ *www.bhrentacar.com.* **Midway Car Rental** ☎ 866/717-6802 *several locations in Los Angeles and Southern California* ⊕ *www. midwaycarrental.com.*

Major Rental Agencies
Alamo ☎ 800/462-5266 ⊕ *www.alamo. com.* **Avis** ☎ 800/331-1212 ⊕ *www.avis.com.* **Budget** ☎ 800/527-0700 ⊕ *www.budget. com.* **Hertz** ☎ 800/654-3131 ⊕ *www.hertz. com.* **National Car Rental** ☎ 877/222-9058 ⊕ *www.nationalcar.com.*

■ TRAIN TRAVEL

One of the most beautiful train trips in the country, Amtrak's *Coast Starlight* begins in Los Angeles and hugs the Pacific Coast to San Luis Obispo before it turns inland for the rest of its journey to Portland and Seattle. The *California Zephyr* travels from Chicago to Oakland via Denver; the *Pacific Surfliner* connects San Diego and San Luis Obispo via Los Angeles and Santa Barbara with multiple departures daily; and the *Sunset Limited* runs from Los Angeles to New Orleans via Arizona, New Mexico, and Texas.

Information Amtrak ☎ 800/872-7245 ⊕ *www.amtrak.com.*

ESSENTIALS

▮ ACCOMMODATIONS

The lodgings we review are the top choices in each price category. ⇨ *For an expanded review of each property, please see ⊕ www.fodors.com.* We don't specify whether the facilities cost extra; when pricing accommodations, ask what's included and what costs extra. ⇨ *For price information, see the planner in each chapter.*

Most hotels require you to give your credit-card details before they will confirm your reservation. If you don't feel comfortable emailing this information, ask if you can fax it or call and give details over the phone. However you book, get confirmation in writing and have a copy of it handy when you check in.

Be sure you understand the hotel's cancellation policy. Some places allow you to cancel without any kind of penalty—even if you prepaid to secure a discounted rate—if you cancel at least 24 hours in advance. Others require you to cancel a week in advance or penalize you the cost of one night. Small inns and B&Bs are most likely to require you to cancel far in advance. Most hotels allow children under a certain age to stay in their parents' room at no extra charge, but others charge for them as extra adults; find out the cutoff age for discounts.

Many B&Bs are entirely nonsmoking, and hotels and motels are decreasing their inventory of smoking rooms; if you require one, ask when you book if any are available.

BED-AND-BREAKFASTS

California has more than 1,000 bed-and-breakfasts. You'll find everything from simple homestays to lavish luxury lodgings, many in historic hotels and homes. The California Association of Boutique and Breakfast Inns has about 300 member properties that you can locate and book through its website.

Reservation Services Bed & Breakfast.com ☎ 512/322-2710, 800/462-2632 ⊕ www. bedandbreakfast.com. Bed & Breakfast Inns Online ☎ 800/215-7365 ⊕ www.bbonline. com. BnB Finder.com ☎ 212/480-0414, 888/547-8226 ⊕ www.bnbfinder.com. California Association of Boutique and Breakfast Inns ☎ 800/373-9251 ⊕ www.cabbi.com.

▮ COMMUNICATIONS

INTERNET

Internet access is widely available in urban areas, but it's usually more difficult to get online in the state's rural areas. Most hotels offer some kind of connection—usually broadband or Wi-Fi. Many hotels charge a daily fee (about $10) for Internet access. Cybercafés are located throughout California.

▮ EATING OUT

California has led the pack in bringing natural and organic foods to the forefront of American cooking. Though rooted in European cuisine, California cooking sometimes has strong Asian and Latin influences. Wherever you go, you're likely to find that dishes are made with fresh produce and other local ingredients.

The restaurants we list are the cream of the crop in each price category. ⇨ *For price information, see the planner in each chapter.*

CUTTING COSTS

▮TIP→ If you're on a budget, take advantage of the "small plates" craze sweeping California by ordering several appetizer-size portions and having a glass of wine at the bar, rather than having a full meal. Also, the better grocery and specialty-food stores have grab-and-go sections, with prepared foods on par with restaurant cooking, perfect for picnicking (remember, it infrequently rains between May and October). At resort areas in the off-season (such as Lake Tahoe in October and May, or San Diego in January), you can often find two-for-one dinner specials at upper-end restaurants; check coupon apps or local papers or with visitor bureaus.

RESERVATIONS AND DRESS

Regardless of where you are, it's a good idea to make a reservation if you can. We only mention reservations specifically when they are essential (there's no other way you'll ever get a table) or when they are not accepted. For popular restaurants, book as far ahead as you can (often 30 days), and reconfirm as soon as you arrive. (Large parties should always call ahead to check the reservations policy.) We mention dress only when men are required to wear a jacket or a jacket and tie.

Online reservation services make it easy to book a table before you even leave home. OpenTable covers many California cities.

Contacts OpenTable ⊕ *www.opentable.com.*

WINES, BEER, AND SPIRITS

Throughout the state, most famously in the Napa and Sonoma valleys, you can visit wineries, many of which have tasting rooms and offer tours. Microbreweries are an emerging trend in the state's cities and in some rural areas in Northern California. The legal drinking age is 21.

▌ HEALTH

Smoking is illegal in all California bars and restaurants, including on outdoor dining patios in some cities. If you have an existing medical condition that may require emergency treatment, be aware that many rural and mountain communities have only daytime clinics, not hospitals with 24-hour emergency rooms.

Outdoor sports are a huge draw in California's moderate climate but caution, especially in unfamiliar areas, is key. Drownings occur each year because beach lovers don't heed warnings about high surfs with their deadly rogue waves. Do not fly within 24 hours of scuba diving.

▌ HOURS OF OPERATION

Banks in California are typically open weekdays from 9 to 6 and Saturday morning; most are closed on Sunday and most holidays. Smaller shops usually operate from 10 to 6, with larger stores remaining open until 8 or later. Hours vary for museums, historical sites, and state parks, and many are closed one or more days a week, or for extended periods during off-season months. It's a good idea to check before you visit a tourist site.

▌ MONEY

Los Angeles, San Diego, and San Francisco tend to be expensive cities to visit, and rates at coastal and desert resorts are almost as high. A day's admission to a major theme park can run as much as $92 per person, though you may be able to get discounts by purchasing tickets in advance online. Hotel rates average $150 to $250 a night (though you can find cheaper places), and dinners at even moderately priced restaurants often cost $20 to $40 per person. Costs in the Gold Country, the Far North, and the Death Valley/Mojave Desert region are considerably less—many fine Gold Country bed-and-breakfasts charge around $100 a night, and some motels in the Far North and the Mojave charge $70 to $90.

CREDIT CARDS

It's a good idea to inform your credit-card company before you travel. Otherwise, unusual activity might prompt the company to put a hold on your card—not a good thing halfway through your trip. Record all your credit-card numbers—as well as the phone numbers to call if your cards are lost or stolen—in a safe place, so you're prepared should something go wrong. Both MasterCard and Visa have general numbers you can call (collect if you're abroad) if your card is lost or not working.

Reporting Lost Cards American Express 🖀 *800/992-3404 in U.S., 715/343-7977 collect from abroad ⊕ www.americanexpress. com.* **Discover** 🖀 *800/347-2683 in U.S., 801/902-3100 collect from abroad ⊕ www. discover.com.* **Diners Club** 🖀 *800/234-6377 in U.S., 514/877-1577 collect from abroad ⊕ www.dinersclub.com.* **MasterCard** 🖀 *800/627-8372 in U.S., 636/722-7111 collect from abroad ⊕ www.mastercard.com.* **Visa** 🖀 *800/847-2911 in U.S., 303/967-1096 collect from abroad ⊕ www.visa.com.*

▌ SAFETY

California is a safe place to visit, as long as you take the usual precautions. In large cities ask the concierge or desk clerk to point out areas on your map that you should avoid. Lock valuables in a hotel safe when you're not using them. (Some hotels have in-room safes large enough to hold a laptop computer.) Keep an eye on your handbag when you're out in public. Security is high (but mostly invisible) at theme parks and resorts.

▌ TAXES

Sales tax in the state of California is 8.25% but local taxes vary and may be as much as an additional 1.5%. Sales tax applies to all purchases except for food bought in a grocery store; food consumed in a restaurant is taxed but take-out food is not. Hotel taxes vary widely by region, from about 8% to 15.5%.

▌ TIME

California is in the Pacific time zone. Pacific daylight time (PDT) is in effect from mid-March through early November; the rest of the year the clock is set to Pacific standard time (PST).

▌ TIPPING

Most service workers in California are fairly well paid compared to those in the rest of the country, and extravagant tipping is not the rule here. Exceptions include wealthy enclaves such as Beverly Hills, La Jolla, and San Francisco as well as the most expensive resort areas.

TIPPING GUIDELINES FOR CALIFORNIA	
Bartender	$1 per drink, or 10%–15% of tab per round of drinks
Bellhop	$1–$5 per bag, depending on the level of the hotel
Hotel Concierge	$5 or more, if he/she performs a service for you
Hotel Doorman	$1–$2 if he/she helps you get a cab
Valet Parking Attendant	$2–$5 when you get your car
Hotel Maid	$2–$3 per person, per day; more in high-end hotels
Waiter	15%–20% (20%–25% is standard in upscale restaurants); nothing additional if a service charge is added to the bill
Skycap at Airport	$1–$3 per bag
Hotel Room-Service Waiter	15%–20% per delivery, even if a service charge was added since that fee goes to the hotel, not the waiter
Taxi Driver	15%–20%, but round up the fare to the next dollar amount
Tour Guide	15% of the cost of the tour, more depending on quality

❚ TOURS

Guided tours are a good option when you don't want to do it all yourself. You travel along with a group (sometimes large, sometimes small), stay in prebooked hotels, eat with your fellow travelers (the cost of meals is sometimes included in the price of your tour, sometimes not), and follow a schedule.

But not all guided tours are an if-it's-Tuesday-this-must-be-Yosemite experience. A knowledgeable guide can take you places that you might never discover on your own, and you may be pushed to see more than you would have otherwise. Tours aren't for everyone, but they can be just the thing for trips to places where making travel arrangements is difficult or time-consuming.

Whenever you book a guided tour, find out what's included and what isn't. A "land-only" tour includes all your travel (by bus, in most cases) in the destination, but not necessarily your flights to and from or even within it. Also, in most cases prices in tour brochures don't include fees and taxes. And remember that you'll be expected to tip your guide (in cash) at the end of the tour.

SPECIAL-INTEREST TOURS
BIKING

Biking is a popular way to see the California countryside, and commercial tours are available throughout the state. Most three- to five-day trips are all-inclusive—you'll stay in delightful country inns, dine at good regional restaurants, and follow experienced guides. The Northern California Wine Country, with its flat valley roads, is one of the most popular destinations. When booking, ask about level of difficulty, as nearly every trip will involve some hill work. Tours fill up early, so book well in advance.

■ TIP→ Most airlines accommodate bikes as luggage, provided they're dismantled and boxed.

Napa and Sonoma Valley Bike Tours. Single-day bike tours through beautiful Napa and Sonoma Wine Country offer a casual pace and frequent winery stops. ✉ *6500 Washington St., Yountville* 🕾 *707/251–8687 Napa tours, 707/996–2453 Sonoma tours* ⊕ *www.napavalleybiketours.com* 🖃 *From $99.*

Bicycle Adventures. Based in Washington state, this outfitter plans all the meal, lodging and travel details of multiday bike trips through some of California's most engaging scenery, including the redwoods, Wine Country, the North Coast, and rugged Death Valley. ✉ *29700 S.E. High Point Way, Issaquah, Washington* 🕾 *800/443–6060, 425/250–5540* ⊕ *www.bicycleadventures.com.*

❚ VISITOR INFORMATION

The California Travel and Tourism Commission's website takes you to each region of California, with digital visitor guides in multiple languages, driving tours, maps, welcome center locations, information on local tours, links to bed-and-breakfasts, and a complete booking center. It also links you—via the Destinations menu—to the websites of city and regional tourism offices and attractions. ⇨ *For the numbers and websites of regional and city visitor bureaus and chambers of commerce, see the Planning section in each chapter.*

Contacts California Travel and Tourism Commission ✉ *Sacramento* 🕾 *916/444–4429 CA Tourism Commission office, 800/862–2543 brochures and information* ⊕ *www.visitcalifornia.com.*

INDEX

A

PHOTO CREDITS

Visuals Photography. 379 (top), Gary Soup/Flickr. 379 (bottom), Albert Cheng/Shutterstock. 380 (top), Sheryl Schindler/SFCVB. 380 (center), Ronen/Shutterstock. 380 (bottom), Robert Holmes. 389, travelstock44/Alamy. 391, Brett Shoaf/Artistic Visuals Photography. 392, San Francisco Municipal Railway Historical Archives. 397, Lewis Sommer/SFCVB. 407, Robert Holmes. 417, aprillilacs, Fodors.com member. 421, Rafael Ramirez Lee/iStockphoto. 426, yummyporky/Flickr. 427 (top), Lisa M. Hamilton. 427 (bottom), Lisa M. Hamilton. 454, Rough Guides/Alamy. 461, Robert Holmes. Chapter 9: The Bay Area: 465 and 466, Robert Holmes. 467, Jyeshern Cheng/iStockphoto. 468, Brett Shoaf/Artistic Visuals Photography. 472, Caro / Alamy. 479, 487, 497, and 505, Robert Holmes. 509, Mark Rasmussen/istockphoto. 513, S. Greg Panosian/iStockphoto. Chapter 10: The Wine Country: 517, Robert Holmes. 518, iStockphoto. 519, Robert Holmes. 520. Warren H. White. 526, Robert Holmes. 527 (top), kevin miller/iStockphoto. 527 (bottom), Far Niente+Dolce+Nickel & Nickel. 528 (top and bottom) and 529 (top), Robert Holmes. 529 (bottom), star5112/Flickr. 530 (top left), Rubicon Estate. 530 (top right and bottom right) and 531 (top and bottom), Robert Holmes. 532 (top), Philippe Roy/Alamy. 532 (center), Agence Images/Alamy. 532 (bottom), Cephas Picture Library/Alamy. 533 (top), Napa Valley Conference Bureau. 533 (second and third from top), Wild Horse Winery (Forrest L. Doud). 533 (fourth from top), Napa Valley Conference Bureau. 533 (fifth from top) Panther Creek Cellars (Ron Kaplan). 533 (sixth from top), Clos du Val (Marvin Collins). 533 (seventh from top), Panther Creek Cellars (Ron Kaplan). 533 (bottom), Warren H. White. 535, di Rosa. 538, Robert Holmes. 547, Far Niente+Dolce+Nickel & Nickel. 549, Terry Joanis/Frog's Leap. 557, Chuck Honek/Schramsberg Vineyard. 561, Castello di Amorosa. 571, 574, 580-81, and 584, Robert Holmes. Chapter 11: The North Coast: 591, Thomas Barrat/Shutterstock. 592 (all), Robert Holmes. 593 (top), Russ Bishop/age fotostock. 593 (bottom), Robert Holmes. 594, Janet Fullwood. 601, 607, and 609, Robert Holmes. Chapter 12: Redwood National Park: 619, iStockphoto. 620 (top), Michael Schweppe/wikipedia.org. 620 (center), Agnieszka Szymczak/iStockphoto. 620 (bottom), Natalia Bratslavsky/Shutterstock. 622, WellyWelly/Shutterstock. Chapter 13: The Inland Empire: 627, Mission Inn Hotel & Spa. 628, Hartford Family Wines. 629 (top), Robert Homes. 629 (bottom), Steve kc/Flickr. 630, Edward Lin/iStockphoto. 639, Glen Ivy Hot Springs. 650, Robert Holmes. 655, Brett Shoaf/Artistic Visuals Photography. Chapter 14: Palm Springs: 657, toby fraley/iStockphoto. 658, JustASC/Shutterstock. 659 (top and bottom), Robert Holmes. 660, iStockphoto. 665, William Royer/iStockphoto. 676, David Falk/iStockphoto. 697, Brett Shoaf/Artistic Visuals Photography. Chapter 15: Joshua Tree National Park: 703, Eric Foltz/iStockphoto. 704 (top), Loic Bernard/iStockphoto. 704 (bottom), Eric Foltz/iStockphoto. 705 (top), Justin Mair/Shutterstock. 705 (bottom), Mariusz S. Jurgielewicz/Shutterstock. 706, Eric Foltz/iStockphoto. Chapter 16: The Mojave Desert: 711, Robert Holmes. 712, amygdala imagery/Shutterstock. 713, Robert Holmes. 714, San Bernardino County Regional Parks. 722, Merryl Edelstein, Fodors.com member. 727, Robert Holmes. 735, Paul Erickson/iStockphoto. Chapter 17: Death Valley National Park: 739, Bryan Brazil/Shutterstock. 741 (top), Igor Karon/Shutterstock. 741 (bottom), iofoto/Shutterstock. 742, Paul D. Lemke/iStockphoto. 746-47, James Feliciano/iStockphoto. 751, Rodney Ee, Fodors.com member. Chapter 18: The Central Valley: 753, Kim Brogan, Fodors.com member. 754, Gary Allard/iStockphoto. 755-775, Robert Holmes. Chapter 19: The Southern Sierra: 777, Randall Pugh, Fodors.com member. 778, Craig Cozart/iStockphoto. 779 (top), David T Gomez/iStockphoto. 779 (bottom left and bottom right), Robert Holmes. 780, christinea78, Fodors.com member. 787, moonjazz/Flickr. 794, Douglas Atmore/iStockphoto. Chapter 20: Yosemite National Park: 797, Sarah P. Corley, Fodors.com member. 798, Yosemite Concession Services. 799 (top), Andy Z./Shutterstock. 799 (bottom), Greg Epperson/age fotostock. 800, Doug Lemke/Shutterstock. 806, Rebalyn, Fodors.com member. 811, Nathan Jaskowiak/Shutterstock. Chapter 21: Sequoia and Kings Canyon National Parks: 817 and 818, Robert Holmes. 819 (top), Greg Epperson/age fotostock. 819 (bottom) and 820, Robert Holmes. 827, urosr/Shutterstock. 833, Robert Holmes. Chapter 22: Sacramento and the Gold Country: 835 and 837 (top and bottom), Robert Holmes. 838, Andy Z./Shutterstock. 846, Marcin Wichary/Flickr. 855, Image Asset Management/age fotostock. 856 (left) and 856 (right), wikipedia.org. 856 (center), Charles Danek. 857, Ambient Images Inc./Alamy. 858 (top), Trailmix.Net/Flickr. 858 (center) oger jones/Flickr. 858 (bottom), L. C. McClure/wikipedia.org. 859 (top left), Russ Bishop/age fotostock. 859 (top center), vera bogaerts/iStockphoto. 859 (top right and bottom left), Walter Bibikow/age fotostock. 859 (bottom right), Charles Danek. 862, Janet Fullwood. 869, RickC/Flickr. Chapter 23: Lake Tahoe: 871, Tom Zikas/North Lake Tahoe. 872 (top), Rafael Ramirez Lee/iStockphoto. 872 (bottom) and 873, Janet Fullwood. 874, Jay Spooner/iStockphoto. 883 (top) Heavenly Mountain Resort. 883 (bottom), Jake Foster/iStockphoto. 884 (top), Lake Tahoe Visitors Authority. 884 (bottom left), iStockphoto. 884 (bottom right), Heavenly Mountain Resort. 887 and 888 (left), Andrew Zarivny/iStockphoto. 888 (right), Harry Thomas/iStockphoto. 889 (top left), Joy Strotz/Shutterstock. 889 (bottom left), iStockphoto. 889 (right), Jennifer Stone/Shutterstock. 894, Jay

Spooner/iStockphoto. 901 Tom O'Neill. 912 Christopher Russell/iStockphoto. Chapter 24: The Far North: 919, NPS. 920, Robert Holmes. 921 (top), Andy Z./Shutterstock. 921 (bottom), NPS. 922, ThreadedThoughts/Flickr. 928, Robert Holmes. 937, kathycsus/Flickr. 943, NPS.

About Our Writers: All photos are courtesy of the writers except for the following: Michele Bigley, courtesy of Tony Belko; John Blodgett, courtesy of Tom Darnall; Cheryl Crabtree, courtesy of Bryn Berg; Denise Leto, courtesy of Kevin Finney; Daniel Mangin, courtesy of J. Rodby; Kathy McDonald, courtesy of Jeff Kirschbaum; Christine Vovakes, courtesy of Michael Vovakes; Bobbi Zane, courtesy of Leena Hanonnen.

NOTES

NOTES

NOTES

NOTES

A veteran traveler, **Claire Deeks van der Lee** feels lucky to call San Diego home. Claire loves playing tourist in her own city, so it was a perfect fit for her to work on the San Diego chapter of this book. Claire has traveled to more than 40 countries, and has contributed to *Everywhere* magazine and several Fodor's guides.

 Freelance writer **Christine Vovakes**—who updated the North Coast, Lake Tahoe, Far North, the Redwoods, and Travel Smart chapters— has contributed to *Fodor's California* since 2004, and also has written for *Fodor's Complete Guide to the National Parks of the West, Fodor's Pacific Northwest*, and *Fodor's Essential USA*. Her travel articles and photographs have appeared in many publications, including *The Washington Post, The Christian Science Monitor, The Sacramento Bee,* and the *San Francisco Chronicle.*

Sharron Wood has contributed to dozens of Fodor's travel guides, writing about everything from hiking in the high Sierra to hitting the nightclubs in San Francisco. When she's not on assignment with Fodor's, she's usually writing about San Francisco restaurants, editing cookbooks, or shaking up cocktails for a houseful of friends in San Francisco. She updated the Yosemite chapter for this edition.

 Bobbi Zane—who updated the Experience California and Inland Empire chapters for this edition—grew up in Southern California. She now lives in historic Julian in San Diego County. Her articles on Palm Springs have appeared in the *Orange County Register* and *Westways* magazine. She has contributed to *Fodor's Complete Guide to the National Parks of the West* and *Fodor's San Diego.* She has also contributed to *Escape to Nature Without Roughing It.*

ABOUT OUR WRITERS

 Michele Bigley spends most of her days exploring California with her two sons and husband. When not hunting for sand dollars in Santa Cruz, hiking through redwood groves, or munching on tacos in San Francisco, she writes articles, books, iPhone apps, and essays about her travels around the globe. Michele updated the San Francisco and Palm Springs chapters.

 Writer **John Blodgett** updated the Joshua Tree National Park, Mojave Desert, and Death Valley National Park chapters. Currently based in Idyllwild, California, he is a former magazine editor, newspaper reporter, and photojournalist. This is the nineteenth Fodor's guidebook he has contributed to.

 Native Californian **Cheryl Crabtree**—who updated the Central Coast, Channel Islands National Park, Monterey Bay, Southern Sierra, and Central Valley chapters—has worked as a freelance writer since 1987. She has contributed to *Fodor's California* since 2003. Cheryl is editor of *Montecito Magazine.* Her articles have appeared in many regional and national publications, including US Airways in-flight magazine and *Santa Barbara Seasons,* and annual visitor magazines in Santa Barbara, Ventura, and Pismo Beach. She also authors regional travel apps for mobile devices and co-authored two California winery books.

Updating our L.A. chapter was a team of crack writers from Fodor's Los Angeles: **Sarah Amandolore, Jim Arnold, Cindy Arora, Michele Bigley, Alene Dawson, Dianne de Guzman,** and **Clarissa Wei.**

 Longtime Fodor's writer, editor, and contributor to our San Francisco chapter, **Denise M. Leto** roams the city out of sheer love for SF, peeking down overgrown alleyways and exploring tucked-away corners from the Tenderloin to the Richmond, often with her three homeschooled kids in tow.

 Daniel Mangin returned to California, where he's maintained a home for three decades, after two stints at the Fodor's editorial offices in New York City, the second one as the editorial director of Fodors.com and the Compass American Guides. While at Compass he was the series editor for the *California Wine Country* guide and commissioned the *Oregon Wine Country* and *Washington Wine Country* guides. With several-dozen wineries less than a half-hour's drive from home, he often finds himself transported as if by magic to a tasting room bar, communing with a sophisticated Cabernet or savoring the finish of a smooth Pinot Noir. For this edition, Daniel updated our Wine Country and Sequoia and Kings Canyon National Park chapters.

 Finding the unexpected is Los Angeles freelance writer and frequent traveler **Kathy A. McDonald's** favorite assignment. A writer with peripatetic beats, she covers film business, design, and destinations, and is a frequent contributor to *Variety, Los Angeles Confidential,* and other publications. Art galleries, modern architecture, and thrift stores entice her; she rarely passes an open house or yard sale without stopping. She updated Orange County.

 Jenie Skoy is a travel writer who has contributed to AOL Travel, *Sunset, USA Today,* and many others. When she's not writing about travel or food, she teaches college-level writing in Salt Lake City, Utah. She loves to hike, fly-fish, play music, and swim in her neighbor's pool. For this edition, she updated the Sacramento and the Gold Country chapter.

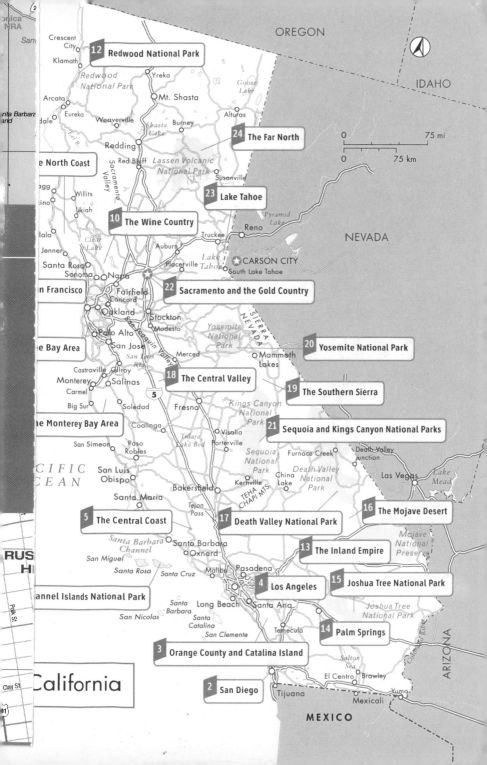

OREGON

IDAHO

Crescent
City
Klamath

12 Redwood National Park

*Redwood
National Park*

Yreka

NEVADA

Mt. Shasta

*Goose
Lake*

Arcata
Eureka
Weaverville
*Shasta
Lake*
Burney

Alturas

24 The Far North

Redding
Red Bluff
*Lassen Volcanic
National Park*

Susanville

23 Lake Tahoe

*Pyramid
Lake*

Willits
Ukiah

10 The Wine Country

Truckee
Auburn
Placerville

Reno

CARSON CITY

*Lake
Tahoe*
South Lake Tahoe

North Coast

gg
no

ala

Jenner

Santa Rosa
Sonoma Napa
Fairfield
Concord

San Francisco

Oakland

Palo Alto
San Jose

Bay Area

22 Sacramento and the Gold Country

Stockton
Modesto

*Yosemite
National
Park*

Mammoth
Lakes

20 Yosemite National Park

*Clear
Lake*

San Joaquin River

Merced

19 The Southern Sierra

Castroville Gilroy
Monterey Salinas
Carmel

18 The Central Valley

Big Sur
Soledad

Fresno

*Kings Canyon
National
Park*

Monterey Bay Area

Coalinga

*Tulare
Lake Bed*

Visalia
Porterville

21 Sequoia and Kings Canyon National Parks

San Simeon

Paso
Robles

*Sequoia
National
Park*

Furnace Creek

*Death Valley
National
Park*

Death Valley
Junction

San Luis
Obispo

Kernville
China
Lake

*TEHA
CHAPI MTS.*

Las Vegas

*Lake
Mead*

PACIFIC
OCEAN

Santa Maria

Bakersfield

Tejon
Pass

5 The Central Coast

Santa Barbara
Oxnard

17 Death Valley National Park

16 The Mojave Desert

*Mojave
National
Preserve*

*Santa Barbara
Channel*

San Miguel

Santa Rosa

Santa Cruz

Malibu

Pasadena

13 The Inland Empire

Channel Islands National Park

Santa
Barbara

Long Beach

Santa Ana

4 Los Angeles

15 Joshua Tree National Park

San Nicolas

Santa
Catalina
San Clemente

Temecula

14 Palm Springs

*Joshua Tree
National Park*

3 Orange County and Catalina Island

*Salton
Sea*

El Centro Brawley

ARIZONA

Colorado River

California

2 San Diego

Tijuana

MEXICO

Mexicali

Yuma

0 _____ 75 mi

0 _____ 75 km

Fodor's CALIFORNIA

Fodor's correspondents highlight the best of California, including San Francisco, Napa and Sonoma, Palm Springs, and Yosemite National Park. Our local experts vet every recommendation to ensure you make the most of your time, whether it's your first trip or your fifth.

★ **MUST-SEE ATTRACTIONS** from Hollywood to Big Sur

★ **PERFECT HOTELS** for every budget

★ **BEST RESTAURANTS** to satisfy a range of tastes

★ **GORGEOUS FEATURES** on coastal drives, wine, and Lake Tahoe

★ **VALUABLE TIPS** on when to go and ways to save

★ **INSIDER PERSPECTIVE** from local experts

★ **COLOR PHOTOS AND MAPS** to inspire and guide your trip

Fodors.com

Find the latest travel trends and deals, and connect with other travelers in our forums.

ISBN 978-0-8041-4273-1